15th Edition

Technology in Action

Complete

Alan Evans • Kendall Martin • Mary Anne Poatsy

 Pearson

330 Hudson Street, NY NY 10013

Vice President, Career & IT Skills: Andrew Gilfillan
Executive Portfolio Manager: Jenifer Niles
Managing Producer: Laura Burgess
Development Editor: Shannon LeMay-Finn
Director of Product Marketing: Maggie Moylan
Director of Field Marketing: Leigh Ann Sims
Field Marketing Manager: Molly Schmidt
Product Marketing Manager: Heather Taylor
Operations Specialist: Maura Garcia
Senior Product Model Manager: Eric Hakanson
Lead, Production and Digital Studio: Heather Darby
Course Producer: Amanda Losonsky

Digital Content Producer: Becca Golden
Senior Art Director: Mary Siener
Associate Director of Design: Blair Brown
Cover Design: Cenveo® Publisher Services
Cover Art: Everything/Shutterstock
Full-Service Project Management: Cenveo® Publisher Services
Composition: Cenveo® Publisher Services
Printer/Binder: LSC/General
Cover Printer: Phoenix Color
Text Font: Helvetica Neue LT W1G, 45 Light

Credits and acknowledgments borrowed from other sources and reproduced, with permission, in this textbook appear on the appropriate page within the text.

Library of Congress Cataloging-in-Publication Data

On file with the Library of Congress.

1 17

ISBN 10: 0-13-483787-8
ISBN 13: 978-0-13-483787-1

Contents at a Glance

Chapter 1
The Impact of Technology in a Changing World 2

Chapter 2
Looking at Computers: Understanding the Parts.. 40

Chapter 3
Using the Internet: Making the Most of the Web's Resources 86

Chapter 4
Application Software: Programs That Let You Work and Play.. 128

Chapter 5
System Software: The Operating System, Utility Programs, and File Management 166

Chapter 6
Understanding and Assessing Hardware: Evaluating Your System 208

Chapter 7
Networking: Connecting Computing Devices.. 250

Chapter 8
Managing a Digital Lifestyle: Media and Ethics.. 288

Chapter 9
Securing Your System: Protecting Your Digital Data and Devices 334

Chapter 10
Behind the Scenes: Software Programming.. 382

Chapter 11
Behind the Scenes: Databases and Information Systems 426

Chapter 12
Behind the Scenes: Networking and Security in the Business World.. 472

Chapter 13
Behind the Scenes: How the Internet Works.. 514

Appendix A
The History of the Personal Computer A-1

Appendix B
Careers in IT B-1

Glossary G-1

Index I-1

Contents

Chapter 1

The Impact of Technology in a Changing World 2

Part 1: Technology in Society 4
Learning Outcome 1.1 **You will be able to discuss the impact of the tools of modern technology on national and global issues.**

Technology in a Global Society 4
Impact of Tools of Modern Technology 4
Objective 1.1 *Describe various technological tools being used to impact national and global issues.*
Global Issues 5
Objective 1.2 *Describe various global social issues that are being affected by technology.*

Technology Connects Us with Others 7
Technology Impacts How and Why We Connect and Collaborate 7
Objective 1.3 *Describe how technology is changing how and why we connect and collaborate with others.*
Technology Impacts How We Consume 8
Objective 1.4 *Summarize how technology has impacted the way we choose and consume products and services.*
HELPDESK: Technology Impacts 8

The Importance of Computer Literacy 9
Computer Literacy 9
Objective 1.5 *Characterize computer literacy and explain why it is important to be computer literate.*
SOUND BYTE: Virtual Computer Tour 9
TRY THIS: Skyping Around the World 13
MAKE THIS: MAKE: A Virtual Assistant 14

Part 2: Emerging Technologies and Ethical Computing 15
Learning Outcome 1.2 **You will be able to describe emerging technologies such as artificial intelligence, and how technology creates new ethical debates.**

Artificial Intelligence 15
Artificial Intelligence Basics 15
Objective 1.6 *Describe artificial intelligence systems and explain their main goals.*
HELPDESK: The Impact of Artificial Intelligence 15
ETHICS IN IT: Ethics in Computing 18

Working with Artificial Intelligence and Other Information Technologies 19
Technology and Career Opportunities 19
Objective 1.7 *Describe how artificial intelligence and other information technologies are providing career opportunities.*
BITS&BYTES: Is It AI or Human? Take a Turing Test! 00
DIG DEEPER: Augmentative and Virtual Realities 23

Ethical Computing 24
Defining Ethics 24
Objective 1.8 *Define ethics and examine various ethical systems.*
SOUND BYTE: How to Debate Ethical Issues 26
Personal Ethics 26
Objective 1.9 *Describe influences on the development of your personal ethics.*
Ethics and Technology 27
Objective 1.10 *Present examples of how technology creates ethical challenges.*
SOLVE THIS: How Technology Is Used on the World Stage and in My Personal Life 39

Chapter 2

Looking at Computers: Understanding the Parts 40

Part 1: Understanding Digital Components 42

Learning Outcome 2.1 **You will be able to describe the devices that make up a computer system.**

Understanding Your Computer 42

Computers Are Data Processing Devices 42
Objective 2.1 *Describe the four main functions of a computer system and how they interact with data and information.*

Binary: The Language of Computers 43
Objective 2.2 *Define bits and bytes, and describe how they are measured, used, and processed.*

SOUND BYTE: Binary Numbers Interactive 43

Types of Computers 45
Objective 2.3 *List common types of computers, and discuss their main features.*

HELPDESK: Understanding Bits and Bytes 45

BITS&BYTES: Today's Supercomputers: Faster Than Ever 49

Input Devices 50

Physical Keyboards and Touch Screens 50
Objective 2.4 *Identify the main types of keyboards and touch screens.*

Mice and Other Pointing Devices 52
Objective 2.5 *Describe the main types of mice and pointing devices.*

DIG DEEPER: How Touch Screens Work 53

BITS&BYTES: Distributed Computing: Putting Your Computer to Work While You Sleep 54

Image, Sound, and Sensor Input 54
Objective 2.6 *Explain how images, sounds, and sensor data are input into computing devices.*

Output Devices 56

Image and Audio Output 56
Objective 2.7 *Describe options for outputting images and audio from computing devices.*

BITS&BYTES: Near Field Communication (NFC): Now Pay (or Get Paid) Anywhere with Your Phone 58

Printers 59
Objective 2.8 *Describe various types of printers, and explain when you would use them.*

BITS&BYTES: Medical Devices and 3D Printing 61

TRY THIS: What's Inside My Computer? 63

MAKE THIS: MAKE: A Mobile App 64

Part 2: Processing, Storage, and Connectivity 65

Learning Outcome 2.2 **You will be able to describe how computers process and store data and how devices connect to a computer system.**

Processing and Memory on the Motherboard 65

The Motherboard and Memory 65
Objective 2.9 *Describe the functions of the motherboard and RAM.*

Processing 66
Objective 2.10 *Explain the main functions of the CPU.*

SOUND BYTE: Smartphones Are Really Smart 66

Storing Data and Information 67

Storage Options on Computing Devices 67
Objective 2.11 *Describe the various means of storing data and information with computing devices.*

ETHICS IN IT: What Is Ethical Computing? 69

TRENDS IN IT: Green Computing (Green IT) 70

Connecting Peripherals to the Computer 71

Computer Ports 71
Objective 2.12 *Describe common types of ports used today.*

HELPDESK: Exploring Storage Devices and Ports 71

Contents   v

Power Management and Ergonomics **72**

Power Controls and Power Management.. 72
Objective 2.13 *Describe how to manage power consumption on computing devices.*

BITS&BYTES: Sleep Better and Avoid Eyestrain: Use Less Blue LIght 74

Setting It All Up: Ergonomics 75
Objective 2.14 *Define ergonomics, and discuss the ideal physical setup for using computing devices.*

SOLVE THIS: Technology Wish List 85

Chapter 3

Using the Internet: Making the Most of the Web's Resources 86

Part 1: Collaborating and Working on the Web **88**

Learning Outcome 3.1 **You will be able to explain how the Internet works and how it is used for collaboration, communication, commerce, and entertainment purposes.**

The Internet and How It Works... **88**

The Origin of the Internet 88
Objective 3.1 *Describe how the Internet got its start.*

How the Internet Works.. 90
Objective 3.2 *Explain how data travels on the Internet.*

Collaborating and Communicating on the Web.. **91**

Collaborating with Web Technologies 91
Objective 3.3 *Evaluate the tools and technologies used to collaborate on the web.*

BITS&BYTES: Secure Messaging Apps.. 93

SOUND BYTE: Blogging 93

Communicating over the Web 96
Objective 3.4 *Summarize the technologies used to communicate over the web.*

Conducting Business on the Web.. **99**

Conducting Business Online.. 99
Objective 3.5 *Describe how business is conducted using the Internet.*

DIG DEEPER: How Cloud Computing Works 100

BITS&BYTES: Looking for Extra Money? Try a Side Hustle... 101

E-Commerce Safeguards 101
Objective 3.6 *Summarize precautions you should take when doing business online.*

HELPDESK: Doing Business Online 102

BITS&BYTES: Making Safe Mobile and Online Payments 103

TRY THIS: Use OneDrive to Store and Share Your Files in the Cloud 105

MAKE THIS: MAKE: A Web-Capable App 106

Part 2: Using the Web Effectively.. **107**

Learning Outcome 3.2 **You will be able to describe the tools and techniques required to navigate and search the web.**

Accessing and Moving Around the Web **107**

Web Browsers.. 107
Objective 3.7 *Explain what web browsers are, and describe their common features.*

URLs, Protocols, and Domain Names.. 109
Objective 3.8 *Explain what a URL is, and discuss its main parts.*

Navigating the Web 110
Objective 3.9 *Describe tools used to navigate the web.*

BITS&BYTES: Maintain Your Privacy While Searching the Web... 111

Searching the Web Effectively.. **112**

Using Search Engines 112
Objective 3.10 *Describe the types of tools used to search the web, and summarize strategies used to refine search results.*

  BITS&BYTES: Digital Assistants and Predictive Search.. 113

  Evaluating Websites.. 115
  Objective 3.11 *Describe how to evaluate a website to ensure it is appropriate to use for research purposes.*

  SOUND BYTE: Finding Information on the Web.. 115

  HELPDESK: Evaluating Websites 115

  TRENDS IN IT: Linked Data and the Semantic Web 116

  BITS&BYTES: Why Isn't Wikipedia Good to Use as a Source for a Research Paper? 117

  Using the Web Ethically **117**

  Digital Activism.. 117
  Objective 3.12 *Demonstrate an understanding of the ethical issues regarding digital activism.*

  Geolocation.. 118
  Objective 3.13 *Demonstrate an understanding of the ethical issues regarding location tracking applications and devices.*

  BITS&BYTES: Human-Implanted Data Chips: Protection or Invasive Nightmare? 119

  ETHICS IN IT: Cyber Harassment.. 120

  SOLVE THIS: Create a Report: Conducting Research on the Web.. 127

Chapter 4

Application Software: Programs That Let You Work and Play 128

Part 1: Accessing, Using, and Managing Software.. **130**

Learning Outcome 4.1 You will be able to explain the ways to access and use software and describe how to best manage your software.

  Software Basics... **130**

  Application vs. System Software.. 130
  Objective 4.1 *Compare application software and system software.*

  Distributing Software 130
  Objective 4.2 *Explain the differences between commercial software and open source software, and describe models for software distribution.*

  BITS&BYTES: Finding Alternative Software.. 131

  Managing Your Software... **131**

  Purchasing Software 131
  Objective 4.3 *Explain the different options for purchasing software.*

  TRENDS IN IT: Mobile Payment Apps: The Power of M-Commerce 132

  HELPDESK: Buying and Installing Software... 133

  Installing and Uninstalling Software 133
  Objective 4.4 *Describe how to install and uninstall software.*

  BITS&BYTES: Ridding Your Computer of "Bloat"... 133

  Upgrading Software.. 134
  Objective 4.5 *Explain the considerations around the decision to upgrade your software.*

  DIG DEEPER: How Number Systems Work... 134

  SOUND BYTE: Where Does Binary Show Up?... 135

  Software Licenses 136
  Objective 4.6 *Explain how software licenses function.*

  ETHICS IN IT: Can I Borrow Software That I Don't Own? 137

  TRY THIS: Citing Website Sources 139

  MAKE THIS: MAKE: A More Powerful App 140

Part 2: Application Software **141**

Learning Outcome 4.2 Describe the different types of application software used for productivity and multimedia.

  Productivity and Business Software **141**

  Productivity Software... 141
  Objective 4.7 *Categorize the types of application software used to enhance productivity, and describe their uses and features.*

BITS&BYTES: Productivity Software Tips and Tricks... 141

BITS&BYTES: How to Open Unknown File Types... 142

BITS&BYTES: Going Beyond PowerPoint.. 146

SOUND BYTE: Programming for End Users 148

Business Software.. 150
Objective 4.8 *Summarize the types of software that large and small businesses use.*

BITS&BYTES: Need to Work as a Team? Try These Collaboration Tools 152

Multimedia and Educational Software... 152

Digital Multimedia Software 152
Objective 4.9 *Describe the uses and features of digital multimedia software.*

Digital Audio Software 154
Objective 4.10 *Describe the uses and features of digital audio software.*

HELPDESK: Choosing Software... 155

App Creation Software 156
Objective 4.11 *Describe the features of app creation software.*

BITS&BYTES: Mirror, Mirror… 157

Educational and Reference Software 157
Objective 4.12 *Categorize educational and reference software, and explain their features.*

SOLVE THIS: Analyzing Benchmark Data 165

Chapter 5

System Software: The Operating System, Utility Programs, and File Management.. 166

Part 1: Understanding System Software.. 168

Learning Outcome 5.1 **You will be able to explain the types and functions of operating systems and explain the steps in the boot process.**

Operating System Fundamentals... 168

Operating System Basics 168
Objective 5.1 *Discuss the functions of the operating system.*

Operating Systems for Personal Use... 169
Objective 5.2 *Explain the most common operating systems for personal use.*

BITS&BYTES: Why Isn't Everyone Using Linux? 170

BITS&BYTES: Operating Systems for the Home... 171

Operating Systems for Machinery, Networks, and Business 171
Objective 5.3 *Explain the different kinds of operating systems for machines, networks, and business.*

ETHICS IN IT: The Great Debate: Is macOS Safer Than Windows?.. 173

What the Operating System Does... 174

The User Interface 174
Objective 5.4 *Explain how the operating system provides a means for users to interact with the computer.*

Hardware Coordination.. 175
Objective 5.5 *Explain how the operating system helps manage hardware such as the processor, memory, storage, and peripheral devices.*

SOUND BYTE: Using Windows Task Manager to Evaluate System Performance 175

Software Application Coordination... 177
Objective 5.6 *Explain how the operating system interacts with application software.*

TRENDS IN IT: Are Personal Computers Becoming More Human? 178

Starting Your Computer 179

The Boot Process... 179
Objective 5.7 *Discuss the process the operating system uses to start up the computer and how errors in the boot process are handled.*

     HELPDESK: Starting the Computer: The Boot Process 181

     TRY THIS: Using Virtual Desktops in Windows 10 184

     MAKE THIS: MAKE: A Notification Alert 185

Part 2: Using System Software **186**

Learning Outcome 5.2 **You will be able to describe how to use system software, including the user interface, file management capabilities, and utility programs.**

    The Windows Interface **186**

     Using Windows 10 186
     Objective 5.8 *Describe the main features of the Windows interface.*

     BITS&BYTES: The Snipping Tool 187

    File Management **189**

     Organizing Your Files 189
     Objective 5.9 *Summarize how the operating system helps keep your computer organized and manages files and folders.*

     BITS&BYTES: Save Files in the Cloud 191

     BITS&BYTES: Tips for Organizing Your Files 192

     HELPDESK: Organizing Your Computer: File Management 193

    Utility Programs **195**

     Windows Administrative Utilities 196
     Objective 5.10 *Outline the tools used to enhance system productivity, back up files, and provide accessibility.*

     DIG DEEPER: How Disk Defragmenting Utilities Work 198

     SOUND BYTE: Hard Disk Anatomy 198

     SOLVE THIS: Mobile Operating Systems: Changing Market Share 207

Chapter 6

Understanding and Assessing Hardware: Evaluating Your System 208

Part 1: Evaluating Key Subsystems **210**

Learning Outcome 6.1 **You will be able to evaluate your computer system's hardware functioning, including the CPU and memory subsystems.**

    Your Ideal Computing Device **210**

     Moore's Law 210
     Objective 6.1 *Describe the changes in CPU performance over the past several decades.*

     Selecting a Computing Device 211
     Objective 6.2 *Compare and contrast a variety of computing devices.*

    Evaluating the CPU Subsystem **213**

     How the CPU Works 213
     Objective 6.3 *Describe how a CPU is designed and how it operates.*

     BITS&BYTES: Liquid Cooling 217

     Measuring CPU Performance 217
     Objective 6.4 *Describe tools used to measure and evaluate CPU performance.*

     DIG DEEPER: The Machine Cycle 219

    Evaluating the Memory Subsystem **220**

     Random Access Memory 220
     Objective 6.5 *Discuss how RAM is used in a computer system.*

     Adding RAM 222
     Objective 6.6 *Evaluate whether adding RAM to a system is desirable.*

     HELPDESK: Evaluating Your CPU and RAM 222

     SOUND BYTE: Installing RAM 223

TRY THIS: Measure Your System Performance 225

MAKE THIS: MAKE: A Location-Aware App 226

Part 2: Evaluating Other Subsystems and Making a Decision **227**

Learning Outcome 6.2 You will be able to evaluate your computer system's storage subsystem, media subsystem, and reliability and decide whether to purchase a new system or upgrade an existing one.

Evaluating the Storage Subsystem **227**

Types of Storage Drives 227
Objective 6.7 *Classify and describe the major types of nonvolatile storage drives.*

SOUND BYTE: Installing an SSD Drive 228

DIG DEEPER: How Storage Devices Work 229

Storage Needs 230
Objective 6.8 *Evaluate the amount and type of storage needed for a system.*

BITS&BYTES: How Much Storage to Buy? 232

Evaluating the Media Subsystems **233**

Video Cards 233
Objective 6.9 *Describe the features of video cards.*

BITS&BYTES: Graphics Cards with SSD on Board 235

TRENDS IN IT: USB 3.1 and USB-C 236

Sound Cards 237
Objective 6.10 *Describe the features of sound cards.*

HELPDESK: Evaluating Computer System Components 237

Evaluating System Reliability and Moving On **239**

Maintaining System Reliability 239
Objective 6.11 *Describe steps you can take to optimize your system's reliability.*

Getting Rid of Your Old Computer 241
Objective 6.12 *Discuss how to recycle, donate, or dispose of an older computer.*

ETHICS IN IT: Free Hardware for All 242

SOLVE THIS: Laptop Alternatives 249

Chapter 7

Networking: Connecting Computing Devices 250

Part 1: How Networks Function **252**

Learning Outcome 7.1 You will be able to explain the basics of networking, including the components needed to create a network, and describe the different ways a network can connect to the Internet.

Networking Fundamentals **252**

Understanding Networks 252
Objective 7.1 *Describe computer networks and their pros and cons.*

HELPDESK: Understanding Networking 253

Network Architectures **254**

Network Designs 254
Objective 7.2 *Explain the different ways networks are defined.*

BITS&BYTES: The Rise of Wearable Technology 256

Network Components **257**

Transmission Media 257
Objective 7.3 *Describe the types of transmission media used in networks.*

SOUND BYTE: Installing a Home Computer Network 257

Basic Network Hardware 260
Objective 7.4 *Describe the basic hardware devices necessary for networks.*

Network Software 261
Objective 7.5 *Describe the type of software necessary for networks.*

TRENDS IN IT: How Smart Is Your Home?.. 262

Connecting to the Internet... **262**

Broadband Internet Connections... 262
Objective 7.6 *Summarize the broadband options available to access the Internet.*

Wireless Internet Access.. 264
Objective 7.7 *Summarize how to access the Internet wirelessly.*

BITS&BYTES: Net Neutrality.. 264

BITS&BYTES: 5G Is Coming—Is It Worth the Wait? 265

BITS&BYTES: Is Dial-Up Still an Option? 266

ETHICS IN IT: Ethical Challenges of the Internet of Things.. 266

TRY THIS: Testing Your Internet Connection Speed 268

MAKE THIS: MAKE: Networked Devices 269

Part 2: Your Home Network.. **270**
Learning Outcome 7.2 **You will be able to describe what is necessary to install and configure a home network and how to manage and secure a wireless network.**

Installing and Configuring Home Networks.. **270**

Planning Your Home Network... 270
Objective 7.8 *Explain what should be considered before creating a home network.*

Connecting Devices to a Network.. 271
Objective 7.9 *Describe how to set up a home network.*

BITS&BYTES: Mesh Networks: An Emerging Alternative 272

BITS&BYTES: Analyzing Network Problems.. 275

Configuring Software for Your Home Network 275
Objective 7.10 *Summarize how to configure home network software.*

DIG DEEPER: P2P File Sharing... 277

Managing and Securing Wireless Networks.. **277**

Troubleshooting Wireless Network Problems 277
Objective 7.11 *Describe the potential problems with wireless networks and means to avoid them.*

Securing Wireless Networks 278
Objective 7.12 *Describe how to secure wireless home network*

SOUND BYTE: Securing Wireless Networks.. 280

HELPDESK: Managing and Securing Your Wireless Network 280

SOLVE THIS: Home Networking Guide... 287

Chapter 8

Managing a Digital Lifestyle: Media and Ethics 288

Part 1: The Impact of Digital Information 290
Learning Outcome 8.1 **You will be able to describe the nature of digital signals and how digital technology is used to produce and distribute digital texts, music, and video.**

Digital Basics **290**

Digital Convergence 290
Objective 8.1 *Describe how digital convergence has evolved.*

Digital vs. Analog... 291
Objective 8.2 *Explain the differences between digital and analog signals.*

Digital Publishing **293**

E-Readers... 293
Objective 8.3 *Describe the different types of e-readers.*

Using e-Texts... 294
Objective 8.4 *Explain how to purchase, borrow, and publish e-texts.*

HELPDESK: Managing Digital Media 294

Digital Music **295**

Creating and Storing Digital Music 295
Objective 8.5 *Describe how digital music is created and stored.*

BITS&BYTES: Digital Music Creation 297

Distributing Digital Music 297
Objective 8.6 *Summarize how to listen to and publish digital music.*

BITS&BYTES: Need Money for Your Band? Try Crowdfunding 298

Digital Media **298**

Digital Photography 298
Objective 8.7 *Explain how best to create, print, and share digital photos.*

BITS&BYTES: Photo Edit on Your Phone 300

SOUND BYTE: Enhancing Photos with Image-Editing Software 300

Digital Video 301
Objective 8.8 *Describe how to create, edit, and distribute digital video.*

BITS&BYTES: Fly-By Drone Video 302

TRENDS IN IT: Digital Asset Managers Needed! 304

TRY THIS: Creating and Publishing a Movie 306

MAKE THIS: MAKE: A Video-Playing App 307

Part 2: Ethical Issues of Living in the Digital Age **308**

Learning Outcome 8.2 You will be able to describe how to respect digital property and use it in ways that maintain your digital reputation.

Protection of Digital Property **308**

Intellectual Property 308
Objective 8.9 *Describe the various types of intellectual property.*

Copyright Basics 309
Objective 8.10 *Explain how copyright is obtained and the rights granted to the owners.*

HELPDESK: Understanding Intellectual Property and Copyright 311

Copyright Infringement 312
Objective 8.11 *Explain copyright infringement, summarize the potential consequences, and describe situations in which you can legally use copyrighted material.*

BITS&BYTES: Software Piracy: It's More Than Just Downloading and Copying 314

BITS&BYTES: Your Tax Dollars at Work: Free Media without Permission! 316

Living Ethically in the Digital Era **317**

Plagiarism 317
Objective 8.12 *Explain plagiarism and strategies for avoiding it.*

Hoaxes and Digital Manipulation 319
Objective 8.13 *Describe hoaxes and digital manipulation.*

SOUND BYTE: Plagiarism and Intellectual Property 319

Protecting Your Online Reputation 322
Objective 8.14 *Describe what comprises your online reputation and how to protect it.*

BITS&BYTES: Celebrity Photographic Rights 324

ETHICS IN IT: Acceptable Use Policies: What You Can and Can't Do 325

SOLVE THIS: Intellectual Property and Copyright Basics 333

Chapter 9

Securing Your System: Protecting Your Digital Data and Devices 334

Part 1: Threats to Your Digital Assets 336

Learning Outcome 9.1 You will be able to describe hackers, viruses, and other online annoyances and the threats they pose to your digital security.

Identity Theft and Hackers **336**

Identity Theft 337
Objective 9.1 *Describe how identity theft is committed and the types of scams identity thieves perpetrate.*

Hacking.. 337
Objective 9.2 *Describe the different types of hackers and the tools they use.*

BITS&BYTES: Hacking for Security 338

Computer Viruses **341**

Virus Basics.. 341
Objective 9.3 *Explain what a computer virus is, why it is a threat to your security, how a computing device catches a virus, and the symptoms it may display.*

SOUND BYTE: Protecting Your Computer 342

Types of Viruses 343
Objective 9.4 *List the different categories of computer viruses, and describe their behaviors.*

Online Annoyances and Social Engineering **345**

Online Annoyances.. 345
Objective 9.5 *Explain what malware, spam, and cookies are and how they impact your security.*

Social Engineering 348
Objective 9.6 *Describe social engineering techniques, and explain strategies to avoid falling prey to them.*

BITS&BYTES: I Received a Data Breach Letter ... Now What?.. 348

Scareware 349

ETHICS IN IT: You're Being Watched ... But Are You Aware You're Being Watched? 350

HELPDESK: Threats to Your Digital Life 350

TRENDS IN IT: Spear Phishing: The Bane of Data Breaches 351

TRY THIS: Testing Your Network Security 353

MAKE THIS: MAKE: A Password Generator 354

Part 2: Protecting Your Digital Property **355**
Learning Outcome 9.2 **Describe various ways to protect your digital property and data from theft and corruption.**

Restricting Access to Your Digital Assets **355**

Firewalls 355
Objective 9.7 *Explain what a firewall is and how a firewall protects your computer from hackers.*

HELPDESK: Understanding Firewalls 357

Preventing Virus Infections... 357
Objective 9.8 *Explain how to protect your computer from virus infection.*

Authentication: Passwords and Biometrics 360
Objective 9.9 *Describe how passwords and biometric characteristics can be used for user authentication.*

BITS&BYTES: CAPTCHA: Keeping Websites Safe from Bots 361

Anonymous Web Surfing: Hiding from Prying Eyes 363
Objective 9.10 *Describe ways to surf the web anonymously.*

BITS&BYTES: Multi-Factor Authentication: Don't Rely Solely on Passwords! 365

Keeping Your Data Safe **365**

Protecting Your Personal Information 365
Objective 9.11 *Describe the types of information you should never share online.*

SOUND BYTE: Managing Computer Security with Windows Tools 365

Backing Up Your Data 366
Objective 9.12 *List the various types of backups you can perform on your computing devices, and explain the various places you can store backup files.*

Protecting Your Physical Computing Assets **370**

Environmental Factors and Power Surges.. 370
Objective 9.13 *Explain the negative effects environment and power surges can have on computing devices.*

Preventing and Handling Theft.. 370
Objective 9.14 *Describe the major concerns when a device is stolen and strategies for solving the problems.*

DIG DEEPER: Computer Forensics: How It Works 372

SOLVE THIS: Computer Security 381

Chapter 10

Behind the Scenes: Software Programming....................382

Part 1: Understanding Programming 384

Learning Outcome 10.1 **You will be able to describe the life cycle of a software project and identify the stages in the program development life cycle.**

Life Cycle of an Information System....................384

Importance of Programming 384
Objective 10.1 *Describe the importance of programming to both software developers and users.*

System Development Life Cycle 384
Objective 10.2 *Summarize the stages of the system development life cycle (SDLC).*

BITS&BYTES: Let Them See Your Work 386

Life Cycle of a Program....................386

The Program Development Life Cycle....................386
Objective 10.3 *Define programming and list the steps in the program development life cycle (PDLC).*

The Problem Statement....................387
Objective 10.4 *Describe how programmers construct a complete problem statement from a description of a task.*

SOUND BYTE: Using the Arduino Microcontroller....................387

HELPDESK: Understanding Software Programming....................388

Algorithm Development 389
Objective 10.5 *Explain how programmers use flow control and design methodologies when developing algorithms.*

BITS&BYTES: Hackathons 392

DIG DEEPER: The Building Blocks of Programming Languages: Syntax, Keywords, Data Types, and
Operators 394

Coding 394
Objective 10.6 *Discuss the categories of programming languages and the roles of the compiler and the integrated development environment (IDE) in coding.*

Debugging 401
Objective 10.7 *Identify the role of debugging in program development.*

BITS&BYTES: Many Languages on Display....................402

Testing and Documentation....................402
Objective 10.8 *Explain the importance of testing and documentation in program development.*

TRY THIS: Programming with Corona....................404

MAKE THIS: MAKE: A Notepad 405

Part 2: Programming Languages 406

Learning Outcome 10.2 **You will understand the factors programmers consider when selecting an appropriate programming language for a specific problem and will be familiar with some modern programming languages.**

Many Programming Languages 406

Need for Diverse Languages 406
Objective 10.9 *Discuss the driving factors behind the popularity of various programming languages.*

SOUND BYTE: Programming with the Processing Language....................406

Selecting the Right Language....................407
Objective 10.10 *Summarize the considerations in identifying an appropriate programming language for a specific setting.*

BITS&BYTES: Coding for Zombies....................407

ETHICS IN IT: When Software Runs Awry 408

Exploring Programming Languages 409

Tour of Modern Languages....................409
Objective 10.11 *Compare and contrast modern programming languages.*

BITS&BYTES: Your Software Portfolio 413

TRENDS IN IT: Emerging Technologies: Unite All Your Video Game Design Tools....................417

Future of Programming Languages 417
Objective 10.12 *State key principles in the development of future programming languages.*

HELPDESK: A Variety of Programming Languages...418

SOLVE THIS: Time Sheets...425

Chapter 11

Behind the Scenes: Databases and Information Systems 426

Part 1: Database Fundamentals...**428**

Learning Outcome 11.1 **You will be able to explain the basics of databases, including the most common types of databases and the functions and components of relational databases in particular.**

Database Advantages **428**

The Need for Databases.. 428
Objective 11.1 *Explain what a database is and why databases are useful.*

HELPDESK: Using Databases... 430

Advantages of Using Databases... 431
Objective 11.2 *Discuss the benefits of using a database.*

Database Types **432**

Relational Databases.. 433
Objective 11.3 *Describe features of relational databases.*

Object-Oriented Databases 434
Objective 11.4 *Describe features of object-oriented databases.*

Multidimensional Databases 434
Objective 11.5 *Describe features of multidimensional databases.*

TRENDS IN IT: Emerging Technologies: Can Your Business Partner Deliver the Goods? Enhanced Databases Can Help You Decide! 435

Database Basics..**435**

Database Components and Functions.. 435
Objective 11.6 *Describe how relational databases organize and define data.*

SOUND BYTE: Creating and Querying an Access Database 439

BITS&BYTES: Music Streaming Services Use Databases 439

Inputting and Managing Data.. 440
Objective 11.7 *Describe how data is inputted and managed in a database.*

DIG DEEPER: Structured Query Language (SQL) 445

BITS&BYTES: Data Dashboards: Useful Visualization Tools 447

TRY THIS: Using Excel's Database Functions 449

MAKE THIS: MAKE: A Family Shopping List... 450

Part 2: How Businesses Use Databases **451**

Learning Outcome 11.2 **You will be able to explain how businesses use data warehouses, data marts, and data mining to manage data and how business information systems and business intelligence are used to make business decisions.**

Data Warehousing and Storage **451**

Data Warehouses and Data Marts.. 451
Objective 11.8 *Explain what data warehouses and data marts are and how they are used.*

HELPDESK: How Businesses Use Databases.. 451

BITS&BYTES: Data Warehouses Are Going to the Cloud... 453

Data Mining.. 453
Objective 11.9 *Describe data mining and how it works.*

BITS&BYTES: Hadoop: How Big Data Is Being Managed 455

ETHICS IN IT: Data, Data Everywhere, but Is It Protected?.. 456

Using Databases to Make Business Decisions **457**

Business Information Systems.. 457
Objective 11.10 *Describe the main types of business information systems and how they are used by business managers.*

BITS&BYTES: Virtual Agents: Expert Systems Replace People on the Web 458

SOUND BYTE: Analyzing Data with Microsoft Power BI Suite 462

TRENDS IN IT: Mobile Business Intelligence 463

SOLVE THIS: College Database 471

Chapter 12

Behind the Scenes: Networking and Security in the Business World 472

Part 1: Client/Server Networks and Topologies 474

Learning Outcome 12.1 You will be able to describe common types of client/server networks, servers found on them, and network topologies used to construct them.

Client/Server Network Basics 474

Networking Advantages 474
Objective 12.1 *List the advantages for businesses of installing a network.*

Comparing Client/Server and Peer-to-Peer Networks 475
Objective 12.2 *Explain the differences between a client/server network and a peer-to-peer network.*

Types of Client/Server Networks 476
Objective 12.3 *Describe the common types of client/server networks as well as other networks businesses use.*

BITS&BYTES: Your Car Network Can Be Hacked 479

Servers and Network Topologies 480

Servers 480
Objective 12.4 *List the common types of servers found on client/server networks.*

HELPDESK: Using Servers 481

TRENDS IN IT: Virtualization: Making Servers Work Harder 482

Network Topologies 483
Objective 12.5 *Describe the common types of network topologies and the advantages and disadvantages of each one.*

SOUND BYTE: Network Topology and Navigation Devices 485

TRY THIS: Sharing Folders on a Home Network Using Windows 490

MAKE THIS: MAKE: An App That Shares 491

Part 2: Setting Up Business Networks 492

Learning Outcome 12.2 You will be able to describe transmission media, network operating system software, and network navigation devices and explain major threats to network security and how to mitigate them.

Transmission Media 492

Wired and Wireless Transmission Media 492
Objective 12.6 *Describe the types of wired and wireless transmission media used in networks.*

BITS&BYTES: Go Green with Mobile Apps 494

Network Adapters and Navigation Devices 494

Network Adapters 494
Objective 12.7 *Describe how network adapters help data move around a network.*

MAC Addresses 496
Objective 12.8 *Define MAC addresses, and explain how they are used to move data around a network.*

Switches, Bridges, and Routers 497
Objective 12.9 *List the various network navigation devices, and explain how they help route data through networks.*

HELPDESK: Transmission Media and Network Adapters 496

Network Operating Systems and Network Security 498

Network Operating Systems 499
Objective 12.10 *Explain why network operating systems are necessary for networks to function.*

BITS&BYTES: Smart Lighting for Smart Homes 499

Client/Server Network Security 500
Objective 12.11 *List major security threats to networks, and explain how network administrators mitigate these threats.*

DIG DEEPER: The OSI Model: Defining Protocol Standards 501

SOUND BYTE: A Day in the Life of a Network Technician 502

ETHICS IN IT: How Should Companies Handle Data Breaches? 504

BITS&BYTES: Are Your Photos Helping Criminals Target You? 505

SOLVE THIS: Cyber Security Flyer and Mail Merge 513

Chapter 13

Behind the Scenes: How the Internet Works 514

Part 1: Inner Workings of the Internet 516

Learning Outcome 13.1 **You will be able to explain how the Internet is managed and the details of how data is transmitted across the Internet.**

Internet Management and Networking 516

Management 516
Objective 13.1 *Describe the management of the Internet.*

Networking Components 517
Objective 13.2 *Explain how the Internet's networking components interact.*

Data Transmission 518
Objective 13.3 *List and describe the Internet protocols used for data transmission.*

BITS&BYTES: A Free Cloud-Based Server for You 518

Internet Identity 521

IP Addresses 521
Objective 13.4 *Explain how each device connected to the Internet is assigned a unique address.*

HELPDESK: Understanding IP Addresses, Domain Names, and Protocols................................ 521

BITS&BYTES: What's Your IP Address? 522

BITS&BYTES: Internet of Things Goes Shopping... 522

SOUND BYTE: Creating Web Pages with Squarespace.. 523

DIG DEEPER: Connection-Oriented Versus Connectionless Protocols....................................... 524

Domain Names 525
Objective 13.5 *Discuss how a numeric IP address is changed into a readable name.*

BITS&BYTES: Server in the Cloud 526

TRY THIS: Ping Me.. 529

MAKE THIS: Make: An Earthquake Detector 530

Part 2: Coding and Communicating on the Internet 531

Learning Outcome 13.2 **You will be able to describe the web technologies used to develop web applications.**

Web Technologies 531

Web Development... 531
Objective 13.6 *Compare and contrast a variety of web development languages.*

BITS&BYTES: CodePen: An Editing Community for Web Designers 532

SOUND BYTE: Client-Side Web Page Development... 535

Application Architecture 535
Objective 13.7 *Compare and contrast server-side and client-side application software.*

BITS&BYTES: Free Code Camp 537

Communications over the Internet 537

Types of Internet Communication 537
Objective 13.8 *Discuss the mechanisms for communicating via e-mail and instant messaging.*

BITS&BYTES: Google Inbox.. 539

Encryption... 540
Objective 13.9 *Explain how data encryption improves security.*

BITS&BYTES: Numbers: We Wouldn't Have Encryption Without Them! 541

ETHICS IN IT: Do We Really Want Strong Encryption? 542

HELPDESK: Keeping E-Mail Secure.. 542

TRENDS IN IT: Cognitive Computing 543

SOLVE THIS: Creating an HTML Document.. 551

Appendix A

The History of the Personal Computer.. A-1

Appendix B

Careers in IT B-1

Glossary G-1

Index I-1

About the Authors

Alan Evans, MS, CPA
aevans@mc3.edu

Alan is currently a faculty member at Moore College of Art and Design and Montgomery County Community College, teaching a variety of computer science and business courses. He holds a BS in accounting from Rider University and an MS in information systems from Drexel University, and he is a certified public accountant. After a successful career in business, Alan finally realized that his true calling is education. He has been teaching at the college level since 2000. Alan enjoys attending technical conferences and exploring new methods of engaging students.

Kendall Martin, PhD
kmartin@mc3.edu

Kendall is a professor of Computer Science at Montgomery County Community College with teaching experience at both the undergraduate and graduate levels at a number of institutions, including Villanova University, DeSales University, Ursinus College, and Arcadia University.

Kendall's education includes a BS in electrical engineering from the University of Rochester and an MS and a PhD in engineering from the University of Pennsylvania. She has industrial experience in research and development environments (AT&T Bell Laboratories) as well as experience with several start-up technology firms.

Mary Anne Poatsy, MBA
mpoatsy@mc3.edu

Mary Anne is a senior faculty member at Montgomery County Community College, teaching various computer application and concepts courses in face-to-face and online environments. She enjoys speaking at various professional conferences about innovative classroom strategies. She holds a BA in psychology and education from Mount Holyoke College and an MBA in finance from Northwestern University's Kellogg Graduate School of Management.

Mary Anne has been in teaching since 1997, ranging from elementary and secondary education to Montgomery County Community College, Gwynedd-Mercy College, Muhlenberg College, and Bucks County Community College, as well as training in the professional environment. Before teaching, she was a vice president at Shearson Lehman Hutton in the Municipal Bond Investment Banking Department.

Dedication

For my wife, Patricia, whose patience, understanding, and support continue to make this work possible … especially when I stay up past midnight writing! And to my parents, Jackie and Dean, who taught me the best way to achieve your goals is to constantly strive to improve yourself through education.

Alan Evans

For all the teachers, mentors, and gurus who have popped in and out of my life.

Kendall Martin

For my husband, Ted, who unselfishly continues to take on more than his fair share to support me throughout this process, and for my children, Laura, Carolyn, and Teddy, whose encouragement and love have been inspiring.

Mary Anne Poatsy

Acknowledgments

First, we would like to thank our students. We constantly learn from them while teaching, and they are a continual source of inspiration and new ideas.

We could not have written this book without the loving support of our families. Our spouses and children made sacrifices (mostly in time not spent with us) to permit us to make this dream into a reality.

Although working with the entire team at Pearson has been a truly enjoyable experience, a few individuals deserve special mention. The constant support and encouragement we receive from Jenifer Niles, Executive Portfolio Product Manager, and Andrew Gilfillan, VP, Editorial Director, continually make this book grow and change. Our heartfelt thanks go to Shannon LeMay-Finn, our Developmental Editor. Her creativity, drive, and management skills helped make this book a reality. We also would like to extend our appreciation to Pearson Content Producers, particularly Laura Burgess, and the vendor teams, who work tirelessly to ensure that our book is published on time and looks fabulous. The timelines are always short, the art is complex, and there are many people with whom they have to coordinate tasks. But they make it look easy! We'd like to extend our thanks to the media and MyLab IT team—Eric Hakanson, Becca Golden, Amanda Losonsky, and Heather Darby for all of their hard work and dedication.

There are many people whom we do not meet at Pearson and elsewhere who make significant contributions by designing the book, illustrating, composing the pages, producing the media, and securing permissions. We thank them all.

And finally, we would like to thank the reviewers and the many others who contribute their time, ideas, and talents to this project. We appreciate their time and energy, as their comments help us turn out a better product each edition. A special thanks goes to Rick Wolff, a wonderfully talented infographic designer who helped by creating the infographics for this text.

Letter from the Authors

Our 15th Edition—A Letter from the Authors

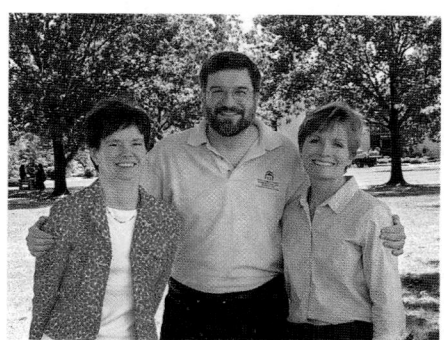

Why We Wrote This Book

The pace of technological change is ever increasing. In education, we have seen this impact us more than ever recently—the Maker movement, MOOCs, touch-screen mobile delivery, and Hangouts are now fixed parts of our environment.

Even the most agile of learners and educators need support in keeping up with this pace of change. We have responded by integrating material to help students develop skills for web application and mobile programming. We see the incredible value of these skills and their popularity with students, and have included Make This exercises for each chapter. These exercises gently bring the concepts behind mobile app development to life. In addition, there is a Solve This exercise in each chapter that reinforces chapter content while also applying Microsoft Office skills. These projects help to promote students' critical thinking and problem-solving skills, which employers highly value.

We have introduced eight new Helpdesk training modules and two new IT Simulations to continue to provide students with an active learning environment in which they can reinforce their learning of chapter objectives. In addition, in this edition we have focused more on artificial intelligence and its impact on how we will use technology ethically. We also continue to emphasize the many aspects of ethics in technology debates. Some of the new Helpdesks and IT Simulations support instruction on how to conduct thoughtful and respectful discussion on complex ethical issues.

Our combined 50 years of teaching computer concepts have coincided with sweeping innovations in computing technology that have affected every facet of society. From iPads to Web 2.0, computers are more than ever a fixture of our daily lives—and the lives of our students. But although today's students have a much greater comfort level with their digital environment than previous generations, their knowledge of the machines they use every day is still limited.

Part of the student-centered focus of our book has to do with making the material truly engaging to students. From the beginning, we have written *Technology in Action* to focus on what matters most to today's student. Instead of a history lesson on the microchip, we focus on tasks students can accomplish with their computing devices and skills they can apply immediately in the workplace, the classroom, and at home.

We strive to keep the text as current as publishing timelines allow, and we are constantly looking for the next technology trend or gadget. We have augmented the text with weekly technology updates to help you keep on top of the latest breaking developments and continue to include a number of multimedia components to enrich the classroom and student learning experience. The result is a learning system that sparks student interest by focusing on the material they want to learn (such as how to integrate computing devices into a home network) while teaching the material they need to learn (such as how networks work). The sequence of topics is carefully set up to mirror the typical student learning experience.

As they read through this text, your students will progress through stages and learning outcomes of increasing difficulty:

1. Thinking about how technology offers them the power to change their society and their world and examining why it's important to be computer fluent
2. Understanding the basic components of computing devices
3. Connecting to and exploring the Internet
4. Exploring application software
5. Learning the operating system and personalizing their computer

6. Evaluating and upgrading computing devices
7. Understanding home networking options
8. Creating digital assets and understanding how to legally distribute them
9. Keeping computing devices safe from hackers
10. Going behind the scenes, looking at technology in greater detail

We strive to structure the book in a way that makes navigation easy and reinforces key concepts. We continue to design the text around learning outcomes and objectives, making them a prominent part of the chapter structure. Students will see the learning outcomes and objectives in the chapter opener, throughout the text itself, as well as in the summary so they understand just what they are expected to learn.

We continue to structure the book in a progressive manner, intentionally introducing on a basic level in the earlier chapters concepts that students traditionally have trouble with and then later expanding on those concepts in more detail when students have become more comfortable with them. Thus, the focus of the early chapters is on practical uses for the computer, with real-world examples to help the students place computing in a familiar context.

For example, we introduce basic hardware components in Chapter 2, and then we go into increasingly greater detail on some hardware components in Chapter 6. The Behind the Scenes chapters venture deeper into the realm of computing through in-depth explanations of how programming, networks, the Internet, and databases work. They are specifically designed to keep more experienced students engaged and to challenge them with interesting research assignments.

In addition to extensive review, practice, and assessment content, each chapter contains several problem-solving, hands-on activities that can be carried out in the classroom or as homework:

- The **Try This** exercises lead students to explore a particular computing feature related to the chapter.
- The **Make This** exercises are hands-on activities that lead students to explore mobile app development.
- The **Solve This** exercises integrate and reinforce chapter concepts with Microsoft Office skills.

Throughout the years we have also developed a comprehensive multimedia program to reinforce the material taught in the text and to support both classroom lectures and distance learning:

- The **Helpdesk training content**, created specifically for *Technology in Action*, enables students to take on the role of a helpdesk staffer fielding questions posed by computer users.
- Exciting **Sound Byte multimedia**—fully updated and integrated with the text—expand student mastery of complex topics.
- **IT Simulations** are detailed, interactive scenarios covering the core chapter topic. As students work through the simulation, they apply what they have learned and demonstrate understanding in an active learning environment.
- The **TechBytes Weekly blog** delivers the latest technology news stories to you for use in your classroom. Each is accompanied by specific discussion topics and activities to expand on what is within the textbook materials.

This book is designed to reach the students of the twenty-first century and prepare them for the role they can take in their own community and the world. It has been an honor to work with you over the past 15 years to present and explain new technologies to students, and to show them the rapidly growing importance of technology in our world.

What's New

Technology in Action, 15th Edition

Welcome to the Fifteenth Edition of *Technology in Action!*

The best-selling *Technology in Action* continues to deliver an engaging approach to teaching the topics and skills students need to be digitally literate. Using practical content, hands-on projects, and interactive simulation lessons, students are engaged in learning.

For *Technology in Action* 15th edition, we have added innovative and important content updates, including *new* coverage of emerging technologies and artificial intelligence, especially in Chapter 1. The technology used throughout the text has been updated and expanded, including 8 *new* Helpdesk training modules and 2 *new* IT Simulations. Each chapter now has *two* Helpdesk trainings, *two* Sound Byte lessons, and *one* IT Sim to provide students with a consistent learning experience from chapter to chapter.

Using these resources and the practical content, students will be prepared for academic, professional, and personal success. And, if they are using MyLab IT, they can earn the *Digital Competency* badge to easily demonstrate their skills to potential employers.

Highlights of What's New

- New and updated content throughout
- New Helpdesk modules in Chapters 1, 7, 8, 9, 10, 11, and 12 ensure that each chapter offers two Helpdesks for a consistent learning experience
- New IT Simulations for Chapter 1 and Chapter 12 to ensure all chapters have one
- Updated content with new artificial intelligence and emerging technologies coverage
- New images and updated quizzes throughout

Explore the Hallmarks and Features of *Technology in Action, 15th Edition*

INSTRUCTION: Engage all types of learners with a variety of instructional resources

- **Pearson Text 2.0** students interact with the learning resources directly and receive immediate feedback.
- **Chapter Overview Videos** provide students with a quick look at what they will learn in the chapter.
- **PowerPoint and Audio Presentations** can be used in class for lecture or assigned to students, particularly online students, for instruction and review.
- **TechBytes Weekly** is a weekly blog that helps you keep your course current by providing interesting and relevant news items and ready-to-use discussion questions.
- **Make This! Projects** provide activities where students build programs that run on their mobile devices. Most of the chapters use App Inventor to build Android apps that can be installed on any Android device or emulated for students using iOS devices. Each project includes instructions and a how-to video.

  Annotated Instructor Chapter Tabs provide teaching tips, homework and assessment suggestions, brief overviews of each chapter's Try This, Make This, and Solve This exercises, as well as select Sound Byte talking points and ethics debate starters.

PRACTICE: Hands-on resources and simulations allow students to demonstrate understanding

- **Try This Projects** are hands-on projects students complete to practice and demonstrate proficiency with important topics. Each project is accompanied by a how-to video.
- **Solve This! Projects** put the concepts students are learning into action through real-world problem solving using Microsoft Word, Access, and Excel. Grader versions of some of these projects are in MyLab IT.
- **Helpdesks** are interactive lessons based on chapter objectives. Students play the role of a helpdesk staffer assisting customers via a live chat, decision-based simulation.
- **Sound Bytes** provide an audio/visual lesson on additional topics related to the chapter, including a brief quiz at the end.
- **IT Simulations** provide 13 individual scenarios that students work through in an active learning environment.

REVIEW: Self-check resources keep learning on track

- **Chapter Overview Videos** for Parts 1 and 2 of the chapter provide an objective-based review of what students should have learned. Videos have a short quiz and can be accessed from mobile devices for a quick review.

- Check Your Understanding Quizzes Part 1 and 2 provide a self-check covering objectives in each part of the chapter so that students can see how well they are learning the content.

ASSESSMENT: Measure performance with ready-to-use resources

- Chapter Quiz provides a way for students to test that they have learned the material from the entire chapter.

- Critical Thinking Questions require that students demonstrate their understanding through written answers that are manually graded.
- Testbank Exams provide customizable prebuilt, autograded, objective-based questions covering the chapter objectives.

15th Edition Content Changes

In addition to these changes, all chapters have been updated with new images, current topics, and state-of-the art technology coverage. Some of the chapter changes are listed here:

Chapter 1

- Learning Outcomes and Learning Objectives have been revised as needed.
- Throughout the chapter, text, figures, and photos have been updated.
- A new section on artificial intelligence has been added to the chapter.
- The section on technology and careers has been updated to shift the focus towards artificial intelligence.
- Two new Helpdesks have been developed for the chapter: Technology Impacts and The Impact of Artificial Intelligence.

Chapter 2

- A new IT Simulation has been added to the chapter.
- Learning Outcomes and Learning Objectives have been revised as needed.
- Throughout the chapter, text, figures, and photos have been updated.
- A new Bits&Bytes, "Sleep Better and Avoid Eyestrain: Use Less Blue Light" has been added.

Chapter 3

- Learning Outcomes and Learning Objectives have been revised as needed.
- Throughout the chapter, text, figures, and photos have been updated.
- A new How Cool Is This on face recognition technology.
- A new Bits&Bytes, "Secure Messaging Apps," has been added.
- A new Bits&Bytes, "Bitcoin: A Form of Virtual Currency," has been added.

Chapter 4

- Learning Outcomes and Learning Objectives have been revised as needed.
- Throughout the chapter, text, figures, and photos have been updated.

Chapter 5

- Learning Outcomes and Learning Objectives have been revised as needed.
- A new Bits&Bytes—""Operating Systems for the Home" has been added.

Chapter 6

- Learning Outcomes and Learning Objectives have been revised as needed.
- Throughout the chapter, text, figures, and photos have been updated.

Chapter 7

- Learning Outcomes and Learning Objectives have been revised as needed.
- Throughout the chapter, text, figures, and photos have been updated.
- The Bits&Bytes "Net Neutrality" has been updated.
- A new Bits&Bytes, "5G Is Coming—Is It Worth the Wait?" has been added.
- A new HelpDesk, "Managing and Securing Wireless Networks" has been added.

Chapter 8

- Learning Outcomes and Learning Objectives have been revised as needed.
- Throughout the chapter, text, figures, and photos have been updated.
- A new Helpdesk, "Managing Digital Media," has been added.

Chapter 9

- Learning Outcomes and Learning Objectives have been revised as needed.
- Throughout the chapter, images and text have been updated
- A new Helpdesk, "Threats to Your Assets," has been added to the chapter.

Chapter 10

- A new Helpdesk, "A Variety of Programming Languages," has been added.
- Learning Outcomes and Learning Objectives have been revised as needed.
- Throughout the chapter, text, figures, and photos have been updated, including coverage of latest programming technologies like Swift and JSON.

Chapter 11

- Learning Outcomes and Learning Objectives have been revised as needed.
- Throughout the chapter, text, figures, and photos have been updated.
- The Bits&Bytes, "Music Streaming Services Use Databases," has been updated.

- A new HelpDesk, "How Businesses Use Databases," has been added.

Chapter 12

- Learning Outcomes and Learning Objectives have been revised as needed.
- Throughout the chapter, text, figures, and photos have been updated.
- A new Helpdesk module "Transmission Media and Network Adapters" has been added.

Chapter 13

- Learning Outcomes and Learning Objectives have been revised as needed.
- Throughout the chapter, text, figures, and photos have been updated.

Visual Walk-Through

Topic Sequence

Concepts are covered in a progressive manner between chapters to mirror the typical student learning experience.

Hardware First Introduced
Chapter 2 is the first time students read about introductory hardware. It's covered at the beginning level because this is students' experience level at this point of the book.

Hardware Taught in More Depth in Additional Chapters
In later chapters, students read about hardware in greater depth because they're more experienced and comfortable working with their computers.

Appendices
Appendices cover the history of the PC and careers in IT.

Clearly Defined Learning Objectives and Outcomes
Provide measurable goals for instructors and students.

Multimedia Cues
Visual integration of multimedia resources, including the Helpdesks, Sound Bytes, and Chapter Overview Videos.

How Cool Is This?
Highlights the latest and greatest websites, gadgets, and multimedia.

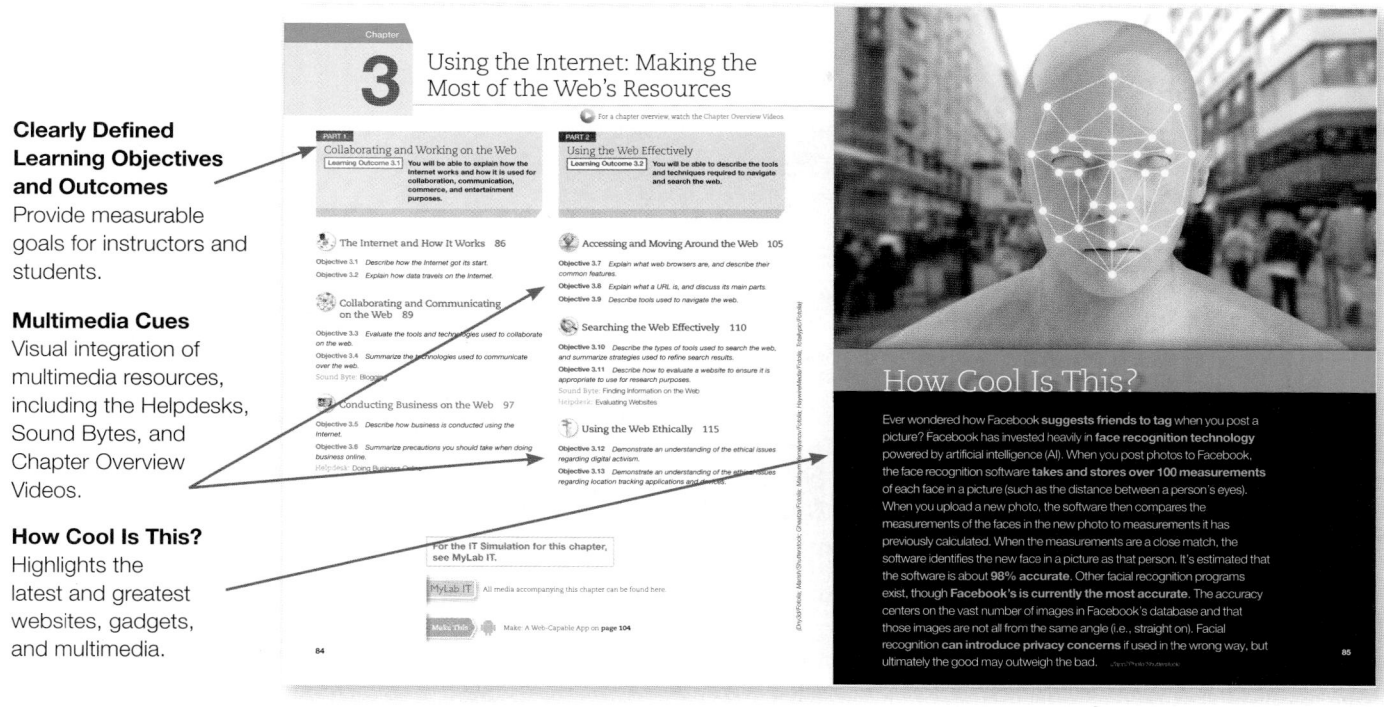

Bits & Bytes
Help make the topics immediately relevant to students' lives.

Dig Deeper
Boxes cover technical topics in depth to challenge advanced students.

Ethics in IT
Boxes examine the ethical dilemmas involved with technology.

Trends in IT
Boxes explore hot topics in computing.

Student Textbook

Try This and Make This
Hands-on activities found between Parts 1 and 2 of each chapter.

End of Chapter Quiz
Multiple Choice, True/False, and Critical Thinking questions at the end of each chapter help students assess their comprehension of chapter material.

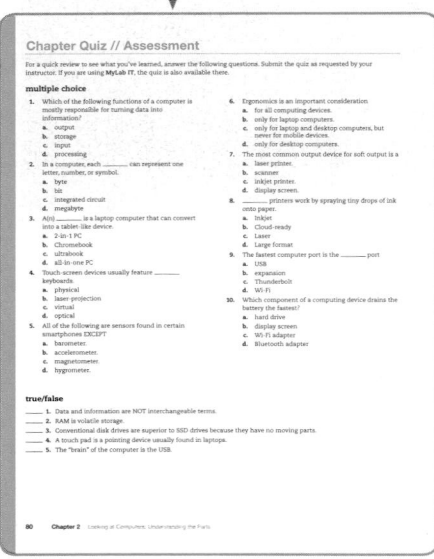

Check Your Understanding
Quizzes Provide an auto-graded self-check covering objectives in each part of the chapter.

Solve This
Exercises that put the concepts students are learning into action using a Microsoft Office application.

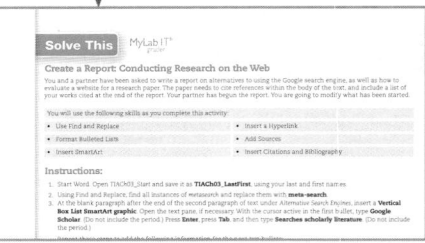

Sound Bytes
Multimedia lessons with video, audio, or animation.

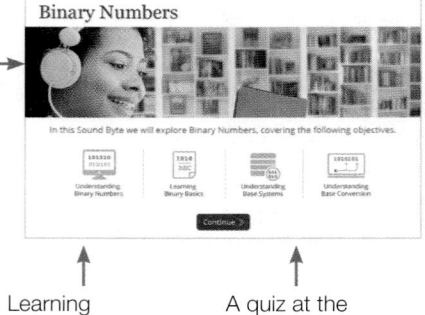

Learning Objectives are integrated throughout the Sound Bytes.

A quiz at the end tests that students have learned key concepts.

Helpdesk
Interactive training that puts the student in the role of a helpdesk staffer fielding questions about technology.

Supervisor available to assist students.

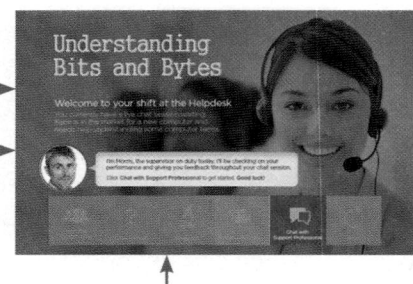

Features textbook references within each Helpdesk and assessment at the end.

MyLab IT

MyLab IT for *Technology in Action* with the Enhanced eBook personalizes learning to help your students better prepare and learn—resulting in more dynamic experiences in the classroom and improved performance in the course. Specific features include:

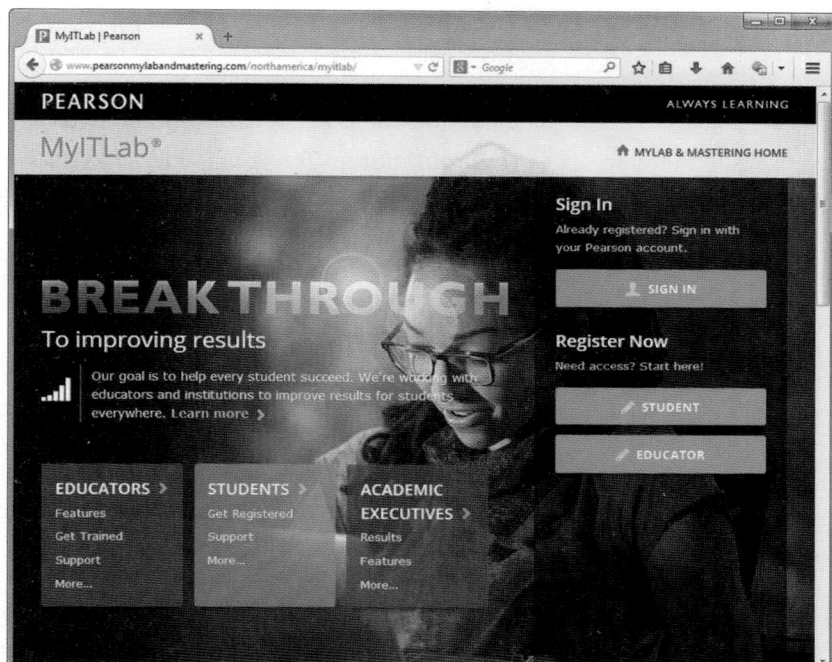

- **Badging:** A Digital Competency badge is offered to allow students to demonstrate their digital knowledge This badge represents that students have the basic digital understanding to enter the workforce and be savvy consumers.

- **Adaptive Learning:** *A way to enable personalized learning at scale.* Not every student learns the same way and at the same rate. MyLab IT with Adaptive Learning continuously assesses student performance and activity in real time, and, using data and analytics, personalizes content to reinforce concepts that target each student's strengths and weaknesses.

- **A powerful homework and test manager:** MyLab IT lets you create, import, and manage online homework assignments, Helpdesk and Soundbyte activities, quizzes, and tests that are automatically graded. The bottom line: MyLab IT means less time grading and more time teaching.

- **Comprehensive online course content:** Filled with a wealth of content that is tightly integrated with your textbook, MyLab IT lets you easily add, remove, or modify existing instructional material. You can also add your own course materials to suit the needs of your students or department. In short, MyLab IT lets you teach exactly as you'd like.

- **Robust Gradebook tracking:** The online Gradebook automatically tracks your students' results on tests, homework, and practice exercises and gives you control over managing results and calculating grades. And, it lets you measure and document your students' learning outcomes.

- **Easily scalable and shareable content:** MyLab IT enables you to manage multiple class sections, and lets other instructors copy your settings so a standardized syllabus can be maintained across your department.

The media is available in MyLab IT, including Helpdesks, Sound Bytes, Chapter Overview Videos, Chapter Grader Projects, and the IT Simulations.

• **The interactive Pearson eText 2.0** in MyLab IT provides an interactive environment that allows students to use technology as they learn. They don't have to stop reading to find the activities such as Helpdesks, Sound Bytes, and Chapter Overview Videos—they just click on them and immediately experience the activity.

• **IT Simulations:** These fully interactive, scenario-based simulations allow students to demonstrate their understanding of the chapter topic in an experiential learning environment.

• **Sound Bytes:** These multimedia lessons provide a multimodal approach to instruction in which topics are presented with audio, video, and interactive activities. The topics covered in the Sound Bytes expand on the coverage in the book to dive into newer technology or more depth on a specific subject.

• **Helpdesks:** These highly interactive, engaging activities provide students with a realistic experience in the role of a helpdesk staffer answering technology questions. These formative assessments cover core objectives in the chapter. As students assume the role of the helpdesk staffer, they apply what they are learning in a new environment. The assessment questions after each Helpdesk provide instructors with a tool to gauge and track students' progress.

• **Make This** projects address the hot area of mobile app creation! Each chapter includes a Make This mobile app project, most of which use App Inventor. By the end of the course, students will have completed 13 small projects that provide them with new skills they can use to create their own apps. And if they don't have an Android device, they can use the emulator and still learn the skills.

• **Solve This** projects put the concepts students are learning into action through real-world problem solving using a Microsoft Office application or other technology tool. For Word and Excel projects, there is also a Grader version in MyLab IT.

• **Chapter Overview Videos:** The Chapter Overview Videos provide an author-narrated video preview/review of each chapter part in an easy-to-use format students can view on their phones, tablets, or computers.

• **With TechBytes Weekly, every week is new!** This weekly newsfeed provides two timely articles to save instructors the prep time required for adding interesting and relevant news items to their weekly lectures. TechBytes Weekly also features valuable links and other resources, including discussion questions and course activities.

Annotated Instructor Chapter Guides

Provided for each chapter are guides that can be printed and inserted in your copy of the text. Sample contents are shown below.

FRONT OF CHAPTER TAB

On the front side of each chapter tab, you'll find the following categories:

IN THE CLASSROOM: Activities you can use in a classroom or in online classes, including:

- **PowerPoint Presentations**
- **Discussion Exercises**
- **Helpdesks**
- **Sound Bytes**

HOMEWORK: Activities used out of class for assessment or preparation for the next chapter, including:

- **Web Resource Projects**
- **Helpdesks**
- **Sound Bytes**

ASSESSMENT:

- **Blackboard**
- **WebCT**
- **TestGen**
- **MyLab IT**
- **Student Text Test Bank**
- **Sound Byte Test Bank**
- **Helpdesk Test Bank**

The back side of each chapter tab includes notes about that chapter's Try This, Make This, and Solve This exercises.

ETHICS TAB

On the Ethics tab, you will find the following:

OPPOSING VIEWPOINTS TABLE: Outlines ethics topics that you can use to debate in the classroom.

KEYWORDS: Provides you with additional words with which to search the Internet for more information related to the ethics topic.

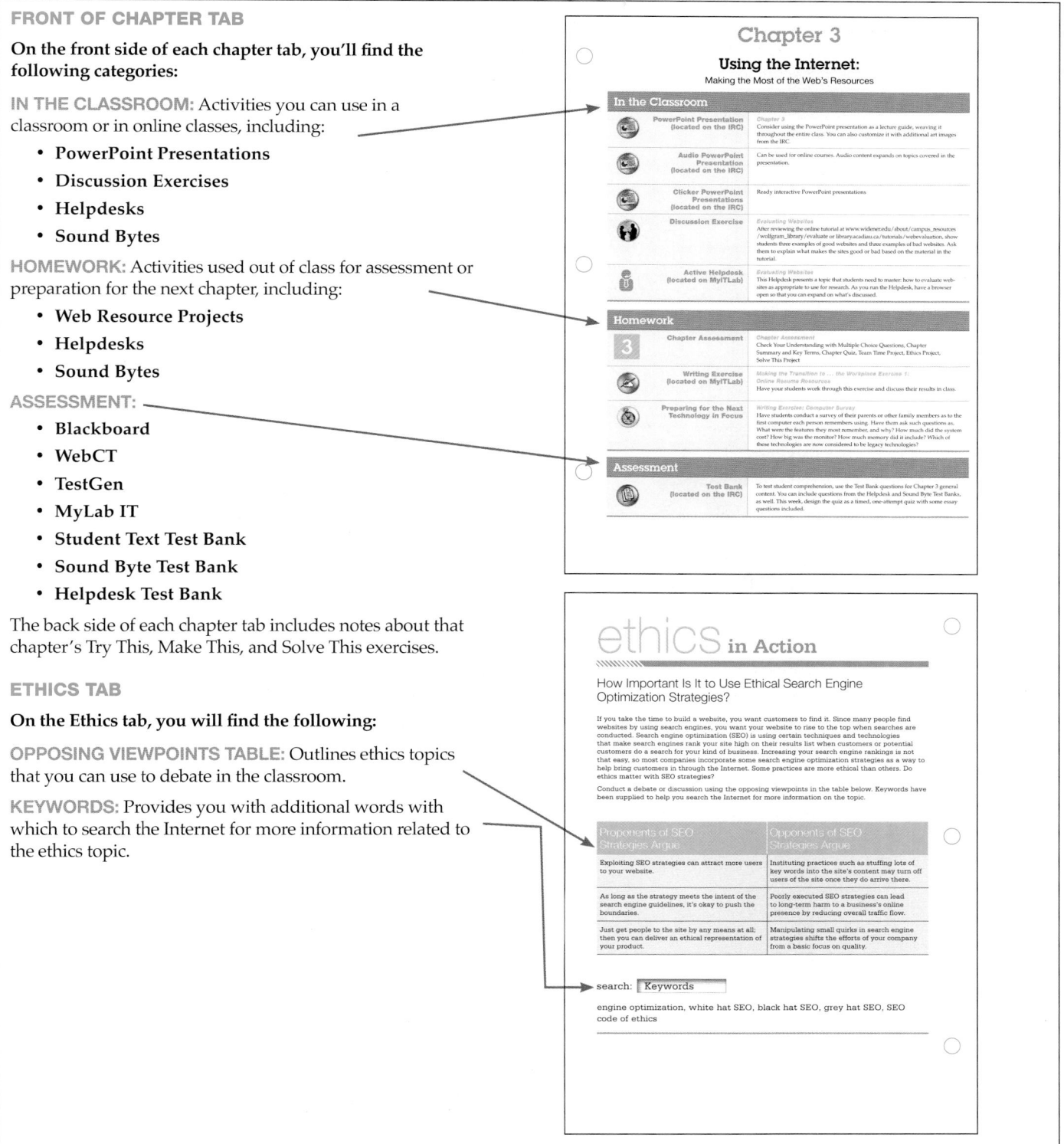

Instructor Resources

- PowerPoint Presentations
- Student Text Test Bank
- Sound Byte Test Bank
- Help Desk Test Bank
- End of Chapter Answer Keys
- Rubrics
- Web Resources

- Image Library
- Sample Syllabi
- Additional Web Projects
- What's New in 15e
- Transition Guide
- TestGen

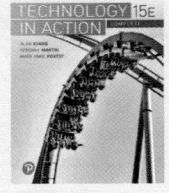

**Technology in Action
Complete, 15/E**
**Alan Evans
Kendall Martin
Mary Anne Poatsy**
ISBN-10: 0-13-483787-8
ISBN-13: 978-0-13-483787-1

Contact your local Pearson sales rep to learn more about the *Technology in Action* instructional system.

For a chapter overview, watch the Chapter Overview Videos.

PART 1

Technology in Society

| Learning Outcome 1.1 | You will be able to discuss the impact of the tools of modern technology on national and global issues. |

 Technology in a Global Society 4

Objective 1.1 *Describe various technological tools being used to impact national and global issues.*

Objective 1.2 *Describe various global social issues that are being affected by technology.*

 Technology Connects Us with Others 7

Objective 1.3 *Describe how technology is changing how and why we connect and collaborate with others.*

Objective 1.4 *Summarize how technology has impacted the way we choose and consume products and services.*

Helpdesk: Technology Impacts

 The Importance of Computer Literacy 9

Objective 1.5 *Characterize computer literacy and explain why it is important to be computer literate.*

Sound Byte: Virtual Computer Tour

PART 2

Emerging Technologies and Ethical Computing

| Learning Outcome 1.2 | You will be able to describe emerging technologies, such as artificial intelligence, and how technology creates new ethical debates. |

 Artificial Intelligence 14

Objective 1.6 *Describe artificial intelligence systems and explain their main goals.*

Helpdesk: The Impact of Artificial Intelligence.

 Working with Artificial Intelligence and Other Information Technologies 18

Objective 1.7 *Describe how artificial intelligence and other emerging technologies are providing career opportunities.*

 Ethical Computing 23

Objective 1.8 *Define ethics and describe various ethical systems.*

Objective 1.9 *Describe influences on the development of your personal ethics.*

Objective 1.10 *Present examples of how technology creates ethical challenges.*

Sound Byte: How to Debate Ethical Issues

For the IT Simulation for this chapter, see MyLab IT.

MyLab IT   All media accompanying this chapter can be found here.

Make This Make: A Virtual Assistant on **page 13**

How Cool Is This?

Want to **make a difference with technology**? The good news is that learning about technology has never been easier. For example, **Massive Open Online Courses (MOOCs)** offer **free instruction** from top universities on programming, algorithm design, and hardware. And **hackathons** organized by various student groups around the country bring together thousands of students to program with one another in marathon weekends, building everything from **crazy contraptions to life-saving devices**. You can follow the projects made at hackathons using tools like **Devpost and GitHub**, where info about hackathons and the actual code produced is freely available. Meanwhile, **civic hacking events**, like one called **Random Hacks of Kindness**, are helping people create apps to track lobbyists in government, to map the locations of murals in a city, and to help organize people to dig out fire hydrants after snowstorms. Want to make a difference in the world? Just get started! *(Luke MacGregor/Bloomberg/Getty Images)*

Technology in Society

> **Learning Outcome 1.1**   **You will be able to discuss the impact of the tools of modern technology on national and global issues.**

Ask yourself: Why are you in this class? Maybe it's a requirement for your degree, or maybe you want to improve your computer skills. But let's step back and look at the bigger picture.

Technology is a tool that enables us all to make an impact beyond our own lives. We've all seen movies that dangle the dream in front of us of being the girl or guy who saves the world—and gets to drive a nice car while doing it!

Technology can be your ticket to doing just that by influencing and participating in projects that will change the world.

Technology in a Global Society

Recent national and global issues are showing that technology is accelerating change around the world and galvanizing groups of people in new ways. Let's look at a few examples.

Impact of Tools of Modern Technology

Objective 1.1   *Describe various technological tools being used to impact national and global issues.*

Social Media Tools

We're all familiar with **social media** tools like Twitter, Facebook, and Instagram that enable people to connect and exchange ideas. These same tools are also bringing together people facing similar problems to fight for social change. For example, the Twitter hashtag #BlackLivesMatter was used to galvanize a movement to protest the use of excessive and even deadly force against African Americans by law enforcement personnel in the United States. Videos streamed live over Facebook from cell phones, and released video captured from officers' body cameras went viral, highlighting the abuses. In this way, technology brought to light an important social issue and was a key means for fostering national discussion.

Britain's Brexit vote (see Figure 1.1)—to exit or remain in the European Union—was fought in large part on social media battlegrounds. The most frequent posters, however, were *bot accounts*, automated programs retweeting news stories and quotes. As you can see, how we conduct informed political discussion in the age of social media is still developing.

Social media tools are also providing a level of instant connection and information distribution that is reshaping the world—both positively and negatively. Although social media has brought important issues to light, as more people get the majority of their news from unsubstantiated, incomplete reports on social media, there can be negative consequences, too. Knowing how to use and critically evaluate social media will be an important skill now and in the future.

Figure 1.1 The Brexit referendum, which resulted in Britain leaving the European Union, was a close decision with fierce debate conducted on social media. *(Momius/Fotolia)*

Crisis-Mapping Tool

Another example of the interaction of technology and society is the software tool Ushahidi. Following a disputed election in Kenya, violence broke out all over the country. Nairobi lawyer Ory Okolloh tried to get word of the violence out to the world through her blog, but she couldn't keep up with the volume of reports. However, two programmers saw her request for help and in a few days created Ushahidi (Swahili for "testimony"). It is a **crisis-mapping tool** that collects information from e-mails, text messages, blog posts, and Twitter tweets and then maps them, instantly making the information publicly available. The developers then made Ushahidi a free platform anyone in the world can use (see Figure 1.2). It has since been used in several international disasters. When a tsunami brought Japan

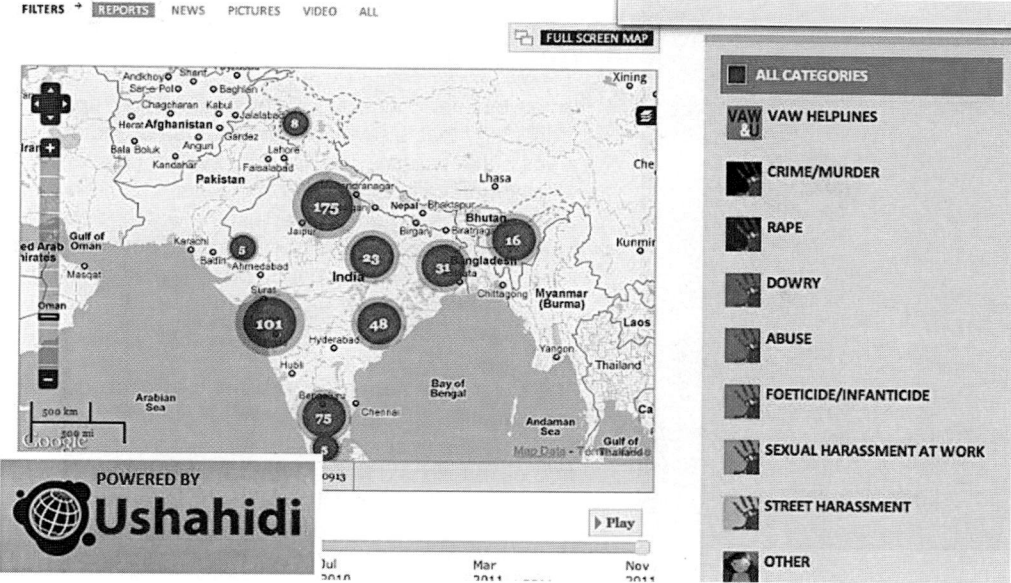

FILTERS → REPORTS NEWS PICTURES VIDEO ALL

ALL CATEGORIES

VAW HELPLINES
CRIME/MURDER
RAPE
DOWRY
ABUSE
FOETICIDE/INFANTICIDE
SEXUAL HARASSMENT AT WORK
STREET HARASSMENT
OTHER

Figure 1.2 Ushahidi crisis-mapping software has been used to identify areas of violence against women in India. *(Ushahidi, Inc., www.ushahidi.com)*

to the brink of a nuclear catastrophe, Ushahidi let anyone with a mobile phone find locations with clean water and food. It has been used to coordinate the anti-apartheid movement in Palestine and to raise awareness about violence against women and children in India. In what other ways will technology help us face times of crisis?

Global Issues

Objective 1.2 *Describe various global social issues that are being affected by technology.*

Trends from mobile devices to new levels of computing power have changed how we live in the world. Let's look at the different global social issues that are being affected by technology.

Health Care

Infectious diseases account for about one-fifth of all deaths worldwide. Researchers say the odds of a flu pandemic occurring in the next century are nearly 100%. Could technology help us develop and deliver vaccines in a way that saves lives? Could our own mobile devices help report the location of illness and help track the geographical pattern of an outbreak? With newer scientific visualization tools, scientists are developing antibodies for flu viruses and even HIV, viruses that are difficult to target because they continually change shape. Computationally intense modeling software is helping researchers increase the pace of vaccine production, saving lives.

As we learn more about the terrible consequences of concussion injuries, technology is playing a part in providing a solution. Researchers now know that even without an actual concussion, athletes can sustain serious damage from repeated impacts of their brain against the skull. Many college teams now use helmets with embedded sensors that can report the precise location and force of an impact to the head, providing team physicians access to important information. Using computer simulation and collecting impact data from sensors in current football helmets, startup company VICIS has been able to design an impact-reducing football helmet.

The Environment

What if every cell phone in the world had built-in atmospheric sensors? Then millions of points of air and water quality data from around the world could be constantly acquired. Tagged with geographical information, the data could alert scientists to new trends in our environment. Ideas like

$$f(x) = \sum_{i=0}^{\infty} \frac{f^{(i)}(0)}{i!} x^i$$

Figure 1.3 The Next Einstein Initiative (NEI) is rallying the support of the world to identify mathematical genius. *(Alistair Cotton/123RF)*

these are being explored by Mark Nieuwenhuijsen of the Center for Research in Environmental Epidemiology in Barcelona, Spain.

Smart Internet-connected water sprinklers are another technology that is saving water in California and other dry areas of the country. The sprinkler system checks the weather forecasts so it won't use water when rain is coming the next day. It can adjust the watering schedule based on the season and can adjust the times of watering to encourage root growth. The system is showing a 30% reduction in water usage.

The Digital Divide

There is a great gap in the levels of Internet access and the availability of technical tools in different regions of the world. The term coined for this difference in ease of access to technology is the **digital divide**. One danger of a digital divide is that it prevents us from using all the minds on the planet to solve the planet's problems. But this challenge created by technology is also being answered by technology.

The Next Einstein Initiative (NEI) is a plan to focus resources on the talented mathematical minds of Africa (see Figure 1.3). By expanding the African Institute for Mathematical Sciences (AIMS) across the continent, the future of Africa can be profoundly changed. Cambridge professor Neil Turok founded AIMS to bring together the brightest young minds across Africa with the best lecturers in the world. The NEI has won funding from Google's Project 10^{100}, an initiative to award \$10 million to a set of five projects selected by open public voting. By capturing the enthusiasm of the world with presentations distributed through TED (**ted.com**) and Project 10^{100}, there is now a push to create 15 additional AIMS centers across Africa.

Figure 1.4 shows additional examples of people putting technology into action to impact the world. How will you join them?

Figure 1.4 Technology in Action: Taking on Global Problems

Person/ Organization	Global Problem	Technology Used	Action	Find Out More ...
Peter Gabriel/The Witness Project	Human rights abuses	Video cameras	Provide video documentation of human rights abuses; the project contributed to the arrest of warlords in the Democratic Republic of the Congo for the recruitment of child soldiers.	The Witness Project: **witness.org**
SolarRoad/ Netherlands	The need for a renewable, nonpolluting energy resource	Solar cells	Solar cells are integrated into the asphalt roadway. They collect solar energy and distribute electricity all day.	Netherlands SolaRoads: **solaroad.nl**
United Nations World Food Programme (WFP)	One in seven people in the world do not get enough food to eat	GIS (geographical information systems) and mobile devices	The WFP can analyze the location and need for food, positioning food where it will help the most.	World Food Programme: **wfp.org**
e-NABLE	Need for inexpensive, easily maintained prosthetic hands	3D printing	This group of engineers, parents, and artists work to print and assemble hands for people they may never meet.	e-NABLE: **enablingthefuture.org**

Technology Connects Us with Others

Technology is also allowing us to redefine very fundamental parts of our social makeup—how we think, how we connect with each other, and how we purchase and consume products.

Technology Impacts How and Why We Connect and Collaborate

Objective 1.3 *Describe how technology is changing how and why we connect and collaborate with others.*

Collaborating for the Benefit of Others

What do you think about in your free time? In the late twentieth century, a common trend was to think about what to buy next—or perhaps what to watch or listen to next. Information and products were being served up at an amazing rate, and the pattern of consumption became a habit. As more and more web applications began to appear that allowed each individual to become a "creator" of the web, a new kind of Internet came into being. It was nicknamed **Web 2.0**, and it had a set of features and functionality that allowed users to contribute content easily and to be easily connected to each other.

Web 2.0 has fostered a dramatic shift across the world, from simply consuming to having the ability to volunteer and collaborate on projects. The term **cognitive surplus** was coined to reflect the combination of leisure time and the tools to be creative. The availability of media tools and the easy connectivity of Web 2.0, along with generosity and a need to share, enable projects like Ushahidi and the Witness Project (see Figure 1.4) to emerge.

Connecting Through Business

One of the most profound ways we can connect with each other is to support other people's dreams. Kickstarter (**kickstarter.com**) helps us connect in this way by allowing people to post their ideas for community projects, games, and inventions and to ask for funding directly. Donors are given rewards for different levels of pledges, such as a signed edition of a book or a special color of a product. This style of generating capital to start a business is known as **crowdfunding**, asking for small donations from a large number of people, often using the Internet. Successful Kickstarter projects have included ice chests with integrated blenders, DNA analysis machines that could inexpensively diagnose disease, and many entertainment projects. In total, over $2.5 billion of funding for businesses has been raised using Kickstarter. Business ideas are not the only projects benefiting from crowdfunding. Sites like GoFundMe allow people in need to crowdfund to raise money for things such as medical bills or tuition.

Technology Impacts How We Consume

Objective 1.4 *Summarize how technology has impacted the way we choose and consume products and services.*

Technology is changing all aspects of how we decide what we'll purchase and how we actually buy goods and services.

Marketing

Marketing strategies are counting on the fact that most people have a cell phone with a camera and Internet access. **Quick response (QR) codes** like the one shown here let any piece of print host a direct link to online information and video content.

Marketers also have to be aware of the phenomenon of **crowdsourcing**—checking in with the voice of the crowd. Consumers are using apps like ScanLife to check people's verdicts on the quality of items. Forward-thinking companies are using this input to improve their products and services. AT&T, for example, has an app called Mark the Spot that lets customers report locations of dropped calls to help the company improve coverage.

Access Versus Ownership

Even the idea of ownership is evolving, thanks to new technologies. Items like cars and bikes can become "subscriptions" instead of large one-time purchases. For example, Zipcar allows hundreds of thousands of people to use shared cars. Citi Bike is catching on in many U.S. cities as a convenient and eco-friendly way to get around a metropolitan area. It has already seen riders take over 25 million trips (see Figure 1.5).

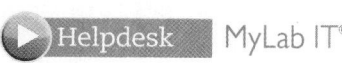

Technology Impacts

In this Helpdesk, you'll play the role of a helpdesk staffer fielding questions about ways in which technology affects society.

Figure 1.5 The Citi Bike program uses digital technology to change our lifestyle from one of ownership to one of subscription. *(Tim Clayton/Contributor/Corbis Sport/Getty Images)*

Figure 1.6 The Sharing Economy

A Day in the Life of the Collaborative Economy

Version 1.2

The growing Collaborative Economy is a peer-based movement that empowers individuals to get what they need from each other.

From crowd-funding new projects, to peer-based money lending, to people sharing physical goods, the collaborative movement stretches across many aspects of our lives and businesses.

We can see it activating all around us. But, is it having a broader impact beyond the limits of our own horizons? This illustration reveals the current, possible daily impact of the Collaborative Economy, making it easy to see the scope and impact of the entire evolving economy in one, single graphic.

Compiled by
Jeremiah Owyang. @jowyang
jeremiah@crowdcompanies.com
Founder of Crowd Companies

Design by Vladimir Mirkovic www.transartdesign.com
August 2014. Creative Commons license: Attribution-NonCommercial.
Access a digital copy of this graphic, and data credits at: http://bit.ly/ColEcoDay

$8.7M of new peer-to-peer loans on LendingClub each day.

55 campaigns successfully funded on Kickster per day

$285k funded on Indiegogo daily

247k sold items on Etsy per day

100,000 items traded on Listia each day.

13M Fon-shared Wifi hot spots available each day.

140k in 2013 people are staying in Airbnb rooms per day.

1,500 deliveries by Munchery per day from a shared kitchen

$217 is the average HomeAway host grosses per day

850 meals delivered on Spoonrocket in SF alone a day

375k On Aug 9th 2014 people stayed at Airbnb

16,666 meals served up on Blue Apron each day

157,143 Uber rides given each day.

66,666 rides on Lyft each day

6,666 jobs posted on Elance-oDesk each day

25,000+ people earning income with TaskRabbit.

10 MILLION miles of travel offered on BlaBlaCar per day.

$2M worth of work done on Elance-oDesk each day

EMPOWERED PEOPLE

MONEY · GOODS · FOOD · SERVICES · TRANSPORTATION · SPACE

PARTICIPATION IN THE COLLABORATIVE ECONOMY: RECENT AND PROJECTED

GOODS
Pre-owned goods — 46%
Loaner products — 11%
Custom products — 18%

FOOD & SERVICES
Professional services — 13%
Personal Services — 16%

TRANSPORTATION
Transportation Services — 9%
Loaner Vehicles — 9%

SPACE
Office Space — 7%
Place to Stay — 13%

MONEY
Moneylending — 10%
Crowdfunding — 12%

2013 Participation
2014 Participation (Projected from intent)

Data from recent report Sharing is the new Buying
with Vision Critical and Crowd Companies, 2014

CROWD COMPANIES
www.crowdcompanies.com

(The Sharing Economy, From A Day in the Life of the Collaborative Economy (INFOGRAPHIC, Ver 1.2) by Jeremiah Owyang.
Used with permission of Jeremiah Owyang.)

These subscription-style business models are spreading now to smaller goods. **Swap.com** helps people trade books, clothes, and video games with one another using the power of peer-to-peer connections—for example, to find those who want to swap used roller blades for a baby crib.

Collaborative consumption implies that we are joining together as a group to use a specific product more efficiently. We are so constantly connected with each other that we have again found the power of community. There are increasing opportunities to redistribute the things we have purchased and to share the services a product provides instead of owning it outright. Add in the pressure of mounting environmental concerns and global financial pressures, and we are migrating toward collaborative consumption (see Figure 1.6).

The Importance of Computer Literacy

Everywhere you go, you see ads for computers and other devices. Do you know what all the words in the ad mean? What is RAM? What is a GPU? What are MB, GB, GHz, and cache? How fast do you need your computer to be, and how much memory should it have? If you're computer literate, you'll be a more informed consumer when it comes time to buy computers, peripherals, and technology services. Understanding computer terminology and keeping current with technology will help you better determine which computers and devices you need.

Computer Literacy

Objective 1.5 *Characterize computer literacy and explain why it is important to be computer literate.*

Let's look at a few examples of what it means to be a savvy computer user and consumer.

Computer literacy. Computer literacy (see Figure 1.7) means you understand the capabilities and limitations of computers and you know how to use them safely and efficiently. If you're not computer literate now, don't worry—the following topics and more are covered in detail in the remaining chapters.

> ▶ **Sound Byte** MyLab IT®
>
> **Virtual Computer Tour**
>
> In this Sound Byte, you'll take a video tour of the inside of a desktop system unit. From opening the cover to locating the power supply, CPU, and memory, you'll become more familiar with what's inside your computer.

Figure 1.7 What Does It Mean to Be Computer Literate?

You can **avoid falling prey to hackers and viruses** because you are aware of how they operate.

You know how to **protect yourself from identity theft**.

You can **separate the real privacy and security risks from things you don't have to worry about**.

You know how to find information and **use the web effectively**.

You can **avoid being overwhelmed by spam, adware, and spyware**.

You know how to **diagnose and fix problems** with your hardware and software.

(Peter Dazeley/The Image Bank/Getty Images; Yuri Arcurs/DigitalVision/Getty Images; Zakai/DigitalVision Vectors/Getty Images; Justin Lewis/Stone/Getty Images; Argus/Fotolia; Ivanastar/E+/Getty Images)

Avoiding hackers and viruses. Do you know what hackers and viruses are? Both can threaten a computer's security. Being aware of how hackers and viruses operate and knowing the damage they can do to your computer can help you avoid falling prey to them.

Protecting your privacy. You've probably heard of identity theft—you see and hear news stories all the time about people whose "identities" are stolen and whose credit ratings are ruined by "identity thieves." But do you know how to protect yourself from identity theft when you're online?

Understanding the real risks. Part of being computer literate means being able to separate the real privacy and security risks from things you don't have to worry about. For example, do you know what a cookie is? Do you know whether it poses a privacy risk for you when you're on the Internet? What about a firewall? Do you know how to configure it for your needs?

Using the web wisely. Anyone who has ever searched the web can attest that finding information and finding good information are two different things. People who are computer literate know how to find the information they want effectively. They also know how to use the web to work well with others. Are you effective in how you use the web?

Avoiding online annoyances. If you have an e-mail account, chances are you've received electronic junk mail, or **spam**. How can you avoid spam? What about adware and spyware—do you know what they are? Do you know the difference between those and viruses, worms, and Trojan horses? Do you know which **software** programs—the instructions that tell the computer what to do—you should install on your computer to avoid online annoyances?

Being able to maintain, upgrade, and troubleshoot your computer. Learning how to care for and maintain your computer and knowing how to diagnose and fix certain problems can save you a lot of time and hassle. Do you know how to upgrade your computer if you want more memory, for example? Do you know which software and computer settings can keep your computer in top shape?

Keeping up to date. Finally, becoming computer literate means knowing which technologies are on the horizon and how to integrate them into your own life. Can you connect your television to your wireless network? What is a media server, and do you need one? Can a USB 3.0 flash drive be plugged into a USB 2.0 port? Do you know about artificial intelligence and how this and other technological advancements might impact your life? Knowing the answers to these and other questions will help you continue to become comfortable with interacting with technology.

This book will help you become computer literate. For example, in Chapter 3, you'll find out how to get the most from the web while staying free from the spam and clutter Internet surfing can leave behind on your computer. Chapter 6 shows you how to determine if your hardware is limiting your computer's performance and how to upgrade or shop for a new system or device. Chapter 9 covers how to keep your computer and your digital life secure. You'll be able to save money, time, and endless frustration by understanding the basics of how computers and computer systems operate.

Before moving on to Part 2:

1. ▶ Watch Chapter Overview Video 1.1.
2. Then take the Check Your Understanding quiz.

Check Your Understanding // Review & Practice

For a quick review to see what you've learned so far, answer the following questions.

multiple choice

1. Ushahidi is an example of what type of social media tool?
   a. blogging
   b. crisis-mapping
   c. video-sharing
   d. content curation

2. The digital divide occurred because
   a. the United States has the fastest Internet access.
   b. not everyone has equal access to the Internet.
   c. crowdfunding is increasing.
   d. everyone now has a smartphone.

3. Cognitive surplus means that we now find many people with
   a. more money than free time.
   b. limited access to the Internet.
   c. mobile devices.
   d. excess time and free tools for collaboration.

4. Crowdfunding helps startup businesses by
   a. selling stock more easily.
   b. using QR codes to advertise and market products.
   c. gathering financial contributions from supporters.
   d. replacing Web 2.0 technology.

5. Collaborative consumption is when people get together to
   a. find the best prices on products.
   b. increase the use of a single product by sharing access to it.
   c. fight diseases of the respiratory tract.
   d. exchange reviews on services and goods they have purchased.

 Go to **MyLab IT** to take an autograded version of the *Check Your Understanding* review and to find all media resources for the chapter.

TechBytes Weekly Go to TechBytes Weekly for current technology news and discussion questions!

Try This

Skyping Around the World

Understanding what your computer can do to improve your life is one of the benefits of being computer literate. In this exercise, we'll show you how to make a free phone call over the Internet using the desktop version of Skype, a popular Voice over Internet Protocol (VoIP) service. (Note: These instructions are for the desktop version of Skype. The interface when using Skype on a mobile device may be different.) For more step-by-step instructions, watch the Chapter 1 Try This video on MyLab IT.

What You Need

Internet Connection	A Device	A Friend

(gst/Shutterstock; Dvougao/DigitalVision Vectors/Getty Images; Filo/DigitalVision Vectors/Getty Images)

Step 1 **Launch the Skype App.** The Skype app is now integrated into Windows. Search for Skype and launch the Windows app. Log in with your Microsoft Account credentials.

Step 2 **Build Your Contact List.** To build your list of contacts, you can go to **Settings** then **Contacts** and select **Use my address book**. Skype will automatically add the people you know to your Skype contact list. In addition, you can search Skype for people using their name, their Skype name, or their e-mail address.

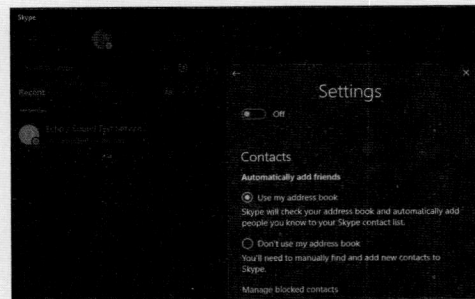

(Courtesy Microsoft, Inc.)

Step 3 **Make a Call.** Now we're ready to call someone! Let's start by calling the people at Skype and making sure everything is hooked up properly. Under your Contacts list, click the **Echo/Sound Test Service**. Then call in by clicking the **Call** button. The Skype service will answer your call, record a short message from you, and play it back to you. You'll know everything is set to go, and you can begin calling the world for free!

(Courtesy Microsoft, Inc.)

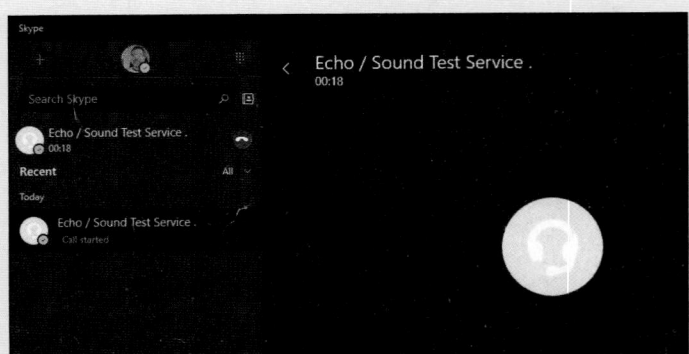

(Courtesy Microsoft, Inc.)

TOOL: IFTTT.com
(If This Then That)

Make: A Virtual Assistant

If This Then That (**IFTTT.com**) is an Internet-based tool that helps you get things done automatically. By using "recipes" within this web-based tool, you can automate tasks you do during the day, such as:

- automatically silencing your phone when you go into class,
- automatically texting your manager when you're on your way to work, or
- notifying you when the president signs a new law.

In this exercise, you'll explore using IFTTT to create recipes like these.

Make the Internet work for you by knowing this one programming statement: IF THIS, THEN THAT.

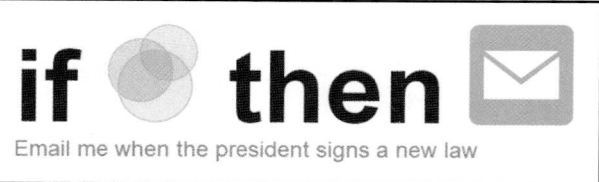

Email me when the president signs a new law

(IFTTT Inc.)

Upload screenshots from your Android device to Dropbox

For the instructions for this exercise, go to MyLab IT.

Emerging Technologies and Ethical Computing

Learning Outcome 1.2 **You will be able to describe emerging technologies, such as artificial intelligence, and how technology creates new ethical debates.**

Can computing devices really think? Are virtual assistants like Alexa intelligent, or do they just mimic thinking? Rapid developments in the field of artificial intelligence have forced us to consider many new ethical debates. It's important to learn about new advancements in technology, such as artificial intelligence, as well as to understand the ethical dilemmas technology presents.

Artificial Intelligence

Artificial intelligence (AI) focuses on creating computer systems that have an ability to perform tasks associated with human intelligence. Let's explore in detail what AI is and how it impacts you every day.

Artificial Intelligence Basics

Objective 1.6 *Describe artificial intelligence systems and explain their main goals.*

What exactly is intelligence? **Intelligence** is the ability to acquire and apply knowledge and skills. Sociologists point to characteristics that make human beings intelligent, such as learning from experiences, reasoning, problem solving, perception, and using language. Animals can exhibit remarkable behavior, such as birds flying south for the winter, but this is attributed to instinct rather than intelligence. Some animals can even solve problems, such as sea otters that use rocks to crack open shellfish so they can consume them. But what separates us from other animals is the ability to combine behaviors as opposed to demonstrating one specific rote behavior (such as flying south for the winter).

What is artificial intelligence? **Artificial intelligence (AI)** is a branch of computer science that focuses on creating computer systems or computer-controlled machines (including robots) able to perform tasks that are usually associated with human intelligence and that are (or were) generally performed by humans. By this definition, any computer program (or computer-controlled device) that accomplishes something normally thought of as intelligence by humans would be considered AI.

Do computers "think" like human beings? In the 1950s, at the dawn of AI research, the goal was to create a machine that could think like a human. Early examples included expert systems that mimicked doctors in diagnosing illnesses. But this goal has shifted somewhat toward machines that generate intelligent output but that do not necessarily mimic the human thought process.

Consider visiting the library. You could tell a human librarian your interests and the librarian could ask you additional questions about your likes and dislikes. Using a unique combination of human logic and intuition, combined with his or her experience with other library patrons, the librarian could recommend books you may enjoy. The Amazon recommendation engine fulfills the same purpose by suggesting books you may like while you're shopping on Amazon. However, the Amazon recommendation engine doesn't mimic a human librarian's thought process but rather analyzes vast amounts of data about you and other shoppers to make its recommendations. It provides intelligent results, but it does not arrive at those results the same way a human would.

Therefore, systems that display artificial intelligence do not have to arrive at their answers in the same way humans do.

What is the focus of current AI research? Today, AI researchers are looking to develop systems inspired by how humans think. Then they use the strengths of computers to build faster, more powerful tools. An example of this is the IBM Watson computer. Watson has defeated the very best human players in the game *Jeopardy!* for example.

▶ Helpdesk   MyLab IT®

The Impact of Artificial Intelligence

In this Helpdesk, you'll play the role of a helpdesk staffer, fielding questions about artificial intelligence.

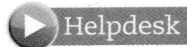

Figure 1.8 Main Areas of AI Research

Natural Language Processing

Understanding
Written and spoken words

Perception

Using sensors to gather data

Knowledge Representation

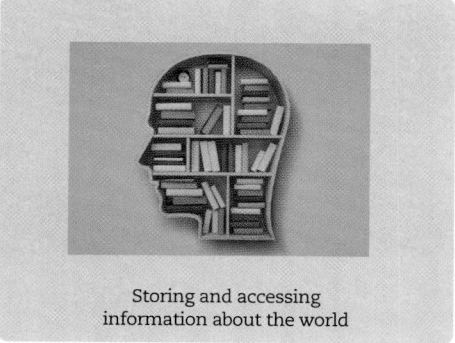

Storing and accessing
information about the world

Planning

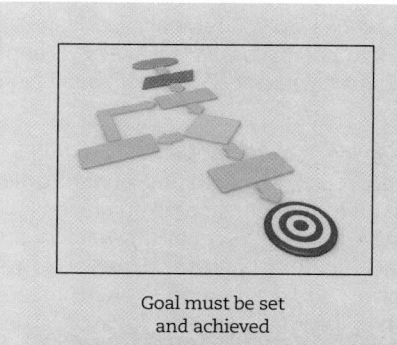

Goal must be set
and achieved

Problem Solving

Using even incomplete information
to achieve solution

Learning

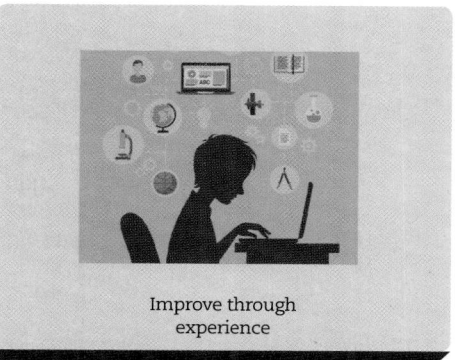

Improve through
experience

(Convisum/123RF; Andrija Markovic/123RF; Galina Peshkova/123RF; Viktor Bondar/123RF; Tomertu/123RF; Sentavio/123RF)

Watson developers noticed that people don't need hard and fast rules to form conclusions. Humans can assemble sets of evidence and then draw reasonably accurate conclusions. For Watson to answer a *Jeopardy!* question, a different approach was used. It examines thousands of pieces of text about a subject and then develops its own level of confidence in its answer. Watson does not think precisely like a human but still generates intelligent answers.

What are the main areas of research for AI? AI's central goals can be grouped into categories (see Figure 1.8). Many AI systems are so complex that they require research in several of these areas simultaneously.

- **Natural language processing (NLP):** NLP works to develop AI systems that understand written and spoken words and can interact with humans using language.
- **Perception:** AI systems have senses just as we do. AI systems use sonar, accelerometers, infrared, magnetic, and other electronic sensors to gather data. Being able to combine all the data from sensors and then construct information from it is a difficult challenge.
- **Knowledge representation:** Knowledge representation involves encoding information about the world into formats that the AI system can understand. Humans possess a vast collection of general knowledge based on their experiences in the world. AI systems need to build knowledge bases to solve problems. Developing a knowledge base and using it efficiently are active areas of research and have been demonstrated effectively by Watson.
- **Planning:** AI systems need to set goals and then achieve them. An AI system might need to plan how to move a blue block out of the way to reach a red one or how to rotate a block as it moves to fit through a narrow opening.
- **Problem solving:** Human beings tend to make intuitive judgments when solving a problem rather than performing a step-by-step analysis. AI programming combines a rules-based approach along with trying to make judgments with incomplete information.
- **Learning:** Like humans, AI algorithms improve through experience. **Supervised learning** is used when the system can be trained with a huge number of examples. When you teach Siri to recognize your voice by reading to it, you're using supervised learning. **Unsupervised learning** is when a system can look at data on its own and build rules for deciding what it is seeing.

A project like a self-driving (autonomous) car requires research in many of these areas. The car must have **computer vision**—the ability to interpret visual information the ways humans do. Although developing computer vision is a daunting problem, consider a situation with a self-driving car approaching a tree and a pedestrian on the side of the road. The AI system needs to be able to tell the difference between the tree and the pedestrian, but it also needs to know many things about each object. Is the tree going to run into the path of the car? The car must scan the scene with sensors, recognize objects, consult a knowledge base to begin to plan, and then execute the plan.

What has enabled us to deploy effective AI systems? Many information technology developments have contributed to the functional AI systems that we have today.

Figure 1.9 Artificial neural networks mimic the functions of neurons in the human brain. *(Cooldesign/123RF)*

Artificial Neural Networks

As noted earlier, **expert systems**, computer programs that try to mimic the experience of human experts such as doctors or lawyers, were among the first attempts at producing AI. **Rules-based systems,** software that asks questions and responds based on preprogrammed algorithms, were the first expert systems designed. These systems asked questions ("Do you have a fever?") and initiated other questions or actions based on the answers ("How long have you had a fever?") and worked adequately for some expert systems. But just a list of rules was not enough to handle more difficult tasks.

Human beings learn from a bottom-up approach—that is, learning from examples rather than going through rote rules. To create AI systems using a bottom-up approach, **artificial neural networks (ANNs)** have been developed. ANNs are constructed based on the structure of the human brain (see Figure 1.9), using loosely connected artificial neurons. When signals (information) are received in sufficient strength, a neuron is activated and the signal travels to other neurons connected to it. Unlike the human brain, the signals and the states of artificial neurons are represented by numbers between 0 and 1. Many modern ANNs feature different layers of neurons that allow for expressing various degrees of complexity rather than just pure Boolean states (like "on" or "off"). ANNs have allowed researchers to tackle complex problems such as speech recognition.

Big Data

Big data describes the vast amounts of both structured and unstructured data that are generated daily. Many AI systems can benefit from analyzing these huge data sets. Humans can't process quickly enough to draw models from gigabytes of data, but that speed is exactly the strength of computing systems.

Cloud Computing

The availability of **cloud computing**, accessing computing resources as needed through the Internet, has made access to stored data more achievable in a mobile environment. Cloud computing resources provided by third-party vendors, such as Amazon Web Services, also make it much more affordable to store and manage big data and potentially integrate it with AI systems.

Advances in Machine Learning

Machine learning (ML) is a type of AI that doesn't need to be specifically programmed but rather can learn from exposure to, and analysis of, data. ML analyzes patterns in data, then uses the patterns to draw conclusions and adjust the actions of the AI system accordingly. By learning, the AI system can adapt itself and become constantly better at its task. For instance, the more you use Alexa, the better it gets at providing you with relevant information because it remembers what you previously asked it and utilizes that information going forward. For example, if you use smart home products and use Alexa to control them, Alexa might give you shopping recommendations based on new smart home products compatible with your installed devices.

Figure 1.10 A deep learning (DL) system would learn to not misclassify this Vespa as a motorcycle by learning to use other unique attributes of a Vespa (such as body shape). *(Mykeyruna/123RF)*

Deep learning (DL) is a subset of the ML field that describes systems capable of learning from their mistakes (just as humans do). DL systems therefore improve their accuracy going forward. For instance, if an AI system is being used to identify objects in pictures, it might misidentify a Vespa motor scooter (see Figure 1.10) as a Honda motorcycle, based on the fact that it has two wheels and holds one or two riders. A DL system would, after being told of the misidentification, learn to use other attributes (such as the unique shape of the body) for distinguishing a Vespa from a motorcycle.

Having a basic understanding about AI systems is necessary to becoming a digitally literate citizen. In the next section, we'll explore various workplace systems that use AI.

Ethics in IT

Ethics in Computing

Should there be rules for conduct in a virtual world? If so, what should they be? What does plagiarism mean in a world where people can easily copy, paste, and upload content of all kinds? Should workplaces be allowed to monitor their employees' computing activities without their knowledge? Should websites be allowed to capture data related to what visitors do on their sites and analyze and sell that data? Should programmers be responsible if their software malfunctions and leads to personal injury or financial loss? Should Internet access be provided for free by communities to their citizens who cannot afford it? Are implantable devices that track the whereabouts of children and vulnerable adults a good thing, or a slippery slope to breaches of privacy? Should artificial intelligence be designed to behave ethically? These are the sorts of ethical questions and challenges that technology poses—questions that did not even exist just a few years ago.

As the reach of technology continues to spread, these are questions that more and more societies must face and develop their own answers to. And because different societies and cultures have different ideas of what it means to behave ethically, there will be many different solutions to ethical questions and interpretations of ethical issues. How we navigate the different cultural responses to ethical challenges therefore becomes more and more important as the pace of technology quickens. For example, how should U.S. companies respond to censorship of their websites in countries such as China? A state in the United States can declare that online gambling is illegal, but what does that mean when its citizens have access to foreign websites hosting gambling (see Figure 1.11)?

Answering challenging ethical questions related to technology is part of being a digitally literate citizen. This text will help you to understand technology and the ethical issues it poses. Later on in this chapter, we look at how you define your own personal ethics with regard to technology. Chapter 3 discusses how geolocation simplifies your life but also might invade your privacy. In Chapter 8, we discuss steps you need to take to establish the right kind of copyright on music, video, and books you create. Taking the time to think deeply about the connection between technology and ethics is one step in being a more knowledgeable and thoughtful global citizen.

Figure 1.11 How do we enforce ethical standards in our global, Internet-enabled environment? *(lucadp/123RF)*

Working with Artificial Intelligence and Other Information Technologies

Information technology (IT) is a field of study focused on the management and processing of information and the automatic retrieval of information. IT careers include working with computers, telecommunications, and software deployment. Career opportunities in IT are on the rise, but no matter what career you choose, new technology in the workplace is creating a demand for new skill levels in technology from employees. A study from the National Research Council concludes that by the year 2030, computers will displace humans in 60% of current occupations. Understanding how AI systems and other technologies can be utilized in the workplace is a desirable skill for all employees to have.

Technology and Career Opportunities

Objective 1.7 *Describe how artificial intelligence and other emerging technologies are providing career opportunities.*

One of the benefits of being digitally literate is that you will undoubtedly be able to perform your job more effectively. It also will make you more desirable as an employee and more likely to earn more and to advance in your career. In fact, your understanding of key concepts in technology can "future-proof" you, letting you easily and quickly react to the next round of new technologies.

Let's look at a whole range of industries and examine how current and emerging technologies, such as AI, are a part of getting work done.

Retail
The amount of data generated each minute of the day is staggering (see Figure 1.12). AI systems deployed in the retail sector are responsible for managing big data and performing data mining

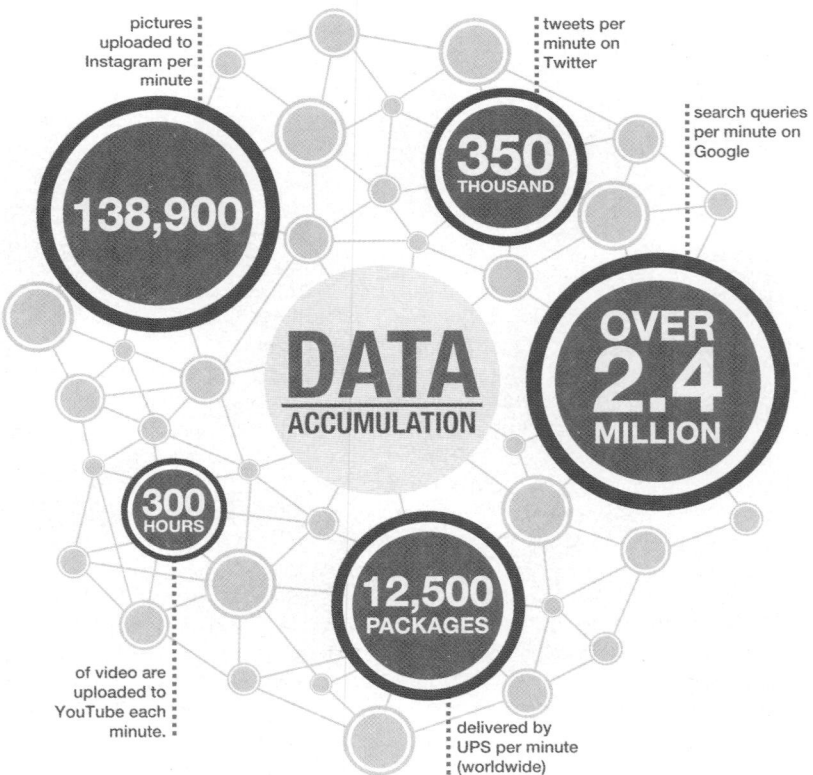

Figure 1.12 Enormous amounts of data are produced every minute. Data mining is performed by sophisticated AI systems such as recommendation engines.

analysis for managers. For example, retailers often study the data gathered from register terminals to determine which products are selling on a given day and in a specific location. In addition to using inventory control systems, which help managers figure out how much merchandise they need to order to replace stock that is sold, managers can use mined data to determine that if they want a certain product to sell well, they must lower its price. Such **data mining** thus allows retailers to respond to consumer buying patterns.

Recommendation engines are AI systems that help people discover things they may like but are unlikely to discover on their own. The secret behind recommendation engines is crunching massive amounts of data effectively—therefore, without big data and data mining, recommendation engines wouldn't exist. With an inventory as vast as Amazon's, the engine needs to learn which recommendations to present to the user and in which order. Presenting effective recommendations and learning to make better recommendations are essential to Amazon's success since it's estimated that 35% of Amazon's sales come from the recommendation list (see Figure 1.13).

Figure 1.13 Recommendation engines powered by AI are key to increasing Amazon's sales. *(Jeramey Lende/Shutterstock)*

Banking and Personal Finance

Credit card fraud is a major problem. Credit card processors and banks use AI systems to analyze huge volumes of transaction data to spot fraud. Banks use software to assess the risk of extending credit to customers by analyzing spending patterns, credit scores and debt repayment. The same software also helps determine what interest rates and terms to offer on loans. Researchers at MIT determined that using AI to evaluate credit risk could help reduce an institution's loan losses by 25%.

Robo advisors, AI powered software that offers investment advice and manages client's portfolios is available at many large brokerage firms. Although some are still hybrid systems that offer human advice when wanted, some investors chose to put their financial planning fully in the hands of software.

Transportation Industries

Autopilots run by AI have been installed on commercial airliners for decades. Although they can't yet replace human pilots, it is estimated that the average commercial flight only requires seven to ten minutes of pilot-directed flight, most of which is during takeoff and landing. It may still be some time before airliners can fly themselves. However, self-driving cars are quickly becoming a reality.

Autonomous (self-driving) vehicles should soon be available commercially on a wide scale. The availability of these vehicles should revolutionize the transportation industry. People will own less vehicles outright and rely more on renting vehicles as needed and delivered automatically where they are required.

Figure 1.14 (a) Robot vacuums are effective at sweeping up a room, but they can't function with the dexterity of human beings. (b) Embodied agents are designed to "think" and master complex dexterity and mobility challenges.
(a) Olga Miltsova/Shutterstock
(b) RikoBest/Shutterstock

Robots and Embodied Agents

Many robots are deployed in industrial settings doing hazardous, repetitive, or boring tasks previously performed by humans. You might even have a robot vacuum in your home cleaning up after you (see Figure 1.14a). The difficult challenges with robots are making ones that are as versatile as humans when it comes to manual dexterity and mobility. This has led to designs that mimic how humans walk and grasp objects, which is also leading to robots that look and act like human beings or **embodied agents** (see Figure 1.14b). Making robots that resemble humans creates many ethical dilemmas, such as whether they need to act exactly like human beings and be programmed to behave ethically. So will we all eventually be replaced by robots? That is highly unlikely. There are many jobs in which human empathy and understanding are highly valued, such as those in medicine, education, and counseling. But we probably will continue to see more robots appearing in our everyday lives.

Education

Intelligent personal assistants (IPAs) are also appearing more widely in classrooms and courseware (see Figure 1.15). IPAs can be created to assist students with designing, updating, and monitoring progress in their individualized learning plans (ILPs). This frees up teachers to work actively with students instead of getting bogged down with paperwork. Pearson has now entered a partnership with IBM to embed its Watson technology directly into Pearson courseware as an IPA. The Watson AI will learn how students are interacting with the courseware, track the pace of their learning, and enable the students to ask questions as they study. Watson will learn to provide better hints, answers, and guidance to students as they study. Watson will also provide feedback to instructors on student learning so that instructors can use their time more efficiently and focus on areas the students are having difficulty mastering.

Figure 1.15 Although robots probably won't be replacing teachers any time soon, intelligent personal assistants are taking more of a role in the classroom. *(Visual Generation/Shutterstock)*

Alan Turing was an early pioneer in computer design and cryptography who inspired many designers of the first digital computers. He proposed a simple test to distinguish between a human and a computer system.

The Turing test (see Figure 1.16) places a person in a room, asking written questions of two other "people." But one person is a live human being (human foil), while the other is a computer system. If the questioner can't tell which one of the respondents is a computer, then Turing felt the computer had reached "intelligence." The computer is permitted to be deceptive; however, the human foil is required to help the questioner reach the correct conclusion.

Figure 1.16 Basic Components of a Turing Test (*Cheskyw/123RF; Fotek/123RF; Ostill/123RF*)

Speeding up the grading of written assignments are AI-powered robo-readers. These software agents can interpret and effectively grade written essays. The Graduate Record Exam (GRE) uses a robo-reader called e-Rater in conjunction with human graders. All essays are graded by both e-Rater and one human grader, and if there is a discrepancy in the grading, then a second human grader reviews the essay.

Plagiarism checkers, like Turnitin, initially relied on brute force comparisons of student work to databases of published material, looking for exact text matches. But with the explosion of data we are now experiencing, this approach is impractical. Modern plagiarism agents use ML and deep learning to spot similar patterns in writing and estimate the likelihood that it was plagiarized. This allows instructors to review only the papers flagged by the AI for suspected plagiarism, which increases the instructor's efficiency.

A classroom teacher can also follow what is happening in the classroom by using the *dashboard*, a screen that shows which topics each student has mastered, which ones they are making progress with, and which ones have them spinning their wheels. Now a teacher can approach a student already knowing exactly what is frustrating them and can avoid the dreaded question, "Oh, what don't you understand?"

As an educator, being digitally literate will help you constructively integrate computer technologies like those discussed here into lesson plans and interactions for your students.

Law Enforcement

Today, AI systems are being used in police cars and crime labs to solve an increasing number of crimes. For example, facial reconstruction systems like the one shown in Figure 1.17 can turn a skull into a finished digital image of a face, allowing investigators to proceed far more quickly with identification than before.

Figure 1.17 Tissue-rendering programs add layers of muscles, fat, and skin to create faces that can be used to identify victims. (*Pixologicsstudio/Science Photo Library/ Glow Images*)

Using AI-powered software, proprietary law enforcement databases, such as the National Center for the Analysis of Violent Crime database, can be analyzed for similarities between crimes in an attempt to detect patterns that may reveal serial crimes. In fact, a law enforcement specialty called computer forensics is growing in importance in order to fight modern crime.

Computer forensics analyzes computer systems with specific techniques to gather potential legal evidence. For example, Steven Zirko was convicted for two Chicago-area murders based on computer forensics work. Computer forensics examiners trained by the Federal Bureau of Investigation (FBI) scoured Zirko's computer and located searches for terms like *hire a hitman*. In many cases, files, videos, and conversations conducted using a computer can be recovered by forensics specialists and can be used as evidence of criminal activity.

Medicine

A career in medicine will connect you to new ways of using technology to better people's lives. Websites like Modernizing Medicine use AI software to search through data on millions of patient visits and treatments provided by thousands of physicians. The website can help doctors quickly diagnose conditions with which they're not familiar and research alternative means of treatment for illnesses to reduce costs and side-effects for patients.

Figure 1.18 3D printing has become a tool for developing more inexpensive, and more stylish, prosthetic devices. *(Cem Ozdel/ Anadolu Agency/Getty Images)*

AI is also being integrated directly into patient information systems. Dashboards on the physician's computer screen can make recommendations about treatments to specific patients after the AI has analyzed their genetic traits and compared them to millions of other patients through records. The AI can recommend drugs for treatment as well as remind physicians about tests that they may need to perform. For instance, some anti-blood-clot medications can't be broken down by individuals with certain genetic traits. The AI might remind the doctor to perform genetic testing on the patient before prescribing anti-blood-clot medication.

The design and construction of prosthetic devices is another area of medicine impacted by modern technology. MIT's Biomechatronics lab has developed software that uses an array of pressure sensors to gauge the softness or stiffness of a patient's remaining tissue to create a better fit for a prosthetic to the limb. Meanwhile, 3D printing is allowing more inexpensive designs for prosthetic arms and legs, and more stylish artificial limbs as well (see Figure 1.18).

Figure 1.19 Digital medications are able to report information back to physicians about how the patient is responding to the medicine. *(Image-BROKER/SuperStock)*

Digital medication has arrived with the Food and Drug Administration's (FDA's) approval of digestible microchips (see Figure 1.19). Looking like regular pills, these medications have embedded sensors that transmit information to the doctor. The sensor itself is the size of a grain of sand. As it is digested, a small voltage is generated and detected by a patch worn on the patient's skin. The patch then transmits to the physician that the pill was taken; it also monitors the patient's heart rate, respiration, and temperature.

Psychology

Fear of speaking in public is common, but for people with autism spectrum disorders, making proper eye contact and reacting to social cues is so difficult it can severely limit their opportunities for jobs and relationships. Researchers at the MIT Media Lab have developed a system to help improve interpersonal skills for people who have autism.

MACH (My Automated Conversation coacH) is a computer system that generates an on-screen person that can, for example, conduct a job interview or appear ready for a first date. The computerized person (see Figure 1.20) nods and smiles in response to the user's speech and movement. This is an example of **affective computing**, developing systems that can recognize and simulate human emotions. MACH users can practice as many times as they wish in a safe environment. They receive an analysis that shows how well they modulated their voices, maintained eye contact, smiled, and how often they lapsed into "umms" and "uhhhs." The software runs on an ordinary laptop, using a webcam and microphone.

Figure 1.20 My Automated Conversation coacH (MACH) generates an on-screen interviewer you can practice with over and over. *(Cultura Limited/SuperStock)*

While engineers work to create computers that can process data faster and faster, psychologists and computer scientists are also working to evolve systems toward a more complete understanding of human behavior. With a career that blends computer science and psychology, you could find yourself at the heart of developing a new kind of relationship between man and machine.

Reality is reality, right? So what is *augmentative reality*? And how is it different from *virtual reality*?

Augmentative reality (AR) is the addition of digital information directly into our reality, either to add more detail or at times to remove unwanted visual effects. How does this happen?

AR combines our normal sense of the world around us with an additional layer of digital information. The extra information can be displayed on a separate device, such as in augmented reality apps for smartphones. Displays in stores can augment your image with the clothing you're interested in, creating a virtual fitting room (see Figure 1.21). Microsoft has announced a product named the HoloLens that will let you manipulate holographic images as part of your reality (see Figure 1.22).

Meanwhile, researcher Stephen Mann at the University of Toronto is working with wearable computers that use "point of eye" (PoE) cameras as AR devices. A PoE camera is designed so that the camera is positioned directly in front of the eye itself. The ultimate PoE camera would be one that is implanted within the eye or eye socket. Mann's research group is exploring this as a way to assist partially sighted or blind people.

Figure 1.21 This high-tech fitting room uses augmented reality technology to allow shoppers to try on clothes virtually. *(Yoshikazu Tsuno/AFP/Getty Images)*

Figure 1.22 The Microsoft HoloLens augments your reality by adding holographic images you can manipulate. *(Used with Permission from Microsoft)*

Instead of adding information to the reality you perceive, **virtual reality (VR)** replaces it with a different world. Virtual reality creates an artificial environment that is immersive and interactive. VR environments can be as simple as a pair of goggles or as elaborate as entire "caves" that you walk into (see Figure 1.23). One "cave" (cave automatic visual environment) is being used at Temple University to study balance in stroke victims.

VR is also coming to the consumer gaming market with the introduction of VR goggles, like Sony's Project Morpheus and the Rift by Oculus (see Figure 1.24). These goggles have high pixel count displays that wrap your full field of view.

So reality may be a bit less absolute than it once seemed. Whether it is being augmented with additional information or replaced by new virtual realms, technology is expanding our sense of what is real.

Figure 1.23 Virtual reality "caves" replace our ordinary reality with a new, immersive environment. *("A Nanoscale Forest Seen Through a Big Lens," 2013. A close-up of a glass fissure computed in a 5-Million atom molecular dynamics nanoscale simulation. Simulation by University of Southern California, computing on the Argonne Leadership Computing Facility at Argonne National Laboratory (ANL), and visualization by ANL and Khairi Reda of the Electronic Visualization Laboratory (EVL) at University of Illinois at Chicago. 3D visualization ported to EVL's CAVE2(TM) Hybrid Reality Environment.) (photo: Lance Long, EVL)*

Figure 1.24 VR goggles like these wrap around your full field of view, creating a totally immersive environment. *(Gabrielle Lurie/AFP/Getty Images)*

 # Ethical Computing

As noted earlier, technology has brought about a new set of ethical challenges. And because technology often moves faster than rules can be formulated to govern it, how technology is used is often left up to the individual and the guidance of his or her personal ethics. And because ethical considerations are complex, reasonable people can have different, yet equally valid, views. In this section, we begin by defining ethics and then examining a set of ethical systems. Next we discuss personal ethics and how technology affects our personal ethics. Finally, we ask you to consider what your personal ethics are and how you make ethical choices.

Defining Ethics

Objective 1.8 *Define ethics and examine various ethical systems.*

Ethics is the study of the general nature of morals and of the specific moral choices individuals make. Morals involve conforming to established or accepted ideas of right and wrong (as generally dictated by society) and are usually viewed as being black or white. Ethical issues often involve subtle distinctions, such as the difference between fairness and equity. Ethical principles are the guidelines you use to make decisions each day, decisions about what you will say, do, and think.

Figure 1.25 Systems of Ethics

Ethical System	Basic Tenets	Examples
Relativism	• There is no universal moral truth. • Moral principles are dictated by cultural tastes and customs.	Topless bathing is prevalent in Europe but generally banned on public beaches in the United States.
Divine Command Theory	• God is all-knowing and sets moral standards. • Conforming to God's law is right; breaking it is wrong.	Christians believe in rules such as the Ten Commandments.
Utilitarianism	• Actions are judged solely by consequences. • Actions that generate greater happiness are judged to be better than actions that lead to unhappiness. • Individual happiness is not important—consider the greater good.	Using weapons of mass destruction ends a war sooner and therefore saves lives otherwise destroyed by conventional fighting.
Virtue Ethics	• Morals are internal. • Strive to be a person who behaves well spontaneously.	A supervisor views the person who volunteered to clean up a park as a better person than the workers who are there because of court-ordered community service.
Deontology (Duty-Based)	• Focus on adherence to moral duties and rights. • Morals should apply to everyone equally.	Human rights (like freedom of religion) should be respected for all people because human rights should be applied universally.

(Solomin Andrey/Fotolia; Olga Galushko/Fotolia; Kentoh/Fotolia; Alexmillos/Fotolia; Scanrail/Fotolia)

There are many systems of ethical conduct. Figure 1.25 lists several major ethical systems. *Relativism* states that there is no universal truth and that moral principles are dictated by the culture and customs of each society. *Divine command theory* follows the principle that God is all knowing and that moral standards are perfectly stated by God's laws, such as the Ten Commandments. *Utilitarianism* judges actions to be right or wrong solely by their consequences. Actions that generate greater happiness are deemed to be better than those actions that lead to less happiness. *Virtue ethics* teaches that we each have an internal moral compass and should try to be a person who spontaneously follows that guide. Finally, the duty-based ethical system, or *deontology,* suggests we should all follow common moral codes and apply those to all humanity.

Systems of Ethics

You may wonder what the difference is between laws and ethics. Laws are formal, written standards designed to apply to everyone. Laws are enforced by government agencies and interpreted by the courts. However, it's impossible to pass laws that cover every possible behavior in which humans can engage. Therefore, ethics provide a general set of unwritten guidelines for people to follow. Unethical behavior isn't necessarily illegal, however. Consider the death penalty. In many U.S. states, putting convicted criminals to death for certain crimes is legal. However, many people consider it unethical to execute a human being for any reason.

Not all illegal behavior is unethical, either. Civil disobedience, which is intentionally refusing to obey certain laws, is used as a form of protest to effect change. Gandhi's nonviolent resistance to the British rule of India, which led to India's establishment as an independent country, and Martin Luther King's protests and use of sit-ins in the civil rights movement are both examples of civil disobedience. What does civil disobedience look like in our hyper-connected age of social media and the Internet?

Note that there is also a difference between unethical behavior and amoral behavior. **Unethical behavior** is not conforming to a set of approved standards of behavior—cheating on an exam, for example. **Amoral behavior** occurs when a person has no sense of right and wrong and no interest in the moral consequences of his or her actions, such as when a murderer shows no remorse for his or her crime.

There is no universal agreement on which is the best system of ethics. Most societies use a blend of different systems. Regardless of the ethical system of the society in which you live, all ethical decisions are greatly influenced by personal ethics.

Sound Byte MyLab IT®

How to Debate Ethical Issues

This Sound Byte will help you consider important aspects of debating difficult issues arising from the ethical use of technology.

Personal Ethics

Objective 1.9   *Describe influences on the development of your personal ethics.*

Each day as you choose your words and actions, you're following a set of **personal ethics**—a set of formal or informal ethical principles you use to make decisions. Some people have a clear, well-defined set of principles they follow. Others' ethics are inconsistent or are applied differently in different situations.

A person's ethics develop in many ways. Naturally, your family plays a major role in establishing the values you cherish in your own life, and these might include a cultural bias toward certain ethical positions (see Figure 1.26). Your religious affiliation is another major influence on your ethics because most religions have established codes of ethical conduct. How these sets of ethics interact with the values of the larger culture is often challenging. Issues such as abortion, the death penalty, and war often create conflict between personal ethical systems and the larger society's established legal–ethical system.

As you mature, your life experiences also affect your personal ethics. Does the behavior you see around you make sense within the ethical principles that your family, your church, or your teachers taught you? Has your experience led you to abandon some ethical rules and adopt others? Have you modified how and when you apply these laws of conduct depending on what's at stake?

Determining Your Personal Ethics

When you have a clear idea of what values are important to you, it may be easier to handle situations in your life that demand ethical action. You can follow these steps to help yourself define a list of personal values:

1. **Describe yourself.** Write down words that describe who you are, based on how others view you. Would a friend describe you as honest, or helpful, or kind? These keywords will give you a hint as to the values and behaviors that are important to you.

2. **List the key principles you believe in.** Make a list of the key principles that influence your decisions. For example, would you be comfortable working in a lab that used animals for medical research? How important is it to you that you never tell a lie? List the key ideas you believe to be important in conducting your life. Do you always behave this way, or are there situations in which your answers might change?

3. **Identify external influences.** Where did your key principles come from—your parents? Your friends? Spiritual advisors? Television and movies? You may want to question some of your beliefs once you actually identify where they came from.

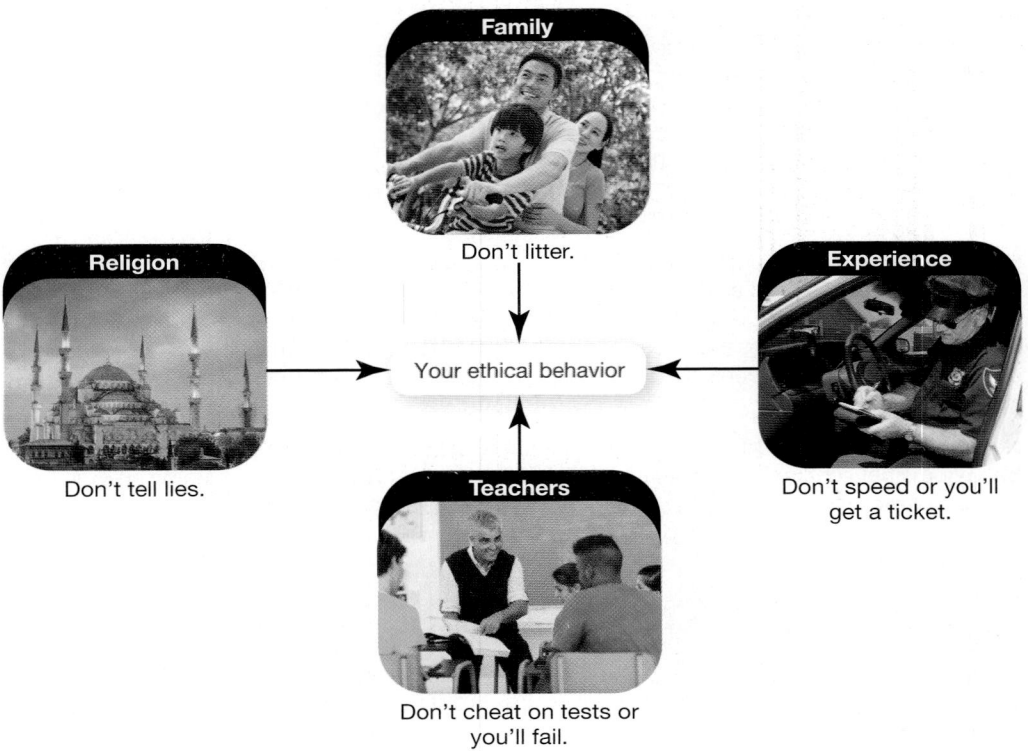

Figure 1.26 Many different forces shape your personal ethics. *(Imtmphoto/Fotolia; Lisa F. Young/Shutterstock; Jovannig/Fotolia; Michael jung/Fotolia)*

4. **Consider why.** After writing down your beliefs, think about why you believe them. Have you accepted them without investigation? Do they stand up in the context of your real-world experiences?

5. **Prepare a statement of values.** Distill what you have written into a short statement. By having a well-defined statement of the values you hold most important in your own life, which you can refer to in times of challenge, it will be easier for you to make ethical decisions.

Ethics and Technology

Objective 1.10   *Present examples of how technology creates ethical challenges.*

You'll encounter many ethical challenges relating to information technology. Your personal ethics—combined with the general ethical environment of society and ethical guidelines your company provides if your decision is related to the workplace—will help to guide your decisions.

Intellectual Property

One obvious area of ethical challenge in technology is intellectual property rights. **Intellectual property** is work that is the result of someone's creativity and knowledge, such as music, writing, and software, and that is protected by copyright law and documented by copyrights, patents, and trademarks. Anti-piracy efforts by various organizations and governments aim to protect intellectual property rights—an issue that has been an ongoing and important one in the technology industry.

With increased use of electronic media, challenges to enforcing copyright laws have increased. Countries such as China and the Philippines are known for their high rates of pirated software use. Businesses and individuals that use such illegal software potentially gain an advantage in the international marketplace. Companies like Microsoft have taken several measures to combat illegal piracy but still haven't managed to effectively reduce the amount of pirated software in certain countries.

Piracy challenges have also placed significant pressures on existing business models for creative arts industries such as film and music. Time will tell whether copyright laws will need to be revised to adapt to the predominant digital culture, whether regulatory agencies will need to improve the methods of controlling piracy, or whether the industries themselves will need to change their business models.

Privacy

Technology is also posing new ethical issues related to privacy. Intelligent personal agents (like Alexa) are constantly listening to you and combing through your data (such as your e-mails and texts) to help determine your needs. Many people are concerned about the loss of privacy from such agents. Social media sites such as Facebook and Twitter are inherently about sharing information with others. Facebook and other social media allow you to set privacy filters on your personal information. You can choose to share information publicly, share it just with your friends, or keep it totally private. Employers now routinely check social media sites to gather publicly shared information on prospective employees. Potential employers sometimes even go so far as to ask job seekers for access to their private social media information. This may give employers access to information related to the applicant's race, religion, age, and sexual orientation that they would not legally be able to ask the applicants about directly. The control and privacy of information will continue to be a fine balancing act for the foreseeable future, with employers trying to gather intelligence about potential employees while appeasing the concerns of privacy advocates.

Social Justice

Technological processing power has led to new issues that impact social justice. Consider *predictive policing*—gathering data from different sources, analyzing it, and then using the results to prevent future crime. Data sources may include crime maps, traffic camera data, surveillance footage, and social media network analysis. But at what point does the possibility of a crime warrant intervention? Is predictive policing just another way to justify racial profiling? Figure 1.27 lists different views on the issue of predictive policing. Where do your views fall?

Another social justice issue affected by technology is whether there are things, such as military secrets and communication related to ongoing negotiations with foreign governments, the public does not have a right to see. Historically, tight controls have been in place over access to such information. With Web 2.0 tools, the entire model for the distribution of information has shifted, and now everyone can create and publish content on the Internet. For example, WikiLeaks (wikileaks.org) is making private and public documents available for viewing on its site. WikiLeaks describes itself as "a public service designed to protect whistle-blowers, journalists, and activists who have sensitive materials to communicate to the public." *Time* magazine said of WikiLeaks, "[I]t could become as important a journalistic tool as the Freedom of Information Act."

Does society have a right to see previously secret documents? And do we all have a responsibility to use technology to help achieve social justice? Where do the boundaries of those rights and responsibilities lie?

Figure 1.27   Point/Counterpoint: Social Justice

Issue: Predictive Policing	**Ethical Question: Should police agencies act on data trends that seem to predict crime?**
Point	• This is just a use of modern technology to enhance law enforcement. • Data trends that show areas of high criminal activity allow the police to use their resources more effectively. • If law enforcement steps in before a crime has been committed, it helps both the potential victim and the potential criminal.
Counterpoint	• This is a high-tech form of racial and socioeconomic profiling and acts to reinforce existing stereotypes. • This decreases our privacy and encourages constant government surveillance of our activities. • It is impossible to create predictive algorithms in a way that is not harmful to law-abiding people living in high crime areas.

(James Steidl/Fotolia)

Figure 1.28 Point/Counterpoint: Liability

Issue: 3D Printing Regulation

Ethical Question: Should 3D printing be regulated?

Point

- The general public expects to buy products that are free from design and material defects. If governments do not regulate 3D printing materials and designs, the public is placed in unnecessary peril.

- Because designs of existing products are easy to produce, there is an increased chance of intellectual property theft.

- Users of 3D printers need to understand the risks, responsibilities, and liabilities of producing products on demand for their use and for resale.

Counterpoint

- Heavily regulating 3D printing will stifle creativity and ingenuity in the design and production of new products.

- Manufacturers can seek legal remedies for violation of design patents under existing laws.

- Consumers should be aware of the principle of "caveat emptor" (let the buyer beware) when using untested or unproven products. People should use untested products cautiously.

(James Steidl/Fotolia)

Liability

3D printing is revolutionizing the way items are manufactured, causing a range of issues involving intellectual property rights and liability. In traditional manufacturing, it is relatively easy to enforce safety laws. Consider the manufacture of bicycle helmets. Traditional manufacturers are held accountable for delivering safely designed products free from defects in workmanship. Products are subjected to safety testing prior to being sold to the public and must conform to legal safety guidelines. If you buy a helmet and are injured while riding your bike because of a defect in the design of or materials used in the helmet, you can sue the manufacturer for damages. Manufacturers protect their designs (intellectual property) by obtaining patents.

3D printers produce objects from design plans generated with various types of software. Anyone who is reasonably proficient with design software can generate a design for an object to be printed. However, a person could also use a 3D scanner to scan an existing object (say a helmet designed and sold by a traditional manufacturer) and use design software to create his or her own plan for how to print it. If the object is patented, this would be a violation of the law. But it certainly makes it easier to steal someone's intellectual property.

Design plans for objects are often shared online. Even if the same design is used, the product quality can be vastly different depending on the type of 3D printer used and the type of plastic selected for printing.

Consider the ethics of printing a helmet from a file you downloaded from a public website. You give it to a friend as a gift. While riding her bicycle, your friend is injured because the design of the helmet was flawed and the materials you used to make it were substandard. Who is responsible for the injuries? You? The manufacturer of the printer? The owner of the printer? The manufacturer of the raw materials used to make the helmet? The creator of the flawed design plans? The person who decided to use an untested product (i.e., your friend)? What if the design you used was created from a patented product? Figure 1.28 lists different views on the issue of 3D printing regulation. Where do your views fall?

Censorship

Various countries have different answers to the question of what information their people should be allowed to see. For instance, India blocked over 800 pornographic sites recently, sparking a huge debate about free speech and personal freedom. The ban was partially lifted in a few days with only sites deemed to be promoting child pornography still blocked. Blocking child pornography is obviously a laudable goal, but other countries block many different types of websites. For example, the Chinese government has demanded that search engine providers like Google self-censor their search engines, restricting search results for sensitive information such as the details of the Tiananmen Square protests and of human rights groups. Figure 1.29 lists different views on the issue of Internet censorship. What do you think?

Figure 1.29 Point/Counterpoint: Censorship

Issue: Censoring the Internet	Ethical Question: Should an American company agree to restrict freedom of information to do business with a more restrictive country?
Point	• It is not the place of a company to try to change laws of foreign countries. Reform must come from within. • Working in China does not mean a company supports all of China's policies. • U.S. companies can ethically stay in China if they make an effort to improve human rights there. U.S. companies operating in China should agree on guidelines that respect human rights.
Counterpoint	• Policies will never change unless there are financial and political incentives to do so. The departure of U.S. companies helps pressure foreign governments to reform. • If companies withdraw from China, it threatens the viability of many other resellers in China. • Countries cannot expect to compete in the global marketplace while refusing to have a global exchange of ideas.

(James Steidl/Fotolia)

Social Activism

Hacktivism (derived from *hack* and *activism*) involves using computers and computer networks in a subversive way to promote an agenda usually related to causes such as free speech, human rights, or freedom of information. Essentially, it is using computer hacking to effect some sort of social change. An example of early hacktivism is "Worms Against Nuclear Killers (WANK)," a computer worm that anti-nuclear activists in Australia unleashed into the networks of NASA in 1989 to protest the launch of a shuttle that carried radioactive plutonium. As computer security has grown more sophisticated, attacks today are usually carried out by groups of hackers (such as Anonymous) or groups of computer scientists funded by nation states for the specific purpose of hacking.

Hacktivism often takes the form of denial-of-service attacks in which websites are bombarded with requests for information until they are overwhelmed and legitimate users can't access the site. At other times, hacktivism takes the form of cyberterrorism, where the objective is to embarrass or harass a company by penetrating its computer networks and stealing (and often publishing) sensitive information. Certain countries are rumored to maintain groups of computer scientists whose main goal is to spy on other countries by hacking into their computer networks. Figure 1.30 lists different views on the issue of hacktivism. What do you think?

Figure 1.30 Point/Counterpoint: Social Activism

Issue: Hacktivism	Ethical Question: Is hacktivism a helpful form of civil disobedience?
Point	• Society as a whole benefits when injustices are exposed. • Civil disobedience is an inalienable right upon which the United States was founded. • Methods of civil disobedience need to keep pace with modern technology in order to have the greatest impact possible.
Counterpoint	• Computer technology provides many opportunities for reaching a wide audience with a message without resorting to illegal activities such as hacking. • Personal data of individuals needs to be protected as a basic right of privacy. • Hacking into computer systems for alleged acts of "civil disobedience" are often hard to distinguish from acts of cyberterrorism.

(James Steidl/Fotolia)

Figure 1.31 Point/Counterpoint: Automated Robotic Machinery

Issue: Ethics of Robotic Machinery	Ethical Question Should owners be able to set the ethical rules of behavior for their own robots?
Point	• As long as choices over robotic ethics don't violate laws, they should be in the hands of individual owners. • Individuals should have the right to set ethical parameters for their robots because they may wish to be even more selfless than society dictates. • Individuals make ethical decisions in times of crisis. Robotic systems should be an extension of the individual's ethical values.
Counterpoint	• If all robots do not contain ethical constraints that prevent harm to human beings, human lives may be lost. • Allowing individuals to adjust the ethics of robotic devices exposes society to risks from careless, thoughtless, or psychotic individuals. • Every robot must have ethical programming that allows them to make decisions regarding the best possible outcomes in life and death situations.

Automated Robotic Machinery

Automobiles now contain sophisticated AI systems to exercise control over the vehicle and respond faster than humans can. For example, using a wide set of sensors, accident-avoidance systems can apply the brakes and even change lanes to help drivers avoid accidents. In the coming years, these systems may exercise even more control of your vehicle, such as the self-driving cars that are under development by Google and major auto manufacturers.

But who controls the ethical constraints by which automated robotic machinery like this operates? Consider a selection between a set of bad choices: You suddenly find that you either have to brake, knowing you will still hit the school bus ahead of you, swerve into oncoming traffic, or swerve to the other side into a tree. Which choice would you make? Which choice would you want your automated car to make? Should owners have a choice of overriding the programming in their vehicles and adjusting the ethical parameters of their robotic systems? What should manufacturers do until laws are passed regarding robo-ethics? Figure 1.31 lists different views on the issue of robotic machinery ethics. Where do your views fall?

Ethical discussions are important in many fields but especially with technology. The pace of change is forcing us to consider implications for our families and countries as well as for our personal ideas of justice and proper conduct. Being able to analyze and then discuss your ethical positions with others are important skills to develop.

> ### Before moving on to the Chapter Review:
>
> 1. ▶ Watch Chapter Overview Video 1.2.
> 2. Then take the Check Your Understanding quiz.

Check Your Understanding // Review & Practice

For a quick review to see what you've learned so far, answer the following questions.

multiple choice

1. _____ is a branch of computer science that focuses on creating computer systems or computer-controlled machines that have an ability to perform tasks usually associated with human intelligence.

   a. Big data

   b. Artificial intelligence

   c. Machine learning

   d. Unsupervised learning

2. AI systems that help people discover things they may like but are unlikely to discover on their own are known as

   a. crowdsourcing systems.

   b. Turing testers.

   c. recommendation engines.

   d. intelligent personal assistants.

3. A working definition of *ethics* is

   a. impossible because it means different things to different people.

   b. the laws of a given society.

   c. the study of the general nature of morals and of the specific moral choices individuals make.

   d. the rules of conduct presented in Christian religions.

4. The set of formal or informal ethical principles you use to make decisions is your

   a. mindset.

   b. instinct.

   c. personal ethics.

   d. personality.

5. All of the following are examples of intellectual property *except*

   a. a recipe from your grandmother.

   b. a brick wall.

   c. a graphic novel.

   d. a photograph.

 Go to **MyLab IT** to take an autograded version of the *Check Your Understanding* review and to find all media resources for the chapter.

TechBytes Weekly Go to TechBytes Weekly for current technology news and discussion questions!

1 Chapter Review

Summary

> **Learning Outcome 1.1** You will be able to discuss the impact of the tools of modern technology on national and global issues.

 ### Technology in a Global Society

Objective 1.1 *Describe various technological tools being used to impact national and global issues.*

- Technology can be the means by which you find your voice in the world and impact others in meaningful ways.
- Social media is impacting elections and other issues worldwide.
- Crisis-mapping tools are an example of technology helping in different kinds of global conflicts and disasters.

Objective 1.2 *Describe various global social issues that are being affected by technology.*

- Global health care issues, like the spread of disease, require international cooperation and technological solutions.
- Environmental issues are global in nature and will require technology to address.
- The digital divide, an uneven distribution of access to computer technology, will make it difficult for us to solve global problems.

 ### Technology Connects Us with Others

Objective 1.3 *Describe how technology is changing how and why we connect and collaborate with others.*

- Web 2.0 is a set of features and functionality that allows Internet users to contribute content easily and to be easily connected to each other.
- Cognitive surplus is the combination of leisure time and access to tools to work on problems and be creative.
- New collaborative tools available on the Internet allow us to work together on projects with much larger groups.

- Crowdfunding is a group of people connecting through the Internet to fund projects by strangers.

Objective 1.4 *Summarize how technology has impacted the way we choose and consume products and services.*

- Marketing is changing because most consumers now shop with Internet access on their phones and can therefore check competing prices and online reviews.
- The idea of ownership is changing because technology is allowing subscription services for products like cars and bikes to be available. Such collaborative consumption means that we are joining together as a group to use specific products more efficiently

 ### The Importance of Computer Literacy

Objective 1.5 *Characterize computer literacy and explain why it is important to be computer literate.*

- If you're computer literate, you understand the capabilities and limitations of computers and know how to use them wisely.
- By understanding how a computer is constructed and how its various parts function, you'll be able to get the most out of your computer.
- You'll be able to avoid hackers, viruses, and Internet headaches; protect your privacy; and separate the real risks of privacy and security from things you don't have to worry about.
- You'll also be better able to maintain, upgrade, and troubleshoot your computer; make good purchasing decisions; and incorporate the latest technologies into your existing equipment.
- Being computer literate also enables you to understand the many ethical, legal, and societal implications of technology today.

Part 2
Emerging Technologies and Ethical Computing

Learning Outcome 1.2 **You will be able to describe emerging technologies, such as artificial intelligence, and how technology creates new ethical debates.**

 ## Artificial Intelligence

Objective 1.6 *Describe artificial intelligence systems and explain their main goals.*

- Artificial intelligence (AI) focuses on creating computer systems that have an ability to perform tasks associated with human intelligence.
- Machines using AI do not necessarily mimic the human thought process.
- Current AI research is focused in the following areas: natural language processing, perception, knowledge representation, planning, problem solving, and learning (both supervised and unsupervised).
- A Turing test can be used to determine whether a system is a computer AI or a human being.

 ## Working with Artificial Intelligence and Other Information Technologies

Objective 1.7 *Describe how artificial intelligence and other emerging technologies are providing career opportunities.*

- Artificial intelligence impacts the full range of careers, from retail and psychology to robotics and medicine.
- Understanding how to use software, how to use and maintain computer hardware, and how to take advantage of Internet resources will help you be a more productive and valuable employee, no matter which profession you choose.

 ## Ethical Computing

Objective 1.8 *Define ethics and describe various ethical systems.*

- Ethics is the study of moral choices.
- There are several different ethical systems. There is no universal agreement on which system is best.
- Unethical behavior is not necessarily unlawful behavior.
- Amoral behavior is when a person has no sense of right and wrong.

Objective 1.9 *Describe influences on the development of your personal ethics.*

- Personal ethics are a set of formal or informal ethical principles you use to make decisions in your life.
- Your personal ethics develop from a number of sources: your family values, your religion, the values of the larger culture, and your life experiences.

Objective 1.10 *Present examples of how technology creates ethical challenges.*

- Technology is posing new ethical challenges with regard to intellectual property, privacy, social justice, liability, censorship, social activism, and automated robotic machinery, among others.

 Be sure to check out **MyLab IT** for additional materials to help you review and learn. And don't forget to watch the Chapter Overview Videos. ▶

Key Terms

affective computing **22**

amoral behavior **26**

artificial intelligence (AI) **15**

artificial neural networks (ANNs) **17**

augmentative reality (AR) **23**

big data **17**

cognitive surplus **7**

cloud computing **17**

collaborative consumption **9**

computer forensics **21**

computer literacy **14**

computer vision **16**

crisis-mapping tool **5**

crowdfunding **8**

crowdsourcing **9**

data mining **20**

deep learning (DL) **17**

digital divide **6**

embodied agents **20**

ethics **24**

expert systems **15**

hacktivism **29**

information technology (IT) **19**

intellectual property **27**

intelligence **15**

knowledge representation **16**

machine learning (ML) **17**

natural language processing (NLP) **16**

personal ethics **26**

QR (quick response) code **9**

recommendation engines **20**

rules-based systems **17**

social media **4**

software **10**

spam **10**

supervised learning **16**

Turing test **21**

unethical behavior **26**

unsupervised learning **16**

virtual reality (VR) **24**

Web 2.0 **7**

Chapter Quiz // Assessment

For a quick review to see what you've learned, answer the following questions. Submit the quiz as requested by your instructor. If you are using **MyLab IT**, the quiz is also available there.

multiple choice

1. Social media
   a. prevents two-way dialog between people.
   b. cannot be immediate enough to react to quickly developing issues.
   c. is incorporated as part of a political strategy by many politicians.
   d. is useful only for personal friendships.

2. Sophisticated modeling software is helping international researchers
   a. create more intricate screenplays and movie scripts.
   b. analyze computer systems to gather potential legal evidence.
   c. market new types of products to a wider audience.
   d. increase the pace of research in finding and producing vaccines.

3. Web 2.0 has led to a shift from just consuming content toward
   a. spending all our time on leisure activities.
   b. producing content.
   c. new standards for HTML.
   d. less sharing of the work we produce.

4. Examples of crowdfunding and crowdsourcing include
   a. Call a Bike and Zipcar.
   b. Bing and Google.
   c. Kickstarter and ScanLife.
   d. Ushahidi and Kiva.

5. Bike-sharing programs like Citi Bike are an example of
   a. principled psychology.
   b. crowdfunding
   c. crowdsourcing.
   d. a subscription-style business model made possible by technology.

6. Being computer literate includes being able to
   a. avoid spam, adware, and spyware.
   b. use the web effectively.
   c. diagnose and fix hardware and software problems.
   d. all of the above.

7. All of the following are current focuses of AI research EXCEPT
   a. natural language processing.
   b. perception.
   c. cognitive surplus.
   d. knowledge representation.

8. Which of the following statements is FALSE?
   a. Unethical behavior is always illegal.
   b. Ethical decisions are usually influenced by personal ethics.
   c. Individuals who have no sense of right or wrong exhibit amoral behavior.
   d. Life experience affects an individual's personal ethics.

9. Which of the following actions would NOT help to identify your personal ethics?
   a. Describe yourself.
   b. Conduct a genealogical study of your extended family.
   c. Identify the influences of your work environment.
   d. Prepare a list of values that are most important to you.

10. Intellectual property
   a. is the result of someone's creative work and design.
   b. can be protected legally by the patent system.
   c. can include works of music, film, or engineering design.
   d. all of the above

true/false

_____ 1. Big data describes the vast amounts of both structured and unstructured data that are generated daily.
_____ 2. The move toward access instead of ownership is a sign of cognitive surplus.
_____ 3. Artificial intelligence systems must think exactly like human beings do.
_____ 4. Web-based databases cannot be used to help investigators solve criminal cases.
_____ 5. Hacktivism is different from cyberterrorism.

critical thinking

1. **What Occupies Your Mind?**

   What we think about is influenced by the information fed to our mind all day long. Web 2.0 has created numerous channels for people to offer their own work for free—open source software, free music, books, and artwork. How has this affected your thinking? Have you created things to share freely with the online world? Has it changed the value you put on music, books, and art?

2. **Career and Computers**

   This chapter lists many ways in which becoming computer literate is beneficial. Think about what your life will be like once you're started in your career. What areas of computing will be most important for you to understand? How would an understanding of computer hardware and software help you in working from home, working with groups in other countries, and contributing your talents?

Team Time

A Culture of Sharing

problem

As more and more peer-to-peer music-sharing services appeared, like BitTorrent and LimeWire, many felt a culture of theft was developing. Some argued there was a mindset that property rights for intellectual works need not be respected and that people should be able to download, for free, any music, movies, or other digital content they wanted.

But there is another view of the phenomenon. Some are suggesting that the amount of constant access to other people—through texting, e-mail, blogging, and the easy exchange of digital content—has created a culture of trust and sharing. This Team Time will explore both sides of this debate as it affects three different parts of our lives—finance, travel, and consumerism.

task

Each of three groups will select a different area to examine—finance, travel, or consumerism. The groups will find evidence to support or refute the idea that a culture of sharing is developing. The finance group will want to explore projects like Kickstarter (**kickstarter.com**) and Kiva (**kiva.org**). The travel group should examine what is happening with Airbnb (**airbnb.com**) to start their research. The team investigating consumerism will want to look at goods-exchange programs like Freecycle (**freecycle.org**).

process

1. Divide the class into three teams.
2. Discuss the different views of a "culture of sharing." With the other members of your team, use the Internet to research up-and-coming technologies and projects that would support your position. People use social media tools to connect into groups to exchange ideas. Does that promote trust? Does easy access to digital content promote theft, or has the value of content changed? Are there other forces like the economy and the environmental state of the world that play a role in promoting a culture of sharing? What evidence can you find to support your ideas?

3. Present your group's findings to the class for debate and discussion.
4. Write a strategy paper that summarizes your position and outlines your predictions for the future. Will the pace of technology promote a change in the future from the position you are describing?

conclusion

The future of technology is unknown, but we do know that it will impact the way our society progresses. To be part of the developments that technology will bring will take good planning and attention, no matter what area of the culture you're examining. Begin now—learn how to stay on top of technology.

Ethics Project

Can Big Data Predict Your Grade?

background

As you move through your academic career, you leave an enormous swath of data: which courses you chose to register for; which ones you looked at but didn't pick; and how you did on each homework assignment, test, and project. Could this massive amount of data be analyzed to predict your grade in a course? To suggest which courses you should take next? Should those predictions be public to your instructor? To you? To financial aid officers?

research topics to consider

- Course Signals
- Degree Compass, Austin Peay State University

process

1. Divide the class into teams. Each team will select a web-based tool that allows access to information.
2. Team members should each think of a situation where a person would benefit from the type of results data mining of Big Data can bring to a campus and a situation where it might be undesirable.

3. Team members should select the most powerful and best-constructed arguments and develop a summary conclusion.
4. Team members should present their findings to the class or submit a PowerPoint presentation for review by the rest of the class, along with the summary conclusion they developed.

conclusion

As technology becomes ever more prevalent and integrated into our lives, ethical dilemmas will present themselves to an increasing extent. Being able to understand and evaluate both sides of the argument, while responding in a personally or socially ethical manner, will be an important skill.

How Technology Is Used on the World Stage and in My Personal Life

In this activity, you'll use Microsoft Word to reflect on how technology is affecting the world as well as you, personally and professionally. Reflect on the content in Chapter 1 as you work through this exercise.

You will use the following skills as you complete this activity:

- Open and Modify a Document Template
- Insert Text
- Apply Styles and Advanced Font Formats
- Apply Themes
- Use Format Painter
- Create a Header and Footer

Instructions

1. Open TIA_Ch1_Start. Save the document as **TIA_Ch1_LastFirst**, using your own Last and First names.

2. Double-click the **Title placeholder** and type **Technology**, then double-click the **Heading placeholder** and type **Introduction**. Replace the remaining placeholder text with the following: **Political and global issues are showing that technology is accelerating change around the world and galvanizing groups of people in new ways. Technology allows us to refine how we connect with each other, and it also impacts our daily personal and professional experiences.** Press **Enter**.

3. Type **How Technology Impacts Society**, press **Enter**, and then type a few sentences that describe how technology is impacting global events such as political revolutions, health care, the environment, and the digital divide. In addition, address how businesses are using social media. Press **Enter**.

4. Type **How Technology Impacts Me Personally and Professionally**, press **Enter**, and then type a few sentences that describe how technology is impacting your personal life. You should address the importance of being computer literate. You should also address the kinds of technology being used in the industry of your current or desired career.

5. Click anywhere in the heading *Introduction*, then using **Format Painter**, apply the **Heading 1** format to the paragraph headers: *How Technology Impacts Society* and *How Technology Impacts Me Personally and Professionally*.
   a. Hint: Format Painter is in the Clipboard group on the Home tab.

6. Change the Document Theme style to the **Slice Theme**.
   a. Hint: Document Themes are found on the Design tab, in the Document Formatting group.

7. Select the title *Technology*, then format the font as **Small caps**. **Center align** the title.
   a. Hint: Click the dialog box launcher in the Font group on the Home tab to access the Small caps font effect.

8. Apply the **Whisp header style** to the document. Click to add Today's date in the Date header and delete the Document title header. Add a **File Path** to the document footer. Select the footer text and change the font size to **8**. Close the Header and Footer.
   a. Hint: Headers are found on the Insert tab in the Header & Footer group. File Path is found in Document Info in the Insert group on the Header & Footer Tools Design tab.

9. Save the document and submit based on your instructor's directions.

For a chapter overview, watch the Chapter Overview Videos.

PART 1

Understanding Digital Components

Learning Outcome 2.1 **You will be able to describe the devices that make up a computer system.**

 Understanding Your Computer   40

Objective 2.1 *Describe the four main functions of a computer system and how they interact with data and information.*

Objective 2.2 *Define bits and bytes, and describe how they are measured, used, and processed.*

Objective 2.3 *List common types of computers, and discuss their main features.*

Sound Byte: Binary Numbers Interactive

Helpdesk: Understanding Bits and Bytes

 Input Devices   48

Objective 2.4 *Identify the main types of keyboards and touch screens.*

Objective 2.5 *Describe the main types of mice and pointing devices.*

Objective 2.6 *Explain how images, sounds, and sensor data are input into computing devices.*

 Output Devices   54

Objective 2.7 *Describe options for outputting images and audio from computing devices.*

Objective 2.8 *Describe various types of printers, and explain when you would use them.*

PART 2

Processing, Storage, and Connectivity

Learning Outcome 2.2 **You will be able to describe how computers process and store data and how devices connect to a computer system.**

 Processing and Memory on the Motherboard   63

Objective 2.9 *Describe the functions of the motherboard and RAM.*

Objective 2.10 *Explain the main functions of the CPU.*

Sound Byte: Smartphones Are Really Smart

 Storing Data and Information   65

Objective 2.11 *Describe the various means of storing data and information with computing devices.*

 Connecting Peripherals to the Computer   69

Objective 2.12 *Describe common types of ports used today.*

Helpdesk: Exploring Storage Devices and Ports

 Power Management and Ergonomics   70

Objective 2.13 *Describe how to manage power consumption on computing devices.*

Objective 2.14 *Define ergonomics, and discuss the ideal physical setup for using computing devices.*

For the IT Simulation for this chapter, see MyLab IT.

 All media accompanying this chapter can be found here.

 Make: A Mobile App on **page 62**

(Edelweiss/Fotolia, Tetra Images/Getty Images, Cigdem/Fotollia, Vizafoto/Fotolia, BillionPhotos.com/Fotolia, Rukanoga/Fotolia, Sebastian Kaulitzki/Shutterstock, imageBROKER/Alamy Stock Photo.

How Cool Is This?

Now that virtual reality is the hottest new trend, what will our cameras need to do in the future? How about take stunning **360-degree photos**! One of the first 360 devices on the market was the Panono 360° camera, which captures **36 images at once** and uses software to stitch them together into a single image. The device is shaped like a ball, and you can even throw it in the air and capture images. More mainstream is the Ricoh Theta S, which uses only two cameras (one on each side of the candy bar–sized device) to capture either **360-degree still or video images**. So sometime soon, expect smartphones that have this capability. Your future Instagram posts may just show the **entire world around you!**

Understanding Digital Components

Learning Outcome 2.1   You will be able to describe the devices that make up a computer system.

After reading Chapter 1, you can see why becoming computer literate is important. But where do you start? You've no doubt gleaned some knowledge about computers just from being a member of society. However, even if you've used a computer before, do you really understand how it works, what all its parts are, and what those parts do?

Understanding Your Computer

Let's start our look at computers by discussing what a computer does and how its functions make it such a useful machine.

Computers Are Data Processing Devices

Objective 2.1   *Describe the four main functions of a computer system and how they interact with data and information.*

What exactly does a computer do? Strictly defined, a **computer** is a data processing device that performs four major functions:

1. **Input:** It gathers data or allows users to enter data.
2. **Process:** It manipulates, calculates, or organizes that data into information.
3. **Output:** It displays data and information in a form suitable for the user.
4. **Storage:** It saves data and information for later use.

What's the difference between data and information? In casual conversations, people often use the terms *data* and *information* interchangeably. However, for computers, the distinction between data and information is an important one. In computer terms, **data** is a representation of a fact, a figure, or an idea. Data can be a number, a word, a picture, or even a recording of sound. For example, the number 7135553297 and the names Zoe and Richardson are pieces of data. Alone, these pieces of data probably mean little to you. **Information** is data that has been organized or presented in a meaningful fashion. When your computer provides you with a contact listing that indicates that Zoe Richardson can be reached at (713) 555-3297, the data becomes useful—that is, it becomes information.

▶ For information about the history of computers, see the History of Computers video.

How do computers interact with data and information? Computers are excellent at **processing** (manipulating, calculating, or organizing) data into information. When you first arrived on campus, you probably were directed to a place where you could get an ID card. You most likely provided a clerk with personal data that was entered into a computer. The clerk then took your picture with a digital camera (collecting more data). All of the data was then processed so that it could be printed on your ID card (see Figure 2.1). This organized output of data on your ID card is useful information.

Input data ⟶ Processing data into information ⟶ Output information

Figure 2.1 Computers process data into information. *(Mocker_bat/Fotolia)*

Binary: The Language of Computers

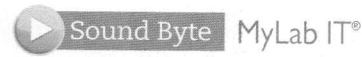

Binary Numbers Interactive

This Sound Byte helps remove the mystery surrounding binary numbers. You'll learn about base conversion between decimal, binary, and hexadecimal numbers using colors, sounds, and images.

Objective 2.2 *Define bits and bytes, and describe how they are measured, used, and processed.*

How do computers process data into information? Unlike humans, computers work exclusively with numbers (not words). To process data into information, computers need to work in a language they understand. This language, called **binary language**, consists of just two digits: 0 and 1. Everything a computer does, such as processing data, printing a file, or editing a photo, is broken down into a series of 0s and 1s. Each 0 and 1 is a **binary digit**, or **bit** for short. Eight binary digits (or bits) combine to create one **byte**. In computers, each letter of the alphabet, each number, and each special character (such as @) consists of a unique combination of eight bits, or a string of eight 0s and 1s. So, for example, in binary language, the letter *K* is represented as 01001011. This is eight bits or one byte.

How does a computer keep track of bits and bytes? Computers understand only two states of existence: on and off. Inside a computer, these two states are defined using the numbers 1 and 0. **Electrical switches** are the devices inside the computer that are flipped between the two states of 1 and 0, signifying on and off. In fact, a computer system can be viewed as an enormous collection of on/off switches. These on/off switches are combined in different ways to perform addition and subtraction and to move data around the system.

You use various forms of switches every day. A light switch is either on, allowing current to flow to the light bulb, or off. Another switch you use is a water faucet. As shown in Figure 2.2, shutting off the faucet could represent the value 0, whereas turning it on could represent the value 1.

What types of switches does a computer use? Early computers used transistors. **Transistors** are electrical switches built out of layers of a special type of material called a semiconductor. A **semiconductor** is any material that can be controlled either to conduct electricity or to act as an insulator (to prohibit electricity from passing through). Silicon, which is found in sand, is the semiconductor material used to make transistors.

By itself, silicon doesn't conduct electricity particularly well, but if specific chemicals are added in a controlled way to the silicon, it behaves like an on/off switch. The silicon allows electric current to flow when a certain voltage is applied; otherwise, it prevents electric current from flowing.

Figure 2.2 Water faucets can be used to illustrate binary switches.

Advances in technology began to require more transistors than circuit boards could handle. Something was needed to pack more transistor capacity into a smaller space. Thus, integrated circuits were developed.

What are integrated circuits? **Integrated circuits** (or **chips**) are tiny regions of semiconductor material that support a huge number of transistors (see Figure 2.3). Most integrated circuits are no more than a quarter inch in size yet can hold billions of transistors. This advancement has enabled computer designers to create small yet powerful **microprocessors**, which are the chips that contain a **central processing unit** (**CPU**, or **processor**). The CPU can be considered the "brains" of the computer, since this is where the processing of data into information takes place. Today, more than 2 billion transistors can be manufactured in a space as tiny as your little fingernail!

What else can bits and bytes be used for? Not only are bits and bytes used as the language that tells the computer what to do, they are used to represent the quantity of data and information that the computer inputs and outputs. Word files, digital pictures, and software are represented inside computing devices as a series of bits and bytes. These files and applications can be quite large, containing billions of bytes.

Figure 2.3 An integrated circuit is packaged in a small case but holds billions of transistors. *(krasyuk/Fotolia)*

To make it easier to measure the size of such files, we need units of measure larger than a byte. Kilobytes, megabytes, and gigabytes are therefore simply larger amounts of bytes. As shown in Figure 2.4, a **kilobyte (KB)** is approximately 1,000 bytes, a **megabyte (MB)** is about 1 million bytes, and a **gigabyte (GB)** is around 1 billion bytes. Today, personal computers are capable of storing **terabytes (TB)** (around 1 trillion bytes) of data, and many business computers can store up to a **petabyte (PB)** (1,000 terabytes) of data. The Google search engine processes more than 1 PB of user-generated data per hour!

Figure 2.4 How Much Is a Byte?

1 Byte (B)
= a single letter
= a single wood block
1-inch cube

1 tweet = 200 Bytes
= a shoebox of blocks
(140 are main message. Source: Twitter)

1 small Instagram picture
≈ **50 Kilobytes (Kb)**
≈ 50,000 bytes
≈ a typical car's cabin filled with blocks

3 minute MP3 song
≈ **5 Megabytes (Mb)**
≈ 5,000,000 bytes
≈ a standard shipping container full of blocks

1 movie,
1080p HD, compressed
≈ **5 Gigabytes (Gb)**
≈ 5,000,000,000 bytes
≈ 32.75 Olympic swimming
pools full of blocks

Twitter's typical daily volume of
500,000,000 tweets × 200 bytes
≈ **200 Gigabytes (Gb)**
≈ 200,000,000,000 bytes
≈ half-fill the Vehicle Assembly Building
at the Kennedy Space Center
(Sources: Twitter, NASA)

Wikipedia
≈ **10 Terabytes (Tb)**
≈ 10,000,000,000,000 bytes
≈ a layer covering
Rhode Island 2.5 times
(June 2015, all pages with edit
history, uncompressed.
Source: Wikipedia)

Facebook's server capacity
≈ **100 Petabytes (Pb)**
≈ 100,000,000,000,000,000 bytes
≈ coating North America 2.8 times
(Media only. February 2012. Source: Facebook)

How does a computer process bits and bytes? A computer uses hardware and software to process data into information that lets you complete tasks such as writing a letter or playing a game. **Hardware** is any part of the computer you can physically touch. **Software** is the set of computer programs that enables the hardware to perform different tasks. **Application software** is what you use to help you carry out tasks such as writing a research paper. **System software** enables your computer's hardware devices and application software to work together. The most common type of system software is the **operating system (OS)**—the program that controls how your computer functions. Most likely, your computer's operating system is a version of Microsoft Windows or Apple's macOS.

Types of Computers

Objective 2.3 *List common types of computers, and discuss their main features.*

What types of computers are popular for personal use? There are two basic designs of computers: portable and stationary. For portable computers, three main categories exist: cell phones, tablets, and laptops.

Cell Phones

Are cell phones really computers? All cell phones have the same components as any computer: a processor (central processing unit, or CPU), memory, and input and output devices, as shown in Figure 2.5. Cell phones also require their own operating system (OS) software and have their own application software. So, in effect, all cell phones are indeed computers.

What makes a cell phone a smartphone? **Smartphones** use a CPU and an interface so powerful that they can take on many of the same tasks as much more expensive computers: videoconferencing, recording and editing high-definition (HD) video, and broadcasting live-streaming video. Most providers, like AT&T or Verizon, label a smartphone as one that has sufficient power so that you can use Internet features easily. You often have to purchase a data plan with a smartphone. Smartphones like the iPhone and tablets like the iPad illustrate the true power of **digital convergence**—they incorporate a range of features that used to be available only in separate, dedicated devices (see Figure 2.6):

- Internet access
- Personal information management (PIM) features
- Voice recording features
- The ability to play and organize music files
- GPS services
- Digital image and video capture
- Computing power to run programs like word processors and video-editing software

Understanding Bits and Bytes

In this Helpdesk, you'll play the role of a helpdesk staffer, fielding questions about the difference between data and information, what bits and bytes are, and how bytes are measured.

Music player

Digital camera

GPS

Remote control

Figure 2.6 A single device like a tablet can play the role of many separate devices, illustrating the concept of digital convergence. *(Rostislav Sedlacek/Fotolia; Science Photo Library/Shutterstock; OnBlast/ Shutterstock; Andrey Popov/ Shutterstock; Amakar/Fotolia)*

Figure 2.5 Inside your cell phone, you'll find a CPU; a memory chip; input devices such as a microphone and a touch screen; and output devices such as a display screen. *(Copyright 2014 iFixit)*

Isn't every phone a smartphone now? Although many cell phones on the market are considered smartphones, less powerful cell phones are still available. Called **feature phones**, these inexpensive phones have modest processors, simpler interfaces, and often no touch screen. As more features are integrated into every cell phone product, though, it becomes difficult to distinguish a smartphone from a feature phone. We'll use the term *cell phone* to refer to all cellular phones and *smartphone* to refer to the more powerful type of cell phone that can run more complex applications.

Tablets

A **tablet computer**, such as the Apple iPad or Amazon Fire, is a portable computer integrated into a multitouch-sensitive screen. Tablet computers use an on-screen keyboard, but you can also connect external keyboards to tablets.

How do tablets compare with smartphones? Tablets are very light, portable devices, although not as light as smartphones. The top-selling tablets include the Apple iPad and the Samsung Galaxy, but there are over 75 tablets on the market. One difference between tablets and smartphones is that you can't make cellular phone calls from most tablets. In addition, whereas smartphones usually have displays that are less than 5 inches, tablets come with screen sizes between 7 and 10 inches. However, manufacturers are beginning to make even larger phones, offering a **phablet** model of phone, with screen sizes of almost 6 inches.

In most other regards, smartphones and tablets are similar. They have the following features:

- Similar operating systems: Common operating systems, such as iOS, Android, or Windows 10, operate on smartphones and tablets.
- Similar processors: The processing power of smartphones and tablets is often the same.
- Touch-screen interfaces: Smartphones and tablets are both equipped with touch-screen interfaces.
- Long battery life: Most tablets and smartphones run at least 10 hours on a single charge.
- Similar software applications: Most apps available for one device are available in a compatible version for the other type of device.
- Similar Internet connectivity: Both can offer cellular and wireless access to the Internet.
- Bluetooth: Most smartphones and tablets on the market today are Bluetooth-enabled, meaning they include a small Bluetooth chip that allows them to transfer data wirelessly to any other Bluetooth-enabled device. Bluetooth is a wireless transmission standard that lets you connect devices such as smartphones, tablets, and laptops to devices such as keyboards and headsets. **Bluetooth technology** uses radio waves to transmit data signals over distances up to approximately 1,200 feet for Bluetooth 5 devices.

Can tablets function as a communication device? Although tablets are currently not able to make cell phone calls, they can easily place audio or video phone calls if connected to a Wi-Fi network. An application like Skype that makes Internet phone calls is required for that. There are also apps available that allow tablets to handle texting. WhatsApp, for example, supports free national and international texting from a range of devices, including tablets.

Laptops and Their Variants

A **laptop** (or **notebook**) **computer** is a portable computer that has a keyboard, monitor, and other devices integrated into a single compact case. This was the first type of portable computer, but as our demand for lighter and more portable computers accelerated, tablets and smartphones were developed. There are several variations of laptops, including 2-in-1 PCs, ultrabooks, and Chromebooks.

What is a 2-in-1 PC? A **2-in-1 PC** is a laptop computer that can convert into a tablet-like device (see Figure 2.7). In laptop mode, there is a physical keyboard, while in tablet mode you use an on-screen keyboard. On some models, such as Microsoft Surface devices, the touch screen is detachable from the keyboard so it can be carried and used as an independent tablet. On others, such as the Lenovo Yoga, there is a hinge so that the keyboard can be folded behind the screen. Usually, there are no DVD or CD drives on 2-in-1 computers.

Why would I want a 2-in-1 instead of a tablet? Although more expensive than a tablet, 2-in-1s have a more powerful CPU so they can function as a laptop. Also, whereas a tablet runs a mobile OS, like Android or iOS, a 2-in-1 uses a full traditional OS, like Windows, and can therefore run the same software applications as a laptop. In addition, a 2-in-1 has a physical keyboard when you need it. Many people find a single 2-in-1 can replace the need to carry both a tablet and a laptop.

Figure 2.7 The Microsoft Surface is an example of a 2-in-1 type of device: a touch-screen tablet and a detachable keyboard merged into one unit. *(Drew Angerer/Getty Images News/Getty Images)*

How are ultrabooks different from laptops? **Ultrabooks** are a category of full-featured computers that focus on offering a very thin, lightweight computing solution. Examples include the Apple Macbook Air and the Asus Zenbook. Ultrabooks don't offer DVD or CD drives, for example, allowing a very thin profile. Some do not even offer traditional USB ports, instead using the more compact USB-C connector so that they are only about 13 mm at the thickest point. Most ultrabooks offer SSD drives and so have very fast response times on startup and restoring from a low power state. They weigh in at under 3 pounds even though they feature the same operating systems and CPUs as heavier, larger laptops. They also include full-size keyboards and 13- to 15-inch screens.

What is a Chromebook? A **Chromebook** is a special breed of laptop that uses the Google Chrome OS and is designed to be connected to the Internet at all times. Documents and apps are stored primarily in the cloud as opposed to locally. Because the Chrome OS places less demand on computing hardware than a conventional operating system (such as Windows or macOS), it can run the Chrome browser much more efficiently. If you do most of your work within a browser and need a lightweight, inexpensive computer, a Chromebook might be what you are seeking. However, remember that to use a Chromebook most effectively, you should have an active Internet connection.

Choosing a Portable Device

With all these choices, how do I know which device is best for me? Use these guidelines to determine what particular device best fits your personal needs:

- **Power:** How much computational power do you need?
- **Screen size and resolution:** These cannot be changed later, so make sure the quality and size of screen will fit your needs for the years you'll keep the device.
- **Style of keyboard:** Do you want a touch-based interface? Is a physical keyboard important, or is an on-screen keyboard sufficient? Does the feel of the keyboard work for you?
- **Battery life:** Some devices can operate for 15 hours continuously, others less than 5. Investigate whether the battery can be upgraded and how much weight that would add.
- **Weight:** Does an additional 2 pounds matter? (Lighter devices usually cost more.) Remember to include the weight of any charging brick you would need to carry when you travel as you consider the tradeoff in price for a lighter device.
- **Number of devices:** Is this your only computing device? As technology prices fall, you may be able to have more than one device. You might find an affordable solution that includes both a very mobile device and a second more powerful one.

Figure 2.8 summarizes the various mobile device categories.

Smartphone
- 0.25 lbs
- Mobile OS

Tablet
- Less than 2 lbs
- Mobile OS

2-in-1
- 1 to 3 lbs
- Traditional OS

Ultrabook
- Less than 3 lbs
- Traditional OS

Laptop
- 5 to 8 lbs
- Traditional OS

Figure 2.8 A full spectrum of mobile devices is available. *(Sean Gallup/Getty Images; Josep Lago/AFP/Getty Images; Ethan Miller/Getty Images; Chris Tzou/ Bloomberg/Getty Images; Peter Dazeley/Photographer's Choice/Getty Images)*

Stationary Computers

What are the main stationary computers available to consumers? A **desktop computer** is intended for use at a single location, so it's stationary (see Figure 2.9a). Most desktop computers consist of a separate case or tower (called the **system unit**) that houses the main components of the computer and to which peripheral devices are attached. A **peripheral device** is a component, such as a monitor or keyboard, that connects to the computer.

An **all-in-one computer**, such as the Apple iMac, eliminates the need for a separate tower because these computers house the computer's processor and memory in the monitor (see Figure 2.9b). Many all-in-one models also incorporate touch-screen technology.

What are the advantages of a desktop computer? Desktop computers are easier to upgrade than laptops or other portable computers (which often cannot be upgraded at all). Upgrades to components such as video cards are often important for gamers and graphic artists. Also, large screens are beneficial in many working environments (such as graphic design) and if a computer doesn't need portability you can use a larger monitor without a problem. Finally, miniaturization of components is usually costly. Therefore, you can often get more computing power for your dollar when you buy a desktop computer.

Are there any other types of computers? Although you may never come into direct contact with the following types of computers, they are still very important and do a lot of work behind the scenes of daily life:

- A **mainframe** is a large, expensive computer that supports many users simultaneously. Mainframes are often used in businesses that manage large amounts of data, such as insurance companies, where many people are working at the same time on similar operations, such as claims processing. Mainframes excel at executing many computer programs at the same time.
- A **supercomputer** is a specially designed computer that can perform complex calculations extremely rapidly. Supercomputers are used when complex models requiring intensive mathematical calculations are needed (such as weather forecasting or atomic energy research). Supercomputers are designed to execute a few programs as quickly as possible, whereas mainframes are designed to handle many programs running at the same time but at a slower pace.
- An **embedded computer** is a specially designed computer chip that resides in another device, such as your car, a drone, or the electronic thermostat in your home. Embedded computers are self-contained computer devices that have their own programming and that typically don't receive input from you or interact with other systems.

Figure 2.9 (a) A desktop computer has a system unit that holds the main components. (b) An all-in-one computer does not need a separate system unit. *(Adempercem/Fotolia; Best pixels/Shutterstock)*

Each part of your computer has a specific purpose that coordinates with one of the functions of the computer—input, processing, output, or storage (see Figure 2.10). Additional devices, such as Wi-Fi adapters and routers, help a computer communicate with the Internet and other computers to facilitate the sharing of documents and other resources. Let's begin our exploration of hardware by looking at your computer's input devices.

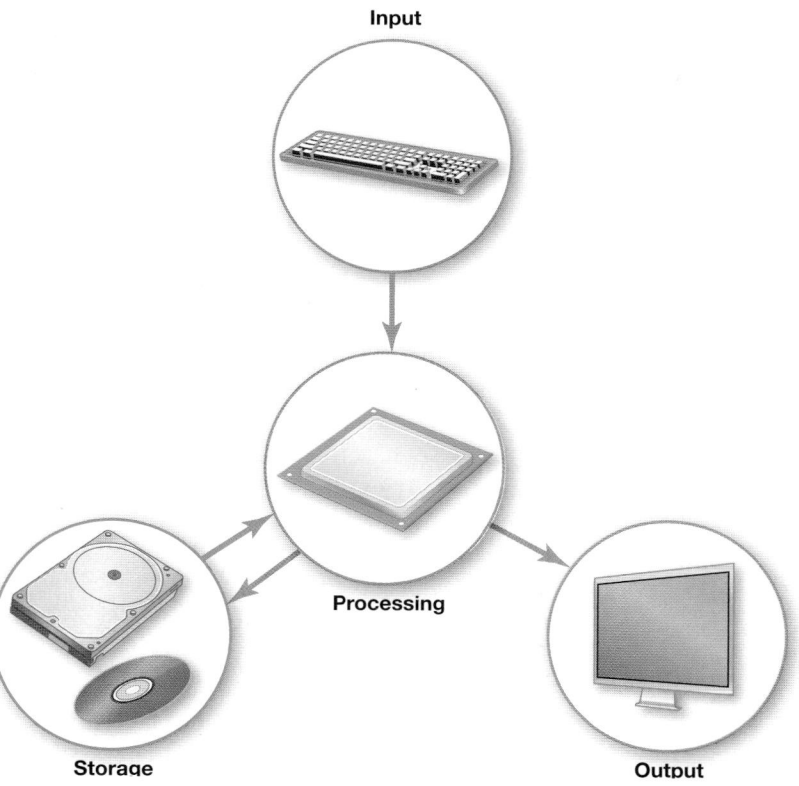

Input

Processing

Storage

Output

Figure 2.10   Each part of the computer serves a special function.

Bits&Bytes   Today's Supercomputers: Faster Than Ever

Supercomputers are the biggest and most powerful type of computer. Scientists and engineers use these computers to solve complex problems or to perform massive computations. Some supercomputers are single computers with multiple processors, whereas others consist of multiple computers that work together. The Sunway TaihuLight was recently ranked as the world's fastest supercomputer (see Figure 2.11). It features a whopping 10,649,600 computing cores and runs the Linux operating system. The computer is expected to perform research in fields such as climate, weather and earth systems modeling, advanced manufacturing, life sciences research, and data analytics.

Figure 2.11   Deployed at the National Supercomputing Center in Wuxi, China, the Sunway TaihuLight is the world's fastest supercomputer—for now! Check **TOP500.org** for the latest rankings.
(*Xinhua/Alamy Stock Photo*)

Input Devices

An **input device** lets you enter data (text, images, and sounds) and instructions (user responses and commands) into your computer. Let's look at some of the most popular input devices used today.

Physical Keyboards and Touch Screens

Objective 2.4   *Identify the main types of keyboards and touch screens.*

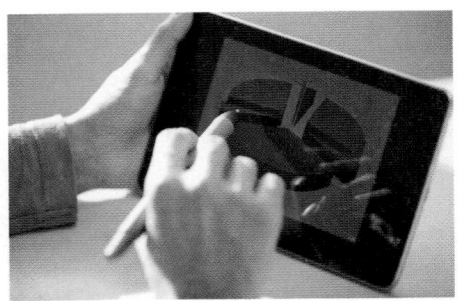

Figure 2.12 Touch screens respond to commands initiated by touching with a finger or a stylus. *(Arman Zhenikeyev/Alamy Stock Photo)*

What is the most common way to input data and commands? A **keyboard** is an input device you use to enter typed data and commands. However, as discussed earlier, computing devices such as smartphones, tablets, and many laptops now respond to touch. **Touch screens** are display screens that respond to commands initiated by touching them with your finger or a **stylus**—a device that looks like a pen and that you use to tap commands or draw on a screen (see Figure 2.12). Touch-screen devices use a **virtual keyboard** that displays on screen when text input is required. These keyboards show basic keyboard configurations but allow you to switch to other special keys. Virtual keyboards can also support dozens of languages and different character sets.

Are all keyboards the same? Whether virtual or physical, the most common keyboard layout is a standard **QWERTY keyboard**. This keyboard layout gets its name from the first six letters in the top-left row of alphabetic keys and is the standard English-language keyboard layout. The QWERTY layout was originally designed for typewriters and was meant to slow typists and prevent typewriter keys from jamming. Although the QWERTY layout is considered inefficient because it slows typing speeds, efforts to change to more efficient layouts, such as that of the Dvorak keyboard (see Figure 2.13), have not been met with much public interest.

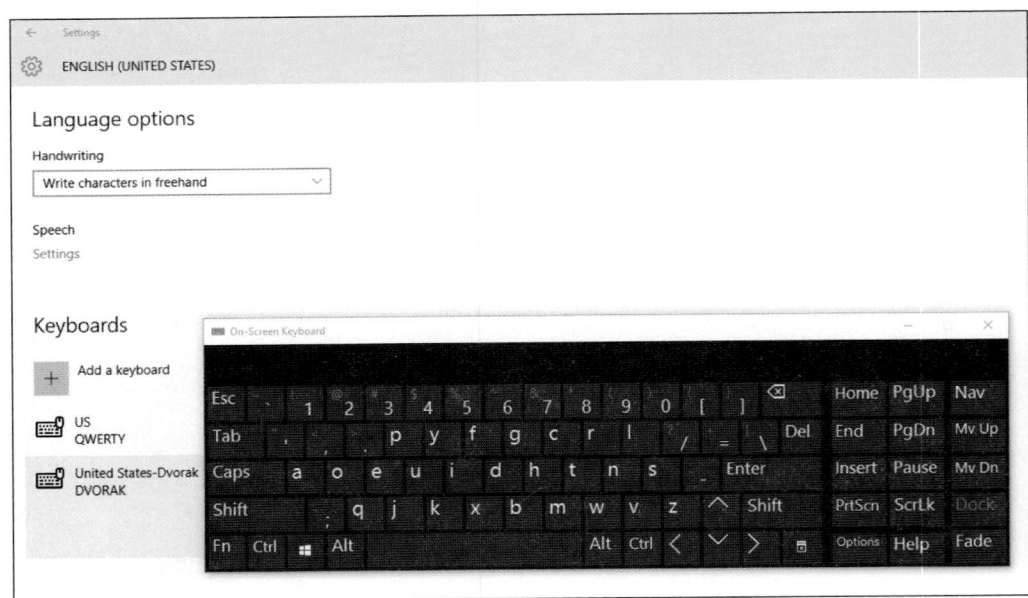

Figure 2.13 The Dvorak keyboard is an alternative keyboard layout that puts the most commonly used letters in the English language on "home keys"—the keys in the middle row of the keyboard. The Dvorak keyboard's design reduces the distance your fingers travel for most keystrokes, increasing typing speed. You can customize the layout of your keyboard using the Windows operating system.

> *To change your keyboard layout in Windows 10, click **Settings** from the Start menu, click **Time & language**, then click **Region & language**. Select **Windows display language**, select **Options**, click **Add a keyboard**, and then select **United States-Dvorak**. (Windows 10, Microsoft Corporation)*

How can I use my keyboard most efficiently? All keyboards have the standard set of alphabetic and numeric keys that you regularly use when typing. As shown in Figure 2.14, many keyboards for laptop and desktop computers have additional keys that perform special functions. Knowing how to use the special keys shown in Figure 2.14 will help you improve your efficiency.

What alternatives are there to a virtual keyboard? Virtual keyboards are not always convenient when a great deal of typing is required. Most computing devices can accept physical keyboards as an add-on accessory. Wired keyboards plug into a data port on the computing device. Wireless keyboards send data to the computer using a form of wireless technology that uses radio frequency (RF). A radio transmitter in the keyboard sends out signals that are received either by a receiving device plugged into a port on the device or by a Bluetooth receiving device located in the computing device. Often, Bluetooth keyboards for tablets are integrated with a case to protect your tablet (see Figure 2.15a).

Flexible keyboards are a terrific alternative if you want a full-sized keyboard for your laptop or tablet. You can roll one up, fit it in your backpack, and plug it into a USB port when you need it. Another compact keyboard alternative is a laser-projection keyboard (see Figure 2.15b), which is about the size of a matchbox. They project an image of a keyboard onto any flat surface, and sensors detect the motion of your fingers as you "type." Data is transmitted to the device via Bluetooth. These keyboards work with the latest smartphones and tablets.

Figure 2.14 Keyboards have a variety of keys that help you work more efficiently. (Note that on Macs, Function keys are slightly different, the Control function is the Apple key or Command key, and the Alt function is the Option key.)

Figure 2.15 (a) Cases with integrated physical keyboards make tablets more typing friendly. (b) Laser-projection keyboard devices project the image of a QWERTY keyboard on any surface. Sensors detect typing motions, and data is transmitted to your device via Bluetooth technology. *(Photo courtesy of Logitech www.logitech.com; Hammacher Schlemmer/Splash News/Newscom)*

Mice and Other Pointing Devices

Objective 2.5 *Describe the main types of mice and pointing devices.*

What input is a mouse responsible for? A **mouse** is the most common pointing device used to enter user responses and commands. One of the mouse's most important functions is to position the cursor. The **cursor** is an onscreen icon (often shown by a vertical bar or an arrow) that helps the user keep track of exactly what is active on the display screen. For instance, in word processing software, the cursor allows you to see exactly where the next character will be typed in a sentence based on its position. To move the cursor to another point on a touch screen you just tap the screen with your finger. Or to select an item on the screen, you just tap it with your finger. But laptops and desktop computers that are not touch enabled need other types of devices (like mice) for positioning the cursor and selecting icons.

What kinds of mice are there? The most common mouse type is the **optical mouse**. An optical mouse uses an internal sensor or laser to detect the mouse's movement. The sensor sends signals to the computer, telling it where to move the pointer on the screen. Optical mice don't require a mouse pad, though you can use one to enhance the movement of the mouse on an uneven surface or to protect your work surface from being scratched.

Figure 2.16 The RAT Pro^X Precision Gaming Mouse looks more like it belongs in Star Wars than on your desk! But it offers the ultimate in customizability for serious gamers or users with special needs. *(Mad Catz, Inc.)*

Most mice have two or three buttons that let you execute commands and open shortcut menus. (Mice for Macs sometimes have only one button.) Many customizable mice have additional programmable buttons and wheels that let you quickly maneuver through web pages or games (see Figure 2.16). These mice are also customizable to fit any size hand and grip style by allowing for length and width adjustments. Aside from gamers, many people use customizable mice to reduce susceptibility to repetitive strain injuries or if they suffer from physical limitations that prevent them from using standard mice.

How do wireless mice connect to a computing device? Wireless mice usually connect the same way that wireless keyboards do—either through an integrated Bluetooth chip or a Bluetooth receiver that plugs into a USB port. Wireless mice have receivers that often fit inside the battery compartment of the mouse for easy storage when not in use.

Touch-screen technology was developed in 1971 and used primarily with ATMs and fast-food order displays. The technology for monitors and other displays was made popular by the iPod Touch in 2007 and is now in smartphones, tablets, laptops, and desktop monitors. But how do touch-screen monitors know where you're touching? How do they know what you want them to do?

The basic idea behind touch screens is pretty straightforward—when you place your finger or stylus on a screen, it changes the physical state of the screen and registers your touch. The location of your touch is then translated into a command. Three basic systems are used to recognize a person's touch: *resistive, capacitive,* and *surface acoustic wave*. All of these systems require the basic components of a touch-responsive glass panel, controller, and software driver, combined with a display and computer processor.

The *resistive system* maps the exact location of the pressure point created when a user touches the screen. The *capacitive system* (see Figure 2.17) uses the change in the electric charge on the glass panel of the monitor, which is created by the user's touch, to generate a location. The third technology, *surface acoustic wave system*, uses two transducers (electrical devices that convert energy from one form to another) that are placed along the x and y axes of the monitor's glass plate. Reflectors, which are also placed on the glass, are used to reflect an electric signal sent from the sending transducer to the receiving transducer. The receiving transducer determines whether the signal has been disturbed by a touch event and locates the touch instantly. With all three systems, the display's software driver then translates the touch into something the operating system can understand, similar to how a mouse driver translates a mouse's movements into a click or drag.

Because the resistive system uses pressure to register a touch, it doesn't matter if the touch is created by a finger or another device. On the other hand, a capacitive system must have conductive input, so generally a finger is required. The surface acoustic wave system allows touches by any object.

The iPhone introduced another complexity to the touch-screen system—a multitouch user interface. In addition to just pressing the screen in one location, multitouch technology can process multiple simultaneous touches on the screen. For example, pinching or spreading out your thumb and finger together makes the display zoom out and in, respectively. The features of each touch, such as size, shape, and location, are also determined.

A touch-sensitive screen, like the one used with the iPhone and iPad and with many other smartphones and tablets, arranges the capacitors in a coordinate system so the circuitry can sense changes at each point along the grid (see Figure 2.18). Consequently, every point on the grid generates its own signal when touched and can do so even as another signal is being generated simultaneously. The signals are then relayed to the device's processor. This allows the device to determine the location and movement of simultaneous touches in multiple locations.

After detecting the position and type of touch occurring on the display, the device's processor combines this information with the information it has about the application in use and what was being done in the application when the touch occurred. The processor relays that information to the program in use, and the command is executed. All this happens seemingly instantaneously.

Figure 2.17 Some basic touch screens use a capacitive system to detect touches and translate them into meaningful commands that are understood by the computer's operating system.

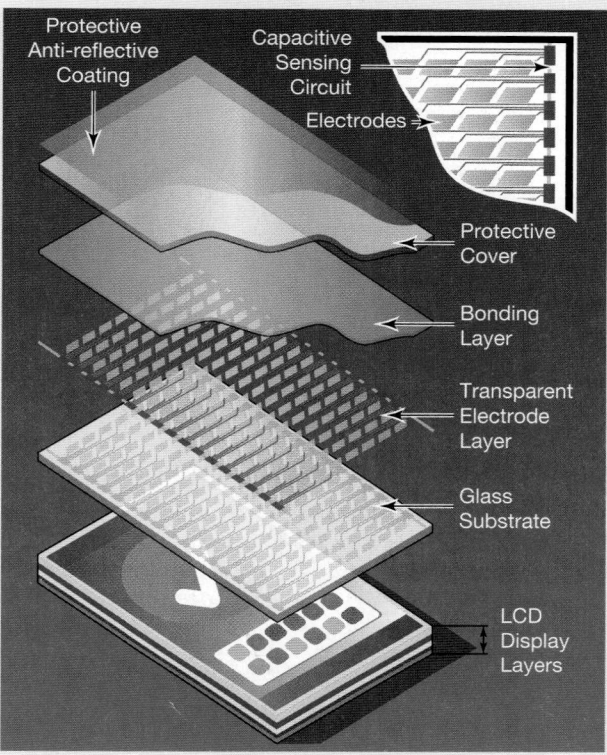

Figure 2.18 Multitouch screens use a coordinate-based grid to arrange the capacitors so the circuitry can detect and respond to multiple touches occurring at the same time.

Why would I want to use a mouse with a touch-screen device? If you're using a physical keyboard with your touch-screen device, it's often easier to perform actions with a mouse rather than taking your hands off the keyboard and reaching to touch the screen. In addition, there are new kinds of mice, called *touch mice*, that are designed with touch-screen computers in mind. Unlike traditional mice, there are no specifically defined buttons. The top surface of a touch mouse is the button. You use one, two, or three fingers to perform touch-screen tasks such as scrolling, switching through open apps, and zooming. Touch mice also allow you to perform traditional mouse tasks, such as moving the cursor when you move the mouse.

What pointing devices do laptops use? Most laptops have an integrated pointing device, such as a **touch pad** (or **trackpad**)—a small, touch-sensitive area at the base of the keyboard. Mac laptops include multitouch trackpads, which don't have buttons but are controlled by various one-, two-, three-, and four-finger actions. For example, scrolling is controlled by brushing two fingers along the trackpad in any direction. Most touch pads are sensitive to taps, interpreting them as mouse clicks. Most laptops also have buttons under or near the pad to record mouse clicks.

What input devices are used with games? **Game controllers** such as joysticks, game pads, and steering wheels are also considered input devices because they send data to computing devices. Game controllers, which are similar to the devices used on gaming consoles such as the Xbox One and the PlayStation, are also available for use with computers. They have buttons and miniature pointing devices that provide input to the computer. Most game controllers, such as those for Rock Band and the Wii U, are wireless to provide extra mobility.

Image, Sound, and Sensor Input

Objective 2.6 *Explain how images, sounds, and sensor data are input into computing devices.*

What are popular input devices for images? Digital cameras, camcorders, and mobile device cameras capture pictures and video and are considered input devices. Stand-alone devices can connect to your computer with a cable, transmit data wirelessly, or transfer data automatically through the Internet.

Flatbed scanners also input images. They work similarly to a photocopy machine; however, instead of generating the image on paper, they create a digital image, which you can then print, save, or e-mail. Flatbed scanners are often used in conjunction with **optical character recognition (OCR) software**, which digitizes and saves text in digital form. Many businesses and libraries use OCR software to reduce volumes of reports and books to manageable digital files.

The digital cameras in cell phones are also often used to scan information. For example, many health and fitness apps, like MyFitnessPal, capture data by using the cell phone's camera to scan UPC codes on food products. The devices used at supermarkets and retail stores to scan the UPC codes on your purchases are also a type of scanner that inputs information into another computer: the point-of-sale terminal (cash register).

A **webcam** is a front-facing camera that attaches to a desktop computer or is built into a computing device. Although webcams are able to capture still images, they're used mostly for capturing and transmitting live video. Videoconferencing software lets a person using a device equipped with a webcam and a microphone transmit video and audio across the Internet. Video apps such as Skype (see the Try This in Chapter 1) and Google Hangouts make it easy to videoconference with multiple people (see Figure 2.19).

Figure 2.19 Videoconferencing relies on two input devices: a webcam and a microphone.
(Andriy Popov/123RF)

How do my computing devices benefit from accepting sound input? Inputting sound to your computer requires using a **microphone** (or **mic**)—a device that lets you capture sound waves (such as your voice) and transfer them to digital format on your computer. Laptops, tablets, and smartphones come with built-in microphones. In addition to letting others hear you in a videoconference, equipping your device to accept sound input enables you to conduct audio conferences, chat with people over the Internet, record podcasts, and even control computing devices with your voice.

How can I use my voice to control my computing device? **Voice recognition software** allows you to control your devices by speaking into a microphone instead of using a keyboard or mouse. Apps like Dragon Naturally Speaking are available as stand-alone apps, but voice recognition features are built into the Windows and macOS operating systems as well.

Popular extensions of voice recognition software are **intelligent personal assistants** such as Apple's Siri, Google Assistant, and Microsoft's Cortana (see Figure 2.20). These so-called software agents respond to voice commands and then use your input, access to the Internet, and location-aware services to perform various tasks, such as finding the closest pizza parlor to your present location.

What types of add-on microphones are available? For specialized situations, built-in microphones don't always provide the best performance. You may want to consider adding other types of microphones, such as those shown in Figure 2.21, to your system for the best results.

Microphone icon

Figure 2.20 Just tap the microphone icon and ask Microsoft's intelligent personal assistant Cortana a question. She communicates using natural language processing techniques.

Figure 2.21   Types of Microphones

Microphone Type	Attributes	Best Used For
Close Talk 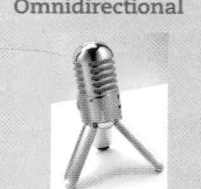	• Attached to a headset (allows for listening) • Leaves hands free	• Videoconferencing • Phone calls • Speech recognition software
Omnidirectional	• Picks up sounds equally well from all directions	• Conference calls in meeting rooms
Unidirectional	• Picks up sounds from only one direction	• Recordings with one voice (podcasts)
Clip-on (Lavalier) 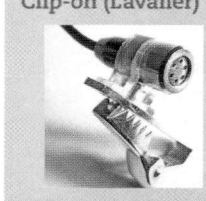	• Clips to clothing • Available as wireless	• Presentations requiring freedom of movement • Leaves hands free for writing on white board

(Fotolia; Sumnersgraphicsinc/Fotolia; Feliks Gurevich/Shutterstock; Joseph Branston/PC Format Magazine via Getty Images)

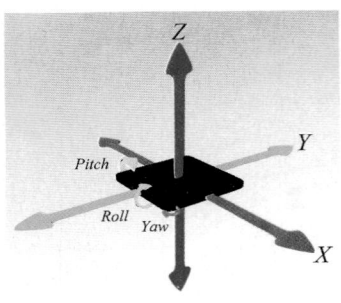

Figure 2.22 The accelerometer is a sensor in your phone (or tablet) that provides input as to the orientation of your device along the three main axes. *(CHIH HSIEN HANG/123RF)*

What other types of input devices are found in computers? Smartphones and tablets are now arrayed with a variety of sensors. Broadly speaking, a **sensor** is any device that detects or measures something. Sensors feed data into the device and are used by the hardware or apps that rely on the input provided. The following sensors can be found in almost all smartphones and many tablets today (although your particular device may not contain every one):

- *Accelerometer*: measures acceleration that the device is experiencing. It also helps determine the orientation of the device along three axes (see Figure 2.22), which allows the device to determine if it is in landscape or portrait orientation.
- *Gyroscope*: provides orientation information but with greater precision than the accelerometer.
- *Magnetometer*: detects magnetic fields. Compass and metal detecting apps use this sensor.
- *Proximity sensor*: used in phones to determine when the phone is placed next to your ear so the phone knows to shut off the display while you are talking.
- *Light sensor*: measures ambient light brightness so the device can adjust the brightness of the display.
- *Barometer*: measures atmospheric pressure to determine how high the device is above sea level. This improves GPS accuracy and also enables counting floors more accurately when step climbing.
- *Thermometer*: measures ambient temperature either inside or outside the device. Mainly used to monitor overheating of delicate electronic components inside the device.
- *Pedometer*: used to record the number of steps taken while having the device in your possession.
- *Fingerprint sensor*: used to record and read fingerprint data to secure the device.
- *Heart rate monitor*: measures pulse rate by detecting pulsating blood vessels inside your finger.

Want to access the sensors in your smartphone? Try our Make This activities in the middle of each chapter to learn how to build your own Android apps that can gather information from the sensors in your smartphone.

Output Devices

An **output device** lets you send processed data out of your computer in the form of text, pictures (graphics), sounds (audio), or video. Let's look at some popular output devices.

Image and Audio Output

Objective 2.7 *Describe options for outputting images and audio from computing devices.*

Computing devices need options for outputting data so you can transfer it to other locations. Sometimes you need only soft copies of data, such as a graph displayed on your screen. Other times you need a hard copy, such as a printed page. Let's explore the most common output device: the display screen.

Image Output

What are the different types of display screens? A **display screen** (sometimes referred to as a **monitor** on desktops and laptops) displays text, graphics, and videos. The most common type of monitor for laptop and desktop computers is a **liquid crystal display (LCD)**. An LCD monitor, also called a *flat-panel monitor*, is light and energy efficient. Some newer monitors use **light-emitting diode (LED)** technology, which is more energy efficient and may have better color accuracy and thinner panels than LCD monitors.

Organic light-emitting diode (OLED) displays use organic compounds that produce light when exposed to an electric current. Unlike LCDs and LEDs, OLEDs do not require a backlight to function and therefore draw less power and have a much thinner display, sometimes as thin as 3 mm. They are also brighter and more environmentally friendly than LCDs. Because of their lower power needs, OLED displays run longer on a single battery charge than do LEDs, which is why OLED technology is probably the technology used in your smartphone, tablet, and digital camera.

Companies like LG are now working on transparent and flexible OLED display screens (see Figure 2.23). These screens allow you to see what is behind the screen while still being able to display information on the screen. These types of screens present interesting possibilities for augmentative reality. As described in Chapter 1, *augmentative reality (AR)* is a view of a real-world environment whose elements are augmented (or supplemented) by some type of computer-generated sensory input such as video, graphics, or GPS data. For instance, if you had a transparent screen on your smartphone and held it up to view street signs that were in English, you could possibly have your phone display the signs in another language. Currently, applications like this exist (such as Pokémon Go) but require the use of a camera as well as your screen. But transparent screens will eliminate the need for the camera.

Figure 2.23 Because they don't need a backlight, OLED displays can be made transparent and flexible. *(YONHAP/EPA/Newscom)*

How do display screens work? Display screens are grids made up of millions of tiny dots, called **pixels**. When these pixels are illuminated by the light waves generated by a fluorescent panel at the back of your screen, they create the images you see on the screen or monitor. Each pixel on the newest 4K resolution TVs and monitors is actually made up of four yellow, red, blue, and green subpixels. Some newer TVs further split the subpixels into upper and lower, which can brighten and darken independently. LCD monitors are made of two or more sheets of material filled with a liquid crystal solution (see Figure 2.24). A fluorescent panel at the back of the LCD monitor generates light waves. When electric current passes through the liquid crystal solution, the crystals move around and either block the fluorescent light or let the light shine through. This blocking or passing of light by the crystals causes images to form on the screen. The various combinations of yellow, red, blue, and green make up the components of color we see on our monitors.

What factors affect the quality of a display screen? Some portable devices don't provide a choice of screens. The current iPhone has whatever screen Apple chooses to use. But when choosing a laptop or a monitor for a desktop, you have options to compare.

The most important factors to consider are aspect ratio and resolution. The **aspect ratio** is the width-to-height proportion of a monitor. Traditionally, aspect ratios have been 4:3, but newer monitors are available with an aspect ratio of 16:9 to accommodate HD video. The screen **resolution**, or the clearness or sharpness of the image, reflects the number of pixels on the screen. An LCD monitor may have a native (or maximum) resolution of 1600 × 1200, meaning it contains 1600 vertical columns with 1200 pixels in each column. The higher the resolution, the sharper and clearer the image, but generally, the resolution of an LCD monitor is dictated by the screen size and aspect ratio. Although you can change the resolution of an LCD monitor beyond its native resolution, the images may become distorted. Generally, you should buy a monitor with the highest resolution available for the screen size (measured in inches).

Is a bigger screen size always better? The bigger the screen, the more you can display, and depending on what you want to display, size may matter. In general, the larger the screen, the larger the number of pixels it can display. For example, a 27-inch monitor can display 2560 × 1440 pixels, whereas a 21.5-inch monitor may only be able to display 1680 × 1050 pixels. However, new monitors have at least the 1920 × 1080 resolution (based on the HDTV resolution) required to display Blu-ray movies.

Larger screens can also allow you to view multiple documents or web pages at the same time. However, buying two smaller monitors might be cheaper than buying one large monitor. For either option—a big screen or two separate screens—check that your computer has the video hardware needed to support the display devices.

Rear glass · Colored light · Polarizer · Front glass · Unpolarized white light from backlight · Polarizer · Liquid crystals · Color filters

Figure 2.24 A magnification of a single pixel in a 4K LCD monitor.

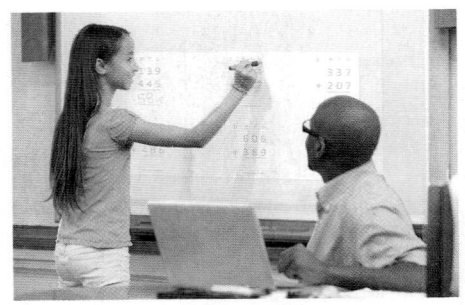

Figure 2.25 Interactive white boards are now common output/input devices found in classrooms and conference rooms.
(Monkey Business Images/Shutterstock)

Should I buy a new Ultra HD monitor or a device that contains one? Ultra HD (otherwise known as 4K) monitors are the emerging standard in conjunction with the release of Ultra HDTV. Ultra HD monitors boast 3840 × 2160 resolution, which provides screens with four times as many pixels as HD devices. More pixels generally provide a sharper picture on a large screen.

So should you replace your HD monitor with an Ultra HD? Probably not yet. Ultra HD monitors are expensive, and there is not much streaming video available yet in the Ultra HD format. But as more programming becomes available and prices of Ultra HD monitors and devices fall, it may soon make sense to consider a higher resolution. Or, you may just hang on and wait for 8K monitors (7680 × 4320 resolution) and TVs, which may be available on the consumer market shortly. The technology to record 8K already exists—in fact, the BBC recorded much of the 2012 Summer Olympics in 8K format.

How do I show output to a large group of people? You can always connect your computing device to an HDTV if you have one large enough to be seen by the entire group. Another option is a **projector**, which lets you project images from your device onto a wall or screen. Small and lightweight portable projectors are ideal for businesspeople who make presentations at client locations. Entertainment projectors include stereo speakers and multimedia connectors, making them a good option for use in the home to display TV programs, DVDs, or video games.

In classrooms and conference rooms, projectors are often combined with another output device, the **interactive white board** (see Figure 2.25). A projector projects the computer's display onto the interactive white board's surface. The touch-sensitive board doubles as an input device and allows users to control and provide input to the computer using a pen, finger, or stylus. Notes and annotations can be captured and saved from the white board to the attached computer.

Audio Output

What are the output devices for sound? All portable computing devices include integrated **speakers**, the output devices for sound. These speakers are sufficient for playing audio clips you find on the web and usually for letting you make videoconference or phone calls over the Internet. However, if you plan to digitally edit audio files or are particular about how your music sounds, you may want a more sophisticated speaker system, such as one that includes subwoofers (special speakers that produce only low bass sounds) and surround-sound speakers. A **surround-sound system** is a set of speakers and audio processing equipment that envelops the listener in a 360-degree field of sound. Wireless speaker systems are widely available, enabling you to connect portable devices to quality speakers easily.

Headphones or **earbuds** connect wirelessly or plug into the same jack on your computing device to which external speakers connect. Studies of users of portable devices have shown that hearing might be damaged by excessive volume, especially when using earbuds because they fit into the ear canals, so limit the volume when you use these devices.

Bits&Bytes | **Near Field Communication (NFC): Now Pay (or Get Paid) Anywhere with Your Phone**

Paid for anything in a retail store with your phone lately? To accomplish this, your phone (and other devices) use a set of communication protocols called **near field communication (NFC)**. Devices equipped with NFC can communicate with each other when they are held in close proximity. When paying with your phone, NFC enables the input of payment information (your credit/debit card number) into a merchant's computer system.

But how can an artist selling his or her work at an art show in a park, for example, accept mobile payments? Now companies like Square are deploying readers (see Figure 2.26) that connect wirelessly to Apple and Android devices (like phones or tablets) and allow customers to pay using NFC-enabled devices. Now you can sell your products and services anywhere and still accept all the latest payment technologies!

Figure 2.26 Portable NFC communication devices for accepting payments are now available. *(Mika Images/Alamy Stock Photo)*

Printers

Objective 2.8 *Describe various types of printers, and explain when you would use them.*

What are the different types of printers? Another common output device is the **printer**, which creates hard copies (copies you can touch) of text and graphics. There are two primary categories of printers common in the home and office: inkjet and laser.

What are the advantages of inkjet printers? Inkjet printers (see Figure 2.27) are popular because they're affordable and produce high-quality printouts quickly and quietly. Inkjet printers work by spraying tiny drops of ink onto paper and are great for printing black-and-white text as well as color images. In fact, when loaded with the right paper, higher-end inkjet printers can print images that look like professional-quality photos. One thing to consider when buying an inkjet printer is the type and cost of the ink cartridges the printer needs. Some printers use two cartridges: black and color. Others use four or more cartridges: typically, cyan, magenta, yellow, and black. The four-color printing process many inkjets use is known as **CMYK** (this acronym stands for cyan, magenta, yellow, and key, which is usually represented by black).

Why would I want a laser printer? A **laser printer** uses laser beams and static electricity to deliver toner (similar to ink) onto the correct areas of the page (see Figure 2.28). Heat is used to fuse the toner to the page, making the image permanent. Laser printers are often used because they print faster than inkjet printers and produce higher-quality printouts. Black-and-white and color laser printers are both affordable for home use. If you print a high volume of pages, consider a laser printer. When you include the price of ink or toner in the overall cost, color laser printers can be more economical than inkjets.

What's the best way to print from portable devices such as tablets and smartphones? Wireless printers are great for printing from portable devices. Wireless printers are also a good option for home networks, as they let several people print to the same printer from different devices and any location in the home. There are two types of wireless printers: Wi-Fi and Bluetooth. Both Wi-Fi and Bluetooth printers have a range of up to approximately 300 feet. Wi-Fi, however, sends data more quickly than Bluetooth.

Figure 2.27 Inkjet printers are popular among home users, especially since high-end inkjet printers can print high-quality photographic images.
(Tankist276/Shutterstock)

Figure 2.28   How Laser Printers Work

Laser printer

laser beam

laser

rotating hexagonal mirror

lenses

path of laser beam

toner hopper

toner roller

paper tray

blank paper

1. Residual toner removed from drum by scraping or by passing under a discharging and erasing lamp.

2. Uniform high-voltage negative charge applied to drum.

negative charger

fuser roller

photoreceptor drum

3. Laser beam selectively discharges the image areas onto the rotating drum, reversing the strong negative charge to a weak positive charge.

negatively charged toner particles

printed side of paper

positive charger

4. Negatively charged toner particles adhere to only the areas given a positive charge by the laser.

5. Paper receives a strong positive charge.

6. Negatively charged toner particles on the drum are transferred to the paper.

7. Toner particles are fused or melted onto the paper.

(Encyclopaedia Britannica/Universal Images Group North America LLC/Alamy)

Figure 2.29 Cloud-ready printers need only an Internet connection and then can be accessed from any mobile device.

If you're using a device running Apple's iOS (such as an iPhone), AirPrint makes printing easy. AirPrint is a feature of iOS that facilitates printing to AirPrint-compatible wireless printers, and many printers produced today are AirPrint compatible. For non-Apple devices, newer wireless printers come with their own app that enables printing from portable devices. After installing the app on your device, you can send print jobs to the wireless printer.

Another option is Google Cloud Print, a service that lets you configure your printers so you can access them from mobile devices. Google Cloud Print uses **cloud-ready printers** (see Figure 2.29) that are available from manufacturers such as HP, Kodak, and Epson. These printers connect directly to the Internet and register themselves with Google Cloud Print. Once a printer is registered with Cloud Print, printing jobs can be sent to it from mobile devices (such as tablets and smartphones) using the Internet. Conventional printers that you already own can also be registered with Cloud Print, although they require connection to the Internet through a computer.

Are there any other types of specialty printers? Although you'll probably use laser or inkjet printers most often, you might encounter other types of printers (shown in Figure 2.30):

- An **all-in-one printer** combines the functions of a printer, scanner, copier, and fax into one machine. Popular for their space-saving convenience, all-in-one printers may use either inkjet or laser technology.
- A **large format printer** generates oversize images such as banners, posters, and infographics that require more sophisticated color detail. Some of these printers use up to 12 different inks to achieve high-quality color images.
- A **3D printer** is used to print three-dimensional objects. For example, parts can be built on the spot when needed using a 3D printer. 3D printers build such objects one layer at a time from the bottom up. They begin by spreading a layer of powder on a platform. Then, depending on the technology, the printer uses nozzles similar to those in an inkjet printer to spray tiny drops of glue at specific places to solidify the powder, or the powder is solidified through a melting process. The printer repeats this process until the object is built. This technology has spurred the manufacturing of a variety of consumer goods, from toys to clothing.

Figure 2.30 Specialty printers: (a) all-in-one printer, (b) large format printer, (c) 3D printer. *(Interior Design/Shutterstock; Koktaro/Shutterstock; hopsalka/123RF)*

How do I choose the best printer? If you're planning to print color photos and graphics, an inkjet printer or a color laser printer is a must, even though the cost per page will be higher. If you'll be printing mostly black-and-white text–based documents or will be sharing your printer with others, a black-and-white laser printer is best because of its speed and overall economy for volume printing. It's also important to determine whether you want just a printer or a device that prints and scans, copies, or faxes. In addition, you should decide whether you need to print from mobile devices.

Once you've narrowed down the type of printer you want, you can use the criteria listed in Figure 2.31 to help you determine the best model to meet your needs.

Figure 2.31   Major Printer Attributes

Attribute	Considerations
Speed	• Print speed is measured in *pages per minute (PPM)*. • Black-and-white documents print faster than color documents. • Laser printers often print faster than inkjets.

Resolution	• Resolution refers to a printer's image clarity.
	• Resolution is measured in *dots per inch (dpi)*.
	• Higher dpi = greater level of detail and clarity.
	• Recommended dpi:
	  • Black-and-white text: 300
	  • General purpose images: 1200
	  • Photos: 4800

Color Output	• Printers with separate cartridges for each color produce the best quality output. • Inkjet and laser color printers generally have four cartridges (black, cyan, magenta, and yellow). • Higher-quality printers have six cartridges (the four above plus light cyan and light magenta). • With separate cartridges, you only need to replace the empty one.
Cost of Consumables	• Consumables are printer cartridges and paper. • Printer cartridges can exceed the cost of some printers. • Consumer magazines such as *Consumer Reports* can help you research costs.

Freshidea/Fotolia; Michael Nivelet/Fotolia; Thomas Amby/Fotolia; Tomislav Forgo/Fotolia

Before moving on to Part 2:

1. Watch Chapter Overview Video 2.1.
2. Then take the Check Your Understanding quiz.

Check Your Understanding // Review & Practice

For a quick review to see what you've learned so far, answer the following questions.

multiple choice

1. Which of the following is one of the four major functions of a computer?

   a. indexing

   b. processing

   c. verification

   d. handling

2. Which of the following statements is TRUE?

   a. All cell phones are now smartphones.

   b. Smartphones have more computing power than desktop computers.

   c. Smartphones do not contain a CPU.

   d. Smartphones are considered a type of computer.

3. Which of the following can be both an input device and an output device?

   a. display screen

   b. keyboard

   c. mouse

   d. laser printer

4. The number of pixels that can be displayed on the screen at one time is known as what?

   a. pixel density

   b. viewing angle

   c. color depth

   d. screen resolution

5. What type of printer heats toner to adhere it to the paper?

   a. inkjet

   b. laser

   c. 3D

   d. impact

MyLab IT   Go to **MyLab IT** to take an autograded version of the *Check Your Understanding* review and to find all media resources for the chapter.

TechBytes Weekly   Go to TechBytes Weekly for current technology news and discussion questions!

Try This

What's Inside My Computer?

Understanding what capabilities your current computer has is one of the first steps toward computer literacy. In this exercise, you'll learn how to explore the components of your Windows computer. For step-by-step instructions, watch the Chapter 2 Try This video on MyLab IT.

Step 1 To gather information about the storage devices on your computer, click **File Explorer** from the Taskbar or from the Start menu. Then in the navigation pane, click **This PC** to display information about your computer's devices.

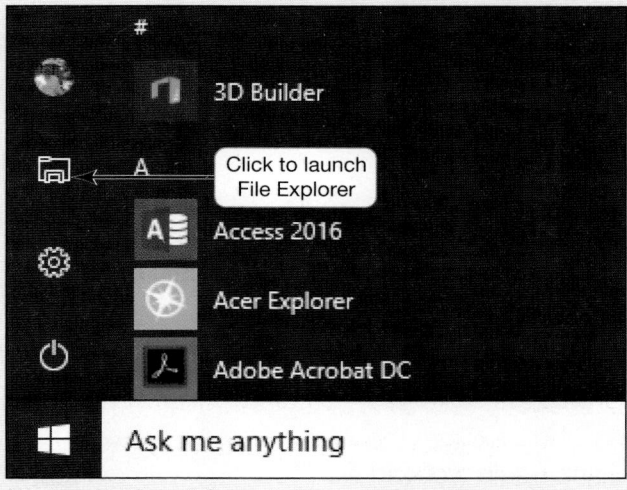

(Windows 10, Microsoft Corporation)

Step 2 The **This PC** dialog box displays information about internal storage devices (such as internal hard drives), optical storage devices (such as DVD drives), and portable storage devices (such as flash drives and external hard drives). To display the System screen, click the **Computer tab** on the ribbon, and then click **System properties**.

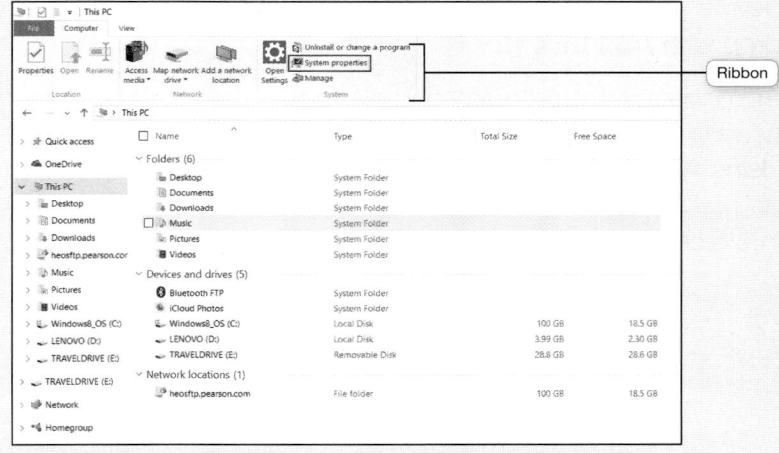

(Windows 10, Microsoft Corporation)

Step 3 You can gather quite a bit of information from the About option on the Settings System screen, such as:

- Version of Windows
- Type of processor
- Speed of the processor
- Amount of RAM installed
- System type (32-bit or 64-bit)

(Windows 10, Microsoft Corporation)

Make: A Mobile App

Want to build your own Android app from scratch? You can, with a simple tool called **App Inventor**. To get started, have ready:

1. A computer connected to a Wi-Fi network

2. The Chrome browser

3. A Google account

4. The MIT AI2 Companion app

5. [optional] An Android device connected to the same Wi-Fi network

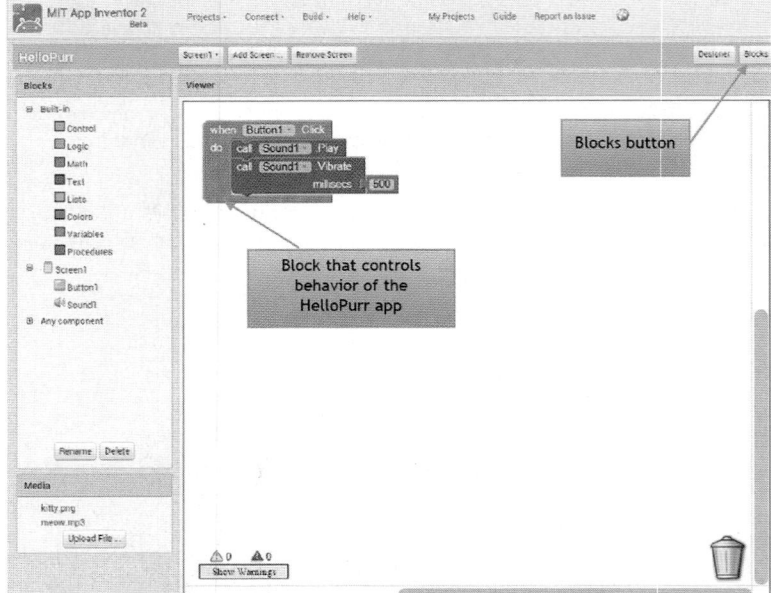

(Copyright MIT, used with permission.)

In this exercise, you'll explore the **App Inventor** tool and begin working with your first simple app. As you'll see, making your device work for you is as easy as drag and drop with **App Inventor**.

App Inventor is a programming platform used to create apps for Android devices. Using App Inventor, you can easily drag and drop components to design your app's interface and its behavior.

(Copyright MIT, used with permission.)

For the detailed instructions for this exercise, go to MyLab IT.

Processing, Storage, and Connectivity

Learning Outcome 2.2   **You will be able to describe how computers process and store data and how devices connect to a computer system.**

So far, we have explored the components of your computer that you use to input and output data. But where does the processing take place, and where is the data stored? And how does your computer connect with peripherals and other computers?

 # Processing and Memory on the Motherboard

The main processing functions of your computer take place in the CPU and memory, both of which reside on your computer's motherboard. In the following sections, we'll explore the components of the motherboard and how memory helps your computer process data.

The Motherboard and Memory

Objective 2.9   *Describe the functions of the motherboard and RAM.*

What exactly is a motherboard? The **motherboard** is the main circuit board that contains the central electronic components of the computing device, including the computer's processor (CPU), its memory, and the many circuit boards that help the computer function. On a desktop, the motherboard (see Figure 2.32) is located inside the system unit, the metal or plastic case that also houses the power source and all the storage devices (such as the hard drive). In a laptop, tablet, or phone, the system unit is combined with the monitor and the keyboard into a single package. Portable device motherboards are smaller, flatter, and lack expansion slots (see the image of the cell phone motherboard in Figure 2.5.).

What exactly is RAM? **Random access memory (RAM)** is the place in a computer where the programs and data that the computer is currently using are stored. RAM is much faster to read

Figure 2.32   A motherboard for a desktop computer contains the socket for the computer's processor (CPU), slots for memory (RAM) modules, ports, and slots for expansion cards. *(GIGA-BYTE Technology Co., Ltd.)*

from and write to than the hard drive and other forms of storage. The processor can request the RAM's contents, which can be located, opened, and delivered to the CPU for processing in a few nanoseconds (billionths of a second). If you look at a desktop motherboard, you'll see RAM as a series of small cards (called memory cards or memory modules) plugged into slots on the motherboard.

Because the entire contents of RAM are erased when you turn off the device, RAM is a temporary or **volatile storage** location. To save data permanently, you need to save it to your hard drive or to another permanent storage location, such as a flash drive or cloud storage.

Does the motherboard contain any other kinds of memory besides RAM? In addition to RAM, the motherboard contains a form of memory called **read-only memory (ROM)**. ROM holds all the instructions the device needs to start up when it's powered on. Unlike data stored in RAM, which is volatile storage, the instructions stored in ROM are permanent, making ROM a **nonvolatile storage** location, which means the data isn't erased when the power is turned off.

What other functionality is contained on the motherboard? The motherboard on desktop computers also includes slots for **expansion cards** (or **adapter cards**), which are circuit boards that provide additional functionality. Typical expansion cards found in the system unit are sound and video cards. A **sound card** provides a connection for the speakers and microphone, whereas a **video card** provides a connection for the monitor. High-end gaming desktops use expansion cards to provide video and sound capabilities, making it easy for owners to upgrade to the latest video cards on the market. Laptops, tablets, and phones have video and sound capabilities integrated into their motherboards.

Other parts of the motherboard provide a means for network and Internet connections. A **network interface card (NIC)**, which enables your computer to connect with other computers or to a cable modem to facilitate a high-speed Internet connection, is often integrated into the motherboard. Wireless network interface modules provide connectivity to Wi-Fi networks. And connectivity ports such as USB and Thunderbolt ports are also integrated into the motherboard.

On cell phone motherboards you'll also find a GPS (global positioning system) receiver, which is used to receive radio waves from satellites that help you pinpoint your location. The GPS receivers were initially installed in cell phones to allow the 911 emergency call operators to pinpoint the location of cell phones for people needing assistance. However, now many location-dependent apps, like Google Maps and Pokémon Go, make use of the GPS information.

How does GPS work? Built and operated by the U.S. Department of Defense, the **global positioning system (GPS)** is a network of 24 satellites (plus 3 working spares) that constantly orbit Earth. GPS receivers use an antenna to pick up the signals from these satellites and use special software to transform those signals into latitude and longitude. Using the information obtained from the satellites, GPS receivers determine geographical location anywhere on the planet to within 3 feet. The exact accuracy depends on such things as atmospheric conditions and interference from obstacles like mountains or buildings.

Processing

Objective 2.10 *Explain the main functions of the CPU.*

What is the CPU? As noted earlier, the *central processing unit* (*CPU* or *processor*) is sometimes referred to as the "brains" of the computer because it controls all the functions performed by the computer's other components and processes all the commands issued to it by software instructions.

How is processor speed measured? Processor speed is measured in units of hertz (Hz). Hertz is a measurement of machine cycles per second. A machine cycle is the process of the CPU getting the data or instructions from RAM and decoding the instructions into something the computer can understand. Once the CPU has decoded the instructions, it executes them and stores the result back in system memory. Current systems run at speeds measured in **gigahertz (GHz)** or billions of machine cycles per second. Therefore, a 3.8 GHz processor performs work at a rate of 3.8 billion machine cycles per second. Modern CPUs can perform as many as tens of billions of tasks per second without error, making them extremely powerful components. It's important to realize, however, that CPU processor speed alone doesn't determine the performance of the CPU.

What else determines processor performance? Although speed is an important consideration when determining processor performance, CPU performance is also affected by other factors. One factor is the number of cores, or processing paths, a processor has. Initially, processors could handle only one instruction at a time. Now, processors are designed so that they can have two, four, or even ten different paths, allowing them to process more than one instruction at a time (see Figure 2.33). Applications such as virus protection software and the operating system, which are always running behind the scenes, can have their own processor paths, freeing up the other paths to run other applications such as a web browser, Word, or iTunes more efficiently.

How can I tell what processor is best for me? The "best" processor will depend on your particular needs and is not always the processor with the highest processor speed and the greatest number of cores. Intel, one of the leading manufacturers of computer processor chips, provides a website (**ark.intel.com**) that assists in comparing the performance of different models of CPUs.

Figure 2.33 With multi-core processors, CPUs can work in parallel, processing two or more separate programs at the same time instead of switching back and forth between them.

Storing Data and Information

Because RAM is volatile storage, it can't be used to store information indefinitely. To save your data and information permanently, you need to save it to a nonvolatile storage device, such as a hard drive, cloud storage location, DVD, or flash drive.

Storage Options on Computing Devices

Objective 2.11   *Describe the various means of storing data and information with computing devices.*

Local Storage Devices

Are there different kinds of hard drives? The **hard disk drive** (**HDD** or **hard drive**) is your desktop's or laptop's primary device for permanent storage of software and documents. The hard drive is a nonvolatile storage device. (Note that because of space limitations, tablets and phones do not have hard drives. The nonvolatile storage used in these devices is various types of memory chips.)

An **internal hard drive** resides within the desktop or laptop system unit and usually holds all permanently stored programs and data. Today's internal hard drives (see Figure 2.34) have capacities of as much as 8 TB or more. **External hard drives** offer similar storage capacities but reside outside the system unit and connect to the computer via a port.

The most common type of hard drive has moveable parts—spinning platters and a moving arm with a read/write head—that can fail and lead to disk failure. However, the **solid-state drive (SSD)** is now a popular option for ultrabooks and laptop storage. SSDs have no moving parts, so they're more efficient, run with no noise, emit little heat, and require little power. In addition, they're less likely to fail after being bumped or dropped. Replacing a conventional hard drive in an older laptop with an SSD can often significantly improve the computer's performance.

Permanent storage devices are located in your desktop or laptop computer in a space called a **drive bay**. There are two kinds of drive bays:

Figure 2.34 Internal hard drives (shown here open…normally they are sealed) are a desktop and laptop computer's primary nonvolatile storage. *(Mbongo/Fotolia)*

1. *Internal drive bays* cannot be seen or accessed from outside the system unit. Generally, internal drive bays are reserved for internal hard drives.
2. *External drive bays* can be seen and accessed from outside the system unit. External drive bays house DVD and Blu-ray drives, for example. On desktop computers, sometimes there are empty external drive bays that can be used to install additional drives. These extra spaces are covered by a faceplate on the front panel. Laptop computers generally do not give you the ability to add additional drives. Such expansion is done by attaching an external drive to the computer through a USB port.

Figure 2.35 Smaller, portable external hard drives enable you to take a significant amount of data and programs on the road with you. *(Inga Nielsen/Shutterstock)*

Figure 2.37 Micro SD flash cards add memory to some phones. *(digitalr/123RF)*

Portable Storage Options

How can I take my files with me? For large portable storage needs, there are portable external hard drives that are small enough to fit into your pocket and that have storage capacities of 4 TB (or more). These devices are lightweight and enclosed in a protective case. They attach to your computer via a USB port (see Figure 2.35).

A **flash drive** (sometimes referred to as a **jump drive**, **USB drive**, or **thumb drive**) uses solid-state flash memory, storing information on an internal memory chip. When you plug a flash drive into your computer's USB port, it appears in the operating system as another disk drive. You can write data to it or read data from it as you would a hard drive. Because a flash drive contains no moving parts, it's quite durable. It's also tiny enough to fit in your pocket. Despite their size, flash drives can have significant storage capacity—currently as much as 1 TB or more. Often, flash drives are combined with other devices such as pens or keychains for added convenience.

Another convenient means of portable storage is a **flash memory card**, such as an SD card. Like the flash drive, memory cards use solid-state flash memory. Most desktops and laptops include slots for flash memory cards, but if your computer is not equipped, there are memory card readers that you can plug into a USB port. Flash memory cards let you transfer digital data between your computer and devices such as digital cameras, smartphones, tablets, video cameras, and printers. Although incredibly small—some are even smaller than a postage stamp—these memory cards have capacities that exceed the capacity of a DVD. Figure 2.36 compares the storage capacities of hard drives and flash drives.

How does my cell phone store data? Today's cell phones use various combinations of memory chips to store data. They do not contain hard drives.

Can I increase the storage capacity of my smartphone? Many smartphones let you add additional memory through micro SD flash cards (see Figure 2.37). Micro SD cards are easy to install inside a phone, and some models have external slots for an SD card. Not all smartphones allow memory upgrades in this way, however. For example, iPhones don't allow you to add memory.

Figure 2.36	Hard Drive and Flash Drive Storage Capacity	
Drive Type	**Image**	**Typical Capacity**
Solid-state drive (SSD)		1 TB or more
External portable hard drive		4 TB or more
Mechanical internal hard drive		8 TB or more
Flash drive		1 TB or more
Flash memory card		128 GB

(Scanrail1/Shutterstock; Ruslan Ivantsov/Shutterstock; D. Hurst/Alamy Stock Photo; Cphoto/Fotolia; Zuma Press/Alamy Stock Photo)

What Is Ethical Computing?

You've probably heard news stories about people using computers to unleash viruses or commit identity theft. You may also have read about students who were prosecuted for illegally sharing copyrighted material, such as songs and videos. These are both examples of *unethical* behavior while using a computer. However, what constitutes *ethical* behavior while using a computer?

As we discussed in Chapter 1, *ethics* is a system of moral principles, rules, and accepted standards of conduct (see Figure 2.38). So what are the accepted standards of conduct when using computers? The Computer Ethics Institute has developed the Ten Commandments of Computer Ethics, widely cited as a benchmark for companies developing computer usage and compliance policies for employees. These guidelines are applicable for schools and students as well. The following ethical computing guidelines are based on the Computer Ethics Institute's work:

Ethical Computing Guidelines

1. Avoid causing harm to others when using computers.
2. Do not interfere with other people's efforts at accomplishing work with computers.
3. Resist the temptation to snoop in other people's computer files.
4. Do not use computers to commit theft.
5. Agree not to use computers to promote lies.
6. Do not use software (or make illegal copies for others) without paying the creator for it.
7. Avoid using other people's computer resources without appropriate authorization or proper compensation.
8. Do not claim other people's intellectual output as your own.
9. Consider the social consequences of the products of your computer labor.
10. Only use computers in ways that show consideration and respect for others.

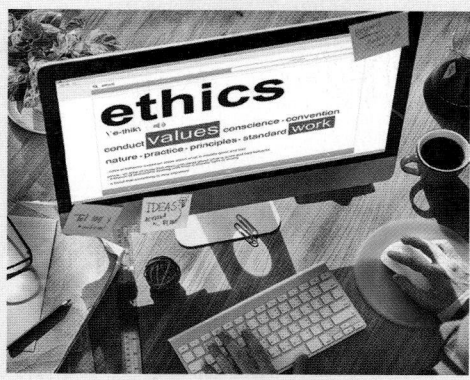

Figure 2.38 Striving to behave ethically isn't just for "real-life" interactions. It applies when using computer devices too. *(Rawpixel.com/Fotolia)*

The United States has enacted laws that support some of these guidelines, such as Guideline 6, the breaking of which would violate copyright laws, and Guideline 4, which is enforceable under numerous federal and state larceny laws. Other guidelines, however, require more subtle interpretation as to what behavior is unethical because there are no laws designed to enforce them.

Consider Guideline 7, which covers unauthorized use of resources. The school you attend probably provides computer resources for you to use for coursework. But if your school gives you access to computers and the Internet, is it ethical for you to use those resources to run an online business on the weekends? Although it might not be technically illegal, you're tying up computer resources that other students could use for their intended purpose: learning and completing coursework. (This behavior also violates Guidelines 2 and 10.)

Throughout the chapters in this book, we touch on many topics related to these guidelines. So keep them in mind as you study, and think about how they relate to the actions you take as you use computers in your life.

Cloud Storage

How can I easily access my files from different devices? You may use multiple devices, such as a smartphone, laptop, and a tablet, at different times. Invariably, you'll need access to a file that is stored on a device other than the one you're using. If your devices are connected to the Internet, cloud storage provides a convenient option.

Cloud storage refers to using a service that keeps your files on the Internet (in the "cloud") rather than storing your files solely on a device. Using a cloud storage service requires that you install software or an app on your device. Popular cloud storage options include Google Drive, Microsoft's OneDrive, and Dropbox. For example, after installing the Dropbox software on your devices, any files you save in the Dropbox folder are accessible by all your other devices via the Internet. You can also share folders in Dropbox with other Dropbox users, making it ideal for group collaboration.

Most cloud storage providers give users an option of some amount of free storage, but the amount of space varies. All cloud storage providers offer additional storage space for a fee.

Optical Storage

What other kinds of storage devices are available? **Optical drives** are devices that use lasers to read from and write to CDs, DVDs, or Blu-ray discs. As we have moved toward streaming media services

Figure 2.39   Optical Storage Media Capacities

Medium Type	Typical Capacity
Blu-ray (dual layer)	50 GB
Blu-ray	25 GB
DVD DL (dual layer)	8.5 GB
DVD	4.7 GB
CD	700 MB

and cloud-based delivery of software, optical drives have not been included in laptops and ultrabooks to save weight and space. However, if you still need to use optical drives, inexpensive portable drives that attach via USB ports are readily available.

Data is saved to optical discs as tiny pits that are burned into the disc by a high-speed laser. **Compact discs (CDs)** were initially created to store audio files. **Digital video** (or **versatile**) **discs (DVDs)** are the same size and shape as CDs but can store up to 14 times more data.

What if you want even more storage capacity? Blu-ray discs (BDs), which are similar in size and shape to CDs and DVDs, can hold as much as 50 GB of data—enough to hold approximately 4.5 hours of movies in HD digital format. Many desktop systems are now available with BD-ROM drives and Blu-ray burners. Figure 2.39 shows the storage capacities of the various optical storage media.

Trends In IT   Green Computing (Green IT)

"Going green" is a goal for many modern businesses. **Green computing** (or **green IT**) is a movement to encourage environmentally sustainable computing. The main goal is to reduce the overall carbon footprint of a company through the strategic use of computing resources and environmentally friendly computing devices. A business's *carbon footprint* is the total amount of greenhouse gases produced directly and indirectly to support the activities of the business. Carbon footprints are expressed in equivalent tons of carbon dioxide (CO_2). CO_2 is the main greenhouse gas contributing to global warming. Reduction of greenhouse gas emissions is critical to sustaining a healthy environment.

The main goals of green computing are as follows:

1. Reducing the use of hazardous processes or materials in the production of computing equipment

2. Promoting the use of recyclable or biodegradable materials to facilitate safe disposal of products
3. Buying products that use energy efficiently
4. Using technology to reduce employee travel
5. Reducing the use of energy and consumption of materials through shared computing resources

Sharing computing resources can make a vast difference in the consumption of resources and electricity. This is one of the reasons cloud storage is becoming so popular. Rather than having 20 individual companies, each maintaining a large group of computers to hold data, savings can be achieved by having one company maintain computer resources that are able to serve the 20 other companies. However, it's not all up to businesses to practice green computing. Figure 2.40 lists a few ways you can participate:

Figure 2.40   Green Computing Problems and Solutions

Issue	Electricity	Commuting	Use Technology Longer
Problems	• Electricity is often generated using fossil fuels, which produce greenhouse gas emissions. • Devices are not energy efficient.	• Cars generate greenhouse gases. • Many people commute to work alone.	• Items are replaced before their useful life is over. • Old items are discarded instead of continuing to be used. • Technology is not disposed of or recycled properly.
Solutions	• Buy energy-efficient computing equipment with high Energy Star ratings. • Turn off computing devices when not in use. • Use appropriate power management settings to use less power when operating devices.	• Use technology to telecommute to your job. • Use public transportation to commute, which uses energy more efficiently than cars. • Use a green vehicle (bicycle, electric car) for your commute.	• Upgrade your technology only when absolutely necessary. • Donate your old technology to someone who will continue to use it (friends, family, charitable organization). • Dispose of electronic devices only at approved e-waste recycling facilities.

Connecting Peripherals to the Computer

Throughout this chapter, we have discussed peripheral devices that input, store, and output data and information. We will now look at how these types of devices are connected to computers so they can exchange data.

Computer Ports

Objective 2.12 *Describe common types of ports used today.*

What is the fastest data transfer port available on today's computing devices? A **port** is a place through which a peripheral device attaches to the computer so that data can be exchanged between it and the operating system. Although peripherals may connect to devices wirelessly, ports are still often used for connections. Thunderbolt is the newest input/output technology on the market. **Thunderbolt ports** (see Figure 2.41) are very useful for laptops and ultrabooks because one Thunderbolt port can allow you to connect up to six different peripherals to your computer. Thunderbolt 3 ports can achieve blazingly fast transfer speeds of up to 40 Gb/s. Apple was the first computer manufacturer to integrate the ports into their hardware, although other manufacturers are following suit.

What is the most common port on digital devices? A **universal serial bus (USB) port** is the port type most commonly used to connect input and output devices to the computer. This is mainly because of the ready availability of USB-compatible peripherals. USB ports can connect a wide variety of peripherals to computing devices, including keyboards, printers, mice, smartphones, external hard drives, flash drives, and digital cameras. The new USB 3.1 standard provides transfer speeds of 10 Gbps and charges devices faster than previous USB ports. USB ports come in a variety of standard and proprietary configurations (see Figure 2.42), plus the new Type-C connector (and port), which is supplanting older connector types as USB 3.1 continues to roll out (see Figure 2.43).

Which ports help me connect with other computers and the Internet? A **connectivity port** can give you access to networks and the Internet. To find a connectivity port, look for a port that resembles a standard phone jack but is slightly larger. This port is called an **Ethernet port**. Ethernet ports transfer data at speeds up to 10,000 Mbps. You can use an Ethernet port to connect your computer to either a cable modem or a wired network.

Figure 2.41 Thunderbolt ports are slim and speedy making them popular on today's ultrabooks and laptops. *(David Paul Morris/Bloomberg/Getty Images)*

▶ Helpdesk MyLab IT®

Exploring Storage Devices and Ports

In this Helpdesk, you'll play the role of a helpdesk staffer, fielding questions about the computer's main storage devices and how to connect various peripheral devices to the computer.

Figure 2.42 USB connectors come in a wide variety of styles. *(TaraPatta/Shutterstock)*

Figure 2.43 Some Apple computers now feature the new USB-C port that supports data transfer, video output, and charging all in a single port. *(epa european pressphoto agency b.v./Alamy Stock Photo)*

(a) (b)

☐ TETHER TOOLS

HDMI Micro
TYPE D

HDMI Mini
TYPE C

HDMI (Full Size)
TYPE A

Figure 2.44 (a) HDMI is the industry standard digital connector type for HD monitors, TVs, and home theater equipment. (b) Cables with the appropriate connectors are available to facilitate connection of your mobile devices to your HDTV for enhanced viewing.
(Feng Yu/Shutterstock; Used with permission from Tether Tools.)

Figure 2.45 If you don't have enough USB ports to support your USB devices, consider getting an expansion hub, which can add four or more USB ports to your system.
(Norman Chan/Fotolia)

How do I connect monitors and multimedia devices? Other ports on the back and sides of the computer include audio and video ports. Audio ports are where you connect headphones, microphones, and speakers to the computer. Whether you're attaching a monitor to a desktop computer or adding a second, larger display to a laptop computer, you'll use a video port.

HDMI ports are now the most common video port on computing devices. A **high-definition multimedia interface (HDMI) port** is a compact audio–video interface that allows both HD video and uncompressed digital audio to be carried on one cable. Because HDMI can transmit uncompressed audio and video, there's no need to convert the signal, which could ultimately reduce the quality of the sound or picture. All currently available monitors, Blu-ray players, TVs, and game consoles have at least one HDMI port (see Figure 2.44a).

If your computing device is equipped with an HDMI port, you can also choose to connect your computer directly to an HDTV using an HDMI cable. The most common HDMI connector types are shown in Figure 2.44b. Full size (or type A) connectors are found on most TVs and laptops. Tablets and phones are more likely to have a mini (type C) or micro (type D) HDMI port.

What if I don't have all the ports I need? If you're looking to add the newest ports to an older desktop computer or to expand the number of ports on it, you can install special expansion cards into an open expansion slot on the motherboard to provide additional ports.

Another alternative for adding ports to any computer is adding an expansion hub (shown in Figure 2.45). An expansion hub is a device that connects to one port, such as a USB port, to provide additional ports. It works like the multiplug extension cords used with electrical appliances.

Power Management and Ergonomics

Conserving energy and setting up workspaces so they are comfortable are goals of many businesses. However, these are also goals to strive for at your home. In this section, we'll explore optimizing the power consumption of computing devices as well as the proper workspace setup to minimize injuries.

Power Controls and Power Management

Objective 2.13 *Describe how to manage power consumption on computing devices.*

Which components of a computing device drain the battery fastest? The number one culprit is the display. The backlights of LCD (and even OLED) displays draw a lot of power. You may love that new HD display in your phone, but your battery doesn't love it!

Wi-Fi and Bluetooth adapters also draw a lot of power because they're continuously scanning for compatible devices. In addition, any peripheral plugged into a port on your computer is most likely drawing power from the computer to function.

Certain apps are big culprits of battery drain also. Many apps continuously sync with the cloud and push alerts to you. So even though you may not be looking at an app (a *foreground* use) it is still drawing power (*background* use). Fortunately, you can determine which apps draw the most power:

- For Android devices, click Settings > Device > Battery or Settings > Power > Battery Use and you'll see a list of apps and how much battery power they're consuming.
- For iOS devices, click Settings > Battery and wait for the battery usage list to populate. Click the clock icon to display information on foreground and background power use.
- For Windows 10 (older versions of Windows lack this feature), launch Settings from the Start menu, select System, select Battery, then click the Battery usage by app link.

Consider uninstalling apps that draw a lot of background power if you rarely use them. For apps you do use frequently, consider disabling or turning off sync and alert features in the app when your battery level is low.

How does my computer battery get its charge? The **power supply** comes in the form of a brick with a cord that plugs into your portable device to charge the battery. The power supply transforms the wall voltage to the voltages required by the battery or the computer chips (if you are operating your device on a/c power). Desktop computers have their power supply housed within the system unit.

What is the best way to turn my computer off? In Windows and macOS, you can turn your computer completely off by displaying the power options and choosing the Shut down option (see Figure 2.46). If your computer's operating system is unresponsive, holding the power button down will force a shutdown to occur.

Can I "rest" my computer without turning it off completely? With many devices, an effective method of power conservation is Sleep. When your computer enters **Sleep mode**, all of the documents, applications, and data you were using remain in RAM (memory), where they're quickly accessible when you wake your computer.

In Sleep mode, the computer enters a state of greatly reduced power consumption, which saves energy and prolongs battery life. To put your computer into Sleep mode in Windows, display the Start menu, select Power, then select the Sleep option. To wake up your computer, press a key or the physical power button. In a few seconds, the computer will resume with the same programs running and documents displayed as when you put it to sleep.

What's the Restart option for? Windows and macOS power options both provide a restart option. Restarting the system while it's powered on is called a **warm boot**. You might need to perform a warm boot if the operating system or other software application stops responding, if you've received Windows updates, or if you've installed new apps. It takes less time to perform a warm boot than to power down completely and then restart all your hardware. Powering on your computer from a completely turned off state is called a **cold boot**.

Should I turn off my computer every time I'm finished using it? Some people argue that turning your computer on and off throughout the day subjects its components to stress because the heating and cooling process forces the components to expand and contract repeatedly. Other people say it's more environmentally friendly and less expensive to shut down your computer when you're not using it.

All modern operating systems include power-management settings that allow the most power-hungry components of the system (the hard drive and monitor) to shut down after a short idle period. The power-management options of Windows 10 (see Figure 2.47), Android, iOS, and macOS provide you with flexibility to conserve power and battery life. Therefore, it's rarely necessary to shut your devices completely off, even when they're charging.

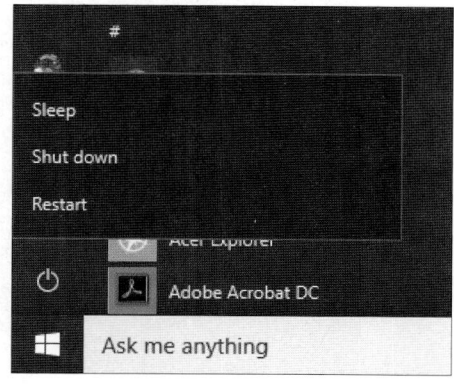

Figure 2.46 The Power option on the Windows Start menu presents several power options.
> *For a warm boot, choose **Restart**. To power down the computer completely, choose **Shut down**. To put your computer into a lower power mode, select **Sleep**.*
(Windows 10, Microsoft Corporation)

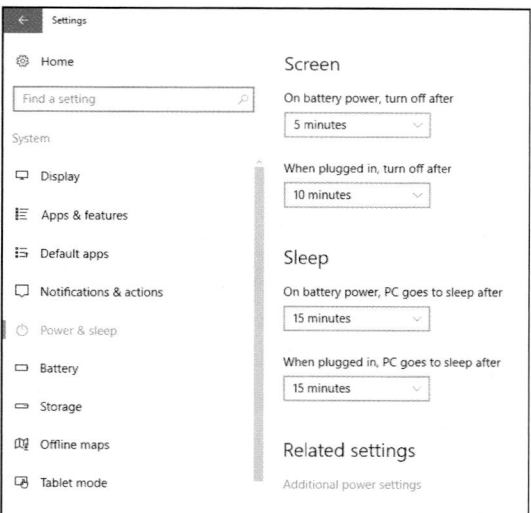

Figure 2.47 In Windows 10, you can set the options to your particular tastes to conserve power.
> *To access Power & sleep Settings, from the Start menu, select **Settings**, then **System**, then select **Power & sleep**.*
(Windows 10, Microsoft Corporation)

Define power buttons and turn on password protection

Choose the power settings that you want for your computer. The changes you make to the settings on this page apply to all of your power plans.

🛡 Change settings that are currently unavailable

Power and sleep buttons and lid settings

	🔋 On battery	🔌 Plugged in
⏻ When I press the power button:	Sleep ∨	Sleep ∨
◐ When I press the sleep button:	Sleep ∨	Sleep ∨
📖 When I close the lid:	Sleep ∨	Sleep ∨

Do nothing
Sleep
Hibernate
Shut down

Shutdown settings

☑ Turn on fast startup (recommended)
This helps start your PC faster after shutdown. Restart isn't affected. Learn More

☑ Sleep
Show in Power menu.

Figure 2.48 You can determine what happens when you press the power button on your computer or close the lid through the Power Options System Settings screen.

*> To access Power Options System Settings, from the Start menu, select **Settings, System, Power & sleep, Additional power settings**, and then select **Choose what closing the lid does**.* (Windows 10, Microsoft Corporation)

If you don't ever want to completely turn off your Windows laptop computer, you can change what happens when you press the power button or close the lid. By accessing the Power Options System Settings window (see Figure 2.48), you can decide if you want your computer to Sleep, Hibernate, or Shut down when you press the power button. The **Hibernate** option is similar to Sleep except that your data is stored on your hard drive instead of in RAM and your computer is powered off. This uses much less battery power than Sleep and is a good choice if you won't be using your laptop for a long time and won't have the opportunity to charge it. However, Sleep is still a good option if you just won't be using your computer for a short time. You may want to set your computer so it sleeps when you close the lid but hibernates when you press the power button, giving you quick access to either option.

Bits&Bytes   Sleep Better and Avoid Eyestrain: Use Less Blue Light

Under normal conditions, your computing device screens emit a lot of blue light. Your eyes mistake this light for that of the sun. This disrupts your biological clock and makes your brain think it needs to stay awake. To lessen this problem, most operating systems now include a setting that allows your screen to use less blue light, replacing it with warmer, softer colors. This reduces eyestrain and helps you fall asleep faster. So check out Night Light (Windows), Night Shift (iOS), and Night Mode (Android) and fall asleep faster.

Figure 2.49 Blue light keeps you awake, but you can set your OS to use less blue light. *(Vadym Malyshevskyi/123RF)*

Setting It All Up: Ergonomics

Objective 2.14 *Define ergonomics, and discuss the ideal physical setup for using computing devices.*

What is ergonomics? Ergonomics is the science that deals with the design and location of machines and furniture so that the people using them aren't subjected to an uncomfortable or unsafe experience. In terms of computing, ergonomics refers to how you set up your computer and other equipment to minimize your risk of injury or discomfort.

Why is ergonomics important? Studies suggest that teenagers, on average, spend 7.5 hours per day using computing devices. The repetitive nature of long-term computing activities can place stress on joints, tendons, and muscles, causing repetitive stress injuries such as carpal tunnel syndrome and tendonitis. These injuries can take months or years to develop to a point where they become painful, but if you take precautionary measures now, you may prevent years of pain later.

How can I avoid injuries when I'm working at my computer? As Figure 2.50 illustrates, it's important to arrange your computer, chair, body, and keyboard in ways that will help you avoid injury, discomfort, and eyestrain. The following additional guidelines can help keep you comfortable and productive:

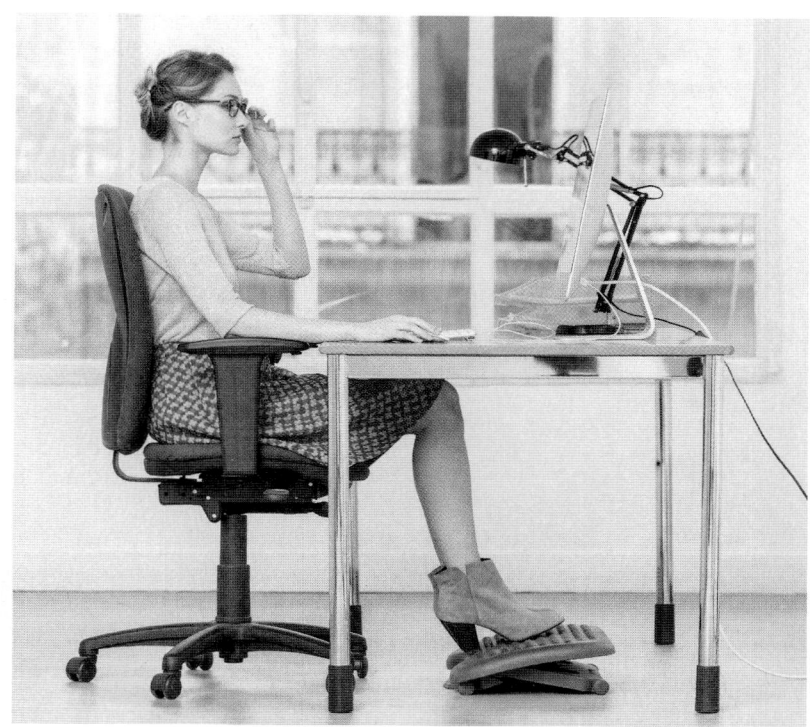

Figure 2.50 Using proper equipment that is adjusted correctly helps prevent repetitive strain injuries while working at a computer. *(Phanie/Alamy Stock Photo)*

- **Position your monitor correctly.** Studies suggest it's best to place your monitor at least 25 inches from your eyes. Experts recommend that you position your monitor either at eye level or at an angle 15–20 degrees below your line of sight. If you have a laptop, this means placing the laptop on a stand (or stack of books) to achieve the correct height.

- **Purchase an adjustable chair.** Adjust the height of your chair (or use a footrest) so that your feet touch the floor. The back support needs to be adjustable so that it supports your lumbar (lower back) region. If your chair doesn't adjust, place a pillow behind your back to provide support.

- **Assume a proper position while typing.** Improperly positioned keyboards are one of the leading causes of repetitive stress injuries. Your wrists should be flat (not bent) with respect to the keyboard, and your forearms should be parallel to the floor. Additionally, your wrists should not be resting on the keyboard while typing. When using a laptop on a stand, attach an external keyboard to achieve the proper typing position. You can adjust the height of your chair or install a height-adjustable keyboard tray to ensure a proper position. Specially designed ergonomic keyboards such as the one shown in Figure 2.51 can also help you achieve the proper wrist position.

- **Take breaks.** Remaining in the same position for long periods increases stress on your body. Shift your position in your chair and stretch your hands and fingers periodically. Likewise, staring at the screen for long periods can lead to eyestrain and dry eyes, so rest your eyes periodically by taking them off the screen and focusing them on an object at least 8 feet away.

- **Ensure the lighting is adequate.** Ensuring that you have proper lighting in your work area minimizes eyestrain. Eliminate sources of direct glare (light shining directly into your eyes) or reflected glare (light shining off the computer screen) and ensure there is enough light to read comfortably. If you still can't eliminate glare from your screen, you can buy an antiglare screen to place over your monitor.

Figure 2.51 Ergonomic keyboards have curved keyboards and wrist rests to help you maintain the proper hand position while typing to reduce the risk of repetitive strain injuries. *(Dmitriy Melnikov/Fotolia)*

Is ergonomics important when using mobile devices? Working with mobile computing devices presents interesting challenges when it comes to injury prevention. For example, many users work with laptops resting on their laps, placing the monitor outside the optimal line of sight and thereby increasing neck strain. Figure 2.52 provides guidelines on preventing injuries when computing on the go.

What devices are available for people with disabilities? **Assistive** (or **adaptive**) **technologies** are products, devices, equipment, or software that are used to maintain, increase, or improve the functional capabilities of individuals with disabilities. For visually impaired users and individuals who can't type with their hand, voice recognition is a common option. For those users whose visual limitations are less severe, keyboards with larger keys are available.

People with motor control issues may have difficulty with pointing devices. To aid such users, special trackballs are available that can be manipulated with one finger and can be attached to almost any surface, including a wheelchair. When arm motion is severely restrained, head-mounted pointing devices can be used. Generally, these involve a camera mounted on the computer monitor and a device attached to the head (often installed in a hat). When the user moves his or her head, the camera detects the movement and moves the cursor. In this case, mouse clicks are controlled by a switch that can be manipulated by the user's hands or feet or even by using an instrument that fits into the mouth and senses the user blowing into it.

Figure 2.52 Preventing Injuries While on the Go

	Smartphone Repetitive Strain Injuries	Portable Media Player Hearing Damage	Small-Screen Vision Issues	Lap Injuries	Tablet Repetitive Strain Injuries
Malady	Repetitive strain injuries (such as de Quervain's disease) from constant typing of instant messages	Hearing loss from high-decibel sound levels in earbuds	Blurriness and dryness caused by squinting to view tiny screens on mobile devices	Burns on legs from heat generated by laptop	Pain caused by using tablets for prolonged periods in uncomfortable positions
Preventative measures	Restrict length and frequency of messages, take breaks, and perform other motions with your thumbs and fingers during breaks to relieve tension.	Turn down volume (you should be able to hear external noises, such as people talking), use software that limits sound levels (not to exceed 60 decibels), and use external, over-ear style headphones instead of earbuds.	Blink frequently or use eye drops to maintain moisture in eyes, after 10 minutes take a break and focus on something at least 8 feet away for 5 minutes, use adequate amount of light, and increase the size of fonts.	Place a book, magazine, or laptop cooling pad between your legs and laptop.	Restrict the length of time you work at a tablet, especially typing or gaming. Use the same ergonomic position you would use for a laptop when using a tablet.

Before moving on to the Chapter Review:

1. ▶ Watch Chapter Overview Video 2.2.
2. Then take the Check Your Understanding quiz.

Check Your Understanding // Review & Practice

For a quick review to see what you've learned so far, answer the following questions.

multiple choice

1. Which of the following is NOT found on a motherboard?
   a. RAM
   b. hard drive
   c. sound card
   d. CPU

2. Which of these is considered the "brains" of the computer?
   a. CPU
   b. ROM
   c. RAM
   d. USB

3. Which of these is an example of optical storage media?
   a. thumb drive
   b. SSD
   c. DVD
   d. a flash memory card

4. Which of the following is NOT a port?
   a. HDMI
   b. Thunderbolt
   c. USB
   d. CPU

5. Which power control option performs a warm boot?
   a. Sleep
   b. Restart
   c. Log off
   d. Shut down

 Go to **MyLab IT** to take an autograded version of the *Check Your Understanding* review and to find all media resources for the chapter.

TechBytes Weekly Go to TechBytes Weekly for current technology news and discussion questions!

2 Chapter Review

Summary

Learning Outcome 2.1 You will be able to describe the devices that make up a computer system.

 ### Understanding Your Computer

Objective 2.1 *Describe the four main functions of a computer system and how they interact with data and information.*

- The computer's four major functions are: (1) input: gather data or allow users to enter data; (2) process: manipulate, calculate, or organize that data; (3) output: display data and information in a form suitable for the user; and (4) storage: save data and information for later use.
- Data is a representation of a fact or idea. The number 3 and the words *televisions* and *Sony* are pieces of data.
- Information is data that has been organized or presented in a meaningful fashion. An inventory list that indicates that 3 Sony televisions are in stock is processed information. It allows a retail clerk to answer a customer query about the availability of merchandise. Information is more powerful than raw data.

Objective 2.2 *Define bits and bytes, and describe how they are measured, used, and processed.*

- To process data into information, computers need to work in a language they understand. This language, called *binary language*, consists of two numbers: 0 and 1. Each 0 and each 1 is a binary digit or bit. Eight bits create one byte.
- In computers, each letter of the alphabet, each number, and each special character consists of a unique combination of eight bits (one byte)—a string of eight 0s and 1s.
- For describing large amounts of storage capacity, the terms *megabyte* (approximately 1 million bytes), *gigabyte* (approximately 1 billion bytes), *terabyte* (approximately 1 trillion bytes), and *petabyte* (1,000 terabytes) are used.

Objective 2.3 *List common types of computers, and discuss their main features.*

- A tablet computer is a portable computer integrated into a flat multitouch-sensitive screen.
- A laptop or notebook computer is a portable computer that has a keyboard, monitor, and other devices integrated into a single compact case.
- A 2-in-1 PC is a laptop computer that can convert into a tablet-like device.
- An ultrabook is a lightweight laptop computer featuring low-power processors and solid-state drives.
- Chromebook computers use the Google Chrome OS. Documents and apps are stored primarily in the cloud.
- Desktop computers consist of a separate case (called the system unit) that houses the main components of the computer plus peripheral devices.

 ### Input Devices

Objective 2.4 *Identify the main types of keyboards and touch screens.*

- You use physical or virtual keyboards to enter typed data and commands. Most keyboards use the QWERTY layout.
- Touch screens are display screens that respond to commands initiated by a touch with a finger or a stylus.
- Wireless keyboards mainly use Bluetooth connectivity and provide alternatives to virtual keyboards on portable computing devices.

Objective 2.5 *Describe the main types of mice and pointing devices.*

- Mice are used to enter user responses and commands.
- Optical mice use a laser to detect mouse movement.
- Some mice can be adjusted to provide better ergonomics for users.
- Laptops have integrated pointing devices called touch pads (trackpads).

Objective 2.6 *Explain how images, sounds, and sensor data are input into computing devices.*

- Images are input into the computer with flatbed scanners, digital cameras, camcorders, and mobile device cameras.
- Live video is captured with webcams and digital video recorders.
- Microphones capture sounds. There are many different types of microphones, including desktop, headset, and clip-on models.
- Smartphones and tablets have a variety of sensors that detect or measure a variety of inputs (such as acceleration that the device is experiencing).

 Output Devices

Objective 2.7 *Describe options for outputting images and audio from computing devices.*

- Monitors display soft copies of text, graphics, and video.
- Liquid crystal display (LCD) and light-emitting diode (LED) are the most common types of computer monitors.

- OLED displays use organic compounds to produce light and don't require a backlight, which saves energy.
- Aspect ratio and screen resolution are key aspects to consider when choosing a monitor.
- Speakers, headphones, and earbuds are the output devices for sound.
- More sophisticated systems include subwoofers and surround sound.

Objective 2.8 *Describe various types of printers, and explain when you would use them.*

- Printers create hard copies of text and graphics.
- There are two primary categories of printers: inkjet and laser. Laser printers usually print faster and deliver higher-quality output than inkjet printers. However, inkjet printers can be more economical for casual printing needs.
- Specialty printers are also available, such as all-in-one printers, large format printers, and 3D printers.
- When choosing a printer, you should be aware of factors such as speed, resolution, color output, and cost of consumables.

Part 2
Processing, Storage, and Connectivity

Learning Outcome 2.2 **You will be able to describe how computers process and store data and how devices connect to a computer system.**

 Processing and Memory on the Motherboard

Objective 2.9 *Describe the functions of the motherboard and RAM.*

- The motherboard, the main circuit board of the system, contains a computer's CPU, which coordinates the functions of all other devices on the computer.
- The motherboard also houses slots for expansion cards, which have specific functions that augment the computer's basic functions. Typical expansion cards are sound and video cards. In portable devices, sound and video are usually integrated directly into the motherboard.
- RAM, the computer's volatile memory, is also located on the motherboard. RAM is where data and instructions are held while the computer is running.

Objective 2.10 *Explain the main functions of the CPU.*

- The CPU controls all the functions performed by the computer's other components. The CPU also processes all commands issued to it by software instructions.

- The performance of a CPU is affected by the speed of the processor (measured in GHz) and the number of processing cores.

 Storing Data and Information

Objective 2.11 *Describe the various means of storing data and information with computing devices.*

- The internal hard drive is your computer's primary device for permanent storage of software and files. The hard drive is a nonvolatile storage device, meaning it holds the data and instructions your computer needs permanently, even after the computer is turned off.
- SSD drives have no moving parts so they are more energy efficient and less susceptible to damage.
- External hard drives are essentially internal hard drives that have been made portable by enclosing them in a protective case and making them small and lightweight.

- Cloud storage refers to nonvolatile storage locations that are maintained on the Internet (in the "cloud"). Examples are OneDrive, Google Drive, and Dropbox.
- Storing your data in the cloud allows you to access it from almost any computing device that is connected to the Internet.
- Optical drives that can read from and write to CD, DVD, or Blu-ray discs are another means of permanent, portable storage. Data is saved to CDs, DVDs, and Blu-ray discs as pits that are burned into the disc by a laser.
- Flash drives are another portable means of storing data. Flash drives plug into USB ports.
- Flash memory cards let you transfer digital data between your computer and devices such as digital cameras, smartphones, video cameras, and printers.

 ## Connecting Peripherals to the Computer

Objective 2.12   *Describe common types of ports used today.*

- The fastest type of port used to connect devices to a computer is the Thunderbolt port.
- The most common type of port used to connect devices to a computer is the USB port.
- Connectivity ports, such as Ethernet ports, give you access to networks and the Internet.
- HDMI ports are the most common multimedia port. They are used to connect monitors, TVs, and gaming consoles to computing devices and handle both audio and video data.

- Audio ports are used to connect headphones, microphones, and speakers to computing devices.
- Expansion hubs can be plugged into existing ports to provide additional ports of the same type.

 ## Power Management and Ergonomics

Objective 2.13   *Describe how to manage power consumption on computing devices.*

- Turning off your computer when you won't be using it for long periods of time saves energy. In Windows 10, you can turn your computer off by accessing the Power option on the Start menu, then selecting Shut down.
- If you are not using your computer for short periods of time, selecting the Sleep option will help your computer save energy but allows it to be quickly "awakened" for use.

Objective 2.14   *Define ergonomics, and discuss the ideal physical setup for using computing devices.*

- Ergonomics refers to how you arrange your computer and equipment to minimize your risk of injury or discomfort.
- Achieving proper ergonomics includes positioning your monitor correctly, buying an adjustable chair, assuming a proper position while typing, making sure the lighting is adequate, and not looking at the screen for long periods. Other good practices include taking frequent breaks and using specially designed equipment such as ergonomic keyboards.
- Ergonomics is also important to consider when using mobile devices.

 Be sure to check out **MyLab IT** for additional materials to help you review and learn. And don't forget to watch the Chapter Overview Videos. ▶

Key Terms

2-in-1 PC **44**

3D printer **58**

all-in-one computer **46**

all-in-one printer **58**

application software **42**

aspect ratio **55**

assistive (adaptive) technology **74**

binary digit (bit) **41**

binary language **41**

Bluetooth technology **44**

Blu-ray disc (BD) **68**

byte **41**

central processing unit (CPU, or processor) **41**

Chromebook **45**

cloud-ready printer **58**

cloud storage **67**

CMYK **57**

cold boot **71**

compact disc (CD) **68**

computer **40**

connectivity port **69**

cursor **50**

data **40**

desktop computer **46**

digital convergence **43**

digital video (or versatile) disc (DVD) **68**

display screen (monitor) **54**

distributed (grid) computing **52**

drive bay **65**

earbuds **56**

electrical switch **41**

embedded computer **46**

ergonomics **73**

Ethernet port **69**

expansion cards (or adapter cards) **64**

external hard drive **65**

feature phone **44**

flash drive (jump drive, USB drive, or thumb drive) **66**

flash memory card **66**

flatbed scanner **52**

game controller **52**

gigabyte (GB) **41**

gigahertz (GHz) **64**

global positioning system (GPS) **64**

green computing (green IT) **68**

hard disk drive (HDD, or hard drive) **65**

hardware **42**

headphones **56**

Hibernate **72**

high-definition multimedia interface (HDMI) port **70**

information **40**

inkjet printer **57**

input device **48**

integrated circuit (chip) **41**

intelligent personal assistant **53**

interactive white board **56**

internal hard drive **65**

keyboard **48**

kilobyte (KB) **41**

laptop (or notebook) computer **44**

large format printer **58**

laser printer **57**

light-emitting diode (LED) **54**

liquid crystal display (LCD) **54**

mainframe **46**

megabyte (MB) **41**

microphone (mic) **53**

microprocessor **41**

motherboard **63**

mouse **50**

near field communication (NFC) **56**

network interface card (NIC) **64**

nonvolatile storage **64**

operating system (OS) **42**

optical character recognition (OCR) software **52**

optical drive **67**

optical mouse **50**

organic light-emitting diode (OLED) display **54**

output device **54**

peripheral device **46**

petabyte (PB) **41**

phablet **44**

pixel **55**

port **69**

power supply **71**

printer **57**

processing **40**

projector **56**

QWERTY keyboard **48**

random access memory (RAM) **63**

read-only memory (ROM) **64**

resolution **55**

semiconductor **41**

sensor **54**

Sleep mode **71**

smartphone **43**

software **42**

solid-state drive (SSD) **65**

sound card **64**

speakers **56**

stylus **48**

supercomputer **46**

surround-sound system **56**

system software **42**

system unit **46**

tablet computer **44**

terabyte (TB) **41**

Thunderbolt port **69**

touch pad (trackpad) **52**

touch screen **48**

transistor **41**

ultrabook **45**

universal serial bus (USB) port **69**

video card **64**

virtual keyboard **48**

voice recognition software **53**

volatile storage **64**

warm boot **71**

webcam **52**

Chapter Quiz // Assessment

For a quick review to see what you've learned, answer the following questions. Submit the quiz as requested by your instructor. If you are using **MyLab IT**, the quiz is also available there.

multiple choice

1. Which of the following functions of a computer is mostly responsible for turning data into information?
   a. output
   b. storage
   c. input
   d. processing

2. In a computer, each _____ can represent one letter, number, or symbol.
   a. byte
   b. bit
   c. integrated circuit
   d. megabyte

3. A(n) _____ is a laptop computer that can convert into a tablet-like device.
   a. 2-in-1 PC
   b. Chromebook
   c. ultrabook
   d. all-in-one PC

4. Touch-screen devices usually feature _____ keyboards.
   a. physical
   b. laser-projection
   c. virtual
   d. optical

5. All of the following are sensors found in certain smartphones EXCEPT
   a. barometer.
   b. accelerometer.
   c. magnetometer.
   d. hygrometer.

6. Ergonomics is an important consideration
   a. for all computing devices.
   b. only for laptop computers.
   c. only for laptop and desktop computers, but never for mobile devices.
   d. only for desktop computers.

7. The most common output device for soft output is a
   a. laser printer.
   b. scanner
   c. inkjet printer.
   d. display screen.

8. _____ printers work by spraying tiny drops of ink onto paper.
   a. Inkjet
   b. Cloud-ready
   c. Laser
   d. Large format

9. The fastest computer port is the _____ port
   a. USB
   b. expansion
   c. Thunderbolt
   d. Wi-Fi

10. Which component of a computing device drains the battery the fastest?
    a. hard drive
    b. display screen
    c. Wi-Fi adapter
    d. Bluetooth adapter

true/false

_____ 1. Data and information are NOT interchangeable terms.

_____ 2. RAM is volatile storage.

_____ 3. Conventional disk drives are superior to SSD drives because they have no moving parts.

_____ 4. A touch pad is a pointing device usually found in laptops.

_____ 5. The "brain" of the computer is the USB.

critical thinking

1. Computers of the Future

Embedded computers keep turning up in new places. They can be found in cars, household appliances, smoke detectors, and thermostats, too, enabling us to interact with even more of these "smart" devices every day. What common objects do you think might benefit from an embedded computer? What capabilities can you envision?

2. New Display Features

The display screen of the future may be paper-thin, flexible, and transparent. Companies like Samsung and LG are already working on it. What uses can you envision for this new technology? What advantages and disadvantages do you foresee? Do you have any suggestions for the manufacturers to help make this successful?

Team Time

Portable Computing Options

problem

You've joined a small business that's beginning to evaluate its technology setup. Because of the addition of several new sales representatives, customer service reps, and other administrative employees, the company needs to reconsider the various computing devices that they need. Salespeople are out in the field, as are the customer service technicians. You've been asked to evaluate options for portable computing devices.

task

Split your class into teams of three and assign the following tasks:

- Member A explores the benefits and downfalls of smartphones.
- Member B explores the benefits and downfalls of tablets.
- Member C explores the benefits and downfalls of ultrabooks.

process

1. Think about what the portable computing needs are for the company and what information and resources you'll need to tackle this project.

2. Research and then discuss the components of each method you're recommending. Are any of these options better suited for the particular needs of certain types of employees (sales representatives versus administrative staff)? Consider the types of battery life needed and the appropriate screen size for common tasks. How significant a factor is device weight?

3. Consider the different types of employees in the company. Would a combination of devices be better than a single solution? If so, what kinds of employees would use which type of device?

4. As a team, write a summary position paper. Support your recommendation for the company. Each team member should include why his or her portable device will or will not be part of the solution.

conclusion

There are advantages and disadvantages to any portable computing device. Being aware of the pros and cons and knowing which device is best for a particular scenario or employee will help you to become a better consumer as well as a better computer user.

Ethics Project

Green Computing

Ethical conduct is a stream of decisions you make all day long. In this exercise, you'll research and then role-play a complicated ethical situation. The role you play may or may not match your own personal beliefs, but your research and use of logic will enable you to represent whichever view is assigned. An arbitrator will watch and comment on both sides of the arguments, and together, the team will agree on an ethical solution.

background

Green computing—conducting computing needs with the least possible amount of power and impact on the environment—is on everyone's minds. Although it's hard to argue with an environmentally conscious agenda, the pinch to our pocketbooks and the loss of some comforts sometimes make green computing difficult. Businesses, including colleges, need to consider a variety of issues and concerns before jumping into a complete green overhaul.

research areas to consider

- End-of-life management: e-waste and recycling
- Energy-efficient devices
- Renewable resources used in computer manufacturing
- Costs of green computing
- Government funding and incentives

process

1. Divide the class into teams.
2. Research the areas cited above and devise a scenario in which your college is considering modifying its current technology setup to a more green information technology (IT) strategy.
3. Team members should write a summary that provides background information for their character—for example, environmentalist, college IT administrator, or arbitrator—and that details their character's behaviors to set the stage for the role-playing event. Then, team members should create an outline to use during the role-playing event.
4. Team members should arrange a mutually convenient time to meet, using a virtual meeting tool or by meeting in person.
5. Team members should present their case to the class or submit a PowerPoint presentation for review by the rest of the class, along with the summary and resolution they developed.

conclusion

As technology becomes ever more prevalent and integrated into our lives, more and more ethical dilemmas will present themselves. Being able to understand and evaluate both sides of the argument, while responding in a personally or socially ethical manner, will be an important skill.

Technology Wish List

You are in need of a significant technology upgrade, and your parents have told you they will help you finance your purchases by loaning you the money. You'll need to repay them with a modest 2.5% interest rate over two years. The only catch is that they want you to create a list of all the new devices that you need, note the cost, and provide a website for each device where they can find more information. Then, they want you to calculate how much you'll need to give them each month to pay them back.

You'll use the following Excel skills as you complete this activity:

- Merge and Center
- Modify Workbook Themes
- Apply Number Formats
- Use the SUM, PMT, and COUNTA Functions

- Modify Column Widths
- Insert a Hyperlink
- Create a Formula
- Wrap Text

Instructions:

1. Open *TIA_Ch2_Start* and save as **TIA_Ch2_LastFirst**.
2. Format the title in cell A1 with the **Title Cell Style**, and format the column headers in cells A3:F3 with the **Heading 3 Cell Style**.
   a. Hint: To format cell styles, on the Home tab, in the Styles group, click **Cell Styles**.
3. **Merge and Center** cell A1 across columns A through F, and **Center align** the column headers in cells A3:F3.
   a. Hint: To Merge and Center text, on the Home tab, in the Alignment group, click **Merge & Center**.
4. Modify column widths so that Column A is **25** and Column D is **45**.
   a. Hint: To modify column widths, on the Home tab, in the Cells group, click **Format**, and then select **Column Width**.
5. In cells B4:E9, fill in the table with the Brand and Model of the six devices that you would like to purchase. The device type is filled out for you. In the *Reason* column, write a brief note as to why this device will help you. (You'll format the text so it all displays later.) Enter the cost of the device in the Cost column. Don't include tax and/or shipping.
6. Change the Workbook Theme to **Integral**.
   a. Hint: To apply the Theme, on the Page Layout tab, in the Themes group, click **Themes**.
7. In cells F4:F9, create a **Hyperlink** to a webpage that features each respective product so your grandparents can have access to more information if they need it. Ensure that each hyperlink includes the URL to the exact webpage for the device in the Address box, but displays the Make/Model of the device in the worksheet.
   a. Hint: To insert a hyperlink, on the Insert tab, in the Links group, click **Hyperlink**. In the Insert Hyperlink dialog box, enter the URL in the Address box and enter the Make/Model in the Text to display box.
8. Wrap the text in cells C4:C9, D4:D9, and F4:F9 so all text displays.
   a. Hint: To wrap text, on the Home tab, in the Alignment group, click **Wrap Text**.
9. Format the values in cells E4:E9 with the **Accounting Number format with two decimals**.
10. In cell A10, type **Subtotal**, then in cell E10, use a **SUM function** to calculate the total cost of all devices. Format the results in the **Accounting Number format with two decimals**.
11. In cell A11, type **Estimated Tax**, then in cell E11, create a formula that references the subtotal in cell E10 and multiplies it by a tax of 6%. Format the results in the **Accounting Number format with two decimals**.
12. In cell A12, type **Estimated Shipping**, then in cell E12, create a formula to calculate the shipping charge by using the **COUNTA function** to determine the number of devices being purchased and then multiplying that by a $10 shipping charge. Format the results in **Accounting Number Format with two decimals**.
13. In cell A13, type **Total Cost**, then in cell E13, use the **SUM function** to create a formula that adds up the *Subtotal*, *Estimated Tax*, and *Estimated Shipping* costs. Format the results in **Accounting Number Format with two decimals**. Format the cells A13:E13 with the **Total Cell Style**.
14. **Right align** cells A10:A13.
15. In cell D14, type **Estimated Monthly Payment**, and then in cell E14, use the **PMT function** to calculate the monthly payment owed to your parents to pay back the total purchase amount in two years at a 2.5% annual interest rate.
16. Save the workbook and submit based on your instructor's directions.

3

Using the Internet: Making the Most of the Web's Resources

 For a chapter overview, watch the Chapter Overview Videos.

(Dny3d/Fotolia; Marish/Shutterstock; Gheatza/Fotolia; Maksym Yemelyanov/Fotolia; HaywireMedia/Fotolia; Totallypic/Fotolia)

PART 1

Collaborating and Working on the Web

Learning Outcome 3.1 You will be able to explain how the Internet works and how it is used for collaboration, communication, commerce, and entertainment purposes.

PART 2

Using the Web Effectively

Learning Outcome 3.2 You will be able to describe the tools and techniques required to navigate and search the web.

 The Internet and How It Works 86

Objective 3.1 *Describe how the Internet got its start.*

Objective 3.2 *Explain how data travels on the Internet.*

 Collaborating and Communicating on the Web 89

Objective 3.3 *Evaluate the tools and technologies used to collaborate on the web.*

Objective 3.4 *Summarize the technologies used to communicate over the web.*

Sound Byte: Blogging

 Conducting Business on the Web 97

Objective 3.5 *Describe how business is conducted using the Internet.*

Objective 3.6 *Summarize precautions you should take when doing business online.*

Helpdesk: Doing Business Online

 Accessing and Moving Around the Web 105

Objective 3.7 *Explain what web browsers are, and describe their common features.*

Objective 3.8 *Explain what a URL is, and discuss its main parts.*

Objective 3.9 *Describe tools used to navigate the web.*

 Searching the Web Effectively 110

Objective 3.10 *Describe the types of tools used to search the web, and summarize strategies used to refine search results.*

Objective 3.11 *Describe how to evaluate a website to ensure it is appropriate to use for research purposes.*

Sound Byte: Finding Information on the Web

Helpdesk: Evaluating Websites

 Using the Web Ethically 115

Objective 3.12 *Demonstrate an understanding of the ethical issues regarding digital activism.*

Objective 3.13 *Demonstrate an understanding of the ethical issues regarding location tracking applications and devices.*

For the IT Simulation for this chapter, see MyLab IT.

MyLab IT   All media accompanying this chapter can be found here.

Make This   Make: A Web-Capable App on page 104

How Cool Is This?

Ever wondered how Facebook **suggests friends to tag** when you post a picture? Facebook has invested heavily in **face recognition technology** powered by artificial intelligence (AI). When you post photos to Facebook, the face recognition software **takes and stores over 100 measurements** of each face in a picture (such as the distance between a person's eyes). When you upload a new photo, the software then compares the measurements of the faces in the new photo to measurements it has previously calculated. When the measurements are a close match, the software identifies the new face in a picture as that person. It's estimated that the software is about **98% accurate**. Other facial recognition programs exist, though **Facebook's is currently the most accurate**. The accuracy centers on the vast number of images in Facebook's database and that those images are not all from the same angle (i.e., straight on). Facial recognition **can introduce privacy concerns** if used in the wrong way, but ultimately the good may outweigh the bad.

Zoonar/Photo (Shutterstock)

Collaborating and Working on the Web

Learning Outcome 3.1 **You will be able to explain how the Internet works and how it is used for collaboration, communication, commerce, and entertainment purposes.**

You most likely know at least a little bit about how to use the web's resources to communicate and collaborate with others and how business is conducted over the web. In this section, we'll explore these and related topics. But first, let's start with a brief overview of the Internet.

The Internet and How It Works

It's hard to imagine life without the Internet. The Internet is actually a network of networks that connects billions of computer users globally, but its beginnings were much more modest.

The Origin of the Internet

Objective 3.1 *Describe how the Internet got its start.*

Why was the Internet created? The concept of the **Internet**—the largest computer network in the world—was developed in the late 1950s while the United States was in the midst of the Cold War with the Soviet Union (see Figure 3.1). At that time, the U.S. Department of Defense needed a computer network that wouldn't be disrupted easily in the event of an attack.

ASCII Code - Character to Binary

0	0011 0000	I	0100 1001	b	0110 0010	v	0111 0110
1	0011 0001	J	0100 1010	c	0110 0011	w	0111 0111
2	0011 0010	K	0100 1011	d	0110 0100	x	0111 1000
3	0011 0011	L	0100 1100	e	0110 0101	y	0111 1001
4	0011 0100	M	0100 1101	f	0110 0110	z	0111 1010
				g	0110 0110		

1958

The **Advanced Research Projects Agency (ARPA)** is established for the U.S. Department of Defense. This agency creates the ARPANET—the beginnings of the Internet.

1963

ASCII code is developed as the standard for computers from different manufacturers to exchange data.

1969

Researchers at UCLA **send the first message via a networked computer system** to researchers at Stanford University.

1964

A **new network scheme** is developed with multiple paths so if one communication path was destroyed (from a potential Soviet Union attack), the rest of the network would still be able to communicate.

Figure 3.1 How the Internet Began *(Cristi180884/Shutterstock)*

At the same time, researchers for the Department of Defense were trying to get different computers to work with each other using a common communications method that all computers could use. The Internet was created to respond to these two concerns: establishing a secure form of communications and creating a means by which *all* computers could communicate.

Who invented the Internet? The modern Internet evolved from an early U.S. government-funded "internetworking" project called the Advanced Research Projects Agency Network (ARPANET). ARPANET began as a four-node network involving UCLA, Stanford Research Institute, the University of California at Santa Barbara, and the University of Utah in Salt Lake City. The first real communication occurred in 1969 between the computer at Stanford and the computer at UCLA. Although the system crashed after the third letter of "Login" was transmitted, it was the beginning of a revolution. Many people participated in the creation of the ARPANET, but two men, Vinton Cerf and Robert Kahn, are generally acknowledged as the "fathers of the Internet." These men earned this honor because in the 1970s, they were primarily responsible for developing the communications protocols (standards) still in use on the Internet today.

So are the web and the Internet the same thing? Because the **World Wide Web** (**WWW** or the **web**) is what we use the most, we sometimes think of the Internet and the web as being interchangeable. However, the web is only a subset of the Internet, dedicated to broadcasting HTML pages; it is the means by which we access information over the Internet. The web is based on the Hypertext Transfer Protocol (HTTP), which is why you see an http:// at the beginning of web addresses. What distinguishes the web from the rest of the Internet is its use of the following:

- Common communications protocols that enable computers to talk to each other and display information in compatible formats
- Special links that enable users to navigate from one place to another on the web

Who created the web? The web began in 1991. It was based on a protocol developed by Tim Berners-Lee, a physicist at the European Organization for Nuclear Research (CERN), who wanted a method for linking his research documents so that other researchers could access them. In conjunction with Robert Cailliau, Berners-Lee developed the basic architecture of the web and

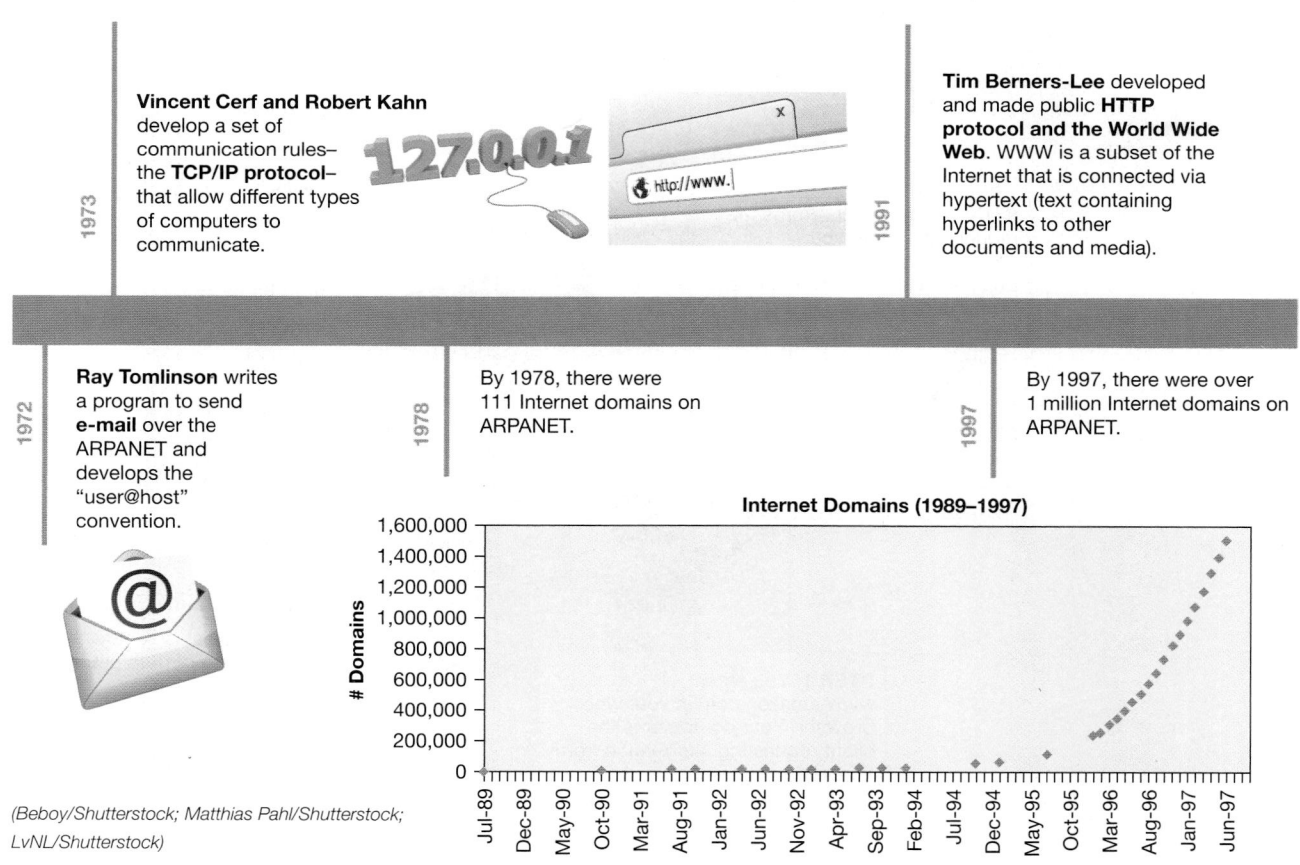

1973

Vincent Cerf and Robert Kahn develop a set of communication rules– the **TCP/IP protocol**– that allow different types of computers to communicate.

1991

Tim Berners-Lee developed and made public **HTTP protocol and the World Wide Web**. WWW is a subset of the Internet that is connected via hypertext (text containing hyperlinks to other documents and media).

1972

Ray Tomlinson writes a program to send **e-mail** over the ARPANET and develops the "user@host" convention.

1978

By 1978, there were 111 Internet domains on ARPANET.

1997

By 1997, there were over 1 million Internet domains on ARPANET.

Internet Domains (1989–1997)

(y-axis, # Domains): 1,600,000 / 1,400,000 / 1,200,000 / 1,000,000 / 800,000 / 600,000 / 400,000 / 200,000 / 0

(x-axis): Jul-89, Dec-89, May-90, Oct-90, Mar-91, Aug-91, Jan-92, Jun-92, Nov-92, Apr-93, Sep-93, Feb-94, Jul-94, Dec-94, May-95, Oct-95, Mar-96, Aug-96, Jan-97, Jun-97

(Beboy/Shutterstock; Matthias Pahl/Shutterstock; LvNL/Shutterstock) created the first web browser, software that lets you display and interact with text and other media on the web. The original browser could handle only text. Then, in 1993, the Mosaic browser, which could display graphics as well as text, was released. The once-popular Netscape Navigator browser evolved from Mosaic and heralded the beginning of the web's monumental growth.

How the Internet Works

Objective 3.2   *Explain how data travels on the Internet.*

How does the Internet work? All computers and other devices such as tablets and smartphones that are connected to the Internet create a network of networks. These Internet-connected devices communicate with each other in turns, just as we do when we ask a question or reply with an answer. Thus, a computer (or other device) connected to the Internet acts in one of two ways: Either it's a **client**, a computer that asks for data, or it's a **server**, a computer that receives the request and returns the data to the client. Because the Internet uses clients and servers, it's referred to as a **client/server network**.

When a client computer puts out a request for information from the server computer, the request travels along transmission lines. These transmission lines are similar to our highway system of roads, with some roads having different speed limits. The transmission lines with the fastest speeds are referred to as **Internet backbones**.

How do computers talk to each other? Suppose you want to order something from Amazon.com. Figure 3.2 illustrates what happens when you type www.amazon.com into your web browser and when Amazon's home page displays on your computer monitor. As you can see, the data request from your computer (the client computer) is sent via Internet communication pathways to a server computer. The server computer (in this case, Amazon's server) processes the request and returns the requested data to your client computer via Internet communication pathways. The data reply most likely takes a different route than did the data request. The web browser on your client computer interprets the data and displays it on its monitor.

How does the data get sent to the correct computer? Each time you connect to the Internet, your computer is assigned a unique identification number. This number, called an **Internet Protocol (IP) address**, is a set of four groups of numbers separated by periods, such as 123.45.245.91, and is commonly referred to as a dotted quad or dotted decimal. IP addresses are the means by which computers connected to the Internet identify each other. Similarly, each website is assigned a unique IP address. However, because the numbers that

STEP 4: The server returns the requested data to your computer using the fastest pathway, which may be different from the one the request took.

Amazon.com's server

STEP 3: Your data flows along the backbone and on to smaller pathways until it reaches its destination, which is the server computer for Amazon's website.

HTML

STEP 5: The web browser interprets the data and displays it on your monitor.

Client

STEP 2: The request is sent to the server via a system of data pathways, similar to a roadway system.

URL

STEP 1: You enter www.amazon.com in your web browser. Your computer is the client requesting information from Amazon.com's website.

Figure 3.2 How the Internet's Client/Server Model Works *(Sashkin/Fotolia; Peshkov/Fotolia)*

make up IP addresses are difficult for people to remember, websites are given text versions of their IP addresses. So, Amazon's website has an IP address of 72.21.211.176 and a name of www.amazon.com. When you enter "www.amazon.com" into your browser, your computer (with its unique IP address) looks for Amazon's IP address (72.21.211.176). Data is exchanged between Amazon's server computer and your computer using these unique IP addresses.

Collaborating and Communicating on the Web

Collaborating, or working together to achieve a common goal, is often done in the classroom, in business, and even at home. The advancement in web technologies has facilitated the collaboration process in many ways, especially enabling participants to collaborate from distant locations. In this section, we'll explore some popular means of collaborating on the web.

Collaborating with Web Technologies

Objective 3.3   *Evaluate the tools and technologies used to collaborate on the web.*

How do we collaborate on the web? Over time, our use of the web has evolved from passively browsing web pages that were created for us, to actively creating our own web content and sharing and collaborating on it with others. This collaborative, user-created web, sometimes classified as the social web, in which the user is also a participant, is possible due to **Web 2.0** technologies. Web 2.0 technologies enable us to collaborate with others on documents through web applications such as Google Drive, to collaborate on projects with tools such as Slack and Bootcamp, to rate and recommend products or services with Yelp, to make business connections on social networks such as LinkedIn, and to share a video on YouTube or a favorite image on Pinterest. These means of Web 2.0 communication are collectively called **social media** and include social networking, project collaboration and file sharing tools, blogs, podcasts, webcasts, and media sharing.

Social Networking

Is there more to social networking than Facebook, Snapchat, and Twitter? As you probably know, **social networking** refers to using the web to communicate and share information among your friends and others. Professional, business-oriented online networks such as LinkedIn are helpful for members seeking clients, business opportunities, jobs, or job candidates. Like a true business network, these sites can help you meet other professionals through connections with people you already know. In addition, businesses use social networking for marketing and communicating directly with their customers. For example, companies may post special deals and offers on their Facebook page or solicit responses from followers that may help with product development or future marketing campaigns.

Figure 3.3 lists various sites that are considered social networking sites. As you can see, there is more to social networking than just Facebook, Snapchat, and Twitter.

What are some dos and don'ts of social networking? When social networking sites first became popular, there was concern over privacy issues, especially for school-aged children who put personal information on their pages without considering the possibility of that information being misused by a stalker or identity thief. Although those concerns still exist, many of the most popular social networking sites have improved their privacy policies, thereby reducing, but not eliminating, such concerns. Still, users must be cautious about the type of content they post on these sites. Consider these precautions as you use social networking sites:

- Keep your personal information personal. The year you were born, your physical address, and the routines of your life (sports games, practices, work schedules) should not be broadcast to the general public.
- Know who your friends are, and know who can see the information you post. Review your privacy settings periodically, as sites change and update their privacy practices frequently.
- Do not post information such as your favorite teacher or your first pet's name because these are often used as security questions to verify your identity.

Figure 3.3 Types of Social Networking Sites

Social Communication

- Facebook
- Tumblr
- Twitter
- Snapchat
- Viber
- WhatsApp

Media Sharing

- Instagram
- YouTube
- Pinterest
- Flickr
- Periscope
- Vine
- Bandcamp
- Spotify

Business Networking and Collaboration

- LinkedIn
- Slack
- Kickstarter
- StartupNation

Information Sharing

- Delicious
- SlideShare
- StumbleUpon
- Reddit
- Digg

Social Commerce and Payment

- Venmo
- PayPal
- SquareCash
- Groupon
- LivingSocial
- GoFundMe

Social Travel

- Uber
- Airbnb
- TripAdvisor
- Waze

Health and Fitness

- MapMyFitness
- Fitocracy
- MyFitnessPal
- Happier

(Lovemask/Fotolia; Vectorchef/Fotollia; RealVector/Fotolia; Vladvm50/Fotolia; Copics/Fotolia; Ylivdesign/Fotolia; Scott Dunlap/Fotolia)

- Use caution when posting images, and know what images others are posting of you. Although privacy settings may offer some comfort, some images may be available for viewing through search engines and may not require site registration to be seen. Online images may become public property and subject to reproduction, and you might not want some—or any—of those images to be distributed.

Many employers and colleges use social networks as a means of gaining information about potential applicants before granting an interview or extending admission or a job offer. In fact, there have been instances of people being fired from their jobs and being expelled from school for using social media, such as Facebook, Twitter, and blogs, in a questionable way. Generally, questionable content on social media includes negative discussion about the poster's job, employer, or colleagues, or inappropriate content about the poster. The responsibility for your content rests with you. Even though you may have strong privacy settings, you can't control what those who you allow to see your content do with it. Therefore, treat all information posted on the web as public, and avoid posting damaging words and pictures. Bottom line: Make sure your profile, images, and site content project an image that positively and accurately represents you.

Project Collaboration and File Sharing Tools

What tools are used when collaborating on a project? Rather than needing to pass documents back and forth via e-mail and possibly losing track of which version is the most recent, file sharing tools are very useful. Web-based document products such as Google Docs and Microsoft Office Online have features to promote online collaboration. These products offer wiki-like capabilities that allow users to add, remove, or edit a document's content in real time. A **wiki** is a document created collaboratively by multiple users, resulting in an emergent "common" output rather than multiple outputs of individual writers. Wikis allow all who have access to the wiki page to post their ideas and modify the content of the current version of a single document. Wikis provide the extra benefit of users being able to access, review, and even revert to past versions at any time.

What other web tools are used to help with project collaborations? In addition to using wikis and wiki-like documents, other tools such as videoconferencing, screen sharing, and project management tools are used to facilitate collaboration. Full-featured business enterprise solutions are available, but for smaller collaborative projects, such as those you might encounter in a group project for school or in a small business environment, there are a wide variety of web-based options to choose from, many of which are free. **Project management tools** incorporate tasks and calendars so the individual components as well as the entire project can stay on schedule. Trello, for example, is a free project management tool that organizes projects onto boards and specific tasks onto cards. Cards can contain checklists, images, labels, discussion notes, and the like. All cards are searchable, shareable, and can have reminders. Slack is another popular project management tool that incorporates text messaging, file sharing, and other collaborative features.

When working with a group whose members are not in the same location, screen sharing or video-conferencing software can be helpful. Products such as Join.me and Screenleap offer free screen-sharing solutions, and Skype and Google Hangouts are handy solutions for videoconferencing.

In addition, built into the latest versions of Microsoft Word and PowerPoint is the capability to present online (see Figure 3.4). When you initiate Present Online, a link is generated that you share with the desired recipients, and then anyone who uses the link can see the slide show or document while you are presenting online.

Blogs

Why do people write blogs? A **blog** (short for **weblog**) is a personal log or journal posted on the web. Anyone can create a blog, and there are millions of blogs available to read, follow, and comment on. Blogs are generally written by a single author and are arranged as a listing of entries on a single page, with the most recent blog entry appearing at the top of the list. In addition, blogs are public, and readers can post comments on your blog, often creating an engaging, interactive experience. Blogs have searchable and organized content, making them user friendly. They're accessible from anywhere using a web browser.

Many people use blogs as a sort of personal scrapbook. Whenever the urge strikes, they report on their daily activities. Many other blogs focus on a particular topic. For example, the Movie Blog (**themovieblog.com**) contains reviews and opinions about movies, and Engadget (**engadget.com**) is a blog devoted to discussing technogadgets. Even some mobile apps have integrated blogs, such as the one affiliated with MyFitnessPal that gives weight loss tips and healthy recipes. Many corporations, such as Walmart and Best Buy, have blogs written by employees. BlogCatalog (**blogcatalog.com**) is a blog directory that can help you find blogs that fit your interests.

Are all blogs text-based? The traditional form of a blog is primarily text-based but may also include images and audio. A **video log** (**vlog** or **video blog**) is a blog that uses video as the primary content (although it can also contain text, images, and audio). Vlogs are a popular means of personal expression, and many can be found by searching YouTube (**youtube.com**).

 Sound Byte MyLab IT®

Blogging

In this Sound Byte, you'll see why blogs are one of today's most popular publishing mediums. You'll also learn how to create and publish your own blog.

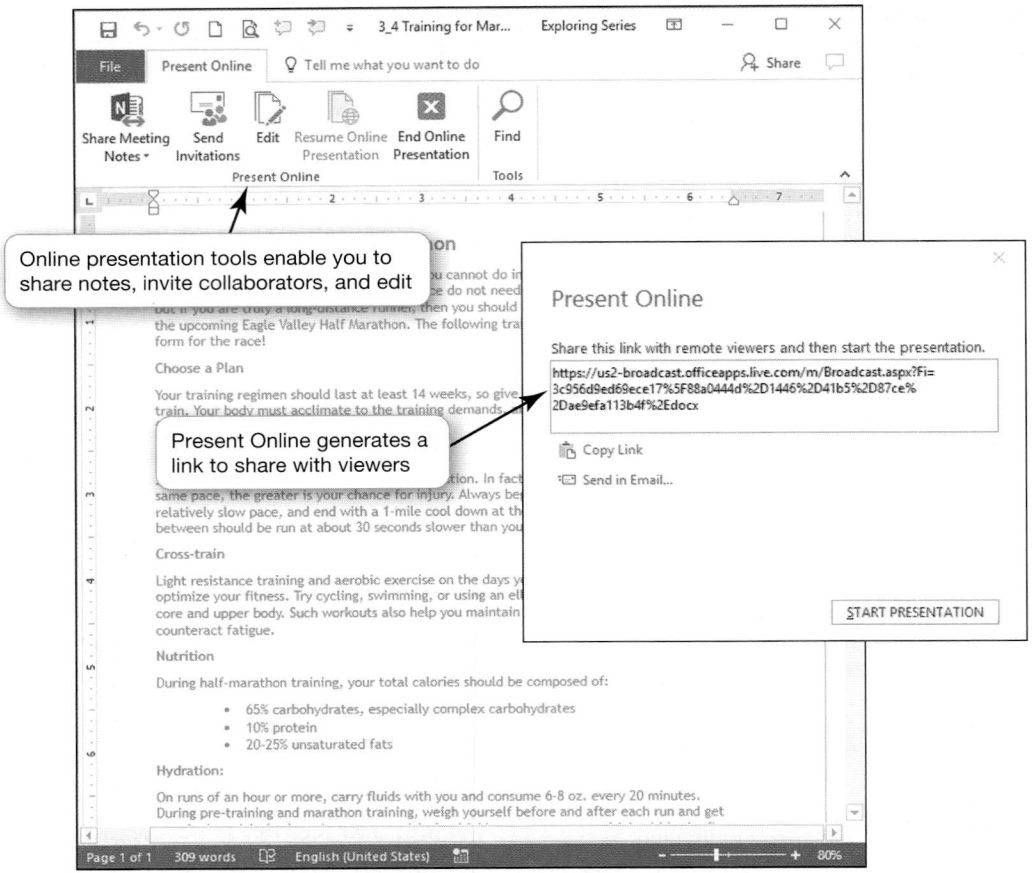

Figure 3.4 You can present a Word document or PowerPoint presentation to an online audience using built-in technology in Microsoft Office. *(Word 2016, Microsoft Corporation)*

How do I create a blog? Many websites provide the tools you need to create your own blog. Two sites that offer free blog hosting are Blogger (**blogger.com**) and WordPress (**wordpress. com**). Such tools also let you add features like pictures or subpages to your blog. You can also choose to host your blog yourself so that the URL reflects your name or the name of your business. If you choose this option, you'll need your own website and a URL so people can access it.

Are there any problems with blogs? The popularity of blogs has brought about spam blogs (splogs), which are artificially created blog sites filled with fake articles or stolen text (a tactic known as blog scraping). Splogs, which contain links to other sites associated with the splog's creator, have the intention of either increasing traffic to, or increasing search engine rankings for, these usually disreputable or useless websites. Although not really harmful, splogs are another unwanted form of content that continues to flourish on the web.

Are Twitter and Tumblr considered blogs? Twitter and Tumblr are examples of **microblogs**, where users post short text with usually frequent updates. With Twitter, the posts are limited to 140 characters. Twitter and Tumblr also allow users to post multimedia and other content. Posts can be public or restricted to a certain audience.

Podcasts

Figure 3.5 Many online news and radio sites offer podcasts of their programs. *(Dwd-Media/Alamy Stock Photo)*

How can I distribute audio or video files over the Internet to a wide audience?
A **podcast** is a form of digital media composed of a series of audio or video files that are distributed over the Internet (see Figure 3.5). There are podcasts for radio shows, audiobooks, magazines, and even educational programs, which you can download to any device that can play audio files. What makes podcasts different from other audio files found on the web is that podcasts deliver their content using **Really Simple Syndication (RSS)**. RSS is a format that sends the latest content of the podcast series automatically to an **aggregator** such as iTunes or Feedspot.

Figure 3.6 Podcast Directories and Aggregators

iTunes (itunes.com)

- Software makes it easy to play, manage, and share your favorite podcasts

PodSearch (podsearch.com)

- Broad collection of podcasts

Stitcher (stitcher.com)

- Customize podcast playlists

YouTube (youtube.com)

- Good source for video blogs (vlogs)

An aggregator locates all the RSS series to which you've subscribed and automatically downloads only the new content to your computer or media player. If you have several favorite websites or podcasts, rather than checking each site for updated content, aggregators collect all the site updates in one place. These updates or changes to the content are then delivered automatically if you subscribe to the podcast, instead of requiring you to search for the latest content and download it manually.

Where can I find podcasts? Most online news and radio sites offer podcasts of their programs. Although many podcasts are news related, others offer entertaining and educational content. For example, you can access lessons on yoga, foreign language classes, or DIY tips. Many schools supply students with course content updates through podcasts, and instructors sometimes create podcasts of their lectures. Figure 3.6 lists some websites where you can find podcasts.

Can I create my own podcast? It's simple to create a podcast. To record the audio content all you need is a computer with a microphone, and if you want to make a video podcast, you also need a webcam or video camera. Although high-end equipment will produce more sophisticated output, you certainly can use whatever equipment you might own. You may also need additional software to edit the audio and video content, depending on how professional you wish the podcast to be. After you've recorded and edited the podcast content, you need to export it to MP3 format. The free program Audacity (**audacity.sourceforge.net**) lets you both edit audio files and export them to MP3 format. All that's left for you is to create an RSS feed (tricky, but doable) and then upload the content to a site that hosts podcasts, such as iTunes, PodSearch, or Stitcher.

Webcasts

What is a webcast? A **webcast** is the (usually live) broadcast of audio or video content over the Internet. Unlike podcasts, which are prerecorded and made available for download, most webcasts are distributed in "real time," meaning that they're live or one-time events. Some webcasts are archived so they can be viewed at a later date. Webcasts are not updated automatically, like podcasts.

Webcasts use continuous audio and video feeds, which let you view and download large audio and video files. Webcasts can include noninteractive content, such as a simultaneous broadcast of a radio or television program, but some webcasts invite interactive responses from the viewing or listening audience. For example, ConcertWindow (**concertwindow.com**) enables musicians to broadcast live to their fans, and ORLive (**orlive.com**) provides surgical webcasts that demonstrate the latest surgical innovations and techniques. Webcasts also are used in the corporate world to broadcast annual meetings and in the educational arena to transmit seminars.

Media Sharing Platforms

Where can I share music, pictures, and videos on the web? Social media sharing sites such as Flickr, Instagram, YouTube, and SoundCloud enable anyone to create and share multimedia. Flickr was created to store and share photos online. Although not as "social" as some other sites, Flickr enables users to tag not only their images but also others' images, thus providing a strong search capability to quickly locate images with similar tags. Instagram is primarily a mobile app that allows users to take photos on their phones or tablets, add a caption, and then instantly upload them. SoundCloud is both a distribution platform and a music streaming service. Fledgling musicians can upload original music to share, and music enthusiasts can track and follow new and favorite artists. SoundCloud has a strong online community of followers. YouTube enables users to upload videos offering a variety of content from educational pieces to cute or funny videos. Many YouTube videos become so popular and are shared or recommended to be seen by so many that they go "viral."

Communicating over the Web

Objective 3.4   *Summarize the technologies used to communicate over the web.*

Why do I still need e-mail? Despite the popularity of social media, **e-mail** (short for **electronic mail**)—a written message sent or received over the Internet—still remains the most widely used form of communication on the Internet. E-mail is the primary method of electronic communication worldwide because it's fast and convenient. And because it's asynchronous, users do not need to be communicating at the same time. They can send and respond to messages at their own convenience. E-mail is also convenient for exchanging files via attachments.

How private is e-mail? Although e-mail is a more private exchange of information than public social networking sites, e-mails are not really private. Consider the following:

- Because e-mails can be printed or forwarded to others, you never know who may read your e-mail.
- Most e-mail content is not protected, so you should never use e-mail to send personal or sensitive information, such as bank account or Social Security numbers. Doing so could lead to your identity being stolen.
- Employers have access to e-mail sent from the workplace, so use caution when putting negative or controversial content in e-mail from your workplace.
- Even after you've deleted a message, it doesn't really vanish. Many Internet service providers and companies archive e-mail, which can be accessed or subpoenaed in the event of a lawsuit or investigation.

What are some tips on e-mail etiquette? When you write a casual e-mail to friends, you obviously don't need to follow any specific e-mail guidelines. But when you send e-mail for professional reasons, you should use proper e-mail etiquette. The following are a few guidelines (see Figure 3.7):

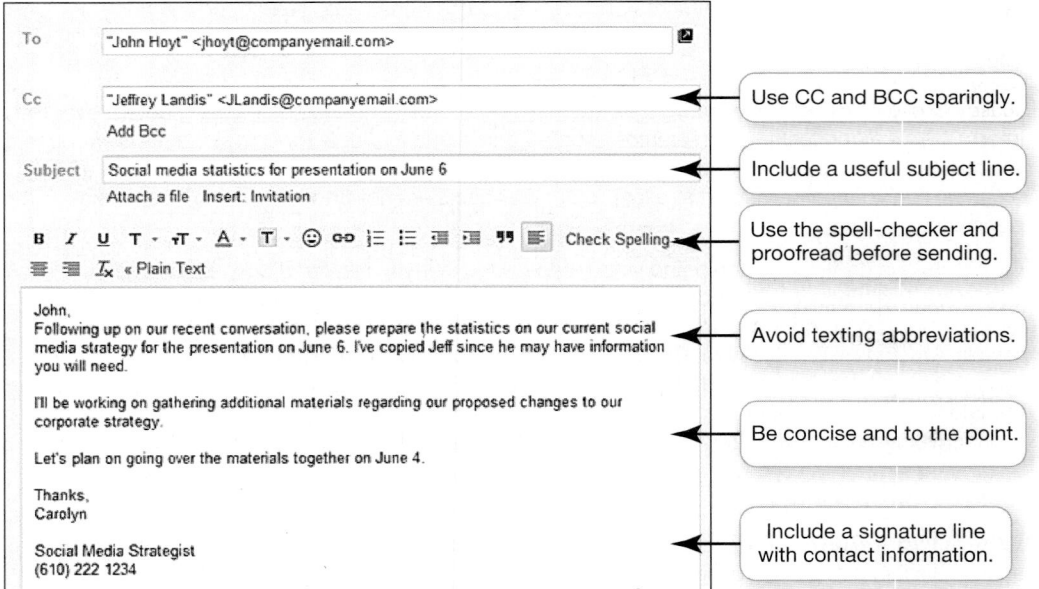

Figure 3.7 Using simple guidelines of e-mail etiquette can promote a professional image and make your message more effective. *(Word 2016, Microsoft Corporation)*

- Be concise and to the point.
- Use the spell-checker and proofread your e-mail before sending it.
- Avoid using abbreviations such as u, r, LOL, and BTW.
- Include a meaningful subject line to help recipients prioritize and organize e-mails.
- Add a signature line that includes your contact information.
- Include only those people on the e-mail who truly need to receive it.

Following such guidelines maintains professionalism, increases efficiency, and might even help protect a company from lawsuits.

Are there different types of e-mail systems? There are two different types of e-mail systems:

1. **Web-based e-mail**, such as Yahoo! Mail, Gmail, or Inbox, is managed with your web browser and allows you to access your e-mail with an Internet connection.
2. An **e-mail client** requires a program, such as Microsoft Outlook, to be installed on your computer. When you open the program, your e-mail is downloaded to your computer.

The primary difference between the two is access. Web-based e-mail allows you to access e-mail from any Internet-connected device, but you can't use your e-mail when you're offline. With an e-mail client, you view your e-mail on the computer on which the e-mail client software has been installed, but you can then view and manage your e-mail while you're offline. E-mail clients often have advanced functionalities such as calendar, meetings, and task management. Both systems can be used together for the "best of both worlds." You can have a Gmail account, for example, so that you can read your e-mail from any computer connected to the Internet, and you can also have Outlook installed on your primary computer, set up the program to display your Gmail account, and have access to additional functionality (see Figure 3.8).

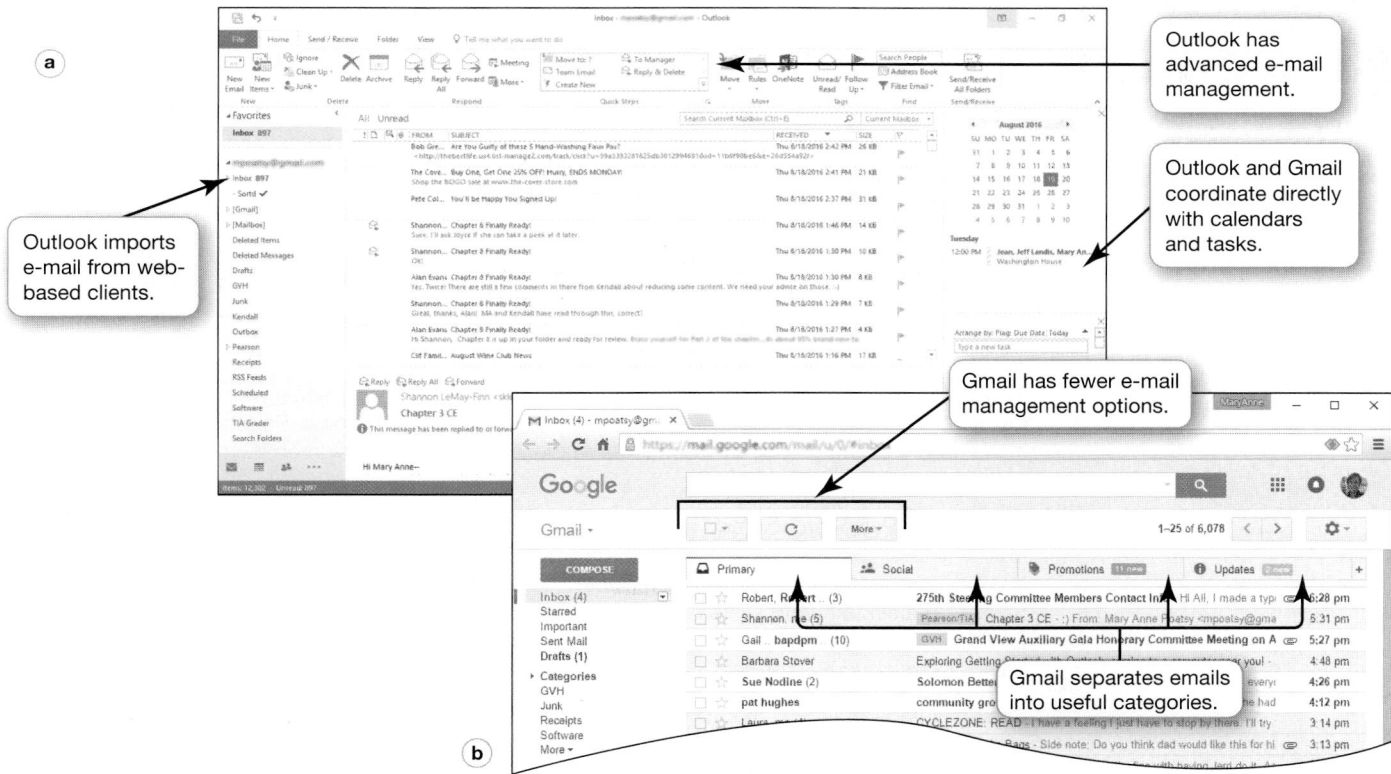

Outlook has advanced e-mail management.

Outlook and Gmail coordinate directly with calendars and tasks.

Outlook imports e-mail from web-based clients.

Gmail has fewer e-mail management options.

Gmail separates emails into useful categories.

Figure 3.8 (a) Client-Based and (b) Web-Based E-Mail Systems *(Word 2016, Microsoft Corporation; Courtesy Google Inc.)*

Who uses instant messaging? **Instant messaging (IM)**, a way of communicating in real time over the Internet, was a primary means of chatting with friends in real time. But with the proliferation of texting and social networking, instant messaging has begun to lose its attraction as a social tool. However, instant messaging still is an important means of quick and efficient communication in the business world. In fact, some IM services, such as Cisco Jabber and Oracle Beehive, have been developed primarily for business use.

Some IM systems provide mechanisms to hold conversations with more than one person, either through simultaneous individual conversations or with group chats. And some programs even let you conduct video chats using a webcam. Other advantages of using IM for business communications is that you can monitor who is allowed to contact you, and people can communicate with you only if they know your exact e-mail or IM address.

Google+ and Hangouts, Skype, and Yahoo! Messenger are proprietary IM services, meaning you can IM or chat only with those who share the same IM service and are on your contact or buddy list. Another option is to chat with those you've "friended" on Facebook through Facebook Messenger. There are also universal chat services, such as WhatsApp, that you install on your device and that allow you to chat with users of all popular IMs, regardless of the service they use. WhatsApp also uses encryption to ensure your messages are safely received.

What is texting and how is it different from instant messaging? Although both IM and texting provide means to chat, there are differences. Instant messaging is synchronous: Both parties need to be participating at the same time, whereas texting is asynchronous in that you do not need to immediately respond to a text once it is received. **Texting** uses the Short Message Service (SMS) to send short messages between mobile devices. Some texting services that use Multimedia Message Service (MMS) can include images or videos. Snapchat is a popular texting app that allows users to send brief videos or images. A differentiating aspect to Snapchat is that once a message is opened, the video or image is available to be viewed for only a brief amount of time and is generally not able to be saved.

Can I make phone calls over the Internet? Using apps such as Skype, FaceTime, or Google Hangouts, users can communicate using audio (voice) and video. These services use **VoIP (Voice over Internet Protocol)**, a fully digital phone service that allows calls to be transmitted over the Internet rather than over traditional phone lines or cellular networks (see Figure 3.9).

Figure 3.9 VoIP technology lets your computing device behave like a phone or video phone, using the Internet instead of the telephone system to transmit data.
(David Malan/The Image Bank/Getty Images)

Traditional telephone communications use analog voice data and telephone connections. In contrast, VoIP uses technology similar to that used in e-mail to transmit your voice data digitally over the Internet. VoIP calls can be placed from anywhere you have Internet access. Creating a VoIP account with Skype is simple (see the Try This in Chapter 1). Skype requires that both callers and receivers have the free Skype software installed on their computer, tablet, or smartphone. With Skype you can place a call, make an HD-video call, and even share screens between users. Calls to other Skype users are free, and you can place low-cost calls to non-Skype users. Major ISPs, like Comcast and Verizon, also provide VoIP phone services as an option you can package with your Internet or cable television plan. Sometimes these services require standalone VoIP phones, sometimes called IP phones.

What are the advantages and disadvantages of VoIP? For people who make many long-distance phone calls, the advantage of VoIP is that it is free or low cost. Portability is another advantage: As long as you are connected to the Internet, you can sign on to your VoIP service and make your call.

Although VoIP is affordable and convenient, it does have drawbacks. Some people regard sound quality and reliability issues as VoIP's primary disadvantages. Additionally, when using VoIP at home, you lose service if power is interrupted. Another issue with VoIP is security risks. Having a hacker break in to a VoIP system to make unauthorized calls is a serious but avoidable problem. Encryption services that convert data into a form not easily understood by unauthorized people are being deployed to help protect calls made over the Internet.

The advantage of VoIP is that as long as you have an Internet connection, you can make a call. In instances when Internet access is free, making long-distance or international connections with VoIP is a much more affordable option to keep in touch with friends and family far away.

Figure 3.10 lists the popular methods of online collaboration and communication that we've discussed.

Figure 3.10 Methods of Online Collaboration and Communication

Social Networking	Project Collaboration and File Sharing	Blogs	Podcasts	Webcasts
• Web 2.0 technology • Lets you build an online network of friends • Lets you share media content	• Web-based document products such as Google Docs • Screen sharing • Project management • Videoconferencing • Wikis	• Written by a single author • Chronologic entries • Searchable content • May include images, audio, and video	• Audio/video files delivered via RSS • New RSS content collected with aggregator • Can download and view content on portable media player	• Most often live, streamed broadcasts

Media Sharing	E-Mail	Instant Messaging	Texting	VoIP
• Platforms to host and share images, videos, and music • Some have more social networking aspects than others	• Most common form of online communication • Asynchronous (not having to be done at the same time)	• Real-time exchange • Can be used with multiple persons simultaneously • Video/audio chats available	• Uses Short Messaging Service (SMS) to send asynchronous messages between mobile devices • Can include images or video	• Voice communication via Internet • Free or low-cost calls • Some reliability issues

(Lowe Standards/Fotolia; Maglara/Shutterstock; Ayzek/Shutterstock; www.3drenderedlogos com/Shutterstock; Batshevs/Shutterstock; Marnikus/Shutterstock; Beboy/Fotolia; LiveStock/Shutterstock; Goolliver25/Fotolia; Yuriy Vlasenko/Shutterstock)

 Conducting Business on the Web

You can buy nearly anything on the web, including big-ticket items such as homes and cars. Now, with mobile apps, there is even greater ability to conduct business from virtually any location, at any time. In this section, we'll take a look at e-commerce and mobile commerce.

Conducting Business Online

Objective 3.5   *Describe how business is conducted using the Internet.*

What are the different types of e-commerce? **E-commerce**—short for **electronic commerce**—is the process of conducting business online. Typically, e-commerce is identified by whom the business is being conducted between:

1. **Business-to-consumer (B2C)** transactions take place between businesses and consumers. Such transactions include those between customers and completely online businesses (such as **Amazon.com**) and those between customers and stores that have both an online and a physical presence, such as Target (**target.com**). Such businesses are referred to as click-and-brick businesses. Some click-and-bricks allow online purchases and in-store pickups and returns.

Have you ever done any of the following?

- Posted pictures on Instagram that your friends accessed from their iPhone
- Used Dropbox or OneDrive to store your files instead of carrying around a flash drive
- Used Google Docs or Microsoft Office Online to collaborate on a team project
- Used Carbonite to back up your data online

By doing any of these activities, you have participated in cloud computing. So what exactly is cloud computing?

Cloud computing refers to storing data, files, and applications on the web and being able to access and manipulate these files and applications from any Internet-connected device. Being able to work from the cloud eliminates the need to have everything stored on your own computer's drives and lets you access your pictures, music, files, and programs from any device as long as you have access to the Internet. In addition, cloud computing makes it easier to collaborate and communicate with others, and it can cut down on administrative tasks for organizations maintaining large amounts of computer hardware and software.

There are two sides to cloud computing: (see Figure 3.11)

1. The *front end* is the side we see as users. It involves a web browser like Google Chrome, Microsoft Edge, or Mozilla Firefox.
2. The *back end* consists of various data centers and server farms that house the files and programs you access "on the cloud." These data centers and server farms are warehouses full of computers and servers, and they are being created all over the world, providing us with "cloud storage." The computers in the data centers or server farms are designed to work together, adjusting to the varying degrees of demand placed on them at any time.

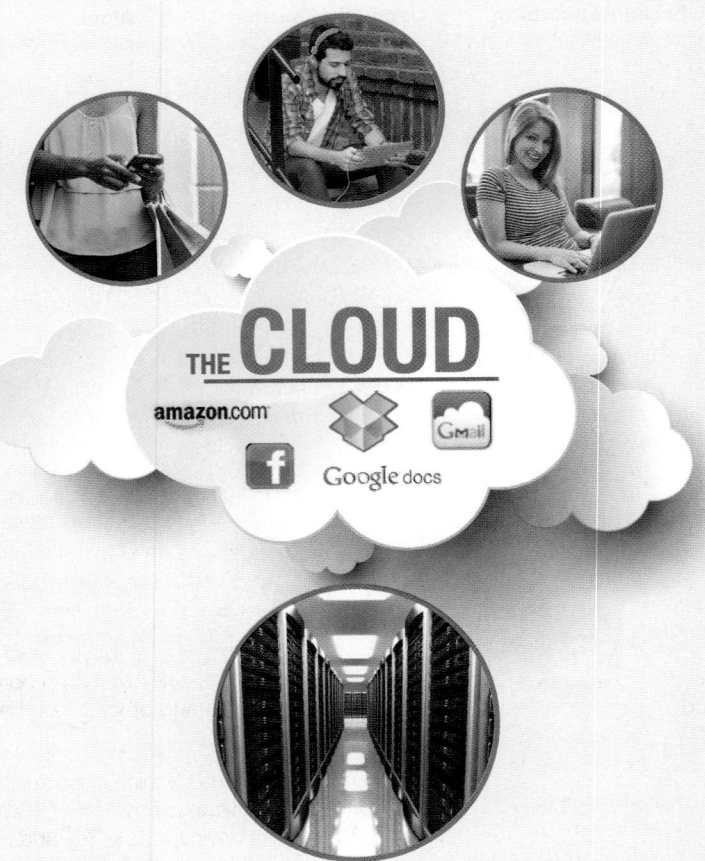

Figure 3.11 There are two sides to cloud computing: the side we see as users and the banks of computers and servers that house the files and programs we access. *(Diego cervo/Fotolia; Fotolia; WavebreakMediaMicro/Fotolia; Alexandr Mitiuc/Fotolia; Anatolii Babii/Alamy Stock Photo; Digitallife/Alamy Stock Photo; PhotoEdit/Alamy Stock Photo; Facebook, Inc.; Google and the Google logo are registered trademarks of Google Inc., used with permission.)*

Google is one of the first true explorers in the cloud, building applications such as Google Drive, Gmail, and the Chrome web browser in an effort to create a completely virtual operating environment. A fully functioning operating environment would enable users to sign in on any computer and have "their" computer setup (desktop configurations and images, programs, files, and other personalized settings) display. Additionally, cloud computing would reduce the need for all of us to have the fastest computers with the most memory and storage capabilities. Instead, we could all have simple front-end terminals with basic input and output devices because the computers on the back end will be providing all the computing muscle.

The Chromebook is Google's first attempt at a notebook where all the applications and files are stored on the web. Little is installed or saved to a hard drive, not even the operating system! All programs are accessed and all work is done through the web-based browser, so sending e-mail, editing photos, and working on documents are all done via web-based applications. Because the Chromebook requires an Internet connection to get most tasks done, users must be near a Wi-Fi connection or pay for a data plan.

There are some considerations with cloud computing:

- *Security and privacy:* Right now, the security of information stored on the web is built on trusting that the passwords we set and the security systems that the data centers put in place are able to keep our information away from unauthorized users. Caution is always warranted, as nothing is completely safe and private.
- *Backup:* Because even the devices in these large data centers and server farms inevitably will break down, the cloud computing systems have redundant systems to provide backup. However, for critical files that you must have, it might be a good idea not to completely rely on the cloud, but to have your own offline backup system as well.
- *Access issues:* With cloud computing, you access your files and programs only through the Internet. If you couldn't access the Internet due to a power failure or system failure with your Internet service provider, you wouldn't be able to access your files. Storing your most critical files and programs offline will help reduce the inconvenience and loss of productivity while access to the Internet is being restored.

Before relying on cloud computing, weigh the above concerns against the convenience of having your information when and where you want it and the ability to promote better collaboration.

2. **Business-to-business (B2B)** transactions occur when businesses buy and sell goods and services to other businesses. An example is Omaha Paper Company (**omahapaper.com**), which distributes paper products to other companies.

3. **Consumer-to-consumer (C2C)** transactions occur when consumers sell to each other through sites such as eBay (**ebay.com**), Craigslist (**craigslist.org**), and Etsy (**etsy.com**).

Social commerce is a subset of e-commerce that uses social networks to assist in marketing and purchasing products. If you're on Facebook, you've no doubt noticed the many businesses that have Facebook pages asking you to "Like" them. Consumers are voicing their opinions on Facebook and other social media sites about products and services by providing ratings and reviews, and studies show that such peer recommendations have a major influence on buying behavior. When you see your friend on Facebook recommend a product or service, you're more likely to click through to that retailer and check out the product.

Other peer-influenced e-commerce trends include group-buying and individual customization. Groupon and LivingSocial are two popular deal-of-the-day group purchase websites that offer discounted deals. CafePress and Zazzle sell T-shirts and other items that are customized with your own graphic designs.

E-commerce encompasses more than just online shopping opportunities from your desktop or laptop computers. **Mobile commerce** (or **m-commerce**) is conducting commercial transactions online through a smartphone, tablet, or other mobile device. Apple Pay and other digital payment systems are becoming quite popular, as well as making payments using mobile apps such as at Starbucks. Many businesses offer mobile loyalty cards, which facilitate pushing coupons and offers to customers using location-based services when the customer is nearby. Some fast-food places and restaurants such as Panera and Dominos enable you to place an order via their mobile app for in-store pick-up or delivery. Mobile commerce also includes services that enable users to check their bank and credit card account balances, deposit checks, pay bills online, and manage investment portfolios. Tickets and boarding passes can also be sent to smartphones, adding another level of convenience.

E-Commerce Safeguards

Objective 3.6 *Summarize precautions you should take when doing business online.*

Just how safe are online transactions? When you buy something online, you may use a credit card; therefore, money is exchanged directly between your credit card company and the online merchant's bank. Because online shopping eliminates a salesclerk or other human intermediary from the transaction, it can actually be safer than traditional retail shopping.

What precautions should I take when shopping online? In addition to using some basic common computing sense such as having a firewall and up-to-date antivirus software on your computer, and using strong passwords for all your online accounts, there are several important guidelines to follow to ensure your online shopping experience is a safe one (see Figure 3.12):

- Look for visual indicators that the website is secure. Check that the beginning of the URL changes from "http://" to "https://"—with the s standing for secure, indicating that the **secure sockets layer** protocol has been applied to manage the security of the website. Also, look for a small icon of a closed padlock in the address bar (in both Microsoft Edge and Firefox) and a green-colored text or a green address bar—indications that the site may be secure. (However, note that even if a site has these indicators, it still might not be safe. Consider the validity of the site before making a purchase.)

Figure 3.12 Online Shopping Precautions

When shopping at home, use a firewall and antivirus software for general computer protection.

Don't shop on public Wi-Fi networks, as they may contain spyware.

Check for visual indicators such as https:// in the URL, a closed padlock icon, and green text or a green address bar.

Look for third-party verification from TRUSTe or the Better Business Bureau symbol.

Use a credit card, not a debit card, to protect transactions, or use a third-party payer such as PayPal or Apple Pay.

Create a strong password for all online accounts (one that includes numbers and other symbols such as @).

Deals that are too good to be true are usually just that.

Read and understand the fine print on warranties, return policies, and the retailer's privacy statements.

(Beboy/Shutterstock; Photoinnovation/Shutterstock; Roy Wylam/Alamy Stock Photo; Newscom; Maxx-Studio/Shutterstock; Isak55/Shutterstock; Alhovik/Shutterstock; Shutterstock)

- Shop at well-known, reputable sites. If you aren't familiar with a site, investigate it with the Better Business Bureau (**bbb.org**) or at Bizrate (**bizrate.com**). Make sure the company has a phone number and street address in addition to a website. You can also look for third-party verification such as that from TRUSTe or the Better Business Bureau. But let common sense prevail. Online deals that seem too good to be true are generally just that—and may be pirated software or illegal distributions.

- Pay by credit card, not debit card. Federal laws protect credit card users, but debit card users don't have the same level of protection. If possible, reserve one credit card for Internet purchases only; even better, use a prepaid credit card that has a small credit limit. For an extra layer of security, find out if your credit card company has a service that confirms your identity with an extra password or code that only you know to use when making an online transaction or that offers a one-time-use credit card number. Also, consider using a third-party payment processor such as PayPal or Apple Pay. PayPal also offers a security key that provides additional security to your PayPal account.

- When you place an order, check the return policy, save a copy of the order, and make sure you receive a confirmation number. Make sure you read and understand the fine print on warranties, return policies, and the retailer's privacy statements. If the site disappears overnight, this information may help you in filing a dispute or reporting a problem to a site such as the Better Business Bureau.

- Avoid making online transactions when using public computers. Public computers may have spyware installed, which are programs that track and log your keystrokes and can retrieve your private information. Similarly, unless you have specific protection on your own mobile device, avoid making wireless transactions on public hotspots.

Whether you're doing business or collaborating and communicating with friends or colleagues, the Internet makes these activities more accessible. The Internet can potentially make these experiences and activities more enriched as well, although you must take precautions for the safest of experiences.

► Helpdesk | MyLab IT®

Doing Business Online

In this Helpdesk, you will play the role of a helpdesk staffer, fielding questions about e-commerce and e-commerce safeguards.

Bitcoin is a form of virtual currency (also known as cryptocurrency) that eliminates intermediaries or banks to conduct transactions, thus enabling direct anonymous transactions between users. Payments are sent peer-to-peer from the payee to the recipient with no transaction fees and without the need to supply personal information. The time and amount of every finalized bitcoin transaction are kept on a massive public online ledger known as the *blockchain*. The public nature of the blockchain makes it difficult for bitcoin transactions to be manipulated by anyone. However, the value of the currency is extremely volatile and can fluctuate widely within hours of a day. If you want to hold and spend bitcoins, you must create a bitcoin wallet, which stores the information needed to complete bitcoin transactions. The security of bitcoin wallets is evolving, but there is a real risk of a wallet being hacked and the contents of the wallet stolen. Although the anonymity of the currency initially encouraged illicit transactions, the use of bitcoins for legitimate purposes is taking hold. Mainstream retailers such as Home Depot, Microsoft, Expedia, and Overstock.com are accepting bitcoins, as are many small businesses. Although Bitcoin has the largest user base and market capitalization, it's not the only virtual currency. Alternatives include Litecoin, Ethereum, Zcash, Dash, Ripple, and Monero.

Zapp2Photo/Shutterstock

Figure 3.13 Bitcoin is a type of virtual currency.

Before moving on to Part 2:

1. ▶ Watch Chapter Overview Video 3.1.
2. Then take the Check Your Understanding quiz.

Check Your Understanding // Review & Practice

For a quick review to see what you've learned so far, answer the following questions.

multiple choice

1. Which is NOT an event associated with the beginning of the Internet?

   a. The first e-mail program was written by Ray Tomlinson.

   b. Amazon.com was one of the first websites on the Internet.

   c. TCP/IP protocol was developed that allowed different computers to communicate with each other.

   d. The U.S. Department of Defense creates ARPA.

2. In an Internet exchange of data, which type of computer asks for data?

   a. server

   b. requester

   c. client

   d. servicer

3. Which technology is being used in creating a document with Google Docs?

   a. e-mail

   b. blog

   c. wiki

   d. microblog

4. Which of the following would be best for *synchronous* text-based communication?

   a. instant messaging

   b. e-mail

   c. texting

   d. blogging

5. Which of the following would be an example of a C2C business?

   a. BestBuy

   b. Target

   c. Google

   d. Etsy

MyLab IT — Go to **MyLab IT** to take an autograded version of the *Check Your Understanding* review and to find all media resources for the chapter.

TechBytes Weekly — Go to TechBytes Weekly for current technology news and discussion questions!

Try This

Use OneDrive to Store and Share Your Files in the Cloud

You probably have your favorite ways of moving your files around. Perhaps you have a USB drive or you e-mail files to yourself. With these solutions, there can be confusion as to which is the most current version of the file if you've worked on it on multiple devices at different times. You also run the risk of losing your USB drive or deleting the e-mail attachment by mistake. These methods also make exchanging files difficult if you want to share your files or collaborate with a group.

A simpler solution is to use a web-based or cloud storage and sharing service such as OneDrive, Dropbox, or Google Drive. In this Try This, we'll explore OneDrive. You can access OneDrive through Microsoft's Office Online or with an Office 365 subscription. For more step-by-step instructions, watch the Chapter 3 Try This video on MyLab IT.

Step 1   **Sign in to OneDrive:** Go to **onedrive.com**. Sign in to your Microsoft account. If you don't have a Microsoft account, creating one is easy.

Step 2   **Create a Folder and Add Files:** Once in OneDrive, you can create a folder and then begin to add files.

- To create a folder: Click **New** at the top of the page, click **Folder**, and then give your new folder a name. Click **Create**, then select the new folder to open it.
- To add a file: Click **Upload** at the top of the page, select **Files**, then locate the file and click **Open**. To upload more than one file, press and hold **Ctrl** while you select each file.

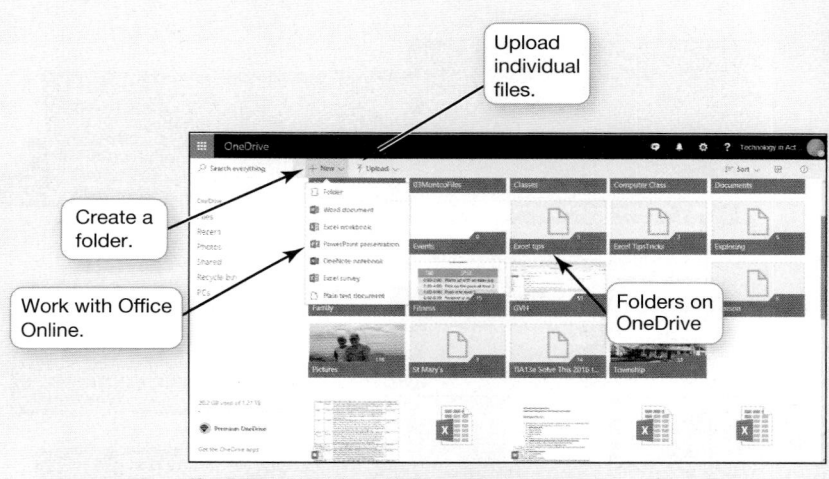

(OneDrive 2016, Microsoft Corporation)

Step 3   **Share a File or Folder:** To share a file or folder, complete the following steps:

1. Right-click the file or folder that you want to share and click **Share**, or click **Share** in the top menu after selecting the desired file or folder.
2. Click **Get a Link** to generate a hyperlink you can copy then send to others, or click **Email** to send an e-mail message containing the hyperlink.
3. Editing privileges are established by default, so if you want to restrict editing privileges, click **Anyone with this link can edit this item**, then click to **uncheck** the **Allow editing** box.
4. To see what files that have been shared with you, click **Shared** in the left menu.

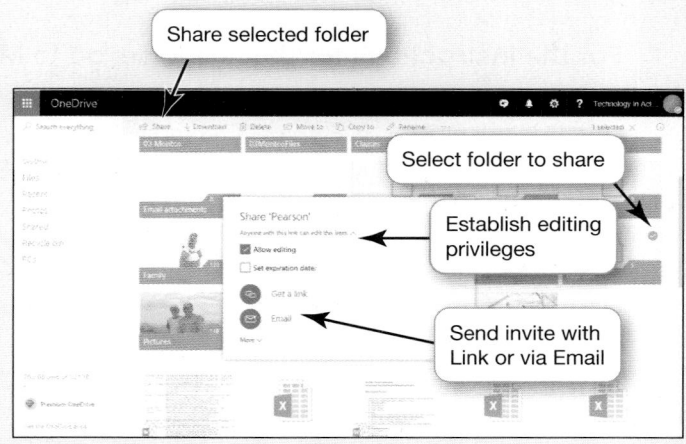

(OneDrive 2016, Microsoft Corporation)

Make: A Web-Capable App

Want your app to be able to display a web page?

In this exercise, you will continue your mobile app development by adding a new power to your apps: web browsing.

It is as easy as using the WebViewer component in **App Inventor**. Drag a WebViewer component onto your Designer screen, then control it with the Blocks for WebViewer. These allow you to go back, forward, to the home page, or to any specific URL.

The WebViewer component allows you to control a live browser inside your mobile app.

(Copyright MIT, used with permission)

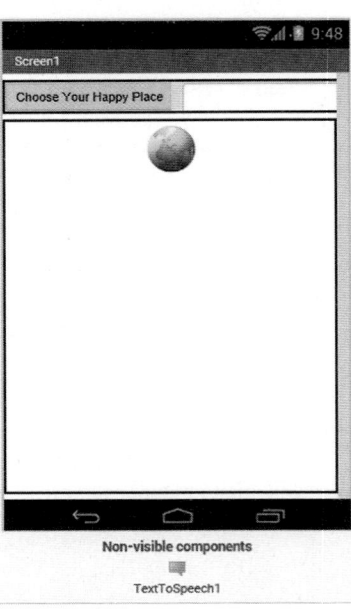

(Copyright MIT, used with permission)

For the instructions for this exercise, go to MyLab IT.

Using the Web Effectively

Learning Outcome 3.2 **You will be able to describe the tools and techniques required to navigate and search the web.**

You no doubt know how to use the web—to buy products, send e-mail, visit Facebook, and use Google—but do you know how to use it effectively? In this section, we'll look at ways to make your online experience more enjoyable, more productive, and more efficient.

Accessing and Moving Around the Web

None of the activities for which we use the web could happen without an important software application: a web browser.

Web Browsers

Objective 3.7 *Explain what web browsers are, and describe their common features.*

What is a web browser exactly? A **web browser** is software that lets you locate, view, and navigate the web. Most browsers today are graphical browsers, meaning they can display pictures (graphics) in addition to text and other forms of multimedia such as sound and video. The most common browsers are displayed in Figure 3.14. Microsoft Edge has replaced Internet Explorer as the default browser for Windows. This transition happened with the introduction of Windows 10.

What features do web browsers offer? The most popular browsers share similar features that make the user experience more efficient (see Figure 3.15). For example, browsers include an **omnibox**, a combined search and address bar, so you can both type a website URL or search the web from the address bar. Other common features include the following:

- Tabbed browsing: Web pages are loaded in "tabs" within the same browser window. Rather than having to switch among web pages in several open windows, you can flip between the tabs in one window. You may also save a group of tabs as a Favorites group if there are several tabs you often open at the same time.
- Pinned tabs: You can "pin" tabs to lock your most used tabs to the left of the tab bar. Pinned tabs are smaller in size and can't be closed by accident. They will display automatically when the browser opens.

Figure 3.14 Common Web Browsers *(Tommy (Louth)/Alamy; Microsoft Edge, Microsoft Corporation; Lucia Lanpur/Alamy; 2020WEB/Alamy)*

Figure 3.15 Tabbed and privacy browsing and an address bar that doubles as a search bar are common features in today's browsers. *(Homepage, Internal Revenue Service, Homepage, Aeronautics and Space Administration)*

- Tear-off tabs: An opened tab can be dragged or moved away from its current window so it's then opened in a new window.
- Thumbnail previews: Another convenient navigation tool that most browsers share is providing thumbnail previews of all web pages in open tabs. Microsoft Edge also enables you to display newsfeed items as well.
- Tab isolation: With this feature, tabs are independent of each other, so if one crashes, it does not affect the other tabs.
- SmartScreen filter: Most browsers offer built-in protection against phishing, malware, and other web-based threats.
- Privacy browsing: Privacy features (such as InPrivate Browsing in Microsoft Edge or Incognito in Chrome) let you browse the web without retaining a history trail, temporary Internet files, cookies, or usernames and passwords. These features are especially helpful when you use public computers at school or the public library, for example.
- Add-ons and extensions: Add-ons (also known as extensions) are small programs that customize and increase the functionality of the browser. Examples include Video Download-Helper, which converts web videos like those found on YouTube to files you can save, as well as a Facebook toolbar that integrates Facebook functionality into your browser.
- Session Restore: Brings back all your active web pages if the browser or system shuts down unexpectedly.

Are there features in each browser that differentiate one from the other? Although Chrome, Edge, Firefox, and Safari share many similar features, each browser has features that are less universally common. For example, Google Chrome, with the largest market share of mobile and desktop web browsers, enables you to mute tabs that produce sounds. If you have multiple people using Chrome on the same device, you can set up individual profiles so each can maintain his or her own bookmarks and browsing preferences. Additionally, Chrome has many custom extensions that let you do things like control your music, take screenshots, and share sites with friends. You can even customize Chrome with your own theme.

Microsoft Edge has some unique features as well. You can make "Webnotes" by annotating a web page and then share them using Onenote or Evernote, or save them for later use. Edge is also integrated with Microsoft's personal assistant Cortana, which shares web content with you based on your indicated preferences and interests. Finally, you can save online content to read later, and if the "noise" of a web page is distracting to you, you can use Reading View for a cleaner, simpler layout.

Can I have the same browser experience on any computer I use? It's not uncommon for users to have access to, and use, several different computers in their work, school, and personal lives. At a bare minimum, many switch between a set of personal devices, including a laptop, smartphone, or tablet. Chrome and Firefox are accessible on any device and operate well with any operating system. Each lets you sync personal information and open tabs and bookmarks between different computers so you have access to the same information on any device.

Currently, Edge is accessible only on Windows devices, and to access your personal settings, you must first log in to your Microsoft account. That means you may not have access to saved passwords, shipping, payment, and other personal information that you might enter into an online form from a non-Windows computer because you would not have access to Edge.

URLs, Protocols, and Domain Names

Objective 3.8 *Explain what a URL is, and discuss its main parts.*

What do all the parts of a URL mean? You gain initial access to a particular website by typing its unique address, or **Uniform Resource Locator** (**URL**, pronounced "you-are-ell"), in your browser. A website comprises many different web pages, each of which is a separate document with its own unique URL. Like a regular street address, a URL is made up of several parts that help identify the web document it stands for (see Figure 3.16):

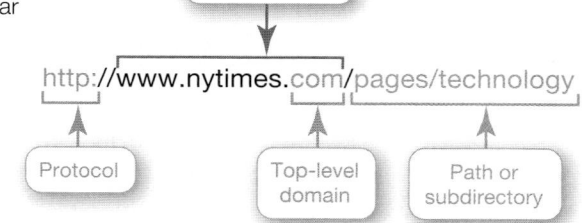

Figure 3.16 The Parts of a URL

- the *protocol* (set of rules) used to retrieve the document;
- the **domain name**; which includes the *top level domain*
- the *path* or subdirectory.

What's the protocol? You're probably most familiar with URLs that begin with http, which is short for **Hypertext Transfer Protocol (HTTP)**. HTTP is the protocol that allows files to be transferred from a **web server**—a computer that hosts the website you're requesting—so that you can see it on your computer. The HTTP protocol is what the web is based on. Since it is so universal, most current browsers no longer require you to enter the http:// protocol or the "www."

Is HTTP the only protocol I need to use? HTTP is the most common protocol, but it's not the only one. HTTP is part of the Internet protocol suite, a group of protocols that govern how information is exchanged on a network. Another protocol in that group is the **File Transfer Protocol (FTP)**. As its name implies, FTP was originally designed to transfer files from a computer to a web server. Today, FTP is often used when you have large files to upload or download. To connect to most FTP servers, you need a user ID and password. To upload and download files from FTP sites, you can use a browser or file transfer software such as CuteFTP, Fetch, or FileZilla.

BitTorrent, like FTP, is a protocol used to transfer files, though it's not part of the Internet protocol suite. To use BitTorrent, you install a software client program. It uses a peer-to-peer networking system so that sharing occurs between connected computers that also have the BitTorrent client installed. BitTorrent was developed in 2001 and is popular especially among users who want to share music, movies, and games. Use caution, however, when accessing BitTorrent content. Because it is a peer-to-peer system, it's possible for copyrighted material to be shared illegally.

What's in a domain name? The domain name identifies the site's **host**, the location that maintains the computers that store the website files. For example, **www.berkeley.edu** is the domain name for the University of California at Berkeley website. The suffix in the domain name after the dot (such as "com" or "edu") is called the **top-level domain**. This suffix indicates the kind of organization to which the host belongs. Some browsers don't require you to enter the domain if it is a .com—the browser enters the domain automatically. For example, you can just type in Amazon in Microsoft Edge and the browser automatically fills in the .com. Figure 3.17 lists the most frequently used top-level domains.

Each country has its own top-level domain. These are two-letter designations such as .za for South Africa, and .de for Germany. A sampling of country codes is shown in Figure 3.18. Within a country-specific domain, further subdivisions can be made for regions or states. For instance, the .us domain contains subdomains for each state, using the two-letter abbreviation of the state.

What's the information after the domain name that I sometimes see? When the URL is the domain name, such as **www.nytimes.com**, you're requesting a site's home page. However, sometimes a forward slash and additional text follow the domain name, such as in **www.nytimes.com/pages/technology**. The information after each slash indicates a particular

Figure 3.17 Common Top-Level Domains and Their Authorized Users

Domain Name	Who Can Use It
.biz	Businesses
.com	Originally for commercial sites, but now can be used by anyone
.edu	Degree-granting institutions
.gov	Local, state, and federal U.S. governments
.info	Information service providers
.mil	U.S. military
.net	Originally for networking organizations, but no longer restricted
.org	Organizations (often not-for-profits)

file or **path** (or **subdirectory**) within the website. Using the URL in Figure 3.16 you would connect to the technology page on the *New York Times* site.

Navigating the Web

Objective 3.9   *Describe tools used to navigate the web.*

What's the best way to get around in a website? As its name implies, the web is a series of interconnected paths, or links. You've no doubt moved around the web by clicking on **hyperlinks**, specially coded elements that let you go from one web page to another within the same website or to another site altogether (see Figure 3.19). Generally, text that operates as a hyperlink appears in a different color (often blue) and is usually underlined, but sometimes images also act as hyperlinks. When you hover your cursor over a hyperlink, the cursor changes to a hand with a finger pointing upward.

What other tools can I use to navigate a website? To move back or forward one page at a time, you can use the browser's Back and Forward buttons (see Figure 3.19).

To help navigate more quickly through a website, some sites provide a **breadcrumb trail**—a navigation aid that shows users the path they have taken to get to a web page, or where the page is located within the website. It usually appears at the top of a page. Figure 3.19 shows an example of a breadcrumb trail. "Breadcrumbs" get their name from the fairy tale "Hansel and Gretel," in which the characters drop breadcrumbs on the trail to find their way out of a forest. By clicking on earlier links in a breadcrumb trail, you can go directly to a previously visited web page without having to use the Back button to navigate back through the website.

Most browsers offer caret browsing, which lets you use your keyboard to grab text instead of swiping across with a mouse. To activate caret browsing, press F7 on your keyboard while you have the browser open. You might have to add an extension (Google Chrome) or enable a preference (Firefox) before you can activate the feature. Then, you can use your mouse pointer as an insertion

Figure 3.18 Examples of Country Codes

Country Code	Country
.au	Australia
.ca	Canada
.jp	Japan
.uk	United Kingdom

Note: For a full listing of country codes, refer to **www.iana.org/domains/root/db/**.

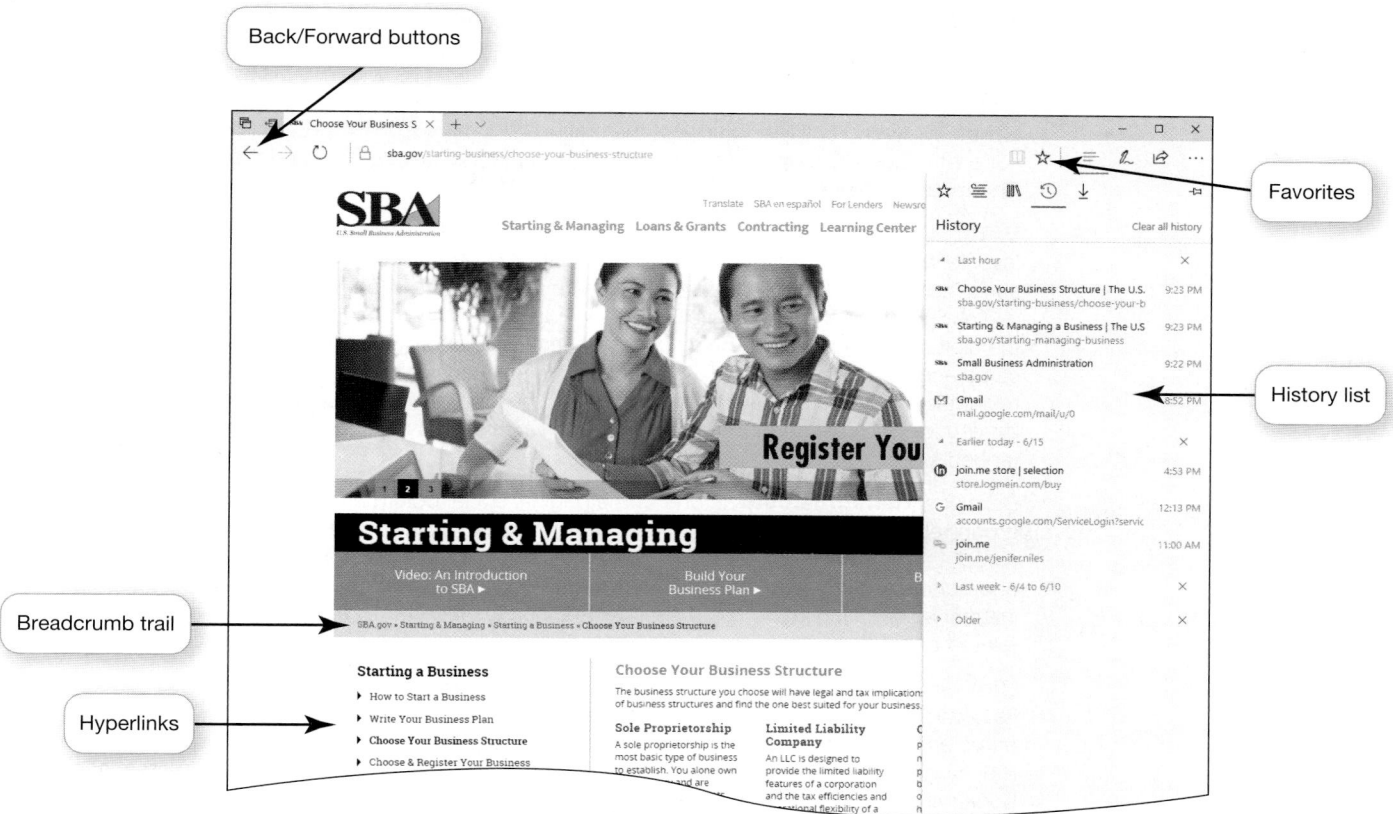

Figure 3.19 Navigating a Web Page *(U.S. Small Business Administration)*

pointer (similar to working in Word) and the arrow keys to move around. Press Shift and an arrow key to select text. Press F7 again to turn off caret browsing. This method offers more precise text selection and is very handy when you frequently copy and paste text from web pages.

What's the best way to mark a site so I can return to it later? If you want an easy way to return to a specific web page, you can use your browser's **Bookmarks** feature (Microsoft Edge calls this feature **Favorites**). This feature places a marker of the site's URL in an easily retrievable list in your browser's toolbar. To organize the sites into categories, most browsers offer tools to create folders.

Favorites and Bookmarks are great for quickly locating those sites you use most, but they're accessible to you only when you're on your own computer. Most browsers provide features that let you export the list of bookmarks to a file you can import to another computer or another browser. Another way to access your Bookmarks and Favorites from any computer is to use MyBookmarks (**mybookmarks.com**)—a free Internet service that stores your Bookmarks and Favorites online.

Bits&Bytes   Maintain Your Privacy While Searching the Web

Privacy is important to many people, but creating a private online experience is not always an easy task. Although you can use the privacy or incognito mode in some web browsers, these only disable your browsing history and web cache so that data generated from your searches can't be retrieved later. DuckDuckGo (**duckduckgo.com**) is different—this search engine doesn't collect your personal browsing information to share with third parties for marketing purposes. And although most search engines sell your search term information to third parties, which then use that information to generate display ads and recommendations on pages you visit, DuckDuckGo doesn't sell your search terms to other sites. Moreover, DuckDuckGo doesn't save your search history. Using DuckDuckGo eliminates third-party sharing of your personal information.

How can I get to a site if it hasn't been bookmarked? If you forget to add a site as a bookmark or favorite, but would like to return to a site you've previously visited, try using the History list. A browser's History list shows all the websites and pages you have visited over a certain period of time. These sites are organized according to date and can go back several months, depending on your browsing activity. To access the History list in Microsoft Edge or Chrome, click the three horizontal lines in the upper right-hand corner of the browser window and then click History in Chrome or the History icon in Microsoft Edge.

What is tagging? Tagging (also known as **social bookmarking**) is like bookmarking your favorite website, but instead of saving it to your browser for only you to see, you're saving it to a social bookmarking site so that you can share it with others. A social bookmark or tag is a term that you assign to a web page, digital image, or video. A tag can be something you create to describe the digital content, or it can be a suggested term provided by the website. For example, if you came across a web page with a great article on inexpensive places to go for spring break, you might tag the article with the term *vacations*. Others on the same social bookmarking site who are looking for websites about vacations may use *vacations* as the search term and find the article you tagged.

Delicious (**delicious.com**) is one of the original social bookmarking sites. Delicious lets you group related links and organize them into "bundles." So if you've collected several links to websites about different places to go to over spring break, you can collect all those links into one bundle about vacations. Or if you want to see what links others may have found about interesting vacations, you could search Delicious with the term *vacations* to see other vacation-related bundles.

Other social bookmarking sites include Reddit, StumbleUpon, and Pinterest. Reddit encourages its community to vote on links and stories, so the most popular rise to the top. StumbleUpon offers a Stumble! button that, when clicked, provides new web content that you can like or dislike, which eventually contours the Stumble results more to your interests. Unlike other social bookmarking sites, Pinterest enables you to share only images. You can post images that you find online or that you directly upload. You do not need a Pinterest account to look at other's pins and boards.

Searching the Web Effectively

You've most likely "Googled" something today, and if you did, your search is one of over 5 billion daily searches. Let's take a look at how to search the web effectively.

Using Search Engines

Objective 3.10   *Describe the types of tools used to search the web, and summarize strategies used to refine search results.*

How do search engines work? Google is the world's most popular **search engine**—a set of programs that searches the web for **keywords** (specific words you wish to look for or *query*) and then returns a list of the sites on which those keywords are found. Search engines have three components:

1. The first component is a program called a *spider*, which constantly collects data on the web, following links in websites and reading web pages. Spiders get their name because they crawl over the web using multiple "legs" to visit many sites simultaneously.

2. As the spider collects data, the second component of the search engine, an *indexer program*, organizes the data into a large database.

3. When you use a search engine, you interact with the third component: the *search engine software*. This software searches the indexed data, pulling out relevant information according to your search.

The resulting list appears in your web browser as a list of hits—sites that match your search.

Voice-activated digital assistants such as Siri, Cortana, and Google Now have become a standard on smartphones. In addition, Cortana and Siri are available on desktops with Windows 10 and macOS Sierra, respectively. Each offers voice-activated capabilities to search files and the web, get directions, and create reminders. Google Now and Cortana have predictive search capabilities, meaning they're able to recognize a user's repeated actions and searches and, using stored data, they can then offer relevant and predictive information. This might include alerts for upcoming flights, news stories relevant to your interests, travel time to your next appointment, and other information deemed relevant to you.

Why don't I get the same results from all search engines? Each search engine uses a unique program, or algorithm, to formulate the search and create the resulting index of related sites. In addition, search engines differ in how they rank the search results. Most search engines rank search results based on the frequency of the appearance and location of the queried keywords in websites. This means that sites that include the keywords in their URL or site name will most likely appear at the top of the results list. An important part of a company's marketing strategy is *search engine optimization*, which is designing the website to ensure it ranks near the top of search results.

Are there search engines that offer more specialized results? Search engines also differ as to which sites they search. For instance, Google and Bing search nearly the entire web, whereas specialty search engines search only sites that are relevant to a particular topic or industry. Specialty search engines exist for almost every industry or interest. DailyStocks (**dailystocks.com**) is a search engine used primarily by investors that searches for corporate information. Search Engine Watch (**searchenginewatch.com**) has a list of many specialty search engines, organized by industry. Google also has several specialized search engines, as shown in Figure 3.20. These can be accessed by clicking on the Google Apps button in Google's main page, then clicking More from Google options. Google's specialized search options include the following:

- *Shopping* lets you search by product rather than by company. So if you're interested in buying a digital camera, Shopping lists cameras by popularity and provides information on the stores that carry the cameras, along with the average price.
- *Finance* gives you access to real-time stock quotes and charts as well as financial news. You can also track your portfolio holdings.
- *Books* features a comprehensive index of full-text books. You can create different bookshelves for your Google Books and magazines.

Figure 3.20 Google's Specialized Search Tools *(Courtesy Google Inc.)*

If you can't decide which search engine is best, you may want to try a metasearch engine. **Metasearch engines**, such as Dogpile (**dogpile.com**), search other search engines rather than individual websites.

Can I use a search engine to search just for images and videos? With the increasing popularity of multimedia, search engines such as Google, Bing, and Yahoo! let you search the web for digital images and audio and video files. After putting in your search term, select Video from Google's top menu to display only the search results that are videos. You can further narrow down the video selection by using the filtering tools. Blinkx (**blinkx.com**) is a video search engine that helps you sift through all the video posted on the web.

How else can I customize my searches? Many other specialty search strategies and services are available. Both Google and Bing have menus at the top of each site to search specifically for movies, videos, maps, and more. In addition, both search engines allow you to restrict search results by time. Google provides additional search customization capabilities providing specific searches for Books, Flights, and Apps. The Search Tools feature in Google provides additional search functionality specific to the type of search being conducted (see Figure 3.21a). For example, when searching for videos, you can continue to customize by time, quality, or duration; if searching for images, Search Tools enables you to restrict the search by Size, Color, Type, Time, or Usage rights. By clicking on the Settings link on Google's search page, you can access an

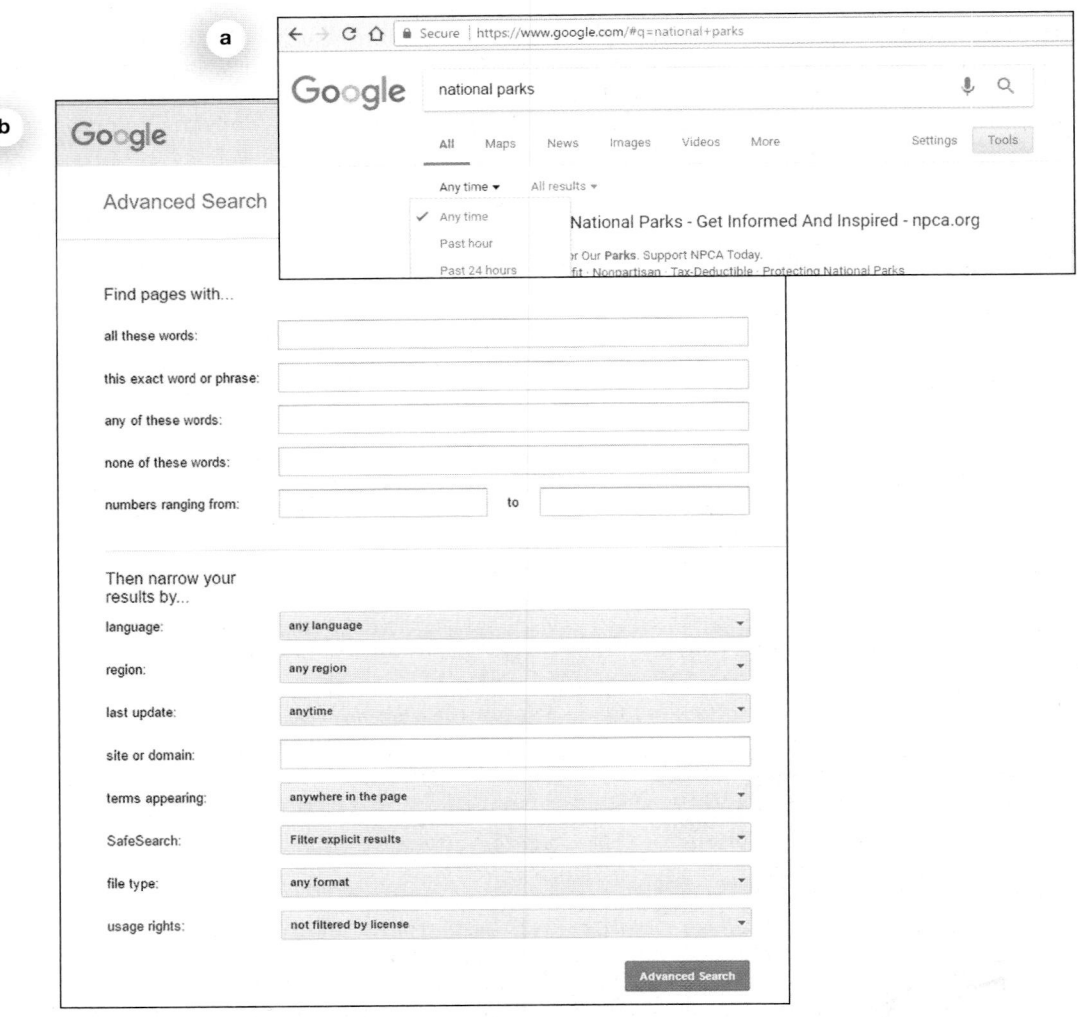

Figure 3.21 (a) Google Search tools and (b) Advanced Search form offer ways to narrow search results. *(Courtesy Google Inc.)*

Advanced Search form (see Figure 3.21b) through which you can narrow your search results by language, region, specific terms, usage rights, or file type. Although many of the features in Advanced Search can be found elsewhere in Google's search tools, it's often convenient to have them located in one spot.

Can I refine my key terms for better results? You've probably searched for something on Google and gotten back a list of hits that includes thousands—even millions—of web pages that have no relevance to the topic you're interested in. Initially, Boolean operators were needed to help refine a search. **Boolean operators** are words such as *AND*, *NOT*, and *OR* that describe the relationships between keywords in a search. With the simple addition of a few words or constraints, you can narrow your search results to a more manageable and more meaningful list. Other strategies can help refine your searches when entering your search keywords:

- **Search for a phrase.** To search for an exact phrase, place quotation marks around your keywords. The search engine will look for only those websites that contain the words in that exact order. For example, if you want information on the movie *Captain America: Civil War* and you type these words without quotation marks, your search results will contain pages that include any of the words captain, America, civil, or war, although not necessarily in that order. Typing "Captain America: Civil War" in quotation marks guarantees that search results will include this exact phrase.

- **Search within a specific website**. To search just a specific website, you can use the search keyword, then site: followed by the website's URL. For example, searching with *processor site*: www.wired.com returns results about processors from the **wired.com** website. The same method works for entire classes of sites in a given top-level domain or country code.

- **Use a wild card**. The asterisk (*) is a wild card, or placeholder, feature that is helpful when you need to search with unknown terms. Another way to think about the wild card search feature is as a "fill in the blank." For example, searching with *Congress voted * on the * bill* might bring up an article about the members of Congress who voted no on the healthcare bill or a different article about the members of Congress who voted yes on the energy bill.

Evaluating Websites

Objective 3.11 *Describe how to evaluate a website to ensure it is appropriate to use for research purposes.*

How can I make sure a website is appropriate to use for research? When you're using the Internet for research, you shouldn't assume that everything you find is accurate and appropriate to use. The following is a list of questions to consider before you use an Internet resource; the answers to these questions will help you decide whether you should consider a website to be a good source of information:

- **Authority:** Who is the author of the article or the sponsor of the site? If the author is well known or the site is published by a reputable news source (such as *The New York Times*), then you can feel more confident using it as a source than if you are unable to locate such information. Note: Some sites include a page with information about the author or the site's sponsor.

- **Bias:** Is the site biased? The purpose of many websites is to sell products or services or to persuade rather than inform. These sites, though useful in some situations, present a biased point of view. Look for sites that offer several sets of facts or consider opinions from several sources.

- **Relevance:** Is the information on the site current? Material can last a long time on the web. Some research projects (such as historical accounts) depend on older records. However, if you're writing about cutting-edge technologies, you need to look for the most recent sources. Therefore, look for a date on information to make sure it's current.

- **Audience:** For what audience is the site intended? Ensure that the content, tone, and style of the site match your needs. You probably wouldn't want to use information from a site geared toward teens if you're writing for adults, nor would you use a site that has a casual style and tone for serious research.

- **Links:** Are the links available and appropriate? Check out the links provided on the site to determine whether they're still working and appropriate for your needs. Don't assume that the links provided are the only additional sources of information. Investigate other sites on your topic as well. You should also be able to find the same information on at least three different websites to help verify the information is accurate.

Sound Byte MyLab IT®

Finding Information on the Web

In this Sound Byte, you'll learn how and when to use search engines and subject directories. Through guided tours, you'll learn effective search techniques, including how to use Boolean operators and metasearch engines.

Helpdesk MyLab IT®

Evaluating Websites

In this Helpdesk, you'll play the role of a helpdesk staffer, fielding questions about how websites can be evaluated as appropriate to use for research.

Think about all the types of data on the web that you access manually, such as appointment times, transportation and entertainment schedules, and store locations and hours. This type of data is referred to as *structured data*—data that can be defined by a particular category (or field) and a specific data type (such as number, text, or date). Structured data is easily entered, stored, queried, and analyzed and is usually found in databases.

However, the web currently is not set up to manipulate the structured data that resides on web pages. The web was initially set up to link documents together and for people to read web pages. Right now, search engines function by recognizing keywords such as *office hours* and *dentist*, but they can't determine, for example, in which office and on what days Dr. Smith works and what his available appointment times are. The capacity to have **linked data**, data that is formally defined and that can be expressed in relationships, does not currently exist. However, the movement to define the data and to link or create relationships between data has begun.

The Linking Open Data project is an ongoing effort to convert existing data into a usable format and link them together. The process ensures that the same categorization structures are used so that similar information shares the same attributes, ensuring consistency of metadata throughout the web. The project has begun with formatting and linking the structured information from Wikipedia but intends to broaden the sources of data as the project evolves. This web of linked data is being coined as the **semantic web**. The semantic web is an evolving extension of the web in which data is defined in such a way to make it more easily processed by computers. Ultimately, each website would have text and pictures (for people to read) and metadata (for computers to read) describing the information on the web (see Figure 3.22).

By using a so-called "agent," linked data would enable computers to find that type of information, coordinate it with your other schedules and preferences, and then make the appointment for you. Linked data will also assist you in comparing products, prices, and shipping options by finding the best product option based on specified criteria and then placing the order for you. Additionally, the agent could record the financial transaction into your personal bookkeeping software and arrange for a technician to help install the software, if needed.

Although some of the semantic web's functionalities are beginning to emerge in technologies such as the digital assistants Siri, Google Now, and Cortana, the majority of its functionality and implementation are still in development. The greatest challenge is recoding all the data currently available on the web into the type of metadata that computers can recognize. The very grandeur of that task means that we won't see a fully functional semantic web until sometime in the distant future. In the meantime, we can continue to benefit from each small step toward that goal.

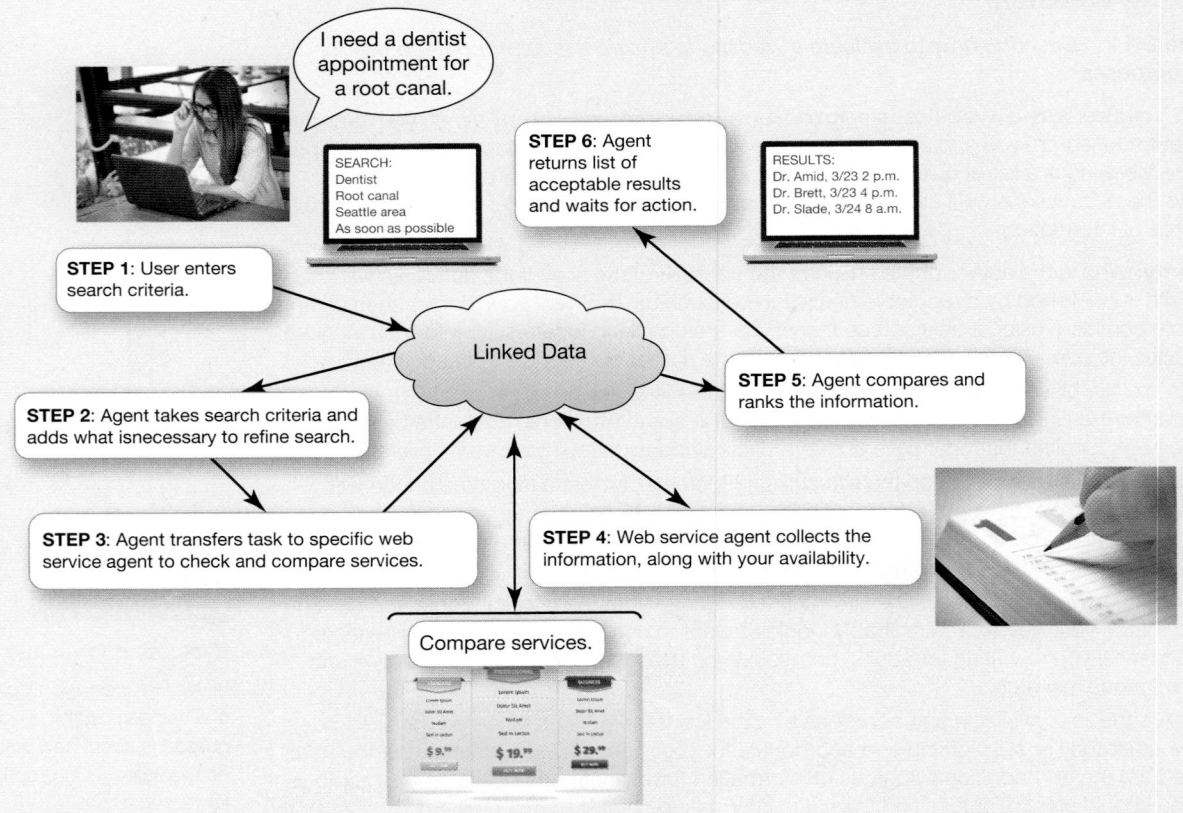

Figure 3.22 Linked Data and the Semantic Web (*Jpkirakun/Fotolia; SergeyIT/Shutterstock; mileswork/Shutterstock*)

Using the Web Ethically

As you've read in this chapter, the web offers a vast array of opportunities for business, communication, and collaboration. It also poses some temptations for inappropriate behavior, often to seek gain at another's expense. In this section, we'll explore several ethical issues that are challenging how we use the web.

Digital Activism

Objective 3.12   *Demonstrate an understanding of the ethical issues regarding digital activism.*

What is digital activism? **Digital activism** describes the use of hashtags and posts to raise awareness and foster discussion about specific issues and causes via social media. You're probably familiar with many hashtag campaigns and their causes:

- The #IceBucketChallenge hashtag campaign raised awareness for Lou Gehrig's disease (ALS) and also resulted in raising over $110 million in an 8-week period, a nearly 35 percent increase in donations for the cause.

- The #BringBackOurGirls hashtag campaign was initiated in Nigeria when 276 schoolgirls were kidnapped there but quickly found its way to the United States, where many joined in and took notice, including celebrities and politicians. Although the political awareness spurred a U.S.-led search for the girls, unfortunately, most of the girls are still missing at the time of this writing. The campaign continues two years later with the goal of bringing awareness to the issue, but the fervor of the initial campaign has decreased significantly.

- After a shooting rampage in Southern California by a man who left a hateful message for women, the #NotAllMen (practice violence against women) hashtag campaign began. What followed was the #YesAllWomen campaign that started a conversation that #YesAllWomen live with the threat of male violence and gender inequality.

- In an effort to offset the rampant consumerism that kicks off the pre-holiday buying frenzy starting with Black Friday, Small Business Saturday, and Cyber Monday, 92nd Street Y and the United Nations Foundation initiated #GivingTuesday. The social initiative, which began in 2012, designates the Tuesday after Thanksgiving as a time for consumers to encourage each other through social media to donate their time, talents, or cash to a cause or an organization. The hashtag campaign has amassed over 3 million uses since its inception. The cause has also expanded beyond U.S. borders, with people around the world making millions of contributions in a 24-hour period.

Each of these hashtag campaigns has had varying degrees of success. The trick is defining success. What was the initial goal of each of these campaigns? Was it to bring awareness to an issue, to instigate action, or to produce some other effect? Often, when digital campaigns go viral, people can join in simply by liking a post on Facebook. Proponents of digital activism celebrate the ability of such hashtag campaigns to raise money and awareness, magnify voices that might not otherwise be heard, and effect change.

Issue: Digital Activism	Ethical Question: Is digital activism effective or does it foster a false sense of involvement?
Point	• Digital activism raises awareness and enables individuals who otherwise might not be heard to have a voice. • Digital activism initiates conversations and generates attention that otherwise might not happen on any other platform. • Digital activism can spur actions such as donations or political involvement.
Counterpoint 	• Digital activism has a limited impact due to the fad-like nature of individuals who participate but have little or no vested interest in the cause. • Digital activism generates attention, but the initial cause or reason may become distorted in the fervor. • Digital activism limits true involvement because people associate passive online actions as "support."

(James Steidl/Fotalia)

However, critics of hashtag activism claim the campaigns foster a false sense of involvement, allowing Facebook and Twitter users to feel they have done something when in reality their social media posts will have no tangible impact. Such critics claim that hashtag campaigns quickly fade from public consciousness in part because they're often initially embraced by people who are following a trend and have little or no true interest in the cause. Figure 3.23 lists different views on the issue of digital activism. Where do your views fall?

Geolocation

Objective 3.13   *Demonstrate an understanding of the ethical issues regarding location tracking applications and devices.*

What is geolocation and what privacy risks does it pose? "Where are you?" is the burning social networking question these days, and your smartphone probably has the answer, since all mobile devices have a GPS chip that can calculate your exact position. **Geolocation**, or the act of targeting consumers by their location, has become a valuable technique that allows businesses to analyze and sculpt customer behaviors and to increase consumer traffic and ultimately revenues. Customers benefit when retailers use geolocation to push ads and coupons to customers who have downloaded the store app, are connected with their mobile device, and are within proximity to the business. Additionally, the massive amounts of geolocation data that is generated and analyzed are being used to improve the customer experience. Starbucks, Snapchat, and Uber are just a handful of apps that have the capacity to track and use your location, with your permission.

Why is this an issue? User location data is often shared with third-party advertising networks and even with law enforcement agencies. Although you can modify or turn off the location aspects in most mobile apps, these measures cannot guarantee that data will not be shared with third parties because the location data is "leaked" in other ways.

Even with app location tracking turned off, your location can be captured when your device is turned on. This feature has been useful to pinpoint users in emergency situations, but the data, if placed in the wrong hands or used for the wrong purposes, can be a violation of your privacy. Retrospectively, historical location data can be discerned from service provider records, and additionally, Wi-Fi hotspots can be used to track mobile devices. Moreover, other features of a smartphone, such as the camera and phone, can capture a user's geolocation data. Therefore, the privacy implications still remain. Although legislation has been initiated, no specific law has been passed to address the privacy concerns of location tracking devices and applications. Although most mobile device users are aware of location data collection practices, they're not aware of what was being collected and how it is, and can be, used. Figure 3.24 lists different views on the issue of geolocation. What do you think?

Figure 3.24 Point/Counterpoint

Issue: Geolocation

Ethical Question: Are geolocation devices a threat to privacy?

Point

- The social norm has shifted and people have become comfortable with sharing more information, including their location.

- Many businesses incorporate geolocation as a primary marketing strategy; the loss of privacy is outweighed by the benefit to consumers.

- Society may need to reevaluate its expectations as to the amount of privacy in people's digital lives.

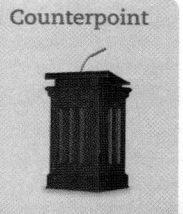

Counterpoint

- The threats and potential risks of using geolocation devices and applications are too great to ignore.

- Privacy settings on apps and GPS devices should be more restrictive.

- Businesses are responsible for educating consumers about how the data they gather through geolocation is used so consumers can make informed choices.

(James Steidl/Fotalia)

Bits&Bytes   Human-Implanted Data Chips: Protection or Invasive Nightmare?

Many of us give up quite a bit of our privacy voluntarily via the devices we carry and the apps we use. So why does the thought of implanting a data chip inside the human body cause so much uproar and dissent?

Human-implantable microchips were approved for use by the Food and Drug Administration in 2004. The basic advantages of implanted chips are that they can receive and transmit information and are extremely difficult to counterfeit. An implanted chip could positively identify you when you make a retail transaction, virtually eliminating fraud. A chip could provide instant access to medical records to facilitate treatment for unconscious accident victims, or track lost or missing children or Alzheimer's patients. And law enforcement could track the movement of convicted criminals out on parole.

Despite the benefits, people see great potential for privacy infringement and potential misuse of data. Would you want your parents (or the government) to know where you are at any time? Would someone be able to read the medical information in your chip without your permission and use it against you? In fact, there is so much resistance from the public to implants that some states such as Wisconsin, California, Georgia, and North Dakota have already enacted legislation to prohibit mandatory data chips implants in the future, even though it is not being considered now.

The debate will most likely rage on as technologies continue to be developed that will allow implanted chips to gather and provide even more data. Whether the public embraces this technology remains to be seen. Would you ever be willing to have a data chip implanted in your body?

Ethics in IT

Cyber Harassment

While the Internet provides an array of benefits and advantages, a darker side has emerged with a growing epidemic of abusive online behaviors collectively referred to as cyber harassment. **Cyber harassment** is used to describe the pursuit of individual(s) by an individual with the intention to frighten, embarrass, "teach the victim a lesson," or seek revenge. Cyber harassment includes acts such as cyberbullying, cyberstalking, trolling, and catfishing.

Cyberbullying and *cyberstalking* involve the use of digital technologies such as the Internet, cell phones, or video to harass, stalk, or bully another. The distinction between cyberbullying and cyberstalking is primarily age. Cyberbullying is generally used when children and adolescents are involved (see Figure 3.25). Cyberbullying and cyberstalking can include actions such as bombarding a victim with harassing instant messages or text messages, spreading rumors or lies on social networking sites, posting embarrassing photos or videos of a victim on the web, or infecting the victim's computer with malware, usually to spy on that person.

The effects of these violations can be devastating. Infamous cases of cyberbullying include Hannah Smith, the English girl who at 14 committed suicide after being repeatedly taunted on social networking sites, and Tyler Clementi, a Rutgers freshman who committed suicide after his roommate showed fellow students videos of him having sex. There are plentiful examples of workplace bullying and celebrity cyberstalking, but often these cases are not as publicized as those involving children.

Trolling is the act of posting inflammatory remarks online for the sheer pleasure of soliciting an angry or negative response. Although both trolling and cyberbullying are generally done anonymously, and with the intention of inflicting fear or anger, the main difference between trolling and cyberbullying is that a troll generally does not personally know his or her target. Trolls derive pleasure from annoying others, and when they are confronted about their behavior, they often shrug off the incident, claiming it was all in good fun. Trolls are more interested in the reaction than the personal confrontation that cyberbullies and cyberstalkers seek. When confronted by a troll, the best thing to do is to not react at all and to leave the conversation as quickly as possible.

Catfishing is another type of Internet harassment where some individual scams others into a false romantic relationship. Catfishers create fake profiles and trick others into thinking they are someone else entirely. The fabricated relationships are developed through online and phone interactions, but never in person. One of the most public

Figure 3.25 Cyberbullying involves the use of digital technologies both to bully and to disseminate acts of bullying. *(highwaystarz/Fotalia)*

catfish scams involved Notre Dame football player Manti Te'o, who fell in love with a fictitious girl. The resulting tragic realization of the scam played out in public for Te'o. "Catfish," a documentary that highlights a true catfishing situation, and a reality TV series of that same name continues to bring attention to this type of scam.

There is currently no federal law prohibiting cyberbullying, but a recently passed law against cyberstalking may cover this area. According to the Cyberbullying Research Center (**cyberbullying.org**), currently all states have anti-bullying laws or policies on the books. However, only 48 state laws cover electronic harassment, and a mere 22 state laws cover cyberbullying. Many legislatures are reluctant to pass laws that instruct parents on how to raise their children because this tends to raise issues about personal freedom. Therefore, anti-cyberbullying laws tend to place the burden of detection on the schools or the workplace. For instance, the Massachusetts law requires schools to provide age-appropriate education on bullying to students, to train school employees in detection and prevention of bullying, and to have plans developed for detecting and reporting bullying.

Before moving on to the Chapter Review:

1. ▶ Watch Chapter Overview Video 3.2.
2. Then take the Check Your Understanding quiz.

Check Your Understanding // Review & Practice

For a quick review to see what you've learned so far, answer the following questions.

multiple choice

1. Which feature of a browser enables you to secure a tab permanently?

    a. tabbed browsing

    b. pinned tabs

    c. tear-off tabs

    d. tab isolation

2. Which of the following is not an Internet protocol?

    a. HTTP

    b. FTP

    c. BitTorrent

    d. ARPANET

3. What is the navigation aid that shows users the path they have taken to get to a web page located within a website?

    a. Favorites

    b. Bookmarks

    c. breadcrumb trail

    d. social bookmarks

4. Which search strategy should you use to search for a specific phrase?

    a. Use a wild card around the phrase.

    b. Include Boolean operators in the phrase.

    c. Use asterisks around the phrase.

    d. Use quotation marks around the phrase.

5. When using the Internet for research, you

    a. can assume if there is no author listed, the site is not appropriate for research.

    b. can assume everything is accurate and appropriate.

    c. should evaluate sites for bias and relevance.

    d. should look for sites with only a few links.

 Go to **MyLab IT** to take an autograded version of the *Check Your Understanding* review and to find all media resources for the chapter.

TechBytes Weekly Go to TechBytes Weekly for current technology news and discussion questions!

3 Chapter Review

Summary

Part 1
Collaborating and Working on the Web

Learning Outcome 3.1 You will be able to explain how the Internet works and how it is used for collaboration, communication, commerce, and entertainment purposes.

 The Internet and How It Works

Objective 3.1 *Describe how the Internet got its start.*

- The Internet is the largest computer network in the world, connecting millions of computers.
- Government and military officials developed the early Internet as a reliable way to communicate in the event of war. Eventually, scientists and educators used the Internet to exchange research.
- Today, we use the Internet and the web (which is a part of the Internet) to shop, research, communicate, and entertain ourselves.

Objective 3.2 *Explain how data travels on the Internet.*

- A computer (or other device) connected to the Internet acts as either a client (a computer that asks for information) or a server (a computer that receives the request and returns the information to the client).
- Data travels between clients and servers along a system of communication lines or pathways. The largest and fastest of these pathways form the Internet backbone.
- To ensure that data is sent to the correct computer along the pathways, IP addresses (unique ID numbers) are assigned to all computers connected to the Internet.

 Collaborating and Communicating on the Web

Objective 3.3 *Evaluate the tools and technologies used to collaborate on the web.*

- Collaboration on the web uses technologies broadly described as Web 2.0. Web 2.0 communication tools are known as social media and include social networking, project collaboration and file sharing tools, blogs, podcasts, webcasts, and media sharing.

- Social networking enables you to communicate and share information with friends as well as meet and connect with others.
- File sharing tools, such as web-based document products, promote online collaboration. A wiki is a document created collaboratively by multiple users, resulting in an emergent common output.
- Project management tools incorporate texting, tasks, and calendar features for individual team members as well as for the project.
- Other useful web tools for group collaboration online are screen sharing and videoconferencing applications.
- Blogs are journal entries posted to the web that are generally organized by a topic or area of interest and are publicly available.
- Video logs are personal journals that use video as the primary content in addition to text, images, and audio.
- Podcasts are audio or video content available over the Internet. Users subscribe to receive updates to podcasts.
- Webcasts are broadcasts of audio or video content over the Internet.
- Media sharing platforms enable users to create, store, and share multimedia.

Objective 3.4 *Summarize the technologies used to communicate over the web.*

- E-mail allows users to communicate electronically without the parties involved being available at the same time.
- Instant-messaging services are programs that enable you to communicate in real time with others who are online.

 Conducting Business on the Web

Objective 3.5 *Describe how business is conducted using the Internet.*

- E-commerce is the business of conducting business online.

- E-commerce includes transactions between businesses (B2B), between consumers (C2C), and between businesses and consumers (B2C).

Objective 3.6 *Summarize precautions you should take when doing business online.*

- Precautions include using firewalls and up-to-date antivirus software, and employing strong passwords for online accounts.

- Check to see if the website is secure, shop at reputable websites, pay by credit card not debit card, check the return policy and save a copy of the receipt, and avoid making online transactions on public computers.

Part 2
Using the Web Effectively

Learning Outcome 3.2 **You will be able to describe the tools and techniques required to navigate and search the web.**

 ### Accessing and Moving Around the Web

Objective 3.7 *Explain what web browsers are, and describe their common features.*

- Once you are connected to the Internet, in order to locate, navigate to, and view web pages, you need software called a web browser.
- The most common web browsers are Google Chrome, Microsoft Edge, Firefox, and Safari.

Objective 3.8 *Explain what a URL is, and discuss its main parts.*

- You gain access to a website by typing in its address, called a Uniform Resource Locator (URL).
- A URL is composed of several parts, including the protocol, the domain, the top-level domain, and paths (or subdirectories).

Objective 3.9 *Describe tools used to navigate the web.*

- One unique aspect of the web is that you can jump from place to place by clicking on specially formatted pieces of text or images called hyperlinks.
- You can also use the Back and Forward buttons, History lists, and breadcrumb trails to navigate the web.
- Favorites, live bookmarks, and social bookmarking help you return to specific web pages without having to type in the URL and help you organize the web content that is most important to you.

 ### Searching the Web Effectively

Objective 3.10 *Describe the types of tools used to search the web, and summarize strategies used to refine search results.*

- A search engine is a set of programs that searches the web using specific keywords you wish to query and then returns a list of the websites on which those keywords are found.

- Search engines can be used to search for images, podcasts, and videos in addition to traditional text-based web content.
- Metasearch engines search other search engines.

Objective 3.11 *Describe how to evaluate a website to ensure it is appropriate to use for research purposes.*

- To evaluate whether it is appropriate to use a website as a resource, determine whether the author of the site is reputable, whether the site is intended for your particular needs, that the site content is not biased, that the information on the site is current, and that all the links on the site are available and appropriate.

 ### Using the Web Ethically

Objective 3.12 *Demonstrate an understanding of the ethical issues regarding digital activism.*

- Digital activism describes the use of hashtags and posts to raise awareness and foster discussion about specific issues and causes on social media.
- Digital activism can be useful to raise awareness and enable people to voice their opinions.
- Digital activist causes can become popular more because of the immediate fervor rather than the underlying cause.

Objective 3.13 *Demonstrate an understanding of the ethical issues regarding location tracking applications and devices.*

- Privacy is the right to be left alone, but it is often difficult to achieve with social media.
- Apps with geolocation technology garner much information about your location. Users should be aware of why companies need to track a user's location, and what the companies will do with that location data.

 Be sure to check out **MyLab IT** for additional materials to help you review and learn. And don't forget to watch the Chapter Overview Videos.

Key Terms

aggregator **92**

blog (weblog) **91**

Bookmarks **109**

Boolean operators **113**

breadcrumb trail **108**

business-to-business (B2B) **99**

business-to-consumer (B2C) **97**

catfishing **118**

client **88**

client/server network **88**

cloud computing **98**

consumer-to-consumer (C2C) **99**

cyber harassment **118**

digital activism **115**

domain name **107**

e-commerce (electronic commerce) **97**

e-mail (electronic mail) **94**

e-mail client **95**

Favorites **109**

File Transfer Protocol (FTP) **107**

geolocation **116**

host **107**

hyperlink **108**

Hypertext Transfer Protocol (HTTP) **107**

instant messaging (IM) **96**

Internet **86**

Internet backbone **88**

Internet Protocol (IP) address **88**

keyword **110**

linked data **114**

metasearch engine **112**

microblog **92**

mobile commerce (m-commerce) **99**

omnibox **105**

path (subdirectory) **108**

podcast **92**

project management tools **91**

Really Simple Syndication (RSS) **92**

search engine **110**

secure sockets layer **99**

semantic web **114**

server **88**

social commerce **99**

social media **89**

social networking **89**

tagging (social bookmarking) **110**

texting **96**

top-level domain **107**

trolling **118**

Uniform Resource Locator (URL) **107**

video log (vlog or video blog) **91**

VoIP (Voice over Internet Protocol) **96**

Web 2.0 **89**

web-based e-mail **95**

web browser **105**

web server **107**

webcast **93**

wiki **90**

World Wide Web (WWW or the web) **87**

Chapter Quiz // Assessment

For a quick review to see what you've learned, answer the following questions. Submit the quiz as requested by your instructor. If you are using **MyLab IT**, the quiz is also available there.

multiple choice

1. The Internet was created to provide
    a. a secure form of communications.
    b. a common communication means for all computers.
    c. both a and b
    d. neither a nor b

2. Which of the following describes an IP address?
    a. It is referred to as a dotted quad.
    b. It identifies any computer connecting to the Internet.
    c. It identifies a website.
    d. all of the above

3. Ordering a mocha latte and paying for it from the Starbucks smartphone app is using what type of Internet commerce?
    a. B2B
    b. C2C
    c. social commerce
    d. mobile commerce

4. What web browser feature would be particularly useful when using public computers?
    a. pinned tabs
    b. privacy browsing
    c. session restore
    d. all of the above

5. In the URL **http://www.whitehouse.gov/blog**, which part is considered the protocol?
    a. .gov
    b. www.whitehouse.gov
    c. http
    d. /blog

6. Search engines that search other search engines are called
    a. megasearch engines.
    b. betasearch engines.
    c. gigasearch engines.
    d. metasearch engines.

7. If you would like to return to a website that you visited last week but can't remember the URL, you should look at:
   a. a breadcrumb list
   b. the Recycle Bin
   c. the History list
   d. any of the above

8. Ensuring that the content, tone, and style of a website match your needs is checking for:
   a. Audience
   b. Authority
   c. Bias
   d. Relevance

9. Which of the following would NOT be a good precaution to take when making online purchases?
   a. use a prepaid credit card
   b. pay by credit card, not debit card
   c. use a third-party processor such as PayPal
   d. pay by debit card, not credit card

10. You want to search the web for information on the movie *Captain America: Civil War*. What would be the best way to enter the key terms to get the most specific results?
    a. Captain America *
    b. "Captain America: Civil War"
    c. * Civil War
    d. Captain America Civil War

true/false

_____ **1.** Geolocation requires a GPS chip in a mobile device.

_____ **2.** Webcasts are delivered only as prerecorded audio and video content.

_____ **3.** The "S" in HTTPS stands for secure and indicates that the secure sockets layer protocol has been applied to the website.

_____ **4.** Digital activism is an exercise platform.

_____ **5.** A blog is usually written by multiple authors.

critical thinking

1. **The Power of Google**

   Google is the largest and most popular search engine on the Internet today. Because of its size and popularity, some people claim that Google has enormous power to influence a web user's search experience solely by its website-ranking processes. What do you think about this potential power? How could it be used in negative or harmful ways?

   a. Some websites pay search engines to list them near the top of the results pages. These sponsors, therefore, get priority placement. What do you think of this policy?

   b. What effect (if any) do you think that Google has on website development? For example, do you think website developers intentionally include frequently searched words in their pages so that they will appear in more hit lists?

2. **Mobile E-Commerce Safety**

   The text lists several ways to ensure your online transactions are secure and to reduce the risk of things going awry as you shop and sell online. However, surveys indicate that many feel that shopping from a mobile device, such as a smartphone, presents additional risks. Do you agree there are additional risks when conducting e-commerce from a mobile device? Why or why not?

Team Time

Collaborating with Technology

problem

Collaborating on projects with team members is a regular part of business and academia. Many great tools are available that facilitate online collaboration, and it's important to be familiar with them. In this Team Time, each team will create a group report on a specific topic, using online collaboration tools, and compare and rate the tools and the collaboration process.

process

Split your group into teams. To appreciate fully the benefits of online collaboration, each team should have at least five or six members. Each group will create a team report on a topic that is approved by your instructor. As part of the report, one group member should record the process the group took to create the report, including a review of the tools used and reflections on the difficulties encountered by the group.

1. Conduct a virtual meeting. Agree on an online meeting and video collaboration tool such as Skype, Google Hangouts, or Apple FaceTime and conduct a group chat. In this phase, outline your group project strategy and delegate work responsibilities.
2. Share documents and collaborate online. Your group must create one document that is accessible to every member at all times. Explore document-sharing sites such as Google Drive, Evernote, OneDrive, or Dropbox and collaboratively create your group document. All members are responsible for reviewing the entire document.

conclusion

After all the team group reports have been completed and shared, discuss the following with your class: What is the benefit of using online collaboration technology to create group projects? How did collaboration technologies help or hinder the team process?

Ethics Project

Internet Privacy

In this exercise, you'll research a complicated ethical situation. The position you are asked to take may or may not match your own personal beliefs, but your research and use of logic will enable you to represent whichever view is assigned. Together the team will agree on an ethical solution.

problem

Our smartphones and other devices that connect to the Internet enable us to share our information, such as where we are, what we've eaten, who we're friends with, when we've exercised, and what we're interested in. In essence, we've become a very public society. And studies show that for the most part, we don't care about being so open. But, should we? It's not just our friends and family that we're sharing this information with. Governments and companies are listening, too, and we've learned that often they can't be trusted in how they collect and use our data. In many cases, we agree to privacy terms when we want to use a device or software. We've come to accept that there is a tradeoff between being able to use a device or software and giving up some level of privacy. But is this the way it should be? Can we have smart devices that offer us great conveniences while preserving our fundamental right to privacy? Who is ultimately responsible for controlling our privacy: we or the companies that make the devices?

research areas to consider

- Internet privacy
- Internet of Things
- Geolocation
- Social media and privacy

process

1. Divide the class into teams and assign each team a device that is connected to the Internet or an app that is used to share information. Each team is to research the aspect of privacy from the perspective of digital device or software owners who enjoy the social networking feature of the device/software, and from the perspective of business management who has developed the device/software and is collecting and using the owners' location, usage, and other data.
2. Team members should write a summary of the position their team assumes, outlining the pros and cons of their position.
3. Team members should present their case to the class or submit a PowerPoint presentation for review by the rest of the class, along with the summary and resolution they developed.

conclusion

As the use of social media and the Internet of Things becomes more prevalent, our definition of privacy and need for privacy may begin to erode. Being able to determine the benefits and potential sacrifices to our privacy is important in this Internet-connected society in which we live.

Create a Report: Conducting Research on the Web

You and a partner have been asked to write a report on alternatives to using the Google search engine, as well as how to evaluate a website for a research paper. The paper needs to cite references within the body of the text, and include a list of your works cited at the end of the report. Your partner has begun the report. You are going to modify what has been started.

You will use the following skills as you complete this activity:

- Use Find and Replace
- Format Bulleted Lists
- Insert SmartArt

- Insert a Hyperlink
- Add Sources
- Insert Citations and Bibliography

Instructions:

1. Start Word. Open *TIACh03_Start* and save it as **TIACh03_LastFirst**, using your last and first names.

2. Using Find and Replace, find all instances of *metasearch* and replace them with **meta-search**.

3. At the blank paragraph after the end of the second paragraph of text under *Alternative Search Engines*, insert a **Vertical Box List SmartArt graphic**. Open the text pane, if necessary. With the cursor active in the first bullet, type **Google Scholar**. (Do not include the period.) Press **Enter**, press **Tab**, and then type **Searches scholarly literature**. (Do not include the period.)

    Repeat these steps to add the following information for the next two bullets:

    Dogpile
    Meta-search engine that searches Google, Yahoo!, and Bing
    Specialty Search Engines
    Search only sites that are relevant to a topic or industry

    a. Hint: To insert a SmartArt graphic, on the Insert tab, in the Illustrations group, click **SmartArt**.

4. Change the SmartArt graphic colors to **Colorful—Accent Colors**. Move the Google Scholar box and bullet point to the bottom of the SmartArt. Change the SmartArt Style to **Intense Effect**.

    a. Hint: To change the colors, on the SmartArt Tools Design tab, in the SmartArt Styles group, click **Change Colors**. To move the box and bullet point, select the content, then in the Create Graphic group, click **Move Down** two times. To change the style, in the SmartArt Styles group, click the **More button** for Styles.

5. In the second to last sentence of the first paragraph in the *Alternative Search Engines* section, select the text **specialty search engines**. Then, create a hyperlink to the web page **bestonlineuniversities.com/2011/20-useful-specialty-search-engines-for-college-students/**.

6. At the end of the first paragraph in the *Evaluating Websites* section, immediately to the left of the period, insert a citation to a new website. Before entering information, click the check box for **Show All Bibliography Fields**. Use the following information:

    Author: **Kapoun, Jim**
    Name of Web Page: **Five criteria for evaluating web pages**
    Name of Website: **Olin & Uris Libraries, Cornell University**
    Year: **2010**
    Month: **May**
    Day: **10**
    URL: http://guides.library.cornell.edu/evaluating_Web_pages

7. In the *Evaluating Websites* section, create a bulleted list with the five points beginning with *Authority, Bias or Objectivity, Relevance, Audience, and Coverage*. Use a checkmark as the bullet point.

8. Press **Ctrl+End** to go to the end of the document, press **Enter** twice, and then insert a Works Cited Bibliography. Change the citation style to **APA Sixth Edition**.

9. Save the document, and then close Word.

10. Submit the document as directed.

Application Software: Programs That Let You Work and Play

 For a chapter overview, watch the Chapter Overview Videos.

PART 1

Accessing, Using, and Managing Software

Learning Outcome 4.1 | **You will be able to explain the ways to access and use software and describe how to best manage your software.**

 Software Basics 128

Objective 4.1 *Compare application software and system software.*

Objective 4.2 *Explain the differences between commercial software and open source software, and describe models for software distribution.*

 Managing Your Software 129

Objective 4.3 *Explain the different options for purchasing software.*

Objective 4.4 *Describe how to install and uninstall software.*

Objective 4.5 *Explain the considerations around the decision to upgrade your software.*

Objective 4.6 *Explain how software licenses function.*

Helpdesk: Buying and Installing Software

Sound Byte: Where Does Binary Show Up?

PART 2

Application Software

Learning Outcome 4.2 | **Describe the different types of application software used for productivity and multimedia.**

 Productivity and Business Software 139

Objective 4.7 *Categorize the types of application software used to enhance productivity, and describe their uses and features.*

Objective 4.8 *Summarize the types of software that large and small businesses use.*

Sound Byte: Programming for End Users

 Multimedia and Educational Software 150

Objective 4.9 *Describe the uses and features of digital multimedia software.*

Objective 4.10 *Describe the uses and features of digital audio software.*

Objective 4.11 *Describe the features of app creation software.*

Objective 4.12 *Categorize educational and reference software and explain their features.*

Helpdesk: Choosing Software

For the IT Simulation for this chapter, see MyLab IT.

MyLab IT | All media accompanying this chapter can be found here.

Make This Make: A More Powerful App on **page 138**

(ronstik/123RF; Rawpixel.com/Shutterstock; Timo Darco/Fotolia; Laurent Davoust/123RF; amorphis/Fotolia)

How Cool Is This?

Biosensors for smartphones are here! The Galaxy Note includes a sensor that can be used to measure your **blood oxygen saturation**. Development is under way for add-ons that allow a phone's optical sensors to **detect biological agents** including molecules, viruses, and toxins. And soon smartphones will be able to **measure blood glucose levels** noninvasively, which would be a great boon for people with diabetes. With more sensors, your phone could provide you with **complete readings of your vitals** after your workout (blood oxygen, blood pressure, electrocardiogram [EKG], pulse). Or you could immediately receive an **air quality report** of your home, warning you about contaminants that could compromise your health (such as high radon levels). Smartphones are on the way to becoming a personal laboratory, monitoring your health and fitting right into your pocket. *(Amorphis/Fotolia)*

Accessing, Using, and Managing Software

Learning Outcome 4.1   You will be able to explain the ways to access and use software and describe how to best manage your software.

Although a computer's hardware is critical, a computer system does nothing without software. In this section, we'll discuss the way software operates and how you can manage your software to make sure it is current and being used legally.

Software Basics

It's important to understand what software is, how it's created, and the different models used to distribute it.

Application vs. System Software

Objective 4.1   *Compare application software and system software.*

What is software? Technically speaking, the term **software** refers to a set of instructions that tells the computer what to do. An instruction set, also called a **program**, provides a means for us to interact with and use the computer, even if we lack specialized programming skills.

What is the difference between application and system software? Your computer has two main types of software. **Application software** is the software you use to do tasks at home, school, and work. **System software** is software that helps run the computer and coordinate instructions between application software and the computer's hardware devices. System software includes the operating system (such as Windows and macOS) and utility programs (programs in the operating system that help manage system resources). We discuss system software in detail in Chapter 5.

Other types of software, such as web browsers, virus protection, and backup and recovery software, are used every day. We'll discuss these types of software elsewhere in this book.

Distributing Software

Objective 4.2   *Explain the differences between commercial software and open source software, and describe models for software distribution.*

How is software created? There are two main ways software is created. **Proprietary (or commercial) software** is created by companies for profit and then sold to you. You're probably familiar with buying products like Adobe Photoshop. These are examples of proprietary software. **Open source software** is software that is available free of charge and with few licensing and copyright restrictions. One advantage of open source software is that a community of passionate users continues to make changes to the software based on user feedback. However, unlike proprietary applications, open source applications offer little or no formal support. Instead, they're supported from their community of users across websites and newsgroups. Figure 4.1 illustrates how some specific software products fit into each of these categories.

How is software distributed? Software is distributed in three main ways:

1. **Local installation:** With **locally installed software**, you pay a one-time fee for either an electronic download or a disc of the software, which you then install on your device. Because the software resides on your hard drive, you can run the software anytime, whether you're connected to the Internet or not. You'll have the option to upgrade to the next version when that version is released and you'll likely need to pay again to purchase the upgraded version. Desktop tax preparation software is an example of software distributed in this way.

2. **SaaS:** With **Software as a Service (SaaS)**, the vendor hosts the software online and you access and use the software over the Internet without having to install it on your computer's hard drive. Because the program resides on a company's server and you run the program through your browser, you can run the program only when you're connected to the Internet. However, because the manufacturer updates the program on its server, you

Figure 4.1 Open Source vs. Commercial Software

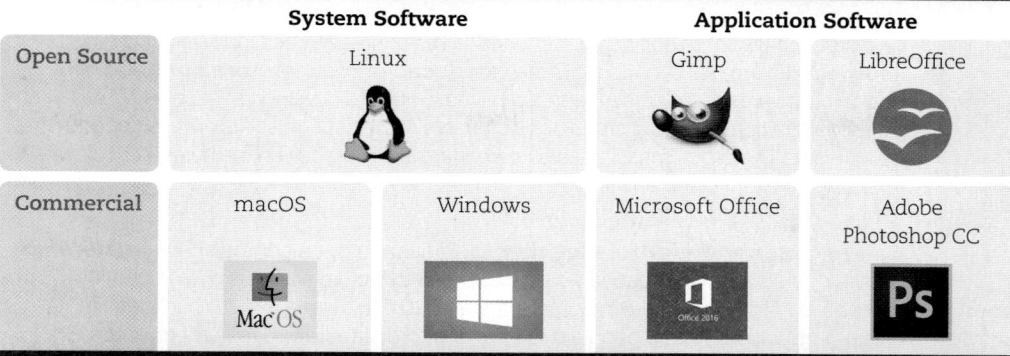

	System Software		Application Software	
Open Source	Linux		Gimp	LibreOffice
Commercial	macOS	Windows	Microsoft Office	Adobe Photoshop CC

(The Linux Foundation; GIMP, Jakub Steiner (Jimmac); The Apache Software Foundation; Apple Inc.; Microsoft Corporation; Microsoft Corporation; © 2017 Adobe Systems Incorporated. All rights reserved. Adobe, Adobe Premiere, Dreamweaver and Photoshop is/are either [a] registered trademark[s] or a trademark[s] of Adobe Systems Incorporated in the United States and/or other countries.)

don't have to worry about manually upgrading the software yourself. Google Docs and Microsoft Office Online are examples of programs that are distributed in this way. SaaS programs are often free of charge but not as full featured as locally installed versions.

3. **Subscription:** With **subscription software**, you pay a fee to use the software for a certain period of time. It is then available for you to download and install on your computer. As soon as updates are available, the manufacturer pushes these new features to you. You can use the software without being on the Internet but can only receive updates when you're connected to the Internet. The Adobe Creative Cloud applications and the Microsoft Office 365 subscription service are examples of software distributed in this way.

Bits&Bytes   Finding Alternative Software

Free open source software products that are very similar to commercially sold versions are often available. But how do you find them? The site AlternativeTo (**alternativeto.net**) can help.

Whether you're looking for mobile apps or software for any of the major operating systems, AlternativeTo can help you find the latest and best reviewed software options.

Managing Your Software

It's important to know how to choose the best software for your computing device, how to get it onto your computer correctly, and how to remove it. We discuss all of these topics next.

Purchasing Software

Objective 4.3 *Explain the different options for purchasing software.*

Where is the best place to buy software? Depending on which device you're purchasing software for, there are many different software outlets. If you have a machine with an optical drive (a DVD or Blu-ray reader), you may want to go to a brick and mortar store for your software. Software for gaming consoles is still sold on discs, for example. However, the most popular way to purchase software now is through an online download. Manufacturers' websites offer their full product line as electronic downloads, with the option to add an optical disc as a backup. Software for mobile devices is sold electronically through centralized stores for each operating system. Apple runs the iTunes store, and Google administers the Google Play site. These sites see over 78 billion downloads a year (see Figure 4.2).

Figure 4.2 Software for mobile devices is sold electronically through centralized stores like iTunes or Google Play. (Bloomicon/Shutterstock)

Is discounted software for students available? If you're a student, you can buy substantially discounted software that is no different from regularly priced software. Campus computer stores and college bookstores offer discounted prices to students who possess a valid student ID. Online software suppliers such as Journey Education Marketing (**journeyed.com**) and Academic Superstore (**academicsuperstore.com**) also offer popular software to students at reduced prices. Software developers, such as Microsoft and Adobe, also often offer their products to students at a discount, so it's always good to check their websites before purchasing software or hardware. In addition, be sure to check with your college or school. Many times they have agreements with large vendors like Microsoft for free or reduced pricing for their students.

Can I get software for free legally? In addition to open source software, **freeware** is copyrighted software that you can use for free. Explore sites like FileHippo (**filehippo. com**) to see how many good freeware programs are available. However, while much legitimate freeware exists, some unscrupulous people use freeware to distribute viruses and malware. Be cautious when installing freeware, especially if you're unsure of the provider's legitimacy.

New models for freely distributing software are also appearing. For example, if you use Amazon devices like the Fire tablet, you can get free applications through Amazon Underground. Developers are paid by Amazon for every minute each app is used.

Can I try new software before it's released? Some software developers offer beta versions of their software free of charge. A **beta version** is an application that is still under development. By distributing free beta versions, developers hope users will report errors, or bugs, they find in their programs. Many beta versions are available for a limited trial period and are used to help developers respond to issues before they launch the software on the market.

Are there risks associated with installing beta versions? By their very nature, beta products are unlikely to be bug free, so you always run the risk of something going awry with your system by installing and using beta versions. Unless you're willing to deal with potential problems, it may be best to wait until the last beta version is released—often referred to as the *gold version*. By that time, most of the serious bugs have been worked out.

As a precaution, you should be comfortable with the reliability of the source before downloading a beta version of software. If it's a reliable developer whose software you're familiar with, you can be more certain that a serious bug or virus isn't hiding in the software. Similarly, you should be sure that the software you're downloading is meant for your system and that your system has met all the necessary hardware and operating system requirements.

Trends In IT Mobile Payment Apps: The Power of M-Commerce

Most people own a mobile device, so it's no surprise that companies regard *mobile commerce* (or m-commerce)—using applications on smartphones and tablets to buy and sell products—as a trend that shouldn't be ignored.

Although mobile commerce hasn't taken over traditional methods of e-commerce just yet, the number of purchases from mobile devices continues to rise. Projections indicate that by 2019, m-commerce will top 1 trillion dollars a year. The emergence of tablets and better functioning m-commerce apps has improved the mobile shopping experience.

The ability to make mobile payments is driving m-commerce. Mobile payment apps, such as Android Pay, Apple Pay, and Samsung Pay, make it convenient to pay just by waving your smartphone at an NFC-compatible terminal. (Near field communication, or NFC, is a set of protocols that facilitate communication between two devices.) Mobile payment apps have been available for several years, but why have they been slow to catch on?

People initially feared that the mobile payment apps were less secure than paying with a conventional credit/debit card. But with the large data breaches occurring at such retail stores as Target, conventional payment methods are no longer viewed as

more secure. And most mobile payment apps use *tokenization*, which substitutes *tokens*, one-use-only numbers, for your credit card numbers to process retail transactions. This makes them more secure than just swiping your credit card. Your credit card number remains safe, even if the retailer's system is hacked,

Figure 4.3 Merchant apps allow you to pay for products and manage loyalty rewards. (Anna Hoychuk/Shutterstock)

because the retailer never actually has your credit card number.

Aside from general payment apps like Apple Pay, many merchants create their own mobile apps, which, in addition to paying for services, can be used to manage coupons, gift cards, and customer loyalty programs (see Figure 4.3). Some merchant apps also use tokenization to safeguard your information.

So wave that phone with confidence when buying your next latte. Your data should be safer than when you swipe your credit card.

Installing and Uninstalling Software

Objective 4.4 *Describe how to install and uninstall software.*

How do I know the software I buy will work on my computer? If you're buying software, it's your responsibility to check for compatibility with your system. Every software program has a set of **system requirements** that specify the minimum recommended standards for the operating system, processor, primary memory (random access memory, or RAM), and storage. These requirements are printed on the software packaging or are available at the manufacturer's website. Before installing software on your computer, ensure that your system setup meets the minimum requirements as specified by the developer.

What steps should I take before installing a new program? Before installing any software, it's always good to make sure your virus protection software is up to date. It's equally important that you back up your system as well as create a **restore point**. A restore point doesn't affect your personal data files but saves all the apps, updates, drivers, and information needed to restore your computer system to the exact way it's configured at that time. That way, if something does go awry, you can return your system to the way it was before you started. You can create a restore point by using Windows 10 System protection tools. To create a restore point, open the Control Panel by right-clicking the Start icon on the taskbar. Next click *System and Security*, and then click *System*. In the left pane, click *System protection* to display the System Properties dialog box. On the System Protection tab, click the *Create* button, type a description for the restore point (such as "Before installing [name of software]"), and click *Create*. You will be notified when the restore point is created.

What's the difference between a custom installation and a full installation? The exact installation process will differ slightly depending on whether you're installing the software from a disc, purchasing it from an app marketplace, or downloading it from the web. If you're using an option that requires files to be installed locally, the installation wizard will ask you to decide between a full installation and a custom installation. A **full installation** (sometimes referred to as a **typical installation**) copies all the most commonly used files and programs to your computer's hard drive. By selecting **custom installation**, you can decide which features you want installed on your hard drive. Installing only the features you want saves space on your hard drive.

How do I uninstall a program? An application contains many different files—library files, help files, and other text files—in addition to the main file you use to run the program. By deleting only the main file, you're not ridding your system of all the pieces of the program. Windows 10 makes it easy to uninstall a program: On the Start menu, right-click the app and select *Uninstall*.

If my computer crashes, can I get the preinstalled software back? Although some preinstalled software is not necessary to replace if your computer crashes, other software such as the operating system is critical to reinstall. Most manufacturers use a separate partition on the hard drive to hold an image, or copy, of the preinstalled software. However, it's not always possible to reboot from the partitioned hard drive, especially when your computer crashes, so one of the first things you should do after you purchase a new computer is create a **recovery drive**. A recovery drive contains all the information needed to reinstall your operating system if it should become corrupted. Often the manufacturer will have placed a utility on your system to create this.

 Helpdesk MyLab IT®

Buying and Installing Software

In this Helpdesk, you'll play the role of a helpdesk staffer, fielding questions about how to best purchase software or to get it for free, how to install and uninstall software, and where you can go for help when you have a problem with your software.

Bits&Bytes   Ridding Your Computer of "Bloat"

Manufacturers often include software on new computers that you don't want or need. Called *bloatware*, this software can slow down your computer and degrade its performance. How do you avoid it or get rid of it? Microsoft offers "Signature Editions" of popular PCs and tablets that are free from bloatware. However, if you purchase a computer with bloatware, you can install an application such as Should I Remove It? (**shouldiremoveit.com**), which actually helps you decide which programs you should remove. Or, if you'd rather do it yourself, consider some of these tips:

- *Uninstall preinstalled antivirus software:* If you have antivirus software on your old computer, you may be able to transfer the unexpired portion of your software license to your new computer. If this is the case, you can uninstall the preinstalled trial version on your new computer.

- *Remove manufacturer-specific software:* Some computer manufacturers install their own software. Some of these programs can be useful, but others are help features and update reminders that are also found in your operating system. You can remove any or all of these support applications and instead just check the manufacturer's website periodically for updates or new information.

If not, you can use the Recovery utility included in Windows to create a recovery drive. You access these tools in Windows 10 by typing *Recovery* in the Cortana search box, and then selecting *Create a recovery drive*. When the Recovery Drive dialog box opens, click Next. Then insert a blank flash drive into a USB port and follow the steps in the wizard. Once the recovery drive has been made, label the flash drive and put it away in a safe place.

How do I recover software that I installed on my device if it crashes? For mobile devices, this can be simple but time-consuming. Most app marketplaces keep track of the software you've purchased. If your device crashes, you can log in to the marketplace and reinstall software you've previously purchased. We'll cover backup and recovery strategies for other software in Chapter 9.

Upgrading Software

Objective 4.5   *Explain the considerations around the decision to upgrade your software.*

When is it time to upgrade software I own? When software is sold by subscription or using the cloud-based SaaS model, you don't need to worry about upgrading because it's handled automatically. However, if you're using software that was installed locally to your hard drive, you'll need to make the upgrade decision yourself. Periodically, software developers improve the

---

Dig Deeper   How Number Systems Work

As we discussed in Chapter 2, to process data into information, computers need to work in a language they understand. This language, called *binary language*, consists of two digits: 0 and 1. Everything a computer does, including running the applications we've been discussing in this chapter, is broken down into a series of 0s and 1s. *Electrical switches* are the devices inside the computer that are flipped between the two states of 1 and 0, signifying on and off. How can simple switches be organized so that they let you use a computer to pay your bills online or write an essay? Let's look at how number systems work so that we can begin to understand this more deeply.

A **number system** is an organized plan for representing a number. Although you may not realize it, you're already familiar with one number system. The **base-10 number system**, also known as **decimal notation**, is the system you use to represent all of the numeric values you use each day. It's called base 10 because it uses 10 digits—0 through 9—to represent any value.

To represent a number in base 10, you break the number down into groups of ones, tens, hundreds, thousands, and so on. Each digit has a place value depending on where it appears in the number. For example, using base 10, in the whole number 6,954, there are 6 sets of thousands, 9 sets of hundreds, 5 sets of tens, and 4 sets of ones. Working from right to left, each place in a number represents an increasing power of 10, as follows:

$$6,954 = (6 * 1,000) + (9 * 100) + (5 * 10) + (4 * 1)$$
$$= (6 * 10^3) + (9 * 10^2) + (5 * 10^1) + (4 * 10^0)$$

Note that in this equation, the final digit 4 is represented as $4 * 10^0$ because any number raised to the zero power is equal to 1.

Anthropologists theorize that humans developed a base-10 number system because we have 10 fingers. However, computer

systems are not well suited to thinking about numbers in groups of 10. Instead, computers describe a number in powers of 2 because each switch can be in one of two positions: on or off. This numbering system is referred to as the **binary number system** (or **base-2 number system**). In the base-10 number system, a whole number is represented as the sum of 1s, 10s, 100s, and 1,000s—that is, sums of powers of 10. The binary system works in the same way but describes a value as the sum of groups of 1s, 2s, 4s, 8s, 16s, 32s, 64s, and so on—that is, powers of 2: 2 to the 0, 1, 2 power, and so on.

Let's look at the number 67. In base 10, the number 67 would be six sets of 10s and seven sets of 1s, as follows:

$$67_{Base\ 10} = (6 * 10^1) + (7 * 10^0)$$

One way to figure out how 67 is represented in base 2 is to find the largest possible power of 2 that could be in the number 67. Two to the eighth power is 256, and there are no groups of 256 in the number 67. Two to the seventh power is 128, but that is bigger than 67. Two to the sixth power is 64, and there is a group of 64 inside a group of 67.

67 has	1	group of	64	**That leaves 3 and**
3 has	0	groups of	32	
	0	groups of	16	
	0	groups of	8	
	0	groups of	4	
	1	group of	2	**That leaves 1 and**
1 has	1	group of	1	**Now nothing is left**

functionality of their software by releasing a software upgrade. Before upgrading, it's important to understand what's included in the upgrade and how stable the new software version is in its performance. Depending on the software, some upgrades may not be sufficiently different from the previous version to make it cost-effective for you to buy the newest version. Unless the upgrade adds features that are important to you, you may be better off waiting to upgrade. You also should consider whether you use the software frequently enough to justify an upgrade and whether your current system can handle the new system requirements of the upgraded version. In between upgrades, developers will make available software updates (sometimes referred to as software patches). Updates are usually downloaded automatically and provide smaller enhancements to the software or fix program bugs.

If I have an older version of software and someone sends me files from a newer version, can I still open them? Software vendors recognize that people work on different versions of the same software. Vendors, therefore, make new versions backward compatible, meaning that the new versions can recognize (open) files created with older versions. However, some software programs are not forward compatible, so these older versions are not able to recognize files created on newer versions of the same software. Files created on newer versions of software can be recognized by older versions if the correct file extension is chosen under Save As Type. For example, a .docx file can be recognized by an older version of Microsoft Word if it is saved as a .doc file (Word 97-2003 document).

So, the binary number for 67 is written as 1000011 in base 2:

$$67_{\text{Base 10}} = 64 + 0 + 0 + 0 + 0 + 2 + 1$$
$$= (1 * 2^6) + (0 * 2^5) + (0 * 2^4) + (0 * 2^3) +$$
$$(0 * 2^2) + (1 * 2^1) + (1 * 2^0)$$
$$= 1000011_{\text{Base 2}}$$

A large integer value becomes a very long string of 1s and 0s in binary. For convenience, programmers often use **hexadecimal notation** to make these expressions easier to use. Hexadecimal is a base-16 number system, meaning it uses 16 digits to represent numbers instead of the 10 digits used in base 10 or the 2 digits used in base 2. The 16 digits it uses are the 10 numeric digits, 0 to 9, plus six extra symbols: A, B, C, D, E, and F. Each of the letters A through F corresponds to a numeric value, so that A equals 10, B equals 11, and so on. Therefore, the value 67 in decimal notation is 1000011 in binary or 43 (= 4 * 16 + 3 * 1) in hexadecimal notation. It is much easier for computer scientists to use the 2-digit 43 than the 7-digit string 1000011.

We've just been converting integers from base 10, which *we* understand, to base 2 (binary state), which the computer understands. Similarly, we need a system that converts letters and other symbols that *we* understand to a binary state the computer understands. To provide a consistent means for representing letters and other characters, certain codes dictate how to represent characters in binary format. Most of today's personal computers use the American National Standards Institute (ANSI, pronounced "AN-see") standard code, called the **American Standard Code for Information Interchange** (ASCII, pronounced "AS-key"), to represent each letter or character as an 8-bit (or 1-byte) binary code.

We've been converting base-10 numbers to a binary format. In such cases, the binary format has no standard length. For example, the binary format for the number 2 is two digits (10), whereas for the number 10 it is four digits (1010). Although binary numbers can have more or fewer than 8 bits, each single alphabetic or special character is 1 byte (or 8 bits) of data. The ASCII code represents the 26 uppercase letters and 26 lowercase letters used in the English language, along with many punctuation symbols and other special characters, using 8 bits. Because the ASCII code represents letters and characters using only 8 bits, it can assign only 256 (or 2^8) different codes. Although this is enough to represent English and many other characters found in the world's languages, the ASCII code can't represent all languages and symbols. Thus, a new encoding scheme, called **Unicode**, was created. By using 16 bits instead of 8 bits, Unicode can represent nearly 1,115,000 code points and currently assigns more than 128,000 unique character symbols. As we continue to become a more global society, it is anticipated that Unicode will replace ASCII as the standard character formatting code.

Sound Byte MyLab IT®

Where Does Binary Show Up?

This Sound Byte helps remove the mystery around binary numbers. You'll learn about base conversion between decimal, binary, and hexadecimal numbers using colors, sounds, and images.

Software Licenses

Objective 4.6 *Explain how software licenses function.*

Don't I own the software I buy? Most people don't understand that, unlike other items they purchase, the software they buy doesn't belong to them. The only thing they're actually purchasing is a license that gives them the right to use the software for their own purposes as the only user of that copy. The application is not theirs to lend.

A **software license**, also known as an **End User License Agreement (EULA)**, is an agreement between you, the user, and the software company (see Figure 4.4). You accept this agreement before installing the software on your machine. It's a legal contract that outlines the acceptable uses of the program and any actions that violate the agreement. Generally, the agreement states who the ultimate owner of the software is, under what circumstances copies of the software can be made, and whether the software can be installed on any other computing device. Finally, the license agreement states what, if any, warranty comes with the software.

Does a license only cover one installation? Some software is purchased with a single license to cover one person's specific use. You can't share these licenses, and you can't "extend" the license to install the software on more than one of your computers. Many manufacturers are now offering licensing bundles to allow several computers in one household to be installed with a legal copy. For example, Apple offers a Family Pack Software License Agreement that permits a user to install the purchased software legally on as many as five computers in the same household, and some versions of Microsoft Office come with a license that allows you to install the software on multiple computers in the same household.

Businesses and educational institutions often buy multiuser licenses that allow more than one person to use the software. Some multiuser licenses are per-seat and limit the number of users overall, whereas others, called concurrent licenses, limit the number of users accessing the software at any given time.

Does open source software require a license? Anyone using open source software has access to the program's code. Therefore, open source software programs can be tweaked by another user and redistributed. A free software license, the GNU General Public License, is required and grants the recipients the right to modify and redistribute the software. Without such a license, the recipient would be in violation of copyright laws. This concept of redistributing modified open source software under the same terms as the original software is known as **copyleft**. Thus, all enhancements, additions, and other changes to copyleft software must also be distributed as free software.

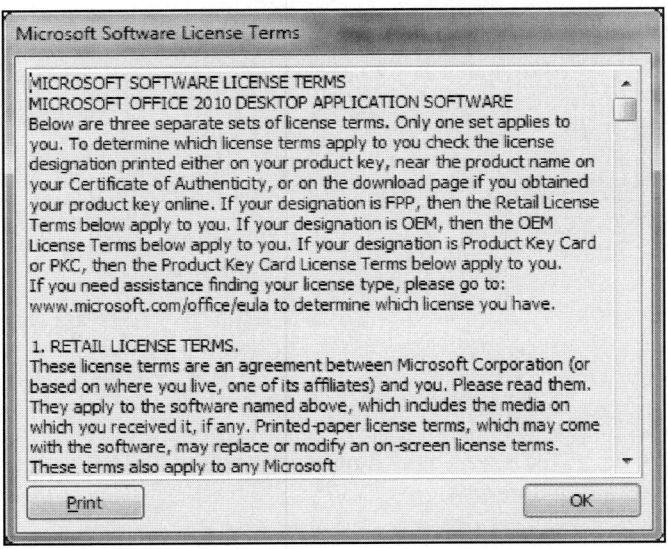

Figure 4.4 You must accept the terms of the software license before using the product. *(Word 2016, Windows 10, Courtesy Microsoft, Inc.)*

Can I Borrow Software That I Don't Own?

As noted earlier, when you purchase software, you're purchasing a license to use it rather than purchasing the actual software. That license tells you how many times you can install the software, so it's important to read it. If you make more copies of the software than the license permits, you're participating in **software piracy** (see Figure 4.5).

Historically, the most common way software has been pirated has been by borrowing installation discs from others and installing the software on other computers. Larger-scale illegal duplication and distribution by counterfeiters are quite common as well. In addition, the Internet provides various ways to copy and distribute pirated software illegally.

Is it really a big deal to copy a program or two? As reported by the Business Software Alliance, nearly half of all software used is pirated. Not only is pirating software unethical and illegal, the practice has financial impacts on all software consumers. The financial loss to the software industry is estimated to be over $62 billion a year. This loss decreases the amount of money available for further software research and development, while increasing the up-front costs to legitimate consumers.

To determine whether you have a pirated copy of software installed on your computer, conduct a software audit. The Business Software Alliance website (**bsa.org**) has several free third-party software audit tools that help you identify and track software installed on your computer and networks. These programs check the serial numbers of the software installed on your computer against software manufacturer databases of officially licensed copies and known fraudulent copies. Any suspicious software installations are flagged for your attention.

As of yet, there's no such thing as an official software police force, but if you're caught with pirated software, severe penalties do exist. A company or individual can pay up to $150,000 for each software title copied. In addition, you can be criminally prosecuted for copyright infringement, which carries a fine of up to $250,000, a five-year jail sentence, or both.

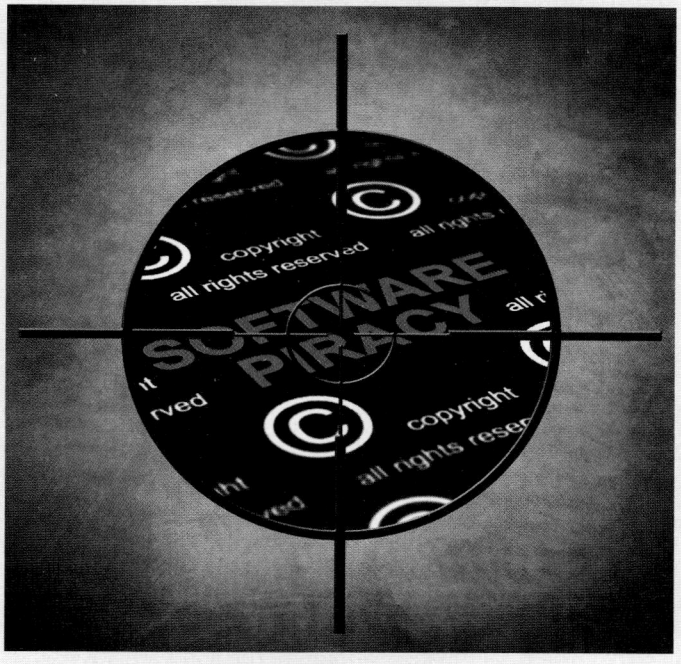

Figure 4.5 Making more copies than the software license permits is pirating and is illegal. *(Alexskopje/123RF)*

Efforts to stop groups involved with counterfeit software are in full force. Software manufacturers also are becoming more aggressive in programming mechanisms into software to prevent illegal installations. For instance, with many products, installation requires you to activate the serial number of your software with a database maintained by the software manufacturer. Failure to activate your serial number or attempting to activate a serial number used previously results in the software going into a "reduced functionality mode" after a certain number of uses. This usually precludes you from doing useful things like saving files created with the software.

Before moving on to Part 2:

1. ▶ Watch Chapter Overview Video 4.1.
2. Then take the Check Your Understanding quiz.

Check Your Understanding // Review & Practice

For a quick review to see what you've learned so far, answer the following questions.

multiple choice

1. Software that helps run the computer's hardware devices and coordinates instructions between applications is called
   a. a web server.
   b. system software.
   c. application software.
   d. beta software.

2. Software built by companies and sold to users is called
   a. open source software.
   b. beta software.
   c. freeware.
   d. proprietary software.

3. Beta software is never
   a. system software.
   b. application software.
   c. the final finished version of the software.
   d. open source software.

4. Which of the following would NOT be of any help before installing beta software?
   a. creating a restore point
   b. defragging the hard drive
   c. backing up your system
   d. ensuring your virus protection software is updated

5. The minimum set of recommended standards for a program is known as the
   a. system requirements.
   b. operating system.
   c. setup guide.
   d. installation specs.

 Go to **MyLab IT** to take an autograded version of the *Check Your Understanding* review and to find all media resources for the chapter.

TechBytes Weekly Go to TechBytes Weekly for current technology news and discussion questions!

Try This

Citing Website Sources

You've been assigned a research paper, and your instructor requires citations. In the past, you might have resorted to using websites such as Son of Citation Machine (**citationmachine.net**) to create your citations. As you'll see in this Try This, there are tools built right into Microsoft Word that do the same thing. (Note: For more step-by-step instructions and also for information on how to build a bibliography, watch the Try This video on MyLab IT.)

Step 1 Click at the end of the sentence or phrase that you want to cite. Set the Bibliography style to the format you wish to follow, for example MLA or APA. On the References tab, in the Citations & Bibliography group, click **Insert Citation**. To add the source information, click **Add New Source**.

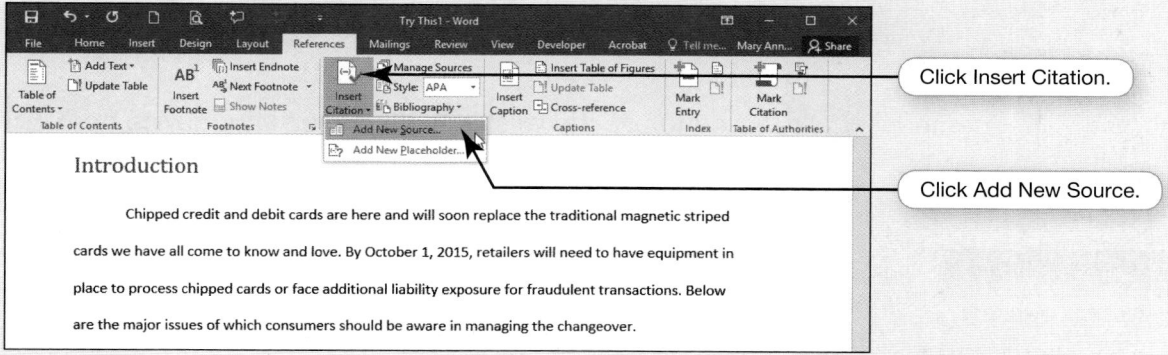

(Courtesy Microsoft, Inc.)

Note: To create a citation and fill in the source information later, click **Add New Placeholder**.

Step 2 Begin to fill in the source information by clicking the arrow next to Type of Source. Click OK when done.

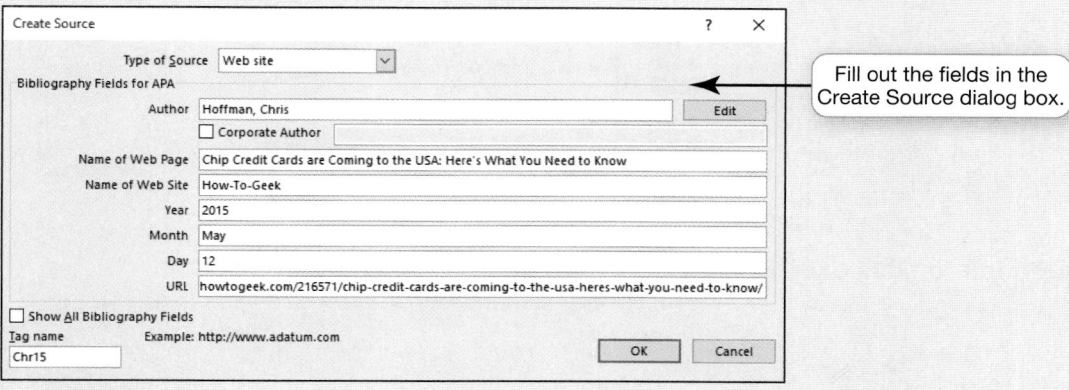

(Courtesy Microsoft, Inc.)

Step 3 The citation will appear in your document.

(Courtesy Microsoft, Inc.)

Make: A More Powerful App

Want your app to be able to open a file from the SD card on your phone, fire up the YouTube app, or display a location in the Maps app?

In this exercise, you'll use the ActivityStarter component of App Inventor to incorporate the software already on your device into your mobile app.

(Copyright MIT, used with permission)

It's as easy as using the Connectivity drawer of the Designer in App Inventor. Drag the ActivityStarter component onto your Designer screen, then control it with the Blocks for ActivityStarter. Your apps now have the power of all the software on your device behind them!

The ActivityStarter component allows you to use the existing software on your device from within your mobile app.

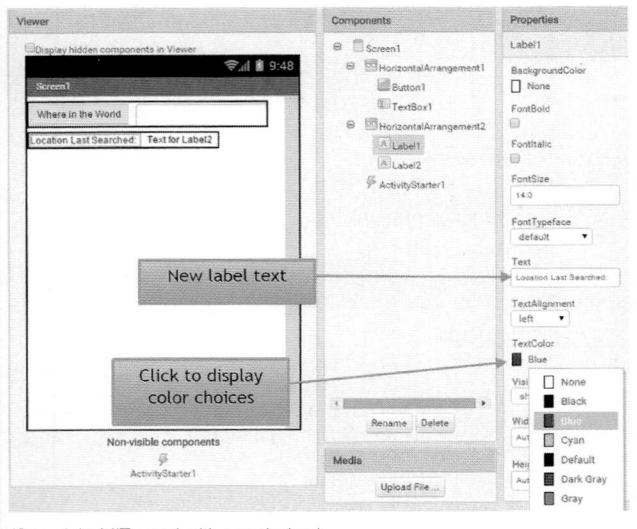

(Copyright MIT, used with permission.)

(Copyright MIT, used with permission.)

For the instructions for this exercise, go to MyLab IT.

Application Software

Learning Outcome 4.2 **Describe the different types of application software used for productivity and multimedia.**

One reason computers are invaluable is that they make it easier to complete our daily tasks. While many programs help you be more productive, there are also programs that entertain you with audio, video, and images, as well as games, animations, and movies.

In this section, we'll look at applications that help enhance your productivity, support your business projects, and let you create multimedia.

Productivity and Business Software

Let's start by taking a look at productivity and business software.

Productivity Software

Objective 4.7 *Categorize the types of application software used to enhance productivity, and describe their uses and features.*

What is productivity software? **Productivity software** lets you perform various tasks required at home, school, and business. The main types of productivity software include programs for word processing, spreadsheet analysis, presentation software, database management, note-taking, and personal information management. In addition, financial planning software and tax preparation software are available for personal use.

How do I choose among the many different programs available? When you're looking for a specific product, say, a word processing program, you have many choices. As discussed earlier, you can choose between commercial products and open source products or choose to install the program on your local device or use it purely online. Figure 4.6 guides you through these many choices.

Microsoft Office is a very successful set of productivity programs and is offered as installed software or as a fully online version, Microsoft Office Online. Google Docs is a strong competitor for purely online products. The open source option LibreOffice is free to download and install and is supported by an active community.

Next we'll examine each type of program to understand its key features.

Figure 4.6   Productivity Software

PROGRAM	WORD PROCESSING	SPREADSHEET	PRESENTATION	DATABASE	NOTE-TAKING	PIM/E-MAIL
Installed: Proprietary						
Microsoft Office	Word	Excel	PowerPoint	Access	OneNote	Outlook
Apple iWork	Pages	Numbers	Keynote			
Installed: Open Source						
LibreOffice	Writer	Calc	Impress	Base		
Web-Based						
Microsoft Office Online	Word	Excel	PowerPoint		OneNote	Outlook
Google Docs	Docs	Sheets	Slides			Gmail
Zoho	Writer	Sheet, Books	Show	Creator	Notebook	
ThinkFree	Write	Calc	Show		Note	

Word Processing Software

What are the most common word processing applications? You've probably used **word processing software** to create and edit documents such as research papers, class notes, and résumés. Microsoft Word is the most popular word processing program that you can buy and install on your computer. If you're looking for a more affordable alternative, you might want to try an open source program such as Writer, from LibreOffice (**libreoffice.org**). When saving a document in Writer, the default file format has an OpenDocument (.odt) file extension. However, by using the Save As command, you can save files in other formats, such as .docx for Word.

What are the special features of word processing programs? Word processors come with basic tools such as spelling and grammar checking, a thesaurus, and the find-and-replace tool. They also include other useful tools. You can translate words and phrases into other languages and can automatically summarize key points in a text document. There are tools that help you format your bibliographical references and organize them into a database so you can reuse them in other papers quickly. You can also enhance the look of your document by creating an interesting background or by adding a "theme" of coordinated colors and styles (see Figure 4.7).

Bits&Bytes   How to Open Unknown File Types

Normally, when you double-click a file to open it, the program associated with the file opens automatically. For example, when you double-click a file with a .doc or .docx extension, the file opens in Microsoft Word. However, if the file has no extension or Windows has no application associated with that file type, a *How do you want to open this file?* dialog box appears and asks what program you want to use to open the file. In other cases, a document may open with a program other than the one you want to use. This is because many applications can open several file types, and the program you expected the file to open in isn't the program currently associated with that file type. To assign a program to a file type or to change the program to open a particular file type, follow these instructions:

1. Use the search and navigation tools in File Explorer to locate the file you want to change. (For example, you can search for all Word files by searching for *.doc or *.docx.) Right-click on the file, and then point to **Open with**.
2. A list of programs installed on your computer appears. Click the program you want to use to open this file type. If you're sure the selected program is the one that should always be used for this file type, select **Choose another app,** which opens the **How do you want to open this file?** dialog box. Check the **Always use this app to open [extension] files**, and click the default program from the list.

When you double-click that file in the future, the file will open in the program you selected.

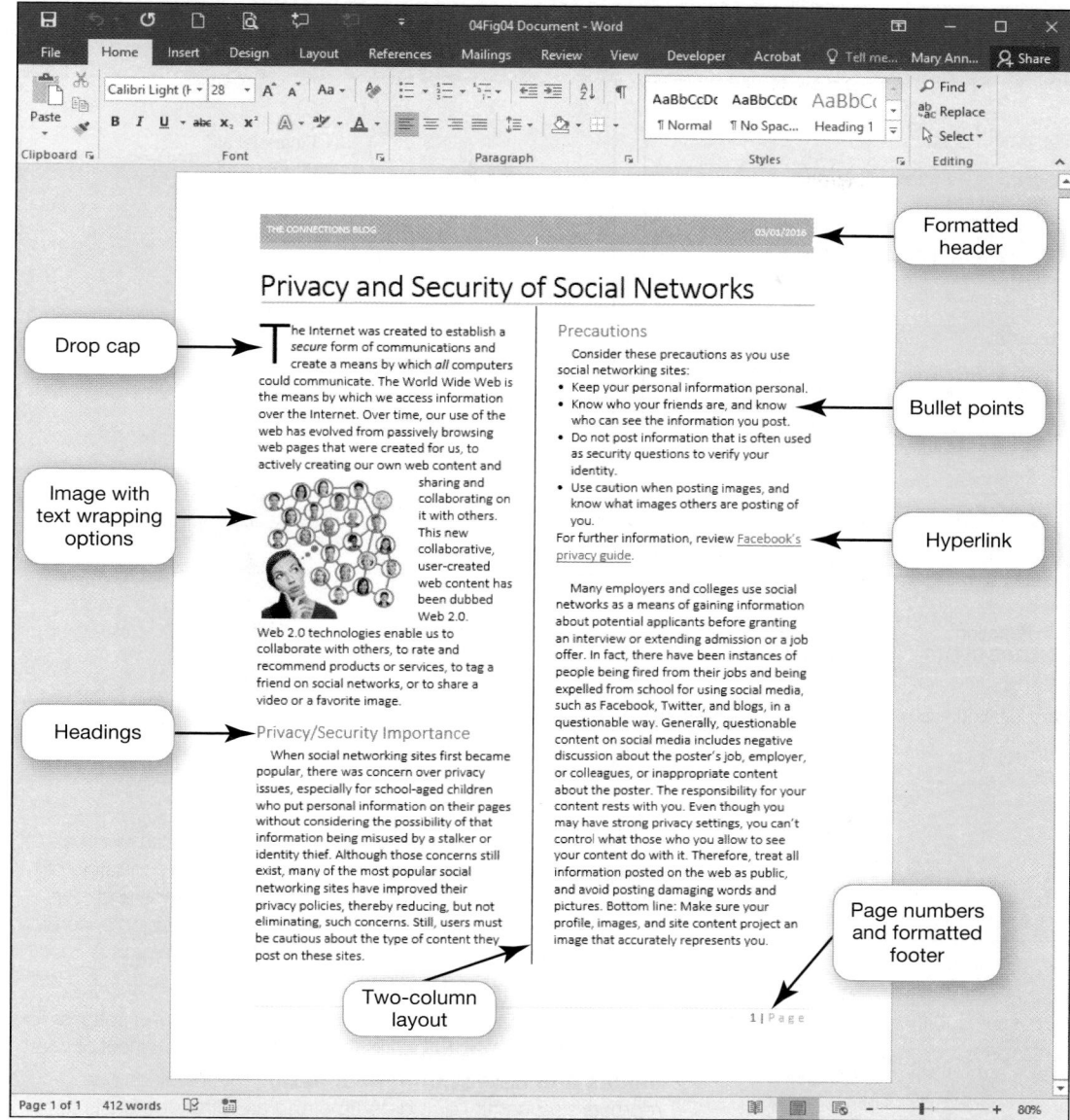

FIGURE 4.7 Nearly every word processing application has formatting features that let you give your documents a professional look. *(Word 2016, Windows 10, Courtesy Microsoft Inc.; Robert Kneschke/Fotolia)*

Spreadsheet Software

Why would I use spreadsheet software? **Spreadsheet software** lets you make calculations and perform numerical analyses. For example, you can use it to create a simple budget, as shown in Figure 4.8a. Microsoft Excel and LibreOffice Calc are two examples of spreadsheet software. (Web-based options are available within Google Docs and Office Online.) One benefit of spreadsheet software is that it can automatically recalculate all formulas and functions in a spreadsheet when values for some of the inputs change. For example, as shown in Figure 4.8b, you can insert an additional row in your budget ("Membership") and change a value (for September Financial aid), and the results for "Total Expenses" and "Net Income" recalculate automatically.

Because automatic recalculation lets you immediately see the effects different options have on your spreadsheet, you can quickly test different assumptions. This is called *what-if analysis*. Look again at Figure 4.8b and ask, "If I don't get as much financial aid next semester, what impact will that have on my total budget?" The recalculated cells in rows 18 and 19 help answer your question. In addition to financial analysis, many spreadsheet applications have limited database capabilities to sort, filter, and group data.

FIGURE 4.8 Spreadsheet software lets you easily calculate and manipulate numerical data with the use of built-in formulas. *(Excel 2016, Windows 10, Courtesy Microsoft, Inc.)*

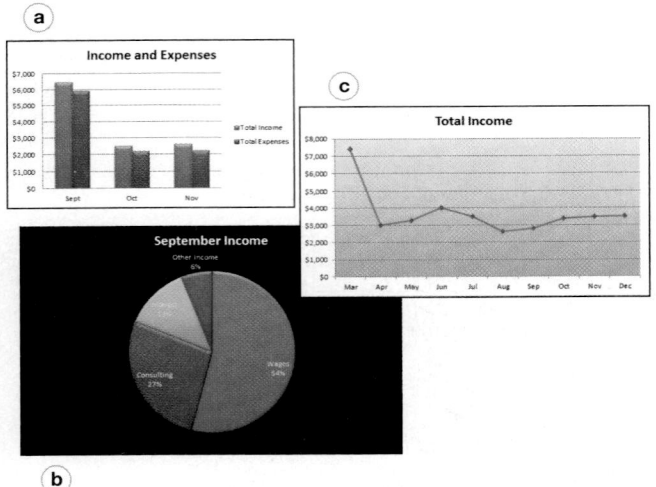

FIGURE 4.9 (a) Column charts show comparisons. (b) Pie charts show how parts contribute to the whole. (c) Line charts show trends over time.

How do I use spreadsheet software? The basic element in a spreadsheet program is the *worksheet*, which is a grid consisting of columns and rows. As shown in Figure 4.8a, the columns and rows form individual boxes called *cells*. Each cell can be identified according to its column and row position. For example, a cell in column A, row 1 is referred to as cell A1. You can enter several types of data into a cell:

- **Text:** Any combination of letters, numbers, symbols, and spaces. Text is often used as labels to identify the contents of a worksheet or chart.
- **Values and dates (numerical data):** These values can represent a quantity or a date/time and are often the basis for calculations.
- **Formulas:** Equations that use addition, subtraction, multiplication, and division operators, as well as values and cell references. For example, in Figure 4.8a, you would use the formula = D8-D17 to calculate net income for November.
- **Functions:** These help you develop your formulas. Adding a group of numbers (SUM) or determining the monthly loan payment (PMT) can be done using built-in functions. This frees you from needing to know the detailed mathematics behind the calculation. In Figure 4.8a, to calculate the total of all expenses for September, you could use the built-in summation function =SUM(B10:B16).

What kinds of graphs and charts can I create with spreadsheet software? Most spreadsheet applications let you create a variety of charts, including basic column charts, pie charts, and line charts, with or without 3D effects (see Figure 4.9). In addition to these basic charts, you can make stock charts (for investment analysis) and scatter charts (for statistical analysis) or create custom charts. Another feature in Excel is *sparklines*—small charts that fit into a single cell and make it easy to show data trends (see Figure 4.10a). To analyze the very large data sets common in Big Data analysis, Excel has added newer chart types like treemaps, sunburst, and waterfall charts (see Figure 4.10b).

Presentation Software

How can software help with my presentations? You've no doubt sat through presentations where the speaker used **presentation software** such as Microsoft PowerPoint (see Figure 4.11) or Apple's Keynote to create a slide show. Because these applications are simple to use, you can produce high-quality presentations without a lot of training. You can embed online videos, add effects, and even trim video clips without the need for a separate video-editing program.

What are some tips to make a great presentation? Some standard guidelines will help improve your presentation but not interfere with your creativity:

- **Use images**: Images can convey a thought or illustrate a point. Make sure any text over an image can be read easily.

- **Be careful with color**: Choose dark text on a light background or light text on a dark background. Avoid using text and background colors that clash.

- **Use bullets for key points**: Limit the number to four to six bulleted points per slide. Avoid full sentences and paragraphs.

- **Consider font size and style**: Keep the font size large enough to read from the back of the room. Avoid script or fancy font styles. Use only one or two font styles per presentation.

- **Keep animations and/or background audio to a minimum**: They can be distracting.

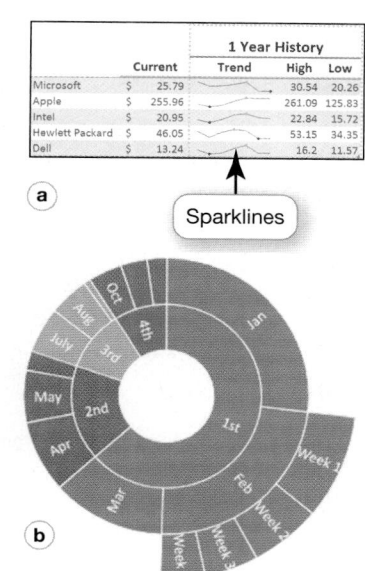

(a) Sparklines

(b)

Figure 4.10 (a) Sparklines and (b) sunbursts are two of many new charting tools in Excel. *(Excel 2016, Windows 10, Microsoft Corporation; Excel 2016, Windows 10, Microsoft Corporation)*

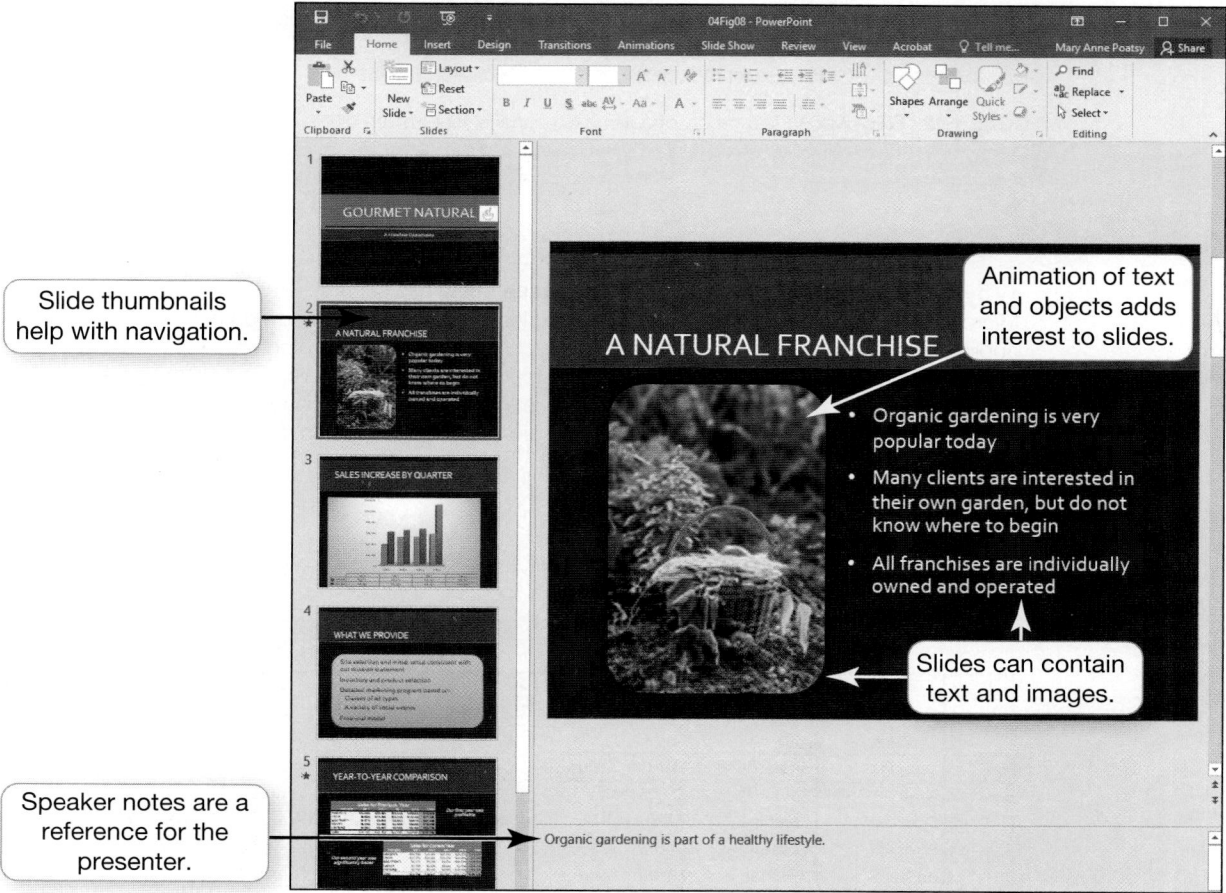

Slide thumbnails help with navigation.

Animation of text and objects adds interest to slides.

Slides can contain text and images.

Speaker notes are a reference for the presenter.

Figure 4.11 You can use Microsoft PowerPoint to create dynamic presentations. *(PowerPoint 2016, Windows 10, Courtesy Microsoft, Inc.; DIA/Fotolia)*

Going Beyond PowerPoint

PowerPoint is generally the go-to application for creating presentations. However, several applications offer a compelling alternative to PowerPoint. One cool option is Prezi (**prezi.com**), a web-based program that produces presentations in an innovative way. Rather than using a set of slides, Prezi uses a large canvas in which you connect ideas. PowToon (**www.powtoon.com**) provides a library of cartoon-like characters that are easily animated to give your presentations more of a "storytelling" aspect.

Microsoft also has two new products: Sway and Office Mix. Sway is a stand-alone app that allows you to create presentations that are stored in the cloud and linked to your Microsoft account. Sway facilitates importing content from a variety of sources to allow you to tell a compelling story and is designed primarily for creating web-based presentations. Office Mix is a PowerPoint add-in that gives you the power to integrate quizzes, polls, voice, video, and digital ink into your PowerPoint presentations to make them into interactive online videos (see Figure 4.12).

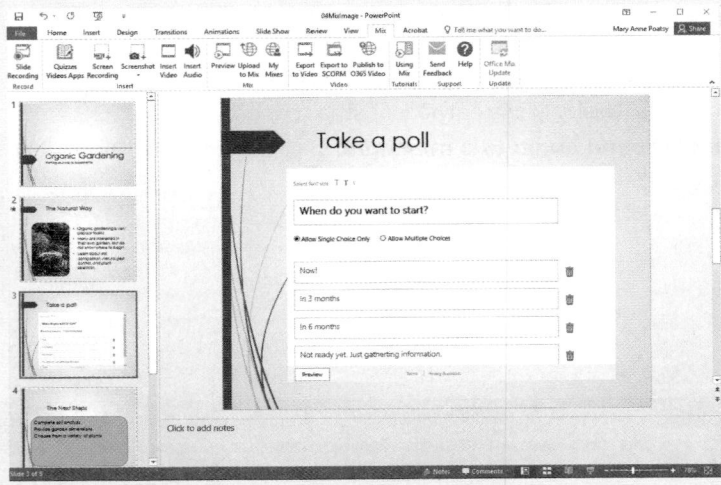

FIGURE 4.12 Office Mix adds a variety of options to enhance your PowerPoint presentations. *(PowerPoint 2016, Windows 10, Courtesy Microsoft, Inc.)*

Database Software

Why is database software useful? Database software such as Oracle, MySQL, and Microsoft Access are powerful applications that let you store and organize data. Spreadsheet applications are easy to use for simple tasks such as sorting, filtering, and organizing data. However, you need to use a more robust, fully featured database application to manage larger and more complicated data that is organized in more than one table; to group, sort, and retrieve data; and to generate reports. Traditional databases are organized into *fields*, *records*, and *tables*, as shown in Figure 4.13.

ID	FirstName	LastName	Company	Street	City	State	ZipCode
1	Susan	Scantosi	eWidget Plus	363 Rogue Street	St. Louis	MO	63136
2	Thomas	Mazeman	BooksRUs	2165 Piscotti Avenue	Springfield	IL	62702
3	Douglas	Seaver	Printing Solutions	7700 First Avenue	Topeka	KS	66603
4	Amir	Raviv	TechStands	1436 Riverfront Road	St. Louis	MO	63136
5	Franklin	Scott	WorksSuite	8789 Ploughman Ave	Tulsa	OK	74101
6	Ronald	Komeika	Creekside Financial	1264 Pond Hill Road	Toledo	OH	43601
7	Barbara	Mitchell	Market Tenders	9823 Bridge Street	La Porte	IN	46350

Field: a data category

Record: a group of related fields

Table: a group of related records

Figure 4.13 In databases, information is organized into fields, records, and tables. *(Excel 2013, Windows 8.1, Courtesy Microsoft, Inc.)*

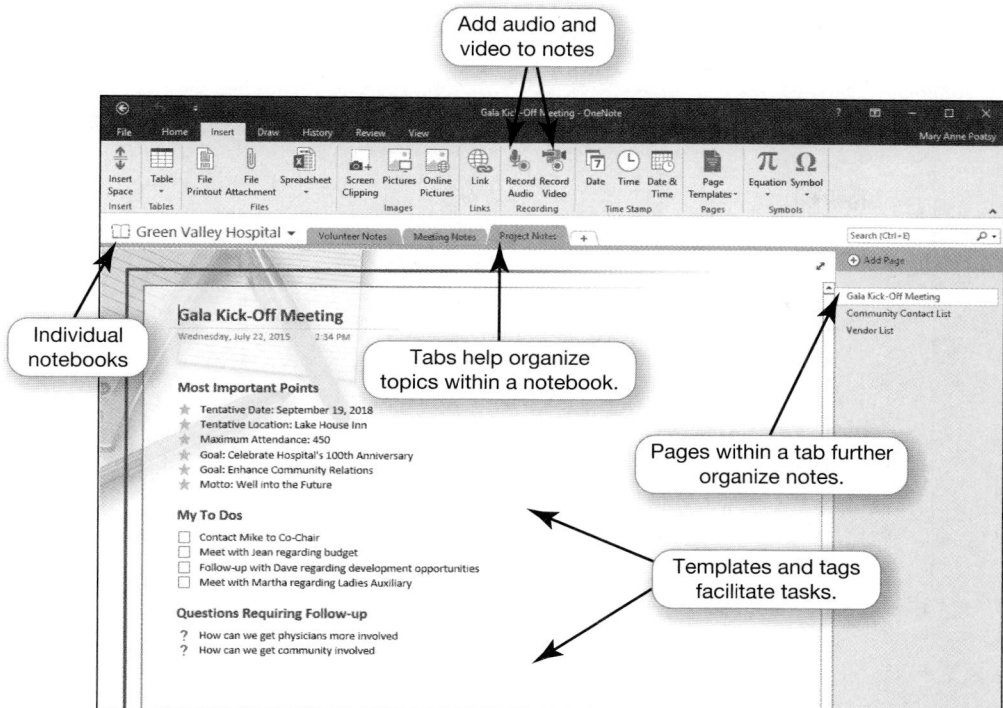

Figure 4.14 Microsoft OneNote is a great way to collect and organize notes and other information. The files are readily searchable and easy to share. *(OneNote 2016, Windows 10, Courtesy Microsoft, Inc.)*

How do businesses use database software? Most websites rely on databases to keep track of products, clients, invoices, and personnel information. Often, some of that information is available to a home computer user. For example, at Amazon, you can access the history of all the purchases you've ever made on the site. Shipping companies let you search their online databases for tracking numbers, allowing you to get instant information on the status of your packages. These functions require well-designed databases.

Note-Taking Software

Is there software to help me take notes? Microsoft OneNote is a popular note-taking and organizational tool you can use for research, brainstorming, and collaboration, as well as just organizing random bits of information. Using OneNote, you can organize your notes into tabbed sections (see Figure 4.14). In addition, you can access your OneNote notes from other Microsoft Office applications. For example, if you're writing a research paper in Word, click the OneNote icon in the Word ribbon to open OneNote, where you can add your notes—perhaps a reference to a website where you found some research. Later, if you open OneNote and click on that reference, it will bring you to the exact spot in the Word document where you made the reference.

You can also add audio or video recordings of lectures to OneNote, and you can search for a term across all the digital notebooks you created during the semester to find common ideas, such as key points that might appear on a test. There is also a OneNote mobile app.

Several very good, free online note-taking options are also available to help you take notes or to just jot down a quick reminder. Evernote (**evernote. com**), for example, lets you take notes via the web, your phone, or your computer and then syncs your notes between your devices. You can then share your notes with other Evernote users for easy collaboration. Figure 4.15 lists some other popular alternative note-taking applications.

Figure 4.15 Beyond Microsoft OneNote: Alternative Note-Taking Applications

Evernote (evernote.com)
- Web-based
- Notes can be shared for easy collaboration
- Syncs notes between all devices

AudioNote (luminantsoftware.com)
- Synchronized note taking and audio recording
- Allows text or handwritten notes
- Highlights notes during playback

Simplenote (simplenote.com)
- Web-based, open source
- Notes organized by tags
- Mobile apps available

Notability (gingerlabs.com)
- PDF annotations
- Advanced word processing
- Linked audio recordings to notes
- Auto-sync notes between devices

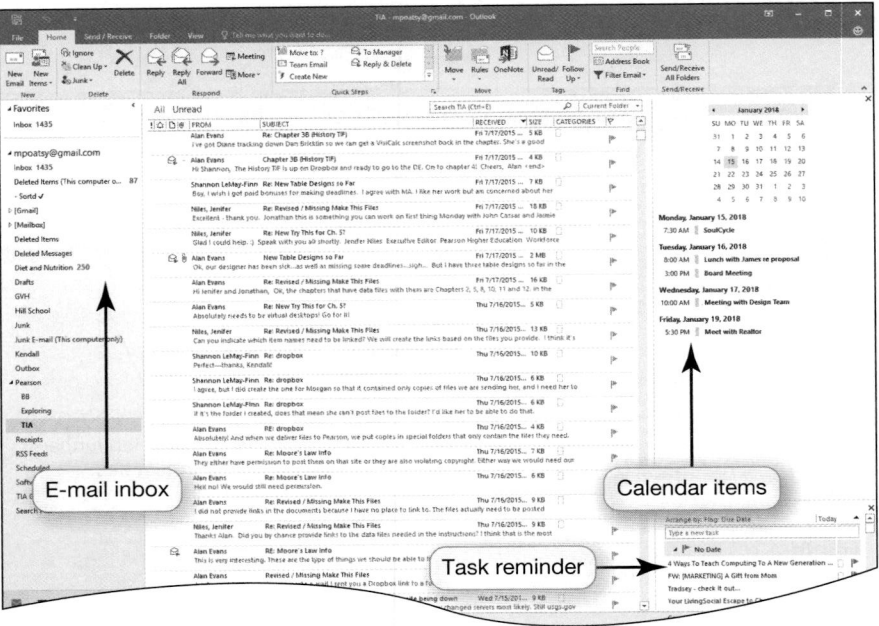

FIGURE 4.16 Microsoft Outlook includes common PIM features, such as a summary of appointments, a list of tasks, and e-mail messages. *(Outlook 2016, Windows 10, Courtesy Microsoft, Inc.)*

Personal Information Manager Software

How can software help me manage my e-mail, time, contact lists, and tasks? Most people need some form of **personal information manager (PIM) software** to help manage e-mail, contacts, calendars, and tasks in one place. Microsoft Outlook (see Figure 4.16) is a widely used PIM program. If you share a network at home or at work and are using the same PIM software as others on a common network, a PIM program simplifies sharing calendars and scheduling meetings.

Many web-based e-mail clients, such as Yahoo! and Google, also include coordinating calendar and contacts similar to those of Microsoft Outlook. Google's calendar and contacts sync with Outlook so you can access your Outlook calendar information by logging into Google. This gives you access to your schedule anywhere you have access to a computer and an Internet connection.

A wide variety of other to-do lists and simple organizers work with mobile and computing devices. For example, Toodledo (**toodledo.com**) is a free program that coordinates well with Microsoft Outlook, and OmniFocus (**omnifocus.com**) is a more full-featured option for Mac devices, including a slick interface for Apple Watch.

Productivity Software Features

What tools can help me work more efficiently with productivity software? Whether you're working on a word processing document, spreadsheet, database, or slide presentation, you can make use of several tools to increase your efficiency:

- A **wizard** walks you through the steps necessary to complete a task. At each step, the wizard asks you questions. Based on your responses, the wizard helps you complete that portion of the task. When you install software, you're often guided by a wizard.

- A **template** is a predesigned form. Templates are included in many productivity applications. They provide the basic structure for a particular kind of document, spreadsheet, database, or presentation. Templates can include specific page layout designs, formatting and styles relevant to that particular document, and automated tasks (macros).

- A **macro** is a small program that groups a series of commands so that they will run as a single command. Macros are best used to automate a routine task or a complex series of commands that must be run frequently. For example, a teacher may write a macro to sort the grades in her gradebook in descending order and to highlight grades that add up to less than a C average. Every time she adds the results of an assignment or a test, she can set up the macro to run through this series of steps.

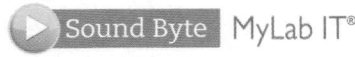

Programming for End Users

In this Sound Byte, you'll be guided through the creation of a macro in Microsoft Office. You'll learn how Office enables you to program with macros in order to customize and extend the capabilities it offers.

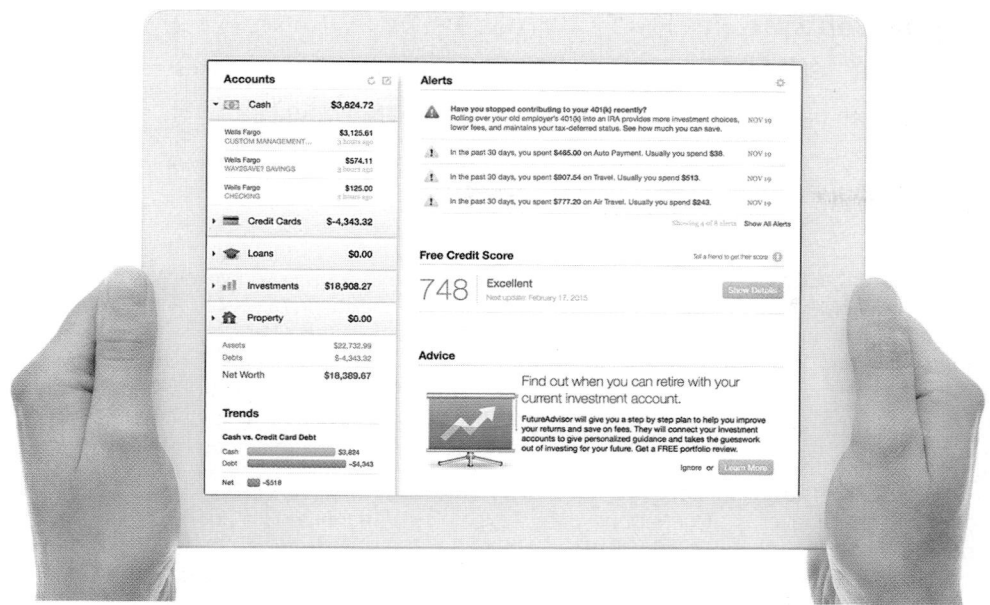

Figure 4.17 Mint (mint.com) is an online financial management tool. An extensive online community provides helpful tips and discussions with other people in similar situations. *(Reprinted with permission © Intuit Inc. All rights reserved.)*

Personal Financial Software

How can I use software to keep track of my finances? **Financial planning software** helps you manage your daily finances. Financial planning programs include electronic checkbook registers and automatic bill payment tools. With these features, you can make recurring monthly payments, such as rent or student loans, with automatically scheduled online payments. The software records all transactions, including online payments, in the checkbook register. In addition, you can assign categories to each transaction and then use these categories to create budgets and analyze your spending patterns.

Intuit's installed and web-based products, Quicken and Mint (**mint.com**), are the market leaders in financial planning software (see Figure 4.17). Both are great at tracking and analyzing your spending habits and at offering advice on how to better manage your finances. With either, you also can track your investment portfolio. With Mint, you can monitor and update your finances from any computer with a private and secure setting. You can also access Mint on a smartphone or tablet, so access to your financial information is always convenient. Mint also provides access to a network of other users with whom to exchange tips and advice.

What software can I use to prepare my taxes? **Tax preparation software**, such as Intuit TurboTax and H&R Block Tax Software, lets you prepare your state and federal taxes on your own. Both programs offer a complete set of tax forms and instructions, as well as videos that contain expert advice on how to complete each form. Each company also offers free web-based versions of federal forms and instructions. In addition, error-checking features are built into the programs to catch mistakes. These can help you file worry-free because they can also run a check for audit alerts, file your return electronically, and offer financial planning guidance to help you plan and manage your financial resources effectively in the following year (see Figure 4.18).

Figure 4.18 Tax preparation software lets you prepare and file your taxes on mobile devices. *(pkphotograhy/123RF)*

Some financial planning applications also coordinate with tax preparation software. Both Quicken and Mint, for example, integrate seamlessly with TurboTax, so you never have to go through your debit card statements and bills to find tax deductions, tax-related income, or expenses. Many banks and credit card companies also offer online services that download a detailed monthly statement into Quicken and Mint. Remember, however, that the tax code changes annually, so you must obtain an updated version of the software each year.

Business Software

Objective 4.8 *Summarize the types of software that large and small businesses use.*

Do businesses use different kinds of software than individuals? Many businesses rely on the types of software we've discussed so far in the chapter. However, specialized software is used in both large and small businesses.

Small Business Software

What kinds of software are helpful for small business owners? If you have a small business or a hobby that produces income, you know the importance of keeping good records and tracking your expenses and income. **Accounting software** helps small business owners manage their finances more efficiently by providing tools for tracking accounts receivable and accounts payable. In addition, these applications offer inventory management, payroll, and billing tools. Intuit QuickBooks is an example of an accounting application. It includes templates for invoices, statements, and financial reports so that small business owners can create common forms and reports.

If your business requires the need for newsletters, catalogs, annual reports, or other large, complicated publications, consider using **desktop publishing (DTP) software**. Although many word processing applications include some of the features that are hallmarks of desktop publishing, specialized DTP software, such as Adobe InDesign, allows professionals to design books and other publications that require complex layouts.

What software do I use to create a web page? **Web authoring software** allows even novices to design interesting and interactive web pages without knowing any HTML code. Web authoring applications often include wizards, templates, and reference materials to help novices complete most web authoring tasks. More experienced users can take advantage of these applications' advanced features to make the web content current, interactive, and interesting. Adobe Dreamweaver is an installed program that both professionals and casual web page designers use. Squarespace is an online-based option that is full featured and easy to use.

Note that if you need to produce only the occasional web page, you'll find that many applications include features that let you convert your document into a web page. For example, in some Microsoft Office applications, you can choose to save a file as a web page.

Software for Large and Specialized Businesses

What types of software do large businesses use? An application exists for almost every aspect of business. There are specialized programs for project management software, customer relationship management (CRM), enterprise resource planning (ERP), e-commerce, marketing and sales, finance, point of sale, security, networking, data management, and human resources, to name just a few. Figure 4.19 lists many of the common types of business-related software. Some applications are tailored to the specific needs of a particular company or industry. Software designed for a specific industry, such as property management software for real estate professionals, is called **vertical market software**.

What software is used to make 3D models? Engineers use **computer-aided design (CAD)** programs such as Autodesk's AutoCAD to create automated designs, technical drawings, and 3D model visualizations. Here are some cool applications of CAD software:

- Architects use CAD software to build virtual models of their plans and readily visualize all aspects of design before actual construction.
- Engineers use CAD software to design everything from factory components to bridges. The 3D nature of these programs lets engineers rotate their models and adjust their designs if necessary, eliminating costly building errors.
- CAD software (and other 3D modeling software) is used to generate designs for objects that will be printed using 3D printers.
- The medical engineering community uses CAD software to create anatomically accurate solid models of the human body, developing medical implants quickly and accurately.

Figure 4.19 Common Types of Large Business-Related Software

Project Management

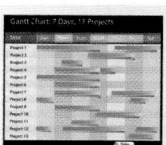

Creates scheduling charts to plan and track specific tasks and to coordinate resources

Customer Relationship Management (CRM)

Stores sales and client contact information in one central database

Enterprise Resource Planning (ERP)

Controls many "back office" operations and processing functions such as billing, production, inventory management, and human resources management

E-Commerce

Facilitates website creation and hosting services, shopping cart setup, and credit card–processing services

Computer-Aided Design (CAD)

Creates automated designs, technical drawings, and 3D model visualizations for architecture, automotive, aerospace, and medical engineering industries

Vertical Market

Addresses the needs of businesses in a specific industry or market such as the real estate, banking, and automotive industries

(Cacaroot/Fotolia; Maksym Yemelyanov/Fotolia; Spiral media/Fotolia; Khanisorn Chalermchan/123RF; Adimas/Fotolia; Nmedia/Shutterstock)

The list of CAD applications keeps growing as more and more industries realize the benefits CAD can bring to their product development and manufacturing processes.

What kind of software can be used for home or landscape planning? Many software packages enable users to plan the layout of homes and landscapes. A simple, web-based, fairly full-featured, and free 3D modeling application is Trimble's SketchUp Make. SketchUp Make (**sketchup.com**) lets you create a 3D image of your dream home (see Figure 4.20).

Figure 4.20 SketchUp Make is a free, web-based 3D modeling application that can be used for home and landscape design. (Shutterstock)

Need to Work as a Team? Try These Collaboration Tools

You're part of a group working together on a project and need to keep track of project goals and achievements, as well as communicate with your team members. What should you do? Consider using some of these collaboration tools:

- UberConference (**uberconference.com**) is an app that facilitates group conference calls. You can easily share your screen with others in the conference, add another person during the conference, record the conference, and mute noisy callers. You can see everyone who is on the call and even view their social networking profiles. The free version accommodates up to 10 callers.
- Slack (**slack.com**) is a messaging app that lets you organize your conversations into different channels. You can also transfer files, and links to cloud services like Google Drive and Dropbox. The files you link into the conversation are searchable along with your conversations. It runs on mobile apps as well as in a web browser so you can stay in touch anywhere you work.
- Trello (**trello.com**) is a visually oriented app used for managing projects. Unlike traditional project management apps, it features a board filled with lists, and each list is filled with cards representing tasks to be completed. It is easy to add checklists and due dates to cards as well as upload files to them. You can easily transfer cards between lists to show progress on various aspects of a project. You can invite as many people to your board as you want. You can then assign people immediately to cards to divide up work tasks. You can easily see an overview of your entire

project just by glancing at your Trello board. The free version of the app offers a very powerful feature set (see Figure 4.21).
- Scribblar (**scribblar.com**) is a multiuser whiteboard with live audio chat, which is great for holding virtual brainstorm sessions.

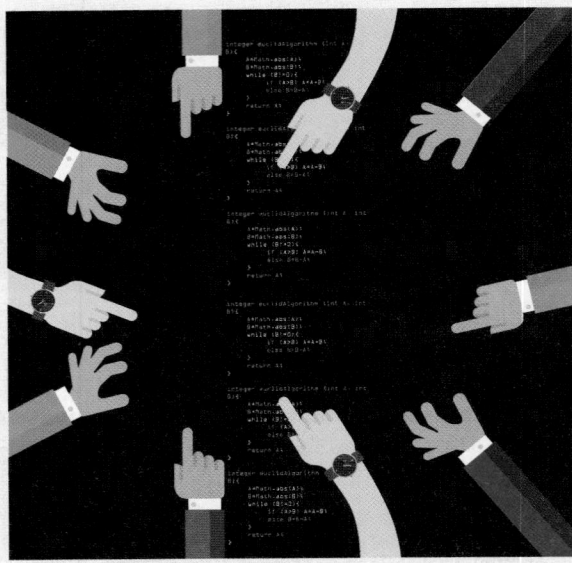

Figure 4.21 Collaboration tools make it easier to work effectively as a team. *(Bakhtiar Zein/Shutterstock)*

Multimedia and Educational Software

While many programs help you increase your productivity, there are also programs that entertain you with audio, video, and digital images and through games, animations, and movies. This section discusses multimedia and educational software, both for your mobile devices and for professional projects (see Figure 4.22).

Digital Multimedia Software

Objective 4.9 *Describe the uses and features of digital multimedia software.*

What is multimedia software? **Multimedia software** includes digital image- and video-editing software, digital audio software, and other specialty software required to produce computer games, animations, and movies (see Figure 4.22). Many mobile and desktop software programs allow everyone, from beginner to professional, to create animations, videos, audio clips and images.

What software enables you to take photographs and edit them? Mobile devices come with an installed camera app. These apps give you control over standard elements like the use of flash, filtering options, and useful modes like panorama or virtual 360 shots. By purchasing specialized camera apps, you can use additional features like the ability to create a video collage or apply selective focus.

Figure 4.22   There are many varieties of multimedia and educational software.

Editing is an important part of creating appealing photo images. Each camera app has editing features that remove red eye and adjust qualities like saturation, contrast, and hue. Specialized apps like Snapseed or Enlight let you do even more. You can merge images, add artistic effects like a pencil sketch look, or apply a filter to make the image look like a watercolor on canvas.

Professionals and advanced amateur photographers often use fully featured **image-editing desktop software** like Adobe Photoshop and Corel PaintShop Pro. A free alternative is Gimp (**gimp.org**), a download that has most of the features offered by the for-pay applications. Desktop photo-editing software offers sophisticated tools (see Figure 4.23) for tasks like layering and masking images (hiding parts of layers to create effects such as collages). Designers use these more sophisticated tools to create the enhanced digital images found commercially in logos and advertisements.

How do I organize all the photos I take? Each mobile operating system has a photo app that stores and sorts images by date, by location, and by tags. These apps can be taught the faces of people you know and then automatically identify and group photos by people. Some apps go further and let you search your photo collection by a term you supply. So searching on "food" will let you pull together all the photos you've taken of meals you've photographed.

You may want to consider moving your photos and videos off your mobile device and storing them in a cloud storage system. Each mobile OS is designed to work smoothly with a specific cloud system (Apple uses iCloud and Android devices automatically save to Google Photos), but you can use any cloud service you like. Tools like If This Then That (IFTTT) allow you to easily create recipes that will automatically backup your mobile images to Dropbox, for example. (To learn more about using If This Then That, see the Make This activity in Chapter 1.)

What software do I need to create and edit digital videos? The same camera apps that come preinstalled on mobile devices record video. They typically include features that let you record in slow motion, in fast motion, and in time lapse. While it's easy to upload videos directly to YouTube or Facebook unedited, you can use **digital video-editing software** to refine your videos. Although the most expensive products (such as Adobe Premiere Pro and Apple's Final

Figure 4.23 You can create collages of your favorite images using Google Photos. *(Google and the Google logo are registered trademarks of Google Inc., used with permission.)*

Figure 4.24 Video editing programs such as Apple iMovie make it easy to create and edit movies then share them on social media. *(Anthony Devlin/PA Wire/AP Images)*

Cut Pro) offer the widest range of special effects and tools, more moderately priced video-editing programs often have enough features to keep the casual user happy. Apple iMovie and VivaVideo, for example, both have intuitive drag-and-drop features and numerous templates and effects that make it simple to create professional-quality movies with little or no training (see Figure 4.24).

What kind of software should I use to create illustrations? Drawing (or illustration) software lets you create and edit 2D, line-based drawings. You can use it to create technical diagrams or original nonphotographic drawings and illustrations using software versions of traditional artistic tools such as pens, pencils, and paintbrushes. You also can drag geometric objects from a toolbar onto the canvas area to create images and can use paint bucket, eyedropper, and spray can tools to add color and special effects to the drawings.

Adobe Illustrator (see Figure 4.25) includes tools that let you create professional-quality creative and technical illustrations such as muscle structures in the human body. Its warping tool allows you to bend, stretch, and twist portions of your image or text. Because of its many tools and features, Illustrator is the preferred drawing software program of most graphic artists. Be sure to also explore Inkscape, an open source program similar to Illustrator. For touch-based devices there is a great collection of software for creating vector art. Apps like Paper and Concepts turn your tablet into a terrific tool for creating illustrations.

Digital Audio Software

Objective 4.10 *Describe the uses and features of digital audio software.*

What's the difference between all the digital audio file types on my computer? You probably have a variety of digital audio files stored on your computer, such as downloaded music files, audiobooks, and podcasts. These types of audio files have been compressed so they're more manageable to transfer to and from your computer and over the Internet. MP3, short for MPEG-1 Audio Layer 3, is a type of audio compression format and is the most common compressed digital format, but there are other compressed formats, such as AAC and WMA.

Figure 4.25 Adobe Illustrator is the industry standard for creating vector art and illustrations. *(Courtesy Adobe Systems, Inc.)*

You may also see uncompressed audio files on your computer, such as WAV or AIFF files. Uncompressed files—the files found on audio CDs, for example—have not had any data removed, so the quality is a perfect representation of the audio as it was recorded. Unfortunately, the file size is much larger than that of compressed files. Compressed formats remove data such as high frequencies that the human ear does not hear in order to make the files smaller and easier to download and store. MP3 format, for example, makes it possible to transfer and play back music on smartphones and other music players. A typical CD stores between 10 and 15 songs in uncompressed format, but with files in MP3 format, the same CD can store between 100 and 180 songs. The smaller file size not only lets you store and play music in less space but also allows quick and easy distribution over the Internet. Ogg Vorbis (or just Ogg) is a free, open source audio compression format alternative to MP3. Some say that Ogg produces a better sound quality than MP3.

What do I use to create my own audio files? Many digital audio applications let you create and record your own audio files. **Digital audio workstation software (DAWs)** lets you create individual tracks to build songs or soundtracks with virtual instruments, voice recorders, synthesizers, and special audio effects, and these will end up as uncompressed MIDI (Musical Instrument Digital Interface) files. Examples of DAWs include Apple GarageBand and Ableton Live. You can use these programs to record audio from live sources as well, such as riffs from your electric guitar or vocals.

How do I edit audio files? **Audio-editing software** includes tools that make editing audio files as easy as editing text files. Software such as the open source Audacity (**audacity. sourceforge.net**) lets you perform basic editing tasks like cutting dead air space from the beginning or end of a song or clipping a portion from the middle. You can also add special sound effects, such as reverb or bass boost, and remove static or hiss from MP3 files. These applications support recording sound files from a microphone or any source you can connect through the input line of a sound card.

> **▶ Helpdesk** MyLab IT®
>
> **Choosing Software**
>
> In this Helpdesk, you'll play the role of a helpdesk staffer, fielding questions about the different kinds of multimedia software, educational and reference software, and entertainment software.

App Creation Software

Objective 4.11 *Describe the features of app creation software.*

I'm not a programmer but could I build my own mobile app? Yes, there are many types of **app creation software**, programming environments that can produce apps that run on various mobile devices. Many are approachable for beginners. MIT's App Inventor (which we use in the Make This exercises in this book) is an open source web application that makes it easy for beginners to create functional apps for Android devices (see Figure 4.26). Featuring a drag-and-drop interface, the application enables users to quickly begin developing powerful apps without actually knowing how to write program code.

Scratch is another MIT programming environment that facilitates the creation of interactive stories, games, and animations that you can then share with an online community. The programming interface of Scratch is somewhat similar to that of App Inventor. Many elementary schools use Scratch to introduce young children to the ideas behind computer programming.

Corona SDK (**coronalabs.com**) is a powerful, free programming environment that has been used to develop games and business apps. Corona comes with a large library of application programming interfaces (APIs) that can be used as building blocks to make writing computer code less time-consuming (although you'll actually have to learn the Lua programming language). The Composer GUI is a visual editor for Corona, which makes it even easier to create apps without doing as much actual coding. Corona supports all major platforms including iOS, Android, and Windows Phone.

Apple also has a powerful development environment for iOS, macOS, and watchOS, called Swift. Swift uses more concise code than some other programming environments. It has a feature that allows you to visually see the results of each line of code as you write it. Many professional developers like using Swift because the code works side-by-side with Objective-C, which is a major programming language used in many businesses.

To get started in Swift, download the Swift Playgrounds app. This is a fun set of puzzles, games, and challenges that guide you into the world of programming for iOS. Despite the power of the Swift environment, it's still very approachable for students.

I really just want to make video games. Is that a reasonable goal? Yes, video games represent an industry that generates billions in revenue each year, so designing and creating video games is a desirable career path. Professionally created video games involve artistic storytelling and design, as well as sophisticated programming. Major production houses such as Electronic Arts use applications not easily available to the casual home enthusiast. However, you can use the editors and game engines available for games such as EverQuest, Oblivion, and Unreal Tournament to create custom levels and characters to extend the game.

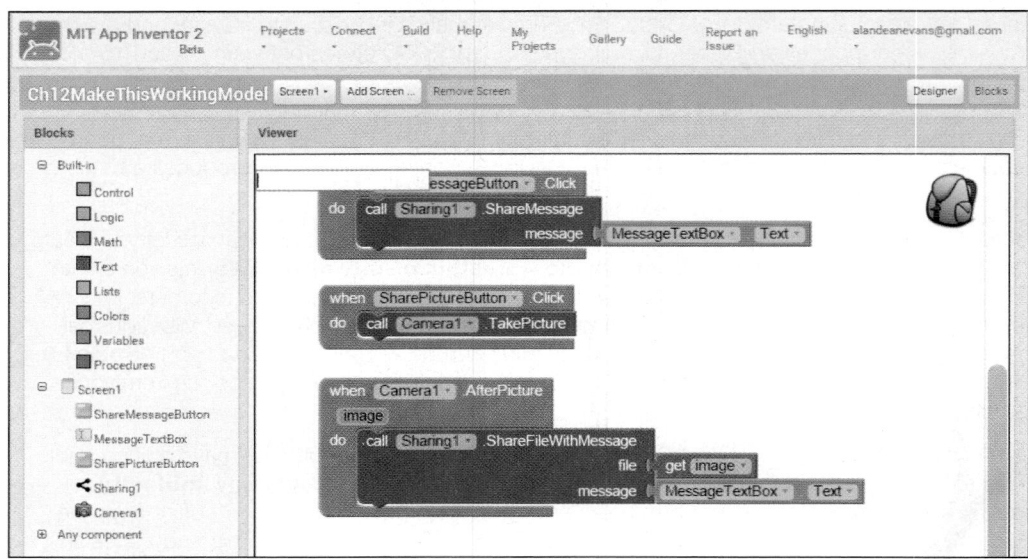

Figure 4.26 MIT's App Inventor is an open source web application that enables beginners to create apps. *(Copyright MIT, used with permission)*

Sometimes when you download software, especially open source software, you must choose a download location. Each location in the list is a mirror site. A *mirror site* is a copy of a website or set of files hosted at a remote location. Software developers sometimes use geographically distributed mirror sites so that users can choose the mirror site closest to their location to expedite the download time. Mirror sites are also used as backups, so if a server goes down for some reason, users can access the software from a different site, ensuring the software is always accessible. Developers also use mirror sites to help offset issues associated with a sudden influx of traffic that would otherwise overload a single server.

If you want to try your hand at creating your own video games right now at home, multimedia applications such as Unity and RPG Maker provide the tools you need to explore game design and creation. The program GameMaker (**yoyogames.com**) is a free product that lets you build a game without any programming; you drag and drop key elements of the new game creation into place. Alice (**alice.org**) is another free environment to check out; it lets you easily create 3D animations and simple games.

Educational and Reference Software

Objective 4.12   *Categorize educational and reference software and explain their features.*

What fun educational and reference software should I check out? If you want to learn more about a subject, you can turn to the web for many instructional videos and documents. But sometimes, it's best to use software for more complete or detailed instructions. Educational and reference software is available to help you master, study, design, create, or plan. As shown in Figure 4.27, there are software products that teach new skills such as typing, languages, cooking, and playing the guitar.

Figure 4.27   Educational and Reference Software: A Sample of What's Available

Test Preparation

Designed to improve your performance on standardized tests

Simulation

Allows you to experience a real situation through a virtual environment

Instructional

Designed to teach you almost anything from playing a musical instrument to learning a language or cooking

Trip Planning

Generates maps and provides driving instructions; some incorporate hotel, restaurant, and other trip information

Home Design/Improvement

Provides 2D or 3D templates and images to let you better visualize indoor and outdoor remodeling projects and landscaping ideas

Course Management

Web-based software system that creates a virtual learning experience, including course materials, tests, and discussion boards

Brain Training

Features games and activities to exercise your brain to improve your memory, processing speed, attention, and multitasking capabilities

Genealogy

Helps chart the relationships between family members through multiple generations

(Aduchinootonosama/123RF; Greg Pease/The Image Bank/Getty Images; iQoncept/Shutterstock; Almagami/Shutterstock; Zack C/Shutterstock; Scott Maxwell LuMaxArt/Shutterstock; Julien tromeur/Fotolia; Sasimoto/Fotolia)

Students who will be taking standardized tests like the SAT often use test preparation software. In addition, many computer and online brain-training games and programs are designed to improve the health and function of your brain. Lumosity (**lumosity.com**) is one such site that has a specific "workout" program that you can play on your PC or smartphone. Brain Age (**brainage.com**) has software for the Nintendo DS and is designed for players of all ages.

What types of programs are available to train people to use software or special machines? Many programs provide tutorials for popular computer applications (you may even use one in your course provided with MyLab IT). These programs use illustrated systematic instructions to guide users through unfamiliar skills in an environment that acts like the actual software, without the software actually being installed.

Some training programs, known as **simulation programs**, allow you to experience or control the software as if it were an actual event. Such simulation programs include commercial and military flight training, surgical instrument training, and machine operation training. One benefit of simulated training programs is that they safely allow you to experience potentially dangerous situations such as flying a helicopter during high winds. Consequently, users of these training programs are more likely to take risks and learn from their mistakes—something they could not afford to do in real life. Simulated training programs also help prevent costly errors. Should something go awry, the only cost of the error is restarting the simulation program.

Do I need special software to take courses online? Although some courses are run from an individually developed website, many online courses are run using **course management software** such as Blackboard, Moodle, and Canvas. In addition to traditional classroom tools such as calendars and grade books, these programs provide special areas for students and instructors to exchange ideas and information through chat rooms, discussion forums, and e-mail. In addition, collaboration tools such as whiteboards and desktop sharing facilitate virtual office hour sessions. Depending on the content and course materials, you may need a password or special plug-ins to view certain videos or demos.

Before moving on to the Chapter Review:

1. ▶ Watch Chapter Overview Video 4.2.
2. Then take the Check Your Understanding quiz.

Check Your Understanding // Review & Practice

For a quick review to see what you've learned so far, answer the following questions.

multiple choice

1. Examples of database software programs include
   a. Photoshop, InDesign, and Illustrator.
   b. Moodle, Blackboard, and Canvas.
   c. PowerPoint, Word, and Access.
   d. Oracle, MySQL, and Microsoft Access.

2. The software that allows you to edit digital images, videos, as well as digital audio is called
   a. multimedia software.
   b. encryption algorithms.
   c. distributed software.
   d. productivity software.

3. Which of the following is an uncompressed audio file format?
   a. WAV
   b. AAC
   c. MP3
   d. WMA

4. Which of the following software packages can be used to create mobile applications?
   a. LibreOffice
   b. App Engine
   c. Microsoft Windows
   d. App Inventor

5. Which of the following is considered a benefit of using simulation programs?
   a. They allow users to experience potentially dangerous situations without risk.
   b. They help to prevent costly errors.
   c. They allow users to experience or control the software as if it were an actual event.
   d. All of the above

 Go to **MyLab IT** to take an autograded version of the *Check Your Understanding* review and to find all media resources for the chapter.

TechBytes Weekly Go to TechBytes Weekly for current technology news and discussion questions!

4 Chapter Review

Summary

Part 1
Accessing, Using, and Managing Software

Learning Outcome 4.1 You will be able to explain the ways to access and use software and describe how to best manage your software.

Software Basics

Objective 4.1 *Compare application software and system software.*

- The term *software* refers to a set of instructions that tells the computer what to do.
- *Application software* is the software you use to do everyday tasks at home, school, and work. Microsoft Word and the Edge browser are examples of application software.
- *System software* is the software that helps run the computer and coordinates instructions between application software and the computer's hardware devices. System software includes the operating system and utility programs.

Objective 4.2 *Explain the differences between commercial software and open source software, and describe models for software distribution.*

- There are two basic types of software that you can install on your computer:
  - *Proprietary (or commercial) software* is software you buy.
  - *Open source software* is program code that is free and publicly available with few licensing and copyright restrictions. The code can be copied, distributed, or changed without the stringent copyright protections of software products you purchase.
- Software is delivered in three main ways:
  - *Local installation* means that software is installed on your computing device. These programs generally do not require an Internet connection to function.
  - *SaaS* (Software as a Service) is a model for delivery of software whereby the vendor hosts the software online and you access and use the software over the Internet without having to install it on your computer's hard drive.

- *Subscription* is a model whereby the user pays a fee to use the software. The software is downloaded and installed locally but is routinely updated by connection to the manufacturer's server.

Managing Your Software

Objective 4.3 *Explain the different options for purchasing software.*

- Although most software today is downloaded from the web, it can also be purchased at retail stores or directly from software developers.
- *Freeware* is copyrighted software that you can use for free.
- *Beta software* comprises apps that are still under development but are released to the public to gather feedback on design features and errors.

Objective 4.4 *Describe how to install and uninstall software.*

- When installing software, you're often given the choice between a full (typical) or custom installation. Before installing any software, it's important that you back up your system as well as create a *restore point*.
- When uninstalling software, it's best to use the uninstall feature that comes with the operating system. To uninstall an app in Windows 10, on the Start menu, right-click the app and select Uninstall.

Objective 4.5 *Explain the considerations around the decision to upgrade your software.*

- Before installing software on your computer, ensure that your system setup meets the *system requirements*. System requirements specify the minimum recommended standards for the operating system, processor, primary memory (RAM), and hard drive capacity.

Objective 4.6 *Explain how software licenses function.*

- A *software license*, also known as an *End User License Agreement (EULA)*, is an agreement between you, the user, and the software company that owns the software.

- When you purchase software, you're actually purchasing the license to use it and therefore must abide by the terms of the licensing agreement you accept when installing the program.
- Software licenses permit installation on a specific number of devices.

Part 2
Application Software

Learning Outcome 4.2   Describe the different types of application software used for productivity and multimedia.

 ### Productivity and Business Software

Objective 4.7 *Categorize the types of application software used to enhance productivity, and describe their uses and features.*

- *Productivity software* programs include the following:
  ○ Word processing: to create and edit written documents
  ○ Spreadsheet: to do calculations and numerical and what-if analyses easily
  ○ Presentation: to create slide presentations
  ○ Database: to store and organize data
  ○ Note-taking: to take notes and easily organize and search them
  ○ Personal information manager (PIM): to keep you organized by putting a calendar, address book, notepad, and to-do lists within your computer
- *Financial planning software* helps you manage your daily finances. Examples include Quicken and Mint.
- *Tax preparation software*, such as Intuit TurboTax and H&R Block Tax Software, lets you prepare your state and federal taxes on your own instead of hiring a professional.

Objective 4.8 *Summarize the types of software that large and small businesses use.*

- *Accounting software* helps small business owners manage their finances more efficiently by providing tools for tracking accounts receivable and accounts payable.
- *Desktop publishing (DTP) software* is used to create newsletters, catalogs, annual reports, or other large, complicated publications.
- *Web authoring software* allows even novices to design interesting and interactive web pages without knowing any HTML code.
- There are also specialized programs for project management software, customer relationship management (CRM), enterprise resource planning (ERP), e-commerce, marketing and sales, finance, point of sale, security, networking, data management, and human resources, to name just a few.

 ### Multimedia and Educational Software

Objective 4.9 *Describe the uses and features of digital multimedia software.*

- *Image-editing desktop software* includes tools for basic modifications to digital photos, such as removing red eye; modifying contrast, sharpness, and color casts; or removing scratches or rips from scanned images of old photos.
- *Digital video-editing software* is used to apply special effects, change the sequence of scenes, or combine separate video clips into one movie.
- *Drawing (or illustration) software* facilitates the creation and editing of 2-D, line-based drawings. It is used for the creation of technical diagrams and original non-photographic drawings.

Objective 4.10 *Describe the uses and features of digital audio software.*

- *Digital audio workstation software (DAWs)* lets you create individual tracks to build songs or soundtracks with virtual instruments, voice recorders, synthesizers, and special audio effects, and these will end up as uncompressed MIDI files.
- *Audio-editing software* includes tools that make editing audio files as easy as editing text files.

Objective 4.11 *Describe the features of app creation software.*

- *App creation software* provides professionals and novices alike with the ability to create their own apps.
- Although used widely in game development, app creation software can be used to create many other types of apps that have business applications.

Objective 4.12 *Categorize education and reference software, and explain their features.*

- *Test preparation software* is designed to improve your performance on standardized tests.
- *Simulation software* allows you to experience or control the software as if it were an actual event. Often this allows you to experience dangerous situations safely.

- *Course management software* creates a virtual learning experience for students and houses course materials, tests, and discussion boards.

 Be sure to check out **MyLab IT** for additional materials to help you review and learn. And don't forget to watch the Chapter Overview Videos. ▶

Key Terms

accounting software **148**

American Standard Code for Information Interchange **133**

app creation software **154**

application software **128**

audio-editing software **153**

base-10 number system (decimal notation) **132**

beta version **130**

binary number system (base-2 number system) **132**

computer-aided design (CAD) **148**

copyleft **134**

course management software **156**

custom installation **131**

database software **144**

desktop publishing (DTP) software **148**

digital audio workstation software (DAWs) **153**

digital video-editing software **151**

drawing (or illustration) software **152**

End User License Agreement (EULA) **134**

financial planning software **147**

freeware **130**

full installation **131**

hexadecimal notation **133**

image-editing desktop software **151**

locally installed software **128**

macro **146**

multimedia software **150**

number system **132**

open source software **128**

personal information manager (PIM) software **146**

presentation software **143**

productivity software **139**

program **128**

proprietary (commercial) software **128**

recovery drive **131**

restore point **131**

simulation programs **156**

software **128**

Software as a Service (SaaS) **128**

software license **134**

software piracy **135**

spreadsheet software **141**

subscription software **129**

system requirements **131**

system software **128**

tax preparation software **147**

template **146**

typical installation **131**

Unicode **133**

vertical market software **148**

web authoring software **148**

wizard **146**

word processing software **140**

Chapter Quiz // Assessment

For a quick review to see what you've learned, answer the following questions. Submit the quiz as requested by your instructor. If you are using **MyLab IT**, the quiz is also available there.

multiple choice

1. Software that includes programs to help you at work, home, and school is called
   a. application software.
   b. productivity software.
   c. Software as a Service (SaaS).
   d. open source software.

2. When a vendor hosts software on a website and you don't need to install the software on your device, this is known as:
   a. freeware.
   b. open source software.
   c. beta software.
   d. Software as a Service (SaaS).

3. Beta software is made available because
   a. new programmers have been hired.
   b. wireless networking must be added.
   c. a company is making an early release to test bugs.
   d. the company needs more profits.

4. When installing software you will often see a question that asks
   a. if you have paid for the software.
   b. what kind of mobile device you own.
   c. if you want a full (typical) or a custom installation.
   d. how long you plan on keeping the software.

5. The minimum recommended standards for the operating system, processor, primary memory (RAM), and storage capacity for certain software are called
   a. redistributing standards.
   b. system requirements.
   c. hardware.
   d. ministan.

6. Which of the following describes copyleft?
   a. terms enabling the redistribution of open source software
   b. terms enabling the redistribution of proprietary software
   c. political philosophy of the corporation
   d. terms restricting the use of leftover copies of software

7. Calendars, tasks, and e-mail can be found in which application?
   a. Excel
   b. Outlook
   c. OneNote
   d. Access

8. Which of the following is an example of financial management software?
   a. Lumosity
   b. AudioAcrobat
   c. Photos
   d. Quicken

9. Image-editing software allows you to
   a. compute complex formulas.
   b. remove red eye.
   c. create drafting blueprints.
   d. conduct product simulations.

10. Digital audio software can be used to
    a. compute complex formulae.
    b. compose songs or soundtracks with virtual instruments.
    c. create drafting blueprints.
    d. perform mathematical simulations.

true/false

_____ 1. Google Docs is an example of Software as a Service.

_____ 2. App creation software includes tools like Adobe Photoshop.

_____ 3. Course management software creates a virtual learning experience for students and houses course materials, tests, and discussion boards.

_____ 4. When you buy software, you can use it only as specified in the EULA.

_____ 5. A macro is a program released early to the public for testing and evaluation.

critical thinking

1. **Living on the Cloud**

   Cloud computing is becoming more popular, and many users are working from the cloud and not even realizing it. Open Google Docs and Office Online and compare these applications with an installed counterpart (e.g., Excel Online and Google Sheets versus Excel). What similarities and differences do you find between the online applications and the installed version? Envision a time when all software is web-based and describe how being totally on the cloud might be an advantage. What disadvantages might a cloud-based environment present?

2. **App Marketplaces and Software Piracy**

   Since app marketplaces work so well with mobile devices, it is difficult to find alternate sources of software. Will this end software piracy, since mobile apps are not distributed on DVDs and have to be purchased within one specified place? Should software for laptops and desktops be distributed only through app marketplaces to prevent piracy? What else might be done to combat software piracy? Explain your answers.

Team Time

Software for Startups

problem

You and your friends have decided to start Recycle Technology, a not-for-profit organization that would recycle and donate used computer equipment. In the first planning session, your group recognizes the need for certain software to help you with various parts of the business, such as tracking inventory, designing notices, mapping addresses for pickup and delivery, and soliciting residents by phone or e-mail about recycling events, to name a few.

task

Split your class into as many groups of four or five as possible. Make some groups responsible for locating free or web-based software solutions and other groups responsible for finding proprietary solutions. Another group could be responsible for finding mobile app solutions. The groups will present and compare results with each other at the end of the project.

process

1. Identify a team leader who will coordinate the project and record and present results.
2. Each team is to identify the various kinds of software that Recycle Technology needs. Consider software that will be needed for all the various tasks required to run the organization, such as communication, marketing, tracking, inventory management, and finance.
3. Create a detailed and organized list of required software applications. Depending on your team, you will specify either proprietary software or open source software.

conclusion

Most organizations require a variety of software to accomplish different tasks. Compare your results with those of other team members. Were there applications that you didn't think about, but that other members did? How expensive is it to ensure that even the smallest company has all the software required to carry out daily activities, or can the needs be met with free, open source products?

Ethics Project

Open Source Software

Ethical conduct is a stream of decisions you make all day long. In this exercise, you'll research and then role-play a complicated ethical situation. The role you play might or might not match your own personal beliefs, but your research and use of logic will enable you to represent the view assigned. An arbitrator will watch and comment on both sides of the arguments, and together, the team will agree on an ethical solution.

topic: proprietary software vs. open source software

Proprietary software has set restrictions on use and can be very expensive, whereas open source software is freely available to use as is or to change, improve, and redistribute. Open source software has become acceptable as a cost-effective alternative to proprietary software—so much so that it's reported that the increased adoption of open source software has caused a drop in revenue to the proprietary software industry. But determining which software to use involves more than just reviewing the IT budget.

research areas to consider

- Open source software
- Proprietary software
- Copyright licensing
- Open source development

process

1. Divide the class into teams.
2. Research the areas cited above and devise a scenario in which someone is a proponent for open source software but is being rebuffed by someone who feels that "you get what you pay for" and is a big proponent of using proprietary software.
3. Team members should write a summary that provides background information for their character—for example: open source proponent, proprietary developer, or arbitrator—and that details their character's behaviors, to set the stage for the role-playing event. Then, team members should create an outline to use during the role-playing event.
4. Team members should present their case to the class or submit a PowerPoint presentation for review by the rest of the class, along with the summary and resolution they developed.

conclusion

As technology becomes ever more prevalent and integrated into our lives, more and more ethical dilemmas will present themselves. Being able to understand and evaluate both sides of the argument, while responding in a personally or socially ethical manner, will be an important skill.

Analyzing Benchmark Data

You work for a design firm that uses many of the software applications in the Adobe Creative Suite, especially Photoshop, Illustrator, and InDesign. You have been asked to evaluate whether it would be worthwhile to upgrade the software to the latest version. In addition to reviewing any new or revised features, you also want to provide an analysis on any improvements in product efficiency and performance, so you have repeated doing the same skills with the current and new data and have recorded the results. Now you just need to analyze it.

You will use the following skills as you complete this activity:

- AutoFill Data
- Insert AVERAGE Function
- Add Borders
- Align and Wrap Text
- Apply Conditional Formatting
- Create Bar Chart

Instructions

1. Open *TIA_Ch4_Start* and save as **TIA_Ch4_LastFirst**.

2. In cell F1, type **Current Average**, and in cell J1, type **New Average**.

3. In cell F2, use the **AVERAGE function** to compute the average of range C2:E2. In cell J2, use the **AVERAGE function** to compute the average of range G2:I2.

4. Select **cell F2**, then drag the **Fill Handle** to cell F13. Select **cell J2**, then drag the **Fill Handle** to cell J13.

5. Select **range C2:J13**, then format the cell contents with **Number format with one decimal**.

6. Select **cell A2**, and **Merge and Center** across **cells A2:A5**. Then adjust the orientation of the text to **Rotate Text Up. Middle Align** cell contents and **Bold** text.

7. Use **Format Painter** to copy these formats to cell A6 and cell A10.

8. Select **range A2:J5**, then apply **Thick Outside Borders**. Repeat with **ranges A6:J9** and **A10:J13**.

9. Select **range F1:F13**, then apply **Thick Outside Borders**. Repeat with range J1:J13.

10. Select **range J2:J13**, then apply a **Conditional Format** that will format cells that are Less Than those cells in range F2:F13 with Green Fill and Dark Green Text.
    a. Hint: In the Format cells that are LESS THAN box, enter **=F2** (*not* F2). The rest of the cells in the range will update automatically.

11. Create a Clustered Bar Chart using ranges B1:B13, F1:F13, J1:J13.
    a. Hint: Hold down the **Ctrl button** as you select ranges F1:F13 and J1:J13.

12. Add the title **Benchmark Comparison: New and Current Versions of CS Software** to the Clustered Bar Chart, and add a Horizontal Axis title and type **Seconds**. Position and resize the chart so it fills range A16:J34.

13. Save the workbook and submit based on your instructor's directions.

System Software: The Operating System, Utility Programs, and File Management

 For a chapter overview, watch the Chapter Overview Videos.

PART 1

Understanding System Software

Learning Outcome 5.1 **You will be able to explain the types and functions of operating systems and explain the steps in the boot process.**

 Operating System Fundamentals 166

Objective 5.1   *Discuss the functions of the operating system.*

Objective 5.2   *Explain the most common operating systems for personal use.*

Objective 5.3   *Explain the different kinds of operating systems for machines, networks, and business.*

 What the Operating System Does 172

Objective 5.4   *Explain how the operating system provides a means for users to interact with the computer.*

Objective 5.5   *Explain how the operating system helps manage hardware such as the processor, memory, storage, and peripheral devices.*

Objective 5.6   *Explain how the operating system interacts with application software.*

Sound Byte: Using Windows Task Manager to Evaluate System Performance

 Starting Your Computer 177

Objective 5.7   *Discuss the process the operating system uses to start up the computer and how errors in the boot process are handled.*

Helpdesk: Starting the Computer: The Boot Process

PART 2

Using System Software

Learning Outcome 5.2 **You will be able to describe how to use system software, including the user interface, file management capabilities, and utility programs.**

 The Windows Interface 184

Objective 5.8   *Describe the main features of the Windows interface.*

 File Management 187

Objective 5.9   *Summarize how the operating system helps keep your computer organized and manages files and folders.*

Helpdesk: Organizing Your Computer: File Management

 Utility Programs 193

Objective 5.10   *Outline the tools used to enhance system productivity, back up files, and provide accessibility.*

Sound Byte: Hard Disk Anatomy

For the IT Simulation for this chapter, see MyLab IT.

MyLab IT   All media accompanying this chapter can be found here.

 Make: A Notification Alert on **page 183**

How Cool Is This?

Tony Stark built the Iron Man suit using a **hologram**. Princess Leia delivered her message to Obi-Wan Kenobi as a hologram. Now, thanks to Microsoft, you might be able to use holograms in your own home. What's a hologram? Holograms are **three-dimensional photographic images** that appear to be **freestanding images**. They are created using two two-dimensional images of the same object taken from different angles and superimposed to display what appears to the brain to be one image. Microsoft is incorporating this holographic technology with **HoloLens**. HoloLens are wireless lenses that will enable you to **interact freely with holograms**. What can you do with holograms? The possibilities are still being explored, but think of how you might interact with a touch-screen device, and then remove the need to physically touch the device. Instead, you'll interact with a holographic image. It might not be long before you're using holographic technology for your next project. *(Monkey Business Images/Shutterstock)*

Understanding System Software

Learning Outcome 5.1	You will be able to explain the types and functions of operating systems and explain the steps in the boot process.

As discussed in the previous chapter, your computer uses two basic types of software: application software and system software. *Application software* is the software you use to do everyday tasks at home and at work. *System software* is the set of programs that helps run the computer and coordinates instructions between application software and the computer's hardware devices. From the moment you turn on your computer to the time you shut it down, you're interacting with system software.

Operating System Fundamentals

Every computer, from smartphones to supercomputers, has an operating system. Even game consoles, cars, and some appliances have operating systems. The role of the operating system is critical; a computer can't operate without it.

Operating System Basics

Objective 5.1 *Discuss the functions of the operating system.*

What does the operating system do? System software consists of two primary types of programs: the *operating system* and *utility programs*. The **operating system (OS)** is a group of programs that controls how your computer functions. The operating system has three primary functions:

- It manages the computer's hardware, including the processor, memory, and storage devices, as well as peripheral devices such as the printer.
- It provides a consistent means for application software to work with the central processing unit (CPU).
- It is responsible for the management, scheduling, and coordination of tasks.

You interact with your OS through the **user interface**—the *desktop*, *icons*, and *menus* that let you communicate with your computer.

A **utility program** is a small program that performs many of the general housekeeping tasks for your computer, such as system maintenance and file compression. A set of utility programs is bundled with each OS, but you can also buy stand-alone utility programs that often provide more features. We'll discuss utility programs in more detail later in the chapter.

Are all operating systems alike? You're probably familiar with Microsoft **Windows** and **macOS**, the operating systems developed by Microsoft and Apple, respectively, but other operating systems exist. Laptops, tablet computers, and smartphones need operating systems designed to manage their smaller and condensed components, so mobile operating systems such as iOS were developed. However, as devices begin to converge in terms of functionality and operating systems become more powerful, developers such as Microsoft and Apple are making mobile and desktop operating systems that have similar functionality (such as macOS and iOS) or single operating systems (such as Windows 10) that can run on a variety of devices. Figure 5.1 lists some common operating systems.

When operating systems were originally developed, they were designed for a single user performing one task at a time (that is, they were *single-user, single-task operating systems*). However, modern operating systems allow a single user to **multitask**—to perform more than one process at a time. And operating systems such as Windows and macOS provide networking capabilities as well, essentially making them *multiuser, multitasking operating systems*.

Figure 5.1   Common Operating Systems

Operating System Name	Windows (Windows 10)	macOS	iOS	Android	Linux
Developed By	Microsoft	Apple	Apple	Google	Open source
Available On	Laptops, tablets, desktops, all-in-ones, smartphones	Laptops, desktops, all-in-ones	Tablets, iPhones, iPod touches	Smartphones, tablets	Laptops, desktops, tablets

(Top Photo Corporation/Alamy; Andrew Burton/Getty Images News/Getty Images; David Paul Morris/Bloomberg/Getty Images; Mtkang/Yay Media As/Alamy Stock Photo; Tibbbb/Fotolia)

Operating systems can be categorized by the type of device in which they're installed, such as robots and specialized equipment with built-in computers, mainframes and network computers, mobile devices, and personal computers. Next, we'll look at these different types of operating systems.

Operating Systems for Personal Use

Objective 5.2   *Explain the most common operating systems for personal use.*

What are the most popular operating systems for personal computers? Microsoft Windows, Apple macOS, and Linux (an open source OS) are the top three operating systems for personal computers. Although each OS has unique features, they share many features as well.

What common features are found in personal computer operating systems? All personal computer operating systems include a window-based interface with icons and other graphics that facilitate point-and-click commands. In addition, as we discuss later in this chapter, personal computer operating systems include many utilities, such as virus protection, file management, and system management tools, to help the computer run more efficiently. The most current versions of Windows and macOS also incorporate natural language search and assistance as well as virtual desktops. Although macOS doesn't have touchscreen capabilities like Windows, iOS offers this capability for iPhones and iPads.

What kind of OS do mobile devices use? Smartphones and tablets use a **mobile operating system**. Mobile operating systems include many features of personal computer operating systems but are modified to be more functional on smaller handheld devices. Today's mobile operating systems offer personal assistants with predictive search capabilities, the ability to use a wide variety of apps, a search engine, a camera, as well as texting and e-mail capabilities. Some even enable note-taking on their touch-screen displays. Mobile operating systems also support Bluetooth and Wi-Fi as standard as well as near field communication (NFC) for wireless transfers and mobile payments.

The main OS for Apple mobile devices is called iOS. Android is the mobile OS for devices designed by Google, Samsung, and other companies. **Windows 10,** although not as popular on smartphones, runs on all types of devices—smartphones, tablets, laptops, and desktops—though it can't run on Apple-specific devices.

Are any operating systems web-based? **Google Chrome OS** (see Figure 5.2), is a web-based OS. With the Chrome OS, very few files are installed on your computing device. Rather, the main functionality of the OS is provided through a web browser. Chrome OS is only available on certain devices called *Chromebooks* from Google's manufacturing partners. Chrome OS should not be confused with the Google Chrome browser. The browser is application software that can run on many different operating systems.

How do other operating systems use the "cloud"? Now that wireless Internet access has become more commonplace, operating systems have features that are tied to cloud computing. For example, using your Microsoft account, Windows 10 stores your settings so

Figure 5.2   The Google Chrome OS is web-based and has a very minimalist look. *(Google and the Google logo are registered trademarks of Google Inc., used with permission. Google Inc.)*

you can see your familiar desktop and applications on any device you log into. Moreover, you can access and store files online from OneDrive, Windows' cloud-based storage system. Similarly, macOS allows you to sign in to any Apple device with your Apple ID, which provides access to Apple's iCloud system. Both systems store your content online and automatically push it out to all your associated devices.

What is Linux? **Linux** is an open source OS designed for use on personal computers and web servers. Open source software is freely available for anyone to use or modify. Linux began in 1991 as a project of Finnish university student Linus Torvalds. It has since been tweaked by scores of programmers as part of the Free Software Foundation GNU Project (**gnu.org**).

Linux has a reputation as a stable OS that is not subject to crashes or failures. Because the code is open and available to anyone, Linux can be modified or updated quickly by hundreds of programmers around the world.

Where can I get Linux? Linux is available for download in various packages known as **distributions** or **distros**. Distros include the underlying Linux kernel (the code that provides Linux's basic functionality) and special modifications to the OS, and may also include additional open source software (such as Apache OpenOffice). A good place to start researching distros is **distrowatch.com**. This site tracks Linux distros and provides helpful tips for beginners on choosing one.

Does it matter what OS is on my computer? Computers and other devices usually come with an OS already installed. An OS is designed to run on specific CPUs. CPUs have different designs, which can require modifying the OS software to allow it to communicate properly with each CPU. The combination of an OS and a specific processor is referred to as a computer's **platform**.

Most application software is OS dependent. You need to make sure you get the correct version of the application software for your OS. For example, Microsoft offers two separate versions of Office: Microsoft Office 2016 for Mac and Microsoft Office 2016 for Windows. In addition, apps are OS specific. Although you might find the same app in Google Play, the Windows store, or the Apple store, you must download and install the app from the specific store that works with your mobile device's OS.

Can I have more than one OS on my computer? Many people run more than one OS on their computer for a variety of reasons. Windows and Linux can run on most of the hardware being sold today. And, although macOS and iOS run only on Apple equipment—MacBooks, iPads, iPhones, and iPods—Apple devices can support Windows and Linux as well. Your choice of an OS in this case is mostly a matter of price and personal preference. For example, many Mac users install Windows or Linux on their computers to take advantage of Windows-based programs. A standard utility included in macOS called Boot Camp lets you boot into either Windows or macOS. And if you want to run both macOS and Windows at the same time, you can create "virtual drives" using virtualization software such as Parallels or VMware Fusion.

Bits&Bytes · Why Isn't Everyone Using Linux?

Proprietary software such as Windows and macOS is developed by corporations and sold for profit. Open source software, such as Linux, is free, and because users have access to the specific code, they can make any changes they want. In fact, the community of open source software users responds to bugs and problems so quickly that the program is relatively bug-free.

So, if an OS such as Linux is free and relatively stable, why do proprietary OSs, which users must pay for, have such a huge market share? One reason is that corporations and individuals have grown accustomed to having technical support. It's almost impossible to provide technical support for open source software because anyone can modify it. However, some proprietary forms of Linux do provide support. Red Hat offers a free, open source OS called Fedora. In addition, Red Hat has modified the original Linux source code and markets a version, Red Hat Enterprise Linux, as a proprietary program. Purchasers of Red Hat Enterprise Linux receive a warranty and technical support.

In Windows, you can create a separate section of your hard drive (called a *partition*) and install Linux on it while leaving your original Windows installation untouched. After installing Linux, when your computer starts, you're offered a choice of which OS to use.

When should I update my OS? The decision to update to the newest features of your OS depends on which OS you're using. Previously, an update decision for Microsoft and Apple users would be based on whether users wanted to install the newest version because of any significantly different or enticing features offered in the new version. However, with the release of Windows 10, Microsoft now delivers automatic OS updates, including new features, apps, and patches, as necessary, and there are no plans to release any new versions. This means that you shouldn't expect there to be a Windows 11, 12, or anything else.

Apple continues to release periodic new versions of its desktop and mobile operating systems. The newest versions as of this writing are iOS 10 and macOS High Sierra. (Note that Apple has rebranded its desktop OS from OS X to macOS.) These versions for Apple mobile and desktop OSs are pushed to the user, and the user can decide to install the updates. Updates to the Android mobile OS get pushed to users but at the discretion of the device manufacturer. For example, when a new version of Android is released, Samsung may release it immediately for the Galaxy smartphone but may not release it for another Galaxy device, whereas LG may choose to delay the release for all its smartphones. If having the latest update on your Android device is important to you, check the device-maker for its update policy before you buy your next device.

Operating Systems for Machinery, Networks, and Business

Objective 5.3   *Explain the different kinds of operating systems for machines, networks, and business.*

Why do machines with built-in computers need an OS? Machinery that performs a repetitive series of specific tasks in an exact amount of time requires a **real-time operating system (RTOS)**. Also referred to as *embedded systems*, RTOSs require minimal user interaction. This type of OS is a program with a specific purpose, and it must guarantee certain response times for particular computing tasks; otherwise, the machine is useless. The programs are written specifically for the needs of the devices and their functions. Devices that must perform regimented tasks or record precise results, such as measurement instruments found in the scientific, defense, and aerospace industries, require RTOSs. Examples include digital storage oscilloscopes and the Mars Reconnaissance Orbiter.

You also encounter RTOSs every day in devices such as point of sale systems, fuel-injection systems in car engines, automobile "infotainment" systems, as well as some common appliances. RTOSs are also found in many types of robotic equipment, such as the robotic cameras television stations use that glide across a suspended cable system to record sports events from many angles (see Figure 5.3).

What kind of operating systems do networks use? A **multiuser operating system** (or **network operating system**) lets more than one user access the computer system at a time by handling and prioritizing requests from multiple users. Networks (groups of computers connected to each other so that they can communicate and share resources) need a multiuser OS because

Figure 5.3 Real time operating systems can be found in devices such as TV sky cameras, cars, medical equipment, and point of sale machines. *(John Pyle/Cal Sport Media/Newscom; Syda Productions/Shutterstock; Elfstrom/ E+/Getty Images; Sergiy Zavgorodny/Shutterstock)*

many users simultaneously access the server (the computer that manages network resources such as printing and communications). The latest versions of Windows and macOS can be considered network operating systems because they enable multiple computers in a home or small business to connect to each other and share resources.

In larger networks, a more robust network OS is required to support workstations and the sharing of databases, applications, files, and printers among multiple computers in the network. This network OS is installed on servers and manages all user requests. For example, on a network where users share a printer, the network OS ensures that the printer prints only one document at a time in the order the requests were made. Examples of network operating systems include Windows Server, Linux, and UNIX.

What is UNIX? UNIX is a multiuser, multitasking OS that's used as a network OS, although it can also be found on PCs. Developed in 1969 by Ken Thompson and Dennis Ritchie of AT&T's Bell Labs, the UNIX code was initially not proprietary—in other words, no company owned it. Rather, any programmer was allowed to use the code and modify it to meet his or her needs. UNIX is now a brand that belongs to the company The Open Group, but any vendor that meets the testing requirements and pays a fee can use the UNIX name. Individual vendors then modify the UNIX code to run specifically on their hardware.

What other kinds of computers require a multiuser OS? Mainframes and supercomputers also require multiuser operating systems. Mainframes routinely support hundreds or thousands of users at time, and supercomputers are often accessed by multiple people working on complex calculations. Examples of mainframe operating systems include UNIX, Linux on System z, and IBM's z/OS, whereas the vast majority of supercomputers use Linux.

Ethics in IT

The Great Debate: Is macOS Safer Than Windows?

Many Mac users feel they're impervious to viruses and malware (software that can disable or interfere with the use of a device) because those are "just Windows problems." This means that Mac users often run their computers with only the basic protection provided by Apple in its operating system software. Are Mac users wild risk takers, or are they actually safe from hackers? As with many issues, it's a little bit of both.

Threats Are Out There

Windows users have been bombarded by malware and virus attacks for decades. When you bought your last Windows device, it invariably came with a trial version of third-party antivirus/anti-malware software. Running a Windows computer without antivirus/anti-malware software is just asking for trouble.

However, over the past several years, the attacks against Macs have also increased. Why weren't Macs attacked frequently in the past? Most malware is designed to steal sensitive information such as credit card numbers. When thieves expend the time, money, and effort to develop malware, they want to ensure that it targets the largest population of potential victims. As macOS gains market share, Mac users are becoming a larger group of potential targets. In fact, in many affluent nations, Mac ownership has reached 20% of the market. And since Macs tend to cost more than Windows machines, it can be argued that Mac users may have more disposable income than other computer buyers. And wealthy people always make attractive targets for thieves.

But Isn't macOS Safer Than Windows by Design?

To a certain extent, this is true. macOS does have certain design features that tend to prevent the installation and spread of malware. Apple has also designed current versions of iOS and macOS to prevent the installation of unapproved software (i.e., software not available on Apple's approved online outlets like the App Store). In addition, apps sold on the App Store are required to be designed using the access control technology known as *App Sandbox*.

When most software programs or apps are running, they have broad latitude to interact with the OS. Usually, they have all the rights that the user has over the OS. So if hackers can design an exploit that takes advantage of a security flaw in an app, they can potentially gain extensive control over the computer using the access that the user has to the OS. As noted, Apple requires all approved apps to be "sandboxed." When an app is sandboxed, the developer defines what the app needs to do in order to interact with the OS. The OS then grants only those specific rights and privileges to the app and nothing else. By doing this, it severely limits what hackers can do in an OS if they breach the security of an app. It's like being in a high-walled sandbox (or playpen) as a child. You can play within the confines of your space, but you can't make mischief outside certain limits.

So I'll Buy a Mac and Be Safe Forever, Right?

Although it's more difficult to design exploits for macOS and iOS, it's not impossible. And a great deal of cybercrime relies on social engineering techniques like those used in scareware scams. *Scareware* is software designed to make it seem as if there is something wrong with your computer. The author of the scareware program then "persuades" you to buy a solution to the problem, acquiring your credit card number in the process. Scareware victims can be both Mac and PC users, so even if you own a Mac, you need to be aware of such scams and avoid falling prey to them (see Chapter 9).

The Solution: Extra Security Precautions

The current versions of macOS, iOS, and Windows all include some level of security tools and precautions. Here are a few things you should do to protect yourself:

1. **Make sure your software is set to download and install updates automatically.** As OS developers discover holes in their software's security, they provide updates to repair these problems.
2. **Use third-party antivirus/anti-malware software (even on a Mac).** Although no product will detect 100% of malware, detecting some is better than detecting none.
3. **Be aware of social engineering techniques.** Use vigilance when surfing the Internet so you don't fall prey to scams.

So, no OS is 100% safe. But if you're informed and proceed with caution, you can avoid a lot of schemes perpetrated by hackers and thieves.

What the Operating System Does

As shown in Figure 5.4, the OS is like an orchestra's conductor. It coordinates and directs the flow of data and information through the computer system. In this section, we explore the operations of the OS in detail.

The User Interface

Objective 5.4   *Explain how the operating system provides a means for users to interact with the computer.*

How does the OS control how I interact with my computer? The OS provides a user interface that lets you interact with the computer. The first personal computers used *Microsoft Disk Operating System* (*MS-DOS* or just *DOS*), which had a command-driven interface, as shown in Figure 5.5a. A **command-driven interface** is one in which you enter commands to communicate

Manages computer
hardware and peripherals

Provides a consistent interaction
between applications and the CPU

Provides a user interface

The Operating System

Manages memory and storage

Manages the processor

Figure 5.4 The OS is the orchestra conductor of your computer, coordinating its many activities and devices. *(StockPhotosArt/Shutterstock; Ra2studio/ Shutterstock; Shutterstock; Pearson; Ragnarock/Shutterstock; Arno van Dulmen/Shutterstock; Pearson Education, Inc. Shcherbakov Roman/Shutterstock)* with the computer system. The DOS commands were not always easy to understand; as a result, the interface proved to be too complicated for the average user. Therefore, PCs were used primarily in business and by professional computer operators.

The command-driven interface was later improved by incorporating a menu-driven interface, as shown in Figure 5.5b. A **menu-driven interface** is one in which you choose commands from menus displayed on the screen. Menu-driven interfaces eliminated the need for users to know every command because they could select most of the commonly used commands from a menu. However, they were still not easy enough for most people to use.

What kind of interface do operating systems use today? Current computer and mobile operating systems such as Microsoft Windows and macOS use a **graphical user interface** or **GUI** (pronounced "gooey"). Unlike command- and menu-driven interfaces, GUIs display graphics and use the point-and-click technology of the mouse and cursor (or human finger), making them much more user-friendly.

Linux-based operating systems do not have a single default GUI interface. Instead, users are free to choose among many commercially available and free interfaces, such as GNOME and KDE, each of which provides a different look and feel.

Hardware Coordination

Objective 5.5 *Explain how the operating system helps manage hardware such as the processor, memory, storage, and peripheral devices.*

How does the OS manage the processor? When you use your computer, you're usually asking the processor, or CPU, to perform several tasks at once. For example, you might be creating a PowerPoint presentation, printing a Word document, and watching a show on Hulu—all at the same time, or at least what appears to be at the same time. Although the CPU is powerful, it still needs the OS to arrange the execution of all these activities in a systematic way.

To do so, the OS assigns a slice of its time to each activity that requires the processor's attention. The OS must then switch among different processes billions of times a second to make it appear that everything is happening seamlessly. Otherwise, you wouldn't be able to watch a movie and print at the same time without experiencing delays in the process.

How exactly does the OS coordinate all the activities? When you create and print a document in Word while also watching a Blu-ray movie, for example, many different devices in the computer are involved, including your keyboard, mouse, Blu-ray drive, and printer. Every keystroke, every mouse click (or touch on the screen), and each signal to the printer and from the Blu-ray drive creates an action, or **event**, in the respective device (keyboard, mouse, Blu-ray drive, or printer) to which the OS responds.

Sometimes these events occur sequentially (such as when you type characters one at a time), but other events involve two or more devices working concurrently (such as the printer printing while you type and watch a movie). Although it looks as though all the devices are working at the same time, the OS in fact switches back and forth among processes, controlling the timing of events on which the processor works.

For example, assume you're typing and want to print a document. When you tell your computer to print your document, the printer generates a unique signal called an **interrupt** that tells the OS that it's in need of immediate attention. Every device has its own type of interrupt, which is associated with an **interrupt handler**, a special numerical code that prioritizes the requests. These requests are placed in the interrupt table in the computer's primary memory (RAM). The OS processes the task assigned a higher priority before processing a task assigned a lower priority. This is called **preemptive multitasking**.

In our example, when the OS receives the interrupt from the printer, it suspends the CPU's typing activity and Blu-ray activity and puts a "memo" in a special location in RAM called a *stack*. The memo is a reminder of what the CPU was doing before it started to work on the printer request. The CPU then retrieves the printer request from the interrupt table and begins to process it. On completion of the printer request, the CPU goes back to the stack, retrieves the memo it placed about the keystroke or Blu-ray activity, and returns to that task until it is interrupted again, in a very quick and seamless fashion, as shown in Figure 5.6.

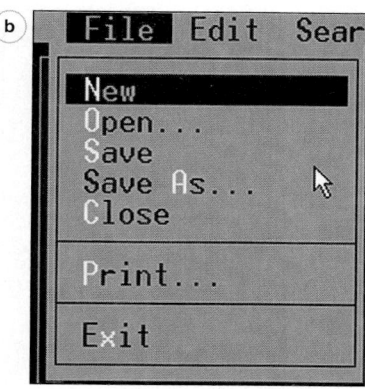

Figure 5.5 (a) A command-driven interface. (b) A menu-driven interface. *(Windows 10, Microsoft Corporation)*

Sound Byte MyLab IT®

Using Windows Task Manager to Evaluate System Performance

In this Sound Byte, you'll learn how to use the utilities provided by Windows to evaluate system performance. You'll also learn about shareware utilities that expand on the capabilities the Task Manager utility provides.

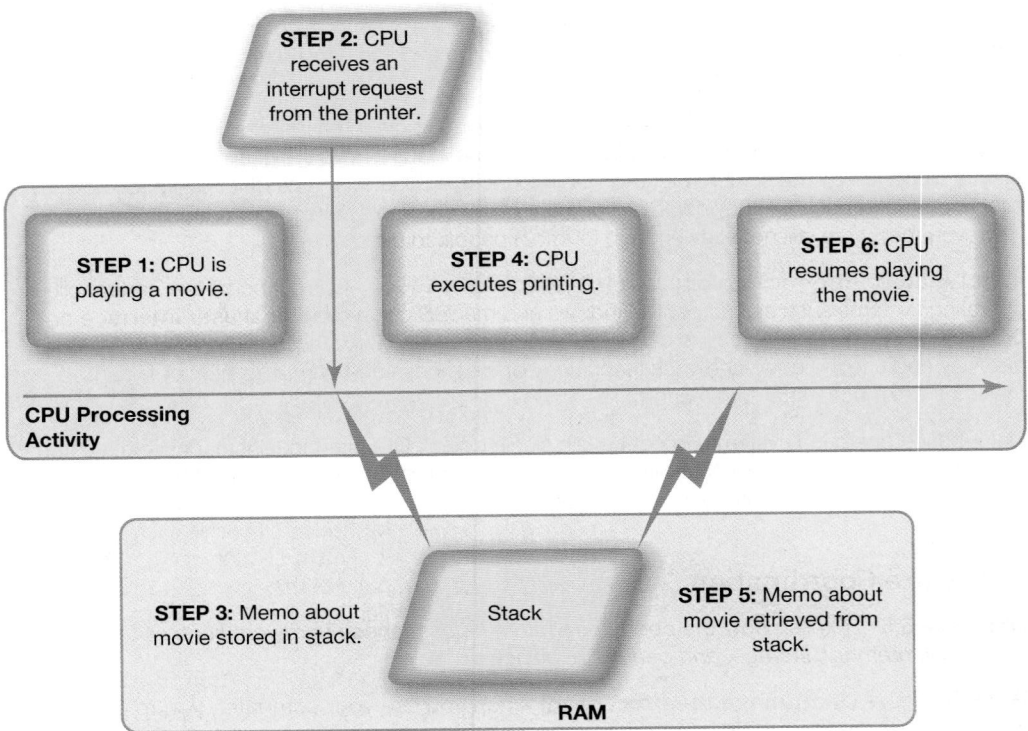

Figure 5.6 How Preemptive Multitasking Works

STEP 2: CPU receives an interrupt request from the printer.

STEP 1: CPU is playing a movie.

STEP 4: CPU executes printing.

STEP 6: CPU resumes playing the movie.

CPU Processing Activity

STEP 3: Memo about movie stored in stack.

Stack

STEP 5: Memo about movie retrieved from stack.

RAM

What happens if more than one document is waiting to be printed? The OS also coordinates multiple activities for printers and other peripheral devices. When the processor receives a request to send information to the printer, it first checks with the OS to ensure that the printer is not already in use. If it is, the OS puts the request in another temporary storage area in RAM, called the *buffer*. The request then waits in the buffer until the **spooler**, a program that helps coordinate all print jobs currently being sent to the printer, indicates the printer is available. If more than one print job is waiting, a line (or *queue*) is formed so that the printer can process the requests in order.

Memory and Storage Management

How does the OS manage the computer's memory? As the OS coordinates the activities of the processor, it uses RAM as a temporary storage area for instructions and data the processor needs. The processor then accesses these instructions and data from RAM when it's ready to process them. The OS is, therefore, responsible for coordinating the space allocations in RAM to ensure there is enough space for all the pending instructions and data. The OS then clears the items from RAM when the processor no longer needs them.

What happens if the applications I'm using require more RAM than what's installed? RAM has limited capacity. As you add and upgrade software and increase your usage of the computer system, you might find that the amount of RAM you have is no longer sufficient for your needs. When there isn't enough RAM for the OS to store the required data and instructions, the OS borrows from the more spacious hard drive. This process of optimizing RAM storage by borrowing hard drive space is called **virtual memory**. As shown in Figure 5.7, when more RAM is needed, the OS swaps out from RAM the data or instructions that haven't recently been used and moves them to a temporary storage area on the hard drive called the **swap file** (or **page file**). If the data or instructions in the swap file are needed later, the OS swaps them back into active RAM and replaces them in the hard drive's swap file with less active data or instructions. This process of swapping is known as **paging**.

Can I ever run out of virtual memory? Only a portion of the hard drive is allocated to virtual memory. You can manually change this setting to increase the amount of hard drive space allocated, but eventually your computer will become sluggish as it is forced to page more often. This condition of excessive paging is called **thrashing**. The solution to this problem is to increase the amount of RAM in your computer, if there is excess capacity available, so that it won't be necessary for it to send data and instructions to virtual memory.

How does the OS manage storage? If it weren't for the OS, the files and applications you save to the hard drive and other storage locations would be an unorganized mess. Fortunately, the OS

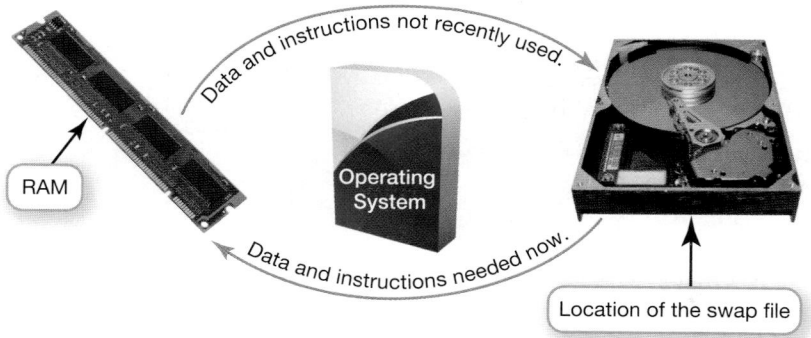

Figure 5.7 Virtual memory borrows excess storage capacity from the hard drive when there isn't enough capacity in RAM. *(Shutterstock; Pearson Education, Inc.; Ragnarock/Shutterstock)*

Location of the swap file

has a file management system that keeps track of the name and location of each file you save and the programs you install. We'll talk more about file management later in this chapter.

Hardware and Peripheral Device Management

How does the OS manage the hardware and peripheral devices? Each device attached to your computer comes with a special program called a **device driver** that facilitates communication between the device and the OS. Because the OS must be able to communicate with every device in the computer system, the device driver translates the device's specialized commands into commands the OS can understand, and vice versa. Devices wouldn't function without the proper device drivers because the OS wouldn't know how to communicate with them.

Do I always need to install drivers? Today, most devices, such as flash drives, mice, keyboards, and digital cameras, come with the driver already installed in Windows. The devices whose drivers are included in Windows are called Plug and Play devices. **Plug and Play (PnP)** is a software and hardware standard designed to facilitate the installation of new hardware in PCs by including in the OS the drivers these devices need in order to run. Because the OS includes this software, incorporating a new device into your computer system seems automatic. PnP lets you plug a new device into your computer, turn it on, and immediately play (use) the device (see Figure 5.8).

What happens if the device is not PnP? Sometimes you may have a device, such as a printer, that does not have a driver incorporated into Windows. You'll then be prompted to install or download from the Internet the driver required for that device. If you obtain a device secondhand without the device driver, or if you're required to update the device driver, you can often download the necessary driver from the manufacturer's website. You can also go to websites such as DriverZone (**driverzone.com**) to locate drivers.

Can I damage my system by installing a device driver? Occasionally, when you install a driver, your system may become unstable. Programs may stop responding, certain actions may cause a crash, or the device or the entire system may stop working. Although this is uncommon, it can happen. Fortunately, to remedy the problem, Windows has a Roll Back Driver feature that removes a newly installed driver and replaces it with the last one that worked (see Figure 5.9).

Figure 5.8 A Windows message showing a successful driver installation the first time an external hard drive was connected to the computer. *(Windows 8.1, Microsoft Corporation)*

Software Application Coordination

Objective 5.6 *Explain how the operating system interacts with application software.*

How does the OS help application software run on the computer? Every computer program, no matter what its type or manufacturer, needs to interact with the CPU using computer code. For programs to work with the CPU, they must contain code the CPU recognizes. Rather than having the same blocks of code for similar procedures in each program, the OS includes the blocks of code—each called an **application programming interface (API)**—that application software needs in order to interact with the CPU. Microsoft DirectX, for example, is a group of multimedia APIs built into the Windows OS that improves graphics and sounds when you're playing games or watching videos on your PC.

What are the advantages of using APIs? To create applications that can communicate with the OS, software programmers need only refer to the API code blocks when they write an application. They don't need to include the entire code sequence. APIs not only prevent redundancies in software code but also make it easier for software developers to respond to changes in the OS. Software companies also take advantage of APIs to ensure applications in software suites (such as Microsoft Office) have a similar interface and functionality. And since these applications share common APIs, data exchange is facilitated between two programs, such as inserting a chart from Excel into a Word document.

Figure 5.9 The Roll Back Driver feature in Windows removes a newly installed driver and replaces it with the last one that worked.
> To access Device Manager, right-click the **Start** button and select **Device Manager**. To display the device's property dialog box, double-click on a device. Click the **Driver** tab. (Windows 10, Microsoft Corporation)

Trends In IT   Are Personal Computers Becoming More Human?

Watch nearly any sci-fi movie or show and you'll see that making computers more human-like has long been a dream. Now, that dream is becoming a reality with advances in the field of artificial intelligence. For example, IBM's artificial intelligence supercomputer Watson was put to the test in a *Jeopardy* challenge and beat two of the show's greatest human champions. Although we've grown to expect great processing capabilities from computers, the *Jeopardy* challenge was different. Watson, like its human competitors, needed to discern specific pieces of data from complex questions (or answers) in the *Jeopardy* game. Computers hadn't been capable of processing these types of complex situations previously.

What's behind Watson's abilities? The computer's ability to generate answers from complex questions is a matter of synthesizing large amounts of unstructured data with natural language processing and machine learning. **Natural language processing** is a field of artificial intelligence that uses software to analyze, understand, and generate human languages naturally, enabling users to communicate with computers as if they were humans. **Machine learning** is another form of artificial intelligence that provides computers with the ability to learn without being explicitly programmed. In other words, machine learning enables computer programs (much like human brains) to grow and adapt when exposed to new data. Machine learning uses data to detect patterns and adjust programmed actions accordingly.

Familiar systems are beginning to use these advanced forms of artificial intelligence. Facebook, for example, personalizes News Feeds based on how users react to posts. Modern operating systems now incorporate personal digital assistants (Siri, Cortana, and Google Now) to facilitate searches using voice commands. Amazon's Echo is a stand-alone device that uses natural language processing to receive and respond to voice commands. In doing so, Echo can coordinate smart-home devices, fire up playlists, or read your daily to-do list. The Watson technology is also being leveraged to discern personalities from Twitter posts and to translate multi-language conversations in real time.

Google has made great advances in using machine learning with photo recognition. A program called PlaNet is able to recognize where a photo was taken just by the details in the photo. Obviously, it's easy to determine the location of photos that include the Golden Gate Bridge or Wrigley Field, but PlaNet is able to determine the location of photos without such distinctive landmarks, such as an image of an open field or a random tree-lined street, with relative accuracy. If you want to challenge yourself to a similar task, visit GeoGuessr (**geoguessr.com**) and you'll quickly realize how difficult a task this is (see Figure 5.10).

While PlaNet is still in its infancy, Google currently uses natural language processing to enable you to search your stored photos based on characteristics. For example, typing "my photos of birds" brings up all the images from your Google photos that contain an image of a bird—without you having to previously tag the image. Finding images based on a characteristic, such as "tree" or "bird," is a conceptual task that computers haven't been able to handle before. The next step, however, goes further, using facial recognition to bring up photos of "Uncle Ted" or "grandpa." With this type of intelligence built into computers, the futuristic visions of sci-fi are not so futuristic anymore.

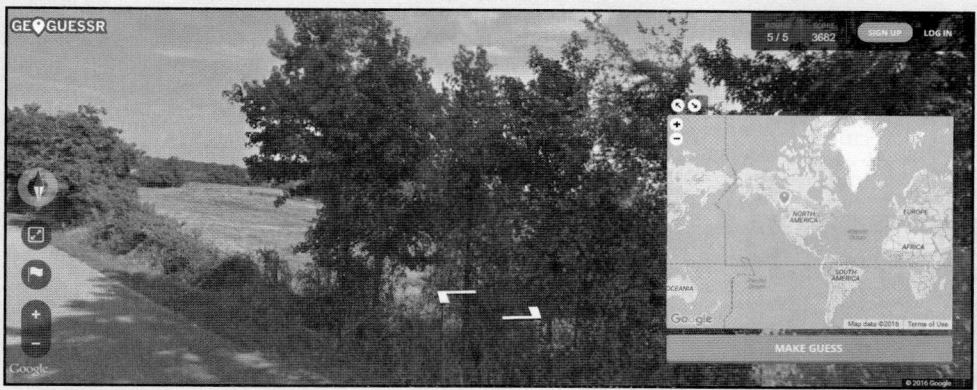

Figure 5.10 Can you guess the location of this photo? Google is creating a program to do just that. You can try your hand at how hard this is by playing GeoGuessr. (*Google and the Google logo are registered trademarks of Google Inc., used with permission.*)

Starting Your Computer

Many things happen quickly between the time you turn on your computer and the time it's ready for you to start using it. As we discussed earlier, data and instructions, including the OS, are stored in RAM while your computer is on. When you turn off your computer, RAM is wiped clean of all its data, including the OS. How does the computer know what to do when you turn it on if there is nothing in RAM? It runs through a *boot process*, a special start-up procedure that loads the OS into RAM.

The Boot Process

Objective 5.7 *Discuss the process the operating system uses to start up the computer and how errors in the boot process are handled.*

What are the steps involved in the boot process? As illustrated in Figure 5.11, the **boot process** consists of four basic steps. The term *boot*, from *bootstrap loader* (a small program used to start a larger program), alludes to the straps of leather, called *bootstraps*, that people used to use to help them pull on their boots. This is also the source of the expression "pull yourself up by your bootstraps." Let's look at each step of the boot process in detail.

Step 1: Activating BIOS

What's the first thing that happens after I turn on my computer? In the first step of the boot process, the CPU activates the **basic input/output system (BIOS)**. BIOS is a program that manages the exchange of data between the OS and all the input and output devices attached to the system. BIOS is also responsible for loading the OS into RAM from its permanent location on the hard drive. BIOS itself is stored on a read-only memory (ROM) chip on the motherboard. Unlike data stored in RAM, data stored in ROM is permanent and is not erased when the power is turned off.

CPU

ROM chip

STEP 1: CPU activates BIOS.
- Basic input/output system
- Stored permanently in ROM

STEP 2: Power-on self-test (POST).
- Tests components of the computer
- Compares results with configuration information in CMOS

STEP 3: Load OS to RAM.
- OS loaded from hard drive
- Kernel is *memory resident*

STEP 4: Configuration and customization settings checked and Start screen displays.

Figure 5.11 The Boot Process *(Ragnarock/Shutterstock; Arno van Dulmen/Shutterstock; Windows 10, Microsoft Corporation)*

Step 2: Performing the Power-On Self-Test

How does the computer determine whether the hardware is working properly? The first job BIOS performs is to ensure that essential peripheral devices are attached and operational—a process called the **power-on self-test (POST)**. The BIOS compares the results of the POST with the various hardware configurations permanently stored in CMOS (pronounced "see-moss"). CMOS, which stands for *complementary metal-oxide semiconductor*, is a special kind of memory that uses almost no power. A small battery provides enough power so that the CMOS contents won't be lost after the computer is turned off. CMOS contains information about the system's memory, types of disk drives, and other essential input and output hardware components. If the results of the POST compare favorably with the hardware configurations stored in CMOS, the boot process continues.

Step 3: Loading the OS

How does the OS get loaded into RAM? Next, BIOS goes through a preconfigured list of devices in its search for the drive that contains the **system files**, the main files of the OS. When the system files are located, they load into RAM.

Once the system files are loaded into RAM, the **kernel** (or **supervisor program**) is loaded. The kernel is the essential component of the OS. It's responsible for managing the processor and all other components of the computer system. Because it stays in RAM the entire time your computer is powered on, the kernel is said to be *memory resident*. Other, less critical, parts of the OS stay on the hard drive and are copied over to RAM on an as-needed basis so that RAM is managed more efficiently. These programs are referred to as *nonresident*. Once the kernel is loaded, the OS takes over control of the computer's functions.

Step 4: Checking Further Configurations and Customizations

Is that it? Finally, the OS checks the registry for the configuration of other system components. The **registry** contains all the different configurations (settings) used by the OS and by other applications. It contains the customized settings you put into place, such as mouse speed, as well as instructions as to which programs should be loaded first.

How do I know if the boot process is successful? The entire boot process takes only a few minutes to complete. If the entire system is checked out and loaded properly, the process completes by displaying the lock screen. After logging in, the computer system is now ready to accept your first command.

Why do I sometimes need to enter a login name and password at the end of the boot process? The verification of your login name and password is called **authentication**. The authentication process blocks unauthorized users from entering the system. You may have your home computer set up for authentication, especially if you have multiple users accessing it. All large networked environments, like your college, require user authentication for access.

On a Windows 10 computer, after your computer has completely booted up, you are brought to the lock screen where you are to log into your **Microsoft account**. Your Microsoft account is a combination of an e-mail address and a password. Because configuration settings are stored online and associated with a particular Microsoft account, your settings will load onto any computer you sign into. Additionally, it is easy for multiple people to share any Windows 10 computer and have access to their individual settings and preferences.

Handling Errors in the Boot Process

What should I do if my computer doesn't boot properly? Sometimes during the boot process, BIOS skips a device (such as a keyboard) or improperly identifies it. Your only indication that this problem has occurred is that the device won't respond after the system has been booted. When this or other problems occur during the boot process, try one of the following suggestions:

- Sometimes, something simple goes awry during the boot process, so the problem might be resolved by simply powering the computer off and powering it back on again.
- If you've recently installed new software or hardware, try uninstalling it. (Make sure you uninstall through *Apps & features* in System Settings to remove the software.) If the problem no longer occurs when rebooting, you can reinstall the device or software.
- Try accessing the Windows Advanced Options Menu (accessible by pressing the F8 key during the boot process). If Windows detects a problem in the boot process, it will add Last Known Good Configuration to the Windows Advanced Options Menu. Every time your computer boots successfully, a configuration of the boot process is saved. When you choose to boot with the Last Known Good Configuration, the OS starts your computer by using the registry information that was saved during the last successful shut down.
- Try resetting your computer (in Update & Security Settings).

What happens when a PC is "reset"? Sometimes Windows does not boot properly or the system does not respond properly. You may even see messages related to "fatal exceptions." **Reset this PC** is a utility program in Windows 10 that attempts to diagnose and fix errors in your Windows system files that are causing your computer to behave improperly (see Figure 5.12). When a PC is reset, the following occurs:

- Your data files (documents, music, videos, etc.) and personalization settings are not removed or changed.
- Apps that you have downloaded from the Windows Store are kept intact.
- Apps that you have downloaded from the Internet or installed from DVDs will be removed from your PC. Therefore, you'll need to reinstall them after the reset.

Helpdesk MyLab IT®

Starting the Computer: The Boot Process

In this Helpdesk, you'll play the role of a helpdesk staffer, fielding questions about how the operating system helps the computer start up.

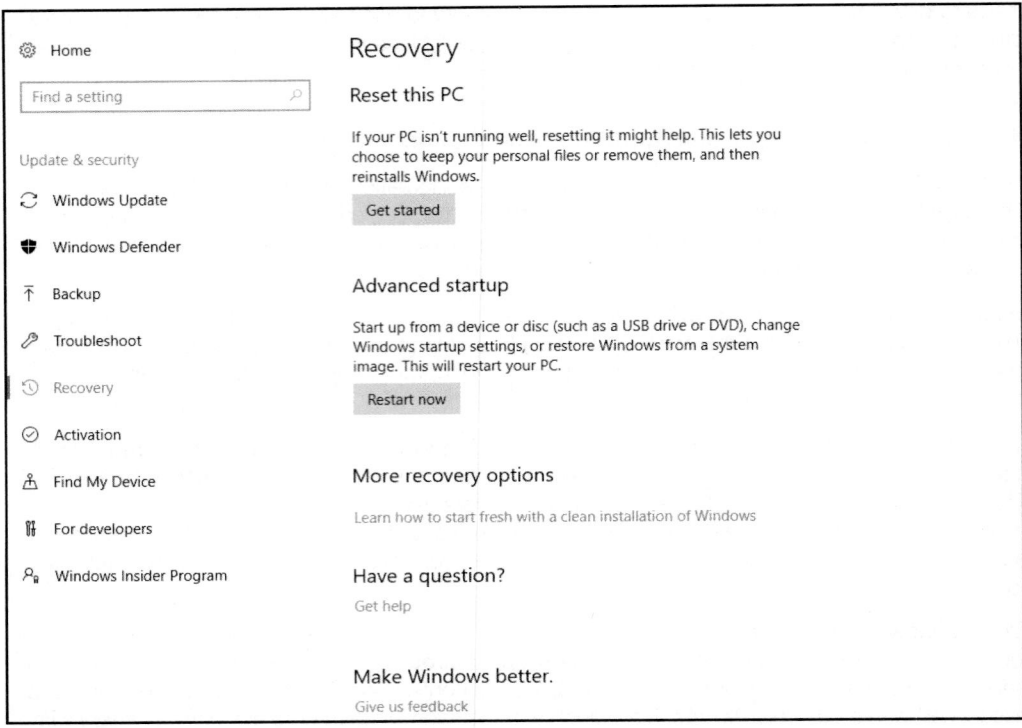

Figure 5.12 The Recovery control in Windows 10 provides access to the Reset this PC option.
*> To access the Recovery control, from the Start menu, click **Settings**, then click **Update & security**. On the Update & security screen, select **Recovery**. (Windows 10, Microsoft Corporation)*

It's recommended that you back up your PC prior to resetting it as a precautionary measure. Finally, if all other attempts to fix your computer fail, try *Go back to an earlier build* to revert to a past configuration. System Recovery is covered in more detail later in this chapter.

Before moving on to Part 2:

1. ▶ Watch Chapter Overview Video 5.1.
2. Then take the Check Your Understanding quiz.

Check Your Understanding // Review & Practice

For a quick review to see what you've learned so far, answer the following questions.

multiple choice

1. Which is NOT an example of a mobile operating system?
   a. iOS
   b. Windows 10
   c. Android
   d. macOS

2. You're most likely to find an RTOS
   a. on an iPad.
   b. in a robotic camera.
   c. on a supercomputer.
   d. on a mainframe.

3. Operating systems that have windows and icons have which type of user interface?
   a. command-driven
   b. menu-driven
   c. graphical user
   d. magnetic tape–based

4. The OS can optimize RAM storage by using
   a. virtual memory.
   b. thrashing.
   c. an interrupt handler.
   d. a spooler.

5. The blocks of code that are needed for programs to work with the CPU are called
   a. application device managers.
   b. application programming interface.
   c. application project interface.
   d. none of the above.

 Go to **MyLab IT** to take an autograded version of the *Check Your Understanding* review and to find all media resources for the chapter.

TechBytes Weekly Go to TechBytes Weekly for current technology news and discussion questions!

Try This

Using Virtual Desktops in Windows 10

Virtual desktops are a great way to organize your working space into different displays when you're multitasking between projects, job and school, or just work and entertainment. This exercise will walk you through the process of organizing your files into virtual desktops. For more step-by-step instructions, watch the Try This video.

Step 1 Click **Task View** on the taskbar to bring up the Task View interface. This interface consists of a display area that shows large thumbnails of all open windows running on your system. If you haven't created any virtual desktops, this is all you'll see. To organize open windows into specific groups, you need to create virtual desktops.

Step 2 While in Task View, click **+New desktop** in the lower right corner. This adds another virtual desktop, Desktop 2.

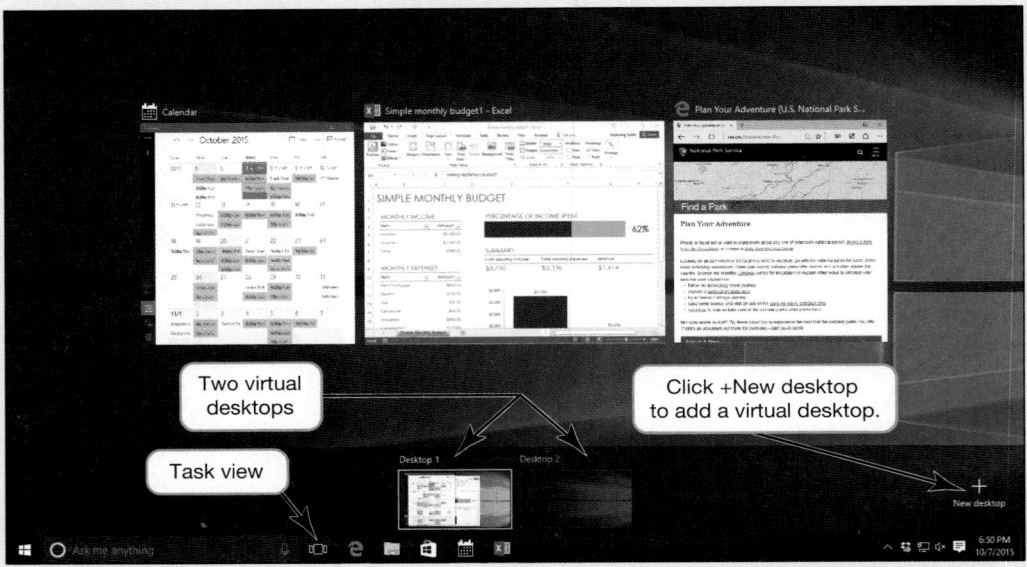

Two virtual desktops

Task view

Click +New desktop to add a virtual desktop.

(Windows 10, Microsoft Corporation)

Step 3 To move programs from Desktop 1 to the newly created Desktop 2, click **Task View**, then click and drag any window to Desktop 2. Alternatively, you can right-click a window, select **Move to**, and then select **Desktop 2**. While in Task View, when you hover the mouse over the desktop thumbnail, all open windows in that desktop display.

Step 4 To move between desktops, press **Ctrl + Windows key + an arrow key**, or open Task View and click the desired desktop to switch. To delete desktops, click **Task View**, point to the thumbnail of the desktop you want to delete, and then click the **(X)** that displays above the desktop thumbnail.

Make: A Notification Alert

Does your app need to communicate with or provide feedback to the user? With the Notifier component of **App Inventor**, you can make your program generate message boxes or ask for a response from the user.

In this exercise, you'll use the Notifier component of **App Inventor** to show a message box, post a user choice with two buttons for response, or post an alert. Your apps can now use more of the features of the Android operating system to communicate!

The Notifier component allows you to communicate with alerts, message boxes, and text choice popups within your mobile app.

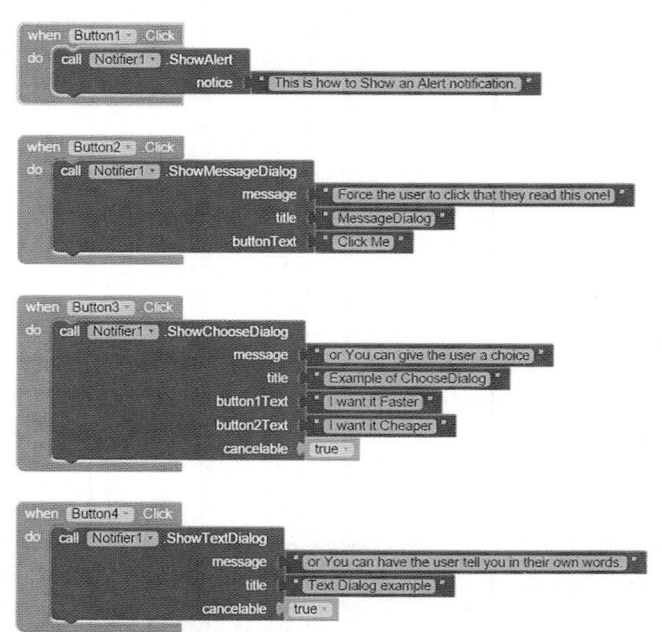

(Copyright MIT, used with permission)

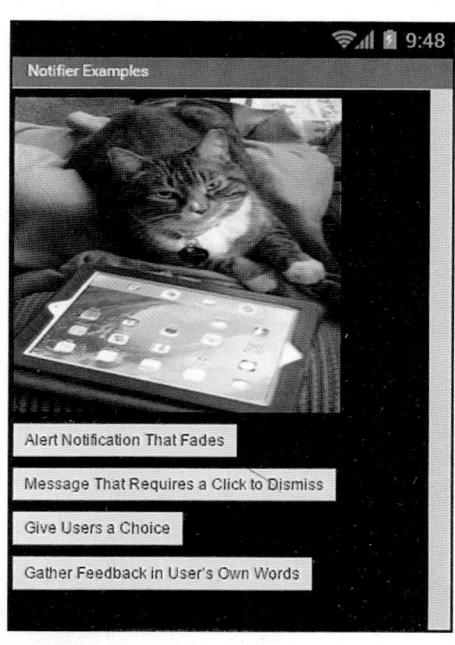

(Copyright MIT, used with permission)

For the instructions for this exercise, go to MyLab IT.

Using System Software

Learning Outcome 5.2   You will be able to describe how to use system software, including the user interface, file management capabilities, and utility programs.

Now that you know how system software works, let's explore how specific operating systems and their tools function.

The Windows Interface

As noted earlier, one of the functions of the operating system is to provide a user interface that lets you communicate with your computer. As was explained earlier, today's operating systems use a graphical user interface. We describe the Windows 10 user interface in this section, but it's very similar to the user interfaces for the macOS and Linux operating systems.

Using Windows 10

Objective 5.8   *Describe the main features of the Windows interface.*

What are the main features of the Windows 10 desktop? After logging into your Microsoft account by entering or confirming your e-mail address and entering a password, you're brought to the primary working area: the **desktop**. At the bottom of the Windows 10 desktop is the **taskbar**, which displays open and favorite applications for easy access. You can point to an icon to preview windows of open files or programs, or move your mouse over a thumbnail to preview a full-screen image. You can also right-click an icon to view a Jump List—a list of the most recently or commonly used files or commands for that application.

How do I find and open applications? The **Start menu** provides access to all applications and apps installed on your device as well as access to settings and power options. You open the Start menu by clicking the Windows icon (or Start button) on the far left side of the taskbar or by pressing the Windows key on the keyboard.

The Start menu is divided into two sections (see Figure 5.13). The right side has block tiles that provide easy access to your most frequently used software and Windows apps (such as Weather, Mail,

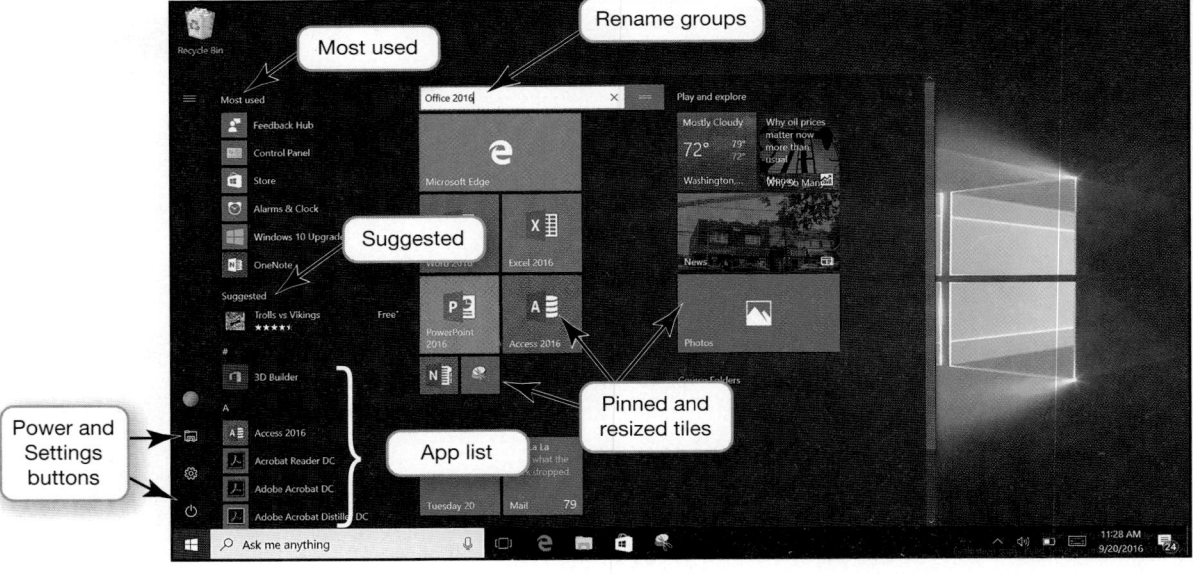

Figure 5.13 The Windows 10 Start menu provides access to your most used programs and apps. You can customize the Start menu by adding, resizing, and grouping tiles. *(Windows 10, Microsoft Corporation)*

and Photos). In addition to programs, tiles can represent files and folders. If there are more tiles on the Start menu than displayed, a scroll bar becomes available. The left side of the Start menu provides access to your most used programs as well as to File Explorer, Pictures, Settings, Power, and a list of all the installed apps and programs on your computer.

Can I modify the Start menu? You can customize the Start menu to meet your needs (refer to Figure 5.13). It's easy to add, remove, resize, move, and group application tiles on the Start menu. You can choose which applications are tiles on the Start menu through a process called **pinning**. Just right-click any application in the app list or in the Most used list, and chose Pin to Start.

Once on the Start menu, a tile can be resized by right-clicking the tile, pointing to Resize, and then selecting the desired size. Most apps can be sized to Small, Medium, Wide, and Large, although some are limited to only Small or Medium. You can rearrange apps on the Start menu by dragging them to a new location. You can also arrange several tiles near each other to create a group. Point to the top of the group to display a name box where you can type a group name. If there is a tile on the Start menu you don't need, just right-click it (or touch and hold), and select Unpin from Start.

You can also customize the left section of the Start menu. Right-click any app in the Most used section to get Pin to Start, More, and Uninstall options. If you click on More, Pin to taskbar and other options that vary by app appear. Just under Most used, you may see a Suggested Apps section that displays apps from the Windows store that might be of interest to you. If you don't want to see these suggestions, go to Personalization in Settings, click Start, and turn off *Occasionally show suggestions in Start*. You can also determine which folders display on the left side of the Start menu. The default is File Explorer and Settings, but there are others to choose from, including Music, Pictures, or Documents.

Because of the potential for customization, the Start menu on your computer will most likely be different from your friend's Start menu. However, because your Windows 10 settings and preferences are saved in your Microsoft account, you'll see your own personal settings, preferences, and applications reflected on the Start menu when you log on to any Windows 10 computer.

How can I change the appearance of my desktop and lock screen? You can also personalize the desktop and lock screen (the screen where you enter a password to resume using your computer) to suit your tastes. For example, you can choose to have a picture, a slide show, or a single color display on the desktop and lock screen. You can also determine whether you'd like other information to display on the lock screen, such as the weather, time, or your e-mail or calendar. Choosing a theme sets a color and font scheme for your entire system.

How can I see more than one window on my screen at a time? Windows 7 introduced "snapping" windows: fixing open programs into place on either the left or the right side of the screen, to easily display two apps at the same time. Windows 10 goes a bit further with more snapping options. Once you snap a window into place, thumbnails of all the other windows display. Clicking any thumbnail will snap that window into place. You can also snap windows to the corners, thus having up to four windows displayed at the same time.

How can I see open windows and quickly move between them? A new feature on the Windows 10 taskbar is Task View, which allows you to view all the tasks you're working on in one glance. To see all open windows at once, click Task View on the taskbar. This is similar to using Alt+Tab.

Can I group my open programs and windows into task-specific groups? When faced with situations in which you're working with multiple documents for multiple projects, it might be easier to group the sets of documents together for each project and just switch between projects. You can do that now in Windows 10 with a feature called **virtual desktops**, which allow you to organize groups of windows into different displays (see Figure 5.14). For example, you can put in

Bits&Bytes   The Snipping Tool

The Snipping Tool is a Windows tool found in the Windows Accessories folder in the apps list that enables you to capture, or snip, a screen display so that you can save, annotate, or share it. You can capture screen elements as a rectangular snip, free-form snip, window snip, or as a full-screen snip. You can also draw on or annotate the screen capture, save it, or send it to others. In Windows 10, a new feature to the Snipping Tool is a delay timer so you can pause the capturing process for up to five seconds to set up screenshots of dialog boxes, menus, or other features that don't stay displayed when you initiate the Snipping Tool.

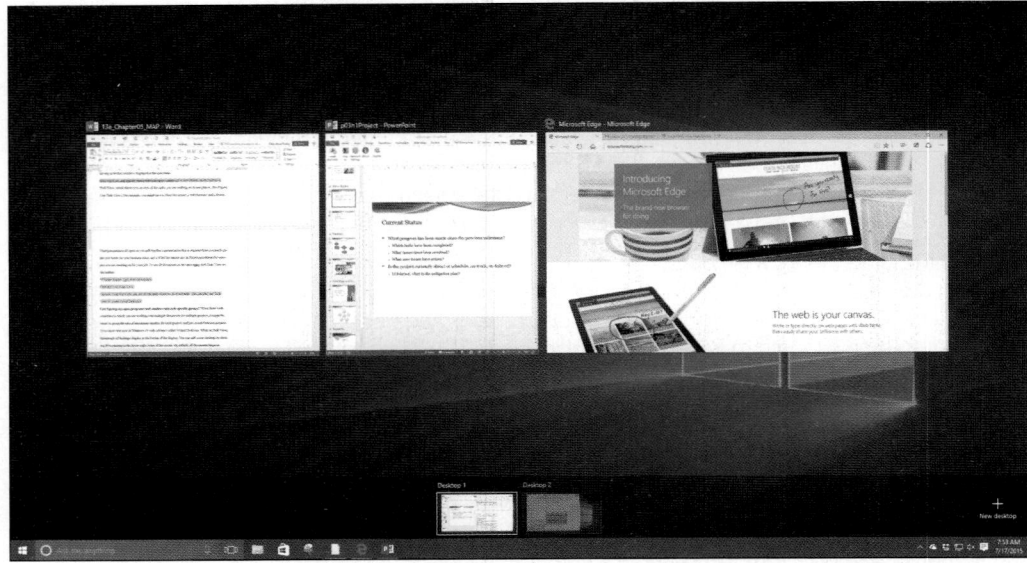

Figure 5.14 Virtual desktops enable you to organize your open files into separate working spaces. *(Windows 10, Microsoft Corporation)*

one desktop an open Word document, web browser, and PowerPoint presentation that you need for your business class, and in a second desktop, a Word document and an Excel spreadsheet for a project you're working on for your job. There is no limit as to the number of desktops you can create. You can see all virtual desktops by clicking Task View. For more information on how to work with virtual desktops in Windows 10, see the Try This on p. 182.

Mac and Linux User Interfaces

How does the Mac user interface compare with that of Windows 10? Although the macOS and the Windows operating systems aren't compatible, they're extremely similar in terms of functionality. For example, as is the case with Windows, macOS programs appear in resizable windows and use menus and icons. Although macOS doesn't have a Start menu, macOS features a Dock with icons on the bottom for your most popular programs (see Figure 5.15), which is very similar to the Windows taskbar. Although Windows 10 can be deployed on all types of devices, as noted earlier, Apple runs two separate operating systems: macOS for desktops and laptops and iOS for the iPhone and iPad. However, the latest versions of macOS feature tight integration between macOS and portable devices running iOS. Apple wants to make transferring data and tasks from one device to another seamless.

Is a Linux user interface similar to that of macOS and Windows? Different distros of Linux feature different user interfaces. But most of them, like Ubuntu (see Figure 5.16), are based on familiar Windows and macOS paradigms, such as using icons to launch programs and having apps run in a window environment.

Figure 5.15 macOS Sierra is Apple's latest operating system for desktop and laptop computers. *(Screen shot(s) reprinted with permission from Apple, Inc.)*

Figure 5.16 The Ubuntu Linux user interface resembles the Windows desktop. *(Ubuntu is a trademark of Canonical Limited and is used with the permission of Canonical Limited. Pearson is not endorsed by or affiliated with Canonical Limited or the Ubuntu project.)*

File Management

So far we've discussed how the OS manages the processor, memory, storage, and devices, and how it provides a way for applications and users to interact with the computer. An additional function of the OS is to enable **file management**, which provides an organizational structure to your computer's contents. In this section, we discuss how you can use this feature to make your computer more organized and efficient.

Organizing Your Files

Objective 5.9 *Summarize how the operating system helps keep your computer organized and manages files and folders.*

How does the OS organize computer contents? Windows organizes the contents of your computer in a hierarchical **directory** structure composed of *drives*, *libraries*, *folders*, *subfolders*, and *files*. The hard drive, represented as the C: drive, is where you permanently store most of your files. Each additional storage drive, such as an optical drive, flash drive, or external hard drive, is given a unique letter (*D*, *E*, *F*, and so on). The C: drive is like a large filing cabinet in which all files are stored. As such, the C: drive is the top of the filing structure of your computer and is referred to as the **root directory**. All other folders and files are organized within the root directory. There are areas in the root directory that the OS has filled with files and folders holding special OS files. The programs within these files help run the computer and generally shouldn't be accessed. In addition, sometimes the manufacturer will store files used to reinstate your computer back to the original factory state. Those files should not be accessed unless necessary.

What exactly are files, folders, and libraries? In an OS, a **file** is a collection of program instructions or data that is stored and treated as a single unit. Files can be generated from an application such as a Word document or an Excel workbook. In addition, files can represent an entire application, a web page, a set of sounds, an image, or a video. Files can be stored on the hard drive, a flash drive, online, or on any other permanent storage medium. As the number of files you save increases, it becomes more important to keep them organized in folders and libraries. A **folder** is a collection of files.

How can I easily locate and see the contents of my computer? In Windows, **File Explorer** is the main tool for finding, viewing, and managing the contents of your computer. It shows the location and contents of every drive, folder, and file. As illustrated in Figure 5.17, File Explorer is divided into two panes or sections:

1. The *Navigation pane* on the left shows the contents of your computer. It displays commonly accessed files and folders in the Quick Access area, files stored online in OneDrive, and other storage areas in My PC such as Documents, Music, Pictures, and Videos.
2. When you select a folder, drive, or library from the Navigation pane, the contents of that particular area are displayed in the *File list* on the right.

For those folders that have been shared with others using an online storage system such as OneDrive or Dropbox, there is a new feature in Windows 10 that displays a shared icon instead of the traditional yellow folder icon.

When you save a file for the first time, you give the file a name and designate where you want to save it. For easy reference, the OS includes libraries where files are saved unless you specify otherwise. In Windows, the default libraries are Documents for document files, Music for audio files, Pictures for graphics files, and Videos for video files. These are in the This PC section of File Explorer.

You can determine the location of a file by its **file path**. The file path starts with the drive in which the file is located and includes all folders, subfolders (if any), the file name, and the extension. For example, if you were saving a picture of Andrew Carnegie for a term paper for a U.S. History course, the file path might be C:\Documents\HIS182\Term Paper\Illustrations\ACarnegie.jpg.

As shown in Figure 5.18, "C:" is the drive on which the file is stored (in this case, the hard drive), and "Documents" is the file's primary folder. "HIS182," "Term Paper," and "Illustrations" are

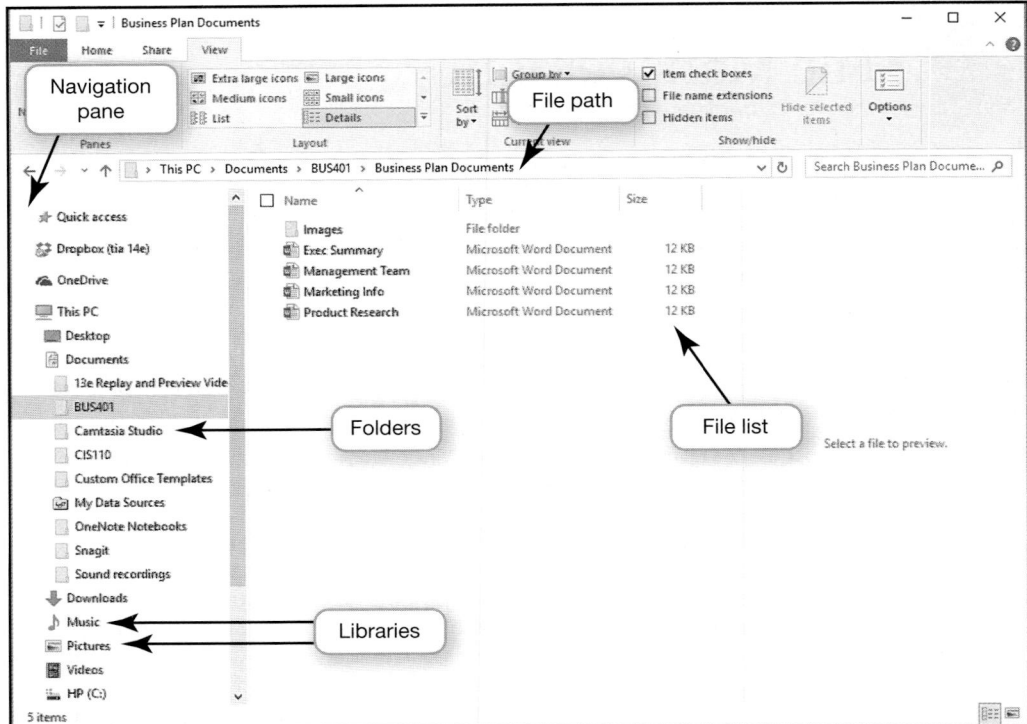

Figure 5.17 File Explorer lets you see the contents of your computer.
> Click **File Explorer** from the Start menu or from the taskbar.
(Windows 10, Microsoft Corporation)

successive subfolders within the "Documents" main folder. Last comes the file name, "ACarnegie," separated from the file extension (in this case, "jpg") by a period. The backslash character (\), used by Windows, is referred to as a **path separator**. macOS files use a colon (:), whereas UNIX and Linux files use the forward slash (/) as the path separator.

Are there different ways I can view and sort my files and folders? Clicking on the View tab in File Explorer offers you different ways to view the folders and files.

1. *Details view:* This is the most interactive view. As shown in Figure 5.20, files and folders are displayed in list form, and the additional file information is displayed in columns alongside the name of the file. You can sort and display the contents of the folder by clicking any of the column headings, so you can sort the contents alphabetically by name or type or hierarchically by date last modified or file size. Right-click the column heading area to modify the display of columns.

2. *Icons view:* There are a number of icon views that display files and folders in sizes ranging from small to extra-large. In most icon views, the folders are displayed as *Live Icons*. Live Icons allow you to preview the actual contents of a specific folder without opening the folder. Large Icons view is the best view to use if your folder contains picture files because you can see a bit of the actual images peeking out of the folder. It's also good to use if your folder contains PowerPoint presentations because the title slide of the presentation will display, making it easier for you to distinguish among presentations.

You can change the views by using the controls in the Layout group on the View tab, or by clicking between Details view and Large Icons view from the bottom right corner of File Explorer. The View tab also enables you to display a Preview pane or a Details pane. The Preview pane displays the first page of the selected document, and the Details pane displays the file or folder's properties.

Figure 5.18 Understanding File Paths

Save Files in the Cloud

If you're still using a flash drive, consider saving to the cloud instead. Cloud storage sites such as Microsoft's OneDrive, Google Drive, and Dropbox provide easy solutions. The advantage of saving files to the cloud is that your files are accessible from any Internet-connected device—including your smartphone. Using cloud storage will ensure the availability of your files when you need them. Moreover, files and folders stored in the cloud are easily shared with others to facilitate collaboration. OneDrive and iCloud are proprietary cloud storage systems for Windows and macOS, respectively. Google Drive is another popular cloud storage system that also integrates with a suite of cloud-based productivity applications. Dropbox integrates with Windows and macOS as well as on Apple and Android mobile devices.

Figure 5.19 OneDrive and Dropbox are integrated in Windows File Explorer for easy cloud-based file storage. *(Windows 10, Microsoft Corporation)*

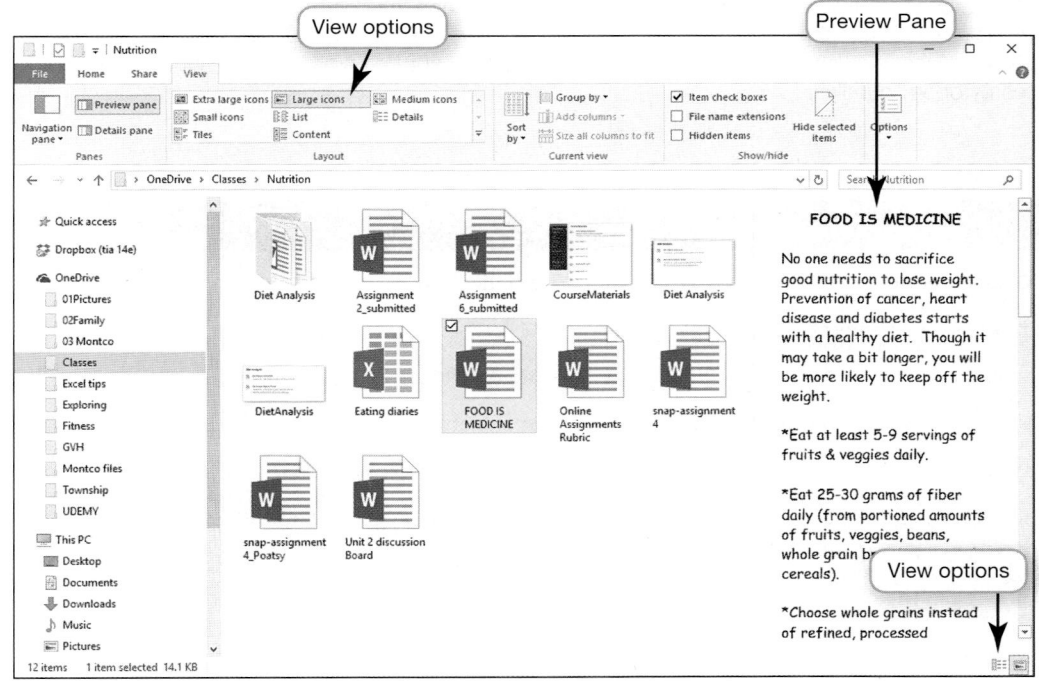

Figure 5.20 The View tab in File Explorer enables you to use different views to display the contents of files and folders. The Preview pane on the right lets you see the first page of your document without first opening it. *(Windows 10, Microsoft Corporation)*

Creating folders is the key to organizing files because folders keep related documents together. For example, you might create one folder called "Classes" to hold your class work. Inside the "Classes" folder, you could create subfolders for each of your classes (such as ENG 325 and BUS 401). Inside each of those subfolders, you could create further subfolders for each class's assignments, homework, and so on.

Grouping related files into folders makes it easier for you to identify and find files. Which would be easier—going to the BUS 401 folder to find a file or searching through the hundreds of individual files in the Documents library hoping to find the right one? Grouping files in a folder also allows you to move files more efficiently, so you can quickly transfer critical files needing frequent backup, for instance.

Naming Files

Are there special rules I have to follow when I name files? The first part of a file, or the **file name**, is generally the name you assign to the file when you save it. For example, "bioreport" may be the name you assign a report you have completed for a biology class.

In a Windows application, an **extension**, or **file type**, follows the file name and a period or dot (.). Like a last name, this extension identifies what kind of family of files the file belongs to, or which application should be used to read the file. For example, if "bioreport" is a spreadsheet created in Microsoft Excel 2016, it has an .xlsx extension and its name is "bioreport.xlsx." You can choose to display file extensions by checking or unchecking the File name extensions box in the Show/hide group on the View tab in File Explorer.

Figure 5.21 lists some common file extensions and the types of documents they indicate.

Why is it important to know the file extension? When you save a file created in most applications running under the Windows OS, you don't need to add the extension to the file name; it is added automatically for you. Mac and Linux operating systems don't require file extensions. This is because the information as to the type of application the computer should use to open the file is stored inside the file itself. However, if you're using the Mac or Linux OS and will be sending files to Windows users, you should add an extension to your file name so that Windows can more easily open your files.

Figure 5.21   Common File Name Extensions

Extension	Type Of Document	Application
.docx	Word processing document	Microsoft Word 2007 and later
.xlsx	Workbook	Microsoft Excel 2007 and later
.accdb	Database	Microsoft Access 2007 and later
.pptx	Presentation	Microsoft PowerPoint 2007 and later
.pdf	Portable Document Format	Adobe Acrobat or Adobe Reader
.rtf	Text (Rich Text Format)	Any program that can read text documents
.txt	Text	Any program that can read text documents
.htm or .html	HyperText Markup Language (HTML) for a web page	Any program that can read HTML
.jpg	Joint Photographic Experts Group (JPEG) image	Most programs capable of displaying images
.zip	Compressed file	Various file compression programs

If you try to open a file with an unknown extension, Windows 10 displays a dialog box that offers several suggested programs that can be used (see Figure 5.22). If you're certain of the type of file you're opening and know the program you'll want to use in the future to open similar types of files, select the option to always use the selected program. However, if you're at all unsure of the program to use or don't want to set a default program for this type of file, make sure that option is not selected.

Are there things I shouldn't do when naming my files? It's important that you name your files so that you can easily identify them. File names can have as many as 255 characters, so don't be afraid to use as many characters as you need. A file name such as "BIO 101 Research Paper First Draft.docx" makes it very clear what that file contains.

Keep in mind, however, that all files must be uniquely identified, unless you save them in different folders or in different locations. Therefore, although files may share the same file name (such as "bioreport.docx" or "bioreport.xlsx") or share the same extension ("bioreport.xlsx" or "budget.xlsx"), no two files stored in the same folder can share *both* the same filename and the same file extension. In addition, some characters can't be used in a file name, such as a quotation mark, and the file will not be saved until the file name is modified.

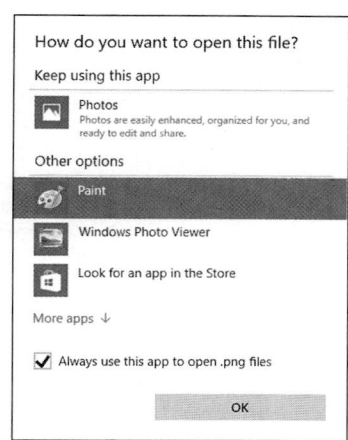

Figure 5.22 When you open a file with an unknown file type, you can choose the app you want to use. *(Windows 10, Microsoft Corporation)*

Copying, Moving, and Deleting Files and Folders

How can I move and copy files and folders? You can move or copy a file or folder to another location using the Cut or Copy commands, respectively, on the ribbon or by right-clicking the file and selecting an option from the shortcut menu. After selecting Cut or Copy, select the new location, and then select Paste from the ribbon or right-click the new location folder and select Paste. Alternatively, you can drag and drop a file or folder to a new location. One method is to open two File Explorer windows side by side and drag a file or folder from one window to the other. Another method is to drag a file or folder from the File list to a new location displayed in the Navigation pane. When dragging a file or folder, the default action is to move the file or folder. If you'd rather make a copy, press Ctrl while you drag the file or folder to its new location.

Where do deleted files go? The **Recycle Bin** is a folder on the desktop, represented by an icon that looks like a recycling bin, where files deleted from the hard drive reside until you permanently purge them from your system. Unfortunately, files deleted from other storage locations or files stored in the cloud don't go to the Recycle Bin but are deleted from the system immediately.

Mac systems have something similar to the Recycle Bin, called Trash, which is represented by a wastebasket icon. To delete files on a Mac, drag the files to the Trash icon.

How do I permanently delete files from the Recycle Bin? Files placed in the Recycle Bin or the Trash remain in the system until they're permanently deleted. To delete files from the Recycle Bin permanently, select Empty Recycle Bin after right-clicking the desktop icon. On Macs, select Empty Trash from the Finder menu in macOS.

What happens if I need to recover a deleted file? Getting a file back after the Recycle Bin has been emptied still may be possible using one of two methods:

- File History is a Windows 10 utility that automatically backs up files and saves previous versions of files to a designated drive (such as an external hard drive). If you're using File History, you can restore previously deleted files or even previous versions of files you've changed. (We'll discuss File History in more detail later in the chapter.)
- Additionally, OneDrive (which is incorporated into Windows 10) and other cloud-based storage systems, such as Dropbox and Google Drive, maintain histories of files and you can not only recover a deleted file, but also roll back files edit by edit.

When the Recycle Bin is emptied, only the reference to the file is deleted permanently, so the OS has no easy way to find the file. The file data actually remains on the hard drive until it's written over by another file. You may be able to use a program such as FarStone's RestoreIT or Norton Online Backup to try to retrieve files you think you've permanently deleted. These programs reveal files that are still intact on the hard drive and help you recover them.

Helpdesk MyLab IT®

Organizing Your Computer: File Management

In this Helpdesk, you'll play the role of a helpdesk staffer, fielding questions about the desktop, window features, and how the OS helps keep the computer organized.

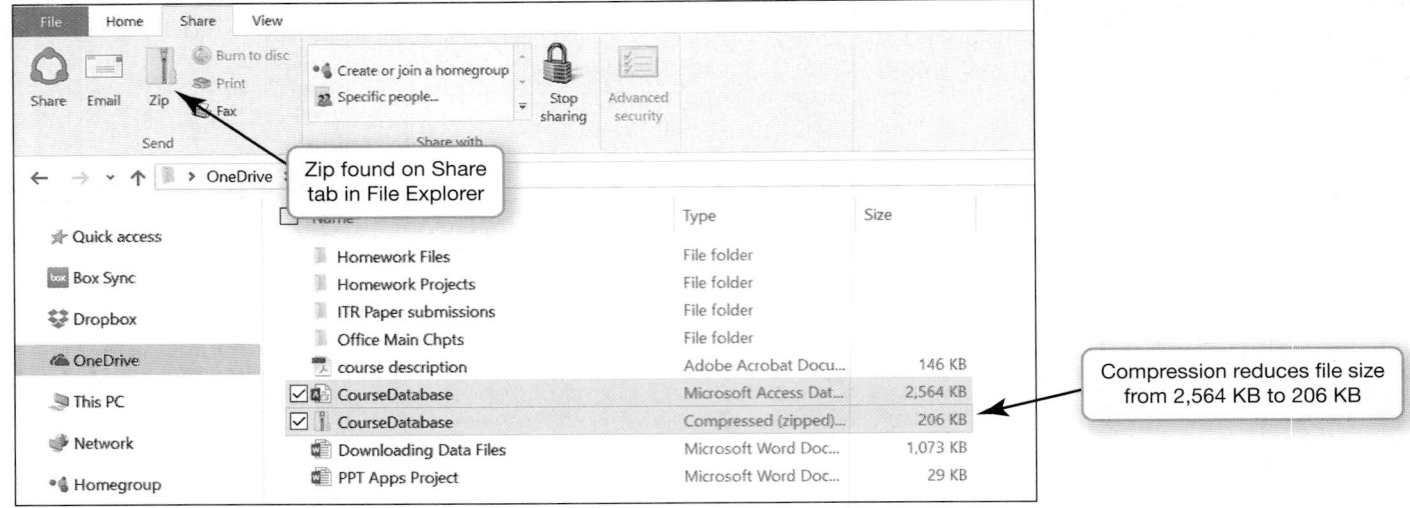

Figure 5.23 File compression is a built-in utility of the Windows OS. Compressing the file reduces the size from 2,564 KB to 206 KB.

> *To compress a file or folder, open File Explorer, click the* **Share** *tab, and then click* **Zip**. *(Windows 10, Microsoft Corporation)*

File Compression

Why would I want to compress a file? File compression makes a large file more compact, making it easier and faster for you to send large attachments by e-mail, upload them to the web, or save them onto a flash drive or other storage medium. You can also compress a group of files together, so you can manage one compressed folder rather than manipulating individual files. As shown in Figure 5.23, Windows has a built-in **file compression utility** that can be accessed through File Explorer. You can also obtain several stand-alone freeware and shareware programs, such as WinZip (for Windows) and StuffIt (for Windows or Mac), to compress your files. Often file compression is referred to as "zipping" a file.

How does file compression work? Compression takes out redundancies in a file to reduce the file size. Most compression programs look for repeated patterns of letters and replace these patterns with a shorter placeholder. The repeated patterns and the associated placeholder are cataloged and stored temporarily in a separate file called the *dictionary*. For example, in the following sentence, you can easily see the repeated patterns of letters.

The rain in Spain falls mainly on the plain.

Although this example contains obvious repeated patterns (ain and the), in a large document, the repeated patterns will be more complex. The compression program's algorithm (a set of instructions designed to complete a solution in a step-by-step manner), therefore, runs through the file several times to determine the optimal repeated patterns needed to obtain the greatest compression.

How effective are file compression programs? Current compression programs can reduce text files by 50% or more, depending on the file. However, some files, such as PDF files, already contain a form of compression, so they don't need to be compressed further. Image files such as JPEG, GIF, and PNG files discard small variations in color that the human eye might not pick up. Likewise, MP3 files permanently discard sounds that the human ear can't hear. These graphic and audio files don't need further compression.

How do I restore a file I've compressed? When you want to restore the file to its original state, you need to *decompress* the file. In File Explorer, when you click on a Compressed (or zipped) folder, the Compressed Folders Tools tab displays (see Figure 5.24). Click Extract all to open the Extract Compressed (Zipped) Folders dialog box. Browse to locate where you want to save the extracted files, or just click Extract to accept the default location (which is generally the location of the zipped folder).

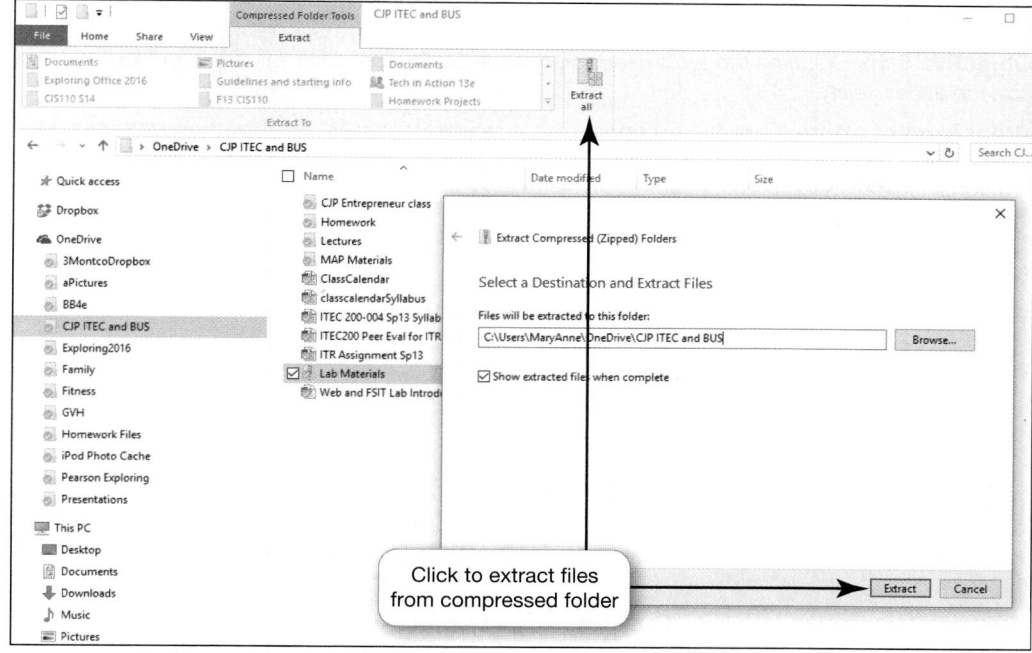

Figure 5.24 Extracting files from a zipped folder is simply done through the Extract all feature in File Explorer. *(Windows 10, Microsoft Corporation)*

Within the figure:
Click to extract files from compressed folder

Utility Programs

The main component of system software is the operating system. However, *utility programs*—small applications that perform special functions on the computer—are also an essential part of system software. Utility programs come in three flavors:

1. Those included with the OS (such as System Restore)
2. Those sold as stand-alone programs (such as Norton antivirus)
3. Those offered as freeware (such as anti-malware software like Ad-Aware from Lavasoft)

Figure 5.25 lists some of the various types of utility programs available within Windows as well as some alternatives available as stand-alone programs.

Figure 5.25 Utility Programs Available Within Windows and as Stand-Alone Programs

Windows Utility Program	Stand-Alone Alternatives	What It Does
Disk Cleanup	McAfee Total Protection	Removes unnecessary files from your hard drive
Defragment and Optimize Drives	Norton Utilities, iDefrag	Rearranges files on your hard drive to allow for faster access of files
Task Manager and Resource Monitor	Process Explorer	Displays performance measures for processes; provides information on programs and processes running on your computer
File History, File Recovery	Acronis True Image, Norton Online Backup	Backs up important files, makes a complete mirror image of your current computer setup
System Restore	FarStone RestoreIT, Acronis True Image	Restores your system to a previous, stable state

Windows Administrative Utilities

Objective 5.10 *Outline the tools used to enhance system productivity, back up files, and provide accessibility.*

What kind of utilities are in the operating system? In general, the basic utilities designed to manage and tune your computer hardware are incorporated into the OS. The stand-alone utility programs typically offer more features or an easier user interface for backup, security, diagnostic, or recovery functions.

System Performance Utilities

What utilities can make my system work faster? **Disk Cleanup** is a Windows utility that removes unnecessary files from your hard drive. These include files that have accumulated in the Recycle Bin as well as temporary files—files created by Windows to store data temporarily while a program is running. Windows usually deletes these temporary files when you exit the program, but sometimes it forgets to do this or doesn't have time because your system freezes or incurs a problem that prevents you from properly exiting a program.

Disk Cleanup also removes temporary Internet files (web pages stored on your hard drive for quick viewing) as well as offline web pages (pages stored on your computer so you can view them without being connected to the Internet). If not deleted periodically, these unnecessary files can slow down your computer.

How can I control which files Disk Cleanup deletes? When you run Disk Cleanup, the program scans your hard drive to determine which folders have files that can be deleted and calculates the amount of hard drive space that will be freed up by doing so. You check off which type of files you would like to delete, as shown in Figure 5.26.

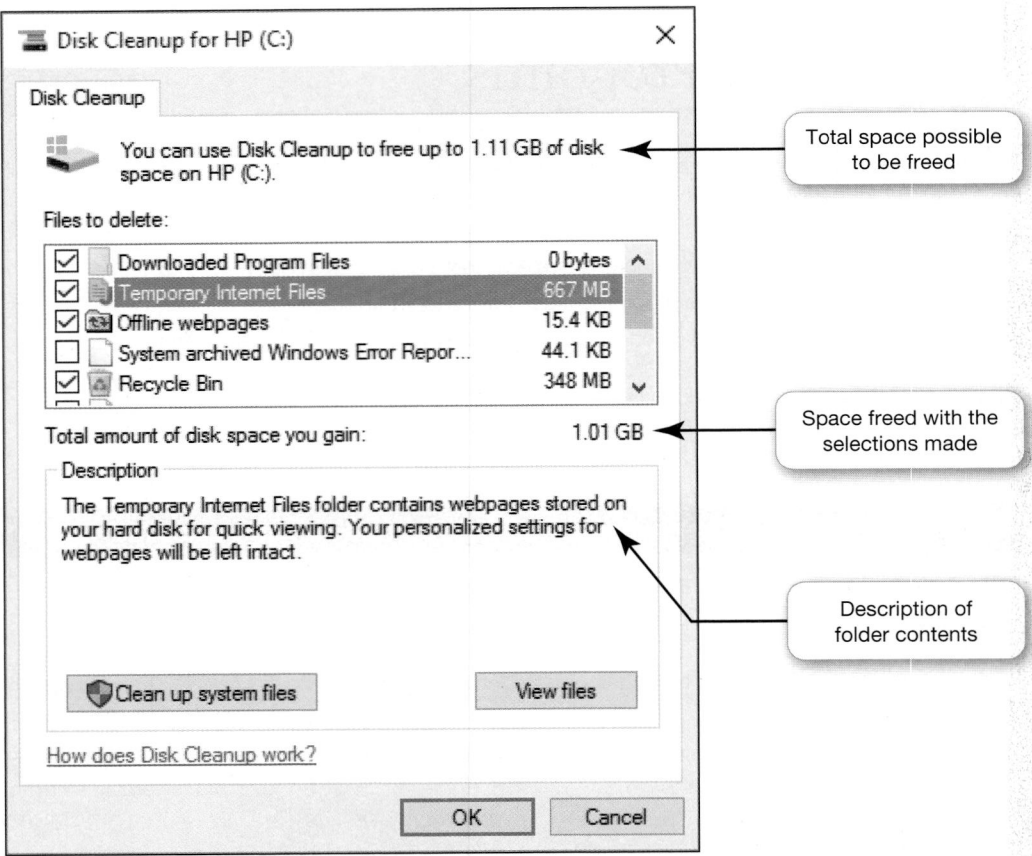

Figure 5.26 Using Disk Cleanup will help free space on your hard drive.
> To access Disk Cleanup, click the **Start** button, scroll to **Windows Administrative Tools**, and click **Disk Cleanup**. *(Windows 10, Microsoft Corporation)*

Figure 5.27 You can use Task Manager to close nonresponsive programs.
> To access Task Manager, right-click the taskbar and select **Task Manager**. (Windows 10, Microsoft Corporation)

How can I check on a program that's stopped running? If a program has stopped working, you can use the Windows **Task Manager** utility (see Figure 5.27) to check on the program or to exit the nonresponsive program. The Processes tab of Task Manager lists all the programs you're using and indicates their status. "Not responding" will be shown next to a program that stopped improperly. You can terminate programs that aren't responding by right-clicking the app name and selecting End task from the shortcut menu.

If you're working on a Mac, Force Quit can help you close out nonresponsive applications. You can access Force Quit by clicking the Apple menu, or simply by pressing Command + Option + Esc. Alternatively, you can press and hold the Option and Ctrl keys and click the nonresponsive program's icon on the dock.

How can I improve my computer's performance? After you have used your computer for a while, uploading, creating, changing, and deleting content, the hard drive becomes fragmented: Parts of files get scattered (fragmented) around the hard disk, making the hard disk do extra work, which can slow down your computer. **Disk defragmentation** rearranges fragmented data so that related file pieces are unified. The Defragment and Optimize Drives utility is found in the Windows Administrative Tools folder in the apps list. Before you defragment your hard drive, you should first determine if the disk needs to be defragmented by selecting Analyze. If your disk is more than 10% fragmented, you should run the disk defragmenter utility. Note that disk defragmentation doesn't apply to solid state drives (SSDs) because they don't have sectors. See the Dig Deeper *How Disk Defragmenting Utilities Work* for more information.

Disk defragmenting programs group together related pieces of files on the hard drive, allowing the OS to work more efficiently. To understand how disk defragmenting utilities work, you first need to understand the basics of how a hard disk drive stores files. A hard disk drive is composed of several platters, or round, thin plates of metal, covered with a special magnetic coating that records the data. The platters are about 3.5 inches in diameter and are stacked onto a spindle. There are usually two or three platters in any hard disk drive, with data stored on one or both sides. Data is recorded on hard disks in concentric circles called **tracks**. Each track is further broken down into pie-shaped wedges, each called a **sector** (see Figure 5.28). The data is further identified by **clusters**, which are the smallest segments within the sectors.

When you want to save (or write) a file, the bits that make up your file are recorded onto one or more clusters of the drive. To keep track of which clusters hold which files, the drive also stores an index of all sector numbers in a table. To save a file, the computer looks in the table for clusters that aren't already being used. It then records the file information on those clusters. When you open (or read) a file, the computer searches through the table for the clusters that hold the desired file and reads that file. Similarly, when you delete a file, you're actually not deleting the file itself but rather the reference in the table to the file.

So, how does a disk become fragmented? When only part of an older file is deleted, the deleted section of the file creates a gap in the sector of the disk

Figure 5.28 On a hard disk platter, data is recorded onto tracks, which are further divided into sectors and clusters.

Figure 5.29 Defragmenting the hard drive arranges file fragments so that they are located next to each other. This makes the hard drive run more efficiently.

where the data was originally stored. In the same way, when new information is added to an older file, there may not be space to save the new information sequentially near where the file was originally saved. In that case, the system writes the added part of the file to the next available location on the disk, and a reference is made in the table as to the location of this file fragment. Over time, as files are saved, deleted, and modified, the bits of information for various files fall out of order and the disk becomes fragmented.

Disk fragmentation is a problem because the OS isn't as efficient when a disk is fragmented. It takes longer to locate a whole file because more of the disk must be searched for the various pieces, slowing down your computer.

Defragmenting tools take the hard drive through a defragmentation process in which pieces of files scattered over the disk are placed together and arranged sequentially on it. Also, any unused portions of clusters that were too small to save data in before are grouped, increasing the available storage space on the disk. Figure 5.29 shows before and after shots of a fragmented disk that has gone through the defragmentation process.

The Defragment and Optimize Drives utility in Windows 10 is set by default to automatically defragment the hard drive on a regular basis. Macs don't have a defragmentation utility built into the system. Those users who feel the need to defragment their Mac can use iDefrag, an external program from Coriolis Systems.

For more about hard disks and defragmenting, check out the Sound Byte "Hard Disk Anatomy."

▶ Sound Byte MyLab IT®

Hard Disk Anatomy

In this Sound Byte, you'll watch a series of animations that show various aspects of a hard drive, including the anatomy of a hard drive, how a computer reads and writes data to a hard drive, and the fragmenting and defragmenting of a hard drive.

File and System Backup Utilities

How can I protect my data in the event something malfunctions in my system? As noted earlier, when you use the **File History** utility, you can have Windows automatically create a duplicate of your libraries, desktop, contacts, and website favorites and copy it to another storage device, such as an external hard drive (see Figure 5.30). A backup copy protects your data in the event your hard drive fails or files are accidentally erased. File History also keeps copies of different versions of your files. This means that if you need to go back to the second draft of your history term paper, even though you are now on your fifth draft, File History should allow you to recover it. File History needs to be turned on by the user and requires an external hard drive (or network drive) that is always connected to the computer to function. You can choose to back up all folders on the C: drive, or select certain ones that you use most often or contain the most sensitive files to back up.

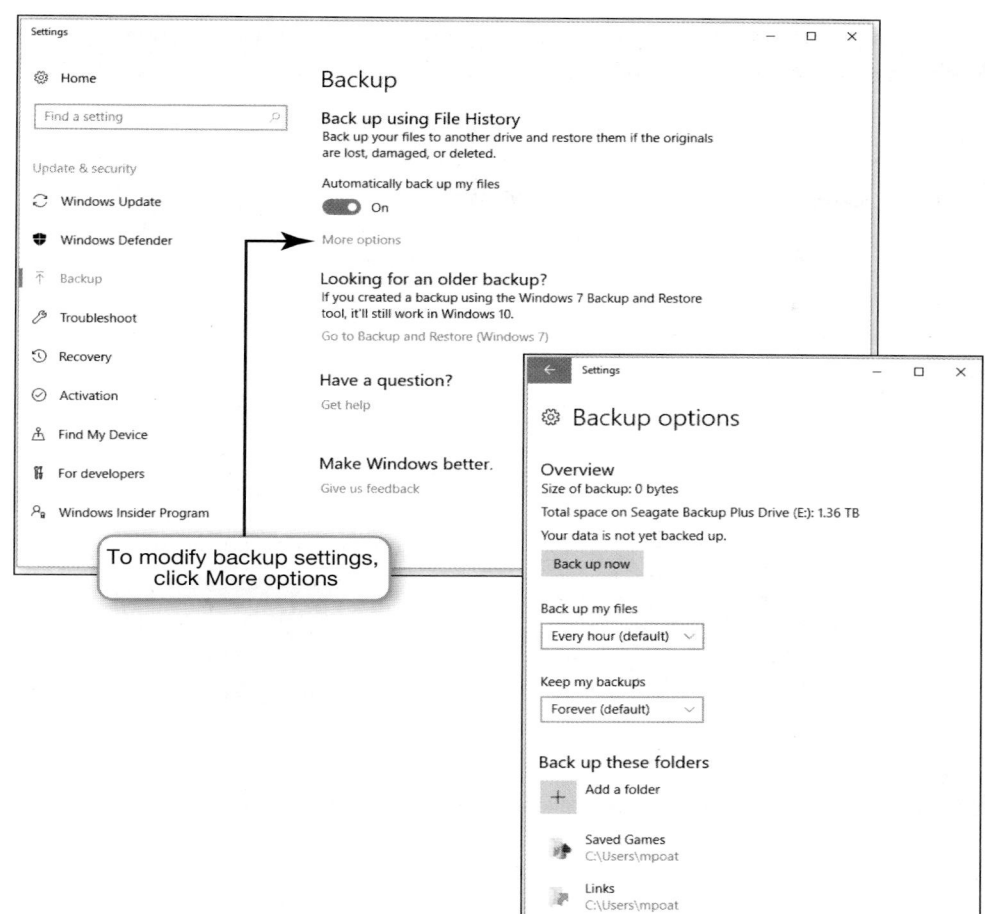

Figure 5.30 File History backs up files to an external hard drive.
> *To turn on File History, choose* **Settings**, *select* **Update & security**, *and then select* **Backup**. *To modify File History and Backup settings, click* **More options**. *(Windows 10, Microsoft Corporation)*

To modify backup settings, click More options

Windows 10 also includes recovery tools that allow you to complete backups of your entire system (system image) that you can later restore in the event of a major hard drive crash.

How can I recover my entire system? Suppose you've just installed a new software program and your computer freezes. After rebooting the computer, when you try to start the application, the system freezes once again. You uninstall the new program, but your computer continues to freeze after rebooting. What can you do now?

Windows has a utility called **System Restore** that lets you roll your system settings back to a specific date when everything was working properly. A **system restore point**, which is a snapshot of your entire system's settings, is generated prior to certain events, such as installing or updating software, or automatically once a week if no other restore points were created in that time. You also can create a restore point manually at any time.

Should problems occur, if the computer was running just fine before you installed new software or a hardware device, you could restore your computer to the settings that were in effect before the software or hardware installation (see Figure 5.31). System Restore doesn't affect your personal data files (such as Word documents or e-mail), so you won't lose changes made to these files.

Figure 5.31 The System Restore Wizard shows restore points set manually by a user and automatically by Windows when updates were installed. Setting a restore point is good practice before installing any hardware or software.
> *To access System Restore, right-click the* **Start** *button, choose* **System**, *select* **System protection**, *and then click* **System Restore**. *The System Restore Wizard displays, with the restore points shown on the second page of the Wizard. (Windows 10, Microsoft Corporation)*

Figure 5.32 Windows Ease of Access Tools

Magnifier

- Creates a separate window that displays a magnified portion of the screen

Narrator

- Reads what is on screen
- Can read the contents of a window, menu options, or text you have typed

Speech Recognition

- Allows you to dictate text and control your computer by voice

On-Screen Keyboard

- Allows you to type with a pointing device

High Contrast

- Color schemes invert screen colors for vision-impaired individuals

Easier to Read!

*To locate Ease of Access, click the **Start** button, click **Settings**, then select **Ease of Access**.*
(Imagery Majestic/Fotolia; Anatoly Maslennikov/Fotolia; iqoncept/123RF; Pockgallery/Shutterstock; Windows 10, Microsoft corporation)

macOS includes a backup utility called Time Machine that automatically backs up your files to a specified location. Apple also offers backup hardware called AirPort Time Capsules, which are hard disk drives with wireless connectivity, designed to work with Time Machine and record your backup data. Because Time Machine makes a complete image copy of your system, it can also be used to recover your system in the case of a fatal error. (For more information on backing up your files, see Chapter 9.)

Accessibility Utilities

What utilities are designed for users with special needs? Microsoft Windows includes Ease of Access settings, which provide a centralized location for assistive technology and tools to adjust accessibility settings. The Ease of Access tools, which are accessible from Settings, include tools to help users with disabilities, shown in Figure 5.32. The tools shown in the figure are just a sampling of the available tools.

Whether you use Windows, macOS, Linux, or another operating system, a fully featured OS is available to meet your needs. As long as you keep the operating system updated and regularly use the available utilities to fine-tune your system, you should experience little trouble from your OS.

Before moving on to the Chapter Review:

1. ▶ Watch Chapter Overview Video 5.2.
2. Then take the Check Your Understanding quiz.

Check Your Understanding // Review & Practice

For a quick review to see what you've learned so far, answer the following questions.

multiple choice

1. The process of adding a Windows 10 app to the Start menu is known as
   a. clipping.
   b. pinning.
   c. visualizing.
   d. screening.

2. The Windows app used for locating files and folders is
   a. Disk Manager.
   b. Finder.
   c. Library Explorer.
   d. File Explorer.

3. Which view in File Explorer can you use to sort files by column heading?
   a. details
   b. small icons
   c. tiles
   d. large icons

4. Which of the following is used to reduce the file size of a file or folder?
   a. defragmenter
   b. extraction
   c. compression
   d. shrinker

5. Which utility is used to exit from a nonresponsive program?
   a. System Refresh
   b. Disk Cleanup
   c. Task Manager
   d. File Explorer

Go to **MyLab IT** to take an autograded version of the *Check Your Understanding* review and to find all media resources for the chapter.

TechBytes Weekly   Go to TechBytes Weekly for current technology news and discussion questions!

5 Chapter Review

Summary

Learning Outcome 5.1 You will be able to explain the types and functions of operating systems and explain the steps in the boot process.

 ### Operating System Fundamentals

Objective 5.1 *Discuss the functions of the operating system.*

- System software is the set of software programs that helps run the computer and coordinates instructions between application software and hardware devices. It consists of the operating system (OS) and utility programs.
- The OS controls how your computer system functions. It manages the computer's hardware, provides a means for application software to work with the CPU, and is responsible for the management, scheduling, and coordination of tasks.
- Utility programs are programs that perform general housekeeping tasks for the computer, such as system maintenance and file compression.
- Modern operating systems allow for multitasking—to perform more than one process at a time.

Objective 5.2 *Explain the most common operating systems for personal use.*

- Microsoft Windows is the most popular OS. The most recent release is Windows 10. macOS is designed to work on Apple computers, and Linux is an open source OS based on UNIX and designed primarily for use on personal computers.
- Some operating systems allow interaction with touch-screen interfaces. All personal use operating systems incorporate elements to share and store files on the Internet.
- An OS is designed to run on specific CPUs. The combination of an OS and a CPU is a computer's platform. Application software is OS dependent.
- Smartphones and tablets have their own specific mobile operating systems, which allow the user to multitask.

Objective 5.3 *Explain the different kinds of operating systems for machines, networks, and business.*

- Real-time operating systems (RTOSs) require no user intervention.
- A multiuser operating system (network operating system) provides access to a computer system by more than one user at a time.
- UNIX is a multiuser, multitasking OS that is used as a network OS, though it can be used on PCs.
- Mainframes and supercomputers are specialty computers that require mainframe operating systems.

 ### What the Operating System Does

Objective 5.4 *Explain how the operating system provides a means for users to interact with the computer.*

- The OS provides a user interface that enables users to interact with the computer.
- Most OSs today use a graphical user interface (GUI). Common features of GUIs include windows, menus, and icons.

Objective 5.5 *Explain how the operating system helps manage hardware such as the processor, memory, storage, and peripheral devices.*

- When the OS allows you to perform more than one task at a time, it is multitasking. To provide for seamless multitasking, the OS controls the timing of the events on which the processor works.
- As the OS coordinates the activities of the processor, it uses RAM as a temporary storage area for instructions and data the processor needs. The OS coordinates the space allocations in RAM to ensure that there is enough space for the waiting instructions and data. If there isn't sufficient space in RAM for all the data and instructions, then the OS allocates the least necessary files to temporary storage on the hard drive, called *virtual memory*.

- The OS manages storage by providing a file management system that keeps track of the names and locations of files and programs.
- Programs called *device drivers* facilitate communication between devices attached to the computer and the OS.

Objective 5.6 *Explain how the operating system interacts with application software.*

- All software applications need to interact with the CPU. For programs to work with the CPU, they must contain code that the CPU recognizes.
- Rather than having the same blocks of code appear in each application, the OS includes the blocks of code to which software applications refer. These blocks of code are called *application programming interfaces* (APIs).

 Starting Your Computer

Objective 5.7 *Discuss the process the operating system uses to start up the computer and how errors in the boot process are handled.*

- When you start your computer, it runs through a special process called the *boot process*.
- The boot process consists of four basic steps: (1) The basic input/output system (BIOS) is activated when the user powers on the CPU. (2) In the POST check, the BIOS verifies that all attached devices are in place. (3) The OS is loaded into RAM. (4) Configuration and customization settings are checked.
- An authentication process occurs at the end of the boot process to ensure an authorized user is entering the system.
- Sometimes errors occur in the boot process. Try rebooting the computer or resetting the computer if the problem persists.

Part 2
Using System Software

Learning Outcome 5.2 **You will be able to describe how to use system software, including the user interface, file management capabilities, and utility programs.**

 The Windows Interface

Objective 5.8 *Describe the main features of the Windows interface.*

- In Windows 10, the Start menu provides access to your computer's apps, tools, and commonly used programs and the desktop is the main working area.
- You can customize the Start menu by pinning and resizing tiles and organizing tiles into groups.
- Virtual desktops are used to organize open programs into different working areas.

 File Management

Objective 5.9 *Summarize how the operating system helps keep your computer organized and manages files and folders.*

- Files and folders are organized in a hierarchical directory structure composed of drives, libraries, folders, subfolders, and files.
- The C: drive represents the hard drive and is where most programs and files are stored.
- File Explorer is the main tool for finding, viewing, and managing the contents of your computer.
- File Explorer helps you manage your files and folders by showing the location and contents of every drive, folder, and file on your computer.

- There are specific rules to follow when naming files.
- The Recycle Bin is the temporary storage location for deleted files from the hard drive.
- File compression reduces the size of a file by temporarily storing components of a file, and then when the file is extracted (uncompressed) the removed components are brought back into the file.

 Utility Programs

Objective 5.10 *Outline the tools used to enhance system productivity, back up files, and provide accessibility.*

- Task Manager is used to exit nonresponsive programs.
- Disk Cleanup removes unnecessary files from your hard drive. If not deleted periodically, these unnecessary files can slow down your computer.
- Disk defragmentation utilities rearrange fragmented data so that related file pieces are unified. When a disk is fragmented, it can slow down your computer.
- File History automatically creates a duplicate of your hard drive (or parts of your hard drive) and copies it to another storage device, such as an external hard drive. You can use File History to recover deleted or corrupted files.

- System Restore lets you roll your system settings back to a specific date (restore point) when everything was working properly.

- Windows Ease of Access settings include tools that help adjust computer settings for those users with disabilities.

 Be sure to check out **MyLab IT** for additional materials to help you review and learn. And don't forget to watch the Chapter Overview Videos. ▶

Key Terms

application programming interface (API) **175**
authentication **179**
basic input/output system (BIOS) **177**
boot process **177**
cluster **196**
command-driven interface **172**
desktop **184**
device driver **175**
directory **187**
Disk Cleanup **194**
disk defragmentation **195**
distributions (distros) **168**
event **173**
extension (file type) **190**
file **187**
file compression utility **192**
File Explorer **187**
File History **196**
file management **187**
file name **190**
file path **187**
folder **187**

Google Chrome OS **167**
graphical user interface (GUI) **173**
interrupt **173**
interrupt handler **173**
kernel (supervisor program) **178**
Linux **168**
machine learning **176**
macOS **166**
menu-driven interface **173**
Microsoft account **179**
mobile operating system **167**
multitask **166**
multiuser operating system (network operating system) **169**
natural language processing **176**
operating system (OS) **166**
paging **174**
path separator **188**
pinning **185**
platform **168**
Plug and Play (PnP) **175**
power-on self-test (POST) **178**
preemptive multitasking **173**

real-time operating system (RTOS) **169**
Recycle Bin **191**
registry **179**
Reset this PC **179**
root directory **187**
sector **196**
spooler **174**
Start menu **184**
swap file (page file) **174**
system files **178**
System Restore **197**
system restore point **197**
Task Manager **195**
taskbar **184**
thrashing **174**
track **196**
UNIX **170**
user interface **166**
utility program **166**
virtual desktops **185**
virtual memory **174**
Windows **166**
Windows 10 **167**

Chapter Quiz // Assessment

For a quick review to see what you've learned, answer the following questions. Submit the quiz as requested by your instructor. If you are using **MyLab IT**, the quiz is also available there.

multiple choice

1. Which of the following would you NOT see on a Windows 10 Start menu?
   a. Task View
   b. Power
   c. apps list
   d. tiles

2. When an OS processes tasks in a priority order, it is known as
   a. preemptive interrupting.
   b. interruptive multitasking.
   c. multitasking handling.
   d. preemptive multitasking.

3. An example of an open source OS is
   a. Linux.
   b. macOS.
   c. Windows.
   d. DOS.

4. Which of the following is not considered an accessibility utility?
   a. Magnifier
   b. System Restore
   c. Narrator
   d. Speech Recognition

5. Which of the following devices would use a real-time operating system?
   a. iPhone
   b. Roomba Vacuum
   c. Microsoft Surface tablet
   d. all of the above

6. Special programs that facilitate interaction between hardware devices and the OS are called
   a. APIs.
   b. utility programs.
   c. device drivers.
   d. hardware players.

7. The first personal computers that used MS-DOS as the operating system had which kind of user interface?
   a. command-driven
   b. menu-driven
   c. graphical
   d. GUI

8. A feature in Windows 10 that is used to organize open windows into task-specific groups is called
   a. Program Manager.
   b. Virtual View.
   c. Snap Assist.
   d. Virtual Desktops.

9. When a printer receives a command, it generates a unique signal to the OS, which is called a(n)
   a. interrupt.
   b. event.
   c. slice.
   d. none of the above.

10. The C: drive on a Windows PC is like a large filing cabinet and is referred to as the
    a. main directory.
    b. root directory.
    c. library directory.
    d. main path.

true/false

_____ 1. Different versions of Linux are known as distros.

_____ 2. Modern desktop operating systems are considered single-user multitasking operating systems.

_____ 3. The power-on self-test ensures all peripheral devices are attached and operational.

_____ 4. System restore points can only be created by Windows automatically on a regular schedule.

_____ 5. Files deleted from a flash drive are sent to the Recycle Bin and could be recovered, if necessary.

critical thinking

1. **Protecting Embedded Systems**

   As more devices and appliances make use of RTOSs, the necessity of protecting them from hackers becomes increasingly critical. Developers are working to improve the security of the software and to safeguard communications between such devices. How concerned are you about the security of RTOSs in cars, smart homes, and wearable technology? Is enough being done to ensure the safety of these devices? What else can be done?

2. **Ease of Access**

   Windows and macOS both include a number of features and utilities designed for users with special needs. Compare the offerings of each OS. Are there options offered by one OS that are not available in the other? Which OS do you think has the best selection? Can you think of any areas that have not been addressed by this assistive technology? Research software from third-party developers to see if there are other tools that would also be useful. Should these tools be included in the OS? Why or why not?

Team Time

Choosing the Best OS

problem

You're the owner of a technology consulting firm. Your current assignments include advising start-up clients on their technology requirements. The companies include a nonprofit social service organization, a small interior design firm, and a social media advertising agency. One of the critical decisions for each company is the choice of OS.

task

Recommend the appropriate OS for each company.

process

1. Break up into teams that represent the three primary operating systems: Windows, macOS, or Linux.
2. As a team, research the pros and cons of your OS. What features does it have that would benefit each company? What features does it not have that each company would need? Discuss why your OS would be the appropriate (or inappropriate) choice for each company.
3. Develop a presentation that states your position with regard to your OS. Your presentation should have a recommendation and include facts to back it up.
4. As a class, decide which OS would be the best choice for each company.

conclusion

Because the OS is the most critical piece of software in the computer system, the selection should not be taken lightly. The OS that is best for a nonprofit social service organization may not be best for an interior design firm. A social media advertising agency may have different needs altogether. To ensure a good fit, it's important to make sure you consider all aspects of the work environment and the type of work being done.

Ethics Project

Upgrade Your World

In this exercise, you'll research and then role-play a complicated ethical situation. The role you play may or may not match your own personal beliefs, but your research and use of logic will enable you to represent whichever view is assigned.

problem

With the release of Windows 10, Microsoft began the "Upgrade Your World" project, to work with 10 global nonprofit groups and 100 local nonprofits (10 in 10 countries). The organizations were selected because they addressed a key societal issue and had demonstrated a consistent record of creating meaningful change in their community and the world. Each local nonprofit will receive a $50,000 cash investment plus technology from Microsoft. If Microsoft decided to extend the program to another local nonprofit, which nonprofit organization in your area would you choose and why?

research areas to consider

- Windows 10 features
- Upgrade Your World project
- The global and local Upgrade Your World nonprofits

process

1. Divide the class into teams.
2. Research the areas cited above and determine a local nonprofit that you think would be deserving of an Upgrade Your World grant.
3. Team members should write a summary that provides background information for their nonprofit suggestion.
4. The team members will present their case to the class or submit a PowerPoint presentation for review by the rest of the class, along with the summary and resolution they developed. The class should determine the pros and cons of awarding the local nonprofit nominee the Upgrade Your World grant, and reach an agreeable conclusion as to which nonprofit would be the best choice to suggest to Microsoft.

conclusion

As deserving as most nonprofits seem to be, some may benefit more than others, and ultimately serve the community better than others, after receiving a substantial grant such as that from Upgrade Your World. Being able to understand and evaluate a decision, while responding in a personally or socially ethical manner, will be an important skill.

Solve This   MyLab IT®
grader

Mobile Operating Systems: Changing Market Share

Using Excel 2016, you will display the market share statistics of mobile operating systems using line, column, and pie charts.

You will use the following skills as you complete this activity:

- Create a Line Chart
- Create and Format a Pie Chart
- Create and Format a Column Chart

- Add Shape to Chart
- Insert Sparklines

Instructions

1. Open *TIA_Ch5_Start* and save as **TIA_Ch5_LastFirst**.

2. Create a 2-D Line chart from the range A3:G7. Modify the chart as follows:
   a. Add a title: **Change in Mobile OS Market Share 2011–2016**. *2011–2016* should be on a separate line. Change the font size of *2011–2016* to **10**.
   b. Move the chart to a separate worksheet. Rename the new worksheet **Line Chart**, and place after the Data worksheet.
   c. Filter out the *Others* data so only *Android*, *iOS*, and *Windows* data displays.
   d. Add a **Line Callout 1 shape** to the chart with the line pointing where the Android and the iOS lines intersect. Add text to the callout: **2014: When Android surpassed iOS**.
      Hint: Line Callout 1 is in the Callouts section in the Insert Shape group on the Chart Tools Format tab.

3. Create a 2-D Pie chart from the ranges A3:A7 and G3:G7.
   a. Hint: Press the **Ctrl key** while selecting nonadjacent ranges. Modify the chart as follows:
   b. Add a title: **2016 Mobile OS Market Share**.
   c. Use **Quick Layout 1** to add data % and Series data labels to each pie slice.
   d. Resize the chart so it fits in the range A12:H30.

4. Create a Clustered Column chart that compares just Android and iOS data for 2011-2016. Modify the chart as follows:
   a. Add a title: **Android versus iOS Market Share**.
   b. Format the chart with **Style 8**.
   c. Move the chart to a separate worksheet. Rename the new worksheet **Column Chart**, and place it after the *Line Chart* worksheet.

5. On the Data worksheet, add **Line Sparklines** to cell range H4:H7 using the data in range B4:G7. Add a **High Point** to each Sparkline. Increase the width of column H to 12.

6. Save the document and submit based on your instructor's directions.

6

Understanding and Assessing Hardware: Evaluating Your System

 For a chapter overview, watch the Chapter Overview Videos.

PART 1

Evaluating Key Subsystems

Learning Outcome 6.1 **You will be able to evaluate your computer system's hardware functioning, including the CPU and memory subsystems.**

 Your Ideal Computing Device 208

Objective 6.1 *Describe the changes in CPU performance over the past several decades.*

Objective 6.2 *Compare and contrast a variety of computing devices.*

 Evaluating the CPU Subsystem 211

Objective 6.3 *Describe how a CPU is designed and how it operates.*

Objective 6.4 *Describe tools used to measure and evaluate CPU performance.*

 Evaluating the Memory Subsystem 218

Objective 6.5 *Discuss how RAM is used in a computer system.*

Objective 6.6 *Evaluate whether adding RAM to a system is desirable.*

Helpdesk: Evaluating Your CPU and RAM
Sound Byte: Installing RAM

PART 2

Evaluating Other Subsystems and Making a Decision

Learning Outcome 6.2 **You will be able to evaluate your computer system's storage subsystem, media subsystem, and reliability and decide whether to purchase a new system or upgrade an existing one.**

 Evaluating the Storage Subsystem 225

Objective 6.7 *Classify and describe the major types of nonvolatile storage drives.*

Objective 6.8 *Evaluate the amount and type of storage needed for a system.*

Sound Byte: Installing an SSD Drive

 Evaluating the Media Subsystems 231

Objective 6.9 *Describe the features of video cards.*

Objective 6.10 *Describe the features of sound cards.*

Helpdesk: Evaluating Computer System Components

 Evaluating System Reliability and Moving On 237

Objective 6.11 *Describe steps you can take to optimize your system's reliability.*

Objective 6.12 *Discuss how to recycle, donate, or dispose of an older computer.*

For the IT Simulation for this chapter, see MyLab IT.

MyLab IT All media accompanying this chapter can be found here.

Make This Make: A Location-Aware App on **page 224**

(Wavebreakmedia Micro/Fotolia; lucadp/Fotolia; Joppo/Shutterstock; Scanrail1/Shutterstock; Leigh Prather/Shutterstock; Ivelin Radkov/Alamy Stock Photo;)

How Cool Is This?

Want to create something really cool? The **Arduino microcontroller** project has fueled an abundance of DIY (do-it-yourself) electronics projects and created an energized community of do-it-yourselfers. This small **printed circuit board** is based on a microcontroller and includes everything you need: You just plug it in and begin your DIY project. The **open source hardware** is licensed under the Creative Commons license, so schematics are freely available to be changed or re-created as you wish.

The **LilyPad** variation of the Arduino, designed by MIT engineer Leah Buechley, is often used to create **wearable projects**. Conductive thread runs from the Arduino output pins to LEDs, and the finished garments are washable. The LilyPad project seen here, a glove that remotely controls a robotic hand, was designed at a hackathon in Warsaw, Poland. **Hackathons** are workshops that help people learn to design software and electronic hardware. *(epa european pressphoto agency b.v./Alamy)*

Evaluating Key Subsystems

> **Learning Outcome 6.1** You will be able to evaluate your computer system's hardware functioning, including the CPU and memory subsystems.

It can be tough to know if your computer is the best match for your needs. New technologies emerge so quickly, and it's hard to determine whether they're expensive extras or tools you need. Do you need USB 3.1 instead of USB 3.0? Doesn't it always seem as though your friend's computer is faster than yours? Maybe you could get more out of newer technologies, but should you upgrade the system you have or buy a new machine? In this chapter, you'll learn how to measure your system's performance and gauge your needs so that you end up with a system you love.

Your Ideal Computing Device

There never seems to be a perfect time to buy a new computer. It seems that if you can just wait a year, computers will be faster and cost less. But is this actually true?

Moore's Law

Objective 6.1 *Describe the changes in CPU performance over the past several decades.*

How quickly does computer performance improve? As it turns out, it is true that if you wait just a while, computers will be faster and cost less. In fact, a rule of thumb often cited in the computer industry, called **Moore's Law**, describes the pace at which central processing units (CPUs) improve. Named for Gordon Moore, the cofounder of the CPU chip manufacturer Intel, this rule predicts that the number of transistors inside a CPU will increase so fast that CPU processing power will double about every two years. (The number of transistors on a CPU chip helps determine how fast it can process data.)

This rule of thumb has held true for over 50 years. Figure 6.1 shows a way to visualize this kind of exponential growth. If CPU capacity were put into terms of population growth, a group of 2,300 people at the start of CPU development would now be a country of over 1 billion!

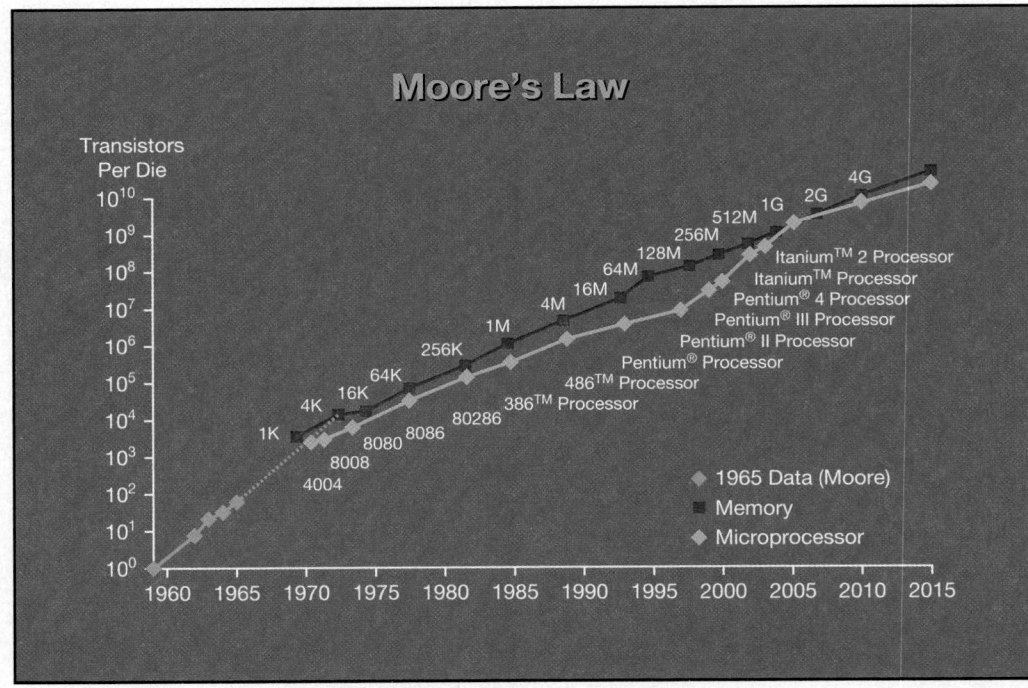

Figure 6.1 Moore's Law illustrates the amazing pace of growth in CPU capabilities.

In addition to the CPU becoming faster, other system components also continue to improve dramatically. For example, the capacity of memory chips such as dynamic random access memory (DRAM)—the most common form of memory found in personal computers—increases about 60% every year. Meanwhile, hard drives have been growing in storage capacity by some 50% each year.

Will Moore's Law always be true? Probably not. Moore himself has predicted that around the year 2020, CPU chips will be manufactured in a different way, thus changing or eliminating the effects of Moore's Law altogether. The scale to which reliable functioning transistors can be produced with silicon has limits (both functional and monetary). Intel is currently producing chips with features just 14 nanometers (nm) wide. It has postponed its switch to a 10-nm width in part due to the costs of constructing the fabrication facilities. Intel and other chip companies are investigating alternative elements for chips such as carbon (in both nanotube and graphene form), indium antimonide (InSb), and indium gallium arsenide (InGaAs). The main advantage with these substances is that they offer higher switching speeds than silicon, at lower power consumption rates. Therefore, the goal may shift toward better performing transistors rather than sheer quantity.

With technology demands switching to mobile devices and the Internet of Things, the goals of computing chip design have also changed. The drive for conventional CPUs used to be all about increasing computing capacity. Now chip designers are more concerned about low power processors (to conserve battery power) and integrating components such as RAM, cellular, Wi-Fi, and sensors (like accelerometers) into chips. So although Moore's Law isn't quite dead, the way the industry looks at increases in computing power and functionality of chips is changing.

Selecting a Computing Device

Objective 6.2   *Compare and contrast a variety of computing devices.*

OK, things change fast. How do I know which device is best for me? Consider what kind of user you are and what needs you have. For example, are you a power user who wants a machine for doing video editing and high-end gaming? Or are you a more casual user, mainly using a device for word processing and Internet access? Or are you on the move and need to bring your computer with you everywhere? Figure 6.2 shows a few different types of users—which type (or types) are you?

Now ask yourself, does your current computer match your needs? As we evaluate the pieces of your system in this chapter, it'll become clear whether your current device will need a few upgrades or whether you may need to acquire a new machine.

What are the main types of devices available? As we discussed in Chapter 2, a huge number of choices are on the market (see Figure 6.3):

- Smartphones
- Tablets (like the iPad or Galaxy)
- Ultrabooks (like the MacBook Air)
- 2-in-1s (which can serve as a tablet but also have a full keyboard)
- Laptops (or notebooks)
- Desktops

The main distinction among the available options is based on your need for mobility versus your need for processing power. If you're on the move all the time, don't use keyboard-intensive apps (like word processing), just need to check e-mail and the Internet, and want to have the lightest solution possible, a smartphone may be best for you. But if you use productivity software and need the convenience of a larger screen and a physical keyboard, you might want an ultrabook. At less than three pounds, they're great on weight but don't include an optical drive for DVDs/Blu-rays or as much storage space as conventional laptops. Even lighter are tablets like the iPad, but they have less processing power and, again, may not be able to run all the software you need.

Figure 6.2   What Kind of Technology User Are You?

Casual User
- Uses the computer primarily for Internet access
- Uses some software applications locally, like Microsoft Office
- Uses videos and software but does not create them

Power User
- Needs fast, powerful processing
- Needs fast storage and lots of it
- Creates videos and software programs

Mobile User
- Needs a lightweight device
- Needs a long battery life
- Is happy to sacrifice some capabilities for less weight

(Ilaszlo/Shutterstock, ColorBlind Images/The Image Bank/Getty Images, Ollyy/Shutterstock)

Figure 6.3 Range of Computing Devices

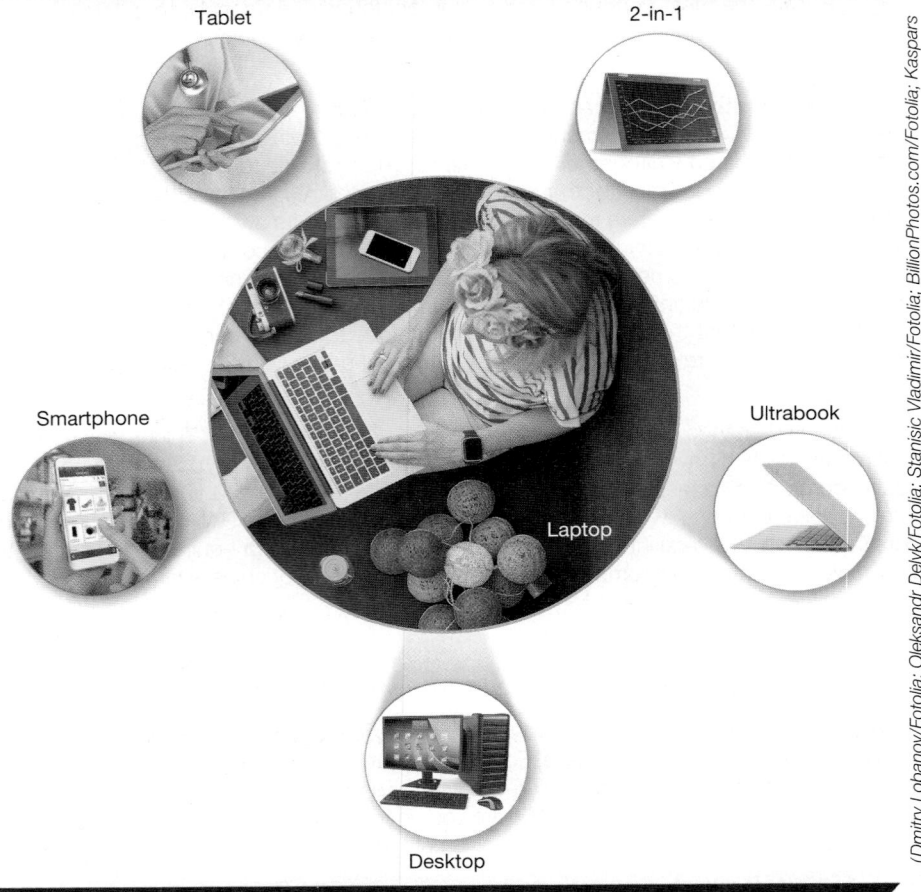

Tablet

2-in-1

Smartphone

Ultrabook

Laptop

Desktop

(Dmitry Lobanov/Fotolia; Oleksandr Delyk/Fotolia; Stanisic Vladimir/Fotolia; BillionPhotos.com/Fotolia; Kaspars Grinvalds/Fotolia; Petr Ciz/Fotolia; Oleksandr Delyk/Fotolia)

Why would anyone consider buying a desktop? Desktop systems are invariably a better value than lighter, more mobile computers. You'll find you get more computing power for your dollar, and you'll have more opportunity to upgrade parts of your system later. In addition, desktops often ship with a 24-inch or larger monitor, whereas lighter computers offer screens between 10 and 17 inches.

Figure 6.4 Computer Subsystems

CPU

Memory

Storage

Media (video and sound)

(Maxim_Kazmin/Fotolia; Cigdem/Fotolia; Maxim_Kazmin/ Fotolia; BillionPhotos.com/Fotolia)

Desktop systems are also more reliable. Because of the vibration that a laptop experiences and the added exposure to dust, water, and temperature fluctuations that portability brings, laptops often have a shorter lifespan than desktop computers. You'll have less worry over theft or loss with a desktop, too. Manufacturers do offer extended warranty plans that cover laptop computers for accidental damage and theft; however, such plans can be costly.

How long should I plan on keeping my computing device? You should be able to count on two years, and maybe even four or five years. The answer depends in part on how easy it is to upgrade your system. Take note of the maximum amount of memory you can install in your device. Also, check whether you can upgrade your device's graphics capabilities down the road. In this chapter, we will focus primarily on laptops and desktops, as they provide you with the most options for upgrading a current device without replacing it.

How do I evaluate the performance of my current device? We'll begin by conducting a **system evaluation**. To do this, we'll look at your computer's subsystems (see Figure 6.4), see what they do, and check how they perform during your typical workday. Then we'll compare that with what is available on the market, and the path forward for you will become clearer. Even if you're not in the market for a new computer, conducting a system evaluation will help you understand what you might want down the road.

Evaluating the CPU Subsystem

Let's start by considering your system's processor, or CPU. The CPU is located on the system motherboard and is responsible for processing instructions, performing calculations, and managing the flow of information through your computer. The dominant processors on the market are the Core family from Intel, featuring the i9, i7, and i5 (see Figure 6.5).

How the CPU Works

Objective 6.3 *Describe how a CPU is designed and how it operates.*

How can I find out what CPU my computer has? If you're running Windows, the System About window will show you the type of CPU you have installed. For example, the computer in Figure 6.6 has an Intel i5 CPU running at 2.6 GHz. AMD is another popular manufacturer of CPUs; you may have one of its processors, such as the A-series or the FX series. More detailed information about your CPU, such as its number of cores and amount of cache memory, is not shown on this screen. Let's dive into that.

How does the CPU actually process data? Any program you run on your computer is actually a long series of binary code describing a specific set of commands the CPU must perform. These commands may be coming from a user's actions or may be instructions fed from a program while it executes. Each CPU is somewhat different in the exact steps it follows to perform its tasks, but all CPUs must perform a series of similar general steps. Every time the CPU performs a program instruction, it goes through this series of steps:

1. **Fetch:** When any program begins to run, the 1s and 0s that make up the program's binary code must be "fetched" from their temporary storage location in random access memory (RAM) and moved to the CPU before they can be executed.

2. **Decode:** Once the program's binary code is in the CPU, it is decoded into commands the CPU understands.

3. **Execute:** Next, the CPU actually performs the work described in the commands. Specialized hardware on the CPU performs addition, subtraction, multiplication, division, and other mathematical and logical operations.

4. **Store:** The result is stored in one of the **registers**, special memory storage areas built into the CPU, which are the most expensive, fastest memory in your computer. The CPU is then ready to fetch the next set of bits encoding the next instruction.

Figure 6.5 The Intel i9, i7, and i5 CPU chips run many of the laptop and desktop offerings on the market today. *(David Caudery/PC Format Magazine/Future/Getty Images)*

Figure 6.6 The System About window identifies your computer's CPU as well as its speed. This computer has an Intel i5 running at 2.6 GHz.
> To view the System About window, right-click the **Start** button. From the menu that displays, choose **System.**.
(Windows 10, Microsoft Corporation)

RAM

1002
1003
1004
1005
1006
1007
1008
1009
1010

CPU

Fetch

Registers

R1
R2
R3
R4
R5
R6
R7
R8
R9
R10

Decode

Arithmetic Logic Unit (ALU)

+ -
* /

Control Unit

Execute

Store

Figure 6.7 The CPU Machine Cycle

This process is called a **machine cycle** (see Figure 6.7). No matter what program you're running and no matter how many programs you're using at one time, the CPU performs these four steps over and over at incredibly high speeds. (We discuss the machine cycle steps in more detail in the Dig Deeper feature in this chapter.)

What are the main components within a CPU? The CPU is composed of two units: the **arithmetic logic unit (ALU)** and the **control unit**. The ALU is responsible for performing all the arithmetic calculations (addition, subtraction, multiplication, and division). It also makes logic and comparison decisions, such as comparing items to determine if one is greater than, less than, or equal to another.

The control unit of the CPU manages the switches inside the CPU. The CPU, like any part of the computer system, is designed from a collection of switches. How can the simple on/off switches of the CPU "remember" the fetch-decode-execute-store sequence of the machine cycle? It is programmed by CPU designers to remember the sequence of processing stages for that CPU and how each switch in the CPU should be set (i.e., on or off) for each stage. With each beat of the system clock, the control unit moves each switch to the correct on or off setting and then performs the work of that stage.

To move from one stage of the machine cycle to the next, the motherboard uses a built-in **system clock**. This internal clock is actually a special crystal that acts like a metronome, keeping a steady beat and controlling when the CPU moves to the next stage of processing.

These steady beats or "ticks" of the system clock, known as the **clock cycle**, set the pace by which the computer moves from process to process. The pace, known as **clock speed**, is measured in hertz (Hz), which describes how many times something happens per second. Today's system clocks are measured in gigahertz (GHz), or a billion clock ticks per second. Therefore, in a 3-GHz system, there are 3 billion clock ticks each second.

What makes one CPU different from another? You pay more for a computer with an Intel i9 than one with an Intel i7 because of its increased processing power. A CPU's processing power is determined by the following:

• Its clock speed
• How many cores it has
• Its amount of cache memory

How does a CPU with a higher clock speed help me? The faster the clock speed, the more quickly the next instruction is processed. CPUs currently have clock speeds of up to 4 GHz.

Some users push their hardware to perform faster, **overclocking** their processor. Overclocking means that you run the CPU at a faster speed than the manufacturer recommends. It produces more heat, meaning a shorter lifespan for the CPU, and usually voids any warranty, but in gaming systems, you'll see this done quite often.

How does increasing the number of cores in a CPU help me? A **core** on a CPU contains the parts of the CPU required for processing an instruction. With multiple-core technology, two or more complete processors live on the same chip, enabling the independent execution of two or more sets of instructions at the same time.

If you had clones of yourself sitting next to you working, you could get twice as much (or more) done: That is the idea of multi-core processing. With multi-core processing, applications that are always running behind the scenes, such as virus protection software and your operating system (OS), can have their own dedicated processor, freeing the other processors to run other applications more efficiently. This results in faster processing and smoother multitasking. Chips with quad-core processing capabilities (see Figure 6.8) have four separate parallel processing paths inside them, so they're almost as fast as four separate CPUs. It's not quite four times as fast because the system must do some extra work to decide which processor will work on which part of the problem and to recombine the results each CPU produces.

Figure 6.8 Intel Quad Core processors have four cores that are able to run four programs simultaneously.

Eighteen-core processors, like the Intel Core i9-7980XE, are now available and feature 18 separate processing paths. Multi-processor systems are often used when intensive computational problems need to be solved in such areas as computer simulations, video production, and graphics processing. Extreme gamers also use them in home computers.

Are multi-core CPUs the only way to handle simultaneous processing? Certain types of problems are well suited to a parallel-processing environment, although this approach is not used in personal computing. In **parallel processing**, there is a large network of computers, with each computer working on a portion of the same problem simultaneously. To be a good candidate for parallel processing, a problem must be able to be divided into a set of tasks that can be run simultaneously. For example, a problem where millions of faces are being compared with a target image for recognition is easily adapted to a parallel setting. The target face can be compared with many hundreds of faces at the same time. But if the next step of an algorithm can be started only after the results of the previous step have been computed, parallel processing will present no advantages.

What other factors can affect processing speed? The CPU's **cache memory** is a form of RAM that gets data to the CPU for processing much faster than bringing the data in from the computer's RAM. There are three levels of cache memory, defined by their proximity to the CPU:

- Level 1 cache is a block of memory built on the CPU chip itself for storage of data or commands that have just been used. That gets the data to the CPU blindingly fast!
- Level 2 cache is located on the CPU chip but is slightly farther away and so takes somewhat longer to access than Level 1 cache. It contains more storage area than Level 1 cache.
- Level 3 cache is also located on the CPU chip itself but is slower to reach and larger in size than Level 2 cache.

Generally, the more expensive the CPU, the more cache memory it will have. As an end user of computer programs, you do nothing special to use cache memory. Unfortunately, because it's built into the CPU chip or motherboard, you can't upgrade cache; it's part of the original design of the CPU. Therefore, as with RAM, when buying a computer, it's important to consider the one with the most cache memory, everything else being equal.

Besides multiple cores and cache memory, what else can be done to increase the processing power of a CPU? As an instruction is processed, the CPU runs sequentially through the four stages of processing: fetch, decode, execute, and store. **Pipelining** is a technique that allows the CPU to work on more than one instruction (or stage of processing) at the same time, thereby boosting CPU performance.

For example, without pipelining, it may take four clock cycles to complete one instruction (one clock cycle for each of the four processing stages). However, with a four-stage pipeline, the computer can process four instructions at the same time. The ticks of the system clock (the clock

a Instruction Cycle, Non-Pipelined

| Instruction 1 | Fetch | Decode | Execute | Store | | | | |

| Instruction 2 | | | | | Fetch | Decode | Execute | Store |

Clock Ticks

0   1   2   3   4   5   6   7

b Instruction Cycle, Pipelined

Instruction 1 — Fetch | Decode | Execute | Store

Instruction 2 — Fetch | Decode | Execute | Store

Instruction 3 — Fetch | Decode | Execute | Store

Instruction 4 — Fetch | Decode | Execute | Store

Clock Ticks

0   1   2   3   4   5   6   7

Figure 6.9 Instead of (a) waiting for each instruction to complete, (b) pipelining allows the system to work on more than one set of instructions at one time.

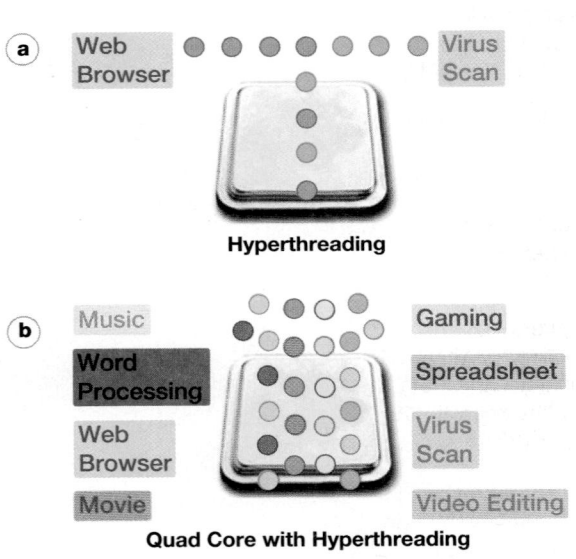

a Web Browser ••••••• Virus Scan

Hyperthreading

b Music   Gaming
Word Processing   Spreadsheet
Web Browser   Virus Scan
Movie   Video Editing

Quad Core with Hyperthreading

Figure 6.10 (a) Hyperthreading allows work on two processes to happen in one core at the same time. (b) So, a four-core hyperthreaded processor can be working on eight programs at one time.

cycle) indicate when all instructions move to the next process. Using pipelining, a four-stage processor can potentially run up to four times faster because some instruction is finishing every clock cycle rather than waiting four cycles for each instruction to finish. In Figure 6.9a, a non-pipelined instruction takes four clock cycles to be completed, whereas in Figure 6.9b, the four instructions have been completed in the same time using pipelining.

There is a cost to pipelining a CPU, however. The CPU must be designed so that each stage (fetch, decode, execute, and store) is independent. This means that each stage must be able to run at the same time that the other three stages are running. This requires more transistors and a more complicated hardware design.

CPUs began to expand their processing power further when **hyperthreading** was introduced in 2002. Hyperthreading provides quicker processing of information by enabling a new set of instructions in a different program (or thread) to start executing before the previous set has finished. This process takes advantage of certain delays that occur in reading and writing memory to registers with pipelining. As shown in Figure 6.10a, hyperthreading allows two different programs to be processed at one time, but they're sharing the computing resources of the chip.

All of the Intel Core processors have multiple cores *and* hyperthreading (see Figure 6.10b). The Intel i9-7980XE has 18 cores, each one using hyperthreading, so it simulates having 36 processors!

A critical aspect of the design of a computer system is to manage how the heat will be removed. One approach is to water-cool the system (see Figure 6.11). A tube containing liquid is placed in contact with heat-producing parts of the system, such as the CPU. The liquid picks up heat and carries it to a radiator, just as in a car. A fan blows across the fins of the radiator and efficiently disperses the heat. High-performance computers like the Aventum 3 from Digital Storm feature complex water-cooling systems because of the massive amount of heat they generate. Want to try water cooling in a computer you're building but nervous about water inside your system? Sealed water-cooling solutions are also available so you never have to pour water near the inside of your computer.

Figure 6.11 PC with liquid cooling system. *(Raw Group/Shutterstock)*

Measuring CPU Performance

Objective 6.4 *Describe tools used to measure and evaluate CPU performance.*

So how do I compare different CPUs? You'll often see models of the same computer with just a different CPU varying in cost by $200 or more. Is the price difference worth it? It's hard to know because so many factors influence CPU performance. Picking the best CPU for the kind of work you do is easier if you research some performance benchmarks. **CPU benchmarks** are measurements used to compare performance between processors. Benchmarks are generated by running software programs specifically designed to push the limits of CPU performance. Articles are often published comparing CPUs, or complete systems, based on their benchmark performance. Investigate a few, using sites like **cpubenchmark.net**, before you select the chip that's best for you.

How can I tell whether my current CPU is meeting my needs? One way to determine whether your CPU is right for you is to watch how busy it is as you work. You can do this by checking out your **CPU usage**—the percentage of time your CPU is working.

Your computer's OS has utilities that measure CPU usage. These are incredibly useful, both for considering whether you should upgrade and for investigating if your computer's performance suddenly seems to drop off for no apparent reason.

On Windows systems, the Task Manager utility lets you access this data (see Figure 6.12). The **CPU usage graph** records your CPU usage for the past minute. (Note that if you have multiple cores and hyperthreading, you'll see only one physical processor listed, but it will show that you have several virtual processors.) Of course, there will be periodic peaks of high CPU usage, but if your CPU usage levels are greater than 90% during most of your work session, a faster CPU will contribute a great deal to your system's performance.

To walk through using the Task Manager, check out the Try This on page 223. macOS has a similar utility named Activity Monitor located in the Utilities folder in the Applications subfolder.

How often should I watch the CPU load? Keep in mind that the workload your CPU experiences depends on how many programs are running at one time. Even though the CPU may meet the specs for each program separately, how you use your machine during a typical

Task Manager

File Options View

| Processes | Performance | App history | Startup | Users | Details | Services |

CPU
17% 2.86 GHz

Memory
3.9/7.9 GB (49%)

Disk 0 (C:)
0%

Bluetooth
Not connected

Wi-Fi
S: 0 R: 0 Kbps

Ethernet
Not connected

CPU
Intel(R) Core(TM) i5-3230M CPU @ 2.60GHz

% Utilization   100%

60 seconds   0

Utilization	Speed		Maximum speed:	2.60 GHz
17%	**2.86 GHz**		Sockets:	1
			Cores:	2
Processes	Threads	Handles	Logical processors:	4
92	**1115**	**40968**	Virtualization:	Enabled
			L1 cache:	128 KB
Up time			L2 cache:	512 KB
1:18:35:33			L3 cache:	3.0 MB

→ Peak CPU utilization

→ Current CPU utilization

→ Actual number of CPU cores

→ Number of virtual processors

Figure 6.12 The Performance tab of the Windows Task Manager utility shows you how busy your CPU is.
> *To access the Performance tab, right-click the **Start** button. From the menu, select **Task Manager**, and then click the **Performance** tab.*
(Windows 10, Microsoft Corporation)

Figure 6.13 Evaluating the CPU

Clock Speed
• Power users: Clock speed is very important; consider whether overclocking is worth sacrificing CPU longevity
• Casual/Mobile users: Clock speed is not as important

Multiple Cores
• Power users: Get as many cores as possible
• Casual users: Fewer cores is acceptable
• Mobile users: Low power draw is more critical than number of cores

Cache Memory
• Power users: Paying for more cache memory is a good investment
• Casual/Mobile users: Save your money

CPU Benchmark
• Use benchmarks to get an exact measure of the difference between two CPUs

(Maxim_Kazmin/Fotolia)

day may tax the CPU. If you're having slow response times or decide to measure CPU performance as a check, open the Task Manager and leave it open for a full day. Check in at points when you have a lot of open windows and when you have a lot of networking or disk-usage demand.

So a better CPU means a better-performing system? Your CPU affects only the processing portion of the system performance, not how quickly data can move to or from the CPU. Your system's overall performance depends on many factors, including the amount of RAM installed as well as hard drive speed. Your selection of CPU may not offer significant improvements to your system's performance if there is a bottleneck in processing because of insufficient RAM or hard drive performance, so you need to make sure the system is designed in a balanced way. Figure 6.13 lists factors to consider as you decide which specific CPU is right for you.

As you learned earlier, the *machine cycle* refers to the four stages performed by the CPU to process and store data. In this Dig Deeper, we'll take an in-depth look at each of these stages.

Stage 1: The Fetch Stage

The data and program instructions the CPU needs are stored in different areas in the computer system. Data and program instructions move between these areas as they're needed by the CPU for processing. Programs are permanently stored on the hard drive because it offers nonvolatile storage. However, when you launch a program, it—or sometimes only its essential parts— is transferred from the hard drive into RAM.

Steve Young/Fotolia

The program moves to RAM because the CPU can access the data and program instructions stored in RAM more than 1 million times faster than if they're left on the hard drive. In part, this is because RAM is much closer to the CPU than the hard drive is. Another reason for the delay in transmission of data and program instructions from the hard drive to the CPU is the relatively slow speed of mechanical hard drives. The read/write heads have to sweep over the spinning platters, which takes time. Even nonmechanical *solid state drives (SSDs)* have slower access speeds than RAM. RAM is a type of memory that gives very fast direct access to data.

As specific instructions from the program are needed, they're moved from RAM into registers (the special storage areas located on the CPU itself), where they wait to be executed.

The CPU's storage area isn't big enough to hold everything it needs to process at the same time. If enough memory were located on the CPU chip itself, an entire program could be copied to the CPU from RAM before it was executed. This would add to the computer's speed and efficiency because there would be no delay while the CPU stopped processing operations to fetch instructions from RAM to the CPU. However, including so much memory on a CPU chip would make these chips extremely expensive. In addition, CPU design is so complex that only a limited amount of storage space is available on the CPU itself.

The CPU doesn't actually need to fetch every instruction from RAM each time it goes through a cycle. As mentioned earlier, another layer of storage, called cache memory, has even faster access to the CPU than RAM. Cache memory blocks are holding places for recently or frequently used instructions or data that the CPU needs the most. When these instructions or data are stored in cache memory, the CPU can retrieve them more quickly than if it

had to access them in RAM. The CPU first looks for the instructions or data in Level 1 cache. If it doesn't find them there, it looks in Level 2 or Level 3 cache. If the needed information is not found in cache, the CPU retrieves it from RAM.

Stage 2: The Decode Stage

The main goal of the decode stage is for the CPU's control unit to translate (or decode) the program's instructions into commands the CPU can understand. The collection of commands that a specific

Andrea Danti/Fotolia

CPU can execute is called the *instruction set* for that system. Each CPU has its own unique instruction set. The control unit interprets the code's bits according to the instruction set the CPU designers laid out for that particular CPU. The control unit then knows how to set up all the switches on the CPU so that the proper operation will occur.

Because humans are the ones who write the initial instructions, all the commands in an instruction set are written in a language called *assembly language*, which is easier for humans to work with than binary language. Many CPUs have similar assembly commands in their instruction sets. CPUs differ in the choice of additional assembly language commands selected for the instruction set. Each CPU design team works to develop an instruction set that is both powerful and speedy.

However, because the CPU knows and recognizes only patterns of 0s and 1s, it can't understand assembly language directly, so these human-readable instructions are translated into binary code. The control unit uses these long strings of binary code called *machine language* to set up the hardware in the CPU for the rest of the operations it needs to perform. Machine language is a binary code for computer instructions. Similar to each letter or character having its own unique combination of 0s and 1s assigned to it, a CPU has a table of codes consisting of combinations of 0s and 1s for each of its commands. If the CPU sees a particular pattern of bits arrive, it knows the work it must do. Figure 6.14 shows a few commands in both assembly language and machine language.

Figure 6.14   Representations of Sample CPU Commands

Human Language for Command	CPU Command in Assembly Language (Language Used by Programmers)	CPU Command in Machine Language (Language Used in the CPU's Instruction Set)
Add	ADD	1110 1010
Subtract	SUB	0001 0101
Multiply	MUL	1111 0000
Divide	DIV	0000 1111

Stage 3: The Execute Stage

The arithmetic logic unit (ALU) is the part of the CPU designed to perform mathematical operations such as addition, subtraction, multiplication, and division and to test the comparison of values such as greater than, less than, and equal to. For example, in calculating an average, the ALU is where the addition and division operations would take place.

Taras Livyy/Fotolia

The ALU also performs logical OR, AND, and NOT operations. For example, in determining whether a student can graduate, the ALU would need to ascertain whether the student had taken all required courses AND obtained a passing grade in each of them. The ALU is specially designed to execute such calculations flawlessly and with incredible speed.

The ALU is fed data from the CPU's registers. The amount of data a CPU can process at a time is based in part on the amount of data each register can hold. The number of bits a computer can work with at a time is referred to as its *word size*. Therefore, a 64-bit processor can process more information faster than a 32-bit processor.

Stage 4: The Store Stage

In the final stage, the result produced by the ALU is stored back in the registers. The instruction itself will explain which register should be used to store the answer.

Once the entire instruction has been completed, the next instruction will be fetched, and the fetch-decode-execute-store sequence will begin again.

John Takai/Fotolia

Evaluating the Memory Subsystem

Let's now take a peek at the memory subsystem of your computer. The memory subsystem can have a terrific impact on your system's processing speed if it is well matched to the power of your CPU. In this section, we'll look at how to measure that and how to upgrade if you need to.

Random Access Memory

Objective 6.5   *Discuss how RAM is used in a computer system.*

What is RAM? Random access memory (RAM) is your computer's temporary storage space. It really is the computer's short-term memory. When the computer is running, the RAM remembers everything that the computer needs in order to process data, such as data that has been entered and software instructions. But when the power is off, the data stored in RAM disappears. So RAM is an example of **volatile storage**. This is why systems always include both RAM and **nonvolatile storage** devices for permanent storage of instructions and data. For example, read-only memory (ROM) is a type of nonvolatile storage that holds the critical startup instructions. Hard drives provide the largest nonvolatile storage capacity in the computer system in laptops and desktops. In mobile devices that lack hard drives, memory chips function as nonvolatile storage.

Why not use a hard drive to store the data and instructions? It's about 1 million times faster for the CPU to retrieve a piece of data from RAM than from a mechanical hard drive. The time it takes the CPU to grab data from RAM is measured in nanoseconds (billionths of seconds), whereas pulling data from a fast mechanical hard drive takes an average of 10 milliseconds (ms), or thousandths of seconds. Even if you are using an SSD, which is about eight times faster than a conventional hard drive, it is still much faster to retrieve data from RAM.

Figure 6.15 shows the various types of memory and storage distributed throughout your system: memory that is actually part of the CPU (such as CPU registers and cache), RAM, virtual memory, optical drives, solid state drives (SSDs), and mechanical hard drives. Each of these has its own tradeoff of speed versus price. Because the fastest memory is so much more expensive, systems are designed with much less of it. This principle is influential in the design of a balanced computer system and can have a tremendous impact on system performance.

Figure 6.15 A computer system's memory has many different levels, ranging from the small amounts in the CPU to the much slower but more plentiful storage of a mechanical hard drive.

Are there different types of RAM? Yes, but in most lower-end systems, the type of RAM used is double data rate 3 (DDR3) memory modules. High-performance systems use DDR4 memory, available in several different speeds (2400 MHz, 2800 MHz, and 3200 MHz). The higher the speed, the better the performance. High-performance video graphics cards often use GDDR5 memory, which has an even faster data transfer rate.

RAM appears in the system on **memory modules** (or **memory cards**), small circuit boards that hold a series of RAM chips and fit into special slots on the motherboard. Most memory modules in today's systems are packaged as a dual inline memory module (DIMM), a small circuit board that holds several memory chips (see Figure 6.16).

How can I tell how much RAM is installed in my computer? The amount of RAM actually sitting on memory modules in your computer is your computer's **physical memory**. The easiest way to see how much RAM you have is to look in the System window. (On a Mac, choose the Apple menu and then About This Mac.) This is the same window you looked in to determine your system's CPU type and speed, and is shown in Figure 6.6. RAM capacity is measured in gigabytes (GB), and most machines sold today have at least 4 GB of RAM.

Figure 6.16 A DIMM memory module holds a series of RAM chips and is wrapped with an aluminum heatsink plate to pull away heat. *(Scanrail/123RF)*

How can I tell how my RAM is being used? To see exactly how your RAM is being used, open the Resource Monitor and click on the Memory tab (see Figure 6.17). The Resource Monitor gives additional details on CPU, disk, network, and memory usage inside your system, and you can use it to see how you're using all the RAM you paid for.

Windows uses a memory-management technique known as **SuperFetch**. SuperFetch monitors the applications you use the most and preloads them into your system memory so that they'll be ready to be used when you want them. For example, if you have Microsoft Word running, Windows stores as much of the information related to Word in RAM as it can, which speeds up how fast your application responds. This is because pulling information from RAM is much faster than pulling it from the hard drive. You can watch this process at work using the Resource Monitor. Figure 6.17 shows how the 4 GB of installed RAM is being used:

* 1.1 GB is reserved to run the hardware systems.
* 0.98 GB is running programs.
* 1.7 GB is holding cached data and files ready for quick access.
* 0.2 GB is currently unused.

This is a system that would benefit from additional memory.

Figure 6.17 The Resource Monitor's Memory tab shows a detailed breakdown of how the computer is using memory.
> *To access the Resource Monitor, from the Start menu, click **Windows Administrative Tools**, click **Resource Monitor**, and then click the **Memory** tab.*
(Windows 10, Microsoft Corporation)

How much RAM do I need? At a minimum, your system needs enough RAM to run the OS. Running the 64-bit version of Windows 10 requires a minimum of 2 GB of RAM. However, because you run more applications at one time than just the OS, you'll want to have more RAM than just what's needed for the OS. For example, Figure 6.18 shows how much RAM is recommended for the OS, a web browser, and some software.

It's a good idea to have more than the minimum amount of RAM you need now so you can use more programs in the future. Remember, too, that "required" means these are the minimum values recommended by manufacturers; having more RAM often helps programs run more efficiently. High-end systems can come with 64 GB of RAM. The rule of thumb: When buying a new computer, buy as much RAM as you can afford.

Adding RAM

Objective 6.6 *Evaluate whether adding RAM to a system is desirable.*

Is there a limit to how much RAM I can add to my computer? The motherboard is designed with a specific number of slots into which the memory cards fit, and each slot has a limit on the amount of RAM it can hold. Some systems ship with the maximum amount of RAM installed, whereas others have room for additional RAM. To determine your specific system limits,

Figure 6.18 Sample RAM Allocation

Application	RAM Recommended
Windows 10 (high resolution)	2 GB
Microsoft Office Professional 2016	2 GB
Microsoft Edge	1 GB
iTunes 12	2 GB
Adobe Photoshop Elements 14	2 GB
Total RAM recommended to run all programs simultaneously	9 GB

check the system manufacturer's website. Also, memory seller sites like Crucial (**crucial.com**) can also help you determine how much RAM your computer model contains, whether you can add more, and the type of memory to add.

In addition, the OS running on your machine imposes its own RAM limit. For example, the maximum amount of RAM for the 32-bit version of Windows 10 is 4 GB, whereas the maximum memory limit using the 64-bit version of Windows 10 Pro is 512 GB.

Is it difficult or expensive to add RAM? Adding RAM is fairly easy (see Figure 6.19). Be sure that you purchase a memory module that's compatible with your computer. Also be sure to follow the installation instructions that come with the RAM module. Typically, you simply line up the notches and gently push the memory module in place.

RAM is a relatively inexpensive system upgrade. The cost of RAM does fluctuate in the marketplace as much as 400% over time, though, so if you're considering adding RAM, you should watch the prices of memory in online and print advertisements.

 Sound Byte MyLab IT®

Installing RAM

In this Sound Byte, you'll learn how to select the appropriate type of memory to purchase, how to order memory online, and how to install it yourself. As you'll discover, the procedure is a simple one and can add great performance benefits to your system.

Figure 6.19 Adding RAM to a computer is quite simple and relatively inexpensive. On a laptop, you often gain access through a panel on the bottom.
(Editorial Image, LLC/Alamy Stock Photo; Editorial Image, LLC/Alamy Stock Photo)

Before moving on to Part 2:

1. Watch Chapter Overview Video 6.1.
2. Then take the Check Your Understanding quiz.

Check Your Understanding // Review & Practice

For a quick review to see what you've learned so far, answer the following questions.

multiple choice

1. Moore's Law describes the pace at which _____ improve.
   a. RAM chips
   b. clock cycles
   c. CPUs
   d. cache modules

2. Which of the following is NOT a stage in the machine cycle?
   a. Fetch
   b. Calculate
   c. Decode
   d. Store

3. CPU _____ are measurements used to compare performance between processors.
   a. RAM speeds
   b. usage graphs
   c. cache cycles
   d. benchmarks

4. The limit to how much RAM you can add to your system
   a. depends on the design of the motherboard.
   b. depends on the operating system running on your system.
   c. depends on the amount of memory each memory card slot supports.
   d. all of the above

5. Adding RAM to your computer
   a. won't improve its performance.
   b. is too difficult for most people to do without professional help.
   c. is too expensive to make it practical.
   d. may be limited by how much RAM the computer can accommodate.

MyLab IT   Go to **MyLab IT** to take an autograded version of the *Check Your Understanding* review and to find all media resources for the chapter.

TechBytes Weekly   Go to TechBytes Weekly for current technology news and discussion questions!

Try This

Measure Your System Performance

Using the Windows Task Manager and the Resource Monitor can provide you with a lot of useful information about your computer system. Let's make sure you can use these Windows tools to keep an eye on your system performance. For more step-by-step instructions, watch the Try This video on MyLab IT.

Step 1 Hold the **Windows key** and press **X**. From the pop-up menu, select **Task Manager**. Click **More Details (if necessary)**, and then click the **Processes tab**.

Step 2 If you leave this window open while you work, you can pop in and check the history of how your CPU, disk, memory, and network are performing. Let's start by clicking on the **Performance tab**, and then looking at CPU utilization. This computer is only occasionally going over 30%, so the system isn't limited by CPU performance.

Step 3 Clicking on **Memory** in the left panel shows that we have 8 GB of DDR3 memory installed in this computer. Notice that memory usage is consistent at about 3.6 GB. We have memory available, so this system isn't limited by memory capacity with its current workload.

Step 4 Clicking on **Disk** in the left panel shows that here we have one disk drive, a 1 TB internal hard drive. The lower graph shows the history of data moving back and forth to the disk, the disk transfer rate. The larger upper graph shows how active the disk is—what percentage of time it is reading and writing. This system was not doing any disk-intensive operations when the screenshot was captured. If the active time is consistently high, upgrading to a faster, larger disk will have a big performance impact.

(Windows 10, Microsoft Corporation)

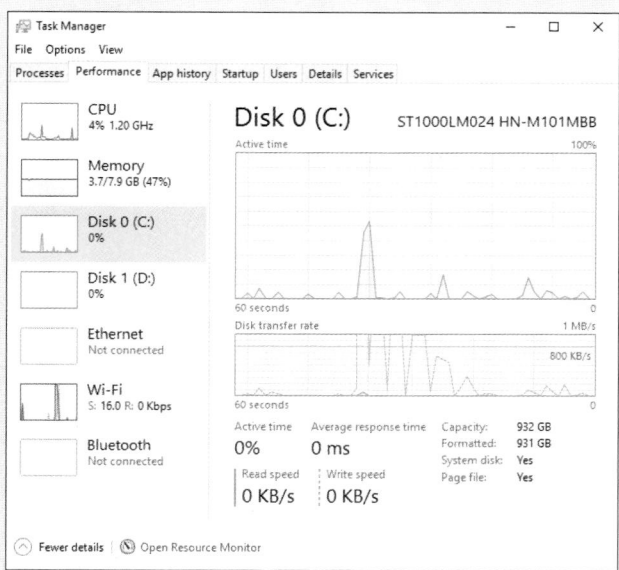

(Windows 10, Microsoft Corporation)

Make: A Location-Aware App

Your smartphone comes equipped with a number of built-in sensors that can, for example, read accelerations (to tell if your phone is shaking), location (using GPS satellites), and even atmospheric pressure. App Inventor can work with sensor data and supports a wide set of sensors used in the Lego Mindstorms kits to recognize color or respond to touch and sound.

(Copyright MIT, used with permission.)

In this exercise, you'll use the LocationSensor component in App Inventor to combine information about your environment into your apps.

The LocationSensor component allows you to work with live GPS data within your mobile app.

(Copyright MIT, used with permission)

For the instructions for this exercise, go to MyLab IT.

Evaluating Other Subsystems and Making a Decision

> **Learning Outcome 6.2** **You will be able to evaluate your computer system's storage subsystem, media subsystem, and reliability and decide whether to purchase a new system or upgrade an existing one.**

The audio and video subsystems of your computer affect much of your enjoyment of the machine. Equally important is the storage subsystem, which allows you to save all that content you're generating. Let's evaluate those subsystems and consider what state-of-the-art audio/video would add to your computing experience. Then let's consider how to make sure your system is reliable—nothing interferes with enjoying technology like a misbehaving computer!

Evaluating the Storage Subsystem

Remember, there are two ways data is stored on your computer: temporary storage and permanent storage. RAM is a form of temporary (or volatile) storage. The information residing in RAM is not stored permanently. It's critical to have the means to store data and software applications permanently, which we discuss in this section.

Types of Storage Drives

Objective 6.7 *Classify and describe the major types of nonvolatile storage drives.*

Permanent storage options include internal hard drives, SSDs, optical drives, and external hard drives. When you turn off your computer, the data that has been written to these devices will be available the next time the machine is powered on. These devices therefore provide nonvolatile storage.

Mechanical Hard Drives

What makes the hard drive such a popular storage device? With storage capacities exceeding 8 terabytes (TB), a mechanical **hard drive** has the largest capacity of any storage device. And because it offers the most storage per dollar, the hard drive is also a more economical device than other options.

Today, most desktop system units are designed to support more than one internal hard drive. The Apple Mac Pro has room for four hard drives, and the Thermaltake Level 10 can support six hard drives. Each one simply slides into place when you want to add more storage. To save weight, most laptops have space for only one hard drive.

How is data stored on a hard drive? A hard drive is composed of several coated, round, thin plates of metal stacked on a spindle. Each plate is called a **platter**. When data is saved to a hard drive platter, a pattern of magnetized spots is created on the iron oxide coating of each platter. When the spots are aligned in one direction, they represent a 1; when they're aligned in the other direction, they represent a 0. These 0s and 1s are bits (or binary digits) and are the smallest pieces of data that computers can understand. When data stored on the hard drive platter is retrieved (or read), your computer translates these patterns of magnetized spots into the data you have saved.

How quickly does a hard drive find information? The hard drive's **access time**, the time it takes a storage device to locate its stored data and make it available for processing, is faster than that of optical drives. Mechanical hard drive access times are measured in milliseconds (ms). For large-capacity drives, access times of approximately 12 to 13 milliseconds are typical. For comparison, a DVD drive can take over 150 milliseconds to access data.

Figure 6.20 The new M.2 form factor allows the production of very fast, thin, and light SSD drives that resemble a stick of chewing gum. *(Andrush/Shutterstock)*

Solid State Drives

Do mechanical hard drives have the fastest access times? A **solid state drive (SSD)** uses electronic memory and has no mechanical motors or moving parts. Having no mechanical motors allows SSDs to offer incredibly fast access times, reaching data in only a tenth of a millisecond (0.1 ms). That's about 100 times faster than mechanical hard drives. SSDs also have a great advantage when booting up because a mechanical hard drive has to wait for motors to bring the plates up to the final rotation speed. The startup time of SSDs is so fast, in fact, that most desktop and laptop systems offer an option to use at least one SSD. This "system drive" may only be 20 GB large, but it holds the operating system and means the wake-up time for the system will be very fast. In addition, SSDs run with no noise, generate very little heat, and require very little power, making them a popular option in laptops.

Storage capacities for SSDs now range up to around 15 TB, but such a large SSD is very expensive. Typical systems now often offer an SSD of 256 GB or 512 GB and then a mechanical hard drive, or two, to provide TBs of inexpensive slower storage space. But with prices of SSD drives continuing to fall, perhaps soon just having a single SSD drive may be affordable and provide the storage you need.

In the quest for ever thinner and lighter laptops, the newest type of SSD drive is in the M.2 form factor. First-generation SSD drives were contained in relatively large (2.5-inch or 3.5-inch) cases to fit the industry standard hard drive bays in desktops and laptops. But inside these SSD cases was mostly empty space. Now newer motherboards use the M.2 connector (see Figure 6.20) and the drives that connect to it are only about 22 mm wide and range in length from 42 to 80 mm. The drives look like sticks of chewing gum that have sprouted memory modules and a controller chip. This allows the SSD drives to be integrated into the motherboard, which saves space and weight and should allow future tablet computers to feature SSD drives. In addition, the M.2 drives have even faster data transfer rates than the previous generation of drives.

Solid State Hybrid Drives

Another relatively new storage option is the **solid state hybrid drive (SSHD)**. An SSHD drive is a combination of both a mechanical hard drive and an SSD into a single device (see Figure 6.21). SSHD drives offer a small amount of SSD storage space, perhaps 8 GB. If it is enough to store the operating system, however, it can have a huge impact on the system boot time. For laptops that will accept only one drive, these drives are a great option if you need large amounts of affordable storage space, as they're currently cheaper than SSD drives.

Optical Drives

How do optical drives work? **Optical drives** are disc drives that use a laser to store and read data. Data is saved to a compact disc (CD), digital video disc (DVD), or Blu-ray disc (BD) (collectively called **optical media**) within established tracks and sectors, just like on a hard drive. But optical discs store data as tiny pits that are burned into the disc by a high-speed laser. These pits are extremely small, less than 1 micron (a millionth of a meter).

Cover
Interface Connector
Magnetic Platters
Spindle
Actuator Arm with Read/Write Heads

Logic Board with Controller Circuits
Actuator

SSD Controller Chip
Drive Cache Memory Chips
SSD NAND Memory Chips

Logic Board

Bottom Cover

Figure 6.21 The SSHD is a single unit that contains both an SSD electronic drive and a mechanical hard drive. *(Zern Liew/Shutterstock)*

Data is read from a disc by a laser beam, with the pits and nonpits (called *lands*) translating into the 1s and 0s of the binary code that computers understand. CDs and DVDs use a red laser to read and write data. Blu-ray discs get their name because they are read with a blue laser light, which has a shorter wavelength and can focus more tightly and pack more information on a disc. Blu-ray drives are the fastest optical devices and deliver the high-definition quality video that larger displays and monitors demand.

Should I bother having an optical disc drive? Traditionally, optical media delivered music and movies, but these are now available through streaming services. Likewise, in the past, software was often installed from a DVD, but now you can buy almost all software through an online download. Therefore, most laptops and many desktops have stopped including optical drives. For example, ultrabooks and 2-in-1s are so thin and lightweight they often leave out an optical drive but may include a slot for an SD memory card to allow you to transfer files. You can buy external optical drives, but if you have a need for optical drives, you're probably better off purchasing a laptop computer with an optical drive.

Dig Deeper — How Storage Devices Work

The thin metal platters that make up a mechanical hard drive are covered with a special magnetic coating that enables the data to be recorded onto one or both sides of the platter. Hard drive manufacturers prepare the disks to hold data through a process called *low-level formatting*. In this process, concentric circles, each called a **track**, and pie-shaped wedges, each called a **sector**, are created in the magnetized surface of each platter, setting up a gridlike pattern that identifies file locations on the hard drive. A separate process called *high-level formatting* establishes the catalog that the computer uses to keep track of where each file is located on the hard drive. (More detail on this process is presented in the Dig Deeper feature in Chapter 5.)

Hard drive platters spin at a high rate of speed, some as fast as 15,000 revolutions per minute (rpm). Sitting between the platters are special "arms" that contain read/write heads (see Figure 6.22).

A **read/write head** moves from the outer edge of the spinning platter to the center, as frequently as 50 times per second, to retrieve (read) and record (write) the magnetic data to and from the hard drive platter. As noted earlier, the average total time it takes for the read/write head to locate the data on the platter and return it to the CPU for processing is called its *access time*. A new hard drive should have an average access time of approximately 12 ms.

Access time is mostly the sum of two factors—seek time and latency:

1. The time it takes for the read/write heads to move over the surface of the disk, moving to the correct track, is called the **seek time**. (Sometimes people incorrectly refer to this as access time.)
2. Once the read/write head locates the correct track, it may need to wait for the correct sector to spin to the read/write head. This waiting time is called **latency** (or **rotational delay**).

The faster the platters spin (or the faster the rpm), the less time you'll have to wait for your data to be accessed. Currently, most hard drives for home systems spin at 7,200 rpm.

The read/write heads don't touch the platters of the hard drive; rather, they float above them on a thin cushion of air at a height of 0.5 microinch. As a matter of comparison, a human hair is 2,000 microinches thick and a particle of dust is larger than a human hair. Therefore, it's critical to keep your hard drive free from all dust and dirt because even the smallest particle could find its way between the read/write head and the disk platter, causing a **head crash**—a stoppage of the hard drive that often results in data loss.

Figure 6.22 A mechanical hard drive is a stack of platters enclosed in a sealed case. Special arms fit between each platter. The read/write heads at the end of each arm read data from and save data to the platters. *(Skaljac/Shutterstock)*

SSDs free you from worry about head crashes at all. The memory inside an SSD is constructed with electronic transistors, meaning there are no platters, no motors, and no read/write arms. Instead, a series of cells are constructed in the silicon wafers. If high voltage is applied, electrons move in and you have one state. Reverse the voltage and the electrons flow in another direction, marking the cell as storing a different value. The limiting factor for an SSD's lifespan is how many times data can be written to a cell. But the current generation of SSDs is proving to have very strong performance over time. Intel, one manufacturer of SSDs, says its drives will last five years when being written to heavily (20 GB per day).

However, the higher cost of SSD drives means they can only provide smaller amounts of storage. One compromise solution is the *SSHD*, a single drive that has both a small (perhaps 8 GB) SSD as well as a high-capacity mechanical hard drive. The faster SSD space can be used to store the operating system so that boot-up times are greatly reduced. These drives will continue to be popular as a cost-effective combination of nonvolatile storage.

Capacities for mechanical hard drives can exceed 8,000 GB (8 TB), and SSD drives are now capable of storing 15 TB (although they are very expensive at that capacity). Increasing the amount of data stored in mechanical drives is achieved either by adding more platters or by increasing the amount of data stored on each platter. SSD capacities continue to increase as the density of transistors on silicon wafers increases. And the new M.2 form factor allows for the production of very thin SSD drives. Modern technology continues to increase the quantities of data that can be stored in small places.

Storage Needs

Objective 6.8 *Evaluate the amount and type of storage needed for a system.*

How do I know how much storage capacity I have? Typically, hard drive capacity is measured in gigabytes (GB) or terabytes (1 TB = 1,000 GB). Accessing This PC from File Explorer will display the hard drives, their capacity, and usage information, as shown in Figure 6.23. To get a slightly more detailed view, select a drive and then right-click and choose Properties.

How much storage do I need? You need enough space to store the following:

- The OS
- The software applications you use, such as Microsoft Office, music players, and games
- Your data files
- Your digital music library, photos, videos of television shows and movies, and so on

Figure 6.24 shows an example of storage calculation. If you plan to have a system backup on the same drive, be sure to budget for that room as well. However, note that if you're going to store your data files only online instead of on your computer, you may not need much hard drive space. For example, if you stream all the movies you watch from Netflix, keep all your data files in Microsoft OneDrive, and use online software like Google Docs to edit, you may need very little hard drive space. Many ultrabooks like the Dell XPS 13 or the Apple MacBook Air are configured with 128-GB drives. In fact, many Chromebooks have only a 16-GB drive.

If you still need more local storage than your internal hard drive provides, you can also add an external hard drive to your system. These use a USB port to connect. If you're looking to buy an external hard drive, the USB 3.1 standard is about 10 times faster than USB 2.0, so if your system supports USB 3.1, that's the better choice.

What is RAID technology? A **redundant array of independent disks (RAID)** is a set of strategies for using more than one drive in a system (see Figure 6.25). RAID 0 and RAID 1 are the most popular options for consumer machines. If you purchase two smaller drives, you can combine them using RAID technology.

Figure 6.23 In Windows, the free and used capacity of each device in the computer system is shown in the This PC window. The General tab of the Properties dialog box gives you more detailed information.
> *To view storage device details, launch File Explorer, and then click* **This PC***. To view more details, right-click the* **C drive***, and select* **Properties***. (Windows 10, Microsoft Corporation)*

Figure 6.24 Sample Hard Drive Space Requirements

Application/Data	Hard Drive Space Required	Heavy Cloud Storage User
Windows 10	20 GB	20 GB
Microsoft Office 2016 Professional	3.5 GB	3.5 GB
Adobe Photoshop Elements 14	4 GB	4 GB
Adobe Premiere Pro CC	10 GB	10 GB
Video library of movies	80 GB about 40 HD movies)	Streamed through online services
Music library	50 GB (about 7,000 songs)	Stored in cloud (iCloud or Amazon Cloud Drive)
Photographs	5 GB	Stored in iCloud or Dropbox
Total storage in use	172.5 GB	37.5 GB
Full backup	172.5 GB	Stored in cloud using Carbonite
Total required	345 GB	37.5 GB

When you run two hard drives in **RAID 0**, the time it takes to write a file is cut in half. If disk performance is very important—for example, when you're doing video editing or sound recording—using two files in RAID 0 could be important. RAID 0 is faster because every time data is written to a hard drive, it's spread across the two physical drives (see Figure 6.25a). The write begins on the first drive, and while the system is waiting for that write to be completed, the system jumps ahead and begins to write the next block of data to the second drive. This makes writing information to disk almost twice as fast as using just one hard drive. The downside is that if either of these disks fails, you lose all your data because part of each file is on each drive. So RAID 0 is for those most concerned with performance.

Figure 6.25 (a) A RAID 0 configuration speeds up file read/write time. (b) A RAID 1 configuration gives you an instant backup. *(Sergey Nivens/Fotolia; Ragnarock/Shutterstock)*

No matter what kind of device you purchase, you'll have to decide how much storage you're willing to pay for. Does your Nexus 10 tablet need 16 GB? 32 GB? Should the SSD drive in your ultrabook be 128 GB? 256 GB? 512 GB? When you make your decision, keep in mind three factors:

1. Check whether you can add storage later using an SD card. If you can use a few SD cards to store music or photos, that will be a cheaper option.

2. Check how much usable storage is available in the device. For example, a 128-GB drive might offer less than 90 GB of available storage space after the operating system, the manufacturer software, and backup storage space are accounted for.

3. Even though you can use cloud storage to expand your options, keep in mind that you need a base amount of local storage for installing apps. If you need to use a large variety of apps, make sure you'll have room to install them all.

If you're really paranoid about losing data, you should consider having two drives in RAID 1. In a **RAID 1** configuration, all the data written to one drive is instantly perfectly mirrored and written to a second drive (see Figure 6.25b). This provides you with a perfect, instant-by-instant backup of all your work. It also means that if you buy two 1-TB drives, you only have room to store 1 TB of data because the second 1-TB drive is being used as the "mirror."

RAID 0 and RAID 1 configurations are available on many desktop systems and are even beginning to appear on laptop computers.

So how do my storage devices measure up? Figure 6.26 summarizes the factors you should consider in evaluating your storage subsystem. Don't forget that you can always extend the storage subsystem in your Internet-connected devices by utilizing cloud storage options. If you constantly switch between devices, cloud storage is most likely your best option.

Figure 6.26   Evaluating Storage

Storage

Mechanical Hard Drive
- How much storage space do you need?
- Do you need a RAID 0 configuration for better performance?
- Do you want a RAID 1 configuration for immediate constant backup?

Solid-State Drive
- Do you want a very fast start-up of the system at boot-up and from sleep mode?
- Are you okay having a second hard disk drive for larger storage space?

Solid-State Hybrid Drive
- Do you want the speed advantage at boot-up of an SSD, the large storage capacity of a mechanical hard drive, and only one drive?

Optical Drive
- Do you need to read or produce DVD/CDs?
- Do you need to read or produce Blu-ray discs?

Cloud Storage
- Do you need access to your files from multiple devices?
- Do you need to access your files when you travel?

(Maxim Kazmin/Fotolia)

Evaluating the Media Subsystems

Enjoying interactive media through your computer demands both good video processing hardware and good audio processing hardware. Video quality depends on two components: your video card and your monitor. If you're considering using your computer to display complex graphics, edit high-definition videos, or play graphics-rich games with a lot of fast action, you may want to consider upgrading your video subsystem. Let's start our look at the media subsystems by examining video cards.

Video Cards

Objective 6.9 *Describe the features of video cards.*

What exactly is a video card? A **video card** (or **video adapter**) is an expansion card that's installed inside the system unit to translate binary data into the images you view on your monitor. Modern video cards like the ones shown in Figure 6.27 let you connect video equipment using a number of different ports:

- HDMI ports for high-definition TVs, Blu-ray players, or gaming consoles
- DVI ports for digital LCD monitors
- DisplayPorts for digital monitors or projectors

How much memory does my video card need? All video systems include their own RAM, called **video memory**. Several standards of video memory are available, including graphics double data rate 3 (GDDR3) memory and the newer **graphics double data rate 5 (GDDR5)** memory. Newer GDDR5X video memory chips offer faster data rates (twice as fast) than earlier chips and improvements in energy efficiency.

The amount of video memory on your video card makes a big impact on the resolution the system can support and on how smoothly and quickly it can render video. Most new laptop computers come with video cards equipped with a minimum of 1 GB of video memory. For the serious gamer, 2 GB or more is essential, and cards with 16 GB are available (at very high prices). These high-end video cards allow games to generate smoother animations and more sophisticated shading and texture.

How can I tell how much memory my video card has? You'll find information about your system's video card in the Advanced Display Settings of the Screen Resolution window. On a Windows computer, to get to the Screen Resolution window, right-click on your desktop and select Display settings. Select Display in the System Settings window, click the Advanced display settings link, and then click the Display adapter properties link. A dialog box will appear that shows you the type of video card installed in your system, as well as its memory capacity.

How does the CPU handle intensive video calculations? Because displaying graphics demands a lot of computational work from the CPU, video cards come with their own **graphics processing unit (GPU)**. The GPU is a separate processing chip specialized to handle 3D graphics and image and video processing with incredible efficiency and speed. When the CPU is asked to process graphics, it redirects those tasks to the GPU, significantly speeding up graphics processing. Figure 6.28 shows how the CPU can run much more efficiently when a GPU does all the graphics computations.

Figure 6.27 Video cards require their own fan for cooling. They support multiple monitors and multiple styles of ports like HDMI, DVI, and DisplayPort. *(YamabikaY/ Shutterstock)*

Figure 6.28 The GPU is specialized to handle processing of photos, videos, and video game images. It frees up the CPU to work on other system demands.

In addition, special lighting effects can be achieved with a modern GPU. Designers can change the type of light, the texture, and the color of objects based on complex interactions. Some GPU designs incorporate dedicated hardware to allow high-definition movies to be decoded or special physics engines to model water, gravity, and rigid body movements.

Why do some people use more than one video card in the same system? For users who are primarily doing text-based work, one video card is certainly enough. Computer gamers and users of high-end visualization software, however, often take advantage of the ability to install more than one video card at a time. Two or even three video cards can be used in one system. When the system is running at very high video resolutions, such as 1920 × 1200 or higher, multiple video cards working together provide the ultimate in performance.

The two major video chip set manufacturers, NVIDIA and AMD, have each developed their own standards supporting the combining of multiple video cards. For NVIDIA, this standard is named SLI; for AMD, it is called CrossFireX. If you're buying a new desktop system and might be interested in employing multiple video cards, be sure to check whether the motherboard supports SLI or CrossFireX.

Can I run a few monitors from one video card? Working with multiple monitors is useful if you often have more than one application running at a time (see Figure 6.29) or even if you just want to expand your gaming experience. Some video cards can support up to six monitors from a single card. The AMD Radeon graphics cards, for example, let you merge all six monitors to work as one screen or to combine them into any subset—for example, displaying a movie on two combined screens, Excel on one monitor, Word on another, and a browser spread across the final two.

Can I have a 3D experience from a computer monitor? 3D panels are available for desktop monitors and for some laptops. The 3D wireless vision glasses included with the panels make existing games or 3D movies display in stereoscopic 3D.

Figure 6.29 AMD Radeon technology supports six monitors, which can be combined in any way. *(Satopon/Fotolia)*

Rendering graphics for digital movies like *Finding Dory* by Pixar is very processor intensive. Pixar maintains a huge collection of computers, called a *render farm*, just for the purpose of rendering the graphics. Rendering means generating the graphics in final full-color form for viewing. Even with a render farm, it still takes 20 to 29 hours to render a single frame of a movie. Depending on their format, movies run at 24 to 60 frames per second. Therefore, it currently takes years of render farm time to render a movie in final form.

AMD answered demand by releasing the Radeon Pro SSG video card, which allows owners to install up to 1 TB of NAND flash memory directly into the graphics card. This essentially combines an SSD with a video card. This design allows massive amounts of data to be processed locally on the video card without having to use system RAM. This should provide a huge performance boost in high-resolution rendering work required by the movie industry. However, you probably won't find them in home computers any time soon, as they cost around $10,000. With the demand for animated movies on the rise, you can bet that movie studios like Pixar will upgrade their render farms with these cards.

How do I know if I'm putting too much demand on my video card? If your monitor takes a while to refresh when you're editing photos or playing a graphics-rich game, then the video card could be short on memory or the GPU is being taxed beyond its capacity. You can evaluate this precisely using the software that came with your card. For example, AMD Overdrive software monitors the GPU usage level, the current temperature, and the fan speed.

Review the considerations listed in Figure 6.30 to see if it might be time to upgrade your video card. On a desktop computer, replacing a video card is fairly simple: Just insert the new video card in the correct expansion slot on the motherboard. For laptop computers, it's usually not practical (or even possible in some cases) to upgrade the video card, as it's integrated directly into the motherboard. Usually your best option is to purchase a new laptop that has a more powerful video card.

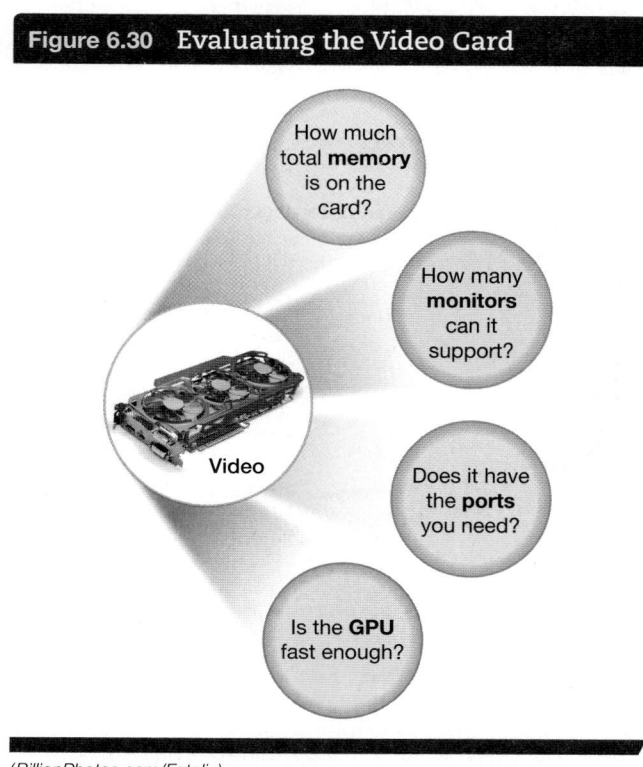

Figure 6.30   Evaluating the Video Card

How much total **memory** is on the card?

How many **monitors** can it support?

Video

Does it have the **ports** you need?

Is the **GPU** fast enough?

(BillionPhotos.com/Fotolia)

When the USB standard was introduced, a number of different ports began to fade from use. With USB, one port could be used to connect a keyboard, a mouse, a flash drive, an external hard drive, and a camera. For sure, USB seemed to be the perfect standard.

But as the need for larger file transfers grew with larger HD video files and higher-resolution image files, the USB standard needed to keep improving to offer faster data transfer rates. The USB connector also needed to be redesigned to different sizes so it could be used in phones, cameras, and thinner ultrabooks. This resulted in a collection of USB 1.0, 2.0, and 3.0 devices along with USB 1.0 and 2.0 ports, blue USB 3.0 ports, tiny mini USB ports, and even tinier micro USB ports. And, of course, each connector was oriented in a certain way, so we found ourselves spinning the cable around to try to find the right orientation to actually fit the connector into the port.

The USB standard faced competition as well, with the Thunderbolt technology appearing on Apple products. Thunderbolt 3 supports fast transfer rates of 40 Gb/s, zooming past the limit of the USB 3.0, which is 4.8 Gb/s. How fast is that? Intel, the company that developed the technology, claims that Thunderbolt can transfer a full-length HD movie in under 30 seconds, or copy in just 10 minutes a library of music that would take a solid year to play through.

Intel used fiber optics—the transmission of digital data through pure glass cable as thin as human hair—to develop Thunderbolt. And Thunderbolt supplies much more power to devices than the USB 3.0 standard allows. It also has a very slim connector design, allowing laptop designers to make their systems even thinner. And Thunderbolt can be used to connect displays!

But now here comes the most recent release of the USB standard, USB 3.1. It addresses all of these issues. The USB 3.1 speed

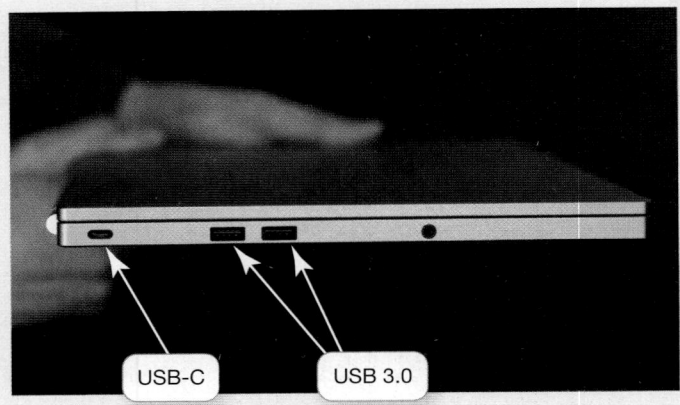

Figure 6.32 The Google Pixel computer has one USB-C port on each side but also includes two USB 3.0 ports. *(Jeff Chiu/AP Images)*

limit matches the 10 Gb/s of Thunderbolt 1, making it twice as fast as USB 3.0. It also can transfer up to 100 watts of power, compared to just 10 watts for USB 3.0. This means a USB 3.1 port could be used to replace even the power charging port of a laptop. If the USB 3.1 standard is implemented using a USB-C connector, then we have the best of all worlds. The USB-C connector, shown in Figure 6.31, is thin, small, and reversible, so the connector will slide into the port in either up or down orientation.

What will this mean to laptop designers? Apple redesigned its popular MacBook laptop with a radical port layout: a single USB 3.1 C port. The Google Pixel computer still has two of the familiar USB 3.0 ports, but it has added a USB 3.1 C port to each side of the machine (see Figure 6.32). Look for a USB 3.1 C port on your next phone, camera, and laptop!

USB-C KEY ASPECTS

ENTIRELY NEW DESIGN
Made for Emerging Product Designs

SUPPORTS SCALABLE POWER CHARGING

FUTURE SCALABILITY
Designed to Establish Future USB Needs

USABILITY ENHANCEMENTS
Reversible Plug Orientation and Cable Direction

NEW SMALLER SIZE

Figure 6.31 USB-C brings a reversible, durable plug capable of charging with 100 watts of power. *(Crystal Eye Studio/Shutterstock)*

Sound Cards

Objective 6.10 *Describe the features of sound cards.*

What does the sound card do? A **sound card** is an expansion card that enables the computer to drive the speaker system. Sound cards are now routinely integrated into the motherboard on most computers and provide excellent quality sound for most users. However, if you often use your computer to play games, music, and video, you may want to upgrade your speakers or add a higher-quality sound card (which is usually only an option in a desktop computer).

Why do I get such good-quality sound from today's sound cards? Most computers include a **3D sound card**. 3D sound technology is better at convincing the human ear that sound is omnidirectional, meaning that you can't tell from which direction the sound is coming. This tends to produce a fuller, richer sound than stereo sound. However, 3D sound is not surround sound.

What is surround sound, then? Surround sound is a type of audio processing that makes the listener experience sound as if it were coming from all directions by using multiple speakers. The current surround-sound standard is from Dolby. There are many formats available, including Dolby Digital EX and Dolby Digital Plus for high-definition audio. Dolby TrueHD is the newest standard. It features high-definition and lossless technology, which means that no information is lost in the compression process.

To create surround sound, another standard, Dolby Digital 7.1, takes digital sound from a medium (such as a Blu-ray disc) and reproduces it in eight channels. Seven channels cover the listening field with placement to the left front, right front, left rear, right rear, and center of the audio stage, as well as two extra speakers to the side, as shown in Figure 6.33. The eighth channel holds extremely low-frequency (LFE) sound data and is sent to a subwoofer, which can be placed anywhere in the room.

Evaluating Computer System Components

In this Helpdesk, you'll play the role of a helpdesk staffer, fielding questions about the computer's storage, video, and audio devices and how to evaluate whether they match your needs as well as how to improve the reliability of your system.

Figure 6.33 Dolby Digital 7.1 surround sound gives you a better quality audio output. *(Zern Liew/Shutterstock)*

Figure 6.34 Sample Home Recording Studio Setup *(AbsentAnna/Fotolia; Sashkin/ Fotolia; Mikita_Kavalenkau/Getty Images; Aleksangel/Fotolia; Mariusz Blach/Fotolia; Maksym Yemelyanov/Fotolia; Fotolia)*

The name 7.1 surround indicates that there are seven speakers reproducing the full audio spectrum and one speaker handling just lower-frequency bass sounds. There is also a 5.1 surround-sound standard, which has a total of six speakers—one subwoofer, a center speaker, and four speakers for right/left in the front and the back. If you have a larger space or want precise location of sounds, use the newer 7.1 system.

To set up surround sound on your computer, you need two things:

1. A set of surround-sound speakers and, for the greatest surround-sound experience,
2. A sound card that is Dolby Digital compatible.

What if I don't like the sound from my laptop speakers? The limited size for speakers in a laptop and the added weight of circuitry to drive them means most people use headphones or ear buds for great audio instead of speakers. However, some laptops have built-in higher-quality speakers, like the Alienware line featuring Klipsch speakers and the HP series offering Beats speakers.

What setup do I need if I want to use my computer for recording my band? You can connect MIDI instruments, high-quality microphones, and recording equipment to your computer through an **audio MIDI interface** box. MIDI is an electronics standard that allows different kinds of electronic instruments to communicate with each other and with computers. The audio interface box attaches to your computer through a USB port and adds jacks for connecting guitars and microphones. You can edit and mix tracks through many different software packages, like Ableton Live or GarageBand. Figure 6.34 shows a simple home recording studio setup.

Figure 6.35 lists the factors to consider when deciding whether your audio subsystem meets your needs.

Figure 6.35 Evaluating the Audio Subsystem

Audio

Do you want to upgrade your **speaker** quality?

Do you need an **audio MIDI interface** box?

Do you want **surround sound**?

(gonin/Fotolia)

Evaluating System Reliability and Moving On

Many computer users decide to buy a new system because they're experiencing problems such as slow performance, freezes, and crashes. Over time, even normal use can cause your computer to build up excess files and to become internally disorganized. This excess, clutter, and disorganization can lead to deteriorating performance or system failure, but fortunately can usually be easily fixed. If you think your system is unreliable, see if the problem is one you can fix before you buy a new machine. Proper upkeep and maintenance also may postpone an expensive system upgrade or replacement.

Maintaining System Reliability

Objective 6.11   *Describe steps you can take to optimize your system's reliability.*

What can I do to ensure my system stays reliable? Here are several procedures you can follow to ensure your system performs reliably (see also Figure 6.36):

- **Install a reliable antivirus package.** Make sure it's set to update itself automatically and to run a full system scan frequently.
- **Run spyware and adware removal programs.** These often detect and remove different pests and should be used in addition to your regular antivirus package.
- **Clear out unnecessary files.** Temporary Internet files can accumulate quickly on your hard drive, taking up unnecessary space. Running the Disk Cleanup utility is a quick and easy way to ensure your temporary Internet files don't take up precious hard drive space. Likewise, you should delete any unnecessary files from your hard drive regularly because they can make your hard drive run more slowly.
- **Run the Disk Defragmenter utility on your hard drive.** When your hard drive becomes fragmented, its storage capacity is negatively affected. When you defragment (defrag) your hard drive, files are reorganized, making the hard drive work more efficiently. But remember that this only makes sense for mechanical drives. With no motors, there is no need to defrag an SSD drive.
- **Automate the key utilities.** The utilities that need to be run more than once, like Disk Cleanup, Disk Defragmenter, and the antivirus, adware, and spyware programs, can be configured to run automatically at any time interval you want. You can use Windows Task Scheduler or third-party programs like Norton Security Suite to set up a sequence of programs to run one after the other every evening while you sleep, so you can wake up each day to a reliable, secure system.

What can I do when my system crashes? Computer systems are complex. It's not unusual to have your system stop responding occasionally. If rebooting the computer doesn't help, you'll need to begin troubleshooting:

1. **If your system isn't responding, try a System Restore**. Windows automatically creates restore points before any major change to the system takes place, such as when you install a new program or change a device driver. Type Restore Point in the Cortana search box, select Create a restore point, and then click the Create button to manually create a restore point at any time. You can then select any restore point and bring your system back to the state it was in at that point. From the System Properties dialog box (accessed through the instructions above), select System Restore on the System Protection tab to learn more about restoring your system.

Figure 6.36   Utilities to Keep Your System Reliable

To Avoid This Problem	Use This Tool	For More Info
Your hard drive is running low on space, making it run slowly	Disk Cleanup utility	Chapter 5
Your system is slowing down; browsers or other programs are behaving strangely	Antivirus software; spyware and adware removal software	Chapter 9
Files are spread across many spots on the hard drive, making the hard drive run slowly	Disk Defragmenter utility	Chapter 5
System not responding	Windows Refresh	Chapter 5

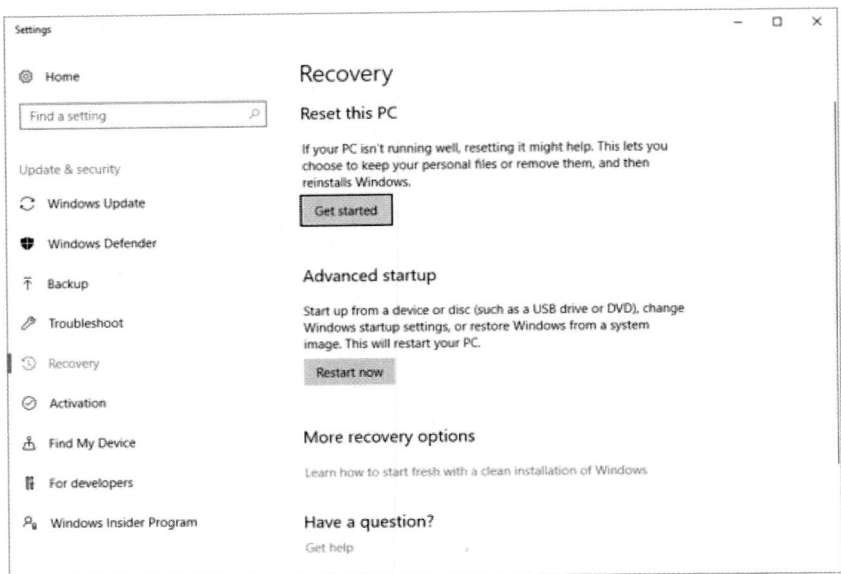

Figure 6.37 The Reset this PC feature in Windows 10 can help when your computer stops responding.

To access Recovery, from Settings, select Update & security. (Microsoft Corporation)

For Mac systems, the macOS Time Machine provides automatic backup and enables you to look through and restore (if necessary) files, folders, libraries, or the entire system.

2. **If a System Restore wasn't enough to fix the problem, consider a Windows Reset on your system.** This Windows utility, shown in Figure 6.37, removes all the changes you've made to the system and brings it back to the state it came to you from the factory. It removes all the applications from third-party vendors, but it won't remove personal files like your music, documents, or videos.

3. **Check that you have enough RAM.** You learned how to do this in the "Evaluating the Memory Subsystem" section earlier in this chapter. Systems with insufficient RAM often crash.

4. **If you see an error code in Windows, visit the Microsoft Knowledge Base (support. microsoft.com).** This online resource helps users resolve problems with Microsoft products. For example, it can help you determine what an error code indicates and how you may be able to solve the problem.

5. **Search with Google.** If you don't find a satisfactory answer in the Knowledge Base, try copying the entire error message into Google and searching the larger community for solutions.

Can my software affect system reliability? Having the latest version of software makes your system much more reliable. You should upgrade or update your OS, browser software, and application software as often as new patches (or updates) are reported for resolving errors. Sometimes these errors are performance related; sometimes they're potential system security breaches.

If you're having a software problem that can be replicated, use the Steps Recorder to capture the exact steps that lead to it. In Windows, type "ste" in the Cortana search box and select the Steps Recorder desktop app. Now run the Steps Recorder and go through the exact actions that create the problem you're having. At any particular step, you can click the Add Comment button and add a comment about any part of the screen. The Steps Recorder then produces a documented report, complete with images of your screen and descriptions of each mouse movement you made. You can then e-mail this report to customer support to help technicians resolve the problem.

How do I know whether updates are available for my software? You can configure Windows so that it automatically checks for, downloads, and installs any available updates for itself, the Microsoft Edge browser, and other Microsoft applications such as Microsoft Office. Type "update" in the Cortana search box and select Check for updates in System Settings. Click *Advanced options* and customize your update strategy.

Many other applications now also include the ability to check for updates. Check under the Help menu of the product, and you'll often find a Check for Updates command.

So is it time to buy a new computer? Now that you've evaluated your computer system, you need to shift to questions of value. How close does your system come to meeting your needs? Can you even upgrade your existing system (tablets and phones usually have very few upgrade options)? How much would it cost to upgrade your current system to match what you'd ideally like your computer to do, not only today but also a few years from now? How much would it cost to purchase a new system that meets these specifications?

To know whether upgrading or buying a new system would have better value for you, you need to price both scenarios. Conduct a thorough system evaluation (see (Figure 6.38) to gather the data to help you decide. Purchasing a new system is an important investment of your resources, and you want to make a well-reasoned, well-supported decision.

Getting Rid of Your Old Computer

Objective 6.12 *Discuss how to recycle, donate, or dispose of an older computer.*

What should I do with my old computer? If the result of your system evaluation is that you need a new computer, you're probably thinking with excitement of your next new system. But what can you do with your old machine? You have options. If your old system still works, be sure to consider what benefit you might obtain by having two systems. Would you have a use for the older system?

Also, before you decide to throw it away, consider the environmental impact (see (Figure 6.39). Mercury in LCD screens, cadmium in batteries and circuit boards, and flame retardants in plastic housings all are toxic. An alarming, emerging trend is that discarded machines are beginning to create an e-waste crisis.

So how can I recycle my old computer? Instead of throwing your computer away, you may be able to donate it to a nonprofit organization. Here are a few ways to do this:

- Many manufacturers, such as Dell, offer recycling programs and have formed alliances with nonprofit organizations to help distribute your old technology to those who need it.

Figure 6.38 Key Items in System Evaluation

CPU
- What is your CPU usage level?

RAM
- Do you have at least 4 GB?

Storage
- Do you need an SSD drive for fast start-up?
- Do you have a fast-access mechanical drive for large storage space?
- Do you need RAID 0 or RAID 1 storage drives for extra-fast performance or mirroring?

Video
- Do you have enough graphics memory?
- Is your GPU powerful enough?
- Do you have HDMI ports?
- How many monitors do you need to run simultaneously?

Audio
- Do you have 7.1 or 5.1 surround sound?

(Oleksandr Delyk/Fotolia; Hugh Threlfall/Alamy Stock Photo; Nikkytok/Shutterstock; Fotolia)

Figure 6.39 An electronics garbage dump can cause environmental concerns like the leaching of lead, mercury, and other hazardous substances into the ground. *(Ton Koene/AGE Fotostock)*

Ethics in IT

Free Hardware for All

The open source software movement has flourished over the past decade. In response to increasing prices and the limitations placed on commercially available software, programmers began to donate time to design, develop, and support software systems. These products, like Gimp (a photo-editing tool), were then made freely available.

In the world of hardware, a similar but different approach called the open source hardware movement has flourished. Because hardware projects require materials and tools to assemble, products distributed as open source are not free in terms of cost, but they are free from any restrictions on how you modify them. Inexpensive hardware devices now span the range from the Digispark, an $8 microcontroller the size of a quarter, to the $40 Raspberry Pi, a full Linux-based computer the size of a credit card. Sample open source hardware projects include video game systems, 3D printers, and even do-it-yourself medical devices.

Is open hardware good for the world? Does it undermine the intellectual property of others who want to create hardware resources and sell them for a profit? What is the impact on developing countries if they have immediate access to hardware designs instead of being required to purchase these items from a for-profit company? Follow the future of open source hardware by keeping an eye on ezines like Make (**makezine.com**), developer and supplier sites like Adafruit (**adafruit.com**), and tutorial headquarters like Instructables (**instructables.com**).

- Sites like Computers with Causes (**computerswithcauses.org**) organize donations of both working and nonworking computers, printers, and mice.
- You can also take your computer to an authorized computer-recycling center in your area. The Telecommunications Industry Association provides an e-cycling information site you can use to find a local e-cycling center (**ecyclingcentral.com**).

For companies that need to retire large quantities of computers, the risk of creating an environmental hazard is serious. Firms like GigaBiter (gigabiter.com) offer a solution. GigaBiter eliminates security and environmental risks associated with electronic destruction by first delaminating the hard drive and then breaking down the computer e-waste into recyclable products. The result of the final step is a sand-like substance that is 100% recyclable.

Can I donate a computer safely, without worrying about my personal data? Before donating or recycling a computer, make sure you carefully remove all data from your hard drive. Built into Windows is an option to help with this. In the Cortana search box, type Reset and select Reset this PC. Upon clicking the Get started button, you will have the option to keep or remove your files and then reinstall Windows.

Becoming a victim of identity theft is a serious risk. Credit card numbers, bank information, Social Security numbers, tax records, passwords, and personal identification numbers (PINs) are just some of the types of sensitive information that we casually record to our computers' hard drives. Just deleting files that contain proprietary personal information is not protection enough. Likewise, reformatting or erasing your hard drive does not totally remove data, as was proved by two MIT graduate students. They bought more than 150 used hard drives from various sources. Although some of the hard drives had been reformatted or damaged so that the data was supposedly nonrecoverable, the two students were able to retrieve medical records, financial information, pornography, personal e-mails, and more than 5,000 credit card numbers!

The U.S. Department of Defense suggests a seven-layer overwrite for a "secure erase." This means that you fill your hard drive seven times over with a random series of 1s and 0s. Fortunately, several programs exist for doing this. For PCs running Windows, look for utility programs like File Shredder or Eraser. Wipe is available for Linux, and ShredIt X can be used for Mac OS X. These programs provide secure hard drive erasures, either of specific files on your hard drive or of the entire hard drive.

Before moving on to the Chapter Review:

1. ▶ Watch Chapter Overview Video 6.2.
2. Then take the Check Your Understanding quiz.

Check Your Understanding // Review & Practice

For a quick review to see what you've learned so far, answer the following questions.

multiple choice

1. SSDs are classified as which type of storage?
   a. volatile
   b. GPU
   c. nonvolatile
   d. cache

2. When would you want to consider RAID 1 technology?
   a. when you need the fastest solution for writing data
   b. if you think that SSDs are too expensive
   c. when you need an instant backup of your work
   d. when you want to have only one hard disk drive

3. Which is NOT a type of video port?
   a. HDMI
   b. DVI
   c. GPU
   d. DisplayPort

4. Dolby Digital 7.1 creates
   a. ultra-sharp high-definition video.
   b. a digital signal from an audio input.
   c. 7-channel surround sound.
   d. 8-channel surround sound.

5. Your Windows computer can be reset to factory specifications by using a utility called Windows
   a. Return.
   b. Refresh.
   c. Restore.
   d. Reboot.

Go to **MyLab IT** to take an autograded version of the *Check Your Understanding* review and to find all media resources for the chapter.

TechBytes Weekly

Go to TechBytes Weekly for current technology news and discussion questions!

6 Chapter Review

Summary

Learning Outcome 6.1   You will be able to evaluate your computer system's hardware functioning, including the CPU and memory subsystems.

Your Ideal Computing Device

Objective 6.1   *Describe the changes in CPU performance over the past several decades.*

- Moore's Law describes the pace at which CPUs improve by holding more transistors. This rule predicts that the number of transistors inside a CPU will double about every two years.

Objective 6.2   *Compare and contrast a variety of computing devices.*

- A huge number of computing choices are on the market, including smartphones, tablets, ultrabooks, netbooks, 2-in-1s, laptops, and desktops.
- The kind of technology user you are will determine what kind of device you need.

Evaluating the CPU Subsystem

Objective 6.3   *Describe how a CPU is designed and how it operates.*

- The CPU is composed of two units: the *control unit* and the *arithmetic logic unit (ALU)*. The control unit coordinates the activities of all the other computer components. The ALU is responsible for performing all the arithmetic calculations (addition, subtraction, multiplication, and division). Every time the CPU performs a program instruction, it goes through the same series of steps (a machine cycle): fetch, decode, execute, and store.
- The clock speed of a CPU dictates how many instructions the CPU can process each second.
- A core contains the parts of the CPU required for processing. Modern CPUs have multiple cores.
- Hyperthreading allows two sets of instructions to be run by a single CPU core.

- Pipelining is a technique that allows the CPU to work on more than one instruction (or stage of processing) at the same time, thereby boosting CPU performance.
- The CPU's cache memory is a form of RAM that is part of the CPU chip itself, so retrieving data is much faster than bringing the data in from the computer's RAM.

Objective 6.4   *Describe tools used to measure and evaluate CPU performance.*

- CPU benchmarks are measurements used to compare performance between processors.
- CPU usage is the percentage of time the CPU is busy doing work.
- On Windows systems, the Task Manager utility lets you access this data.

Evaluating the Memory Subsystem

Objective 6.5   *Discuss how RAM is used in a computer system.*

- Random access memory (RAM) is your computer's temporary storage space. RAM is an example of volatile storage. RAM appears in the system on memory modules. There are several types of RAM, including DDR3, and DDR4.
- Physical memory is the amount of RAM installed in the system.
- The Resource Monitor shows how much memory is in use at any time.

Objective 6.6   *Evaluate whether adding RAM to a system is desirable.*

- Adding RAM is simple to do and relatively inexpensive. However, there is a limit to how much RAM can be installed in a device.

Part 2
Evaluating Other Subsystems and Making a Decision

Learning Outcome 6.2 You will be able to evaluate your computer system's storage subsystem, media subsystem, and reliability and decide whether to purchase a new system or upgrade an existing one.

 ## Evaluating the Storage Subsystem

Objective 6.7 *Classify and describe the major types of nonvolatile storage drives.*

- Major types of nonvolatile storage include mechanical hard drives, SSDs, SSHDs, and optical drives.
- Mechanical hard drives are the least expensive and the slowest to access information.
- SSD drives are electronic, so they have no moving parts, produce no heat, and are many times faster than hard drives. However, they are more expensive.
- An SSHD drive is a combination of both a mechanical hard drive and an SSD into a single device.
- Optical drives, like Blu-ray and DVDs, use a laser to read pits and bumps on plastic discs.

Objective 6.8 *Evaluate the amount and type of storage needed for a system.*

- Your storage needs will depend on the number and types of programs and data you use. Your local storage needs may be significantly reduced if you utilize cloud storage for your data files.
- It may be better to have several drives connected, either in RAID 0 for more speed or in RAID 1 for instantaneous backup protection.

 ## Evaluating the Media Subsystems

Objective 6.9 *Describe the features of video cards.*

- A video card translates binary data into images that are displayed on a monitor.
- A video card has specialized video memory that is very fast. Some systems have multiple video cards for even greater performance.
- A video card has a graphics processing unit (GPU), which helps the CPU by handling the graphics workload.
- Certain individual video cards can support multiple monitors.

Objective 6.10 *Describe the features of sound cards.*

- A sound card can support 3-D sound as well as surround sound like Dolby 7.1.
- Dolby 7.1 surround sound has one speaker for low-frequency tones and seven additional speakers for a full, immersive experience.
- An audio MIDI interface unit allows you to connect musical instruments, microphones, and headphones to your computer.

 ## Evaluating System Reliability and Moving On

Objective 6.11 *Describe steps you can take to optimize your system's reliability.*

- There are many regular maintenance steps you should take to keep your system reliable. They include using an antivirus program, adware removal software, clearing out unnecessary files, and running a disk defragmenter.

Objective 6.12 *Discuss how to recycle, donate, or dispose of an older computer.*

- A used computer can be recycled through several manufacturers or through nonprofit organizations.
- To safely recycle or donate a computer, you must first remove all applications and personal data. There are options in Windows to help with this.

 Be sure to check out **MyLab IT** for additional materials to help you review and learn. And don't forget to watch the Chapter Overview Videos. ▶

Key Terms

3D sound card **235**

access time **225**

arithmetic logic unit (ALU) **212**

audio MIDI interface **236**

cache memory **213**

clock cycle **212**

clock speed **212**

control unit **212**

core **213**

CPU benchmarks **215**

CPU usage **215**

CPU usage graph **215**

graphics double data rate 5 (GDDR5) **231**

graphics processing unit (GPU) **231**

hard drive **225**

head crash **227**

hyperthreading **214**

latency (rotational delay) **227**

machine cycle **211**

memory module (memory card) **219**

Moore's Law **208**

nonvolatile storage **218**

optical drive **226**

optical media **226**

overclocking **213**

parallel processing **213**

physical memory **219**

pipelining **213**

platter **225**

RAID 0 **229**

RAID 1 **230**

random access memory (RAM) **218**

read/write head **227**

redundant array of independent disks (RAID) **228**

registers **211**

sector **227**

seek time **227**

solid state drive (SSD) **226**

solid state hybrid drive (SSHD) **226**

sound card **235**

SuperFetch **219**

surround sound **235**

system clock **212**

system evaluation **210**

track **227**

video card (video adapter) **231**

video memory **231**

volatile storage **218**

Chapter Quiz // Assessment

For a quick review to see what you've learned, answer the following questions. Submit the quiz as requested by your instructor. If you are using **MyLab IT**, the quiz is also available there.

multiple choice

1. Moore's Law refers to the
   a. amount of memory on a memory chip.
   b. overall system processing capability.
   c. speed of DRAM.
   d. number of transistors inside a CPU chip.

2. When the CPU actually performs the work described in the commands during a machine cycle, this stage is known as
   a. Fetch.
   b. Decode.
   c. Store.
   d. Execute.

3. Computers are designed with
   a. only volatile memory.
   b. only nonvolatile memory.
   c. neither volatile nor nonvolatile memory.
   d. both volatile and nonvolatile memory.

4. A good way to assess your CPU usage is to
   a. check the Performance tab of the Task Manager.
   b. listen for the sound of a spinning hard disk drive.
   c. check the number reported by the system defrag utility.
   d. feel the temperature of the CPU with your hand.

5. _____ is a set of strategies for using more than one drive in a system.
   a. A machine cycle
   b. GPU
   c. RAID
   d. VPU

6. GDDR5 and GDDR3 are types of
   a. ROM.
   b. HDMI.
   c. video memory.
   d. GPUs.

7. If you want to use your computer for recording your band, you would benefit most from a(n)
   a. HDMI interface.
   b. MIDI interface.
   c. RAID interface.
   d. overclocking interface.

8. Before donating your Windows computer, you should perform a Windows
   a. Restore.
   b. Refresh.
   c. Reclaim.
   d. Reset.

9. The fastest memory in a computer is
   a. ROM.
   b. cache.
   c. RAM.
   d. HDMI.

10. Windows creates "restore points" so that you can
    a. return your system to the way it was before you installed new software.
    b. add additional hard disk storage space.
    c. extend your warranty.
    d. protect your system from hackers.

true/false

_____ 1. Desktop systems are invariably a worse value than lighter, more mobile computers.

_____ 2. SSD drives are preferable to conventional hard drives because they transfer data more quickly.

_____ 3. In Windows, if you experience unreliable behavior, try a System Reclaim before doing a Windows Refresh.

_____ 4. There is a limit to how much RAM you can add to modern computers.

_____ 5. Moore's Law describes the pace at which graphics processing units (GPUs) improve.

critical thinking

1. **Measure Up**

   Briefly describe the way you would evaluate whether the CPU, memory, and storage of your system were meeting your needs. What tools would you need? What operating system programs help you evaluate performance?

2. **A Green Machine**

   Review the impacts on the environment of your computer during its entire life cycle. How do the production, transportation, and use of the computer affect the increase of greenhouse gas emissions? How does the selection of materials and packaging impact the environment? What restricted substances (like lead, mercury, cadmium, and PVC) are found in your machine? Could substitute materials be used? How would the ultimate "green machine" be designed?

Team Time

Many Different Devices for Many Different Needs

problem

Even within one discipline, there are needs for a variety of types of computing solutions. Consider the communications department in a large university. There are some groups involved in video production, some groups producing digital music, and some groups creating scripts.

process

1. Split the class into teams. Select one segment of the communications department that your team will represent: video production, digital music, or scripting. The video production team requires its labs to be able to support the recording, editing, and final production and distribution of digital video. The digital music group wants to establish a recording studio (after the model of the Drexel University recording label, Mad Dragon Music Group, at **maddragonmusic.com**). The scripting group needs to support a collaborative community of writers and voice-over actors.

2. Analyze the computing needs of that segment, with particular focus on how it needs to outfit its computer labs.

3. Price the systems you would recommend and explain how they will be used. What decisions have you made in order to guarantee they will still be useful in three years?

4. Write a report that summarizes your findings. Document the resources you used and generate as much enthusiasm as you can for your recommendations.

conclusion

Being able to evaluate a computer system and match it to the current needs of its users is an important skill.

Ethics Project

Benchmarking

In this exercise, you'll research and then role-play a complicated ethical situation. The role you play might not match your own personal beliefs; regardless, your research and use of logic will enable you to represent the view assigned. An arbitrator will watch and comment on both sides of the arguments, and, together, the team will agree on an ethical solution.

problem

We've seen that for complex systems like computers, performance often is determined by using benchmarks, software suites that test a full area of performance. The results of these tests become a major force in marketing and selling the product.

There have been a number of claims of unethical conduct in the area of benchmarking. Companies have been accused of using out-of-date testing software to skew their results. Some companies have manipulated the settings on the machine to artificially raise their score (for example, turning off the display before testing for battery life). Some companies make sure the systems sent out to magazines and other evaluators have better-performing components than you might get off the shelf. Where is the line between gaining a competitive edge and lying when it comes to hardware assessment?

research areas to consider

- BAPCo
- MobileMark
- 2009 Nobel Prize for Physics

process

1. Divide the class into teams. Research the areas cited above from the perspective of either an Intel engineer working on a new CPU, an engineer working on a competing CPU, or a benchmark designer.
2. Team members should write a summary that provides documentation for the positions their character takes on the issue of equitable testing of hardware. Then, team members should create an outline to use during the role-playing event.
3. Team members should present their case to the class or submit a PowerPoint presentation for review, along with the summary they developed.

conclusion

As technology becomes ever more prevalent and integrated into our lives, more and more ethical dilemmas will present themselves. Being able to understand and evaluate both sides of the argument, while responding in a personally or socially ethical manner, will be an important skill.

Laptop Alternatives

You are in need of a new laptop that is lightweight, but that has enough power to edit the videos you produce for your YouTube channel. You have asked a few of your friends for some suggestions. One friend put together a list of possible computers in an Excel workbook; the other friend created a list as a text file. You will import the text file into the Excel 2016 table, sort the data, and then filter the data to display only those computers you are interested in. With Excel 2016, you will use tables to sort, filter, and display data.

You will use the following skills as you complete this activity:

- Import Data from Text File
- Format as Table
- Sort Data

- Apply Filters
- Change Cell Fill Color

Instructions

1. Open *TIA_Ch6_Start* and save as **TIA_Ch6_LastFirst**.

2. Select **cell A30**, then import the text file, *TIA_Ch6_TableText*, accepting all defaults.
   a. Hint: To Import a text file, on the Data tab, in the Get External Data group, click **From Text**. You will end up with 40 rows of data.

3. Format range A1:M41 as a table, with **Table Style Medium 13**. Select **Yes** when asked to convert the selection to a table and remove all external connections.
   a. Hint: To format a range as a table, on the Home tab, in the Styles group, select **Format as Table**, then select the desired style.

4. Sort the data by **Style (A to Z)**, then by **Processor Speed (Largest to Smallest)**, then by **RAM (GB) (Largest to Smallest)**.
   a. Hint: To Sort data with multiple levels, on the Data tab, in the Sort & Filter group, click **Sort**, then click **Add Level**. Select the desired column in each sort drop down list. Make sure *My data has headers* checkbox is selected.

5. Filter the data to display Ultrabooks with Intel Core i5 processors and Solid-State Drives (SSDs).
   a. Hint: To Filter data, ensure Filter is selected on the Data tab, in the Sort & Filter group. Then click the arrow for each column to be filtered, and then add or delete checkmarks for the desired category.

6. Copy the header row and four rows that display after all filters have been applied. Open a new worksheet, and paste the copied data in cell A1. Rename the new worksheet **Choices**. Click the **Data worksheet**, and press **Esc** to clear the selection.

7. Click the **Choices worksheet**, change the width of columns C, H, I, J, K, L to **9**, and change the width of columns D, E, G, and M to **12**. Select **cells A1:M1** and **Wrap Text**.
   a. Hint: To change the width of nonadjacent columns, select the first column heading, then hold down the **Ctrl key** while selecting the remaining column headings. Click **Format** in the Cells group, and then select **Column Width**.

8. Select **cells A3:M3**, and change the Fill Color to **Yellow**.

9. In cell A8, type **The HP Ultrabook is my choice, as it has the most RAM, greatest storage capacity, and the best wireless standard of the four choices.**

10. Save the workbook and submit based on your instructor's directions.

Chapter

7 Networking: Connecting Computing Devices

 For a chapter overview, watch the Chapter Overview Videos.

PART 1
How Networks Function

Learning Outcome 7.1 You will be able to explain the basics of networking, including the components needed to create a network, and describe the different ways a network can connect to the Internet.

PART 2
Your Home Network

Learning Outcome 7.2 You will be able to describe what is necessary to install and configure a home network and how to manage and secure a wireless network.

 Networking Fundamentals   250

Objective 7.1   *Describe computer networks and their pros and cons.*

Helpdesk: Understanding Networking

 Network Architectures   252

Objective 7.2   *Explain the different ways networks are defined.*

 Network Components   255

Objective 7.3   *Describe the types of transmission media used in networks.*

Objective 7.4   *Describe the basic hardware devices necessary for networks.*

Objective 7.5   *Describe the type of software necessary for networks.*

Sound Byte: Installing a Home Computer Network

 Connecting to the Internet   260

Objective 7.6   *Summarize the broadband options available to access the Internet.*

Objective 7.7   *Summarize how to access the Internet wirelessly.*

 Installing and Configuring Home Networks   268

Objective 7.8   *Explain what should be considered before creating a home network.*

Objective 7.9   *Describe how to set up a home network.*

Objective 7.10   *Summarize how to configure home network software.*

 Managing and Securing Wireless Networks   275

Objective 7.11   *Describe the potential problems with wireless networks and means to avoid them.*

Objective 7.12   *Describe how to secure wireless home networks.*

Sound Byte: Securing Wireless Networks

Helpdesk: Managing and Securing Wireless Networks

For the IT Simulation for this chapter, see MyLab IT.

MyLab IT   All media accompanying this chapter can be found here.

Make This   Make: Networked Devices on **page 267**

(Sergey Nivens/Fotolia, Nicotombo/Fotolia, AKS/Fotolia, Vlad Kochelaevskiy/123RF, Hywards/Fotolia, Mipan/Fotolia)

How Cool Is This?

The **Internet of Things (IoT)**—a multitude of devices connected to the Internet wirelessly—is here to stay. Today, **Bluetooth** is used to connect such devices to each other, but the true smart home of the future will have most devices connected to the Internet through **Wi-Fi**. But a current problem with Wi-Fi is that the **signal diminishes** as more devices connect to a wireless network. The **Wi-Fi Alliance**, the organization that manages Wi-Fi standards, has announced a solution: a new Wi-Fi standard called **HaLow** that operates on the 801.11ah standard. HaLow has **twice the range** of current Wi-Fi and is also **more robust** to easily penetrate walls or other barriers, which is perfect for connecting IoT devices throughout a home. The HaLow standard is expected to be certified in 2018, so watch for devices coming to the market supporting the 802.11ah standard soon. *(Aimage/123rf)*

How Networks Function

Learning Outcome 7.1	You will be able to explain the basics of networking, including the components needed to create a network, and describe the different ways a network can connect to the Internet.

You access wired and wireless networks all the time—when you use an ATM, print out a document, or use the Internet (the world's largest network). It's important to understand the fundamentals of networking, such as how networks are set up, what devices are necessary to establish a network, and how you can access a network so that you can share, collaborate, and exchange information.

Networking Fundamentals

A typical family engages in many activities that involve sharing and accessing files over and from the Internet and using a variety of Internet-connected devices (see Figure 7.1). What makes all this technology transfer and sharing possible? A computer network!

Understanding Networks

Objective 7.1 *Describe computer networks and their pros and cons.*

What is a network? A computer **network** is simply two or more computers that are connected via software and hardware so they can communicate with each other. Each device connected to a network is referred to as a **node**. A node can be a computer, a peripheral such as a printer or a game console, or a network device such as a router (see Figure 7.2).

Jackie watches a video she took while on vacation.

Andy plays PlayStation online and uploads a video he made for school.

Mom watches a lecture from her online course while she prepares a snack.

Dad watches a streaming movie and checks fantasy football scores on his iPad.

Andrea takes pictures of her dog and uploads them directly to Facebook.

Figure 7.1 With a home network, all family members can connect their computing devices whenever and wherever they want.

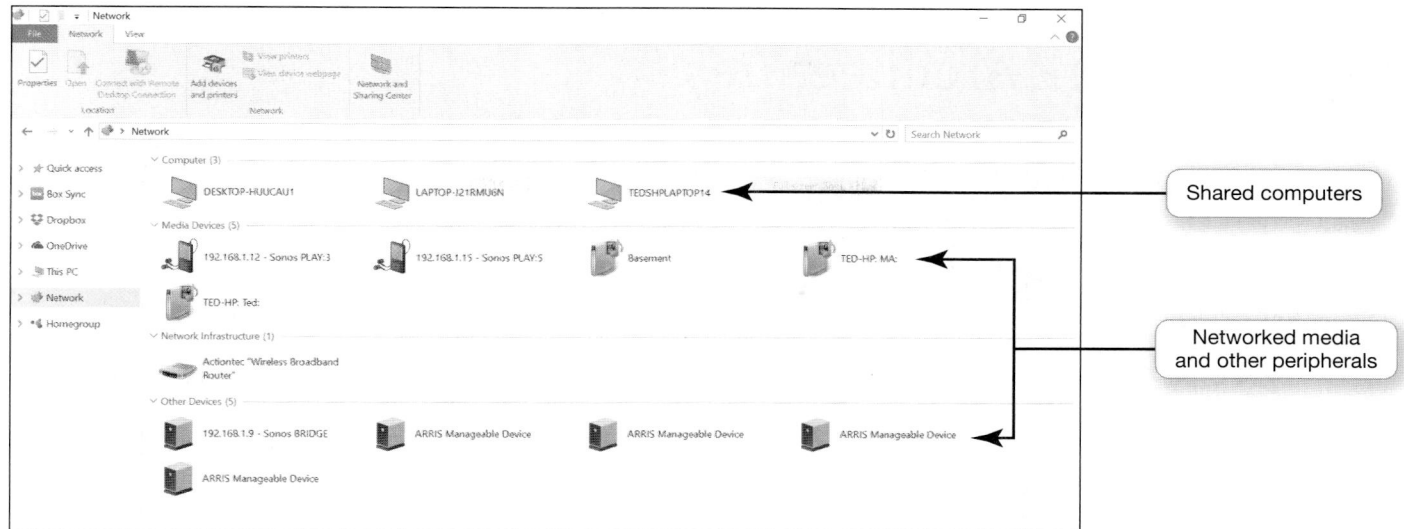

Figure 7.2 File Explorer shows computers, media, and other devices (such as set-top boxes) that are networked for sharing. *(Windows 10, Microsoft Corporation)*

What are the benefits of networks? There are several benefits to having computers networked:

- **Sharing an Internet connection:** A network lets you share the high-speed Internet connection coming into your home.
- **Sharing printers and other peripherals:** Networks let you share printers and other peripheral devices. For example, say you have a laptop that isn't connected to a printer. To print a document from your laptop without a network, you would need to transfer the file to another computer using a flash drive or another device that's connected to the printer, or carry your laptop to the printer and connect your laptop to it. With a network, you can print directly from your device even if it's not physically connected to the printer.
- **Sharing files:** You can share files between networked computers without having to use portable storage devices such as flash drives to transfer the files. In addition, you can set sharing options in Windows or macOS that let the user of each computer on the network access files stored on any other computer on the network.
- **Common communications:** Computers running different operating systems can communicate on the same network.

Are there disadvantages to setting up networks? The only disadvantage of setting up a network is the initial time it takes to set up the network. Once it's set up, there is very little ongoing maintenance and administration for a home network. However, large networks involve an initial purchase of equipment to set them up. They also need to be administered, which can be costly and time consuming. **Network administration** involves tasks such as:

- Installing new computers and devices,
- Monitoring the network to ensure it is performing efficiently,
- Updating and installing new software on the network, and
- Configuring, or setting up, proper security for a network.

How fast does data move through networks? **Data transfer rate** (also called **bandwidth**) is the maximum speed at which data can be transmitted between two nodes on a network. **Throughput** is the actual speed of data transfer that is achieved. Throughput is always less than or equal to the data transfer rate. Data transfer rate and throughput are usually measured in megabits per second (Mbps) and gigabits per second (Gbps). One of the main factors that determine how fast data moves is the type of network, which we'll discuss later in this chapter.

Helpdesk MyLab IT®

Understanding Networking

In this Helpdesk, you'll play the role of a helpdesk staffer, fielding questions about home networks—their advantages, their main components, and the most common types—as well as about wireless networks and how they're created.

Network Architectures

The network you have in your home differs greatly in terms of its size, structure, and cost from the one on your college campus. This difference is based in part on how the networks are designed or configured. In this section, we'll look at a variety of network classifications.

Network Designs

Objective 7.2 *Explain the different ways networks are defined.*

What are the ways that networks can be classified or defined? **Network architectures**, or network designs, can be classified by the following:

- The distance between nodes
- The way in which the network is managed (or administered)
- The set of rules (or protocol) used to exchange data between network nodes

Distance

How does the distance between nodes define a network? Networks can range from the smallest network of just one person, in one room with multiple connected devices, to the largest network that spans between cities and even the world. The following are common types of networks (see Figure 7.3):

- A **personal area network (PAN)** is a network used for communication among devices close to one person, such as smartphones and tablets using wireless technologies such as Bluetooth and Wi-Fi.

WAN
Wide Area
Network

MAN
Metropolitan
Area Network

HAN
Home Area
Network

LAN
Local Area
Network

PAN
Personal Area
Network

Figure 7.3 Networks can be classified by the distance between their nodes. *(Fenton one/Shutterstock; CataVic/Shutterstock; SiuWing/Shutterstock; Lucadp/Shutterstock)*

- A **local area network (LAN)** is a network in which the nodes are located within a small geographical area. Examples include a network in a computer lab at school or at a fast-food restaurant.
- A **home area network (HAN)** is a specific type of LAN located in a home. HANs are used to connect all of a home's digital devices, such as computers, peripherals, phones, gaming devices, digital video recorders (DVRs), and televisions.
- A **metropolitan area network (MAN)** is a large network designed to provide access to a specific geographical area, such as an entire city. Many U.S. cities are now deploying MANs to provide Internet access to residents and tourists. Some MANs employ WiMAX wireless technology that extends local Wi-Fi networks across greater distances.
- A **wide area network (WAN)** spans a large physical distance. The Internet is the largest WAN, covering the globe. A WAN is also a networked collection of LANs. If a school has multiple campuses located in different towns, each with its own LAN, connecting the LANs of each campus by telecommunications lines allows the users of the LANs to communicate. All the connected LANs would be described as a single WAN.

Levels of Administration

How does the level of administration define a network? A network can be administered, or managed, in two main ways—centrally or locally (see Figure 7.4):

- *Central administration*: In a centrally administered network, tasks performed from one computer can affect the other computers on the network. A **client/server network** is an example. In a client/server network, a client is a computer on which users accomplish tasks and make requests, whereas the server is the computer that provides information or resources to the client computers as well as central administration for network functions such as printing. Most networks that have 10 or more nodes are client/server networks.

Figure 7.4 Client/Server and P2P Networks *(Sashkin/Fotolia, Tuulijumala/Fotolia, Scanrail/Fotolia, Scanrail/Fotolia, Maksym Dykha/Fotolia, Scanrail/Fotolia)*

Wearable technology, as its name indicates, is technology incorporated into things you wear. The devices become a part of your personal area network (PAN) as they transfer data via Bluetooth to a mobile app or your computer. Popular wearable devices include fitness trackers, such as those from Garmin and Fitbit, and interactive digital fabrics, such as Athos Gear, which have built-in sensors that monitor specific activity as well as your heart rate while you're working out. In addition to health and fitness monitoring, some wearable devices, such as the Apple Watch, let you connect to your e-mail and calendar, among other personal productivity tools (see Figure 7.5). The medical industry is also implementing wearable devices, such as those to monitor cardiac patients for heart rate and blood pressure. Nearly 50% of American adults already own some form of a wearable device, and the trend is increasing at a remarkable rate. Do you have any wearable technology as a part of your PAN?

Figure 7.5 Smartwatches are a form of wearable technology that can monitor your activity and let you connect to personal productivity tools like your e-mail and calendar as well as sync to your mobile device. *(DM studio/Shutterstock)*

- *Local administration*: In a locally administered network, the configuration and maintenance of the network must be performed on each individual computer attached to the network. A **peer-to-peer (P2P) network** is an example. In a P2P network, each node connected on the network can communicate directly with every other node on the network. Thus, all nodes on this type of network are peers (equals). When printing, for example, a computer on a P2P network doesn't have to go through the computer that's connected to the printer. Instead, it can communicate directly with the printer. Because they're simple to set up, cost less than client/server networks, and are easier to configure and maintain, P2P networks are the most common type of home network. Very small schools and offices may also use P2P networks.

Ethernet Protocols

What network standard is used in my home network? The vast majority of home and corporate networks are Ethernet networks. An **Ethernet network** is so named because it uses the Ethernet protocol as the means (or standard) by which the nodes on the network communicate.

The Ethernet protocol was developed by the Institute of Electrical and Electronics Engineers (IEEE), which develops many standard specifications for electronic data transmission that are adopted throughout the world. Establishing standards for networking is important so that devices from different manufacturers will work well together.

There are different standards for wired and wireless networks. The standard for wired Ethernet networks is 802.3, also known as **gigabit Ethernet (GbE)**. Wireless networks (referred to as **Wi-Fi**) are based on the IEEE 802.11 standard. The current version of wireless Ethernet is 802.11ac. Previous versions included 802.11n, 802.11g, 802.11b, and 802.11a.

How is the 802.11ac version different from the previous versions? The newer wireless Ethernet standard, 802.11ac, is faster and has a better signal range than the 802.11n standard. The 802.11n standard, often referred to as dual band, operates at either a 2.4 GHz or a 5 GHz frequency. Prior standards operated only at the 2.4 GHz frequency and often competed with the many other wireless devices (such as wireless landline phones) that run on the same frequency. The 802.11ac standard operates at a 5 GHz frequency. This means the 802.11ac standard is more resistant to signal interference from other wireless devices in the home.

Are there new and emerging standards? 802.11ad, also known as WiGig, is a new wireless option that delivers speeds up to 7 gigabits per second (Gbps) at 60 GHz frequencies. However, WiGig won't replace Wi-Fi because it works for short distances. 802.11ac and 802.11ad are best when put to work in tandem: 802.11ad providing very fast transmission speeds for a room-sized area—perfect for delivering streaming media or quick data transfers between devices—and 802.11ac for all other wireless transmissions. Two other standards, 802.11af (Super Wi-Fi or White-Fi) and 802.11ah (HaLow or Low Power Wi-Fi), are being developed to help accommodate the anticipated continued dependence on wireless devices.

Will devices using older Wi-Fi standards still work on a newer network? Devices using older standards, such as 802.11n, will still work with newer 802.11ac and 802.11ad network devices. The ability of current devices to use earlier standards in addition to the current standard is known as **backward compatibility**. It's important to note that the speed of a network connection is determined by the slowest speed of any network device, so while an older Wi-Fi device might work, it will operate with slower data transfer rates and may run into some frequency interference.

Are there different standards for wired Ethernet? The most commonly used wired Ethernet standard for home networks is the gigabit Ethernet (GbE) standard. A data transfer rate of up to 1 Gbps is possible using this standard. Computers generally ship with gigabit Ethernet cards installed in them.

For even faster data transfer speeds, 10, 40, and even 100 gigabit Ethernet is available, providing maximum data transfer rates of 10, 40, and 100 Gbps, respectively. However, these networks are not currently meant for home use. The 10 and 40 GbE are intended for businesses, whereas 100 GbE is used for the major transmission lines of the Internet known as the Internet backbone.

Network Components

To function, all networks must include:

- A means to connect the nodes on the network (transmission media)
- Special hardware devices that allow the nodes to communicate with each other and to send data
- Software that allows the network to run (see Figure 7.6)

Transmission Media

Objective 7.3 *Describe the types of transmission media used in networks.*

How do nodes connect to each other? All network nodes are connected to each other and to the network by transmission media. **Transmission media** establish a communications channel between the nodes on a network. They can be either wired or wireless. The media used depend on the requirements of a network and its users.

What wired transmission media is used on a network? Wired networks use various types of cable (wire) to connect nodes. The type of network and the distance between nodes determine the type of cable used:

- **Unshielded twisted-pair (UTP) cable** (see Figure 7.7a) is composed of four pairs of wires twisted around each other to reduce electrical interference. UTP is slightly different from

Figure 7.6 Network Components *(RealVector/Shutterstock, Doomu/Fotolia, Ifong/Shutterstock, Adrian Lyon/Alamy Stock Photo, Norman Chan/Shutterstock)*

twisted-pair cable, which is what is used for telephone cable. Twisted-pair cable is made up of copper wires that are twisted around each other and surrounded by a plastic jacket.

- **Coaxial cable** (see Figure 7.7b) consists of a single copper wire surrounded by layers of plastic. If you have cable TV, the cable running into your TV or cable box is most likely coaxial cable.
- **Fiber-optic cable** (see Figure 7.7c) is made up of plastic or glass fibers that transmit data at extremely fast speeds.

Figure 7.7 Wired Transmission Media

a	b	c
Unshielded twisted-pair cable	Coaxial cable	Fiber-optic cable

(Deepspacedave/Shutterstock, Zwola Fasola/Shutterstock, Zentilia/Shutterstock)

Figure 7.8 UTP cable types used in networks have different data transfer rates. *(Emran/Shutterstock)*

What type of transmission media is most common in wired home networks? The most popular transmission media option for wired Ethernet home networks is UTP cable. You can buy UTP cable in varying lengths with Ethernet connectors (called RJ-45 connectors) already attached. Ethernet connectors resemble standard phone connectors (called RJ-11 connectors) but are slightly larger and have contacts for eight wires (four pairs) instead of four wires.

Is there just one kind of UTP cable? There are three types of UTP cable commonly found in wired Ethernet networks (see Figure 7.8). Cat 5e and Cat 6 cable are more common in home networks, while Cat 6a is designed for bigger networks that require more speed.

1. **Cat 5e:** **Cat 5e cable** is the cheapest of the three types and is sufficient for many home networking tasks. It was designed for 100 Mbps–wired Ethernet networks that were popular before gigabit Ethernet networks became the standard.

2. **Cat 6:** **Cat 6 cable** is designed to achieve data transfer rates that support a gigabit Ethernet network. Although using Cat 5e cable is sufficient, using Cat 6 cable is probably the better choice for home networking cable, though it's more expensive and more difficult to work with than Cat 5e cable.

3. **Cat 6a:** Cat 6a cable is designed for ultrafast Ethernet networks that run at speeds as fast as 10 Gbps. Installing a 10 gigabit Ethernet network in the home is probably unnecessary because today's home applications (even gaming and streaming media) don't require this rate of data transfer.

What transmission media is used on a wireless network? Wireless (or Wi-Fi) networks use radio waves to connect computing devices to other devices and to the Internet instead of using wires.

Can the same network have both wired and wireless nodes? One network can support nodes with both wireless and wired connections. A home network might include a desktop or printer that uses a wired connection, and then use the wireless connection for the host of portable devices such as laptops and smartphones. Wireless connections are also used for stationary devices such as printers, TVs, and some smart home devices such as thermostats and security systems.

Why might a portable device use a wired connection? When you want to achieve the highest possible throughput on your portable device, you may want to use a wired connection, if one is available. Wired connections let you take advantage of the faster throughput achieved by wired connectivity. Wireless signals have slower throughput than wired connections for the following reasons:

- Wireless bandwidth is shared among devices.
- Wireless signals are more susceptible to interference from magnetic and electrical sources.
- Other wireless networks (such as your neighbor's network) can interfere with the signals on your network.
- Certain building materials (such as concrete and cinderblock) and metal (such as a refrigerator) can decrease throughput.
- Throughput varies depending on the distance between your networking equipment.
- Wireless networks usually use specially coded signals to protect their data, whereas wired connections don't protect their signals. This process of coding signals can slightly decrease throughput, although once coded, data travels at usual speeds.

Figure 7.9 A simplified explanation of the function of switches is that, together with NICs, they act like traffic signals or traffic cops. They enforce the rules of the data road on an Ethernet network and help prevent data packets from crashing into each other.

Basic Network Hardware

Objective 7.4   *Describe the basic hardware devices necessary for networks.*

What hardware is needed for different nodes on a network to communicate? For the different nodes on a network to communicate with each other and access the network, each node needs a **network adapter**. All desktop and laptop computers as well as smartphones, tablets, and many peripherals sold today contain network adapters. This type of integrated network adapter is referred to as a **network interface card (NIC)**. Different NICs are designed to use different types of transmission media. Most NICs included in computing devices today are built to use wireless media, but many can use wired media as well.

What equipment do I need in order to connect to the Internet and share data through the network? A **modem** connects your network to the Internet. This brings the Internet signal to your home, but you need a way to share that signal with all the devices in your home. That's done with **network navigation devices**, such as a router or a switch. A **router** transfers packets of data between two or more networks. On a home network, you need a router to transfer data between your home network and the Internet, which is considered a separate network. To add Wi-Fi to your home network, use a router that features wireless capabilities. A **switch** acts like a traffic signal on a network (see Figure 7.9). Switches receive data packets and send them to their intended nodes on the same network (not between different networks). During the transmission process, data packets can suffer collisions; subsequently, the data in them is damaged or lost and the network doesn't function efficiently. The switch keeps track of the data packets and, in conjunction with NICs, helps the data packets find their destinations without running into each other. The switch also keeps track of all the nodes on the network and sends the data packets directly to the node for which they're headed. This keeps the network running efficiently.

Most modern network equipment has simplified to one device that combines a modem and a router with integrated switches. The specific type of modem will depend on the type of broadband service you have. Your Internet service provider will rent the appropriate modem to you or specify what type of modem you have to buy to work properly with the Internet service provider's technology.

Besides computers, what can be connected to a network? The short answer: almost anything. The **Internet of Things (IoT)** is not a new concept—it has been around since the new millennium. The IoT is defined as the interconnection of uniquely identifiable embedded computing devices that transfer data over a network without requiring human-to-human or human-to-computer interaction (see Figure 7.10). "Things" can be anything—machines, appliances, buildings, vehicles, even animals, people, plants, and soil. In addition to all the smart TVs, refrigerators, and thermostats we hear so much about, a thing can be a heart monitor implant that can warn of an oncoming problem or a device in an automobile that monitors driving behaviors so insurance companies can better assess risk. Ultimately, the Internet of Things is about connecting companies, people, and technology in real time via an extension of the Internet into the physical world. By the year 2020, there will be an estimated 30 billion connected devices.

Figure 7.10   The Internet of Things

The Things You Can Do

Home entertainment.
The DVR is just for starters.

Security cameras.
Watch your house with cameras in each room.

Appliances.
Trigger or time any function, or set it to alert you.

Security locks.
Let people into your home remotely.

Lighting.
Turn lights on or off remotely, for hands-free safety.

Smoke detector.
Get a fire alert on your phone.

Thermostat.
Heat choices when you want, for energy savings.

Irrigation.
Program lawn sprinklers for best times of the day.

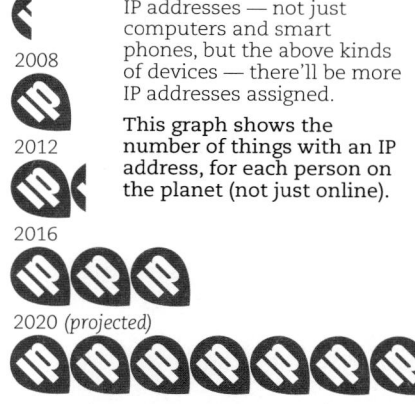

2000

2004

2008

2012

2016

2020 (projected)

Each "thing" on the Internet has its own unique address.

It's called an IP (Internet Protocol) address. As more things people own will have IP addresses — not just computers and smart phones, but the above kinds of devices — there'll be more IP addresses assigned.

This graph shows the number of things with an IP address, for each person on the planet (not just online).

That's how many IP addresses are used. So how many IP addresses *can there be*?

Since the beginning of the internet, they've been using a method called IPv4: four clumps of digits, broken up with periods. That method let us have a total of

4,294,967,296
IP addresses, or about 1 for every 2 people on the planet (not just online) in 2016.

But soon, it was clear there were way too few combinations. So on June 16, 2012, they established IPv6, which is six clumps of digits.

With that new standard, the potential number of IP addresses is now

340,282,366,920,938,463,463, 374,607,431,768,211,456
...or, **over 45 octillion (45×10^{27})** for each person on the planet (not just online) in 2016.

← And we'll only use enough for **seven per person** by 2020! Think we'll run out, ever?

Network Software

Objective 7.5   *Describe the type of software necessary for networks.*

What network software do home networks require? Because home networks are P2P networks, they need operating system software that supports P2P networking. Windows, macOS, and Linux all support P2P networking. You can connect computers running any of these operating systems to the same home network.

Is the same network software used in client/server networks? No, nodes on client/server networks are different than P2P networks. They communicate through a centralized server instead of communicating directly with each other. Communicating through a server is more efficient in a network with a large number of nodes, but it requires more complex software than is necessary for P2P networks. Therefore, the servers on client/server networks have specialized **network operating system (NOS)** software installed. This software handles requests for information, Internet access, and the use of peripherals for the rest of the network nodes. Examples of NOS software include Windows Server and SUSE Linux Enterprise Server.

The concept of a **smart home**—where devices and appliances are automated or controlled by apps installed on your smartphone or tablet (see Figure 7.11)—is in full play today, thanks to the power and availability of strong wireless networks and Bluetooth.

With smart home automation, you can dictate how and when a device should engage or respond. For some devices and appliances, just set a schedule and the rest is automated. Other devices and appliances work using some type of sensor and react to changes in their surrounding environment, such as motion, light, or temperature. For example, some smart home thermostats learn your habits (such as waking and sleeping patterns) and heating and cooling preferences over time and create automatic settings. Some smart home draperies and blinds open and close in reaction to the timing of sunrise and sunset using geolocation settings.

Smart home automation can also alert you to unpredictable events, such as water leaks and unexpected visitors to your home. But smart home technology isn't only about security and efficiency. It's also used to help control your entertainment devices as well.

At the heart of many smart homes are hubs that are used to control a variety of devices from different manufacturers. A hub receives different wireless signals from smart devices and then translates those into one Wi-Fi signal that your router can understand. In addition, the hub consolidates the controls required by each device and provides one single app for you to interact with, thus simplifying your experience. Other hubs, such as the Belkin WeMo, control devices more locally. Plug a device (e.g., a lamp or coffee maker) into the WeMo and you can control it from your phone or tablet. An alternative to a hub is a single home automation platform, such as those offered by Google, Microsoft, Lowe's, and AT&T.

You can create your own automation by using the IFTTT (If This Then That) app (**IFTTT.com**) or the open source application

Figure 7.11 You can remotely monitor your home through a dashboard on your mobile device with smart home technology. *(scyther5/123RF)*

openHAB and an IoT device (such as a WeMo motion detector, Nest thermostat, or Philips light bulb).

As of yet, no single standard has been adopted for home automation. Some devices work on Wi-Fi, while others work on Bluetooth. Some smart devices interact with apps on mobile devices, whereas others interact with each other directly. There have been some attempts at single platforms, such as Google's Android@Home platform and Microsoft's Home 2.0 program, but neither of these programs, nor anything else, has been accepted as the standard. Also, while costs have come down significantly on many smart home devices, the overall cost is not completely affordable to most, especially as a complete smart home solution.

Still, the smart home technology industry is estimated to increase to $100 billion by 2020. Most likely the smart home is here to stay.

Connecting to the Internet

One of the main reasons for setting up a network is to share an Internet connection. Broadband is the preferred way to access the Internet, but in some situations, other connections may be necessary.

Broadband Internet Connections

Objective 7.6 *Summarize the broadband options available to access the Internet.*

What exactly is broadband Internet access? **Broadband**, often referred to as high-speed Internet, refers to a type of connection that offers a means to connect to the Internet with fast throughput. Broadband has a data transmission rate that ranges from 1 to 500 Mbps. Some businesses and large organizations have a dedicated connection to the Internet, but most homeowners and small businesses purchase Internet access from **Internet service providers (ISPs)**. ISPs may be specialized providers, like Juno, or companies like Comcast that provide additional services, such as phone and cable TV.

Figure 7.12 Comparing Common Wired Broadband Internet Connection Options

Broadband Type	Transmission Medium	Speed Considerations	Average and Maximum Download Speeds
Cable	Coaxial cable, similar to cable TV wire	Cable connections are shared, so speed can drop during high-usage periods	Average speed of 10 Mbps, with maximum of 30 Mbps
DSL (Digital Subscriber Line)	Copper wire phone line	Speed drops as distance from the main signal source increases	Average speed of 3.7 Mbps, with maximum of 15 Mbps
Fiber-Optic	Strands of optically pure glass or plastic	Transmits data via light signals, which do not degrade over long distances	Average speed of 50 Mbps, with maximum of 500 Mbps

What types of broadband are available? As shown in Figure 7.12, the standard wired broadband technologies in most areas are cable, DSL (digital subscriber line), and fiber-optic service. Satellite broadband is used mostly in rural or mountain areas where DSL, cable, or fiber-optic service is unavailable or very costly.

How does cable Internet work? Cable Internet is a broadband service that transmits data over the coaxial cables that also transmit cable television signals; however, cable TV and cable Internet are separate services. Cable TV is a one-way service in which the cable company feeds programming signals to your television. To bring two-way Internet connections to homes, cable companies had to upgrade their networks with two-way data-transmission capabilities.

How does DSL work? DSL (digital subscriber line) uses twisted-pair cable, the same as that used for regular telephones, to connect your computer to the Internet. The bandwidth of the wires is split into three sections, like a three-lane highway. One lane is used to carry voice data. DSL uses the remaining two lanes to send and receive data separately at much higher frequencies than voice data. Although DSL uses a standard phone line, having a traditional phone line in your house doesn't mean you have access to DSL service. Your local phone company must have special DSL technology to offer you the service.

How does fiber-optic service work? Fiber-optic service uses fiber-optic lines, which are strands of optically pure glass or plastic that are as thin as a human hair. They're arranged in bundles called optical cables and transmit data via light signals over long distances. Because light travels so quickly, this technology can transmit an enormous amount of data at superfast speeds. When the data reaches your house, it's converted to electrical pulses that transmit digital signals your computer can "read." Note that fiber-optic cable is not usually run inside the home. On a fiber-optic network, twisted-pair or coaxial cable is still used inside the home to transport the network signals.

How does satellite Internet work? To take advantage of **satellite Internet**, you need a satellite dish that is placed outside your home and connected to your computer with coaxial cable, the same type of cable used for cable TV. Data from your computer is transmitted between your personal satellite dish and the satellite company's receiving satellite dish by a satellite that sits in geosynchronous orbit thousands of miles above Earth (see Figure 7.13).

How do I choose which broadband connection option is best for me? Depending on where you live, you might not have a choice of the broadband connection available. Check with your local cable TV provider, phone company, and satellite TV provider(s) to determine what broadband options are available and what the transfer rates are in your area.

Often, the most difficult decision is choosing between high-speed plans offered by the same company. For instance, at the time of printing, Verizon offered several fiber-optic plans that featured download speeds from 25 to 500 Mbps. Although 25 Mbps is fine for everyday browsing, e-mail, and shopping, it may not be fast enough for streaming HD movies or satisfying the needs of multiple devices on the Internet at the same time. Finally, you may also need to consider what other services you want bundled into your payment, such as phone or TV. Consulting with friends and neighbors about the plan they have and whether it's meeting their needs can help you decide on the right plan for you.

Figure 7.13 Internet data is transmitted between your personal satellite dish and the satellite company's receiving satellite dish by a satellite that sits in geosynchronous orbit thousands of miles above the Earth. *(Rendeeplumia/Fotolia)*

Wireless Internet Access

Objective 7.7 *Summarize how to access the Internet wirelessly.*

How can I access the Internet wirelessly at home? To access the Internet wirelessly at home without relying on your cellular network, you need to establish Wi-Fi on your home network by using a router that features wireless capabilities. You also need the right equipment on your mobile device. Virtually all laptops, smartphones, game systems, and personal media players sold today are Wi-Fi enabled and come with wireless capability built in.

How can I access Wi-Fi when I'm away from home? When you're away from home, you need to find a Wi-Fi hotspot. Many public places, such as libraries, hotels, and fast-food shops, offer free Wi-Fi access. Websites like Wi-Fi-FreeSpot (**wififreespot.com**) or apps such as WiFiGet help you locate a free hotspot wherever you're planning to go. Your ISP provider may also provide free hotspot service.

Mobile Hotspot

Figure 7.14 You can turn your smartphone into a mobile hotspot. *(Android, Google and the Google logo are registered trademarks of Google Inc., used with permission.)*

Alternatively, you can connect to the Internet using a **mobile hotspot**. Mobile hotspots let you tether, or connect, more than one device to the Internet but require access to a data plan. Although you can buy a separate mobile hotspot device, most smartphones have built-in functionality, enabling you to turn your smartphone into a mobile hotspot (see Figure 7.14). If you have several mobile devices that need wireless Internet access, this may be the most economical and functional way to access the Internet while on the road when you can't access Wi-Fi. Check with your provider, though, because they may charge an extra fee for tethering.

When you're not in a Wi-Fi hotspot but still need to access the Internet, you may want to consider mobile broadband. **Mobile broadband** connects you to the Internet through the same cellular network that cell phones use to get 3G or 4G Internet access.

How do I get mobile broadband? Just as you have an Internet service provider (ISP) for Internet access for your desktop or laptop computer, you must have a **wireless Internet service provider** (or **wireless ISP**) to connect your smartphone to the Internet. Phone companies (such as T-Mobile, Verizon, and AT&T) double as wireless ISPs.

3G and 4G can be thought of as "Wi-Fi everywhere" in that they provide Internet access to your mobile devices in the same way they provide voice service to your mobile phone. 3G and 4G refer to the third and fourth generations, respectively, of cell-phone networks. **4G** is the latest service standard and offers the fastest data-access speeds over cell-phone networks.

How do I purchase Internet time? Providers measure your Internet usage not according to how much time you're on the Internet but according to how much data you download and upload. An Internet connectivity plan is known as a **data plan**. You pay one monthly price and are allowed data transfers up to some fixed limit per month, such as 2 GB or 5 GB. If you exceed your data limit in a month, the fee for the extra data usage is usually very expensive.

Understanding your data usage is complicated. A cellular data plan is for Internet data transfer, not texting. Providers require a separate texting plan. Note that all the data transfer you do using Wi-Fi (instead of the 3G/4G network) does not count as part of your data plan usage.

Bits&Bytes   Net Neutrality

Until recently, small web-based businesses would have the same opportunity of being accessed on the Internet as a new on-demand movie from Verizon or an online sale at Target. This is because of *net neutrality* where Internet access and use has been treated equally with no differentiation by the type of user, the content that's being uploaded, or the mode of communication. Big Internet service providers, such as Comcast and Spectrum, have pushed for a tiered structure: a premium tier with priority access to a faster Internet and a lower tier with less priority and slower speeds. Access to the faster tier would be more costly than access to the lower tier. In this new structure,

providers like Comcast could charge content companies, like Netflix or Facebook, a fee to avoid being given slower access speeds for their customers. Smaller users who might not afford the better access would have less priority and slower access, thus putting them at a disadvantage. Proponents claim that a tiered priority system will promote competition and innovation. Opponents claim that paying for faster access will put small Internet startups at a disadvantage and ultimately stifle innovation. In 2015, the U.S. Federal Communications Commission (FCC) voted to maintain net neutrality, keeping the Internet open and free. That decision was overturned in 2017.

5G (or 5th-generation) wireless data is in the works, with proposed services up to 100 times faster than current wireless connections. It's anticipated that 5G networks could manage connections for 7 trillion devices, enabling everyone on Earth to have around 1,000 connected devices before the network gets overloaded. Additionally, 5G could save up to 90% on energy consumption over current standards. The bad news: you may need to wait until 2020 for this capability.

How big a data plan do I need to buy? Before subscribing to a data plan, you should assess your needs. When you are out of reach of a Wi-Fi network, how often do you:

* download apps, stream music, or play online games?
* watch streaming video?
* download files attached to e-mails or from your company website?
* use apps that are communicating with the Internet?

Begin by estimating how much data you transfer up and down from the Internet each month. To do so, you can use an online estimator supplied by your provider like the one shown in Figure 7.15.

The Android OS allows you to see a graph of your data usage and set alarms at specific levels. iOS keeps track of your cellular data usage too. This feature resets automatically each month so you know how much data transfer you have left. Most mobile operating systems keep track of data usage for you.

Be sure you select a data plan that provides adequate service at a good price. There are plans that allow a group of people to share data and pull from a single pool. Some plans transfer unused data over to the next month; some do not. Shop carefully.

How does mobile broadband Internet compare with wired Internet access? 3G performs similarly to a standard DSL connection (roughly 3 Mbps). 3G is more reliable than Wi-Fi and is less susceptible to interference. 3G blankets most major urban areas with connectivity.

According to the standards set for 4G, the data transfer rate you would get while in a moving vehicle is approximately 100 Mbps; from a fixed location, you can expect up to a 1 Gbps data transfer rate. Some of the early 4G systems released in the market support less than the required 1 Gbps rate and are not fully compliant with the 4G standards and so are being tagged as 4G LTE. They are still faster than 3G, however.

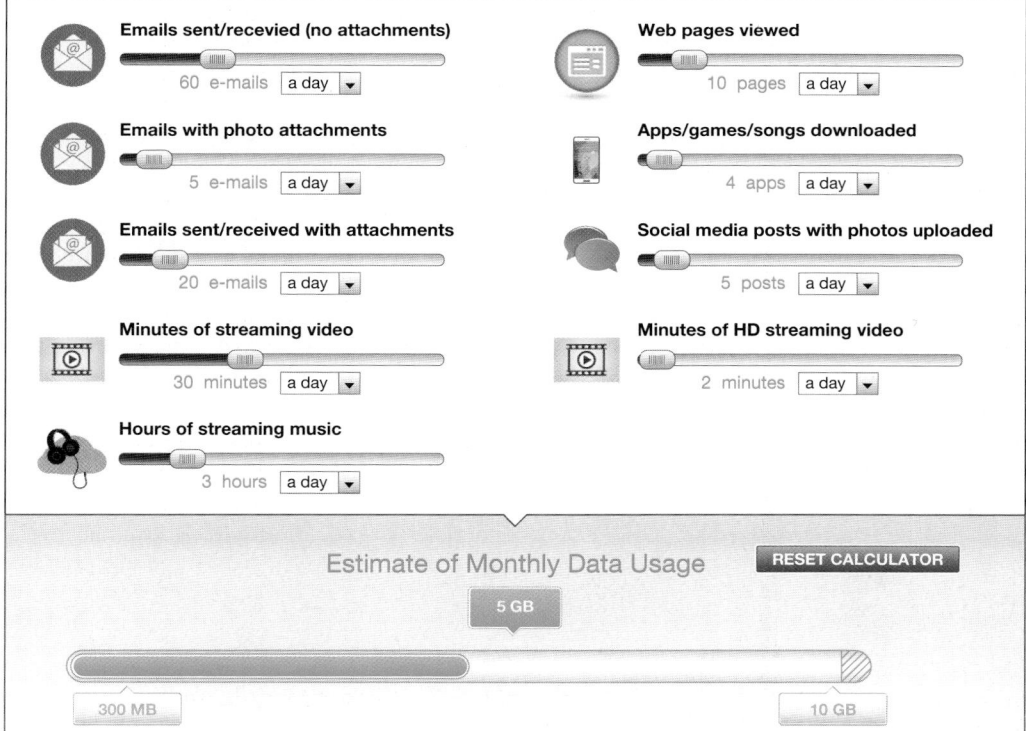

Figure 7.15 Online tools can help you estimate your monthly data usage.

Although about 90% of Internet users in the United States use high-speed Internet connections such as DSL, cable, or fiber-optic, there are still some areas (usually rural) where broadband service isn't available. A dial-up connection needs only a standard phone line and a modem to access the Internet. Therefore, some people choose to use a dial-up connection when there's no high-speed service in their area. Additionally, a dial-up connection is the least costly way to connect to the Internet, so for those who don't use the Internet frequently, the extra cost of broadband may be unnecessary.

The major downside to dial-up is speed. Dial-up modems transfer data about 600 times slower than a fiber-optic broadband connection. Also, dial-up uses a traditional phone line to connect to the Internet; therefore, unless you have a separate phone line just for your dial-up connection, when you're using dial-up, you tie up your phone line.

Ethics in IT

Ethical Challenges of the Internet of Things

We interact with the Internet of Things (IoT)—knowingly and sometimes unknowingly—on a daily basis in all aspects of our lives. As we become more connected to the Internet through our vast array of devices, we also become part of the information infrastructure, each of us essentially acting as nodes on the Internet of Things. Although the interconnectivity of the IoT brings with it many benefits, it also poses ethical concerns, including those related to privacy and equal access.

Let's consider privacy issues. As we use our Internet-connected devices, we generate huge amounts of data. Many organizations are acquiring and using that data to help with decision making, resource allocation, and operations. Although we may be used to having Internet advertisers take our search data and send us targeted advertising, how would you feel about companies using information gleaned from an IoT-connected device? For example, say you wear a fitness tracker, such as a Fitbit or an Apple Watch. The sensors in these activity monitors are connected wirelessly to smartphones and to the Internet to enable users to track their workout activities. How would you feel if the data collected by your Fitbit or Apple Watch was then shared by your mobile phone carrier with a third-party marketer? How would you feel if you were in a restaurant or grocery store and received text messages providing discounts or coupons for low-calorie offerings from those third-party marketers, simply because your behavior implied that weight loss is one of your goals? Although some might welcome these opportunities, others might consider the offerings an invasion of their privacy.

The Internet of Things also adds to the ethical dilemma of the digital divide—the technological gap between those who can and cannot afford to own these devices. At the very core of the dilemma is the ability for users to access the Internet at all. Significant work has been done to provide developing countries with access to the Internet. But now, the IoT adds new considerations, not only discriminating against certain groups of people who do not have access to the Internet but also those who cannot afford IoT devices. There have been discussions about providing free nationwide wireless Internet access to bridge this gap, but the creation and delivery of that type of service is complicated and fraught with political and corporate debate, preventing any type of public access anytime soon.

As the Internet of Things continues to grow, we will be faced with these issues and certainly others as well. Can you think of other ethical issues the Internet of Things might create?

Before moving on to Part 2:

1. Watch Chapter Overview Video 7.1.

2. Then take the Check Your Understanding quiz.

Check Your Understanding // Review & Practice

For a quick review to see what you've learned so far, answer the following questions.

multiple choice

1. Which of the following is a reason to establish a network?

   a. to share an Internet connection

   b. to share peripherals

   c. to share files

   d. all of the above

2. The type of network used for communication among a laptop and smartphone using Bluetooth is a

   a. PAN.

   b. MAN.

   c. LAN.

   d. WAN.

3. The device used to connect a network to the Internet is called a

   a. switch.

   b. modem.

   c. gateway.

   d. router.

4. The fastest broadband Internet service is usually

   a. DSL.

   b. fiber-optic.

   c. cable.

   d. satellite.

5. Which of the following allows you to connect to the Internet wirelessly?

   a. Wi-Fi

   b. 4G LTE

   c. Mobile hotspot

   d. all of the above

 Go to **MyLab IT** to take an autograded version of the *Check Your Understanding* review and to find all media resources for the chapter.

TechBytes Weekly   Go to TechBytes Weekly for current technology news and discussion questions!

Try This

Testing Your Internet Connection Speed

Your ISP may have promised you certain downloading and uploading data speeds. How can you tell if you're getting what was promised? Numerous sites on the Internet, such as SpeedOf.Me and speedtest.net, test the speed of your Internet connection. You can see how your results compare with others, as well as determine whether you're getting the results promised by your ISP. In this Try This, we will test your Internet connection speed using SpeedOf.Me. For more step-by-step instructions, watch the Try This video on MyLab IT.

Step 1 Type **SpeedOf.Me** in any browser. SpeedOf.Me is an HTML5 Internet speed test, so it will work on PCs, Macs, and Android devices. Click Start Test to begin.

Step 2 SpeedOf.Me tests upload and download speeds using sample files of varying sizes, starting with a 128 KB sample until it reaches a sample size that takes more than 8 seconds to upload or download (with the largest possible sample size being 128 MB). The results are based on the last sample file. As the test runs, graphics illustrate the process, with the final results displaying when the test is finished.

Step 3 A history chart displays at the bottom of the screen, showing the results of any tests you have run on that particular device over time. If you want to share your results, you can use the Share button to post them to your favorite social media site or by e-mail.

Download Speed: Time taken to move data from the server to your computer

Upload Speed: Time taken to move data from your computer to the server

Bands represent series of sample files sent

(Courtesy SpeedOf.Me)

Make: Networked Devices

One of the nice features of programming in **App Inventor** is that you can instantly see changes on your target device as you work. The two devices connect using Wi-Fi. But what is going on behind the scenes to allow this?

In this exercise, you'll explore how the AI Companion software works with the AI program to connect your systems. You'll see how useful networking utilities like Ping and Telnet are to investigate how network firewalls are set up.

The App Inventor Companion app and program communicate across Wi-Fi to make your programming easier.

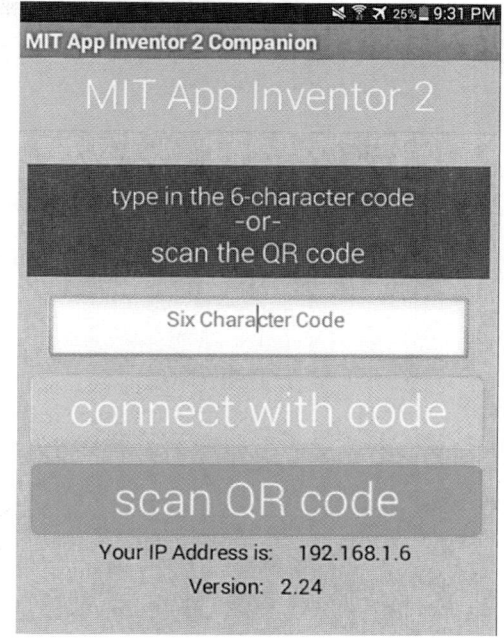

(Copyright MIT, used with permission)

```
Command Prompt                              —    □    ×

Microsoft Windows [Version 10.0.10240]
(c) 2015 Microsoft Corporation. All rights reserved.

C:\Users\fly_n>ping 192.168.1.11

Pinging 192.168.1.11 with 32 bytes of data:
Request timed out.
Request timed out.
Reply from 192.168.1.4: Destination host unreachable.
Reply from 192.168.1.4: Destination host unreachable.

Ping statistics for 192.168.1.11:
    Packets: Sent = 4, Received = 2, Lost = 2 (50% loss),

C:\Users\fly_n>_
```

(Windows 10, Microsoft Corporation)

For the instructions for this exercise, go to MyLab IT.

Your Home Network

You know what a network is and the advantages of having one. In this section, we look at installing or updating a home network and keeping it safe.

Installing and Configuring Home Networks

Now that you understand the basic components of a network and your Internet connection options, you're ready to install a network in your home. If you already have a network in your home, it's useful to examine your network settings and configuration to make sure they're still meeting your needs, especially if you've added new devices.

Only a few years ago, most home networks included just a few computers and a printer. However, a network that can manage those devices is often very different from one that can support the smartphones, gaming consoles, tablets, smart TVs, and IoT devices many homes have added to their networks since. If you're using any of these additional devices and you haven't updated your network equipment or setup in a while, it may be time to do so.

Planning Your Home Network

Objective 7.8 *Explain what should be considered before creating a home network.*

Where do I start? One of the first things you should do to evaluate your network is list all the devices that will connect to it. Consider not only the obvious devices, such as computers, laptops, tablets, and printers, but also smartphones, DVR boxes, smart TVs, wireless stereo equipment, and any other appliance that connects to the Internet wirelessly. You might be surprised at how many devices you list. Then include any devices you think you may add in the near future. Once you have a complete list, determine whether your router can support all your devices. For more than 15 connected devices, you should have at least an 802.11ac router.

What wireless Ethernet standard should my network be using? For a home network to run most efficiently and to provide the fastest experience, it's best that all network nodes— computers, network adapters (NICs), routers, and so on—use the latest wireless Ethernet standard. Devices that support the 802.11n standard have been around for a while, so if you've bought a laptop or other portable device in the past few years, it most likely has an 802.11n NIC. Your router may also be supporting the 802.11n standard.

However, most newer devices support the 802.11ac standard. If you have the fastest 802.11ac NIC in your laptop but the router is the slower 802.11n standard, then data will be sent at the speeds supported by the lower standard. If you haven't updated your router in a while, you may want to consider getting an 802.11ac router (see Figure 7.16) to get the fastest connection speeds.

Additionally, to provide the speediest short-range connections between devices you may want to employ the newer standard, 802.11ad (WiGig). For longer-range connections, the 802.11ac standard will work best. Most new routers that offer 802.11ad also offer 802.11ac, so it can be used for both Wi-Fi, and WiGig.

How can I tell what wireless standard my router supports? You may be able to tell what standard your router is supporting just by looking at it. Many routers have the wireless standard indicated on the device. If you're still not sure, you can search for more information on your router by entering the model number into a search engine. If your router is provided by your ISP and it's an older standard, you should consider having your ISP provide you with a new router.

Figure 7.16 802.11ac wireless routers offer the fastest connection speeds and a greater wireless signal range. *(AlexLmx/Shutterstock)*

How can I tell what network adapters are installed in my computer? To see which network adapters are installed in your Windows computer, use the Device Manager utility (see Figure 7.17), which lists all the adapters. If you can't tell which wireless standard the adapter supports from the list, search the Internet for information on your specific adapter to determine its capability. The Device Manager can also alert you if there's a problem with the adapter.

Connecting Devices to a Network

Objective 7.9 *Describe how to set up a home network.*

How should a basic home network be set up? Because most newer modems have integrated routers, and only a few wired connections may be needed, setting up a home network is fairly straightforward. As shown in Figure 7.18, the modem/router is the central device of a home network. The Ethernet cable should connect directly to the modem/router using the WAN or Internet port, and all computer devices—such as laptops, tablets, smartphones, HDTVs, gaming consoles, and printers—are connected to the modem/router via a wired connection to the LAN ports or wirelessly.

Is there a limit to the number of wired devices I can have in my network? Most home routers have three or four LAN ports on the back to support wired connections. This is usually

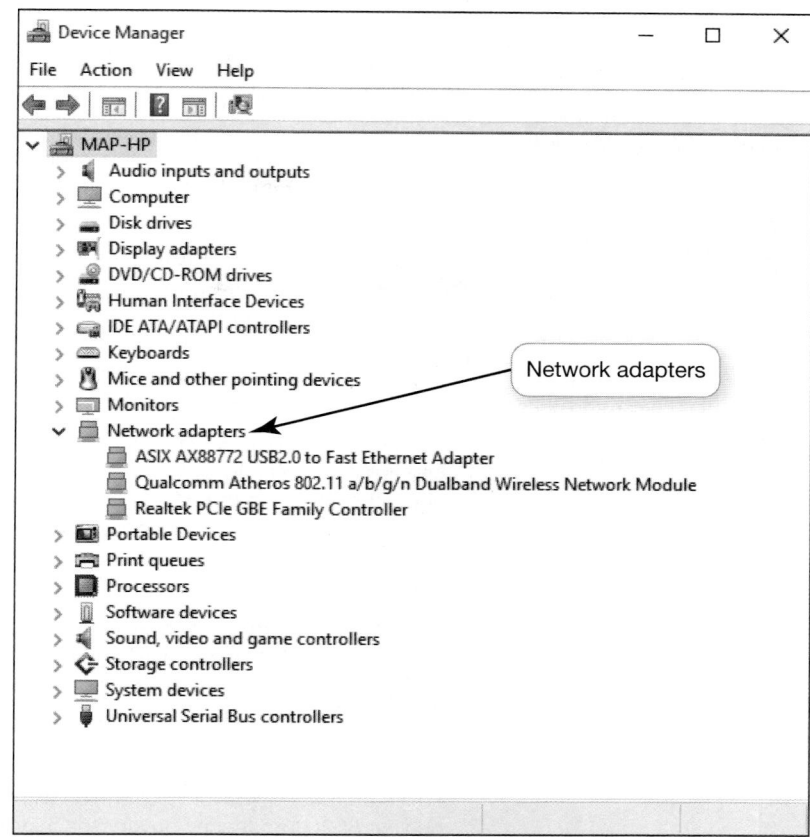

Figure 7.17 The Windows Device Manager shows the wireless and wired network adapters installed on a computer.
> *To access the Device Manager, access* **Settings**, *click* **Devices**, *and then select* **Device manager** *at the bottom of the window. (Windows 10, Microsoft Corporation)*

Figure 7.18 A Small Network with a Wired/Wireless Modem/Router Attached *(Laurentiu Iordache/Fotolia, Beboy/Shutterstock, Oleksiy Maksymenko/Alamy, Sergey Peterman/Shutterstock, Iko/Shutterstock)*

Router

Switch

Figure 7.19 You can add ports to your network by connecting a switch to your router. *(Alarich/Shutterstock, Leslie Wilk/Alamy Stock Photo)*

sufficient for the general house that has at least one computer, maybe a printer, and perhaps some entertainment devices that are connected directly to the router. If you need additional ports for plugging in wired connections to your network, you can buy a stand-alone switch and plug it into one of the ports on your router (see Figure 7.19). This will give you additional ports for making wired connections. However, don't mistakenly buy another router with an embedded switch and try adding that to your network. The two routers will cause conflicts as they fight for control over network navigation.

How many wireless devices can connect to a router in a home network? Most home wireless routers can support up to 253 wireless connections at the same time, although most home networks have far fewer. Regardless of how many devices your home network has, they all share bandwidth when they're connected to a router. Therefore, the more devices actively transmitting data that you connect to a single router, the smaller the portion of the router's bandwidth each device receives.

To look at this another way, say you have a pizza that represents your router's bandwidth. You can cut the pizza into six or eight pieces (that is, you can connect either six or eight devices to the network). If you cut the pizza into eight pieces, each person who gets a slice receives a smaller portion than if you had cut the pizza into six pieces. Similarly, when you connect eight devices to the network, each device has less bandwidth than it would if only six devices were connected to the network.

Are wireless routers for Windows and macOS networks different? All routers that support the 802.11n standard and the newer 802.11ac standard should work with computers running the more recent versions of Windows or macOS. However, Apple has designed routers that are optimized for working with Apple computers. So if you're connecting Apple computers to your network, you may want to use the Apple AirPort Extreme router for larger home networks or the AirPort Express for smaller networks. Windows devices can also connect to an AirPort router, so it's a great choice for households with both Apples and PCs. The AirPort Extreme uses the newest 802.11ac technology for the fastest data transfers.

How do I know what's connected to my router? To determine what's connected to your router, you need to log in to an account associated with your router's IP address. You can find your router's IP address on the router manufacturer's website. Once you know it, type it into a web browser. You may need to enter a user name and password, but eventually you'll get to a configuration page that lists what wired and wireless devices are in your network. You may be surprised at all the various devices associated with your network.

Figure 7.20 shows a router network listing with wired (desktop computer) and wireless (DVR, laptop, iPhone, and iPad) devices connected in a home network. You'll notice that each device also has an IP address. You can think of your network as an apartment building. The router's IP address is the building's street address, while the IP addresses of the individual devices connected to the router are the apartment numbers. Each device needs an IP address so the router knows to which device to send information.

Bits&Bytes | **Mesh Networks: An Emerging Alternative**

Have you ever heard of a *mesh network*? This emerging technology uses small radio transmitters instead of wireless routers as its network nodes. What is so great about mesh networks is that only one node needs to physically connect to a network connection, and then all other nodes can share wirelessly with each other. This connection sharing between nodes can extend almost endlessly, since one wired node can share its Internet connection wirelessly with other nearby nodes, and then those nodes can share their connection wirelessly with nodes closest to them—thus creating a "mesh" of connectivity. The truly wireless aspect of mesh networks poses several advantages to the wireless networks that are in place today: They're easier to install

because fewer wires need to be run; they can accommodate more nodes; and they enable wireless networks to be created in outdoor and unstructured venues.

In developing nations as well as in some areas in the United States, mesh networks have helped provide access to the Internet in a more timely and inexpensive manner than waiting for the physical connections to be established. Mesh networks can also help promote cellular communications during times of disasters when traditional communications are halted. And if you have an Android mobile phone, you can participate in the Serval Mesh, which allows users to send and receive information without depending on established cellular networks.

Figure 7.20 Wired and wireless connections can use the same router. *(Windows 10, Microsoft Corporation)*

Specialized Home Networking Devices

What can I attach to my network to facilitate file sharing and backup of data? Network-attached storage (NAS) devices are specialized devices designed to store and manage all network data. Although data can always be stored on individual hard drives in computers on a network, NAS devices provide for centralized data storage and access.

Figure 7.21 A network-attached storage device provides centralized data storage and access. *(Leslie Wilk/ Alamy Stock Photo)*

Popular for years on business networks, NAS devices are now being widely marketed for home networks (see Figure 7.21). You can think of them as specialized external hard drives. NAS devices connect directly to the network through a router or switch. Specialized software is installed on computers attached to the network to ensure that all data saved to an individual computer is also stored on the NAS device as a backup.

For Apple computers, the AirPort Time Capsule is a wireless router combined with a hard drive that facilitates the backup of all computers connected to the network. The AirPort Time Capsule looks very similar to the AirPort router, and it works in conjunction with the Time Machine backup feature of macOS. If you buy an AirPort Time Capsule, you won't need to buy an AirPort router (or other router) because the AirPort Time Capsule also fulfills this function on your network. When the Air-Port Time Capsule is installed on your network, Macs connected to the network will ask the user if they want to use the AirPort Time Capsule as their source for Time Machine backups. The AirPort Time Capsule is another type of NAS device.

Besides NAS devices, are there other storage devices I could use on my network? A more sophisticated type of NAS device is a home network server. **Home network servers** are specialized devices designed to store files, share files across the network, and back up files on computers connected to the network. All computers connected to the network can access the server.

Home network servers often look like oversized external hard drives. They're configured with operating systems like Windows Server and connect directly as a node on your network. Home servers have more sophisticated functionality than NAS devices and often handle the following tasks:

- Automatically back up all computers connected to the network
- Act as a repository for files to be shared across the network
- Function as an access gateway to allow any computer on the network to be accessed from a remote location via the Internet (see Figure 7.22)

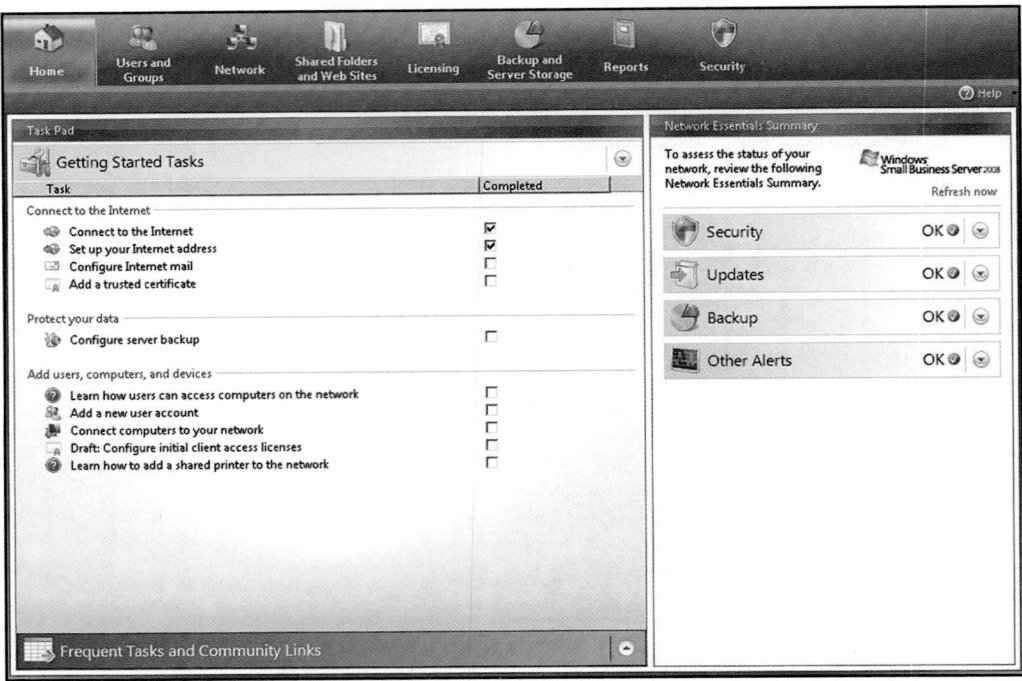

Figure 7.22 Home network servers are often configured with software such as Windows Server. *(Windows Server, Microsoft Corporation)*

Note that even though these devices are servers, they don't convert a home P2P network into a client/server network because these servers don't perform all the functions performed on client/server networks.

What kinds of digital entertainment devices can connect directly to the network? A **network-ready device** (or Internet-ready device) can be connected directly to a network through either a wired or wireless connection. Most game consoles, Blu-ray players, DVRs, smart TVs, and home theater systems are network ready. A device that isn't network ready requires that the device be connected directly to another computer via a cable on the network.

Why should I connect digital entertainment devices to my network? One reason for connecting entertainment devices to your network is to access and share digital content between devices. Connecting these devices to your network also connects them to the Internet so you can access online entertainment content, including movies, videos, and music.

You can also use gaming devices to play multiplayer games with players in the next room or all over the world. The content you access is either downloaded or streamed to your devices. Newer smart TVs and other smart devices (such as Blu-ray players, game consoles, and home theater systems) are continually adding apps and video services so that you can play games, view on-demand and online videos, listen to Internet radio, and access social networking sites (see Figure 7.23). Some smart devices also feature an integrated web browser that lets you access the web directly, without the use of apps.

What if I don't have a smart TV? You can get the same services on your existing television by using a Blu-ray player that features integrated wireless connectivity to receive streaming media from various ISPs. For best video viewing, look for a Blu-ray player that has high-definition resolution and the capability to display 3D video. Some set-top boxes also provide the same types of connectivity as a Blu-ray player. Alternatively, you can use devices such as Apple TV or Google Chromecast that enable you to send Internet-based media to your traditional TV.

Figure 7.23 Smart TVs have their own apps and let you directly access the web. *(scanrail/123RF)*

If you have areas in your home where you have little or no Wi-Fi coverage, try using a Wi-Fi analyzer to gather information before embarking on ways to improve your coverage. Free apps such as

WiFi Analyzer (Android) or Wi-Fi Inspector (Windows) provide signal strength and other details that might be helpful in remedying the problem.

Configuring Software for Your Home Network

Objective 7.10   *Summarize how to configure home network software.*

How do I set up a Windows home network for the first time? In Windows, the process of setting up a network is fairly automated, especially if you're using the same version of Windows on all your computers. The Windows examples in this section assume all computers are running Windows 10. Before configuring the computers to the network, do the following:

1. Make sure there is a network adapter on each node.
2. For any wired connections, plug all the cables into the router, nodes, and so on.
3. Make sure the modem/router is connected to the Internet. If you have separate devices, then make sure that your modem is connected to the Internet and that the router is connected to the modem.
4. Turn on your equipment in the following order:
   a. Your modem/router (or if individual devices, the modem and then the router, allowing each device about one minute each to power up)
   b. All computers and peripherals (printers, scanners, and so on)

You can add other devices, such as TVs, Blu-ray players, and gaming consoles, to the network after you configure the computers.

After you've completed the previous steps, launch the Windows network setup wizards from the Network and Sharing Center, which you access via the Network & Internet group in Settings (see Figure 7.24):

- If your computer has a wired connection to the network, you should automatically be connected. You should give the network the same secured name you give to your router (see the "Troubleshooting Wireless Network Problems" section in this chapter).
- If you're connecting wirelessly, ensure that your Wi-Fi is turned on by selecting Wi-Fi in the Network & Internet group in Settings. Then, from the Notification area on the taskbar, click Internet access. A panel opens, displaying the wired and wireless connection options. You'll need to enter your security passphrase to connect to your wireless network initially.

How do I share files with other computers on my network? For ease of file and peripheral sharing, Windows has the HomeGroup network sharing feature. HomeGroup makes it easier to

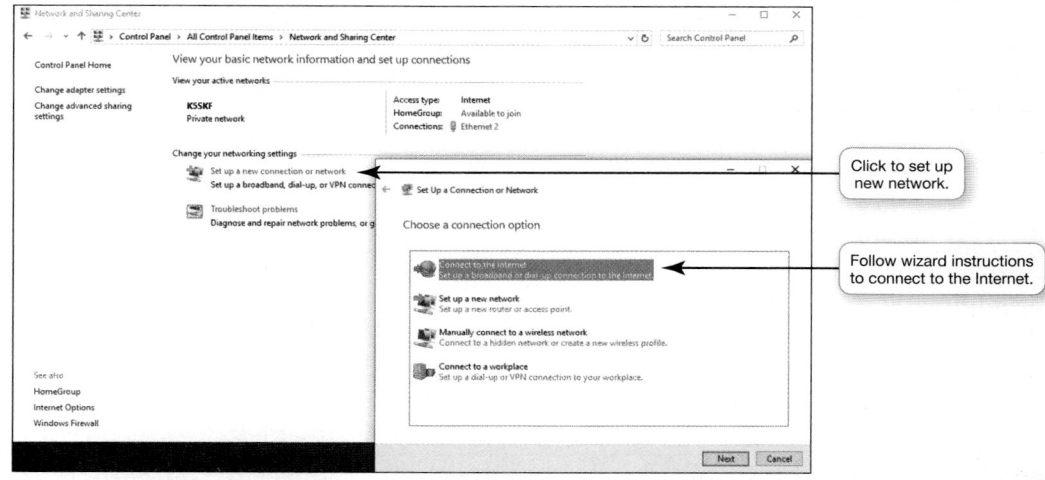

Figure 7.24 Connecting a Windows 10 computer to a network for the first time is fairly automated. *(Windows 10, Microsoft Corporation)*

allow computers on a Windows network to share peripherals and information. To create a homegroup, it's important that you first shut down all other computers on the network, leaving only the computer you'll use to create the new HomeGroup powered on. Then, complete the steps outlined in Figure 7.25.

What if I don't have the same version of Windows on all my computers? Computers with various versions of Windows can coexist on the same network. Always set up the computers running the newest version of Windows first. Then consult the Microsoft website for guidance on how to configure computers with previous versions of Windows.

What if I need to share files between Macs and Windows PCs on the same network? Many families have Windows PCs as well as Macs. In order to share files between Mac and Windows PCs, you can use the Service Message Block (SMB) protocol. SMB is a file sharing protocol incorporated into all operating systems that enables users at non-Windows computers to access data in Windows machines. To enable file sharing in macOS, open the Sharing pane and select the option for File Sharing. Your Mac automatically initiates the SMB protocol to communicate.

Figure 7.25 Creating a HomeGroup in Windows

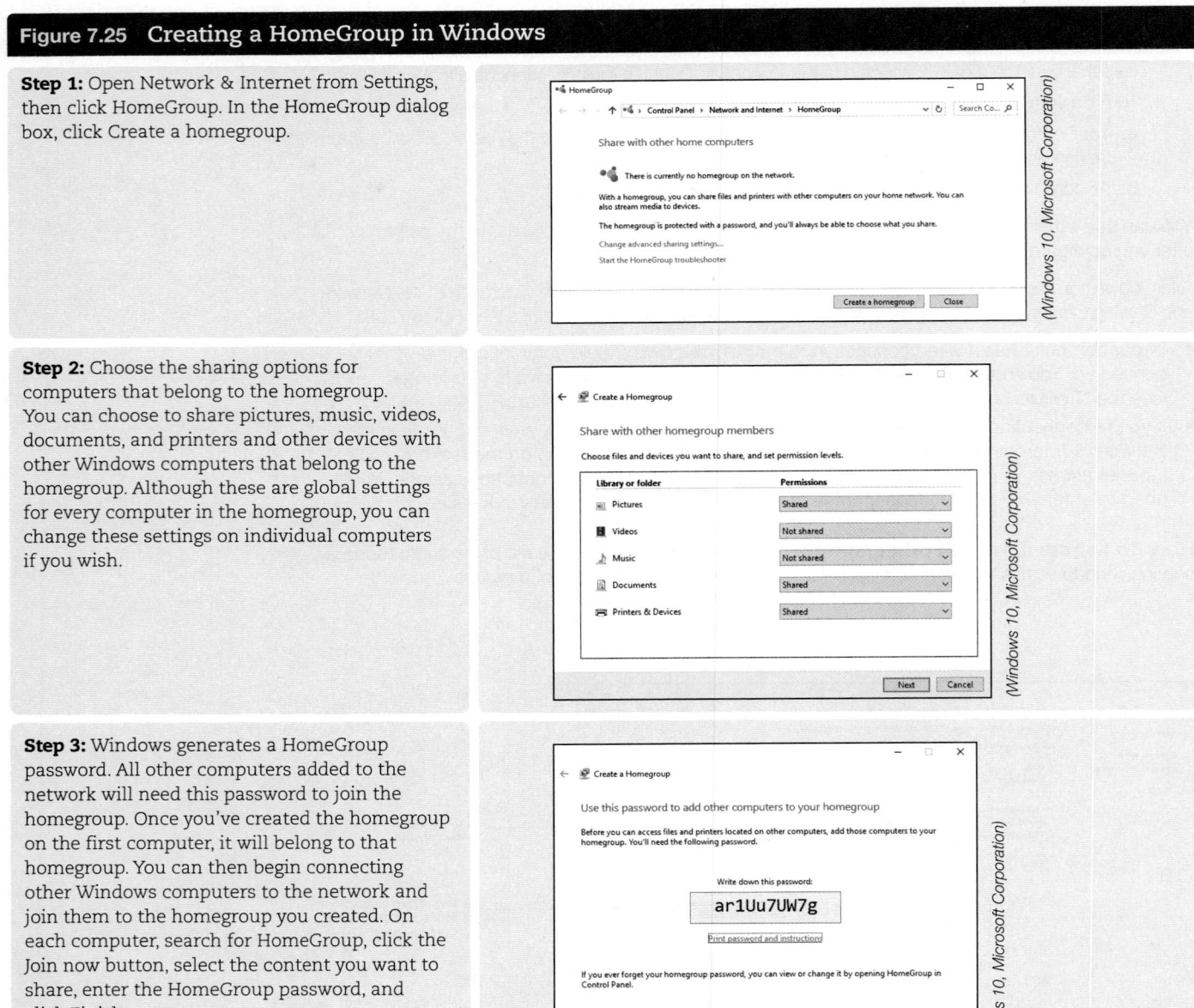

Step 1: Open Network & Internet from Settings, then click HomeGroup. In the HomeGroup dialog box, click Create a homegroup.

Step 2: Choose the sharing options for computers that belong to the homegroup. You can choose to share pictures, music, videos, documents, and printers and other devices with other Windows computers that belong to the homegroup. Although these are global settings for every computer in the homegroup, you can change these settings on individual computers if you wish.

Step 3: Windows generates a HomeGroup password. All other computers added to the network will need this password to join the homegroup. Once you've created the homegroup on the first computer, it will belong to that homegroup. You can then begin connecting other Windows computers to the network and join them to the homegroup you created. On each computer, search for HomeGroup, click the Join now button, select the content you want to share, enter the HomeGroup password, and click Finish.

(Windows 10, Microsoft Corporation)

The process of users transferring files between computers is referred to as **peer-to-peer (P2P) sharing** (see Figure 7.26). Any kind of file can be made available to share with others. Often media files, songs, and movies are made easily obtainable on P2P sites. These sites don't have a central computer acting to index all this information. Instead, they operate in a true P2P sharing environment in which computers connect directly to other computers. This makes them a prime source of unwanted viruses and spyware.

Some blame peer-to-peer networks for the growth of piracy on the Internet. As more sites have made it easier to illegally download music using P2P networks, music sales have dropped significantly. The recording industry is still trying to counter losing these sales. The heavy amount of traffic on P2P sites also played into the debate on Internet neutrality. Internet service providers like Comcast were choosing to throttle, or limit, the speed of data transfer for P2P file exchanges. Users complained this was an illegal use of a public resource and all data should be treated equally by such Internet service providers.

P2P networks defend their legality in that they don't run a central server but only facilitate connections between users. Therefore, they have no control over what the users choose to trade. There are legitimate uses of these new avenues of distribution. For example, *BitTorrent (BT) Bundles* are packages of free audio, video, and print content provided for download by musicians through BitTorrent. You can unlock additional content by paying or supplying your e-mail address.

Figure 7.26 Peer-to-peer (P2P) networks do not have a central computer distributing information but instead send information between each member. *(So47/Fotolia)*

Tracks that are easy to remix are provided so fans can create and share their own extensions to the work.

How do I connect a mobile device to a wireless network? Connecting a mobile device, regardless of its operating system, to a wireless network is an easy process these days. When you boot up your device, a list of available networks that the NIC in your device detects will display. On Macs, the list pops up in the network login screen. On Windows devices, you can click on the Internet access icon in the system tray to display available networks. If there's a padlock icon next to the network name, this means that the network is secure and requires a password. Enter the password for the network in the password box, and click the Join button. For unsecure networks, you don't need a password. Checking the "Remember this network" check box makes any network a preferred network, enabling the computer to connect to the network automatically when that network is available. You can have multiple preferred networks, such as your home, school, work, and local coffee shop networks.

Managing and Securing Wireless Networks

All networks require some maintenance and management, but there are some situations that are particular to wireless networks. In addition, wireless networks require additional security measures. In this section, we'll look at how to troubleshoot typical wireless network problems and how to protect wireless networks from common security threats.

Troubleshooting Wireless Network Problems

Objective 7.11   *Describe the potential problems with wireless networks and means to avoid them.*

What types of problems can I run into when installing wireless networks? The maximum range of 802.11n or 802.11ac wireless devices is about 350 feet. But as you go farther away from your router, the throughput you achieve decreases. Obstacles between wireless nodes also decrease throughput. Walls, floors, and large metal objects (such as refrigerators) are the most common sources of interference with wireless signals.

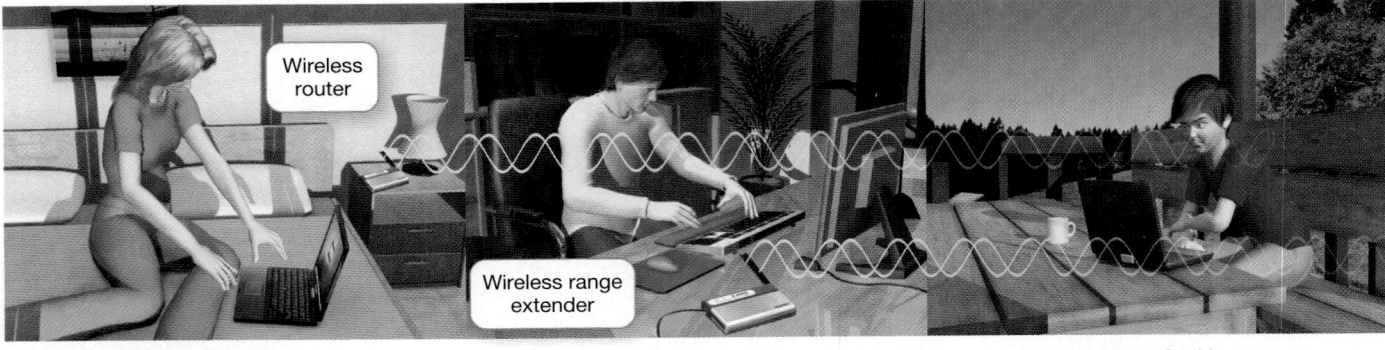

Wireless router

Wireless range extender

Computer A with wireless network adapter

Computer B with wireless range extender

Laptop C with wireless network adapter

Figure 7.27 Because a wireless range extender is installed in the den, Laptop C on the back porch can now connect to the wireless network.

What if a node on the network seems slow? Repositioning the node within the same room (sometimes even just a few inches from the original position) can affect communication between nodes. If this doesn't work, move the device closer to the router or to another room in your house. You might also try repositioning the antennas on your router. If these solutions don't work, consider adding additional equipment to your network.

What equipment will help improve a wireless signal throughout the network? There are two types of devices that you can use to amplify your wireless signal to extend to parts of your home that are experiencing poor connectivity: access points and extenders. An **access point** is connected with cable to the main router. The disadvantage of using an access point is the need for a wired connection between the access point and the router, which may not always be possible. Alternatively, a **wireless range extender** is a wireless network device that repeats your wireless signal. For example, as shown in Figure 7.27, Laptop C on the back porch can't connect to the wireless network, even though Computer B in the den can. By placing a wireless range extender in the den, where there is still good connectivity to the wireless network, the wireless signal is amplified and beamed farther out to the back porch. This allows Laptop C to make a good connection to the network. The downside of using an extender over an access point is that it shares the wireless connection, and can potentially slow the entire network.

Securing Wireless Networks

Objective 7.12 *Describe how to secure wireless home networks.*

Why is a wireless network more vulnerable than a wired network? Packets of information on a wireless network are broadcast through the airwaves. Savvy hackers can intercept and decode information from your transmissions that may allow them to bypass standard protections, such as a firewall, that you have set up on your network. All computers that connect to the Internet, whether or not they're on a network, need to be secured from intruders. This is usually accomplished by using a firewall, which is a hardware or software solution that helps shield your network from prying eyes. (We discuss firewalls at length in Chapter 9.) Wireless networks present special vulnerabilities; therefore, you should take additional steps to keep your wireless network safe.

With a wired network, it's fairly easy to tell if someone is using your network. However, most wireless 802.11 networks have wide ranges that may extend outside your house. This makes it possible for a hacker to access your network without your knowledge. Also, in some areas where residences are close together, wireless signals can reach a neighbor's residence. Most wireless network adapters are set up to access the strongest wireless network signal detected. **Piggybacking** is connecting to a wireless network without the permission of the owner. This practice is illegal in many jurisdictions but often happens inadvertently between neighbors.

Why should I be worried about someone logging onto my wireless network without my permission? If your neighbor is using your network connection, his or her usage could be slowing down your connection speed. Some neighbors might even be computer savvy enough to penetrate your unprotected wireless network and steal personal information, just as any other hacker could. And any cyberattack or illegal behavior a hacker initiates from your wireless network could get you in trouble with the authorities.

How can I secure my wireless network? To secure a wireless network, take the additional precautions described as follows:

1. **Use encryption and security protocols.** Most routers ship with security protocols such as Wired Equivalent Privacy (WEP), Wi-Fi Protected Access (WPA), or Wi-Fi Protected Access Version 2 (WPA2). Each use encryption (a method of translating your data into code) to protect data in your wireless transmissions. WPA2 is the most secure, but WPA may be compatible with more client devices. WEP still offers protection, but offers the least protection of the three.

2. **Change your network name (SSID).** Each wireless network has its own name to identify it, known as the **service set identifier (SSID)**. Unless you change this name when you set up your router, the router uses a default network name that all routers from that manufacturer use (such as "Wireless" or "Netgear"). Hackers know the default names and access codes for routers. If you haven't changed the SSID, it's advertising the fact that you probably haven't changed any of the other default settings for your router either.

3. **Disable SSID broadcast.** Most routers are set up to broadcast their SSIDs so that other wireless devices can find them. If your router supports disabling SSID broadcasting, turn it off. This makes it more difficult for a hacker to detect your network and nearly impossible for a neighbor to inadvertently connect to your network. Keep in mind that you will have to re-enable this setting when adding new components to the network.

4. **Change the default password on your router.** Routers have default user names and passwords. Hackers can use these to access your router and break into your network. Change the password on your router to something hard to guess. Use at least twelve characters that are a combination of letters, symbols, and numbers.

5. **Create a passphrase.** When you enable these protocols, you're forced to create a security encryption key (passphrase). When you attempt to connect a node to a security-enabled network for the first time, you're required to enter the security key. The security key or passphrase (see Figure 7.28) is the code that computers on your network need to decrypt (decode) data transmissions. Without this key, it's extremely difficult, if not impossible, to decrypt the data transmissions from your network. The Windows 10 Networks panel shows all wireless networks within range. Moving your cursor over the network name reveals details about the

Figure 7.28 By accessing your router, you can configure the security protocols available on your router and change the SSID. *(Windows 10, Microsoft Corporation)*

network, such as whether it's a secured network. Clicking on a network name allows you to connect to it or prompts you for more information, such as the SSID name and security key.

6. **Implement media access control.** Each network adapter on your network has a unique number (like a serial number) assigned to it by the manufacturer. This is called a media access control (MAC) address, and it's a number printed right on the network adapter. Many routers allow you to restrict access to the network to only certain MAC addresses. This helps ensure that only authorized devices can connect to your network.

7. **Limit your signal range.** Many routers allow you to adjust the transmitting power to low, medium, or high. Cutting down the power to low or medium could prevent your signal from reaching too far away from your home, making it tougher for interlopers to poach your signal.

8. **Apply firmware upgrades.** Your router has read-only memory that has software written to it. This software is known as **firmware**. As bugs are found in the firmware (which hackers might exploit), manufacturers issue patches, just as the makers of operating system software do. Periodically check the manufacturer's website and apply any necessary upgrades to your firmware.

9. **Disable remote access.** Some routers have a setting to allow remote access. This makes it easier for the manufacturer to offer technical support. However, hackers can use this to get into your home network. You can always turn on this feature when needed.

10. **Keep your router firmware up to date.** It's a good idea to check the manufacturer's website periodically for any updates to the router's software.

If you follow these steps, you'll greatly improve the security of your wireless network. In Chapter 9, we'll explore many other ways to keep your computer safe from malicious individuals on the Internet and ensure that your digital information is secure.

Before moving on to the Chapter Review:

1. Watch Chapter Overview Video 7.2.
2. Then take the Check Your Understanding quiz.

Check Your Understanding // Review & Practice

For a quick review to see what you've learned so far, answer the following questions.

multiple choice

1. What would you use to see what network adapters are installed in your Windows computer?

    a. Programs and Utilities manager

    b. Device Manager utility

    c. Ethernet Manager utility

    d. Home Network manager

2. How can you tell what wireless devices are connected to your router?

    a. Look at the device's wireless settings.

    b. Log in to the router's IP address and check the configuration page.

    c. Look at what's plugged into the router.

    d. all of the above

3. Which Windows feature facilitates sharing peripherals and info on a home network?

    a. HomeGroup

    b. GroupShare

    c. NetworkShare

    d. HomeShare

4. Which of the following would help improve a wireless signal throughout a network?

    a. Access point

    b. Network Internet card

    c. Network switch

    d. Wireless router

5. Why would you want to disable SSID broadcast?

    a. to make it more difficult for hackers to detect your network

    b. to make it difficult for a neighbor to connect to your network

    c. neither A nor B

    d. both A and B

MyLab IT   Go to **MyLab IT** to take an autograded version of the *Check Your Understanding* review and to find all media resources for the chapter.

TechBytes Weekly   Go to TechBytes Weekly for current technology news and discussion questions!

7 Chapter Review

Summary

Part 1
How Networks Function

Learning Outcome 7.1 You will be able to explain the basics of networking, including the components needed to create a network, and describe the different ways a network can connect to the Internet.

 ### Networking Fundamentals

Objective 7.1 *Describe computer networks and their pros and cons.*

- A computer network is simply two or more computers that are connected using software and hardware so they can communicate.
- Advantages of networks include allowing users to share an Internet connection, share printers and other peripheral devices, share files, and communicate with computers regardless of their operating system.
- Disadvantages for larger networks are that they require administration and that they may require costly equipment.

 ### Network Architectures

Objective 7.2 *Explain the different ways networks are defined.*

- Networks can be defined by the distance between nodes:
  - A personal area network (PAN) is used for communication among personal mobile devices using Bluetooth or Wi-Fi wireless technologies.
  - A local area network (LAN) connects nodes that are located in a small geographical area.
  - A home area network (HAN) is a specific type of LAN located in a home.
  - A metropolitan area network (MAN) is a large network in a specific geographical area.
  - A wide area network (WAN) spans a large physical distance.
- Networks can also be defined by the level of administration:
  - *Central:* A client/server network contains two types of computers: a client computer on which users

perform specific tasks and a server computer that provides resources to the clients and central control for the network. Most networks that have 10 or more nodes are client/server networks.
  - *Local:* Peer-to-peer (P2P) networks enable each node connected to the network to communicate directly with every other node. Most home networks are P2P networks.
- Ethernet networks are the most common networks used in home networking. Most Ethernet networks use a combination of wired and wireless connections, depending on the data throughput required. Wired connections usually achieve higher throughput than wireless connections. Wired Ethernet home networks use the gigabit Ethernet standard.
- Wireless Ethernet networks are identified by a protocol standard: 802.11a/b/g/n/ac. 802.11ac is the newest standard. WiGig (802.11ad) is a new wireless link between devices. WiGig is similar to but faster than Bluetooth.

 ### Network Components

Objective 7.3 *Describe the types of transmission media used in networks.*

- Wired networks use various types of cable to connect nodes, including unshielded twisted-pair cable, coaxial cable, and fiber-optic cable. The type of network and the distance between the nodes determine the type of cable used.
- Wireless networks use radio waves.

Objective 7.4 *Describe the basic hardware devices necessary for networks.*

- All devices must have a network adapter. All devices sold today contain an integrated network interface card.

- Network navigation devices, such as routers and switches, are necessary for computers to communicate in a network.

Objective 7.5 *Describe the type of software necessary for networks.*

- Home networks need operating system software that supports peer-to-peer networking. Windows, macOS, and Linux all support P2P networking.
- Servers on client/server networks use network operating systems (NOS).

 ## Connecting to the Internet

Objective 7.6 *Summarize the broadband options available to access the Internet.*

- Broadband connections include the following types:
  - Cable transmits data over coaxial cable, which is also used for cable television.
  - DSL uses twisted-pair wire, similar to that used for telephones.
  - Fiber-optic cable uses glass or plastic strands to transmit data via light signals.
  - Satellite is a connection option for those who do not have access to faster broadband technologies. Data is transmitted between a satellite dish and a satellite that is in a geosynchronous orbit.

Objective 7.7 *Summarize how to access the Internet wirelessly.*

- Wi-Fi allows users to connect to the Internet wirelessly but is not as fast as a wired connection.
- Mobile broadband is a 3G or 4G service delivered by cell-phone networks.

Part 2

Your Home Network

Learning Outcome 7.2   You will be able to describe what is necessary to install and configure a home network and how to manage and secure a wireless network.

 ## Installing and Configuring Home Networks

Objective 7.8 *Explain what should be considered before creating a home network.*

- Most home network routers should support both wireless and wired access to the Internet.
- For a home network to run efficiently, all nodes such as NICs and routers should use the same Ethernet standard.
- The Device Manager utility in Windows lists all adapters installed on your computer.

Objective 7.9 *Describe how to set up a home network.*

- All devices are connected to your router, either wirelessly or with a wired connection. Wired connections deliver better throughput than wireless.
- To add additional ports to your network, you can connect a switch to your router.
- Network-attached storage (NAS) devices let you store and share data files such as movies and music, as well as provide a central place for file backups.
- Home network servers can be used instead of an NAS device if your needs require more sophisticated functionality than NAS devices.
- Devices such as gaming consoles each have their own setup procedures for connecting to wireless networks but usually require the same information as that needed for connecting a computer to a secured wireless network.

Objective 7.10 *Summarize how to configure home network software.*

- The latest versions of Windows make it easy to set up wired and wireless networks.
- Create a Windows HomeGroup to share files and peripherals on a Windows network.
- Use SMB protocol to share files in networks with both Windows PCs and Macs.

 ## Managing and Securing Wireless Networks

Objective 7.11 *Describe the potential problems with wireless networks and means to avoid them.*

- You may not get the throughput you need through a wireless connection. Therefore, you may need to consider a wired connection for certain devices.
- Distance from the router, as well as walls, floors, and large metal objects between a device and the router, can interfere with wireless connectivity.
- To solve connectivity problems, access points or wireless range extenders can amplify signals to improve connectivity in areas of poor signal strength.

Objective 7.12 *Describe how to secure wireless home networks.*

- Wireless networks are even more susceptible to hacking than wired networks because the signals of most wireless networks extend beyond the walls of your home.
- Neighbors may unintentionally (or intentionally) connect to the Internet through your wireless connection, and hackers may try to access it.

- To prevent unwanted intrusions into your network, you should change the default password on your router to make it tougher for hackers to gain access, use a hard-to-guess SSID (network name), disable SSID broadcasting to make it harder for outsiders to detect your network, enable security protocols such as WPA or WEP, create a network passphrase, implement media access control, limit your signal range, and apply firmware upgrades.

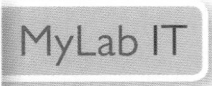 Be sure to check out **MyLab IT** for additional materials to help you review and learn. And don't forget to watch the Chapter Overview Videos. ▶

Key Terms

4G **262**

access point **276**

backward compatibility **255**

broadband **260**

cable Internet **261**

Cat 5e cable **257**

Cat 6 cable **257**

client/server network **253**

coaxial cable **256**

data plan **262**

data transfer rate (bandwidth) **251**

DSL (digital subscriber line) **261**

Ethernet network **254**

fiber-optic cable **256**

fiber-optic service **261**

firmware **278**

gigabit Ethernet (GbE) **254**

home area network (HAN) **253**

home network server **271**

Internet of Things (IoT) **258**

Internet service provider (ISP) **260**

local area network (LAN) **253**

metropolitan area network (MAN) **253**

mobile broadband **262**

mobile hotspot **262**

modem **258**

network **250**

network adapter **258**

network administration **251**

network architecture **252**

network-attached storage (NAS) device **271**

network interface card (NIC) **258**

network navigation device **258**

network operating system (NOS) **259**

network-ready device **272**

node **250**

peer-to-peer (P2P) network **254**

peer-to-peer (P2P) sharing **275**

personal area network (PAN) **252**

piggybacking **276**

router **258**

satellite Internet **261**

service set identifier (SSID) **277**

smart home **260**

switch **258**

throughput **251**

transmission media **255**

twisted-pair cable **255**

unshielded twisted-pair (UTP) cable **255**

wide area network (WAN) **253**

Wi-Fi **254**

wireless Internet service provider (wireless ISP) **262**

wireless range extender **276**

Chapter Quiz // Assessment

For a quick review to see what you've learned, answer the following questions. Submit the quiz as requested by your instructor. If you're using MyLab IT, the quiz is also available there.

multiple choice

1. Which of the following would NOT be a benefit of networking computers?
   a. sharing an Internet connection
   b. sharing software licenses
   c. sharing printers and other peripherals
   d. sharing files

2. Bethany is in her home, watching a video she took on vacation, while her brother is playing FIFA Soccer on his Xbox, and her dad is checking stock quotes on his iPad. What kind of network does this family have?
   a. Client/server network
   b. P2P network
   c. both a and b
   d. neither a and b

3. What two devices are often combined into one device in a small network to connect the network to the Internet and to share the connection between devices on the network?
   a. router hub and switch
   b. switch and hub
   c. modem and switch
   d. modem and router

4. Which of the following is a factor when determining the type of data plan you might need?
   a. the amount of time spent streaming music and videos
   b. how many web pages you view
   c. how many photos you upload to social media
   d. all the above

5. Which of the following should you NOT do to secure a wireless network?
   a. Implement media access control.
   b. Disable SSID broadcasting.
   c. Create a security encryption passphrase.
   d. Keep the default network name and router password.

6. What is the type of broadband Internet in which the connection is degraded by adding multiple users?
   a. cable
   b. satellite
   c. DSL
   d. fiber-optic

7. Which of the following might cause interference or poor connectivity between nodes on a wireless network?
   a. concrete walls
   b. nodes that are too far apart
   c. some appliances
   d. all of the above

8. Before creating a home network, you should do which of the following?
   a. List all the devices that will connect to the network.
   b. Gather together all the devices you need to connect to the network.
   c. Set up a HomeGroup sharing connection.
   d. all of the above

9. The type of network that would be necessary to connect the networks of two college campuses would be:
   a. LAN
   b. MAN
   c. WAN
   d. PAN

10. Which of the following does NOT accurately describe fiber-optic broadband?
   a. It uses strands of pure glass or plastic.
   b. It transmits data at the speed of light.
   c. Data is converted into electrical pulses.
   d. Speed drops as the distance from the main signal source increases.

true/false

_____ 1. You can attach more than four wired devices to a network by using a switch.

_____ 2. P2P networks require specialized network operating system software.

_____ 3. Actual data throughput is usually higher on wireless networks than on wired networks.

_____ 4. To facilitate sharing peripherals and files on a Windows network, you need to establish a HomeGroup.

_____ 5. Satellite Internet is the fastest broadband option.

critical thinking

1. **Using Online Storage**

   Sneakernet is jargon for physically transporting files from one location to another, as in using a flash drive. Think about the advantages and disadvantages of using flash drives versus online storage systems, such as Dropbox, Google Drive, and OneDrive. Defend your preferred method of storing and sharing files.

2. **Internet of Things**

   Think about the term "Internet of Things" in which things (objects, animals, and people) are connected to the Internet and can automatically transfer data over a network. Our society is already filled with many examples of "smart nodes"—such as cars, appliances, and entertainment devices—that are connected to the Internet. What are the advantages and disadvantages of developing a more robust Internet of Things and continuing to add more smart nodes?

Team Time

Providing Wireless Internet Access to the Needy

problem

Not everyone can afford wireless Internet access, and this can put families, especially ones with school-aged children, at a disadvantage.

task

You're volunteering for a charity that wants to install wireless networks in the homes of needy families. The project is funded by charitable grants, with the objective of providing basic broadband Internet access and networking capabilities at no cost to the recipients.

process

Break the class into three teams. Each team will be responsible for investigating one of the following issues:

1. **Internet service providers:** Research broadband Internet providers that serve the town where your school is located. Compare maximum upload and download speeds as well as costs. Be sure to consider the cost of the modems—whether they're purchased or rented. Select what your group considers the best deal.

2. **Networking equipment and network-ready peripherals:** Each home needs to be provided with an 802.11ac-capable wireless router (or modem/router) and a network-ready all-in-one printer. Research three options for these devices, considering price as well as functionality.

3. **Security:** Work in conjunction with the group researching routers to determine the best router to purchase, since it needs to support a security protocol such as WPA2. Consider other types of protection needed, such as antivirus software and firewalls.

Present your findings to your class and come to a consensus about the solution you would propose for the charity.

conclusion

Providing technology to underserved populations on a cost-effective basis will go a long way toward closing the digital divide.

Ethics Project

Firing Employees for Expressing Views on Social Media Sites

In this exercise, you'll research and then role-play a complicated ethical situation. The role you play may or may not match your own personal beliefs; regardless, your research and use of logic will enable you to represent the view assigned. An arbitrator will watch and comment on both sides of the arguments, and together the team will agree on an ethical solution.

problem

Employers often are intolerant of employees who express negative opinions or expose inside information about their employers on social media sites. Given that most jurisdictions in the United States use the doctrine of employment at will (employees can be fired at any time for any reason), many employers are quick to discipline or terminate employees who express opinions with which the company disagrees. When such cases come to court, the courts often find in favor of the employers.

research areas to consider

- Ellen Simonetti and Delta Airlines
- Fired for blogging about work
- Free speech
- Joyce Park or Michael Tunison

process

1. Divide the class into teams. Research the areas above and devise a scenario in which someone has complained about an employee blogging about a sensitive company issue, such as cleanliness at a food manufacturing facility.

2. Team members should assume the role of an employee or a human resources manager that represents each side of this scenario. Another team member can opt to be an arbitrator who would present an objective point of view for each character. To set the stage for the role-playing event, each team member should write a summary that provides background information for their role and that details their character's behaviors.

3. Team members should present their case to the class or submit a PowerPoint presentation for review, along with the summary and resolution they developed.

conclusion

As technology becomes ever more prevalent and integrated into our lives, more and more ethical dilemmas will present themselves. Being able to understand and evaluate both sides of the argument, while responding in a personally or socially ethical manner, will be an important skill.

Solve This MyLab IT®
grader

Home Networking Guide

You write a newsletter, *The Everyday Technologist*, which specializes in technology tips and tricks for the casual everyday technology user. Your current newsletter is a guide to home networks. The basic document has been created, and now, using Word 2016, you need to add formatting and images to make the guide more visually appealing.

You will use the following skills as you complete this activity:

- Apply Text Effects
- Insert WordArt
- Insert Columns
- Insert Section Breaks
- Insert Column Break
- Insert Images
- Apply Text Wrapping
- Use Custom Margins

Instructions

1. Open *TIA_Ch7_Start* and save as **TIA_Ch7_LastFirst**
2. Select the title **Home Networking Guide**, and convert the text to a WordArt Object using **Gradient Fill—Blue, Accent 5, Reflection**.
3. With the WordArt object still selected, click **Layout Options**, and select **Top and Bottom**. Then, click **See more...** at the bottom of the Layout Options window, and in the Layout dialog box, in the *Horizontal* section, select the **Alignment option**, and then choose **Centered** from the dropdown box.
4. Apply the **Fill—Orange, Accent 2, Outline—Accent 2 Text Effect** to the three headings: *Hardware*, *Wireless versus Wired*, and *Powerline Adapters*. Increase the font size of each heading to 18.
5. Create custom margins so all margins are 0.7".
6. Position the cursor before the heading *Hardware*. Insert a **Section Break (Continuous)**, and then apply **Two Column** formatting.
7. Place the cursor at the end of the second bullet point paragraph in the *Hardware* section. Insert the image TIA_Ch7_Modem Router. Change the Layout Option of the image to **Square**. Resize the image so the height is **0.9"** and the width is **1.2"**, and then move the image so that the two top lines of the Router paragraph display above the image, and the left side of the image is flush with the left margin.
8. Place the cursor at the beginning of the Powerline adapters paragraph. Insert the image TIA_Ch7_Powerline. Change the Layout Option to **Tight**. Change the height of the image to **1"**, and then move the image so the right side is flush with the right margin of the document and centered vertically in the Powerline adapters paragraph.
9. Place the cursor at the beginning of *Current Wireless (Wi-Fi) Standards*. Insert a column break. Format the text with bold and italics.
10. Save the document and submit based on your instructor's directions.

8 Managing a Digital Lifestyle: Media and Ethics

 For a chapter overview, watch the Chapter Overview Videos.

PART 1

The Impact of Digital Information

| Learning Outcome 8.1 | You will be able to describe the nature of digital signals and how digital technology is used to produce and distribute digital texts, music, and video. |

PART 2

Ethical Issues of Living in the Digital Age

| Learning Outcome 8.2 | You will be able to describe how to respect digital property and use it in ways that maintain your digital reputation. |

 Digital Basics 288

Objective 8.1 *Describe how digital convergence has evolved.*

Objective 8.2 *Explain the differences between digital and analog signals.*

 Digital Publishing 291

Objective 8.3 *Describe the different types of e-readers.*

Objective 8.4 *Explain how to purchase, borrow, and publish e-texts.*

Helpdesk: Managing Digital Media

 Digital Music 293

Objective 8.5 *Describe how digital music is created and stored.*

Objective 8.6 *Summarize how to listen to and publish digital music.*

 Digital Media 296

Objective 8.7 *Explain how best to create, print, and share digital photos.*

Objective 8.8 *Describe how to create, edit, and distribute digital video.*

Sound Byte: Enhancing Photos with Image-Editing Software

 Protection of Digital Property 306

Objective 8.9 *Describe the various types of intellectual property.*

Objective 8.10 *Explain how copyright is obtained and the rights granted to the owners.*

Objective 8.11 *Explain copyright infringement, summarize the potential consequences, and describe situations in which you can legally use copyrighted material.*

Helpdesk: Understanding Intellectual Property and Copyright

 Living Ethically in the Digital Era 315

Objective 8.12 *Explain plagiarism and strategies for avoiding it.*

Objective 8.13 *Describe hoaxes and digital manipulation.*

Objective 8.14 *Describe what comprises your online reputation and how to protect it.*

Sound Byte: Plagiarism and Intellectual Property

For the IT Simulation for this chapter, see MyLab IT.

MyLab IT — All media accompanying this chapter can be found here.

 Make This — Make: A Video-Playing App on **page 305**

(Kuroji/Fotolia, Tetra Images/Getty Images, Future Music Magazine/Getty Images, Olly/Fotolia, Jakub Jirsák/Fotolia, John Williams/Shutterstock)

How Cool Is This?

Ever heard of CLIP? If not, you soon will, as it's maturing into a technology that's set to launch a **hardware revolution**. First-generation 3D printing consisted of "extruded plastic printing"—melting plastic down and then layering it with a very fine nozzle. **CLIP** (continuous liquid interface production) 3D printers go beyond extruded plastic, using a **new, more accurate technique**. The printer's laser draws on the surface of a **pool of liquid plastic** resin. The small spots where the laser hits harden. Layer by layer, a specific shape can be formed. In its accuracy and resolution, this approach far exceeds that of earlier 3D printers, and **different colors, transparencies**, and **flexibility** can be incorporated to create much more sophisticated printable parts. Visit sites like **Thingiverse** (thingiverse.com) to see the growing collection of objects you can print out at home. *(Leonello Calvetti/Science Photo Library/Getty Images)*

The Impact of Digital Information

Learning Outcome 8.1 **You will be able to describe the nature of digital signals and how digital technology is used to produce and distribute digital texts, music, and video.**

Do you realize how many revolutionary changes are happening in all kinds of media as we continue to use digital formats? The entertainment industry has become an all-digital field. The publishing, music, photography, and film industries have all seen radical changes in how content is created and distributed to an audience. In this section, we will examine what digital really is and explore how digital technology has changed the production and distribution of media.

Digital Basics

How did we end up in a world in which we're all connected to our devices and able to communicate with each other whenever and almost wherever we want? Part of the story relates to the concept of *digital convergence*, as we'll explore in this section.

Digital Convergence

Objective 8.1 *Describe how digital convergence has evolved.*

What is digital convergence? **Digital convergence** refers to our ability to use a single device to meet all of our media, Internet, entertainment, and phone needs. For example, you see digital convergence in the evolution of smartphones, which now let you do just about anything a computer can do. You can also see the push to digital convergence in the migration of digital devices into environments like the cabin of cars (see Figure 8.1a).

Even some refrigerators, like the one shown in Figure 8.1b, include LCD touch-screen displays and network adapters so that they can display recipes from websites as well as place a call to the service center and schedule their own repair visit for you. These devices are all a part of the so-called *Internet of Things (IoT)*.

In fact, devices are beginning to converge so much that an organization—the Digital Living Network Alliance (**dlna.org**)—exists to standardize them. As our appliances, cars, and homes become designed to communicate over a common network, how we manage our media, control our living spaces, and communicate with others will continue to change. Let's start by looking at the foundation for all our computing devices: digital signals.

(a)

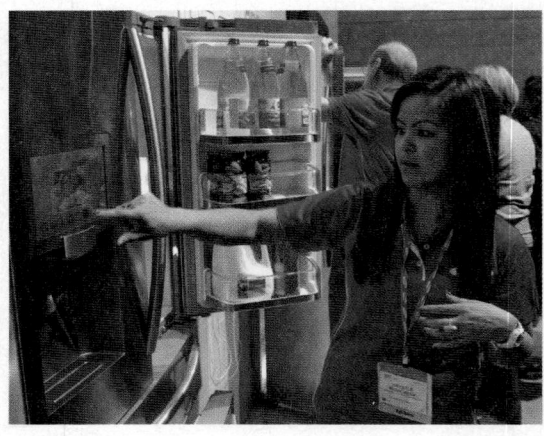

(b)

Figure 8.1 (a) Auto electronics have now converged with tablet technology. The Tesla S features a 17-inch touch-screen display that controls all of the car's electronics systems, providing Internet access, mobile communications, and navigation features, including sensors that detect vehicles in your blind spot. (b) Some refrigerators are now equipped with touch screens that connect to the Internet. *(David Paul Morris/Bloomberg/Getty Images, Steve Marcus/Reuters/Alamy Stock Photo)*

Digital vs. Analog

Objective 8.2 *Explain the differences between digital and analog signals.*

What does it mean to be "digital"? Any kind of information can be **digitized**—measured and converted to a stream of numerical values. Consider sound. It's carried to your ears by sound waves, which are actually patterns of pressure changes in the air. Images are our interpretation of the changing intensity of light waves around us. These sound and light waves are called **analog** waves or continuous waves. They illustrate the loudness of a sound or the brightness of the colors in an image at a given time. They're continuous signals because you would never have to lift your pencil off the page to draw them; they're just long, continuous lines.

First-generation recording devices such as vinyl records and analog television broadcasts were designed to reproduce these sound and light waves. A needle in the groove of a vinyl record vibrates in the same pattern as the original sound wave. Analog television signals are actually waves that tell an analog TV how to display the same color and brightness as is seen in the production studio.

However, it's difficult to describe a wave, even mathematically. The simplest sounds, such as that of middle C on a piano, have the simplest shapes, like the one shown in Figure 8.2a. However, something like the word *hello* generates a highly complex pattern, like the one shown in Figure 8.2b.

What advantages do digital formats have over analog ones? Digital formats describe signals as long strings of numbers. This digital representation gives us a simple way to describe sound and light waves exactly so that sounds and images can be reproduced perfectly any time they're wanted. In addition, we already have easy ways to distribute digital information, such as streaming movies or sending photos in a text message. Digital information can be reproduced exactly and distributed easily. These reasons give digital advantages over an analog format.

When the market for communication devices for entertainment media—like photos, music, and video—switched to a digital standard, we began to have products with new capabilities. Small devices can now hold huge collections of a variety of information. Users can create their own digital assets instead of just being consumers of digital media. We can interact with our information any time we like in ways that, prior to the conversion to digital media, had been too expensive or too difficult to learn. The implications of the shift to digital media are continually evolving.

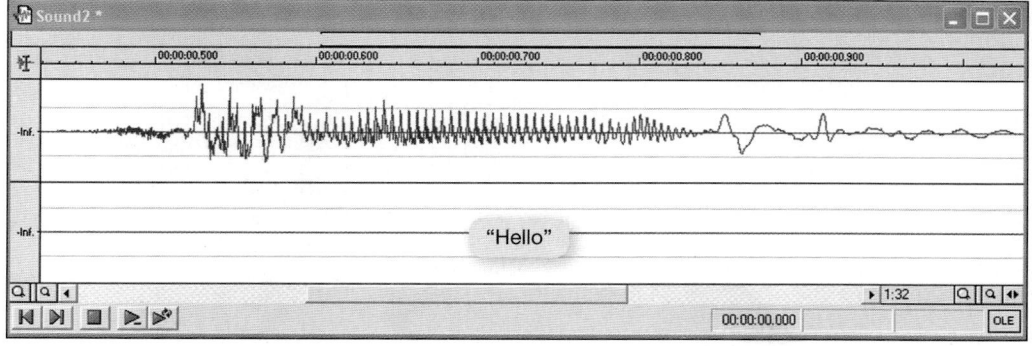

Figure 8.2 (a) This is an analog wave showing the simple, pure sound of a piano playing middle C. (b) This is the complex wave produced when a person says "Hello." *(Windows 10, Microsoft Corporation)*

Figure 8.3 Analog Versus Digital Entertainment

	Analog	Digital
Publishing	Magazines, books	E-books, e-zines
Music	Vinyl record albums and cassette tapes	CDs, MP3 files, and streaming music stations
Photography	35-mm single-lens reflex (SLR) cameras Photos stored on film	Digital cameras, including digital SLRs Photos stored as digital files
Video	8-mm, VHS, and Hi8 camcorders Film stored on tapes	HD digital video (DV) cameras Film stored as digital files; distributed on DVD and Blu-ray discs and streamed
Radio	AM/FM radio	HD Radio, SiriusXM satellite radio
Television	Analog TV broadcast	High-definition digital television (HDTV)

So how has digital impacted entertainment? Today, all forms of entertainment have migrated to the digital domain (see Figure 8.3).

Phone systems and TV signals are now digital streams of data. MP3 files encode digital forms of music, and cameras and video equipment are all digital. In Hollywood, feature films are shot with digital equipment. Movie theaters receive a hard drive storing a copy of a new release to show using digital projection equipment. Satellite radio systems such as SiriusXM and HD Radio are broadcast in digital formats.

How is analog converted to digital? The answer is provided by a process called *analog-to-digital conversion*. In analog-to-digital conversion, the incoming analog signal is measured many times each second. The strength of the signal at each measurement is recorded as a simple number. The series of numbers produced by the analog-to-digital conversion process gives us the digital form of the wave. Figure 8.4 shows analog and digital versions of the same wave. In Figure 8.4a, you see the original, continuous analog wave. You could draw that wave without lifting your pencil. In Figure 8.4b, the wave has been digitized and is no longer a single line; instead, it's represented as a series of points or numbers.

In the next sections, we'll discuss different types of digital media you interact with or create.

Figure 8.4 (a) A simple analog wave. (b) A digitized version of the same wave.

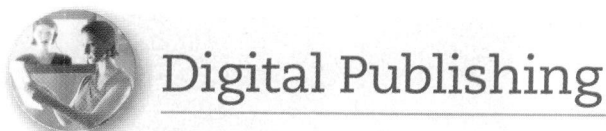

Digital Publishing

The publishing industry is migrating to digital materials. How does this impact books?

E-Readers

Objective 8.3 *Describe the different types of e-readers.*

Are printed books dead? **Electronic text (e-text)** is textual information captured digitally so that it can be stored, manipulated, and transmitted by electronic devices. With the increasing usage of e-text, the market for printed materials is changing. In fact, Amazon now sells more Kindle e-books than printed books each year. Mainstream authors who traditionally relied on print publishing, such as Stieg Larsson and James Patterson, have each sold over 1 million e-books. John Locke, a self-published author, has also sold over 1 million e-books, giving hope to fledging writers everywhere. But the conversion to digital books is not a 100 percent shift. In the U.S. book market, e-books seem to be settling in at between 20% and 30% of total book sales.

What electronic devices are trying to replace books? **E-readers** (see Figure 8.5) are devices that display e-text and have supporting tools, like note-taking, bookmarks, and integrated dictionaries. They're selling at a brisk pace with a range of offerings on the market, including versions of the Amazon Kindle and the Barnes and Noble NOOK.

Tablets, like the Amazon Fire, are also helping to popularize the e-book and electronic versions of magazines and newspapers. And while traditional print publisher's sales are falling (including their e-book sales), independently published e-book sales are rising at a fast pace.

Figure 8.5 E-readers are popularizing the digital e-book.
(Kristoffer Tripplaar/Alamy Stock Photo)

What features make digital text and e-readers popular? One big allure of digital publishing is distribution. Even a 1,000-page book can be delivered to your e-reader in under a minute. An array of titles is available—over 4.5 million books in the Amazon Kindle store alone. In addition, millions of texts without copyright are available for free.

The basic features of e-readers offer many advantages over paper books:

- Integrated dictionaries pull up a definition when you highlight a word. The Kindle, for example, comes with nine different foreign language dictionaries—a help in reading foreign works.
- Note-taking and highlighting are supported, and you can search the text for your own notes or for specific terms. You can also share the notes you make with others.
- URL links or links to a glossary are often live.
- Bookmarks are pushed through cloud technology so you can read on one device and pick up with your most current bookmark on another.
- E-books and audio books of the same title can be linked, so you can switch from reading a book to listening to the book without losing your place.
- For comics and graphic novels, you can magnify panels to read them fully.

Do I need a dedicated device just for reading e-texts? Free software download versions of the Kindle and the NOOK are available that run on either Windows or Apple computers. You can also download texts that have no copyrights and read them directly on a computer either as a PDF file or by using browser add-ons like MagicScroll Web Reader for Google Chrome. In fact, MagicScroll can display any web page in e-book format for easier reading.

How is digital text displayed? Two popular technologies are used for representing digital text:

- *Electronic ink*: **Electronic ink (E ink)** is a sharp grayscale representation of text. The "page" is composed of millions of microcapsules with white and black particles in a clear fluid. Electronic signals can make each spot appear either white or black. E ink devices reflect the light that shines on the page, like paper. E ink gives great contrast and is much easier to read in direct sunlight because there's no glare. High-end e-readers also offer a built-in front light so you can read in any light. Examples of devices using E ink include the Amazon Kindle Paperwhite (see Figure 8.6a).

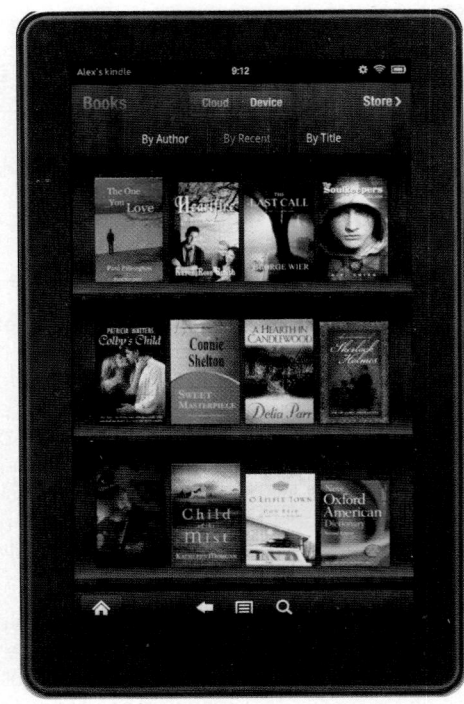

Figure 8.6 The two main technologies for e-text display are (a) E ink grayscale displays, like on the Amazon Kindle, and (b) high-resolution backlit color screens, like on the Amazon Fire.
(David McNew/Getty Images News/ Getty Images, Oleksiy Maksymenko Photography/Alamy Stock Photo)

(a)   (b)

- *Backlit monitors*: Another option is the high-resolution backlit monitors seen in tablets like the Amazon Fire (see Figure 8.6b). These screens illuminate themselves instead of depending on room lighting. They display color materials, like magazines, with clarity. The glass does reflect glare, though, which makes them hard to use in direct sunlight. Some people experience more fatigue when reading from a backlit device than when using E ink. Also note that E ink readers have a battery life of a month or two on a charge, whereas high-resolution color readers hold a charge for 8 to 10 hours.

What kinds of file formats are used in electronic publishing? Digital formats for publishing vary. Amazon uses a proprietary format (.azw extension), so books purchased for a Kindle aren't transportable to a device that isn't running Kindle software. An open format, ePub, is also supported by some e-readers, and ePub reader extensions (plug-ins) exist for all major browsers, as well as stand-alone ePub reader apps.

Using e-Texts

Objective 8.4 *Explain how to purchase, borrow, and publish e-texts.*

Where do I buy e-books? A number of vendors are associated with e-reader devices:

- Amazon Kindle devices connect directly to the Amazon Kindle store.
- Barnes and Noble NOOK devices work with the Barnes and Noble e-bookstore.
- Many publishers sell e-books online that can be read on any kind of device.
- Textbooks can be purchased in e-book format directly from the publisher. Another option is a company like VitalSource, which offers 180-day non-expiring subscriptions to digital texts. When the subscription ends, the book disappears from your device.

What if I just want to borrow a book from a library? Libraries now offer e-books and audio books (see Figure 8.7). There is never a late fee; the book just times out and disappears from your device when the borrowing period expires. Software like the Libby app (**libbyapp.com**) lets you search to find which area library has the book you want. Libraries have a specific number of copies of each e-book title available, so you may be added to a wait list if all the copies are checked out. However, friction exists between publishers and libraries on how to handle lending electronically. It's so convenient that some publishers are refusing to allow their e-books to be distributed through libraries.

▶ Helpdesk MyLab IT®

Managing Digital Media

In this Helpdesk, you'll play the role of a helpdesk staffer, fielding questions about e-readers and e-texts.

Can I borrow an e-book from a friend? Lending of e-books is becoming a popular feature of e-reader systems. Both Barnes and Noble and Amazon support lending books for up to two weeks.

Where can I find free e-books? A great source of free reading is Project Gutenberg (**gutenberg.org**), a collection of over 49,000 free books in ePub, Kindle, and PDF format. It contains books that are free in the United States because their copyrights have expired. The catalog includes many classic titles like *Moby Dick* by Herman Melville or science fiction novels by H. G. Wells.

How can I publish my own works? Self-publishing is much easier in the age of digital texts. Many options are available:

- Self-publish into the Amazon Kindle Store in a matter of minutes and earn up to 70% royalty on sales. The Kindle Direct Publishing site (**kdp.amazon.com**) has information on self-publishing using the Kindle format.
- Use a company like Smashwords (**smashwords.com**). It accepts a Microsoft Word document from you and then makes your book available through a number of vendors like the Apple iBooks store and the Barnes & Noble e-store. Your book can also be distributed as an app to mobile marketplaces like Google Play or the Apple App Store.
- Use a site like Lulu (**lulu.com**) to learn about social marketing and other techniques for promoting your book. In addition, it offers services from editors, designers, and marketers and can also allow you to offer your e-book for sale as a physical book.

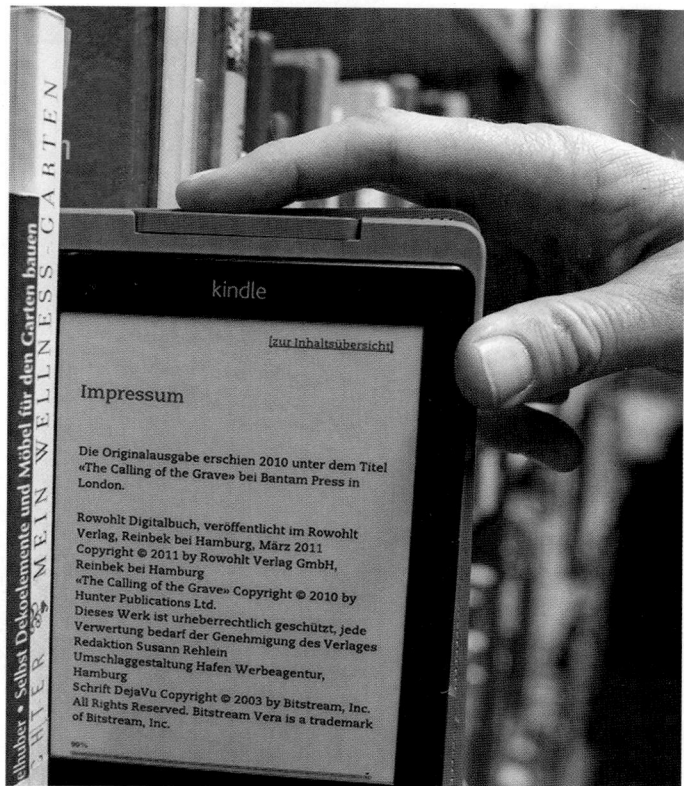

Figure 8.7 E-books and audio books can be borrowed for free at most public libraries. *(Alex Ehlers/DPA/Picture-alliance/Newscom)*

 # Digital Music

Digital music has upended the recording industry, with new models of distributing music, streaming services, and issues of copyright protection. In this section, we'll look at the mechanics of creating and distributing digital music.

Creating and Storing Digital Music

Objective 8.5   *Describe how digital music is created and stored.*

How is digital music created? To record digital music, the sound waves created by instruments need to be turned into a string of digital information. Figure 8.8 shows the process of digitally recording a song:

1. Playing music creates analog waves.
2. A microphone feeds the sound waves into a chip called an *analog-to-digital converter (ADC)* inside the recording device.
3. The ADC digitizes the waves into a series of numbers.
4. This series of numbers can be saved in a file and then recorded onto digital media or sent electronically.
5. On the receiving end, a playback device such as a mobile device or a DVD player is fed that same series of numbers. Inside the playback device is a *digital-to-analog converter (DAC)*, a chip that converts the digital numbers to a continuous analog wave.
6. That analog wave tells the receiver how to move the speaker cones to reproduce the original waves, resulting in the same sound as the original.

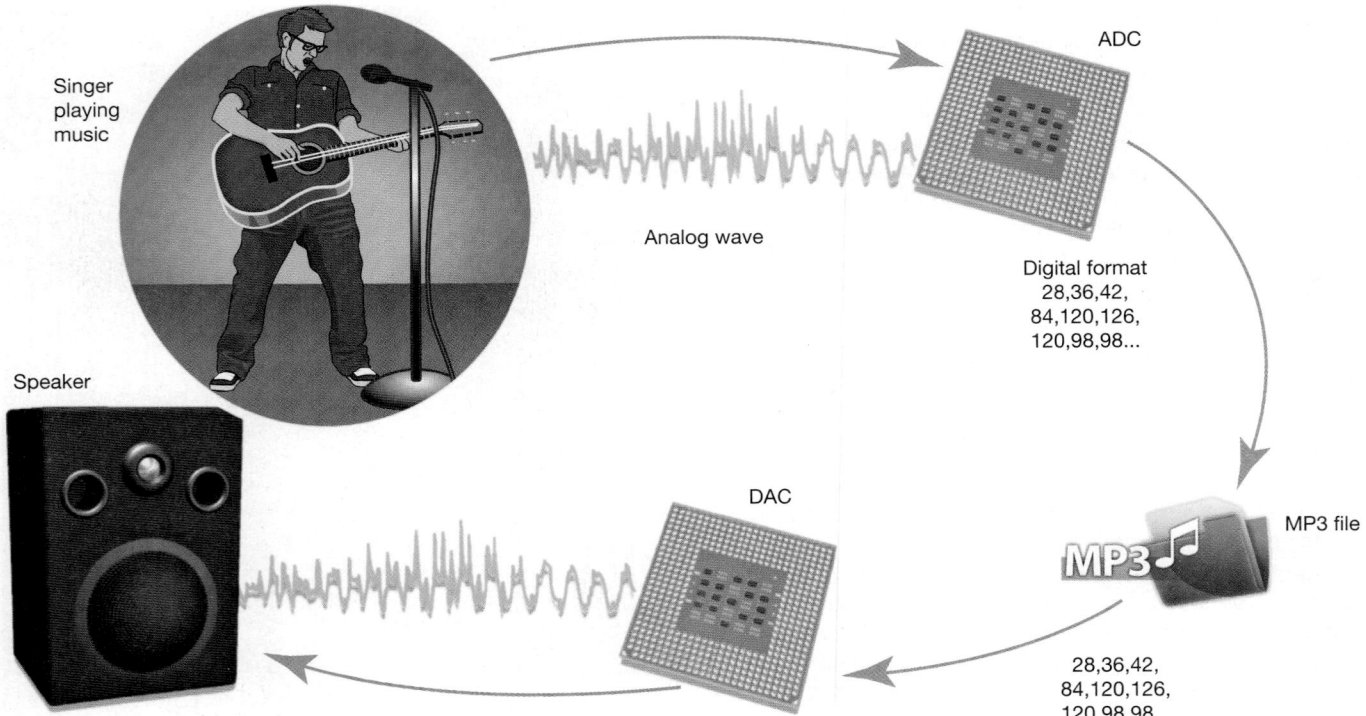

ADC

Singer
playing
music

Analog wave

Digital format
28,36,42,
84,120,126,
120,98,98...

Speaker

DAC

MP3 file

MP3♫

28,36,42,
84,120,126,
120,98,98...

Figure 8.8 During the complete recording process, information changes from analog form to digital data and then back again to analog sound waves.

More precisely, the digital wave will be *close* to exact. How accurate it is, or how close the digitized wave is in shape to the original analog wave, depends on the sampling rate of the ADC. The **sampling rate** specifies the number of times the analog wave is measured each second. The higher the sampling rate, the more accurately the original wave can be recreated. The improved sound quality higher sampling can afford also depends on the quality of the output device and speakers, of course. However, higher sampling rates also produce more data and therefore result in bigger files. For example, sound waves on CDs are sampled at a rate of approximately 44,000 times a second. This produces a huge list of numbers for even a single minute of a song.

What file types store digital music? You're no doubt familiar with the MP3 format used to store digital music, but many others exist, such as AAC and WMA. If you buy a song from the iTunes Store, for example, you receive an AAC-format file (although these files can be converted to other formats within iTunes). Many formats, such as DivX, MPEG-4 (which usually has an .mp4 extension), WMV, and Xvid, hold both video and audio information. All file formats compete on sound and video quality and *compression*, which relates to how small the file can be and still provide high-quality playback. Check what kind of files your audio device understands before you store music on it.

How do I know how much digital media my device can hold? The number of songs or hours of video your device can hold depends on how much storage space it has. Some mobile devices also use flash memory or SD cards storing from 2 to 64 GB.

Another factor that determines how much music a player can hold is the quality of the MP3 files. The size of an MP3 file depends on the digital sampling of the song. The same song could be sampled at a rate anywhere between 64 kbps and 320 kbps. The size of the song file will be five times larger if it's sampled at 320 kbps rather than 64 kbps. The higher the sampling rate, the better quality the sound—but the larger the file.

How do you control the size of an MP3 file? If you're *ripping*, or converting, a song from a CD to a digital MP3 file, you can select the sampling rate yourself. You decide by considering what quality sound you want as well as how many songs you want to fit onto your device. For example, 1 GB of storage could hold about 700 minutes of music if you've ripped songs at 192 kbps. The same 1 GB could store three times as much music if it were sampled at 64 kbps.

Ever heard of a digital audio workstation? If you're not in the music world, you may not have. *Digital audio workstations (DAWs)* are programs used to create songs. They use digitally sampled instruments to mimic drum sets, orchestral instruments, and piano—almost any real or imagined musical device. One popular DAW, Ableton Live, can be controlled by a piece of hardware called Push. Notes are played by tapping on the hardware's pressure-sensitive pads, generating new creative ideas in the music it produces.

(Neil Godwin/Future Music Magazine/Getty Images)

What if I want to access more music than my device has room for? Some devices allow you to add storage capacity by purchasing removable flash memory or SD cards. You could also choose to use a service that streams the music to you over Wi-Fi or 3G/4G networks. Spotify, Tidal, Google Play Music, and Apple Music are subscription services that let you listen to tracks in their catalogs. The music isn't yours to own, however—if you cancel your subscription, you no longer have access to the music. But because it's streamed to you, it doesn't take up space on your device. Some streaming services offer options that let you download music so that you can still play the songs on your playlist even if you don't have Internet access.

How do I transfer files to my music device? To move large volumes of data between your computer and music device, you can connect the devices using a USB port. Cloud services automatically push music to your mobile device. For example, when you purchase a song from iTunes, it's automatically pushed to all your registered iTunes devices—your Mac, your Windows computer (with iTunes installed), your iPad, and your iPhone.

Distributing Digital Music

Objective 8.6   *Summarize how to listen to and publish digital music.*

What's the best way to listen to digital music? You have a number of options for listening to music other than with headphones:

- Many audio receivers come with a port or dock so you can connect a mobile device to them as an audio input source.
- Networked audio/video receivers have the hardware and software required to connect to your home network and use streaming services like Pandora or Spotify to play music (see Figure 8.9).
- New cars are equipped with an auxiliary input to the speaker system to support connecting a mobile device; others have a fully integrated software system (like Apple CarPlay) that displays and runs your playlists, connecting wirelessly to your device over Bluetooth.
- Systems like Sonos (see Figure 8.10) can mate wirelessly with a mobile device and broadcast sound throughout the house.

Figure 8.9 Networked audio receivers can run Internet streaming services like Spotify and can connect to home servers. *(Anton Mishchenko/123RF)*

Figure 8.10 Sonos is a multiroom system that streams music wirelessly throughout your home. *(Robert Schlesinger/DPA/Picture-alliance/Newscom)*

If I don't pay for a music download, is it illegal? Although you're required to pay for most music you download, some artists post songs for free. Business models are evolving as artists and recording companies try to meet audience needs while also protecting their intellectual property rights. Several approaches exist. One is to deliver *tethered downloads*, in which you pay for the music and own it but are subject to restrictions on its use. Another approach is to offer *DRM-free* music, which is music without any **digital rights management (DRM)**. DRM is a system of access control that allows only limited use of material that's been legally purchased. It may be that the song can run only on certain devices or a movie can be viewed only a certain number of times. A DRM-free song can be placed on as many computers or players as you wish.

Will streaming music services eliminate radio stations? The Internet allows artists to release new songs to their fans (on sites such as SoundCloud) without relying on radio airtime. This opens up channels for artists to reach an audience and changes the amount of power radio stations have in the promotion of music. Many radio stations have increased listenership by making their stations available through Internet sites and by broadcasting in high-definition quality.

What if I want to publicize my band's music? Digital music has made the distribution of recordings simple using sites like SoundCloud (**soundcloud.com**), CD Baby (**cdbaby.com**), and ReverbNation (**reverbnation.com**). You can quickly create a web page for your band, post songs, and start building a fan base through social media. ReverbNation sends you reports detailing who's listening to your music and what they're saying about it. ReverbNation is also a way to connect with independent recording labels and to find places that want to book your band.

How can I get my band's music on streaming sites like Spotify? Streaming sites usually use artist aggregators like TuneCore and CD Baby rather than dealing with independent artists. Once your music is uploaded to the aggregator, it can be made available to fans on streaming media services at no cost to you.

Digital Media

Photography and video have also moved to digital formats, impacting the movie industry and creating new styles of visual performance.

Digital Photography

Objective 8.7   *Explain how best to create, print, and share digital photos.*

What is analog photography? Before digital cameras hit the market, most people used 35-mm single-lens reflex (SLR) cameras. When you take a picture using a traditional SLR camera, a shutter opens, creating an aperture (a small window) that allows light to hit the film inside. Chemicals coating the film react when exposed to light. Later, additional chemicals develop the image on the film, and it's printed on special light-sensitive paper. A variety of lenses and processing techniques, equipment, and filters are needed to create printed photos taken with traditional SLR cameras.

What's different about digital photography? Digital cameras don't use film. Instead, they capture images on electronic sensors called *charge-coupled device (CCD) arrays* and then convert those images to digital data, series of numbers that represent the color and brightness of millions of points in the image. Unlike traditional cameras, digital cameras allow you to see your images the instant you shoot them. Most camera models can now record digital video as well as digital photos. Images and video are usually stored on flash memory cards in the camera.

Don't most people use the camera on their smartphone to take photos? For casual photos, the answer is yes. The cameras on smartphones have improved significantly in resolution. But for taking high-quality photos, phone cameras fall short because they often employ smaller image sensors and inferior lenses compared to stand-alone cameras. In addition, many features that serious photographers rely on aren't available in smartphone cameras, such as different types of autofocus and image stabilization algorithms. So if you're a serious amateur photographer or want to sell your work, invest in a digital stand-alone camera.

Figure 8.11 Digital SLR cameras can accommodate a range of separate auto-focus lenses. *(B@rmaley/Fotolia)*

How do I select a digital camera? If you want a stand-alone digital camera, you have a number of camera models from which to choose. Some digital cameras are *fixed-lens cameras*, meaning they come with one lens that you can't change. However, digital SLRs let you switch among different lenses, as shown in Figure 8.11.

In addition to allowing you to switch lenses, the size of the image sensor that actually captures the light is critical. Larger sensors demand larger cameras and lenses. Professional digital SLR cameras use a full-frame sensor, whereas smartphones use a compact sensor and use a wider-angle lens to capture the full scene, making them less powerful.

Although having such flexibility in selection of lenses and a larger sensor are great advantages, most digital SLR cameras are larger, heavier, and use more battery power than fixed-lens models. Think about how you'll be using your camera and decide which model will serve you best. One resource is Digital Photography Review (**dpreview.com**), a site that compares cameras (including those in phones) and provides feedback from owners.

What determines the quality of a digital image? The overall image quality is determined by many factors:

- Lens quality
- Image sensor size
- File format and compression used
- Color management software included
- The camera's resolution

A digital camera's **resolution**, or the number of data points it records for each image captured, is measured in megapixels (MP). The word *pixel* is short for *picture element*, which is a single dot in a digital image. So-called point-and-shoot models typically offer resolutions from 12 to 20 MP. Professional digital SLR cameras, such as the Canon EOS 5DS, can take photos at resolutions as high as 50.6 MP.

If you're interested in making only 5″ × 7″ or 8″ × 10″ prints, a lower-resolution camera is fine. However, low-resolution images become grainy and pixelated when pushed to larger sizes. For example, if you tried to print an 11″ × 14″ enlargement from an 8 MP image taken using your smartphone camera, you'd see individual dots of color instead of a sharp image. The 16- to 24-MP cameras on the market have plenty of resolution to guarantee sharp images even with enlargements as big as 11″ × 14″.

What file formats are used for digital images? Digital cameras let you choose from several file types in order to compress the image data into less memory space. When you choose to compress your images, you'll lose some of the detail, but in return you'll be able to fit more images on your flash card. The most common file types supported by digital cameras are raw uncompressed data (RAW) and Joint Photographic Experts Group (JPEG):

- *RAW files* have different formats and extensions, depending on the camera manufacturer. The RAW file records all the original image information, so it's larger than a compressed JPEG file.
- *JPEG files* can be compressed just a bit, keeping most of the details, or compressed a great deal, losing some detail. Most cameras let you select from a few JPEG compression levels.

Sound Byte MyLab IT®

Enhancing Photos with Image-Editing Software

In this Sound Byte, you'll learn tips on how to best use image-editing software. You'll learn how to remove red eye from photos and how to incorporate borders, frames, and other enhancements.

Often, cameras also support a very low-resolution option that provides images that aren't useful for printing but are so small that they're easy to e-mail or download quickly. Even people with slow Internet connections are able to quickly download and view such images on screen. Low-resolution images are often used on mobile-friendly websites because the expectation is that the images will be viewed on smaller screens and need to download quickly to save on data.

What's the best way to transfer my photos from my stand-alone camera to my computer? Many cameras support wireless connections so you can transfer images without connecting cables. If that isn't available, you can connect the camera to your computer through a USB port or transfer the flash card from your camera directly to a built-in memory card reader on your computer.

How do I share my photos? You've probably shared photos on Facebook or Instagram. Both iOS and Android have photo-sharing features that provide access to photos or video you capture from your devices. iCloud Photo Sharing is an option within Apple's iCloud storage that allows you to organize photos and videos into albums and share them. Google Photos (**photos.google.com**) is an even better option. The Google Photos app (available for Android, iOS, Windows, and macOS) automatically uploads photos from your device to the Google Photos website and syncs them to all your other devices. From the website, you can easily share photos. This is especially handy when you upgrade to new devices because you can maintain access to all the images captured with your old devices.

You can also connect your device wirelessly to your TV and deliver slide shows of your photos, complete with musical soundtracks you've selected. If you've networked your home, a TV connected to your network can display all the photos and videos stored on any computer on your network.

Can I make my old photos digital? You can use an all-in-one printer, which contains a flatbed scanner, to turn your old photos into digital files. If lower resolution is acceptable, scanning apps are available that use your phone camera. Most scanner software lets you store the converted images as TIFF files or in compressed JPEG files. Some scanners include hardware that lets you scan film negatives or slides as well, or even insert a stack of photos to be scanned in sequence.

What are the best options for printing digital photos? If you want to print photos, you have two main options:

1. **Use a photo printer:** The most popular and inexpensive ones are inkjet printers. Some inkjet printers can print high-quality color photos, although they vary in speed, quality, and features. Dye-sublimation printers are another option for printing only photos. However, some models print only specific sizes, such as 4″ × 6″ prints, so be sure the printer you buy fits your needs.

2. **Use a photo-printing service:** Most photo-printing labs, including film-processing departments at stores such as Target, offer digital printing services. The paper and ink used at these labs are higher quality than what's available for home use and produce heavier, glossier prints that won't fade. You can send your photos directly to local merchants such as CVS and Target for printing using the merchant's websites that allow uploading from your device or Facebook. Online services, such as Flickr (**flickr.com**) and Shutterfly (**shutterfly.com**), store your images and allow you to create hard-copy prints, greeting cards, photo books, calendars, and gifts (like mugs and T-shirts).

Digital Video

Objective 8.8 *Describe how to create, edit, and distribute digital video.*

What devices, sites, and other sources provide digital video content? Digital video surrounds us:

- Television is broadcast in digitally formatted signals.
- The Internet delivers digital video through YouTube, communities like Vimeo (**vimeo.com**), and webcasting sites like Ustream (**ustream.tv**).
- Many pay services are available to deliver digital video. These include on-demand streaming from cable providers, iTunes, Netflix, Hulu, and Amazon.

How do I record my own digital video? Although you can buy dedicated digital camcorders to record digital video, most smartphones now record HD video. Webcams (integrated into laptops) also work as inexpensive devices for creating digital video. You can transfer video files to your computer and, using video-editing software, edit the video at home. You can write your final product to a disc or upload it to a web-based video channel.

What if I decide to add special effects and a sound track? Video-editing software such as Adobe Premiere presents a storyboard or timeline you can use to manipulate your video file, as shown in Figure 8.12. You can review your clips frame by frame or trim them at any point. You can add titles, audio tracks, and animations; order each segment on the timeline; and correct segments for color balance, brightness, or contrast. Examine online tutorial resources such as Izzy Video podcasts (**izzyvideo.com**) and No Film School (**nofilmschool.com**) to learn how to make the most impact with the editing and effects you apply to your video footage.

Figure 8.12 Adobe Premiere allows you to build a movie from video clips (and still photos) and add soundtracks and special effects.
(© 2017 Adobe Systems Incorporated. All rights reserved. Adobe, Adobe Premiere, Dreamweaver and Photoshop is/are either [a] registered trademark[s] or a trademark[s] of Adobe Systems Incorporated in the United States and/or other countries.)

	File Extension	Notes
...le	.qt .mov	You can download the QuickTime player without charge from **apple.com/quicktime**. The Pro version allows you to build your own QuickTime files.
...oving Picture Experts Group (MPEG)	.mpg .mpeg .mp4	The MPEG-4 video standard was adopted internationally in 2000; it's recognized by most video player software.
Windows Media Video	.wmv	This is a Microsoft file format recognized by Windows Media Player (included with the Windows OS).
Microsoft Video for Windows	.avi	This is a Microsoft file format recognized by Windows Media Player (included with the Windows OS).

What kinds of files will I end up with? Once you're done editing your video, you can save or export it in a variety of formats. Figure 8.13 shows some of the popular video file formats in use, along with their file extensions.

(Cyrus McCrimmon/The Denver Post/Getty Images)

Figure 8.14 Compact cameras like the GoPro are small enough to make them part of any activity.

Your choice of file format for your video will depend on what you want to do with it. For example, the QuickTime streaming file format is a great choice if your file is large and you plan to post it on the web. The Microsoft AVI format is a good choice if you're sending your file to a wide range of users because it's the standard video format for Windows Media Player and is recognized by most popular free media players used in Windows 10 like 5KPlayer and GOM Player.

Different compression algorithms will have different results on your particular video. Try several to see which one does a better job of compressing your file. A **codec** (compression/*dec*ompression) is a rule, implemented in either software or hardware, that squeezes the same audio and video information into less space. Some information will be lost using compression, and there are several different codecs to choose from, each claiming better performance than its competitors. Commonly used codecs include MPEG-4, H.264, and DivX. There's no one codec that's always superior—a codec that works well for a simple interview may not do a good job compressing a live-action scene.

What's the quickest way to get my video out to viewers? Webcasting, or broadcasting your video live to an audience, is a simple option. Use either your phone or a compact camera like a GoPro (see Figure 8.14) and apps like Meerkat and Periscope to stream live video. Snapchat Stories is also a popular option for distributing casual videos. These apps have features like interactive chat next to the video feed so viewers can interact with you while you're live. On many apps, both the chat and video can be captured and archived for viewers who missed the live broadcast.

Bits&Bytes   Fly-By Drone Video

Thanks to recent technological advancements, aerial video is easier than ever to capture. Quadcopters, flying remote-controlled devices with four propellers and equipped with digital video cameras, are popular. They transmit video to a phone or tablet so the pilot sees exactly what the flying device is seeing. A huge do-it-yourself community is dedicated to making the hardware and software needed by quadcopters. Visit **dronecode.org** and **ardupilot.com** for inspiration—and lots of free code!

(Maria Dryfhout/123RF)

You may want to produce a more polished video. You can then upload it to video-sharing sites like YouTube or Vimeo. Of course, it's illegal for you to upload videos you don't own. You also can't take a piece of a copyrighted video and post it publicly. The second part of this chapter presents legal and ethical situations that are important for you to be aware of as a content creator in the digital age.

How is HD different from "plain" digital? HD stands for **high definition**. It's a standard of digital television signal that guarantees a specific level of resolution and a specific *aspect ratio*, the ratio of the width of an image to its height. For example, an aspect ratio of 16:9 might mean an image is 16″ wide and 9″ high. A 1080p HDTV displays 1,920 vertical lines and 1,080 horizontal lines of video on the screen, which is over six times as many pixels as a standard-definition TV. The newest standard, UHDTV (ultra-high-definition television), is also known as 4K or 2160p. A 2160p UHDTV has a resolution of 3840 × 2160 pixels. The aspect ratio used is 16:9 in both formats, which makes the screen wider than it is tall, giving it the same proportions as the rectangular shape of a movie screen (see Figure 8.15). This allows televisions to play movies in widescreen format instead of "letterboxing" the film with black bars on the top and bottom.

What types of connectivity are provided on modern TV sets? A typical HDTV or UHDTV set has multiple HDMI connectors, allowing game consoles, Blu-ray players, computing devices, and cable boxes to be connected and to produce the highest-quality output. HDMI is a single cable that carries all the video and audio information.

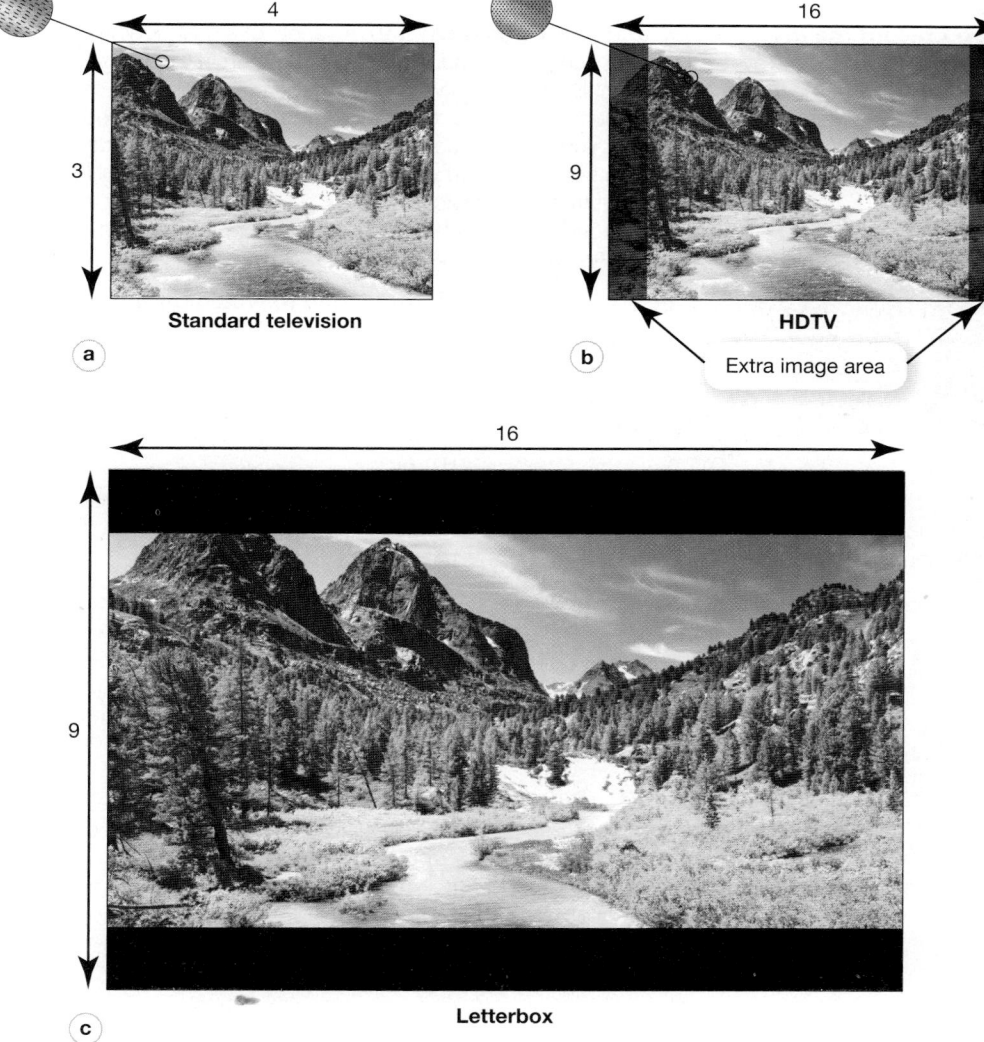

Figure 8.15 (a) Standard-definition TV has a more "square" aspect ratio, whereas (b) HDTV and UHDTV matches the 16:9 ratio used in the motion picture industry without the need for (c) letterboxing.
(Pichugin Dmitry/Shutterstock)

Some companies routinely generate valuable digital assets. Managing these assets to ensure they're being properly monetized is now a full-time job. *Digital asset management (DAM)* is an up-and-coming field for media-savvy graduates.

The creative industries were the first to realize they needed DAM. Photographers and graphic designers generate a tremendous amount of content in various formats. Images may need to be saved in different file formats and at different resolutions. The rights granted to third parties for the use of images needs to be tracked. Creation of new digital assets needs to be managed.

However, many other businesses realize the need for DAM as they roll out cohesive brand strategies that need consistency in imagery both on the web and in printed media. Organizing,

cataloging, tracking, and sharing image and video files are often done with DAM software, such as WebDAM and Libris.

So what skills does it take to become a digital asset manager? Obviously, an understanding of the creation process of digital assets is the first step. Experience managing projects and workflows is also important. The ability to work well with different types of people in the creative, IT, and marketing departments is also a plus. And because many assets are created with Adobe Creative Cloud products, experience with these software packages would make your transition into the job much easier.

So if you enjoy working with digital content creators and have the ability to organize complex workflows, your next job might just be a lot of DAM fun.

You can also connect your devices to your TV wirelessly. Roku, Apple TV, Amazon Fire TV, and Google's Chromecast let you view content from your device or stream content from the Internet on the big screen without connecting cables.

Can I record the digital video that comes over my TV? A variety of digital video recorders (DVRs) are available, provided by cable companies and independent vendors. Models like TiVo even recommend new shows you might like based on what you've been watching. You can also install personal video recording (PVR) software on your computer. Programs like Kodi (**kodi.tv**), an open source software media center, let you use your computer to view the program guide, select shows to record, and then watch them from anywhere you have Internet access. Unlike Netflix or other streaming services, Kodi doesn't include content; rather it depends on sources of free content or content from services you may already have.

Can I get digital video to watch on my portable device? Most cable providers have apps, like Fios TV to Go from Verizon, that facilitate watching TV shows on your mobile devices. Most DVR units let you transfer recorded shows to files on your PC and format them for viewing on a mobile device. Devices like Slingbox take the video from your TV and broadcast it to you over the Internet. With Slingbox, you can be in another room, or another country, and control and watch your home TV on your laptop or smartphone (see Figure 8.16).

Figure 8.16 Slingbox can send your digital television content to your tablet, notebook, or phone, wherever you may be. *(Handout/MCT/Newscom)*

Before moving on to Part 2:

1. ▶ Watch Chapter Overview Video 8.1.
2. Then take the Check Your Understanding quiz.

Check Your Understanding // Review & Practice

For a quick review to see what you've learned so far, answer the following questions.

multiple choice

1. An analog signal is different from a digital signal because it
   a. is easier to transmit.
   b. has only specific discrete values.
   c. is easier to duplicate.
   d. is continuous.

2. The open format for publishing e-books that is optimized for mobile devices is
   a. raw.
   b. ePub.
   c. azw.
   d. pdf.

3. The number of times the analog wave is measured each second when digitizing music is the
   a. MP3 rate.
   b. bit rate.
   c. sampling rate.
   d. DRM rate.

4. Which of the following is NOT a factor that determines the quality of a digital image?
   a. lens quality
   b. file format used
   c. image sensor size
   d. pixel coverage

5. Adobe Premiere
   a. is a website where you can store digital photos.
   b. is a type of video-editing software.
   c. is included as part of Windows 10.
   d. is used for editing still photographs.

 Go to **MyLab IT** to take an autograded version of the *Check Your Understanding* review and to find all media resources for the chapter.

TechBytes Weekly Go to TechBytes Weekly for current technology news and discussion questions!

Try This

Creating and Publishing a Movie

You've just taken some video and photos at the zoo, and you'd like to organize the media and put it on your YouTube channel. What should you do? In this Try This, we'll explore Ezvid. For more step-by-step instructions, watch the Chapter 8 Try This video in MyLab IT. Before starting, do the following:

a. Make sure you have video clips and photos available. If you don't have any, you can find free images and video clips at sites like **videezy.com**.

b. Download Ezvid, a free video editor, from **ezvid.com**. Click on the **Free Screen Recorder** link to download the installation file. Once installed, type **Ezvid** in the search box to launch.

Step 1 Click the **add pictures or video** button. In the dialog box that displays, browse to where your media files are saved, select the files you wish to import, and then click the **Open** button. The files you've selected will appear on the Media timeline.

Step 2 Click and drag your media to the spot in the timeline where you want it to appear.

Step 3 To create a text slide, click the **add text** button. In the dialog box that displays, type the text you want to appear; change the text color, background color, and font; and then click the **finish** button to add the text slide to your timeline. Click and drag the text slide where you want it to appear.

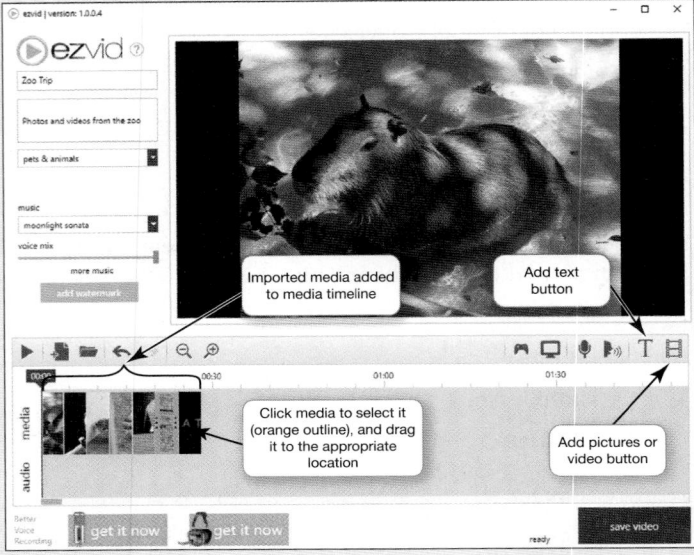

(From Ezvid Inc. Copyright © by Ezvid Inc. Used by permission of Ezvid Inc.)

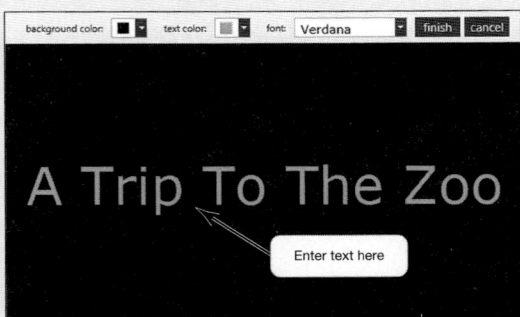

(From Ezvid Inc. Copyright © by Ezvid Inc. Used by permission of Ezvid Inc.)

Step 4 To adjust the length of time a piece of media displays, click the media and then adjust the width of the clip. Add a video title, description, and category in the appropriate boxes. Select a music track from the ones provided or use your own.

Step 5 To preview your movie, click **Play**. When you're satisfied, click the **save video** button. If you start a new project or close Ezvid, your project will automatically be saved.

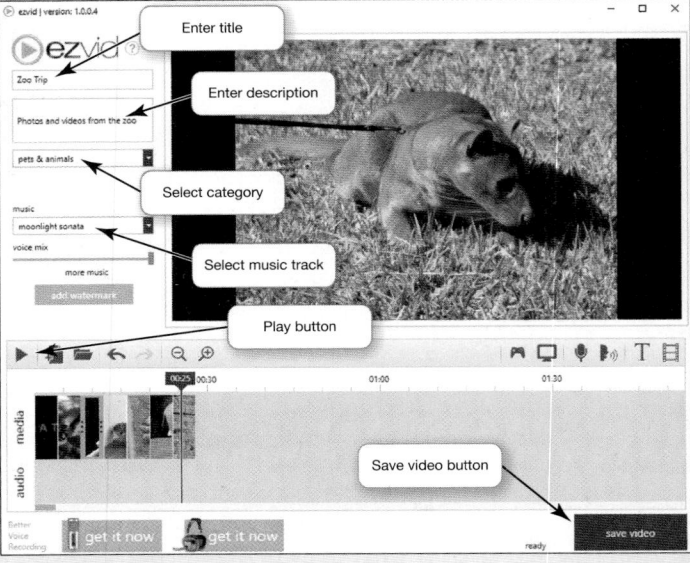

(From Ezvid Inc. Copyright © by Ezvid Inc. Used by permission of Ezvid Inc.)

Make: A Video-Playing App

Do you want to run video clips inside your app?

In this exercise, you'll continue your mobile app development by using the Video Player component in **App Inventor** to run video clips inside your app. Using the component, you can play clips stored on your device, clips that you've recorded with the built-in camera, or clips on the Internet.

The Video Player has controls to pause, play, and fast forward or rewind and lets you manipulate the size of the video screen as well as the volume. So decide how you will make your applications more media-intensive using the Video Player component in App Inventor!

The Video Player component allows you to display video inside your app.

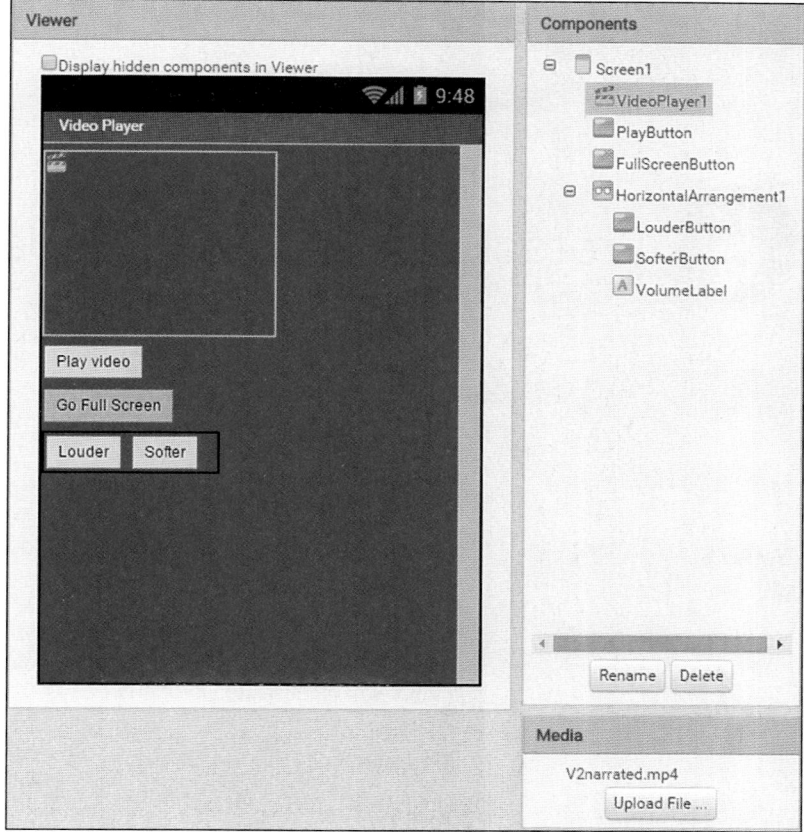

(Copyright MIT, used with permission.)

(Copyright MIT, used with permission)

For the instructions for this exercise, go to MyLab IT.

Ethical Issues of Living in the Digital Age

In Part 1 of this chapter, you learned about ways to create digital assets. Unfortunately, the proliferation of the digital lifestyle has made it easier to misuse or misappropriate another's digital property. In the following sections, you'll learn how to protect your digital rights and how to avoid infringing on the rights of others.

Protection of Digital Property

You can easily locate a picture of almost anything by searching Google Images. If you have to prepare a research paper on global warming, you can find millions of sources on the subject, including professionally written articles. Does that mean you can freely use all these resources you locate? No, you can't, because they're most likely someone else's property. Just as you wouldn't take someone's bike parked outside your dorm, you can't just take property you find on the Internet.

Property comes in two general types: real and personal. **Real property** is considered immoveable, such as land or a home, and it's often called *real estate*. **Personal property**, which is stuff you own, comes in two types: tangible and intangible. We're all familiar with **tangible personal property**, which is something that has substance like your smartphone or car. **Intangible personal property** can't be touched—or potentially even seen—yet it still has value. If someone steals your iPad, the action is easily recognizable as theft. However, what if someone tries to steal your ideas? This action moves into the realm of one of the biggest problems in cyberspace: the theft of intangible personal property or intellectual property.

Intellectual Property

Objective 8.9 *Describe the various types of intellectual property.*

What is intellectual property? **Intellectual property (IP)** is a product of a person's mind and is usually considered an expression of human creativity. Examples of IP are books (or any type of writing), art, music, songs, movies (or any type of video), patents for inventions, formulas (or methods of production), and computer software. IP is considered intangible personal property.

It's important to distinguish intellectual property from the physical medium that carries it. A music CD is not IP. The music that is contained on a CD is the IP, whereas the CD itself is merely a delivery device. Likewise, a poem is IP, but the piece of paper on which it's written is not.

Types of Intellectual Property

How is intellectual property categorized? IP is divided into five broad categories: *copyright, patents, trademarks, service marks,* and *trade dress.* Each category has its own laws of protection.

Copyright protection can be granted to creators of "original works of authorship." In the United States, copyrightable works include:

- Literary works, including computer software
- Musical works, including any accompanying words
- Dramatic works, including any accompanying music
- Pantomimes and choreographic works
- Pictorial, graphic, and sculptural works
- Motion pictures and other audiovisual works
- Sound recordings
- Architectural works

Patents grant inventors the right to stop others from manufacturing, using, or selling (including importing) their inventions for a period of 20 years from the date the patent is filed. Generally, patents aren't renewable but may be extended under certain circumstances.

A **trademark** is a word, phrase, symbol, or design—or a combination of these—that uniquely identifies and differentiates the goods of one party from those of another. A **service mark** is essentially the same as a trademark, but it applies to a service as opposed to a product. The Nike swoosh and McDonald's Golden Arches are trademarks, whereas the FedEx logo is a service mark.

Similar to a trademark, a *trade dress* applies to the visual appearance of a product or its packaging. The unique shape of the iconic Coca Cola bottle is an example of trade dress.

Most digital assets you create will be protected by copyright. In this section, we'll discuss the basic tenets of copyright and how it protects you.

Copyright Basics

Objective 8.10 *Explain how copyright is obtained and the rights granted to the owners.*

When does copyright protection begin? Copyright begins when a work is created and fixed into a digital or physical form. For example, if you record a video of your cat, as soon as you save the video to your phone, the video is subject to copyright protection. There is no need for the video to be registered or even published for it to be protected by copyright.

If I own copyright to a work I created, what exactly do I own? Copyright holders own rights that grant them the ability to exclusively do things with the copyrighted work. U.S. law grants these rights to a copyright holder:

- **Reproducing the work**: Applies to copying the entire work or just part of the work. For instance, you might sell prints of one of your paintings on Etsy.
- **Preparing derivative works based on the original work**: This means developing any media based on the original work regardless of what form the original is in. *Iron Man* was originally a character in a Marvel comic book, but he now appears in movies and video games.
- **Distributing the work to the public**: This usually involves selling the work. However, the copyright holder could also loan, rent, or give away the work.
- **Public performance of the work**: This applies to any audiovisual work such as plays, movies, and songs. In the case of audio recordings, this also means digital audio transmission.
- **Public display of the work**: This right usually applies to works of art such as paintings, photographs, and sculptures, but this also includes posting images on the Internet.

Figure 8.17 shows ways you could capitalize on a video of your band that you created by exercising your rights granted by copyright.

Can I copyright anything I create? U.S. copyright law does not protect all ideas, but rather the *unique expression* of an idea. You can't copyright common phrases, such as "bad boy" or "good girl"; discoverable facts, such as water boils at 212 degrees Fahrenheit; or old proverbs, such as "To err is human, to forgive divine." However, you can copyright a creative twist on an old phrase, such as the one in Figure 8.18.

Generic settings and themes of a story also can't be copyrighted. J. R. R. Tolkien wrote *The Lord of the Rings* trilogy, which is about a boy who overcomes hardships to save the world from an evil being. In an e-book or video game you create, you're not allowed to use the same characters and plot lines Tolkien used, but you could write about the basic idea of a lone person overcoming the forces of evil.

How long does copyright last? Current U.S. law grants copyright for the life of the author (creator) plus 70 years for original works. After you die, any copyrights you own are transferred to your heirs. Therefore, if you write a best-selling e-book in 2020 and die in 2092, your heirs can continue to earn money from the book until the year 2162.

Figure 8.17 Exercising Your Rights with a Video of Your Band

Public Performance
- Post the video on YouTube

Reproduction
- Burn DVDs

Distribution to the Public
- Sell DVDs at your concerts

Derivative Work
- Capture audio tracks from the video soundtrack

Public Display
- Place a still image from the video on a poster

(lpopba/Fotolia, Denis Dryashkin/Fotolia, Pixelrobot/Fotolia, Djvstock/Fotolia, Log88off/Fotolia)

Figure 8.18 You can copyright this clever twist on an old proverb.

Can rights to a copyrighted work be sold? Rights can be sold or granted for free to various individuals or entities in perpetuity or for a limited time. For instance, if your band is going to appear at a bar, you might grant the bar owner the right to play your band video in his bar for a specific period of time leading up to your performance. Or, you might grant the right to produce and sell DVDs of your performance to a distributor such as CD Baby (**cdbaby.com**).

If I work for a company and develop intellectual property, do I own it? The answer to this question depends on the terms of your employment contract. *Works made for hire* or *works of corporate authorship* occur when a company or person pays you to create a work and the company or person owns the copyright when it's completed. Most companies in which IP is developed require employees to sign agreements that any IP developed while working for the company becomes the company's property.

Is buying a copyrighted work the same as buying the copyright? Usually you only buy a physical or digital copy, not the actual copyright. When you buy software, usually what you've purchased is a license to install the software and use it on a specific number of devices. When you purchase music, you've bought the right to listen to the music in a private setting, such as on your phone. When you download a movie or subscribe to Netflix, again you've purchased the right to view the content privately.

However, buying copyrighted works is covered by a rule of law known as the *first sale doctrine*. You have the right to sell, lend, give away, or otherwise dispose of the item you purchase. This principle gives you the right to sell your book to another student at the end of the semester.

Are all works protected by copyright? Works without copyright protection are considered to be in the **public domain**. Works in the public domain are considered public property and therefore, anyone can modify, distribute, copy, or sell them for profit. Some works that were created never had a copyright holder. Examples are traditional folk songs or stories, the origins of which are unknown and can't be attributed to a specific individual. Copyrighted works can lose their copyright protection after their term of protection expires.

It can be difficult to determine when works enter the public domain. Therefore, you should probably consider a work to be in the public domain only if there is provable, objective evidence that it's in the public domain or it's clearly identified as being in the public domain. The safest assumption is that all intellectual property you find on the Internet is protected by copyright, *unless otherwise stated*.

Protecting Your Work with Copyrights

As we discussed in Part 1 of this chapter, you're potentially creating intellectual property on a regular basis. If your work is valuable and you're using it to earn a living, you definitely want to take appropriate steps to protect your copyright.

Isn't copyright protection automatic? Copyright does accrue as soon as you create the intellectual property and set it down in digital or physical form. However, registering copyright provides certain advantages, including the ability to sue someone for violating your copyright.

How do I register works for copyright protection? Instructions and forms for registering work for copyright protection can be found on the U.S. Copyright Office website (**copyright.gov**). Registration can be done online and requires payment of a small fee. Although you can file online, the Library of Congress might still require you to submit a hard copy of your work. It can take up to eight months to receive your notice of registration, but your registration is effective when the Copyright Office receives your registration form.

Posting a copyright notice with your work is also a deterrent to copyright infringement, as it establishes the work is copyrighted. A simple format is to use the word copyright (or the copyright symbol—©), the year the work was first published, the copyright holder's name, and optionally, the location of the copyright holder.

Do I have to pay to register each photo in my portfolio? A copyright registration form can be filed for a collection of works. The stipulation is that the works must be published as a collection. A group of related images, songs, videos, poems, or short stories, or a collection of blog postings prior to registration meets this criterion.

What if I don't mind people using my work, but I don't want to constantly answer permission requests? **Copyleft**—a play on the word copyright—is a term for various licensing plans that enable copyright holders to grant certain rights to the work while retaining other rights.

License Conditions

Creators choose a set of conditions they wish to apply to their work.

(i) Attribution (by)

All CC licenses require that others who use your work in any way must give you credit the way you request, but not in a way that suggests you endorse them or their use. If they want to use your work without giving you credit or for endorsement purposes, they must get your permission first.

(ↄ) ShareAlike (sa)

You let others copy, distribute, display, perform, and modify your work, as long as they distribute any modified work on the same terms. If they want to distribute modified works under other terms, they must get your permission first.

($) NonCommercial (nc)

You let others copy, distribute, display, perform, and (unless you have chosen NoDerivatives) modify and use your work for any purpose other than commercially unless they get your permission first.

(=) NoDerivatives (nd)

You let others copy, distribute, display and perform only original copies of your work. If they want to modify your work, they must get your permission first.

Figure 8.19 The Creative Commons has a variety of licenses, one of which should be right for you. *(Creative Commons attribution 4.0 International license)*

Usually, the rights (such as modifying or copying a work) are granted with the stipulation that when users redistribute their work (based on the original work), they agree to be bound by the same terms of the copyleft plan used by the original copyright holder. The General Public License (GNU) is a popular copyleft license used for software. For other works, the Creative Commons, a non-profit organization, has developed a range of licenses that can be used to control rights to works (see Figure 8.19). It provides a simple algorithm to assist you with selecting the proper license for your work (**creativecommons.org/share-your-work**).

What are the advantages and drawbacks of licenses designed by Creative Commons? The advantage to using Creative Commons licenses is that people won't constantly send you permission requests to use your work. The licenses explain how your work can be used. Also, many advocates of copyleft policies feel that creativity is encouraged when people are free to modify other people's work instead of worrying about infringing on copyright.

Opponents of Creative Commons licenses complain that the licenses have affected their livelihoods. If millions of images are on Google Photos with Creative Commons licenses that permit free commercial use, professional photographers might have a tougher time selling their work. Furthermore, Creative Commons licenses are irrevocable. If you make a mistake and select the wrong license for your work, or you later find out a work is valuable and you've already selected a license that allows commercial use, you're out of luck.

Understanding the meaning of copyright, and copyleft, is important so that you respect the rights of others and so that you can simplify your life in granting permission rights to the works you create.

Helpdesk   MyLab IT®

Understanding Intellectual Property and Copyright

In this Helpdesk, you'll play the role of a helpdesk staffer, fielding questions about the basics of intellectual property and how individuals can protect their digital assets with copyright.

Copyright Infringement

Objective 8.11 *Explain copyright infringement, summarize the potential consequences, and describe situations in which you can legally use copyrighted material.*

What happens if you use copyrighted material without permission of the copyright holder? A violation of the holder's rights is known as **copyright infringement**. Illegally copying or using software, music, video, and photos tops the list of digital rights violations on the Internet. Here are a few examples of copyright infringement that you may recognize:

- Taking someone else's photo from the Internet and posting it on Instagram
- Copying a CD of someone else's music and giving it to a friend
- Using a peer-to-peer file sharing service or torrent to download a movie
- Copying a copyrighted software app and giving it to your friend

What happens to people who infringe on someone's copyright? Infringing on copyright risks a potentially long and costly legal battle. At best, you might receive a slap on the wrist, but worst-case scenarios involve large fines and prison terms. Penalties vary depending on the type of property being infringed and the country whose laws are in effect.

Is posting a picture on a social media site really copyright infringement? If you don't own the copyright to the picture or the rights to display a copyrighted image, then it's copyright infringement. Although you may not have read a social media site's user agreement, most sites, like Pinterest, have users agree not to post material to which they don't own copyright. Of course, if a website provides a Pinterest link for you to share material, you could argue that they're giving you implicit permission to share their material.

How do courts decide when copyright has been infringed? When judges consider cases of infringement, they generally examine the extent to which there is a substantial similarity between the copyrighted work and the infringing work. Obviously, if you copy an image from the Internet or burn a copy of a music CD, that is an exact copy and is clearly infringement. What if you wrote a story with a similar plot to an episode of your favorite TV show? The courts will have to determine how similar the characters and plot are to the copyrighted work and if infringement exists.

Why would anyone risk copyright infringement? Severe monetary penalties exist for copyright infringement, so why take a chance? Here are a few reasons people have indicated they risk copyright infringement:

- **Low likelihood of getting caught**: If you download three songs from a file-sharing website, are you likely to get caught? Probably not, but that doesn't make it ethical. You're still depriving an artist of his or her livelihood. However, some people commit such acts if they think they can escape notice.
- **Everyone is doing it**: If people think "everyone else does it so why should I miss out?" they might take a chance, especially if the likelihood of getting caught is low.
- **No one would come after an individual**: Many people believe that only large corporations are sued for copyright infringement. But thousands of individuals have been sued by the record and motion picture industries for illegal file sharing. Most of these cases were settled out of court for amounts ranging from $3,000 to $4,000, but court awards have gone higher. The Recording Industry of America (RIAA) and movie studios tend to target *supernodes*— people who offer thousands of music or video files on P2P networks for sharing—for their legal action, but they can just as easily target you for downloading a movie or a CD of songs.
- **I'm only downloading one song, picture, etc....it isn't worth that much**: Whether you're stealing one candy bar from a convenience store or a box of them from a truck, they're both crimes. Because copyright infringement is prohibited by law, copying one song is still stealing.

Is putting a URL that points to a copyrighted website on my social media page copyright infringement? A URL is a direction for finding a specific page on the Internet. It isn't debatable or open to interpretation; therefore, it's considered a fact. Because facts can't be copyrighted, you can list all the textual URLs you want on your website without committing copyright infringement. However, be sure you don't take copyrighted material, such as a logo or character, to use as a visual link to a website. For instance, using a picture of Mickey Mouse to link to the Disney website may constitute infringement.

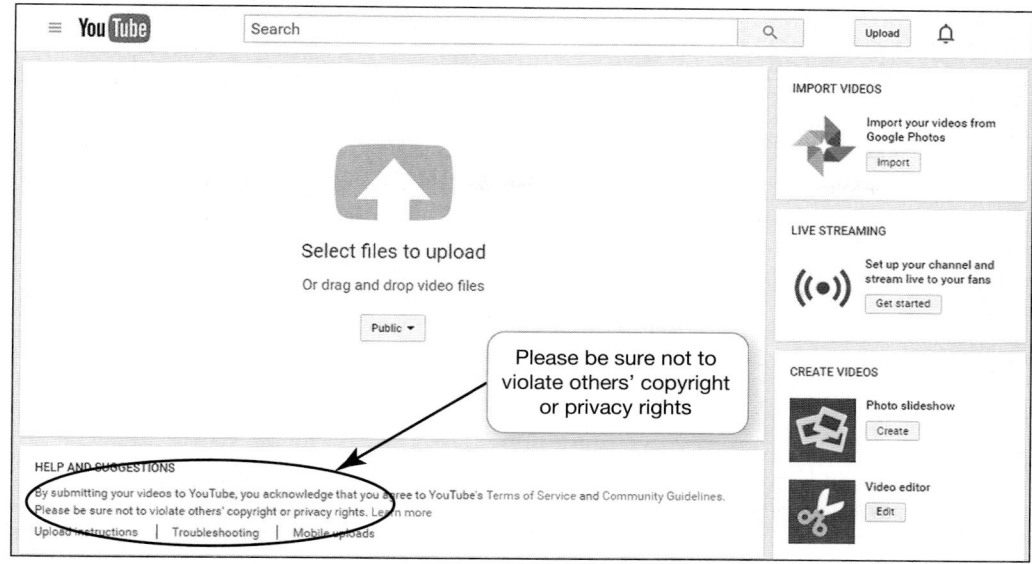

Figure 8.20 Although you might have missed it, when you upload videos to YouTube, you agree to respect copyright and privacy. *(Courtesy Google Inc.)*

Music and Video Issues

I uploaded clips from TV shows to YouTube. Could I be liable for copyright infringement? Although many people think that YouTube would be responsible for any infringement, anyone who uploads copyrighted material could be held responsible. Although you might not pay attention when uploading videos, you do agree not to infringe on copyright when uploading the files, as shown in Figure 8.20. Therefore, YouTube has potential legal recourse to recover damages from users who ignore the terms of use on its website. If you've uploaded copyrighted material without permission to YouTube or any other file-sharing site, you should remove it immediately.

Why would a band object to uploading a music video to YouTube? Wouldn't it be free publicity for them? Each time someone plays a video that's uploaded illegally to a website, the performer (singer or band), the songwriter, and the music publisher potentially lose money. A song played on a website is considered a live performance. Songwriters and music publishers are entitled to a royalty every time a song is played live, on the radio, on a streaming service (like Spotify), or anywhere on the Internet. Normally, radio stations and streaming services pay royalty fees to Performing Rights Organizations (PROs). The PROs then forward the royalties to the songwriters, music publishers, and other copyright holders. Because you're not paying royalties to a PRO when you view the video on YouTube, someone is losing money.

How significant is the loss of revenue from music and video infringement? A recent study from Columbia University concluded that 45% of U.S. citizens pirate movies on a regular basis. Many popular movies are illegally downloaded tens of millions of times. If everyone pays $4 to watch the movie from a legitimate streaming source, the movie studio could have earned millions of more dollars. Clearly, illegal file swapping is costing people and companies a significant amount of revenue.

Software Issues

How are the rights of software copyright holders usually violated? Illegally using copyrighted software is known as **software piracy**. If you've ever given a friend a copy of a copyrighted software program or downloaded copyrighted software from a file-sharing site, you've committed infringement.

You need to exercise caution when buying software online to ensure that it's a real, fully licensed copy. Otherwise you might not be able to use the software you bought. Most modern software requires a serial number or product key for installation. Typically, the first time you launch the software after installation, this serial number is checked against a database to ensure the software hasn't been installed on more computers than the license allows. This is a form of digital rights management (DRM). If you're buying illegally copied software on the Internet, you might not be able to activate it because too many other people have already used the same serial number.

How widespread is software piracy? In some countries, such as Indonesia and China, software piracy is rampant. Piracy rates approach 90 percent in some areas of the world. Although less of a problem in the United States on a percentage basis, the United States still leads the world in lost revenue from software piracy.

Photographic Issues

Why is photographic infringement widespread on the Internet? Because it's so easy! Need a picture of the Eiffel Tower for your presentation? Google's image search makes it simple to find a picture. Copy and paste it into your presentation and you're done. Congratulations, you've probably just infringed on someone's copyright!

Who owns the copyright to a photo? When the photo is taken, the photographer owns the copyright, assuming the photographer was taking photos in a public place or had permission from the property owner. If the photographer was working on a "work for hire" basis, usually the copyright belongs to his or her employer.

Do people in the photo have any rights? Being photographed without your consent generally falls under the realm of privacy. The Fourth Amendment to the U.S. Constitution and various other laws and court cases have recognized Americans' rights to certain amounts of privacy. Usually, if a photographer includes you in a photo (see Figure 8.21) that he or she intends to sell for publication, you'll be asked to sign a **model release**, which usually grants the photographer the right to use an image of the model (or subject of the photo) commercially.

(Alan Evans)

If a picture of you is published without your consent, you might have the basis for a lawsuit. However, be aware that there are times when you agree to allow your photo to be taken and used commercially (usually for publicity), such as when you enter a contest, buy a ticket for an amusement park, or enter an event such as a marathon. So read the conditions on sign-up forms and tickets to ensure you understand any rights you're surrendering.

How do you know if a photo on the Internet is copyrighted? Usually information is attached to a photo to indicate it's copyrighted, in the public domain, or that all rights are reserved. If there's no information attached, the safest course of action is to assume that the photo is protected by copyright and you'd need permission to use the photo. Figure 8.22 shows an example of copyright information for a photo on the Flickr website.

Figure 8.21 There is no problem taking a picture of this statue of Lincoln on display in a public park. But if you want to use the photo for commercial purposes, you need to obtain a model release from the man chatting with Lincoln.

Using Copyrighted Material Legally

Under what circumstances can I use copyrighted material? Many websites that contain copyrighted material also contain lengthy legal documents that delineate the **terms of use** for the material that you download from the site (see Figure 8.23). It's important to read the terms of use *before* using any copyrighted material on the site. Failure to read the terms of use doesn't absolve you from liability for using copyrighted material without permission.

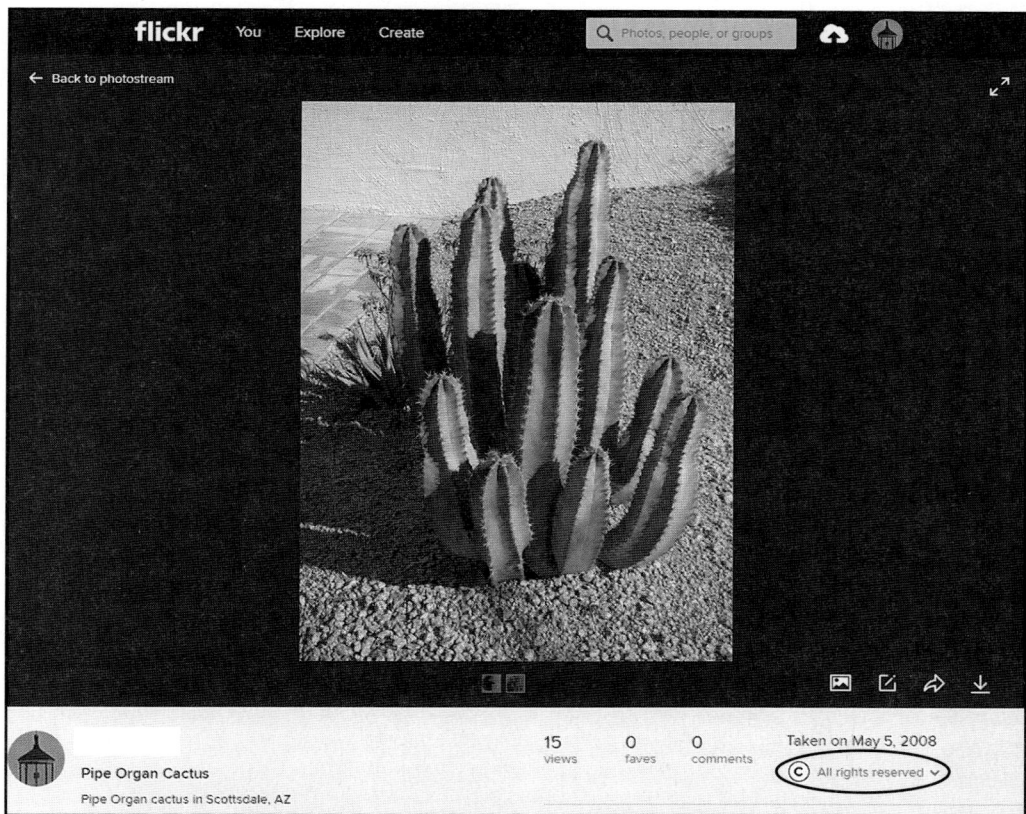

Figure 8.22 Although you can download this photo from Flickr, all rights are reserved so you cannot use it without obtaining permission. *(Courtesy Yahoo, Inc.)*

What if a website does not have terms of use? Ferreting out the terms of use on a site can sometimes be tricky. Look for links that say Terms of Use, Restrictions, Copyright, Rules, Media Room, Usage Guidelines, FAQ, or Contact Us. Sometimes, the usage terms aren't displayed until you attempt to download copyrighted material. If you've done a thorough search and can't find them, contact the organization that maintains the website and ask about the site's terms of use.

Can I use copyrighted material if it isn't permitted in the terms of use or there are no terms of use? Copyright holders can always grant permission to use copyrighted material to an individual or organization. Depending on the material used and the specific nature of the usage, a payment may be required to secure the rights to the copyrighted work. Sometimes though, simply asking permission is enough to get you the rights to use the work for a specific purpose free of charge.

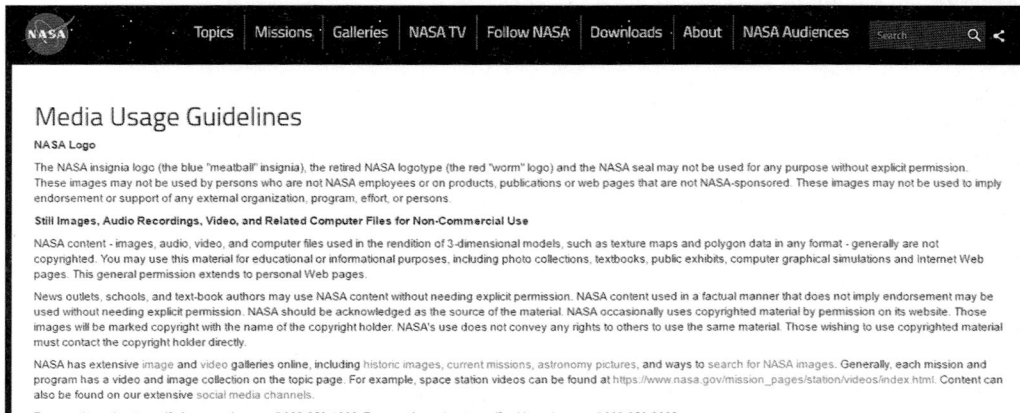

Figure 8.23 The terms of use page from **nasa.gov** clearly spells out your rights regarding photos downloaded from its website. NASA's media usage guidelines are very generous. *(National Aeronautics and Space Administration)*

Need an image or a video but don't want to pay for it? Many (if not all) images posted on U.S. government websites have generous usage guidelines. Need a V-2 rocket photo (see Figure 8.24)? Head to **nasa.gov**. NASA's collection of media is free to use for educational and informational purposes without explicit permission. You can even use NASA media for commercial purposes if it doesn't imply endorsement of your product or company by NASA. Need a photo of Arches National Park? Check out the U. S. Geological Survey site (**library.usgs .gov/photo**). Any images posted on the site generated by employees of the USGS are considered in the public domain. Picture of a grizzly bear? The U.S. Fish and Wildlife Service can help you out (**digitalmedia.fws.gov**). So make your tax dollars work for you by saving money on permissions fees for media!

Figure 8.24   U.S. government websites have a wealth of media, like this rocket, that is free to use. *(NASA)*

Figure 8.25   Contacts for Various Types of Media

Books and Periodicals
- Author or publisher

Website Content
- Webmaster, website owner, or author

Photos, Sculpture, Paintings, or Other Art
- Artist or photographer, publisher (print media), gallery management (on display)

Movies or Video
- Uploader (original video on website), production company, film distributor, screenwriter

(Monticellllo/Fotolia, Bannosuke/Fotolia, Sakunee977/Fotolia, Axsimen/Fotolia)

Whom do I contact for permission? Identifying the appropriate contact from which to obtain permission depends on the nature of the intellectual property. Sometimes it can be difficult to tell who actually owns the copyright, or the particular rights you need, to a piece of media. The creator may not be the copyright holder any longer. He or she may have sold the rights to another party. Figure 8.25 provides suggestions about permission contacts.

What information should I provide in a permission request? Be sure to include these points:

- **Who you are**: Include your contact information (name, address, phone number, and e-mail) and whether you're requesting permission personally or on behalf of an organization.
- **Which work you're requesting permission to use**: Describe the work completely as well as how much of the work you'll be using.
- **Complete details of your usage of the work**: Indicate why you're using the work, if the work is being used as part of a money-making project, where the work will be used (website, book, magazine, etc.), how frequently the work will be used, and if you're making modifications to the work.
- **The timing of the request**: Indicate the date you intend to begin using the work and suggest a deadline for responding to the request.

Be sure you receive a written response to your request authorizing the usage you requested. Never assume that a lack of response indicates a tacit approval on the part of the copyright holder. Remember, copyright holders are under no obligation to grant your request or even to respond to it.

Fair Use

Are there any instances in which I can use copyrighted work without permission of the copyright holder? **Fair use** provides for people to use portions of a copyrighted work for specific purposes without receiving prior permission from the copyright holder. However, there are no specific rules on exactly what amount of use constitutes fair use, which means each case has to be decided on its own merits.

What types of activities constitute fair use? The following are examples of fair use activities permitted in the United States:

- Quotation of excerpts in a review or criticism
- Summary of an address or article, with brief quotations, in a news report
- Reproduction by a teacher or student of a small part of a work to illustrate a lesson; this is commonly known as **educational fair use**

Figure 8.26 Suggested Educational Fair Use Guidelines

Media	Quantity
Motion media	Up to 10% or 3 minutes, whichever is less
Text material	Up to 10% or 1,000 words, whichever is less
Music, lyrics, and music videos	Up to 10%, but in no event more than 30 seconds, of the music and lyrics from an individual musical work (or in the aggregate of extracts from an individual work)
Illustrations and photographs	a. One artist: No more than 5 images b. Collections of works: No more than 10% or 15 images, whichever is less
Numerical data sets (databases and spreadsheets)	Up to 10% or 2,500 fields or cell entries, whichever is less

Does being a student who uses educational (academic) fair use give me a defense for using any copyrighted material I want? Because there are no fixed guidelines on the quantity of material that can be used and still be considered fair use, guidelines have been developed to assist teachers and students. The Consortium of College and University Media Centers developed suggested guidelines for various types of media, excerpts of which are summarized in Figure 8.26.

Again, these are only suggested guidelines and depending on the individual case, you may be able to make a successful argument under the fair use doctrine to use a greater percentage of a given work. Many educational institutions publish their own guidelines, so inquire about your school's guidelines.

Living Ethically in the Digital Era

The rise of digital technology provides new challenges to us all. In this section, we'll explore some of the ethical choices you might be confronted with as you navigate the digital world.

Plagiarism

Objective 8.12 *Explain plagiarism and strategies for avoiding it.*

What exactly is plagiarism? Plagiarism is the act of copying text or ideas from someone else and claiming them as your own. Using ideas from other sources and integrating them into your work is acceptable only if you clearly indicate the content being used (such as through quotation marks) and attribute your source. Changing a few words but keeping the essence of someone else's idea is still plagiarism even if you don't copy the text exactly. Although the following examples don't involve copying words or ideas without attribution, they're still examples of plagiarism under the academic definition:

- **Turning in work that someone else did for you**: Copying the Excel file that was due for homework in your computer literacy class from a classmate is still plagiarism, even though the file isn't a text file.
- **Failing to identify a direct quotation with quotation marks**
- **Copying too much material from other sources**: If a work consists mostly of quotes and ideas from other sources, even though the source has been identified, it's difficult to justify it as original, creative work.

Plagiarism is usually considered an academic offense of dishonesty and isn't punishable under U.S. civil law. Plagiarism is prohibited by almost all academic institutions, and the penalties usually are severe, ranging from receiving a failing grade on the assignment to receiving a failing grade for the course to being dismissed from the institution. Although plagiarism isn't technically copyright infringement, it can easily turn into copyright infringement if too much material is stolen from other sources, such as an entire chapter of a book or an entire research paper. The author may choose to sue you if the market for his or her intellectual property is damaged.

Why is plagiarism such a big issue today when it has been a problem for centuries? Quick access to information on the Internet has made it easier than ever to commit plagiarism. It's possible to copy and paste large quantities of information with just a few mouse clicks.

Another huge problem today is presented by **paper mills**—websites that sell prewritten or custom-written research papers to students. For custom work, you can even specify what type of grade you would like to get. Some students choose to buy papers to earn them a grade of "C" if they think that it's less likely to arouse suspicion from their instructor. It's illegal in most states to sell essays that will be turned in by students as their own work, but the mills get around this by putting disclaimers on their websites that the papers should be used only for research purposes and not as the student's work. Fortunately, tools are available to instructors for detecting this type of plagiarism.

What can my instructor do to detect plagiarism? Sometimes, just reading a student's work is a giveaway. If the level of writing improves dramatically from earlier assignments, most instructors become suspicious. Most colleges allow instructors to test students orally on the content of papers they suspect aren't the student's own work. If a student is unfamiliar with the content of the paper and the sources used, charges of academic dishonesty can be brought against the student.

Typing suspicious phrases from a paper into a search engine is an effective way to find uncredited sources. Also, most school libraries subscribe to searchable databases of periodicals that contain the full text of published articles. This aids instructors in ferreting out plagiarism from printed sources.

Educational institutions also often subscribe to specialized electronic tools such as Turnitin (**turnitin.com**). The subscription enables instructors to upload student papers, which are then checked against databases of published journals and periodicals, previously submitted student papers, and websites—both current sites and archived sites that are no longer live. Customized reports, such as the one shown in Figure 8.27, are generated to determine the amount of suspected plagiarism in the paper. Instructors have the option of letting students upload their papers to check them for inadvertent plagiarism to give them a chance to cite uncredited sources before turning in their final product.

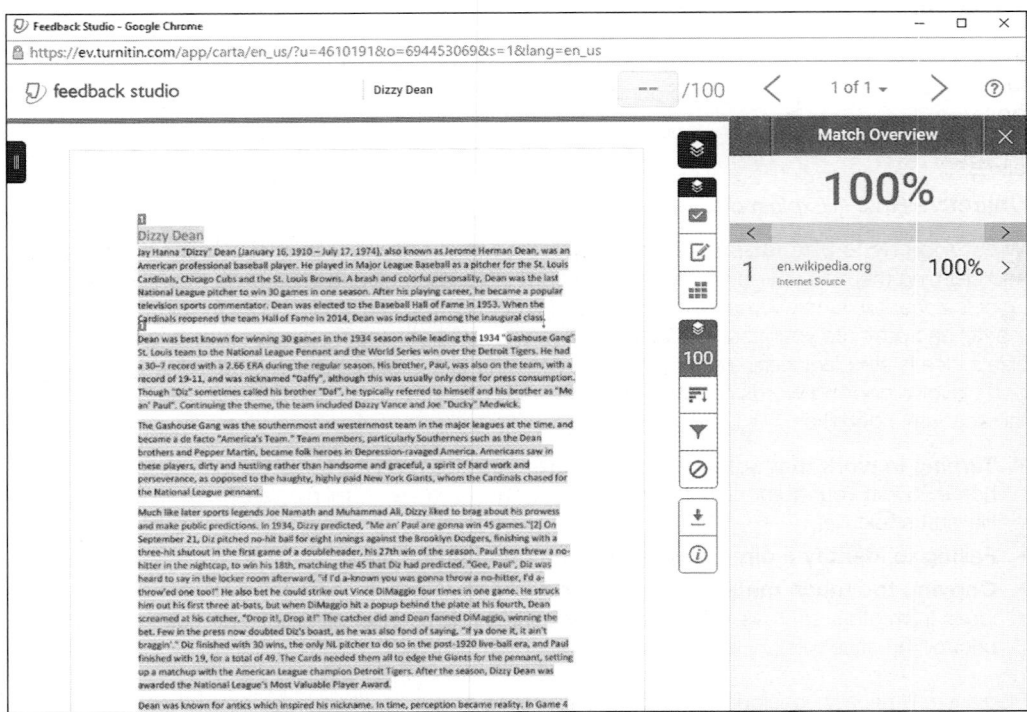

Figure 8.27 The Turnitin feedback report for this paper clearly shows that this paper was plagiarized directly from Wikipedia. *(From Turnitin USA. Copyright © by Turnitin USA. Used by permission of Turnitin USA.)*

How can I avoid committing plagiarism? Learn to follow this simple maxim: *When in doubt, cite your source.* If you're taking an exact quote from a work, cite the source. If you're paraphrasing someone else's idea but still retaining the essence of their original, creative idea, cite the source.

How do I cite a printed source properly? Many different styles of citations have been developed by organizations such as the American Psychological Association (APA) and the Modern Language Association (MLA). Ask your instructor which style is preferred. Regardless of the style, readers of your work need enough information to find the sources you cite. Microsoft Word has built-in features that make creating citations easy (see the Try This feature in Chapter 4 for more information).

So if plagiarism isn't illegal, why do professors get so upset about it? A summary of the issues follows in Figure 8.28.

Hoaxes and Digital Manipulation

Objective 8.13 *Describe hoaxes and digital manipulation.*

Everyone seems to post social media stories warning about a variety of issues, such as the police in your state giving out speeding tickets or the plight of sick children with one last wish. Because anyone can put up a web page on any subject, post to social media, or send off a quick e-mail, how can you distinguish fact from fiction? Determining the reliability of information you encounter in cyberspace can be a challenge, but it's important when you use the Internet as a source of scholarly research. Your professor would not be impressed if you gave a presentation on the illusive North American Jackalope (see Figure 8.29).

Hoaxes and Other Lies

What is a hoax? A **hoax** is anything designed to deceive another person either as a practical joke or for financial gain. Hoaxes perpetrated in cyberspace for financial gain are classified as *cybercrimes*. Hoaxes are most often perpetrated by e-mail and postings on social media.

Many hoaxes become so well known that they're incorporated into society as true events even though they're false. Once this happens, they're known as **urban legends**. An example of an urban legend is the story about a man who wakes up in a bathtub full of ice water to discover he's had his kidney removed.

How can I tell if something on social media is a hoax? Many hoaxes are well written and crafted in such a way that they sound real. Before sharing the post, check it out at sites such as Snopes (**snopes.com**), Hoax-Slayer (**hoax-slayer.com**), or the Museum of Hoaxes (**hoaxes.org**). These sites are searchable, so you can enter a few keywords from the item you suspect may be a hoax and find similar items with an explanation of whether they're true or false.

Figure 8.28 Point/Counterpoint: Plagiarism

Issue: Plagiarism   **Ethical Question: Is plagiarism wrong?**

Point	
	• Taking credit for another's work is always unethical. • Plagiarizing published work (implying it's a higher-quality product) puts an unfair burden on other students who have to compete with the plagiarizer. • Creators of intellectual property deserve full credit for their work.
Counterpoint 	• There are no laws in the U.S. that make plagiarism a crime. • Only academics frown on plagiarism. The "real world" is more concerned with results. • Today's culture fosters an environment of collaborating and sharing. Therefore, how can accessing published information and using it be wrong?

(James Steidl/Fotalia)

Figure 8.29 Hoax websites often look real and are used in computer fluency classes to teach people the value of fact checking.

(Patti McConville/Alamy Stock Photo)

Figure 8.30 Resources for Conducting Scholarly Research

Google Scholar
(scholar.google.com)
- Specialty search engine that returns results from scholarly sources

Academia
(academia.edu)
- A free site where users share scholarly research and follow the research of others

BASE
(base-search.net)
- Operated by Bielefeld University Library—included information is carefully selected and reviewed

RefSeek
(refseek.com)
- Searches over 1 billion documents such as books, encyclopedias, newspapers, professional journals, and websites

How do I know if something in Wikipedia is true?
Wikipedia entries are reviewed by editors, so there's some control over the accuracy of content. But, just as with any other source of information, articles in Wikipedia need to be evaluated based on the criteria described in Chapter 3. Many articles on Wikipedia have extensive footnotes and lists of sources, making it possible to investigate the reliability of the source material. So treat Wikipedia as you would any other web page you might want to rely on; evaluate the content thoroughly before relying on it.

Is there a resource for finding quality sites for scholarly research? Several resources on the Internet, many of which are created (or maintained) by librarians, can be useful for locating websites and scholarly publications that are considered reliable, current, and suitable for academic research. Some of the more popular ones are described in Figure 8.30. Using these sites doesn't mean you don't have to check facts, but it does provide you with an excellent starting point for your research.

Because anyone can post anything to the Internet, what's the harm in posting something that is false (see Figure 8.31)? Not passing on information that is false is part of being an ethical Internet user. It takes more effort to check potential hoaxes and the accuracy of websites. But think of all the time you'll save your friends and family by not sending out endless streams of bogus information. And certainly your research papers will benefit from using accurate information sources.

Figure 8.31 Point/Counterpoint: Posting False Information

Issue: Posting False Information	Ethical Question: Is it unethical to post false information on the Internet?
Point 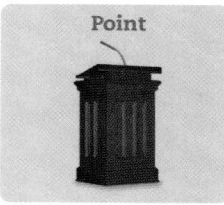	• Creating stories for the purposes of deceiving people is always unethical. • Inaccurate content might be used as the basis for the creation of new content, thereby spreading the contamination even further. • Spreading false information for monetary gain is illegal.
Counterpoint	• Writers create works of fiction every day. Why is creating hoaxes and rumors any different? • People should be able to judge for themselves and do research to figure out when authors are creating false information for amusement or satire. • Advertisers constantly exaggerate about product attributes. Hoaxes help foster healthy skepticism in the public.

(James Steidl/Fotalia)

Digital Manipulation

What is digital manipulation? Now that we have computer apps that can generate life-like images for movies and alter photographs, can we believe anything we see? **Digital manipulation** involves altering media so that the images captured are changed from the way they were originally seen by the human eye.

So manipulation of images started when Photoshop was invented? Hoaxes perpetrated via photographic manipulation have been around since photography was invented. Multiple exposures, compositing negatives, and cutting-and-pasting multiple photos and then reshooting were common methods of manipulation clever photographers used in the past (see Figure 8.32). It was once common practice for images of family members to be cut and pasted into the same photo to make it seem as though they were together for a family portrait when in fact they never had been.

So when is manipulating a photograph or a video unethical? If changes are made to an image for the purpose of deceiving someone or to alter perceptions of reality, this crosses the boundaries into unethical behavior. For instance, there was a famous image floating around the Internet of George W. Bush reading to elementary school children and the book he was holding was made to appear upside down through digital manipulation. It didn't really happen, but many people believed it did!

Some adjustments that photographers make are purely for aesthetic reasons. *Aesthetics* deals with making things pleasing in appearance. When you use a flash, people in the photo often have red eyes. Eliminating the red eye and changing the brightness and contrast of a photo are things you can do right from your camera app. This doesn't alter the reality of the photo; it just improves the appearance. Therefore, this type of digital manipulation isn't considered unethical because it only involves enhancing the photo's aesthetics.

Aren't photos and videos often submitted as evidence in courts? Quite frequently they are and this presents new dilemmas. If a photo or video can be altered, can you rely on it as evidence? Videos are often enhanced for the purpose of bringing out details that are obscured under normal circumstances. Is this fabrication of evidence or just improving aesthetics? Most photos and videos submitted as evidence are examined to determine they haven't been altered. But the techniques for manipulating images are advancing, and soon it may be difficult, if not impossible, to determine whether an image has been altered. Courts are now beginning to wrestle with these issues.

So should you engage in digital manipulation? We explore both sides of the argument in Figure 8.33. But as with any other type of information you find on the Internet, be sure to validate the accuracy of photos and videos before relying on them.

Figure 8.32 Over 100 years before the invention of Photoshop, photo manipulation was alive and well. This purported photo of General Grant at City Point is a composite of three different photographs.
(Library of Congress)

Figure 8.33 Point/Counterpoint: Digital Manipulation

Issue: Digital Manipulation	Ethical Question: Is digital manipulation unethical?
Point 	• Images and videos are meant to represent what happened in the real world and therefore should not be subject to alteration. • Photographic and video evidence in court cases would be useless unless we're able to determine whether they've been altered.
Counterpoint 	• Artists and photographers need to be free to alter the aesthetics of images for artistic purposes. • People should be able to tell when images have been purposely distorted for satirical purposes. Isn't it obvious there is no such thing as an 80-pound housecat?

(James Steidl/Fotalia)

Protecting Your Online Reputation

Objective 8.14 *Describe what comprises your online reputation and how to protect it.*

There is already quite a bit of information about you on the Internet. Chances are you've put most of it out there yourself through sites such as Facebook, Instagram, and Twitter. Most people strive to maintain a good reputation in the real world, but in the twenty-first century, your online reputation is just as important as your real-life one.

What is my online reputation? Your **online reputation** consists of the information available about you in cyberspace that can influence people's opinions of you in the real world. Your online reputation is an extension of your real-life reputation—the view held by the community, the general public, friends, family, and others of your general character. Are you considered an honest person? Do you always speak your mind regardless of the consequences? Are you known for defending the rights of less fortunate individuals? These are examples of factors that contribute to society's view of the type of individual you are.

Information is constantly added to the Internet about many of us, even by people we don't know. It can be challenging to control the information that contributes to your online reputation. If you go to a party and guests take pictures of you, they may post their pictures to sites and identify (or **tag**) you in them. Your friends might write about you on their Facebook or Twitter feed. No matter whether this information is true, false, misleading, embarrassing, or disturbing, it's part of your online reputation.

Why is it so important to protect my online reputation? If you say something or do something you wish you hadn't done in real life, most people will forget about it eventually. However, given the **persistence of information** on the Internet, pictures, videos, and narratives about you might never disappear. Even if you delete something, it probably still exists somewhere. There are numerous examples of politicians tweeting something they later regret and deleting it from their Twitter feed, only to find many people have captured and saved their tweet already.

Sites such as the Internet Archive (**archive.org**) feature utilities such as the Wayback Machine that show you what a website looked like at a previous point in time. Ever wonder what Yahoo! looked like in the early days? A search on the Wayback Machine shows you that in 1996 it looked like Figure 8.34.

Of course, your reputation varies depending on who is interpreting the cyberspace information about you. Your friends might laugh at that picture on Facebook of you at a recent party, but employers routinely browse through social networking sites to evaluate job applicants as part of their hiring decision process. And just keeping your information private isn't a good solution. Many employers don't interview candidates for whom they find a lack of social information online because they view this as a negative or at least a potential concern. Even after you're hired, if your employer finds things that he or she doesn't like on your sites, you might be fired because of it. According to CareerBuilder, 18% of employers surveyed have fired employees due to social media posts.

Figure 8.34 A much simpler Yahoo! home page is preserved for posterity in the Internet Archive. Your web pages might live on forever also. *(Courtesy Yahoo, Inc.)*

How can an employer fire me for writing something on my own time? In the majority of states, the employment at-will principle governs the firing of employees. *Employment at-will* means that unless you're covered by an employment contract or a collective bargaining agreement, such as a union contract, employers can fire you at any time for any reason, unless the reason violates a legal statute such as race or age discrimination. Your employer is not required to provide you with a reason for the firing but can simply tell you not to report for work any longer.

You do have a constitutional right to free speech. However, that doesn't mean your employer is going to agree with your opinions. Therefore, it's a good idea to familiarize yourself with your employer's social media policies. Many employers now have such policies, and they usually prevent you from saying disparaging things about your employer, work environment, customers, and co-workers on social media sites. Also, giving the appearance that your employer supports an activity or political agenda is usually prohibited (see Figure 8.35), so make sure you're aware of the rules at your workplace.

What steps should I take to protect my online reputation? There are many things you can do if you're proactive:

* *Improve and update your personal profiles*: Make sure your profiles on social media sites are accurate. Update them with new information.

Figure 8.35 You have the right to protest, but your employer's social media policy may prohibit you from posting a picture of yourself wearing a company T-shirt while attending the event. *(Photographee.eu/Fotolia)*

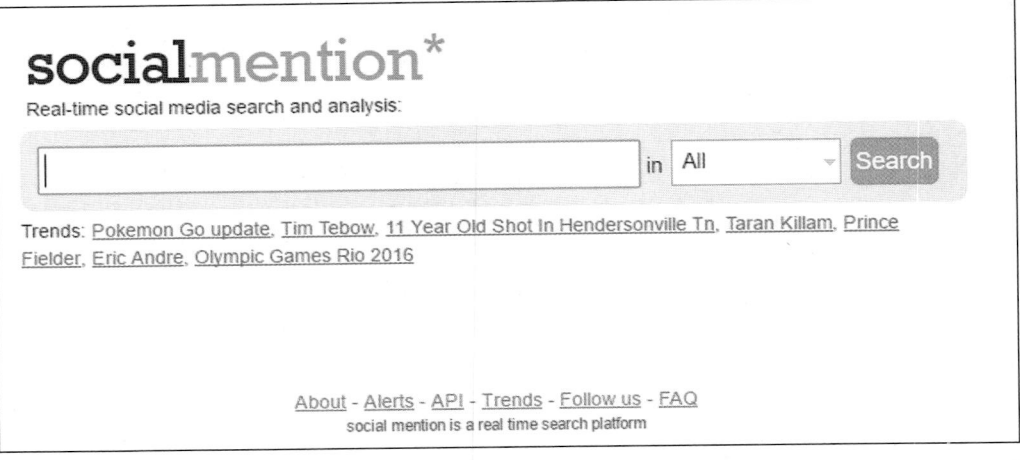

Figure 8.36 SocialMention.com aggregates content from social media sites so you can keep up with any person, topic, or business…even yourself! *(socialmention.com)*

- *Create content on relevant sites*: For instance, if you're an up-and-coming interior designer, post positive comments on relevant sites that assist people with some aspect of design. Make sure your name is associated with things people feel good about reading.
- *Post frequently*: Posting frequently helps minimize negative information, as newer information tends to come up first in search engine results.
- *Be vigilant*: Contact people who've posted negative things about you and see if you can get them to modify or delete them.

You need to examine your own reputation periodically. Google yourself and see what information about you is available on the Internet. If you see something that displeases you, ask the poster or the webmaster to remove the offending material. Don't have time to constantly monitor your reputation? Sites such as **SocialMention.com** (see Figure 8.36) and Trackur (**trackur.com**) provide tools to conduct searches and generate updates regarding information posted about you on social media sites. These tools can also be used to track mentions about specific topics or businesses that interest you.

Keeping your online reputation accurate and not damaging other people's reputations unfairly are integral parts of being an ethical cyber-citizen.

Bits&Bytes Celebrity Photographic Rights

How do paparazzi get away with photographing celebrities without their consent? By the nature of being a celebrity, courts have decided that these individuals surrender a certain amount of privacy. In the United States, photos that are taken for editorial use in a public place generally enjoy constitutional protection under the right of free speech. Paparazzi are free to photograph celebrities in public places for the purposes of selling their photos to news outlets and news publications. However, paparazzi can't sneak into a celebrity's backyard and photograph them through the window.

There are several exceptions to the free speech doctrine though. Photos can't have captions that imply something false or libelous about the person in the photo. If they do, then they aren't legally protected free speech. Also, photos of a celebrity can't be used to promote any goods or services without permission of the celebrity. This is because celebrities have the right of publicity, which grants them control of the commercial use of their name, image, likeness, and other unequivocal aspects of their identity.

Ethics in IT

Acceptable Use Policies: What You Can and Can't Do

With computers and the Internet becoming ubiquitous tools, more and more ethical decisions revolve around how we use technology. Because of the potential for problems related to misuse of technology, most schools and businesses have adopted **acceptable use policies**—guidelines regarding usage of computer systems—relating to the use of their computing resources. Your school most likely has a policy similar to that shown in Figure 8.37 with which you should familiarize yourself. You can usually find it on your institution's website, either under the Information Technology department section or the Student Policies section. If you can't locate it, check with the helpdesk personnel at your school; they can likely direct you to the appropriate web page. Among other things, these policies usually cover the following:

- Keeping your account access (logon ID and password) secure from others
- Not running a side business with college/business assets

- Prohibiting attempts to gain access to portions of the computer systems you are not authorized to use
- Illegally copying legally protected materials, such as software
- Creating, distributing, or displaying threatening, obscene, racist, sexist, or harassing material
- Prohibiting the installation of unauthorized software on the institution's computers
- Conducting any illegal activities with computing systems

If you have a job, you should also familiarize yourself with your employer's policy because it may differ from your school's policy. For instance, most schools consider any work products—such as research papers, poems, musical compositions, and so forth—generated with school computing resources to be the property of the students who created them, unless the students were paid to create the works. With many employers, any work products created using company-provided computing resources are deemed to be the property of the company, not the employees who created them.

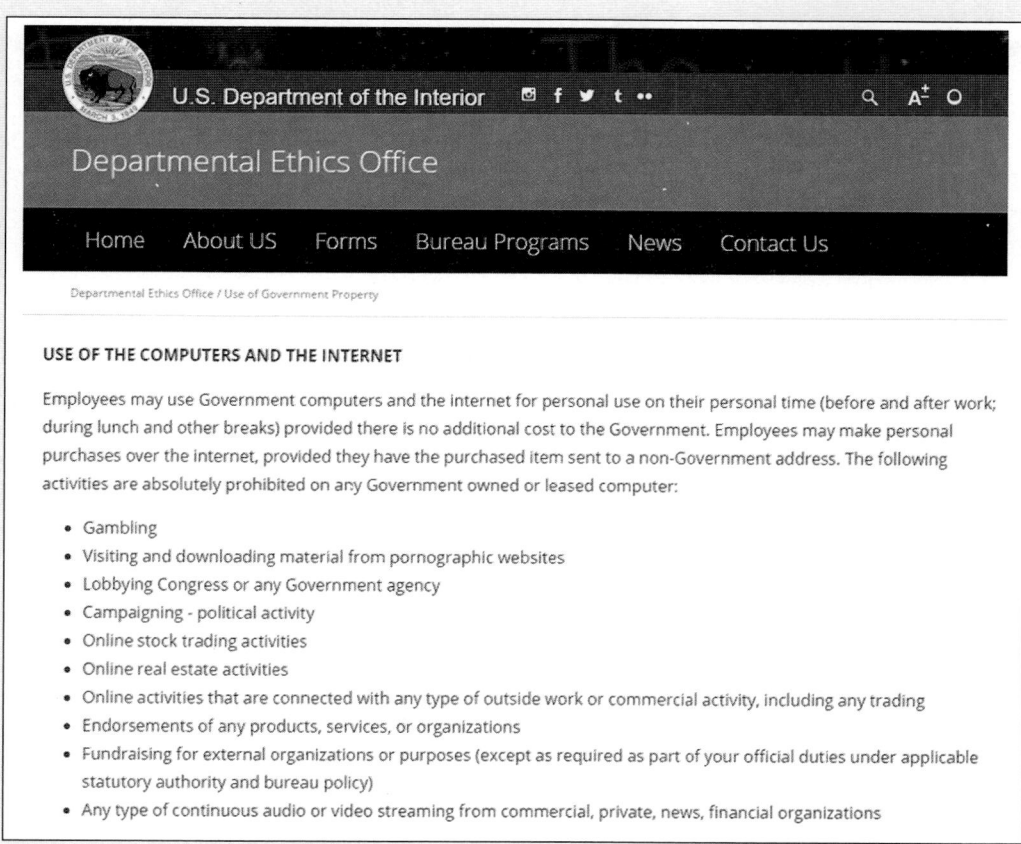

Figure 8.37 A typical acceptable use policy. *(U.S. Department of the Interior)*

Figure 8.38 The Ten Commandments of Computer Ethics

Thou shalt not use a computer to harm other people

Thou shalt not interfere with other people's computer work

Thou shalt not snoop around in other people's computer files

Thou shalt not use a computer to steal

Thou shalt not use a computer to bear false witness

Thou shalt not copy or use proprietary software for which you have not paid

Thou shalt not use other people's computer resources without authorization or proper compensation

Thou shalt not appropriate other people's intellectual output

Thou shalt think about the social consequences of the program you are writing or the system you are designing

Thou shalt always use a computer in ways that ensure consideration and respect for your fellow humans

If your school or employer doesn't have an acceptable use policy, the Computer Ethics Institute (**computerethicsinstitute.org**) has developed a well-known set of guidelines you can follow. They are known as the Ten Commandments of Computer Ethics (see Figure 8.38).

In the absence of clear policies, following the Ten Commandments of Computer Ethics should help you steer clear of most unethical behavior.

Before moving on to Chapter Review:

1. ▶ Watch Chapter Overview Video 8.2.
2. Then take the Check Your Understanding quiz.

Check Your Understanding // Review & Practice

For a quick review to see what you've learned so far, answer the following questions.

multiple choice

1. Which of the following is considered intellectual property?
   a. a song
   b. a sculpture
   c. a movie
   d. all of the above

2. Copyleft
   a. protects you from having others use your work.
   b. is a term for a set of licensing plans.
   c. legalizes unlimited copying of digital music.
   d. all of the above

3. When is posting a picture on social media considered copyright infringement?
   a. when you don't own the copyright to the photo
   b. when you don't have permission from the copyright holder to post the photo
   c. neither A nor B
   d. both A and B

4. Plagiarism is
   a. illegal under U.S civil law.
   b. always copyright infringement.
   c. unethical.
   d. not a big problem in academic institutions.

5. Altering a picture so that it doesn't reflect the reality of what is being shown is known as
   a. digital interpretation.
   b. pixel manipulation.
   c. digital manipulation.
   d. digital intervention.

 Go to **MyLab IT** to take an autograded version of the *Check Your Understanding* review and to find all media resources for the chapter.

TechBytes Weekly Go to TechBytes Weekly for current technology news and discussion questions!

8 Chapter Review

Summary

Learning Outcome 8.1 You will be able to describe the nature of digital signals and how digital technology is used to produce and distribute digital texts, music, and video.

Digital Basics

Objective 8.1 *Describe how digital convergence has evolved.*

- Digital convergence has brought us single devices with the capabilities that used to require four or five separate tools. With more computing power in a mobile processor, a single device can perform a wider range of tasks.

Objective 8.2 *Explain the differences between digital and analog signals.*

- Digital media is based on a series of numerical data—that is, number values that were measured from the original analog waveform. As a string of numbers, a digital photo or video file can be easily processed by modern computers.

Digital Publishing

Objective 8.3 *Describe the different types of e-readers.*

- E-readers are devices that store, manipulate, and transmit textual information digitally. Some use electronic ink for a sharp grayscale representation of text. Others use backlit monitors.

Objective 8.4 *Explain how to purchase, borrow, and publish e-texts.*

- There are a variety of formats for e-text files, including .azw and .epub. E-texts can be purchased from many publishers directly or from online stores. Libraries loan e-texts using products like Overdrive. You can easily publish your own books using services such as the Amazon Kindle Store, Smashwords, or Lulu.

Digital Music

Objective 8.5 *Describe how digital music is created and stored.*

- Digital music is created by combining pure digital sounds with samples of analog sounds. It has meant changes for the recording industry, for performers, and for music listeners. It's now inexpensive to carry a music library, to create new songs, and to distribute them worldwide. The sampling rate determines the fidelity of the final recorded digital sound.

Objective 8.6 *Summarize how to listen to and publish digital music.*

- Digital rights management is a system of access control to digital music. Many services, such as SoundCloud, CD Baby, and ReverbNation, are available for openly sharing and streaming your own content.

Digital Media

Objective 8.7 *Explain how best to create, print, and share digital photos.*

- Digital cameras allow you to instantly capture and transfer images to your devices, computers, and cloud storage sites. The camera's resolution is important, as it tells the number of data points recorded for each image captured.

Objective 8.8 *Describe how to create, edit, and distribute digital video.*

- Using software for video production, you can create polished videos with titles, transitions, a sound track, and special effects.

- A codec is a compression/decompression rule, implemented in either software or hardware, that squeezes the same audio and video information into less space.

- You can also use a webcam to stream live video to sites that will "broadcast" it over the Internet.

Part 2
Ethical Issues of Living in the Digital Age

Learning Outcome 8.2 **You will be able to describe how to respect digital property and use it in ways that maintain your digital reputation.**

 ### Protection of Digital Property

Objective 8.9 *Describe the various types of intellectual property.*

- Intellectual property (IP) is a product of a person's mind. Types of IP include copyrights, patents, trademarks, service marks, and trade dress. Copyright protection can be granted to creators of "original works of authorship."

Objective 8.10 *Explain how copyright is obtained and the rights granted to the owners.*

- Copyright begins when a work is created and fixed into a digital or physical form. Copyright can also be registered to provide additional benefits. Copyright includes the rights to sell, reproduce, and display (or perform) the work publicly.

Objective 8.11 *Explain copyright infringement, summarize the potential consequences, and describe situations in which you can legally use copyrighted material.*

- Using someone's copyrighted work without his or her permission is copyright infringement. Potential consequences include lawsuits and fines. You can use copyrighted material if you obtain permission from the copyright holder, adhere to posted terms of use, or qualify under a *fair use* exception.

 ### Living Ethically in the Digital Era

Objective 8.12 *Explain plagiarism and strategies for avoiding it.*

- Plagiarism is the act of copying text or ideas from someone else and claiming them as your own. Citing your sources in the proper format will help you avoid committing plagiarism.

Objective 8.13 *Describe hoaxes and digital manipulation.*

- A *hoax* is anything designed to deceive another person either as a practical joke or for financial gain. *Digital manipulation* involves altering some sort of media so that the images captured are changed from the way they were originally seen by the human eye. Sites such as snopes.com help tell fact from fiction.

Objective 8.14 *Describe what comprises your online reputation and how to protect it.*

- Your online reputation is information available about you in cyberspace that can influence people's opinions of you in the real world. Keeping content current, being vigilant, and frequently creating content are strategies for protecting your digital reputation.

 Be sure to check out **MyLab IT** for additional materials to help you review and learn. And don't forget to watch the Chapter Overview Videos. ▶

Key Terms

acceptable use policies **323**

analog **289**

codec **300**

copyleft **308**

copyright **306**

copyright infringement **310**

digital convergence **288**

digital manipulation **319**

digital rights management (DRM) **296**

digitized **289**

educational fair use **314**

electronic ink (E ink) **291**

electronic text (e-text) **291**

e-reader **291**

fair use **314**

high definition **301**

hoax **317**

intangible personal property **306**

intellectual property (IP) **306**

model release **312**

online reputation **320**

paper mills **316**

patents **307**

persistence of information **320**

personal property **306**

plagiarism **315**

public domain **308**

real property **306**

resolution **297**

sampling rate **294**

service mark **307**

software piracy **311**

tag **320**

tangible personal property **306**

terms of use **312**

trademark **307**

urban legends **317**

Chapter Quiz // Assessment

For a quick review to see what you've learned, answer the following questions. Submit the quiz as requested by your instructor. If you're using **MyLab IT**, the quiz is also available there.

multiple choice

1. Our ability to use a single device to meet all our digital needs is known as
   a. digital convergence.
   b. digital cohesion.
   c. digital shrinkage.
   d. digital collision.

2. Which of the following is an *open* electronic publishing format?
   a. PDF
   b. azw
   c. ePub
   d. SMS

3. The number of times the analog wave is measured each second is the
   a. DAW rate.
   b. digitization rate.
   c. MP3 rate.
   d. sampling rate.

4. DRM is an acronym for
   a. digital role maker.
   b. digital rights management.
   c. distribution regional media.
   d. digital real movie.

5. Image resolution is
   a. the size of the image in bytes.
   b. only important with analog image capture.
   c. the number of data points recorded in an image.
   d. based on the kind of compression used.

6. Which of the following is a digital video file format?
   a. MPEG-4
   b. PDF
   c. MP3
   d. JPG

7. Which of the following is NOT a category of intellectual property?
   a. copyright
   b. trademark
   c. patent
   d. imprint

8. Using copyrighted works without permission of the copyright holder
   a. is never possible.
   b. is possible under the "fair use" doctrine.
   c. only applies to proprietary software.
   d. is only possible for photographs of public places.

9. A well-known hoax that many people in society now believe to be true is known as

   a. a public domain tale.

   b. a persistence of information story.

   c. an urban legend.

   d. legend convergence.

10. It is important to maintain your online reputation

   a. because of the persistence of information.

   b. because employers often review social media before hiring employees.

   c. to ensure information about you is accurate.

   d. all of the above

true/false

_____ **1.** Analog signals are not continuous.

_____ **2.** Plagiarism is illegal.

_____ **3.** Publishing an e-book is easy enough for almost anyone to do.

_____ **4.** Copyright lasts for only 40 years.

_____ **5.** Copying Microsoft Word and giving it to a friend is "fair use."

critical thinking

1. Registration of Copyright

Although copyright accrues without registration, there are additional benefits to having your copyright registered. Visit copyright.gov and prepare a summary of the advantages of registration and explain how registration would help you pursue an infringement action.

2. Self-Publishing

What impact will the availability of self-publication have on the writing and recording industries? Will it promote a greater amount of quality content or a flood of amateur work? How could this be managed?

Team Time

"And One Will Rule Them All"

problem

Digital convergence posits the dream of one device that can do it all, for everyone. But there are so many different mobile devices saturating the market that many people are left confused.

task

For each scenario described as follows, the group will select the _minimum_ set of devices that would support and enhance the client's life.

process

1. Consider the following three clients:
   - A retired couple who now travels for pleasure a great deal. They want to be involved in their grandchildren's lives and need support for their health, finances, and personal care as they age.
   - A young family with two children, two working parents, and a tight budget.
   - A couple in which each individual is a physician and each adores technology.

2. Make two recommendations for your clients in terms of digital technologies that will enhance their business or their lifestyle. Discuss the advantages and disadvantages of each technology. Consider value, reliability, computing needs, training required, and communication needs as well as expandability for the future.

3. As a group, prepare a final report that considers the recommendations you've made for your clients.

conclusion

With so many digital solutions on the market, recommending options needs to focus on converging to the minimum set of tools that will enhance life without adding complication to it.

Ethics Project

When Everyone Has a Voice

In this exercise, you'll research and then role-play a complicated ethical situation. The role you play might or might not match your own personal beliefs; in either case, your research and use of logic will enable you to represent the view assigned. An arbitrator will watch and comment on both sides of the arguments, and together the team will agree on an ethical solution.

background

Much of the world's population is now equipped with Internet-ready camera phones. Sensors on these phones could measure for viruses or compute pollution indexes, while the cameras could be used to document a range of human behavior. This could create changes in political movements, art, and culture as everyone's experience is documented and shared.

research areas to consider

- Evgeny Morozov RSA Animate
- Smart Insights mobile marketing statistics
- The Witness Project
- Center for Embedded Networked Sensing

process

1. Divide the class into teams.
2. Research the areas cited above and devise a scenario in which mobile access could make an impact politically or environmentally, positively or negatively.
3. To set the stage for the role-playing event, team members should write a summary that provides background information for their character—for example, business owner, politician, reporter, or arbitrator—and that details their character's behaviors. Then team members should create an outline to use during the role-playing event.
4. Team members should arrange a mutually convenient time to meet for the exchange, using a virtual meeting tool or by meeting in person.
5. Team members should present their case to the class or submit a PowerPoint presentation for review by the rest of the class, along with the summary and resolution they developed.

conclusion

As technology becomes ever more prevalent and integrated into our lives, more and more ethical dilemmas will present themselves. Being able to understand and evaluate both sides of the argument, while responding in a personally or socially ethical manner, will be an important skill.

Solve This MyLab IT®
grader

Intellectual Property and Copyright Basics

You have been asked to make a presentation about intellectual property and copyright basics as they apply to digital images. The presentation is almost done, but you need to make a few adjustments. In addition, you'll need to add a few images from a website and give credit to the source.

You'll use the following PowerPoint skills as you complete this activity:

- Apply Theme
- Insert Images from Webpage
- Create and Modify SmartArt
- Apply Design Ideas
- Add and Modify Text
- Rearrange Slides
- Add New Slide
- Apply Slide Transition

Directions

1. Open TIA_Ch8_Start, and save as TIA_Ch8_LastFirst. Select slide 1, and add your first and last names as the subtitle.
2. Apply the **Berlin Theme** to the entire presentation.
   a. Hint: Click the Berlin Theme from the Themes group on the Design tab.
3. Select **Slide 2**. Click just before the second sentence beginning with *IP is considered*, and press **Enter** to create a new bullet point.
4. Create a **New Slide using Title and Content layout** (slide becomes slide 3). Enter **Examples of Intellectual Property** as the title. Insert a **Basic Block List SmartArt** diagram, and enter the following as individual items: **Books**, **Art**, **Photographs**, **Music and Songs**, **Movies and Videos**, **Patents**, **Formulas**, and **Computer Software**.
   a. Hint: Click the arrow to the left of the SmartArt diagram to open the SmartArt text pane to enter text more easily.
5. Change the color of the SmartArt to **Gradient Loop - Accent 2**, and change the color of the font to **Black, Background 1**.
6. Select **Slide 4**. Reposition the second bullet so it becomes the first bullet. Create a sub-bullet for the new second bullet and type **This includes photographs and videos posted to the Internet.** Select copyright infringement in the third bullet, and format with **Bold** and **Italics**.
7. Select **Slide 5**. Enter **Copyright Infringement and Social Media** as the slide title. Increase the font size of the bulleted text to **32**.
8. Select **Slide 6**. Change the title of the slide to **Photographic Copyrights**.
9. Select **Slide 9**. Using any browser, go to **Nasa.gov**, and click **Galleries** from the top menu, then click **Search for NASA Images**. Type **rocket**, in the search bar, then right-click any photo of a rocket and select **Copy**. **Paste** this photo on Slide 9. Repeat the procedure with a second rocket image.
10. Select an appealing layout from the Design Ideas pane.
    a. Hint: If the Design Ideas pane does not automatically display, click Design Ideas from the Designer group on the Design tab.
11. On Slide 9, insert a **Text Box** and type **Images courtesy of Nasa.gov** in the text box. Change the font to **Arial Narrow** and font size to **16**. Place the text box near the photos.
12. Move **Slide 8** so that it is the last slide of the presentation.
13. Apply the **Wipe** transition and the **From Left** effect option to **all slides**.
14. Save the file and submit for grading.

9

Securing Your System: Protecting Your Digital Data and Devices

 For a chapter overview, watch the Chapter Overview Videos.

PART 1

Threats to Your Digital Assets

Learning Outcome 9.1 **You will be able to describe hackers, viruses, and other online annoyances and the threats they pose to your digital security.**

 Identity Theft and Hackers 334

Objective 9.1 *Describe how identity theft is committed and the types of scams identity thieves perpetrate.*

Objective 9.2 *Describe the different types of hackers and the tools they use.*

 Computer Viruses 339

Objective 9.3 *Explain what a computer virus is, why it is a threat to your security, how a computing device catches a virus, and the symptoms it may display.*

Objective 9.4 *List the different categories of computer viruses, and describe their behaviors.*

Sound Byte: Protecting Your Computer

 Online Annoyances and Social Engineering 343

Objective 9.5 *Explain what malware, spam, and cookies are and how they impact your security.*

Objective 9.6 *Describe social engineering techniques, and explain strategies to avoid falling prey to them.*

Helpdesk: Threats to Your Digital Life

PART 2

Protecting Your Digital Property

Learning Outcome 9.2 **Describe various ways to protect your digital property and data from theft and corruption.**

 Restricting Access to Your Digital Assets 353

Objective 9.7 *Explain what a firewall is and how a firewall protects your computer from hackers.*

Objective 9.8 *Explain how to protect your computer from virus infection.*

Objective 9.9 *Describe how passwords and biometric characteristics can be used for user authentication.*

Objective 9.10 *Describe ways to surf the web anonymously.*

Helpdesk: Understanding Firewalls

 Keeping Your Data Safe 363

Objective 9.11 *Describe the types of information you should never share online.*

Objective 9.12 *List the various types of backups you can perform on your computing devices, and explain the various places you can store backup files.*

Sound Byte: Managing Computer Security with Windows Tools

 Protecting Your Physical Computing Assets 368

Objective 9.13 *Explain the negative effects environment and power surges can have on computing devices.*

Objective 9.14 *Describe the major concerns when a device is stolen and strategies for solving the problems.*

For the IT Simulation for this chapter, see MyLab IT.

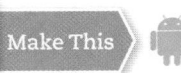 All media accompanying this chapter can be found here.

 Make: A Password Generator on **page 352**

(Robert Mizerek/Fotolia, Wk1003mike/Fotolia, Carlos Amarillo/Shutterstock, James Thew/Fotolia, Ymgerman/Fotolia, Graja/Shutterstock)

How Cool Is This?

Smartphones are now using **iris scanning** to authenticate you and log you in to your phone. Because the unique color and patterns in your iris (the colored ring that surrounds your pupil) develop at a young age and do not change over your lifetime, a scan of your eye can tell that it is you with no password to remember. Meanwhile, banks now use scanners that utilize **finger vein authentication technology**. The scanners read the unique vein patterns inside your finger to **verify your identity**. How does this improve upon fingerprint scans? Fingerprint scanning technology has flaws—impressions of your fingerprints can be left on scanner surfaces and can be duplicated to fool security devices. *(Andrea Danti/Shutterstock)*

Part 1 ▶ For an overview of this part of the chapter, watch **Chapter Overview Video 9.1**.

Threats to Your Digital Assets

Learning Outcome 9.1 **You will be able to describe hackers, viruses, and other online annoyances and the threats they pose to your digital security.**

The media is full of stories about malicious computer programs damaging computers, criminals stealing people's identities online, and attacks on corporate websites bringing major corporations to a standstill. These are examples of **cybercrime**—any criminal action perpetrated primarily through the use of a computer. Cybercriminals are individuals who use computers, networks, and the Internet to perpetrate crime. In this part of the chapter, we'll discuss the most serious types of cybercrime you need to worry about as well as some online annoyances to avoid.

Identity Theft and Hackers

Every year, the Internet Crime Complaint Center (IC3)—a partnership between the FBI and the National White Collar Crime Center (NW3C)—receives hundreds of thousands of complaints related to Internet crime. *Government impersonation scams* involve people pretending to represent official organizations, such as the FBI, the IRS, or Homeland Security, to defraud. *Non-auction/non-delivery scams* involve running auctions (or sales) of merchandise that does not really exist, wherein the perpetrators just collect funds and disappear without delivering the promised goods. *Advance fee fraud* involves convincing individuals to send money as a "good faith" gesture to enable them to receive larger payments in return. The scammers then disappear with the advance fees. *Identity theft* involves the stealing of someone's personal information for financial gain. Other complaints received involve equally serious matters such as computer intrusions (hacking), extortion, and blackmail. Figure 9.1 shows that cybercrime is more common than you may have known. In this section, we'll look at both identity theft and hacking in more detail.

Figure 9.1 **Frequency of Cybercrimes**

Identity Theft

Objective 9.1 *Describe how identity theft is committed and the types of scams identity thieves perpetrate.*

What is identity theft? **Identity theft** occurs when a thief steals personal information such as your name, address, Social Security number, birth date, bank account number, and credit card information and poses as you in financial or legal transactions. Theft of personal data such as bank account numbers and credit/debit card numbers is of most concern to individuals because this information is usually used for fraudulent purposes. Many victims of identity theft spend months, or even years, trying to repair their credit and eliminate fraudulent debts.

What types of scams do identity thieves perpetrate? The nefarious acts cover a wide range:

- Counterfeiting your existing credit and debit cards
- Requesting changes of address on your bank and credit card statements, which makes detecting fraudulent charges take longer
- Opening new credit cards and bank accounts in your name and then writing bad checks and not paying off the credit card balances (ruining your credit rating in the process)
- Obtaining medical services under your name, potentially causing you to later lose coverage if the thief's treatment exceeds the limits of your policy's covered services
- Buying a home with a mortgage in your name, then reselling the house and absconding with the money (leaving you with the debt)

Many people believe that the only way your identity can be stolen is by using a computer. However, the Federal Trade Commission (**ftc.gov**) has identified additional methods thieves use to obtain others' personal information:

- Stealing purses and wallets, in which people often keep personal information such as their ATM PIN codes
- Stealing mail or looking through trash for bank statements and credit card bills
- Posing as bank or credit card company representatives and tricking people into revealing sensitive information over the phone
- Installing skimming devices on ATM machines that record information, such as account numbers and passcodes

Although foolproof protection methods don't exist, there are precautions that will help you minimize your risk, which we'll discuss later in this chapter.

Hacking

Objective 9.2 *Describe the different types of hackers and the tools they use.*

What defines a hacker? Although there's a great deal of disagreement as to what a hacker actually is, especially among hackers themselves, a **hacker** is most commonly defined as anyone who unlawfully breaks into a computer system—either an individual computer or a network (see Figure 9.2).

Are there different kinds of hackers? Some hackers are offended by being labeled as criminals and classify different types of hackers:

- **White-hat hackers** (or **ethical hackers**) break in to systems for nonmalicious reasons, such as to test system security vulnerabilities or to expose undisclosed weaknesses. They believe in making security vulnerabilities known either to the company that owns the system or software or to the general public, often to embarrass a company into fixing a problem.
- **Black-hat hackers** break into systems to destroy information or for illegal gain. The terms white hat and black hat are references to old Western movies in which the heroes wore white hats and the outlaws wore black hats.
- **Grey-hat hackers** are a bit of a cross between black and white—they often illegally break into systems merely to flaunt their expertise to the administrator of the system they penetrated or to attempt to sell their services in repairing security breaches.

The laws in the United States consider *any* unauthorized access to computer systems a crime.

Figure 9.2 Hacking humor.
(Singer, Andy)

The 2016 election season was jarred when federal authorities found that hacker groups working for the Russian government had broken into Democratic National Committee databases, possibly in an attempt to destabilize the presidential election.

Every country collects foreign intelligence, but in the digital age, cybersecurity is increasingly important. There is an open question as to what is the best way to train and recruit talented hackers to work to increase our national cybersecurity.

Could a hacker steal my debit card or bank account number? Hackers often try to break in to computers or websites that contain credit card information. If you perform financial transactions online, such as banking or buying goods and services, you probably do so using a credit or debit card. Credit card and bank account information can thus reside on your hard drive or an online business's hard drive and may be detectable by a hacker.

Aside from your home computer, you have personal data stored on various websites. For example, many sites require that you provide a login ID and password to gain access. Even if this data isn't stored on your computer, a hacker may be able to capture it when you're online by using a *packet analyzer (sniffer)* or a *keylogger* (a program that captures all keystrokes made on a computer).

What's a packet analyzer? Data travels through the Internet in small pieces called packets. The packets are identified with an Internet Protocol (IP) address, in part to help identify the computer to which they are being sent. Once the packets reach their destination, they're reassembled into cohesive messages. A **packet analyzer (sniffer)** is a program deployed by hackers that examines each packet and can read its contents. A packet analyzer can grab all packets coming across a particular network—not just those addressed to a particular computer. For example, a hacker might sit in a coffee shop and run a packet sniffer to capture sensitive data (such as debit/credit card numbers) from patrons using the coffee shop's free wireless network. Wireless networks are vulnerable to this type of exploitation if encryption of data wasn't enabled when the networks were set up. (See Chapter 7 on how to use security protocols to set encryption on your network.)

What do hackers do with the information they "sniff"? Once a hacker has your debit/credit card information, he or she can use it to purchase items illegally or can sell the number to someone who will. If a hacker steals the login ID and password to an account where you have your bankcard information stored (such as eBay or Amazon), he or she can also use your account to buy items and have them shipped to him- or herself instead of to you. If hackers can gather enough information in conjunction with your credit card information, they may be able to commit identity theft.

Although this sounds scary, you can easily protect yourself from packet sniffing by installing a firewall and using a personal VPN to secure all the data you exchange over the Internet. (We discuss these topics later in this chapter.)

Trojan Horses and Rootkits

What other problems can hackers cause if they break into my computer? Hackers often use individuals' computers as a staging area for mischief. To commit widespread computer attacks, for example, hackers need to control many computers at the same time. To this end, hackers often use Trojan horses to install other programs on computers. A **Trojan horse** is a program that appears to be something useful or desirable, like a game or a screen saver, but while it runs it does something malicious in the background without your knowledge (see Figure 9.3).

Figure 9.3 The term *Trojan horse* derives from Greek mythology and refers to the wooden horse that the Greeks used to sneak into the city of Troy and conquer it. Therefore, computer programs that contain a hidden, and usually dreadful, "surprise" are referred to as Trojan horses. *(Ralf Kraft/Fotolia)*

What damage can Trojan horses do? Often, the malicious activity perpetrated by a Trojan horse program is the installation of a backdoor program or a rootkit. **Backdoor programs** and **rootkits** are programs (or sets of programs) that allow hackers to gain access to your computer and take almost complete control of it without your knowledge. Using a backdoor program, hackers can access and delete all the files on your computer, send e-mail, run programs, and do just about anything else you can do with your computer. A computer that a hacker controls in this manner is referred to as a **zombie**. Zombies are often used to launch denial-of-service attacks on other computers.

Denial-of-Service Attacks

What are denial-of-service attacks? In a **denial-of-service (DoS) attack**, legitimate users are denied access to a computer system because a hacker is repeatedly making requests of that computer system through a computer he or she has taken over as a zombie. A computer system can handle only a certain number of requests for information at one time. When it's flooded with requests in a DoS attack, it shuts down and refuses to answer any requests, even if the requests are from a legitimate user. Thus, the computer is so busy responding to the bogus requests for information that authorized users can't gain access.

Could a DoS attack be traced back to the computer that launched it? Yes, launching a DoS attack on a computer system from a single computer is easy to trace. Therefore, most savvy hackers use a **distributed denial-of-service (DDoS) attack**, which launches DoS attacks from more than one zombie (sometimes thousands of zombies) at the same time.

Figure 9.4 illustrates how a DDoS attack works. A hacker creates many zombies and coordinates them so that they begin sending bogus requests to the same computer at the same time. Administrators of the victim computer often have a great deal of difficulty stopping the attack because it comes from so many computers. Often, the attacks are coordinated automatically by botnets. A **botnet** is a large group of software programs (called robots or bots) that runs autonomously on zombie computers. Some botnets have been known to span millions of computers.

Because many commercial websites receive revenue from users, either directly (such as via subscriptions to online games) or indirectly (such as when web surfers click on advertisements), DDoS attacks can be financially distressing for the owners of the affected websites.

Figure 9.4 Zombie computers are used to facilitate a DDoS attack. *(Vovan/Shutterstock, nico_blue/E+/Getty Images, Juffin/ DigitalVision Vectors/Getty images)*

How does a hacker gain access to a computer? Hackers can gain access to computers directly or indirectly. Direct access involves sitting down at a computer and installing hacking software. It's unlikely that such an attack would occur in your home, but it's always a wise precaution to set up your computer so that it requires a password for a user to gain access.

Indirect access involves subtler methods. Many professional hackers use exploit kits. **Exploit kits** are software programs that run on servers and search for vulnerabilities of computers that visit the server. Exploit kits look for security holes in browsers and operating systems that haven't yet been patched by the users. When they detect a vulnerability, they can deliver spyware, bots, backdoor programs, or other malicious software to your computer. Fortunately, most exploit kits take advantage of known vulnerabilities, so if your antivirus software and operating system are up to date, you should be secure. We'll discuss both of these topics later in the chapter.

Hackers also can access a computer indirectly through its Internet connection. Many people forget that their Internet connection is a two-way street. Not only can you access the Internet, but also people on the Internet can access your computer. Think of your computer as a house. Common sense tells you to lock your home's doors and windows to deter theft when you aren't there. Hooking your computer up to the Internet without protection is like leaving the front door to your house wide open. Your computer obviously doesn't have doors and windows, but it does have logical ports.

What are logical ports? You already know what physical ports are: You use them to attach peripherals, as when you plug your USB flash drive into a USB port. **Logical ports** are virtual—that is, not physical —communications paths. Unlike physical ports, you can't see or touch a logical port; it's part of a computer's internal organization. Logical ports allow a computer to organize requests for information. So all information arriving from another computer or network that's related to e-mail will be sent to the logical port associated with e-mail.

Logical ports are numbered and assigned to specific services. For instance, logical port 80 is designated for hypertext transfer protocol (HTTP), the main communications protocol for the web. Thus, all requests for information from your browser to the web flow through logical port 80. Open logical ports, like open windows in a home, invite intruders, as illustrated in Figure 9.5. Unless you take precautions to restrict access to your logical ports, other people on the Internet may be able to access your computer through them. Fortunately, you can thwart most hacking problems by installing a firewall, which we discuss later in the chapter.

FTP (port 21)

E-mail (port 25)

HTTP (port 80)

DNS (port 53)

Telnet (port 23)

WEBSITE REQUEST

Figure 9.5 Open logical ports are an invitation to hackers.

Computer Viruses

Creating and disseminating computer viruses is one of the most widespread types of cybercrimes. Some viruses cause only minor annoyances, whereas others cause destruction or theft of data. Many viruses are designed to gather sensitive information such as credit card numbers.

Virus Basics

Objective 9.3 *Explain what a computer virus is, why it is a threat to your security, how a computing device catches a virus, and the symptoms it may display.*

What is a computer virus? A computer **virus** is a computer program that attaches itself to another computer program (known as the *host* program) and attempts to spread to other computers when files are exchanged. That behavior is very similar to how biological viruses spread, giving this type of threat its name.

What does a computer virus do? A computer virus's main purpose is to replicate itself and copy its code into as many other host files as possible. This gives the virus a greater chance of being copied to another computer system so that it can spread its infection. However, computer viruses require human interaction to spread. Although there might be a virus in a file on your computer, a virus normally can't infect your computer until the infected file is opened or executed.

Why are viruses such a threat to my security? Although virus replication can slow down networks, it's not usually the main threat. The majority of viruses have secondary objectives or side effects, ranging from displaying annoying messages on the computer screen to destroying files or the contents of entire hard drives.

Computer viruses are engineered to evade detection. Viruses normally attempt to hide within the code of a host program to avoid detection. And viruses are not just limited to computers. Smartphones, tablet computers, and other devices can be infected with viruses. Viruses exist that trick users into downloading an infected file to their phones, and then steal their online banking information.

How does my computer catch a virus? If your computer is exposed to a file infected with a virus, the virus will try to copy itself and infect a file on your computer.

Downloading infected audio and video files from peer-to-peer file-sharing sites is a major source of virus infections. Shared flash drives are also a common source of virus infection, as is e-mail. Just opening an e-mail message usually won't infect your computer with a virus, although some new viruses are launched when viewed in the preview pane of your e-mail software. Downloading and running (executing) a file that's attached to the e-mail are common ways that your computer becomes infected. Thus, be extremely wary of e-mail attachments, especially if you don't know the sender. Figure 9.6 illustrates the steps by which computer viruses are often passed from one computer to the next:

1. An individual writes a virus program, attaches it to a music file, and posts the file to a file-sharing site.
2. Unsuspecting Tony downloads the "music file" and infects his computer when he listens to the song.
3. Tony sends his friend Amit an e-mail with the infected "music file" and contaminates Amit's tablet.
4. Amit syncs his phone with his tablet and infects his phone when he plays the music file.
5. Amit e-mails the file from his phone to Lily, one of his colleagues at work. Everyone who copies files from Lily's infected work computer, or whose computer is networked to Lily's computer, risks spreading the virus.

I have an Apple computer, so I don't need to worry about viruses, do I? This is a popular misconception! Everyone, even Apple users, needs to worry about viruses. As the macOS operating system has gained market share, the number of virus attacks against it is on the rise.

STEP 1: Virus creation

STEP 2: Initial virus infection

Hacker's computer

File-sharing server

Tony's computer

STEP 3: Virus spreads to another computer

Amit's smartphone

STEP 4: Amit infects his cell phone

Amit's tablet

Lily's work computer

STEP 5: Other computers susceptible to infection

Figure 9.6 Computer viruses are passed from one unsuspecting user to the next. *(Juffin/DigitalVision Vectors/Getty Images; Stanca Sanda/Alamy Stock Photo; Ian Dagnall/Alamy Stock Photo; Denis Rozhnovsky/Alamy Stock Photo)*

Sound Byte MyLab IT®

Protecting Your Computer

In this Sound Byte, you'll learn how to use a variety of tools to protect your computer, including antivirus software and Windows utilities.

How can I tell if my computer is infected with a virus? Sometimes it can be difficult to definitively tell whether your computer is infected with a virus. However, if your computer displays any of the following symptoms, it may be infected with a virus:

• Existing program icons or files suddenly disappear. Viruses often delete specific file types or programs.
• You start your browser and it takes you to an unusual home page (i.e., one you didn't set) or it has new toolbars.
• Odd messages, pop-ups, or images are displayed on the screen, or strange music or sounds play.
• Data files become corrupt. (However, note that files can become corrupt for reasons other than a virus infection.)
• Programs stop working properly, which could be caused by either a corrupted file or a virus.
• Your system shuts down unexpectedly, slows down, or takes a long time to boot up.

Can I get a virus on my smartphone? Viruses can indeed infect smartphones. Over half of users say they send confidential e-mails using their phones, and one-third of users access bank account or credit card information on their phones, so smartphones are the next most likely realm of attack by cybercriminals. Although viruses plaguing smartphones have not yet reached the volume of viruses attacking PC operating systems, with the proliferation of mobile devices, virus attacks are expected to increase.

Kaspersky and McAfee are among the leading companies currently providing antivirus software for mobile devices. Products are designed for specific operating systems; for example, Kaspersky Mobile Security has versions for Android phones and tablets and Windows phones. Often, businesses will have their information technology department install and configure an antivirus solution like this for all the phones used in the organization.

If no antivirus program is available for your phone's OS, the best precautions are commonsense ones. Check the phone manufacturer's website frequently to see whether your smartphone needs any software upgrades that could patch security holes. In addition, remember that you shouldn't download ring tones, games, or other software from unfamiliar websites.

Types of Viruses

Objective 9.4 *List the different categories of computer viruses, and describe their behaviors.*

What types of viruses exist? Although thousands of computer viruses and variants exist, they can be grouped into broad categories based on their behavior and method of transmission.

Boot-Sector Viruses

What are boot-sector viruses? A **boot-sector virus** replicates itself onto a hard drive's master boot record. The **master boot record** is a program that executes whenever a computer boots up, ensuring that the virus will be loaded into memory immediately, even before some virus protection programs can load. Boot-sector viruses are often transmitted by an infected flash drive left in a USB port. When the computer boots up with the flash drive connected, the computer tries to launch a master boot record from the flash drive, which is usually the trigger for the virus to infect the hard drive.

Logic Bombs and Time Bombs

What are logic bombs and time bombs? A **logic bomb** is a virus that is triggered when certain logical conditions are met, such as opening a file or starting a program a certain number of times. A **time bomb** is a virus that is triggered by the passage of time or on a certain date. For example, the Michelangelo virus was a famous time bomb that was set to trigger every year on March 6, Michelangelo's birthday. The effects of logic bombs and time bombs range from the display of annoying messages on the screen to the reformatting of the hard drive, which causes complete data loss.

Worms

What is a worm? Although often called a virus, a **worm** is subtly different. Viruses require human interaction to spread, whereas worms take advantage of file transport methods, such as e-mail or network connections, to spread on their own. A virus infects a host file and waits until that file is executed to replicate and infect a computer system. A worm, however, works independently of host file execution and is much more active in spreading itself. Some worms even attack peripheral devices such as routers. Worms can generate a lot of data traffic when trying to spread, which can slow down the Internet.

Script and Macro Viruses

What are script and macro viruses? Some viruses are hidden on websites in the form of scripts. A **script** is a series of commands—actually, a miniprogram—that is executed without your knowledge. Scripts are often used to perform useful, legitimate functions on websites, such as collecting name and address information from customers. However, some scripts are malicious. For example, you might click a link to display a video on a website, which causes a script to run that infects your computer with a virus.

A **macro virus** is a virus that attaches itself to a document that uses macros. A macro is a short series of commands that usually automates repetitive tasks. However, macro languages are now so sophisticated that viruses can be written with them. The Melissa virus became the first major macro virus to cause problems worldwide.

E-Mail Viruses

What is an e-mail virus? In addition to being a macro virus, the Melissa virus was the first practical example of an e-mail virus. **E-mail viruses** use the address book in the victim's e-mail system to distribute the virus. In the case of the Melissa virus, anyone opening an infected document triggered the virus, which infected other documents on the victim's computer. Once triggered, the Melissa virus sent itself to the first 50 people in the e-mail address book on the infected computer.

Encryption Viruses

What are encryption viruses? When **encryption viruses** (also known as ransomware) infect your computer, they run a program that searches for common types of data files, such as Microsoft

Figure 9.7   Major Categories of Viruses

Boot-sector Viruses	Logic Bombs/Time Bombs	Worms
Execute when a computer boots up	Execute when certain conditions or dates are reached	Spread on their own with no human interaction needed
Script and Macro Viruses	E-mail Viruses	Encryption Viruses
Series of commands with malicious intent	Spread as attachments to e-mail, often using address books	Hold files "hostage" by encrypting them; ask for ransom to unlock them

Word files, and compresses them using a complex encryption key that renders your files unusable. You then receive a message that asks you to send payment to an account if you want to receive the program to decrypt your files. The flaw with this type of virus, which keeps it from being widespread, is that law enforcement officials can trace the payments to an account and may possibly be able to catch the perpetrators. Figure 9.7 summarizes the major categories of viruses.

Additional Virus Classifications

How else are viruses classified? Viruses can also be classified by the methods they take to avoid detection by antivirus software:

- A **polymorphic virus** changes its own code or periodically rewrites itself to avoid detection. Most polymorphic viruses infect a particular type of file such as .EXE files, for example.
- A **multipartite virus** is designed to infect multiple file types in an effort to fool the antivirus software that is looking for it.
- **Stealth viruses** temporarily erase their code from the files where they reside and then hide in the active memory of the computer. This helps them avoid detection if only the hard drive is being searched for viruses. Fortunately, current antivirus software scans memory as well as the hard drive.

Online Annoyances and Social Engineering

Surfing the web, using social networks, and sending and receiving e-mail have become common parts of most of our lives. Unfortunately, the web has become fertile ground for people who want to advertise their products, track our browsing behaviors, or even con people into revealing personal information. In this section, we'll look at ways in which you can manage, if not avoid, these and other online headaches.

Online Annoyances

Objective 9.5 *Explain what malware, spam, and cookies are and how they impact your security.*

Malware

What is malware? **Malware** is software that has a malicious intent (hence the prefix *mal*). There are three primary forms of malware: adware, spyware, and viruses. Adware and spyware are not physically destructive like viruses and worms, which can destroy data. Known collectively as *grayware*, most malware consists of intrusive, annoying, or objectionable online programs that are downloaded to your computer when you install or use other online content such as a free program, game, or utility.

What is adware? **Adware** is software that displays sponsored advertisements in a section of your browser window or as a pop-up box. It's considered a legitimate, though sometimes annoying, means of generating revenue for those developers who don't charge for their software or information. Fortunately, because web browsers such as Safari, Chrome, and Edge have built-in pop-up blockers, the occurrence of annoying pop-ups has been greatly reduced.

Some pop-ups, however, are legitimate and increase the functionality of the originating site. For example, your account balance may pop up on your bank's website. To control which sites to allow pop-ups on, you can access the pop-up blocker settings in your browser (see Figure 9.8) and add websites for which you allow pop-ups. Whenever a pop-up is blocked, the browser displays an information bar or plays a sound to alert you. If you feel the pop-up is legitimate, you can choose to accept it.

What is spyware? **Spyware** is an unwanted piggyback program that usually downloads with other software you install from the Internet and that runs in the background of your system. Without your knowledge, spyware transmits information about you, such as your Internet-surfing habits, to the owner of the program so that the information can be used for marketing purposes.

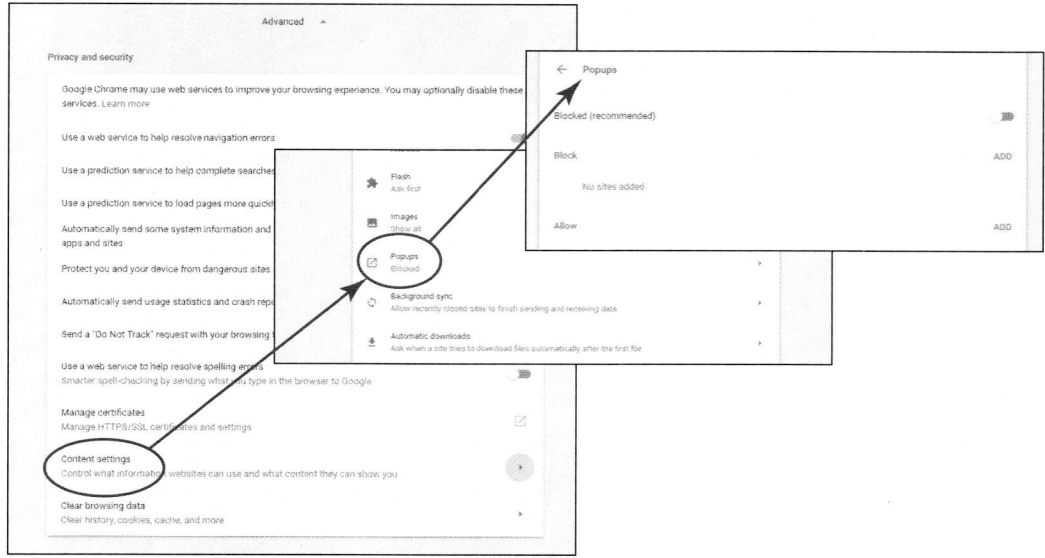

Figure 9.8 Chrome allows you to customize how you manage pop-ups.
> *To display the pop-up management in Chrome, click* **Settings,** *then click* **Advanced,** *then from the* **Privacy and security** *group, select* **Content settings,** *and customize the choices in* **Popups***. (Courtesy Google Inc.)*

Many spyware programs use tracking cookies (small text files stored on your computer) to collect information. One type of spyware program known as a **keystroke logger (keylogger)** monitors keystrokes with the intent of stealing passwords, login IDs, or credit card information.

Can I prevent spyware from spying on me? Anti-spyware software detects unwanted programs and allows you to delete the offending software easily. Most Internet security suites now include anti-spyware software. Because so many variants of spyware exist, your Internet security software may not detect all types that attempt to install themselves on your computer. Therefore, it's a good idea to install one or two additional stand-alone anti-spyware programs on your computer.

Because new spyware is created all the time, you should update and run your anti-spyware software regularly. Windows comes with a program called Windows Defender, which scans your system for spyware and other potentially unwanted software. Malwarebytes Anti-Malware, Ad-Aware, and Spybot - Search & Destroy are other anti-spyware programs that are easy to install and update. Figure 9.9 shows an example of Windows Defender in action.

Spam

How can I best avoid spam? Companies that send out **spam**—unwanted or junk e-mail—find your e-mail address either from a list they purchase or with software that looks for e-mail addresses on the Internet. Unsolicited instant messages are also a form of spam, called spim. If you've used your e-mail address to purchase anything online, open an online account, or participate in a social network such as Facebook, your e-mail address eventually will appear on one of the lists that spammers get.

One way to avoid spam in your primary account is to create a secondary e-mail address that you use only when you fill out forms or buy items on the web. If your secondary e-mail account is saturated with spam, you can abandon that account with little inconvenience. It's much less convenient to abandon your primary e-mail address.

Another way to avoid spam is to filter it. A **spam filter** is an option you can select in your e-mail account that places known or suspected spam messages into a special folder (called "Spam" or "Junk Mail"). Most e-mail services, such as Gmail and Outlook, offer spam filters (see Figure 9.10).

How do spam filters work? Spam filters and filtering software can catch as much as 95% of spam by checking incoming e-mail subject headers and senders' addresses against databases of known spam. Spam filters also check your e-mail for frequently used spam patterns and keywords,

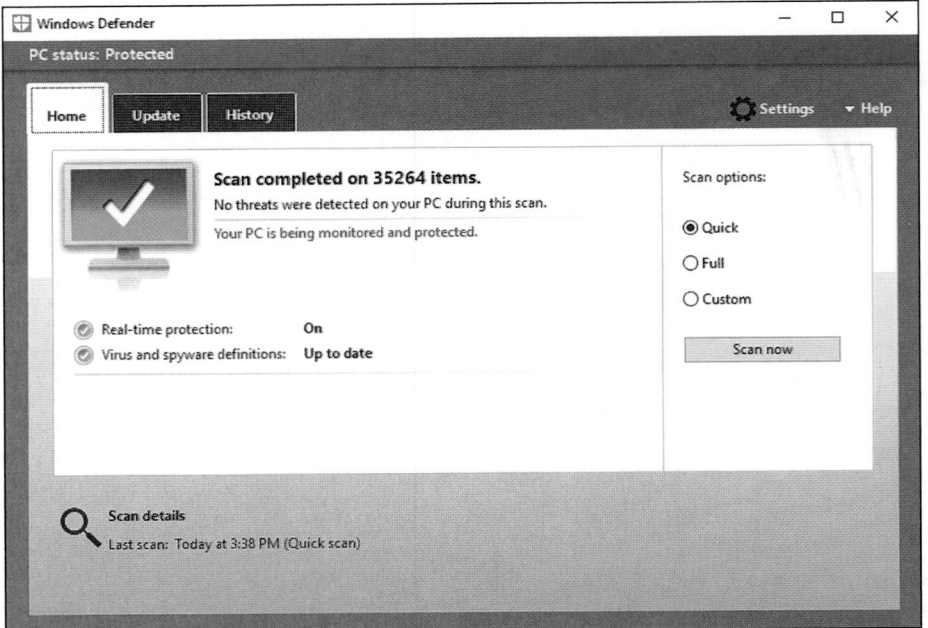

Figure 9.9 Routine scans of a computer by Windows Defender will detect and eliminate spyware and other unwanted types of software. (*Microsoft Windows Defender, Microsoft Corporation.*)

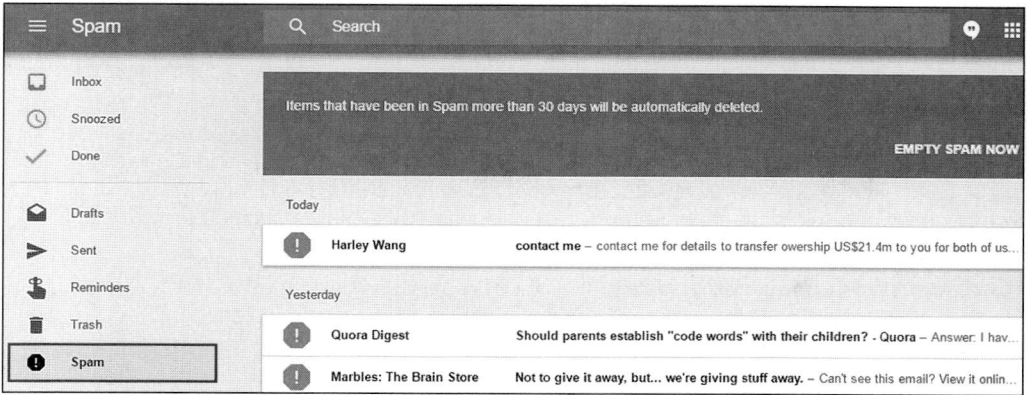

Figure 9.10 In Google Inbox, messages identified as spam are directed into a folder called "Spam" for review and deletion. *(Courtesy Google Inc.)*

such as "for free" and "over 21." Spam filters aren't perfect, and you should check the spam folder before deleting its contents because legitimate e-mail might end up there by mistake. Most programs let you reclassify e-mails that have been misidentified as spam.

How else can I prevent spam? Before registering on a website, read its privacy policy to see how it uses your e-mail address. Don't give the site permission to pass on your e-mail address to third parties. Another strategy is to make sure you don't reply to spam to remove yourself from the spam list. By replying, you're confirming that your e-mail address is active. Instead of stopping spam, you may receive more.

Cookies

What are cookies? Cookies are small text files that some websites automatically store on your hard drive when you visit them. When you log on to a website that uses cookies, a cookie file assigns an ID number to your computer. The unique ID is intended to make your return visit to a website more efficient and better geared to your interests. The next time you log on to that site, the site marks your visit and keeps track of it in its database.

What do websites do with cookie information? Cookies can provide websites with information about your browsing habits, such as the ads you've opened, the products you've looked at, and the time and duration of your visits. Companies use this information to determine the traffic flowing through their website and the effectiveness of their marketing strategy and placement on websites. By tracking such information, cookies enable companies to identify different users' preferences.

Can companies get my personal information when I visit their sites? Cookies do not go through your hard drive in search of personal information such as passwords or financial data. The only personal information a cookie obtains is the information you supply when you fill out forms online.

Do privacy risks exist with cookies? Some sites sell the personal information their cookies collect to web advertisers who are building huge databases of consumer preferences and habits, collecting personal and business information such as phone numbers, credit reports, and the like. The main concern is that advertisers will use this information indiscriminately, thus invading your privacy. And you may feel your privacy is being violated by cookies that monitor where you go on a website.

Should I delete cookies from my hard drive? Cookies pose no security threat because it's virtually impossible to hide a virus or malicious software program in a cookie. Because they take up little room on your hard drive and offer you small conveniences on return visits to websites, there is no great reason to delete them. Deleting your cookie files could actually cause you the inconvenience of reentering data you've already entered into website forms. However, if you're uncomfortable with the accessibility of your personal information, you can periodically delete cookies (as shown in Figure 9.11) or configure your browser to block certain types of cookies.

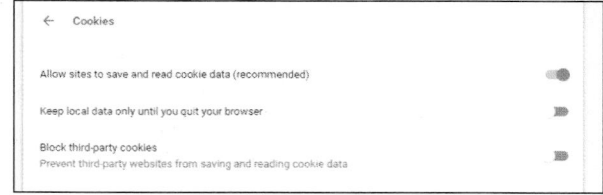

Figure 9.11 Tools are available in your browser (Chrome is shown here) to distinguish between cookies you want to keep and cookies you don't want on your system.
> *From Chrome **Settings**, click **Advanced**. Then in the **Privacy and security** block, click the **Content settings** . . . button. The **Cookies** block allows you to set cookie-handling preferences. (Courtesy Google Inc.)*

Social Engineering

Objective 9.6 *Describe social engineering techniques, and explain strategies to avoid falling prey to them.*

What is social engineering? **Social engineering** is any technique that uses social skills to generate human interaction that entices individuals to reveal sensitive information. Social engineering often doesn't involve the use of a computer or face-to-face interaction. For example, telephone scams are a common form of social engineering because it's often easier to manipulate someone when you don't have to look at them.

How does social engineering work? Most social engineering schemes use a pretext to lure their victims. **Pretexting** involves creating a scenario that sounds legitimate enough that someone will trust you. For example, you might receive a phone call during which the caller says he is from your bank and that someone tried to use your account without authorization. The caller then tells you he needs to confirm a few personal details such as your birth date, Social Security number, bank account number, and whatever other information he can get out of you. The information he obtains can then be used to empty your bank account or commit some other form of fraud. The most common form of pretexting in cyberspace is phishing.

Phishing and Pharming

How are phishing schemes conducted? **Phishing** (pronounced "fishing") lures Internet users to reveal personal information such as credit card numbers, Social Security numbers, or passwords that could lead to identity theft. The scammers send e-mail messages that look like they're from a legitimate business such as a bank. The e-mail usually states that the recipient needs to update or confirm his or her account information. When the recipient clicks on the provided link, they go to a website. The site looks like a legitimate site but is really a fraudulent copy that the scammer has created. Once the e-mail recipient enters his or her personal information, the scammers capture it and can begin using it.

Is pharming a type of phishing scam? Pharming is much more insidious than phishing. Phishing requires a positive action by the person being scammed, such as going to a website mentioned in an e-mail and typing in personal information. **Pharming** occurs when malicious code is planted on your computer, either by viruses or by your visiting malicious websites, which then alters your browser's ability to find web addresses. Users are directed to bogus websites even when they enter the correct address of the real website. You end up at a fake website that looks legitimate but is expressly set up for the purpose of gathering information.

How can I avoid being caught by phishing and pharming scams? Follow these guidelines to avoid falling prey to such schemes:

- Never reply directly to any e-mail asking you for personal information.
- Don't click on a link in an e-mail to go to a website. Instead, type the website address in the browser.
- Check with the company asking for the information and only give the information if you're certain it's needed.
- Never give personal information over the Internet unless you know the site is secure. Look for the closed padlock, https, or a certification seal such as Norton Secured to help reassure you that the site is secure.

Bits&Bytes | I Received a Data Breach Letter ... Now What?

Data breaches are becoming more common, and companies that are the subject of data breaches now routinely notify customers of data breaches—usually by physical letter, but sometimes via e-mail. Here's what you should do if you receive such a letter:

1. Take it seriously. Quite often the recipients of these letters become the victim of identity theft.
2. Contact one of the three big credit bureaus (Equifax, Experian, and TransUnion) and have a fraud alert put on your credit report. This alerts people accessing your credit report that your identity information has been stolen and that the person who is applying for credit in your name might be an imposter.

3. For even better security, contact all three credit bureaus and have a credit freeze put on your credit reports. This prevents anyone (even you) from getting credit in your name. You can always unfreeze your accounts later if you need to apply for credit yourself.
4. Review your credit reports regularly. You are entitled to one free credit report per year from each of the three big agencies. Go to **annualcreditreport.com** and request a report from one of the agencies. Repeat the process every four months from a different agency. Review the reports for any suspicious activity.

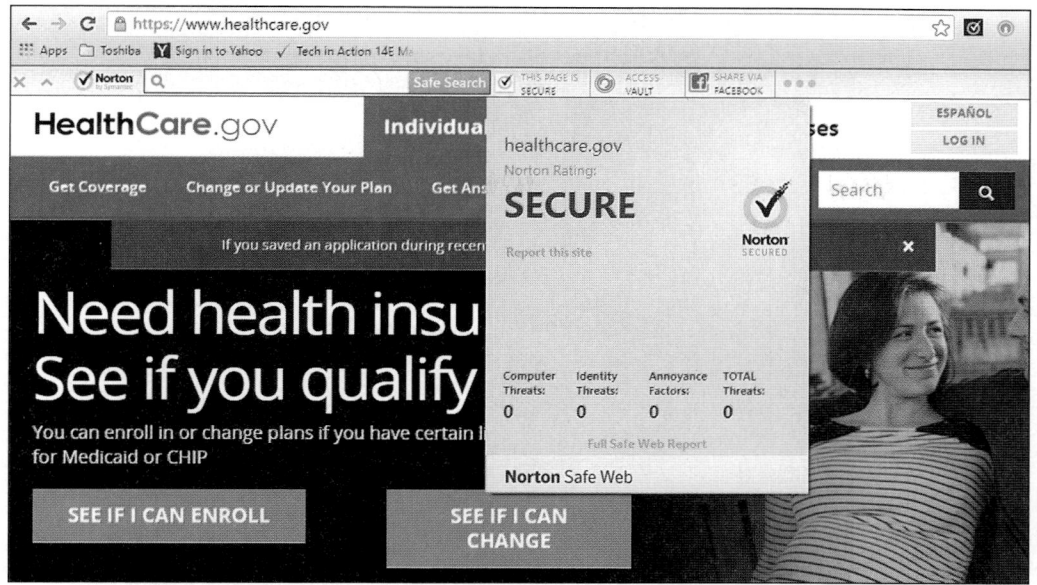

Figure 9.12 Not sure whether you're on the Healthcare.gov website or a cleverly disguised phishing site? Norton Safe Web reassures you that all is well. *(U.S. Centers for Medicare & Medicaid Services)*

- Use phishing filters. The latest versions of Safari, Chrome, and Edge have phishing filters built in, so each time you access a website, the phishing filter checks for the site's legitimacy and warns you of possible web forgeries.
- Use Internet security software on your computer that's constantly being updated.

Most Internet security packages can detect and prevent pharming attacks. The major Internet security packages—for example, McAfee and Norton (see Figure 9.12)—also offer phishing-protection tools. When you have the Norton Toolbar displayed in your browser, you're constantly informed about the legitimacy of the site you are visiting.

Scareware

What is scareware? **Scareware** is a type of malware that downloads onto your computer and tries to convince you that your computer is infected with a virus or other type of malware. Pop-ups, banners, or other annoying types of messages will flash on your screen, saying frightening things like "Your computer is infected with a virus ... immediate removal is required." You're then directed to a website where you can buy fake removal or antivirus tools that provide little or no value. Some scareware even goes so far as to encrypt your files and then demand that you pay to have them unencrypted, which is essentially extortion. In 2017, an international cyberattack like this hit hospitals and businesses in 99 countries at the same time (see Figure 9.13).

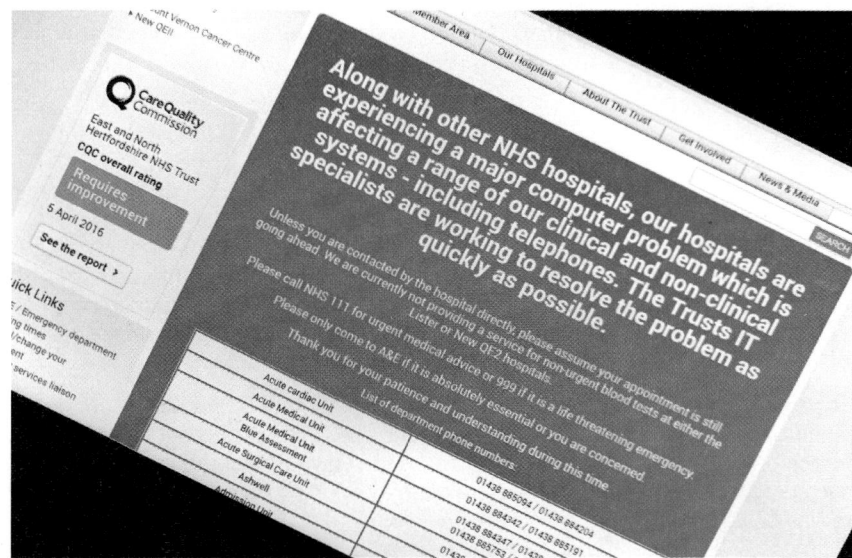

Figure 9.13 In 2017, a massive ransomware attack hit hospitals, businesses, and universities in 99 countries. *(Jeffrey Blackler/Alamy Stock Photo)*

Ethics in IT

You're Being Watched ... But Are You Aware You're Being Watched?

Think you aren't being closely watched by your employer? Think again. A recent survey of employers by the American Management Association and the ePolicy Institute revealed that, of the employers surveyed:

- 73% monitored e-mail messages
- 66% monitored web surfing
- 48% monitored activities using video surveillance
- 45% monitored keystrokes and keyboard time
- 43% monitored computer files in some other fashion

As you can see, there is a high probability that you're being monitored while you work and when you access the Internet via your employer's Internet connection.

The two most frequently cited reasons for employee monitoring are to prevent theft and to measure productivity. Monitoring for theft isn't new—monitoring cameras have been around for years, and productivity monitoring has been used for assembly line workers for decades. However, the Internet has led to a new type of productivity drain of concern to employers. **Cyberloafing** (or **cyberslacking**) means using your computer for nonwork activities while you're being paid to do your job. Examples of cyberloafing activities include playing games and using social networks. Some employees even do multiple nonwork tasks at the same time, which is known as *multishirking*. Estimates of business productivity losses due to cyberloafing top $50 billion annually.

Do you have a right to privacy in the workplace? Laws such as the 1986 Electronic Communications Privacy Act (ECPA), which prohibits unauthorized monitoring of electronic communications, have been interpreted by the courts in favor of employers. The bottom line is that employers who pay for equipment and software have the *legal* right to monitor their usage (see Figure 9.14).

Figure 9.14 It's legal for employers to monitor your computer usage.

(Beatriz J Gascon/Shutterstock)

So, is it *ethical* for employers to monitor their employees? Certainly, it seems fair that employers ensure they're not the victims of theft and that they're getting a fair day's work from their employees, just as employees have an obligation to provide a fair effort for a fair wage. The ethical issue is whether employees are adequately informed of monitoring policies. Employers have an ethical responsibility (and a legal one as well, depending on the jurisdiction) not to place monitoring devices in sensitive locations such as bathrooms and dressing areas. However, in many states, the employer does not legally need to inform employees in advance that they're being monitored. Conscientious employers include monitoring disclosures in published employee policies to avoid confusion and conflict.

The bottom line? Because employers may have a legal right to monitor you in the workplace, operate under the assumption that everything you do on your work computer is subject to scrutiny and behave accordingly.

Helpdesk · MyLab IT®

Threats to Your Digital Life

In this Helpdesk, you'll play the role of a helpdesk staffer, fielding calls about identity theft, computer viruses, and malware.

Scareware is a social engineering technique because it uses people's fear of computer viruses to convince them to part with their money. Scareware is often designed to be extremely difficult to remove from your computer and to interfere with the operation of legitimate security software. Scareware is usually downloaded onto your computer from infected websites or Trojan horse files.

How do I protect myself against scareware? Most Internet security suites, antivirus, and anti-malware software packages now detect and prevent the installation of scareware. But make sure you never click on website banners or pop-up boxes that say "Your computer might be infected, click here to scan your files" because these are often the starting points for installing malicious scareware files on your computer.

Most people have vast amounts of personal data residing in the databases of the various companies with which they conduct business. **Amazon.com** has your credit card and address information. Your bank has your Social Security number, birth date, and financial records. Your local supermarket probably has your e-mail address from when you joined its loyalty club to receive grocery discounts. All this data in various places puts you at risk when companies responsible for keeping your data confidential suffer a data breach.

A **data breach** occurs when sensitive or confidential information is copied, transmitted, or viewed by an individual who isn't authorized to handle the data. Data breaches can be intentional or unintentional. Intentional data breaches occur when hackers break into digital systems to steal sensitive data. Unintentional data breaches occur when companies controlling data inadvertently allow it to be seen by unauthorized parties, usually due to some breakdown in security procedures or precautions.

Unfortunately, data breaches appear to be quite common, as there always seems to be another one in the news. Thousands of data breaches a year are reported by U.S. companies. Over a hundred million records are exposed in a typical year. These breaches pose serious risks to the individuals whose data has been compromised, even if financial data is not involved. The data thieves now have the basis with which to launch targeted social engineering attacks even if they just have contact information, such as e-mail addresses.

With regular phishing techniques, cybercriminals just send out e-mails to a wide list of e-mail addresses, whether they have a relationship with the company or not. For example, a criminal might send out a general phishing e-mail claiming that a person's Citibank checking account had been breached. People receiving this e-mail who don't have any accounts at Citibank should immediately realize this is a phishing attack and ignore the instructions to divulge sensitive data.

But when cybercriminals obtain data on individuals that includes information about which companies those individuals have a relationship with, they can engage in much more targeted attacks known as **spear phishing** (see Figure 9.15). Spear phishing e-mails are sent to people known to be customers of a company and have a much greater chance of successfully getting individuals to reveal sensitive data. If cybercriminals obtain

Figure 9.15 Not that kind of fishing! Spear phishing is a targeted type of social engineering. *(Ehrlif/Shutterstock)*

a list of e-mail addresses of customers from Barclays Bank, for example, they can ensure that the spear phishing e-mails purport to come from Barclays and will include the customer's full name. This type of attack is much more likely to succeed in fooling people than just random e-mails sent out to thousands of people who might not have a relationship with the company mentioned in the phishing letter.

So how can you protect yourself after a data breach? You need to be extra suspicious of any e-mail correspondence from companies involved in the data breach. Companies usually never contact you by e-mail or phone asking you to reveal sensitive information or reactivate your online account by entering confidential information. Usually, these requests come via regular snail mail.

If you receive any e-mails or phone calls from companies you deal with purporting to have problems with your accounts, your best course of action is to delete the e-mail or hang up the phone. Then contact the company that supposedly has the problem by a phone number that you look up yourself either in legitimate correspondence from the company (say, the toll-free number on your credit card statement) or in the phone book. The representatives from your company can quickly tell if a real problem exists or if you were about to be the victim of a scam.

Before moving on to Part 2:

1. ▶ Watch Chapter Overview Video 9.1.
2. Then take the Check Your Understanding quiz.

Check Your Understanding // Review & Practice

For a quick review to see what you've learned so far, answer the following questions.

multiple choice

1. When a hacker steals personal information with the intent of impersonating another individual to commit fraud, it is known as

   a. impersonation theft.

   b. identity theft.

   c. scareware theft.

   d. malware theft.

2. An attack that renders a computer unable to respond to legitimate users because it is being bombarded with data requests is known as a _____ attack.

   a. stealth

   b. backdoor

   c. denial-of-service

   d. scareware

3. A computer virus is like a biological virus because

   a. it attaches to a host and then spreads to other victims.

   b. they can both be difficult to exterminate.

   c. they are easy to catch.

   d. all of the above

4. A series of commands that are executed without your knowledge is a typical attribute of a(n) _____ virus.

   a. script

   b. boot-sector

   c. time bomb

   d. encryption

5. Software that pretends your computer is infected with a virus to entice you into spending money on a solution is known as

   a. trackingware.

   b. spyware.

   c. adware.

   d. scareware.

 Go to **MyLab IT** to take an autograded version of the *Check Your Understanding* review and to find all media resources for the chapter.

TechBytes Weekly   Go to TechBytes Weekly for current technology news and discussion questions!

Testing Your Network Security

A properly installed firewall should keep you relatively safe from hackers. But how do you know if your computer system is safe? Many websites help test your security. In this exercise, we'll use tools provided by Gibson Research Corporation (**grc.com**) to test the strength of your protection.

Step 1 Open a web browser and navigate to **grc.com**. From the pull-down Services menu at the top of the screen, select **ShieldsUP!** On the ShieldsUP! welcome screen, click the **Proceed button**.

Step 2 Click the **Common Ports link** to begin the security test. It will take a few moments for the results to appear, depending on the speed of your Internet connection.

Step 3 You'll now see a report showing your computer's status on the TruStealth analysis test. If you passed, it means that your computer is very safe from attack. However, don't panic if your results say **failed for true stealth analysis**. Consider these common issues:

- A common failure on the TruStealth test is ping reply. This means GRC attempted to contact your computer using a method called ping and it replied to the GRC computer. This is not a serious problem. It just means it's a little easier for a hacker to tell your computer network exists, but that doesn't mean that a hacker can break in. Often, your ISP will insist that your home modem be configured to reply to ping requests to help them run remote diagnostics if there is ever a problem with your modem. As long as your ports are closed (or stealthed), your system should still be secure.
- As long as all ports are either stealth or closed, you're well protected. For the TruStealth analysis, though, if ports are only closed (not stealthed) the report will result in a failure. Only if some ports report as being open do you have to worry that your computer is exposed to hackers. Consult your firewall documentation to resolve the problem.

(Gibson Research Corporation)

Make This > AI TinyDB

Make: A Password Generator

Want to make sure your passwords are randomly selected so they are more secure, but afraid you'll forget what you chose?

In this exercise, you'll continue your mobile app development by using the TinyDB component in **App Inventor** to store information on your phone so it can be recalled by your application the next time it runs. This is called data persistence, and as you'll see, it is very easy to do!

The TinyDB component allows you to store data on your device to use the next time the app opens.

(Copyright MIT, used with permission)

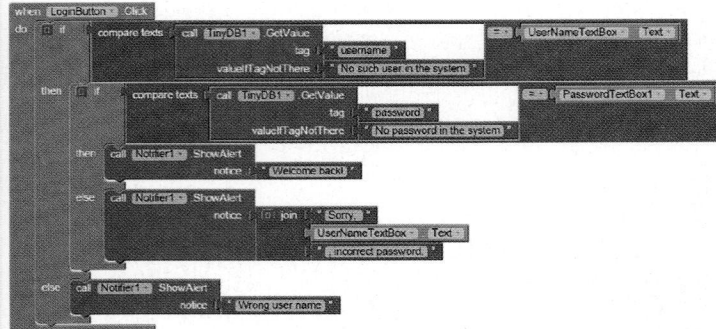

(Copyright MIT, used with permission)

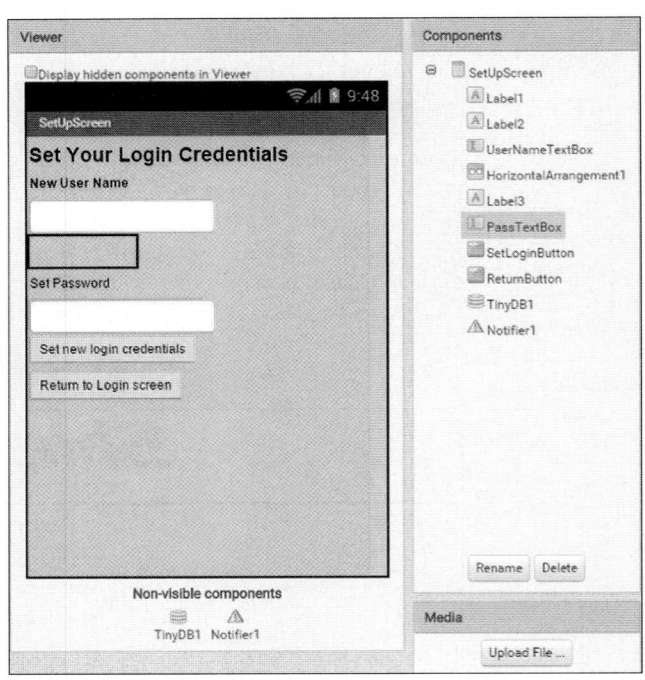

(Copyright MIT, used with permission)

For the instructions for this exercise, go to MyLab IT.

Protecting Your Digital Property

Learning Outcome 9.2	**Describe various ways to protect your digital property and data from theft and corruption.**

Often, we can be our own worst enemies when using computing devices. If you're not careful, you might be taken in by thieves or scam artists who want to steal your digital and physical assets. As we'll discuss in this section, protecting yourself is key, and there are many relatively easy measures you can take to increase your level of security.

Restricting Access to Your Digital Assets

Keeping hackers and viruses at bay is often a matter of keeping them out. You can achieve this by:

- Preventing hackers from accessing your computer (usually through your Internet connection)
- Using techniques to prevent virus infections from reaching your computer
- Protecting your digital information in such a way that it can't be accessed (by using passwords, for example)
- Hiding your activities from prying eyes

In this section, we explore strategies for protecting access to your digital assets and keeping your Internet-surfing activities private.

Firewalls

Objective 9.7 *Explain what a firewall is and how a firewall protects your computer from hackers.*

What is a firewall? A **firewall** is a software program or hardware device designed to protect computers from hackers. It's named after a housing construction feature that slows the spread of fires from house to house. A firewall designed specifically for home networks is called a **personal firewall**. By using a personal firewall, you can close open logical ports and make your computer invisible to other computers on the Internet.

Which is better, a software firewall or a hardware firewall? One type isn't better than the other. Both hardware and software firewalls will protect you from hackers. Although installing either a software or a hardware firewall on your home network is probably sufficient, you should consider installing both for maximum protection. This will provide you with additional safety.

Types of Firewalls

What software firewalls are there? Both Windows and macOS include reliable firewalls. The Windows Action Center is a good source of information about the security status of your computer. The status of your Windows Firewall is shown in the Windows Firewall dialog box (see Figure 9.16). Security suites such as Norton Security and Trend Micro Internet Security Suite also include firewall software. Although the firewalls that come with Windows and macOS will protect your computer, firewalls included in security suites often come with additional features such as monitoring systems that alert you if your computer is under attack.

If you're using a security suite that includes a firewall, the suite should disable the firewall that came with your OS. Two firewalls running at the same time can conflict with each other and cause your computer to slow down or freeze up.

What are hardware firewalls? You can also buy and configure hardware firewall devices, although most routers sold for home networks include firewall protection. Just like software firewalls, the setup for hardware firewalls is designed for novices, and the default configuration on most routers keeps unused logical ports closed. Documentation accompanying routers can assist more-experienced users in adjusting the settings to allow access to specific ports if needed.

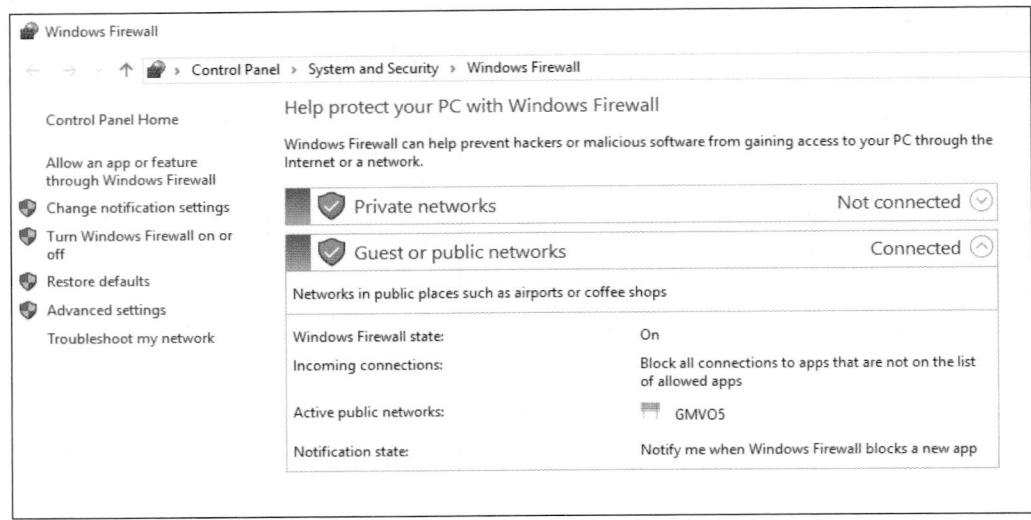

Figure 9.16 The Windows Firewall dialog box provides the status of your firewall.
> *To view the Windows Firewall dialog box, access **Settings**, select **Network & Internet**, select **Wi-Fi**, and then click the **Windows Firewall** link. (Windows 10, Microsoft Corporation)*

How Firewalls Work

How do firewalls protect you from hackers? Firewalls are designed to restrict access to a network and its computers. Firewalls protect you in two major ways: (1) by blocking access to logical ports, and (2) by keeping your computer's network address secure.

How do firewalls block access to your logical ports? Recall that logical ports are virtual communications paths that allow a computer to organize requests for information from other networks or computers. See Figure 9.17 for some logical port numbers and the services they are associated with.

Certain logical ports are very popular in hacker attacks. For example, logical port number 1337 is often used because it looks close to the word "leet," which is hacker talk for "elite," so hackers think it's fun to go after that port.

To block access to logical ports, firewalls examine data packets that your computer sends and receives. Data packets contain the address of the sending and receiving computers and the logical port that the packet will use. Firewalls can be configured so that they filter out packets sent to specific logical ports in a process known as **packet filtering**.

Firewalls can also be configured to completely refuse requests from the Internet asking for access to specific ports. That process is referred to as **logical port blocking**. By using filtering and blocking, firewalls help keep hackers from accessing your computer (see Figure 9.18).

Figure 9.17	Common Logical Ports
Port Number	**Protocol Using the Port**
21	FTP (File Transfer Protocol) control
23	Telnet (unencrypted text communications)
25	SMTP (Simple Mail Transfer Protocol)
53	DNS (domain name system)
80	HTTP (Hypertext Transfer Protocol)
443	HTTPS (HTTP with Transport Layer Security [TLS] encryption)

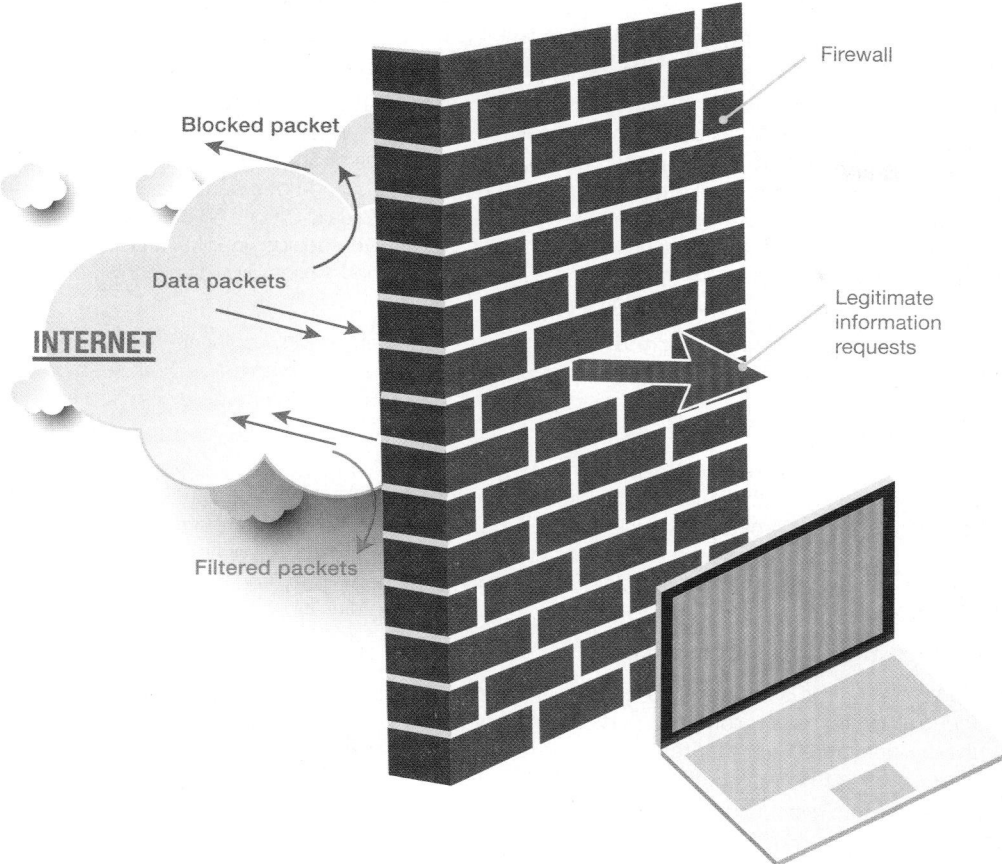

Blocked packet

Firewall

Data packets

INTERNET

Legitimate information requests

Filtered packets

Figure 9.18 Firewalls use filtering and blocking to keep out unwanted data on specific logical ports. That keeps your network safe.

How do firewalls keep your network address secure? Every computer connected to the Internet has a unique address called an Internet Protocol address (IP address). Data is routed to the correct computer on the Internet based on the IP address. This is similar to how a letter finds its way to your mailbox. You have a unique postal address for your home. If a hacker finds out the IP address of your computer, he or she can locate it on the Internet and try to break into it.

Your IP address for your home network is assigned to your router by your Internet service provider (ISP). Then each device on your home network has its own IP address. Firewalls use a process called **network address translation (NAT)** to assign internal IP addresses on a network. The internal IP addresses are used only on the internal network and therefore can't be detected by hackers. For hackers to access your computer, they must know your computer's internal IP address. With a NAT–capable router/firewall installed on your network, hackers are unable to access the internal IP address assigned to your computer, so your computer is safe. Most routers sold for home use are configured as firewalls and feature NAT.

Helpdesk MyLab IT®

Understanding Firewalls

In this Helpdesk, you'll play the role of a helpdesk staffer, fielding questions about how hackers can attack networks and what harm they can cause as well as what a firewall does to keep a computer safe from hackers.

Preventing Virus Infections

Objective 9.8 *Explain how to protect your computer from virus infection.*

What is the best way to protect my devices from viruses? Earlier in the chapter, we discussed the various viruses that hackers may unleash on your system. There are two main ways to protect your computer from viruses: by installing antivirus software and by keeping your software up to date.

Antivirus Software

What antivirus software do I need? **Antivirus software** is specifically designed to detect viruses and protect your computer and files from harm. Symantec, Kaspersky, Trend Micro, and Avast are among the companies that offer highly rated antivirus software packages. Antivirus protection is also included in comprehensive Internet security packages such as Norton Security or Trend Micro Internet Security. These software packages also help protect you from threats other than computer viruses.

My new computer came with antivirus software installed, so shouldn't I already be protected? Computers running Windows come with its built-in antivirus software, Windows Defender. This offers built-in virus protection but does not get as strong ratings as many third-party products. Your new system will probably also come with a trial version of a particular company's antivirus program. That software is free only for a limited time, usually 90 or 180 days. After that, you have to pay to upgrade to the full version of the product if you decide you like it. Before you consider paying for the upgrade though, check with your Internet service provider. Many include free antivirus software with your monthly service plan.

How often do I need to run antivirus software? Although antivirus software is designed to detect suspicious activity on your computer at all times, you should run an active virus scan on your entire system at least once a week. By doing so, all files on your computer will be checked for undetected viruses.

Antivirus programs run scans in the background when your CPU is not being heavily utilized. However, you can also configure the software to run scans at times when you aren't using your system—for example, when you're asleep (see Figure 9.19). (However, it's important to note that your computer must be powered on and not in sleep mode for these virus scans to take place.) Alternatively, if you suspect a problem, you can launch a scan manually and have it run immediately.

How does antivirus software work? The main functions of antivirus software are as follows:

- *Detection:* Antivirus software looks for virus signatures in files. A **virus signature** is a portion of the virus code that's unique to a particular computer virus. Antivirus software scans files for these signatures when they're opened or executed and identifies infected files and the type of virus infecting them.

- *Stopping virus execution:* If the antivirus software detects a virus signature or suspicious activity, such as the launch of an unknown macro, it stops the execution of the file and virus and notifies

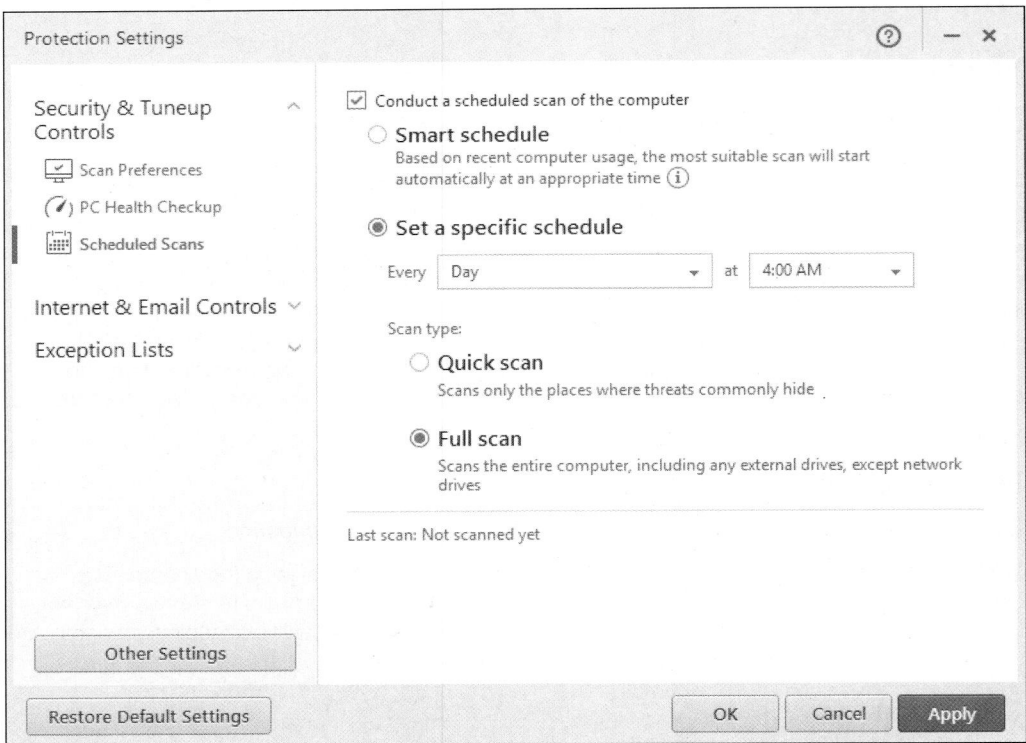

Figure 9.19 In Trend Micro Internet Security, you can set up virus scans to run automatically based on your usage or on a specific schedule. *(Reprinted courtesy of Trend Micro Incorporated)*

you that it has detected a virus. It also places the virus in a secure area on your hard drive so that it won't spread to other files; this procedure is known as **quarantining**. Usually, the antivirus software then gives you the choice of deleting or repairing the infected file. Unfortunately, antivirus programs can't always fix infected files to make them usable again. You should keep backup copies of critical files so that you can restore them in case a virus damages them irreparably.

- *Prevention of future infection:* Most antivirus software will also attempt to prevent infection by inoculating key files on your computer. In **inoculation**, the antivirus software records key attributes about your computer files, such as file size and date created, and keeps these statistics in a safe place on your hard drive. When scanning for viruses, the antivirus software compares the attributes of the files with the attributes it previously recorded to help detect attempts by virus programs to modify your files.

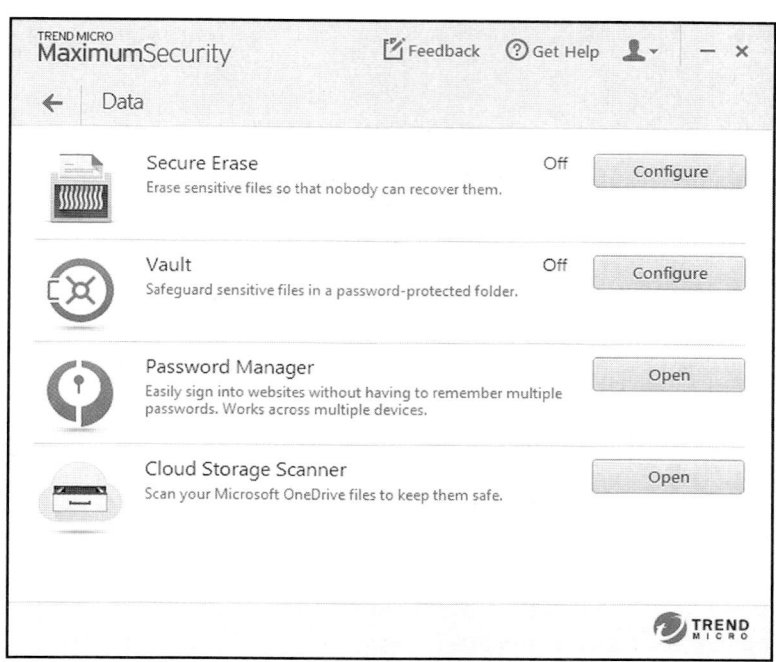

Figure 9.20 Many protection packages, such as Trend Micro Internet Security, offer other types of security features besides basic malware protection. *(Courtesy of Trend Micro Incorporated)*

Does antivirus software stop all viruses? Antivirus software catches *known* viruses effectively. However, new viruses are written all the time. To combat unknown viruses, modern antivirus programs search for suspicious virus-like activities as well as virus signatures. To minimize your risk, you should keep your antivirus software up to date.

How do I make sure my antivirus software is up to date? Most antivirus programs have an automatic update feature that downloads updates for virus signature files every time you go online. Also, the antivirus software usually shows the status of your update subscription so that you can see how much time you have remaining until you need to buy another version of your software. Many Internet security packages offer bonus features such as cloud storage scanners and password managers (see Figure 9.20) to provide you with extra protection.

What should I do if I think my computer is infected with a virus? If you see suspicious behavior from your system, run a complete virus scan. If viruses are detected, you may want to research the situation further to determine whether your antivirus software will eradicate them completely or whether you'll need to take additional manual steps to eliminate the viruses. Most antivirus company websites contain archives of information on viruses and provide step-by-step solutions for removing them if they're particularly stubborn.

How do I protect my phone from viruses? Because smartphones and other mobile devices run operating systems and contain files, they are susceptible to infection by viruses. Cybercriminals are now hiding viruses in legitimate-looking apps for download to mobile devices. Most antivirus software companies now offer antivirus software specifically designed for mobile devices. The Google Play store offers effective free products to protect your Android devices such as 360 Security and Avast! Mobile Security.

Software Updates

Why does updating my operating system (OS) software help protect me from viruses? Many viruses exploit weaknesses in operating systems. Malicious websites can be set up to attack your computer by downloading harmful software onto your computer. According to research conducted by Google, this type of attack, known as a **drive-by download**, affects almost 1 in 1,000 web pages. To combat these threats, make sure your OS is up to date and contains the latest security patches.

Do OS updates only happen automatically? Prior to the release of Windows 10, you updated your Windows OS with an automatic update utility called Windows Update. You had the ability to decide when to download updates and when to install them. (macOS has a similar utility for gathering updates.) With Windows 10, however, you no longer have as many choices. Updates are now downloaded automatically whenever they're provided by Microsoft. You do have the choice to allow Windows to automatically schedule a restart of your computer to apply the updates or pick a more convenient restart time manually (see Figure 9.21).

The Advanced Options screen for Windows Update provides a few other options (see Figure 9.22). The most notable is the ability to receive updates for other Microsoft products (like MS Office). (Note that the ability to defer upgrades is not available on the Windows 10 Home edition—you must install updates as they are delivered by Microsoft.)

Authentication: Passwords and Biometrics

Objective 9.9   *Describe how passwords and biometric characteristics can be used for user authentication.*

How can I best use passwords to protect my computer? You no doubt have many passwords you need to remember to access your digital life. However, creating strong passwords—ones that are difficult for hackers to guess—is an essential piece of security that people sometimes overlook. Password-cracking

Figure 9.21 The Windows Update screen makes it easy for users to stay abreast of software updates and manage restarts.
*> To access the Windows Update screen, access **Settings**, select **Update & security**, then select **Windows Update**. (Windows 10, Microsoft Corporation)*

programs have become more sophisticated. In fact, some commonly available programs can test more than 1 million password combinations per second! Creating a secure password is therefore more important than ever.

Websites that need to be very secure, such as those for financial institutions, usually have strong defenses to prevent hackers from cracking passwords. But sites that need less security, such as casual gaming or social networking sites, might have less protection. Hackers attack poorly defended sites for passwords because many people use the same password for every site they use. Don't let a hacker get your password from a poorly secured gaming site, and then be able to access your bank account with the same password!

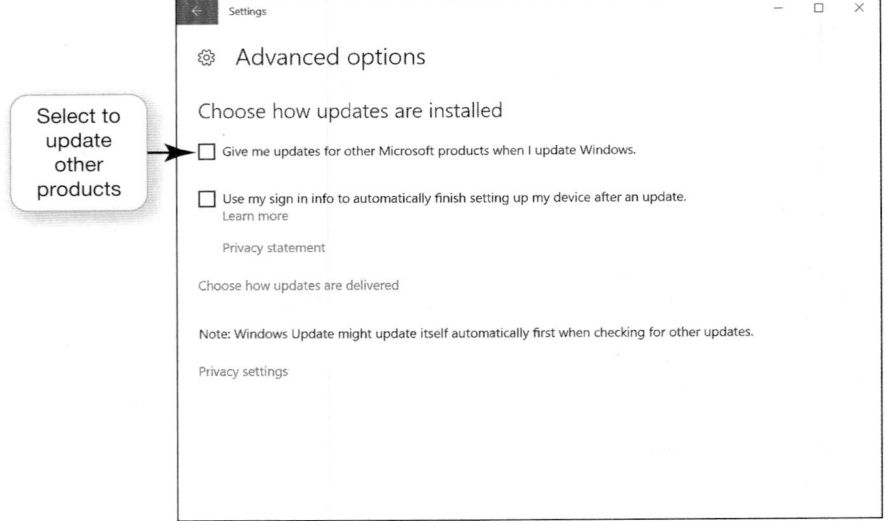

Select to update other products

Figure 9.22 The Windows Update Advanced Options screen provides a few more user controlled update options.
*> To access the Windows Update **Advanced Options** screen, click the Advanced options link near the bottom of the Windows Update screen (Figure 9.21). (Windows 10, Microsoft Corporation)*

Creating Strong Passwords

What constitutes a strong password? Strong passwords are difficult for someone to guess. Follow these guidelines to create strong passwords (see Figure 9.24):

- Don't use easily deduced components related to your life, such as parts of your name, your pet's name, your street address, or the name of the website or institution for which you're creating the password (e.g., don't use "Citibank" for your online banking password).
- Use a password that's at least 14 characters long. Longer passwords are more difficult to deduce. Consider using a passphrase that is even longer.
- Don't use words found in the dictionary.
- Use a mix of upper- and lowercase letters, numbers, and symbols (such as # or %).
- Never tell anyone your password or write it down in a place where others might see it, like in your wallet or a sticky note on your computer screen.
- Change your passwords on a regular basis, such as monthly or quarterly. Your school or your employer probably requires you to change your password regularly. This is also a good idea for your personal passwords.
- Don't use the same password for every account you have.
- If you have trouble thinking of secure passwords, there are many password generators available for free, such as the Strong Password Generator (**strongpasswordgenerator.com**).

Automated programs called *bots* (or web robots) are used to make tasks easier on the Internet. For example, search engines use bots to search and index web pages. Unfortunately, bots can also be used for malicious or illegal purposes because they can perform some computing tasks faster than humans. For example, bots can be used on ticket-ordering sites to buy large blocks of high-demand concert tickets. They are also often used to post spam in the comment sections of blogs. Fortunately, website owners can deploy CAPTCHA software to prevent such bot activities.

CAPTCHA (Completely Automated Public Turing Test to Tell Computers and Humans Apart) programs are used to generate distorted text and require that it be typed into a box. Newer programs, like Google's reCAPTCHA, monitor users' website behavior to determine if you are a human or a bot. reCAPTCHA merely asks you to click a check box and if it displays a green check (see Figure 9.23a), you have passed the bot test. If the app isn't sure if you are a human, it may ask you to type in some

a **b**

Figure 9.23 (a) CAPTCHA programs like reCAPTCHA monitor a user's website behavior and can often determine if a user is human just by having the user check a box. If a green check mark appears, you are human! (b) If the app isn't sure if you're a bot, you may be asked to enter some text. *(Metrue/Shutterstock)*

distorted text (see Figure 9.23b) just like older versions of the program did. If you want to try integrating a CAPTCHA program into your website (to protect your e-mail address), go to **google. com/recaptcha**, which offers free CAPTCHA tools to help you protect your data.

How can I check the strength of my passwords? You can use online password strength testers, such as the Password Meter (**passwordmeter.com**), to evaluate your passwords. The Password Meter provides guidelines for good passwords and shows you how integrating various elements, such as symbols, affects the strength score of your password.

How do I restrict access to my computer? Windows, macOS, and most other operating systems have built-in password (or passcode) protection for files as well as the entire desktop. After a certain period of idle time, your computer is automatically password locked, and your password (or PIN) must be entered to gain access to the computer. This provides excellent protection from casual snooping if you need to walk away from your computer for a period of time. If someone attempts to log on to your computer without your password, that person won't be able to gain access. It's an especially good idea to use passwords on laptop computers, smartphones, and tablets because this provides additional protection of your data if your device is lost or stolen.

Figure 9.24 Strong and Weak Password Candidates

Password	Rating	Good Points	Bad Points
Joysmithl022	Poor	• Contains upper- and lowercase letters • Contains letters and numbers	• Less than 14 characters • Contains name and birth date
test44drive6car	Mediocre	• 15 characters in length	• Contains three words found in the dictionary • Numbers repeated consecutively
8$RanT%5ydTTtt&	Better	• Good length • Contains upper- and lowercase letters • Contains symbols	• Upper- and lowercase letters repeated consecutively • Still contains one dictionary word (rant)
7R3m3mB3R$5%y38	Best	• All good points from above • Dictionary word (remember) has 3s instead of Es	• None

Gesture 1

Gesture 2

Gesture 3

Figure 9.25 Drawing three gestures on your picture (and repeating them once) sets your picture password options in Windows. *(Windows 10, Microsoft Corporation)*

Windows allows you to use gesture passwords on touchscreen devices. You select a picture and then draw three gestures on it—either straight lines, circles, or taps. This combination then works as an additional method for accessing your computer. You can unlock your computer by repeating the gestures (see Figure 9.25). Biometric verification is beginning to appear now as well (discussed below).

Managing Your Passwords

How can I remember all of my complex passwords? Good security practices suggest that you have different passwords for all the different websites that you access and that you change your passwords frequently. The problem with well-constructed passwords is that they can be hard to remember. Fortunately, password-management tools are now available. They take the worry out of forgetting passwords because the password-management software does the remembering for you.

Where can I obtain password-management software? Most current Internet security suites and web browsers make it easy to keep track of passwords by providing password-management tools. When you go to a website that requires a login, the browser will display a dialog box asking if you want the browser to remember the password for the site (see Figure 9.26). The next time you return to the site, it will automatically fill in the information for you. However, there are some passwords that you might not want your browser to store, such as your online banking password. So be selective when using this feature.

Select to have Microsoft Edge store the password for this site.

Figure 9.26 The password dialog box in Microsoft Edge displays whenever you type in a password for a website for which Microsoft Edge hasn't yet stored the password. *(Screenshot of Pearson Higher Education website, Pearson Education, Inc.)*

Biometric Authentication Devices

Besides passwords, how else can I restrict the use of my computer? A **biometric authentication device** is a device that reads a unique personal characteristic such as a fingerprint or the iris pattern in your eye and converts its pattern to a digital code. When you use the device, your pattern is read and compared to the one stored on the computer. Only users having an exact fingerprint or iris pattern match are allowed to access the computer.

Because no two people have the same biometric characteristics (fingerprints and iris patterns are unique), these devices provide a high level of security. They also eliminate the human error that can occur in password protection. You might forget your password, but you won't forget to bring

Figure 9.27 Windows Hello brings facial recognition for login to many laptops and mobile devices.
> *From the* **Start** *menu, select* **Settings**. *Go to* **Accounts**, *then select* **Sign-In options**. *Under* **Windows Hello**,
select **Set Up**. *(Windows 10, Microsoft Corporation)*

your fingerprints when you're working on your computer! Many smartphones now include finger-print readers. Other biometric devices, including voice authentication and facial recognition systems, are now widely offered. Windows 10 offers facial recognition for login, called Hello, in laptops (see Figure 9.27), tablets, and smartphones.

Anonymous Web Surfing: Hiding from Prying Eyes

Objective 9.10 *Describe ways to surf the web anonymously.*

Should I be concerned about surfing the Internet on shared, public, or work computers? If you use shared computers in public places such as libraries, coffee shops, or student unions, you never know what nefarious tools have been installed by hackers. When you browse the Internet, traces of your activity are left behind on that computer, often as temporary files. A wily hacker can glean sensitive information long after you've finished your surfing session. In addition, many employers routinely review the Internet browsing history of employees to ensure workers are spending their time on the Internet productively.

What tools can I use to keep my browsing activities private when surfing the Internet? The current versions of Mozilla Firefox, Microsoft Edge, and Google Chrome include privacy tools (called Private Browsing, InPrivate, and Incognito, respectively) that help you surf the web anonymously (see Figure 9.28). When you choose to surf anonymously, all three browsers open special versions of their browser windows that are enhanced for privacy. When surfing in these windows, records of websites you visit and files you download don't appear in the web browser's history files. Furthermore, any temporary files generated in that browsing session are deleted when you exit the special window.

Are there any other tools I could use to protect my privacy? Portable privacy devices, such as the Kingston Personal Flash Drives (**kingston.com**), provide an even higher level of surfing privacy. Simply plug the device into an available USB port on the machine on which you'll be working. All sensitive Internet files, such as cookies, passwords, Internet history, and browser caches, will be stored on the privacy device, not on the computer you're using. Privacy devices such as these often come preloaded with software designed to shield your IP address from prying eyes, making it difficult (if not impossible) for hackers to tell where you're surfing on the Internet. These privacy devices also have password-management tools that store all of your login information and encrypt it so it will be safe if your privacy device falls into someone else's hands.

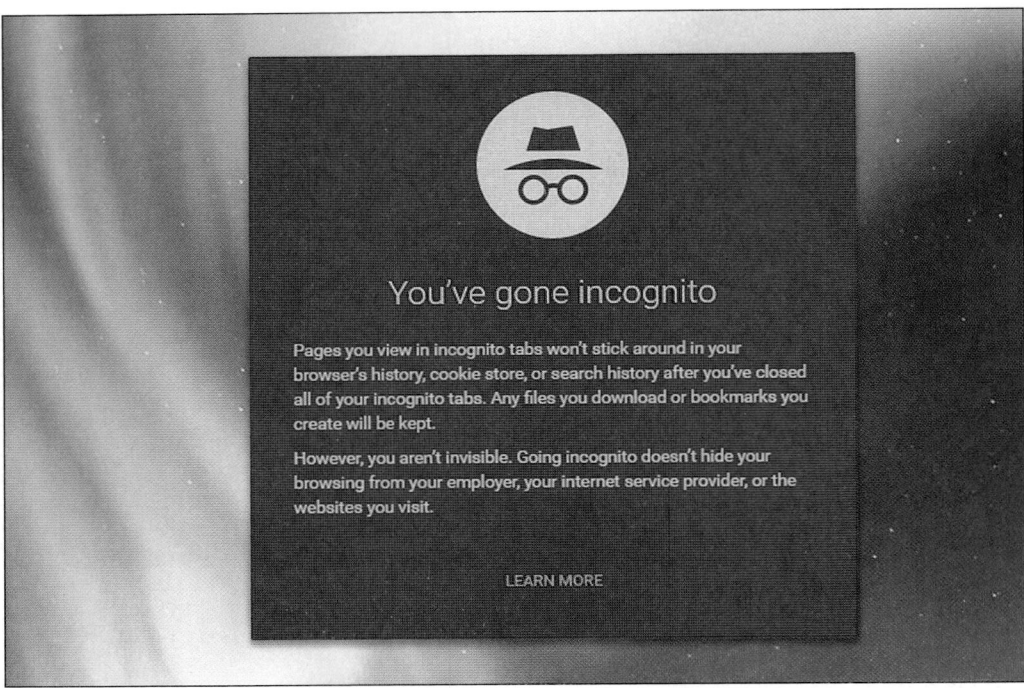

Figure 9.28 Modern browsers include privacy tools to support anonymous web surfing. *(© 2015 Google Inc, used with permission. Google and the Google logo are registered trademarks of Google Inc.)*

Is there anything else I can do to keep my data safe on shared computers? Another free practical solution is to take the Linux OS with you on a flash drive and avoid using the public or work computer's OS. The interfaces of many Linux distros look almost exactly like Windows and are easy to use. There are several advantages to using a Linux-based OS on a public or work computer:

- When you run software from your own storage medium, such as a flash drive, you avoid reading and writing to the hard disk of the computer. This significantly enhances your privacy because you don't leave traces of your activity behind.
- Your risk of picking up viruses and other malicious programs is significantly reduced because booting a computer from a flash drive completely eliminates any interaction with the computer's OS. This, in turn, significantly reduces the chance that your flash drive will become infected by any malware running on the computer.
- Virus and hacking attacks against Linux are far less likely than attacks against Windows. Because Windows has about 90% of the OS market, people who write malware tend to target Windows systems.

Pendrivelinux (**pendrivelinux.com**) is an excellent resource that offers many different versions of Linux for download and includes step-by-step instructions on how to install them on your flash drive. If you're a Mac user, the Elementary OS Luna distro of Linux provides a close approximation of macOS, so you can feel right at home.

How can I protect sensitive data transmissions if I have to use a public wireless network? Virtual private networks (VPNs) are secure networks that are established using the public Internet infrastructure. Using specialized software, servers, and data transmission protocols, VPNs are used to send information on the public Internet in such a manner that the data is as secure as sending it on a private network. VPNs used to be only used by businesses. But with public concerns about information security on the rise, many VPN software providers (such as Private Internet Access and NordVPN) are marketing affordable solutions to individuals. So if you routinely transmit sensitive information, you should consider a personal VPN solution.

Make sure to use some (or all) of these methods to keep your activities from prying eyes and to restrict access to your digital information.

Computer system security depends on authentication—proving users are who they say they are. There are three independent authentication factors:

- Knowledge factor: something the user knows (password, PIN)
- Possession factor: something the user has (ATM card, mobile phone)
- Inherence factor: something only the user is (biometric characteristics, such as fingerprints or iris pattern)

Multi-factor authentication requires two of the three above factors be demonstrated before authorization is granted (see Figure 9.29). At the bank's ATM machine, you present an ATM card (something you have) and then use a PIN code (something you know) to access your account.

For online access, multi-factor authentication often relies on the use of mobile phones. For instance, when you register a Google account, you supply your mobile phone number. If you then want to make changes to your account, you supply the password (something you know). The second step of authentication is Google sending an SMS message with a unique code to your mobile phone. Retrieving the code and entering it online proves you have the phone (something the user has) and serves as the second authentication step.

Multi-factor authentication is much safer than single-factor authentication. So make use of it when it is offered to you to enhance your account security.

Figure 9.29 Multi-Factor Authentication

Possession factor:
Something the user has
(ATM card, mobile phone)

Knowledge factor:
Something the user knows
(password, PIN)

Inherence factor:
Something only the user is
(biometric characteristics, such as fingerprints)

! **Strong Authentication:**
Two of the three factors

(LoloStock/Fotolia, Jamdesign/Fotolia, Jamie/Fotolia)

Keeping Your Data Safe

People are often too trusting or just plain careless when it comes to protecting private information about themselves or their digital data. In this section, we discuss ways to keep your data safe from damage, either accidental or intentional.

Protecting Your Personal Information

Objective 9.11   *Describe the types of information you should never share online.*

If a complete stranger walked up to you on the street and asked you for your address and phone number, would you give it to him or her? Of course you wouldn't! But many people are much less careful when it comes to sharing sensitive information online. And often people inadvertently share information that they really only intended to share with their friends. With cybercrimes like identify theft rampant, you need to take steps to protect your personal information.

What information should I never share on websites? A good rule of thumb is to reveal as little information as possible, especially if the information would be available to everyone. Figure 9.30 gives you some good guidelines.

Your Social Security number, phone number, date of birth, and street address are four key pieces of information that identity thieves use to steal an identity. This information should never be shared in a public area on any website.

How can I tell who can see my information on a social network? Social networking sites like Facebook make privacy settings available in your profile settings. If you've never changed your default privacy settings in Facebook, you're probably sharing information more widely than you should.

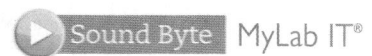

Sound Byte MyLab IT®

Managing Computer Security with Windows Tools

In this Sound Byte, you'll learn how to monitor and control your computer security using features built into the Windows OS.

Figure 9.30 Internet Information-Sharing Precautions

Information Identity Thieves Crave

- Social Security Number
- Full Date of Birth
- Phone Number
- Street Address

Never make this information visible on websites!

Other Sensitive Information

- Full Legal Name
- E-mail Address
- Zip Code
- Gender
- School or Workplace

Only reveal this information to people you know—don't make it visible to everyone!

(Mograph/Fotolia, Kevin Largent/Fotolia)

How can I protect my information on Facebook? To begin, you need to change your privacy settings in your profile from some of the default options. In general, it's a bad idea to make personal information available to the public, although this is a default setting for some items in Facebook. It's a good idea to set most of the options in your profile's Basic Information section to Friends or to Only Me because, presumably, these are personal details you should wish to share only with friends.

In the Contact Information section, restricting this information only to friends or to yourself is imperative. You don't want scammers contacting you via e-mail or snail mail and trying to trick you into revealing sensitive information.

Backing Up Your Data

Objective 9.12 *List the various types of backups you can perform on your computing devices, and explain the various places you can store backup files.*

How might I damage my data? A hacker can gain access to your computer and steal your data, but a more likely scenario is that you'll lose your data unintentionally. You may accidentally delete files or have your flash drive suddenly stop working. You may drop your laptop on the ground, causing the hard drive to break and resulting in complete data loss. A virus from an e-mail attachment you opened may destroy your original file. Your house may catch fire and destroy your computer. Because many of these possibilities are beyond your control, you should have a strategy for backing up your files (see Figure 9.31). **Backups** are copies of files that you can use to replace the originals if they're lost or damaged.

What types of files do I need to back up? Two types of files need backups:

1. **Data files** include files you've created or purchased, such as research papers, spreadsheets, music and photo files, contact lists, address books, e-mail archives, and your Favorites list from your browser.

2. **Program files** include files used to install software. Most manufacturers allow you to re-download the installation files if you need to reinstall the program, but some don't or charge you an extra fee for that service. Making sure you have your own backup of your system protects you in either case.

What types of backups can I perform? There are two important types of backups:

1. A **full backup** means that you create a copy of all your application and data files. This is followed by a schedule of **incremental backups** (or partial backups). These involve only backing up files that have changed or have been created since the last backup was performed.

Figure 9.31 An Effective Backup Strategy

Files to Back Up

- **Program files:** Installation files for productivity software (i.e., Microsoft Office)
- **Data files:** Files you create (term papers, spreadsheets, etc.)

Types of Backups

- **Incremental (partial):** Only backs up files that have changed
- **Image (system):** Snapshot of your entire computer, including system software

Where to Store Backup Files

- Online (in the cloud)
- External hard drives
- Network-attached storage devices or home servers

Figure 9.32 A Comparison of Typical Data Backup Locations

Backup Location	Pros	Cons
Online (in the Cloud)	• Files stored at a secure, remote location • Files/backups accessible anywhere through a browser	• Most free storage sites don't provide enough space for image backups
External Hard Drive	• Inexpensive, one-time cost • Fast backups with USB 3.0 devices connected directly to your computer	• Could be destroyed in one event (fire/flood) with your computer • Can be stolen • Slightly more difficult to back up multiple computers with one device
Network-Attached Storage (NAS) Device and Home Server	• Makes backups much easier for multiple computing devices	• More expensive than a stand-alone external hard drive • Could be destroyed in one event (fire/flood) with your computer • Can be stolen

(Mipan/Fotolia, Prapass Wannapinij/Fotolia, Darkdesigns/Fotolia)

2. An **image backup** (or system backup) means that all system files are backed up, not just the application and data files. An image backup ensures you capture a complete snapshot of everything that makes your computer run—the operating system, the applications, and the data. The idea of imaging is to make an exact copy of the setup of your computer so that in the event of a total hard drive failure, you can copy the image to a new hard drive and have your computer configured exactly the way it was before the crash.

Where should I store my backups? You have three main choices for where to back up your files (see Figure 9.32):

1. *Online (in the cloud):* To be truly secure, backups should be stored online. Because the information is stored online, it's in a secure, remote location, so data isn't vulnerable to the disasters that could harm data stored in your home. Image backups may not fit within the storage limits offered for free by cloud providers. Look for a service that specifically provides mirror image backups, which will include a copy of your full operating system. For example, Carbonite (**carbonite.com**) offers certain plans that include online storage of a full system backup.

2. *External hard drives:* External hard drives, or even large-capacity flash drives, are popular backup options. Although convenient and inexpensive, using external hard drives for backups still presents the dilemma of keeping the hard drive in a safe location. Also, external hard drives can fail, possibly leading to loss of your backed-up data. Therefore, using an external hard drive for backups is best done in conjunction with an online backup strategy for added safety.

3. *Network-attached storage (NAS) devices and home servers:* NAS devices are essentially large hard drives connected to a network of computers instead of to just one computer, and they can be used to back up multiple computers simultaneously. Home servers also act as high-capacity NAS devices for automatically backing up data and sharing files.

How do I create a backup of my data files? Use the Windows 10 File History utility (see Figure 9.33). You may want to connect an external hard drive to your computer or a NAS device (or home server) to your network to store your backup or you may just want to back up to a USB flash drive, depending on how much data you have to store. Once configured, your data files will be backed up as often as you indicate. You can also restore files that you've backed up from the File History utility. With a few clicks you can retrieve any file back to your system.

How often should I back up my data files? File History can be set to automatically save files you've changed every ten minutes or every day, whatever you select. File History keeps previous versions of the file on the backup drive so you can revert to an older copy of the file if you need to do so.

Figure 9.33 You can use the Windows File History utility to back up files and restore files from a previous backup.
> *Access **Settings**, select **Update & security**, then click **Backup**. (Windows 10, Microsoft Corporation)*

How do I create an image backup? Windows also includes the System Image backup utility, which provides a quick and easy way to perform image backups. You can access this utility from the Backup and Restore screen (see Figure 9.34a) by clicking *Create a system image*. Before starting this utility, make sure your external drive or NAS device is connected to your computer or network and is powered on. To create the image backup:

1. Click the *Create a system image* link. Select the location (drive) for your backup files and click *Next* to proceed.
2. On the second screen (see Figure 9.34b), you can select the drives (or partitions of drives) from your computer to be backed up. Notice that all the drives/partitions that are required for Windows to run are preselected for you. Windows will back up all data files and system files on all selected drives/partitions. Click *Next* to proceed.
3. On the third screen, click *Start backup* to start your system image.

After the system image backup runs for the first time, you'll see the results of the last backup and the date of the next scheduled backup on the Backup and Restore (Windows 7) screen (see Figure 9.34a). If the scheduled backup time is not convenient for you, click the *Change settings* link to select an alternative time.

From the Backup and Restore screen, you can also create a system repair disc. A system repair disc contains files that can be used to boot your computer in case of a serious Windows error.

How often should I create an image backup? Because your program and OS files don't change as often as your data files, you can perform image backups on a less frequent basis. You might consider scheduling an image backup of your entire system on a weekly basis, but you should definitely perform one after installing new software.

What about backing up Apple computers? For macOS users, backups are very easy to configure. The Time Machine feature in macOS detects when an external hard drive is connected to

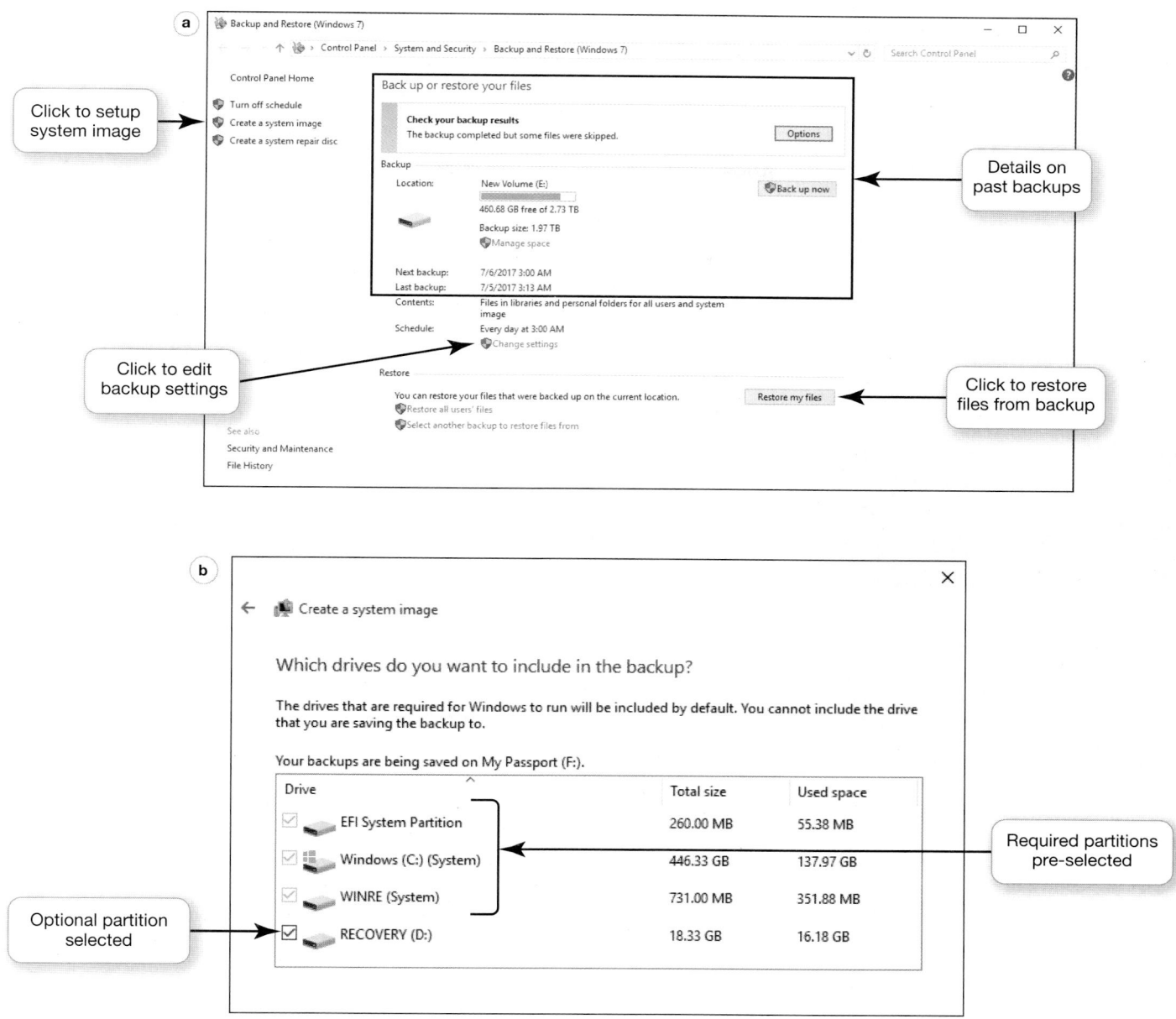

Figure 9.34 (a) The Backup and Restore utility allows you to perform an image backup and restore from one. (b) Select drives or partitions to be included in the system image backup. *(Windows 10, Microsoft Corporation)*

the computer or a NAS device is connected to your network. You're then asked if you want this to be your backup drive. If you answer yes, all of your files (including OS files) are automatically backed up to the external drive or NAS device.

Should I back up my files that are stored on my school's network? Most likely, if you're allowed to store files on your school's network, these files are backed up regularly. You should check with your school's network administrators to determine how often they're backed up and how you would request that files be restored from the backup if they're damaged or deleted. But don't rely on these network backups to bail you out if your data files are lost or damaged. It may take days for the network administrators to restore your files. It's better to keep backups of your data files yourself, especially homework and project files, so that you can immediately restore them. Storing your school projects in an organized portfolio with a cloud service like Dropbox or Google Drive is the best way to keep safe and to be prepared for creating the resumes you'll need in the future.

Protecting Your Physical Computing Assets

It's essential to ensure a safe environment for all your computing devices. This includes protecting them from environmental factors, power surges, power outages, and theft.

Environmental Factors and Power Surges

Objective 9.13 *Explain the negative effects environment and power surges can have on computing devices.*

Why is the environment critical to the operation of my computer equipment? Sudden movements, such as a fall, can damage your computing device's internal components. Make sure that your computer sits on a flat, level surface, and if it's a laptop or a tablet, carry it in a protective case.

Figure 9.35 Surge protectors are critical for protecting your electronic devices. *(JcJg Photography/Fotolia)*

Electronic components don't like excessive heat or excessive cold. Don't leave computing devices and phones in a car during especially hot or cold weather because components can be damaged by extreme temperatures. Unfortunately, computers generate a lot of heat, which is why they have fans to cool their internal components. Chill mats that contain cooling fans and sit underneath laptop computers are useful accessories for dissipating heat. Make sure that you place your desktop computer where the fan's intake vents, usually found on the rear of the system unit, are unblocked so air can flow inside.

Naturally, a fan drawing air into a computer also draws in dust and other particles, which can wreak havoc on your system. Therefore, keep the room in which your computer is located as clean as possible. Finally, because food crumbs and liquid can damage keyboards and other computer components, consume food and beverages away from your computer.

What is a power surge? Power surges occur when electric current is supplied in excess of normal voltage. Old or faulty wiring, downed power lines, malfunctions at electric company substations, and lightning strikes can all cause power surges. A **surge protector** is a device that protects your computer against power surges (see Figure 9.35).

Note that you should replace your surge protectors every two to three years. Also, after a major surge, the surge protector will no longer function and must be replaced. And it's wise to buy a surge protector that includes indicator lights, which illuminate when the surge protector is no longer functioning properly. Don't be fooled by old surge protectors—although they can still function as multiple-outlet power strips, they deliver power to your equipment without protecting it from surges.

Besides my computer, what other devices need to be connected to a surge protector? All electronic devices in the home that have solid-state components, such as TVs, stereos, printers, and smartphones (when charging), should be connected to a surge protector. However, it can be inconvenient to use individual surge protectors on everything. A more practical method is to install a **whole-house surge protector** (see Figure 9.36). Whole-house surge protectors function like other surge protectors, but they protect *all* electrical devices in the house. Typically, you'll need an electrician to install a whole-house surge protector, which costs hundreds of dollars.

Is my equipment 100% safe when plugged into a surge protector? No. Lightning strikes can generate such high voltages that they can overwhelm a surge protector. Unplugging electronic devices during an electrical storm is the only way to achieve absolute protection.

Preventing and Handling Theft

Objective 9.14 *Describe the major concerns when a device is stolen and strategies for solving the problems.*

What if my computing device is stolen? The theft of tablets, smartphones, notebook computers, and other portable computing devices is always a risk. The resale value for used electronic equipment is high, and the equipment can be easily sold online. And because they're

Surge protector

Figure 9.36 A whole-house surge protector is usually installed at the breaker panel or near the electric meter.

portable, laptops, tablets, and phones are easy targets for thieves. The main security concerns with mobile devices are:

1. Keeping them from being stolen
2. Keeping data secure in case they are stolen
3. Finding a device if it is stolen

What type of alarm can I install on my mobile device? Motion alarm software is a good, inexpensive theft deterrent. Free software such as LAlarm (**lalarm.com**) is effective for laptops. Apps such as Motion Alarm and Alarmomatic help secure your iPad or iPhone. Alarm software either detects motion, as when your device is being picked up, or sounds near your device and then sets off an ear-piercing alarm until you enter the disable code.

How can I secure the data on my mobile devices? The easiest way to keep the data secure is to make sure you have a login passcode set for your device. If your device supports biometrics like fingerprint detection for login, that's another way to make sure the contents are safe even if it's stolen.

Even if somehow the thief gets entry into the device, you can protect the data from prying eyes. Encrypting the data on your mobile device can make it practically impossible for thieves to obtain the data. Encryption involves transforming your data using an algorithm that can only be unlocked by a secure passcode. Encrypted data can't be read unless it's decrypted, which requires the passcode. On both iOS and Android devices, the operating system offers a built-in encryption option.

How can my device help me recover it when it is stolen? Software is available that lets your device report back its current location. For iOS devices, Apple offers the Find My iPhone service. Enabling this service provides you with numerous tools to assist you in recovering and protecting your mobile devices. Did you forget where you left your iPad? Just sign in with your Apple ID at the iCloud website to see a map showing the location of your iPad. You can send a message to your device, remotely password lock the device, or wipe all data from the device to completely protect your privacy. For Android devices, the Android Device Manager offers similar features. You can easily type "Find my phone" into the omnibox (the browser search bar) of Google Chrome, and a map with the location of your Android device will be shown (see Figure 9.37). And for Windows 10 devices, there is a similar Find My Device command located in the Update and Security section of Settings.

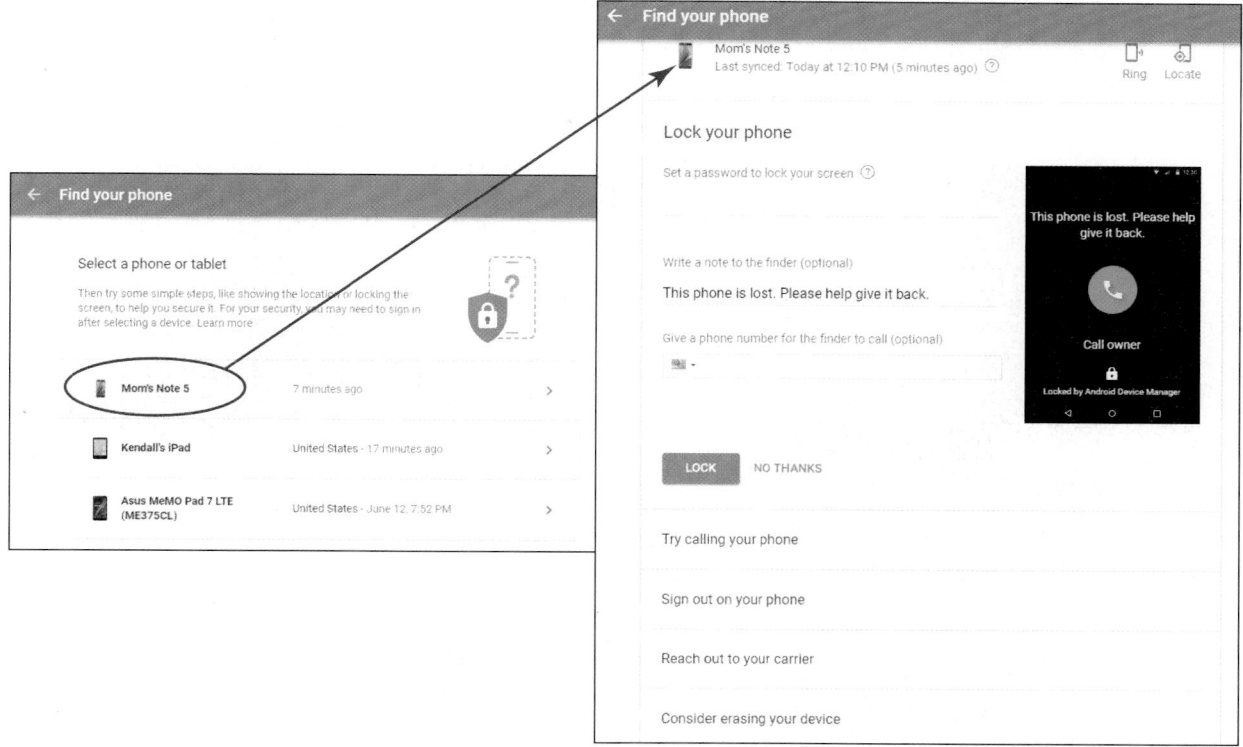

Figure 9.37 The Android Device Manager lets you locate any Android device and take steps to find and return it to its owner.

On law enforcement TV shows, you often see computer technicians working on suspects' computers to assist detectives in solving crimes. It may look simple, but the science of computer forensics is a complex, step-by-step process that ensures evidence is collected within the confines of the law.

Forensic means that something is suitable for use in a court of law. There are many branches of forensic science. For example, forensic pathologists provide evidence about the nature and manner of death in court cases involving deceased individuals. **Computer forensics** involves identifying, extracting, preserving, and documenting computer evidence. Computer forensics is performed by individuals known as *computer forensic scientists*, who rely primarily on specialized software to collect their evidence.

Phase 1: Obtaining and Securing Computer Devices

The first step in a computer forensics investigation is to seize the computer equipment that law enforcement officials believe contains pertinent evidence. Police are required to obtain a warrant to search an individual's home or place of business. Warrants must be very specific by spelling out exactly where detectives can search for evidence and exactly what type of evidence they're seeking. If a warrant indicates that the police may search an individual's home for his laptop computer, they can't then confiscate a tablet computer they notice in his car. It is important to specify in the warrant all types of storage devices where potential evidence might be stored, such as external hard drives, flash drives, and servers.

Once permission to collect the computers and devices containing possible evidence has been obtained, law enforcement officials must exercise great care when collecting the equipment. They need to ensure that no unauthorized persons are able to access or alter the computers or storage devices. The police must make sure the data and equipment are safe; if the equipment is connected to the Internet, the connection must be severed without data loss or damage. It's also important for law enforcement officials to understand that they may not want to power off equipment because potential evidence contained in RAM may be lost. After the devices are collected and secured, the computer forensic scientists take over the next phase of the investigation.

Phase 2: Cataloging and Analyzing the Data

It's critical to preserve the data exactly as it was found, or attorneys may argue that the computer evidence was subject to tampering or altering. Because just opening a file can alter it, the first task is to make a copy of all computer systems and storage devices collected (see Figure 9.38). The investigators then work from the copies to ensure that the original data always remains preserved exactly as it was when it was collected.

After obtaining a copy to work from, forensics professionals attempt to find every file on the system, including deleted files. Files on a computer aren't actually deleted, even if you empty the Recycle Bin, until the section of the hard disk they're stored on is overwritten with new data. Therefore, using special forensic software tools such as SANS Investigative Forensic Toolkit (SIFT) the forensic scientists catalog all files found on the system or storage medium and recover as much information from deleted files as they can. Software like the Forensic Toolkit (FTK) can readily detect hidden files and perform procedures to crack encrypted files or access protected files and reveal their contents.

The most important part of the process is documenting every step. Forensic scientists must clearly log every procedure performed because they may be required to provide proof in court that their investigations did not alter or damage information contained on the systems they examined. Detailed reports should list all files found, how the files were laid out on the system, which files were protected or encrypted, and the contents of each file. Finally, computer forensic professionals are often called on to present testimony in court during a trial.

Criminals are getting more sophisticated and are now employing anti-forensics techniques to foil computer forensic investigators. Although techniques for hiding or encrypting data are popular, the most insidious anti-forensics techniques are programs designed to erase data if unauthorized persons (i.e., not the criminal) access a computer system or if the system detects forensics software in use. When computer forensic investigators detect these countermeasures, they must often use creative methods and custom-designed software programs to retrieve and preserve the data.

Computer forensics is an invaluable tool to law enforcement in many criminal investigations, but only if the correct procedures are followed and the appropriate documentation is prepared.

Figure 9.38 Portable computer forensic devices make it easy to copy storage devices at crime scenes. *(Lance Mueller/Alamy Stock Photo)*

Figure 9.39 Computer Security Checklist

Firewall

- Do all your computers and tablets have firewall software installed and activated before connecting to the Internet?
- Is your router also able to function as a hardware firewall?
- Have you tested your firewall security by using the free software available at grc.com?

Virus and Spyware Protection

- Is antivirus and anti-spyware software installed on all your devices?
- Is the antivirus and anti-spyware software configured to update itself automatically and regularly?
- Is the software set to scan your device on a regular basis (at least weekly) for viruses and spyware?

Software Updates

- Have you configured your operating systems (Windows, OS X, macOS) to install new software patches and updates automatically?
- Is other software installed on your device, such as Microsoft Office or productivity apps, configured for automatic updates?
- Is the web browser you're using the latest version?

Protecting Your Devices

- Are all computing devices protected from electrical surges?
- Do your mobile devices have alarms or tracking software installed on them?

How can I ensure that I've covered all aspects of protecting my digital devices?
Figure 9.39 provides a guide to ensure you haven't missed critical aspects of security. If you've addressed all of these issues, you can feel reasonably confident that your data and devices are secure.

Before moving on to the Chapter Review:

1. ▶ Watch Chapter Overview Video 9.2.
2. Then take the Check Your Understanding quiz.

Check Your Understanding // Review & Practice

For a quick review to see what you've learned so far, answer the following questions.

multiple choice

1. Firewalls work by closing _____ in your computer.
   a. software gaps
   b. logical ports
   c. logical doors
   d. backdoors

2. Antivirus software looks for _____ to detect viruses in files.
   a. virus signatures
   b. virus artifacts
   c. virus bots
   d. virus VPNs

3. _____ involve using a physical attribute such as a fingerprint for authentication.
   a. Backdoors
   b. Biometrics
   c. Rootkits
   d. Trojan horses

4. When you are surfing the web anonymously,
   a. the sites you visit are not stored in the browser history.
   b. temporary files created are immediately deleted.
   c. you are using a browser that has privacy tools.
   d. all of the above

5. A backup of the files required to restore your operating system is known as a(n)
   a. total backup.
   b. image backup.
   c. incremental backup.
   d. global backup.

MyLab IT   Go to **MyLab IT** to take an autograded version of the *Check Your Understanding* review and to find all media resources for the chapter.

TechBytes Weekly   Go to TechBytes Weekly for current technology news and discussion questions!

9 Chapter Review

Summary

Part 1
Threats to Your Digital Assets

Learning Outcome 9.1 You will be able to describe hackers, viruses, and other online annoyances and the threats they pose to your digital security.

 Identity Theft and Hackers

Objective 9.1 *Describe how identity theft is committed and the types of scams identity thieves perpetrate.*

- Identity theft occurs when a thief steals personal information about you and runs up debts in your name. Identify thieves can obtain information by stealing mail, searching through trash, or tricking people into revealing information over the phone or via e-mail. Identity thieves counterfeit existing credit cards, open new credit card and bank accounts, change the address on financial statements, obtain medical services, and buy homes with a mortgage in the victim's name.

Objective 9.2 *Describe the different types of hackers and the tools they use.*

- White-hat hackers break into systems for nonmalicious reasons such as testing security to expose weaknesses. Black-hat hackers break into systems to destroy information or for illegal gain. Grey-hat hackers often break into systems just for the thrill or to demonstrate their prowess.
- Packet analyzers (sniffers) are programs used to intercept and read data packets, and they travel across a network. Trojan horses are programs that appear to be something else but are really a tool for hackers to access your computer. Backdoor programs and rootkits are tools used by hackers to gain access to and take total control of a computer system. Denial-of-service attacks overwhelm computer systems with so many requests for data that legitimate users can't access the system.

 Computer Viruses

Objective 9.3 *Explain what a computer virus is, why it is a threat to your security, how a computing device catches a virus, and the symptoms it may display.*

- A computer virus is a computer program that attaches itself to another computer program and attempts to spread to other computers when files are exchanged. Computer viruses can display annoying messages, destroy your information, corrupt your files, or gather information about you. Computers catch viruses when exposed to infected files. This can occur from downloading infected files, downloading and running infected e-mail attachments, or sharing flash drives that contain infected files. Symptoms of virus infection include: (1) files or app icons disappear; (2) browser is reset to an unusual home page; (3) odd messages, pop-ups, or images are displayed; (4) data files become corrupt; and (5) programs stop working properly.

Objective 9.4 *List the different categories of computer viruses, and describe their behaviors.*

- Boot-sector viruses copy themselves onto the master boot record of a computer and execute when the computer is started. Logic bombs and time bombs are viruses triggered by the completion of certain events or by the passage of time. Worms can spread on their own without human intervention, unlike conventional viruses. Macro viruses lurk in documents that use macros (short series of commands that automate repetitive tasks). E-mail viruses access the address book of a victim to spread to the victim's contacts. Encryption viruses render files unusable by compressing them with complex encryption keys. Polymorphic viruses periodically rewrite themselves to avoid detection. Stealth viruses temporarily erase their code and hide in the active memory of the computer.

 Online Annoyances and Social Engineering

Objective 9.5 *Explain what malware, spam, and cookies are and how they impact your security.*

- Malware is software that has a malicious intent. Adware is software that displays sponsored advertisements in a section of your browser window or as a pop-up box. Spyware collects information about you, without your knowledge, and transmits it to the owner of the program.
- Spam is unwanted or junk e-mail. Spim is unsolicited instant messages, which is also a form of spam. Spam filters in e-mail systems forward junk mail to their own folder. Never reply to spam or click on unsubscribe links, as this usually just generates more spam.
- Cookies are small text files that some websites automatically store on your hard drive when you visit them. Cookies are usually used to keep track of users and personalize their browsing experience. Cookies do not pose a security threat, although some individuals view them as privacy violations.

Objective 9.6 *Describe social engineering techniques, and explain strategies to avoid falling prey to them.*

- Social engineering is any technique that uses social skills to generate human interaction that entices individuals to reveal sensitive information. Phishing lures people into revealing personal information via bogus e-mails that appear to be from legitimate sources and direct people to scammer's websites. Pharming occurs when malicious code is planted on your computer, either by viruses or by your visiting malicious websites, which then alters your browser's ability to find web addresses. Scareware attempts to convince you that your computer is infected with a virus and then tries to sell you a "solution." Most Internet security software packages have scareware, phishing, and pharming protection built in.

Part 2
Protecting Your Digital Property

Learning Outcome 9.2 **Describe various ways to protect your digital property and data from theft and corruption.**

 ## Restricting Access to Your Digital Assets

Objective 9.7 *Explain what a firewall is and how a firewall protects your computer from hackers.*

- A firewall is a software program or hardware device designed to protect computers from hackers. Firewalls block access to your computer's logical ports and help keep your computer's network address secure. Firewalls use packet filtering to identify packets sent to specific logical ports and discard them. Firewalls use network address translation to assign internal IP addresses on networks. The internal IP addresses are much more difficult for hackers to detect.

Objective 9.8 *Explain how to protect your computer from virus infection.*

- Antivirus software is specifically designed to detect viruses and protect your computer and files from harm. Antivirus software detects viruses by looking for virus signatures: code that specifically identifies a virus. Antivirus software stops viruses from executing and quarantines infected files in a secure area on the hard drive. Virus software must be constantly updated to remain effective.

Objective 9.9 *Describe how passwords and biometric characteristics can be used for user authentication.*

- Secure passwords contain a mixture of upper- and lowercase letters, numbers, and symbols and are at least 14 characters long. Passwords should not contain words that are in the dictionary or easy-to-guess personal information. Utilities built into web browsers and Internet security software can be used to manage your passwords.
- A biometric authentication device reads a unique personal characteristic to identify an authorized user. Fingerprint readers, iris scanners, and facial recognition software are common examples of biometric security devices.

Objective 9.10 *Describe ways to surf the web anonymously.*

- Privacy tools built into web browsers help you surf anonymously by not recording your actions in the history files. USB devices containing privacy tools are available that prevent the computer you are using from storing any information about you on the computer. Virtual private networks (VPNs) are secure networks that can be used to send information securely across the public Internet.

 ## Keeping Your Data Safe

Objective 9.11 *Describe the types of information you should never share online.*

- Reveal as little information as possible about yourself. Your Social Security number, phone number, date of birth, and street address are four key pieces of information that identity thieves need to steal an identity.

Objective 9.12 *List the various types of backups you can perform on your computing devices, and explain the various places you can store backup files.*

- An incremental backup involves backing up only files that have changed or have been created since the last backup was performed. An image backup (or system backup) means that all system, application, and data files are backed up, not just the files that changed. You can store backups online (in the cloud), on external hard drives, or on network-attached storage (NAS) devices.

 ## Protecting Your Physical Computing Assets

Objective 9.13 *Explain the negative effects environment and power surges can have on computing devices.*

- Computing devices should be kept in clean environments free from dust and other particulates and should not be exposed to extreme temperatures (either hot or cold). You should protect all electronic devices from power surges by hooking them up through surge protectors, which will protect them from most electrical surges that could damage the devices.

Objective 9.14 *Describe the major concerns when a device is stolen and strategies for solving the problems.*

- The four main security concerns regarding computing devices are (1) keeping them from being stolen, (2) keeping data secure in case they are stolen, (3) finding a device if it is stolen, and (4) remotely recovering and wiping data off a stolen device.
- Software is available for installation on devices that will (1) set off an alarm if the device is moved; (2) help recover the device, if stolen, by reporting the computer's whereabouts when it is connected to the Internet; and (3) allow you to lock or wipe the contents of the device remotely.

 Be sure to check out **MyLab IT** for additional materials to help you review and learn. And don't forget to watch the Chapter Overview Videos. ▶

Key Terms

adware **343**

antivirus software **355**

backdoor program **336**

backup **364**

biometric authentication device **360**

black-hat hacker **335**

boot-sector virus **341**

botnet **337**

computer forensics **370**

cookie **345**

cybercrime **334**

cyberloafing (cyberslacking) **348**

data breach **349**

data file **364**

denial-of-service (DoS) attack **337**

distributed denial-of-service (DDoS) attack **337**

drive-by download **357**

e-mail virus **341**

encryption virus **341**

exploit kits **338**

firewall **353**

full backup **364**

grey-hat hacker **335**

hacker **335**

identity theft **335**

image backup (system backup) **365**

incremental backup (partial backup) **364**

inoculation **357**

keystroke logger (keylogger) **344**

logic bomb **341**

logical port **338**

logical port blocking **354**

macro virus **341**

malware **343**

master boot record **341**

multi-factor authentication **363**

multipartite virus **342**

network address translation (NAT) **355**

packet analyzer (sniffer) **336**

packet filtering **354**

personal firewall **353**

pharming **346**

phishing **346**

polymorphic virus **342**

pretexting **346**

program file **364**

quarantining **357**

rootkit **336**

scareware **347**

script **341**

social engineering **346**

spam **344**

spam filter **344**

spear phishing **349**

spyware **343**

stealth virus **342**

surge protector **368**

time bomb **341**

Trojan horse **336**

virtual private network (VPN) **362**

virus **339**

virus signature **356**

white-hat hacker (ethical hacker) **335**

whole-house surge protector **368**

worm **341**

zombie **336**

Chapter Quiz // Assessment

For a quick review to see what you've learned, answer the following questions. Submit the quiz as requested by your instructor. If you're using MyLab IT, the quiz is also available there.

multiple choice

1. Which of the following is NOT a major type of cybercrime reported to the IC3?
   a. government impersonation scams
   b. malware fraud
   c. identity theft
   d. advance fee fraud

2. Viruses that load from USB drives left connected to computers when computers are turned on are known as
   a. script viruses.
   b. polymorphic viruses.
   c. encryption viruses.
   d. boot-sector viruses.

3. Malicious software (malware) includes the following:
   a. adware.
   b. spyware.
   c. viruses.
   d. all of the above

4. Computer viruses can be spread by
   a. sharing flash drives.
   b. downloading and running a file attached to an email.
   c. downloading a song from a peer-to-peer sharing site.
   d. all of the above

5. A _____ is a program that takes complete control of your computer without your knowledge.
   a. botnet
   b. rootkit
   c. VPN
   d. sniffer

6. A backup of all the data files on your computer can be managed easily using the Windows 10 _____ utility.
   a. Windows Defender
   b. File History
   c. Windows Update
   d. Recovery

7. Authentication techniques that rely on personal biological traits are called
   a. Trojan horses
   b. scanners
   c. botnets
   d. biometrics

8. Antivirus software prevents infection by recording key attributes about your files and checking to see if they change over time in a process called
   a. updating.
   b. quarantine.
   c. signature.
   d. inoculation.

9. A surge protector may look like just another power strip but it also can
   a. detect viruses.
   b. prevent theft.
   c. save your device if a voltage spike is sent through the electrical system.
   d. help manage heat.

10. Firewalls use a process of _____ to assign IP addresses to the devices internal to the network so hackers will not know what they are.
    a. packet filtering
    b. port blocking
    c. VPN
    d. netowrk address translation (NAT)

true/false

_____ 1. Password strength is solely determined by the length of the password.

_____ 2. Your social security number should never be shared on a website, in an email, or through messaging.

_____ 3. Sending e-mails to lure people into revealing personal information is a technique known as phishing.

_____ 4. Encrypting data is not an appropriate measure for mobile devices such as smartphones.

_____ 5. Virtual private networks make it just as secure to send information across a public network as it is on a secure private network.

critical thinking

1. **Protecting Your Data from Data Breaches**

   You most likely have provided personal information to many websites and companies. What information have you provided to companies that you wish you had never disclosed? What types of information have companies asked you to provide that you believe was unnecessary? List specific companies and examples of the extraneous information.

2. **Phishing**

   Have you or anyone you know ever been a victim of a phishing scam? What sorts of scams have you heard about? Research and discuss at least three types of common scams.

Team Time

Protecting a Network

problem

Along with easy access to the web comes the danger of theft of digital assets.

task

A school alumnus is in charge of the county government computer department. The network contains computers running Windows 10, Windows 8, Windows 7, and macOS. He asked your instructor for help in ensuring that his computers and network are protected from viruses, malware, and hackers. He is hoping that there may be free software available that can protect his employees' computers.

process

1. Break the class into three teams. Each team will be responsible for investigating one of the following issues:
   a. **Antivirus software:** Research alternatives that protect computers from viruses. Find three alternatives and support your recommendations with reviews that evaluate free packages.
   b. **Anti-malware software:** Research three free anti-malware alternatives and determine whether the software can be updated automatically. You may want to recommend that the county purchase software to ensure that a minimum of employee intervention is needed to keep it up to date.
   c. **Firewalls:** Determine if the firewall software provided with Windows 10, Windows 8, Windows 7, and macOS is reliable. If it is, prepare documentation (for all four OSs) for county employees to determine if their firewalls are properly configured. If additional firewall software is needed, research free firewall software and locate three options that can be deployed by the county.
   d. Present your findings to the class and provide your instructor with a report suitable for eventual presentation to the manager of the county office network.

conclusion

With the proliferation of viruses and malware, it is essential to protect computers and networks. Free alternatives might work, but you should research the best protection solution for your situation.

Ethics Project

Content Control: Censorship to Protect Children

In this exercise, you'll research and then role-play a complicated ethical situation. The role you play might or might not match your own personal beliefs; in either case, your research and use of logic will enable you to represent the view assigned. An arbitrator will watch and comment on both sides of the arguments, and together the team will agree on an ethical solution.

problem

Many parents use web-filtering software (content-control software) to protect their children from objectionable Internet content. The U.S. federal government requires libraries to use content-control software as a condition to receiving federal funds. Some states, such as Virginia, have passed laws requiring libraries to install filtering software even if they did not receive federal funds. Upon installation of the software, it's up to the library administrators to decide what content is restricted. Therefore, content restriction can vary widely from library to library.

research areas to consider

- U.S. Supreme Court case *United States v. American Library Association*
- Content-control software and First Amendment rights
- Violation of children's free speech rights
- Children's Internet Protection Act (CIPA)

process

1. Divide the class into teams. One team will play the role of parents of elementary school students. Another team will be the library administration and another will be the users of the local town library.
2. Each team will be presenting its position on how access to the Internet should be managed for the local library, where there are many children, as well as adults, using services. The team position needs to be grounded in more than just opinion. Research so your position is supported by specific data, facts, and examples. Consider both the benefits and challenges of your position and how it will impact the other groups' interests.
3. Team members should present their case to the class or submit a PowerPoint presentation for review by the class. Be sure to include a summary statement of your position.

conclusion

As technology becomes ever more prevalent and integrated into our lives, more and more ethical dilemmas will present themselves. Being able to understand and evaluate both sides of the argument, while responding in a personally or socially ethical manner, will be an important skill.

Computer Security

You have been asked to prepare a report on computer security using Word 2016. You have written the majority of the report, but you have to make some final modifications and refinements, such as incorporating the results of some research on good antivirus software, adding a cover page, and generating a table of contents.

You will use the following skills as you complete this activity:

- Create and Modify Tables
- Insert Tab Stops
- Add Watermark
- Insert Cover Page
- Create and Update Table of Contents
- Add Footnote
- Use Find and Replace

Instructions:

1. Open *TIA_Ch9_Start* and save as **TIA_Ch9_LastFirst**.
2. Find all instances of *email* and replace with **e-mail**.
   a. Hint: Click **Replace** in the Editing group on the Home tab, type **e-mail** in the Find what box, and type **e-mail** in the Replace with box. Click **Replace All**.
3. Find the first instance of malware. Place the cursor after the word *malware* (before the period) and insert the footnote: **Malware is defined as software that is intended to gain access to, or damage or disable, computer systems for the purposes of theft or fraud.**
   a. Hint: Use Find in the Editing group on the Home tab to locate malware.
   b. Hint: Click **Insert Footnote** in the Footnotes group on the References tab to insert a footnote.
4. In the Types of Viruses section, highlight the six lines of text that outline the categories of computer viruses and variants. Add a Right Align Tab Stop at 1½˝ and a Left Align Tab Stop at 2˝.
   a. Hint: To set tab stop, display ruler, select tab stop style from Select tab box to the left of the ruler, and click at the desired position on the ruler.
5. Place cursor at the end of the paragraph in the Antivirus Software section. Press **Enter**, then insert a **3×4 Table**. Type **Product Name, Description/Review**, and **Cost** in the top three cells. Adjust the width of the Description/Review column to **3.5˝** and the width of the Cost column to **1"**.
   a. Hint: Click **Table** in the Tables group on the Insert tab, and drag to select the desired grid.
6. Add a row at the top of the table, **Merge Cells**, type **Antivirus Software Reviews**, and **Align Center** the contents. Format the table with **Grid Table 4 - Accent 1 style**.
   a. Hint: Click **Insert Above** in the Rows & Columns group on the Table Tools Layout tab.
7. Open a browser, and go to **www.pcmag.com/reviews/antivirus**. Research four antivirus software programs and place the software name, review, and cost of the software in the respective columns in the table.
   a. Hint: Press **Tab** at the end of the last row to add an additional line to the table to accommodate a fourth review.
8. Press **Ctrl+Home**, then insert the **Banded Cover Page**. Ensure *Computer Security* displays as the title and *your name* displays as the Author. Delete the Company and Address placeholders.
9. Insert **Page Numbers** at the bottom of the page using the **Plain Number 3 format**. Ensure Different First Page is checked. Close Header and Footer.
10. On page 2 of the document, insert a **Page Break** before the report title, Computer Security.
11. Place the cursor at the top of the new blank page, and insert a **Table of Contents** using the Automatic Table 1 format.
    a. Hint: Click **Table of Contents** in the Table of Contents group on the References tab.
12. Press **Ctrl+End**, scroll up and change the heading style of *Firewalls* to **Heading 2**, and then change the heading style of *Software Firewalls* and *Hardware Firewalls* to **Heading 3**.
13. Update the Table of Contents to reflect the changes in headings; ensure you update the entire table.
    a. Hint: Click anywhere in the Table of Contents, and click **Update Table**, and then click **Update entire table**.
14. Add a **Draft 1 Watermark** to the report.
    a. Hint: Click **Watermark** in the Page Background group on the Design tab.
15. Save the document and submit based on your instructor's directions.

10

Behind the Scenes: Software Programming

 For a chapter overview, watch the Chapter Overview Videos.

PART 1

Understanding Programming

Learning Outcome 10.1 You will be able to describe the life cycle of a software project and identify the stages in the program development life cycle.

PART 2

Programming Languages

Learning Outcome 10.2 You will understand the factors programmers consider when selecting an appropriate programming language for a specific problem and will be familiar with some modern programming languages.

 Life Cycle of an Information System 382

Objective 10.1 Describe the importance of programming to both software developers and users.

Objective 10.2 Summarize the stages of the system development life cycle (SDLC).

 Life Cycle of a Program 384

Objective 10.3 Define programming and list the steps in the program development life cycle (PDLC).

Objective 10.4 Describe how programmers construct a problem statement from a description of a task.

Objective 10.5 Explain how programmers use flow control and design methodologies when developing algorithms.

Objective 10.6 Discuss the categories of programming languages and the roles of the compiler and the integrated development environment (IDE) in coding.

Objective 10.7 Identify the role of debugging in program development.

Objective 10.8 Explain the importance of testing and documentation in program development.

Sound Byte: Using the Arduino Microcontroller

Helpdesk: Understanding Software Programming

 Many Programming Languages 404

Objective 10.9 Discuss the driving factors behind the popularity of various programming languages.

Objective 10.10 Summarize the considerations in identifying an appropriate programming language for a specific setting.

Sound Byte: Programming with the Processing Language

Exploring Programming Languages 407

Objective 10.11 Compare and contrast modern programming languages.

Objective 10.12 State key principles in the development of future programming languages.

Helpdesk: A Variety of Programming Languages

For the IT Simulation for this chapter, see MyLab IT.

MyLab IT   All media accompanying this chapter can be found here.

    Make: A Notepad on **page 403**

(Dizain/Shutterstock, DigitalVision Vectors/Dondesigns/Getty Images, Stuart Kinlough/Alamy Stock Photo, Geozacho/123RF)

How Cool Is This?

Most major U.S. cities have made a commitment to make the **data** they use to govern **open and transparent**—to human eyes and to your programs. Websites format information so it is useful for communicating with humans, but **web services** format the information in a way that makes it easy to **communicate the data to your program**. Chicago, Philadelphia, and other major cities have opened up thousands of government records through **Open Data initiatives**. Using this data, users can do such things as create a program to **visualize neighborhood crime statistics**, track their city's snowplows, or compare the current school budget expenditures.

It's not just cities that are becoming more transparent. **Data.gov** opens the U.S. government's data to you. Open government is here. Use it to write a web app or mobile tool that really has an **impact in your community**. Consider your own community. What kind of web app is needed? Get started working on it—the data

Understanding Programming

> **Learning Outcome 10.1**   You will be able to describe the life cycle of a software project and identify the stages in the program development life cycle.

Every day, we face a wide array of tasks. Some tasks are complex and require creative thought and a human touch. But tasks that are repetitive, work with electronic information, and follow a series of clear steps are candidates for automation with computers—automation achieved through programming. In this part of the chapter, we'll look at some of the basics of programming.

Life Cycle of an Information System

A career in programming offers many advantages—jobs are plentiful, salaries are strong, and telecommuting is often easy to arrange. But even if you're not planning a career in programming, knowing the basics of programming is important to help you use computers productively.

Importance of Programming

Objective 10.1   *Describe the importance of programming to both software developers and users.*

Why would I ever need to create a program? Computer programs already exist for many tasks. For example, if you want to write a paper, Microsoft Word has already been designed to translate the tasks you want to accomplish into computer instructions. However, for users who can't find an existing software product to accomplish a task, programming is mandatory. For example, imagine that a farmer needs to have a drone fly a specific pattern inspecting his or her crops, automatically taking photos and sensor readings at specific points to create a weekly report. No software product exists that will accumulate and relay information in just this manner. Therefore, a team of programmers will have to create smart farming software (see Figure 10.1).

If I'm not going to be a programmer, why should I learn about programming? If you plan to use only existing, off-the-shelf software, having a basic knowledge of programming enables you to add features that support your personal needs. For example, most modern software applications let you automate features by using custom-built miniprograms called **macros**. By creating macros, you can execute a complicated sequence of steps with a single command. Understanding how to program macros enables you to add custom commands to, for example, Word or Excel and lets you automate frequently performed tasks, providing a huge boost to your productivity. And if you plan to create custom applications from scratch, having a detailed knowledge of programming will be critical to the successful completion of your projects.

Figure 10.1 Unmanned drones are playing a larger role in transportation, videography, agriculture, and other fields. They require programming to integrate sensor and geographic information. *(John Lund/Blend Images/Getty Images)*

System Development Life Cycle

Objective 10.2   *Summarize the stages of the system development life cycle (SDLC).*

What is an information system? Generally speaking, a system is a collection of pieces working together to achieve a common goal. Your body, for example, is a system of muscles, organs, and other groups of cells working together. An **information system** includes data, people, procedures, hardware, and software that help in planning and decision making. Information systems help run an office and coordinate online-purchasing systems and are behind database-driven applications used by Amazon and Netflix. But how are these complicated systems developed? Through a particular step-by-step process.

Why do I need a process to develop a system? Because teams of people are required to develop information systems, there needs to be an organized process to ensure that development proceeds in an orderly fashion. Software applications also need to be available for multiple operating systems, to work over networked environments, and to be free of errors and well supported. Therefore, a process often referred to as the **system development life cycle (SDLC)** is used.

What steps constitute the SDLC? There are six steps in a common SDLC model, as shown in Figure 10.2. This system is sometimes referred to as a "waterfall" system because each step is dependent on the previous step being completed before it can be started.

1. *Problem and Opportunity Identification:* Corporations are always attempting to break into new markets, develop new customers, or launch new products. At other times, systems development is driven by a company's desire to serve its existing customers more efficiently or to respond to problems with a current system. Whether solving an existing problem or exploiting an opportunity, large corporations typically form a development committee to evaluate systems development proposals. The committee decides which projects to take forward based on available resources such as personnel and funding.

2. *Analysis:* In this phase, analysts explore the problem or need in depth and develop a program specification. The **program specification** is a clear statement of the goals and objectives of the project. The first feasibility assessment is also performed at this stage. The feasibility assessment determines whether the project should go forward. If the project is determined to be feasible, the analysis team defines the user requirements and recommends a plan of action.

3. *Design:* The design phase generates a detailed plan for programmers to follow. The proposed system is documented using flowcharts and data-flow diagrams. Flowcharts are visual diagrams of a process, including the decisions that need to be made along the way. **Data-flow diagrams** trace all data in an information system from the point at which data enters the system to its final resting place (storage or output). The data-flow diagram in Figure 10.3 shows the flow of concert ticket information.

   The design phase details the software, inputs and outputs, backups and controls, and processing requirements of the problem. Once the system plan is designed, a company evaluates existing software packages to determine whether it needs to develop a new piece of software or whether it can buy something already on the market and adapt it to fit its needs.

4. *Development:* It is during this phase that actual programming takes place. This phase is also the first part of the program development life cycle, described in detail later in the chapter. The documentation work is begun in this phase by technical writers.

5. *Testing and Installation:* Testing the program ensures it works properly. It is then installed for official use.

6. *Maintenance and Evaluation:* In this phase, program performance is monitored to determine whether the program is still meeting the needs of end users. Errors that weren't detected in the testing phase but that are discovered during use are corrected. Additional enhancements that users request are evaluated so that appropriate program modifications can be made.

Figure 10.2 Each step of the system development life cycle must be completed before you can progress to the next.

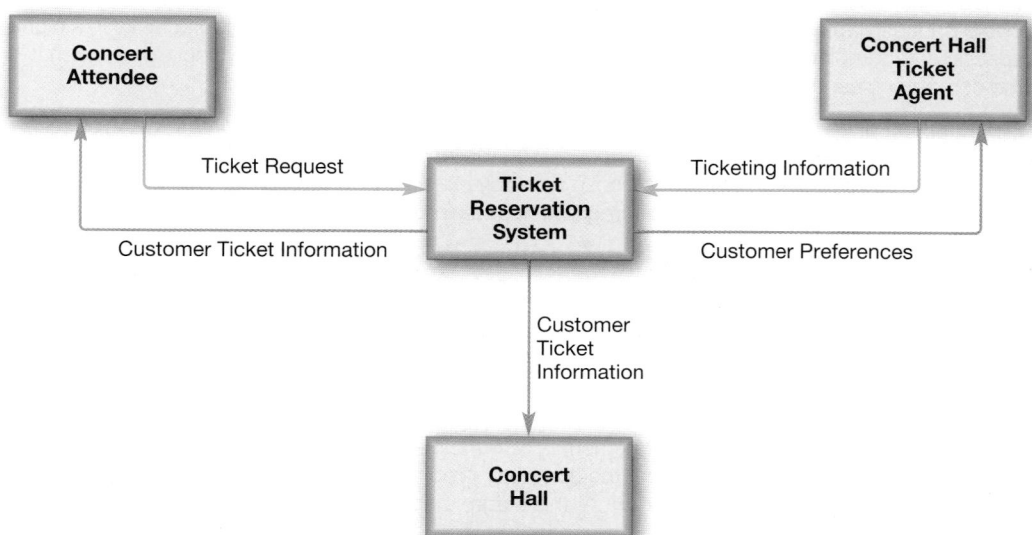

Figure 10.3 Data-flow diagrams illustrate the way data travels in an information system.

Can the SDLC vary from these steps? The waterfall model is an idealized view of software development. Most developers follow some variation of it. For example, a design team may "spiral," where a group that's supporting the work of another group will work concurrently with the other group on development. This contrasts with workflows in which the groups work independently, one after the other. Often, there is a "backflow" up the waterfall, because even well-designed projects can require redesign and specification changes midstream.

Some people criticize the waterfall model for taking too long to provide actual working software to the client. This may contribute to **scope creep**, an ever-changing set of requests from clients for additional features as they wait longer and longer to see a working prototype. Other developmental models are being used in the industry to address these issues (see the Bits & Bytes sidebar "Let Them See Your Work").

Life Cycle of a Program

Programming takes place during the fourth step in the SDLC and requires its own step-by-step process.

The Program Development Life Cycle

Objective 10.3   *Define programming and list the steps in the program development life cycle (PDLC).*

How do programmers tackle a programming project? **Programming** is the process of translating a task into a series of commands that a computer will use to perform that task. It involves identifying which parts of a task a computer can perform, describing those tasks in a highly specific and complete manner, and, finally, translating this description into the language spoken by the computer's central processing unit (CPU).

Programming often begins with nothing more than a problem or a request, such as "Can you tell me how many transfer students have applied to our college?" A proposal will then be developed for a system to solve this problem, if one doesn't already exist. Once a project has been deemed feasible and a plan is in place, the work of programming begins.

What are the steps in the programming process? Each programming project follows several stages, from conception to final deployment. This process is sometimes referred to as the **program development life cycle (PDLC)**:

1. *Describing the Problem:* First, programmers must develop a complete description of the problem. The problem statement identifies the task to be automated and describes how the software program will behave.

2. *Making a Plan:* The problem statement is next translated into a set of specific, sequential steps that describe exactly what the computer program must do to complete the work. The steps are known as an **algorithm**. At this stage, the algorithm is written in natural, ordinary language (such as English).

3. *Coding:* The algorithm is then translated into programming code, a language that is friendlier to humans than the 1s and 0s that the CPU speaks but is still highly structured. By coding the algorithm, programmers must think in terms of the operations that a CPU can perform.

4. *Debugging:* The code then goes through a process of debugging in which the programmers repair any errors found in the code.

5. *Testing and Documentation:* The software is tested by both the programming team and the people who will use the program. The results of the entire project are documented for the users and the development team. Finally, users are trained so that they can use the program efficiently.

Figure 10.4 illustrates the steps of a program development life cycle.

Now that you have an overview of the process involved in developing a program, let's look at each step in more detail.

The Problem Statement

Objective 10.4   *Describe how programmers construct a complete problem statement from a description of a task.*

Why is a problem statement necessary? The **problem statement** is the starting point of programming work. It's a clear description of what tasks the computer program must accomplish and how the program will execute those tasks and respond to unusual situations. Programmers develop problem statements so they can better understand the goals of their programming efforts.

What kind of problems can computer programs solve? As noted previously, tasks that are repetitive, work with electronic information, and follow a series of clear steps are good candidates for computerization. This might sound as if computers help us with only the dullest and most simplistic tasks. However, many sophisticated problems can be broken down into a series of easily computerized tasks. For example, pharmaceutical companies design drugs using complex computer programs that model molecules. Using simulation software to perform "dry" chemistry, chemists can quickly "create" new drugs and determine whether they will have the desired pharmacological effects. Scientists then select the most promising choices and begin to test those compounds in the "wet" laboratory.

What kinds of problems can computers not solve? Computers can't yet act with intuition or be spontaneously creative. They can attack highly challenging problems, such as making weather predictions or playing chess, but only in a way that takes advantage of what computers do best—making fast, reliable computations. Computers don't "think" as humans do. They can only follow instructions and algorithms.

How do programmers create problem statements? The goal in creating a useful problem statement is to have programmers interact with users to describe three things relevant to creating a useful program:

1. **Data** is the raw input that users have at the start of the job.
2. **Information** is the result, or output, that the users require at the end of the job.
3. **Method**, described precisely, is the process of how the program converts the inputs into the correct outputs.

For example, say you want to compute how much money you'll earn working at a parking garage. Your salary is $7.50 per hour for an eight-hour shift, but if you work more than eight hours a day, you get time and a half, which is $11.25 per hour, for the overtime work. To determine how much money you will make in any given day, you could multiply this in your mind, write it on a piece of paper, or use a calculator; alternatively, you could create a simple computer program to do the work for you. In this example, what are the three elements of the problem statement?

1. *Data (Input):* the data you have at the beginning of the problem, which is the number of hours you worked and the pay rate.
2. *Information (Output):* the information you need to have at the end of the problem, which is your total pay for the day.
3. *Method (Process):* the set of steps that take you from your input to your required output. In this case, the computer program would check if you worked more than eight hours. This is important because it would determine whether you would be paid overtime. If you didn't

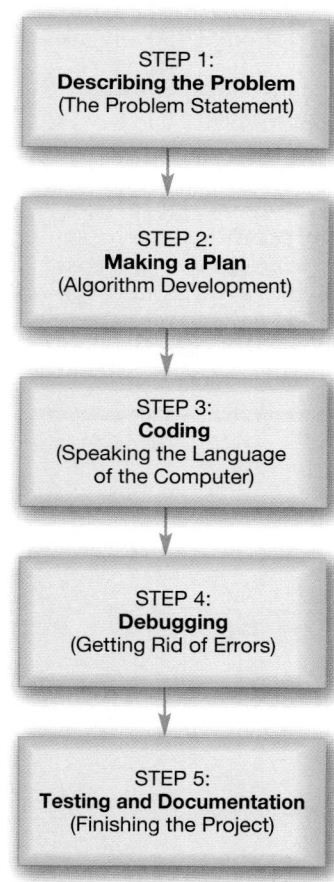

Figure 10.4 The stages that each programming project follows, from conception to final deployment, are collectively referred to as the program development life cycle (PDLC).

Sound Byte MyLab IT®

Using the Arduino Microcontroller

In this Sound Byte, you'll program the Arduino microcontroller to control LED lights and motors.

In this Helpdesk, you'll play the role of a helpdesk staffer, fielding questions about the life cycle of a program, the role a problem statement plays in programming, how programmers create algorithms and move from algorithm to code to the 1s and 0s a CPU can understand, and the steps involved in completing the program.

work overtime, the output would be $7.50 multiplied by the total number of hours you worked ($60.00 for eight hours). If you did work overtime, the program would calculate your pay as eight hours at $7.50 per hour for the regular part of your shift, plus an additional $11.25 multiplied by the number of overtime hours you worked.

How do programmers handle bad inputs? In the problem statement, programmers also must describe what the program should do if the input data is invalid or just gibberish. This part of the problem statement is referred to as **error handling**.

The problem statement also includes a **testing plan** that lists specific input numbers that the programmers would typically expect the user to enter. The plan then lists the precise output values that a perfect program would return for those input values. Later, in the testing process, programmers use the input and output data values from the testing plan to determine whether the program they created works the way it should. We discuss the testing process later in this chapter.

Does the testing plan cover every possible use of the program? The testing plan can't list every input the program could ever encounter. Instead, programmers work with users to identify the categories of inputs that will be encountered, find a typical example of each input category, and specify what kind of output must be generated. In the parking garage pay example, the error-handling process would describe what the program would do if you happened to enter "–8" (or any other nonsense character) for the number of hours you worked. The error handling would specify whether the program would return a negative value, prompt you to reenter the input, or shut down.

We could expect three categories of inputs in the parking garage example. The user might enter:

1. A negative number for hours worked that day
2. A positive number equal to or less than eight
3. A positive number greater than eight

The testing plan would describe how the error would be managed or how the output would be generated for each input category.

Is there a standard format for a problem statement? Most companies have their own format for documenting a problem statement. However, all problem statements include the same basic components: the data that is expected to be provided (inputs), the information that is expected to be produced (outputs), the rules for transforming the input into output (processing), an explanation of how the program will respond if users enter data that doesn't make sense (error handling), and a testing plan. Figure 10.5 shows a sample problem statement for our parking garage example.

Figure 10.5 Complete Problem Statement for the Parking Garage Example

Problem Statement

Program Goal	Compute the total pay for a fixed number of hours worked at a parking garage.
Input	Number of hours worked (a positive number)
Output	Total pay earned (a positive number)
Process	Total pay earned is computed as $7.50 per hour for the first eight hours worked each day. Any hours worked consecutively beyond the first eight are calculated at $11.25 per hour.
Error Handling	The input (number of hours worked) must be a positive real number. If it is a negative number or another unacceptable character, the program will force the user to reenter the information.

Testing Plan	Input	Output		Notes
	8	8*7.50		Testing positive input
	3	3*7.50		Testing positive input
	12	8*7.50 + 4*11.25		Testing overtime input
	–6	Error message/ask user to reenter value		Handling error

Algorithm Development

Objective 10.5 *Explain how programmers use flow control and design methodologies when developing algorithms.*

How does the process start? Once programmers understand exactly what the program must do and have created the final problem statement, they can begin developing a detailed algorithm—a set of specific, sequential steps that describe in natural language exactly what the computer program must do to complete its task. Let's look at some ways in which programmers design and test algorithms.

Do algorithms appear only in programming? Although the term algorithm may sound as though it would fall only under the domain of computing, you design and execute algorithms in your daily life. For example, say you're planning your morning. You know you need to

1. Get gas for your car,
2. Pick up a mocha latte at the café, and
3. Stop by the bookstore and buy a textbook before your 9 A.M. accounting lecture.

You quickly think over the costs and decide it will take $150 to buy all three. In what order will you accomplish all these tasks? How do you decide? Should you try to minimize the distance you'll travel or the time you'll spend driving? What happens if you forget your credit card?

Figure 10.6 presents an algorithm you could develop to make decisions about how to accomplish these tasks. This algorithm lays out a specific plan that encapsulates all of the choices you need to make in the course of completing a particular task and shows the specific sequence in which these tasks will occur. At any point in the morning, you could gather your current data (your inputs)—"I have $20 and my Visa card, but the ATM is down"—and the algorithm would tell you unambiguously what your next step should be.

What are the limitations of algorithms? An algorithm is a series of steps that's completely known: At each point, we know exactly what step to take next. However, not all problems can be described as a fixed sequence of predetermined steps; some involve random and unpredictable events. For example, although the program that computes your parking garage take-home pay each day works flawlessly, programs that predict stock prices are often wrong because many random events (inputs), such as a flood in India or a shipping delay in Texas, can change the outcomes (outputs).

How do programmers represent an algorithm? Programmers have several visual tools at their disposal to help them document the decision points and flow of their algorithms:

- **Flowcharts** provide a visual representation of the patterns the algorithm comprises. Figure 10.6 presents an example of a flowchart used to depict the flow of an algorithm. Specific symbols indicate program behaviors and decision types. Diamonds indicate that a yes/no decision will be performed, and rectangles indicate an instruction to follow. Figure 10.7 lists additional flowcharting symbols and explains what they indicate. Many software packages make it easy for programmers to create and modify flowcharts. Microsoft Visio is one popular flowcharting program.

- **Pseudocode** is a text-based approach to documenting an algorithm. In pseudocode, words describe the actions that the algorithm will take. Pseudocode is organized like an outline, with differing levels of indentation to indicate the flow of actions within the program. There is no standard vocabulary for pseudocode. Programmers use a combination of common words in their natural language and the special words that are commands in the programming language they're using.

Flow Control

How do programmers handle complex algorithms? When programmers develop an algorithm, they convert the problem statement into a list of steps the program will take.

Problems that are complex involve choices, so they can't follow a sequential list of steps. Algorithms therefore include **decision points**, places where the program must choose from a list of actions based on the value of a certain input.

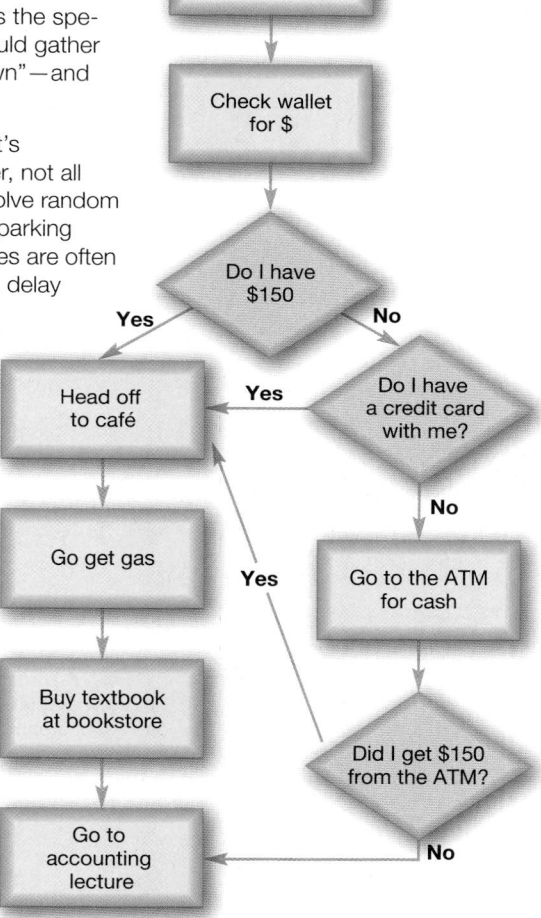

Figure 10.6 An algorithm you might use to plan your morning would include all of the decisions you might need to make and would show the specific sequence in which these steps would occur.

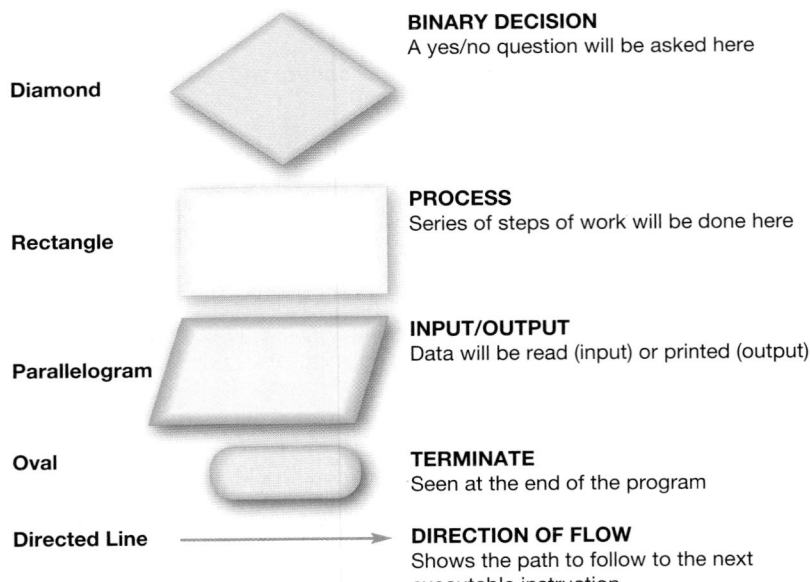

BINARY DECISION
A yes/no question will be asked here

PROCESS
Series of steps of work will be done here

INPUT/OUTPUT
Data will be read (input) or printed (output)

TERMINATE
Seen at the end of the program

DIRECTION OF FLOW
Shows the path to follow to the next executable instruction

Figure 10.7 Standard Symbols Used in Flowcharts

Figure 10.8 shows the steps of the algorithm in our parking garage example. If the number of hours you worked in a given day is eight or less, the program performs one simple calculation: It multiplies the number of hours worked by $7.50. If you worked more than eight hours in a day, the program takes a different path and performs a different calculation.

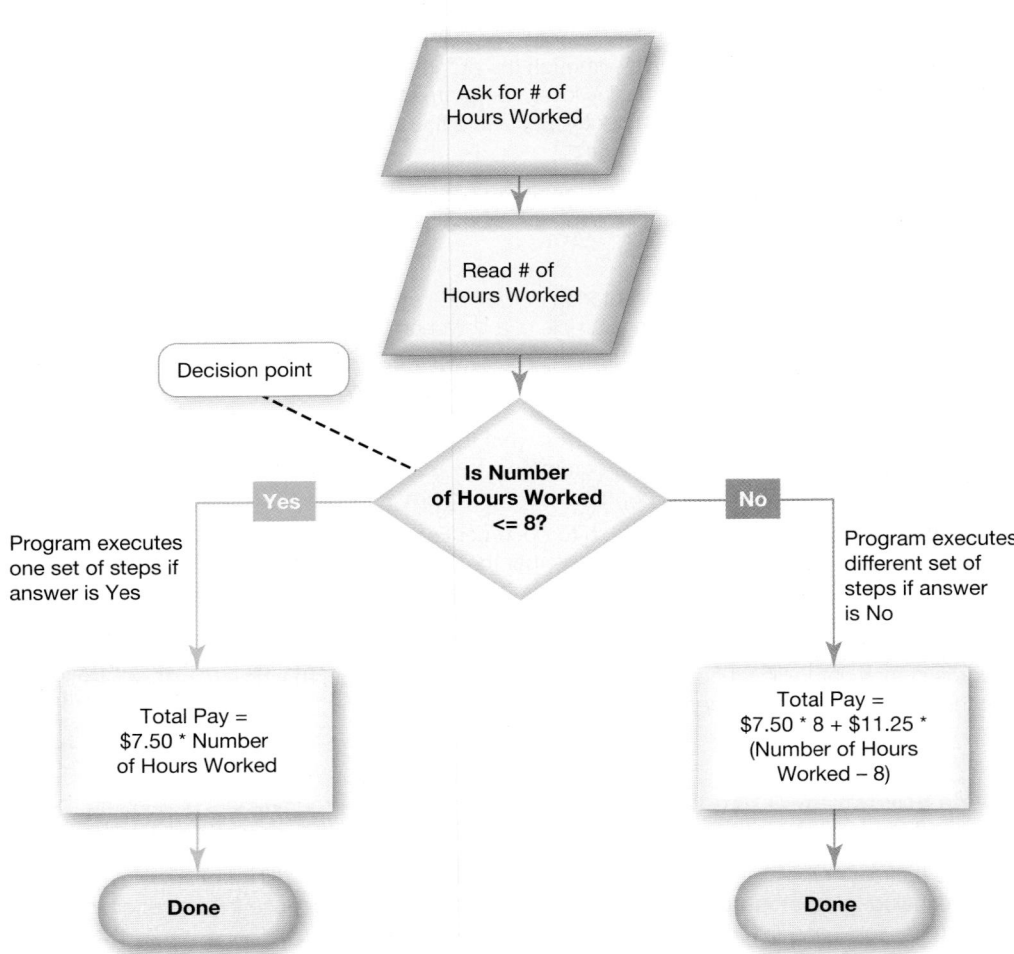

Figure 10.8 Decision points force the program to travel down one branch of the algorithm or another.

What kinds of decision points are there?

There are two main types of decisions that change the flow of an algorithm:

1. *Binary decisions:* One decision point that appears often in algorithms is like a "fork in the road." Such decision points are called **binary decisions** because they can be answered in one of only two ways: yes (true) or no (false). For example, the answer to the question, "Did you work at most eight hours today?" (Is number of hours worked ≤ 8 hours?), shown in Figure 10.8, is a binary decision because the answer can be only yes or no. If the answer is yes, the program follows one sequence of steps; if the answer is no, it follows a different path.

2. *Loops:* A second decision point that often appears in algorithms is a repeating loop. In a **loop**, a question is asked, and if the answer is yes, a set of actions is performed. Once the set of actions has finished, the question is asked again, creating a loop. As long as the answer to the question is yes, the algorithm continues to loop around and repeat the same set of actions. When the answer to the question is no, the algorithm breaks free of the looping and moves on to the first step that follows the loop.

In our parking garage example, the algorithm would require a loop if you wanted to compute the total pay you earned in a full week of work rather than in just a single day. For each day of the week, you would want to perform the same set of steps. Figure 10.9 shows how the idea of looping would be useful in this part of our parking garage program. On Monday, the program would set the Total Pay value to $0.00. It would then perform the following set of steps:

1. Read the number of hours worked that day.
2. Determine whether you qualified for overtime pay.
3. Compute the pay earned that day.
4. Add that day's pay to the total pay for the week.

On Tuesday, the algorithm would loop back, repeating the same sequence of steps it performed on Monday, adding the amount you earned on Tuesday to the Total Pay amount. The algorithm would continue to perform this loop for each day (seven times) until it hits Monday again. At that point, the decision "Are we still in the same week?" would become false. The program would stop, calculate the total pay for the entire week of work, and print the weekly paycheck. As you can see, there are three important features to look for in a loop:

1. A beginning point, or **initial value**. In our example, the total pay for the week starts at an initial value of $0.00.
2. A set of **actions** that will be performed. In our example, the algorithm computes the daily pay each time it passes through the loop.
3. A **test condition**, or a check to see whether the loop is completed. In our example, the algorithm should run the loop seven times, no more and no fewer.

Every higher-level programming language supports both making binary yes/no decisions and handling repeating loops. **Control structures** are keywords in a programming language that allow the programmer to direct the flow of the program based on a decision.

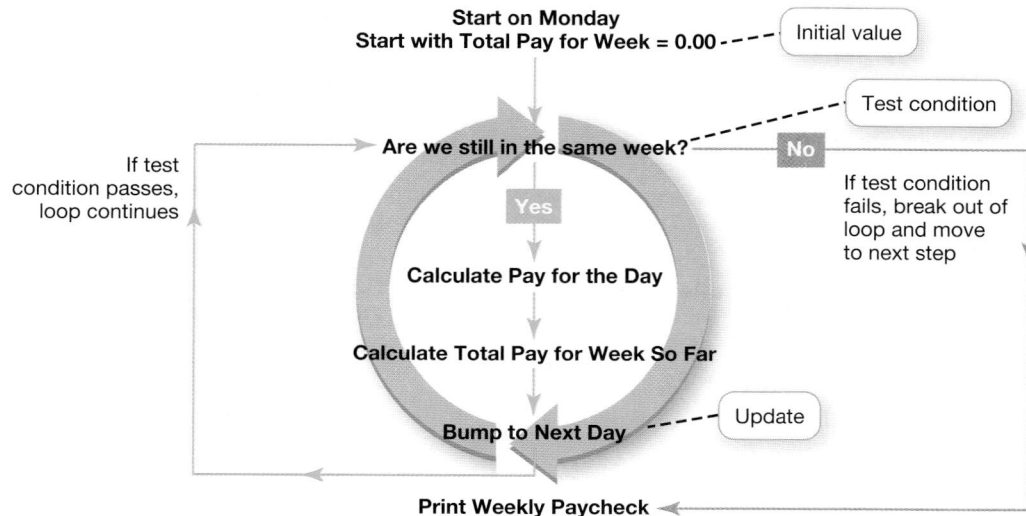

Figure 10.9 We stay in the loop until the test condition is no longer true. We then break free from the loop and move on to the next step in the algorithm, which is outside of the loop.

How do programmers create algorithms for specific tasks? It's difficult for human beings to force their problem-solving skills into the highly structured, detailed algorithms that computing machines require. Therefore, several different methodologies have been developed to support programmers, including top-down design and object-oriented analysis.

Design Methodology: Top-Down Design

What is top-down design? Top-down design is a systematic approach in which a problem is broken into a series of high-level tasks. In top-down design, programmers apply the same strategy repeatedly, breaking each task into successively more detailed subtasks. They continue until they have a sequence of steps that are close to the types of commands allowed by the programming language they'll use for coding. Previous coding experience helps programmers know the appropriate level of detail to specify in an algorithm generated by top-down design.

How is top-down design used in programming? Let's consider our parking garage example again. Initially, top-down design would identify three high-level tasks: Get Input, Process Data, and Output Results (see Figure 10.10a).

Applying top-down design to the first operation, Get Input, we'd produce the more detailed sequence of steps shown in the first step of Figure 10.10b: Announce Program, Give Users Instructions, and Read the Input NumberHoursWorkedToday. When we try to refine each of these steps, we find that they are just print-and-read statements and that almost every programming language will support them. Therefore, the operation Get Input has been converted to an algorithm.

Figure 10.10 (a) A top-down design is applied to the highest level of task in our parking garage example, (b) the tasks are further refined into subtasks, and (c) subtasks are refined into a sequence of instructions—an algorithm.

a

b

GET INPUT

Announce Program

Give Users Instructions

Read the Input NumberHoursWorkedToday

c

PROCESS DATA

Determine If They Qualify for Overtime

Compute Pay

```
if (NumberHoursWorkedToday <= 8)
    Pay = $7.50 * NumberHoursWorkedToday
else
    Pay = $7.50 * 8 +
        $11.25 * (NumberHoursWorkedToday – 8)
```

OUTPUT RESULTS

Print TotalPay

Next, we move to the second high-level task, Process Data, and break it into subtasks. In this case, we need to determine whether overtime hours were worked and to compute the pay accordingly. We continue to apply top-down design on all tasks until we can no longer break tasks into subtasks, as shown in Figure 10.10c.

Design Methodology: Object-Oriented Analysis

What is object-oriented analysis? With **object-oriented analysis**, programmers first identify all the categories of inputs that are part of the problem the program is meant to solve. These categories are called **classes**. With the object-oriented approach, the majority of design time is spent identifying the classes required to solve the problem, modeling them, and thinking about what relationships they need to be able to have with each other. Constructing the algorithm becomes a process of enabling the objects to interact. For example, the classes in our parking garage example might include a TimeCard class and an Employee class.

Classes are defined by

- Information (data) within the class and
- Actions (methods) associated with the class

For example, as shown in Figure 10.11, data for an Employee would include a Name, Address, and Social Security Number, whereas the methods for the Employee would be GoToWork(), Leave-Work(), and CollectPay(). The data of the class describes the class, so classes are often characterized as nouns, whereas methods are often characterized as verbs—the ways that the class acts and communicates with other classes.

Programmers may need to create several different examples of a class. Each of these examples is an **object**. In Figure 10.11, John Doe, Jane Doe, and Bill McGillicutty are each Employee objects (specific examples of the Employee class). Each object from a given class is described by the same pieces of data and has the same methods; for example, John, Jane, and Bill are all Employees and can use the GoToWork(), Leave-Work(), and CollectPay() methods. However, because they all have different pay grades (PayGrade 5, PayGrade 10, and PayGrade 4, respectively) and different Social Security numbers, they are all unique objects.

Why would a developer select the object-oriented approach over top-down design? An important aspect of object-oriented design is that it leads to **reusability**. Object-oriented analysis forces programmers to think in general terms about their problem, which tends to lead to more general and reusable solutions. Because object-oriented design generates a family of classes for each project, programmers can easily reuse existing classes from other projects, enabling them to produce new code quickly.

How does a programmer take advantage of reusability? Programmers must study the relationships between objects. Hierarchies of objects can be built quickly in object-oriented languages using the mechanism of inheritance. **Inheritance** means that a new class can automatically pick up all the data and methods of an existing class and then can extend and customize those to fit its own specific needs.

The original class is called the **base class**, and the new, modified class is called the **derived class**, as illustrated in Figure 10.12. You can compare this with making cookies. For example, you have a basic recipe for sugar cookies (base class: Sugar Cookies). However, in your family, some people like chocolate-flavored sugar cookies (derived class: Chocolate Sugar Cookies), and others like mini-chip sugar cookies (derived class: Mini-Chip Sugar Cookies). All the cookies share the attributes of the basic sugar cookie. However, instead of creating two entirely new recipes—one for chocolate cookies and one for mini-chip cookies— the two varieties inherit the basic sugar cookie (base class) recipe; the recipe is then customized to make the chocolate and mini-chip sugar cookies (derived classes).

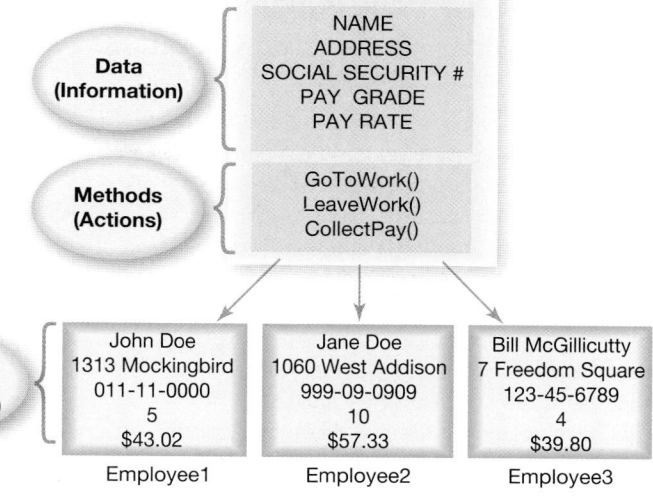

Figure 10.11 The Employee class includes the complete set of information (data) and actions (methods or behaviors) that describe an Employee.

Figure 10.12 In object-oriented programming, a single base class— for example, Soup Stock—helps you quickly create many additional derived classes, such as Lentil Soup or Minestrone Soup. (*Valentina Razumova/Shutterstock*)

Programming languages are evolving constantly. New languages emerge every year, and existing languages change dramatically. Therefore, it would be extremely difficult and time-consuming for programmers to learn every programming language. However, all languages have several common elements: rules of syntax, a set of keywords, a group of supported data types, and a set of allowed operators. By learning these four concepts, a programmer will be better equipped to approach any new language.

The transition from a well-designed algorithm to working code requires a clear understanding of the rules (syntax) of the programming language being used. **Syntax** is an agreed-on set of rules defining how a language must be structured. The English language has a syntax that defines which symbols are words (for example, *gorilla* is a word but *allirog* is not) and what order words and symbols (such as semicolons and commas) must follow.

Likewise, all programming languages have a formal syntax that programmers must follow when creating code **statements**, which are sentences in a code. **Syntax errors** are violations of the strict, precise set of rules that define the programming language. In a programming language, even misplacing a single comma or using a lowercase letter where a capital letter is required will generate a syntax error and make the program unusable.

Keywords are a set of words that have predefined meanings for a particular language. Keywords translate the flow of the algorithm into the structured code of the programming language. For example, when the algorithm indicates where a binary decision must be made, the programmer translates that binary decision into the appropriate keyword(s) from the language.

To illustrate further, in the programming language C++, the binary decision asking whether you worked enough hours to qualify for overtime pay would use the keywords **if else**. At this point in the code, the program can follow one of two paths: If you indicated through your input that you worked fewer than or

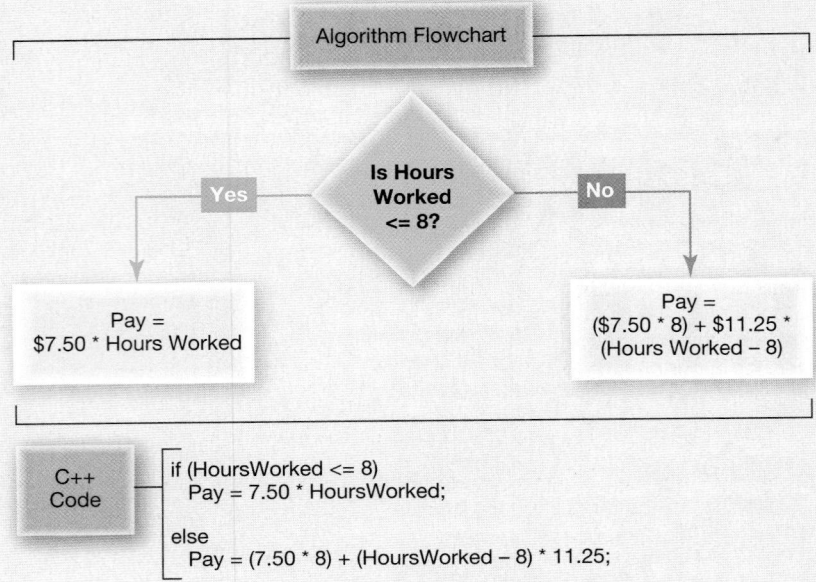

Figure 10.13 The binary decision in the algorithm has been converted into C++ code.

equal to eight hours, the program takes one path; if not (else), it follows another. Figure 10.13 shows this binary decision in the algorithm and the corresponding lines of C++ code that use the "if else" keywords.

Loops are likewise translated from algorithm to code by using the appropriate keyword from the language. For example, in the programming language Visual Basic, programmers use the keywords **For** and **Next** to implement a loop. After the keyword For, an input or output item is given a starting value. Then the statements, or "sentences," in the body of the loop are executed. When the command Next is run, the program returns to the For statement and increments the value of the input or output item by 1. It then tests that the value is still inside the range given. If it is, the body of the loop is executed again. This continues until the value of the input or output item is outside the range listed. The loop is then ended, and the statement that follows the loop is run.

Coding

Objective 10.6 *Discuss the categories of programming languages and the roles of the compiler and the integrated development environment (IDE) in coding.*

How is a person's idea translated into CPU instructions? Once programmers create an algorithm, they select the best programming language for the problem and then translate the algorithm into that language. Translating an algorithm into a programming language is the act of **coding**. Programming languages are somewhat readable by humans but then are translated into patterns of 1s and 0s to be understood by the CPU.

Although programming languages free programmers from having to think in binary language—the 1s and 0s that computers understand—they still force programmers to translate the ideas of the algorithm into a highly precise format. Programming languages are quite limited, allowing programmers to use only a few specific keywords, while demanding a consistent structure.

In the parking garage example, the following lines of Visual Basic code loop to sum up the total pay for the entire week:

```
For Day = 1 to 7
    TotalPay = TotalPay + Pay
Next Day
```

In this statement, the starting value of the input item Day is 1, and the program loops through until Day equals 7. Then, when Day equals 8, we move out of the loop, to the line of code that comes after the loop.

Often, a quick overview of a language's keywords can reveal the unique focus of that language. For example, the language C++ includes the keywords *public*, *private*, and *protected*, which indicate that the language includes a mechanism for controlling security.

Each time programmers want to store data in their program, they must ask the OS for storage space at a RAM location. **Data types** describe the kind of data being stored at the memory location. Each programming language has its own data types (although there is some degree of overlap). For example, C++ includes data types that represent integers, real numbers, characters, and Boolean (true–false) values. These C++ data types show up in code statements as *int* for integer, *float* for real numbers, *char* for characters, and *bool* for Boolean values.

Because it takes more room to store a real number such as 18,743.23 than it does to store the integer 1, programmers use data types in their code to indicate to the OS how much memory it needs to allocate. Programmers must be familiar with all the data types available in the language so that they can assign the most appropriate one for each input and output value, without wasting memory space.

Operators are the coding symbols that represent the fundamental actions of the language. Each programming language has its own set of operators. Many languages include common algebraic operators such as +, –, *, and / to represent the mathematical operations of addition, subtraction, multiplication, and division, respectively. Some languages, however, introduce

Figure 10.14 APL requires programmers to use an APL keyboard that includes the many specialized operators in the language.

new symbols as operators. The language APL (short for A Programmer's Language) was designed to solve multidimensional mathematical problems. APL includes less familiar operators such as rho, sigma, and iota, each representing a complex mathematical operation. Because it contains many specialized operators, APL requires programmers to use a special keyboard (see Figure 10.14).

Programming languages sometimes include other unique operators. The C++ operator >>, for example, is used to tell the computer to read data from the keyboard or from a file. The C++ operator && is used to tell the computer to check whether two statements are both true. "Is your age greater than 20 AND less than 30?" is a question that requires the use of the && operator.

In the following C++ code, several operators are being used. The > operator checks whether the number of hours worked is greater than 0. The && operator checks that the number of hours worked is simultaneously positive AND less than or equal to 8. If that happens, then the = operator sets the output Pay to equal the number of hours multiplied by $7.50:

```
if (Hours > 0 && Hours <= 8)
    Pay = Hours * 7.50;
```

Knowing operators such as these, as well as the other common elements described earlier, helps programmers learn new programming languages.

How exactly do programmers move from algorithm to code? Once programmers have an algorithm, in the form of either a flowchart or a series of pseudocode statements, they identify the key pieces of information the algorithm uses to make decisions:

- What steps are required for the calculation of new information?
- What is the exact sequence of the steps?
- Are there points where decisions have to be made?
- What kinds of decisions are made?
- Are there places where the same steps are repeated several times?

Once programmers identify the required information and the flow of how it will be changed by each step of the algorithm, they can begin converting the algorithm into computer code in a specific programming language.

Categories of Programming Languages

What exactly is a programming language? A **programming language** is a kind of "code" for the set of instructions the CPU knows how to perform. Computer programming languages use special words and strict rules so that programmers can control the CPU without having to know all its hardware details.

What kinds of programming languages are there? Programming languages are classified into several major groupings, sometimes referred to as generations. With each generation of language development, programmers have been relieved of more of the burden of keeping track of what the hardware requires. The earliest languages—assembly language and machine languages—required the programmer to know a great deal about how the computer was constructed internally and how it stored data. Programming is becoming easier as languages continue to become more closely matched to how humans think about problems.

How have modern programming languages evolved? There are five major categories of languages:

1. A **first-generation language (1GL)** is the actual **machine language** of a CPU, the sequence of bits (1s and 0s) that the CPU understands.

2. A **second-generation language (2GL)** is also known as an **assembly language**. Assembly languages allow programmers to write their programs using a set of short, English-like commands that speak directly to the CPU and that give the programmer direct control of hardware resources.

3. A **third-generation language (3GL)** uses symbols and commands to help programmers tell the computer what to do. This makes 3GL languages easier for humans to read and remember. Most programming languages today, including BASIC, FORTRAN, COBOL, C/C++, and Java, are considered third generation.

4. **Fourth-generation languages (4GLs)** include database query languages and report generators. **Structured Query Language (SQL)** is a database programming language that is an example of a 4GL. The following SQL command would check a huge table of data on the employees and build a new table showing all those employees who worked overtime:

   ```
   SELECT EmployeeName, TotalHours FROM EMPLOYEES WHERE
   "TotalHours" Total More Than 8
   ```

5. **Fifth-generation languages (5GLs)** are considered the most "natural" of languages. In a 5GL, a problem is presented as a series of facts or constraints instead of as a specific algorithm. The system of facts can then be queried (asked) questions. Prolog (PROgram-mingLOGic) is an example of a 5GL. A Prolog program could be a list of family relationships and rules such as "Mike is Sally's brother. A brother and a sister have the same mother and father." Once a user has amassed a huge collection of facts and rules, he or she can ask for a list of all Mike's cousins, for example. Prolog would find the answers by repeatedly applying the principles of logic instead of following a systematic algorithm that the programmer provided.

Figure 10.15 shows small code samples of examples of each generation of language.

Figure 10.15 Sample Code for Different Language Generations

Generation	Example	Sample Code
1GL	Machine	**Bits** describe the commands to the CPU. **1110 0101 1001 1111 0000 1011 1110 0110**
2GL	Assembly	**Words** describe the commands to the CPU. **ADD Register 3, Register 4, Register 5**
3GL	FORTRAN, BASIC, C, Java	**Symbols** describe the commands to the CPU. **TotalPay = Pay + OvertimePay**
4GL	SQL	**More powerful commands** allow complex work to be done in a single sentence. **SELECT isbn, title, price, price*0.06 AS sales_tax FROM books WHERE price>100.00 ORDER BY title;**
5GL	Prolog	Programmers can build applications **without specifying an algorithm**. Find all the people who are Mike's cousins as: ?-cousin (Mike, family)

Do programmers have to use a higher-level programming language to solve a problem with a computer? No, experienced programmers sometimes write a program directly in the CPU's assembly language. However, the main advantage of higher-level programming languages—C or Java, for example—is that they allow programmers to think in terms of the problem they're solving rather than having to worry about the internal design and specific instructions available for a given CPU. In addition, higher-level programming languages have the capability to easily produce a program that will run on differently configured CPUs. For example, if programmers wrote directly in the assembly language for an Intel i7 CPU, they would have to rewrite the program completely if they wanted it to run on a Sun workstation with the SPARC64 CPU. Thus, higher-level programming languages offer **portability**—the capability to move a completed solution easily from one type of computer to another.

What happens first when you write a program? All of the inputs a program receives and all of the outputs the program produces need to be stored in the computer's RAM while the program is running. Each input and each output item that the program manipulates, also known as a **variable**, needs to be announced early in the program so that memory space can be set aside. A **variable declaration** tells the operating system that the program needs to allocate storage space in RAM. The following line of code is a variable declaration in the language Java:

```
int Day;
```

The one simple line makes a lot of things happen behind the scenes:

- The variable's name is Day. The "int" that precedes the Day variable indicates that this variable will always be an integer (a whole number such as 15 or –4).
- The statement "int Day;" asks for enough RAM storage space to hold an integer. After the RAM space is found, it is reserved. As long as the program is running, these RAM cells will be saved for the Day variable, and no other program can use that memory until the program ends. From that point on, when the program encounters the symbol Day, it will access the memory it reserved as Day and find the integer stored there.

Can programmers leave notes to themselves inside a program? Programmers often insert a **comment** into program code to explain the purpose of a section of code, to indicate the date they wrote the program, or to include other important information about the code so that fellow programmers can more easily understand and update it.

Comments are written into the code in plain English. The compiler, a program that translates codes into binary 1s and 0s, just ignores comments. Comments are intended to be read only by human programmers. Languages provide a special symbol or keyword to indicate the beginning of a comment. In C++, the symbol // at the beginning of a line indicates that the rest of the line is a comment.

What would completed code for a program look like? Figure 10.16 presents a completed C++ program for our parking garage example. We'll discuss later how you would actually enter this program on your system. This program, which is written in a top-down style, does not make use of objects. Each statement in the program is executed sequentially (that is, in order from the first statement to the last) unless the program encounters a keyword that changes the flow. In the figure:

1. The program begins by declaring the variables needed to store the program's inputs and outputs in RAM.
2. Next, the *for* keyword begins a looping pattern. All of the steps between the very beginning bracket ({) and the end one (}) will be repeated seven times to gather the total pay for each day of the week.
3. The next section collects the input data from the user.
4. The program then checks that the user entered a reasonable value. In this case, a positive number for hours worked must be entered.
5. Next, the program processes the data. If the user worked eight or fewer hours, he or she is paid at the rate of $7.50 per hour, whereas hours exceeding eight are paid at $11.25 per hour.
6. The final statement updates the value of the TotalPay variable. The end bracket indicates that the program has reached the end of a loop. The program will repeat the loop to collect and

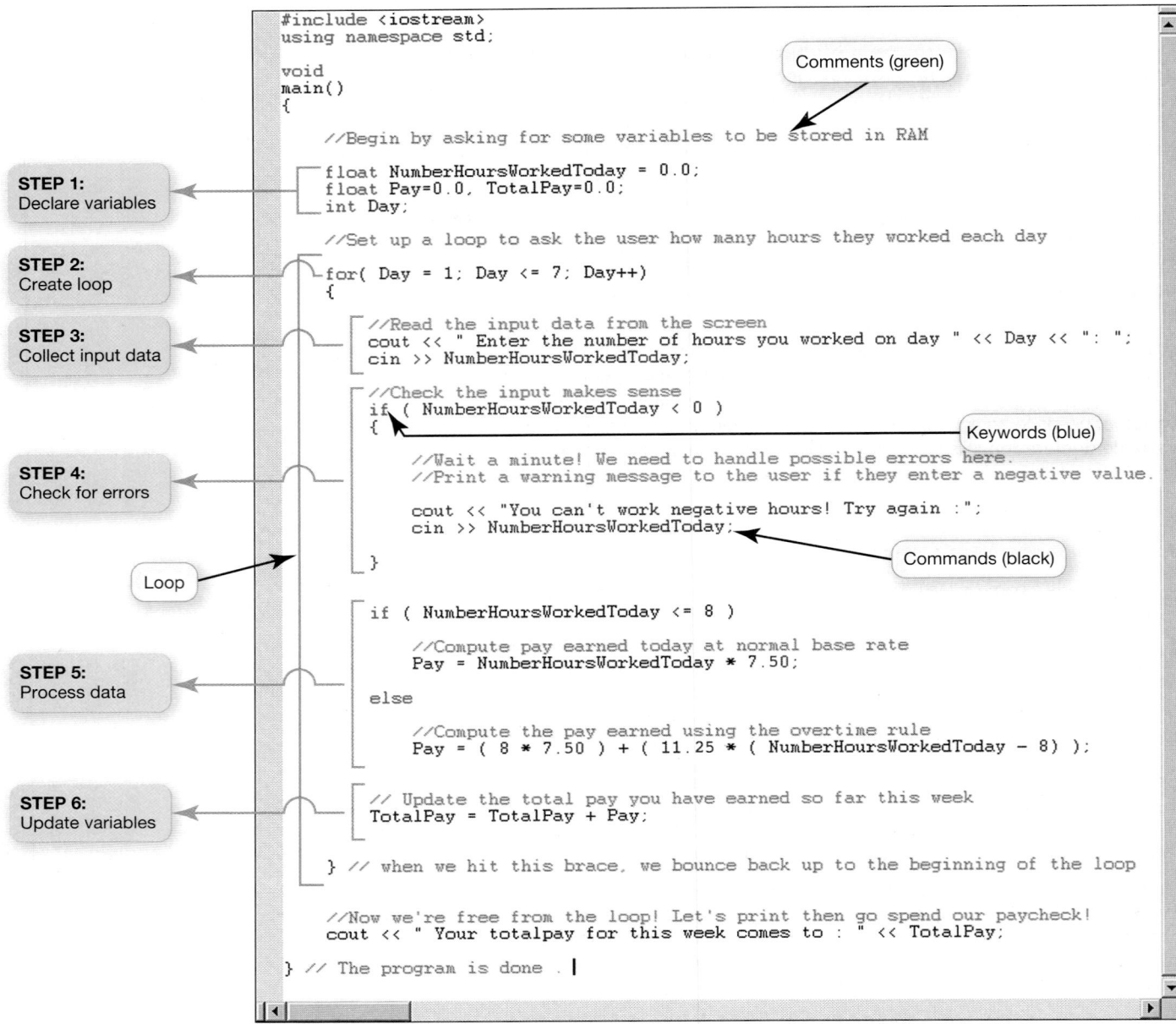

```cpp
#include <iostream>
using namespace std;

void
main()
{
    //Begin by asking for some variables to be stored in RAM

    float NumberHoursWorkedToday = 0.0;
    float Pay=0.0, TotalPay=0.0;
    int Day;

    //Set up a loop to ask the user how many hours they worked each day

    for( Day = 1; Day <= 7; Day++)
    {
        //Read the input data from the screen
        cout << " Enter the number of hours you worked on day " << Day << ": ";
        cin >> NumberHoursWorkedToday;

        //Check the input makes sense
        if ( NumberHoursWorkedToday < 0 )
        {
            //Wait a minute! We need to handle possible errors here.
            //Print a warning message to the user if they enter a negative value.

            cout << "You can't work negative hours! Try again :";
            cin >> NumberHoursWorkedToday;

        }

        if ( NumberHoursWorkedToday <= 8 )

            //Compute pay earned today at normal base rate
            Pay = NumberHoursWorkedToday * 7.50;

        else

            //Compute the pay earned using the overtime rule
            Pay = ( 8 * 7.50 ) + ( 11.25 * ( NumberHoursWorkedToday - 8) );

        // Update the total pay you have earned so far this week
        TotalPay = TotalPay + Pay;

    } // when we hit this brace, we bounce back up to the beginning of the loop

    //Now we're free from the loop! Let's print then go spend our paycheck!
    cout << " Your totalpay for this week comes to : " << TotalPay;

} // The program is done . |
```

Labels on the figure:

Comments (green)

STEP 1: Declare variables

STEP 2: Create loop

STEP 3: Collect input data

Keywords (blue)

STEP 4: Check for errors

Commands (black)

Loop

STEP 5: Process data

STEP 6: Update variables

Figure 10.16 A Complete C++ Program That Solves the Parking Garage Pay Problem

process the information for the next day. When the seventh day of data has been processed, the Day variable will be bumped up to the next value, 8. This causes the program to fail the test (Day <= 7?). At that point, the program exits the loop, prints the results, and quits.

Are there ways in which programmers can make their code more useful for the future? One aspect of converting an algorithm into good code is the programmer's ability to design general code that can easily be adapted to new settings. Sections of code that will be used repeatedly, with only slight modification, can be packaged into reusable "containers" or components. Depending on the language, these reusable components are referred to as functions, methods, procedures, subroutines, modules, or packages.

In our program, we could create a function that implements the overtime pay rule. As it stands in Figure 10.16, the code works only in situations in which the hourly pay is exactly $7.50 and the bonus pay is exactly $11.25. However, if we rewrote this part of the processing rules as a function, we could have code that would work for any base pay rate and any overtime rate. If the base pay

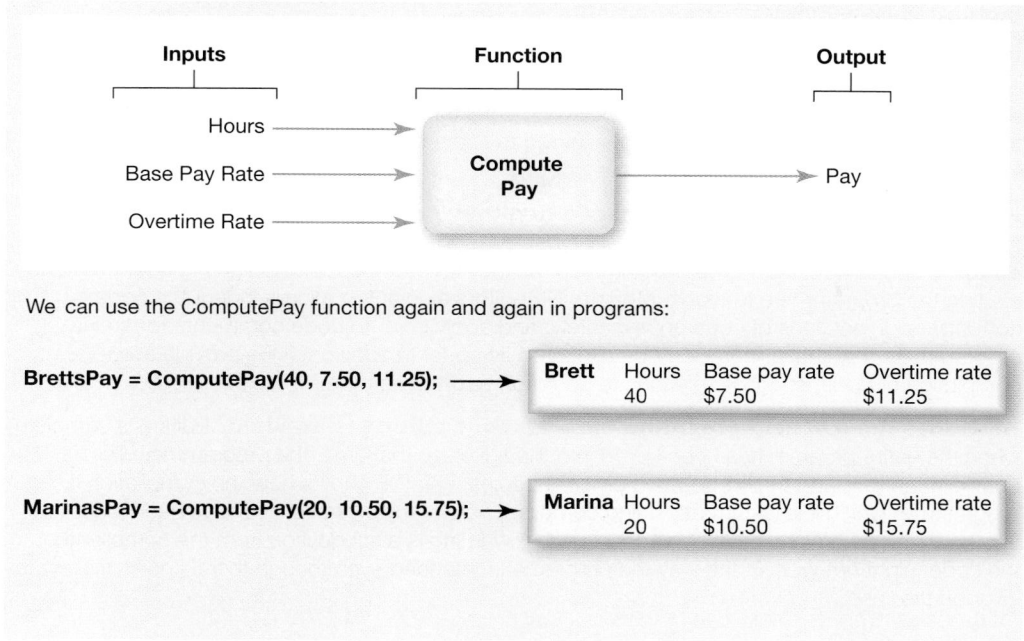

We can use the ComputePay function again and again in programs:

BrettsPay = ComputePay(40, 7.50, 11.25); ⟶

Brett	Hours	Base pay rate	Overtime rate
	40	$7.50	$11.25

MarinasPay = ComputePay(20, 10.50, 15.75); ⟶

Marina	Hours	Base pay rate	Overtime rate
	20	$10.50	$15.75

Figure 10.17 A function is a reusable component that can be used in different settings.

rate or overtime rate changed, the function would use whichever values it was given as input to compute the output pay variable. Such a function, as shown in Figure 10.17, may be reused in many settings without changing any of the code.

The Compiler

How does a programmer move from code in a programming language to the 1s and 0s the CPU can understand? **Compilation** is the process by which code is converted into machine language—the language the CPU can understand. A **compiler** is a program that understands both the syntax of the programming language and the exact structure of the CPU and its machine language. It can "read" the **source code**, which comprises the instructions programmers have written in the higher-level language and can translate the source code directly into machine language—the binary patterns that will execute commands on the CPU. (You can learn more about the binary number system in Chapters 2 and 4.)

Each programming language has its own compiler. It's a program that you purchase and install just like any other software on your system. Separate versions of the compiler are required if you want to compile code that will run on separate processor types. One version of a compiler would create finished programs for a Fujitsu SPARC64 processor, for example, and another version of the compiler would create programs for an Intel i7 CPU.

At this stage, once the compiler has generated the executable program, the programmers have a program to distribute. An **executable program**, the binary sequence that instructs the CPU to run its code, can't be read by human eyes because it consists of pure binary codes. Executable programs are stored as *.exe or *.com files on Windows systems.

Does every programming language have a compiler? Some programming languages don't have a compiler but use an interpreter instead. An **interpreter** translates the source code into an intermediate form, line by line. Each line is then executed as it's translated. The compilation process takes longer than the interpretation process because in compilation, all the lines of source code are translated into machine language before any lines are executed. However, the finished compiled program runs faster than an interpreted program because the interpreter is constantly translating and executing as it goes.

If producing the fastest executable program is important, programmers will choose a language that uses a compiler instead of an interpreter. For development environments in which many changes are still being made to the code, interpreters have an advantage because programmers don't have to wait for the entire program to be recompiled each time they make a change. With interpreters, programmers can immediately see the results of their program changes as they're making them.

Integrated Development Environments

What tools make the coding process easier? Modern programming is supported by a collection of tools that make the writing and testing of software easier. An **integrated development environment (IDE)** is a developmental tool that helps programmers write and test their programs. One IDE can often be configured to support many different languages. Figure 10.18 shows the IDE jGRASP working with Java code.

How does an IDE help programmers when they're typing the code? **Code editing** is the step in which a programmer physically types the code into the computer. An IDE includes an **editor**, a special tool that helps programmers as they enter the code, highlighting keywords and alerting the programmers to typos. Modern IDE editors also automatically indent the code correctly, align sections of code appropriately, and apply color to code comments to remind programmers that these lines won't be executed as code. In addition, IDEs provide auto-completion of code, suggest solutions to common errors, and more.

How does the IDE help programmers after code editing is finished? Editing is complete when the entire program has been keyed into the editor. At that time, the programmer clicks a button in the IDE, and the compilation process begins. The IDE shows how the compilation is progressing, which line is currently being compiled, how many syntax errors have been identified, and how many warnings have been generated. A warning is a suggestion from the compiler that the code might not work in the way the programmer intended even though there's no formal syntax error on the line.

Figure 10.18 The jGRASP IDE is a free tool that helps the programmer visualize the code as it runs to help eliminate logical errors. *(From jGRASP (http://www.jgrasp.org/viewers.html). Copyright © by Auburn University. Used by permission Auburn University)*

A syntax error is a violation of the strict, precise set of rules that define the language. Programmers create syntax errors when they misspell keywords (such as typing BEEGIN instead of BEGIN) or use an operator incorrectly (such as typing x =, y + 2 instead of x = y + 2). Once compilation is finished, the IDE presents all of the syntax errors in one list. The programmer can then click any item in the list to see a detailed explanation of the type of error. When the programmer double-clicks an item in the list, the editor jumps to the line of code that contains the error, enabling the programmer to repair syntax errors quickly.

Debugging

Objective 10.7 *Identify the role of debugging in program development.*

What is debugging? Once the program has compiled without syntax errors, it has met all of the syntax rules of the language. However, this doesn't mean that the program behaves in a logical way or that it appropriately addresses the task the algorithm described. If programmers made errors in the strategy used in the algorithm or in how they translated the algorithm to code, problems will occur. The process of running the program over and over to find and repair errors and to make sure the program behaves in the way it should is termed **debugging** (see Figure 10.19).

Figure 10.19 Debugging—the process of correcting errors in a program—combines logic with an understanding of the problem to be solved. *(nullplus/Shutterstock)*

How do programmers know the program has solved the problem? At this point in the process, the testing plan that was documented as part of the problem statement becomes critically important to programmers. The testing plan clearly lists input and output values, showing how the users expect the program to behave in each input situation. It's important that the testing plan contain enough specific examples to test every part of the program.

In the parking garage problem, we want to make sure the program calculates the correct pay for a day when you worked eight or fewer hours and for a day when you worked more than eight hours. Each of these input values forces the program to make different decisions in its processing path. To be certain the program works as intended, programmers try every possible path.

For example, once we can successfully compile the example code for the parking garage problem, we can begin to use our testing plan. The testing plan indicates that an input of 3 for NumberHoursWorkedToday must produce an output of Pay = 3 * $7.50 = $22.50. In testing, we run the program and make sure that an input value of 3 yields an output value of $22.50. To check that the processing path involving overtime is correct, we input a value of 12 hours. That input must produce Pay = 8 * $7.50 + (12 − 8) * $11.25 = $105.00.

A complete testing plan includes sample inputs that exercise all the error handling required as well as all the processing paths. Therefore, we would also want to check how the program behaves when NumberHoursWorkedToday is entered as −6.

If the testing plan reveals errors, why does the program compile? The compiler can't think through code or decide whether what the programmer wrote is logical. The compiler can only make sure that the specific rules of the language are followed.

For example, if in the parking garage problem we happened to type the if statement as

```
if (NumberHoursWorkedToday > 88)
    //Use the Overtime Pay rule
```

instead of

```
if (NumberHoursWorkedToday > 8)
    //Use the Overtime Pay rule
```

the compiler wouldn't see a problem. It doesn't seem strange to the compiler that you only get overtime after working 88 hours a day. These **logical errors** in the problem are caught only when the program executes.

Another kind of error caught when the program executes is a **runtime error**. For example, it's easy for a programmer to accidentally write code that occasionally divides by zero, a big "no-no" mathematically! That kind of forbidden operation generates a runtime error message.

Are there tools that help programmers find logic errors? Most IDEs include a tool called a **debugger** that helps programmers dissect a program as it runs. The debugger pauses the program while it's executing and allows the programmer to examine the values of all the variables. The programmer can then run the program in slow motion, moving it forward just one line at a time.

This lets the programmer see the exact sequence of steps being executed and the outcome of each calculation. He or she can then isolate the precise place in which a logical error occurs, correct the error, and recompile the program.

Testing and Documentation

Objective 10.8   *Explain the importance of testing and documentation in program development.*

What is the first round of testing for a program? Once debugging has detected all the runtime errors in the code and they have been repaired, it's time for users to test the program. This process is called internal testing. In internal testing, a group within the software company uses the program in every way it can imagine—including how the program was intended to be used and in ways only new users might think up. The internal testing group makes sure the program behaves as described in the original testing plan. Any differences in how the program responds are reported back to the programming team, which makes the final revisions and updates to the code.

The next round of testing is external testing. In this testing round, people like the ones who eventually will purchase and use the software must work with it to determine whether it matches their original vision.

What other testing does the code undergo? Before its final commercial release, software is often provided free or at a reduced cost in a **beta version** to certain test sites or to interested users. By providing users with a beta version of software, programmers can collect information about remaining errors in the code and make a final round of revisions before officially releasing the program. Often, popular software packages like Microsoft Windows and Microsoft Office are available for free beta download for months before the official public release.

What happens if problems are found after beta testing? The manufacturer will make changes before releasing the product to other manufacturers, for installation on new machines, for example. That point in the release cycle is called **release to manufacturers (RTM)**. After the RTM is issued, the product is in **general availability (GA)** and can be purchased by the public.

Users often uncover problems in a program even after its commercial release to the public. These problems are addressed with the publication of software updates or **service packs**. Users can download these software modules to repair errors identified in the program code. Most operating systems now push updates directly to users to make sure key security patches are automatically installed.

After testing, is the project finished? Once testing is complete, but before the product is officially released, the work of **documentation** is still ahead. At this point, technical writers create internal documentation for the program that describes the development and technical details of the software, how the code works, and how the user interacts with the program. In addition, the technical publishing department produces all the necessary user documentation that will be distributed to the program's users. User training begins once the software is distributed. Software trainers take the software to the user community and teach others how to use it efficiently.

Before moving on to Part 2:

1. ▶ Watch Chapter Overview Video 10.1.
2. Then take the Check Your Understanding quiz.

Check Your Understanding // Review & Practice

For a quick review to see what you've learned so far, answer the following questions.

multiple choice

1. Custom-built mini-programs that can execute a complicated series of commands in a tool like Microsoft Word or Excel are called
   a. executables.
   b. compilers.
   c. macros.
   d. debuggers.

2. A data-flow diagram
   a. shows all of the steps of the algorithm.
   b. includes the data, people, and hardware needed to help in decision making.
   c. shows where data is entered and is stored in an information system.
   d. includes design, development, and testing details.

3. The life cycle of a program begins with describing a problem and making a plan. Then the PDLC requires
   a. an algorithm.
   b. process, input, and output.
   c. data, information, and method.
   d. coding, debugging, and testing.

4. In object-oriented analysis, classes are defined by
   a. objects and data.
   b. operators and objects.
   c. data and methods.
   d. behaviors and keywords.

5. Compiling a program turns
   a. top-down design into object-oriented design.
   b. source code into an executable program.
   c. a first-generation language into a fourth-generation language.
   d. none of the above

 Go to **MyLab IT** to take an autograded version of the *Check Your Understanding* review and to find all media resources for the chapter.

TechBytes Weekly Go to TechBytes Weekly for current technology news and discussion questions!

Try This

Programming with Corona

You've already been doing mobile app development in the Make This activities using App Inventor. In this Try This, we'll use the product Corona to create an application that could be run on either an Android or an iOS device. For more step-by-step instructions, watch the Try This video.

NOTE: You need to be confident in installing and uninstalling demo software to your system to proceed. Refer to Chapter 4 if you need more support. Also, be aware that you will be asked to provide an e-mail address to qualify for the free trial version of Corona.

Step 1 First install the application Notepad++. From **notepad-plus-plus.org**, click **Download** to install the editor Notepad++. Launch Notepad++ and click **File->New**.

Step 2 Head to **coronalabs.com**. Enter your email and click the button **Download**, and follow the download instructions.

Step 3 Run the Corona Simulator.

Step 4 In Notepad++, type the following:

```
myText = display.newText("TECH IN ACTION", 400, 400, native.systemFont, 88)
myText:setTextColor(1, 0.1, 0.1)
```

Step 5 In Notepad++, click **File-> Save As**. In the Save As type dropdown, select **LUA source File (*.lua)** and save this file with the name **main**. The file *main.lua* is now created.

Step 6 Move to the Corona Simulator window and click **File->Open Project**. Then navigate to *main.lua* and open it.

You have just written a complete iPhone application! You can also run it on an iPad or any Android phone or tablet. In the Corona Simulation window, click **View->View As** and see how the program output looks on a few different devices.

Step 7 Play with changing the color by altering the values in setTextColor. Try adding the line **myText.rotation = 45**.

Visit **docs.coronalabs.com/api** to see the full set of built-in methods available. Look over the physics library and begin to imagine what you could create!

(Corona Labs Inc.)

Make: A Notepad

Drawing and writing on a touch device is convenient and creative.

In this exercise, you'll continue your mobile app development by using the Canvas component in App Inventor to build a notepad that lets you switch pen colors and draw shapes.

The Canvas component lets you draw on the screen. Combine that with statements like "if" and "for" and you can make more sophisticated behaviors.

Use the Canvas component in App Inventor to combine control statements with drawing commands to create your own images.

(Copyright MIT, used with permission)

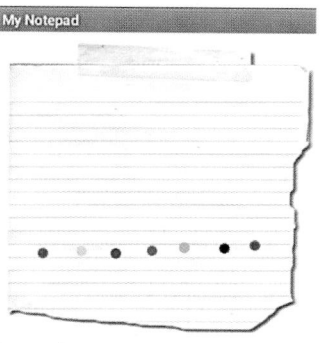

Instructions:
Tap screen to draw a dot or select a color
Drag finger to draw a line
Swipe diagonally bottom to top to clear

(Copyright MIT, used with permission)

(Copyright MIT, used with permission)

For the instructions for this exercise, go to MyLab IT.

Programming Languages

Learning Outcome 10.2 **You will understand the factors programmers consider when selecting an appropriate programming language for a specific problem and will be familiar with some modern programming languages.**

Earlier in the chapter, you learned about the five main categories (generations) of programming languages. In this section, we discuss the specific programming languages that are members of these different generations.

Many Programming Languages

In any programming endeavor, programmers want to create a solution that meets several objectives. The software needs to:

- Run quickly
- Be reliable
- Be simple to expand later when the demands on the system change
- Be completed on time
- Be finished for the minimum possible cost

Because it's difficult to balance these conflicting goals, many programming languages have been developed. Although programming languages often share common characteristics, each language has specific traits that allow it to be the best fit for certain types of projects. The ability to understand enough about each language to match it to the appropriate style of problem is an exceptionally powerful skill for programmers.

Need for Diverse Languages

Objective 10.9 *Discuss the driving factors behind the popularity of various programming languages.*

What languages are popular today? One quick way to determine which languages are popular is to examine job postings for programmers. As of this writing, the languages most in demand include C/C++ and Java. In specific industries, certain languages tend to dominate the work. In the banking and insurance industries, for example, the programming language COBOL is still common, although most other industries rarely use it anymore. Figure 10.20 shows the popularity of different languages in the software industry.

How do I know which language to study first? A good introductory programming course will emphasize many skills and techniques that will carry over from one language to another. You should find a course that emphasizes design, algorithm development, debugging techniques, and project management. All of these aspects of programming will help you in any language environment.

Visual languages like App Inventor or Scratch are often used to introduce key programming concepts. Many colleges and universities have opted to have students begin with Java, C++, or Python. Students interested in the arts often use the language **Processing (processing.org)** as a first experience with coding.

How does anyone learn so many languages? Professional programmers can become proficient at new languages because they've become familiar with the basic components, discussed in this chapter's Dig Deeper feature, that are common to all languages: syntax, keywords, operators, and data types.

▶ Sound Byte MyLab IT®

Programming with the Processing Language

In this Sound Byte, you'll use the Processing language to create interactive art.

Figure 10.20 Programming Language Popularity

Selecting the Right Language

Objective 10.10   *Summarize the considerations in identifying an appropriate programming language for a specific setting.*

How do programmers know which language to select for a specific project? A programming team considers several factors before selecting the language it will use for a specific project:

- *Space available:* Not all languages produce code that takes up the same amount of space. Therefore, the target language should be well matched to the amount of space available for the final program. For example, if the program will be embedded in a chip for use in a cell phone, it's important for the language to create space-efficient programs.

- *Speed required:* Although poorly written code executes inefficiently in any language, some languages can execute more quickly than others. Some projects require a focus on speed rather than size. These projects require a language that produces code that executes in the fastest possible time.

- *Organizational resources available:* Another consideration is the resources available in a manager's group or organization. Selecting a language that's easy to use and that will be easy to maintain if there's a turnover in programmers is an important consideration.

- *Type of target application:* Certain languages are customized to support a specific environment (UNIX or Windows, for instance). Knowing which languages are most commonly used for which environments can be helpful. We'll discuss this more in the next section.

Bits&Bytes   Coding for Zombies

There are an incredible number of free courses available for the latest programming technologies. Rails for Zombies from Code School is one such course. The free interactive coding environment runs right in your browser and teaches you to create a Twitter-like program for Zombies using the Ruby on Rails web application framework. Also, explore course providers like Coursera, Udacity, and Codecademy. They offer courses complete with quizzes, video lectures, and live discussion on topics like Python, Web Programming, and Java.

(Code School)

Ethics in IT

When Software Runs Awry

In the field of software programming, mistakes can be costly. Consider these examples:

- In 1996, Europe's newest unmanned rocket, the Ariane 5, had to be destroyed seconds after launch, along with its cargo of four scientific satellites. Cost: $500 million. The problem occurred when the guidance computer tried to convert rocket velocity from a 64-bit to a 16-bit value. Programmers had not properly coded for this, and an overflow error resulted. When the guidance system shut down, control passed to the backup unit, which also failed because it was running the same algorithm.
- When one switch in the AT&T network had a minor problem in 1990, system software fired off a message to the other 113 AT&T switching centers. This sparked a cascade of shutdowns, bringing down the entire network for nine hours. An estimated 75 million phone calls were missed, and over 200,000 airline reservations were lost. A single line of code in a large software upgrade was in error and led to the shutdown.
- In 2007, Los Angeles International Airport grounded 17,000 planes. For over eight hours, no one was authorized to enter or leave the United States through LAX. Software on a network card was sending faulty data and brought the entire Customs and Border Protection network to a halt.

Could better software engineering practices have prevented these failures? Many different factors contributed to this set of accidents, including the following:

- Simple programming errors
- Inadequate safety engineering
- Poor human–computer interaction design
- Inadequate or inappropriate testing
- Too little focus on safety by the manufacturing organization
- Inadequate reporting structure at the company level

Who should be held responsible for defective software? Is it the corporate management, who did not institute a defined software process? Is it the production managers, who forced tight schedules that demanded risky software engineering practices? What about the software engineers who wrote the defective code? What about the users of the software? Can they be held responsible for accidents? What if they made changes to the system?

Organizations of engineers and software designers have tried to define ethical standards that will minimize the risk of negative impact from their work. The very first article of the code of ethics of the Institute of Electrical and Electronics Engineers (IEEE) alerts engineers to their responsibility for making decisions that protect the health and safety of others. The Association for Computing Machinery (ACM) and the IEEE have established eight principles for ethical software engineering practices:[1]

1. *Public:* Software engineers shall act consistently with the public interest.
2. *Client and Employer:* Software engineers shall act in a manner that is in the best interests of their client and employer consistent with the public interest.
3. *Product:* Software engineers shall ensure that their products and related modifications meet the highest professional standards possible.
4. *Judgment:* Software engineers shall maintain integrity and independence in their professional judgment.
5. *Management:* Software engineering managers and leaders shall subscribe to and promote an ethical approach to the management of software development and maintenance.
6. *Profession:* Software engineers shall advance the integrity and reputation of the profession consistent with the public interest.
7. *Colleagues:* Software engineers shall be fair to and supportive of their colleagues.
8. *Self:* Software engineers shall participate in lifelong learning regarding the practice of their profession and shall promote an ethical approach to the practice of the profession.

Can you think of other steps the software industry could take to make sure its work contributes positively to our society?

[1] "Software Engineering Code of Ethics and Professional Practice," by IEEE-CS/ACM Joint Task Force on Software Engineering Ethics and Professional Practices. Copyright © 2011 by the Institute of Electrical and Electronics Engineers. Reprinted by permission.

Can I just point and click to create an application? Many languages have a development environment that features a drag-and-drop–style interface for designing the visual layout of an application. Programmers use a mouse to lay out the screen and position scroll bars and buttons. The code needed to explain this to the computer is then written automatically. **Visual programming languages**, like Scratch and App Inventor, go even further. They use graphical blocks to represent control elements and variables. Programming consists of clicking together these blocks to define program behavior.

Exploring Programming Languages

How are modern programming languages the same and how are they different? What will future programming languages look like? Let's find out.

Tour of Modern Languages

Objective 10.11 *Compare and contrast modern programming languages.*

All programming languages have many features in common. Let's take a tour of many of the popular languages and learn what makes each one special for particular situations.

Visual Basic

Why do programmers choose Visual Basic? Programmers often like to build a **prototype**, or small model, of their program at the beginning of a large project. Prototyping is a form of **rapid application development (RAD)**, an alternative to the waterfall approach of systems development that was described at the beginning of this chapter. Instead of developing detailed system documents before they produce the system, developers create a prototype first, then generate system documents as they use and remodel the product.

Prototypes for Windows applications are often coded in Microsoft **Visual Basic (VB)**, a powerful programming language used to build a wide range of Windows applications. One strength of VB is its simple, quick interface, which is easy for a programmer to learn and use. It has grown from its roots in the language BASIC (short for Beginner's All-purpose Symbolic Instruction Code) to become a sophisticated and full-featured object-oriented language.

VB is designed for building object-oriented applications for Windows, the web, and mobile devices. The interface of VB makes it easy to drag and drop entire programming components into an application. VB and the .NET Framework are both part of Visual Studio, which provides a complete set of developer tools.

How does the Microsoft .NET Framework help programmers? The Microsoft .NET (pronounced "dot net") Framework is a software development environment designed to let websites "talk" to each other easily. The .NET Framework includes **web services**, programs that a website uses to make information available to other websites. Web services provide a standard way for software to interact. The rules are documented in an **Application Programming Interface (API)**. For example, a web application could use the Google web service to search for information or to check the spelling of a word. The Google web service returns the requested information to your program in a standard format. Figure 10.21 shows just a small list of the many web services available to programmers.

C and C++

What languages do programmers use if the problem requires a lot of "number crunching"? A Windows application that demands raw processing power to execute difficult, repetitive numerical calculations is most often a candidate for C/C++. For example, applications that simulate human cells and drug interactions have to solve elaborate mathematical equations many thousands of times each second and are, therefore, excellent candidates for programming using C/C++. Several companies sell C/C++ design tools equipped with an environment that makes Windows programming as visual as with VB.

Why was the C language developed? The predecessor of **C++**, **C**, was originally developed for system programmers. It was defined by Brian Kernighan and Dennis Ritchie of AT&T Bell Laboratories in 1978 as a language that would make accessing the operating system easier. It provides higher-level programming language features (such as if statements and for loops) but still

Figure 10.21 Web Services

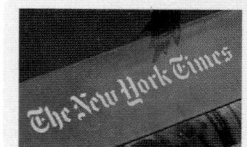

The New York Times **API** offers access to articles, book lists, and movie reviews.

Yahoo Finance API provides stock quotes, historic quotes, exchange rates, and company reports.

Wunderground API provides data on tides, forecasts, hurricanes, and weather alerts.

Chicago Open City gives access to plow locations, crime statistics, public school data, and more. Most cities offer a similar API.

allows programmers to manipulate the system memory and CPU registers directly. This mix of high- and low-level access makes C highly attractive to "power" programmers. Most modern operating systems (Windows, macOS, and Linux) were written in C.

The C++ language takes C to an object-oriented level. Bjarne Stroustrup, the developer of C++, used all the same symbols and keywords as C, but he extended the language with additional keywords, better security, and more support for the reuse of existing code through object-oriented design.

Are C and C++ natural choices for when I'm looking to learn my first language?
Neither C nor C++ was intended as a teaching language. The notation and compactness of these languages make them relatively difficult to master. They're in demand in industry, however, because C/C++ can produce fast-running code that uses a small amount of memory. Programmers often choose to learn C/C++ because their basic components (operators, data types, and keywords) are common to many other languages.

Java and C#

What language do programmers use for applications that need to collect information from networked computers? Java would be a good choice for these types of applications. James Gosling of Sun Microsystems introduced Java in the early 1990s. It quickly became popular because its object-oriented model enables Java programmers to benefit from its large set of existing classes. For example, a Java programmer could begin to use the existing "network connection" class with little attention to the details of how that code itself was implemented. Classes exist for many graphical objects, such as windows and scroll bars, and for network objects such as connections to remote machines. Observing Java's success, Microsoft released a language named **C#** (pronounced "see sharp") that competes with Java.

Can a Java application work on any type of computer? An attractive feature of Java is that it's **architecture neutral**. This means that Java code needs to be compiled only once, after which it can run on many CPUs (see Figure 10.22). The Java program doesn't care which CPU, OS, or user interface is running on the machine on which it lands. This is possible because the target computer runs a Java Virtual Machine (VM), software that can explain to the Java program

Figure 10.22 Java programs can be compiled once and run on many different platforms.
(D. Hurst/Alamy Stock Photo, Ifong/Shutterstock Oleksiy Maksymenko Photography/Alamy Stock Photo)

Figure 10.23 Objective C is the programming language that is most often used to program applications to run under macOS. © *photovibes/Shutterstock.com*

how to function on any specific system. A Java VM installed with Microsoft Edge, for example, allows Edge to execute any **Java applet** (small Java-based program) it encounters on the Internet. Although Java code doesn't perform as fast as C++, the advantage of needing to compile only once before a program can be distributed to any system is extremely important.

Objective C and Swift

What's the most popular language for writing macOS applications? Objective C is the language most often used to program applications to run under macOS (see Figure 10.23). It's an object-oriented style of language, a superset of the C language, so it includes all the keywords of C and then adds more keywords and features. It's often used together with a library called Cocoa. The Cocoa library, or framework, lets users program for the macOS graphical user interface. The Cocoa Touch extension introduces a framework of methods that support gesture recognition for touch devices like the iPhone or iPad.

Swift is a new programming language introduced by Apple for developing for iOS and macOS. Easier to read and maintain, Swift uses a "playground" area where you can quickly write and test ideas before moving the code into the main project.

Is there a favorite IDE for Objective C? Many different IDE tools support Objective C, but macOS ships with a tool named Xcode that's often used to develop Objective C applications for macOS. Xcode is available free from the online Mac App Store.

HTML

What's the most basic formatting language for web applications? A document that will be presented on the web must be written using special symbols called tags. Tags control how a web browser will display the text, images, and other content tagged in **Hypertext Markup Language (HTML)**.

Although knowledge of HTML is required to program for the web, HTML itself isn't a programming language. HTML is just a series of tags that modify the display of text. HTML was the original standard defining these tags. Many good HTML tutorials are available on the web at sites such as Learn the Net (**learnthenet.com**) and the W3 Schools (**w3schools.com**). These sites include lists of the major tags that can be used to create HTML and XHTML documents.

Are there tools that help programmers write in HTML? Several different programs are available to assist in the generation of HTML. Adobe Dreamweaver presents web page designers with an interface that's similar to a word processing program. Web designers can quickly insert

Figure 10.24 Adobe Dreamweaver is a popular tool for creating web pages.

(© 2017 Adobe Systems Incorporated. All rights reserved. Adobe, Adobe Premiere, Dreamweaver and Photoshop is/are either [a] registered trademark[s] or a trademark[s] of Adobe Systems Incorporated in the United States and/or other countries.)

text, images, and hyperlinks, as shown in Figure 10.24. The program automatically inserts the corresponding HTML tags. For simple, static web pages, no programming is required. Online services like Squarespace and Wix allow you to design and maintain a website with powerful features with no direct programming.

Will HTML continue evolving? Yes, the current release of HTML is HTML5. HTML standards are discussed and finalized by committee, and HTML5 is a significant advancement. For example, new HTML5 tags <audio> and <video> allow pages to easily integrate media and let designers more easily support manipulating those elements. HTML5 eliminates the need to install third-party browser plug-ins and supports features like drag-and-drop elements and document editing.

Scripting Languages

Which programming languages do programmers use to make complex web pages? To make their web pages more visually appealing and interactive, programmers use scripting languages to add more power and flexibility to their HTML code. A **scripting language** is a simple programming language that's limited to performing a set of specialized tasks. Scripts allow decisions to be made and calculations to be performed. Several popular scripting languages work well with HTML, including JavaScript, PHP (PHP: Hypertext Preprocessor), and VBScript.

JavaScript is a scripting language that's customized to work with the elements of a web page and is often used to add interactivity to web pages. The syntax, keywords, data types, and operators are similar to those of Java. In addition, JavaScript has a set of classes that represent the objects often used on web pages: buttons, check boxes, and drop-down lists.

The JavaScript button class, for example, describes a button with a name and a type—for example, whether it's a regular button or a Submit or Reset button. The language includes behaviors, such as click(), and can respond to user actions. For example, when a user moves his or her mouse over a button and clicks to select it, the button "knows" the user is there and jumps in and performs a special action (such as playing a sound).

Are there other scripting languages besides JavaScript? PHP, discussed in the following section, is another scripting language that's commonly used. It's a free, open source product that runs very efficiently on multiple platforms, including Windows, UNIX, and Linux. Scripting languages like PHP and JavaScript allow dynamic decision making to be incorporated into the web page design. **Dynamic decision making** means that the page can decide how to display itself based on the choices the reader makes. Programmers who are more familiar with Visual Basic than Java or C++ might use **VBScript**, a subset of Visual Basic.

ASP, JSP, and PHP

How are interactive web pages built? To build websites with interactive capabilities, programmers use **Active Server Pages (ASP)**, **JavaServer Pages (JSP)**, or the scripting language **PHP (PHP: Hypertext Preprocessor)** to adapt the HTML page to the user's selections. The user supplies information that's translated into a request by the main computer at the company that owns the website, often using a database query language such as SQL. Scripting code in ASP, JSP, or PHP controls the automatic writing of the custom HTML page that's returned to the user's computer.

What does additional programming bring to a web page? Modern web applications interact with the user, collecting information and then customizing the content displayed based on the user's feedback. For example, the client/server type application shown in Figure 10.25 shows the web page of the ABC Bike Company collecting a customer bicycle inquiry for red bikes. The program then asks ABC's main server for a list of red bicycles sold by the company. A PHP program running on the server creates a new HTML page and delivers that to the user's browser, telling the customer what red bikes (including details such as model and size) are currently sold by ABC.

STEP 1: User requests information on red bikes.

STEP 2: Server sends request to database server.

STEP 4: Server's PHP program writes HTML page.

STEP 3: Database server returns list.

12345
45678
98764
54321
11223
22334

Customer's computer

ABC Bike Company server

ABC Bike Company database

Figure 10.25 An online store is an example of the client/server type of Internet application.

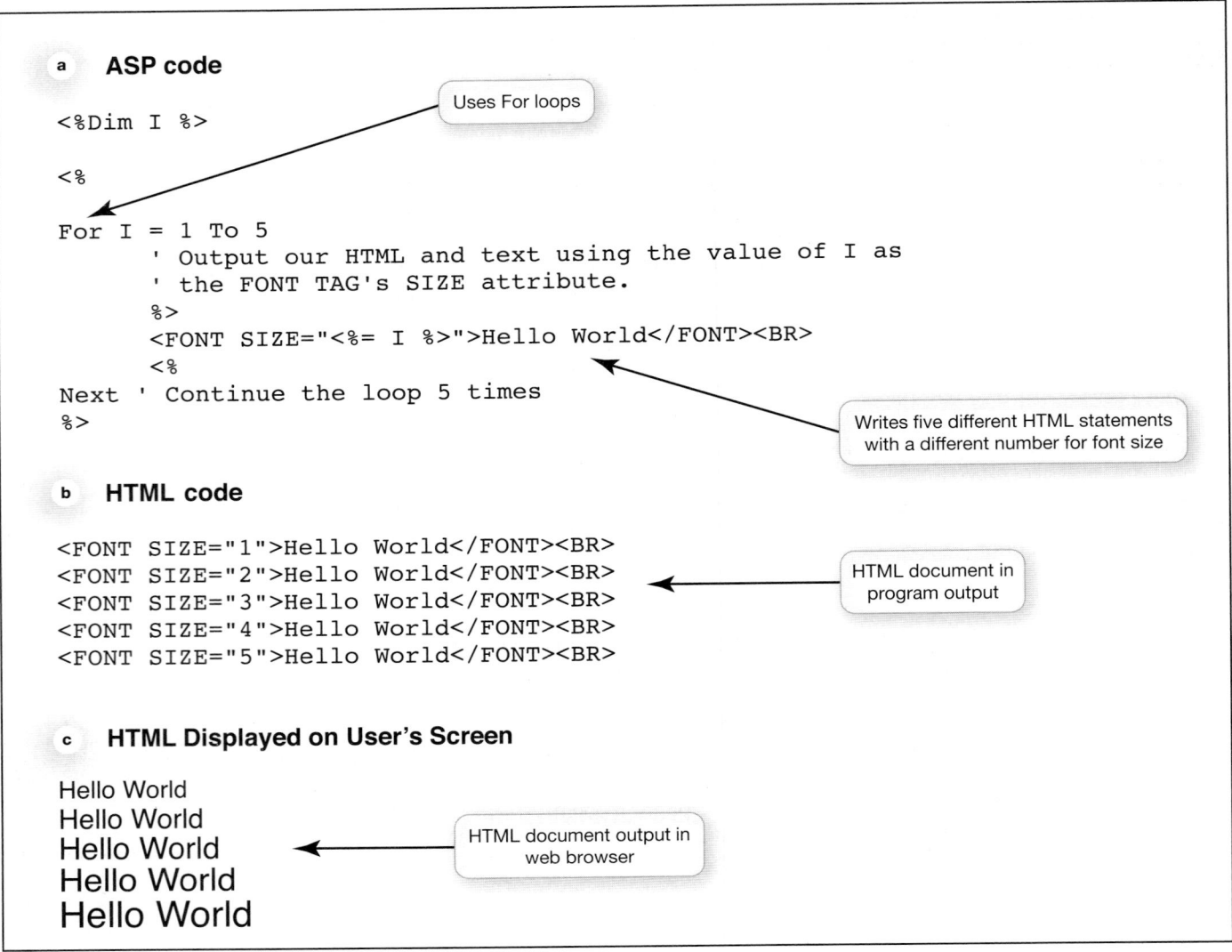

Figure 10.26 An ASP program can (a) write HTML code as its (b) output. (c) This image illustrates how the HTML page would show up in a browser.

Server programs, written in ASP or PHP, can have HTML code as their output. They use what the user has told them (via the list boxes, check boxes, and buttons on the page) to make decisions. Based on those results, the server software decides what HTML to write. A small example of ASP writing its own HTML code is shown in Figure 10.26.

AJAX, XML, and JSON

What if a programmer wants to create a web application that smoothly updates and communicates with other computers? Many websites feature elaborate animations that interact with visitors. They may reach out to several other web resources to gather information or request services like translation. The collection of technologies referred to as **AJAX (Asynchronous JavaScript and XML)** and the continued evolution of HTML5 allow such web applications to update information on a page without requiring the user to do a page refresh or leave the page. By using existing technologies to do more processing in the browser, users have a more responsive experience.

How do programs gather information from other computers? The markup language called **eXtensible Markup Language (XML)** enables designers to define their own data-based tags, making it much easier for a program running on a server computer (a web service) to transfer the key information on its page to another site. When websites communicate with humans, HTML works well because the formatting it controls is important. People respond immediately to the visual styling of textual information; its layout, color, size, and font design all help to transfer the message of the page to the reader. When computer programs want to communicate with each other, however, all of these qualities just get in the way.

With XML, groups can agree on standard systems of tags that represent important data elements. For example, the XML tags <stock> and </stock> might delimit key stock quote information. Mathematicians have created a standardized set of XML tags named MathML for their work, and biometrics groups continue to refine XML standards to describe and exchange data such as DNA and face scans. Without XML, a website that wanted to look up current stock pricing information at another site would have to retrieve the HTML page, sort through the formatting information, and try to recognize which text on the page identified the data needed. **JavaScript Object Notation (JSON)** is another standard for exchanging information between a server computer process and a client. The information is delivered as a series of names and their values, making it easy for programs to parse and easy for humans to read.

Figure 10.27 shows a table of popular programming languages and technologies with their features and the typical settings in which they're used.

Mobile Application Development

How do programmers build applications for mobile devices? Special languages and supporting tools are speeding the development of applications for mobile devices like smartphones and tablets. Programmers need to be able to take advantage of specific features like GPS capability, compasses, software keyboards, and touch-sensitive screens. In addition, the user interface has to take the smaller screen size of mobile devices into account.

What development tools are used for creating mobile apps for Apple's iOS platform? To start a complex project like an iPhone app requires a detailed prototype. Each of the many screens, all the user interface elements, and all the content need to be organized and linked

Figure 10.27 Popular Programming Languages

Programming Language	Features	Typical Setting
C/C++ and C#	• Can create compact code that executes quickly • Provides high- and low-level access	• Used in industrial applications such as banking and engineering
Java	• Is architecture neutral • Is object oriented	• Used to create applets that can be delivered over the web
Objective C	• Has a framework for writing iOS applications	• Used to create applications for macOS and Apple mobile devices
Visual Basic	• Is easy to learn and use • Is object oriented • Has a drag-and-drop interface	• Used in prototype development • Used to design graphical user interfaces

Web Technologies	Features	Typical Setting
AJAX	• Uses a combination of existing technologies like JavaScript, CSS, and XML	• Creates websites that can update without the user refreshing the page
HTML5	• Latest version of HTML	• Introduces tags like <video> and supports drag and drop
VBScript	• Is similar in syntax to Visual Basic • Has classes that represent buttons, drop-down lists, and other web page components	• Creates code that lives on the client machine and adds interaction to web pages
XML	• Enables users to define their own tags	• Facilitates exchange of information from web services
JSON	• Format defined with name/value pairs	• Very common format for exchange of information from web services

smoothly. Often, programmers begin with a prototype, created quickly with drag-and-drop elements using products like Proto.io or Interface Builder. Proto.io (**proto.io**) is a browser-based tool that lets you construct a working simulation of your application. Interface Builder is part of the Apple Xcode development tool; it requires a bit more expertise to use than Proto.io but can also rapidly create a prototype.

When it's time to begin writing the code for an iOS app, programmers turn to Objective C and use the Apple Xcode development toolset. Xcode lets designers code and debug the behavior of the application and simulate the application in a software version of the target device. After the program is running, its performance can be profiled for speed, memory usage, and other possible problems.

Are there different tools for building apps for Android devices? Yes, the Android software development kit (SDK) is required to build apps targeting Android smartphones and tablets. There are many ways programmers work with the Android SDK, including using well-known IDEs like Eclipse with special plug-ins or using the Android Studio, shown in Figure 10.28. Information on the latest version of the Android SDK, as well as tutorials, guides, and other resources, is available at the Android Developers page (**developer.android.com**).

I'm not a programmer, but can I make a simple app? Absolutely. Tools like Corona and App Inventor produce amazing games and apps quickly (see the Try This on page 402 for more information). Tens of millions of apps constructed using Corona have been downloaded, including the overnight sensation Bubble Ball created by 14-year-old Robert Nay (**naygames.com**). The apps you have written using App Inventor in the Make This exercises can be uploaded to the Google Play store for download worldwide.

If your goal is to make a mobile app that's very simple or even specific to one occasion, like a wedding, there are web-based products that make that quick and easy. Magmito (**magmito.com**) supports developing a simple app with text and graphics and requires no programming knowledge.

Does an application need to be rewritten for every kind of mobile device? Programming environments like Corona and Magmito support publishing an application to several different types of devices. Although these tools can be great time savers for very simple applications, for programmers using specific features that make that device unique or for those concerned with extracting ultimate performance, custom programming for each environment still is required.

Figure 10.28 Android Studio integrates all the tools required to program Android applications from scratch, targeting tablets, phones, TVs, wearables, and even Android Auto. *(Courtesy Google Inc.)*

Unity is a game-development environment that supports home video game production by combining many tools into one package, giving you what you need to edit, test, and play your game idea quickly. It can generate real-time shadowing effects, for example, and has preprogrammed scripts integrated. After you've polished your production, Unity allows you to publish for web, mobile, or console platforms. With over 5 million developers using Unity, and over 700 million people playing Unity-made games, the potential of this tool is amazing (see Figure 10.29).

You'll start with the built-in Unity editor so you can quickly assemble a 3D environment. Unity gives you access to its Asset Store right from the editor window. Art assets are supplied so that you instantly have materials to create your own landscape. Tutorials and sample projects are available, as well as character models and textures. Grab a sound effect or some code to simulate a great explosion effect. If you create assets you'd like to distribute, you can put them up for sale within the Asset Store.

Unity incorporates lighting control and shading and the application of textures in order to develop rich terrains. Its built-in physics engine lets objects respond to gravity, friction, and collisions. One example is the "wheel collider," a module that simulates the traction of real car tires. Audio processing is included, with effects like echo, reverb, and a chorus filter, as are tools to make real-time networking available from your game.

Programming is handled through several flexible scripting languages—JavaScript, C#, and an implementation of Python named Boo. It has a visual interface that lets you drag and drop objects to set variables, or you can choose to sync with an external IDE like Visual Studio. There's an integrated debugger so that you can pause your game, check variable values, and quickly repair errors. When it's time to optimize the performance before your final release, you can use the built-in profiler: It reports statistics on where the processing time is being spent so that you can fine tune game play.

Figure 10.29 Unity is a free game engine that can build web, mobile, or console games. *(Screenshot courtesy of Unity Technologies)*

Unity is available in a free downloadable version (**unity3d. com**) and in a pay version, Unity 3D Pro. The Pro version adds features but also can be licensed and used by companies. The free version of Unity can be used to create games that can be sold—there is no royalty or revenue sharing required. And there are modules that let you easily port your code to a number of target platforms: PC, iOS, Android, and the web as well as Xbox 360, PS4, and Wii U.

You'll also find an active community to support you as you learn. There are live online training courses offered and forums for community discussion. There is also a dedicated IRC (Internet Relay Chat) channel for live chatting with Unity users. If you need help distributing your finished game, you can join Union, a service that brings your game to new markets for you.

If you're interested in video game development, architectural visualizations, or just creating interactive animations, download Unity and realize the power of programming.

Future of Programming Languages

Objective 10.12   *State key principles in the development of future programming languages.*

What will the next great language be? It is never easy to predict which language will become the next "great" language. Software experts predict that as software projects continue to grow in size, the amount of time needed to compile a completed project will also grow. It's not uncommon for a large project to require 30 minutes or more to compile. Interpreted languages, however, take virtually no compile time because compilation occurs while the code is being edited. As projects get larger, the capability to be compiled instantaneously will become even more important. Thus, interpreted languages such as Python, Ruby, and Smalltalk could become more important in the coming years.

Will visual programming languages become more popular? Visual programming languages (VPLs) have a history of over 50 years. The idea of "programming without coding," the name of an MIT open source project to promote VPLs, is maturing but is not yet a tool for most professional software development environments. The future may bring a push for the elegance of visual programming. VPLs use visual modeling, creating the code using images to represent each statement, which helps programmers understand complex designs. We have already seen a move

Figure 10.30 Just as there is diversity in human programmers, each programming language has its own "personality."
(Rawpixel.com/Shutterstock)

toward visual modeling in audio production in the development of software for adding effects like echo or reverse to music snippets. Programming environments like Max 7 are visual and have a growing and enthusiastic user base.

Will all languages someday converge into one? Certain characteristics of modern programming languages correspond well with how programmers actually think. These traits support good programming practices and are emerging as common features of most modern programming languages. The object-oriented paradigm is one example. Both Visual Basic and COBOL have moved toward supporting objects.

There will always be a variety of programming languages, each with their own distinct characteristics. As Figure 10.30 shows, this also mirrors the diversity of the programmer community.

Forcing a language to be so general that it can work for any task also forces it to include components that make it slower to compile, produce larger final executables, and require more memory to run. Having a variety of languages and mapping a problem to the best language create the most efficient software solutions.

So what do I do if I want to learn languages that will be relevant in the future? No particular set of languages is best to learn, and there is no one best sequence in which to learn them. The Association for Computing Machinery (**acm.org**) encourages educators to teach a core set of mathematical and programming skills and concepts, but school and university departments are free to offer a variety of languages.

When you're selecting which programming languages to study, some geographical and industry-related considerations come into play. For example, in an area in which a large number of pharmaceutical companies exist, there may be a demand for Massachusetts General Hospital Utility Multi-Programming System (MUMPS). This language is often used to build clinical databases, an important task in the pharmaceutical industry. Review the advertisements for programmers in area newspapers and investigate resources such as ComputerJobs (**computerjobs.com**) to identify languages in demand in your area.

Regardless of whether you pursue a career in programming, having an understanding of how software is created will help you in many IT careers. Software is the set of instructions that allows us to make use of our hardware. Programming skills give you the power to understand, create, and customize a computer system.

Helpdesk MyLab IT®

A Variety of Programming Languages

In this Helpdesk, you'll play the role of a helpdesk staffer, fielding questions about the variety of modern programming languages: what makes one popular, which language is best for a certain situation, and how they all compare.

Before moving on to the Chapter Review:

1. Watch Chapter Overview Video 10.2.
2. Then take the Check Your Understanding quiz.

Check Your Understanding // Review & Practice

For a quick review to see what you've learned so far, answer the following questions.

multiple choice

1. The most popular programming languages include
   a. Pascal and Object Pascal.
   b. R and F#.
   c. MATLAB and Assembly.
   d. Java, C, and C++.

2. Selecting the right programming language for a project depends on
   a. who you have working for you and what they know.
   b. the final requirements for performance and space used.
   c. the environment of the finished project.
   d. all of the above

3. Which is NOT an advantage of Java?
   a. Java is architecture neutral.
   b. Java needs to compile only once prior to distribution.
   c. Java performs faster than C++.
   d. Java supports network communications.

4. Which is TRUE about XML?
   a. XML supports the development of rich multimedia.
   b. XML enables designers to define their own data-based tags.
   c. XML makes it possible to update web pages without refreshing.
   d. XML has classes that represent dropdown lists and other web elements.

5. There is not one "perfect" language for programming because
   a. visual programming is more elegant.
   b. programmers enjoy learning many different languages.
   c. it's easier to maintain a software system if it uses many different languages.
   d. forcing a language to be general purpose also forces it to become inefficient.

MyLab IT   Go to **MyLab IT** to take an autograded version of the *Check Your Understanding* review and to find all media resources for the chapter.

TechBytes Weekly   Go to TechBytes Weekly for current technology news and discussion questions!

10 Chapter Review

Summary

Part 1

Understanding Programming

Learning Outcome 10.1 You will be able to describe the life cycle of a software project and identify the stages in the program development life cycle.

 Life Cycle of an Information System

Objective 10.1 *Describe the importance of programming to both software developers and users.*

- Programming skills allow you to customize existing software products to accomplish required tasks. A beginning-level knowledge of programming will let you create macros, customized miniprograms that speed up redundant tasks.

Objective 10.2 *Summarize the stages of the system development life cycle (SDLC).*

- An information system includes data, people, procedures, hardware, and software. The set of steps followed to ensure that development proceeds in an orderly fashion is the system development life cycle (SDLC). There are six steps in the SDLC waterfall model:
  1. A problem or opportunity is identified.
  2. The problem is analyzed, and a program specification document is created to outline the project objectives.
  3. A detailed plan for programmers to follow is designed using flowcharts and data-flow diagrams.
  4. Using the developed plan, programmers develop the program, and the program is then documented.
  5. The program is tested to ensure that it works and that it's installed properly.
  6. Ongoing maintenance and evaluation ensure a working product.

 Life Cycle of a Program

Objective 10.3 *Define programming and list the steps in the program development life cycle (PDLC).*

- Programming is the process of translating a task into a series of commands that a computer will use to perform that task. The PDLC involves five steps: describing the problem, developing the algorithm, coding, debugging, and testing and documentation.

Objective 10.4 *Describe how programmers construct a problem statement from a description of a task.*

- The problem statement is an explicit description of what tasks the computer program must accomplish and how the program will execute these tasks and respond to unusual situations. The problem statement describes the input data that users will have at the start of the job, the output that the program will produce, and the exact processing that converts these inputs to outputs. The problem statement identifies potential errors and plans to address these errors.

Objective 10.5 *Explain how programmers use flow control and design methodologies when developing algorithms.*

- Programmers create an algorithm by converting a problem statement into a list of steps and identifying where decision points occur. Yes/no binary decisions are common, and often the pattern of a repeating action loop is recognized. Algorithms are documented in the form of a flowchart or in pseudocode. Programmers use either top-down or object-oriented analysis to produce the algorithm.

Objective 10.6 *Discuss the categories of programming languages and the roles of the compiler and the integrated development environment (IDE) in coding.*

- Computer code uses special words and strict rules to enable programmers to control the CPU without having to know all of its hardware details. Programming languages are classified in several major groupings, sometimes referred to as *generations*, with the first generation being machine language—the binary code of 1s and 0s that the computer understands. Assembly language is the next generation; it uses short, English-like commands that speak directly to the CPU and give the programmer direct control of hardware resources. Each successive generation in language development has relieved programmers of some of the burden of keeping track of what the hardware requires and more closely matches how humans think about problems.

- Compilation is the process by which code is converted into machine language, the language the CPU can understand. A compiler is a program that understands both the syntax of the programming language and the exact structure of the CPU and its machine language. It can translate the instructions written by programmers in the higher-level language into machine language, the binary patterns that will execute commands on the CPU. Each programming language has its own compiler.
- An integrated development environment (IDE) is a developmental tool that helps programmers write and test their programs.

Objective 10.7 *Identify the role of debugging in program development.*

- If programmers make errors in the algorithm or in translating the algorithm to code, problems will occur. Programmers debug the program by running it constantly to find errors and to make sure the program behaves the way it should.

Objective 10.8 *Explain the importance of testing and documentation in program development.*

- Once debugging has detected all the code errors and they have been repaired, users—both within the company and outside the company—test the program in every way they can imagine, both as the program was intended to be used and in ways only new users might think up. Before its commercial release, software is often provided at a reduced cost or at no cost in a beta version to certain test sites or to interested users for a last round of testing.
- Once testing is complete, technical writers create internal documentation for the program and external documentation that will be provided to users of the program. User training, which begins once the software is distributed, teaches the user community how to use the software efficiently.

Part 2
Programming Languages

> **Learning Outcome 10.2** **You will understand the factors programmers consider when selecting an appropriate programming language for a specific problem and will be familiar with some modern programming languages.**

 Many Programming Languages

Objective 10.9 *Discuss the driving factors behind the popularity of various programming languages.*

- There are a variety of languages because of the many tradeoffs that must be made between speed of execution, security, ease of programming, interface, and ability to grow and support more features later.

Objective 10.10 *Summarize the considerations in identifying an appropriate programming language for a specific setting.*

- A programming team reviews several considerations before selecting the language to be used. Certain languages are best used for certain problems. The target language should be well matched to the amount of space available for the final program. Some projects require the selection of a language that can produce code that executes in the fastest possible time. Selecting a language with which the programmers are familiar is also helpful.

 Exploring Programming Languages

Objective 10.11 *Compare and contrast modern programming languages.*

- Visual Basic, C/C++, and Java are languages that enable programmers to include control features such as scroll bars, title bars, text boxes, buttons, and expanding and collapsing menus.
- Objective C is a language used in programming applications for mobile devices using iOS and applications that will run under macOS.
- Programmers use HTML tags to structure web pages. HTML5 includes more advanced tags like <audio> and <video>.
- For more complex web development, scripting programs such as JavaScript, PHP, and VBScript are popular.
- AJAX is a programming solution that uses a combination of technologies to create websites that can update without the user refreshing the page.
- XML and JSON allow programmers to create their own tags so that web pages can exchange information, not just formatting details.

Objective 10.12 *State key principles in the development of future programming languages.*

- New languages may lean toward being interpreted instead of compiled because of the speed gained in development. Many languages have moved toward the object-oriented paradigm.

 Be sure to check out **MyLab IT** for additional materials to help you review and learn. And don't forget to watch the Chapter Overview Videos.

Key Terms

actions **389**
Active Server Pages (ASP) **411**
AJAX (Asynchronous JavaScript and XML) **412**
algorithm **384**
Application Programming Interface (API) **407**
architecture neutral **408**
assembly language **394**
base class **391**
beta version **400**
binary decision **389**
C **407**
C++ **407**
C# **408**
class **391**
code editing **398**
coding **392**
comment **395**
compilation **397**
compiler **397**
control structure **389**
data **385**
data-flow diagram **383**
data type **393**
debugger **399**
debugging **399**
decision point **387**
derived class **391**
documentation **400**
dynamic decision making **411**
editor **398**
error handling **386**
executable program **397**
eXtensible Markup Language (XML) **412**

fifth-generation language (5GL) **394**
first-generation language (1GL) **394**
flowchart **387**
For **392**
fourth-generation language (4GL) **394**
general availability (GA) **400**
Hypertext Markup Language (HTML) **409**
if else **392**
information **385**
information system **382**
inheritance **391**
initial value **389**
integrated development environment (IDE) **398**
interpreter **397**
Java **408**
Java applet **409**
JavaScript **410**
JavaScript Object Notation (JSON) **413**
JavaServer Pages (JSP) **411**
keyword **392**
logical error **399**
loop **389**
machine language **394**
macros **382**
method **385**
Next **392**
object **391**
Objective C **409**
object-oriented analysis **391**
operator **393**
PHP (PHP: Hypertext Preprocessor) **411**
portability **395**
problem statement **385**

Processing **404**
program development life cycle (PDLC) **384**
program specification **383**
programming **384**
programming language **394**
prototype **407**
pseudocode **387**
rapid application development (RAD) **407**
release to manufacturers (RTM) **400**
reusability **391**
runtime error **399**
scope creep **384**
scripting language **410**
second-generation language (2GL) **394**
service pack **400**
source code **397**
statement **392**
Structured Query Language (SQL) **394**
Swift **409**
syntax **392**
syntax error **392**
system development life cycle (SDLC) **382**
test condition **389**
testing plan **386**
third-generation language (3GL) **394**
top-down design **390**
variable **395**
variable declaration **395**
VBScript **411**
Visual Basic (VB) **407**
visual programming languages **406**
web service **407**

Chapter Quiz // Assessment

For a quick review to see what you've learned, answer the following questions. Submit the quiz as requested by your instructor. If you're using **MyLab IT**, the quiz is also available there.

multiple choice

1. You do not need to know how to program to
   a. add commands to Microsoft Word that automate complex, repetitive tasks.
   b. create unique software solutions for specialized problems.
   c. use Microsoft Word to type text and select various fonts.
   d. create macros to boost your speed at completing certain jobs.

2. What is the first step of the SDLC?
   a. design
   b. analysis
   c. development
   d. problem identification

3. The steps of the program development life cycle start with
   a. algorithm development.
   b. coding.
   c. describing the problem.
   d. testing.

4. How the program should behave if the input data is invalid is part of
   a. process.
   b. scope creep.
   c. beta testing.
   d. error handling.

5. When designing a program, the developer selects a design approach like
   a. if or for.
   b. top down or object oriented.
   c. Python or C++.
   d. IDE or compiler.

6. An IDE is a tool that has support for
   a. editing and debugging.
   b. flowcharting and creating the project specification.
   c. releasing updates to the public.
   d. scope creep.

7. The following are common to all programming languages:
   a. architecture neutrality
   b. syntax, keywords, and operators
   c. SDLC and PDLC
   d. JSON and APIs

8. In selecting the most appropriate language it is useful to know
   a. how quickly the final code must run.
   b. how much space the final code delivered can occupy.
   c. if there is a specific target environment (say, a specific operating system).
   d. all of the above

9. Java is considered to be *architecture neutral* because it
   a. can be recompiled to run on many CPUs.
   b. can run on many different generations of Windows.
   c. only needs to be compiled once and can run on many different CPUs.
   d. can run in any browser.

10. JSON stands for
    a. Just Short of Notice.
    b. JavaScript Object Notation.
    c. Java Startup Output Naming.
    d. JavaScript Only.

true/false

_____ 1. A logical error can be detected and repaired by the compiler.

_____ 2. An RTM version of software is often released so users can help debug it.

_____ 3. AJAX allows you to create websites that can refresh without the user taking an action.

_____ 4. XML and JSON are both common formats for the exchange of information between web services.

_____ 5. Many programming languages are moving away from the object-oriented paradigm.

critical thinking

1. **Key Classes for Shopping**

   Think of the last time you had a big shopping trip facing you. What would key classes be if you were going to design a software program that helped you manage your shopping excursion? What data and methods would belong in each class?

2. **Programming Languages**

   Is there one programming language that can outperform all others? How would you select the first programming language to learn? Will the number of programming languages you need to know as a professional programmer keep increasing or settle down to just few choices?

Team Time

Working Together for Change

problem

Your team has been selected to write a program that tells a vending machine how to make change. The program needs to deliver the smallest number of coins for each transaction.

task

Divide the class into three teams: Algorithm Design, Coding, and Testing. The responsibilities of each team are outlined as follows.

process

1. The Algorithm Design team must develop a document that presents the problem as a top-down design sequence of steps, and another document that uses object-oriented analysis to identify the key objects in the problem. Each object needs to be represented as data and behaviors. Inheritance relationships between objects should be noted, as well. You can use flowcharts to document your results.
2. The Coding team needs to decide which programming language would be most appropriate for the project. This program needs to be fast and take up little memory. Use the web to gather information to defend your selection. You may also consider using a product such as Visual Logic (**visuallogic.org**) to develop the code for a prototype of the system.
3. The Testing team must create a testing plan for the program, including a table listing combinations of inputs and correct outputs.
4. As a group, discuss how each team would communicate its results to the other teams. Once one team has completed its work, are the team members finished? How would the tools of a site such as GitHub (**github.com**) help your development team?

conclusion

Any programming project requires teams to produce an accurate and efficient solution to a problem. The interaction of team members is vital to successful programming.

Ethics Project

Software That Kills

In this exercise, you'll research and then role-play a complicated ethical situation. The role you play might not match your personal beliefs, but your research and use of logic will enable you to represent the view assigned. An arbitrator will watch and comment on both sides of the argument, and together the team will agree on an ethical solution.

problem

The Therac-25 was a computerized radiation-therapy machine. Between 1985 and 1987, six people were killed or badly harmed due to a flaw in its software. The dose that one patient had received was estimated to be in the 15,000- to 20,000-rad range. This is roughly 100 times more than the expected dose and 15 to 20 times more than a fatal dose. The error-prone software remained on the market for months before the problem was recognized, acknowledged, and solved.

Does this situation indicate criminal conduct? Or is it a situation that needs to be resolved in civil court (for monetary damages)? Is this an example of the price society pays for using complex technology, so no blame should be assigned?

research areas to consider

- Therac-25 case resolution
- 2010 Toyota recalls for unanticipated acceleration
- Software errors in avionic software systems
- ACM ethical guidelines

process

1. Divide the class into teams. Research the areas cited above from the perspective of a software developer, the people impacted, or the arbitrator.
2. Team members should write a summary that provides factual support for their character's position regarding the fair and ethical design and use of technology. Then, team members should create an outline to use during the role-playing event.
3. Team members should present their case to the class or submit a PowerPoint presentation for review by the rest of the class, along with the summary and resolution they developed.

conclusion

As technology becomes ever more prevalent and integrated into our lives, ethical dilemmas will present themselves to an increasing extent. Being able to understand and evaluate both sides of the argument, while responding in a personally or socially ethical manner, will be an important skill.

Time Sheets

You've been asked to automate a time card and to automatically record a log of the weekly payments using Excel 2016. You have made great progress on the time card, and now need to add data validation, VLOOKUPs to automate Employee data entry, an IF function to calculate the daily payments, and a macro to copy the time card data to a payment log.

You will use the following skills as you complete this activity:

- Use Absolute Cell Reference
- Create IF and VLOOKUP Functions
- Record a Macro
- Create a Data Validation
- Fill Date Series
- Use Paste Values

Instructions:

1. Open *TIA_Ch10_Start* and save as **TIA_Ch10_LastFirst**.

2. To display the Developer tab, click **File**, click **Options**, and then click **Customize Ribbon**. In the Customize the Ribbon pane, select the **Developer check box**. Click **OK**.

3. Click the **Time Card worksheet**; in cell B3, type **Ted Hoyt**. In cell B4, create a VLOOKUP function to look up up the value of cell B3 in the range A2:C16 on the Employee Data worksheet, and return the value in the third column of that range. Use False as the Range_Lookup argument.
   Hint: The function will be = VLOOKUP(B3,'Employee Data'!A2:C16,3,FALSE).

4. In cell B5, create a VLOOKUP function to look up the value of cell B3 in the range A2:C16 on the Employee Data worksheet, and return the value from the second column. Use False as the Range_Lookup argument.

5. Click **cell C9** on the Time Card worksheet, type **4/11/2018**, and then use the **Fill Handle** to copy the series of dates in cells C10:C13.

6. Select **range D9:D13**. Click the **Data tab**, then select **Data Validation** in the Data Tools group. In the Data Validation dialog box, on the Settings tab, click the **Allow arrow** and select **Decimal**. Click the **Data arrow**, and select **between**; then type **0** in the Minimum box and **12** in the Maximum box. Click the **Error Alert tab**, ensure a Stop style is selected, type the title: **Invalid Entry**, and an Error message: **Total hours worked cannot exceed 12 hours**.

7. In cell D9, type **16** and press **Enter**. The Data Validation Error box displays. Click **Retry**, then type **10** and press **Enter**. In cells D10:D13, type **8**, **12**, **8**, and **9**, respectively. Note the Overtime Hours fills in automatically, calculating the hours in excess of 8 hours.

8. In cell F9, use an IF function to test if the value in cell D9 is less than or equal to 8. If this condition is true, then multiply cell D9 times cell E4 (the regular rate). If the condition is false, then multiply 8 times E4 and add to that E9*E5 (the overtime rate). Make sure you use absolute cell references in the formula where needed. Use the **Fill Handle** to copy the formula to range F10:F13.

9. Click the **Payment Log worksheet**. Click **cell A1**.

10. Click the **Developer tab**, then click **Record Macro** in the Code group. Name the macro **CopyTimeCard** and assign a shortcut key of Ctrl+t. Click **OK**. With the Macro recorder on, complete the following steps: Click the **Time Card worksheet**, select and copy **range A20:F20**, click the **Payment Log worksheet**, and then press **Ctrl + ↓** to go to the last row with values. Click the **Developer tab**, click **Use Relative References** in the Code group, and then press the **↓ key** to move to the first blank cell in the worksheet. Click **Use Relative References** in the Code group to deselect it. Click the **Home tab**, click the **Paste arrow**, and then select **Values**. Click **cell A1**, select the **Time Card worksheet**, press **Esc**, and then click **cell B3**. Click the **Developer tab**, and then click **Stop Recording** in the Code group.

11. Test the Macro by typing **Brett Martin** in cell B3. In cells D9:D13, type **8**, **10**, **8**, **8**, and **9**, respectively. Click **cell B3**, then press **Ctrl+T** to run the Macro. Click the **Payment Log worksheet** to ensure the Brett Martin data was successfully transferred.

12. Click the **Developer tab**, click **Macros** in the Code group, select the **CopyTimeCard macro**, and click **Edit**. Copy the macro code, close the Macro window, add a new worksheet and paste in cell A1 of the new worksheet. Name the worksheet **Macro**.

13. Save the workbook. Note: Answer Yes when asked to save as a Macro-free workbook. Submit based on your instructor's directions.

For a chapter overview, watch the Chapter Overview Videos.

PART 1

Database Fundamentals

Learning Outcome 11.1 **You will be able to explain the basics of databases, including the most common types of databases and the functions and components of relational databases in particular.**

PART 2

How Businesses Use Databases

Learning Outcome 11.2 **You will be able to explain how businesses use data warehouses, data marts, and data mining to manage data and how business information systems and business intelligence are used to make business decisions.**

 Database Advantages 426

Objective 11.1 *Explain what a database is and why databases are useful.*

Objective 11.2 *Discuss the benefits of using a database.*

Helpdesk: Using Databases

 Database Types 430

Objective 11.3 *Describe features of relational databases.*

Objective 11.4 *Describe features of object-oriented databases.*

Objective 11.5 *Describe features of multidimensional databases.*

 Database Basics 433

Objective 11.6 *Describe how relational databases organize and define data.*

Objective 11.7 *Describe how data is inputted and managed in a database.*

Sound Byte: Creating and Querying an Access Database

 Data Warehousing and Storage 449

Objective 11.8 *Explain what data warehouses and data marts are and how they are used.*

Objective 11.9 *Describe data mining and how it works.*

 Using Databases to Make Business Decisions 455

Objective 11.10 *Describe the main types of business information systems and how they are used by business managers.*

Sound Byte: Analyzing Data with Microsoft Power BI Suite

Helpdesk: How Businesses Use Databases

For the IT Simulation for this chapter, see MyLab IT.

 All media accompanying this chapter can be found here.

 Make: A Family Shopping List on **page 448**

(Marek Uliasz/Alamy Stock Photo, Kheng Ho Toh/Alamy Stock Photo, Juri/Fotolia, Mira/Alamy Stock Photo, Fotolia)

How Cool Is This?

When can **data visualization** become not only more effective but also a **form of art**? When you use **Circos (circos.ca)**, a software package that uses a **circular layout for visualizing data and information**. The data elements (the traditional rows and columns of a table) are represented as segments around the circle, and relationships between elements in the data are indicated by ribbon-like links. The color and thickness of each ribbon link represents the element and the magnitude of the relationship, respectively.

The circular layout **emphasizes patterns in connections and data relationships** more readily than traditional linear layouts. This application was originally designed to visualize genome data, but it has also been effectively used to visualize other types of data, including customer loyalty, urban planning, and human migration patterns. Moreover, the **results can just be interesting works of art.** *(Martin Krzywinski, Genome Sciences Center)*

Database Fundamentals

Learning Outcome 11.1 You will be able to explain the basics of databases, including the most common types of databases and the functions and components of relational databases in particular.

You interact with databases every day: when you retrieve a friend's phone number from your contacts, post to your Facebook page, or add a song to your Spotify playlist. In this part of the chapter, we'll look at the basics of databases and how databases can be used to provide relevant information quickly and easily.

 ## Database Advantages

Many actions we frequently perform, such as using an ATM, shopping online, and registering for classes, generate data that needs to be stored, managed, and used by others. Most likely, a system has been created that receives and stores our inputted data and that enables that data to be processed and used by others, effectively turning data into information. In this section, we look at why databases are needed as well as their specific advantages.

The Need for Databases

Objective 11.1 *Explain what a database is and why databases are useful.*

Why do I need to know about databases? A **database** is a collection of related data that can be stored, sorted, organized, and queried. By creating an organized structure for data, databases make data more meaningful and therefore more useful. Because you interact with databases every day, understanding how databases work and what you can do with databases will help you use the ones you interact with more effectively. For example, *categorizing*, *sorting*, and *filtering* are key attributes of most databases. If a database isn't set up correctly or if you don't know how to use the database, you may not get the type of information you're looking for.

Amazon.com, the electronic commerce company (see Figure 11.1), is an example of a database. When consumers want to view or purchase an item, they can specify the department the item falls

Figure 11.1 Amazon.com and other electronic commerce websites use databases to enhance customer experience and for inventory management. *(IanDagnall Computing/Alamy Stock Photo)*

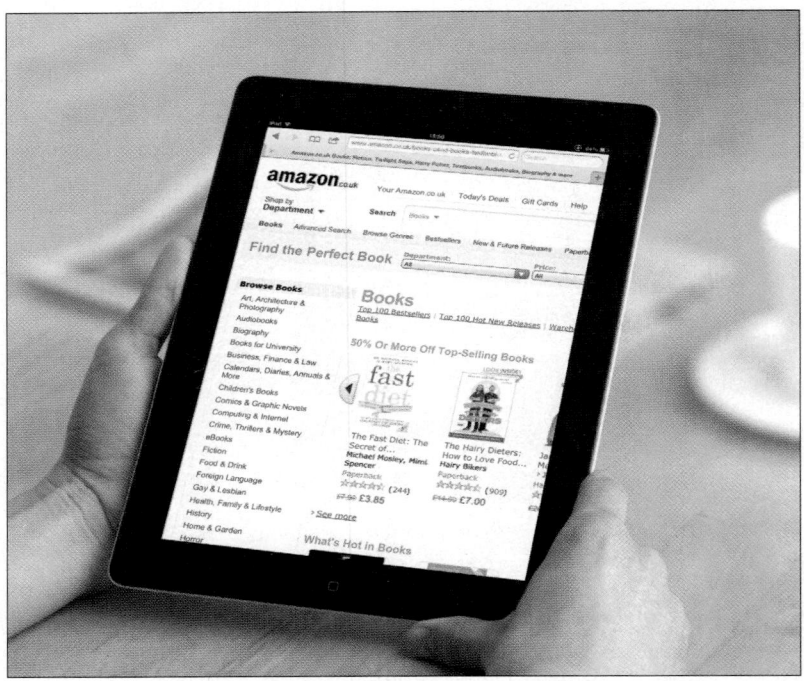

	A	B	C	D
2	**Books To Buy**			
3				
4	Class	Title	Author	Bought
5	American Literature 1	Anthology of American Literature, Volume 1	McMichael et al.	
6	American Literature 1	Moby Dick	Melville	Yes
7	American Literature 1	The Last of the Mohicans	Cooper	Yes
8	English Composition 1	The Academic Writer's Handbook	Rosen	
9	English Composition 1	The Write Stuff: Thinking Through Essays	Sims	Yes
10	Intro to Business	Better Business	Solomon, Poatsy, Martin	Yes

Figure 11.2 A basic list created as a spreadsheet in Microsoft Excel or as a table in Microsoft Word is often sufficient to organize simple data. *(Excel 2016, Microsoft Corporation)*

into, such as books, grocery, or electronics, and then specify one or more subcategories to help narrow the search. If the database doesn't have the right categories for consumers to choose from, they won't easily be able to locate the item they want. Most online retailers use some form of a sophisticated database to enhance the consumer experience but also to help manage inventory.

Do I need databases for managing all types of data? Not every situation in which related data needs to be turned into organized information demands the complexity of a database. For simple tasks, lists are adequate. Most word processing and spreadsheet applications have tools to help you create simple lists. A table you create in Microsoft Word can serve as a list, as can a spreadsheet you create in Microsoft Excel.

Figure 11.2 shows a simple "Books to Buy" list you might create in Excel before beginning college. This list works well because it's simple and suited to just one purpose: to provide you with a list of books you need to buy for a particular semester. If all the information that needs to be tracked were as simple as the information in Figure 11.2, there would be little need for databases.

When is a list not sufficient for organizing data? If complex information needs to be organized or more than one person needs to access it, a list isn't an efficient solution. For example, when you enrolled in college, you provided to a number of people basic information about yourself, including your name and address as well as the classes you wished to take. Your school also tracks other information about you, such as your residence hall assignment and meal plan preferences. Consider the lists shown in Figure 11.3. Figure 11.3a is a list the registrar's office might use to keep track of students and the classes they are taking. Figure 11.3b is a list the housing and dining manager might use to track a student's assigned housing and his or her selected meal plan.

What's the problem with lists? Lists can lead to inefficiencies due to repetition of data and errors from inconsistently entered or updated data. Consider Figure 11.3 again:

- *Duplication*: There is a great deal of duplicated data in the two lists. For example, each time Julio Garza registers for a class, his name and address are entered. He also provides the same data to the housing and dining manager when he makes his residence hall and meal plan selections. Such unnecessary duplication of data in a database, referred to as **data redundancy**, can be problematic, especially when a school has thousands of students. Imagine the time wasted by entering the same data multiple times, semester after semester, as well as the time required for the database to search through the duplicated information. Consider, too, the increased likelihood that someone will make a data-entry mistake. Additionally, if data is entered multiple times, as with most of the students in the list in Figure 11.3a, any reports (such as student bills) generated based on this list could be inaccurate because of the duplicate data. In this case, students could be sent multiple bills for their classes.

- *Inconsistency*: Each time the information in the list changes, multiple lists must be updated. If a student moves, his or her data will need to be updated in all the lists that contain his or her address. It would be easy to overlook one or more lists or even one or more entries in the same list. Moreover, it wouldn't be possible to easily tell which data is correct. This would lead to a state of **data inconsistency**, when different versions of the same data appear in different places in a database. Notice in Figure 11.3 that Susan Finkel's address on the registration list differs from that on the residence hall and meal plan list. It's impossible to tell which address is correct, resulting in data inconsistency.

a

Class Registration List - Spring Semester

Student ID	Last Name	First Name	Home Address	City	State	Zip	Class Code	Class Name	# of Credits
1234567	Finkel	Susan	645 Pine Street	Philadelphia	PA	19012	CIS 110	Computer Literacy	3
1234567	Finkel	Susan	645 Pine Street	Philadelphia	PA	19012	ENG 101	English Comp 1	3
1234567	Finkel	Susan	645 Pine Street	Philadelphia	PA	19012	HIS 103	Western Civ 1	3
1234567	Finkel	Susan	645 Pine Street	Philadelphia	PA	19012	CHE 140	Chemistry	4
1234567	Finkel	Susan	645 Pine Street	Philadelphia	PA	19012	PSY 101	Intro to Psychology	3
4567890	Garza	Julio	421 West 3rd Street	New Witten	SD	57584	CIS 110	Computer Literacy	3
4567890	Garza	Julio	421 West 3rd Street	New Witten	SD	57584	SOC 101	Intro to Sociology	3
4567890	Garza	Julio	421 West 3rd Street	New Witten	SD	57584	PSY 101	Intro to Psych	3
7890123	O'Connor	Leanne	238 Grant Street	Beverly	MA	01915			
2345678	Stinson	Arthur	345 Ryan Drive	Cedar Falls	IA	50613	MAT 161	Pre-Calculus	3
2345678	Stinson	Arthur	345 Ryan Drive	Cedar Falls	IA	50613	ENG 101	English Comp 1	3
2345678	Stinson	Arthur	345 Ryan Drive	Cedar Falls	IA	50613	SOC 101	Intro to Sociology	3
6789012	Zhang	Mei	457 Blanchard St.	Boston	MA	01901	PSY 101	Intro to Psychology	3
6789012	Zhang	Mei	457 Blanchard St.	Boston	MA	01901	HIS 103	Western Civ 1	3
6789012	Zhang	Mei	457 Blanchard St.	Boston	MA	01901	ENG 102	English Comp 2	3

Data Redundancy: Student name entered multiple times and on different lists

Data Inconsistency: Different data on different lists

b

Residence Hall and Meal Plan List

Student ID	Last Name	First Name	Home Address	City	State	Zip	Residence Hall	Room Number	Meal Plan
1234567	Finkel	Susan	10 Green Street	Malvern	PA	19355	Fielder Hall	303	1
4567890	Garza	Julio	421 West 3rd Street	New Witten	SD	57584	Bauer Hall	121	3
7890123	O'Connor	Leanne	238 Grant Street	Beverly	MA	01915	Bauer Hall	214	
2345678	Stinson	Arthur	345 Ryan Drive	Cedar Falls	IA	50613	Berger Quad	317	3
6789012	Zhang	Mei	457 Blanchard St.	Boston	MA	01901	Anders Hall	350	2

Figure 11.3 (a) A class registration list and (b) a list of residence hall assignments are two lists a college might create to keep track of student information. *(Excel 2016, Microsoft Corporation)*

In addition, correct data can be entered into a list but in an inconsistent format. Look at students Julio Garza and Mei Zhang in Figure 11.3a. Both are registered for PSY 101, but two different course names appear: *Intro to Psychology* and *Intro to Psych*. Are these the same course? Which name is correct? Confusion arises when data is inconsistently entered. Establishing data consistency is difficult to do with a list.

Aside from data redundancy and data inconsistency, are there any other problems with using lists instead of databases? Other problems that occur when using simple lists to organize data are as follows:

- *Inappropriate data:* In Figure 11.3b, each student has selected one of the college's three meal plans. What if someone enters a nonexistent meal plan? Not only is this wrong, but it can also be confusing to anyone viewing the list. With a list, there are few checks to make sure that data entered is valid.

- *Incomplete data:* In Figure 11.3a and Figure b, Leanne O'Connor has enrolled in the college but hasn't registered for courses yet or chosen a meal plan. It's difficult to tell by looking at her record whether data relating to her course registration and meal plan is available and just wasn't entered or is truly missing.

Helpdesk MyLab IT®

Using Databases

In this Helpdesk, you'll play the role of a helpdesk staffer, fielding questions about databases, their benefits, their components, and how relational databases organize and manipulate data.

Can't I just exercise caution and set rules for creating and updating lists? Carefully following the rules when you create and update a list like the ones in Figure 11.3 can address many of the problems mentioned, but there's still room for error. Being careful doesn't avoid the problems of data redundancy and data inconsistency. And even if you could surmount these problems, it's difficult to share a list with other users and have the data remain consistent. Therefore, for any complex data that needs to be organized or shared, using a database is the most practical and efficient way to avoid the pitfalls associated with using lists.

Advantages of Using Databases

Objective 11.2 *Discuss the benefits of using a database.*

What are the main advantages of databases? Databases provide several main advantages: They manage large amounts of data efficiently, they enable information sharing, and they promote data integrity.

How can databases manage large amounts of data efficiently? Often, large amounts of data are complex and need to be organized in specific ways in order to be used most efficiently. Figure 11.3 illustrates some issues that can occur when complex data is put in list format. The more data you have, the more likely you are to store that data in multiple lists or tables in a database. A database has mechanisms to manage large amounts of data and to keep it accurate as it's updated and manipulated.

How do databases make information sharing possible? With a database, only one file is maintained. Because of this, databases provide **data centralization**. There is no need for multiple lists and files. A centralized database becomes a shared source that everyone can access (see Figure 11.4). For example, in a college database, each department that needs to use student information accesses it from the same set of data. A centralized database also increases efficiency because there are no files to reconcile with each other. In addition, many databases also provide the ability to control who has access to the data, so the security of data isn't diminished because it's centralized.

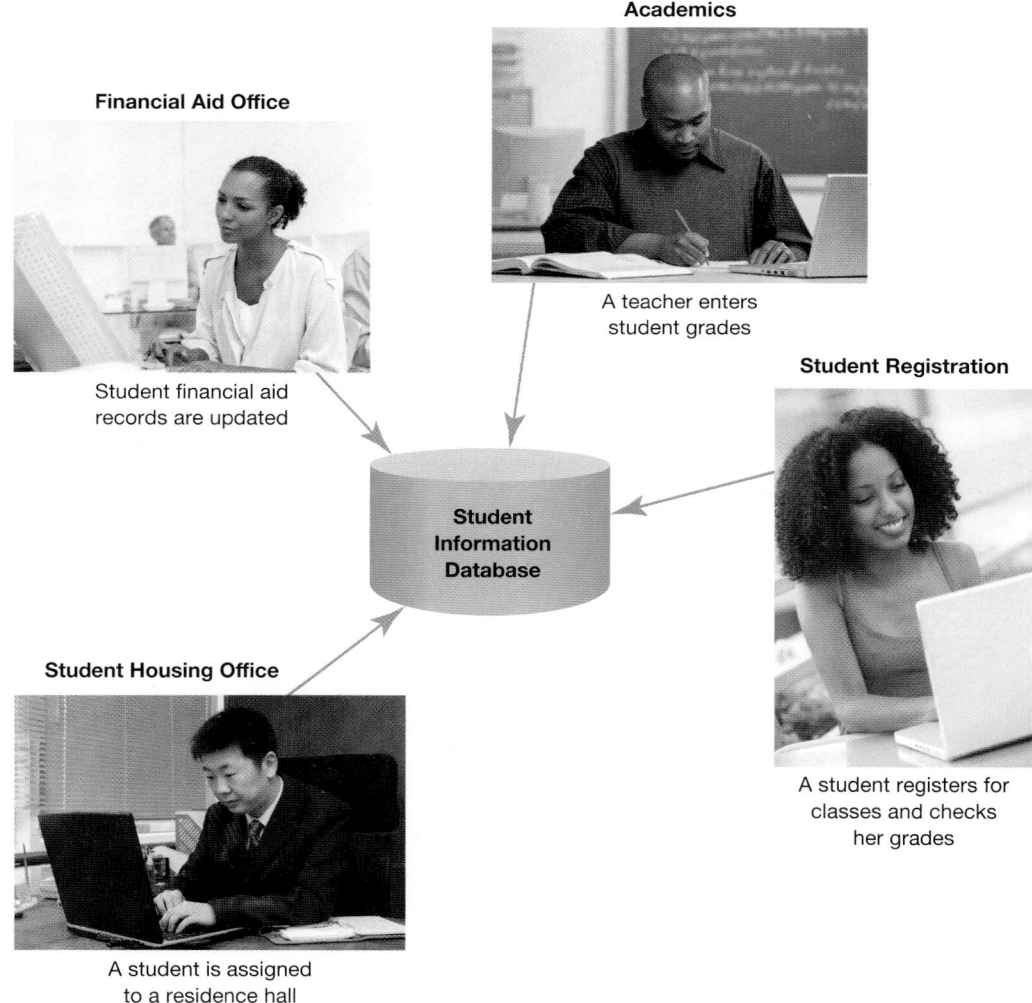

Academics

A teacher enters
student grades

Financial Aid Office

Student financial aid
records are updated

Student Registration

A student registers for
classes and checks
her grades

Student Housing Office

A student is assigned
to a residence hall

Student Information Database

Figure 11.4 A database centralizes data so that only one copy of relevant data must be maintained. All database users therefore access the same up-to-date information. *(Wavebreakmedia/Shutterstock, Avava/ Shutterstock, KK Tan/Shutterstock, MonkeyBusiness Images/Shutterstock)*

How do databases promote data integrity? **Data integrity** means that the data contained in the database is accurate and reliable. Data centralization goes a long way toward ensuring data integrity, but databases have other mechanisms that enforce data integrity. For example, data integrity checks would prevent the entry of employee ID 57 if there already existed an employee with an ID of 57. Similarly, data integrity would prevent an hourly wage of $23 to be applied if the wage range was $10–$22 because $23 falls outside the wage range. Finally, if an address changes, in a centralized database, it needs to be changed in only one place, whereas with multiple lists, it's quite possible that data will be updated in one list and not in another, as was illustrated with a change in address for Susan Finkel in Figure 11.3.

Is there a way to ensure data is organized efficiently? The process to ensure data is organized most efficiently is called data **normalization**. Normalization removes issues such as the data redundancy and inconsistency shown in Figure 11.3 by structuring the data so that student information was in a distinctly separate table and not repeated in the class registration and residence hall tables. Removing redundancy and inconsistency not only improves the integrity of the data but also improves the efficiency of the database.

Are there any disadvantages associated with databases? Databases can be more time consuming and expensive to set up and administer than lists. Great care must be exercised in the design of databases to ensure they'll function as intended. Although average individuals can design small databases, for larger databases, it's helpful to have an experienced **database administrator** (or **database designer**)—an IT professional who is responsible for designing, constructing, and maintaining databases. Database administrators (DBAs) review and manage data on an ongoing basis to ensure the data is flowing smoothly into and out of the database. Figure 11.5 shows a view of the MySQL Enterprise Monitor screen, a tool used primarily by DBAs when reviewing the performance of a database. DBAs can monitor table usage and CPU utilization to help determine whether database performance is acceptable.

Database Types

Many different types of electronic databases have been used since the invention of the computer. The type of database that is used depends on the type of data that needs to be managed. In this section, we look at the three types of database management systems currently in use.

Figure 11.5 The Enterprise Monitor in MySQL helps DBAs review database performance. *(Courtesy Oracle Corporation)*

Relational Databases

Objective 11.3 *Describe features of relational databases.*

What is a relational database? A **relational database**, such as Microsoft Access, operates by organizing data into various tables based on logical groupings. Relational databases are the most commonly used type of database. In our earlier example, all student contact information would be grouped into one table, while the housing and dining information would be grouped into a separate table. Doing so, however, requires that the student contact information is linked to the housing and dining table. In relational databases, a link between tables that defines how the data is related is referred to as a **relationship**. A common field between the two tables is used to create the link. In Figure 11.6, StudentID is the common field in the Residence Assignments and Student Information tables, and ResidenceID is the common field in the Residence Halls and Residence Assignments tables.

Are there different types of relationships in relational databases? A relationship in relational databases can take one of three forms:

1. A **one-to-many relationship** is characterized by a record appearing only once in one table while having the capability of appearing many times in a related table. For example, as shown in Figure 11.6, the "1" next to ResidenceID in the Residence Halls table indicates there is only one instance of each ResidenceID in the Residence Halls table, and the "∞" next to ResidenceID in the Residence Assignments table indicates that many records can have the same ResidenceID in the Residence Assignments table. There is only one instance of each residence hall, but each residence hall will be listed for every student who will be living there. One-to-many relationships are the most common type of relationship in relational databases.

2. A **one-to-one relationship** indicates that for each record in a table there is only one corresponding record in a related table. For example, each student is assigned a room. Because a student can live in only one residence hall at a time, a one-to-one relationship is established, as shown in Figure 11.6 by the "1" next to the StudentID field in both the Residence Assignments table and the Student Information table.

3. A **many-to-many relationship** is characterized by records in one table being related to multiple records in a second table and vice versa. For instance, a table of students could be related to a table of student employers. The employers could employ many students, and students could work for more than one employer.

Relational databases are great for data that can fit into tables and be organized into fields and records. But some data, such as graphics, video, or audio files, are handled better in an object-oriented database.

Figure 11.6 Tables are linked together by a common field, creating a relationship. *(Excel 2016, Microsoft Corporation)*

Object-Oriented Databases

Objective 11.4   *Describe features of object-oriented databases.*

What is an object-oriented database? An **object-oriented database** stores data in objects rather than in tables. Objects contain not only data but also methods for processing or manipulating that data. This allows object-oriented databases to store more types of data than relational databases and to access that data faster.

For example, a student object that contains data about the courses a student is taking might also store the instructions for generating a bill for the student based on his or her course load. Because object-oriented databases store the instructions for doing computations in the same place as they store the data, they can usually process requests for information faster than can relational databases (which would store only the student information).

Why would I use an object-oriented database? Object-oriented databases are more adept at handling **unstructured data** such as audio clips (including MP3 files), video clips, pictures, and extremely large documents. Data of this type is known as a **binary large object (BLOB)** because it's encoded in binary form. In comparison, relational databases are best for the storage of **structured (analytical) data** (such as Bill or 345).

Because businesses today need to store a greater variety of data, object-oriented databases are becoming more popular. Many relational database systems have been expanded to include object-oriented components. For a business to use its data in an object-oriented database, the data needs to undergo a costly conversion process. However, the faster access and reusability of the database objects can provide advantages for large businesses.

Object-oriented databases also need to use a query language to access and manage data. A **query language** is a specially designed computer language used to manipulate data in or extract data from a database. Many object-oriented databases use **Object Query Language (OQL)**, which is similar in many respects to **Structured Query Language (SQL)**, a standard language used to construct queries to extract data from relational databases.

Multidimensional Databases

Objective 11.5   *Describe features of multidimensional databases.*

What is a multidimensional database? A **multidimensional database** stores data that can be analyzed from different perspectives, called dimensions. This distinguishes it from a relational database, which stores data in tables that have only two dimensions (fields and records). Multidimensional databases organize data in a cube format. Each data cube has a *measure attribute*, which is the main type of data that the cube is tracking. Other elements of the cube are known as *feature attributes*, which describe the measure attribute in some meaningful way.

For example, sales of automobiles (measure attribute) could be categorized by various dimensions such as region, automobile model, or sales month—all feature attributes (see Figure 11.7). In addition, the database could be constructed to define different levels within a particular feature attribute, such as state and town within a region.

What are the advantages of multidimensional databases? The two main advantages of multidimensional databases are as follows:

1. They can be customized to provide information to a variety of users based on their needs.
2. They can process data much faster than pure relational databases can.

The need for processing speed is critical at any time, but especially when deploying a large database that's accessed via the Internet. Therefore, large databases such as the one used by eBay or Amazon are usually

Figure 11.7 Multidimensional databases store data in at least three dimensions.

designed as multidimensional databases. Multidimensional databases are used in online analytical processing (OLAP) systems, which we discuss in Part 2 of this chapter.

Emerging Technologies: Can Your Business Partner Deliver the Goods? Enhanced Databases Can Help You Decide!

Suppose you manufacture T-shirts, and to keep costs low, you'd like to explore Vietnamese T-shirt manufacturers. You could use the terms *Vietnamese T-shirt manufacturers* in a search engine, and you'd probably find many leads. The information in the leads available online may be factually correct, but how do you determine how reliable these suppliers are? Alibaba.com and Panjiva are two online business-to-business databases that help to navigate these transactions.

Developed to respond to business needs, Alibaba.com is one of the world's largest online business-to-business databases. Alibaba.com specializes in matching suppliers with buyers for all types of manufactured goods and raw materials. With the global nature of business, databases such as those maintained by Alibaba.com are essential tools that assist businesspeople in managing their global businesses.

Panjiva (**panjiva.com**) is a website that also has a searchable global trade database that tracks the shipments of 10 million

companies. The founders of Panjiva decided to make their database different. They gather data that indicates the reliability of suppliers from sources such as government agencies, independent certification companies, nonprofit organizations, and customers. Using the reliability information, Panjiva then creates ratings for companies (on a scale of 1 to 100) based on specific business performance criteria, such as number of shipments to the U.S. market, the company's environmental record, and their capability to deliver shipments within promised time frames. Companies such as Home Depot that subscribe to Panjiva's database can feel more comfortable about doing business with suppliers that Panjiva has rated for reliability.

Databases with enhanced information are the wave of the future in the business world. So, before you make that next crucial business decision, ask yourself how much you really know about your prospective business partner. If you don't know enough, then find a database that can make you feel more at ease.

Database Basics

Databases are created and managed using specially designed application software (such as Oracle Database or Microsoft Access) to capture and analyze data. Once a database is designed and tested to ensure that it works properly, you can begin creating individual records in (or populating) the database. After the database has been populated with data, users can employ certain methods to extract subsets of data from the database and then output the data in a meaningful and presentable format. In this section, we look at the components that make up a database and how these components function.

Database Components and Functions

Objective 11.6 *Describe how relational databases organize and define data.*

What is needed to manage a database? A **database management system (DBMS)** is the software that allows a computer to perform database functions. The four main operations of a DBMS include:

1. Storing and defining data
2. Viewing (or browsing), adding, deleting, and modifying data
3. Querying (extracting) data
4. Outputting data

Storing and Defining Data

How is data stored and organized in a database? As described earlier, an advantage of databases is that they provide an organized structure for data to make data more meaningful and useful. As shown in Figure 11.8, in a relational database, data is organized using fields, records, and tables:

1. *Fields:* Categories of data are called **fields**. Fields are displayed in columns. Each field is identified by a **field name**, which is a way of describing the information in the field. In Figure 11.8, there are seven different fields (Student ID, Last Name, First Name, Address, City, State, and Zip Code).

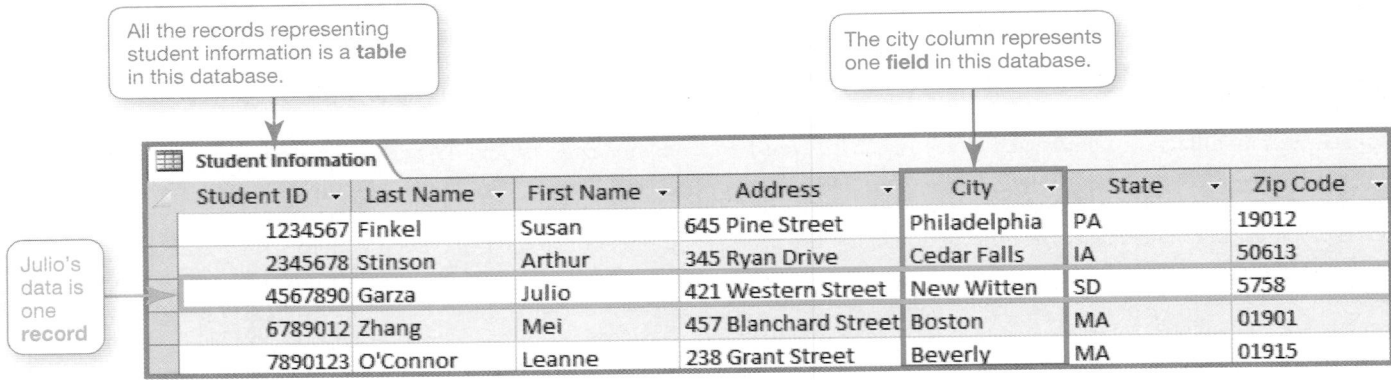

All the records representing student information is a **table** in this database.

The city column represents one **field** in this database.

Julio's data is one record

Student Information

Student ID	Last Name	First Name	Address	City	State	Zip Code
1234567	Finkel	Susan	645 Pine Street	Philadelphia	PA	19012
2345678	Stinson	Arthur	345 Ryan Drive	Cedar Falls	IA	50613
4567890	Garza	Julio	421 Western Street	New Witten	SD	5758
6789012	Zhang	Mei	457 Blanchard Street	Boston	MA	01901
7890123	O'Connor	Leanne	238 Grant Street	Beverly	MA	01915

Figure 11.8 In a database, a category of information is stored in a field. A group of related fields is called a record, and a group of related records is called a table. *(Access 2016, Microsoft Corporation)*

2. *Records:* A group of related fields is called a **record**. For example, in Figure 11.8, a student's ID, name, and complete address comprise a record.

3. *Tables (Files):* A group of related records is called a **table** (or **file**). Tables are usually organized by a common subject. Figure 11.8 shows a table (called Student Information) that contains contact information for students.

How do I know what fields are needed in my database? Careful planning is required to identify each distinct category of data you need to capture. It's often easiest to begin with the anticipated output—that is, what fields will be required in reports. Then, you can work backward to determine what other components of data are needed to support the output and begin to organize the fields into distinct tables. Each field should describe a unique piece of data and should not combine two separate pieces of data. For example, first and last names are separate pieces of data, and you'd want to create a separate field for each rather than having one field for Name. Keeping data into the smallest units possible makes sorting and filtering data more efficient. For instance, suppose you want to send an e-mail to students that addresses all of them by their first name (such as Dear Geri). If Geri's first and last names are in the same field in the database, extracting just her first name for the salutation will be difficult. Similarly, if the name data is combined, it will be difficult to sort by last name (unless the data is inputted with the last name first).

Are there specific rules for establishing field names? The following are some guidelines in establishing field names:

- Field names must be unique within a table. For example, as shown in Figure 11.9, you can't have two fields labeled Name in one table; they must be different, such as FirstName and LastName.

- It's helpful to distinguish similarly named fields in different tables to avoid confusion if those fields appear together in other components of the database. For example, in a college database, there may be separate tables for Student and Faculty. In each table, there will be fields for FirstName and LastName for both students and faculty. Those fields may be used together in the same report that details a student's schedule. To avoid confusion, it would be better to use field names with some notation that identifies the table that the field is from, such as S_LastName and S_FirstName in the Student table and F_LastName and F_FirstName in the Faculty table.

- It is best practice to not use spaces in field names because they can cause errors when the objects are involved in programming tasks. Underscores or PascalCase notation can be used in lieu of spaces.

Can any type of data be entered in any field? When fields are created in the database, the user assigns each field a **data type** (or **field type**). The data type indicates what type of data can be stored in the field and prevents the wrong type of data from being entered into the field. For example, you would not be able to enter an alphabetic character in a field with a number data type.

Figure 11.10 lists the most common data types, with examples of each.

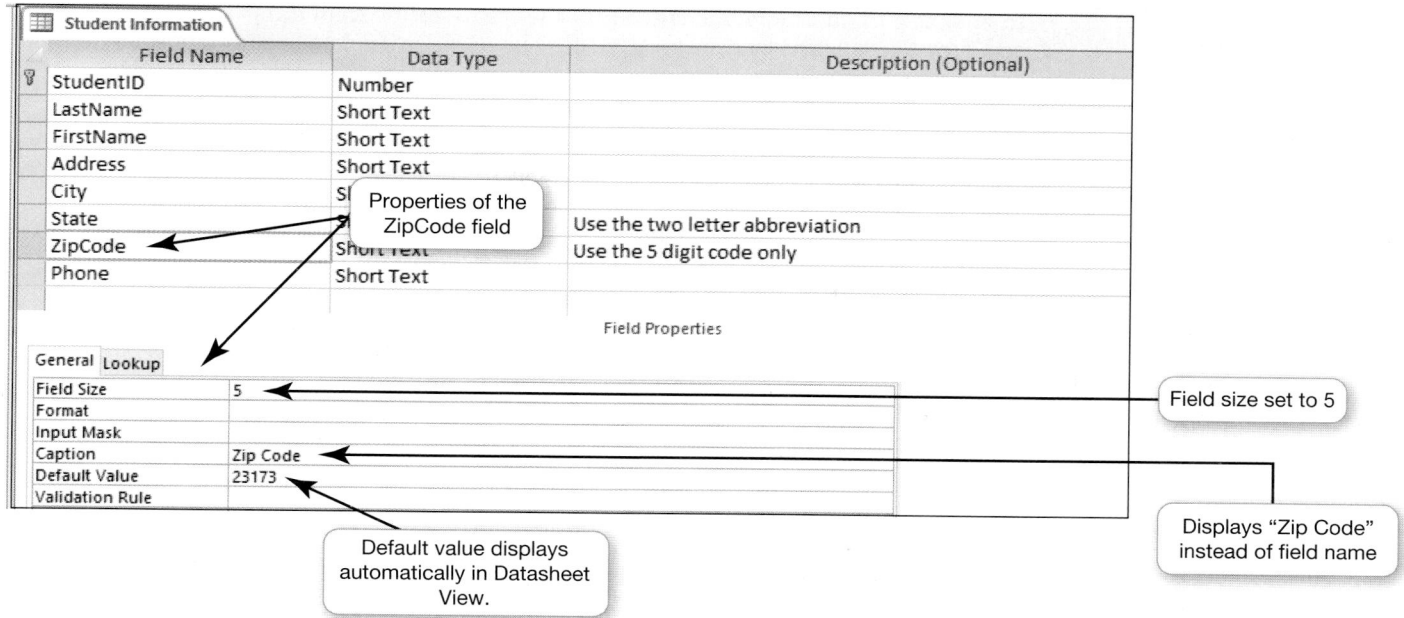

Figure 11.9 The Student Information table, displayed in Design View, shows field names, data types, and other field properties. *(Access 2016, Microsoft Corporation)*

Figure 11.10 Common Data Types in Microsoft Access

Data Type	Used to Store	Examples
Short Text	Letters, symbols, or combinations of letters, symbols, and numbers (up to 255 characters). Short text also contains numbers that can't be used in calculations, such as phone numbers and zip codes.	Cecilia PSY 101 (610) 555-1212
Long Text	Long blocks of text (up to 65,535 characters).	Four score and seven years ago our fathers brought forth on this continent, a new nation, conceived in Liberty, and dedicated to the proposition that all men are created equal.
Number and Currency	Numeric data that can be used in calculations or that is represented as currency.	512 1.789 $1,230
Date/Time	Dates and times in standard notation. Data may be used in calculations, such as calculating the number of days between today and your next birthday.	2/21/2018 10:48:01
Yes/No	Data that has one of two values	True/False
Calculated	Results of a calculation; often involves numeric or date/time data from other fields in the database.	Price * Quantity * .06
OLE Object	Pictures, charts, or files from another Windows-based application.	JPG file Word document
Hyperlink	Alphanumeric data stored as a hyperlink address to a web page, an e-mail address, or an existing file.	pearsonhighered.com techinactionname@email.com

In addition to data type, are there other ways to define field data? In addition to specifying the data type for each field, you can also define field data with other properties, referred to as **field properties**, using Design View. Common field properties include the following:

- **Field size** defines the maximum number of characters that a field can hold. It is important to ensure that the selected field length is long enough to enable storage of the longest possible piece of data that might be entered into the field. Otherwise, data may be truncated (a portion of it chopped off and lost) during data entry. If a field size is set to 5, it can hold a number that has up to 5 digits (from 1 to 99999) or text with five characters. For the ZipCode field in Figure 11.9, the field size property is set to 5 (5 characters), allowing enough space for a five-digit zip code. If the zip code were to include the "zip plus four" system, then the field size would need to be 9 or 10 (allowing for the hyphen). The default field size is determined by the data type, and not all data types (such as Date/Time) require a field size property.

- **Default value** is the value the database automatically uses for the field unless the user enters another value. Default values are useful for field data that's frequently the same. For example, if most students live in Delaware, then setting a default value for the State field to DE saves users from having to enter that value for each student.

- **Caption** enables you to display the field name in a more meaningful or readable manner. As described earlier, PascalCase notation or underscores are often used when creating field names. In addition, field names might include other notations to distinguish similar field names on different tables. In these cases, the field name used to create the table may not be the best to display on forms and reports. The Caption property in Microsoft Access lets you display a field name that is more readable, such as Zip Code instead of ZipCode, as shown in Figure 11.9.

Using Primary Keys

Can fields have the same values in the same table? In most fields, it is possible to have the same value in multiple records. For example, two students can live in the same town or have the same last name. However, to keep records distinct, each record must have one field that has a value unique to that record. This field that provides a unique value for each record is called a **primary key field**. For example, as shown in Figure 11.11, in the Student Information table, the primary key field is Student ID. Notice that each Student ID value in the Student Information table is different. Establishing a primary key and ensuring that its values are unique makes it impossible to have duplicate records, thereby maintaining data integrity.

What makes a good primary key? The most important constraint is that the primary key does not allow duplicate data. Although some numbers, such as Social Security numbers or driver's license numbers, are unique to a person and may be used as primary keys for those specific databases, they do not make great primary keys for other uses. Social Security numbers and other personal identifiers usually aren't a good choice as primary keys for other databases because of the fear of identity theft if the data were misused.

Student Information						
Student ID	Last Name	First Name	Address	City	State	Zip Code
1234567	Finkel	Susan	645 Pine Street	Philadelphia	PA	19012
3456789	Finkel	Susan	25 Maywood Road	Darien	CT	06820
6789012	Zhang	Mei	457 Blanchard Street	Boston	MA	01901
2345678	Stinson	Arthur	345 Ryan Drive	Cedar Falls	IA	50613
4567890	Garza	Julio	421 Western Street	New Witten	SD	05758
2341235	Steuer	James	539	McClean	VA	22101

Same name, different Student ID

Figure 11.11 The StudentID field makes an ideal primary key field because even students with the same name won't have the same ID number. *(Access 2016, Microsoft Corporation)*

In essence, primary keys don't have to be numbers that already represent something. In most instances, the number used to represent a record is some form of serial number that begins with the first record and increases serially as each new record is generated. For example, when you place an order with Amazon.com, your transaction gets a unique order number. This order number is a primary key in Amazon's database. It's essential to have a unique number for each order because it would be difficult to keep track of individual orders without one. Similarly, your student ID number is a unique number, most likely generated in some serial manner. Many database programs have a means of automatically generating a unique identifier that has no meaning outside of the database system. In Microsoft Access, the AutoNumber data type provides the means to generate a serial number as each new record is added.

How is the primary key used to establish relationships between tables? Recall that relational databases link tables together to establish a relationship and join the tables through a common field. The common field in one table is that table's primary key, and the common field in the related table is called the **foreign key** (refer to Figure 11.6). When the relationship is established, you have the option of enforcing **referential integrity** for each relationship.

Referential integrity ensures that relationships between tables remain constant and guarantees the quality of the data in the database. Because data is changed continually in a database, it's important to ensure that the data in related tables is synchronized and that a record isn't added or modified in one table and not the other. For instance, going back to our earlier example, you wouldn't be able to enter a student's record in the Residence Assignments table with a StudentID number that doesn't exist in the Student Information table (the primary key table) if referential integrity is being enforced. You first would need to add the student to the Student Information table and then enter the student in the Residence Assignments table.

How can I keep track of everything in a database? Databases have many components, such as tables, reports, queries, and forms and fields. It's often difficult to keep track of all the components in a database. Therefore, it's useful, especially for large databases, to access the **data dictionary** (or the **database schema**). A database dictionary captures all the database components in a list. The data dictionary is like a map of the database; it not only defines the features of the database (tables, queries, reports, and forms) but also defines the relationships between the tables as well as the features or attributes of the fields in the database.

Bits&Bytes Music Streaming Services Use Databases

When you stream music on your smartphone, you usually don't think about accessing a database, but that's what you're doing when you subscribe to music services such as Spotify, Apple Music, and Tidal. Spotify is a data-driven company incorporating databases in almost everything it does. The company uses massive databases to keep track of and organize over 20 million songs, with thousands of new songs added every day. Moreover, Spotify uses databases to manage its millions of users, their playlists, and their payment and access preferences. Databases are also used to keep track of the monies owed and paid to rights holders. User data is analyzed to create recommended playlists tailored to each user's preferences, and sophisticated algorithms are used to manipulate the data so when songs are shuffled the same artist isn't played in back-to-back songs. Spotify's databases keep track of information such as who is listening to what music, their location, the time music is played, and which tracks are skipped. Spotify is enabling artists and others in the music industry to tap into these databases to gain insight into who is listening to what music, which provides valuable information for artists to improve revenues from touring and merchandising. Now, as you play a song recommendation or shuffle your playlist, you might think of the databases that are being used.

Figure 11.12 Spotify uses databases so you can create and share your playlists or listen to those created by your friends or others. (Pe3k/Shutterstock)

The attributes that define the data in the data dictionary are **metadata**: data that describes other data. Metadata is an integral part of the data dictionary and includes the following:

- The field name
- The *data type* (type of data in the field, such as text, numeric, or date/time)
- The description of the field (optional)
- Any properties (decimals, formatting, etc.) of that particular type of data
- The *field size* (the maximum expected length of data for each field)

Describing the data in this way helps to categorize it and sets parameters for entering valid data into the database (such as a 10-digit number in a phone number field).

Most database management systems keep the data dictionary hidden from users to prevent them from accidentally modifying its contents. In Microsoft Access, the data dictionary can be produced using the Database Documenter command found on the Database Tools tab.

Inputting and Managing Data

Objective 11.7   *Describe how data is inputted and managed in a database.*

How do I get data into the database? You can manually enter data directly into the database, but that is often inefficient and subject to error. Alternatively, because a great deal of data already exists in some type of digital format, such as web-based data, spreadsheets, and data from other databases, most databases can import data from other files, which can save an enormous amount of keying and reduces the amount of data-entry errors.

When importing data, the data must exactly match the format of the database. Most databases usually apply filters to the data to determine whether it's in the correct format. Nonconforming data is flagged (either on-screen or in a report) so that you can modify the data to fit the necessary format.

How can I make manual entry into a database more efficient? Input forms are used to control how new data is entered into a database. Figure 11.13 shows an example of an input form for the Student Information table. Each field has a label that indicates the data to be placed in the field. The data is inputted into the blank boxes. Notes have been added to the form to guide the users. In addition to being used to input new data, input forms are used to make changes to existing data in the database. Because a form can be configured to display individual records, making changes to data by using a form ensures that the change is made to the correct record.

Data Validation

How can I ensure that only valid data is entered into a field? Validation is the process of ensuring that data entered into a field meets specified guidelines. A **validation rule** sets a standard for the data contained in a particular field, and is specified in the field properties. Violations of validation rules usually result in an error message displayed on the screen with a suggested action so that the error can be addressed. Common validation rules include the following:

- *Range check:* A **range check** ensures that the data entered into the field falls within a certain range of values. For instance, you could set a **field constraint** (a property that must be satisfied for an entry to be accepted into the field) to restrict the rate of pay to fall within a certain range. Figure 11.14 shows a range check in the Field Properties pane for an Access database.

A validation rule restricts the entries for a student's rate of pay for his or her campus job to amounts between $7.25 and $15.50. If users tried to enter a rate of pay less than $7.25 or greater than $15.50, they would be notified of a range error and the input would not be accepted, as shown in Figure 11.15.

Student Information Form

Student Information Input Form

Student ID		Enter a 7 digit Student ID number
Last Name		
First Name		
Address		Student's permanent home address
City		
State		Use the 2 letter state abbreviation
Zip Code		

NOTE: All fields must be completed!

Figure 11.13 Input forms are used to enter data into tables. *(Access 2016, Microsoft Corporation)*

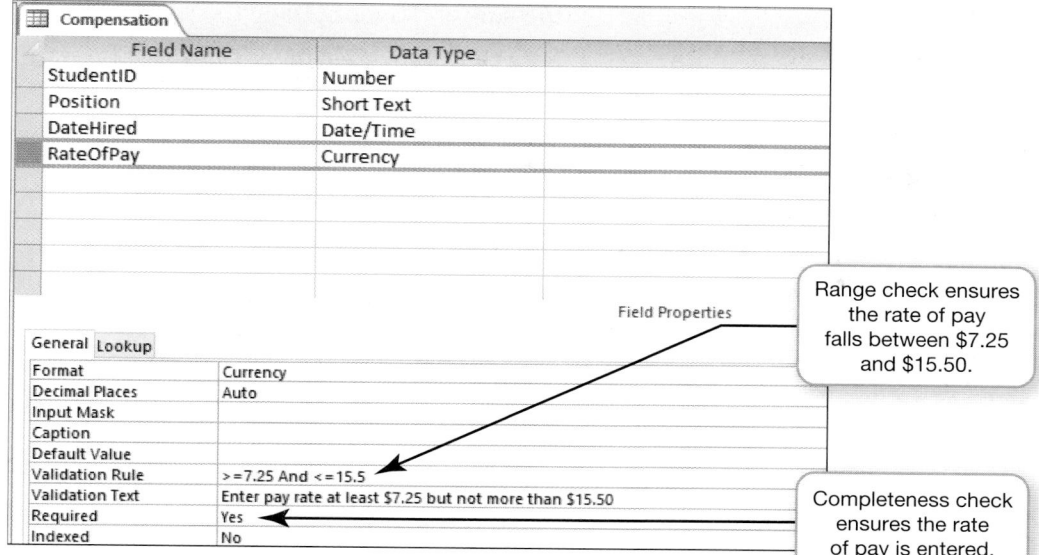

Figure 11.14 Validation rules help ensure correct data is entered. *(Access 2016, Microsoft Corporation)*

Range check ensures the rate of pay falls between $7.25 and $15.50.

Completeness check ensures the rate of pay is entered.

- *Completeness:* A **completeness check** ensures that all required fields have been completed. For example, Figure 11.14 shows the Required property set to Yes, so when data is not entered in the field, as is the case in Figure 11.16, the database performs a completeness check, notices the blank RateOfPay field, and displays an error message to alert the user of the omission.

- *Consistency check:* A **consistency check** compares the values of data in two or more fields to see if those values are reasonable. For example, your birth date and the date you enrolled in school are often in a college's database. It's not possible for you to have enrolled in college before you were born. Furthermore, most college students are at least 16 years old. Therefore, a consistency check on these fields might ensure that your birth date is at least 16 or more years before the date when you enrolled in college.

- *Alphabetic and numeric checks*: An **alphabetic check** confirms that only textual characters are entered in a field. A **numeric check** confirms that only numbers are entered in the field. With a numeric check in place, $J2.5n would not be accepted as the price of a product. Setting the data type will help ensure that the correct type of data is entered into a field and acts as an alphabetic and numeric check.

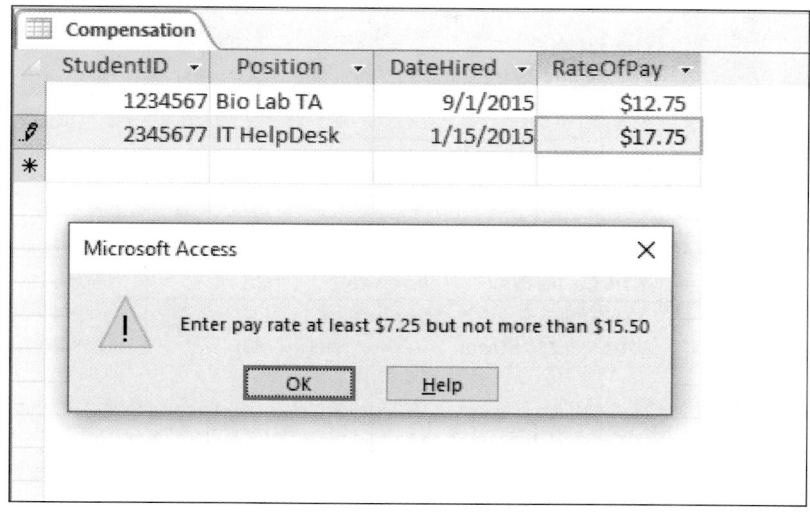

Figure 11.15 Access users see this pop-up when they enter a value that falls outside the stated range of acceptable values. The displayed message is generated from the text typed in the Validation Text property. *(Access 2016, Microsoft Corporation)*

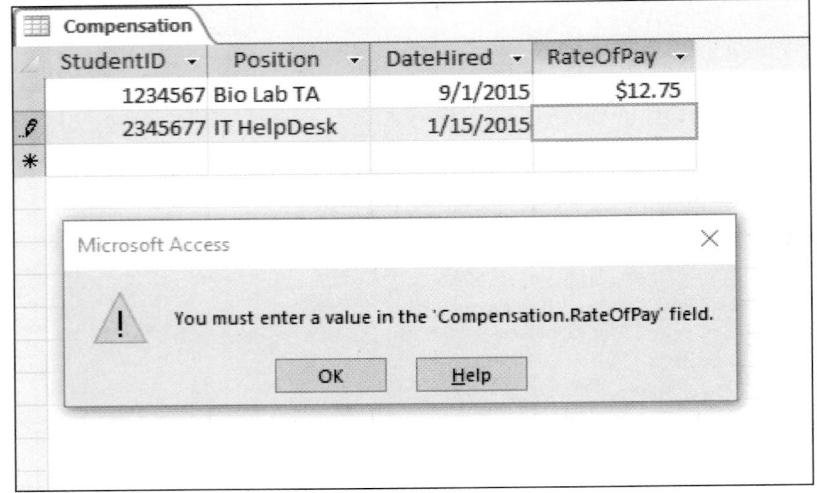

Figure 11.16 Access users see this pop-up when they do not enter a value in a field that has been indicated as being required. *(Access 2016, Microsoft Corporation)*

Viewing and Sorting Data

How can I view data in a database? Displaying the tables on-screen and browsing through all the data is an option with most databases. In many instances, you'll want to view the data only one record at a time and not display all the data in an entire table. Forms are used to display individual records, either alone or in conjunction with other related data.

How can I reorder records in a database? You can easily sort data into ascending or descending order. Figure 11.17a shows an Access database table in which the records were inputted in no particular order. By highlighting a column (in this case, Last Name) and then sorting the data in ascending order, the database displays the records in alphabetical order by last name, as shown in Figure 11.17b.

> Records not sorted in any particular order.

> Click to sort the highlighted column.

> Last Name field sorted in ascending alphabetical order.

Figure 11.17 (a) Shown is an unsorted table. Notice that the Last Name column is selected (highlighted) for sorting. (b) Selecting the sorting option Ascending produces the sorted output with the records sorted in ascending alphabetical order by last name. *(Access 2016, Microsoft Corporation)*

What if I want to display only a certain subset of data in a database? One of the primary benefits of using a database is the ability to manipulate the data so it reveals those records that meet certain criteria. There are two ways to display only those records that match particular criteria:

1. *Use a filter:* A **filter** temporarily displays records that match certain criteria. When you apply a filter, you can't save the results, so filters are useful for quick analyses, and if you don't need to review the results at another time. Additionally, filters can be applied only to fields from the same table, so if you need to combine fields from multiple tables to achieve your subset of data, queries are a better option.

2. *Create a query:* Like a filter, a database **query** is a way of retrieving a particular subset of data that matches certain criteria. Unlike a filter, a query can be used to extract data from one or multiple tables, and queries can be saved and run again whenever necessary to obtain updated results. When you create a query, you choose the fields that should be included in the results and specify the criteria for selecting records. For example, as shown in Figure 11.18a, if you wanted to create a list of students living in the Boyer 1

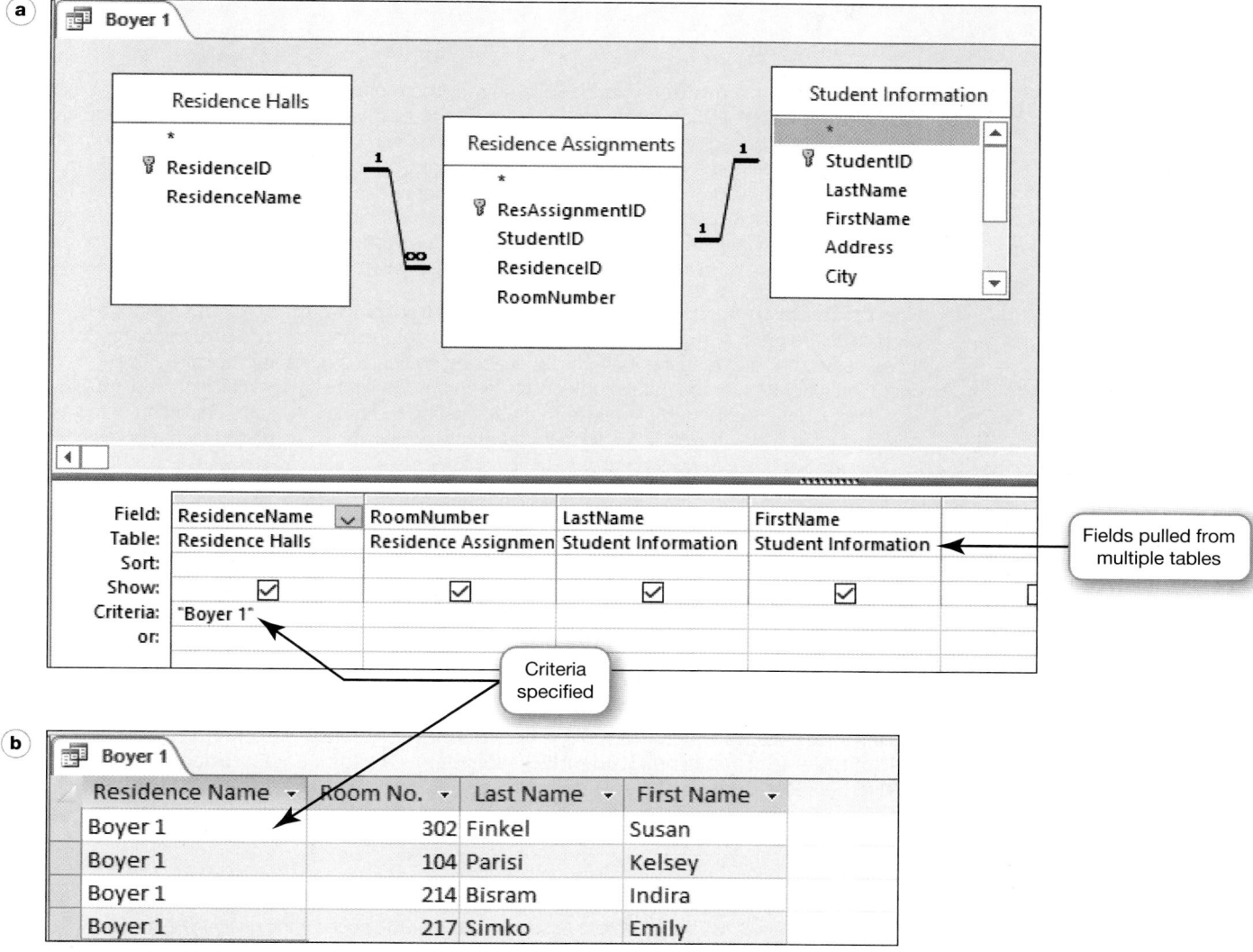

Figure 11.18 (a) When creating a query, you can specify fields from multiple tables as well as specific criteria within a field. (b) The outcome reflects those records meeting the specified criteria. *(Access 2016, Microsoft Corporation)*

dorm and their room numbers, you would pull data from the Student Information table (FirstName and LastName), Residence Halls table (ResidenceName), and Residence Assignments table (RoomNumber). Then you'd need to apply a filter or certain criteria to specify that you want to see only those records pertaining to a specific dorm, in this case Boyer 1. Figure 11.18b displays the results for this query.

How do I develop queries for my database? Modern database systems provide wizards or other mechanisms to guide you through the process of creating queries. Figure 11.18a shows an example of an Access query being created in Design View that allows you to easily select query elements. You can also create a query using a Simple Query Wizard in Microsoft Access. However, when you use the Simple Query Wizard or Design View, you're actually using SQL commands without realizing it. All modern DBMSs contain a query language that the software uses to retrieve and display records. A query language consists of its own vocabulary and sentence structure that you use to frame the requests. Query languages are similar to full-blown programming languages but are usually much easier to learn. The most popular query language used today is SQL.

Rather than relying on the features in Access to create queries, you may create your own SQL queries in Access, modify existing queries at the SQL language level, or view the SQL code that the wizard created. Figure 11.19 shows the SQL code that the query in Figure 11.18 created.

Outputting Data

How do I get data out of a database? The most common form of output for any database is a viewable (or printable) electronic report. You can use data in tables to create reports, or you can generate reports based on queries you create. Although you can print tables and the results of queries directly, when you create a report you can make other adjustments to how the information is displayed, such as grouping like information together and including aggregate information such as totals. Businesses routinely summarize the data within their databases and compile summary data reports. For instance, at the end of each semester, your school generates a grade report for you that shows the grades you received for the classes you took.

Can I transfer data from a database to another software application? Although databases are great at managing data, they are often not the best for data analysis or reporting. In those cases, using spreadsheet or word processing software is more appropriate. Although you could manually reenter the data into the other programs, it is much more efficient, and subject to less error, if data is exported directly from a database to the other program. Exporting data involves putting it into an electronic file in a format that another application can understand. For example, as

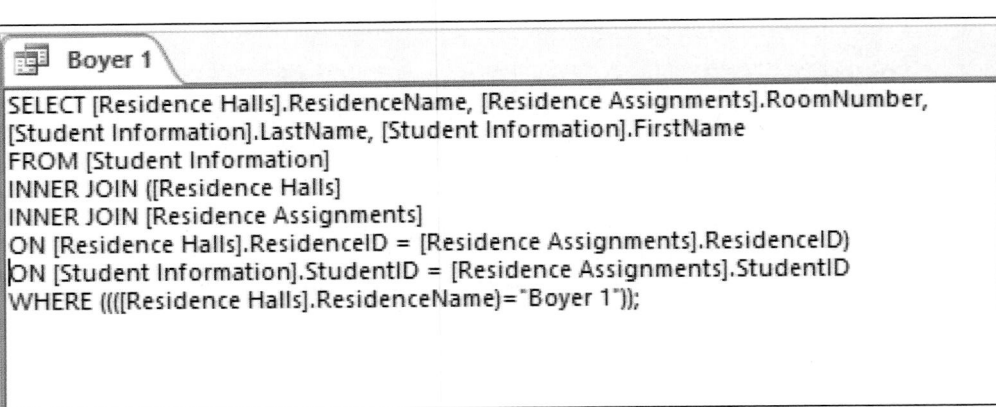

Figure 11.19 The SQL View window in Access shows the SQL code for the query in Figure 11.18. Although it is a relatively simple SELECT statement, it is much easier to create the query using the Access tools provided.
*> To display SQL code for a query, open a query and select **SQL View** from the View drop-down list on the Home tab of the Ribbon. (Access 2016, Microsoft Corporation)*

Structured Query Language (SQL)

To extract records from a database, you use a query language. Almost all relational and object-oriented databases today use Structured Query Language, or SQL. Oracle, Microsoft SQL Server, Microsoft Access, IBM DB2, and MySQL are examples of popular databases that use SQL.

SQL uses relational algebra to extract data from databases. **Relational algebra** is the use of English-like expressions that have variables and operations, much like algebraic equations. Variables include table names, field names, or selection criteria for the data you wish to display. Operations include directions such as *select* (which enables you to pick variable names), *from* (which tells the database which table to use), and *where* (which enables you to specify selection criteria). The two most common queries used to extract data using relational algebra are select queries and join queries.

A **select query** displays a subset of data from a table (or tables) based on the criteria you specify. A typical select query has the following format:

```
SELECT (Field Name 1, Field Name 2,...)
FROM (Table Name)
WHERE (Selection Criteria)
```

The first line of the query contains variables for the field names you want to display. The FROM statement enables you to specify the table name from which the data will be retrieved. The last line (the WHERE statement) is used only when you wish to specify which records need to be displayed (such as all students with GPAs greater than 3.3). If you wish to display all the rows (records) in the table, then you don't use the WHERE statement (see Figure 11.20).

Suppose you want to create a phone list that includes all students from the Student Information table in Figure 11.20a. The SQL query you would send to the database would look like this:

```
SELECT (FirstName, LastName, CellPhone)
FROM (Student Information Table)
```

Figure 11.20b shows the output from this query.

What if you want a phone list that shows only students from Massachusetts? In that case, you would add a WHERE statement to the query, as follows:

```
SELECT (FirstName, LastName, CellPhone)
FROM (Student Information Table)
WHERE (State = MA)
```

a

Student ID	LastName	FirstName	HomeAddress	City	State	Zip Code	CellPhone
1234567	Finkel	Susan	645 Pine Street	Philadelphia	PA	19012	(610) 555-2367
4567890	Garza	Julio	421 Western Street	New Witten	SD	57584	(454) 555-6512
7890123	O'Connor	Leanne	238 Grant Street	Beverly	MA	01915	(303) 555-8723
2345678	Stinson	Arthur	345 Ryan Drive	Cedar Falls	IA	50613	(427) 555-2398
6789012	Zhang	Mei	457 Blanchard Street	Boston	MA	01901	(302) 555-4976

Query applied to this table

```
SELECT (FirstName, LastName, CellPhone)
FROM (Student Information Table)
```

Query applied to this table

```
SELECT (FirstName, LastName, CellPhone)
FROM (Student Information Table)
WHERE (State = MA)
```

Produces this output

b

FirstName	LastName	CellPhone
Susan	Finkel	(610) 555-2367
Julio	Garza	(454) 555-6512
Leanne	O'Connor	(303) 555-8723
Arthur	Stinson	(427) 555-2398
Mei	Zhang	(302) 555-4976

Produces this output

c

FirstName	LastName	CellPhone
Leanne	O'Connor	(303) 555-8723
Mei	Zhang	(302) 555-4976

Figure 11.20 When the query on the left is applied to the (a) Student Information table, it restricts the output to (b) only a phone list. The query on the right, which uses a WHERE statement, further restricts the phone list to (c) only students from Massachusetts. *(Access 2016, Microsoft Corporation)*

This query restricts the output to students who live in Massachusetts, as shown in Figure 11.20c. Notice that the State field in the Student Information table can be used by the query (in this case, as a limiting criterion) but that the contents of the State field aren't required to be displayed in the query results. This explains why the output shown in Figure 11.20c does not show the State field.

When you want to extract data that is in two or more tables, you use a **join query**. The query actually links (or joins) the two tables using the common field in both tables and extracts the relevant data from each. The format for a simple join query for two tables is as follows:

```
SELECT (Field Name 1, Field Name 2)
FROM (Table 1 Name, Table 2 Name)
```

```
WHERE (Table 1 Name.Common Field Name =
Table 2 Name.Common Field Name)
AND (Selection Criteria)
```

Notice how similar this is to a select query, although the FROM statement must now contain two table names. In a join query, the WHERE statement is split into two parts. In the first part (right after WHERE), the relation between the two tables is defined by identifying the common fields between the tables. The second part of the statement (after AND) is where the selection criteria are defined.

The AND means that both parts of the statement must be true for the query to produce results (i.e., the two related fields must exist and the selection criteria must be valid). Figure 11.21 illustrates using a join query for the Student Information and Roster Master tables to produce a class roster for students.

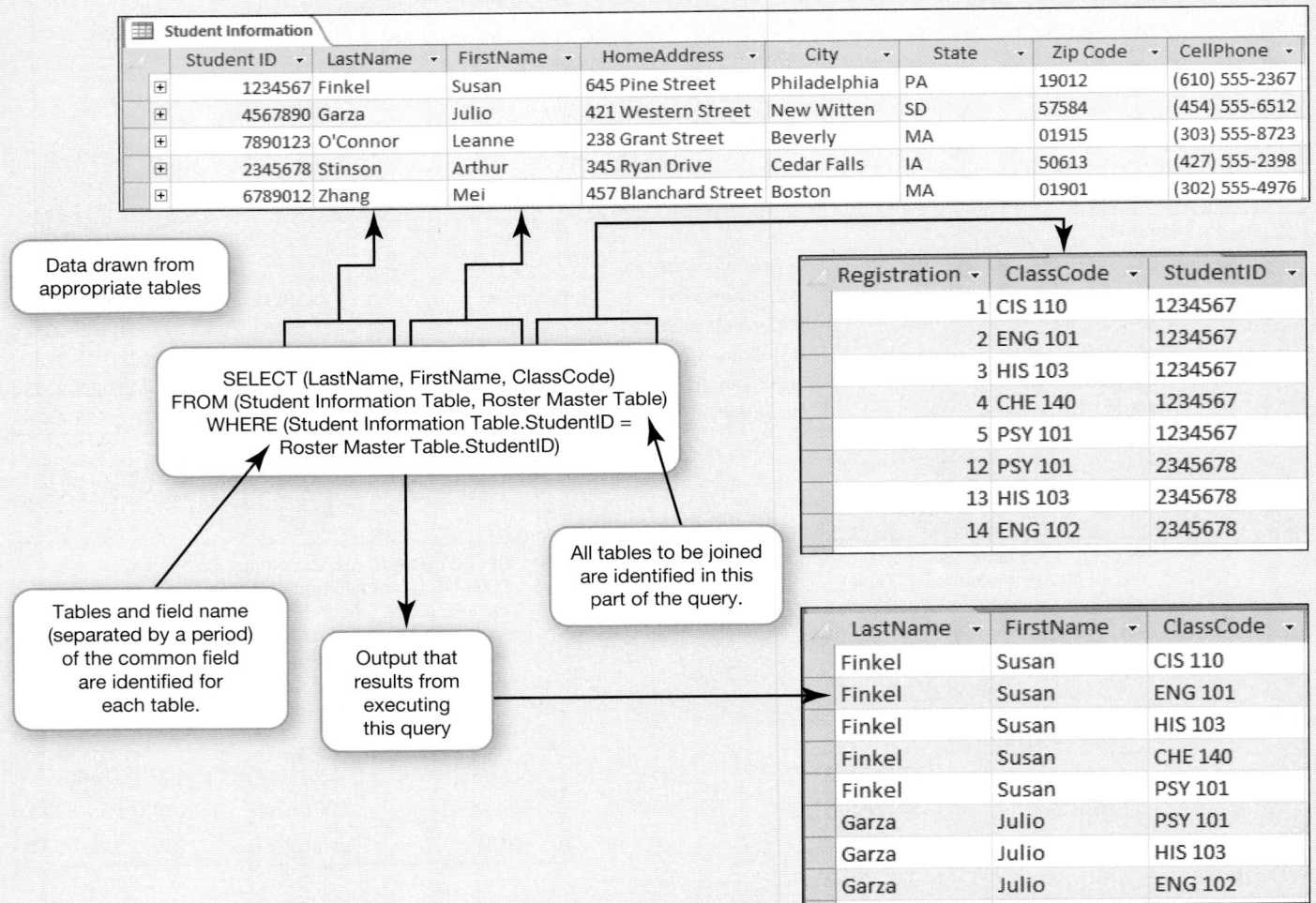

Figure 11.21 This join query will display a student roster for each student in the Student Information table. Notice that the WHERE statement creates the join by defining the common field (in this case, StudentID) in each table. *(Access 2016, Microsoft Corporation)*

shown in Figure 11.22, data can be imported and exported among Microsoft Access and Word and Excel as well as converted to and from other formats such as PDF and XML for use with other applications.

Figure 11.22 Data can be imported and exported between Access and other Microsoft Office applications as well as converted to PDF, XML, and other formats for use with other applications. *(Access 2016, Microsoft Corporation)*

Bits&Bytes

Data Dashboards: Useful Visualization Tools

Data is abundant in today's business world, but all that data is useless unless it's analyzed appropriately and provides insights that lead to better business solutions and decisions. Moreover, in a fast-paced and competitive business environment, having meaningful metrics in one place and updated in real time is powerful for any decision maker. A *data dashboard* is a combination of company metrics, or key performance indicators (KPIs), and is often publicly displayed in real-time so many employees can have access to the information at once. Data dashboards are important tools for good decision making at any level. They can be tailored to display department-specific metrics or can incorporate data from a variety of corporate sources such as sales, customer relationships, website analytics, and accounting. Data dashboards can foster better collaboration between departments and promote better decision making for the entire corporation. In the past, data could only be visualized with charts that used static data. But with cloud-based data and

tools, dashboards can be updating live on screens around the office, providing a means to spot trends or pick up on issues before they become major problems.

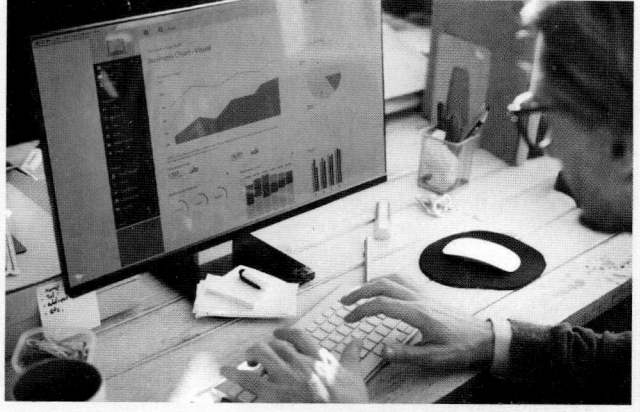

(Rawpixel.com/Fotalia)

Before moving on to Part 2:

1. ▶ Watch Chapter Overview Video 11.1.
2. Then take the Check Your Understanding quiz.

Check Your Understanding // Review & Practice

For a quick review to see what you've learned so far, answer the following questions.

multiple choice

1. Two lists showing different values for the same data in different places of a database is an example of
   a. data redundancy.
   b. data disparity.
   c. data irregularity.
   d. data inconsistency.

2. Which of the following is a TRUE statement when considering using databases instead of lists?
   a. Data can be easily shared among users.
   b. Data-entry errors can be minimized with databases.
   c. Data integrity can be ensured with a database.
   d. all of the above

3. Which type of relationship should be used to connect a Password table to a User Account table?
   a. one-to-many relationship
   b. one-to-one relationship
   c. many-to-many relationship
   d. one-to-none relationship

4. Which type of database organizes data by measure and feature attributes?
   a. multidimensional database
   b. relational database
   c. object-oriented database
   d. all of the above

5. The field that has a unique entry for each record in a database table is called the
   a. foreign key.
   b. logical key.
   c. primary key.
   d. master field.

 Go to **MyLab IT** to take an autograded version of the *Check Your Understanding* review and to find all media resources for the chapter.

TechBytes Weekly Go to TechBytes Weekly for current technology news and discussion questions!

Try This

Using Excel's Database Functions

Databases are great for organizing lots of data, but they can be difficult to understand and to learn how to use. If your data is flat, that is, if it doesn't need to be divided into multiple tables, you can use Excel's database functions to organize your data. In this Try This exercise, you'll learn about some of Excel's useful database functions: sorting one or multiple columns, applying filters, and applying data validation. All the database commands in Excel are on the Data tab. For more step-by-step instructions, watch the Try This video on MyLab IT.

Sorting in Alphabetical Order

You can sort one column of data in alphabetical or numerical order.

Step 1 Place your cursor anywhere in the column you want to sort.

Step 2 In the Sort & Filter group, click **Sort A to Z** or **Sort Z to A**, depending on whether you want to sort in ascending or descending order.

Applying Filters

When you want to isolate a subset of data, you should apply a filter.

Step 1 Click anywhere in the table, then click **Filter** in the Sort & Filter group. Filter arrows will display next to each column heading.

Step 2 Click the filter arrow beside the column heading for the column you want to filter.

Step 3 Remove the checkmark from Select All, and then click the filter value(s) you'd like to apply. Click **OK**.

Step 4 Review the data to ensure the filter has been applied correctly. (Note: To remove the filter, click **Filter** to deselect the option.)

Applying Data Validation

Using the Data Validation tool, you can apply rules to data so that you can ensure the proper data is being entered.

Step 1 Click **Data Validation** in the Data Tools group to display the Data Validation dialog box.

Step 2 On the Settings tab in the Data Validation dialog box, choose the type of data value to be allowed and the value limits in the Data and Maximum boxes. (Note: The criteria in the Data box and other limits will vary.)

Step 3 On the Error Alert tab, select the style of error message you want displayed (Stop, Warning, or Information), and then type the title of the error message and the error message text. Click **OK**.

Step 4 Test the data validation by entering an unacceptable value. When an unacceptable value is entered, an error message displays.

(Excel 2016, Microsoft Corporation)

(Excel 2016, Microsoft Corporation)

Make: A Family Shopping List

In this exercise, you'll create an app that allows each family member to add items to a shopping list from his or her own phone.

This requires the TinyWebDB component in **App Inventor**, which allows you to store information on the Internet so it can be recalled by anyone using your application. Now your app can trade information between all its users!

Your app can store values on the Internet so they are accessible by everyone using your app.

(Copyright MIT, used with permission)

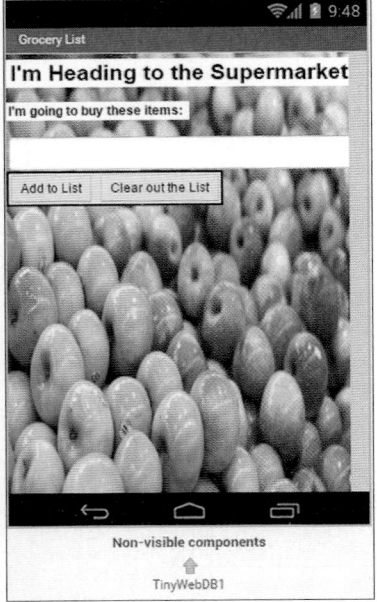

(Copyright MIT, used with permission)

For the instructions for this exercise, go to MyLab IT.

Part 2 ▶ For an overview of this part of the chapter, watch **Chapter Overview Video 11.2**.

How Businesses Use Databases

> **Learning Outcome 11.2** You will be able to explain how businesses use data warehouses, data marts, and data mining to manage data and how business information systems and business intelligence are used to make business decisions.

Large organizations accumulate massive amounts of data, both internal and external. By using *data warehousing*, *data marts*, and *data mining*, these organizations use databases to tap into a wealth of information, improving their internal operations as well as their customer relationships. In this section, we'll look at how they do just that.

Data Warehousing and Storage

At the simplest level, data is stored in a single database on a database server, and you retrieve the data as needed. This works fine for small databases and simple enterprises. Problems can arise when the organization gets much larger, requiring data to be stored in separate department-specific databases. These databases weren't designed to be accessed together to retrieve and combine data from multiple sources, thus eliminating the benefits of accessing data from all databases. Large storage repositories called *data warehouses* and *data marts* are being used help solve this problem.

Data Warehouses and Data Marts

Objective 11.8 *Explain what data warehouses and data marts are and how they are used.*

What is a data warehouse? A **data warehouse** is a large-scale collection of data that contains and organizes in one place all the data from an organization's multiple databases. Individual databases contain a wealth of information, but each database's information usually pertains to one area in the organization. For instance, the order database at Amazon.com contains information about product orders, such as the buyer's name, address, and payment information and the product name or ID. However, the order database doesn't contain information on inventory levels of products, nor does it list suppliers from which out-of-stock products can be obtained. Data warehouses, therefore, consolidate information from various operational systems to present an enterprise-wide view of business operations.

How is data in a data warehouse organized? Data in the data warehouse is organized by *subject*. For example, a large electronics retailer sells many types of electronics, such as TVs and cell phones. Different departments in the retailer are responsible for each type of product and track the products they sell in different databases (one database for TV sales and one for cell phone sales, for example), as shown in Figure 11.23.

These databases capture specific information about each type of electronics. The TV Sales database captures information such as TV features, extended warranty details (and costs), and the cost of the TV because this information is pertinent to determining the ultimate value of TV sales. The Cell Phone Sales database captures information such as data plan details, calling plan features (and costs), and phone costs.

However, data on total electronic devices sold (and the resulting revenue generated) is critical to the management of the electronics retailer no matter what types of products are involved. Therefore, an electronics retailer's data warehouse would have a subject called Electronics Sales Subject (see Figure 11.23) that would contain information about *all* electronic devices sold throughout the company. While the Electronics Sales Subject is a database that contains information from the other databases the company maintains, all data in the Electronics Sales Subject database specifically relates to electronics sales (as opposed to, say, appliances, which the retailer also carries).

From the Electronics Sales Subject database, it's easy for managers to produce comprehensive reports, such as the Total Electronics Sales Report, as shown in Figure 11.23, which can contain information pertaining to all types of electronics sales.

▶ Helpdesk ▮ MyLab IT®

How Businesses Use
Databases
In this Helpdesk, you'll play the role
of a heldesk staffer, fielding
questions about how businesses
use databases.

Figure 11.23 Data from individual databases is drawn together in a data warehouse. Managers can then produce comprehensive reports that would be impossible to create from the individual databases.

Do data warehouses capture data from only one time period? Data warehouse data is **time-variant data**, meaning it doesn't all pertain to one period in time. The warehouse contains current values, such as amounts due from customers, as well as historical data. If you want to examine the buying habits of a certain type of customer, you need data about both current and prior purchases. Having time-variant data in the warehouse gives managers the ability to analyze the past, examine the present in light of historical data, and make projections about the future.

What sources does a data warehouse get its data from? Data warehouses can get data from three sources:

1. *Internal sources:* Sales, billing, inventory, and customer databases all provide a wealth of information. Spreadsheets and other ad hoc analysis tools may contain data that can be loaded into the data warehouse.
2. *External sources:* Vendors and suppliers often provide data regarding product specifications, shipment methods and dates, billing information, and so on.
3. *Clickstream data:* Software used on company websites to capture information about each click that users make as they navigate through the site is referred to as **clickstream data**. Using clickstream data–capture tools, a company can determine which webpages users visit most often, how long users stay on each webpage, which sites directed users to the company site, and user demographics. Such data can provide valuable clues as to what a company needs to improve on its website to stimulate sales.

Data Staging

How does data get into a data warehouse? Although two source databases might contain similar information (such as customer names and addresses), the format of the data is most likely different in each database. Therefore, source data must go through data staging before entering the data warehouse. Data staging is vital because different data must be extracted and then reformatted to fit the data structure defined in the data warehouse's DBMS. **Data staging** consists of three steps:

1. Extraction of the data from source databases
2. Transformation (reformatting) of the data
3. Storage of the data in the data warehouse

Many different software programs and procedures may be needed to extract the data from varied sources and reformat it for storage in the data warehouse. The nature and complexity of the source data determine the complexity of the data-staging process.

How can data stored in the data warehouse be extracted and used? Managers can query the data warehouse in much the same way you would query an Access database. However, because there is more data in the data warehouse, special software is needed to perform such queries. **Online analytical processing (OLAP)** software provides standardized tools for viewing and manipulating data in a data warehouse. The key feature of OLAP tools is that they enable flexible views of the data, which the software user can easily change.

Data Marts

What if a smaller amount of data is needed? Small slices of the data warehouse, each called a **data mart**, are often created so that companies can analyze a related set of data that is grouped together and separated out from the main body of data in the data warehouse. Whereas data warehouses have an enterprise-wide depth, the information in data marts pertains to a single component of the business. Data can be extracted using powerful OLAP query tools, or it can be stored in specialized data marts for use by specific employee groups.

For instance, if you need accurate sales-related information and you don't want to wade through customer service data, accounts payable data, and product shipping data to get it, a data mart that contains information relevant only to the sales department can be created to make the task of finding this data easier. An overview of the data-warehousing process is illustrated in Figure 11.24.

Data Mining

Objective 11.9 *Describe data mining and how it works.*

What is data mining? Just because you have captured data in an organized fashion and have stored it in a format that seems to make sense doesn't mean that an analysis of the data will automatically reveal everything you need to know. Trends can sometimes be hard to spot if the data isn't organized or analyzed in a particular way. To make data work harder, companies employ

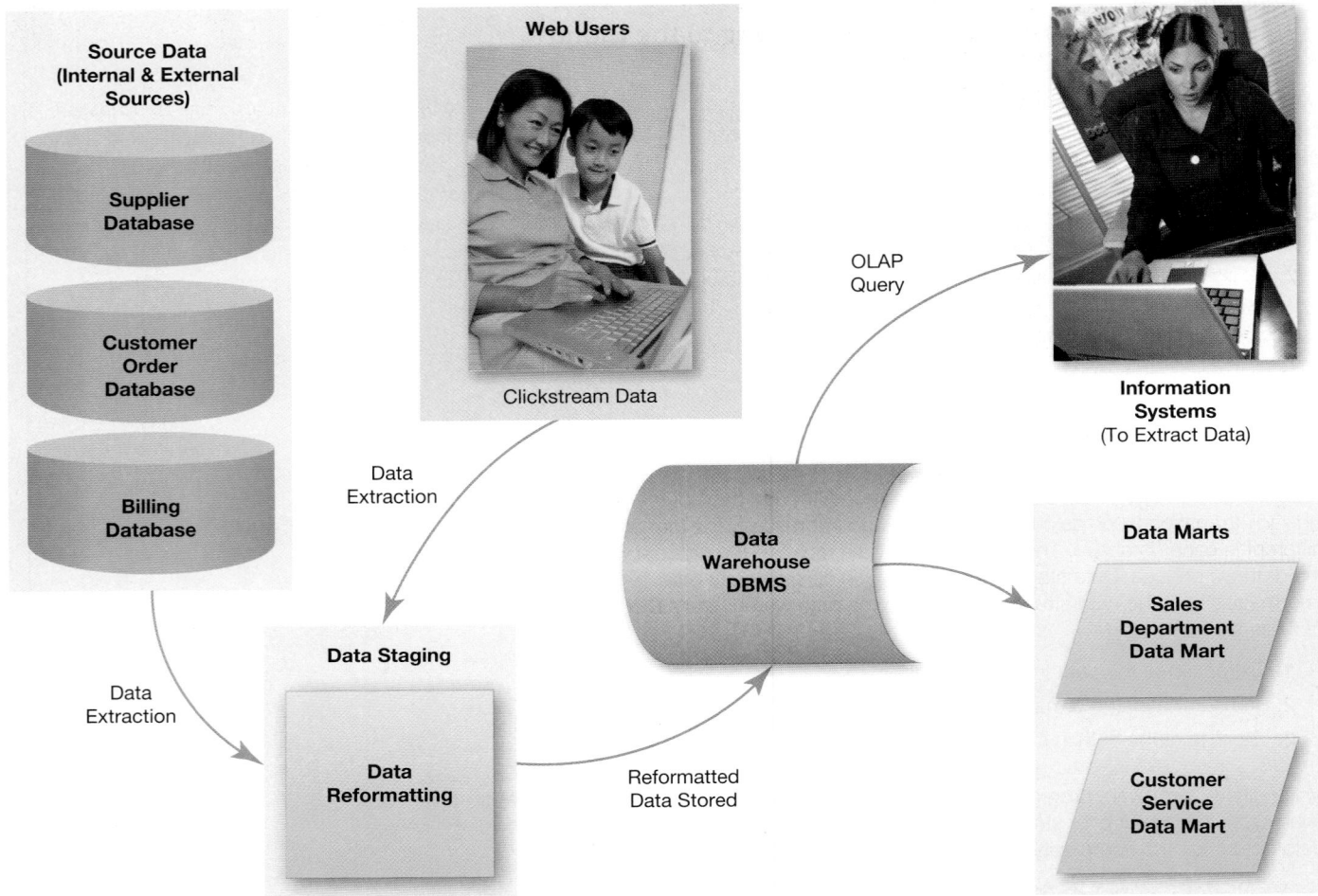

Figure 11.24 An overview of the data warehouse process. *(Sirtravelalot/Shutterstock, Redav/Shutterstock)*

data-mining techniques. **Data mining** is the process by which great amounts of data are analyzed and investigated. The objective is to spot significant patterns or trends within the data that would otherwise not be obvious. For instance, by mining student enrollment data, a school may discover that there's been a consistent increase in new engineering-degree students who are women.

Why do businesses mine their data? The main reason businesses mine data is to understand their customers better. If a company can better understand the types of customers who buy its products and can learn what motivates its customers to do so, it can market effectively by concentrating its efforts on the populations most likely to buy. You may have noticed that products are frequently moved around in supermarkets. This is usually the result of data mining. With electronic scanning of bar codes, each customer's purchase is recorded in a database. By classifying the data and using analytical tools and methods, supermarket managers can determine which products people usually purchase with other products. The store then places these products close to each other so that shoppers can find them easily. For instance, if analysis shows that people often buy potato chips with soft drinks, it makes sense to place these items in the same aisle.

How do businesses mine their data? Data mining enables managers to sift through data in several ways. Each technique produces different information on which managers can then base their decisions.

Managers make their data meaningful through the following techniques described next and listed in Figure 11.25.

- *Classification:* Before mining, managers define data classes they think will be helpful in spotting trends. They then apply these class definitions to all unclassified data to prepare it for analysis. For example, good credit risk and bad credit risk are two data classes managers could establish to determine whether to grant car loans to applicants. Managers would then identify factors, such as credit history and yearly income, that they could use to classify applicants as good or bad credit risks.

- *Estimation:* When managers classify data, the record either fits the classification criteria or it doesn't. Estimation enables managers to assign a value to data based on some criterion. For example, assume a bank wants to send out credit card offers to people who are likely to be granted a credit card. The bank may run the customers' data through a program that assigns a score based on where they live, their household income, and their average bank balance. This provides managers with an estimate of the most likely credit card prospects to target.

- *Affinity grouping (or association rules):* When mining data, managers can determine which data goes together by applying affinity grouping or association rules to the data. For example, suppose analysis of a sales database indicates that two items are bought together 60% of the time. Based on this data, managers might decide that these items should be pictured on the same page of their website.

- *Clustering:* Clustering involves organizing data into similar subgroups, or clusters. It's different from classification in that there are no predefined classes. The data-mining software makes the decision about what to group, and it's up to managers to determine whether the clusters are meaningful. For example, the data-mining software may identify clusters of customers with similar buying patterns. Further analysis of the clusters may reveal that certain socioeconomic groups have similar buying patterns.

- *Description and visualization:* Often, the purpose of data mining is to describe data so that managers can interpret it in new and different ways. For example, if large amounts of data revealed that right-handed women who live in rural environments never take philosophy courses, it would most likely spark a heated discussion about the reasons why. It would certainly provide plenty of opportunities for additional study on the part of psychologists, sociologists, and college administrators!

As we continue to generate data and businesses continue to accumulate data, the development of faster and bigger databases will be a necessity. You can expect to interact with more and more databases every year, even if you don't realize you're doing so.

Figure 11.25 Data-Mining Techniques

Classification
Define data classes to help spot trends, then apply the class definitions to all unclassified data.

Estimation
Assign a value to data based on some criterion.

Affinity Grouping (or Association Rules)
Determine which data goes together.

Clustering
Organize data into similar subgroups, or clusters, without using predefined classes.

Description and Visualization
Describe data so that managers can interpret it in new and different ways.

(Dreaming Andy/Fotolia, Kbuntu/Fotolia, Frank Boston/Fotolia, Gallo Images/Fotolia, Lvnel/Fotolia)

Bits&Bytes   Hadoop: How Big Data Is Being Managed

Hadoop is an open source platform sponsored by the Apache Software Foundation that makes big, complex, and unstructured data easier to manage. It eliminates the constraints placed on how data is traditionally stored and processed by spreading out the data and using many processors that work in parallel. The unique aspects of Hadoop reside in how it stores files and processes data:

- *File storage:* Hadoop facilitates storing files bigger than what can be stored in a centralized database system. Instead of using one server that is common in a centralized database system, Hadoop breaks the data into chunks that it then spreads across to different servers, so it can store many files and very large files.
- *Data processing:* In addition, Hadoop uses a system called MapReduce for processing big data sets. It makes working

with large data sets over a network much more efficient. Rather than moving the data to the software, as is done with traditional data processing systems, MapReduce moves the software to the data. MapReduce sends code to each of the dozens of servers storing the data, and then each server uses multiple processors to process its set of data. Results are then delivered back in a unified result set.

Hadoop is being used in a variety of industries and markets. For example, Hadoop can be used to conduct accurate portfolio evaluation and risk analysis in the financial industry as well as better organize and manage retail data in order to give customers a better response to their searches.

Ethics in IT

Data, Data Everywhere, but Is It Protected?

Every organization is generating, acquiring, processing, and storing massive amounts of data every day. Unfortunately, protecting that data from being mishandled is difficult to do. Inadvertently exposing information to inappropriate or unauthorized individuals is known as a *data breach*. According to Identity Theft Resource Center, As of August 2016, there were more than 600 data breaches exposing nearly 21 million records. The average cost per stolen record is approximately $150. Consider the following:

- In March 2016, Verizon Enterprise Solutions experienced the theft and resale of data from approximately 1.5 million customers. Ironically, Verizon Enterprise Solutions is a unit of the telecommunications company that often helps other large companies respond to data breaches.
- In February 2016, a laptop and several hard drives were stolen from the Office of Child Support Enforcement in Olympia, Washington. Nearly 5 million people may have had personal information, such as Social Security numbers, compromised.
- In October 2015, a patient database at 21st Century Oncology containing insurance data, Social Security numbers, and other sensitive data was hacked. Nearly 2.2 million current and former patients were affected.
- In June 2015, approximately 22 million records of current, former, and prospective federal employees were exposed when hackers targeted the U.S. Office of Personnel Management.

What responsibility do companies have in safeguarding your data? Should they inform you that your data might be shared with other corporations and obtain your permission before sharing it? How should consumers be compensated (and by whom) if their data is misused?

What Can You Do?

Providing information and having it recorded in databases are part of our way of life now. Ask the following questions related to data you're providing:

- **For what purpose is the data being gathered?** When the clerk at the electronics superstore asks for your zip code, ask why he or she wants it.

- **Are the reasons for gathering the data legitimate or important to you?** You might not want to share your information for marketing purposes, but might want to in order to initiate a product warranty. Similarly, disclosing personal information to your pharmacist may be important for receiving good care and therefore is important to you. If you don't see the advantage, then ask more questions or don't reveal the information.
- **How will the collected information be protected?** Ask about data protection policies before you give information. Most websites provide access to their data protection policies when they ask you for information. If an organization does not have a data protection policy, be wary of giving them sensitive information. Data protection does not just refer to keeping data secure; it also means restricting access to the data to employees of the organization who need to use that data. A shipping clerk might need to see your address, for example, but does not need to see your credit card information.
- **Will the collected information be used for purposes other than the purpose for which it was originally collected?** This might be covered in a data protection policy. If it is not, ask about it. Will your information be sold to or shared with other companies? Will it be used for marketing other products to you?
- **Could the information asked for be used for identity theft?** Identity thieves usually need your Social Security number and your birth date to open credit card accounts in your name. Be especially wary when asked for this information, and make sure there is a legitimate need for it. And do you really need an e-mail from someone on your birthday, advertising a product? It really is not worth exposing your birth date to potential misuse.
- **Are organizations safeguarding your data?** Don't just consider new requests for information. Think about organizations, such as banks, that already have your information. Have they been in the news lately because of a major data breach? You might want to consider switching institutions if yours has a poor record of data security.

Think carefully before providing information and be vigilant about monitoring your data when you can. It may make the difference between invasion of privacy and peace of mind.

Using Databases to Make Business Decisions

Making intelligent decisions about developing new products, creating marketing strategies, and buying raw materials requires timely, accurate information. In this section, we look at the different types of database systems that are used to help managers make good business decisions.

Business Information Systems

Objective 11.10   *Describe the main types of business information systems and how they are used by business managers.*

What is an information system? An **information system** is a software-based solution used to gather and analyze data. It is made up of the database, application programs, and manual and machine procedures necessary to process data into meaningful information. For example, an information system is used to deliver up-to-the-minute sales data on shoes to the computer of Zappos's president. Databases are integral parts of information systems because they store the information that makes information systems functional.

All information systems perform similar functions, including acquiring data, processing that data into information, storing the data, and providing the user with a number of output options with which to make the information meaningful and useful (see Figure 11.26). There are several types

Figure 11.26   Information systems acquire data, process that data into information, store the data, and provide the user with a number of output options to make the information useful. *(Wavebreakmedia/Shutterstock, Wavebreakmedia/Shutterstock, Michaeljung/Shutterstock, Raisa Kanareva/Shutterstock, Ryan McVay/Photodisc/Getty Images, Zoomstudio/E+/Getty Images)*

of information systems. Each system responds to a particular need of an organization, and is generally specific to the type of information required. Generally, the information can be categorized as operational, managerial, and strategic. Specifically, information systems include transaction-processing systems (operational), management information systems (managerial), decision support systems (senior managers), and business intelligence systems (executive managers). Businesses operate more efficiently by using one or more information systems. Finally, enterprise resource planning systems integrate data from department-specific information systems across the entire enterprise. This facilitates decision making at many managerial levels, improving efficiency.

Transaction-Processing Systems

What is a transaction-processing system? A **transaction-processing system (TPS)** is an operational-level system that keeps track of everyday business transactions or activities, such as order tracking, order processing, payroll, and cash management. For example, colleges have TPSs in place to track transactions that occur frequently, such as registering students for classes, accepting tuition payments, and printing course catalogs. When computers were introduced to the business world, they often were first put to work hosting TPSs.

How are transactions entered into a TPS? Transactions can be entered in real time or through batch processing:

- For most activities, processing and recording transactions in a TPS occur in real time. **Real-time processing** means that the database is updated while the transaction is taking place. For instance, when you register for classes online, the database immediately records your registration in the class to ensure you have a spot. This **online transaction processing (OLTP)** ensures that the data in the TPS is current.
- **Batch processing** means that transaction data is accumulated until a certain point is reached and then several transactions are processed at once. Batch processing is appropriate for activities that aren't time sensitive. For example, you may not receive a bill for each

---

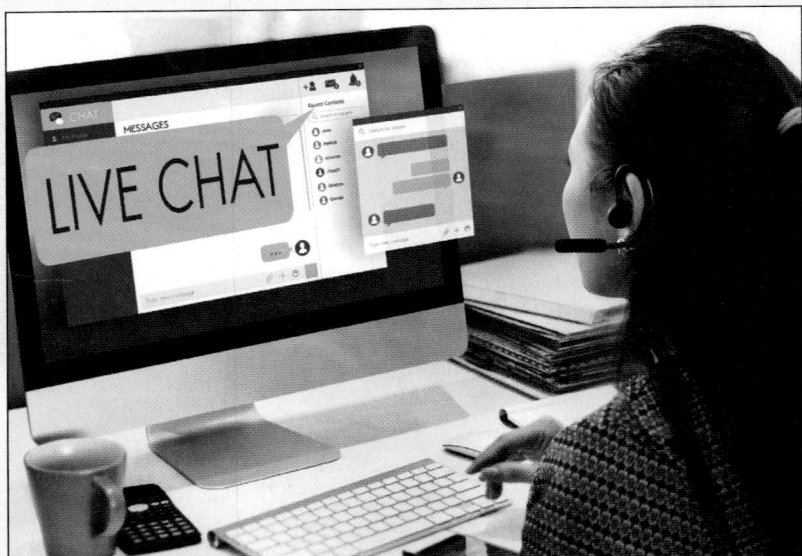

charge you make at the bookstore. Instead, the college may collect your charges and batch them together into one monthly billing. It's more efficient to batch and process all requests periodically.

Various departments in an organization then access the TPSs to extract the information they need to process additional transactions, as shown in Figure 11.28.

Management Information Systems

What is a management information system? A **management information system (MIS)** provides timely and accurate information that enables managers to make critical business decisions. MISs were a direct outgrowth of TPSs. Managers quickly realized that the data contained in TPSs could be an extremely powerful tool only if the information could be organized and outputted in a

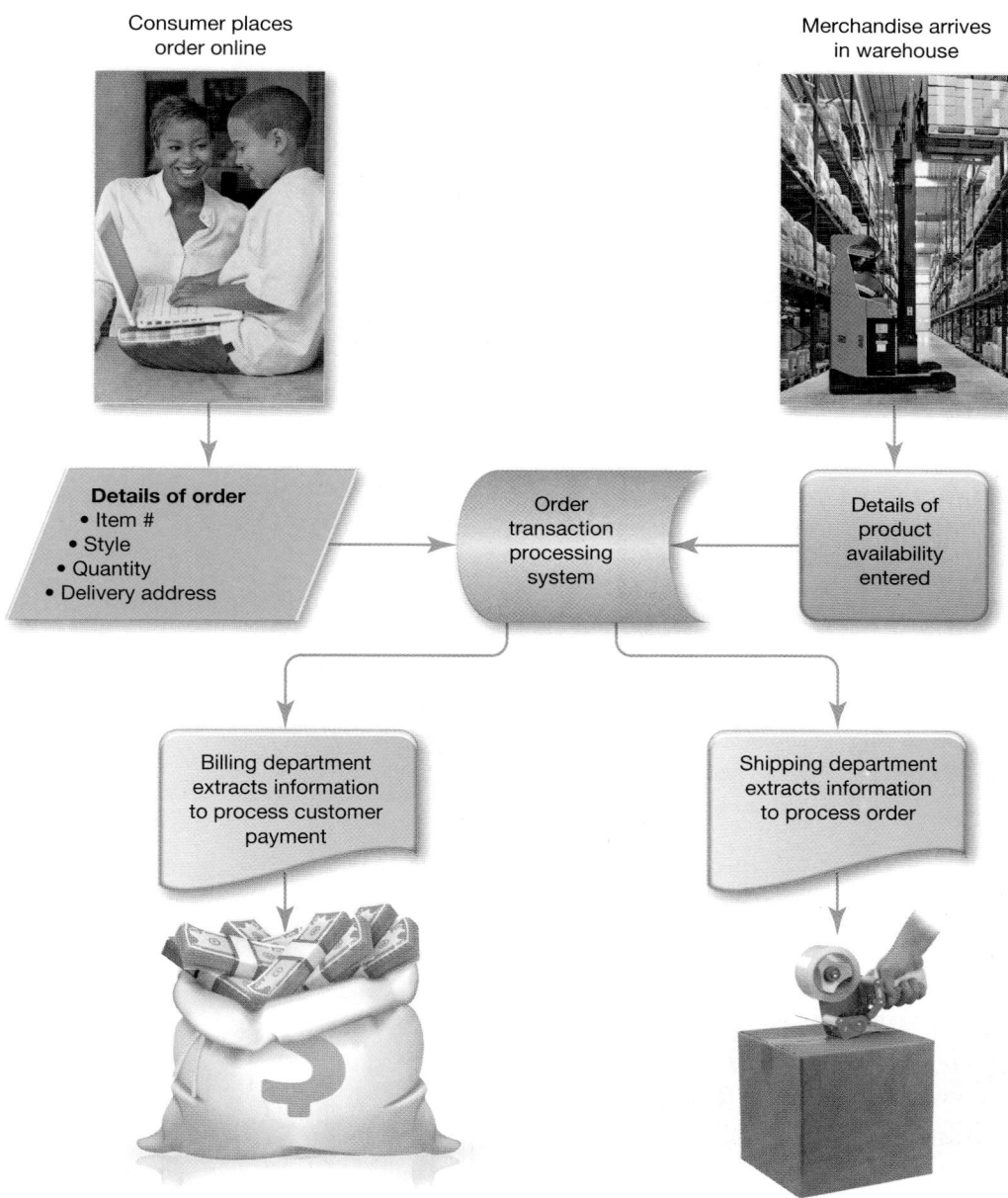

Figure 11.28 Transaction-processing systems help capture and track critical business information needed for successful completion of business transactions such as selling merchandise over the Internet. *(Sirtravelalot/ Shutterstock, Penka Todorova Vitkova/Shutterstock, Natykach Nataliia/Shutterstock, Chuck Rausin/Shutterstock)*

useful form. Periodically, the MIS can create prescheduled reports, which are used by managers to make strategic and tactical decisions. MIS reports are also useful in conducting "what-if" analyses that offer potential results on given sets of variables.

What types of reports are generated by MISs? MISs generate three types of reports:

1. A **detail report** provides a list of the transactions that occurred during a certain time period. For example, during registration at your school, the registrar might receive a detail report that lists the students who registered for classes each day. Figure 11.29a shows an example of a detail report on daily enrollment.

2. A **summary report** provides a consolidated picture of detailed data. These reports usually include some calculations (totals) or visual displays of information (such as charts and graphs). Figure 11.29b shows an example of a summary report displaying total daily credits enrolled by division.

3. An **exception report** shows conditions that are unusual or that need attention by system users. The registrar at your college may get an exception report when all sections of a course are full, indicating that it may be time to schedule additional sections. Figure 11.29c shows an example of such an exception report.

Decision Support Systems

What is a decision support system? A **decision support system (DSS)** is another type of business information system designed to help managers develop solutions for specific problems. With a DSS, managers can make queries of data for specific answers in an effort to evaluate the impact of a decision before it is implemented. For example, a DSS for a marketing department might provide statistical information on customer attributes, such as income levels or buying patterns that would assist managers in making advertising strategy decisions. A DSS not only uses data from databases and data warehouses but also enables users to add their own insights and experiences and apply them to the solution. As shown in Figure 11.30, many data-related systems work together to provide the user of the DSS with a broad base of information on which to base decisions.

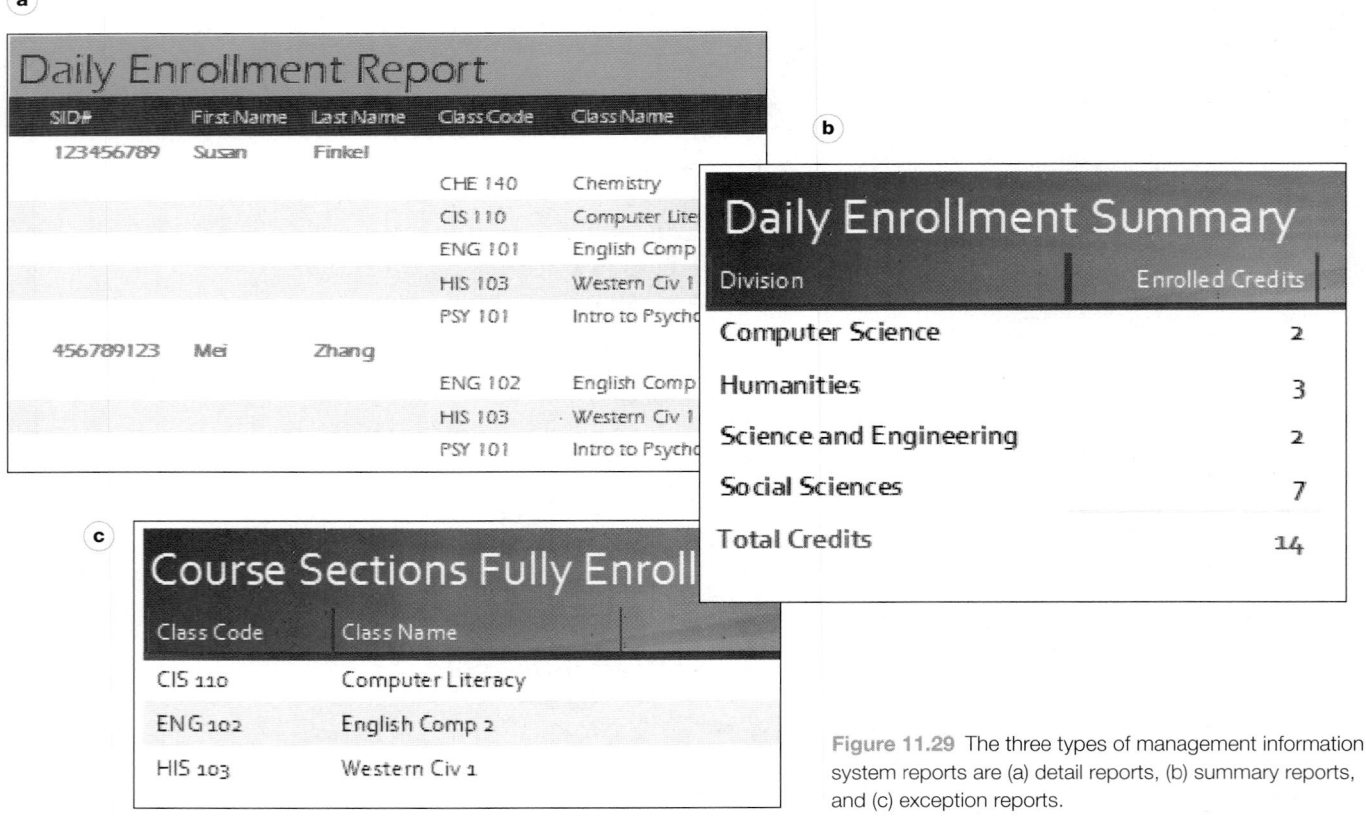

Figure 11.29 The three types of management information system reports are (a) detail reports, (b) summary reports, and (c) exception reports.

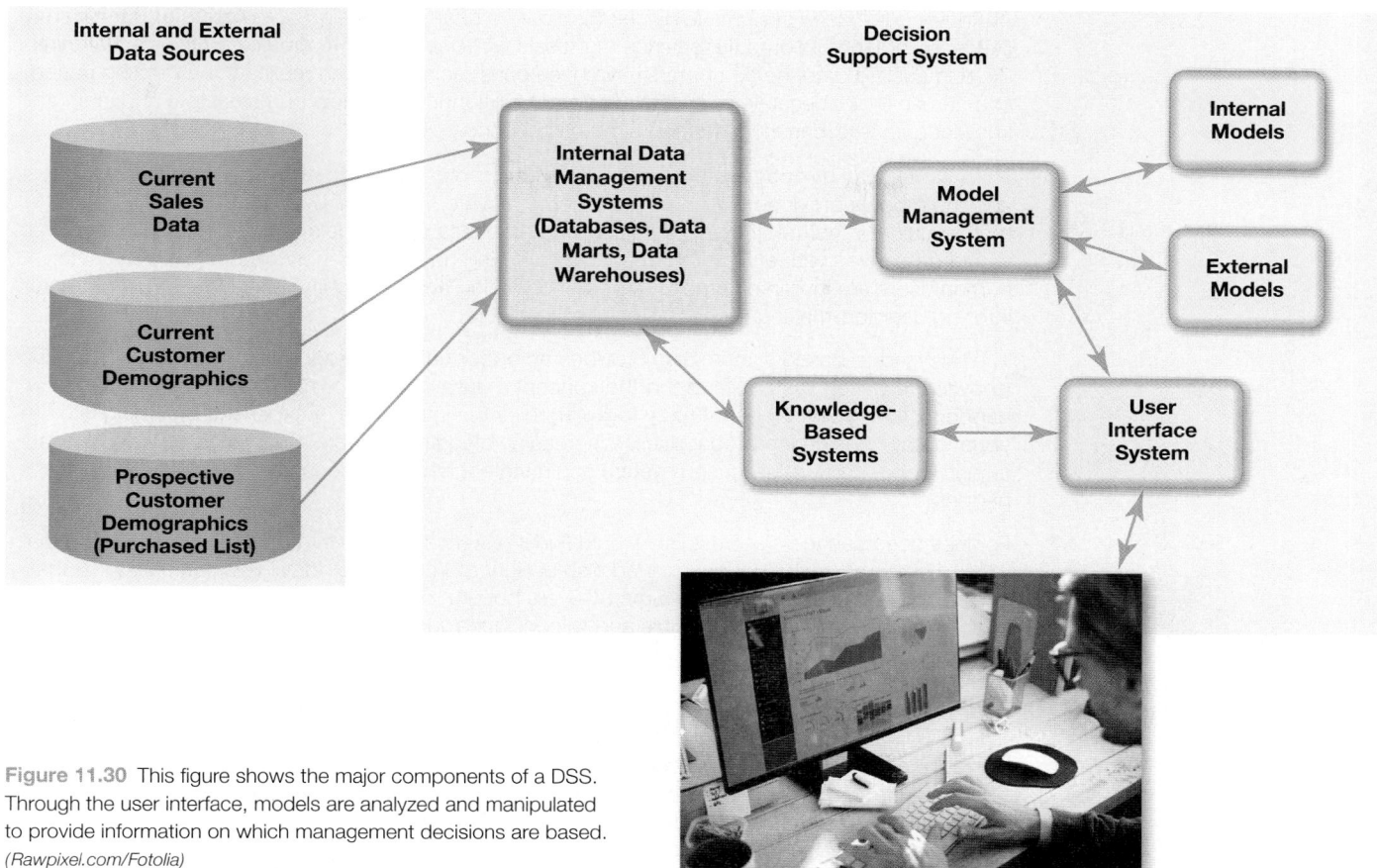

Figure 11.30 This figure shows the major components of a DSS. Through the user interface, models are analyzed and manipulated to provide information on which management decisions are based. (Rawpixel.com/Fotolia)

How does a DSS get data? Internal and external data sources provide a stream of data that is integrated into the DSS for analysis. Internal data sources are maintained by the same company that operates the DSS. For example, internal TPSs can provide a wealth of statistical data about customers, ordering patterns, inventory levels, and so on. An external data source is any source not owned by the company that owns the DSS, such as customer demographic data purchased from third parties, mailing lists, or statistics compiled by the government.

What function does a model management system perform? A **model management system** is software that assists in building management models in a DSS. A management model is an analysis tool that, through the use of internal and external data, provides a view of a particular business situation for the purposes of decision making. Models can be built to describe any business situation, such as the classroom space requirements for next semester or a listing of alternative sales outlet locations. Model management systems typically contain financial and statistical analysis tools that are used to analyze the data provided by models or to create additional models.

What is a knowledge-based system, and how is it used in a DSS? A **knowledge-based system** provides intelligence that supplements the user's own intellect and makes the DSS more effective. It could be an **expert system** that tries to replicate the decision-making processes of human experts in order to solve specific problems. For example, an expert system might be designed to take the place of a physician in a remote location. A physician expert system would ask the patient about symptoms just as a live physician would, and the system would make a diagnosis based on the algorithms programmed into it.

Another type of knowledge-based system is a **natural language processing (NLP) system**. NLP systems enable users to communicate with computer systems using a natural spoken or written language instead of using a computer programming language. Individuals just speak to the computer and it understands what they're saying, without users needing to use specific computer commands. The personal assistants in today's operating systems, such as Siri and Cortana, as well as Amazon's Alexa, are NLP systems.

All knowledge-based systems fall under the science of artificial intelligence. **Artificial intelligence (AI)** is the branch of computer science that deals with the attempt to create computers that think like humans. To date, no computers have been constructed that can replicate the thinking patterns of a human brain, because scientists still do not fully understand how humans store and integrate knowledge and experiences to form human intelligence.

How does a knowledge-based system help in the decision-making process? Databases and the models provided by model management systems tend to be extremely analytical and mathematical in nature. If we relied solely on databases and models to make decisions, answers would be derived with a yes or no mentality, allowing no room for human thought. Fortunately, human users are involved in these systems, providing an opportunity to inject human judgment into the decision-making process.

The knowledge-based system also provides an opportunity to introduce experience into the mix. Knowledge-based systems support the concept of fuzzy logic. Normal logic is highly rigid: If x happens, then y will happen. **Fuzzy logic** enables the interjection of experiential learning into the equation by considering probabilities. Whereas an algorithm in a database has to be specific, an algorithm in a knowledge-based system could state that if *x* happens, 70% of the time *y* will happen.

For instance, managers at Best Buy would find it extremely helpful if their DSS informed them that 45% of customers who bought an iPad also bought a Smart Cover for it. This could suggest that designing a discount program for Smart Covers bought with iPads might spur sales. Fuzzy logic enables a system to be more flexible and to consider a wider range of possibilities than would conventional algorithmic thinking.

Business Intelligence Systems

What is a business intelligence system? **Business intelligence (BI)** is the ability to improve business decision making with databases and other fact-based support systems. A **business intelligence system** is another form of business information system and is used primarily at the executive level. A business intelligence system is a set of technologies used to analyze and interpret large sets of data (often referred to as big data) in order to enable executives and senior managers to make informed decisions about how best to run a business. Often business intelligence systems use data gathered from data warehouses or data marts because they enable access to information gathered from multiple sources. Increased access to data and the ability to transform it into useful information for business analysis purposes can lead managers to identify new opportunities and implement effective business strategies.

Enterprise Resource Planning Systems

What does an enterprise resource planning system do? All businesses have data and information to manage, and large, complex organizations can benefit from managing that information with a central piece of software. An **enterprise resource planning (ERP) system** is a software system that accumulates all information relevant to running a business and makes it readily available to whoever needs it to make decisions. ERP systems use a common database to store and integrate information. This enables the information to be used across multiple areas of an enterprise.

Human resource functions (such as the management of hiring, firing, promotions, and benefits) and accounting functions (such as payroll) are often the first processes integrated into an ERP system. Having such information reside in one database makes the management and compensation of employees more streamlined. If manufacturing operations were also integrated into the ERP system, then the employees and payroll data could be used to determine the cost of running an assembly line or for scheduling workers to run the assembly line.

Sound Byte MyLab IT®

Analyzing Data with Microsoft Power BI Suite

In this Sound Byte, you'll explore how the Microsoft Power BI Suite is used to analyze big data.

The advent of the smartphone brought forth several revolutions that are so standard today that it is hard to remember what life was like before. While entertainment and communication capabilities have been improved by smartphones, tablets, and other mobile devices, so, too, have business intelligence capabilities. As mentioned above, business intelligence uses databases and other fact-based support systems to improve business decision making. Smartphones, tablets, and more universal access to wireless Internet have enabled business intelligence to go mobile. Using mobile business intelligence systems and technologies, companies have access to data at their fingertips and can interact in real time with customers and business partners. Such capabilities can help to improve service and productivity (see Figure 11.31).

There has always been a huge demand for making data more interesting or useful. Think about how useful transforming a spreadsheet full of values into a chart can be to make trends easier to recognize. However, in earlier models of mobile devices, it was virtually impossible to display data visibly. Early mobile business intelligence systems were limited by small screen sizes and text-based delivery. Most reports were delivered in table format, eliminating the benefit of visual data representation that charts offer. In addition, access to the Internet with mobile devices was limited, making it difficult to interact with real-time data.

Presently, not only do mobile business intelligence solutions make data look good with impressive displays and interactive capabilities, but mobile business intelligence systems also make data completely accessible all the time. Mobile delivery of business intelligence can be accomplished via a mobile web browser or a mobile app. Mobile business intelligence products integrate with business intelligence systems, such as knowledge-based and ERP systems, to deliver access to key performance indicators, business metrics, and dashboards on mobile devices. Systems such as Oracle's Business Intelligence Enterprise Edition and SAP's BusinessObjects Explorer have mobile

Figure 11.31 Mobile business intelligence applications on smartphones and other mobile devices enable managers to have access to data all the time. *(ChartsTable789/Shutterstock)*

business intelligence applications that integrate with expansive data sources. Using the capabilities of mobile business intelligence, a corporate executive can, for example, monitor on his or her mobile device a dashboard of key metrics of critical offshore manufacturing facilities while running a meeting thousands of miles away.

Mobile business intelligence solutions are enabling companies to improve business processes, increase employee productivity, and deliver better customer service by providing connections to real-time, on-demand access to business critical information. Additionally, mobile business intelligence is expected to make advancements with collaboration and with using cloud computing, capturing and capitalizing on social data. However, as great as mobile business intelligence seems, there is room for improvement in many areas, especially security and privacy.

Before moving on to the Chapter Review:

1. ▶ Watch Chapter Overview Video 11.2.
2. Then take the Check Your Understanding quiz.

Check Your Understanding // Review & Practice

For a quick review to see what you've learned so far, answer the following questions.

multiple choice

1. Which best describes a data warehouse?
   a. a building that stores computer servers
   b. a software program that assists with file management
   c. a database that organizes data from multiple organizations
   d. a collection of all the data from an organization's databases

2. Extracting, transforming, and storing data are processes associated with which of the following?
   a. transaction processing
   b. data staging
   c. online analytical processing
   d. data scrubbing

3. The process by which great amounts of data are analyzed and investigated is known as
   a. clustering.
   b. data staging.
   c. data mining.
   d. online analytical processing.

4. A system that is designed to help keep track of everyday business activities is a(n)
   a. management information system.
   b. decision support system.
   c. enterprise resource planning system.
   d. transaction-processing system.

5. Which type of information system is used mainly by executive managers and gathers data from data warehouses and data marts?
   a. business intelligence system
   b. decision support system
   c. expert system
   d. voice management system

MyLab IT   Go to **MyLab IT** to take an autograded version of the *Check Your Understanding* review and to find all media resources for the chapter.

TechBytes Weekly   Go to TechBytes Weekly for current technology news and discussion questions!

11 Chapter Review

Summary

Part 1

Database Fundamentals

Learning Outcome 11.1 You will be able to explain the basics of databases, including the most common types of databases and the functions and components of relational databases in particular.

 ### Database Advantages

Objective 11.1 *Explain what a database is and why databases are useful.*

- Databases are electronic collections of related data that can be organized so that data is more easily accessed and manipulated. Properly designed databases cut down on data redundancy and duplicate data by ensuring relevant data is recorded in only one place. This also helps eliminate data inconsistency, which comes from having different data about the same transaction recorded in different places. When databases are used, multiple users can share and access information at the same time.

Objective 11.2 *Discuss the benefits of using a database.*

- Some of the main advantages of using databases include the following: They can manage large amounts of data efficiently, they enable information sharing, and they promote data integrity. Data sharing is made possible because databases provide data centralization, a shared source that everyone can access. Data centralization also promotes better data integrity.

 ### Database Types

Objective 11.3 *Describe features of relational databases.*

- A relational database operates by organizing data into various tables based on logical groupings and then creating a relationship between tables by linking through a common field.
- There are three main types of relationships. A one-to-many relationship has a record appearing only once in a table, while having the capability of appearing many times in a related table. A one-to-one relationship is

when there is only one instance of a record in a table, and only one corresponding record in a related table. A many-to-many relationship has multiple instances of records in both the primary and related tables.

Objective 11.4 *Describe features of object-oriented databases.*

- Object-oriented databases store data in objects rather than in tables, and provide methods for processing or manipulating the data. Object-oriented databases are best for handling unstructured data, such as media files and extremely large documents.

Objective 11.5 *Describe features of multidimensional databases.*

- Multidimensional databases store data that can be analyzed from different dimensions, or perspectives. Multidimensional databases organize data with three dimensions, giving it a cube-like format. In addition to the field and record dimensions of other databases, a measure attribute is also used.

 ### Database Basics

Objective 11.6 *Describe how relational databases organize and define data.*

- Database management systems (DBMSs) are specially designed applications (such as Microsoft Access) that interact with the user, other applications, and the database itself to capture and analyze data. The main operations of a DBMS are creating databases, entering data, viewing (or browsing) data, sorting (or indexing) data, extracting (or querying) data, and outputting data.
- Data is organized using fields, records, and tables. A category of information in a database is stored in a field. Fields are assigned a field name and a data type that indicates what type of data can be stored in the

field. Common data types include short text, long text, numeric, calculated, date/time, yes/no, OLE object, and hyperlink. A group of related fields is a record. A group of related records is a table or file. Field properties reflect data dictionary details. Some common field properties include field size, default value, and captions.

- To keep records distinct, each record must have one field that has a value unique to that record. This unique field is a primary key (or a key field).

Objective 11.7 *Describe how data is inputted and managed in a database.*

- Input forms are used to control how new data is entered into a database as well as how changes are made to data. Data validation helps to ensure that only valid data is entered into a field. Common validation rules include a range check, a completeness check, a consistency check, and an alphabetic or numeric check.
- Queries and filters are used to display a subset of data. A query language is used to extract records from a database. Almost all relational databases today use Structured Query Language (SQL). However, most DBMSs include wizards that enable you to query the database without learning a query language. Reports are used to output data from a database, or data can be transferred to another software application for further distribution or modification.

Part 2

How Businesses Use Databases

Learning Outcome 11.2   You will be able to explain how businesses use data warehouses, data marts, and data mining to manage data and how business information systems and business intelligence are used to make business decisions.

 ## Data Warehousing and Storage

Objective 11.8   *Explain what data warehouses and data marts are and how they are used.*

- A data warehouse is a large-scale collection of data that contains and organizes in one place all the relevant data for an organization. Data warehouses often contain information from multiple databases. Because it can be difficult to find information in a large data warehouse, small slices of the data warehouse, called data marts, are often created.
- The information in data marts pertains to a single department within the organization.
- Data warehouses and data marts consolidate information from a wide variety of sources to provide comprehensive pictures-of-operations or transactions within a business.

Objective 11.9   *Describe data mining and how it works.*

- Data mining is the process by which large amounts of data are analyzed to spot otherwise hidden trends. Through processes such as classification, estimation, affinity grouping, clustering, and description (visualization), data is organized so that it provides meaningful information that can be used by managers to identify business trends.

 ## Using Databases to Make Business Decisions

Objective 11.10   *Describe the main types of business information systems and how they are used by business managers.*

- An information system is a software-based solution used to gather and analyze information. All information systems perform similar functions including acquiring, processing, and storing data, and providing the user with a means to output the results into meaningful and useful information.
- A transaction-processing system (TPS) is used to keep track of everyday business activities.
- A management information system (MIS) provides timely and accurate information that enables managers to make critical business decisions.
- A decision support system (DSS) is designed to help managers develop solutions for specific problems. A model management system is software that assists in building analysis tools for DSSs. A knowledge-based system provides intelligence to make the DSS more effective. There are several kinds of knowledge-based systems. An expert system tries to replicate the decision-making process of human experts to solve specific problems. A natural language processing (NLP) system uses natural spoken or written language rather than a computer

programming language to communicate with a computer. Artificial intelligence (AI) attempts to create computers that think like humans.

- Business intelligence systems are used by executive managers to analyze and interpret data in order to make informed decisions about how best to run a business.

- An enterprise resource planning (ERP) system is a large software system that gathers information from all parts of a business and integrates it to make it readily available for decision making.

 Be sure to check out **MyLab IT** for additional materials to help you review and learn. And don't forget to watch the Chapter Overview Videos. ▶

Key Terms

alphabetic check **439**

artificial intelligence (AI) **459**

batch processing **456**

binary large object (BLOB) **432**

business intelligence (BI) **459**

business intelligence system **459**

caption **436**

clickstream data **450**

completeness check **439**

consistency check **439**

data centralization **429**

data dictionary (database schema) **437**

data inconsistency **427**

data integrity **430**

data mart **451**

data mining **452**

data redundancy **427**

data staging **451**

data type (field type) **434**

data warehouse **449**

database **426**

database administrator (database designer) **430**

database management system (DBMS) **433**

decision support system (DSS) **457**

default value **436**

detail report **456**

enterprise resource planning (ERP) system **460**

exception report **456**

expert system **459**

field **433**

field constraint **438**

field name **433**

field properties **436**

field size **436**

filter **441**

foreign key **437**

fuzzy logic **459**

information system **455**

input forms **438**

join query **444**

knowledge-based system **459**

management information system (MIS) **456**

many-to-many relationship **431**

metadata **438**

model management system **459**

multidimensional database **432**

natural language processing (NLP) system **459**

normalization **430**

numeric check **439**

object-oriented database **432**

Object Query Language (OQL) **432**

one-to-many relationship **431**

one-to-one relationship **431**

online analytical processing (OLAP) **451**

online transaction processing (OLTP) **456**

primary key field **436**

query **441**

query language **432**

range check **438**

real-time processing **456**

record **434**

referential integrity **437**

relational algebra **443**

relational database **431**

relationship **431**

select query **443**

structured (analytical) data **432**

Structured Query Language (SQL) **432**

summary report **456**

table (file) **434**

time-variant data **450**

transaction-processing system (TPS) **456**

unstructured data **432**

validation **438**

validation rule **438**

Chapter Quiz // Assessment

For a quick review to see what you've learned, answer the following questions. Submit the quiz as requested by your instructor. If you're using **MyLab IT**, the quiz is also available there.

multiple choice

1. When is it sufficient to use a list to organize data?
   a. when the data needs to be organized into two or more tables
   b. when the data is simple and can be organized in one table
   c. when more than one person needs to access the data
   d. all of the above

2. A customer information table linked to an orders table in a business database reflects which type of relationship?
   a. one-to-many
   b. many-to-one
   c. many-to-many
   d. one-to-one

3. A process to ensure that data in a database is organized most efficiently is called
   a. centralization.
   b. data staging.
   c. normalization.
   d. integration.

4. Which of the following is NOT considered metadata?
   a. data type
   b. field name
   c. database name
   d. field size

5. Data captured as users navigate through a website is called
   a. staged data.
   b. web-user data.
   c. time-variant data.
   d. clickstream data.

6. The type of database that would be best to store and organize video clips and pictures is which of the following?
   a. object-oriented database
   b. relational database
   c. multidimensional database
   d. all of the above

7. Which of the following is used to create a temporary subset of data that matches certain criteria?
   a. relationship
   b. query
   c. request
   d. filter

8. Which of the following data-mining techniques is used to determine which data goes together?
   a. classification
   b. affinity grouping
   c. clustering
   d. visualization

9. Unnecessary duplication of data in a database is referred to as
   a. data redundancy.
   b. normalized data.
   c. validated data.
   d. data inconsistency.

10. Which of the following is a method of inputting data into a transaction-processing system while the transaction is taking place?
    a. batch processing
    b. input processing
    c. real-time processing
    d. all of the above

true/false

_____ 1. A field labeled PHONE that accepts data such as (610) 555-1212 would use the Number data type.

_____ 2. A query is used to extract a subset of data from a database.

_____ 3. A small slice of a data warehouse is called a data mine.

_____ 4. Data warehouses capture data only from one time period.

_____ 5. A multidimensional database uses two dimensions in which to organize data.

critical thinking

1. Auto Repair Database

You've been asked to establish a new database for the local auto repair shop. The owner has given you the following data categories that he feels should be in the database. Organize the data categories into two tables, label each table with a name, and identify in each table the primary key field.

Customer ID	Car Make	Last Name
Address	Phone	Vehicle ID
Model Year	Model	City
State	First Name	License Plate

Team Time

Redesigning Facebook

problem

Facebook is a database. Facebook management decides what data they require from Facebook account holders and sets up specific areas to display what management considers to be a user's pertinent information. But perhaps you as a user would have designed Facebook differently.

task

Your class has volunteered to work as a focus group for Facebook to assess the usefulness of the information it gathers.

process

1. Divide the class into small groups.
2. Your group members should examine their individual Facebook accounts. What fields in the profile do you consider to be most useful? Which fields are unnecessary and could be eliminated? What fields are missing from the profile that you think would be useful?
3. Investigate your account settings and application settings. What changes would you make to these settings? Are options missing that you would find helpful?
4. Present your group's findings to the class. Compare your suggestions to those of other groups.
5. Prepare a list of recommendations for improvements to the current Facebook home page and settings pages. Clearly indicate how the proposed changes will benefit both users and the management of Facebook (retaining users, being able to better target advertising to users, and so on).

conclusion

To remain competitive, Facebook needs to consider the input of users to ensure that it delivers a product with features its customers want and need.

Ethics Project

Private Information on Public Databases

In this exercise, you'll research and then role-play a complicated ethical situation. The role you play might not match your own personal beliefs, but your research and use of logic will enable you to represent the view assigned. An arbitrator will watch and comment on both sides of the arguments, and, together, the team will agree on an ethical solution.

problem

A tremendous amount of data is accumulated about us in online databases. Much of this material is accessible in databases that are searchable by anyone with Internet access or by anyone willing to pay a small fee. Websites such as **spokeo.com** and **411.com** comb through publicly accessible databases, such as social networking sites, online phone books, as well as business and government websites, to compile information on individuals. Your online information may expose you to risks such as identify theft.

research areas to consider

- Electronic information privacy
- Electronic Privacy Information Center (**epic.org**)
- Protecting your online privacy
- Protecting yourself from data breaches

process

1. Divide the class into teams.
2. Research the areas cited above and devise a scenario in which someone has complained about a website providing information that led to his or her identity being stolen.
3. Team members should determine a character they want to represent in the role-playing event, such as a victim of identity theft, a website owner, or an arbitrator. Then each member should write a summary that provides background information for their character and that details their character's behaviors to set the stage for the role-playing event. Then, team members should create an outline to use during the role-playing event.
4. Team members should present their case to the class or submit a PowerPoint presentation for review by the rest of the class, along with the summary and resolution they developed.

conclusion

As technology becomes ever more prevalent and integrated into our lives, ethical dilemmas will present themselves to an increasing extent. Being able to understand and evaluate both sides of the argument, while responding in a personally or socially ethical manner, will be an important skill.

Solve This

MyLab IT®
grader

At this time, an auto-graded version of this project is not available in **MyLab IT**.

College Database

You help out in the registrar's office at your college. You are being asked to help update the college's database by modifying some of the tables and by creating some queries and reports. You will use Access 2016 to complete this exercise.

You will use the following skills as you complete this activity:

- Create and Modify Data Table
- Import Excel Data
- Create AND Query
- Modify Field Properties
- Establish Table Relationships
- Create Multitable Query

Instructions

1. Open the *TIA_Ch11_Start* file and save the database as **TIA_Ch11_LastFirst**.
2. Open the Faculty table in Design View. Change the Data Type of FullTime to **Yes/No**. Add a primary key to the FacultyID field. Move the DeptID field to be after the Title field.
3. In the Faculty table, modify the Field Size and Caption properties as follows:

Field Name	Field Size	Caption
FacultyFirst	10	First Name
FacultyLast	15	Last Name
DeptID	3	Dept ID
FullTime		Full Time Status

4. Add a new field with the name **HireDate** and the **Date/Time data type**. Save and close the Faculty table.
5. On the External Data tab, click **Excel** in the Import & Link group. Browse to your student data files and select the *Faculty.xlsx* **file**. In the *Specify how and where you want to store the data in the current database* section, click **Append a copy of the records to the table**: and select the **Faculty table**. Accept all other default options in the wizard. Close the Get External Data - Excel Spreadsheet wizard, and then open the Faculty table to ensure the records were imported correctly. 261 records display. Close the Faculty table.
6. Open the Students table in Datasheet view. Adjust the columns so the column sizes best fit the data in each field. Then, in Design view of the Students table, change the data type for the Email field to **Hyperlink**. Add a Default Value of CT for the State field. Save and close the Students table.
7. Create a form using the Form Wizard using all fields from the Students table. Select a **Columnar layout** and name the form **Students**. In the Students form, click in the **Student Last text box**. Then, using the search box in the Navigation bar at the bottom of the Student form, type **Lopez**. Check that the StudentID is 444096, and then update the address field to **4024 Broad Street** to reflect the student's new address. Save and close the Students form.
8. On the Database Tools tab, click **Relationships**. Add the Faculty table, and create a relationship between the Faculty table and the Courses table. Enforce referential integrity. Save and close the Relationships window.
9. Create a query from the Courses table using Query Design. Display the CourseID, Building, Room, Days, Start, and End fields. Enter criteria to display records for courses meeting in the Park building, on Tuesdays and Thursdays after 12:00 P.M. 23 records display. Save the query as **Park TTH**. Run, then close the query.
    a. Hint: Check how Days are displayed in the table, and use the same format for Days in the criteria. Use **12:00** for the Start criteria.
10. Create a query using Query Design that includes CourseID from the Roster table; Course Description from the Courses table; FacultyLast from the Faculty table; StudentLast, StudentFirst, and Email from the Students table. Display only MGT110 IC courses. Save the query as **MGT110 IC Roster**. Run, then close the query.
11. Using the Report Wizard, create a report from the MGT110 IC Roster query. Include all fields except CourseID and FacultyLast. View the data by Courses; do not add additional grouping. Sort by StudentLast in Ascending order. Accept default layout options, and save the report as Rosters.
12. Save and close the database and submit based on your instructor's directions.

12

Behind the Scenes: Networking and Security in the Business World

 For a chapter overview, watch the Chapter Overview Videos.

PART 1

Client/Server Networks and Topologies

Learning Outcome 12.1 **You will be able to describe common types of client/server networks, servers found on them, and network topologies used to construct them.**

PART 2

Setting Up Business Networks

Learning Outcome 12.2 **You will be able to describe transmission media, network operating system software, and network navigation devices and explain major threats to network security and how to mitigate them.**

 Client/Server Network Basics 472

Objective 12.1 *List the advantages for businesses of installing a network.*

Objective 12.2 *Explain the differences between a client/server network and a peer-to-peer network.*

Objective 12.3 *Describe the common types of client/server networks as well as other networks businesses use.*

 Servers and Network Topologies 478

Objective 12.4 *List the common types of servers found on client/server networks.*

Objective 12.5 *Describe the common types of network topologies and the advantages and disadvantages of each one.*

Helpdesk: Using Servers

Sound Byte: Network Topology and Navigation Devices

 Transmission Media 490

Objective 12.6 *Describe the types of wired and wireless transmission media used in networks.*

 Network Adapters and Navigation Devices 492

Objective 12.7 *Describe how network adapters help data move around a network.*

Objective 12.8 *Define MAC addresses, and explain how they are used to move data around a network.*

Objective 12.9 *List the various network navigation devices, and explain how they help route data through networks.*

Helpdesk: Transmission Media and Network Adapters

Network Operating Systems and Network Security 496

Objective 12.10 *Explain why network operating systems are necessary for networks to function.*

Objective 12.11 *List major security threats to networks, and explain how network administrators mitigate these threats.*

Sound Byte: A Day in the Life of a Network Technician

For the IT Simulation for this chapter, see MyLab IT.

MyLab IT   All media accompanying this chapter can be found here.

Make This   Make: An App That Shares **page 489**

(Deepadesigns/Shutterstock, Sashkin/Shutterstock, Stuart Ford/Shutterstock, Destina/Fotolia, Lukas Gojda/123RF)

How Cool Is This?

In science fiction movies, people are often **controlling devices** by touching an interface attached to their bodies. Now researchers at MIT have debuted **DuoSkin**. Using silver and gold metal leaf, **functional devices** can be created that **attach directly to the skin** and resemble jewelry. Think of them as **temporary tattoos** that can control your mobile devices and display and store information. Goodbye smartwatches…hello **smart tattoos**!

(MIT Media Lab)

Client/Server Networks and Topologies

Learning Outcome 12.1 **You will be able to describe common types of client/server networks, servers found on them, and network topologies used to construct them.**

You learned about peer-to-peer networks and home networking in Chapter 7. In this chapter, you'll expand your knowledge about networks by delving into the client/server networks typically used in businesses.

Client/Server Network Basics

Recall that a *network* is a group of two or more computing devices (or nodes) that are configured to share information and resources such as printers, files, and databases. Businesses such as your school or an insurance company gain advantages from deploying networks, similar to the advantages gained with a home network.

Networking Advantages

Objective 12.1 *List the advantages for businesses of installing a network.*

What advantages do businesses gain from networks? Networked computers have many advantages over individual stand-alone computers (see Figure 12.1):

- **Networks enable expensive resources to be shared.** Networks enable people to share peripherals such as printers or share resources such as an Internet connection. Without a network,

Figure 12.1 Benefits of Business Networks

Enable resource sharing
- Expensive peripherals, such as printers, can be shared.
- Networks can share a single internet connection.

Facilitate knowledge sharing
- Data can be accessed by multiple people.

Enable software sharing
- Software can be delivered to client computers from a server.

Enhance communication
- Information sharing is more effective when employees are connected.

each computer would have to be individually connected to a printer and to the Internet. Attaching the computers to a network avoids the cost of providing each computer with duplicate resources.

- **Networks facilitate knowledge sharing.** The databases you learned about in Chapter 11 become especially powerful when deployed on a network. Networked databases can serve the needs of many people at one time and can increase the availability of data. Your college's databases are much more useful when all college employees can look up student records at the same time.

- **Networks enable software sharing.** Installing a new version of software on everyone's desktop in a business with 800 employees can be time-consuming. However, if the computers are networked, all employees can access the same copy of a program from the server. Although the business must still purchase a software license for each user, with a network it can avoid having to install the program on every computer.

- **Networks enable enhanced communication.** Social networking tools, e-mail, and instant messaging are powerful applications when deployed on a network, especially one that's connected to the Internet. Business colleagues can easily exchange information with each other and can share valuable data by transferring files to other users.

Are there disadvantages to using networks? Because business networks are often complex, additional personnel are usually required to maintain them. These people, called **network administrators**, have training in computer and peripheral maintenance and repair, networking design, and the installation of networking software.

Another disadvantage is that operating a network requires special equipment and software. However, most companies feel that the cost savings of peripheral sharing and the ability to give employees simultaneous access to information outweigh the costs associated with network administrators and equipment.

Comparing Client/Server and Peer-to-Peer Networks

Objective 12.2   *Explain the differences between a client/server network and a peer-to-peer network.*

Where do I find client/server networks? Aside from the smallest networks—such as peer-to-peer (P2P) networks, which are typically used in homes and small businesses—the majority of computer networks are based on the client/server model of computing. As you learned in Chapter 7, a **client/server network** (also called a **server-based network**) contains servers as well as client computers. A *server* is a computer that both stores and shares resources on a network, whereas a *client* is a computer that requests those resources.

Recall that in a P2P network, each node connected to the network communicates directly with every other node rather than using a server to exercise central control over the network. Many tasks that individual users must handle on a P2P network can be handled centrally at the server in a client/server network.

For instance, data files are normally stored on a server. Therefore, backups for all users on a business network can be performed by merely backing up all the files on that server. Security, too, can be exercised over the server instead of on each user's computer; this way, the server, not the individual user, coordinates data security. Therefore, client/server networks are said to be **centralized**. P2P networks, on the other hand, are **decentralized**.

Why do businesses use client/server networks? The main advantage of a client/server relationship is that it makes data flow more efficiently than in P2P networks. Servers can respond to requests from a large number of clients at the same time. In addition, servers can be configured to perform specific tasks, such as handling e-mail or database requests, efficiently.

Why aren't P2P networks used more in business settings? P2P networks become difficult to administer when they're expanded beyond 10 users. Each computer may require updating if there are changes to the network, which isn't efficient with large numbers of computers. And as noted previously, security can't be implemented centrally on a P2P network but instead must be handled by each user.

Figure 12.2 shows a small client/server arrangement. The server in this figure provides printing and Internet-connection services for all the client computers connected to the network. The server is performing tasks that would need to be done by each of the client computers in a P2P network. This frees resources on the client computers so that they can more efficiently perform processor-intensive tasks such as viewing a video or accessing a database.

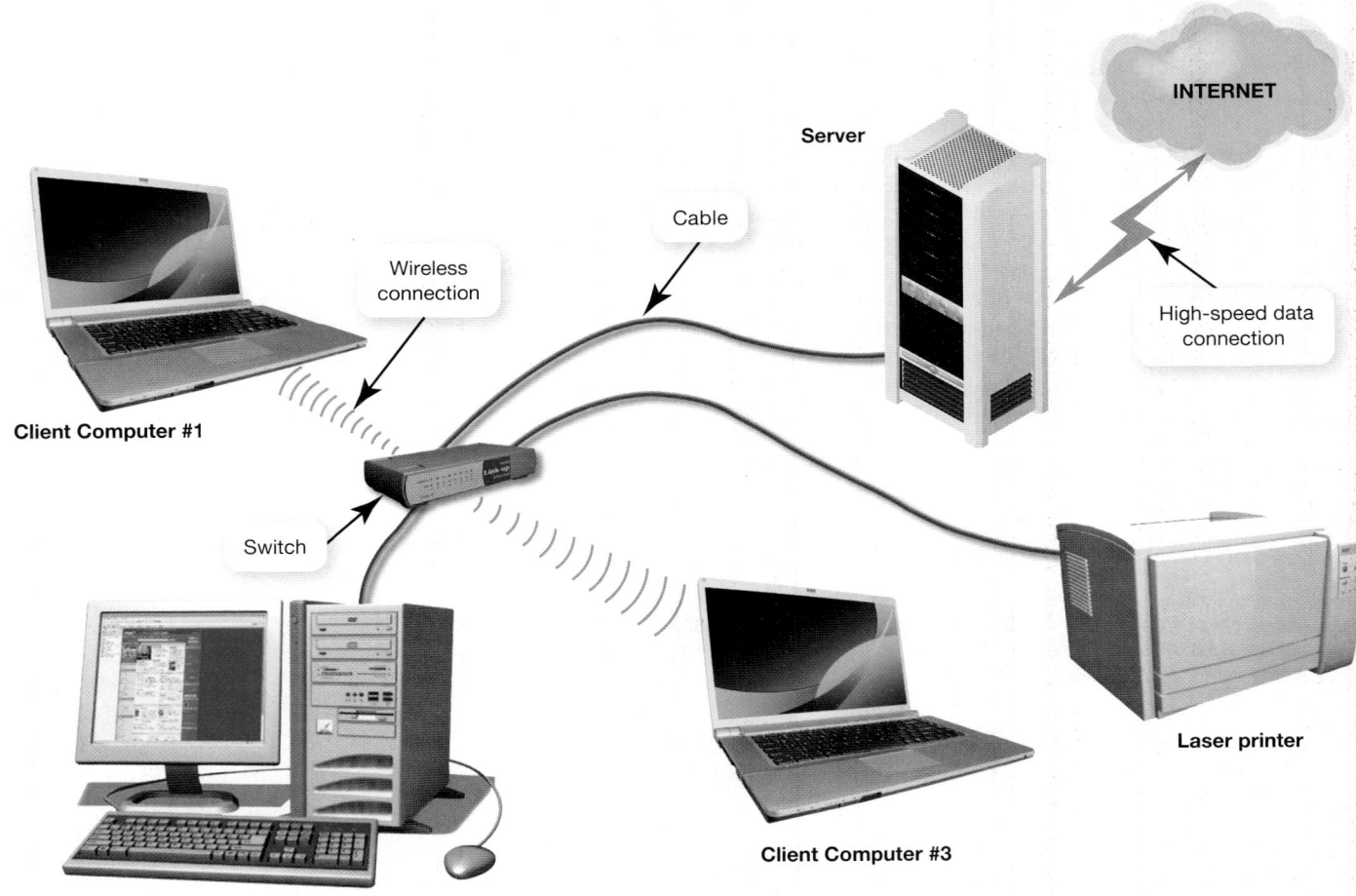

INTERNET

Server

Cable

Wireless
connection

High-speed data
connection

Client Computer #1

Switch

Laser printer

Client Computer #3

Client Computer #2

Figure 12.2 This small client/server network enables users to share a printer and an Internet connection.

Besides having a server, what makes a client/server network different from a P2P network? Client/server networks also have increased scalability. **Scalability** means that more users can be added easily without affecting the performance of the other network nodes. Because servers handle the bulk of the printing, Internet access, and other tasks performed on the network, it's easy to accommodate more users by installing additional servers to help with the increased workload. Installing additional servers on a network is relatively simple and can usually be done without disrupting services for existing users.

Types of Client/Server Networks

Objective 12.3 *Describe the common types of client/server networks as well as other networks businesses use.*

As you learned in Chapter 7, networks are generally classified according to their size and the distance between the physical parts of the network. Figure 12.3 lists the five most common types of client/server network classifications.

What are the most common types of client/server networks encountered in businesses? The two types of client/server networks most commonly encountered in businesses are *local area networks (LANs)* and *wide area networks (WANs)*:

- **Local area network (LAN)**: A LAN is generally a small group of computers and peripherals linked together over a relatively small geographical area. The computer lab at your school or the network serving the floor of the office building where you work is probably a LAN.
- **Wide area network (WAN)**: A WAN comprises large numbers of users over a wider physical area or separate LANs that are miles apart. Businesses often use WANs to connect two or more geographically distant locations. For example, a college might have a west and an east campus

Figure 12.3 Classifications of Client/Server Networks

Network Type	Description	Where Used in Business
PAN (Personal Area Network)	Devices used by one person connected via wireless media	Usually by employees traveling on business
LAN (Local Area Network)	A network consisting of nodes covering a small geographical area	In small businesses or self-contained units of a large business (such as one or more floors of the same office building)
HAN (Home Area Network)	A type of small LAN installed in a home	Not usually deployed by businesses, except small home-based businesses
WAN (Wide Area Network)	Two or more LANs connected together, often over long distances	Connecting business LANs over long distances such as between branches in two cities
MAN (Metropolitan Area Network)	WANs constructed by municipalities to provide connectivity in a specific geographical area	Although not deployed by businesses, employees often use them while traveling

(Drubig Photo/Fotolia, Whitehoune/Fotolia, Maridav/Fotolia, Fotolia, Kamaga/Fotolia)

located in two different towns. The LAN at the west campus is connected to the LAN at the east campus, forming one WAN connected either by dedicated telecommunications lines or by satellite links. Students on both campuses can share data and collaborate through the WAN.

What other sort of networks do businesses use? An **intranet** is a private network set up by a business or an organization that's used exclusively by a select group of employees, customers, suppliers, volunteers, or supporters. It can facilitate information sharing, database access, group scheduling, videoconferencing, and other employee collaborations. An intranet isn't accessible by unauthorized individuals; a firewall protects it from unauthorized access through the Internet.

An area of an intranet that only certain corporations or individuals can access is called an **extranet**. The owner of an extranet decides who will be permitted to access it. For example, a company's customers and suppliers may be permitted to access information on the company's extranet.

Extranets are useful for enabling **electronic data interchange (EDI)**, which allows the exchange of large amounts of business data (such as orders for merchandise) in a standardized electronic format. Walmart has an extranet that allows its employees, vendors, and contractors to easily share information. Other uses of extranets include providing access to catalogs and inventory databases and sharing information among partners or industry trade groups.

How is information kept secure on intranets and extranets? Intranets and extranets often use virtual private networks to keep information secure. A **virtual private network (VPN)** uses the public Internet communications infrastructure to build a secure, private network among various locations. Although WANs can be set up using private leased communications lines, these lines are expensive and tend to increase in price as the distance between points increases. VPNs use special security technologies and protocols that enhance security, enabling data to traverse the Internet as securely as if it were on a private leased line. Installing and configuring a VPN requires special hardware such as VPN-optimized routers and firewalls. In addition, VPN software must be installed on users' computing devices. However, there are many VPN providers (such as Barracuda Networks) that are now offering VPN services to businesses and individuals. This alleviates the aggravation and hassle of installing and maintaining VPN equipment.

How do VPNs work? The main technology for achieving a VPN is called **tunneling**. In tunneling, data packets are placed inside other data packets. The format of these external data packets is encrypted and can be understood only by the sending and receiving hardware, which is known as a *tunnel interface*. The hardware is optimized to seek efficient routes of transmission through the Internet. This provides a high level of security and makes information much more difficult to intercept and decrypt. Using a VPN is the equivalent of hiring a limousine and an armed guard to drive a package (your data) through a private tunnel directly to the destination (see Figure 12.4).

What are the key components of a client/server network? The key components of a client/server network are as follows:

- servers
- network topologies (the layout of the components)
- transmission media
- network adapters
- network navigation devices
- a network operating system

Figure 12.5 shows the components of a simple client/server network. In the following sections, we'll explore each component in more detail.

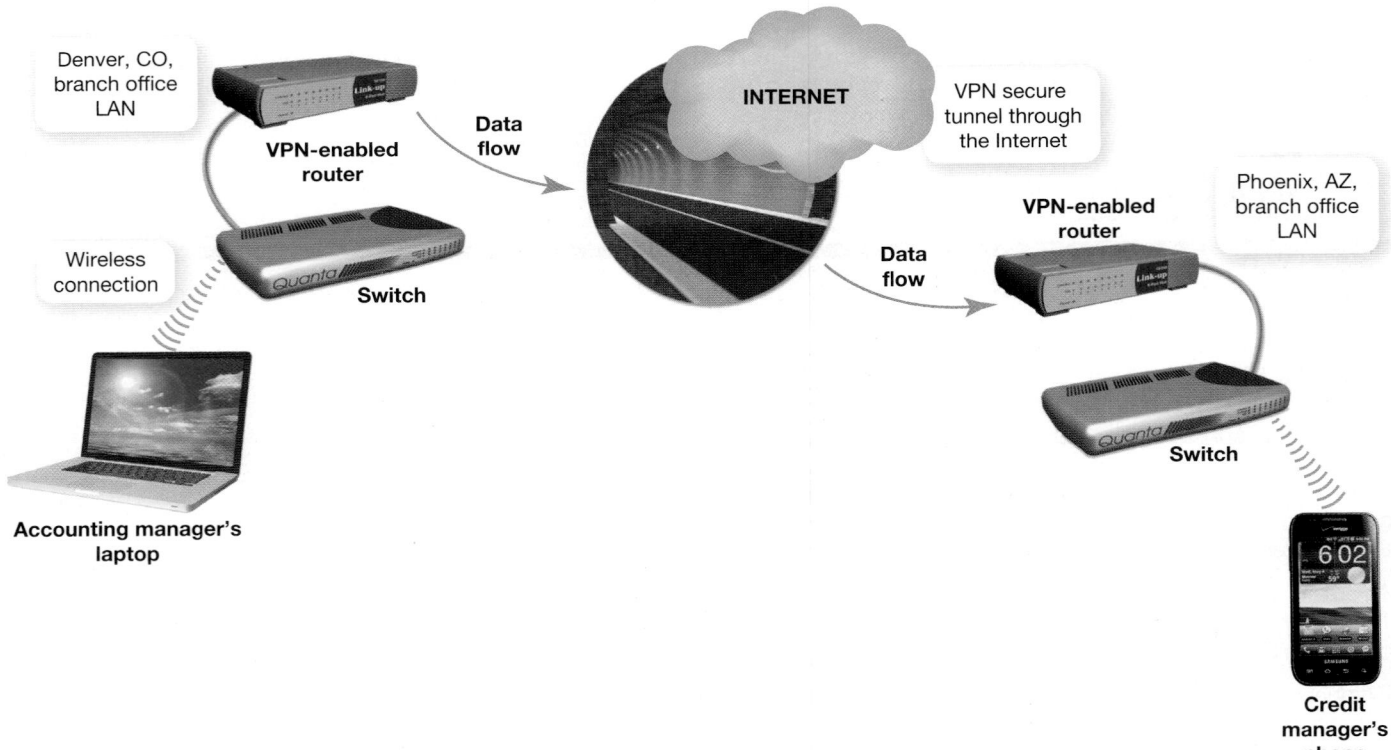

Figure 12.4 Local area networks (LANs) in different cities can communicate securely over the Internet using VPN technology.

Network interface card (NIC)
Installed in each client

Client Computer #2

Network interface card (NIC)
Installed in server

Cable (transmission media)

Client Computer #1

Switch (Network navigation device)

Server

Network operating software
Included in operating system software for client computers

Network operating software
Installed on server

Figure 12.5 The basic components of a typical client/server network. *(Naypong/Fotolia; Julien Eichinger/Fotolia; Maksym Yemelyanov/Fotolia; Maksim Kabakou/Fotolia; Felix Jork/Talex/Fotolia; Fotolia; Ag visuell/Fotolia; Mariusz Prusaczyk/Fotolia)*

Bits&Bytes Your Car Network Can Be Hacked!

Cars today contain multiple microchips (sometimes more than 30) that control the vehicle's various systems. For example, some cars use network communications, such as Wi-Fi and Bluetooth, so that parts of the car can communicate with each other. Collision-avoidance systems and anti-theft systems, controlled by microprocessors, make cars safer and tougher to steal. But what if your car gets hacked?

Hackers have successfully taken over cars' computer systems and caused malfunctions, such as taking control of the cars' entertainment and climate control systems. Fortunately, this hacking has so far been limited to individuals employed by car manufacturers, and to successfully hack the cars usually requires a great deal of time and usually physical access to the vehicle. Nevertheless, manufacturers have begun to recall cars to patch computer security vulnerabilities when they're discovered.

So is a hacker going to take control of your car? Probably not. Most hacking attacks are aimed at generating financial gain, such as by stealing credit card numbers. However, if a driverless vehicle were hacked, it could be used to kidnap the passengers.

But here are a few things you can do to feel more secure about your vehicle's computing systems:

- **Find out if your car has wireless systems:** Ask when buying a new car or read the manual for a car you already own.
- **Inquire whether any systems on your car can be accessed remotely:** Remote shutdown systems on leased or financed vehicles can be activated in the case of repossession by the financing company.
- **Keep your car's computer systems updated:** Dealerships often provide updates during scheduled maintenance, but inquire to see if your vehicle is due for an update.
- **Don't leave password information related to your vehicle systems in the vehicle:** If someone obtains your OnStar password, they could have your car remotely shut down.
- **Don't ignore recall notices:** A recall notice on your car's entertainment system might not sound important, but if it fixes a vulnerability that keeps a hacker out of your vehicle, it could be critical.

Servers and Network Topologies

Servers are the workhorses of the client/server network. They interface with many network users and assist them with a variety of tasks. The number and types of servers on a client/server network depend on the network's size and workload. Small networks (such as the one pictured in Figure 12.2 on page 474) would have just one server to handle all server functions. *Network topology* refers to the physical or logical arrangement of computers, transmission media (cables), and other network components. In the following sections, we'll explore the types of servers found in client/server networks and the typical topologies you may encounter.

Servers

Objective 12.4   *List the common types of servers found on client/server networks.*

What types of servers are found on larger client/server networks? A **dedicated server** is a server used to fulfill one specific function, such as handling e-mail. When more users are added to a network, dedicated servers are also added in order to reduce the load on the main server. Once dedicated servers are deployed, the original main server can become a dedicated server.

What functions do dedicated servers handle? Any task that's repetitive or demands a lot of time from a computer's processor (CPU) is a good candidate to relegate to a dedicated server. Common types of dedicated servers are authentication servers, file servers, print servers, application servers, database servers, e-mail servers, communications servers, web servers, and cloud servers. Servers are connected to a client/server network so that all client computers that need to use their services can access them, as shown in Figure 12.6.

Figure 12.6   Major Categories of Servers

Print Servers	Application Servers	Database Servers	Authentication Servers
Manage all printing jobs for client computers	Serve as a repository for application software	Provide client computers with database access	Keep track of users logged onto the network
File Servers	**E-Mail Servers**	**Communications Servers**	**Web/Cloud Servers**
Store and manage files for network users	Process and deliver incoming and outgoing e-mail	Handle all communications between the network and other networks	Host websites to make them available through the Internet

(Naypong/Fotolia, Julien Eichinger/Fotolia, Maksym Yemelyanov/Fotolia, Maksim Kabakou/Fotolia, Felix Jork/Fotolia, TAex/Fotolia, AG Visuell/Fotolia, Curioso Photography/Fotolia)

Authentication and File Servers

What are authentication and file servers? An **authentication server** is a server that keeps track of who is logging on to the network and which services on the network are available to each user. Authentication servers usually act as overseers for the network. They manage and coordinate the services provided by all other dedicated servers located on the network.

A **file server** is a server that stores and manages files for network users. On the network at your workplace or school, you may be provided with space on a file server to store files you create.

Print Servers

How does a print server function? **Print servers** manage all client-requested printing jobs for all printers on a network, which helps client computers complete more productive work by relieving them of printing duties. When you tell your computer to print a document, it passes off the task to the print server. This frees the CPU on your computer to do other jobs.

How does the printer know which documents to print? A **print queue** (or *print spooler*) is a software holding area for print jobs. When the print server receives a printing request from a client computer, it puts the job into a print queue on the print server. Normally, each printer on a network has its own uniquely named print queue. Jobs receive a number when they enter the queue and go to the printer in the order in which they were received. Thus, print servers organize print jobs into an orderly sequence to make printing more efficient on a shared printer.

Another useful aspect of print servers is that network administrators can set them to prioritize print jobs. Different users and types of print jobs can be assigned different priorities so that higher-priority jobs will be printed first. For instance, in a company in which documents are printed on demand for clients, you would want those print jobs to take precedence over routine employee correspondence.

Application Servers

What function does an application server perform? In many networks, all users run the same application software on their computers. In a network of thousands of personal computers, installing application software on each computer is time-consuming. An **application server** acts as a repository for application software.

When a client computer connects to the network and requests an application, the application server delivers the software to the client computer. Because the software doesn't reside on the client computer itself, this eases the task of installation and upgrading. The application needs to be installed or upgraded only on the application server, not on each client computer.

Database Servers

What does a database server do? A **database server** provides client computers with access to information stored in databases. Often, many people need to access a database at the same time. For example, multiple college advisors can serve students at the same time because the advisors all have access to the student information database. This is made possible because the database resides on a database server that each advisor's computer can access through the network. If the database were on a stand-alone computer instead of a network, only one advisor could use it at a time.

E-Mail Servers

How is e-mail handled on a large client/server network? The sole function of an **e-mail server** is to process and deliver incoming and outgoing e-mail. The volume of e-mail on a large network could quickly overwhelm a server that was attempting to handle other functions as well. On a network with an e-mail server, when you send or receive an e-mail, it goes through the e-mail server, which then handles the routing and delivery of your message.

Communications Servers

What types of communications does a communications server handle? A **communications server** handles all communications between the network and other networks, including managing Internet connectivity. All requests for information from the Internet and all messages being sent through the Internet pass through the communications server. Because Internet traffic is substantial at most organizations, the communications server has a heavy workload.

> ▶ HELPDESK MyLab IT®
>
> **Using Servers**
>
> In this Helpdesk, you'll play the role of a helpdesk staffer, fielding questions about various types of servers and client/server software.
>
>

The communications server often is the only device on the network connected to the Internet. E-mail servers, web servers, and other devices needing to communicate with the Internet usually route all their traffic through the communications server. Providing a single point of contact with the outside world makes it easier to secure the network from hackers.

Web Servers and Cloud Servers

What function does a web server perform? A **web server** is used to host a website so that it will be available through the Internet. Web servers run specialized software such as Apache HTTP Server or Microsoft Internet Information Services (IIS) that enable them to host web pages. Not every large network has a web server; many businesses use a third-party web-hosting company to host their websites instead.

Trends In IT   Virtualization: Making Servers Work Harder

Servers have historically been deployed on client/server networks as dedicated machines that perform one specific task. But today there are good reasons why some businesses may consider having servers perform multiple tasks.

Computers produce a lot of heat and take up physical space. As a company grows, continually adding servers may exceed the available floor space and cooling capacity of a company's data center. And budgets may limit a company's ability to purchase additional dedicated servers when needed.

Dedicated servers are mission critical when those servers handle processor-intensive operations. For instance, a major online retailer would have dedicated web servers handling e-commerce traffic so that customers could purchase items quickly and efficiently. But small businesses don't necessarily require the computing power of a dedicated server for all of their computing needs. In addition, today's powerful multi-core processors allow computers to process data more quickly and efficiently than single-core machines. Sometimes just dedicating a computer to one task, such as an authentication server, might not come close to fully utilizing that server's computing potential. For all of these reasons, *virtualization* was born.

Virtualization involves using specialized software to make individual physical servers behave as though they are more than one physical device (see Figure 12.7). Each virtual server can operate as a separate device and can even run its own operating system (OS). Therefore, you could have a virtual e-mail server running Windows and a virtual web server running Linux on the same physical server.

Creating virtual servers requires running specialized virtualization software on a physical server. The physical server then becomes known as the *host*. Virtual servers running on a host machine are known as *guest servers*. The computing power of the CPU is split between the guests running on the host. Therefore, it wouldn't be practical to run dozens of guest environments on one host because the computing power would become diluted. However, it's very possible to run two or three guest servers on one multi-processor physical server as long as the applications running on the virtual servers aren't overly processor intensive. VMware's vSphere, Microsoft's Hyper-V Server, and XenServer are popular virtualization software packages.

Figure 12.7 Virtualization software allows one physical server to appear to be multiple separate servers capable of handling three different processes.

Virtualization is a great way to provide backup servers at a low cost. Mission-critical servers, such as web servers, need to be running and available to customers at all times. If a web server for an e-commerce business fails, the company is unable to sell products until the server is repaired. With virtual servers, you could have a copy of your web server running virtually on two separate physical machines (such as servers 1 and 2). If server 1 breaks, you could immediately have the virtual copy of your web server on physical server 2 take over, and the company could still be processing orders and conducting business.

Although virtualization isn't the perfect solution for every business situation, it does offer intriguing possibilities and effective solutions for specific needs. Even small companies today are actively exploring virtualization as a way to extend their computing resources and save money.

What is a cloud server? Servers no longer need to be physically located at a company's offices. **Cloud servers** are servers that are maintained by hosting companies, such as Rackspace Hosting, and are connected to networks via the Internet. A company could choose to have any of the server types discussed previously hosted on cloud servers instead of maintaining them locally. Small businesses that don't have a large staff of computer professionals often choose to use cloud servers to save money.

Network Topologies

Objective 12.5   *Describe the common types of network topologies and the advantages and disadvantages of each one.*

Just as buildings have different floor plans depending on their uses, networks have different layouts according to their purpose. As noted above, **network topology** refers to the physical or logical arrangement of computers, transmission media (cables), and other network components. *Physical topology* refers to the layout of the "real" components of the network, whereas *logical topology* refers to the virtual connections among network nodes. Logical topologies usually are determined by network protocols instead of the physical layout of the network or the paths that electrical signals follow on the network.

What are network protocols? A **protocol** is a set of rules for exchanging communications. Although many people think that Ethernet is a type of network topology, it's actually a communications protocol. Therefore, an Ethernet network could be set up using almost any type of physical topology.

In this section, we'll explore the most common network topologies (bus, ring, and star) and discuss when each topology is used. The type of network topology used is important because it can affect a network's performance and scalability. Knowing how the basic topologies work—and knowing the strengths and weaknesses of each one—will help you understand why particular network topologies were chosen on the networks you use.

Bus Topology

What does a bus topology look like? In a **bus** (or **linear bus**) **topology**, all computers are connected in sequence on a single cable, as shown in Figure 12.8. This topology has largely become legacy technology because star topologies are more efficient on Ethernet networks, and a bus topology isn't designed to easily support wireless connections. However, bus topologies are still found in some manufacturing facilities where groups of computer-controlled machines are connected.

Each computer on the bus network can communicate directly with every other computer on the network. **Data collisions**, which happen when two computers send data at the same time and the sets of data collide somewhere in the connection media, are a problem on all networks. When data collides, it's often lost or damaged. A limitation of bus networks is that data collisions can occur fairly easily because a bus network is essentially composed of one main communication medium (a single cable).

Because two signals transmitted at the same time on a bus network may cause a data collision, an **access method** has to be established to control which computer is allowed to use the transmission media at a certain time. Computers on a bus network behave like a group of people having a conversation. The computers "listen" to the network data traffic on the media. When no other computer is transmitting data (that is, when the "conversation" stops), the computer knows it's allowed to transmit data. This means of taking turns "talking" prevents data collisions.

How does data get from point to point on a bus network? The data is broadcast throughout the network via the media to all devices connected to the network. The data is broken into small segments, each called a *packet*. Each packet contains the address of the computer or peripheral device to which it's being sent. Each computer or device connected to the network listens for data that contains its address. When it "hears" data addressed to it, it takes the data off the media and processes it.

The devices (nodes) attached to a bus network do nothing to move data along the network. This makes a bus network a **passive topology**. The data travels the entire length of the medium and is received by all network devices. The ends of the cable in a bus network are capped off by terminators (as shown in Figure 12.8). A **terminator** is a device that absorbs a signal so that it's not reflected back onto parts of the network that have already received it.

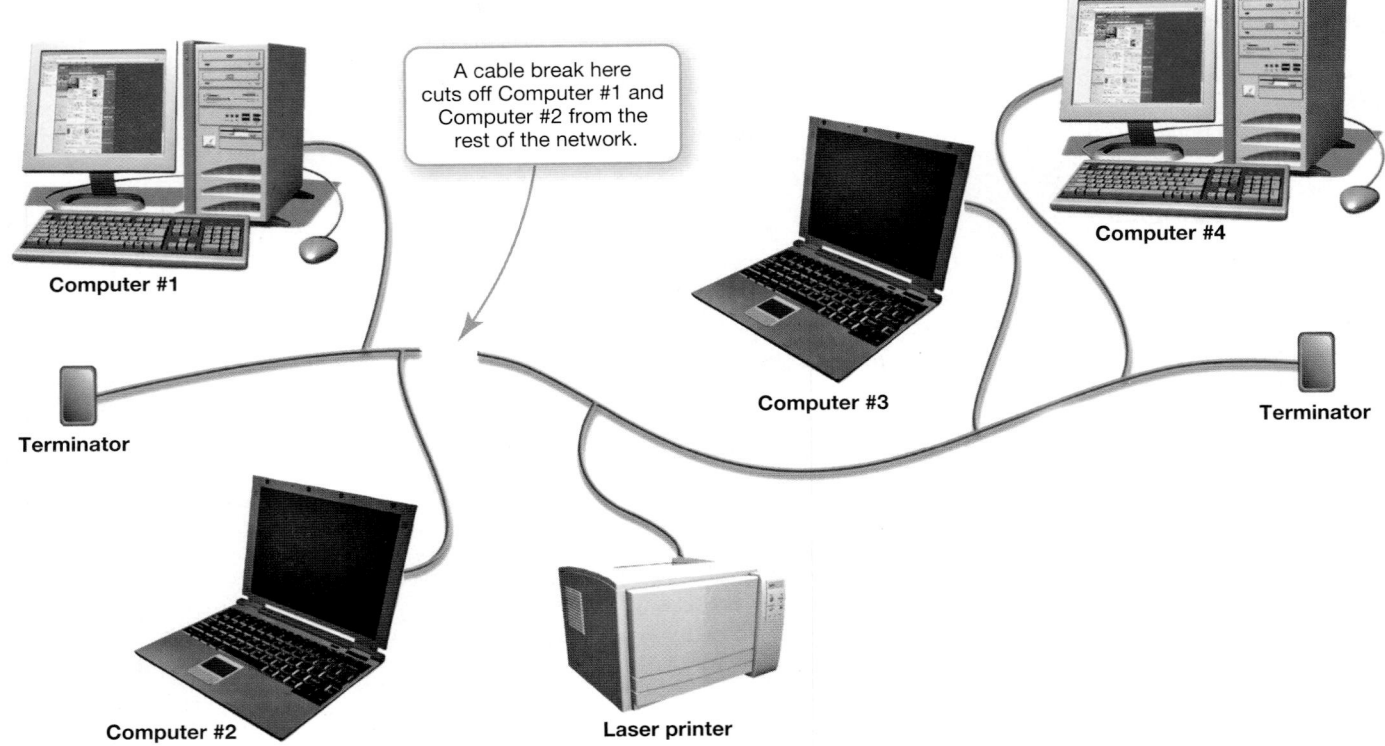

A cable break here cuts off Computer #1 and Computer #2 from the rest of the network.

Computer #1

Computer #4

Terminator

Computer #3

Terminator

Computer #2

Laser printer

Figure 12.8 In a linear bus topology, all computers are connected in a sequence.

What are the advantages and disadvantages of bus networks? The simplicity and low cost of bus network topology are its key advantages. As shown in Figure 12.8, the major disadvantage is that if there is a break in the cable, the bus network is effectively disrupted because some computers are cut off from others on the network. Also, because only one computer can communicate at a time, adding a large number of nodes to a bus network limits performance and causes delays in sending data.

Ring Topology

What does a ring topology look like? Not surprisingly, given its name, the computers and peripherals in a **ring** (or **loop**) **topology** are laid out in a configuration resembling a circle, as shown in Figure 12.9. Data flows around the circle from device to device in one direction only. Because data is passed using a special data packet called a **token**, this type of topology was once commonly called a *token-ring topology*.

How does a token move data around a ring? A token is passed from computer to computer around the ring until it's grabbed by a computer that needs to transmit data. The computer "holds" on to the token until it has finished transmitting data. Only one computer on the ring can "hold" the token at a time, and usually only one token exists on each ring.

If a node has data to send, such as a document that needs to go to the printer, it waits for the token to be passed to it. The node then takes the token out of circulation and sends the data to its destination. When the receiving node receives a complete transmission of the data (in this example, when the document is received by the printer), it transmits an acknowledgment to the sending node. The sending node then generates a new token and starts it going around the ring again. This is called the **token method** and is the access method that ring networks use to avoid data collisions.

A ring topology is an **active topology**, which means that nodes participate in moving data through the network. Each node on the network is responsible for retransmitting the token or the data to the next node on the ring. Large ring networks have the capability to use multiple tokens to help move data faster.

STEP 1: The token travels around the ring until a computer needs to transmit data.

STEP 2: Computer #2 needs to print and grabs the token.

Token Ring

STEP 4: A cable break stops movement of the token and data transmission.

Computer #1

Computer #4

Computer #2

STEP 3: Computer #2 completes the transmission and releases the token.

Computer #3

Printer

Figure 12.9 A ring topology provides a fair allocation of resources.

What are the advantages and disadvantages of a ring topology? A ring topology provides a fairer allocation of network resources than does a bus topology. By using a token, a ring network enables all nodes on the network to have an equal chance to send data. One "chatty" node can't monopolize the network bandwidth as easily as in a bus topology because it must pass the token on after sending a batch of data. In addition, a ring topology's performance remains acceptable even with large numbers of users.

As shown in Figure 12.9, one disadvantage of a ring network is that if one computer fails, the entire network can come to a halt because the failed computer is unavailable to retransmit tokens and data. Another disadvantage is that problems in the ring can be hard for network administrators to find. It's easier to expand a ring topology than a bus topology, but adding a node to a ring causes the ring to cease to function while the node is being installed.

Star Topology

What is the layout for a star topology? A **star topology** is the most widely deployed client/server network topology because it offers the most flexibility for a low price. In a star topology, the nodes connect to a central communications device called a *switch* in a pattern resembling a star, as shown in Figure 12.10. The switch receives a signal from the sending node and retransmits it to

Sound Byte MyLab IT®

Network Topology and Navigation Devices

In this Sound Byte, you'll learn about common network topologies, the types of networks they are used with, and various network navigation devices.

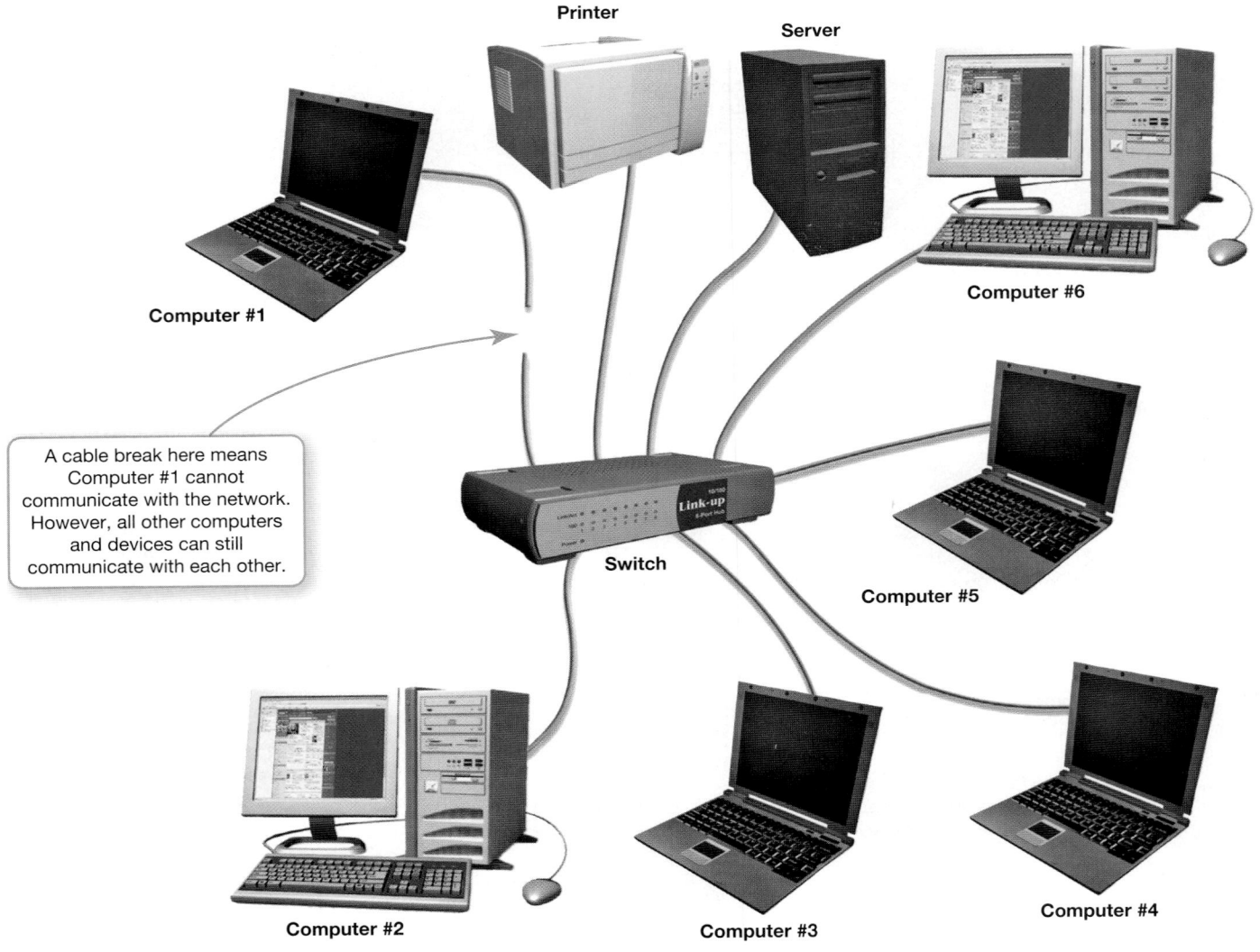

Printer

Server

Computer #1

Computer #6

A cable break here means Computer #1 cannot communicate with the network. However, all other computers and devices can still communicate with each other.

Switch

Computer #5

Computer #2

Computer #3

Computer #4

Figure 12.10 In a star topology, network nodes are connected through a central switch.

the node on the network that needs to receive the signal. Each network node picks up only the transmissions addressed to it. Because the switch retransmits data signals, a star topology is an active topology. The only drawback is that if the switch fails, the network no longer functions. However, it's relatively easy to replace a switch.

How do computers on a star network avoid data collisions? Because most star networks are Ethernet networks, they use the method used on all Ethernet networks to avoid data collisions: **CSMA/CD** (short for *carrier sense multiple access with collision detection*). With CSMA/CD, a node connected to the network uses carrier sense (that is, it "listens") to verify that no other nodes are currently transmitting data signals. If the node doesn't hear any other signals, it assumes that it's safe to transmit data. All devices on the network have the same right (that is, they have multiple access) to transmit data when they deem it safe. It's therefore possible for two devices to begin transmitting data signals at the same time. If this happens, the two signals collide.

What happens when the signals collide? As shown in Figure 12.11, when two nodes (#1 and #2) begin transmitting data signals at the same time (Step 1), signals collide, and a node on the network (#3) detects the collision. Node #3 then sends a special signal called a **jam signal** to all network nodes, alerting them that a collision has occurred (Step 2). The original nodes #1 and #2 then stop transmitting and wait a random amount of time before retransmitting their data signals (Step 3). The wait times need to be random; otherwise, both nodes would start retransmitting at the same time and another collision would occur.

Node #1

STEP 1: Nodes 1 and 2 transmit data at the same time.

Node #2

Jam signal

Data collision

Jam signal

STEP 3: Node 2 retransmits its data after waiting a random interval.

Jam signal

Switch

STEP 2: Node 3 detects a data collision and sends a jam signal.

Node #3

Figure 12.11 Jam signals are used to handle data collisions on an Ethernet network.

What are the advantages and disadvantages of a star topology? The major advantages of a star network are as follows:

- The failure of one computer doesn't affect the rest of the network. This is extremely important in a large network, where having one disabled computer affect the operations of several hundred other computers would be unacceptable.
- It's easy to add nodes to star networks.
- Performance remains acceptable even with large numbers of nodes.
- Centralizing communications through a switch makes troubleshooting and repairs easier. Technicians can usually pinpoint a communications problem just by examining the switch, as opposed to searching for a particular length of cable that has broken in a ring network.

The disadvantage of star networks used to be cost. Because of the complexity of the layout of star networks, they require more cable and used to be more expensive than bus or ring networks. However, the price of cable has fallen and wireless nodes are replacing many wired nodes on networks, removing cost as a barrier in most cases.

Comparing Topologies

Which topology is the best one? Figure 12.12 lists the advantages and disadvantages of bus, ring, and star topologies. Star topologies are the most common, mainly because large networks are constantly adding new users. The ability to add new users easily—by installing an additional switch—without affecting users already on the network is the deciding factor. Bus topologies have become all but extinct now that most home networks utilize a star topology. Ring topologies are still popular in certain businesses where fair allocation of network access is a major requirement of the network.

Figure 12.12 Advantages and Disadvantages of Bus, Ring, and Star Topologies

Topology	Advantages	Disadvantages
Bus	• Uses a minimal amount of cable. • Installation is easy, reliable, and inexpensive.	• Breaks in the cable can disable the network. • Large numbers of users decrease performance because of high volumes of data traffic.
Ring	• Allocates access to the network fairly. • Performance remains acceptable even with many users.	• Adding/removing nodes disables the network. • Failure of one node can bring down the network. • Problems in data transmission can be difficult to find.
Star	• Failure of one node doesn't affect other nodes on the network. • Centralized design simplifies troubleshooting and repairs. • High scalability: Adding computers is easy. • Performance remains acceptable even with many users.	• Requires more cable (and possibly higher installation costs) than a bus or ring topology. • The switch is a single point of failure; if it fails, all computers connected to it are affected.

Can topologies be combined within a single network? Because each topology has its own unique advantages, topologies are often combined to construct business networks. Combining multiple topologies into one network is known as constructing a **hybrid topology**. For instance, fair allocation of resources may be critical for reservation clerks at an airline (thereby requiring a ring network), but the airline's purchasing department may require a star topology.

Before moving on to Part 2:

1. ▶ Watch Chapter Overview Video 12.1.
2. Then take the Check Your Understanding quiz.

Check Your Understanding // Review & Practice

For a quick review to see what you've learned so far, answer the following questions.

multiple choice

1. Which of the following is NOT an advantage of installing a network in a business?
    a. enables peripheral sharing
    b. decentralization of files and data
    c. enables software sharing
    d. centralization of files and data

2. Why are client/server networks usually installed in businesses?
    a. Security is weaker on client/server networks.
    b. They do not require dedicated servers like P2P networks.
    c. Client/server networks are cheaper to install.
    d. They are more scalable than P2P networks.

3. A network consisting of devices used by a single person connected via wireless media is a
    a. PAN.
    b. WAN.
    c. MAN.
    d. LAN.

4. To manage authorized connections to internal networks, which server would a client/server network include?
    a. authentication
    b. database
    c. communications
    d. application

5. The physical or logical arrangement of computers, transmission media (cables), and other network components is known as network
    a. blueprint.
    b. domain.
    c. topology.
    d. protocol.

 Go to **MyLab IT** to take an autograded version of the *Check Your Understanding* review and to find all media resources for the chapter.

TechBytes Weekly Go to TechBytes Weekly for current technology news and discussion questions!

Try This

Sharing Folders on a Home Network Using Windows

Creating a HomeGroup in Windows lets you share folders, files, and devices (such as printers) with all computers on a network that belong to that HomeGroup. When you set up a Windows computer, you're asked to create a HomeGroup and are provided with instructions for having other Windows computers join that HomeGroup. In this tutorial, you'll learn how to share a folder. For more step-by-step instructions, watch the Try This video on MyLab IT.

Step 1 Ensure that all the computers on your network are members of the same HomeGroup. To check if a Windows 10 computer is in a HomeGroup, launch Settings, select **Network and Internet**, then select **HomeGroup**. If you see a screen like the one here, your computer is in a HomeGroup. To add other computers to the same HomeGroup, click the **View or print the homegroup password link** to display the HomeGroup password. Write it down and use it to have your other computers join the HomeGroup.

(Windows 10, Microsoft Corporation)

Step 2 Open File Explorer, navigate to the folder you wish to share with your HomeGroup, and left-click to select it. On the File Explorer ribbon, click the **Share tab**, and then select either **Homegroup (view)** or **Homegroup (view and edit)** to share the folder with your HomeGroup. The Homegroup (view) option allows only other members of the HomeGroup the ability to see and open the files in the folder. The Homegroup (view and edit) option gives other members of the HomeGroup the ability to add or delete files from the folder.

(Windows 10, Microsoft Corporation)

Step 3 Launch File Explorer on another computer in the HomeGroup (a Windows 8 computer is shown here). Under Network in the Navigation pane, find the name of the computer on which you shared the folder. Navigate through the directory structure until you find the shared folder. You should now have access to the files.

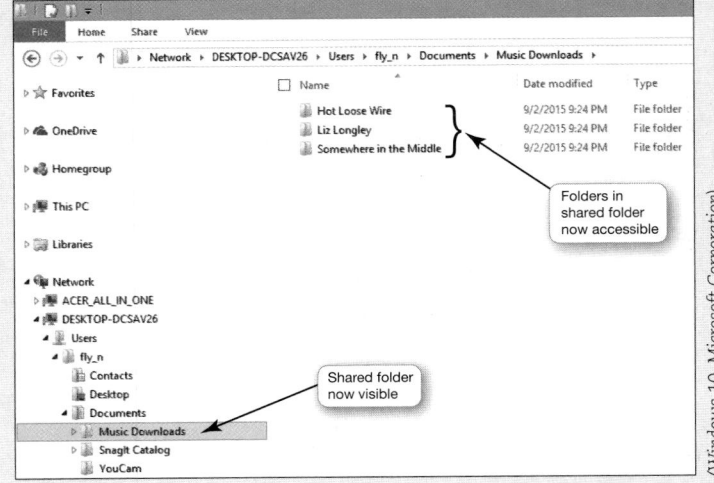

(Windows 10, Microsoft Corporation)

Make: An App That Shares

Want to share something you have created in an app with others?

In this exercise, you'll continue your mobile app development by using the Sharing component of the Social drawer in **App Inventor** to share information.

This component will pull up a list of all the applications on your device that can share a file. Make your work part of a larger community by sharing it!

Use the Sharing component to fire up all the ways your users can exchange information.

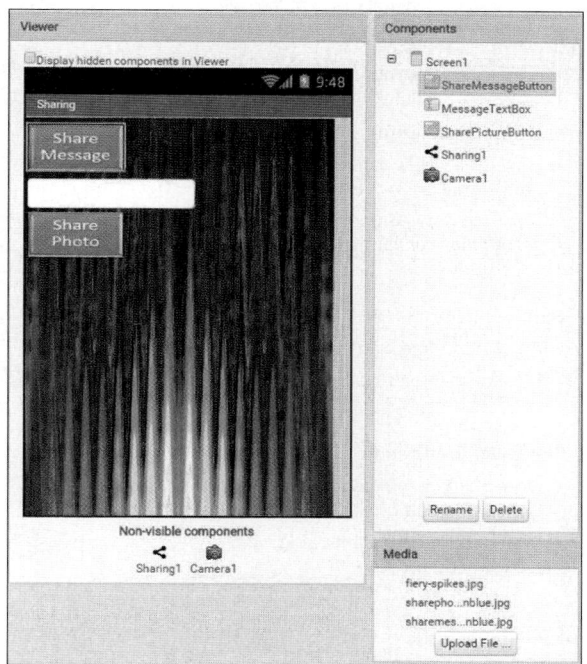

(Courtesy Massachusetts Institute of Technology)

For the instructions for this exercise, go to MyLab IT.

Setting Up Business Networks

Learning Outcome 12.2   **You will be able to describe transmission media, network operating system software, and network navigation devices and explain major threats to network security and how to mitigate them.**

Setting up business networks is similar to configuring home networks. You need to consider the type of transmission media, ensure all nodes have network adapters, and install the appropriate network communication devices.

 # Transmission Media

You may have only wireless transmission media in your home network. But businesses have different needs than home users. Let's start by looking at the transmission media used in business networks.

Figure 12.13 Factors to Consider When Choosing Network Cable

Maximum run length
- How far a cable can run before data signal degrades
- Distance between nodes determines run length needed

Bandwidth
- Amount of data transmitted across medium
- Measured in bits per second (bps)

Flexibility (bend radius)
- How much a cable can be bent before it is damaged
- Lots of corners? Need cable with a high bend radius.

Cable cost
- Cost is different for each cable type
- Budget may limit choice of cable type

Installation cost
- Twisted-pair and coaxial cable are inexpensive to install (low $)
- Fiber-optic cable requires special training and equipment (high $)

Interference
- Twisted-pair most susceptible to interference
- Fiber-optic immune to interference

(Maridav/Fotolia, Victoria/Fotolia, Nicholas Piccillo/Fotolia, Ion Popa/Fotolia, Auremar/Fotolia, Ermess/Fotolia)

Wired and Wireless Transmission Media

Objective 12.6   *Describe the types of wired and wireless transmission media used in networks.*

What exactly do we mean by transmission media? Transmission media, whether for wired or wireless communications technology, make up the physical system that data takes to flow between devices on the network. Without transmission media, network devices would be unable to communicate. Most corporate networks contain a combination of wired and wireless media.

Why are wired connections used in business networks? Wired connections are popular in business networks because they generally provide higher throughput and better security than wireless connections. Desktop computers still provide more computing power for less money than laptops, which makes desktop computers popular choices for business networks. Because desktops aren't often moved around, they're usually connected to a network with a wired connection.

What are the important factors in choosing a cable type? For business networks, the three main cable types that are used are *twisted-pair*, *coaxial*, and *fiber-optic*. Although each cable type is different, the same six factors always need to be considered when choosing a cable type (see Figure 12.13): maximum run length, bandwidth, flexibility (bend radius), cable cost, installation cost, and interference.

What causes interference with data signals? Signals traveling down a cable are subject to two types of interference:

1. *Electromagnetic interference (EMI)*, which is caused when the cable is exposed to strong electromagnetic fields, can distort or degrade signals on the cable. Fluorescent lights and machinery with motors or transformers are the most common sources of EMI emissions.

2. Cable signals also can be disrupted by *radio frequency interference (RFI)*, which is usually caused by broadcast sources (TV and radio signals) located near the network.

Both coaxial cable and twisted-pair cable send electrical impulses down conductive material to transmit data signals, making them more subject to interference. Fiber-optic cable transmits data signals as pulses of light. Because EMI and RFI don't affect light waves, fiber-optic cable is virtually immune to interference.

In the sections that follow, we'll discuss the characteristics of each of the three major types of cable. We'll also discuss the use of wireless media as an alternative to cable.

Twisted-Pair Cable

Why are the wires in twisted-pair cable twisted? **Twisted-pair cable** consists of pairs of copper wires twisted around each other and covered by a protective sheath (jacket). The twists are important because they cause the magnetic fields that form around the copper wires to intermingle, making them less susceptible to outside interference. The twists also reduce the amount of crosstalk interference (the tendency of signals on one wire to interfere with signals on a wire next to it).

If the twisted-pair cable contains a layer of foil shielding to reduce interference, it's called **shielded twisted-pair (STP) cable**. Most home networks use unshielded twisted-pair (UTP) cable that doesn't have the foil shielding. UTP cable is more susceptible to interference than STP cable. Figure 12.14 shows illustrations of both types of twisted-pair cable. Because of its lower price, UTP is used in business networks unless significant sources of interference must be overcome, such as in a production environment where machines create magnetic fields.

Figure 12.14 Anatomy of (a) unshielded twisted-pair (UTP) cable and (b) shielded twisted-pair (STP) cable.

Coaxial Cable

Is coaxial cable still used in business networks? Although not as popular as it once was, coaxial cable is still used in some manufacturing facilities where machinery creates heavy electrical interference. **Coaxial cable** (as shown in Figure 12.15) consists of four main components:

1. A core (usually copper) is in the very center and is used for transmitting the signal.

2. A solid layer of nonconductive insulating material (usually a hard, thick plastic) surrounds the core.

3. A layer of braided metal shielding covers the insulation to reduce interference with signals traveling in the core.

4. An external jacket of lightweight plastic covers the internal cable components to protect them from damage.

Figure 12.15 Coaxial cable consists of four main components: a core, an insulated covering, a braided metal shielding, and a plastic jacket.

Fiber-Optic Cable

What does fiber-optic cable look like? As shown in Figure 12.16, **fiber-optic cable** is composed of the following:

- A glass (or plastic) fiber (or a bundle of fibers called a core) through which the data is transmitted.
- A protective layer of glass or plastic cladding is wrapped around the core to protect it.
- For additional protection, it has an outer jacket (sheath), which is often made of a durable material such as Kevlar (the substance used to make bulletproof vests).

Data transmissions can pass through fiber-optic cable in only one direction. Therefore, at least two fibers (or cores) are contained in most fiber-optic cables to enable transmission of data in both directions.

Figure12.16 Fiber-optic cable is made up of a glass or plastic fiber (or a bundle of fibers), a glass or plastic cladding, and a protective sheath.

Many people want to support green initiatives and sustainability. The U.S. Environmental Protection Agency (EPA) hosts the Developer Central website (**developer.epa.gov/category/apps**) to make it easier to find useful apps that support green lifestyles (see Figure 12.17). The site currently lists existing apps that can help individuals or groups switch to a greener lifestyle or track progress in daily green living activities.

If you can't locate an app that meets your needs, you can review ideas submitted by previous visitors to the website or even submit your own ideas. For even more apps, you can visit Eco Libris's green apps website at **ecolibris.net/greenapps.asp**. Eco Libris maintains a list of its top 100 apps, all of which are free or cost less than $2. So visit one of these sites today and find an app to help you live greener.

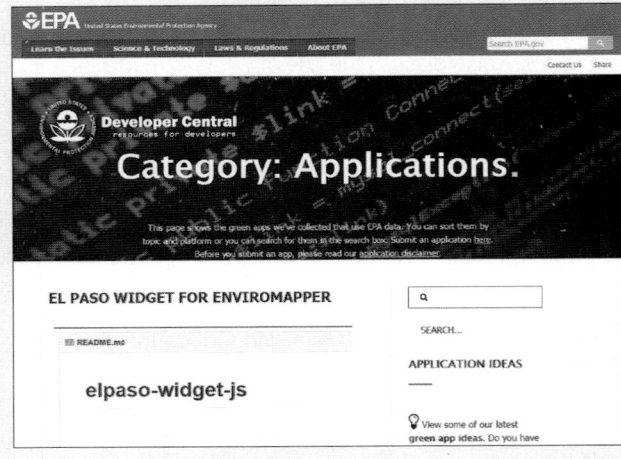

Figure 12.17 The EPA's Developer Central website provides information about apps that help you go green. *(U.S. Environmental Protection Agency)*

Wireless Media Options

What wireless media options are there? Most business networks use the same Ethernet standards as home networks. Therefore, the wireless options for business networks are very similar to those available for home networks. *Wireless access points* are installed to provide coverage wherever employees will be working with portable devices, such as in conference rooms.

Comparing Transmission Media

Which medium is best for business networks? Network engineers specialize in the design and deployment of networks and are responsible for selecting the appropriate network topologies and media types. Their decision as to which transmission medium a network will use is based on the topology selected, the length of the cable runs needed, the amount of interference present, and the need for wireless connectivity.

As noted above, most large networks use a mix of media types. For example, fiber-optic cable may be appropriate for the portion of a network that traverses the factory floor, where interference from magnetic fields is significant. However, UTP cable may work fine in a general office area. Wireless media may be required in areas where employees are likely to connect their portable computing devices or where it's impractical or expensive to run cable.

Network Adapters and Navigation Devices

As mentioned earlier, data flows through the network in packets. Data packets are like postal letters. They don't get to their destinations without some help. In this section, we explore the various conventions and devices that help speed data packets on their way through the network.

Network Adapters

Objective 12.7 *Describe how network adapters help data move around a network.*

What is a network adapter? As noted in Chapter 7, client and server computers and peripherals need an interface to connect with and communicate on the network. **Network adapters** are devices that perform specific tasks to enable nodes to communicate on a network. Network adapters are installed inside computers and peripherals. These adapters are referred to as *network interface cards (NICs)*. Most NICs are now integrated into the motherboard of the computing device as opposed to being a separate plug-in card.

What do network adapters do? Network adapters perform three critical functions:

1. *They generate high-powered signals to enable network transmissions.* Digital signals generated inside the computer are fairly low powered and would not travel well on cable or wireless network media without network adapters. Network adapters convert the signals from inside the computer into higher-powered signals that have no trouble traversing the network media.

2. *They're responsible for breaking the data into packets and for transmitting and receiving data.* They're also responsible for receiving incoming data packets and, in accordance with networking protocols, reconstructing them, as shown in Figure 12.18.

3. *They act as gatekeepers for information flowing to and from the client computer.* Much like a security guard in a gated community, a network adapter is responsible for permitting or denying access to the client computer (the community) and controlling the flow of data (visitors).

You should note that there won't always be the same number of response packets as there are request packets. The number of packets depends on the volume of the data being sent. A simple response may have less data than a complex one.

Are there different types of network adapters? Although there are different types of network adapters, almost without exception Ethernet is the standard communications protocol used on most client/server networks. Therefore, the adapter cards that ship with computers today are Ethernet compliant.

Do wireless networks require network adapters? A computing device that connects to a network using wireless access needs to have a special network adapter card, called a **wireless network interface card (wireless NIC)**, installed in it. Laptop computers and other portable computing devices contain wireless NICs.

To allow wireless connections, a network also must be fitted with devices called wireless access points. A **wireless access point (WAP)** gives wireless devices a sending and receiving connection point to the network.

Figure 12.19 shows an example of a typical small business network with a wireless access point. The access point is connected to the wired network through a conventional cable. When a laptop or other device with a wireless NIC is powered on near a wireless access point, it establishes a connection with the access point using radio waves. Many devices can communicate with the network through a single wireless access point.

STEP 1: You request information from the network database.

STEP 2: The NIC breaks the request into packets and sends the packets to the server.

Request packet #1

Request packet #2

Request packet #3

Response packet #1

Response packet #2

Server

Your computer (client)

Network interface card (NIC)

STEP 4: The NIC reassembles the response packets and displays information on your screen.

STEP 3: The server executes the request, assembles the response into packets, and sends the packets to the client.

Figure 12.18 A network interface card (NIC) is responsible for breaking down data into packets, preparing packets for transmission, receiving incoming data packets, and reconstructing them.

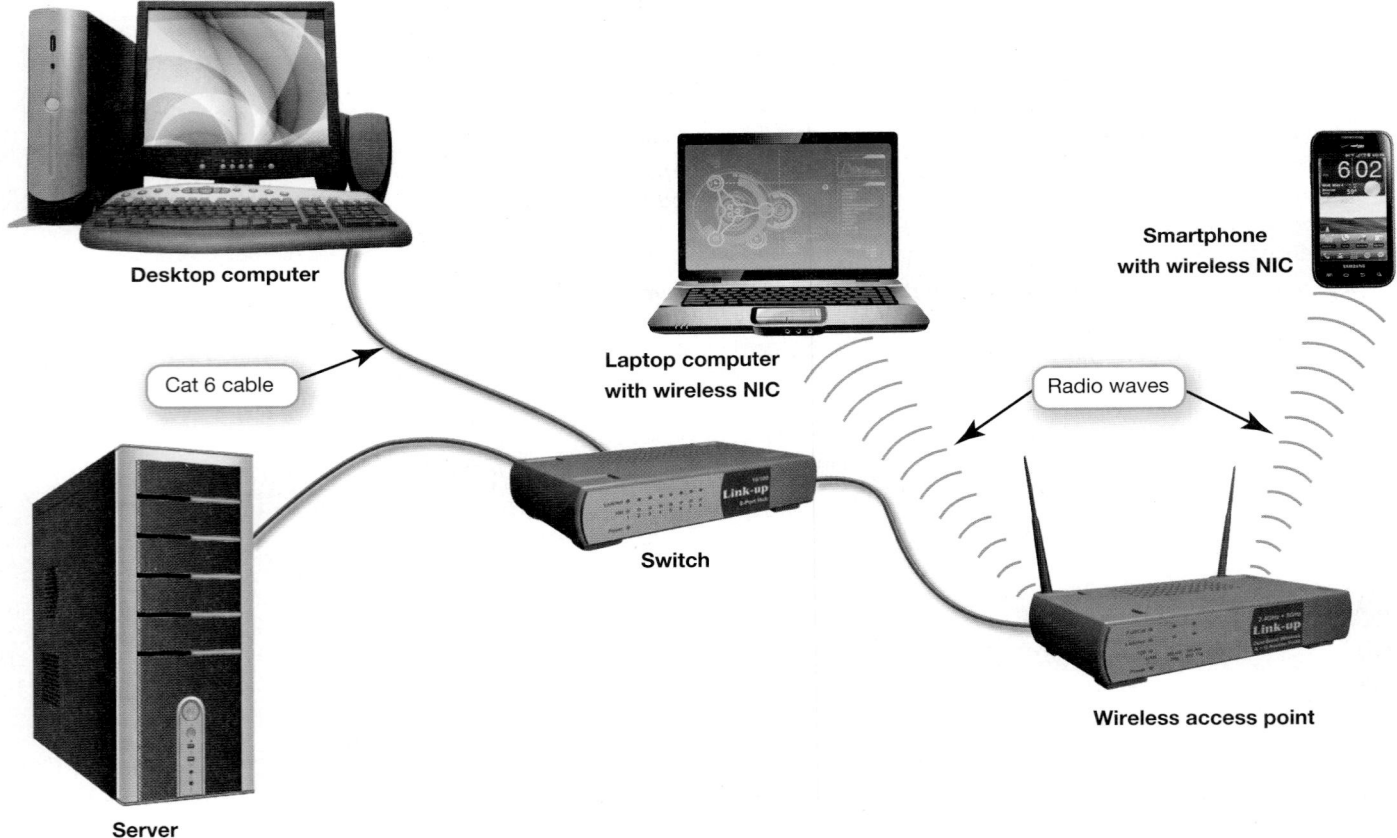

Desktop computer

Cat 6 cable

**Laptop computer
with wireless NIC**

Radio waves

**Smartphone
with wireless NIC**

Switch

Wireless access point

Server

Figure 12.19 This small business network has an added wireless access point.

Do network adapters require software? Special communications software called a **device driver** is installed on all client computers in the client/server network. Device drivers enable the network adapter to communicate with the server's OS and with the OS of the computer in which the adapter is installed.

MAC Addresses

Objective 12.8 *Define MAC addresses, and explain how they are used to move data around a network.*

How do network adapters know where to send data packets? Each network adapter has a physical address, similar to a serial number on an appliance. This address is called a **media access control (MAC) address**, and it's made up of 6 two-position characters, such as 01:40:87:44:79:A5. (Don't confuse this MAC with the Apple computers of the same name.) The first three sets of characters (in this case, 01:40:87) specify the manufacturer of the network adapter, and the second set of characters (in this case, 44:79:A5) makes up a unique address. Because all MAC addresses must be unique, there is an IEEE (Institute of Electrical and Electronics Engineers) committee responsible for allocating blocks of numbers to network adapter manufacturers.

Are MAC addresses the same as IP addresses? MAC addresses and IP (Internet Protocol) addresses are not the same thing. A MAC address is used for identification purposes *internally* on a network. An IP address is the address *external* entities use to communicate with your network. Think of it this way: The postal carrier delivers a package (data packet) to your dorm building based on its street address (IP address). The dorm's mail clerk delivers the package to your room because it has your name on it (MAC address) and not that of your neighbor. Both pieces of information are necessary to ensure that the package (or data) reaches its destination.

How are data packets packaged for transmission? Data packets aren't necessarily sent alone. Sometimes groups of data packets are sent together in a package called a **frame**. A frame is a container that can hold multiple data packets. This is similar to placing several letters going to the same postal address in a big envelope. While the data packets are being assembled into frames, the network operating system (NOS) software assigns the appropriate MAC address to the frame. The NOS keeps track of all devices and their addresses on the network. Much like an envelope that's entrusted to the postal service, the frame is delivered to the MAC address that the NOS assigned to the frame.

What delivers the frames to the correct device on the network? In a small bus network, frames just bounce along the transmission medium until the correct client computer notices that the frame is addressed to it and pulls the signal off the medium. However, this is inefficient in a larger network. Therefore, many types of devices have been developed to deliver data to its destination efficiently. These devices are designed to route signals and exchange data with other networks.

Are MAC addresses useful for anything besides identifying a particular network device? On networks with wireless capabilities, MAC addresses can be used to enhance network security. Because each MAC address is unique, you can input a list of authorized MAC addresses into the router. If someone who is using an unauthorized network adapter attempts to connect to the network, he or she will be unable to make a connection.

Switches, Bridges, and Routers

Objective 12.9 *List the various network navigation devices, and explain how they help route data through networks.*

Which devices are used to route signals through a single network? Switches are used to send data on a specific route through the network. A **switch** makes decisions, based on the MAC address of the data, as to where the data is to be sent and rebroadcasts it to the appropriate network node. This improves network efficiency by helping ensure that each node receives only the data intended for it. Figure 12.20 shows a switch being used to rebroadcast a message.

Message for Computer #3

Switch

Computer #1

Server

Rebroadcast of message for Computer #3

Computer #2

Computer #3

Figure 12.20 Switches rebroadcast messages—but only to the devices to which the messages are addressed.

Figure 12.21 Bridges are devices used to send data between different network collision domains.

Do all Ethernet networks need a switch? Switches are needed on Ethernet networks whether they are installed in a home or a business. (Routers sold for home use have switches built in to them.)

Are switches sufficient for moving data efficiently across all sizes of networks? When a corporate network grows in size, performance can decline because many devices compete for transmission time on the network media. To solve this problem, a network can be broken into multiple segments known as *collision domains*. A **bridge** is a device that's used to send data between different collision domains, depending on where the recipient device is located, as indicated in Figure 12.21. Signals received by the bridge from Collision Domain A are forwarded to Collision Domain B only if the destination computer is located in that domain. (Note that most home networks contain only one segment and therefore do not require bridges.)

What device does a network use to move data to another network? Whereas switches and bridges perform their functions within a single network, as you learned in Chapter 7, a **router** is designed to send information between two networks. To accomplish this, the router must look at higher-level network addresses (such as IP addresses), not MAC addresses. When the router notices data with an address that doesn't belong to a device on the network from which it originated, it sends the data to another network to which it is attached or out to the Internet.

> **Helpdesk** MyLab IT®
>
> **Transmission Media and Network Adapters**
>
> In this Helpdesk, you'll play the role of a helpdesk staffer, fielding questions about transmission media and network adapters.

Network Operating Systems and Network Security

Networks need specialized software so that the devices attached to the networks can communicate with each other. Business networks need even more security than home networks to protect them from hackers. In this section, we'll explore the software that allows networks to function and discuss security measures that help keep networks safe from prying eyes.

Network Operating Systems

Objective 12.10 *Explain why network operating systems are necessary for networks to function.*

What is a network operating system? Merely using media to connect computers and peripherals does not create a client/server network. Special software known as a **network operating system (NOS)** needs to be installed on each client computer and server that's connected to the network to provide the services necessary for them to communicate. The NOS provides a set of common rules (a *protocol*) that controls communication among devices on the network. Modern operating systems, such as Windows and macOS, include NOS client software as part of the basic installation. However, large networks, such as those found in businesses, require more sophisticated NOS server software.

Why is NOS server software needed on large networks? OS software is designed to facilitate communication between the software and hardware components of your computer. NOS software is specifically designed to provide server services, network communications, management of network peripherals, and storage. Popular server software includes Windows Server, Red Hat Enterprise Linux, and SUSE Linux Enterprise Server. NOS software is installed on servers.

To provide network communications, the client computers must run a small part of the NOS in addition to their OS. Windows and macOS contain network communication capabilities; therefore, no other NOS software is usually installed on these client computers.

Do P2P networks need special NOS software? The software that P2P networks require is built into the Windows, Linux, and macOS operating systems. So if you have a simple P2P network, there is no need to purchase specialized NOS software.

How does the NOS control network communications? Each NOS has its own proprietary communications language, file-management structure, and device-management structure. The NOS also sets and controls the protocols for all devices wishing to communicate on the network. Proprietary protocols from one vendor's NOS won't work with another vendor's NOS.

However, because the Internet uses an open protocol (called TCP/IP) for communications, almost all corporate networks use TCP/IP as their standard networking protocol regardless of the manufacturer of their NOS. All modern NOSs support TCP/IP.

Can a network use two different NOSs? Many large corporate networks use several different NOSs at the same time. This is because different NOSs provide different features, some of which are more useful in certain situations than others. For instance, although the employees of a corporation may be using a Windows environment for their desktops and e-mail, the file servers and web servers may be running a Linux-based NOS.

Bits&Bytes — Smart Lighting for Smart Homes

Software as a service (SaaS) is the model of software delivery that is really taking over the industry. But with the Internet of Things (having devices constantly connected to the Internet) picking up momentum, we can use this model to deliver other services efficiently.

Consider smart homes, which have devices connected through networks to the Internet to control lighting, environmental factors (such as heating and cooling), video surveillance, and door locks. Lighting is estimated to account for 25% of world electricity usage. So how can smart lighting devices be used to help reduce costs?

Enter Lighting as a Service (LaaS). In this approach, energy-efficient light fixtures with integrated motion detectors are installed in your home to detect whether a room is occupied. Light sensors can also be installed to detect when there is adequate sunlight in an area and therefore no artificial light is needed. Lighting is then provided as a service only when required. Why keep the lights on in a room if there is no one in it? It's estimated that LaaS could cut lighting-related electricity usage by up to 90%. Now that's a smart home.

Client/Server Network Security

Objective 12.11 *List major security threats to networks, and explain how network administrators mitigate these threats.*

What sources of security threats do all network administrators need to watch for? A major advantage that client/server networks have over P2P networks is that they offer a higher level of security. With client/server networks, users can be required to enter a user ID and a password to gain access to the network. The security can be centrally administered by network administrators, freeing individual users of the responsibility of maintaining their own data security, as they must do on a P2P network. Still, client/server networks are vulnerable to threats. These threats can be classified into three main groups:

1. *Human errors and mistakes:* Everyone makes mistakes. For example, a member of the computer support staff could mistakenly install an old database on top of the current one. Even physical accidents fall into this category; for example, someone could lose control of a car and drive it through the wall of the main data center.

2. *Malicious human activity:* Malicious actions can be perpetrated by current employees, former employees, or third parties. For example, a disgruntled employee could introduce a virus to the network, or a hacker could break into the student database server to steal credit card records.

3. *Natural events and disasters:* Some events—such as floods and fires—are beyond human control. All can lead to the inadvertent destruction of data.

Because networks are vulnerable to such security threats, one of the network administrator's key functions is to keep network data secure. Let's explore the challenges network administrators face in keeping a client/server network secure.

Authentication

How do network administrators ensure that only authorized users access the network? **Authentication** is the process whereby users prove they have authorization to use a computer network. For example, correctly entering the user ID and password on your college network proves to the network that you have authorized access. The access is authorized because the ID was generated by a network administrator when you became an authorized user of the network.

However, authentication can also be achieved through the use of biometric devices (discussed later in this chapter) and through possessed objects. A **possessed object** is any object that users carry to identify themselves and that grants them access to a computer system or computer facility. Examples include identification badges, magnetic key cards, and smart keys (similar to flash drives).

Can hackers use my account to log in to the network? If a hacker knows your user ID and password, he or she can log in and impersonate you. Impersonation can also happen if you fail to log out of a terminal on a network and someone comes along and uses your account. Sometimes network user IDs are easy to figure out because they have a certain pattern, such as your last name and the first initial of your first name.

If a hacker can deduce your user ID, he or she might use a software program that tries millions of combinations of letters and numbers as your password in an attempt to access your account. Attempting to access an account by repeatedly trying different passwords is known as a **brute force attack**. To prevent these attacks from succeeding, network administrators often configure accounts so that they'll disable themselves after a set number of login attempts using invalid passwords have been made.

Access Privileges

How can I gain access to everything on a network? The simple answer is that you can't! When your account is set up on a network, certain access privileges are granted to indicate which systems you're allowed to use. For example, on your college network, your access privileges probably include the ability to access the Internet. However, you definitely weren't granted access to the grade-entering system, because this would enable you to change your grades.

The OSI Model: Defining Protocol Standards

The Institute of Electrical and Electronics Engineers (IEEE) has taken the lead in establishing worldwide networking protocols, including a standard of communications called the **Open Systems Interconnection (OSI)** reference model. The OSI model, which has been adopted throughout the computing world, provides the protocol guidelines for all modern networks. All modern network operating system (NOS) protocols are designed to interact in accordance with the standards set out in the OSI model.

The OSI model divides communications tasks into seven processes called layers. Each layer of an OSI network has a specific function and knows how to communicate with the layers above and below it. Figure 12.22 shows the layers of the OSI model and their functions.

This layering approach makes communications more efficient because specialized pieces of the NOS perform specific tasks. The layering approach is akin to assembly-line manufacturing.

Figure 12.22 Layers of the OSI Model and Their Functions

Application Layer
- Handles all interfaces between the application software and the network
- Translates user information into a format the presentation layer can understand

Presentation Layer
- Reformats data so that the session layer can understand it
- Compresses and encrypts data

Session Layer
- Sets up a virtual (not physical) connection between the sending and receiving devices
- Manages communications sessions

Transport Layer
- Creates packets and handles packet acknowledgment

Network Layer
- Determines where to send the packets on the network

Data Link Layer
- Assembles the data into frames, addresses them, and sends them to the physical layer for delivery

Physical Layer
- Transmits (delivers) data on the network so it can reach its intended address

Producing thousands of cars per day would be difficult if one person had to build a car on his or her own. However, by splitting up the work of assembling a car into specialized tasks and assigning the tasks to people who perform them well, greater efficiency is achieved. By handling specialized tasks and communicating only with the layers above and below them, OSI layers make communications more efficient.

Let's look at how each OSI layer functions by following an e-mail you create and send to your friend through the layers:

- *Application layer:* Handles all interaction between the application software and the network. It translates the data from the application into a format that the presentation layer can understand. For example, when you send an e-mail, the application layer takes the e-mail message you created in Microsoft Outlook, translates it into a format your network can understand, and passes it to the presentation layer.
- *Presentation layer:* Reformats the data so that the session layer can understand it. It also handles data encryption (changing the data into a format that makes it harder to intercept and read) and compression, if required. In our e-mail example, the presentation layer notices that you selected an encryption option for the e-mail message and encrypts the data before sending it to the session layer.
- *Session layer:* Sets up a virtual (not physical) connection between the sending and receiving devices. It then manages the communication between the two. In our e-mail example, the session layer would set up the parameters for the communications session between your computer and the Internet service provider (ISP) where your friend has her e-mail account. The session layer then tracks the transmission of the e-mail until it's satisfied that all the data in the e-mail was received at your friend's ISP.

- *Transport layer:* Breaks up the data into packets and sequences them appropriately. It also handles acknowledgment of packets (that is, it determines whether the packets were received at their destination) and decides whether packets need to be sent again. In our e-mail example, the transport layer breaks up your e-mail message into packets and sends them to the network layer, making sure that all the packets reach their destination.
- *Network layer:* Determines where to send the packets on the network and identifies the best way to route them there. In our e-mail example, the network layer examines the address on the packets (the address of your friend's ISP) and determines how to route the packets so they get to the ISP and can ultimately get to the receiving computer.
- *Data link layer:* Responsible for assembling the data packets into frames, addressing the frames, and delivering them to the physical layer so they can be sent on their way. It's the equivalent of a postal worker who reads the address on a piece of mail and makes sure it's sent to the proper recipient. In our e-mail example, the data link layer assembles the e-mail data packets into frames, which are addressed with the appropriate routing information that it receives from the network layer.
- *Physical layer:* Takes care of delivering the data. It converts the data into a signal and transmits it over the network so that it can reach its intended address. In our e-mail example, the physical layer sends the data over the Internet to its ultimate destination (your friend's ISP).

By following standardized protocols set forth by the OSI model, NOS software can communicate happily with the computers and peripherals attached to the network as well as with other networks.

How does restricting access privileges protect a network? Because network-access accounts are centrally administered on the authentication server, it's easy for the network administrator to set up accounts for new users and grant them access only to the systems and software they need. The centralized nature of the network-access creation and the ability to restrict access to certain areas of the network make a client/server network more secure than a P2P network.

Aside from improper access, how else do data theft and destruction occur? A major problem that portable devices such as flash drives pose is theft of data or intellectual property. Because these devices are so easy to conceal and have such large memory capacity, it's easy for a disgruntled employee to walk out the front door with stacks of valuable documents tucked in his or her pocket. Industrial espionage has never been easier—and no spy cameras are needed!

Flash drives can also introduce viruses or other malicious programs to a network, either intentionally or unintentionally. Secure Network Technologies, a security consulting firm, decided to test a client's security procedures by leaving 20 flash drives at random locations around the client's office. By the end of the day, employees had picked up 15 of the flash drives and plugged them into computers on the company network. The flash drives contained a simple program to display images as well as a Trojan horse program. While the employees were viewing the images, the Trojan horse program enabled the consultants to access the company network and steal or compromise data. It isn't hard to imagine hackers leaving flash drives around your school that could act as "skeleton keys" to your school's network.

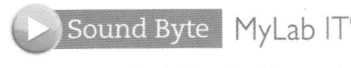 Sound Byte | MyLab IT®

A Day in the Life of a Network Technician

In this Sound Byte, you'll learn firsthand about the exciting, fast-paced job of a computer technician. Interviews with network technicians and tours of networking facilities will provide you with a deeper appreciation for the complexities of the job.

How should network administrators protect their networks from portable storage devices? To head off problems with portable storage devices, the following actions should be taken:

- Educate employees about the dangers posed by portable media devices.
- Create policies regulating the use of portable media devices in the workplace.
- Install security measures such as personal firewalls or antivirus software to protect all computers in the company. The firewalls should be able to prevent malicious programs from running, even if they're introduced to a computer via a flash drive.
- Limit and monitor the use of portable media devices. Microsoft networking software allows network administrators to shut off access to the USB ports on computers; this prevents employees from using flash drives and other USB devices for legitimate purposes.
- Inform employees that their use of portable media devices is being monitored. This alone will often be enough to scare employees away from connecting untrusted devices to the network.

Other software products, such as DeviceLock and Safend Data Protection Suite, can be deployed on a network to provide options such as detailed security policies. Such products can also monitor USB device connections and track which users have connected devices to the network (including devices other than flash drives).

Physical Protection Measures

What physical measures are used to protect a network? Restricting physical access to servers and other sensitive equipment is critical to protecting a network. Where are the servers that power your college network? They're most likely behind locked doors to which only authorized personnel have access. Likewise, the network's switches are securely tucked away in ceilings, walls, or closets, safe from anyone who might tamper with them in an attempt to sabotage the network or breach its security.

As shown in Figure 12.23, a number of different devices can be used to control access:

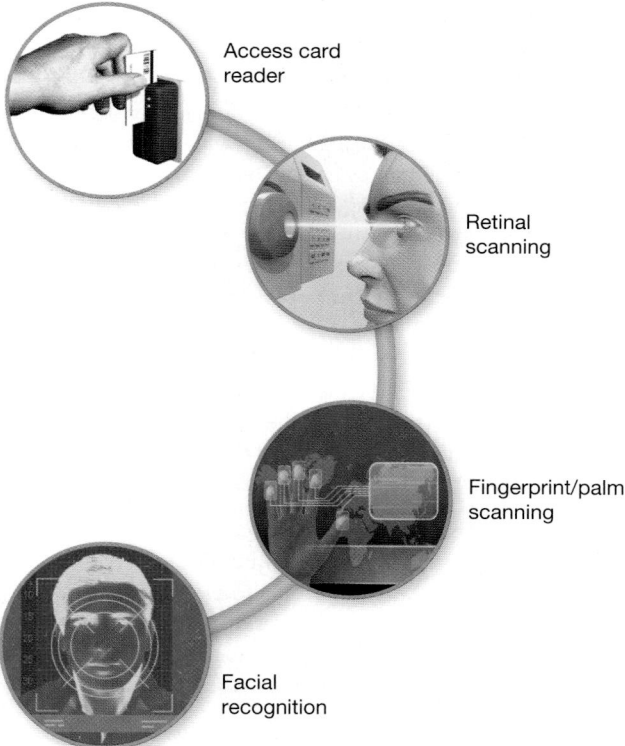

Access card reader

Retinal scanning

Fingerprint/palm scanning

Facial recognition

- An **access card reader** is a relatively cheap device that reads information from a magnetic strip on the back of a credit card–like access card, such as your student ID card. The card reader, which can control the lock on a door, is programmed to admit only authorized personnel to the area. Card readers are easily programmed by adding authorized ID card numbers.
- A **biometric authentication device** uses a unique characteristic of human biology to identify authorized users. Some devices read fingerprints or palm prints when you place your hand on a scanning pad. Other devices shine a laser beam into your eye and read the unique patterns of your retina. Facial-recognition systems store unique characteristics of an individual's face for later comparison and identification. When an authorized individual uses a device for the first time, his or her fingerprints, retinal patterns, or face patterns are scanned and stored in a database.

Financial institutions and retail stores are considering using such devices to attempt to eliminate the growing fraud problems of identity theft and counterfeiting of credit and debit cards. If fingerprint authorization were required at the supermarket to make a purchase, a thief who stole your wallet and attempted to use your credit card would be unsuccessful.

What are the problems with biometric devices? The biometric devices currently on the market don't always function as intended. Facial-recognition and retinal-scanning systems can sometimes be fooled by pictures or videos of an authorized user. Researchers have fooled biometric fingerprint readers by using fingers made out of modeling clay, using the fingers of cadavers, or having unauthorized persons breathe on the sensor, which makes the previous user's fingerprint visible.

Next-generation fingerprint readers will use specially designed algorithms that will detect moisture patterns on a person's fingers. Another approach may involve readers that detect an electrical current when a finger touches the reader, which is possible because the human body conducts electrical current. Future retinal readers may check whether a person blinks or if his or her pupils contract when a bright light shines on them.

Figure 12.23 Access card readers provide a relatively inexpensive solution to security for areas needing low-level security. Biometric authentication devices, such as fingerprint/palm, retinal, and facial-recognition scanners, are used to protect high-security areas such as a server room.

Ethics in IT

How Should Companies Handle Data Breaches?

Data breaches occur all too frequently, and it seems we're always seeing reports in the media about yet another hacker obtaining supposedly private information. Many companies have sensitive data about you. But what is their ethical responsibility to protect your data? And what should a company do for its customers when a data breach occurs?

Data Confidentiality

The objective for any company that possesses sensitive data should be **information assurance**, which means ensuring information systems are adequately secured against tampering. The five key attributes of secure information systems are as follows:

1. *Availability:* The extent to which a data processing system is able to receive and process data. A high degree of availability is usually desirable.
2. *Integrity:* A quality that an information system has if the processing of information is logical and accurate and the data is protected against unauthorized modifications or destruction.
3. *Authentication:* Security measures designed to protect an information system against acceptance of a fraudulent transmission of data by establishing the validity of a data transmission or message or the identity of the sender.
4. *Confidentiality:* The assurance that information isn't disclosed to unauthorized persons, processes, or devices.
5. *Nonrepudiation:* A capability of security systems that guarantees that a message or data can be proven to have originated from a specific person and to have been processed by the recipient. The sender of the data receives a receipt for the data, and the receiver of the data gets proof of the sender's identity. The objective of nonrepudiation is to prevent either party from later denying having handled the data.

From your perspective, you are probably the most concerned about authentication and confidentiality. Companies that have your data shouldn't share it with unauthorized parties and should keep unauthorized people out of their databases. Unfortunately, you have very little control over authentication safeguards. That's the responsibility of the company that holds your data.

Authentication Failures

The data breaches that occur usually represent authentication failures—unauthorized people gaining access to data. Clearly, when this happens, a corporation has failed in its responsibility to protect its customers' data. No system is ever 100% safe against breaches, but most systems are adequately protected against all but the most determined hackers. But what ethical responsibilities does a company have to its customers after a data breach?

The first thing a company should do is admit the problem and inform its customers. The Federal Trade Commission (FTC) recommends the following course of action for companies who experience data breaches:

1. Notify the appropriate law enforcement agencies.
2. Notify other affected businesses, such as banks and credit card companies. These companies can then monitor the affected accounts for fraudulent activity.
3. Notify the individuals affected. The company should explain what happened, what information was compromised, who to contact in the organization, and what customers should do to protect themselves (which will vary based on the information compromised).

How can you be aware of a data breach if the company that suffered it never tells you that your data was exposed? You should monitor websites such as the Privacy Rights Clearinghouse (**privacyrights.org/data-breach**) and Identity Theft Resource Center (**idtheftcenter.org/Data-Breaches/data-breaches.html**), which track data breaches. This might be the fastest way to find out if your information has been compromised so you can take action. The FTC website on identity theft (**consumer.ftc.gov/topics/identity-theft**) provides good guidelines to follow when your data has been exposed.

Granting customers free identity-theft protection is one of the more common forms of compensation offered to placate customers after a data breach, but not every company does it. Some companies merely stop at notifying customers and offer nothing in terms of compensation for the inconvenience.

Although companies may behave ethically after a data breach, your best protection is still your own vigilance!

Are Internet connections on client/server networks vulnerable to hackers? Just like a home network, any company's network that's connected to the Internet can attract hackers. For this reason, a well-defended business network, just like a well-defended home network, includes a firewall. Firewalls can be composed of software or hardware, and many sophisticated firewalls include both. Routers are often equipped to act as hardware firewalls.

Does a firewall on a client/server network work the same way as a personal firewall installed on a home network? Although a firewall on a business network may contain a few extra security options, making it even harder to breach than a personal firewall, the firewalls for business networks work on the same basic principles as a personal firewall. At a minimum, most firewalls work as packet screeners. **Packet screening** involves having an *external screening router* examining incoming data packets to ensure that they originated from or are authorized by valid users on the internal network. Unauthorized or suspect packets are discarded by the firewall before they reach the network.

Packet screening also can be configured for outgoing data to ensure that requests for information to the Internet are from legitimate users. This is done by an *internal screening router* and helps detect Trojan horse programs that may have been installed by hackers. Trojan horses often try to disguise where they're sending data from by using bogus IP addresses on the packets the programs send instead of using an authorized IP address belonging to the network.

With packet screening in place, packets going into and out of the network are checked to ensure they're either from or addressed to a legitimate IP address on the network. If the addresses aren't valid addresses on the network, the firewall (or the screening routers) discards them.

What other security measures does the firewall on a client/server network use? To increase security even further, most large networks add a **bastion host**, which is a heavily secured server located on a special perimeter network between the company's secure internal network and the firewall.

To external computers, the bastion host gives the appearance of being the internal network server. Hackers can waste a lot of time and energy attacking the bastion host. However, even if a hacker breaches the bastion host server, the internal network isn't vulnerable because the bastion host isn't on the internal network. Moreover, during the time the hackers spend trying to penetrate the bastion host, network administrators can detect and thwart their attacks.

How do bastion hosts help protect systems from hackers? Bastion hosts are a type of honey pot. A **honey pot** is a computer system that's set up to attract unauthorized users by appearing to be a key part of a network or a system that contains something of great value.

Bits&Bytes | ## Are Your Photos Helping Criminals Target You?

All cell phones today contain GPS chips. The cameras in phones often use information gathered from the GPS chips to encode information onto photos in the form of geotags. A geotag is a piece of data attached to a photo that indicates your latitude and longitude when you took the photo. Geotagging is useful for applications that can take advantage of this information, but problems arise when you share geotagged photos on the web.

If you post a lot of photos, cybercriminals and cyberstalkers can use the information from the geotags on your photos to figure out the patterns of your movements. They may be able to ascertain when you're at work or that you're currently on vacation, which leads them to determine prime times for

burglarizing your home. Some sites such as Facebook and Twitter have measures in place to limit the amount of geotagged information that can be seen in photos in order to prevent their users from unwittingly revealing personal information. However, many photo-sharing sites don't have such protections in place.

The safest thing to do is not tag your photos with geotags in the first place. It's usually easy to disable location tracking on your smartphone in the settings. If you want to remove tags from photos you already have taken, you can use software such as BatchPurifier LITE or Pixelgarde. Not geotagging your photos will make it tougher for the cybercriminals to figure out your movements.

Figure 12.24 Business firewalls provide sophisticated protection from hackers.

Bastion hosts are often configured as proxy servers. A **proxy server** acts as a go-between, connecting computers on the internal network with those on the external network (the Internet). All requests from the internal network for Internet services are directed through the proxy server. Similarly, all incoming requests from the Internet must pass through the proxy server. It's much easier for network administrators to maintain adequate security on one server than it is to ensure that security is maintained on hundreds or thousands of computers in a college network, for example.

Figure 12.24 shows a network secured by a firewall, a bastion host and proxy server, and a screening router. Now that you know a bit more about business networks, you should be able to comfortably navigate the network at your college or your place of employment and understand why certain security measures have been taken to protect network data.

Before moving on to the Chapter Review:

1. ▶ Watch Chapter Overview Video 12.2.
2. Then take the Check Your Understanding quiz.

Check Your Understanding // Review & Practice

For a quick review to see what you've learned so far, answer the following questions.

multiple choice

1. Fiber-optic cable most likely would be used in a business network when
   a. saving money is more important than speed.
   b. the installation budget is very limited.
   c. very short cable runs are required.
   d. electrical or magnetic interference is present.

2. A MAC address
   a. is the address *external* entities use to communicate with your network.
   b. is used for *internal* identification purposes on a network.
   c. is only used on Apple computers.
   d. is the same thing as an IP address.

3. On client/server networks, bridges
   a. transfer data between two networks.
   b. move data efficiently from node to node on the internal network.
   c. route data between two collision domains on a single network.
   d. are necessary only in networks using the ring topology.

4. NOS software is needed
   a. only if a communications server is deployed on a client/server network.
   b. only on the servers in a client/server network.
   c. on all computers in a client/server network.
   d. only when configuring a network in a star topology.

5. Which of the following is used to increase security on a client/server network?
   a. bridge
   b. bastion host
   c. transmission media
   d. database server

 Go to **MyLab IT** to take an autograded version of the *Check Your Understanding* review and to find all media resources for the chapter.

TechBytes Weekly Go to TechBytes Weekly for current technology news and discussion questions!

12 Chapter Review

Summary

Part 1
Client/Server Networks and Topologies

Learning Outcome 12.1 You will be able to describe common types of client/server networks, servers found on them, and network topologies used to construct them.

 Client/Server Network Basics

Objective 12.1 *List the advantages for businesses of installing a network.*

- Networks enable expensive resources, such as printers, to be shared.
- Networks facilitate knowledge sharing, as multiple people can access information at the same time.
- Software can be shared from network servers, thereby reducing the costs of installation on each user's computer.
- Information sharing is more effective when employees are connected via networks.

Objective 12.2 *Explain the differences between a client/server network and a peer-to-peer network.*

- In a peer-to-peer network, each node connected to the network can communicate directly with every other node on the network. In a client/server network, a separate device (the server) exercises control over the network.
- Data flows more efficiently in client/server networks than in peer-to-peer networks.
- Client/server networks have increased scalability, meaning users can be added to the network easily.

Objective 12.3 *Describe the common types of client/server networks as well as other networks businesses use.*

- Local area networks (LANs) are small groups of computers (as few as two) and peripherals linked together over a small geographical area.
- Wide area networks (WANs) comprise large numbers of users (or of separate LANs) that are miles apart and linked together.
- An intranet is a private network set up by a business or an organization that's used exclusively by a select group of employees, customers, suppliers, volunteers, or supporters.

- Virtual private networks (VPNs) use the public Internet communications infrastructure to build a secure, private network among various locations.

 Servers and Network Topologies

Objective 12.4 *List the common types of servers found on client/server networks.*

- Dedicated servers are used on large networks to increase efficiency.
- Authentication servers control access to the network and ensure that only authorized users can log in.
- File servers provide storage and management of user files.
- Print servers manage and control all printing jobs initiated on a network.
- Application servers provide access to application software.
- Database servers store database files and provide access to users who need the information in the databases.
- E-mail servers control all incoming and outgoing e-mail traffic.
- Communications servers are used to control the flow of information from the internal network to outside networks.
- Web servers are used to host websites.
- Cloud servers provide storage and access to data on the Internet.

Objective 12.5 *Describe the common types of network topologies and the advantages and disadvantages of each one.*

- In a bus topology, all nodes are connected to a single linear cable. Installation is easy, reliable, and inexpensive. Breaks in the cable disable the network, and large numbers of users decrease performance.

- Ring topologies are made up of nodes arranged roughly in a circle. The data flows from node to node in a specific order. Access to the network is allocated fairly among nodes. Failure of one node can bring down the network.

- In a star topology, nodes are connected to a central communication device (a switch) and branch out like points of a star. Failure of one node doesn't affect other nodes and the network is highly scalable. Requires more cable to install and network navigation devices are a single point of failure that can affect many nodes.

Part 2

Setting Up Business Networks

Learning Outcome 12.2 **You will be able to describe transmission media, network operating system software, and network navigation devices and explain major threats to network security and how to mitigate them.**

 Transmission Media

Objective 12.6 *Describe the types of wired and wireless transmission media used in networks.*

- Transmission media make up the physical system that data takes to flow between devices on a network. Twisted-pair cable consists of pairs of wires twisted around each other in order to reduce interference. Coaxial cable is the same type of cable used by your cable TV company to run a signal into your house. Fiber-optic cable uses bundles of glass or plastic fiber to send signals using light waves. It provides the largest bandwidth but is expensive and difficult to install. Wireless media uses radio waves to send data between nodes on a network.

 Network Adapters and Navigation Devices

Objective 12.7 *Describe how network adapters help data move around a network.*

- A network adapter provides three critical functions: (1) It takes low-power data signals generated by the computer and converts them into higher-powered signals that can traverse network media easily. (2) It breaks the data generated by the computer into packets and packages them for transmission across the network media. (3) It acts as a gatekeeper to control the flow of data to and from the computer.

Objective 12.8 *Define MAC addresses, and explain how they are used to move data around a network.*

- A media access control (MAC) address represents the physical address of a network adapter. It is made up of 6 two-position characters, such as 01:40:87:44:79:A5. A frame is a container that can hold multiple data packets. While the data packets are being assembled into frames, the network operating system (NOS) software assigns the appropriate MAC address to the frame. The NOS keeps track of all devices and their addresses on the network.

Objective 12.9 *List the various network navigation devices, and explain how they help route data through networks.*

- Switches are devices that read the addresses of data packets and retransmit a signal to its destination instead of to every device connected to the switch. Bridges are devices used to send data between two different segments (collision domains) of the same network. Routers are used to route data between two different networks, such as between a business network and the Internet.

 Network Operating Systems and Network Security

Objective 12.10 *Explain why network operating systems are necessary for networks to function.*

- Network operating system (NOS) software needs to be installed on each computer and server connected to a client/server network in order to provide the services necessary for the devices to communicate. The NOS provides a set of common rules (called a protocol) that controls communication between devices on the network.

Objective 12.11 *List major security threats to networks, and explain how network administrators mitigate these threats.*

- Human errors and mistakes, malicious human activity (such as unauthorized access), and natural events and disasters are major categories of security threats.
- Access to most networks requires authentication procedures, such as having users enter a user ID and password, to ensure that only authorized users access the network. The system administrator defines access privileges for users so that they can access only specific files.
- Network equipment is physically secured behind locked doors. Access to equipment is often restricted by biometric devices, which use unique physical characteristics of individuals for identification purposes.
- Firewalls, packet screeners, and bastion hosts are employed to keep hackers from successfully attacking networks.
- Data backups help secure data against destruction by natural events and disasters (such as fire).

 Be sure to check out **MyLab IT** for additional materials to help you review and learn. And don't forget to watch the Chapter Overview Videos. ▶

Key Terms

access card reader   **501**
access method   **481**
active topology   **482**
application server   **479**
authentication   **498**
authentication server   **479**
bastion host   **503**
biometric authentication device   **501**
bridge   **496**
brute force attack   **498**
bus (linear bus) topology   **481**
centralized   **473**
client/server network (server-based network)   **473**
cloud server   **481**
coaxial cable   **491**
communications server   **479**
CSMA/CD   **484**
data collision   **479**
database server   **481**
decentralized   **473**
dedicated server   **478**
device driver   **494**

electronic data interchange (EDI)   **475**
e-mail server   **479**
extranet   **475**
fiber-optic cable   **491**
file server   **479**
frame   **495**
honey pot   **503**
hybrid topology   **486**
information assurance   **502**
intranet   **475**
jam signal   **484**
local area network (LAN)   **474**
media access control (MAC) address   **494**
network adapter   **492**
network administrator   **473**
network operating system (NOS)   **497**
network topology   **481**
Open Systems Interconnection (OSI)   **499**
packet screening   **503**
passive topology   **481**
possessed object   **498**

print queue   **479**
print server   **479**
protocol   **481**
proxy server   **504**
ring (loop) topology   **482**
router   **496**
scalability   **474**
shielded twisted-pair (STP) cable   **491**
star topology   **483**
switch   **495**
terminator   **481**
token   **482**
token method   **482**
transmission media   **490**
tunneling   **476**
twisted-pair cable   **491**
virtual private network (VPN)   **476**
virtualization   **480**
web server   **480**
wide area network (WAN)   **474**
wireless access point (WAP)   **493**
wireless network interface card (wireless NIC)   **493**

Chapter Quiz // Assessment

For a quick review to see what you've learned, answer the following questions. Submit the quiz as requested by your instructor. If you are using **MyLab IT**, the quiz is also available there.

multiple choice

1. Which of the following is an advantage of installing a client/server network in a business?
   a. centralization of network adapters
   b. decentralization of peripherals
   c. decentralization of files and data
   d. sharing of peripherals

2. On client/server networks, more users can be added without affecting the performance of other nodes. This is known as network
   a. scalability.
   b. decentralization.
   c. topology.
   d. flexibility.

3. Which server would a client/server network include to control data exchanges with other networks?
   a. database
   b. communications
   c. authentication
   d. application

4. Which of the following is a private network set up by a business that's used exclusively by a select group of employees and suppliers?
   a. WAN
   b. VPN
   c. PAN
   d. intranet

5. Network adapters send data packets based on a(n)
    a. IP address.
    b. router address.
    c. MAC address.
    d. frame address.

6. Providing adequate security on a corporate network involves all of the following issues EXCEPT
    a. authentication.
    b. proprietary software encryption.
    c. restricting access to servers.
    d. limiting physical access to networking equipment.

7. Which network cable type is virtually immune to signal interference?
    a. UTP
    b. STP
    c. coaxial
    d. fiber-optic

8. The process whereby users prove they have authorization to use a computer network is known as
    a. authentication.
    b. decentralization.
    c. proxy control.
    d. repudiation.

9. Which topology tends to provide the fairest allocation of network resources?
    a. bus
    b. star
    c. ring
    d. VPN

10. Which is NOT a key component of a typical client/server network?
    a. transmission media
    b. network navigation devices
    c. terminator
    d. NOS

true/false

_____ **1.** Switches are used to send data on a specific route through an internal network.

_____ **2.** A proxy server is used to host websites on a client/server network.

_____ **3.** MAC adapters perform specific tasks to enable nodes to communicate on a network.

_____ **4.** Most modern operating systems do not include some type of NOS functionality.

_____ **5.** Ring topologies are the most widely used topology.

critical thinking

1. **Acceptable-Use Internet Policies**

    Most schools have drafted acceptable-use policies for computers and Internet access to inform students and employees of the approved uses of college computing assets. Should college employees be allowed to use their computers and Internet access for personal tasks? If so, how much time per day is reasonable for employees to spend on personal tasks? Should student computer and Internet usage be monitored to ensure compliance with the personal use policies? Should the college inform students that they're being monitored?

2. **Monitoring Computer Usage in the Workplace**

    Software tools for monitoring computer usage are available on the Internet, often for free. In most jurisdictions, it's legal for employers to install monitoring software on computers they provide to employees. It's usually illegal for employees to install monitoring software on computers owned by their employers for purposes of monitoring computer usage of coworkers or bosses. Do you think this double standard is fair? What circumstances do you think would justify an employee monitoring other employees' computer usage?

Team Time

Developing a Bring-Your-Own-Device Policy

problem

Employees, especially in developing economies, are often bringing their own computing device (BYOD) to work and using these devices to access company networks, databases, and the Internet. While this can keep equipment costs down, BYOD can present unique challenges for data security.

task

Cool Tees, a local T-shirt company, has experienced a large rise in BYOD by its employees. It is concerned about the security of data that may be on the devices. The Cool Tees CEO has asked you to assist him in constructing a BYOD policy for his company.

process

1. Divide the class into small teams. Research BYOD security issues. Review BYOD policies that are in place for businesses and schools. Consider what types of devices (laptops, phones, tablets, etc.) might be used to access company data. Draft a BYOD policy for Cool Tees employees that sets forth the company's expectations with regard to personal devices.
2. Meet as a class to discuss each group's findings. Do you feel most employees are aware of the security issues related to BYOD? Try to obtain a consensus about which precautions are the most important ones for employees to take to protect the company's data.
3. Have each group prepare a multimedia presentation (PowerPoint, video, etc.) to educate employees about the security risks of BYOD.

conclusion

Having personal computing devices and bringing them to work is fast becoming the norm in the twenty-first century. But the best defense against loss of control of company data is to understand the consequences of accessing data with and storing data on personal computing devices.

Ethics Project

Using Wireless Networks Without Permission

In this exercise, you'll research and then role-play a complicated ethical situation. The role you play might not match your own personal beliefs, but your research and use of logic will enable you to represent the view assigned. An arbitrator will watch and comment on both sides of the argument, and together the team will agree on an ethical solution.

problem

Piggybacking occurs when people use a wireless network without the owner's permission. Although piggybacking is illegal in many jurisdictions, it's often hard to detect. Piggybacking often happens inadvertently when people trying to connect to their own network accidentally connect to their neighbor's network. And because of the close proximity of many businesses, the potential for piggybacking of business wireless networks also exists. Sharing wireless connections between two entities (whether they be two households or two businesses) may violate the terms of service of the Internet service provider.

research areas to consider

- Detecting wireless piggybacking
- Piggybacking laws (legality of piggybacking)
- Securing wireless networks

process

1. Divide the class into teams. Research the areas cited above and devise a scenario in which the owner of a coffee shop has accused the proprietor of the sandwich shop next door of encouraging the sandwich shop's patrons to piggyback on the coffee shop's wireless network.
2. Team members should write a summary that provides background information for their character—for example, coffee shop owner, sandwich shop owner, and arbitrator—and that details their character's behaviors to set the stage for the role-playing event. Then, team members should create an outline to use during the role-playing event.
3. Team members should present their case to the class or submit a PowerPoint presentation for review by the rest of the class, along with the summary and resolution they developed.

conclusion

As technology becomes ever more prevalent and integrated into our lives, ethical dilemmas will present themselves to an increasing extent. Being able to understand and evaluate both sides of the argument, while responding in a personally or socially ethical manner, will be important skills.

Cyber Security Flyer and Mail Merge

You have been asked to modify a flyer that announces an upcoming cyber-security presentation to highlight National Cyber Security Awareness Month. Additionally, you have been told to mail the flyer to some key community members. You will use Mail Merge and other features of Word 2016 to complete this task.

You will use the following skills as you complete this activity:

- Apply Artistic Effect
- Insert Shapes
- Apply Page Borders

- Create Custom Bullets
- Use Mail Merge

Instructions

1. Open *TIA_Ch12_Start* and save as **TIA_Ch12_LastFirst**.
2. Scroll to page 2. Select the image at the top left of the page, click the **Picture Tools Format tab**, click **Artistic Effects** in the Adjust group, and then click the **Film Grain effect**.
3. Click the **Insert tab**, click **Shapes** in the Illustrations group, and then click **Rectangle** from the Rectangles group. Place the cursor in the top left image, and draw a rectangle. In the Size group, modify the size to be 2.2" high and 4.1" wide. Using the arrow keys on the keyboard, nudge the rectangle in any direction so that it is centered within the image.
4. Change the Shape Fill color of the rectangle to **Blue, Accent 5, Lighter 60%**. Type **October is**, press **Enter**, then type **National Cyber Security Awareness Month**. Change the font to **Century Gothic**, and change the font color to **Black, Text 1**. Then change the font size of the first line to **14**, and the remaining text to **28**. Click the **Paragraph dialog box launcher**, then change Spacing Before to **12pt**, and Line spacing: At: to **.85**.
5. With the text box still selected, click the **Drawing Tools Format tab**, click **Shape Effects** in the Shape Styles group, then select **Soft Edges, 5 point**.
6. Select **Cyber Security Presentation** (upper right corner of page 2)**.** Change the font to **Britannic Bold** and the font color to **Dark Red** in the Standard Colors group.
7. Select the first set of bullets, click the **Bullets arrow** in the Paragraph group, click **Define New Bullet**, and then click **Picture**. Click **Browse** next to From a File, and select **TIA_Ch12_Image1** from your student data files location. Select the second set of bullets, and repeat the process to define a new bullet using **TIA_Ch12_Image2**.
8. Click the **Design tab**, then click **Page Borders** in the Page Background group. Click Box in the *Setting* section, and then click the **triple line** in the *Style* section. Ensure that *Whole document* displays in the Apply to: box.
9. On Page 1, select **National Cyber Security Awareness Month!** Click **WordArt** in the Text group on the Insert tab, select **Fill – Blue, Accent 1, Shadow**. Click the **Text Fill arrow**, then click **Dark Red** in the Standard Colors group.
10. In the second paragraph, beginning with *You are invited*, **bold** *Springer Auditorium, October 22, from 12 – 2:30 PM* and change the font color to **Dark Red** in the Standard Colors group.
11. On the Mailings tab, click **Start Mail Merge** in the Start Mail Merge group, select **Letters**. Click **Select Recipients**, and click **Use an Existing List**. Navigate to the student data files, and select **TIA_Ch12_MailList**. Ensure Sheet1 is selected, then click **OK**.
12. Click **Edit Recipient List** in the Start Mail Merge group, click the **City header** to sort the addresses by city, then uncheck the two records from Elk Grove Village. Click **OK**.
13. Place the insertion point at the beginning of the first paragraph, beginning with *We are all living*. In the Write & Insert Fields group, click **Address Block**. Ensure *Joshua Randall Jr.* is selected in the *Specify address elements* section, and accept all other default settings. Click **OK**. Press **Enter**.
14. Place the insertion point at the beginning of the first paragraph, beginning with *We are all living*. In the Write & Insert Fields group, click **Greeting Line**, then in the *Greeting line format* section, ensure that *Dear* displays in the first box, select **Joshua** in the second box, and ensure a comma displays in the third box. Click **OK**. Press **Enter**.
15. Click **Preview Results** and click **Next Record** several times to advance through the letters.
16. Save the file and submit based on your instructor's directions.

13 Behind the Scenes: How the Internet Works

 For a chapter overview, watch the Chapter Overview Videos.

PART 1

Inner Workings of the Internet

Learning Outcome 13.1 You will be able to explain how the Internet is managed and the details of how data is transmitted across the Internet.

 Internet Management and Networking   514

Objective 13.1   *Describe the management of the Internet.*

Objective 13.2   *Explain how the Internet's networking components interact.*

Objective 13.3   *List and describe the Internet protocols used for data transmission.*

Internet Identity   519

Objective 13.4   *Explain how each device connected to the Internet is assigned a unique address.*

Objective 13.5   *Discuss how a numeric IP address is changed into a readable name.*

Helpdesk: Understanding IP Addresses, Domain Names, and Protocols
Sound Byte: Creating Web Pages with Squarespace

PART 2

Coding and Communicating on the Internet

Learning Outcome 13.2 You will be able to describe the web technologies used to develop web applications.

 Web Technologies   529

Objective 13.6   *Compare and contrast a variety of web development languages.*

Objective 13.7   *Compare and contrast server-side and client-side application software.*

Sound Byte: Client-Side Web Page Development

Communications over the Internet   535

Objective 13.8   *Discuss the mechanisms for communicating via e-mail and instant messaging.*

Objective 13.9   *Explain how data encryption improves security.*

Helpdesk: Keeping E-Mail Secure

For the IT Simulation for this chapter, see MyLab IT.

MyLab IT   All media accompanying this chapter can be found here.

 Make This   Make: An Earthquake Detector on **page 528**

(Maksim Pasko/Fotolia, Matthias Pahl/Shutterstock, Olly/Fotolia, Ra2 studio/Fotolia)

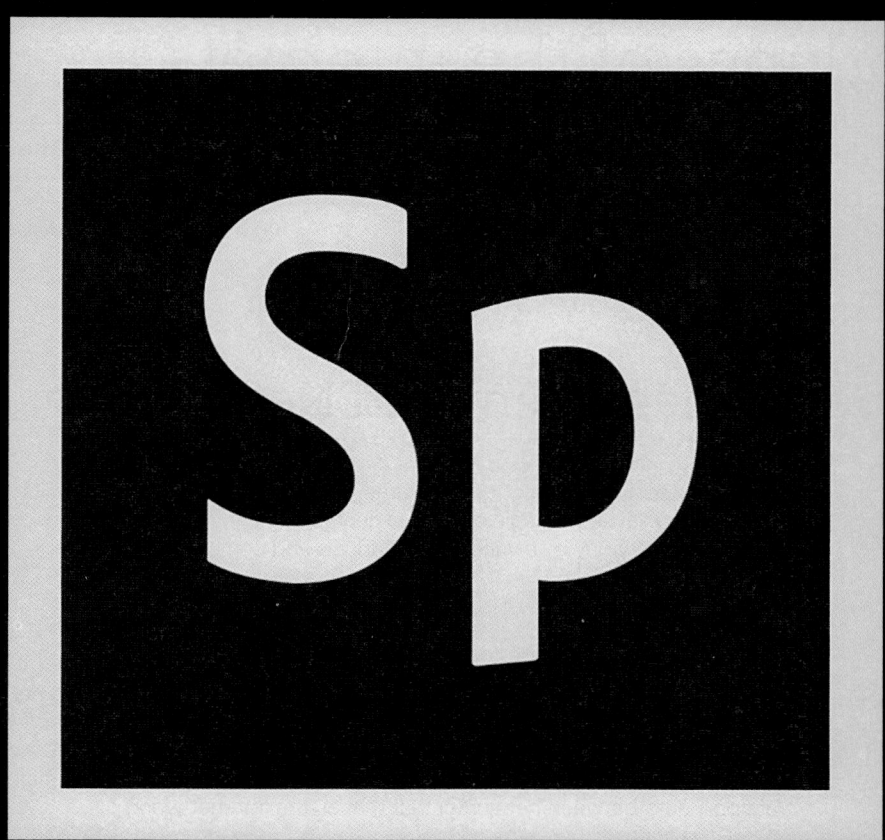

How Cool Is This?

Want to create a clean professional-looking website in just 5 minutes? Try using the free web app **Adobe Spark** (or the mobile app version). You can also use Spark to create a just-right social media posting using its built-in templates and image filters. You can even use Spark to create an animation or video from your own images or those it offers. This Adobe product (**spark.adobe.com**) supports many different **cloud storage options** so you can reach your photos on Dropbox or Creative Cloud. With a click, you can post your creation to Twitter or Facebook. Professional themes and **magazine-style fonts and layout** make your work shine. Hosted for free by Adobe, the final website you create can be linked to from anywhere. Becoming a web developer has never been so easy.

Inner Workings of the Internet

> **Learning Outcome 13.1**   **You will be able to explain how the Internet is managed and the details of how data is transmitted across the Internet.**

We use the Internet so routinely that it may not have occurred to you to ask some fundamental questions about how it's administered. In this part of the chapter, we'll discuss this and other topics.

Internet Management and Networking

To keep a massive network like the Internet functioning at peak efficiency, it must be governed and regulated. However, no single entity is in charge of the Internet. In addition, new uses for the Internet are created every day by a variety of individuals and companies.

Management

Objective 13.1   *Describe the management of the Internet.*

Who owns the Internet? The local networks that constitute the Internet are owned by different entities, including individuals, universities, government agencies, and private companies. Government entities such as the National Science Foundation (NSF), as well as many privately held companies, own pieces of the communications infrastructure (the high-speed data lines that transport data between networks) that makes the Internet work.

Does anyone manage the Internet? Several nonprofit organizations and user groups, each with a specialized purpose, are responsible for the Internet's management. Figure 13.1 shows major organizations that play a role in the governance and development of the Internet.

Many of the functions handled by these nonprofit groups were previously handled by U.S. government contractors because the Internet developed out of a defense project. However, because the Internet serves the global community, assigning responsibilities to organizations with global membership is the best way to guarantee worldwide engagement in determining the direction of the Internet.

Who pays for the Internet? The National Science Foundation (NSF), which is a U.S. government–funded agency, still pays for a large portion of the Internet's infrastructure and funds research and development for new technologies. The primary source of NSF funding is federal taxes. Other countries also pay for Internet infrastructure and development.

Figure 13.1   Major Organizations in Internet Governance and Development

Organization	Purpose	Web Address
Internet Society	Professional membership society that provides leadership for the orderly growth and development of the Internet	**internetsociety.org**
Internet Engineering Task Force (IETF)	A subgroup of the Internet Society that researches new Internet technologies to improve its capabilities and keep the infrastructure functioning smoothly	**ietf.org**
Internet Architecture Board (IAB)	Technical advisory group to the Internet Society and an IETF committee; provides direction for the maintenance and development of Internet protocols	**iab.org**
Internet Corporation for Assigned Names and Numbers (ICANN)	Organization responsible for managing the Internet's domain name system and the allocation of IP addresses	**icann.org**
World Wide Web Consortium (W3C)	Consortium of organizations that sets standards and develops protocols for the web	**w3.org**

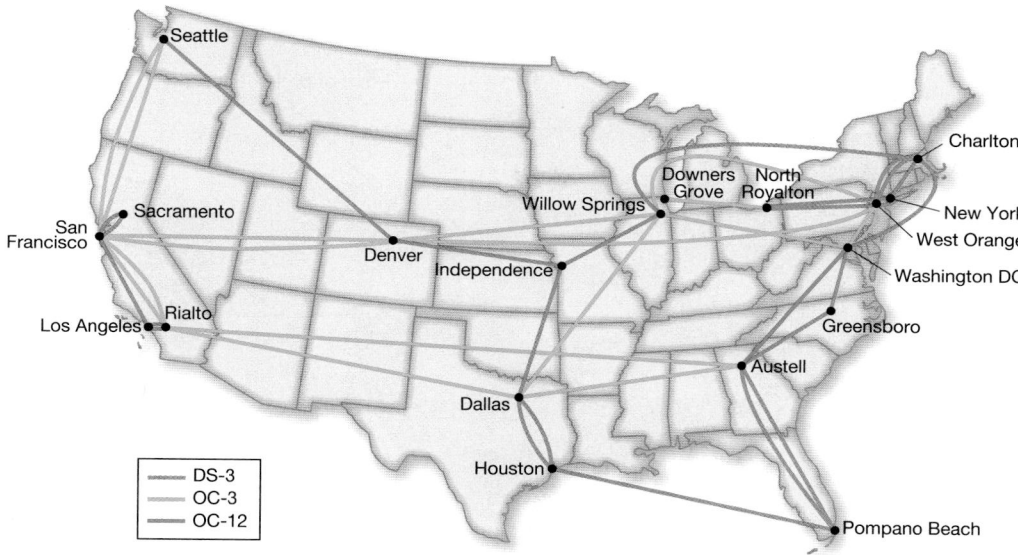

Figure 13.2 A Typical Internet Backbone Provided by a Single Company

Networking Components

Objective 13.2 *Explain how the Internet's networking components interact.*

How are computers connected to the Internet? As a "network of networks," the Internet is similar to the U.S. highway system, where smaller roads feed into larger, faster highways. The main paths of the Internet, along which data travels the fastest, are known collectively as the **Internet backbone**. The Internet backbone is a collection of large national and international networks, most of which are owned by commercial, educational, or government organizations. These backbone providers, which are required to connect to other backbone providers, have the fastest high-speed connections. Figure 13.2 shows a typical Internet backbone provided by a single company. Large U.S. companies that provide backbone connectivity include Verizon, AT&T, and Sprint.

How do the Internet service providers (ISPs) that form the Internet backbone communicate? A backbone is typically a high-speed fiber-optic line, designated as an **optical carrier (OC) line**. OC lines come in a range of speeds, from 0.052 Gbps for OC-1 to the fastest OC-768, which runs at almost 40 Gbps.

Backbone ISPs initially connected with T lines. A **T line** carried digital data over twisted-pair wires. T-1 lines, which were the first to be used, transmit data at a throughput rate of 1.544 Mbps. T-3 lines, which were developed later, transmit data at 45 Mbps.

The bandwidth of the connections between ISPs and end users depends on the amount of data traffic required. Whereas your home might connect to the Internet with cable or fiber-optic lines, the volume of Internet traffic at your college probably requires it to use an OC line to move data to the school's ISP. Large companies usually must connect to their ISPs using high-throughput OC lines.

How are ISPs connected to each other? ISPs like Verizon and Comcast are connected together through an **Internet exchange point (IXP)**. A typical IXP is made up of one or more network switches to which ISPs connect. As you'll recall from Chapter 7, switches are devices that send data on a specific route through a network. By connecting directly to each other through IXPs, networks can reduce their costs and improve the speed and efficiency with which data is exchanged.

How do individuals connect to an ISP? Individual Internet users enter an ISP through a **point of presence (POP)**, which is a bank of modems, servers, routers, and switches (see Figure 13.3) through which many users can connect to an ISP simultaneously. ISPs maintain multiple POPs throughout the geographic area they serve.

What type of network model does the Internet use? The majority of Internet communications follow the **client/server model** of network communications. The clients are devices such as computers, tablets, and smartphones that use browsers to request services such as web pages.

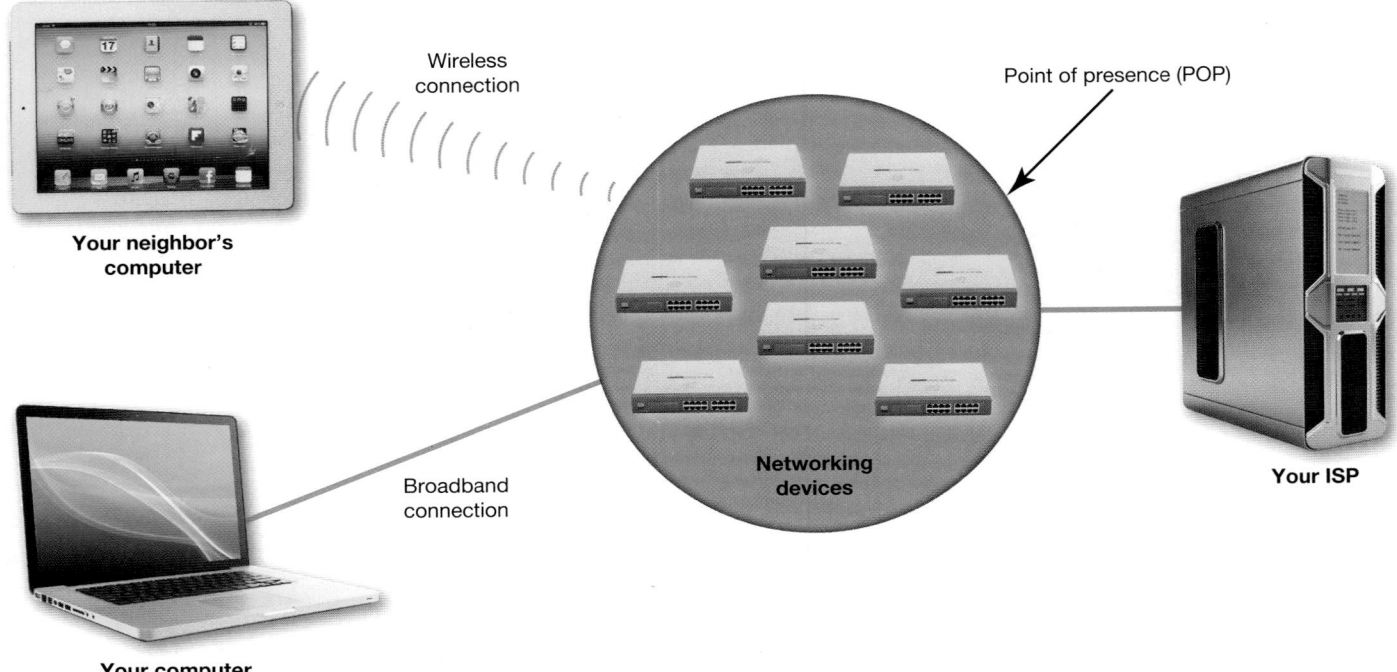

Figure 13.3 Home users connect to their ISPs through a single point of presence that can handle many simultaneous connections.
(Klaus Westermann/Agencja Fotograficzna Caro/Alamy Stock Photo, Ifong/Shutterstock Robert Hyrons/Alamy Stock Photo, Sashkin/Shutterstock)

Various types of servers from which clients can request services are deployed on the networks that make up the Internet:

- **Web servers**: computers that run specialized operating systems, enabling them to host web pages and other information and to provide requested information to clients.
- **Commerce servers**: computers that host software that enables users to buy goods and services over the web. These servers generally use special security protocols to protect sensitive information, such as credit card numbers, from being intercepted.
- **File servers**: computers that are deployed to provide remote storage space or to act as storehouses for files that users can download. Cloud service providers offering online storage services have a huge collection of file servers.

Data Transmission

Objective 13.3 *List and describe the Internet protocols used for data transmission.*

What is a protocol? Just like any other network, the Internet follows a standard set of rules to send information between computers. A **computer protocol** is the set of rules for exchanging electronic information. If the Internet is the information superhighway, then protocols are the rules of the road.

Bits&Bytes **A Free Cloud-Based Server for You**

Interested in trying out web application development but stop in your tracks when you think about setting up and running your own server? No longer! Head to Cloud9 (**c9.io**), where you can set up and run as many Ubuntu workspaces as you need. Each workspace is an easy-to-use Linux desktop that lives in the cloud and that you access through your browser. Use one workspace just to practice your skill on a Linux command line or use the languages Cloud9 supports, like Ruby, C++, or PHP, to start coding your own server in the cloud.

Why were Internet protocols developed? The idea of a protocol is that anyone can use it on his or her computer system and be able to communicate with any other computer using the same protocol. The most common Internet tasks—communicating, collaborating, creating content, seeking information, and shopping—are all executed the same way on any system following accepted Internet protocols.

When common communication protocols are followed, networks can communicate even if they have different topologies, transmission media, or operating systems. To accomplish the early goals of the Internet, protocols needed to be written and agreed on by users. Each protocol had to be an **open system**, meaning its design would be made public for access by any interested party. This was in direct opposition to the **proprietary system** (private system) model that was the norm at the time.

Were there problems developing an open system Internet protocol? Agreeing on common standards was relatively easy. The tough part was developing a new method of communication because the technology available in the 1960s—circuit switching—was inefficient for computer communication.

Circuit Switching

Why don't we use circuit switching to connect two computers? Circuit switching has been used since the early days of the telephone for establishing communication. In **circuit switching**, a dedicated connection is formed between two points (such as two people on phones), and the connection remains active for the duration of the transmission. This method of communication is important when communications must be received in the order in which they're sent, like phone conversations.

When applied to computers, however, circuit switching is inefficient. As a computer processor performs the operations necessary to complete a task, it transmits data in a group, or burst. The processor then begins working on its next task and ceases to communicate with output devices or other networks until it's ready to transmit data in the next burst. Circuit switching is inefficient for computers because either the circuit would have to remain open, and therefore unavailable to any other system, with long periods of inactivity, or it would have to be reestablished for each burst.

Packet Switching

If they don't use circuit switching, what do computers use to communicate? **Packet switching** is the communications methodology that makes computer communication efficient. Packet switching doesn't require a dedicated communications circuit to be maintained. With packet switching, data is broken into smaller chunks called **packets** (or **data packets**). The packets are sent over various routes at the same time. When the packets reach their destination, they're reassembled by the receiving computer. This technology resulted from one of the original goals of creating the Internet: If an Internet node is disabled or destroyed, the data can travel an alternate route to its destination.

What information does a packet contain? Packet contents vary, depending on the protocol being followed. At a minimum, all packets must contain the following:

1. An address to which the packet is being sent
2. The address from where the packet originates
3. The data that's being transmitted, and
4. Reassembly instructions, if the original data is split between multiple packets

Sending a packet is like sending a letter. Assume you're sending a large amount of information in written format from your home in Philadelphia to your aunt in San Diego. The information is too large to fit in one small envelope, so you mail three different envelopes to your aunt. Each envelope includes your aunt's address, your return address, and the information being sent inside it. The pages of the letters in each envelope are numbered so that your aunt will know in which order to read them.

Each envelope may not find its way to San Diego by the same route. However, even if the letters are routed through different post offices, they'll all eventually arrive in your aunt's mailbox. Your aunt will then reassemble the message in the right order and read it. The process of sending a message through the Internet works in much the same way. This process is illustrated in Figure 13.4, which traces an e-mail message sent from a computer in Philadelphia to a computer in San Diego.

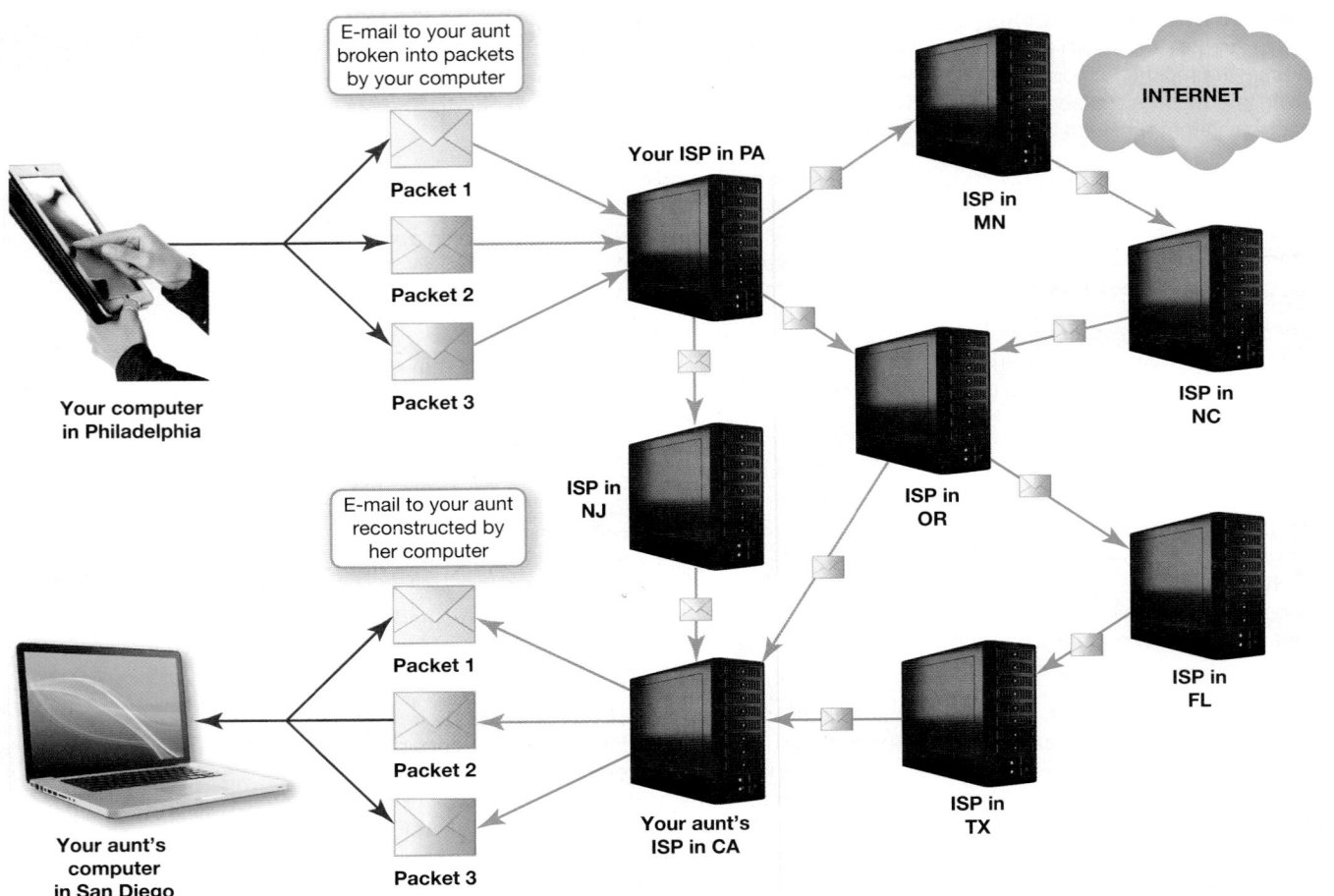

E-mail to your aunt
broken into packets
by your computer

Packet 1

Packet 2

Packet 3

Your computer
in Philadelphia

Your ISP in PA

INTERNET

ISP in
MN

ISP in
NC

ISP in
OR

ISP in
NJ

E-mail to your aunt
reconstructed by
her computer

Packet 1

Packet 2

Your aunt's
computer
in San Diego

Packet 3

Your aunt's
ISP in CA

ISP in
TX

ISP in
FL

Figure 13.4 Each packet sent through the Internet can follow its own route to its final destination. Sequential numbering of packets ensures they're reassembled in the correct order at their destination. *(Nikada/E+/Getty Images, Ifong/Shutterstock, Adventtr/E+/Getty Images)*

Why do packets take different routes, and how do they decide which route to use? The routers that connect ISPs with each other monitor traffic and decide on the most efficient route for packets to take to their destination. The router works in the same way a police officer does while directing traffic. To ensure a smooth flow of traffic, police officers are deployed in areas of congestion, directing drivers along alternate routes to their destinations. The Try This exercise in this chapter uses the Windows utility tracert to show you the details on the exact route your request takes to the destination server.

TCP/IP

What protocol does the Internet use for transmitting data? Although many protocols are available on the Internet, the main suite of protocols used is **TCP/IP**. The suite is named after the original two protocols that were developed for the Internet: the **Transmission Control Protocol (TCP)** and the **Internet Protocol (IP)**. Although most people think that the TCP/IP suite consists of only two protocols, it actually comprises many interrelated protocols, the most important of which are listed in Figure 13.5.

Which particular protocol actually sends the information? The Internet Protocol (IP) is responsible for sending the information from one computer to another. The IP is like a postal worker who takes a letter (a packet of information) that was mailed (created by the sending computer) and sends it on to another post office (router), which in turn routes it to the addressee (the receiving computer). The postal worker never knows whether the recipient actually receives the letter. The only thing the postal worker knows is that the letter was handed off to an appropriate post office that will assist in completing the delivery of the letter.

Figure 13.5 TCP/IP Protocol Suite—Main Protocols

Internet Protocol (IP)	Sends data between computers on the Internet
Transmission Control Protocol (TCP)	Prepares data for transmission and provides for error checking and resending of lost data
User Datagram Protocol (UDP)	Prepares data for transmission; lacks resending capabilities
File Transfer Protocol (FTP)	Enables files to be downloaded to a computer or uploaded to other computers
Telnet	Enables user to log in to a remote computer and work on it as if sitting in front of it
Hypertext Transfer Protocol (HTTP) and HTTP Secure (HTTPS)	Transfers Hypertext Markup Language (HTML) data from servers to browsers; HTTPS is an encrypted protocol for secure transmissions
Simple Mail Transfer Protocol (SMTP)	Used for transmission of e-mail messages across the Internet
Dynamic Host Configuration Protocol (DHCP)	Takes a pool of IP addresses and shares them with hosts on a network on an as-needed basis
Real-time Transport Protocol (RTP)	Network protocol for delivering audio and video over IP

 Internet Identity

Each computer, server, or device connected to the Internet is required to have a unique identification number, or IP address. However, because humans are better at remembering and working with words than with numbers, the numeric IP addresses were given more "human," word-based addresses. Thus, domain names were born. In this section, we'll look at both IP addresses and domain names.

IP Addresses

Objective 13.4 *Explain how each device connected to the Internet is assigned a unique address.*

What is an IP address? You'll recall from Chapter 3 that an **IP address** is a unique identification number that defines each computer, service, or other device connected to the Internet. IP addresses fulfill the same function as street addresses. For example, to send a letter to Rosa Juarez's house in Metamora, Illinois, you have to know her address. Rosa might live at 456 Walnut Street, which isn't a unique address because many towns have a Walnut Street, but 456 Walnut Street, Metamora, IL 61548 is a unique address.

The numeric zip code is the unique postal identification for a specific geographical area. IP addresses must be registered with the **Internet Corporation for Assigned Names and Numbers (ICANN)** to ensure they're unique and haven't been assigned to other users. ICANN is responsible for allocating IP addresses to network administrators.

What does an IP address look like? A typical IP address is expressed as follows:

197.169.73.63

An IP address in this form is called a **dotted decimal number** (or a **dotted quad**). The same IP address in binary form is as follows:

11000101.10101001.01001001.00111111

Each of the four numbers in a dotted decimal number is referred to as an **octet**. This is because each number would have eight positions when shown in binary form. Because 32 positions are available for IP address values (four octets with eight positions each), IP addresses are considered 32-bit numbers. A position is filled by either a 1 or a 0, resulting in 256 (which is 2^8) possible values for each octet, from 0 to 255. The entire 32-bit address can represent 4,294,967,296 values (or 2^{32}), which is quite a few Internet addresses!

 Helpdesk MyLab IT®

Understanding IP Addresses, Domain Names, and Protocols

In this Helpdesk, you'll play the role of a helpdesk staffer, fielding questions about which data transmissions and protocols the Internet uses and why IP addresses and domain names are important for Internet communications.

Curious as to what your IP address is? Go to Google and type "what is my ip" (see Figure 13.6). Google will show your IP address at the top of the search results. If you want additional information, such as the geographical location of an IP address or even the telephone area code associated with it, visit **whatismyipaddress.com**.

Figure 13.6 You can find your IP address using Google. (*Courtesy Google Inc.*)

Will we ever run out of IP addresses? When the original IP addressing scheme, **Internet Protocol version 4 (IPv4)**, was created in 1981, no one foresaw the explosive growth of the Internet in the 1990s. Four billion values for an address field seemed like enough to last forever. However, as the Internet grew, it quickly became apparent that we were going to run out of IP addresses.

Why do we need so many IP addresses? Not only laptops need an IP address. The **Internet of Things (IoT)** is a term for the explosive growth of Internet-enabled devices. Appliances, switches, light bulbs, and smoke detectors all now send and receive messages over the Internet. That means each one needs a unique IP address. As each electronic device begins to have the ability to pull information from the Internet and push out messages, expect changes in our daily lives. Imagine parking lots that know how many spaces are empty and text you directions to a specific free spot. Medical devices will monitor your health and automatically book a doctor appointment when you begin to fall ill. The data we collect will be translated quickly and invisibly into the actions we need to take in the physical world.

How did Internet addresses change to allow more of them? Internet Protocol version 6 (IPv6) is an IP addressing scheme developed by the IETF to make IP addresses longer, thereby providing more available IP addresses. IPv6 uses 128-bit addressing instead of 32-bit addressing. An IPv6 address would have the following format:

$$XXXX:XXXX:XXXX:XXXX:XXXX:XXXX:XXXX:XXXX$$

Each digit X is a **hexadecimal digit**. Hexadecimal is a base-16 number system, and each hexadecimal digit is one of 16 possible values: 0–9 or A–F. Hex addressing provides a much larger field size, which will make available a much larger number of IP addresses (approximately 340 followed by 36 zeros). This should provide a virtually unlimited supply of IP addresses and will allow many

The Amazon Dash button is one example of how the Internet of Things is impacting daily life.

The Dash button can be configured to send an order for a specific product in to Amazon with just a click, so sticking a Dash button in the spot where you'll remember you're running low makes it easy to keep items in stock. Click the Dash button and the product shows up on your doorstep the next day. You can buy a Dash button from Amazon for a wide range of household and grocery products.

Hacks already have appeared to allow a Dash button to do more than just order from Amazon. After all, a Dash button is really just a battery and a Wi-Fi radio. When you push the button it wakes up, jumps on your home network, and sends a message to an Amazon server. You can watch for the Dash to join your network and use that as a trigger for your own events, like updating a number in a Google spreadsheet. Want to keep track of how many times you run the dishwasher in a week? Hacks to the Dash button let you do just that.

Amazon Dash buttons order products with a single click. (*James W Copeland/Shutterstock*)

different kinds of non-PC devices, such as cell phones and home appliances, to join the Internet more easily in the future. All modern operating systems can handle both IPv4 and IPv6 addresses. Although the majority of routing on the Internet still takes place using IPv4 addresses, the conversion to IPv6 addressing should accelerate now that we're running out of IPv4 addresses.

How does my device get an IP address? IP addresses are assigned either statically or dynamically:

- **Static addressing** means that the IP address for a computer never changes and is most likely assigned manually by a network administrator or an ISP.
- **Dynamic addressing**, in which your computer is assigned a temporary address from an available pool of IP addresses, is more common.

A connection to an ISP could use either method. If your ISP uses static addressing, then you were assigned an IP address when you applied for your service and had to configure your computer manually to use that address. More often, though, an ISP assigns a computer a dynamic IP address, as shown in Figure 13.7.

Sound Byte MyLab IT®

Creating Web Pages with Squarespace

In this Sound Byte, you'll use Squarespace, an online web page development tool, to design a modern interactive web page with no need for coding or web development tools.

Day 1

Connecting to ISP

Your computer

Connected, your IP is ... 192.168.1.2

Your ISP

Day 2

Connecting to ISP

Your computer

Connected, your IP is ... 192.168.8.7

Your ISP

Figure 13.7 With dynamic IP addressing, your IP address changes every time you connect to the Internet. *(Ifong/Shutterstock, Juffin/ DigitalVision Vectors/Getty Images)*

How exactly are dynamic addresses assigned? Dynamic addressing is normally handled by the **Dynamic Host Configuration Protocol (DHCP)**, which belongs to the TCP/IP protocol suite. DHCP takes a pool of IP addresses and shares them with hosts on the network on an as-needed basis. ISPs don't need to maintain a pool of IP addresses for all their subscribers because not everyone is logged on to the Internet at one time. Thus, when a user logs on to an ISP's server, the DHCP server assigns that user an IP address for the duration of the session. Similarly, when you log on to your computer at work in the morning, DHCP assigns an IP address to your computer. These temporary IP addresses may or may not be the same from session to session.

What are the benefits of dynamic addressing? Although having a static address would seem to be convenient, dynamic addressing provides a more secure environment by keeping hackers out of computer systems. Imagine how hard it would be for burglars to find your home if you changed your address every day!

Dig Deeper Connection-Oriented Versus Connectionless Protocols

The Internet Protocol is responsible only for sending packets on their way. The packets are created by either the TCP or the **User Datagram Protocol (UDP)**. You don't decide whether to use TCP or UDP. The choice of protocol is made for you by the developers of the computer programs you're using or by the other protocols that interact with your data packet (such as those listed in Figure 13.5).

As explained earlier, data transmission between computers is highly efficient if connections don't need to be established (as in circuit switching). However, there are benefits to maintaining a connection, such as reduced data loss. The difference between TCP and UDP is that TCP is a *connection-oriented* protocol, whereas UDP is a *connectionless* protocol.

A **connection-oriented protocol** requires two computers to exchange control packets, thereby setting up the parameters of the data-exchange session, before sending packets that contain data. This process is referred to as **handshaking**. TCP uses a process called a **three-way handshake** to establish a connection, as shown in Figure 13.8:

1. Your computer establishes a connection to the ISP and announces it has e-mail to send.
2. The ISP server responds that it's ready to receive the e-mail.
3. Your computer then acknowledges the ready state of the server and begins to transmit the e-mail.

A **connectionless protocol** doesn't require any type of connection to be established or maintained between two computers exchanging information. Just like a letter that's mailed, the data packets are sent without notifying the receiving computer or receiving any acknowledgment that the data was received. UDP is the Internet's connectionless protocol.

Besides establishing a connection, TCP provides for reliable data transfer, ensuring that all the data packets are delivered to the receiver free from errors and in the correct order. TCP achieves reliable data transfer by using acknowledgments and providing for the retransmission of data, as shown in Figure 13.9.

Assume that two systems, X and Y, have established a connection. When Y receives a data packet that it can read from X, it sends back a **positive acknowledgment (ACK)**. If X doesn't receive an ACK in an appropriate period of time, it resends the packet. If the packet is unreadable (damaged in transit), Y sends a **negative acknowledgment (NAK)** to X, indicating the packet wasn't received in understandable form. X then retransmits that packet. Acknowledgments ensure that the receiver has received a complete set of data packets. If a packet is unable to get through after being resent several times, the user is generally presented with an error message, indicating the communications were unsuccessful.

You may wonder why you wouldn't always want to use a protocol that provides for reliable data transfer. On the Internet, speed is often more important than accuracy. For certain

STEP 1:
I want to send e-mail.

STEP 2:
Okay, I'm ready to receive.

STEP 3:
Here's the e-mail message for Aunt Sally.

Your ISP's server

communication using a three-way handshake. *(Lfong/Shutterstock, Juffin/*

Domain Names

Objective 13.5 *Discuss how a numeric IP address is changed into a readable name.*

I've been on the Internet, so why have I never seen IP addresses? As you learned in Chapter 3, a domain name is a name that takes the place of an IP address, making it easier for people to remember. For example, **google.com** is a domain name. The server where Google's main website is deployed has an IP address (such as 173.194.205.101, but it's much easier for you to remember to tell your browser to go to **google.com**.

How are domains organized? Domains are organized by level. As you'll recall from Chapter 3, the portion of the domain name after the dot is the top-level domain (TLD). The TLDs are standardized pools such as .com and .org established by ICANN (see Figure 13.10).

applications (such as e-mail), it's important that your message be delivered completely and accurately. For streaming multimedia, it's not always important to have every frame delivered accurately because most streaming media formats provide for correction of errors caused by data loss. However, it's extremely important for streaming media to be delivered at a high rate of speed. Therefore, a protocol such as TCP, which uses handshakes and acknowledgments, would probably not be appropriate for transmitting a movie trailer over the Internet; in this instance, the Real-time Transport Protocol (RTP) would be better.

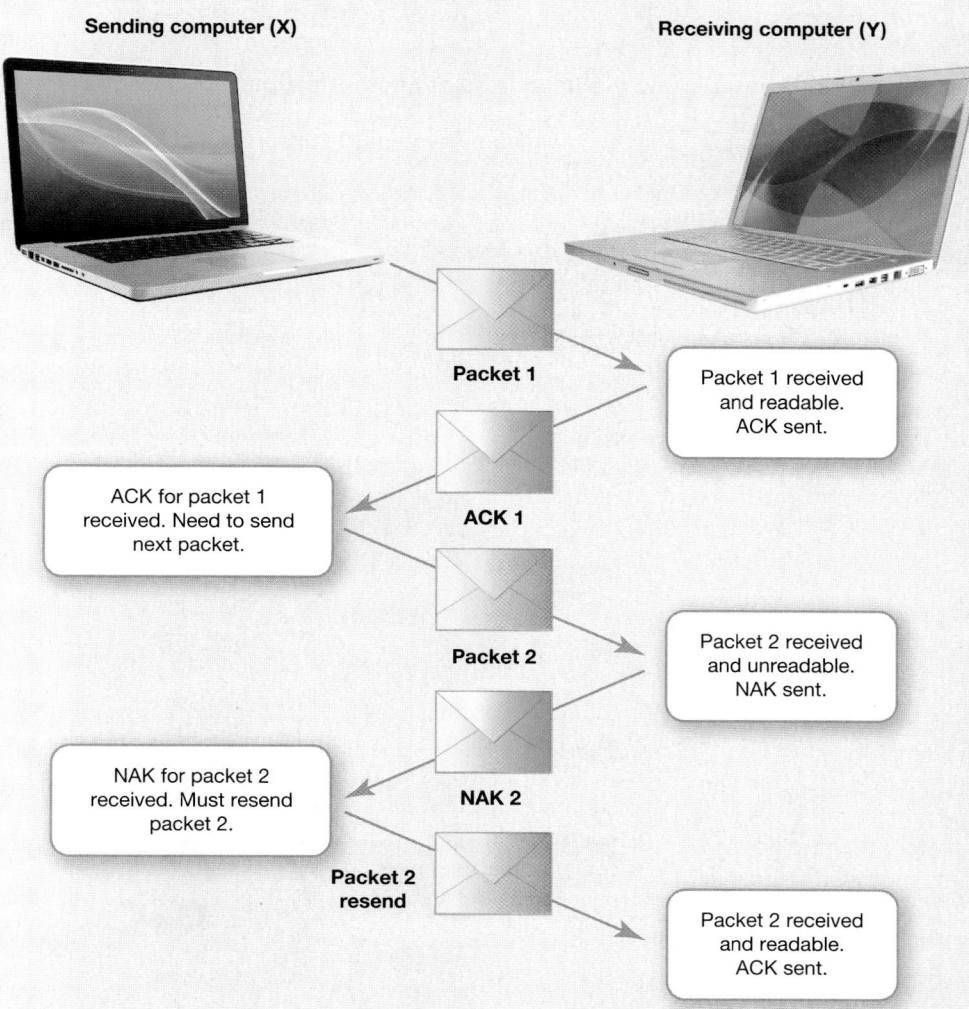

Figure 13.9 Positive (ACK) and negative (NAK) packet acknowledgments provide reliable data transfer. *(Lfong/Shutterstock, LdF/E+/Getty Images)*

Sending computer (X)

Receiving computer (Y)

Packet 1

Packet 1 received and readable. ACK sent.

ACK for packet 1 received. Need to send next packet.

ACK 1

Packet 2

Packet 2 received and unreadable. NAK sent.

NAK for packet 2 received. Must resend packet 2.

NAK 2

Packet 2 resend

Packet 2 received and readable. ACK sent.

.com
.net
.tv .info
.int
.org
.gov
.biz
.edu
.eu

DOMAIN NAMES

Within each top-level domain are many second-level domains. A **second-level domain** is a domain that's directly below a top-level domain. For example, in **dropbox.com**, dropbox is the second-level domain to the .com TLD. A second-level domain needs to be unique within its own TLD but not necessarily unique to all top-level domains. For example, mynewIdeaWebsite.com and mynewIdeaWebsite.org could be registered as separate domain names.

Who controls domain name registration? ICANN assigns companies or organizations to manage domain name registration. Because names can't be duplicated within a TLD, one company is assigned to oversee each TLD and to maintain a listing of all registered domains. VeriSign is the current ICANN-accredited domain name registrar for the .com and .net domains. VeriSign provides a database that lists all the registered .com and .net domains and their contact information. You can look up any .com or .net domain at Network Solutions (**networksolutions.com**) to see whether it's registered and, if so, who owns it.

Country-specific domains (such as .au for Australia) are controlled by groups in those countries. You can find a complete list of country-code TLDs on the Internet Assigned Numbers Authority website (**iana.org**).

Figure 13.10 The number of generic top-level domains has grown to include .museum and .job. ICANN is responsible for organizing TLD names. *(Rondabroc.com/Fotolia)*

How does my computer know the IP address of another computer? When you enter a URL in your browser, your computer converts the URL to an IP address. To do this, your computer consults a database maintained on a **domain name system (DNS) server** that functions like a phone book for the Internet.

Your ISP's web server has a default DNS server (one that's convenient to contact) that it goes to when it needs to translate a URL to an IP address (illustrated in Figure 13.11).

It uses the following steps:

1. Your browser requests information from a website (for example, ABC.com).
2. Your ISP doesn't know the address of ABC.com, so your ISP must request the address from its own default DNS server.
3. The default DNS server doesn't know the IP address of ABC.com either, so it queries one of the 13 root DNS servers maintained throughout the Internet. Each **root DNS server** knows the location of all the DNS servers that contain the master listings for an entire top-level domain.

Bits&Bytes   Server in the Cloud

If you want to build a web application (a program that allows a user to send and receive information to a web browser), you may start by buying and maintaining a server computer in your home to host it. That means you have to get up in the middle of the night if the hard drive crashes, or risk angry user e-mails in the morning! What if your site becomes wildly popular and suddenly you need to expand to three or four servers to handle the load?

Using the free Google App Engine service avoids such problems. The server for your application is hosted by Google and

is automatically scaled up or down as the demand for it changes. Using App Engine frees you from the worries of maintaining hardware, too. And you can test out your ideas and then go live to users at no cost and only pay for services once your usage begins to take off. Your application can live at a domain name you make up, or you can serve your app from an available name off the **appspot.com** domain. Explore more about Google App Engine at **cloud.google.com/appengine**.

STEP 1: Your browser requests information from ABC.com.

STEP 2: Your ISP's server asks the DNS server to turn that into an IP address.

STEP 3: If the DNS server doesn't know the IP address, it asks the root server for that IP address.

Your computer

Your ISP's web server

Your ISP's default DNS server

Root server for .com domain

STEP 6: Your computer routes request to correct IP address.

STEP 5: The DNS server stores that IP address so it will remember it next time. It then passes it along to the web server.

STEP 4: The root server provides the IP address.

Figure 13.11   DNS Servers in Action *(Ifong/Shutterstock, Juffin/DigitalVision Vectors/Getty Images, Sashkin/Shutterstock, Alex Mit/Shutterstock)*

4. The root server provides the default DNS server with the appropriate IP address of ABC.com.
5. The default DNS server stores the correct IP address for ABC.com for future reference and returns it to your ISP's web server.
6. Your computer then routes its request to ABC.com and stores the IP address in cache for later use.

How can you make your browser translate IP addresses faster? The **Internet cache** is a section of your hard drive that stores information you may need again, such as IP addresses and frequently accessed web pages. The caching of domain name addresses also takes place in domain name system (DNS) servers. This helps speed up Internet access time because a DNS server doesn't have to query master DNS servers for top-level domains (TLDs) constantly.

However, caches have limited storage space, so entries are held in the cache only for a fixed period of time and are then deleted. The time component associated with cache retention is known as the time to live (TTL). Without caches, surfing the Internet would take a lot longer.

Remember you can't always tell whether your browser is loading the current version of a page from the web or a copy from your Internet cache. If a website contains time-sensitive information (such as a snow day alert on a college website), clicking the browser's Reload or Refresh button will ensure that the most current copy of the page loads into your browser.

Before moving on to Part 2:

1. Watch Chapter Overview Video 13.1.
2. Then take the Check Your Understanding quiz.

Check Your Understanding // Review & Practice

For a quick review to see what you've learned so far, answer the following questions.

multiple choice

1. The Internet is managed by
   a. the U.S. government.
   b. no one.
   c. the National Science Foundation.
   d. several non-profit organizations.

2. In the client/server model, clients are phones or computers and servers are computers
   a. with software allowing you to make purchases.
   b. hosting web pages.
   c. that are storehouses for files.
   d. all of the above

3. Packet switching sends information between two points
   a. by finding one route between the two points and sending the data.
   b. by breaking it into small chunks and sending the chunks across different routes.
   c. by encrypting the data, then sending it.
   d. differently for each company using it.

4. The rise of the Internet of Things has meant
   a. we need longer IP addresses than are available in IPv4.
   b. there are more machines with wireless network adapters.
   c. light bulbs can join your Wi-Fi network at home.
   d. all of the above

5. A(n) _____ takes the place of an IP address because it's easier for humans to recall than a long string of numbers.
   a. DNS
   b. domain name
   c. XML
   d. HTML

 Go to **MyLab IT** to take an autograded version of the *Check Your Understanding* review and to find all media resources for the chapter.

TechBytes Weekly Go to TechBytes Weekly for current technology news and discussion questions!

Try This

Ping Me

Several programs that help you understand networking are part of your Windows operating system but aren't on your desktop. In this Try This, we'll use the **ping command** and the **tracert command** to get some detailed info about the Internet. For more step-by-step instructions, watch the Try This video.

Step 1 In Windows, in the search box, type **command**. Click **Command Prompt** from the search results.

Step 2 Type **ping google.com**, and press **Enter**. Ping is a utility that sends a packet of information to a specific computer and measures the time it takes to travel a round trip to the destination and back. You can use ping to test an IP address or a computer name. Ping will send a few packets and then report back to you the minimum, maximum, and average round-trip times in milliseconds.

Step 3 Now let's try another utility, tracert. Type **tracert google.com**, and press **Enter**. Tracert traces the route that the packet takes from your computer to the destination computer and back. Here, we see it starting off on a home system and jumping on to a computer that ISP Verizon operates in the Philadelphia area. The packet makes one more hop on the Verizon system, then jumps onto backbone network IAD8.ALTER.NET, and then begins to step down to local computers until it reaches Google [74.125.228.6]. Tracert displays the total number of hops to reach the destination. Here, we see it took 10 hops to reach **google.com**. It also shows the round-trip time for a packet to travel to each hop. Tracert sends three packets to each point and reports the round-trip time for each one. Note that the specifics you see when you run tracert will be different because you are starting at a different location.

> The packet starts at a home computer, 192.168.1.1.

> Here, the packet has moved onto part of the Internet backbone, IAD8.ALTER.NET.

> The first column tells which hop the packet is on in its journey.

(Windows 10, Microsoft Corporation)

Step 4 Now let's try to reach a location far away from home base. At the prompt, type **tracert www.cityoflondon.gov.uk**, and press **Enter**. Here, a computer in Philadelphia is trying to reach a computer in London, **cityoflondon.gov.uk**. The packet moves to a Verizon computer in Philadelphia, then travels to Washington D.C. Next, there is a much longer trip time, 85 ms. This is probably as the packet

> Hops 9 and 10 take 85 ms each. These are probably traversing the ocean.

> Here is the destination IP address, 86.54.118.84 (CityofLondon.gov.uk). After that, the firewall of CityofLondon.gov.uk begins to reject the packets.

(Windows 10, Microsoft Corporation)

moves across the Atlantic Ocean. The packet finally reaches **cityoflondon.gov.uk** [86.54.118.84]. [Note: You may see some timeouts along the way. You can exit the tracert command by hitting Ctrl-C.] By using ping and tracert, you can see exactly where a connection is failing.

Make: An Earthquake Detector

Want your apps to talk to other computers and grab current information from them? Web services allow you to do just that. Thousands of free web services are available to you, like one that shows current stock prices or one that tells the most recent earthquake activity.

In this exercise, you'll continue your mobile app development by using the Web component of the Connectivity drawer in **App Inventor** to have a conversation with a web service. You will send a request for the specific information you want, then process it with the **when Web1 .GotText** event handler.

Using web services, your app can talk with other computers and collect useful information.

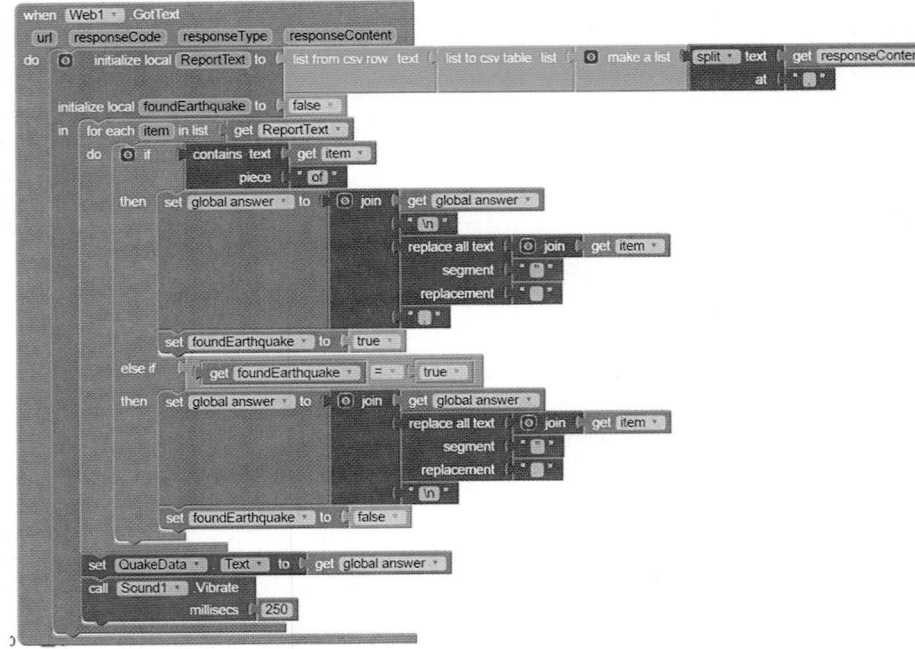

(Copyright MIT, used with permission.)

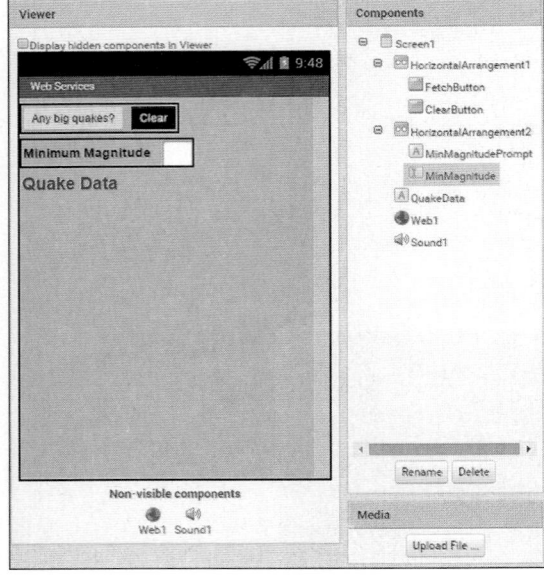

(Copyright MIT, used with permission.)

For the instructions for this exercise, go to MyLab IT.

Coding and Communicating on the Internet

Learning Outcome 13.2   **You will be able to describe the web technologies used to develop web applications.**

The web uses special languages such as HTML and protocols such as HTTP to facilitate communication between computers that use different system and application software. Communication between any two points on the Internet is possible because of HTML and communication protocols. In this part of the chapter, we'll explore these topics.

 Web Technologies

Let's examine in more detail the programming languages and communication protocols that support the Internet. We introduced some of these ideas in Chapter 10. Now we'll explore them in a bit more depth.

Web Development

Objective 13.6   *Compare and contrast a variety of web development languages.*

Websites require more than just simple formatting commands. They are interactive and display high-quality audio and video. This is all controlled with a variety of development tools and languages.

HTML

How are web pages formatted? Web pages are text documents formatted using HTML (Hypertext Markup Language). HTML isn't a programming language; rather, it's a set of rules for marking up blocks of text so that a browser knows how to display them.

Blocks of text in HTML documents are surrounded by pairs of **HTML tags** (such as <b> and </b>, which indicate bolding). HTML tags surround and define HTML content. Each pair of tags and the text between them are collectively referred to as an **element**. The elements are interpreted by the browser, and appropriate effects are applied to the text. The following is an element from an HTML document:

```
<i>This should be italicized.</i>
```

The browser would display this element as:

This should be italicized.

The first tag, <i>, tells the browser that the text following it should be italicized. The ending </i> tag indicates that the browser should stop applying italics. Note that multiple tags can be combined in a single element:

```
<b><i>This should be bolded and italicized.</i></b>
```

The browser would display this element as:

This should be bolded and italicized.

Tags for creating hyperlinks appear as follows:

```
<a href="www.pearsonhighered.com">Pearson Higher Education</a>
```

The code <a href="www.pearsonhighered.com"> defines the link's destination. The </a> tag is the anchor tag and creates a link to another resource on the web. Here, the link is to the **www.pearsonhighered.com** web page. The text between the open and close of the anchor tag, Pearson Higher Education, is the link label. The link label is the text (or image) that's displayed on the web page as clickable text for the hyperlink.

Web pages are a collection of types of files. There is the HTML file that governs formatting and basic structure, the CSS file that refines the formatting, and often a set of JavaScript code that runs animations or other interactivity on the page. CodePen (codepen.io) is a web-based platform for working with all three kinds of files at once. As a community, developers post code for pages or effects they have created so you can use them to expand your skills.

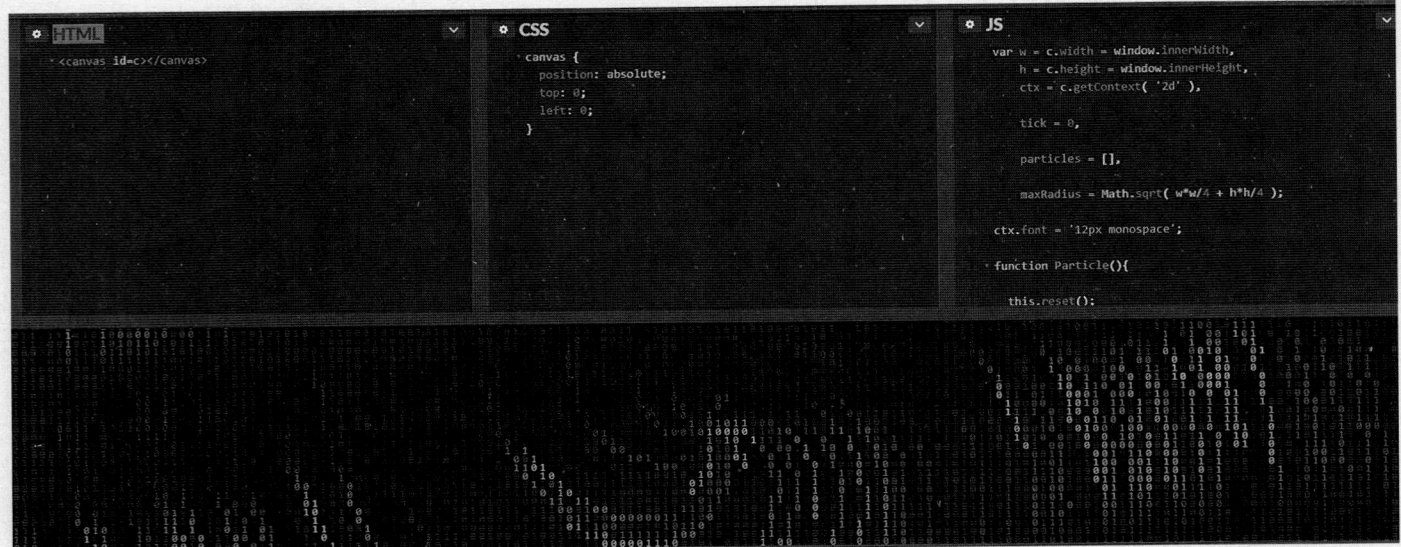

Tools like CodePen make it easier to develop client-side web application code. *(Courtesy of CodePen Inc., Reprinted by permission.)*

How do I see the HTML coding of a web page? HTML documents are merely text documents with tags applied to them. If you want to look at the HTML coding behind any web page, just right-click and select View Source from the shortcut menu, and the HTML code for that page will display, as shown in Figure 13.12.

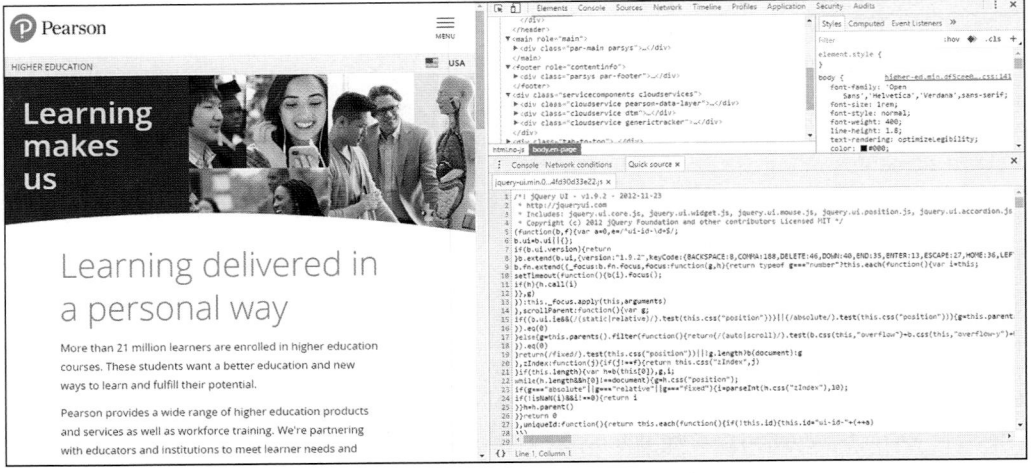

Figure 13.12 You can view the source code of a website using built-in browser tools.
> *In Chrome, select **More tools**, then select **Developer tools**. (Screenshot of Pearson Higher Education website, Pearson Education, Inc.)*

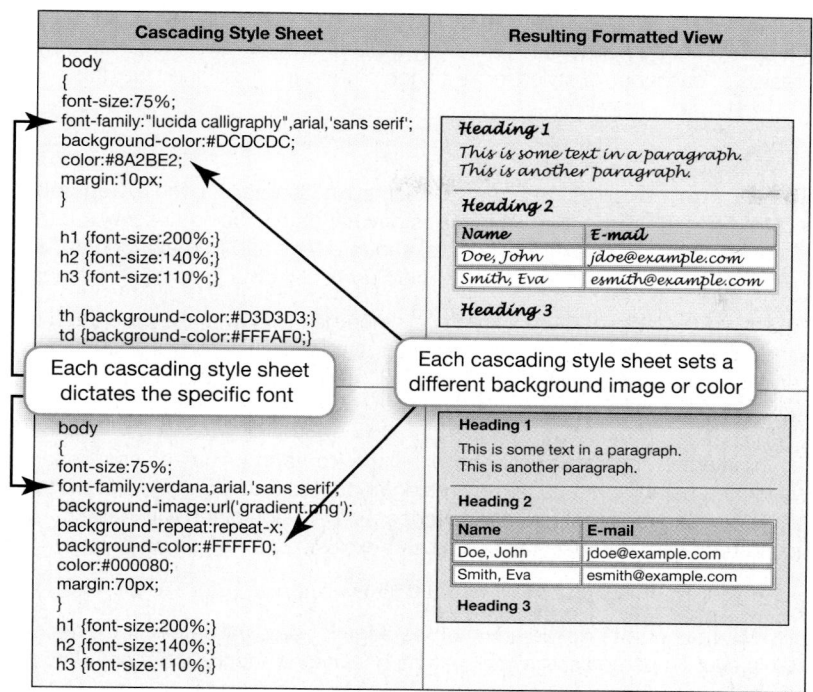

Cascading Style Sheet	Resulting Formatted View

```
body
{
font-size:75%;
font-family:"lucida calligraphy",arial,'sans serif';
background-color:#DCDCDC;
color:#8A2BE2;
margin:10px;
}

h1 {font-size:200%;}
h2 {font-size:140%;}
h3 {font-size:110%;}

th {background-color:#D3D3D3;}
td {background-color:#FFFAF0;}
```

Each cascading style sheet dictates the specific font

Each cascading style sheet sets a different background image or color

Heading 1

This is some text in a paragraph.
This is another paragraph.

Heading 2

Name	*E-mail*
Doe, John	*jdoe@example.com*
Smith, Eva	*esmith@example.com*

Heading 3

```
body
{
font-size:75%;
font-family:verdana,arial,'sans serif';
background-image:url('gradient.png');
background-repeat:repeat-x;
background-color:#FFFFF0;
color:#000080;
margin:70px;
}
h1 {font-size:200%;}
h2 {font-size:140%;}
h3 {font-size:110%;}
```

Heading 1

This is some text in a paragraph.
This is another paragraph.

Heading 2

Name	E-mail
Doe, John	jdoe@example.com
Smith, Eva	esmith@example.com

Heading 3

Figure 13.13 Cascading style sheets allow developers to create formatting templates. Just as all the pages of this book have a similar look and feel, one style sheet can control the formatting of many web pages.

What is the current HTML standard? As we discussed in Chapter 10, HTML5 is the current version of the HTML standard. HTML5 modernizes a number of features in HTML, such as:

- Reducing the need for external plug-ins (like Flash)
- Supporting better error handling
- Supporting advanced animation and audio effects
- Making it easier to draw graphics

To see an example of what HTML5 makes possible in a browser, play with the drawing tool at **muro.deviantart.com**.

How can developers easily change the formatting of HTML elements? A **cascading style sheet (CSS)** is a list of rules that defines in one single location how to display HTML elements. Style rules enable a web developer to define a kind of formatting for each HTML element and apply it to all those elements on a set of web pages. Essentially, a template is created on which the formatting for many web pages within a site will be based. When a global change is necessary, the developer only needs to change the style on the style sheet, and all the elements in the web document will update automatically (see Figure 13.13).

For example, a web page has an <h1> heading tag, and all <h1> tags in the web page are formatted with a white background and an orange border. Before cascading style sheets, if you wanted to change the border color from orange to yellow, you had to change the border color of each individual <h1> tag. With cascading style sheets, the change from orange to yellow needs to happen only once on the style sheet; all the <h1> tags on the web pages then update to yellow without individual changes needing to be made.

Where does the cascading come in? In web documents, there are different layers of styles:

- External: stored in a separate file
- Embedded: stored inside the current HTML document
- Inline: stored within a single line inside the HTML document

Therefore, it's possible that different rules can be created for the same type of element located in different places (external, embedded, or inline). In other words, in an external style sheet, there might be a rule that defines the background color for all paragraphs as blue. In an embedded style sheet, a rule for the background color for all paragraphs might be white. And in an inline style sheet, the background color might be light pink. Eventually, all these style sheets must be merged to form one style sheet for the document. This creates conflicts among rules. Therefore, each type of rule is understood to have a specific weight so that when the rules are collected and merged, the rule or style with a higher weight overrides the rule or style with a lower weight. This hierarchy of competing styles creates a "cascade" of styles ranked according to their assigned weights.

XML and JSON

How is XML different from HTML? As you learned in Chapter 10, the **eXtensible Markup Language (XML)** describes the content in terms of what data is being described rather than how it's to be displayed. Instead of being locked into standard tags and formats for data, users can build their own markup languages to accommodate particular data formats and needs.

For example, say you want to capture a credit card number. In HTML, the paragraph tags (<p> and </p>) are used to define text and numeric elements. Almost any text or graphic can fall between these tags and be treated as a paragraph. The HTML code could appear as:

```
<p>1234567890123456</p>
```

The browser will interpret the data contained within the <p> and </p> tags as a separate paragraph. However, the paragraph tags tell us nothing about the data contained within them. A better approach lies in creating tags that actually describe the data contained within them. Using XML, we could create a "credit card number" tag that's used exclusively for credit card data:

```
<credit_card_number>1234567890123456</credit_card_number>
```

In addition, HTML tags don't provide any methodology for data validation. If we needed a tag for an age field, we know a person's age can only be between 0 and 120, but any data may be inserted between <p> and </p> tags. How would we know if the age was valid? XML schema diagrams (XSDs) allows you to specify all kinds of data validation for a specific XML tag. An XSD schema definition that restricts age to be in the range 0, 120 would read:

```
<xs:simpleType name= "age">
 <xs:restriction base="xs:integer">
   <xs:minInclusive value="0"/>
   <xs:maxInclusive value="120"/>
 </xs:restriction>
</xs:simpleType>
```

What custom XML packages are available? XML has spawned quite a few custom packages for specific communities. A few examples are listed in Figure 13.14. These packages illustrate the goal of XML—information exchange standards that can be easily constructed and customized to serve a growing variety of online applications.

Is XML the only format websites use to speak to each other? There is another very popular format used to transfer information between computers named **JSON**. It stands for JavaScript Object Notation and is a data interchange standard that is easy for humans to read and write. JSON is faster and easier to use than XML. It consists of name and value pairs like:

```
"firstName" : "Kendall"
```

HTTP

Which Internet protocol does a browser use to send requests? The **Hypertext Transfer Protocol (HTTP)** was created especially for the transfer of hypertext documents across the Internet. (Recall that hypertext documents are documents in which text is linked to other documents or media.)

Figure 13.14 XML Custom Packages

XML Custom Package	Sample Tags
MathML	<times>, <power>, <divide>
X3D	<viewpoint>, <shape>, <scene>
MusicXML	<score>, <beat>, <measure>, <clef>

STEP 2: Server executes script

STEP 1: Click the "Click Here to Join Mailing List" button.

STEP 3: Form sent to browser

STEP 4: Information on form sent to server

Your computer

bookworlds.com

Figure 13.15 Information Flow When a Browser Action Executes a Program on a Web Server *(Ifong/Shutterstock, Shashkin/Shutterstock)*

How does a browser safeguard secure information? **Hypertext Transfer Protocol Secure (HTTPS)** ensures that data is sent securely over the web. HTTPS is actually an acronym that's the combination of HTTP and **Secure Sockets Layer (SSL)**, a network security protocol. **Transport Layer Security (TLS)** is an updated extension of SSL. These protocols provide data integrity and security for transmissions over the Internet. Commerce servers use security protocols to protect sensitive information from interception by hackers.

Application Architecture

Objective 13.7 *Compare and contrast server-side and client-side application software.*

Web application software typically consists of two parts: the client-side software, which lives on the user's computer, and the server-side programs, which live on the server computer. Let's look more closely at both aspects of web application development.

Server-Side Applications

What are server-side applications? The web is a client/server network. The type of program that runs on a web server rather than on your computer is referred to as a **server-side program**. Server-side program execution can require many communication sessions between the client and the server to achieve the goal, but server-side programs can perform very complex operations.

What are popular server-side interfaces? Several methods of designing programs are available that execute on the server and give a web page more sophisticated capabilities. PHP and .NET are very popular choices for coding server-side programs. A very popular choice for those beginning to explore programming server-side code is to use JavaScript, using the library Node.js.

How do the two programs communicate? Let's examine a specific example: to collect a user's answers in a form and then create and send out an e-mail message with that information.

Begin by looking at Figure 13.15:

Step 1. A button on bookworlds.com's website may say, "Click Here to Join Mailing List."

Step 2. Clicking the button may execute a script file, called "mailinglist.js," from the web server hosting the site.

Step 3. This file generates a form that's sent to your browser. The form includes fields for a name and e-mail address and a Submit button.

Step 4. After you fill in the fields and click the Submit button, the mailinglist.js program sends the information back to the server. The server then records the information in a database.

Client-Side Applications

What are client-side applications? A **client-side program** is a program that runs on the client computer and requires no interaction with a web server. Once a web server processes a web page and sends the page to the client computer that requested it, the receiving computer can't get new data from the server unless a new request is made. If interactivity is required on a web page, this exchange of data between the client and server can make the interactivity inefficient and slow.

Sound Byte | MyLab IT®

Client-Side Web Page Development

In this Sound Byte, we'll use a popular tool named CodePen to examine client-side web applications that use HTML, CSS, and JavaScript to create amazing results.

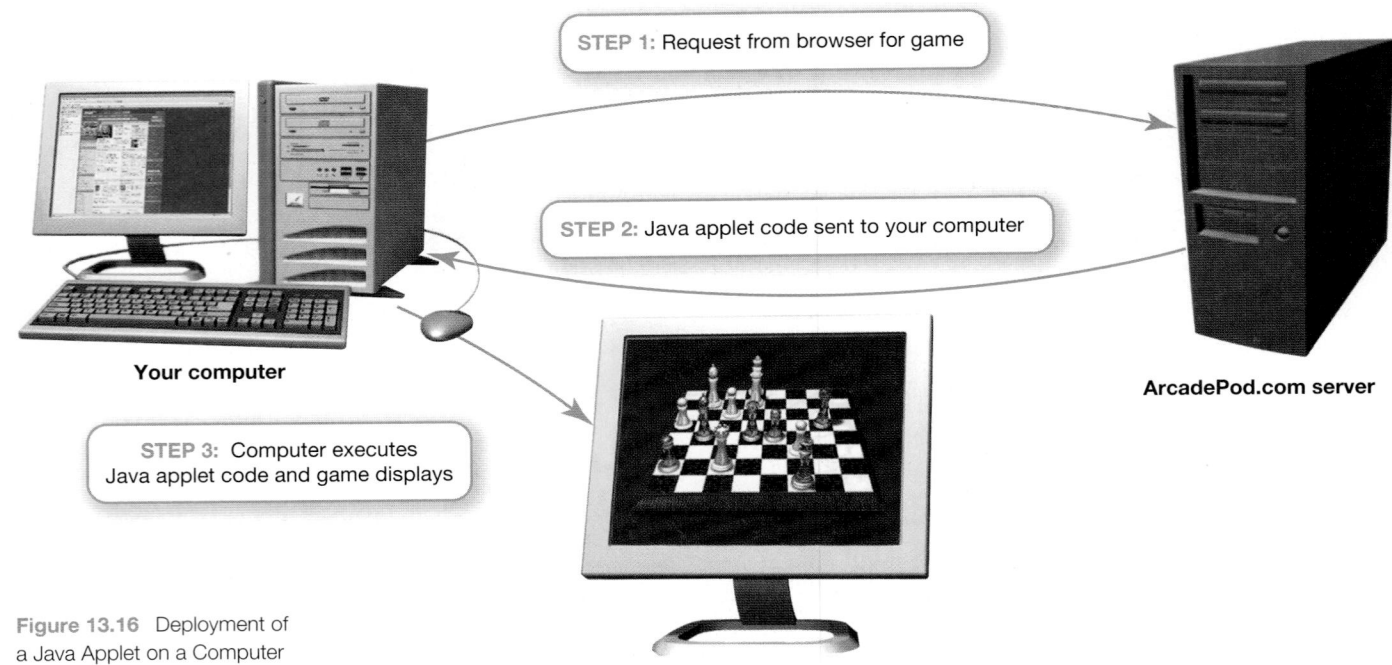

STEP 1: Request from browser for game

STEP 2: Java applet code sent to your computer

Your computer

STEP 3: Computer executes
Java applet code and game displays

ArcadePod.com server

Figure 13.16 Deployment of
a Java Applet on a Computer

Often it's more efficient to run programs on your computer (the client). Therefore, client-side programs are created.

How is client-side programming done? There are two main approaches to client-side programming:

1. An **HTML embedded scripting language**, which tucks programming code directly within the HTML of a web page. The most popular embedded language is JavaScript.
2. An **applet**, which is a small application actually located on the server. When requested, the applet is downloaded to the client. It's there ready to run when needed, without additional data transfers between the client and server. The Java language is the most common language used to create applets for use in browsers.

Isn't there a delay as an applet downloads? You may experience some delay in functionality while waiting for a Java applet to download to your computer, but once the applet arrives, it can execute all its functions without further communication with the server. Let's look at an example, as shown in Figure 13.16:

Step 1. Your browser makes contact with a game on the game site ArcadePod (**arcadepod.com**) and makes your request to play a game.

Step 2. The web server returns the Java applet that contains all the code to run the game on your computer.

Step 3. Your computer executes the applet code, and the game runs on your computer.

What are some scripting technologies? Dynamic HTML (DHTML) is a combination of technologies—HTML, cascading style sheets, and JavaScript—that's used to create lively and interactive websites. DHTML technologies allow a web page to change (that is, to be dynamic) after it's been loaded. Such change generally occurs in response to user actions, such as when you click your mouse or mouse over objects on a page. DHTML also brings special effects to otherwise static web pages without requiring users to download and install plug-ins or other special software.

What is JavaScript? JavaScript is a commonly used scripting language for creating DHTML effects. JavaScript is often confused with the Java programming language because of the similarity in their names. However, though they share some common elements, the two languages are different.

With JavaScript, HTML documents can be made responsive to mouse clicks and typing. For example, JavaScript is often used to validate the information you input in a web form, for example, to make sure you filled in all required fields.

When JavaScript code is embedded in an HTML document, it's downloaded to the browser with the HTML page. All actions dictated by the embedded JavaScript commands are executed on the client computer. Without JavaScript and other scripting languages, web pages would be lifeless.

How does JavaScript control the components of a web page? Just as cascading style sheets organize and combine the attributes of objects on a web page, JavaScript uses the **Document Object Model (DOM)** to organize the objects and page elements. The Document Object Model defines every item on a web page—including graphics, tables, and headers—as an object. Then with DOM, as with cascading style sheets, web developers can easily change the look and feel of these objects.

Where is web programming headed? Web pages can interact with servers at times other than when a page is being fetched. Web pages can have an ongoing exchange of information, communicating with the server and updating information on the page without requiring the user to do a page refresh or leave the page. AJAX is the acronym for Asynchronous JavaScript and XML, a group of technologies that facilitates the creation of this style of web applications. There are a huge number of web application frameworks now available, like Ruby on Rails. These packages make it simpler to create an application that talks to a web server, queries a database, and then presents information in a nicely formatted template.

Communications over the Internet

In this section, we explore electronic communications media and how to keep your information exchanges efficient and secure.

Types of Internet Communication

Objective 13.8 *Discuss the mechanisms for communicating via e-mail and instant messaging.*

Two of the most common communication methods on the Internet are e-mail and instant messaging.

E-Mail

Who invented e-mail? In 1971, Ray Tomlinson, a computer engineer who worked on the development of the ARPANET, the precursor to the Internet, created e-mail. E-mail grew from a simple program that Tomlinson wrote to enable computer users to leave text messages for each other on a single machine. The logical extension of this was sending text messages between machines on the Internet. E-mail became the most popular application on ARPANET; by 1973, it accounted for 75% of all data traffic.

How does e-mail travel the Internet? Just like other kinds of data that flow along the Internet, e-mail has its own protocol. The **Simple Mail Transfer Protocol (SMTP)** is responsible for sending e-mail along the Internet to its destination. SMTP is part of the Internet Protocol suite. As in most other Internet applications, e-mail is a client/server application. On the way to its destination, your mail will pass through **e-mail servers**—specialized computers whose sole function is to store, process, and send e-mail.

STEP 1: You send an e-mail message to your friend Cheyenne.

Your computer

STEP 2: Your ISP's e-mail server consults the DNS server for Cheyenne's domain address.

Your ISP's e-mail server

DNS server

STEP 3: The DNS server provides the domain IP address.

INTERNET

STEP 4: The e-mail server forwards your e-mail through the Internet to Cheyenne's ISP's e-mail server.

Cheyenne's ISP's e-mail server

STEP 5: The next time Cheyenne checks her e-mail, she gets your e-mail.

Cheyenne's computer

Figure 13.17 A Sample Route an E-Mail Takes on the Internet *(Ifong/Shutterstock, Sashkin/Shutterstock, LdF/E+/Getty Images)*

Where are e-mail servers located? If your ISP provides you with an e-mail account, it runs an e-mail server that uses SMTP. For example, as shown in Figure 13.17, say you're sending an e-mail message to your friend Cheyenne. Cheyenne uses Verizon as her ISP. Therefore, your e-mail to her is addressed to Cheyenne@verizon.net.

Let's follow that e-mail:

Step 1. When you send the e-mail message, your ISP's e-mail server receives it.

Step 2. The e-mail server reads the domain name (verizon.net) and communicates with a DNS server to determine the location of verizon.net.

Step 3. The DNS server turns the domain name into the associated IP address.

Step 4. The e-mail message is forwarded to verizon.net, and it arrives at an e-mail server maintained by Cheyenne's ISP.

Step 5. The e-mail is then stored on Cheyenne's ISP's e-mail server. The next time Cheyenne checks her e-mail, she'll receive your message.

How are we able to send files as attachments? SMTP was designed to handle text messages. When the need arose to send files by e-mail, the **Multipurpose Internet Mail Extensions (MIME)** specification was introduced. All e-mail client software now uses this protocol to attach files. E-mail is still sent as text, but the e-mail client using the MIME protocol now handles the encoding and decoding for the users. When attaching a file, your e-mail client transparently encodes and decodes the file for transmission and receipt.

Gmail has long been the free web-based e-mail product from Google. It still exists, but Google has introduced a newer product, Inbox, that has features that can help you manage your e-mail.

- **Bundles:** Inbox comes with a set of "bundles" like Promos, Finance, and Social. This means that Inbox automatically sorts your incoming e-mail into these groups. It makes your inbox much more organized, and you can quickly glance through the titles of all the e-mails in a bundle then move them all to the Done folder with just one click.

- **Reminders and snooze:** If you enter a reminder into Google Now, say, by clicking the microphone on your Android phone and saying, "Remind me to send flowers to Mom on Wednesday," a Reminder will appear right in your inbox. If you don't want to look at it every day but just on Tuesday, you can "snooze" it and tell it when to reappear.

- **Pin an e-mail:** You can "pin" e-mails to your Inbox that are important and that you want highlighted until you finish a task. With a click you can clear out the other mail and just see the pinned items. So Inbox functions as a to-do list as well as an e-mail manager.

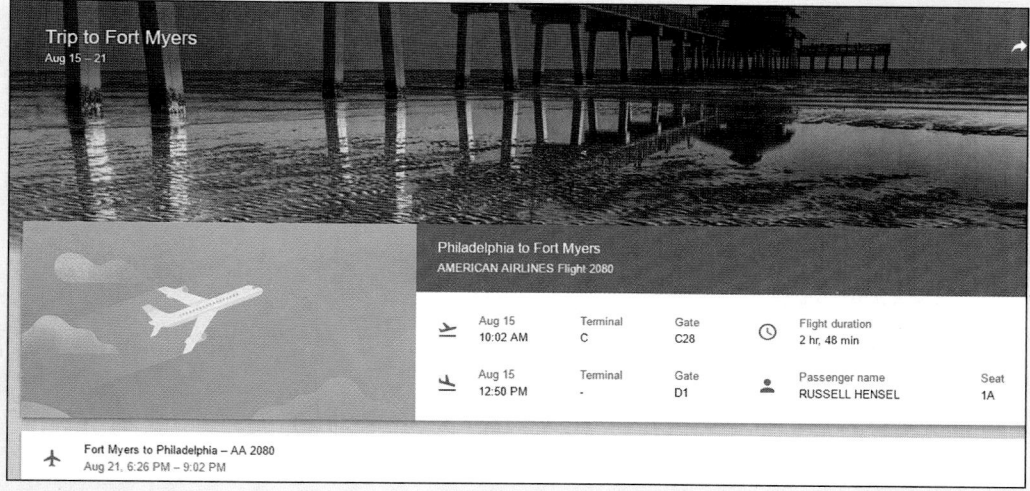

With a very visual style, Inbox has won over many Gmail users. *(Courtesy Google Inc.)*

Instant Messaging

What do you need to run instant messaging? Instant messaging (IM) requires the use of a client program that connects to an IM service. WhatsApp and Facebook Messenger are two popular IM services in use today.

How does instant messaging work? The client software running on your device makes a connection with the chat server and provides it with connection information for your device (such as the IP address), as shown in Figure 13.18.

Because both your device and your friend's device have the connection information (the IP addresses) for each other, the server isn't involved in the chat session. Chatting takes place directly between the two devices over the Internet.

Is sending an IM secure? Most IM services do not use a high level of encryption for their messages—if they bother to use encryption at all. In addition to viruses, worms, and hacking threats, IM systems are vulnerable to eavesdropping, in which someone using a packet sniffer "listens in" on IM conversations. Although several measures are under way to increase the security of this method of real-time communication, major vulnerabilities still exist. And employers can install monitoring software to record IM sessions. Therefore, it's not a good idea to send sensitive information using IM because it's susceptible to interception and possible misuse by hackers.

STEP 1: Contact chat server to see who is online

Your tablet running IM software

STEP 2: IP addresses of your buddies sent to your computer

Chat server

INTERNET

STEP 3: Chat with your buddy commences via his IP address

Your buddy's smartphone running the same IM software

Figure 13.18 How an Instant Messaging Program Works
(Tom Wang/Shutterstock, Sashkin/Shutterstock, Tyler Olson/Shutterstock)

Encryption

Objective 13.9 *Explain how data encryption improves security.*

Can other people read my e-mail? E-mail is highly susceptible to being read by unintended parties because it's sent in plain text. Additionally, copies of your e-mail messages may exist, temporarily or permanently, on numerous servers as the messages make their way through the Internet. To protect your sensitive e-mail messages, encryption practices are available.

How do I encrypt my e-mail? Many e-mail services offer built-in encryption. Hushmail (**hushmail.com**) and Comodo SecureEmail (**comodo.com**) offer free versions of their secure e-mail services. You can sign up on their websites and experiment with sending encrypted e-mail. And you don't need to abandon your current e-mail accounts—just use your secure account when you require secure communications.

How does encryption work? **Encryption** refers to the process of coding your e-mail so that only the person with the key to the code (the intended recipient) can decode (or decipher) the message. There are two basic types of encryption:

1. Private-key encryption
2. Public-key encryption

E-mail encryption, SSL encryption, and just about anything we do to achieve privacy on the Internet requires random numbers. Encryption is accomplished using random number sequences, which are sequences of numbers in which no patterns can be recognized. Even for an e-commerce transaction that uses SSL encryption to encode your credit card number, as many as 368 bits of random data might be needed. Only 128 bits are needed for the encryption key, but other random data is needed to create authentication codes and to prevent replay attacks. Replay attacks occur when hackers attempt to copy packets traveling across the Internet and to extract data (such as encryption codes) from them. The hackers then can reuse the data to gain access to networks or transactions.

So where do all these random numbers come from? Generating true random sequences is more difficult than it sounds. Most random number generators are really pseudo-random because they're all based on some sort of pattern to generate the numbers. However, the site **random.org** is dedicated to providing true random numbers for web applications such as encryption algorithms. The numbers are generated based on atmospheric noise, which is truly random. The noise is gleaned from radios not tuned to a particular station, so they're broadcasting static. Anyone can access the website and download random numbers to be used for encryption or other vital services such as lottery drawings. For more information, check out **random.org**.

What is private-key encryption? In **private-key encryption**, only the two parties involved in sending the message have the code. This could be a simple shift code where letters of the alphabet are shifted to a new position (see Figure 13.19).

For example, in a two-position right-shift code, the letter a becomes c, b becomes d, and so on. Alternatively, it could be a more complex substitution code (a = h, b = r, c = g, etc.). The main problem with private-key encryption is key security. If someone steals a copy of the code or is savvy about decoding, the code is broken.

What is public-key encryption? In **public-key encryption**, two keys, known as a **key pair**, are created. You use one key for coding and the other for decoding. The key for coding is generally distributed as a **public key**. You can place this key on your website, for instance. Anyone wishing to send you a message can then download your public key and code the message using your public key.

When you receive the message, you use your **private key** to decode it. You're the only one who ever possesses the private key, and therefore it's highly secure. The keys are generated in such a way that they can work only with each other. The private key is generated first. The public key is then generated using a complex mathematical formula, often using values from the private key. The computations are so complex that they're considered unbreakable. Both keys are necessary to decode a message. If one key is lost, the other key can't be used by itself.

Which type of encryption is used on the Internet? Public-key encryption is the most commonly used encryption on the Internet. Public-key packages such as **Pretty Good Privacy (PGP)** are available for download at sites such as CNET Downloads (**download.cnet.com**), and you can usually use them free of charge (although there are now commercial versions of PGP). After obtaining the PGP software, you can generate key pairs to provide a private key for you and a public key for the rest of the world.

What does a key look like? A key is a binary number. Keys vary in length, depending on how secure they need to be. A 12-bit key has 12 positions and might look like this:

```
100110101101
```

Longer keys are more secure because they have more values that are possible. A 12-bit key provides 4,096 different possible values, whereas a 40-bit key allows for 1,099,511,627,776 possible values. The key and the message are run through a complex algorithm in the encryption program that converts the message into unrecognizable code. Each key turns the message into a different code.

A = C	N = P
B = D	O = Q
C = E	P = R
D = F	Q = S
E = G	R = T
F = H	S = U
G = I	T = V
H = J	U = W
I = K	V = X
J = L	W = Y
K = M	X = Z
L = N	Y = A
M = O	Z = B

The word **COMPUTER** using the two-position code at the left now becomes:

E Q O R W V G T

This is difficult to interpret without the code key at the left.

Figure 13.19 Writing the word *COMPUTER* using a two-position right-shift encryption code results in *EQORWVGT*.

Ethics in IT

Do We Really Want Strong Encryption?

Encryption has fueled the enormous growth of electronic commerce. Because people feel safe in transmitting private data like credit card numbers across the Internet, online banking, shopping, and communication have exploded. But ardent shoppers are not the only people relying on encryption to keep their information hidden.

Criminals are also increasing their use of encryption. "Going dark" is the term for encrypting the phone and e-mail accounts that carry the details of their illegal transactions. For federal agencies, it becomes more and more difficult to gather the evidence needed for a conviction as easy-to-use encryption software spreads. The encryption standards are now so strong that there is no way to break into some encrypted messages. Apple announced with the release of iOS 8 that the default encryption its products support could not be broken by Apple. So if a government agency received a warrant for specific records, Apple could not possibly comply and hand over readable information.

This exact scenario occurred when the FBI began investigating a terrorist attack that took place in San Bernadino, California. The couple who carried out the attack were both killed in the subsequent shootout with police. The FBI wanted to access the iPhone used by the shooter to search for additional background on the crime. Neither the FBI nor the National Security Agency (NSA) was able to enter the phone. Apple's security system meant that if anyone tried to enter the phone with the incorrect password more than ten times, all data on the phone would be erased.

Concern about just such an event has pushed national security officials and law enforcement agencies to lobby for tech companies to undermine their own encryption schemes. But if the encryption were weakened, allowing some mechanism for it

Figure 13.20 Should security experts be forced by law to leave a way to break their encryption systems? *(johan2011/123RF)*

to be broken upon request, there would be no information that was completely "secure." This idea of a "backdoor" or a "key under the doormat" allowing every secure message to be broken has been controversial for years, and the debate continues (see Figure 13.20).

The FBI was granted a court order forcing Apple to create a new operating system that could be used to allow law enforcement to enter the phone. Apple refused. As tensions grew, it suddenly was announced that the Department of Justice had found a way into the phone. *The Washington Post* reported that the FBI had hired professional hackers to do the job.

The opposition, which includes many security experts as well as civil libertarians, points to the fact this would be bad for commercial business. Deliberately making security products less secure may be useful to some government agencies but exposes all users to possible security leaks by hackers.

So do you want strong encryption? And just how strong?

▶ Helpdesk   MyLab IT®

Keeping E-Mail Secure

In this Helpdesk, you'll play the role of a helpdesk staffer, fielding questions about how e-mail works and how messages are kept secure.

Is a private key really secure? Because of the complexity of the algorithms used to generate key pairs, it's impossible to deduce the private key from the public key. However, that doesn't mean your coded message can't be cracked. As you learned in Chapter 12, a brute force attack occurs when hackers try every possible key combination to decode a message. This type of attack can enable hackers to deduce the key and decode the message.

What kind of key is considered safe? In the early 1990s, 40-bit keys were thought to be completely resistant to brute force attacks and were the norm for encryption. However, in 1995, a French programmer used a unique algorithm of his own and 120 workstations simultaneously to attempt to break a 40-bit key. He succeeded in just eight days. After this, 128-bit keys became the standard. However, using supercomputers, researchers have had some success cracking 128-bit encryption. Therefore, strong encryption now calls for 256-bit keys. It's believed that even with the most powerful computers in use today, it would take hundreds of billions of years to crack a 256-bit key.

Do corporations use special encryption? Businesses often pay for encryption services that also provide other features such as confirmation of message delivery, message tracking, and overwriting of e-mail messages when they're deleted to ensure that copies don't exist. Companies such as ZixCorp (**zixcorp.com**) provide these higher levels of service to businesses.

Trends In IT   Cognitive Computing

We're used to thinking of computers as pure calculators, good at performing fixed tasks with specific instructions very quickly. But computers have begun to mimic how our minds work. This is referred to as *cognitive computing*.

Imagine a computer program that can read through your Facebook posts, your tweets, and the online essays in your blog and then "think" about them. Instead of just returning a word count or computing the writing level of your work, what if it could return the most dominant emotion of your writing—perhaps anger with a strong undercurrent of fear? IBM's Watson tone analyzer program does that now (try it out by searching for the Watson tone analyzer demo).

One of the hallmarks of cognitive computing is strong natural language processing (see the Trends in IT in Chapter 5). Cognitive computing combines natural language processing with advanced machine learning algorithms, pattern recognition, and data mining to be able to extract new insights from information faster and on a grander scale than we can as humans. One application uses a vast array of legal information to create an "artificially intelligent" lawyer, who can conduct legal research at blazing speeds. Another project is looking at creating spontaneous networks of idle cars, which have cameras, sensors, and computers onboard already, so they can communicate. Together these connected cars could produce information about where the nearest open parking space is, if there is a gas leak nearby, or even locate missing persons.

The applications are not just static either. They can learn over time from their past mistakes and improve their performance. Veterinarians are using IBM's artificial intelligence supercomputer Watson to digest hundreds of thousands of pages of medical journals, textbooks, and current research to assist in diagnosing animal illness (see Figure 13.21). As more information is added and more cases are presented, the software builds better techniques for diagnosis. Meanwhile, businesses are using cognitive computing to spot trends and coordinate feedback from a variety of sources to adjust their products. We may soon have to work hard to outthink our laptops.

Figure 13.21 IBM's Watson is able to communicate with natural language and deduce emotion, tone, and mood from visual and textual data. *(Caroline Seidel/Dpa picture alliance archive/Alamy Stock Photo)*

Before moving on to the Chapter Review:

1. ▶ Watch Chapter Overview Video 13.2.
2. Then take the Check Your Understanding quiz.

Check Your Understanding // Review & Practice

For a quick review to see what you've learned so far, answer the following questions.

multiple choice

1. JSON, JavaScript Object Notation, is useful because it
    a. allows web services to exchange information.
    b. uses PGP to encrypt data.
    c. makes the Document Object Model usable in HTML.
    d. is hexadecimal codes that execute quickly on computers.

2. Cascading style sheets allow you to quickly change
    a. from server-side processing to client-side processing.
    b. the rules for applying formatting to an HTML document.
    c. to a more secure transport protocol.
    d. from HTML to XML.

3. JavaScript
    a. is the same language as Java.
    b. is commonly used to make HTML documents more dynamic.
    c. is obsolete.
    d. provides high-level security for e-mail.

4. The protocol used to send e-mail over the Internet is
    a. HTTP.
    b. DHTML.
    c. SMTP.
    d. DNS.

5. A key pair is a set of two keys you use to
    a. encrypt and decrypt an e-mail message.
    b. open doors into websites so you can pass through a firewall.
    c. execute a CSS script.
    d. attach a photo to an e-mail message.

 Go to **MyLab IT** to take an autograded version of the *Check Your Understanding* review and to find all media resources for the chapter.

TechBytes Weekly Go to TechBytes Weekly for current technology news and discussion questions!

13 Chapter Review

Summary

Part 1
Inner Workings of the Internet

Learning Outcome 13.1 You will be able to explain how the Internet is managed and the details of how data is transmitted across the Internet.

Internet Management and Networking

Objective 13.1 *Describe the management of the Internet.*

- Management of the Internet is carried out by several nonprofit organizations and user groups such as the Internet Society, the Internet Engineering Task Force (IETF), the Internet Architecture Board (IAB), the Internet Corporation for Assigned Names and Numbers (ICANN), and the World Wide Web Consortium (W3C). Each group has different responsibilities and tasks. Currently, the U.S. government funds a majority of the Internet's costs. Other countries also pay for Internet infrastructure and development.

Objective 13.2 *Explain how the Internet's networking components interact.*

- The largest paths of the Internet, along which data travels the most efficiently and quickly, make up the Internet backbone. Homes and all but the largest businesses connect to the Internet through regional or local connections, which then connect to the Internet through the entities that make up the Internet backbone. The largest businesses, educational centers, and some government agencies make up the Internet backbone.
- Optical carrier (OC) lines are high throughput and are used to connect large corporations to their ISPs.
- Service providers use an Internet exchange point (IXP) to connect directly to each other, reducing cost and latency time.
- Individual users enter their ISP through a point of presence (POP), a bank of routers and switches through which many users can connect simultaneously.

Objective 13.3 *List and describe the Internet protocols used for data transmission.*

- Data is transmitted along the Internet using packet switching. Data is broken up into discrete units known as *packets*, which can take independent routes to the destination before being reassembled.
- A computer protocol is a set of rules for exchanging electronic information. Although many protocols are available on the Internet, the main suite of protocols used to move information over the Internet is TCP/IP. The suite is named after the original two protocols that were developed for the Internet: the Transmission Control Protocol (TCP) and the Internet Protocol (IP). TCP is responsible for preparing data for transmission, but IP actually sends data between computers on the Internet.

Internet Identity

Objective 13.4 *Explain how each device connected to the Internet is assigned a unique address.*

- An IP address is a unique number assigned to all computers connected to the Internet. The IP address is necessary so that packets of data can be sent to a particular location (computer) on the Internet.

Objective 13.5 *Discuss how a numeric IP address is changed into a readable name.*

- A domain name is merely a name that stands for a certain IP address and that makes it easier for people to remember it. DNS servers act as the phone books of the Internet. They enable your computer to find out the IP address of a domain by looking up its corresponding domain name.

Part 2
Coding and Communicating on the Internet

Web Technologies

Objective 13.6   *Compare and contrast a variety of web development languages.*

- The Hypertext Transfer Protocol (HTTP) is the protocol used on the Internet to display web pages in your browser.
- The Hypertext Markup Language (HTML) is a set of rules for marking up blocks of text so that a browser knows how to display them. Most web pages are generated with at least some HTML code. Blocks of text in HTML documents are surrounded by a pair of tags (such as <b> and </b> to indicate bolding). These tags and the text between them are referred to as *elements*. The current HTML standard is HTML5, which offers much better support for media like audio and video.
- Because HTML wasn't designed for information exchange, eXtensible Markup Language (XML) was created. Instead of locking users into standard tags and formats for data, XML enables users to create their own markup languages to accommodate particular data formats and needs. JSON is another standard supporting the exchange of information between web services.

Objective 13.7   *Compare and contrast server-side and client-side application software.*

- Software is developed both on the server side and on the client side to make web pages more responsive and interactive. Server-side programming includes

Node.js and PHP. Client-side programs can run faster because they don't need to wait for information exchanges with the server. Embedded JavaScript and Java applets are two common approaches for writing client-side programs.

Communications over the Internet

Objective 13.8   *Discuss the mechanisms for communicating via e-mail and instant messaging.*

- Simple Mail Transfer Protocol (SMTP) is the protocol responsible for sending e-mail over the Internet. E-mail is a client/server application. E-mail passes through e-mail servers, whose functions are to store, process, and send e-mail to its ultimate destination. ISPs and portals such as Gmail maintain e-mail servers to provide e-mail functionality to their customers. Your ISP's e-mail server uses DNS servers to locate the IP addresses for the recipients of the e-mail you send.
- Instant messaging (IM) software communicates with a chat server to quickly deliver communications to your friends who are online. It's not secure and can be vulnerable to eavesdropping.

Objective 13.9   *Explain how data encryption improves security.*

- Encryption software, such as Pretty Good Privacy (PGP), is used to code messages so that they can be decoded only by authorized recipients.

 Be sure to check out **MyLab IT** for additional materials to help you review and learn. And don't forget to watch the Chapter Overview Videos. ▶

Key Terms

applet **534**

cascading style sheet (CSS) **531**

circuit switching **517**

client/server model **515**

client-side program **533**

commerce server **516**

computer protocol **516**

connectionless protocol **522**

connection-oriented protocol **522**

Document Object Model (DOM) **535**

domain name system (DNS) server **524**

dotted decimal number (dotted quad) **519**

dynamic addressing **521**

Dynamic Host Configuration Protocol (DHCP) **522**

dynamic HTML (DHTML) **534**

element **529**

e-mail server **535**

encryption **538**

eXtensible Markup Language (XML) **532**

file server **516**

handshaking **522**

hexadecimal digit **520**

HTML embedded scripting language **534**

HTML tag **529**

Hypertext Transfer Protocol (HTTP) **532**

Hypertext Transfer Protocol Secure (HTTPS) **533**

Internet backbone **515**

Internet cache **525**

Internet Corporation for Assigned Names and Numbers (ICANN) **519**

Internet exchange point (IXP) **515**

Internet of Things (IoT) **520**

Internet Protocol (IP) **518**

Internet Protocol version 4 (IPv4) **520**

Internet Protocol version 6 (IPv6) **520**

IP address **519**

JavaScript **534**

JSON **532**

key pair **539**

Multipurpose Internet Mail Extensions (MIME) **536**

negative acknowledgment (NAK) **522**

octet **519**

open system **517**

optical carrier (OC) line **515**

packet (data packet) **517**

packet switching **517**

point of presence (POP) **515**

positive acknowledgment (ACK) **522**

Pretty Good Privacy (PGP) **539**

private key **539**

private-key encryption **539**

proprietary system **517**

public key **539**

public-key encryption **539**

root DNS server **524**

second-level domain **524**

Secure Sockets Layer (SSL) **533**

server-side program **533**

Simple Mail Transfer Protocol (SMTP) **535**

static addressing **521**

T line **515**

TCP/IP **518**

three-way handshake **522**

Transmission Control Protocol (TCP) **518**

Transport Layer Security (TLS) **533**

User Datagram Protocol (UDP) **522**

web server **516**

Chapter Quiz // Assessment

For a quick review to see what you've learned, answer the following questions. Submit the quiz as requested by your instructor. If you are using **MyLab IT**, the quiz is also available there.

multiple choice

1. The Internet is primarily funded by
   a. your state income taxes.
   b. voluntary contributions.
   c. your federal income taxes.
   d. Google.

2. The collection of large national and international networks used to establish the Internet is called the
   a. Internet backbone.
   b. highway system.
   c. OC.
   d. T1.

3. The information in a data packet includes
   a. the data and the circuit identifier.
   b. the data and the destination.
   c. just the data.
   d. different types of information depending on the type of message being sent.

4. IPv6 uses 128 bits to assign a(n)
   a. data packet to each transmission.
   b. memory address to the CPU.
   c. destination Internet address to each e-mail.
   d. address to every device connected to the Internet.

5. HTTPS is different than HTTP because
   a. of how it transforms or reformats the data.
   b. it extracts data from source databases.
   c. it is a combination of HTTP and the Secure Sockets Layer (SSL).
   d. it stores data in the data warehouse.

6. A private key is important
   a. to reboot system hardware.
   b. to reset your public key if you lose a password.
   c. because it enables you to use MIME.
   d. to decode an encrypted message.

7. Encryption is used to
   a. shrink the amount of space it takes to store e-mail.
   b. code your e-mail so only one person can decipher it.
   c. transfer e-mail more quickly.
   d. make shopping on the Internet more available.

8. An applet is
   a. a program distributed by Apple Inc.
   b. a small application located on a server computer.
   c. a hardware device that encrypts e-mail messages.
   d. a programming language used to help create dynamic web pages.

9. SMTP is the set of rules used to
   a. shrink the amount of space it takes to store e-mail.
   b. send e-mail along the Internet to its destination.
   c. encrypt e-mail messages.
   d. make shopping on the Internet more available.

10. The set of instructions that define how to display the HTML elements in your site is
    a. XML.
    b. CSS.
    c. AJAX.
    d. PHP.

true/false

_____ 1. If you use an Internet cache, then the information displayed in your browser is automatically refreshed.

_____ 2. Your Internet service provider has a default DNS server to translate a URL into an IP address.

_____ 3. Instant messaging is secure because of the type of encryption used.

_____ 4. MIME is the protocol that supports sending files as e-mail attachments.

_____ 5. The term *dotted quad* means you have four dots in a row in your Java source code.

critical thinking

1. **Who's in Charge?**

   Should there be an agency in charge of the Internet? How would business, government, and education be impacted if the Internet were suddenly no longer available? Does this warrant establishing a governing body to regulate and monitor the Internet?

2. **The Future of Web Programming**

   Where is web programming headed? It will be driven by the needs of users, so think about what kinds of things you need web pages to do for you that they currently cannot do. Should biometric identification replace passwords, for example?

Team Time

Using Crowdsourcing in a Business

background

Determining the right merchandise to sell is critical. Having a website that's designed to use crowdsourcing—either to gather information about products you carry, such as customer reviews or to determine what merchandise you're going to stock—provides you with a competitive advantage. In this Team Time, you'll consider how to take advantage of crowdsourcing in running a business.

task

Three individuals starting new businesses have requested help in designing their websites and customer interaction programs. The businesses are (a) a coffee shop that offers live music; (b) a clothing company; and (c) a company that sells iPhone accessories. You need to help these businesses choose a crowdsourcing strategy.

process

Break the class into small teams. Each team should select one of the businesses described previously. Each team should prepare a report as follows:

1. Decide on the types of products that will be sold by the company. For each category of product, decide what attributes you feel customers will comment on when giving input on products.
2. Decide if the company will solicit feedback from potential customers on all products or whether the company will offer a core selection of products without soliciting feedback. Divide the products into two lists: core products and products subject to crowdsourcing.
3. Determine a social networking strategy for the company. How will customers be driven to the company website to participate in the crowdsourcing for incentives, discount coupons, contests, and such?
4. Develop a PowerPoint presentation to summarize your findings and present your proposed solution to the class.

conclusion

E-commerce websites are relatively easy to deploy, but risk exists when financing and stocking products. Crowdsourcing feedback can help businesses minimize the risk of stocking unwanted products.

Ethics Project

Privacy at School

In this exercise, you'll research and then role-play a complicated ethical situation. The role you play might not match your own personal beliefs; regardless, your research and use of logic will enable you to represent the view assigned. An arbitrator will watch and comment on both sides of the arguments, and together the team will agree on an ethical solution.

problem

Parents are especially concerned about protecting their children's privacy rights. School administrators are quickly learning that they need to craft policies that set appropriate boundaries and guidelines for monitoring students. Should school districts be allowed to monitor students? Should school districts be required to inform students and parents of any monitoring that takes place?

research areas to consider

- Lower Merion school district in Pennsylvania using webcams to monitor students in their homes
- Schools using the Geo Listening service to monitor students' social media posts
- The Family Educational Rights and Privacy Act (FERPA)

process

1. Divide the class into teams. Research the areas cited above and devise a scenario in which a school district has been monitoring students without their knowledge and has potentially violated their privacy.
2. Team members should write a summary that provides background information for their character—for example, student, parent, school official, or arbitrator—and that details their character's behaviors to set the stage for the role-playing event. Then, team members should create an outline to use during the role-playing event.
3. Team members should present their case to the class or submit a PowerPoint presentation for review by the rest of the class, along with the summary and resolution they developed.

conclusion

As technology becomes ever more prevalent and integrated into our lives, ethical dilemmas will present themselves to an increasing extent. Being able to understand and evaluate both sides of the argument, while responding in a personally or socially ethical manner, will be an important skill.

Creating an HTML Document

You work part time for a small computer repair and education center. As part of your job you need to be able to edit HTML files. Your boss has started a brief document about the basics of HTML that she'll be using for a training class. She would like you to add the HTML tags so she can put it on the website. You'll be using Notepad to complete this exercise.

You will use the following skills as you complete this activity:

* Apply HTML tags
* View an HTML document in a browser

Instructions

1. Open Notepad.
   * In Windows, type Notepad in the Search box on the taskbar. Click Notepad Desktop app.
2. Click **File**, then click **Open**, and navigate to your student data files. Click **TIA_CH13_Start.txt**.
3. Press **Ctrl+Home** on your keyboard to place the cursor at the top of the document.
4. Type **<!DOCTYPE html>** and press **Enter**. Type **<html>** and press **Enter**. Type **<body>** and press **Enter**. These tags define the document as an HTML document.
5. Place the cursor at the beginning of the first paragraph that starts with *HTML stands for*, and type **What is HTML?**, then press **Enter**.
6. Place the cursor at the beginning of the second paragraph that starts with *You can easily create* and type **Creating an HTML Document**, then press Enter.
7. At the beginning of the third paragraph, type **Formatting Tags**, then press **Enter**, and at the beginning of the fourth paragraph, type **Viewing an HTML Page**, then press **Enter**.
8. Place the cursor at the beginning of the first header, *HTML Beginning Tutorial*. Add a header start tag by typing **<h1>**. Press **End**, then type the end tag **</h1>**.
9. Place the cursor at the beginning of the second header, *What is HTML?*. Add a third level header start tag by typing **<h3>**. Press **End**, then add an end tag by typing **</h3>**.
10. Add third-level header tags for the other three headers by repeating step 9 for each.
11. Place the cursor at the beginning of the first paragraph beginning with *HTML stands for*, then add paragraph tags to the beginning and end of the paragraph by typing **<p>** at the start of the paragraph, and **</p>** at the end of the paragraph. Repeat for the remaining three paragraphs.
12. Press **Ctrl+Home**, then click **Edit** on the menu bar, and use Find to locate the first occurrence of the word *tags*. With the cursor at the beginning of *tags*, add a bold formatting start tag by typing ****. Place the cursor at the end of the word *tags*, then add a bold formatting end tag by typing ****.
13. In the same paragraph, add start and end bold tags to the phrases *Start tags* and *end tags*.
14. Place the cursor between the 3 and the > in the first <h3> tag. Press **Space**, then type **style="color:blue"**.
15. Repeat step 14 for the remaining three headers.
16. Place the cursor before the paragraph end tag at the end of the third paragraph and type **For more information on creating HTML pages work through this <a href="http://www.w3schools.com/html/"> HTML Tutorial.</a>**
17. Press **Ctrl+End**, then type **</body>**, and press **Enter**.
18. Type **</html>**.
19. Click **File**, click **Save As**, then type **TIA_CH13_LastFirst.html**. (Make sure you type .html). Navigate to where you are saving your student files, then click Save. Close Notepad.
20. Open File Explorer, then navigate to where you saved the *TIA_CH13_LastFirst.html* file. Double-click the file to open it in your default browser. Check to ensure all headings have been formatted correctly, select words and phrases have bolding formats applied, and all paragraphs start and end appropriately. Click the hyperlink to ensure that it works.
21. Close the browser and submit the *TIA_CH13_LastFirst.html* file for grading.

The History of the Personal Computer

 For an overview of how the PC got its start, watch the History of the PC video.

Learning Outcome A.1 You will be able to describe the history of personal computer hardware and software development.

Have you ever wondered how big the first personal computer was or how much the first laptop weighed? Computers are such an integral part of our lives that we don't often stop to think about how far they've come or where they got their start. In just over 40 years, computers have evolved from expensive, huge machines that only corporations could own to small, powerful devices that almost anyone can have. In this appendix, we look at the history of the personal computer.

Early Personal Computers

Our journey through the history of the personal computer starts in 1975. At that time, most people weren't familiar with the mainframes and supercomputers that large corporations and the government owned. With price tags exceeding the cost of buildings, and with few (if any) practical home uses, these monster machines weren't appealing to or attainable by average Americans.

(B Christopher/Alamy Stock Photo, SSPL/The Image Works, Marilyn K. Yee/Archive Photos/New York Times Co./Getty Images, Steve Castillo/AP Images, Science & Society Picture Library/Getty Images, Jerry Mason/Science Source)

Figure A.1 Timeline of Early Personal Computer Development

The Altair 8800

- Only 256 bytes of memory
- No keyboard or monitor
- Switches on front used to enter data in machine code (1s and 0s)
- Lights on front indicated results of a program

Commodore PET

- Featured in *Popular Science* magazine
- Popular in business settings in Europe

1975

October 1977

1976

June 1977

Apple I

Steve Jobs and Steve Wozniak form Apple Computer

- Featured color monitor, sound, and game paddles
- 4 KB of RAM
- Operating system stored in ROM
- Optional floppy disk to load programs (mostly games)

Apple II

The First Personal Computer: The Altair

Objective A.1 *Describe the earliest personal computer ever designed.*

In 1975, the first personal computer, the **Altair 8800** (see Figure A.1), was born. At $395 for a do-it-yourself kit or $498 for a fully assembled unit (about $2,253 in today's dollars), the price was reasonable enough that computer fanatics could finally own their own computers.

The Altair was primitive by today's standards—no keyboard, no monitor, and completely not user friendly. Despite its limitations, computer enthusiasts flocked to the machine. Many who bought it had been taught to program, but until that point, they had access only to big, clumsy computers at their jobs. With the Altair, they could create their own programs at home. Within 3 months, 4,000 orders were placed for the machine.

The release of the Altair marked the start of the personal computer boom. In fact, two men whose names you might have heard were among the first Altair owners—Bill Gates and Paul Allen were so enamored by the "minicomputer" that they wrote a compiling program (a program that translates user commands into commands the computer can understand) for it. The two later convinced the Altair's developer to buy their program, marking the start of a company called Microsoft. We'll get to that story later. First, let's see what their rivals were up to.

The Apple I and II

Objective A.2 *Describe the distinguishing features of the Apple I and Apple II.*

Around the time the Altair was released, Steve Wozniak, an employee at Hewlett-Packard, was dabbling with his own computer design. **Steve Jobs**, who was working for computer game manufacturer Atari at the time, liked Wozniak's prototypes and made a few suggestions. Together, the two built a personal computer, the **Apple I**, in Wozniak's garage (see Figure A.1) and formed the Apple Computer Company in 1976.

TRS-80

- Introduced by Radio Shack
- Monochrome display
- 4 KB of RAM
- Circuitry hidden under keyboard
- Wildly popular with consumers—sold 10,000 units in the first month

November 1977

IBM PC (5150)

- Marketed to businesses and consumers
- 64 KB to 256 KB of RAM
- Floppy disk drives optional
- Hard disks not supported in early models

August 1981

April 1981

- First "portable" computer
- Weighed 24.5 pounds
- 5-inch screen
- 64 kilobytes of RAM
- Two floppy disk drives
- Preinstalled with spreadsheet and word processing software

Osborne

One year later, in 1977, the **Apple II** was born (see Figure A.1). The Apple II included a color monitor, sound, and game paddles. Priced around $1,300 (about $5,245 in today's dollars), one of its biggest innovations was that the operating system was stored in read-only memory (ROM). Previously, the operating system had to be rewritten every time the computer was turned on. The friendly features of the Apple II operating system encouraged less technically oriented computer enthusiasts to write their own programs.

An instant success, the Apple II would eventually include a spreadsheet program, a word processor, and desktop publishing software. These programs gave personal computers like the Apple functions beyond gaming and special programming and led to their popularity.

Enter the Competition

Around the time Apple was experiencing success with its computers, a number of competitors entered the market. The largest among them were Commodore, Radio Shack, Osborne, and IBM. The **Commodore PET** (see Figure A.1) was aimed at the business market and did well in Europe, while Radio Shack's **TRS-80** (see Figure A.1) was clearly aimed at the U.S. consumer market. Just 1 month after its release in 1977, it had sold about 10,000 units.

The Osborne: The Birth of Portable Computing

Objective A.3 *Describe the first portable computer.*

The Osborne Company introduced the first portable computer, the **Osborne**, in 1981 (see Figure A.1). Although portable, the computer weighed 24.5 pounds. It featured a minuscule 5-inch screen and carried a price tag of $1,795 (about $4,884 today). The Osborne was an overnight success, and its sales quickly reached 10,000 units per month. However, despite the computer's popularity, the Osborne Company eventually closed. Compaq bought the Osborne design and in 1983 produced its own portable computer.

IBM PCs

Objective A.4 *Describe the development of the IBM PC.*

Until 1980, IBM primarily made mainframe computers, which it sold to large corporations, and hadn't taken the personal computer seriously. In 1981, however, IBM released its first personal computer, the **IBM PC** (see Figure A.1). Because many companies were familiar with IBM mainframes, they adopted the IBM PC. The term PC soon became the term used to describe all personal computers.

IBM marketed its PC through retail outlets such as Sears to reach home users, and it quickly dominated that market. In January 1983, *Time* magazine, playing on its annual person of the year issue, named the computer "1982 Machine of the Year."

Other Important Advancements

It wasn't just personal computer hardware that was changing. At the same time, advances in programming languages and operating systems and the influx of application software were leading to more useful and powerful machines.

The Importance of BASIC

Objective A.5 *Explain why BASIC was an important step in revolutionizing the software industry.*

The software industry began in the 1950s with programming languages such as FORTRAN, ALGOL, and COBOL. These languages were used mainly by businesses to create financial, statistical, and engineering programs. However, in 1964 John Kemeny and Thomas Kurtz designed the **Beginners All-Purpose Symbolic Instruction Code (BASIC)** at Dartmouth College and revolutionized the software industry. BASIC was a language that beginning programming students could easily learn. It thus became enormously popular—and the key language of the PC. In fact, Bill Gates and Paul Allen (see Figure A.2) used BASIC to write their program for the Altair, which led to the creation of Microsoft, a company that produced computer software.

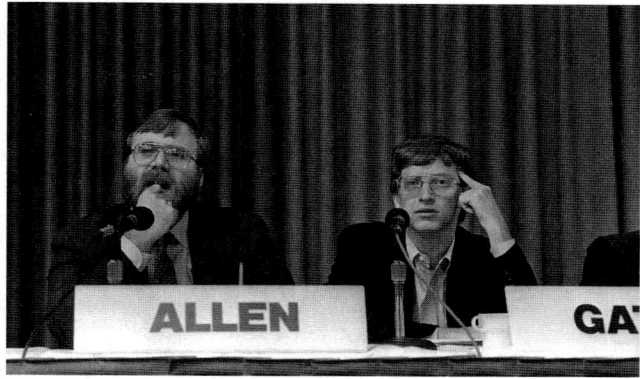

Figure A.2 Bill Gates and Paul Allen are the founders of Microsoft. *(Ann E. Yow-Dyson/Archive Photos/Getty Images)*

The Advent of Operating Systems

Objective A.6 *Explain why the development of the operating system was an important step in PC development.*

Because data on the earliest personal computers was stored on audiocassettes, many programs weren't saved or reused. This meant that programs had to be rewritten whenever they were needed. In 1978, Steve Wozniak designed a 5.25-inch floppy disk drive so that programs could be saved easily and operating systems developed.

Operating systems are written to coordinate with the specific processor chip that controls the computer. At that time, Apples ran on a Motorola chip, whereas PCs (IBMs and so on) ran on an Intel chip. **Disk Operating System (DOS)**, developed by Wozniak and introduced in 1977, was the OS that controlled the first Apple computers. The **Control Program for Microcomputers (CP/M)**, developed by Gary Kildall, was the OS designed for the Intel 8080 chip (the processor for PCs).

In 1980, when IBM was entering the personal computer market, it approached Bill Gates at Microsoft to write an OS program for the IBM PC. Gates recommended that IBM investigate the CP/M OS, but IBM couldn't arrange a meeting with the founder, Gary Kildall. Microsoft reconsidered the opportunity to write an OS program and developed **MS-DOS** for IBM computers. Eventually, virtually all PCs running on the Intel chip used MS-DOS as their OS (see Figure A.3). Microsoft's reign as one of the dominant players in the personal computer landscape had begun.

Figure A.3 This 1983 Hewlett-Packard computer used an early version of the MS-DOS operating system as well as the Lotus 1-2-3 spreadsheet program. *(Everett Collection/SuperStock)*

The Software Application Explosion: VisiCalc and Beyond

Objective A.7 *List early application software that was developed for the PC.*

Because the floppy disk was a convenient way to distribute software, its inclusion in personal computers set off an application software explosion. In 1978, Harvard Business School student Dan Bricklin recognized the potential for a personal computer spreadsheet program. He and his friend Bob Frankston created the program **VisiCalc**, which became an instant success. Finally, ordinary home users could see the benefit of owning a personal computer. More than 100,000 copies of VisiCalc were sold in its first year.

After VisiCalc, other electronic spreadsheet programs entered the market. **Lotus 1-2-3** came on the market in 1983, and **Microsoft Excel** entered the scene in 1985. These products became so popular that they eventually put VisiCalc out of business.

Meanwhile, word processing software was also gaining a foothold in the industry. Until then, there were separate, dedicated word processing machines; personal computers, it was believed, were

Figure A.4 Application Software Development

Year	Application
1978	**VisiCalc:** First electronic spreadsheet application **WordStar:** First word processing application
1980	**WordPerfect:** Best DOS-based word processor, was eventually sold to Novell and later acquired by Corel
1983	**Lotus 1-2-3:** Added integrated charting, plotting, and database capabilities to spreadsheet software **Word for MS-DOS:** Introduced in the pages of *PC World* magazine on the first magazine-inserted demo disk
1985	**Excel:** One of the first spreadsheets to use a graphical user interface **PageMaker:** The first desktop publishing software

for computation and data management only. However, once **WordStar**, the first word processing application, became available for personal computers in 1979, word processing became another important use for the personal computer. Competitors such as **Word for MS-DOS** (the precursor to Microsoft Word) and **WordPerfect** soon entered the market. Figure A.4 lists some of the important dates in application software development.

The Graphical User Interface and the Internet Boom

Other important advancements related to personal computers came in the form of the graphical user interface and the Internet.

Xerox and Apple's Lisa and Macintosh

Objective A.8 *Describe the features of the Lisa and Macintosh computers and their predecessor, the Xerox Alto.*

A **graphical user interface (GUI)**, which uses icons to represent programs and actions, allows users to interact with the computer more easily. Until that time, users had to use complicated command- or menu-driven interfaces. Apple was the first company to take full commercial advantage of the GUI, but the GUI was not invented by a computer company.

In 1972, a few years before Apple launched its first personal computer, photocopier manufacturer **Xerox** was designing a personal computer of its own. Named the **Alto** (see Figure A.5), the computer included a word processor, based on the What You See Is What You Get (WYSIWYG) principle, that incorporated a file management system with directories and folders. It also had a mouse and could connect to a network. None of the other personal computers of the time had these features. For a variety of reasons, Xerox never sold the Alto commercially. Several years later, it developed the Star Office System, which was based on the Alto. Despite its convenient features, the Star never became popular because no one was willing to pay the $17,000 asking price.

Xerox's ideas were ahead of their time, but many of the ideas present in the Alto and Star would soon catch on. In 1983, Apple introduced the **Lisa**—the first successful personal computer brought to market that used a GUI (see Figure A.6). Legend has it that Jobs had seen the Alto during a visit to Xerox in 1979 and was influenced by its GUI. He therefore incorporated a similar user interface into the Lisa, providing features such as windows, drop-down menus, icons, a file system with folders and files, and a point-and-click device called a mouse. The only problem with the Lisa was its price. At $9,995 (about $24,047 in today's dollars), few buyers were willing to take the plunge.

Figure A.5 The Alto was the first computer to use a GUI, and it provided the basis for the GUI that Apple used. However, because of marketing problems, the Alto never was sold. *(Josie Lepe/San Jose Mercury News/MCT/Newscom)*

One year later, in 1984, Apple introduced the **Macintosh**, shown in Figure A.7. The Macintosh was everything the Lisa was and then some, at about a third of the cost. The Macintosh was also the first personal computer to utilize 3.5-inch floppy disks with a hard cover, which were smaller and sturdier than the previous 5.25-inch floppies.

Figure A.6 The Lisa was the first computer to introduce a GUI to the market. Priced too high, it never gained the popularity it deserved. *(SSPL/The Image Works)*

Figure A.7 The Macintosh became one of Apple's best-selling computers, incorporating a GUI along with other innovations such as the 3.5-inch floppy disk drive. *(INTERFOTO/History/Alamy Stock Photo)*

The Internet Boom

Objective A.9   *List the first successful web browsers.*

The GUI made it easier for users to work on the computer. The Internet provided another reason for people to buy computers. Now people could conduct research and communicate in a new way. In 1993, the web browser **Mosaic** was introduced. This browser allowed users to view multimedia on the web, causing Internet traffic to increase by nearly 350%.

Meanwhile, companies discovered the Internet as a means to do business, and computer sales took off. IBM-compatible PCs became the computer system of choice when, in 1995, Microsoft introduced **Internet Explorer**, a browser that integrated web functionality into Microsoft Office applications, and **Windows 95**, the first Microsoft OS designed to be principally a GUI OS.

About one year earlier, in 1994, a team of developers launched the **Netscape Navigator** web browser, which soon became a predominant player in browser software. However, pressures from Microsoft became too strong, and in 1998, Netscape announced it would no longer charge for the product and would make the code available to the public.

Making the Personal Computer Possible: Early Computers

Billions of personal computers have been sold over the past four decades. But the computer is a compilation of parts, each of which is the result of individual inventions. Let's look at some early machines that helped to create the personal computer we know today.

The Pascalene Calculator and the Jacquard Loom

Objective A.10   *Discuss the features of the Pascalene calculator and the Jacquard loom that inspired modern computer elements.*

From the earliest days of humankind, we have been looking for a more systematic way to count and calculate. Thus, the evolution of counting machines led to the development of the computer we know today. The **Pascalene** was the first accurate mechanical calculator. This machine, created by the French mathematician **Blaise Pascal** in 1642, used revolutions of gears, like odometers in cars, to count by tens. The Pascalene could be used to add, subtract, multiply, and divide. The basic design of the Pascalene was so sound that it lived on in mechanical calculators for more than 300 years.

Nearly 200 years later, Joseph Jacquard revolutionized the fabric industry by creating a machine that automated the weaving of complex patterns. Although not a counting or calculating machine,

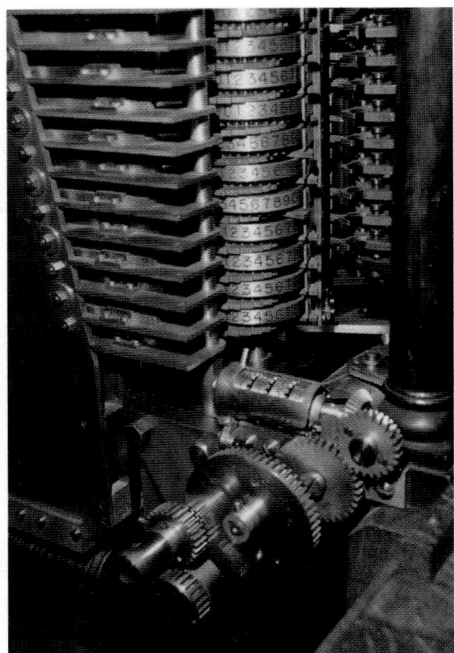

Figure A.8 The Jacquard loom used holes punched in stiff cards to make complex designs. This technique would later be used in punch cards that controlled the input and output of data in computers. *(Janek Skarzynski/Newscom)*

Figure A.9 The Analytical Engine, designed by Charles Babbage, was never fully developed but included components similar to those found in today's computers. *(Chris Howes/Wild Places Photography/Alamy Stock Photo)*

the **Jacquard loom** (shown in Figure A.8) was significant because it relied on stiff cards with punched holes to automate the weaving process. Much later, this punch-card process would be adopted as a means for computers to record and read data.

Babbage's Engines and the Hollerith Tabulating Machine

Objective A.11 *Discuss the contributions of Babbage's engines and the Hollerith Tabulating Machine to modern computing.*

In 1834, Charles Babbage designed the first automatic calculator, called the **Analytical Engine** (see Figure A.9). The machine was actually based on another machine called the **Difference Engine**, which was a huge steam-powered mechanical calculator that Babbage designed to print astronomical tables. Although the Analytical Engine was never developed, Babbage's detailed drawings and descriptions of the machine include components similar to those found in today's computers, including the store (akin to RAM) and the mill (a central processing unit) as well as input and output devices. This invention gave Charles Babbage the title of the "father of computing."

Meanwhile, Ada Lovelace, who was the daughter of poet Lord Byron and a student of mathematics (which was unusual for women of the time), was fascinated with Babbage's engines. She translated an Italian paper on Babbage's machine and, at the request of Babbage, added her own extensive notes. Her efforts are thought to be the best description of Babbage's engines.

In 1890, Herman Hollerith, while working for the U.S. Census Bureau, was the first to take Jacquard's punch-card concept and apply it to computing with his **Hollerith Tabulating Machine**. Until that time, census data had been tabulated manually in a long, laborious process. Hollerith's tabulating machine automatically read data that had been punched onto small punch cards, speeding up the tabulation process. Hollerith's machine became so successful that he left the Census Bureau in 1896 to start the Tabulating Machine Company. His company later changed its name to International Business Machines, or IBM.

The Z1, the Atanasoff–Berry Computer, and the Harvard Mark I

Objective A.12 *Discuss the features of the Z1, the Atansoff–Berry Computer, and the Mark I.*

German inventor Konrad Zuse is credited with a number of computing inventions. His first, in 1936, was a mechanical calculator called the Z1. The Z1 is thought to be the first computer to include certain features integral to today's systems, such as a control unit and separate memory functions.

In 1939, John Atanasoff, a professor at Iowa State University, and his student Clifford Berry built the first electrically powered digital computer, called the **Atanasoff–Berry Computer (ABC)**, shown in Figure A.10. The computer was the first to use vacuum tubes, instead of the mechanical switches used in older computers, to store data. Although revolutionary at the time, the machine weighed 700 pounds, contained a mile of wire, and took about 15 seconds for each calculation. (In comparison, today's personal computers can perform billions of calculations in 15

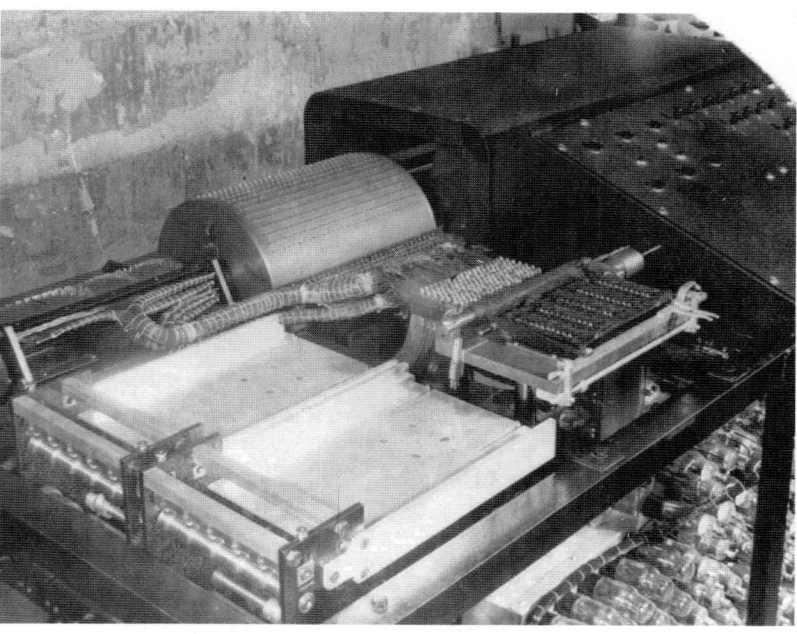

Figure A.10 The Atanasoff–Berry Computer laid the design groundwork for many computers to come. *(Frederick News Post/AP Images)*

seconds.) Most importantly, the ABC was the first computer to use the binary system and to have memory that repowered itself upon booting. The design of the ABC would be central to that of future computers.

From the late 1930s to the early 1950s, Howard Aiken and Grace Hopper designed the Mark series of computers used by the U.S. Navy for ballistic and gunnery calculations. Aiken, an electrical engineer and physicist, designed the computer, while Hopper did the programming. The Harvard Mark I, finished in 1944, could add, subtract, multiply, and divide.

However, many believe Hopper's greatest contribution to computing was the invention of the **compiler**—a program that translates English-language instructions into computer language. The team was also responsible for a common computer-related expression. Hopper was the first to "debug" a computer when she removed a moth that had flown into the Harvard Mark I and had caused the computer to break down (see Figure A.11). After that, problems that caused a computer not to run were called bugs.

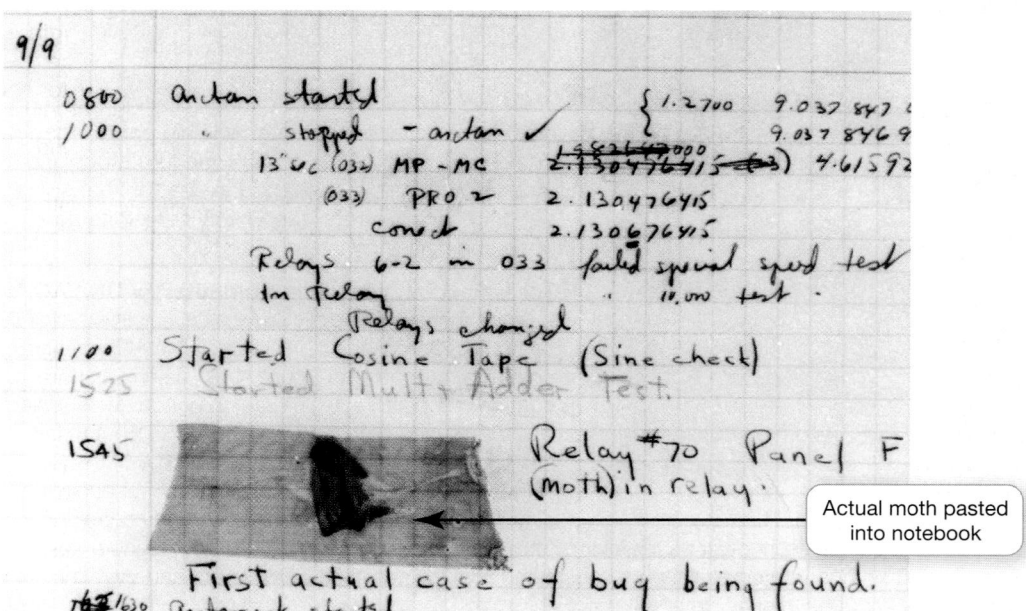

Actual moth pasted into notebook

Figure A.11 Grace Hopper coined the term *computer bug* when a moth flew into the Harvard Mark I, causing it to break down. *(Naval History & Heritage Command)*

Figure A.12 The ENIAC took up an entire room and required several people to manipulate it. *(INTERFOTO/ History/Alamy Stock Photo)*

The Turing Machine, the ENIAC, and the UNIVAC

Objective A.13 *Discuss the major features of the Turing Machine, the ENIAC, and the UNIVAC.*

Meanwhile, in 1936, British mathematician **Alan Turing** created an abstract computer model that could perform logical operations. The **Turing Machine** was not a real machine but rather a hypothetical model that mathematically defined a mechanical procedure (or algorithm). Additionally, Turing's concept described a process by which the machine could read, write, or erase symbols written on squares of an infinite paper tape. This concept of an infinite tape that could be read, written to, and erased was the precursor to today's RAM.

The **Electronic Numerical Integrator and Computer (ENIAC)**, shown in Figure A.12, was another U.S. government–sponsored machine developed to calculate the settings used for weapons. Created by John W. Mauchly and J. Presper Eckert at the University of Pennsylvania, it was put into operation in 1944. Although the ENIAC is generally thought of as the first successful high-speed electronic digital computer, it was big and clumsy. The ENIAC used nearly 18,000 vacuum tubes and filled approximately 1,800 square feet of floor space. Although inconvenient, the ENIAC served its purpose and remained in use until 1955.

The **Universal Automatic Computer**, or **UNIVAC**, was the first commercially successful electronic digital computer. Completed in 1951, the UNIVAC operated on magnetic tape (see Figure A.13), setting it apart from its competitors, which ran on punch cards. The UNIVAC gained notoriety when, in a 1951 publicity stunt, it was used to predict the outcome of the Stevenson–Eisenhower presidential race. After analyzing only 5% of the popular vote, the UNIVAC correctly identified Dwight D. Eisenhower as the victor. After that, UNIVAC soon became a household word. The UNIVAC and computers like it were considered **first-generation computers** and were the last to use vacuum tubes to store data.

Figure A.13 UNIVACs were the first computers to use magnetic tape for data storage. *(CBS Photo Archive/Getty Images)*

Figure A.14 Transistors were one-tenth the size of vacuum tubes, were faster, and produced much less heat. *(Borissos/Fotolia)*

Transistors and Beyond

Objective A.14   *Describe the milestones that led to each "generation" of computers.*

Only one year after the ENIAC was completed, scientists at the Bell Telephone Laboratories in New Jersey invented the **transistor**—another means to store data (see Figure A.14). The transistor replaced the bulky vacuum tubes of earlier computers and was smaller and more powerful than tubes. It was used in almost everything, from radios to phones. Computers that used transistors were referred to as **second-generation computers**. Still, transistors were limited as to how small they could be made.

A few years later, in 1958, Jack Kilby, while working at Texas Instruments, invented the world's first **integrated circuit**—a small chip capable of containing thousands of transistors. This consolidation in design enabled computers to become smaller and lighter. The computers in this early integrated-circuit generation were considered **third-generation computers**.

Other innovations in the computer industry further refined the computer's speed, accuracy, and efficiency. However, none was as significant as the 1971 introduction by the Intel Corporation of the **microprocessor chip**—a small chip containing millions of transistors (see Figure A.15). The microprocessor functions as the CPU, or brains, of the computer. Computers that use a microprocessor chip are called **fourth-generation computers**. Over time, Intel and Motorola became the leading manufacturers of microprocessors. Today, the Intel Core i7 is one of Intel's most powerful processors.

As you can see, personal computers have come a long way since the Altair and have a number of inventions and people to thank for their amazing popularity. What will the future bring?

Figure A.15 Today's microprocessors can contain billions of transistors. *(Tudor Voinea/Shutterstock)*

Check Your Understanding // Review & Practice

For a quick review of what you've learned, answer the following questions.

multiple choice

1. What was the name of the first web browser?
   a. Internet Explorer
   b. Netscape
   c. Mosaic
   d. Firefox

2. Which operating system was specifically developed for the first IBM PC?
   a. MS-DOS
   b. COBOL
   c. CP/M
   d. VisiCalc

3. Which invention replaced vacuum tubes in computers?
   a. the integrated circuit
   b. magnetic tape
   c. the microprocessor chip
   d. the transistor

4. Which computer was touted as the first personal computer?
   a. Lisa
   b. Commodore PET
   c. Altair
   d. Osborne

5. What was the importance of the Turing machine to today's computers?
   a. It described a system that was a precursor to today's notebook computer.
   b. It described a process to read, write, and erase symbols on a tape and was the precursor to today's RAM.
   c. It was the first computer to have a monitor.
   d. It was the first electronic calculator and a precursor to the computer.

6. Which computer first stored its operating system in ROM?
   a. Lisa
   b. Apple I
   c. Apple II
   d. Macintosh

7. What was the first word processing application?
   a. WordStar
   b. WordPerfect
   c. Word for MS-DOS
   d. Alto

8. Which company introduced the first "portable" computer?
   a. Apple
   b. Osborne
   c. IBM
   d. Xerox

9. For what is the Atanasoff–Berry Computer best known?
   a. It was the first computer used as a mechanical calculator.
   b. It was the first computer to use the binary system.
   c. It was the first computer to incorporate a magnetic tape system.
   d. It was the first computer to use vacuum tubes instead of mechanical switches.

10. Which was a programming language that beginning students could learn easily?
    a. FORTRAN
    b. COBOL
    c. BASIC
    d. ALGOL

11. The term "PC" was derived from what manufacturer's personal computer?
    a. IBM
    b. Osborne
    c. Commodore
    d. Altair

12. What was the first successful computer that featured a GUI?
    a. Altair
    b. Osborne
    c. Lisa
    d. Harvard Mark IV

13. The Jacquard loom introduced what significant innovation that would be adopted by later computers?

    a. keyboard

    b. monitor

    c. tape storage

    d. punch cards

14. Who is known as the "father of computing"?

    a. Bill Gates

    b. Blaise Pascal

    c. Charles Babbage

    d. Steve Jobs

B Careers in IT

It's hard to imagine an occupation in which computers aren't used in some fashion. Even such previously low-tech industries as waste disposal and fast food use computers to manage inventories and order commodities. In this appendix, we explore various information technology (IT) career paths open to you.

Rewards of Working in Information Technology

Objective B.1   *List the reasons why IT fields are attractive to students pursuing bachelor's degrees.*

There are many great reasons to work in the exciting, ever-changing field of IT. In this section, we'll explore some reasons why IT fields are so attractive to graduates looking for entry-level positions.

(Carol and Mike Werner/Alamy Stock Photo)

IT Workers Are in Demand

If you're investigating a career with computers, the first question you may have is "Will I be able to get a job?" Consider the following:

- According to projections by the U.S. Department of Labor's Bureau of Labor Statistics, computer-related jobs are expected to be among the fastest-growing occupations through 2024 (see Figure B.1).
- In 2017, *U.S. News & World Report* published a list of the best careers to consider based on employment opportunity, good salary, work–life balance, and job security. Computer systems analyst, software developer, web developer, computer network architect, and IT manager were included among the top 35 careers.
- According to the National Association of Colleges and Employers (NACE) Winter 2017 Salary Survey, the average starting salary for computer science majors with bachelor's degrees was projected to be $65,540 and was the second-highest average salary on the list, just below engineering majors.

The number of students pursuing computer science degrees also has been increasing over the past several years. Fields of specialization such as game development, information security, and mobile app development are very popular. Yet, shortages of computing professionals in the United States are still projected over the next 5 to 10 years. What does all this mean? In terms of job outlook, now is a perfect time to consider an IT career.

IT Jobs Pay Well

As you can see from Figure B.1, median salaries in IT careers are robust. But what exactly affects your salary in an IT position? Your skill set and your experience level are obvious answers, but the size of an employer and its geographical location are also factors. Large companies tend to pay more, so if you're pursuing a high salary, set your sights on a large corporation. But remember that making a lot of money isn't everything—be sure to consider other quality-of-life issues, such as job satisfaction. Of course, choosing a computer career isn't a guarantee you'll get a high-paying job. Just as in any other profession, you'll need appropriate training and on-the-job experience to earn a high salary.

So how much can you expect to start out earning? Although starting salaries for some IT positions, such as computer support specialists, are more on the modest side ($52,160), starting salaries for students with bachelor's degrees in IT are fairly robust.

Figure B.1 High-Growth IT Jobs*

Occupation	Median Pay ($)	10-Year Growth Rate (%)	Total New Jobs
Web developers	66,130	27	39,500
Computer systems analysts	87,220	21	118,600
Information security analysts	92,600	18	14,800
Software developers	102,280	17	186,600
Computer support specialists	52,160	12	88,800
Database administrators	84,950	11	13,400
Computer and information research scientists	111,840	11	2,700
Computer network architects	101,210	9	12,700
Network and computer systems administrators	79,700	8	30,200

*Excerpted from Occupational Outlook Handbook, *2017 Edition, U.S. Bureau of Labor Statistics.*

Figure B.2 Although many companies outsource IT jobs to third-party companies, this does not mean the jobs necessarily go offshore.

To obtain the most accurate information, you should research salaries yourself in the geographical area where you expect to work. **Salary.com** provides a free salary wizard to help you determine what IT professionals in your area are making compared with national averages. You can add information such as your degree and the size of the company to your search selection to fine-tune the figures further.

Figure B.2 shows that for an entry-level programming position in Denver, you could expect to earn a salary of between $47,436 and $72,702 with a bachelor's degree. Hundreds of IT job titles are listed in **Salary.com**, so you can tailor your search to the specific job, location, and industry in which you're interested.

IT Jobs Are Not Going "Offshore"

In the global economy in which we now operate, job outlook includes the risk of jobs being outsourced, possibly to other countries. **Outsourcing** is a process whereby a business hires a third-party firm to provide business services (such as customer-support call centers) that were previously handled by in-house employees. **Offshoring** occurs when the outsourcing firm is located (or uses employees) outside the United States.

India, China, and Romania and other former Eastern Bloc countries are major players in providing outsourcing services for U.S. companies. The big lure of outsourcing and offshoring is cost savings: Considering that the standard of living and salaries are much lower in many countries than they are in the United States, offshoring is an attractive option for many U.S. employers.

However, outsourcing and offshoring don't always deliver the cost savings that CEOs envision. Demand for personnel overseas has led to increased costs (primarily due to wage increases) for service providers in foreign markets. Furthermore, other, less tangible factors can outweigh the cost savings from outsourcing. Communications problems can arise between internal and external employees, for example, and cultural differences between the home country and the country doing the offshoring can result in software code that needs extensive rework by in-house employees. Data also can be less secure in an external environment or during the transfer between the company and an external vendor. Although outsourcing and offshoring won't be going away, companies are approaching these staffing alternatives with more caution and are looking more to U.S. companies to provide resources.

So, many IT jobs are staying in the United States. According to *InformationWeek* magazine, most jobs in the following three categories (see Figure B.3) will stay put:

1. Customer interaction: jobs that require direct input from customers or that involve systems with which customers interface daily
2. Enablers: jobs that involve getting key business projects accomplished, often requiring technical skills beyond the realm of IT and good people skills

Figure B.3 Jobs That Will Likely Remain Onshore

Customer Interaction	Enablers	Infrastructure Jobs
Web application developers	Business process analysts	Network security
Web interface designers	Application developers (when customer interaction is critical)	Network installation technicians
Database and data warehouse designers/developers	Project managers (for systems with users who are located predominantly in the United States)	Network administrators (engineers)
Customer relationship management (CRM) analysts		Wireless infrastructure managers and technicians
Enterprise resource planning (ERP) implementation specialists		Disaster recovery planners and responders

3. Infrastructure jobs: jobs that are fundamental to moving and storing the information that U.S.-based employees need to do their jobs

In addition, jobs that require specific knowledge of the U.S. marketplace and culture, such as social media managers, are also very likely not to be offshored.

Women Are in High Demand in IT Departments

Currently, women make up about 26% of the IT workforce (per the National Center for Women and Information Technology). This presents a huge opportunity for women who have IT skills, because many IT departments are actively seeking to diversify their workforces. In addition, although a salary gender gap (the difference between what men and women earn for performing the same job) exists in IT careers, it's smaller than in most other professions.

You Have a Choice of Working Location

In this case, location refers to the setting in which you work. IT jobs can be office-based, field-based, project-based, or home-based. Because not every situation is perfect for every individual, you can look for a job that suits your tastes and requirements. Figure B.4 summarizes the major job types and their locations.

You Constantly Meet New Challenges

In IT, the playing field is always changing. New software and hardware are constantly being developed. You'll need to work hard to keep your skills up to date. You'll spend a lot of time in training and self-study, trying to learn new systems and techniques. Many individuals thrive in this type of environment because it keeps their jobs from becoming dull or routine.

You Work in Teams

When students are asked to describe their ideal jobs, many describe jobs that involve working in teams. Despite what some people think, IT professionals are not locked in lightless cubicles, basking in the glow of their monitors and working alone on projects. Most IT jobs require constant interaction with other workers, usually in team settings. People skills are highly prized by IT departments. If you have good leadership and team-building skills, you'll have the opportunity to exercise them in an IT job.

You Don't Need to Be a Mathematical Genius

Certain IT careers such as programming involve a fair bit of math. But even if you're not mathematically inclined, you can explore many other IT careers. IT employers also value such attributes as creativity, marketing, and artistic style, especially in jobs that involve working on the Internet or with social media.

Figure B.4 Where Do You Want to Work?

Type of Job	Location and Hours	Special Considerations
Office-Based	Report for work to the same location each day and interact with the same people on a regular basis; requires regular hours of attendance (such as 9 A.M. to 5 P.M.)	May require working beyond "normal" working hours; may also require workers to be on call 24/7
Field-Based	Travel from place to place as needed and perform short-term jobs at each location	Involves a great deal of travel and the ability to work independently
Project-Based	Work at client sites on specific projects for extended periods of time (weeks or months)	Can be especially attractive to individuals who like workplace situations that vary on a regular basis
Home-Based (Telecommuting) 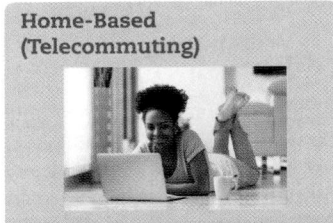	Work from home	Involves very little day-to-day supervision and requires an individual who is self-disciplined

IT Skills Are Transferable

Most computing skills are transferable from industry to industry. A networking job in the clothing manufacturing industry uses the same primary skill set as a networking job for a supermarket chain. Therefore, if something disastrous happens to the industry you're in, you should be able to switch to another industry without having to learn an entirely new skill set. Combining business courses with IT courses will also make you more marketable when changing jobs. For example, as an accounting major, if you minor in IT, employers may be more willing to hire you because working in accounting today means constantly interfacing with management information systems and manipulating data.

Challenges of IT Careers

Objective B.2 *Explain the various challenges of IT careers.*

Although there are many positive aspects of IT careers, there can be some challenges. The discussions that follow aren't meant to discourage you from pursuing an IT career but merely to make you aware of exactly what challenges you might face in an IT department.

Stress

Most IT jobs are hectic (see Figure B.5). Whereas the average American works 42 hours a week, a survey by *InformationWeek* revealed that the average IT staff person works 45 hours a week and is

Figure B.5 Stress comes from multiple directions in IT jobs. *(Khakimullin Aleksandr/Shutterstock, Monkey Business Images/Shutterstock, Rawpixel/Shutterstock, TORWAISTUDIO/Shutterstock, Ollyy/Shutterstock)*

on call for another 24 hours. On-call time (hours an employee must be available to work in the event of a problem) has been increasing because most IT systems require 24/7 availability.

Women Are in the Minority

A majority of IT jobs are filled by men, so some women view IT departments as *Dilbert*-like microcosms of antisocial geeks and don't feel as though they would fit in. Unfortunately, it is true that in most IT departments, women are underrepresented. As companies begin to push to address this imbalance, new opportunities are emerging for women with technical skill sets.

Lifelong Learning Is Required

Although the constantly changing nature of IT can alleviate boredom, keeping up with the changes can also cause some stress. You'll need to take training courses, do self-study, and perhaps take additional college courses, such as getting a graduate degree, to keep up with the vast shifts in technology.

Choosing Your Realm of IT

Objective B.3 *List and describe the various IT careers for which you can train.*

Figure B.6 shows an organizational chart for a modern IT department at a large corporation that should help you understand the variety of careers available and how they interrelate. The chief information officer (CIO) has overall responsibility for the development, implementation, and maintenance of information systems and their infrastructure. Usually, the CIO reports to the chief operating officer (COO).

The responsibilities below the CIO are generally grouped into two units:

1. Development and integration (responsible for the development of systems and websites)
2. Technical services (responsible for the day-to-day operations of the company's information infrastructure and network, including all hardware and software deployed)

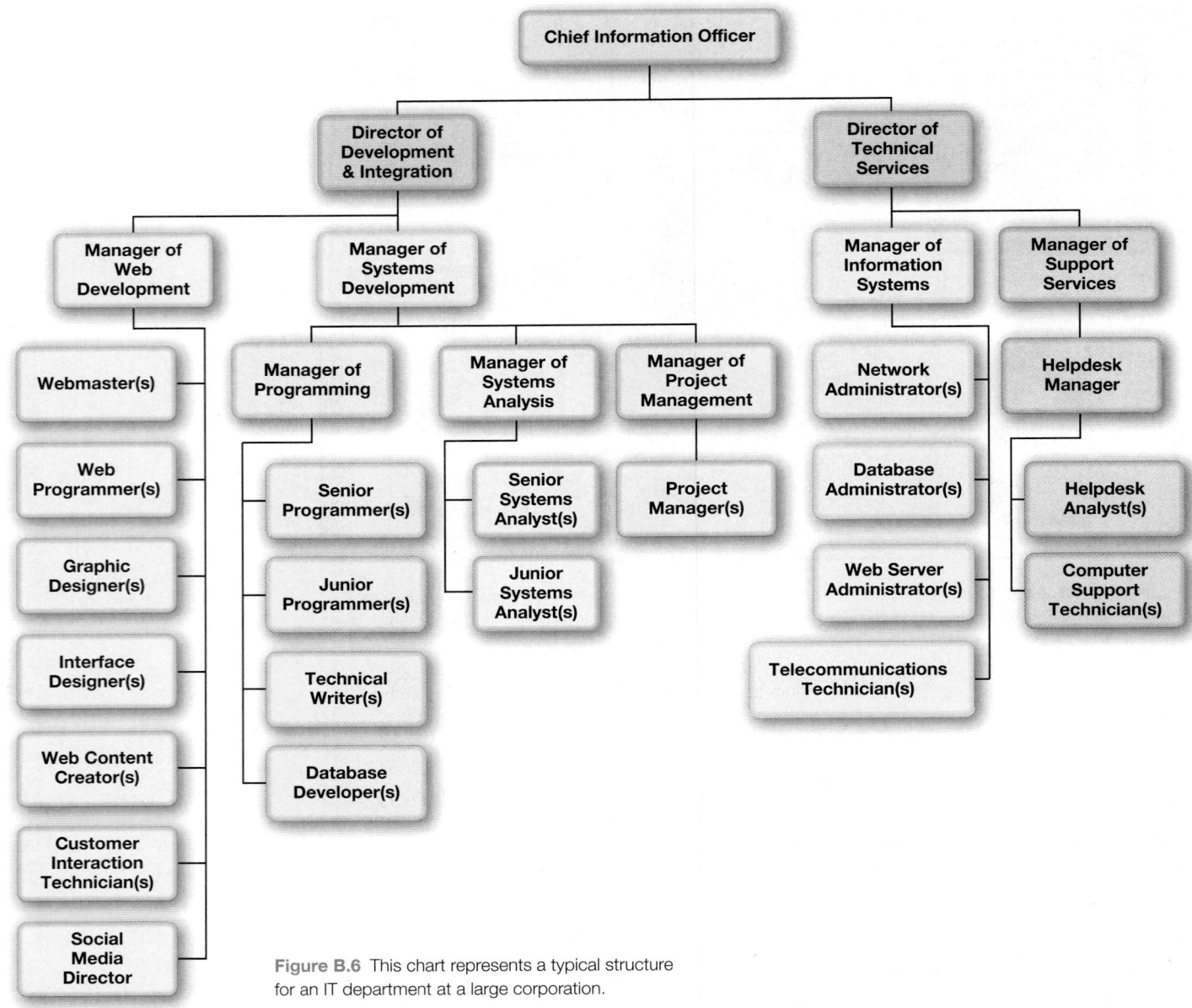

Figure B.6 This chart represents a typical structure for an IT department at a large corporation.

In large organizations, responsibilities are distinct and jobs are defined more narrowly. In medium-sized organizations, there can be overlap between position responsibilities. At a small company, you might be the network administrator, database administrator, computer support technician, and social media manager all at the same time. Let's look at the typical jobs found in each department.

Working in Development and Integration

Two distinct paths exist in this division:

1. Web development
2. Systems development

Because everything involves the web today, there's often a great deal of overlap between these paths.

Web Development. When most people think of web development careers, they usually equate them with being a webmaster. Webmasters used to be individuals who were solely responsible for all aspects of a company's website. However, today's webmasters usually are supervisors with responsibility for certain aspects of web development. At smaller companies, they may also be responsible for tasks that other individuals in a web development group usually do, such as the following:

- **Web content creators** generate the words and images that appear on the web. Journalists, other writers, editors, and marketing personnel prepare an enormous amount of web content, whereas **video producers**, **graphic designers**, and **animators** create web-based multimedia. Web content creators have a thorough understanding of their own fields as well as HTML, PHP, and JavaScript.
- **Interface designers** work with graphic designers and animators to create a look and feel for the site and make it easy to navigate.
- **Web programmers** build web pages to deploy the materials that the content creators develop. They wield software tools such as Adobe Dreamweaver and InDesign to develop the web pages. They also create links to databases using products such as Oracle and SQL Server to keep information flowing between users and web pages. They must possess a solid understanding of client- and server-side web languages (HTML, XML, Java, JavaScript, ASP, PHP, Silverlight, and Perl) and of development environments such as the Microsoft .NET Framework.
- **Customer interaction technicians** provide feedback to a website's customers. Major job responsibilities include answering e-mail, sending requested information, funneling questions to appropriate personnel (technical support, sales, and so on), and providing suggestions to web programmers for site improvements. Extensive customer service training is essential to work effectively in this area.
- **Social media directors** are responsible for directing the strategy of the company on all social media sites where the company maintains a presence. Often, while supervising customer interaction technicians, social media directors make sure that customers have a quality experience while interacting with company employees and customers on sites such as Facebook, Twitter, and Yelp. Responding to comments left on such sites, developing promotional strategies, and designing functionality of the company's social media sites are common job responsibilities.

As you can see in Figure B.7, many different people can work on the same website. Web programming jobs often require a four-year college degree in computer science, whereas graphic designers often are hired with two-year art degrees.

Figure B.7 It takes a team to create and maintain a website.
(United States Department of Agriculture)

Systems Development. Ask most people what systems developers do and they'll answer "programming." However, programming is only one aspect of systems development. Because large projects involve many people, there are many job opportunities in systems development, most of which require four-year college degrees in computer science or management information systems:

- **Systems analysts** gather information from end users about problems and existing information systems. They document systems and propose solutions to problems. Having good people skills is essential to success as a systems analyst. In addition, systems analysts work with programmers during the development phase to design appropriate programs to solve the problem at hand. Therefore, many organizations insist on hiring systems analysts who have solid business backgrounds and programming experience (at least at a basic level).

- **Programmers** attend meetings to document user needs, and they work closely with systems analysts during the design phase of program development. Programmers need excellent written communication skills because they often generate detailed systems documentation for end-user training purposes. Because programming languages are mathematically based, it is essential for programmers to have strong math skills and an ability to think logically.

- **Project managers** manage the overall systems development process: assigning staff, budgeting, reporting to management, coaching team members, and ensuring deadlines are met. Project managers need excellent time management skills because they're often pulled in several directions at once. They usually have prior experience as programmers or systems analysts. Many project managers obtain master's degrees to supplement their undergraduate degrees.

In addition to these key players, the following people are also involved in the systems development process:

- **Technical writers** generate systems documentation for end users and for programmers who may make modifications to the system in the future.

- **Network administrators** help the programmers and analysts design compatible systems, because many systems are required to run in certain environments (UNIX or Windows, for instance) and must work in conjunction with other programs.

- **Database developers** design and build databases to support the software systems being developed.

Large development projects may have all of these team members on the project. Smaller projects may require an overlap of positions, such as a programmer also acting as a systems analyst. As shown in Figure B.8, team members work together to build a system.

Working in Technical Services

Technical services jobs are vital to keeping IT systems running. The people in these jobs install and maintain the infrastructure behind the IT systems and work with end users to make sure they can interact with the systems effectively. There are two major categories of technical services careers:

1. Information systems
2. Support services

Note that these also are the least likely IT jobs to be outsourced because hands-on work with equipment and users is required on a regular basis.

- **Programmers build the software that solves problems.**

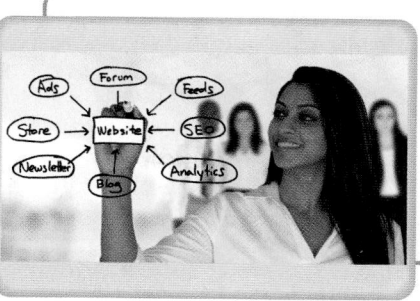

- **Systems analysts document systems and propose solutions.**

- **Project managers supervise, organize, and coach team members.**

- **Database developers ensure data is accessible when it's needed.**

Figure B.8 There are many important team members in systems development. *(Dmitry Nikolaev/Fotolia, Rob/Fotolia, cheekywemonkey/Fotolia, Trueffelpix/Shutterstock)*

Information Systems. The information systems department keeps the networks and telecommunications up and running at all times. Within the department, you'll find a variety of positions.

- **Network administrators** (sometimes called network engineers) are involved in every stage of network planning and deployment (see Figure B.9). They decide what equipment to buy and what media to use, they determine the network's topology, and they help install the network (by supervising contractors or doing it themselves). Network administrators plan disaster-recovery strategies (such as what to do if a fire destroys the server room). When equipment and cables break, network administrators must fix the problem. They also obtain and install updates to network software and evaluate new equipment to determine whether the network should be upgraded. In addition, they monitor the network's performance and often develop policies regarding network usage, security measures, and hardware and software standards.

- **Database administrators (DBAs)** install and configure database servers and ensure that the servers provide an adequate level of access to all users.

    - **Web server administrators** install, configure, and maintain web servers and ensure that the company maintains Internet connectivity at all times.

    - **Telecommunications technicians** oversee the communications infrastructure, including training employees to use telecommunications equipment. They are often on call 24 hours a day.

Support Services. As a member of the support services team, you interface with users (external customers or employees) and troubleshoot their computer problems. Support service positions include the following:

    - **Helpdesk analysts** staff the phones, respond to Internet live chats, or respond to e-mails and solve problems for customers or employees, either remotely or in person. Often, helpdesk personnel are called on to train users on the latest software and hardware.

- **Computer support technicians** go to a user's location and fix software and hardware problems. They also often have to chase down and repair faults in the network infrastructure.

As important as these people are, they may receive a great deal of abuse by angry users whose computers are not working. When working in support services, you need to be patient and not be overly sensitive to insults!

Figure B.9 At smaller companies, network administrators may be fixing a user's computer in the morning, installing and configuring a new network operating system in the afternoon, and troubleshooting a server problem (shown here) in the evening. *(Mikhail Starodubov/Shutterstock)*

The video gaming industry in the United States has surpassed the earning power of the Hollywood movie industry. In 2016, the U.S. video game industry brought in sales of $30.2 billion worth of video game software, hardware, and accessories, whereas Hollywood took in just over $11.3 billion. Although some aspects of game development, such as scenery design and certain aspects of programming, are being sent offshore, the majority of game development requires a creative team whose members need to work in close proximity. Therefore, it's anticipated that most game development jobs will stay in the United States.

Consoles such as the Xbox One and the PlayStation 4 generate demand for large-scale games. The popularity of mobile devices such as smartphones and tablets is driving demand for lower-end, casual game applications. Casual games are games that can be played relatively quickly or occasionally, such as MMO (massively multiplayer online) strategy games like Clash of Clans (see Figure B.10). Demand for family-friendly games without violence, sex, and profanity is on the rise. With all this demand, there are many opportunities for careers in game development.

Game development jobs usually are split along two paths: designers and programmers.

- **Game designers** tend to be artistic and are responsible for creating 2D and 3D art, game interfaces, video sequences, special effects, game levels, and scenarios. Game designers must master software packages such as Autodesk 3ds Max, Autodesk Maya, NewTek LightWave 3D, Adobe Photoshop, and Adobe Flash.
- **Game programmers** are responsible for coding the scenarios developed by the designers. Using languages and toolsets such as Objective-C, Unity, Apple Xcode, C, C++, Assembly, and Java, programmers build the game and ensure that it plays accurately.

Aside from programmers and designers, play testers and quality-assurance professionals play the games with the intent

Figure B.10 Clash of Clans, which has you build a village and recruit soldiers to fend off neighboring marauders, is an example of a popular casual game available for mobile platforms. *(Kevin Britland/Alamy Stock Photo)*

of breaking them or discovering bugs within the game interfaces or worlds. **Play testing** is an essential part of the game development process because it assists designers in determining which aspects of the game are most intriguing to players and which parts of the game need to be repaired or enhanced.

No matter what job you may pursue in the realm of gaming, you'll need to have a two- or four-year college degree. If you're interested in gaming, look for a school with a solid animation or 3D art program or a computer game–programming curriculum. Programming requires a strong background in math and physics to enable you to realistically program environments that mimic the real world. Proficiency with math (especially geometry) also helps with design careers.

For more information on gaming careers, check out the International Game Developers Association site (**igda.org**) and the Game Career Guide (**gamecareerguide.com**).

Technical services jobs often require a two-year college degree or training at a trade school or technical institute. At smaller companies, job duties tend to overlap between the helpdesk and technician jobs. These jobs are in demand and require staffing in local markets, so they are staying onshore. You can't repair a computer's power supply if you are located in another country!

Preparing for a Job in IT

Objective B.4   *Explain the various ways you can prepare for a career in IT.*

A job in IT requires a robust skill set and formal training and preparation. Most employers today have an entry-level requirement of a college degree, a technical institute diploma, appropriate professional certifications, experience in the field, or a combination of these. How can you prepare for a job in IT?

1. **Get educated.** Two- and four-year colleges and universities normally offer three degrees to prepare students for IT careers: computer science, management information systems, and information technology (although titles vary). Alternatives to colleges and universities

Employees with certifications generally earn more than employees who aren't certified. However, most employers don't view a certification as a substitute for a college degree or a trade school program. You should think of certifications as an extra edge beyond your formal education that will make you more attractive to employers. To ensure you're pursuing the right certifications, ask employers which certifications they respect, or explore online job sites to see which certifications are listed as desirable or required.

are privately licensed technical (or trade) schools. Generally, these programs focus on building skill sets rapidly and qualifying for a job in a specific field. The main advantage of technical schools is that their programs usually take less time to complete than college degrees. However, to have a realistic chance of employment in IT fields other than networking or web development, you should attend a degree-granting college or university.

2. **Investigate professional certifications.** Certifications attempt to provide a consistent method of measuring skill levels in specific areas of IT. Hundreds of IT certifications are available, most of which you get by passing a written exam. Software and hardware vendors (such as Microsoft and Cisco) and professional organizations (such as the Computing Technology Industry Association) often establish certification standards. Visit **microsoft.com**, **cisco.com**, **comptia.org**, and **sun.com** for more information on certifications.

3. **Get experience.** In addition to education, employers want you to have experience, even for entry-level jobs. While you're still completing your education, consider getting an internship or part-time job in your field of study. Many schools will help you find internships and allow you to earn credit toward your degree through internships.

4. **Do research.** Find out as much as you can about the company and the industry it's in before going on an interview. Start with the company's website, and then expand your search to business and trade publications such as *Businessweek* and *Inc.* magazines.

Getting Started in an IT Career

Objective B.5   *Explain the various ways you can find a career in IT.*

Training for a career is not useful unless you can find a job at the end of your training. Here are some tips on getting a job:

1. **Use the career resources at your school.** Many employers recruit at schools, and most schools maintain a placement office to help students find jobs. Employees in the placement office can help you with résumé preparation and interviewing skills and can provide you with leads for internships and jobs.

2. **Develop relationships with your instructors.** Many college instructors still work in or previously worked in the IT industry. They can often provide you with valuable advice and industry contacts.

3. **Start networking.** Many jobs are never advertised but instead are filled by word of mouth. Seek out contacts in your field and discuss job prospects with them. Find out what skills you need, and ask them to recommend others in the industry with whom you can speak. Professional organizations such as the Association for Computing Machinery (ACM) offer one way to network. These organizations often have chapters on college campuses and offer reduced membership rates for students. Figure B.11 lists major professional organizations you should consider investigating.

   If you're a woman and are thinking about pursuing an IT career, many resources and groups cater to female IT professionals and students (see Figure B.12). The oldest and best-known organization is the Association for Women in Computing, founded in 1978.

4. **Check corporate websites for jobs.** Many corporate websites list current job opportunities. For example, Google provides searchable job listings by geographical location. Check the sites of companies in which you are interested and then do a search on the sites for job openings or, if provided, click their employment links.

Figure B.11   Professional Organizations

Organization Name	Purpose	Website
Association for Computing Machinery (ACM)	Oldest scientific computing society; maintains a strong focus on programming and systems development	acm.org
Association for Information Systems (AIS)	Organization of professionals who work in academia and specialize in information systems	aisnet.org
Association of Information Technology Professionals (AITP)	Heavy focus on IT education and development of seminars and learning materials	aitp.org
Institute of Electrical and Electronics Engineers (IEEE)	Provides leadership and sets engineering standards for all types of network computing devices and protocols	ieee.org
Information Systems Security Association (ISSA)	Not-for-profit, international organization of information security professionals and practitioners	issa.org

Figure B.12   Resources for Women in IT

Organization Name	Purpose	Website
Anita Borg Institute	Organization whose aim is to "increase the impact of women on all aspects of technology"	anitaborg.org
Association for Women in Computing (AWC)	A not-for-profit organization dedicated to promoting the advancement of women in computing professions	awc-hq.org
The Center for Women in Technology (CWIT)	An organization dedicated to providing global leadership in achieving women's full participation in all aspects of IT	cwit.umbc.edu
Women in Technology International (WITI)	A global trade association for tech-savvy, professional women	witi.com

5. **Visit online employment sites.** Most of these sites allow you to store your résumé online, and many sites allow employers to browse résumés to find qualified employees. Begin looking at job postings on these sites early in your education because these job postings detail the skill sets employers require. Focusing on coursework that will provide you with desirable skill sets will make you more marketable. Figure B.13 lists employment sites as well as sites that offer other career resources.

The outlook for IT jobs should continue to be positive in the future. We wish you luck with your education and job search.

Figure B.13   Resources for IT Employment

Site Name	URL
CareerBuilder	careerbuilder.com
ComputerJobs.com	computerjobs.com
ComputerWork.com	computerwork.com
Dice	dice.com
Gamasutra	gamasutra.com
JustTechJobs	justtechjobs.com
LinkedIn	linkedin.com
Monster	monster.com
TechCareers	techcareers.com

Check Your Understanding // Review & Practice

For a quick review of what you've learned, answer the following questions.

multiple choice

1. The individuals responsible for generating images for websites are referred to as
   a. network administrators.
   b. web programmers.
   c. graphic designers.
   d. interface designers.

2. What type of job involves working at client locations and the ability to work with little direct supervision?
   a. home-based
   b. system-based
   c. office-based
   d. field-based

3. Which position is *not* typically a part of the information systems department?
   a. telecommunications technician
   b. helpdesk analyst
   c. network administrator
   d. web server administrator

4. Outsourcing is thought to be an attractive option for many companies because of
   a. the emphasis on employee training.
   b. increased data security.
   c. the cost savings that can be realized.
   d. decreased travel and entertainment costs.

5. Which of the following IT positions is responsible for directing a company's strategy on sites such as Facebook, Twitter, and Yelp?
   a. project manager
   b. social media director
   c. customer interaction technician
   d. social web analyst

6. Which of the following statements about IT careers is FALSE?
   a. Most IT jobs require little interaction with other people.
   b. Women who have IT skills have ample opportunities for securing IT employment.
   c. Many IT jobs are staying in the United States.
   d. IT employers typically prefer experience over certification.

7. Which task is NOT typically performed by a network administrator?
   a. developing network usage policies
   b. installing networks
   c. web programming
   d. planning for disaster recovery

8. Which of the following is NOT a challenge in an IT career?
   a. Stress often accompanies IT jobs.
   b. You usually work alone.
   c. Women are in the minority.
   d. Lifelong learning is the norm.

true/false

_____ **1.** IT certifications are considered important to most employers.

_____ **2.** Online employment sites cannot provide guidance as to coursework you should take.

Glossary

2-in-1 PC A laptop computer that can convert into a tablet-like device.

3D printer Used to print three-dimensional models.

3-D sound card An expansion card that enables a computer to produce omnidirectional or three-dimensional sounds.

4G Stands for 4th Generation. The latest mobile communication standard with faster data transfer rates than 3G.

A

acceptable use policies Guidelines regarding usage of computer systems.

access card reader A device that reads information from a magnetic strip on the back of a credit card-like access card.

access method A method to control which computer is allowed to use transmission media at a certain time.

access point Device that is connected by a cable to the main router that amplifies a wireless signal to otherwise unreachable locations.

access time The time it takes a storage device to locate its stored data.

accounting software An application program that helps business owners manage their finances more efficiently by providing tools for tracking accounting transactions such as sales, accounts receivable, inventory purchases, and accounts payable.

Active Server Pages (ASP) Programming language used to build websites with interactive capabilities; adapts an HTML page to the user's selections.

active topology In a network, a type of topology where the nodes participate in moving data through the network.

adware A program that downloads on your computer when a user installs a freeware program, game, or utility. Generally, adware enables sponsored advertisements to appear in a section of a browser window or as a pop-up ad.

affective computing A type of computing that relates to emotion or that deliberately tries to influence emotion.

aggregator A software program that finds and retrieves the latest update of web material (usually podcasts) according to your specifications.

AJAX (Asynchronous JavaScript and XML) A collection of technologies that allow the creation of web applications that can update information on a page without requiring the user to refresh or leave the page.

algorithm A set of specific, sequential steps that describe exactly what the computer program must do to complete the required work.

all-in-one computer A desktop system unit that houses the computer's processor, memory, and monitor in a single unit.

all-in-one printer A device that combines the functions of a printer, scanner, copier, and fax.

alphabetic check In a database, confirms that only textual characters are entered in a field.

American Standard Code for Information Interchange (ASCII) The American National Standards Institute (ANSI, pro-nounced "AN-see") standard code, called the American Standard Code for Information Interchange (ASCII, pronounced "AS-key"), to represent each letter or character as an 8-bit (or 1-byte) binary code.

amoral behavior When a person has no sense of right and wrong and no interest in the moral consequences of his or her actions.

analog Waves that illustrate the loudness of a sound or the brightness of the colors in an image at a given moment in time.

antivirus software Software specifically designed to detect viruses and protect a computer and files from harm.

app creation software Programming environments that can produce apps that run on various mobile devices.

applet A small application located on a server; when requested, the applet is downloaded to the client.

application programming interface (API) A set of software routines that allows one software system to work with another.

application server A server that acts as a repository for application software.

application software The set of programs on a computer that helps a user carry out tasks such as word processing, sending e-mail, balancing a budget, creating presentations, editing photos, taking an online course, and playing games.

architecture neutral A feature of Java whereby code needs to be compiled only once, after which the code can be run on many different CPUs.

arithmetic logic unit (ALU) The part of the CPU that performs arithmetical and logic calculations.

artificial intelligence (AI) The branch of computer science that deals with the attempt to create computers that think like humans.

artificial neural networks (ANNs) Computer systems constructed based on the structure of the human brain using loosely connected artificial neurons.

aspect ratio The width-to-height proportion of a monitor.

assembly language A computer language that allows programmers to write programs using a set of short, English-like commands that speak directly to the CPU and that give the programmer direct control of hardware resources.

assistive (adaptive) technology Any device, software feature, or app that is designed to improve the functional capabilities of individuals with disabilities.

audio MIDI interface Interface technology that allows a user to connect musical instruments and microphones to their computer.

audio-editing software Programs that perform basic editing tasks on audio files such as cutting dead air space from the beginning or end of a song or cutting a portion from the middle.

augmentative reality/augmented reality A combination of our normal sense of the objects around us with an overlay of information displayed.

authentication The process of identifying a computer user, based on a login or username and password. The computer system determines whether the computer user is authorized and what level of access is to be granted on the network.

authentication server A server that keeps track of who's logging on to the network and which services on the network are available to each user.

B

backdoor program A program that enables a hacker to take complete control of a computer without the legitimate user's knowledge or permission.

backup A copy of a computer file that can be used to replace the original if it's lost or damaged.

backward compatibility The accommodation of current devices being able to use previously issued software standards in addition to the current standards.

base class In object-oriented analysis, the original class.

base-10 number system (decimal notation) The system you use to represent all of the numeric values you use each day. It's called base 10 because it uses 10 digits—0 through 9—to represent any value.

basic input/output system (BIOS) A program that manages the data between a computer's operating system and all the input and output devices attached to the computer; also responsible for loading the operating system (OS) from its permanent location on the hard drive to random access memory (RAM).

bastion host A heavily secured server located on a special perimeter network between the company's secure internal network and its firewall.

batch processing The accumulation of transaction data until a certain point is reached, at which time several transactions are processed at once.

beta version A version of the software that's still under development. Many beta versions are available for a limited trial period and are used to help the developers correct any errors before they launch the software on the market.

Big Data Very large data sets that are analyzed to reveal patterns, trends, and associations.

binary decision A type of decision point in an algorithm that can be answered in one of only two ways: yes (true) or no (false).

binary digit (bit) A digit that corresponds to the on and off states of a computer's switches. A bit contains a value of either 0 or 1.

binary language The language computers use to process data into information, consisting of only the values 0 and 1.

binary large object (BLOB) Audio clips, video clips, pictures, and extremely large documents.

binary number system (base-2 number system) A method of representing a number in powers of 2.

biometric authentication device A device that uses some unique characteristic of human biology to identify authorized users.

black-hat hacker A hacker who uses his or her knowledge to destroy information or for illegal gain.

blog (weblog) A personal log or journal posted on the web; short for *web log*.

Bluetooth technology A type of wireless technology that uses radio waves to transmit data over short distances often used to connect peripherals such as printers and keyboards to computers or headsets to cell phones.

Blu-ray disc (BD) A method of optical storage for digital data, developed for storing high-definition media. It has the largest storage capacity of all optical storage options.

Bookmarks Features in some browsers that place markers of websites' Uniform Resource Locators (URLs) in an easily retrievable list.

Boolean operators A word used to refine logical searches. For Internet searches, the words AND, NOT, and OR describe the relationships between keywords in the search.

boot process The process for loading the operating system (OS) into random access memory (RAM) when the computer is turned on.

boot-sector virus A virus that replicates itself into the master boot record of a flash drive or hard drive.

botnet A large group of software applications (called *robots* or *bots*) that run without user intervention on a large number of computers.

breadcrumb trail A navigation aid that shows users the path they have taken to get to a web page or where the page is located within the website; it usually appears at the top of a page.

bridge A device that is used to send data between different collision domains in a network, depending on where the recipient device is located.

broadband A high-speed Internet connection such as cable, satellite, or digital subscriber line (DSL).

brute force attack An attempt to access an account by repeatedly trying different passwords.

bus (linear bus) topology A system of networking connections in which all devices are connected in sequence on a single cable.

business intelligence (BI) The ability to improve business decision making with databases and other fact-based support systems.

business intelligence system Systems used to analyze and interpret data in order to enable managers to make informed decisions about how best to run a business.

business-to-business (B2B) E-commerce transactions between businesses.

business-to-consumer (B2C) E-commerce transactions between businesses and consumers.

byte Eight binary digits (bits).

C

C A programming language originally developed for system programmers.

C++ A programming language; takes C to an object-oriented level.

C# A Microsoft programming language developed to compete with Java.

cable Internet A broadband service that transmits data over coaxial cables.

cache memory Small blocks of memory, located directly on and next to the central processing unit (CPU) chip, that act as holding places for recently or frequently used instructions or data that the CPU accesses the most.

caption A property in a database that enables the field name to display in a more meaningful or readable manner.

cascading style sheet (CSS) A list of rules that defines in one single location how to display HTML elements.

catfishing A type of Internet harassment where some individual scams others into a false romantic relationship.

Cat 5e cable A UTP cable commonly found in wired Ethernet networks, designed for 100 Mbps-wired Ethernet networks.

Cat 6 cable A UTP cable type that provides more than 1 Gbps of throughput.

central processing unit (CPU or processor) The part of the system unit of a computer that is responsible for data processing; it is the largest and most important chip in the computer. The CPU controls all the functions performed by the computer's other components and processes all the commands issued to it by software instructions.

centralized A characteristic of client/server networks where the server, not the individual nodes, provide services such as data security.

Chromebook Any laptop or tablet running the Chrome OS as its operating system.

circuit switching Where a dedicated connection is formed between two points (such as two people on telephones) and the connection remains active for the duration of the transmission.

class A category of input identified in object-oriented analysis; classes are defined by information and actions.

clickstream data Software used on company websites to capture information about each click that users make as they navigate through the site.

client A computer that requests information from a server in a client/server network (such as your computer when you are connected to the Internet).

client/server model A model of network communications where a client device such as a computer, tablet, or smartphone uses browsers to request services from networks that make up the Internet.

client/server network A type of network that uses servers to deliver services to computers that are requesting them (clients).

client-side program A program that runs on the client computer and that requires no interaction with a web server.

clock cycle Steady beats or "ticks" of the system clock.

clock speed The steady and constant pace at which a computer goes through machine cycles, measured in hertz (Hz).

cloud computing The process of storing data, files, and applications on the web, which allows access to and manipulation of these files and applications from any Internet-connected device.

cloud server A server that is maintained by a hosting company and that is connected to networks via the Internet.

cloud storage A service that keeps files on the Internet (in the "cloud") rather than storing files solely on a local device.

cloud-ready printer Printers that connect directly to the Internet and register themselves with Google Cloud Print.

cluster The smallest increment in which data is stored on hard disks; hard disks are divided into *tracks*, then *wedges*, then *sectors*, then clusters.

CMYK A color model in which all colors are described as a mixture of four base colors (cyan, magenta, yellow, and black).

coaxial cable A single copper wire surrounded by layers of plastic insulation, metal sheathing, and a plastic jacket; used mainly in cable television and cable Internet service.

code editing The step of programming in which a programmer types the code to be executed.

codec A rule, implemented in either software or hardware, which squeezes a given amount of audio and video information into less space.

coding Translating an algorithm into a programming language.

cold boot The process of starting a computer from a powered-down or off state.

collaborative consumption Joining together as a group to use a specific product more efficiently.

command-driven interface Interface between user and computer in which the user enters commands to communicate with the computer system.

comment A note left by a programmer in the program code to explain the purpose of a section of code, to indicate the date the program was written, or to include other important information about the code so that other programmers can more easily understand and update it.

commerce server Computers that host software that enables users to buy goods and services over the web.

communications server A server that handles all communications between the network and other networks, including managing Internet connectivity.

compact disc (CD) A method of optical storage for digital data; originally developed for storing digital audio.

compilation The process by which code is converted into machine language—the language the CPU can understand.

compiler A program that understands both the syntax of the programming language and the exact structure of the CPU and its machine language.

completeness check In a database, ensures that all required fields have been completed.

computer A data-processing device that gathers, processes, outputs, and stores data and information.

computer forensics The application of computer systems and techniques to gather potential legal evidence; a law enforcement specialty used to fight high-tech crime.

computer literacy Being familiar enough with computers that a user knows how to use them and understands their capabilities and limitations.

computer protocol A set of rules for exchanging electronic information.

computer vision The ability of a computing device to interpret visual information the way humans do.

computer-aided design (CAD) A 3-D modeling program used to create automated designs, technical drawings, and model visualizations.

connectionless protocol A protocol that a host computer can use to send data over the network without establishing a direct connection with any specific recipient computer.

connection-oriented protocol A protocol for exchanging information that requires two computers to exchange control packets, thereby setting up the parameters of the data-exchange session, before sending packets that contain data.

connectivity port A port that enables a computing device to be connected to other devices or systems such as networks, modems, and the Internet.

consistency check In a database, compares the values of data in two or more fields to see if those values are reasonable.

consumer-to-consumer (C2C) E-commerce transactions between consumers through online sites such as eBay.

control structure General term used for a keyword in a programming language that allows the programmer to direct the flow of the program based on a decision.

control unit Unit of the CPU that manages the switches inside the CPU.

cookie A small text file that some websites automatically store on a client computer's hard drive when a user visits the site.

copyleft A simplified licensing scheme that enables copyright holders to grant certain rights to a work while retaining other rights.

copyright A creator's exclusive rights to use a work of intellecutal property, such as making copies or selling it.

copyright infringement Any violation of someone's rights under copyright laws, such as reproducing their work without permission.

core A complete processing section from a central processing unit, embedded into one physical chip.

course management software A program that provides traditional classroom tools, such as calendars and grade books, over the Internet, as well as areas for students to exchange ideas and information in chat rooms, discussion forums, and e-mail.

CPU benchmarks Measurements used to compare performance between processors.

CPU usage The percentage of time the central processing unit (CPU) is working.

CPU usage graph Records central processing unit (CPU) usage for several seconds.

crisis-mapping tool A tool that collects information from e-mails, text messages, blog posts, and Twitter tweets and maps them, making the information instantly publicly available.

crowdfunding Asking for small donations from a large number of people, often using the Internet; a style of generating capital to start a business through social media.

crowdsourcing Obtaining information or input for a project (such as development of a product) by obtaining the opinions of many different people.

CSMA/CD The method used on Ethernet networks to avoid data collisions; short for *carrier sense multiple access with collision detection*. A node connected to the network uses carrier sense to verify that no other nodes are currently transmitting data signals.

cursor An onscreen icon (often shown by a vertical bar or an arrow) that helps the user keep track of exactly what is active on the display screen

custom installation The process of installing only those features of a software program that a user wants on the hard drive.

cybercrime Any criminal action perpetrated primarily through the use of a computer.

cyber harassment Using technology to harass or intimidate another individual.

cyberloafing Doing anything with a computer that's unrelated to a job (such as playing video games) while one's supposed to be working. Also called *cyberslacking*.

D

data Numbers, words, pictures, or sounds that represent facts, figures, or ideas; the raw input that users have at the start of a job.

data breach When sensitive or confidential information is copied, transmitted, or viewed by an individual who is not authorized to handle the data.

data centralization When data is maintained in only one file.

data collision When two computers send data at the same time and the sets of data collide somewhere in the transmission media.

data dictionary (database schema) A map of a database that defines the features of the fields in the database.

data file A file that contains stored data.

data inconsistency Data for a record being different in two different lists.

data integrity When the data in a database is accurate and reliable.

data mart Small slices of a data warehouse grouped together and separated from the main body of data in the data warehouse so that related sets of data can be analyzed.

data mining The process by which great amounts of data are analyzed and investigated. The objective is to spot significant patterns or trends within the data that would otherwise not be obvious.

data plan A connectivity plan or text messaging plan in which data charges are separate from cell phone calling charges and are provided at rates different from those for voice calls.

data redundancy Duplicated data in a list.

data staging The act of formatting data from source databases before fitting it into a data warehouse; it consists of three steps: extraction, transformation, and storage.

data transfer rate (bandwidth) The maximum speed at which data can be transmitted between two nodes on a network; measured in megabits per second (Mbps) or gigabits per second (Gbps).

data type (field type) (1) Describes the kind of data being stored at the memory location; each programming language has its own data types (although there is some degree of overlap). (2) In a database, indicates what type of data can be stored in a field and prevents the wrong type of data from being entered into the field.

data warehouse A large-scale collection of data that contains and organizes in one place all the data from an organization's multiple databases.

database A digital collection of related data that can be stored, sorted, organized, and queried.

database administrator (database designer) An information technology professional responsible for designing, constructing, and maintaining databases.

database management system (DBMS) A specially designed application software used to create and manage databases.

database server A server that provides client computers with access to information stored in databases.

database software An electronic filing system best used for larger and more complicated groups of data that require more than one table and the ability to group, sort, and retrieve data and generate reports.

data-flow diagram Diagrams that trace all data in an information system from the point at which data enters the system to its final resting place (storage or output).

debugger A tool in an integrated development environment that helps programmers analyze a program as it runs.

debugging The process of running a program over and over to find and repair errors and to make sure the program behaves in the way it should.

decentralized A characteristic of peer-to-peer networks where the individual nodes provide services such as data security.

decision point A place where a program must choose from a list of actions based on the value of a certain input.

decision support system (DSS) A type of business intelligence system designed to help managers develop solutions for specific problems.

dedicated server A server used to fulfill one specific function, such as handling e-mail.

deep learning (DL) AI systems capable of learning from their mistakes (just as humans do). DL systems therefore improve their accuracy going forward.

default value The value a database automatically uses for a field unless the user enters another value.

denial-of-service (DoS) attack An attack that occurs when legitimate users are denied access to a computer system because a hacker is repeatedly making requests of that computer system that tie up its resources and deny legitimate users access.

derived class In object-oriented analysis, the modified class.

desktop The primary working area of Windows 10.

desktop computer A computer that is intended for use at a single location. A desktop computer consists of a case that houses the main components of the computer, plus peripheral devices.

desktop publishing (DTP) software Programs for incorporating and arranging graphics and text to produce creative documents.

detail report A report generated by a management information system that provides a list of the transactions that occurred during a certain time period.

device driver Software that facilitates the communication between a device and its operating system.

digital activism The use of hashtags and posts to raise awareness and foster discussion about specific issues and causes via social media.

digital audio workstation software (DAW) Software used to record and edit music.

digital convergence The use of a single unifying device to handle media, Internet, entertainment, and telephony needs.

digital divide The discrepancy between those who have access to the opportunities and knowledge that computers and the Internet offer and those who do not.

digital manipulation Altering media so that the images captured are changed from the way they were originally seen by the human eye.

digital rights management (DRM) A system of access control that allows only limited use of material that has been legally purchased.

digital video (or versatile) disc (DVD) A method of optical storage for digital data that has greater storage capacity than compact discs.

digital video-editing software A program for editing digital video.

digitized Information measured and converted (from analog data) to a stream of numerical values.

directory A hierarchical structure that include files, folders, and drives used to create a more organized and efficient computer.

Disk Cleanup A Windows utility that removes unnecessary files from the hard drive.

disk defragmentation The process of regrouping related pieces of files on the hard drive, enabling faster retrieval of the data.

display screen (monitor) A common output device that displays text, graphics, and video as soft copies (copies that can be seen only on screen).

distributed (grid) computing A software system in which components located on networked computers interact to achieve a common goal.

distributed denial-of-service (DDoS) attack An automated attack that's launched from more than one zombie computer at the same time.

distributions (distros) Linux download packages.

Document Object Model (DOM) Used by JavaScript to organize objects and page elements.

documentation Description of the technical details of the software, how the code works, and how the user interacts with the program; in addition, all the necessary user documentation that will be distributed to the program's users.

domain name A part of a Uniform Resource Locator (URL). Domain names consist of two parts: the site's host and a suffix that indicates the type of organization (example: popsci.com, where *popsci* is the domain name and *com* is the suffix).

domain name system (DNS) server A server that maintains a database of domain names and converts domain names to Internet protocol addresses.

dotted decimal number (dotted quad) The form of an Internet protocol address, where sets of numerals are separated by decimals, i.e., 197.169.73.63.

drawing software (illustration software) Programs for creating or editing two-dimensional line-based drawings.

drive bay A special shelf inside a computer that is designed to hold storage devices.

drive-by download The use of malicious software to attack a computer by downloading harmful programs onto a computer, without the user's knowledge, while they are surfing a website.

DSL (digital subscriber line) A type of connection that uses telephone lines to connect to the Internet and that allows both phone and data transmissions to share the same line.

dynamic addressing A way of assigning Internet protocol addresses where a computer is assigned a temporary address from an available pool of addresses.

dynamic decision making The ability of a web page to decide how to display itself based on the choices the reader makes.

Dynamic Host Configuration Protocol (DHCP) A protocol for assigning dynamic internet protocol addresses.

dynamic HTML (DHTML) A combination of technologies—HTML, cascading style sheets, and JavaScript—used to create lively and interactive websites.

E

earbuds Listening devices that connect to computing devices so sound can be heard.

e-commerce (electronic commerce) The process of conducting business online for purposes ranging from fund-raising to advertising to selling products.

editor A special tool in an integrated development environment (IDE) that helps programmers as they enter code.

educational fair use Extension of fair use guidelines that grants additional exceptions to copyright infringement for teachers and students when the material is used for educational purposes.

electronic data interchange (EDI) The exchange of large amounts of data in a standardized electronic format.

electronic ink (E Ink) A very crisp, sharp grayscale representation of text achieved by using millions of microcapsules with white and black particles in a clear fluid.

electronic text (e-text) Textual information stored as digital information so that it can be stored, manipulated, and transmitted by electronic devices.

electrical switches The devices inside the computer that are flipped between the two states of 1 and 0, signifying on and off. I

element In HTML, a pair of tags and the text between them.

e-mail (electronic mail) Internet-based communication in which senders and recipients correspond.

e-mail client A software program that runs on a computer and is used to send and receive e-mail through an Internet service provider's server.

e-mail server A server whose function is to process and deliver incoming and outgoing e-mail.

e-mail virus A virus transmitted by e-mail that often uses the address book in the victim's e-mail system to distribute itself.

embedded computer A specially designed computer chip that resides inside another device, such as a car. These selfcontained computer devices have their own programming and typically neither receive input from users nor interact with other systems.

embodied agents Robots that look and act like human beings.

encryption The process of coding e-mail so that only the person with the key to the code (the intended recipient) can decode the message.

encryption virus A malicious program that searches for common data files and compresses them into a file using a complex encryption key, thereby rendering the files unusable.

End User License Agreement (EULA) An agreement between the user and the software developer that must be accepted before installing the software on a computer.

enterprise resource planning (ERP) system A business intelligence system that accumulates in a central location all information relevant to running a business and makes it readily available to whoever needs it to make decisions.

e-reader A device that can display e-text and that has supporting tools, like note taking, bookmarks, and integrated dictionaries.

ergonomics How a user sets up his or her computer and other equipment to minimize risk of injury or discomfort.

error handling The part of a problem statement where programmers describe what the program should do if the input data is invalid or just gibberish.

Ethernet network A network that uses the Ethernet protocol as the means (or standard) by which the nodes on the network communicate.

Ethernet port A port that transfers data at speeds of up to 10,000 Mbps; used to connect a computer to a modem or to a network.

ethics The study of the general nature of morals and the choices individuals make.

event The result of an action, such as a keystroke, mouse click, or signal to the printer, in the respective device (keyboard, mouse, or printer) to which the operating system responds.

exception report A report generated by a management information system that shows conditions that are unusual or that need attention by system users.

executable program The binary sequence that instructs the CPU to run the programmer's code.

expansion cards (or adapter cards) A circuit board with specific functions that augment the computer's basic functions and provide connections to other devices; examples include sound cards and video cards.

expert system A system that tries to replicate the decision-making processes of human experts in order to solve specific problems.

exploit kits A software toolkit used to take advantage of security weaknesses found in apps or operating systems, usually to deploy malware.

eXtensible Markup Language (XML) A markup language that enables designers to define their own data-based tags, making it much easier for a website to transfer the key information on its page to another site; it defines what data is being described rather than how it's to be displayed.

extension (file type) In a file name, the three letters that follow the user-supplied file name after the dot (.); the extension identifies what kind of family of files the file belongs to, or which application should be used to read the file.

external hard drive A hard drive that is enclosed in a protective case to make it portable; the drive is connected to the computer with a data transfer cable and is often used to back up data.

extranet An area of an intranet that only certain entities or individuals can access; the owner of the extranet decides who will be permitted to access it.

F

fair use Guidelines allowing people to use portions of a copyrighted work for specific purposes without receiving prior permission from the copyright holder.

Favorites A feature in Microsoft Internet Explorer that places a marker of a website's Uniform Resource Locator (URL) in an easily retrievable list in the browser's toolbar. (Called Bookmarks in some browsers.)

feature phone Inexpensive cell phones with modest processors, simple interfaces, and, often, no touch screens.

fiber-optic cable A cable that transmits data via light waves along glass or plastic fibers.

fiber-optic service Internet access that is enabled by transmitting data at the speed of light through glass or plastic fibers.

field The component of a database in which the database stores each category of information.

field constraint A property that must be satisfied for an entry to be accepted into the field.

field name A way of describing the information in the field.

field properties In an Access database table, the field name, data type, and other data elements.

field size Defines the maximum number of characters that a field can hold in a database.

fifth-generation language (5GL) A computer language in which a problem is presented as a series of facts or constraints instead of as a specific algorithm; the system of facts can then be queried; considered the most "natural" of languages.

file A collection of related pieces of information stored together for easy reference.

file compression utility A program that takes out redundancies in a file in order to reduce the file size.

File Explorer The main tool for finding, viewing, and managing the contents of your computer by showing the location and contents of every drive, folder, and file; called Windows Explorer prior to Windows 8.

File History A Windows utility that automatically creates a duplicate of your libraries, desktop, contacts, and favorites and copies it to another storage device, such as an external hard drive.

file management The process by which humans or computer software provide organizational structure to a computer's contents.

file name The first part of the label applied to a file; generally the name a user assigns to the file when saving it.

file path The exact location of a file, starting with the drive in which the file is located and including all folders, subfolders (if any), the file name, and the extension (example: C:\ Users\username\Documents\ Illustrations\ EBronte.jpg).

file server A server that stores and manages files for network users or that acts as a storehouse for files that users can download.

File Transfer Protocol (FTP) A protocol used to upload and download files from one computer to another over the Internet.

filter In a database, temporarily displays records that match certain criteria.

financial planning software Programs for managing finances, such as Intuit's Quicken, which include electronic checkbook registers and automatic bill-payment tools.

firewall A software program or hardware device designed to prevent unauthorized access to computers or networks.

firmware System software that controls hardware devices.

first-generation language (1GL) The machine language of a CPU; the sequence of bits that the CPU understands.

flash drive (jump drive, USB drive, or thumb drive) A drive that plugs into a universal serial bus (USB) port on a computer and that stores data digitally.

flash memory card A form of portable storage; this removable memory card is often used in digital cameras, smartphones, video cameras, and printers.

flatbed scanner Used to create a digital image from a tangible image (like a paper photo).

flowchart Visual diagram of a process, including the decisions that need to be made along the way.

folder A collection of files stored on a computer.

For In Visual Basic, programmers use the keyword For to implement a loop; after the keyword For, an input or output item is given a starting value, and then the statements in the body of the loop are executed.

foreign key In a relational database, the common field between tables that's not the primary key.

fourth-generation language (4GL) A computer language type that includes database query languages and report generators.

frame Groups of data packets that are sent together in a package.

freeware Any copyrighted software that can be used for free.

full backup A file backup that encompasses all files on a computer Irregardless of whether they have changed since the last backup.

full installation The process of installing all the files and programs from the distribution media to the computer's hard drive.

fuzzy logic Enables the interjection of experiential learning into knowledge-based systems by allowing the consideration of probabilities.

G

game controllers Devices such as joysticks, game pads, and steering wheels are considered input devices because they send data to computing devices.

general availability (GA) The point in the release cycle, where, after release to manufacturers, software is available for purchase by the public.

geolocation The method of identifying the geographical location of a person or device, usually by utilizing information processed through the Internet.

gigabit Ethernet (GbE) The most commonly used wired Ethernet standard deployed in devices designed for home networks; provides bandwidth of up to 1 Gbps.

gigabyte (GB) About a billion bytes.

gigahertz (GHz) One billion hertz.

global positioning system (GPS) A system of 21 satellites (plus 3 working spares), built and operated by the U.S. military, that constantly orbit the earth. The satellites provide information to GPS–capable devices to pinpoint locations on the earth.

Google Chrome OS A web-based OS.

graphical user interface (GUI) Unlike the command- and menu-driven interfaces used in earlier software, GUIs display graphics and use the point-and-click technology of the mouse and cursor, making them much more user friendly.

graphics double data rate 5 (GDDR5) A standard of video memory.

graphics processing unit (GPU) A specialized logic chip that's dedicated to quickly displaying and calculating visual data such as shadows, textures, and luminosity.

green computing (green IT) A movement that encourages environmentally sustainable computing (or IT).

grey-hat hacker A cross between black and white—a hacker who will often illegally break into systems merely to flaunt his or her expertise to the administrator of the system he or she penetrated or to attempt to sell his or her services in repairing security breaches.

H

hacker Anyone who unlawfully breaks into a computer system (whether an individual computer or a network).

hacktivism Using computers and computer networks in a subversive way to promote an agenda.

handshaking In a connection-oriented protocol, the process of exchanging control packets before exchanging data packets.

hard disk drive (HDD or hard drive) The computer's nonvolatile, primary storage device for permanent storage of software and data.

hardware Any part of a computer or computer system you can physically touch.

head crash Impact of the read/write head against the magnetic platter of the hard drive; often results in data loss.

headphones Devices for listening to sounds on computing devices.

hexadecimal digit A digit with 16 possible values: 0–9 and A–F.

hexidecimal notation A base-16 number system, meaning it uses 16 digits to represent numbers instead of the 10 digits used in base 10 or the 2 digits used in base 2. The 16 digits it uses are the 10 numeric digits, 0 to 9, plus six extra symbols: A, B, C, D, E, and F.

Hibernate A power-management mode that saves the current state of the current system to the computer's hard drive.

high definition A standard of digital TV signal that guarantees a specific level of resolution and a specific *aspect ratio*, which is the rectangular shape of the image.

high-definition multimedia interface (HDMI) port A compact audio–video interface standard that carries both high-definition video and uncompressed digital audio.

hoax Anything designed to deceive another person either as a practical joke or for financial gain.

home area network (HAN) A network located in a home that's used to connect all of its digital devices.

home network server A device designed to store media, share media across the network, and back up files on computers connected to a home network.

honey pot A computer system that's set up to attract unauthorized users by appearing to be a key part of a network or a system that contains something of great value.

host The portion of a domain name that identifies who maintains a given website. For example, berkeley.edu is the domain name for the University of California at Berkeley, which maintains that site.

HTML embedded scripting language A programming language that tucks programming code directly within the HTML of a web page; the most popular example is JavaScript.

HTML tag Tags that surround and define HTML content (such as <b> and</b>, which indicate bolding).

hybrid topology Combining multiple topologies on one network.

hyperlink A type of specially coded text that, when clicked, enables a user to jump from one location, or web page, to another within a website or to another website altogether.

Hypertext Markup Language (HTML) A series of tags that define how elements on a website should be displayed in a browser.

Hypertext Transfer Protocol (HTTP) The protocol that allows files to be transferred from a web server so that you can see them on your computer by using a browser.

Hypertext Transfer Protocol Secure (HTTPS) The Internet protocol that ensures data is sent securely over the web.

hyperthreading A technology that permits quicker processing of information by enabling a new set of instructions to start executing before the previous set has finished.

identity theft The process by which someone uses personal information about someone else (such as the victim's name, address, and Social Security number) to assume the victim's identity for the purpose of defrauding another.

if else In C++, a binary decision in the code where the program can follow one of two paths: If the decision is made one way, the program follows one path; if made the other way (else), the program follows another path.

image backup (system backup) A copy of an entire computer system, created for restoration purposes.

image-editing software Programs for editing photographs and other images.

incremental backup (partial backup) A type of backup that only backs up files that have changed since the last time files were backed up.

information Data that has been organized or presented in a meaningful fashion; the result, or output that users require at the end of a job.

information assurance Ensuring that information systems contain accurate information and are adequately secured against tampering.

information system A system that includes data, people, procedures, hardware, and software that help in planning and decision making; a software-based solution used to gather and analyze information.

information technology (IT) The set of techniques used in processing and retrieving information.

inheritance In object-oriented analysis, the ability of a new class to automatically pick up all the data and methods of an existing class and then extend and customize those to fit its specific needs.

initial value A beginning point.

inkjet printer A nonimpact printer that sprays tiny drops of ink onto paper.

inoculation A process used by antivirus software; compares old and current qualities of files to detect viral activity.

input device: A hardware device used to enter, or input, data (text, images, and sounds) and instructions (user responses and commands) into a computer.

input forms Used to control how new data is entered into a shared database.

instant messaging (IM) A program that enables users to communicate online in real time with others who are also online.

intangible personal property Property that can't be touched—or potentially even seen—yet it still has value.

integrated circuits (or chips) Tiny regions of semiconductor material that support a huge number of transistors.

integrated development environment (IDE) A developmental tool that helps programmers write and test their programs;

one IDE can be configured to support many different languages.

intellectual property Refers to products derived from the mind, such as works of art and literature, inventions, and software code.

intelligence The ability to acquire and apply knowledge and skills.

intelligent personal assistant Software designed to perform tasks or services for individuals.

interactive white board An input/output device that projects the computer's display onto the interactive white board's surface.

internal hard drive A hard drive that resides within the computer's system unit and that usually holds all permanently stored programs and data.

Internet A network of networks that's the largest network in the world, connecting billions of computers globally.

Internet backbone The main pathway of high-speed communications lines over which all Internet traffic flows.

Internet cache A section of the hard drive that stores information that may be needed again, such as Internet protocol addresses and frequently accessed web pages.

Internet Corporation for Assigned Names and Numbers (ICANN) The organization that registers Internet protocol addresses to ensure they're unique and haven't been assigned to other users.

Internet exchange point (IXP) A way of connecting Internet service providers (ISPs) that's made up of one or more network switches to which the ISPs connect.

Internet of Things (IoT) The interconnection of uniquely identifiable embedded computing devices that transfer data over a network without requiring human-to-human or human-to-computer interaction.

Internet Protocol (IP) One of the original two protocols that were developed for the Internet (the other was TCP).

Internet Protocol (IP) address The means by which all computers connected to the Internet identify each other. It consists of a unique set of four numbers separated by dots, such as 123.45.178.91.

Internet Protocol version 4 (IPv4) The original Internet protocol addressing scheme, created in 1981.

Internet Protocol version 6 (IPv6) An Internet protocol (IP) addressing scheme that makes IP addresses longer, thereby providing more available addresses.

Internet service provider (ISP) A company that specializes in providing Internet access. ISPs may be specialized providers, like Juno, or companies that provide other services in addition to Internet access (such as phone and cable television).

interpreter For a programming language, translates the source code into an intermediate form, line by line; each line is then executed as it's translated.

interrupt A signal that tells the operating system that it's in need of immediate attention.

interrupt handler A special numerical code that prioritizes requests from various devices. These requests then are placed in the interrupt table in the computer's primary memory.

intranet A private network set up by a business or an organization that's used exclusively by a select group of employees, customers, suppliers, volunteers, or supporters.

IP address *See Internet Protocol address.*

J

jam signal A special signal sent to network nodes alerting them that a data collision has occurred.

Java An object-oriented programming language that has a large set of existing classes.

Java applet A small Java-based program.

JavaScript An Internet protocol (IP) addressing scheme that makes IP addresses longer, thereby providing more available addresses.

Javascript Object Notation (JSON) A syntax for exchanging information between computers.

JavaServer Pages (JSP) Programming language used to build websites with interactive capabilities; adapts the HTML page to the user's selections.

join query A query used to extract data that's in two or more tables in a database.

K

kernel (supervisor program) The essential component of the operating system that's responsible for managing the processor and all other components of the computer system. Because it stays in random access memory (RAM) the entire

time the computer is powered on, the kernel is called memory resident.

key pair The two keys used in public-key encryption.

keyboard A hardware device used to enter typed data and commands into a computer.

keystroke logger (keylogger) A type of spyware program that monitors keystrokes with the intent of stealing passwords, login IDs, or credit card information.

keyword (1) A specific word a user wishes to query (or look for) in an Internet search. (2) A specific word that has a predefined meaning in a particular programming language.

kilobyte (KB) A unit of computer storage equal to approximately 1,000 bytes.

knowledge representation Encoding information about the world into formats that an AI system can understand.

knowledge-based system A business intelligence system that provides intelligence that supplements the user's own intellect and makes the decision support system more effective.

L

laptop (or notebook) computer A portable computer with a keyboard, a monitor, and other devices integrated into a single compact case.

large format printer A printer that prints on oversized paper. Often used for creating banners and signs.

laser printer A nonimpact printer known for quick and quiet production and high-quality printouts.

latency The process that occurs after the read/write head of the hard drive locates the correct track and then waits for the correct sector to spin to the read/write head.

light-emitting diode (LED) An energy-efficient technology used in monitors. It may result in better color accuracy and thinner panels than traditional LCD monitors.

linked data Data that is formally defined and that can be expressed in relationships.

Linux An open-source operating system based on UNIX. Because of the stable nature of this operating system, it's often used on web servers.

liquid crystal display (LCD) The technology used in flat-panel computer monitors.

local area network (LAN) A network in which the nodes are located within a small geographic area.

locally installed software Software that is installed on your device's internal storage.

logic bomb A computer virus that runs when a certain set of conditions is met, such as when a program is launched a specific number of times.

logical error An error in a program that produces unintended or undesired output, where the syntax is correct but some other human error has occurred.

logical port A virtual communications gateway or path that enables a computer to organize requests for information (such as web page downloads and e-mail routing) from other networks or computers.

logical port blocking A condition in which a firewall is configured to ignore all incoming packets that request access to a certain port so that no unwanted requests will get through to the computer.

loop A type of decision point in an algorithm. In a loop, a question is asked, and if the answer is yes, a set of actions is performed. Once the set of actions has finished, the question is asked again, creating a loop. If the answer to the question is *no*, the algorithm breaks free of the loop and moves on to the first step that follows the loop.

M

machine cycle The series of steps a central processing unit goes through when it performs a program instruction.

machine language The sequence of bits that the CPU understands.

machine learning A form of artificial intelligence that provides computers with the ability to learn without being explicitly programmed.

macOS The first commercially available operating system to incorporate a graphical user interface (GUI) with user-friendly point-and-click technology.

macro A small program that groups a series of commands to run as a single command.

macro virus A virus that's distributed by hiding it inside a macro.

mainframe A large, expensive computer that supports hundreds or thousands of users simultaneously and executes many different programs at the same time.

malware Software that's intended to render a system temporarily or permanently useless or to penetrate a computer system completely for purposes of information gathering. Examples include spyware, viruses, worms, and Trojan horses.

management information system (MIS) A type of business intelligence system that provides timely and accurate information that enables managers to make critical business decisions.

many-to-many relationship In a relational database, records in one table are related to multiple records in a second table, and vice versa.

master boot record A small program that runs whenever a computer boots up.

media access control (MAC) address The physical address, similar to a serial number, of each network adapter.

megabyte (MB) A unit of computer storage equal to approximately 1 million bytes.

memory module (memory card) A small circuit board that holds a series of random access memory (RAM) chips.

menu-driven interface A user interface in which the user chooses a command from menus displayed on the screen.

metadata Data that describes other data.

metasearch engine A search engine, such as Dogpile, that searches other search engines rather than individual websites.

method The process of how a program converts inputs into the correct outputs.

metropolitan area network (MAN) A wide area network (WAN) that links users in a specific geographic area (such as within a city or county).

microblog Social media in which users post short text with usually frequent updates.

microphone (mic) A device that allows you to capture sound waves, such as those created by your voice, and to transfer them to digital format on your computer.

microprocessors The chips that contain a central processing unit (CPU, or processor).

Microsoft account Registered user profile with specific user id and password to log into Windows account from any machine and access familiar desktop and applications.

mobile broadband Connection to the Internet through the same cellular network that cell phones use to get 3G or 4G Internet access.

Mobile commerce (m-commerce) Conducting commercial transactions online

through a smartphone, tablet, or other mobile device.

mobile hotspot Devices that enable you to connect more than one device to the Internet; they require access to a data plan. Most smartphones have this capability built-in.

mobile operating system An operating system that includes many features of personal computer operating systems but are modified to be more functional on handheld devices.

model management system Software that assists in building management models in decision support systems; an analysis tool that, through the use of internal and external data, provides a view of a particular business situation for the purposes of decision making.

model release A release which usually grants the photographer the right to use an image of the model (or subject of the photo) commercially.

modem A device that connects a network to the Internet.

Moore's Law A prediction, named after Gordon Moore, the co-founder of Intel; states that the number of transistors on a central processing unit chip will double every two years.

motherboard A special circuit board in the system unit that contains the central processing unit, the memory (RAM) chips, and the slots available for expansion cards; all of the other boards (video cards, sound cards, and so on) connect to it to receive power and to communicate.

mouse A hardware device used to enter user responses and commands into a computer.

multidimensional database A database that stores data from different perspectives, called dimensions, and organizes data in cube format.

multi-factor authentication A process that requires two of the three assigned factors be demonstrated before authentication is granted.

multimedia software Programs that include image-, video-, and audio-editing software, animation software, and other specialty software required to produce computer games, animations, and movies.

multipartite virus Literally meaning "multipart" virus; a type of computer virus that attempts to infect computers using more than one method.

Multipurpose Internet Mail Extensions (MIME) Specification for sending files as attachments to e-mail.

multitask The ability of an operating system to perform more than one process at a time.

multiuser operating system (network operating system) An operating system that enables more than one user to access the computer system at one time by efficiently juggling all the requests from multiple users.

N

natural language processing A feature of AI systems that allow the system to understand written and spoken words and to interact with humans using language.

natural language processing (NLP) system A knowledge-based business intelligence system that enables users to communicate with computer systems using a natural spoken or written language instead of a computer programming language.

near field communication (NFC) A set of communication protocols that enable devices to communicate with each other when they are held in close proximity. NFC is commonly used for mobile payments.

negative acknowledgment (NAK) In data exchange, the communication sent from one computer or system to another stating that it did not receive a data packet in readable form.

network A group of two or more computers (or nodes) that are configured to share information and resources such as printers, files, and databases.

network adapter A device that enables the computer (or peripheral) to communicate with the network using a common data communication language, or protocol.

network address translation (NAT) A process that firewalls use to assign internal Internet protocol addresses on a network.

network administration Involves tasks such as (1) installing new computers and devices, (2) monitoring the network to ensure it's performing efficiently, (3) updating and installing new software on the network, and (4) configuring, or setting up, proper security for a network.

network administrator Person who maintains networks for a business or organization.

network architecture The design of a computer network; includes both physical and logical design.

network-attached storage (NAS) device A specialized computing device designed to store and manage network data.

network interface card (NIC) An expansion card that enables a computer to connect other computers or to a cable modem to facilitate a high-speed Internet connection.

network navigation device A device on a network such as a router or switch that moves data signals around the network.

network operating system (NOS) Software that handles requests for information, Internet access, and the use of peripherals for network nodes, providing the services necessary for the computers on the network to communicate.

network topology The physical or logical arrangement of computers, transmission media (cable), and other network components.

network-ready device A device (such as a printer or an external hard drive) that can be attached directly to a network instead of needing to attach to a computer on the network.

Next In Visual Basic, programmers use the keyword Next to implement a loop; when the Next command is run, the program returns to the For statement and increments the value of the input or output item by 1 and then runs a test cycle.

node A device connected to a network such as a computer, a peripheral (such as a printer), or a communications device (such as a modem).

nonvolatile storage Permanent storage, as in read-only memory (ROM).

normalization A process to ensure data is organized most efficiently in a database.

number system An organized plan for representing a number.

numeric check In a database, confirms that only numbers are entered in a field.

O

object An example of a class in objectoriented analysis.

Object Query Language (OQL) A query language used by many object-oriented databases.

Objective C The programming language most often used to program applications to run under OS X.

object-oriented analysis A type of analysis in which programmers first identify all the categories of inputs that are part of the problem the program is meant to solve.

object-oriented database A database that stores data in objects rather than in tables.

octet A reference to each of the four numbers in a dotted decimal number internet protocol address, so called because each number would have eight numerals in binary form.

omnibox A combined search and address bar, so you can both type a website URL or search the web from the address bar.

one-to-many relationship In a relational database, a record appears only once in one table while having the capability of appearing many times in a related table.

one-to-one relationship In a relational database, each record in a table has only one corresponding record in a related table.

online analytical processing (OLAP) Software that provides standardized tools for viewing and manipulating data in a data warehouse.

online reputation Information available about you in cyberspace that can influence people's opinions of you in the real world.

online transaction processing (OLTP) The real-time processing of database transactions online.

open source software Program code made publicly available for free; it can be copied, distributed, or changed without the stringent copyright protections of proprietary software products.

open system A system having the characteristic of being public for access by any interested party; as opposed to a *proprietary system*.

Open Systems Interconnection (OSI) A networking protocol established by the Institute of Electrical and Electronics Engineers (IEEE) that provides guidelines for modern networks.

operating system (OS) The system software that controls the way in which a computer system functions, including the management of hardware, peripherals, and software.

operator A coding symbol that represents a fundamental action of the programming language.

optical character recognition (OCR) software Software that digitizes and saves text in digital form.

optical drive A hardware device that uses lasers or light to read from, and even write to, CDs, DVDs, or Blu-ray discs.

optical media Portable storage devices, such as CDs, DVDs, and Blu-ray discs, that use a laser to read and write data.

optical mouse A mouse that uses an internal sensor or laser to control the

mouse's movement. The sensor sends signals to the computer, telling it where to move the pointer on the screen.

organic light-emitting diode (OLED) displays Displays that use organic compounds to produce light when exposed to an electric current. Unlike LCDs, OLEDs do not require a backlight to function and therefore draw less power and have a much thinner display, sometimes as thin as 3 mm.

output device A device that sends processed data and information out of a computer in the form of text, pictures (graphics), sounds (audio), or video.

overclocking Running the central processing unit at a speed faster than the manufacturer recommends.

P

packet (data packet) A small segment of data that's bundled for sending over transmission media. Each packet contains the address of the computer or peripheral device to which it's being sent.

packet analyzer (sniffer) A computer hardware device or software program designed to detect and record digital information being transmitted over a network.

packet filtering A process in which firewalls are configured so that they filter out packets sent to specific logical ports.

packet screening Having a screening router examine data packets to ensure they originated from or are authorized by valid users on a network.

packet switching A communications methodology that makes computer communication efficient; in packet switching, data is broken into smaller chunks called packets.

paging The process of swapping data or instructions that have been placed in the swap file for later use back into active random access memory (RAM). The contents of the hard drive's swap file then become less active data or instructions.

paper mills Websites that sell prewritten or customwritten research papers to students.

parallel processing A large network of computers, with each computer working on a portion of the same problem simultaneously

passive topology In a network, a type of topology where the nodes do nothing to move data along the network.

patents Grant inventors the right to stop others from manufacturing, using, or selling (including importing) their inventions for a period of 20 years from the date the patent is filed.

path (subdirectory) The information after the slash that indicates a particular file or path (or subdirectory) within the website.

path separator The backslash mark (\) used by Microsoft Windows and DOS in file names. Mac files use a colon (:), and UNIX and Linux use the forward slash (/) as the path separator.

peer-to-peer (P2P) network A network in which each node connected to the network can communicate directly with every other node on the network.

peer-to-peer (P2P) sharing The process of users transferring files between computers.

peripheral device A device such as a monitor, printer, or keyboard that connects to the system unit through a data port.

persistence of information The tendency for pictures, videos, and narratives to continue to exist in cyberspace even after you delete them.

personal area network (PAN) A network used for communication among devices close to one person, such as smartphones, laptops, and tablets, using wireless technologies such as Bluetooth.

personal ethics The set of formal or informal ethical principles that an individual uses to guide their ethical decisions.

personal firewall A firewall specifically designed for home networks.

personal information manager (PIM) software Programs such as Microsoft Outlook or Lotus Organizer that strive to replace the various management tools found on a traditional desk such as a calendar, address book, notepad, and to-do lists.

personal property Things of value that you own (such as a car or laptop).

petabyte 10^{15} bytes of digital information.

phablet Model of phone, with screen sizes of almost 6 inches.

pharming Planting malicious code on a computer that alters the browser's ability to find web addresses and that directs users to bogus websites.

phishing The process of sending e-mail messages to lure Internet users into revealing personal information such as credit card or Social Security numbers or other sensitive information that could lead to identity theft.

PHP (PHP: Hypertext Preprocessor) Programming language used to build websites with interactive capabilities; adapts the HTML page to the user's selections.

physical memory The amount of random access memory (RAM) that's installed in a computer.

piggybacking The process of connecting to a wireless network without the permission of the owner of the network.

pinning The process through which you choose which applications are visible on the Windows Start screen.

pipelining A technique that allows the CPU to work on more than one instruction (or stage of processing) at the same time, thereby boosting CPU performance.

pixel A single point that creates the images on a computer monitor. Pixels are illuminated by an electron beam that passes rapidly back and forth across the back of the screen so that the pixels appear to glow continuously.

plagiarism The act of copying text or ideas from someone else and claiming them as your own.

platform The combination of a computer's operating system and processor. The two most common platform types are the PC and the Apple.

platter A thin, round, metallic storage plate stacked onto the hard drive spindle.

Plug and Play (PnP) The technology that enables the operating system, once it is booted up, to recognize automatically any new peripherals and to configure them to work with the system.

podcast A clip of audio or video content that's broadcast over the Internet using compressed audio or video files in formats such as MP3.

point of presence (POP) A bank of modems, servers, routers, and switches through which Internet users connect to an Internet service provider.

polymorphic virus A virus that changes its virus signature (the binary pattern that makes the virus identifiable) every time it infects a new file. This makes it more difficult for antivirus programs to detect the virus.

port An interface through which external devices are connected to the computer.

portability The capability to move a completed solution easily from one type of computer to another.

positive acknowledgment (ACK) In data exchange, the confirmation sent from one

computer or system to another saying that the computer has received a data packet that it can read.

positive psychology A field that attempts to discover the causes of happiness rather than to address the treatment of mental dysfunctions.

possessed object Any object that users carry to identify themselves and that grants them access to a computer system or facility.

power supply Regulates the wall voltage to the voltages required by computer chips; it's housed inside the system unit.

power-on self-test (POST) The first job the basic input/output system (BIOS) performs, ensuring that essential peripheral devices are attached and operational. This process consists of a test on the video card and video memory, a BIOS identification process (during which the BIOS version, manufacturer, and data are displayed on the monitor), and a memory test to ensure memory chips are working properly.

preemptive multitasking When the operating system processes the task assigned a higher priority before processing a task that has been assigned a lower priority.

presentation software An application program for creating dynamic slide shows, such as Microsoft PowerPoint or Apple Keynote.

pretexting The act of creating an invented scenario (the pretext) to convince someone to divulge information.

Pretty Good Privacy (PGP) A public-key package for encryption available for download on the Internet.

primary key field In a database, a field that has a value unique to a record.

print queue A software holding area for print jobs. Also called a print spooler.

print server A server that manages all client-requested printing jobs for all printers on a network.

printer A common output device that creates tangible or hard copies of text and graphics.

private key The key for decoding retained as private in public-key encryption.

private-key encryption A type of encryption where only the two parties involved in sending the message have the code.

problem statement The starting point of programming work; a clear description of what tasks the computer program must accomplish and how the program will

execute those tasks and respond to unusual situations.

processing Manipulating or organizing data into information.

productivity software Programs that enable a user to perform various tasks generally required in home, school, and business. Examples include word processing, spreadsheet, presentation, personal information management, and database programs.

program A series of instructions to be followed by a computer to accomplish a task.

program development life cycle (PDLC) The process of performing a programming project, which consists of five stages: describing the problem, making a plan, coding, debugging, and testing and documentation.

program file Files that are used in the running of software programs and that do not store data.

program specification A clear statement of the goals and objectives of the project.

programming The process of translating a task into a series of commands a computer will use to perform that task.

programming language A kind of "code" for the set of instructions the CPU knows how to perform.

project management tools Software designed to help assess the progress of a project as it moves towards completion.

projector A device that can project images from your computer onto a wall or viewing screen.

proprietary (commercial) software Custom software application that's owned and controlled by the company that created it.

proprietary system A system having the characteristic of being closed to public access (private), as opposed to an *open system*.

protocol A set of rules for conducting communications.

prototype A small model of a program built at the beginning of a large project.

proxy server A server that acts as a go-between, connecting computers on an internal network with those on external networks (like the Internet).

pseudocode A text-based approach to documenting an algorithm.

public domain Copyrightable works whose copyright has expired, or that never had copyright protection.

public key The key for coding distributed to the public in public-key encryption.

public-key encryption A type of encryption where two keys, known as a *key pair*, are created. One key is used for coding and the other for decoding. The key for coding is distributed as a public key, while the private key is retained for decoding.

Q

quarantining The placement (by antivirus software) of a computer virus in a secure area on the hard drive so that it won't spread infection to other files.

query In a database, a way of retrieving information that defines a particular subset of data; can be used to extract data from one or more tables.

query language A specially designed computer language used to manipulate data in or extract data from a database.

QR (quick response) code Technology that lets any piece of print in the real world host a live link to online information and video content.

QWERTY keyboard A keyboard that gets its name from the first six letters on the top-left row of alphabetic keys on the keyboard.

R

RAID 0 The strategy of running two hard drives in one system, cutting in half the time it takes to write a file.

RAID 1 The strategy of mirroring all the data written on one hard drive to a second hard drive, providing an instant backup of all data.

random access memory (RAM) The computer's temporary storage space or shortterm memory. It's located in a set of chips on the system unit's motherboard, and its capacity is measured in megabytes or gigabytes.

range check Ensures that the data entered into the field of a database falls within a certain range of values.

rapid application development (RAD) An alternative program-development method; instead of developing detailed system documents before they produce the system, developers first create a prototype, then generate system documents as they use and remodel the product.

read/write head The mechanism that retrieves (reads) and records (writes) the magnetic data to and from a data disk.

read-only memory (ROM) A set of memory chips, located on the motherboard,

which stores data and instructions that cannot be changed or erased; it holds all the instructions the computer needs to start up.

real property Immoveable property such as land or a home, (often called *real estate*).

Really Simple Syndication (RSS) An XML–based format that allows frequent updates of content on the World Wide Web.

real-time operating system (RTOS) A program with a specific purpose that must guarantee certain response times for particular computing tasks or else the machine's application is useless. Real-time operating systems are found in many types of robotic equipment.

real-time processing The processing of database transactions in which the database is updated while the transaction is taking place.

recommendation engines AI systems that help people discover things they may like but are unlikely to discover on their own.

record A group of related fields in a database.

recovery drive A drive that contains all the information needed to reinstall your operating system if it should become corrupted. Often the manufacturer will have placed a utility on your system to create this.

Recycle Bin A folder on a Windows desktop in which deleted files from the hard drive are held until permanently purged from the system.

redundant array of independent disks (RAID) A set of strategies for using more than one hard drive in a computer system.

referential integrity In a relational database, a condition where, for each value in the foreign key table, there's a corresponding value in the primary key table.

registers Special memory storage areas built into the CPU, which are the most expensive, fastest memory in your computer.

registry A portion of the hard drive containing all the different configurations (settings) used by the Windows operating system as well as by other applications.

relational algebra The use of English-like expressions that have variables and operations, much like algebraic equations, to extract data from databases using Structured Query Language.

relational database A database type that organizes data into related tables based on logical groupings.

relationship In a relational database, a link between tables that defines how the data is related.

release to manufacturers (RTM) The point in the release cycle, where, after beta testing, a manufacturer makes changes to the software and releases it to other manufacturers, for installation on new machines, for example.

Reset this PC A utility program in Windows 10 that attempts to diagnose and fix errors in Windows system files that are causing a computer to behave improperly.

resolution The clearness or sharpness of an image, which is controlled by the number of pixels displayed on the screen.

restore point A type of backup that doesn't affect your personal data files but saves all the apps, updates, drivers, and information needed to restore your computer system to the exact way it's configured at that time. That way, if something does go awry, you can return your system to the way it was before you started.

reusability In object-oriented analysis, the ability to reuse existing classes from one project for another project.

ring (loop) topology A type of network topology where computers and peripherals are laid out in a configuration resembling a circle.

root directory The top level of the filing structure in a computer system. In Windows computers, the root directory of the hard drive is represented as C:\.

root DNS server A domain name system (DNS) server that contains the master listings for an entire top-level domain.

rootkit Programs that allow hackers to gain access to your computer and take almost complete control of it without your knowledge. These programs are designed to subvert normal login procedures to a computer and to hide their operations from normal detection methods.

router A device that routes packets of data between two or more networks.

rules-based systems Software that asks questions and responds based on preprogrammed algorithms. Early attempts at expert systems were rules-based.

runtime error An error in a program that occurs when a programmer accidentally writes code that divides by zero, a mathematical error.

S

sampling rate The number of times per second a signal is measured and converted to a digital value. Sampling rates are measured in kilobits per second.

satellite Internet A way to connect to the Internet using a small satellite dish, which is placed outside the home and is connected to a computer with coaxial cable. The satellite company then sends the data to a satellite orbiting the Earth. The satellite, in turn, sends the data back to the satellite dish and to the computer.

scalability A characteristic of client/server networks where more users can be easily added without affecting the performance of other network nodes.

scareware A type of malware that's downloaded onto your computer and that tries to convince you that your computer is infected with a virus or other type of malware.

scope creep An ever-changing set of requests from clients for additional features as they wait longer and longer to see a working prototype.

script A list of commands (mini-programs or macros) that can be executed on a computer without user interaction.

scripting language A simple programming language that's limited to performing a set of specialized tasks.

search engine A set of programs that searches the web for specific words (or keywords) you wish to query (or look for) and that then returns a list of the websites on which those keywords are found.

second-generation language (2GL) A computer language that allows programmers to write programs using a set of short, English-like commands that speak directly to the central processing unit and that give the programmer direct control of hardware resources; also called *assembly language*.

second-level domain A domain that's directly below a top-level domain.

sector A section of a hard drive platter, wedge-shaped from the center of the platter to the edge.

Secure Sockets Layer (SSL) A network security protocol that provides for the encryption of data transmitted using the Internet. The current versions of all major web browsers support SSL.

seek time The time it takes for the hard drive's read/write heads to move over the surface of the disk to the correct track.

select query In Structured Query Language, displays a subset of data from a table (or tables) based on the criteria specified.

semantic web (Web 3.0) An evolving extension of the World Wide Web in which

information is defined in such a way as to make it more easily readable by computers.

semiconductor Any material that can be controlled to either allow it to conduct electricity or act as an insulator.

sensor Any device that detects or measures something. Computing devices, especially smartphones, contain many sensors.

server A computer that provides resources to other computers on a network.

server-side program A type of program that runs on a web server rather than on a computer.

service mark Essentially the same as a trademark, but it applies to a service as opposed to a product.

service pack A software update.

service set identifier (SSID) A network name that wireless routers use to identify themselves.

shielded twisted-pair (STP) cable Twisted-pair cable that contains a layer of foil to reduce interference.

Simple Mail Transfer Protocol (SMTP) The protocol responsible for sending e-mail along the Internet to its destination; part of the Internet Protocol suite.

simulation programs Software, often used for training purposes, which allows the user to experience or control an event as if it's reality.

Sleep mode A low-power mode for computing devices that saves electric power consumption and saves the last-used settings. When the device is "woken up," work is resumed more quickly than when cold booting the device.

smart home A dwelling in which devices and appliances are automated or controlled by apps.

smartphone Phone with features of a computer including a wide assortment of apps, media players, high-quality cameras, and web connectivity.

social commerce A subset of e-commerce that uses social networks to assist in marketing and purchasing products.

social engineering Any technique that uses social skills to generate human interaction for the purpose of enticing individuals to reveal sensitive information.

social media Websites or apps that allow users to create and share content and/or participate in social networking with others.

social networking A means by which people use the Internet to communicate and share information among their immediate friends and to meet and connect with others through common interests, experiences, and friends.

software The set of computer programs or instructions that tells the computer what to do and that enables it to perform different tasks.

Software as a Service (SaaS) Software that's delivered on demand over the Internet.

software license An agreement between the user and the software developer that must be accepted before installing the software on a computer.

software piracy Violating a software license agreement by copying an application onto more computers than the license agreement permits.

solid-state drive (SSD) A storage device that uses the same kind of memory that flash drives use but that can reach data in only a tenth of the time a flash drive requires.

solid-state hybrid drive (SSHD) A drive that is a combination of both a mechanical hard drive and an SSD in a single device.

sound card An expansion card that attaches to (or is integrated into) the motherboard inside the system unit and that enables the computer to produce sounds; also provides a connection for the speakers and microphone.

source code The instructions programmers write in a higher-level language.

spam Unwanted or junk e-mail.

spam filter An option you can select in your e-mail account that places known or suspected spam messages into a folder other than your inbox.

speakers Output devices for sound.

spear phishing A targeted phishing attack that sends e-mails to people known to be customers of a company. Such attacks have a much greater chance of successfully getting individuals to reveal sensitive data.

spooler A program that helps coordinate all print jobs being sent to the printer at the same time.

spreadsheet software An application program such as Microsoft Excel or Lotus 1-2-3 that enables a user to do calculations and numerical analyses easily.

spyware An unwanted piggyback program that downloads with the software you want

to install from the Internet and then runs in the background of your system.

star topology The most widely deployed client/server network topology, where the nodes connect to a central communications device called a switch in a pattern resembling a star.

Start menu A feature in Windows 10 that provides access to all applications in one convenient screen.

statement A sentence in a code.

static addressing A way of assigning internet protocol addresses where the address for a computer never changes and is most likely assigned manually by a network administrator or an Internet service provider.

stealth virus A virus that temporarily erases its code from the files where it resides and hides in the active memory of the computer.

structured (analytical) data Data such as "Bill" or "345," as opposed to *unstructured data*.

Structured Query Language (SQL) A database programming language used to construct queries to extract data from relational databases; one example of a fourth-generation language.

stylus A pen-shaped device used to tap or write on touch-sensitive screens.

subscription software A model whereby the user pays a fee to use the software. The software is downloaded and installed locally but is routinely updated by connection to the manufacturer's server.

summary report A report generated by a management information system that provides a consolidated picture of detailed data; these reports usually include some calculation or visual displays of information.

supercomputer A specially designed computer that can perform complex calculations extremely rapidly; used in situations in which complex models requiring intensive mathematical calculations are needed (such as weather forecasting or atomic energy research).

SuperFetch A memory-management technique used by Windows. Monitors the applications you use the most and preloads them into your system memory so that they'll be ready to go.

supervised learning Training an AI system using a huge number of examples.

surge protector A device that protects computers and other electronic devices from power surges.

surround sound A type of audio processing that makes the listener experience sound as if it were coming from all directions.

surround-sound speaker A system of speakers set up in such a way that it surrounds an entire area (and the people in it) with sound.

swap file (page file) A temporary storage area on the hard drive where the operating system "swaps out" or moves the data or instructions from random access memory (RAM) that haven't recently been used. This process takes place when more RAM space is needed.

Swift A programming language introduced by Apple for developing for iOS and macOS.

switch A device for transmitting data on a network. A switch makes decisions, based on the media access control address of the data, as to where the data is to be sent.

syntax An agreed-on set of rules defining how a language must be structured.

syntax error A violation of the strict set of rules that define the programming language.

system clock This internal clock is actually a special crystal that acts like a metronome, keeping a steady beat and controlling when the CPU moves to the next stage of processing.

system development life cycle (SDLC) A process used to develop information systems; it consists of the following six steps: problem and opportunity identification, analysis, design, development, testing and installation, and maintenance and evaluation.

system evaluation The process of looking at a computer's subsystems, what they do, and how they perform to determine whether the computer system has the right hardware components to do what the user ultimately wants it to do.

system files The main files of an operating system.

system requirements The set of minimum storage, memory capacity, and processing standards recommended by the software manufacturer to ensure proper operation of a software application.

System Restore A utility in Windows that restores system settings to a specific previous date when everything was working properly.

system restore point In Windows, a snapshot of your entire system's settings used for restoring your system to a prior point in time.

system software The set of programs that enables a computer's hardware devices and application software to work together; it includes the operating system and utility programs.

system unit The metal or plastic case that holds all the physical parts of the computer together, including the computer's processor (its brains), its memory, and the many circuit boards that help the computer function.

T

T line A communications line that carries digital data over twisted-pair wires.

table (file) A group of related records in a database.

tablet computer A mobile computer, such as the Apple iPad or Samsung Galaxy Tab, integrated into a flat multitouch-sensitive screen. It uses an onscreen virtual keyboard, but separate keyboards can be connected via Bluetooth or wires.

tag Electronically identifying someone in a photo or post.

tagging (social bookmarking) Assigning a keyword or term to a web resource such as a web page, digital image, or video.

tangible personal property Property that has substance like your smartphone or car.

Task Manager A Windows utility that shows programs currently running and permits you to exit nonresponsive programs when you click End Task.

taskbar In later versions of Windows operating systems, a feature that displays open and favorite applications for easy access.

tax preparation software An application program, such as Intuit's TurboTax or H&R Block's At Home, for preparing state and federal taxes. Each program offers a complete set of tax forms and instructions as well as expert advice on how to complete each form.

TCP/IP The main suite of protocols used for transmitting data over the Internet. Named after Transmission Control Protocol (TCP) and the Internet Protocol (IP).

template A form included in many productivity applications that provides the basic structure for a particular kind of document, spreadsheet, or presentation.

terabyte (TB) 1,099,511,627,776 bytes or 2^{40} bytes.

terminator A device that absorbs a signal so that it's not reflected back onto parts of the network that have already received it.

terms of use Legal documents (or disclaimers) that delineate how copyrighted material can be used.

test condition A check to see whether the loop in an algorithm is completed.

testing plan The part of the problem statement that lists specific input numbers the programmers would typically expect the user to enter; the plan then lists the precise output values that a perfect program would return for those input values.

texting Using the Short Message Service (SMS) to send short messages between mobile devices.

third-generation language (3GL) A computer language that uses symbols and commands to help programmers tell the computer what to do, making 3GL languages easier for humans to read and remember; examples of 3GL languages include BASIC, FORTRAN, COBOL, C/C++, and JAVA.

thrashing A condition of excessive paging in which the operating system becomes sluggish.

three-way handshake In Transmission Control Protocol, the process used to establish a connection between two computers before exchanging data. The steps in a three-way handshake are as follows: One computer establishes a connection to the Internet service provider (ISP) and announces it has e-mail to send, the ISP server responds that it's ready to receive, and the computer acknowledges the ready state of the server and begins to transmit the e-mail.

throughput The actual speed of data transfer that's achieved. It's usually less than the data transfer rate.

Thunderbolt port A high speed input/output port.

time bomb A virus that's triggered by the passage of time or on a certain date.

time-variant data Data that doesn't pertain to one time period.

token A special data packet used to pass data on a network.

token method The access method used by ring networks to avoid data collisions.

top-down design A systematic approach in which a problem is broken into a series of high-level tasks.

top-level domain The suffix, often of three letters (such as .com or .edu), in the domain name that indicates the kind of organization the host is.

touch pad (trackpad) A small, touchsensitive surface at the base of a laptop keyboard that's used to direct the cursor.

touch screen A type of monitor (or display in a smartphone or tablet computer) that accepts input from a user touching the screen.

track A concentric circle that serves as a storage area on a hard drive platter.

trademark A word, phrase, symbol, or design—or a combination of these—that uniquely identifies and differentiates the goods (or services) of one party from those of another.

transaction-processing system (TPS) A type of business intelligence system for keeping track of everyday business activities.

transistor Electrical switches built out of layers of a special type of material called a semiconductor.

Transmission Control Protocol (TCP) One of the original two protocols developed for the Internet.

transmission media The radio waves or the physical system (cable) that transports data on a network.

Transport Layer Security (TLS) An updated extension of *Secure Sockets Layer*.

Trojan horse A computer program that appears to be something useful or desirable (such as a game or a screen saver), but at the same time does something malicious in the background without the user's knowledge.

trolling The act of posting inflammatory remarks online for the sheer pleasure of soliciting an angry or negative response.

tunneling The main technology for achieving a virtual private network; the placement of data packets inside other data packets.

Turing test A simple test to distinguish between a human and a computer system. Named after Alan Turing, a computing pioneer.

twisted-pair cable Cable made of copper wires that are twisted around each other and are surrounded by a plastic jacket (such as traditional home phone wire).

typical installation A type of installation procedure that copies all the most commonly used files and programs to your computer's hard drive.

U

ultrabook A full-featured but lightweight laptop computer that features a low-power processor and a solid-state drive; it tries to reduce its size and weight to extend battery life without sacrificing performance.

unethical behavior Not conforming to a set of approved standards of behavior—cheating on an exam, for example

unicode An encoding scheme which uses 16 bits instead of 8 bits. Unicode can represent nearly 1,115,000 code points and currently assigns more than 128,000 unique character symbols.

Uniform Resource Locator (URL) A website's unique address; an example is microsoft.com.

universal serial bus (USB) port A port that can connect a wide variety of peripheral devices to the computer, including keyboards, printers, mice, smartphones, external hard drives, flash drives, and digital cameras.

UNIX An operating system originally conceived in 1969 by Ken Thompson and Dennis Ritchie of AT&T's Bell Labs. In 1974, the UNIX code was rewritten in the standard programming language C. Today there are various commercial versions of UNIX.

unshielded twisted-pair (UTP) cable The most popular transmission media option for Ethernet networks. UTP cable is composed of four pairs of wires that are twisted around each other to reduce electrical interference.

unsupervised learning When an AI system can look at data on its own and build rules for deciding what it is seeing.

urban legends When hoaxes become so well known that they're incorporated into society as true events even though they're false.

unstructured data Audio clips, video clips, pictures, and extremely large documents. Also called *binary large object (BLOB)*.

User Datagram Protocol (UDP) An Internet Protocol that creates data packets across the Internet.

user interface Part of the operating system that enables individuals to interact with the computer.

utility program A small program that performs many of the general housekeeping tasks for the computer, such as system maintenance and file compression.

V

validation The process of ensuring that data entered into a field of a database meets specified guidelines.

validation rule In a database, generally defined as part of the data dictionary and

specified in the field properties for each field; violations result in an error message and a suggested action.

variable Each input and output item the program manipulates.

variable declaration Tells the operating system that the program needs to allocate storage space in RAM.

VBScript A subset of Visual Basic, used to introduce dynamic decision making into web pages.

vertical market software Software that's developed for and customized to a specific industry's needs (such as a wood inventory system for a sawmill) as opposed to software that's useful across a range of industries (such as word processing software).

video card (video adapter) An expansion card that's installed inside a system unit to translate binary data (the *1*s and *0*s the computer uses) into the images viewed on the monitor.

video log (vlog or video blog) A personal online journal that uses video as the primary content in addition to text, images, and audio.

video memory Random access memory that's included as part of a video card.

virtual desktops A Windows 10 feature that allows you to organize groups of windows into different displays.

virtual keyboard A keyboard that displays on screen when text input is required.

virtual memory The space on the hard drive where the operating system stores data if there isn't enough random access memory to hold all of the programs you're currently trying to run.

virtual private network (VPN) A network that uses the public Internet communications infrastructure to build a secure, private network among various locations.

virtual reality (VR) An artificial environment that is immersive and interactive.

virtualization Using specialized software to make individual physical servers behave as though they are more than one physical device.

virus A computer program that attaches itself to another computer program (known as the host program) and attempts to spread itself to other computers when files are exchanged.

virus signature A portion of the virus code that's unique to a particular computer virus

and that makes it identifiable by antivirus software.

Visual Basic (VB) A programming language used to build a wide range of Windows applications.

visual programming languages Programming language that uses graphical blocks to represent control elements and variables.

voice recognition software Software that allows you to control your computing devices by speaking into the microphone instead of using a keyboard or mouse.

VoIP (Voice over Internet Protocol) A technology that facilitates making telephone calls across the Internet instead of using conventional telephone lines.

volatile storage Temporary storage, such as in random access memory. When the power is off, the data in volatile storage is cleared out.

W

warm boot The process of restarting a computing device while it's powered on.

Web 2.0 Tools and web-based services that emphasize online collaboration and sharing among users.

web authoring software Programs you can use to design interactive web pages without knowing any HyperText Markup Language (HTML) code.

web-based e-mail A type of e-mail system that's managed by a web browser and that allows access to e-mail from the web.

web browser (browser) Software installed on a computer system that allows individuals to locate, view, and navigate the web.

web server A computer running a specialized operating system that enables it to host web pages (and other information) and to provide requested web pages to clients.

web service Part of the Microsoft .NET Framework, programs that a website uses to make information available to other websites.

webcam A small camera that sits on top of a computer monitor or that's built into a laptop computer and is usually used to transfer live video.

webcast The (usually live) broadcast of audio or video content over the Internet.

white-hat hacker (ethical hacker) A hacker who breaks into systems just for the challenge of it (and who doesn't wish to steal or wreak havoc on the systems). Such hackers tout themselves as experts who are performing a needed service for society by helping companies realize the vulnerabilities that exist in their systems.

whole-house surge protector A surge protector that's installed on (or near) the breaker panel of a home and that protects all electronic devices in the home from power surges.

wide area network (WAN) A network made up of local area networks (LANs) connected over long distances.

Wi-Fi The 802.11 standard for wireless data transmissions established by the Institute of Electrical and Electronics Engineers (IEEE).

wiki A type of website that allows anyone visiting the site to change its content by adding, removing, or editing the content.

Windows Microsoft's operating system that incorporates a user-friendly, visual interface.

Windows 10 Newest release of Microsoft's operating system that provides an interface optimized for touch-screen devices and is designed to run across all devices: phones, tablets, laptops, and desktops.

wireless access point (WAP) Gives wireless devices a sending and receiving connection point to the network.

wireless Internet service provider (wireless ISP): An ISP that provides service to wireless devices such as smartphones.

wireless network interface card (wireless NIC) A special network adapter card that allows a computing device to connect to a network using wireless media.

wireless range extender A device that amplifies your wireless signal to get it out to parts of your home that are experiencing poor connectivity.

wizard A step-by-step guide that walks a user through the necessary steps to complete a complicated task.

word processing software Programs used to create and edit written documents such as papers, letters, and résumés.

World Wide Web (WWW or the web) The part of the Internet used the most. What distinguishes the web from the rest of the Internet are (1) its use of common communication protocols (such as Transmission Control Protocol/Internet Protocol, or TCP/IP) and special languages (such as the HyperText Markup Language, or HTML) that enable different computers to talk to each other and display information in compatible formats and (2) its use of special links (called hyperlinks) that enable users to jump from one place to another in the web.

worm A program that attempts to travel between systems through network connections to spread infections. Worms can run independently of host file execution and are active in spreading themselves.

Z

zombie A computer that is controlled by a hacker who uses it to launch attacks on other computer systems.

Index

A

ABC (Atanasoff-Berry Computer), A8, A8f
Ableton Live, 153, 295
Academia, 318f
Academic Superstore, 130
accelerometer, 54f
acceptable use policies, 323–324,
    323f, 324f
access
    client/server network privileges with,
        498, 500–501
    cloud computing considerations with, 98
    to computers, hackers gaining, 338
    Internet and, 105–110
    logical ports and firewalls blocking,
        354, 354f
    ownership versus, 7–9, 8f
    restricting, 359–360
access card readers, 501f
access car readers, 501
accessibility utilities, 198, 198f
access method, 481
access points, 276
access time, of hard disk drives, 225, 227
accounting software, 148
ACK (positive acknowledgment), 522, 523f
ACM (Association for Computing
        Machinery), 406, 416, B12, B13f
Active Server Pages (ASP), 411–412, 412f
active topology, 482
ActivityStarter, of App Inventor, 138
adapter cards, 64
adaptive (assistive) technologies, 74
ADC (analog-to-digital converter), 293
add-ons, 106
Adobe Creative Cloud, 129
Adobe Dreamweaver, 409–410, 410f
Adobe Illustrator, 152, 153f
Adobe InDesign, 148
Adobe Photoshop, 151
Adobe Premiere, 299, 299f
Adobe Spark, 513
Advanced Research Projects Agency
        Network (ARPANET), 86f, 87, 87f, 535
advance fee fraud, 334
adware, 9f, 237, 343, 343f
aerial digital video, drones for, 300, B9
aesthetics, 319
affective computing, 21
affinity grouping, in data mining, 453, 453f
aggregators, 92–93
agile methodology, 384
AI. See artificial intelligence
Aiken, Howard, A8
Airbnb, 35–36, 99
AirPort Time Capsule, 271
AirPrint, 58
AIS (Association for Information Systems),
    B13f
AITP (Association of Information Technology
    Professionals), B13f

AJAX (Asynchronous JavaScript), 412,
    413f, 535
alarms, on mobile devices, 369
Alexa, 169
algorithm development, in PDLC, 387–391,
    387f–391f
algorithms, 384
    binary decisions and, 389, 389f
    coding and, 393
    in daily life, 387, 387f
    decision points and, 387, 388f,
        389, 389f
    flowcharts for, 387, 387f, 388f
    limitations of, 387
    loops and, 389, 389f
    object-oriented analysis for, 391, 391f
    pseudocode for, 387
    top-down design for, 390–391, 390f
Alibaba, 433
Alice, 155
Allen, Paul, A2, A4, A4f
all-in-one computer, 46, 46f
all-in-one printers, 58, 58f
alphabetic check, 439
Altair 8800, A1f, A2
AlternativeTo, 129
Alto, A5, A5f
ALU (arithmetic logic unit), 212, 218
Amazon, 19, 19f, 88f, 97, 426–427, 426f
Amazon Dash buttons, 520, 520f
Amazon Echo, 176
Amazon Fire, 291, 292f
Amazon Kindle, 291–293, 292f
Amazon Redshift, 451
Amazon Underground, 130
AMD, 232
AMD Radeon, 232–233, 232f
American National Standards Institute
    (ANSI), 133
American Psychological Association
    (APA), 317
American Standard Code for Information
    Interchange (ASCII), 86f, 133
amoral behavior, 25
analog photography, 296–297
analog-to-digital conversion, 290, 290f
analog-to-digital converter (ADC), 293
analog waves, 289–290, 289f, 290f
analytical data. See structured data
Analytical Engine, A7, A7f
Android, 167f
Android Developers, 414
Android Pay, 130
Android Studio, 414, 414f
animators, A8
Anita Borg Institute, B13f
ANNs (artificial neural networks), 16
ANSI (American National Standards
    Institute), 133
anti-malware, 171
antivirus software, 171, 355–357

APA (American Psychological Association),
    317
APIs (application programming interfaces),
    154, 175, 407
APL (A Programmer's Language), 393, 393f
app creation software, 154–155, 154f
App Inventor, 62
    ActivityStarter of, 138
    Canvas in, 403
    Companion app for, 267
    explanation of, 154, 154f
    Location Sensor in, 224
    Notifier in, 183
    Sharing in, 489
    TinyDB in, 352
    TinyWebDB in, 448
    Video Player of, 305
    web services in, 528
    WebViewer in, 104
Apple GarageBand, 153
Apple I, A1f, A2
Apple iCloud Photo Sharing, 298
Apple II, A1f, A3
Apple iMovie, 152f
Apple iOS, 167f
Apple Keynote, 143
Apple Lisa, A5, A6f
Apple Macintosh, A5, A6f
Apple macOS. See macOS
Apple Pay, 99–100, 130
applets, 534, 534f
Apple TV, 272
Apple Watch, 254, 264
application programming interfaces (APIs),
    154, 175, 407
application servers, 478f, 479
application software, 42–43, 128, 139–156,
        166. See also productivity software
    development, A5f
    OS coordination with, 175
App Sandbox, 171
Appspot, 524
A Programmer's Language (APL), 393, 393f
AR (augmented reality), 22, 22f, 55
ArcadePod, 534
architecture neutral, 408
Arduino microcontroller, 207
arithmetic logic unit (ALU), 212, 218
ARPANET (Advanced Research Projects
        Agency Network), 86f, 87, 87f, 535
artificial intelligence (AI)
    of Amazon, 19, 19f
    basics, 14–16
    computers and, 14, 176–177, 460
    defining, 14
    law enforcement for, 20–21, 20f
    neural networks in, 16, 16f
    research in, 15f
    Turing test for, 20, 20f
    working with, 18–22
artificial neural networks (ANNs), 16

ASCII (American Standard Code for Information Interchange), 86f, 133
ASP (Active Server Pages), 411–412, 412f
aspect ratio, 55
assembly language, 217, 394, 394f
assistive (adaptive) technologies, 74
Association for Computing Machinery (ACM), 406, 416, B12, B13f
Association for Information Systems (AIS), B13f
Association for Women in Computing (AWC), B13f
Association of Information Technology Professionals (AITP), B13f
association rules, in data mining, 453, 453f
Asynchronous JavaScript (AJAX), 412, 413f, 535
Atanasoff, John, A8
Atanasoff-Berry Computer (ABC), A8, A8f
attachments, e-mail with, 536
Audacity, 93, 153
audio-editing software, 153
audio MIDI interface, 236, 236f
AudioNote, 145f
audio output, 56
audio subsystems, 236f
augmentative reality (AR), 22, 22f, 55
authentication, 179, 498, 502
authentication servers, 478f, 479
AWC (Association for Women in Computing), B13f

B
B (bytes), 41, 42f
B2B (business-to-business), 99
B2C (business-to-consumer), 97
backdoor programs, 336
backlit monitors, 292, 292f
backups
    cloud computing considerations with, 98
    definition of, 364
    file types needing, 364
    frequency of, 365
    image, 365–366, 367f
    for MacOS, 366–367
    on school's network, 367
    storage locations for, 365, 365f
    strategy for, 364f
    types of, 364–365
backward compatibility, 255
bandwidth, 251
bank account information, hackers and, 336
banking, 19
Barnes and Noble Nook, 291–292
base-2 number system (binary number system), 132–133
base-10 number system (decimal notation), 132
base class, 391
Base site, 318f
BASIC (Beginners All-Purpose Symbolic Instruction Code), A4, A4f
basic input/output system (BIOS), 177, 178f
bastion hosts, 503–504
batch processing, 456
battery drain, 71
BDs (Blu-ray discs), 68, 68f, 173, 226–227

Beginners All-Purpose Symbolic Instruction Code (BASIC), A4, A4f
Belkin WeMo, 260
benchmarking, 215, 246
Berners-Lee, Tim, 87f
beta versions, of software, 130, 400
Better Business Bureau, 100
BI (business intelligence), 460–461
bias, 113
big data, 16, 18–19
binary decisions, 389, 389f
binary digits, 41
binary language, 41
binary large object (BLOB), 432
binary number system (base-2 number system), 132–133
Bing, 111–112
biometric authentication devices, 333, 360–361, 361f, 501, 501f
BIOS (basic input/output system), 177, 178f
biosensors, for smartphones, 127
bitcoin, 101, 101f
bits, 41
BitTorrent, 35, 107, 275
BitTorrent (BT) Bundles, 275
Bizrate, 100
black-hat hackers, 335
#BlackLivesMatter, 4
Blaise Pascal, A6
Blinkx, 112
bloatware, 131
BLOB (binary large object), 432
blockchain, 101
BlogCatalog, 91
Blogger, 92
blogs, 91–92, 97f
blue light, 72f
Bluetooth technology, 44, 49, 50f, 249
Blu-ray, 173
Blu-ray discs (BDs), 68, 68f, 226–227
Blu-ray player, 272
bookmarking, social, 110
Bookmarks, 109
Boolean operators, 113
boot process, 177–180, 178f
boot-sector viruses, 341, 342f
botnets, 337
bots, 4, 359, 359f
Brain Age, 156
breadcrumb trail, 108
Brexit vote, 4, 4f
bridges, 496, 496f
bring-your-own-device (BYOD) policies, 510
broadband Internet, 260–263, 261f
brute force attack, 498
Bs (bytes), 41
BT (BitTorrent) Bundles, 275
Buechley, Leah, 207
business
    crowdsourcing in, 547
    encryption and, 541
    firewalls for, 504, 504f
    on internet, 97–101
    network advantages, disadvantages and, 472–473, 472f
    operating systems for, 169–170
    P2P networks and, 473, 474f

software, 148–149, 149f
transmission media for, 492
business information systems, 455–460
business intelligence (BI), 460–461
business intelligence systems, 460
Business Software Alliance, 135, 312
business-to-business (B2B), 99
business-to-consumer (B2C), 97
bus topology, 481–482, 482f, 486f
BYOD (bring-your-own-device) policies, 510
bytes (B), 41, 42f

C
C, 404, 407–408, 413f
C#, 408, 413f
C++, 404, 407–408, 413f
C2C (consumer-to-consumer), 99
cable Internet, 261, 261f
cache memory, 213
CAD (computer-aided design), 148–149, 149f
Canvas, in App Inventor, 403
capacitive touch screen system, 51, 51f
CAPTCHA, 359, 359f
caption, 436
Carbonite, 98, 365
careers, technology and, 18–21. See also information technology; IT careers
caret browsing, 108–109
car networks, hacking, 477
cascading style sheet (CSS), 531–532, 531f
Category 5e cable, 257, 257f
Category 6a cable, 257, 257f
Category 6 cable, 257, 257f
catfishing, 118
CCD (charge-coupled device) arrays, 296
CD Baby, 296, 308
CDs (compact discs), 68, 68f, 226–227
cell phones, 43–44, 43f. See also smartphones
    alarms on, 369
    data plans for, 262–263
    data storage on, 66
    digital photography on, 297–298, 330
    mobile broadband for, 262
    political change and, 330
    texting and, 96, 97f
    viruses on, 357
    wireless network connection for, 275
censorship, ethics and, 28, 29f
Center for Women in Technology (CWIT), B13f
central administration, of networks, 253, 253f
centralization, data, 429, 429f
centralized P2P network, 473
central processing unit (CPU), 41, 43, 178f. See also CPU subsystems
    APIs and, 175
    definition of, 64
    speed and performance measurement of, 64–65, 65f
    video calculations and, 231–232
Cerf, Vinton, 87
certifications, for IT careers, B12
charge-coupled device (CCD) arrays, 296
charts, 142, 143f
Chicago Open City, 407f

chief information officer (CIO), B6–B7
chips, 41
Chromebook, 45, 98
CIO (chief information officer), B6–B7
Circos, 425
circuit switching, 517
Cisco Jabber, 96
citation, of website sources, 137, 317
Citi Bike, 7, 8f
Citizendium, 115
Clash of Clans, B11f
classes, 391, 391f
classification, in data mining, 452–453, 453f
clickstream data, 450
client, 88
client-based e-mail, 95, 95f
client/server application, 410, 411f
client/server model, 515
client/server networks, 88, 253, 253f
   access privileges for, 498, 500–501
   authentication and, 498
   basics of, 472–476
   firewalls for, 503–504
   key components of, 476, 477f
   peer-to-peer networks compared to, 473–474, 474f
   physical protection measures for, 501, 501f
   scalability of, 474
   security, 498–504
   server types in, 478–481, 478f
   types of, 474–476, 475f
client-side programs, 533–534
CLIP (continuous liquid interface production) 3D printers, 287
clip-on microphones, 53f
clock cycle, 212
clock speed, 212–213
close talk microphones, 53f
Cloud9, 516
cloud-based data warehouses, 451
cloud computing, 16
   front end and back end of, 98
   operating systems in, 167–168
   privacy, backup, and access considerations with, 98
   two sides to, 98f
cloud-ready printers, 58, 58f
cloud servers, 478f, 481
cloud storage, 67, 98, 513
clustering, in data mining, 453, 453f
clusters, disk defragmentation, 196
CMOS (complementary metal-oxide semiconductor), 178, 178f
CMYK, 57
coaxial cable, 256, 256f, 490–491, 490f, 491f
COBOL, 404
codec, 300
code editing, 398–399
Code for America, 390
CodePen, 530
Code School, Rails for Zombies from, 405
code statements, 392
coding. See also programming languages
   algorithms and, 393
   compiler and, 397
   completed example of, 395–396, 396f

definition of, 392
   integrated development environment and, 398–399, 398f
   interpreter and, 397
   in PDLC, 392–399
   reusability and, 396–397, 397f
cognitive computing, 541
cognitive surplus, 7
cold boot, 71
collaboration, on Internet, 7, 89–94, 97f, 150, 150f
collaborative consumption, 8f, 9
command-driven interface, 172–173, 173f
comments, programming languages and, 395
commerce servers, 516
commercial software (proprietary software), 128, 129f, 162
Commodore PET, A1f, A3
communication, over Internet, 94–96, 97f, 535–541
communications servers, 478f, 479–480
Comodo SecureEmail, 538
compact discs (CDs), 68, 68f, 226–227
Companion app, for App Inventor, 267
compilation, 397
compiler, 397, A8
complementary metal-oxide semiconductor (CMOS), 178, 178f
completeness check, 439, 439f
compression, 294
computer ads, 9f
computer-aided design (CAD), 148–149, 149f
computer bug, A8, A8f
Computer Ethics Institute, 324, 324f
computer forensics, 21, 370
computer forensic scientists, 370
ComputerJobs, 416
computer literacy, 9–10, 9f, 18–21
computer protocol, 516–517
computers
   artificial intelligence and, 14, 176–177, 460
   boot process for, 177–180, 178f
   buying new, 239
   capabilities of, 61
   connecting peripherals to, 69–70
   crashes and, 236–237
   definition of, 40
   donating old, 240
   environmental impact of disposing, 239
   ergonomics for, 73–74, 73f
   factors for keeping, 210
   first-generation, A9
   fourth-generation, A10
   functions of, 40
   hackers gaining access to, 338
   language of, 41–42, 432
   Moore's law and buying new, 208–209, 208f
   passwords for protecting, 358
   ports, 69–70, 69f, 70f
   power controls and management for, 70–72
   power surges and, 368, 368f
   privacy on shared, 361
   problem statement for, 385

   processing of, 40, 40f
   recycling old, 239, 239f
   resetting, 179, 180f
   restarting, 71
   second-generation, A10
   selecting devices of, 209–210
   shutting down, 71
   starting, 177–180
   subsystems, 210f
   system evaluation for, 210, 223
   system reliability evaluation for, 236–238, 236f, 237f, 238f
   theft and, 368–371, 369f, 371f
   third-generation, A10
   troubleshooting, 10
   types of, 43–47, 209, 210f
computer security checklist, 371f
computer support technicians, B10
Computers with Causes, 240
computer viruses. See viruses
computer vision, 16
computing, ethics in, 17
ConcertWindow, 93
connectionless protocol, 522
connection-oriented protocol, 522
connectivity ports, 69
consistency check, 439
consumer-to-consumer (C2C), 99
content control for children, ethics and, 378
continuous liquid interface production (CLIP) 3D printers, 287
Control Program for Microcomputers (CP/M), A4
control structures, 389
control units, 212
cookies, 345, 345f
copyleft, 134, 308–309
copyright infringement
   definition and examples of, 310
   fair use and, 314–315, 315f
   legal usage avoiding, 312–314
   penalties for, 310
   photographic issues with, 312, 312f, 313f
   reasons for risking, 310
   software piracy and, 311–312
   terms of use and, 312–313, 313f
   YouTube issues with, 311, 311f
Copyright Office, U.S., 308
copyrights, 307f
   corporate authorship and, 308
   Creative Commons licenses and, 309, 309f
   duration of, 307
   fair use and, 314–315, 315f
   granting, selling, 307–308
   legal usage of, 312–314
   limits, rights of, 307
   origin of, 307
   permission requests for, 314
   public domain and, 308
   registering for, 308
   terms of use and, 312–313, 313f
   works under, 306
Corel PaintShop Pro, 151
cores, in CPU subsystems, 213, 213f
Corona, 402, 414
Corona SDK, 154

corporate authorship, intellectual property and, 308
Cortana, 106, 111
country codes, 107, 108f
course management software, 156
CP/M (Control Program for Microcomputers), A4
CPU. *See* central processing unit
cpubenchmark.net, 215
CPU benchmarks, 215, 246
CPU commands, 217f
CPU subsystems
    clock speed of, 212–213
    comparison of, 215
    components of, 212
    cores in, 213, 213f
    data processing of, 211, 212f
    evaluating, 211–216
    internal working of, 211–214
    measuring performance of, 215–216, 216f
    processing power, speed of, 212–214
CPU usage, 215
CPU usage graph, 215
Craigslist, 99
Creative Commons licenses, 309, 309f
credit card information, hackers and, 336
credit reports, 346
crisis-mapping tool, 4–5, 5f
CrossFireX, 232
crowdfunding, 7, 296
crowdsourcing, 547
Crucial, 221
CSMA/CD method, 484
CSS (cascading style sheet), 531–532, 531f
cursor, 50
customer interaction technicians, A8
custom installation, 131
CVS, 298
CWIT (Center for Women in Technology), B13f
cyberattacks, 276
cyberbullying, 118, 118f
Cyberbullying Research Center, 118
cybercrime, 317, 334, 334f. *See also* hackers; identity theft
cyber harassment, 118
cyberloafing, 348
cyberslacking, 348
cyber spying, A9
cyberstalking, 118

D

DAC (digital-to-analog converter), 293
DailyStocks, 111
DAM (digital asset management), 302
dashboard, data, 445
data
    cell phone storage of, 66
    centralization, 429, 429f
    clickstream, 450
    collection, ethics of, 454
    CPU subsystems processing, 211, 212f
    dashboard, 445
    database organization, storage of, 433–434, 434f
    data warehouse organization of, 449, 450f

extracting, querying, 441–442, 441f, 442f
    government transparency with, 381
    hard disk drives storage of, 225
    inappropriate, incomplete, 428, 428f
    inconsistency, 427, 428f
    information compared to, 40
    inputting, managing, 437–442
    integrity, 430
    Internet and transmission of, 516–518
    linked, 114, 114f
    normalization, 430
    outputting, 442, 445, 445f
    processing, 453
    redundancy, 427, 428f
    relationships, 431, 431f
    sorting, viewing, 440
    storage options for, 65–68
    structured, 114, 432
    time-variant, 450
    unstructured, 432
    validation of, 438–439, 439f
    viewing and sorting, 440f
    visualization, 425
database administrators (DBAs), 430, A10
database designers, 430
database developers, B9
database management system (DBMS), 433
databases
    advantages of, 429–430, 429f, 430f
    components and functions of, 433–437
    data organization, storage in, 433–434, 434f
    data types in, 393, 434, 435f
    data validation in, 438–439, 439f
    definition of, 426
    enhanced information for, 433
    ethics of private information on public, 468
    extracting, querying data in, 441–442, 441f, 442f
    field, field names in, 433–434, 434f
    field properties in, 436
    filters in, 441
    input forms in, 438, 438f
    inputting, managing data in, 437–442
    lists compared to, 427–428, 427f, 428f
    Microsoft Excel functions for, 447
    multidimensional, 432, 432f
    need for, 426–428
    object-oriented, 432
    outputting data in, 442, 445, 445f
    primary keys in, 436–437
    records in, 434, 434f
    relational, 431, 431f
    sorting, viewing data in, 440
    tables in, 434, 434f
    types of, 430–432
    viewing and sorting data in, 440f
database schema, 437
database servers, 478f, 479
database software, 143–145, 144f
data breaches, 346, 349, 502
data collisions, 481
data dictionary, 437
data files, backups for, 364
data-flow diagrams, 383, 383f
data marts, 451

data mining, 18–19, 18f, 451–453, 453f
data packets, 517
data plans, 262–263
data staging, data warehouses and, 451
data transfer rate, 251
data types, 393, 434, 435f
data warehouses
    cloud-based, 451
    data staging and, 451
    definition of, 449
    organization of data in, 449, 450f
    overview of, 452f
    sources in, 450
    time-variant data in, 450
DAWS (digital audio workstation software), 153, 295
DBAs (database administrators), 430, B10
DBMS (database management system), 433
DDos (distributed denial-of-service) attacks, 337, 337f
debugger, 399–400
debugging, in PDLC, 399–400, 399f
decentralized P2P network, 473
decimal notation (base-10 number system), 132
decision points, algorithms and, 387, 388f, 389, 389f
decision support systems (DSS), 458–459, 458f, 459f
decode stage, of machine cycle, 217
dedicated servers, 478–481, 478f
deep learning (DL), 16, 16f
default value, 436
Delicious site, 110
denial-of-service (DoS) attack, 337
deontology, 24, 24f
derived class, 391, 391f
description and visualization, in data mining, 453, 453f
desktop, in Windows 10, 184–185
desktop computers, 46–47, 46f, 209–210
desktop publishing (DTP) software, 148
detail report, 458, 458f
Developer Central, 492
device drivers, 175, 176f, 494
DevPost, 390, 411
DHCP (Dynamic Host Configuration Protocol), 519f, 522
DHTML (dynamic HTML), 534
dial-up Internet connection, 264
Difference Engine, A7
Digispark, 240
digital activism, 115–116, 116f
digital asset management (DAM), 302
digital audio software, 152–153
digital audio workstation software (DAWS), 153, 295
digital convergence, 43, 288, 329
digital divide, 6
digital format
    analog compared to, 289–290, 289f, 290f
    definition of, 289
    entertainment, impact of, 290
    entertainment and impact of, 290f
Digital Living Network Alliance, 288
digital manipulation, 319, 320f

digital media
    digital photography, 296–298
    digital video, 299–302
digital medications, 21f
digital music
    creation of, 293–295, 294f
    device storage capacity and, 294–295
    distributing, 295–296
    file types for, 294
    Internet streaming of, 296, 437
    listening options for, 295, 295f
digital photography
    analog photography compared to, 296–297
    camera selection for, 297
    on cell phones, 297–298, 330
    digital manipulation of, 319, 320f
    editing, 298
    file formats in, 297–298
    image quality in, 297
    political change and, 330
    printing, 298
    sharing, 298
Digital Photography Review, 297
digital property, 306–315
digital publishing, 291–293, 291f, 292f
digital rights management (DRM), 296, 311
digital SLR cameras, 297
digital subscriber line (DSL), 261, 261f
digital-to-analog converter (DAC), 293
digital video
    creating, publishing, 304
    digital manipulation of, 319, 320f
    drones for aerial, 300, B9
    editing, effects for, 299, 299f
    formats for, 300, 300f
    HD, 301
    Internet broadcasting of, 300–301
    recording, 299
    sources of, 299
    televisions for, 301–302
digital video discs (DVDs), 68, 68f, 226–227
digital video-editing software, 151–152, 152f
digital video recorders (DVRs), 302
digitized information, 289
DIMM (dual inline memory modules), 219, 219f
directory, 187
disabilities, assistive technologies for, 74
Disk Cleanup utility, 194, 194f
disk defragmentation, 195–196, 196f
Disk Operating System (DOS), 172–173, A4, A5f
display screen, 54. *See also* monitors
distributed computing, 52
distributed denial-of-service (DDoS) attacks, 337, 337f
distributions (distros), 168
distrowatch.com, 168
divine command theory, 24, 24f
DL (deep learning), 16, 16f
DNS (domain name system) servers, 524–525, 525f
documentation, in PDLC, 400
Document Object Model (DOM), 535
Dogpile, 112
Dolby Digital 7.1, 235–236, 235f

Dolby TrueHD, 235
DOM (Document Object Model), 535
domain names, 107–108, 108f
    definition of, 523
    DNS servers and, 524–525, 525f
    Internet cache and, 525
    organization of, 523–524, 524f
    registration of, ICANN and, 524
    second-level domains and, 524
domain name system (DNS) servers, 524–525, 525f
donating old computers, 240
DOS (Disk Operating System), 172–173, A4, A5f
DoS (denial-of-service) attack, 337
dotted decimal number (dotted quad), 519
DRAM (dynamic random access memory), 209
drawing (illustration) software, 152, 153f
drive bays, 65
drive-by download, 357
driverless cars, A9
DriverZone, 175
DRM (digital rights management), 296, 311
drones, for aerial digital video, 300, B9
Dropbox, 67, 98, 189f, 524
DSL (digital subscriber line), 261, 261f
DSS (decision support systems), 458–459, 458f, 459f
DTP (desktop publishing) software, 148
dual inline memory modules (DIMM), 219, 219f
DuckDuckGo, 109
DuoSkin, 471
DVDs (digital video discs), 68, 68f, 226–227
Dvorak keyboard, 48, 48f
DVRs (digital video recorders), 302
dynamic addressing, of IP addresses, 521–522, 521f
dynamic decision making, 411
Dynamic Host Configuration Protocol (DHCP), 519f, 522
dynamic HTML (DHTML), 534
dynamic random access memory (DRAM), 209

E

earbuds, 56
Ease of Access tools, 198, 198f
eBay, 99
e-books, 291–293
Eco Libris, 492
e-commerce (electronic-commerce), 97, 99–100, 100f
ECPA (Electronic Communications Privacy Act), 348
e-cycling centers, 240
EDI (electronic data interchange), 475
editors, IDE, 398–399
education
    artificial intelligence for, 20–21
    computer technology and, 19–20
    software discounts for, 130
educational and reference software, 155–156, 155f
educational fair use, 314–315, 315f
802.11ac standard, 254–255, 268, 268f
802.11ad standard, 255, 268

802.11af standard, 255
802.11ah standard, 255
802.11n standard, 254, 268
E ink (electronic ink), 291–292, 292f
Elance, 99
electrical switches, 41
electromagnetic interference (EMI), 490
electronic-commerce (e-commerce), 97, 99–100, 100f
Electronic Communications Privacy Act (ECPA), 348
electronic data interchange (EDI), 475
electronic ink (E ink), 291–292, 292f
Electronic Numerical Integrator and Computer (ENIAC), A9, A9f
electronic text (e-text), 291–293, 292f
elements, 529
e-mail, 87f, 97f
    client-based, 95, 95f
    encryption and, 538
    etiquette for, 94–95, 94f
    files and attachments with, 536
    flow of, 535
    invention of, 535
    popularity of, 94
    privacy and, 94
    viruses, 341, 342f
    web-based, 95, 95f
e-mail servers, 478f, 479, 535
    location of, 536, 536f
    types of, 536
embedded computers, 46
embodied agents, 19, 19f
EMI (electromagnetic interference), 490
employee monitoring, ethics and, 348, 348f
employees, expressing views on social media, 284, 321
employment-at-will, 321, 321f
e-Nable, 6f
encryption
    businesses and, 541
    e-mail and, 538
    ethics and, 540
    keys, 277
    private-key, 539–540, 539f
    public-key, 539
    random numbers for, 539
    types of, 538
    viruses, 341–342, 342f
End User License Agreement (EULA), 134, 134f
Engadget, 91
enhanced information, for databases, 433
ENIAC (Electronic Numerical Integrator and Computer), A9, A9f
enterprise resource planning (ERP) systems, 460
entertainment, digital impact on, 290, 290f
environment
    computer disposal and, 239
    technology and, 5–6
environmental factors, computer equipment operations and, 368, 368f
Environmental Protection Agency (EPA), 492, 492f
ePub, 292
e-readers, 291–292, 291f
ergonomics, for computers, 73–74, 73f

ERP (enterprise resource planning) systems, 460
error handling, 386
estimation, in data mining, 453, 453f
e-text (electronic text), 291–293, 292f
Ethernet connectors, 257
Ethernet network, 254–255
Ethernet ports, 69
ethical computing, 67
ethics
    acceptable use policies and, 323–324, 323f, 324f
    censorship and, 28, 29f
    in computing, 17
    content control for children and, 378
    cyber harassment and, 118
    data breaches and, 502
    data collection and, 454
    defining, 23, 67
    digital activism and, 115–116, 116f
    digital manipulation and, 319, 320f
    employee monitoring and, 348, 348f
    encryption and, 540
    geolocation and, 116, 117f
    hacktivism and, 29, 29f
    hoaxes and, 317–318, 319f
    intellectual property and, 26–27
    Internet and, 115–118
    Internet of Things and, 264
    IT and, 17, 67, 118, 135, 171, 323–324, 348, 406, 502, 540
    liability and, 28, 28f
    online reputation and, 320–322
    open source hardware and, 240
    personal, 25–26, 26f
    piggybacking and, 510
    plagiarism and, 315–317, 317f
    privacy and, 27
    privacy at school and, 548
    of private information on public databases, 468
    programming and, 406, 422
    robotic machinery and, 30, 30f
    safety of MacOS, Microsoft Windows, 171
    social justice and, 27, 27f
    software piracy and, 135
    systems of, 24f, 25
    technology and, 17, 23–30
etiquette, for e-mail, 94–95, 94f
Etsy, 99
EULA (End User License Agreement), 134, 134f
events, 173
Evernote, 106, 145, 145f
Excel. See Microsoft Excel
exception report, 458, 458f
executable program, 397
execute stage, of machine cycle, 218
expansion cards, 64
expert system, 16, 459
exploit kits, 338
eXtensible Markup Language (XML), 412–413, 413f, 532, 532f
extensions, file, 106, 190–191
external drive bays, 65
external hard drives, 65, 365
extranet, 475

eyestrain, avoiding, 72
ezines, 240
Ezvid, 304

F
Facebook, 4, 85, 89–90, 116, 176, 298, 320
    personal information on, 364
    redesigning, 467
Facebook chat, 96
facial recognition programs, 85
fair use, 314–315, 315f
Family Pack Software License Agreement, 134
fatal expectations, 179
Favorites, 109
FBI (Federal Bureau of Investigation), 21
FDA (Federal Drug Administration), 21, 21f
feature phones, 44
Federal Bureau of Investigation (FBI), 21
Federal Drug Administration (FDA), 21, 21f
Federal Trade Commission (FTC), 335, 502
fetch stage, of machine cycle, 217
fiber-optic cable, 256, 256f, 490–491, 490f, 491f
fiber-optic service, for Internet, 261, 261f
field constraint, 438
field names, 433–434, 434f
field properties, 436
fields, 433–434, 434f
field size, 436
field types, 434, 435f
fifth-generation language (5GL), 394, 394f
File Explorer, in Windows 10, 187, 188f, 189f, 193f
file extensions, 106
FileHippo, 130
File History, in Windows 10, 196–197, 197f, 365, 366f
file management, 187–192
files
    backups and types of, 364
    compression, 192, 192f
    compression utility, 192
    copying, deleting, moving, 191
    definition of, 187
    e-mail with, 536
    extensions, 190–191
    locating, 187–188
    names, 190–191, 190f
    organizing, 187–192
    path, 187
    recovering deleted, 191
    saving in cloud, 189, 189f
    sorting, viewing, 188, 189f
    storage, 453
    tips for organizing, 190
    types, 190
file servers, 478f, 479, 516
File Transfer Protocol (FTP), 107, 519f
filters, in databases, 441
financial planning software, 147, 147f
"Find my phone," 369, 369f
fingerprint scanning, 333
fingerprint sensor, 54
Fios TV, 302
Firefox, 105f, 107
firewalls, 10, 276, 351

bastion hosts and, 503–504
business, 504, 504f
for client/server network, 503–504
definition of, 353
hackers, protection by, 354
logical port access blocked by, 354, 354f
network address security with, 355
packet screening and, 503
personal, 353
types of, 353, 354f
firmware, 278
first-generation computers, A9
first-generation language (1GL), 394, 394f
Fish and Wildlife Service, U.S., 314
Fitbit, 254
5GL (Fifth-generation language), 394, 394f
5G wireless data, 263
fixed-lens cameras, 297
flash drives, 66, 66f
flash memory cards, 66, 66f
flatbed scanners, 52
flexible keyboards, 49
Flickr, 93, 298, 312, 313f
flowcharts, 383, 383f, 387, 387f, 388f
folders, 187, 191
"For" command, 392
foreign keys, 437
Forensic Toolkit (FTK), 370, 370f
4GL (fourth-generation language), 394, 394f
4G service, 262–263
fourth-generation computers, A10
fourth-generation language (4GL), 394, 394f
frames, MAC addresses and, 495
freeCodeCamp, 535
Freecycle, 36
freeware, 130
FTC (Federal Trade Commission), 335, 502
FTK (Forensic Toolkit), 370, 370f
FTP (File Transfer Protocol), 107, 519f
full backups, 364
full installation, 131
fuzzy logic, 460

G
GA (general availability), 400
Gabriel, Peter, 6f
Galaxy Note, 127
game controllers, 52
game designers, B11
game development careers, B11
GameMaker, 155
game programmers, B11
games, input devices with, 52
Gates, Bill, A2, A4, A4f
GB (gigabytes), 41, 42f
GCFLearnFree.org, 139
GDDR5 (graphics double data rate 5), 231
general availability (GA), 400
geolocation, 116, 117f
Geological Survey, U.S., 314
GHz (gigahertz), 64
Gibson Research Corporation, 351
gigabit Ethernet, 254–255
gigabytes (GB), 41, 42f
gigahertz (GHz), 64
Gimp, 151
GitHub, 411

GitHub Pages, 411
global positioning system (GPS), 64, 116
Gmail, 95, 537
GNU General Public License, 134
GNU Project, 168
GoFundMe, 8
Google, 262, 520, 520f, 523
Google+, 96
Google App Engine, 524
Google Chrome, 105f, 106–107
Google Chromecast, 272
Google Chrome OS, 167, 167f
Google Cloud Print, 58
Google Docs, 90, 98, 129, 141, 228
Google Drive, 67, 98
Google GeoGuessr, 176–177, 177f
Google Hangouts, 96
Google Inbox, 345f
Google Now, 111
Google Photos, 152f, 298
Google PlaNet, 176–177
Google Play, 129, 130f, 414
Google Scholar, 318f
Google search, 110, 111f, 112, 112f
GoPro, 300, 300f
Gosling, James, 408
government impersonation scams, 334
GPS (global positioning system), 64, 116
GPU (graphics processing unit), 231–232, 231f
graphical user interface (GUI), 173, A5–A6, A5f, A6f
graphic designers, A8
graphics double data rate 5 (GDDR5), 231
graphics processing unit (GPU), 231–232, 231f
graphs, 142, 143f, 215
green computing (green IT), 68, 68f
grey-hat hackers, 335
grid computing, 52
guest servers, 480
GUI (graphical user interface), 173, A5–A6, A5f, A6f
gyroscope, 54

H

hackathons, 3, 207, 390
hackers, 9f, 10, 335f
    backdoor programs, rootkits and, 336
    bank account information, credit cards and, 336
    brute force attack by, 498
    car networks and, 477
    computer access gained by, 338
    definition of, 335
    denial-of-service attacks, 337
    distributed denial-of-service attacks, 337, 337f
    exploit kits used by, 338
    firewall protection from, 354
    logical ports and, 338, 338f, 354, 354f, 355f
    recruiting, training, 336
    Trojan horses and, 336, 336f, 503
    types of, 335
hacktivism, ethics and, 29, 29f
Hadoop, 453
HaLow, 249, 255
HAN. See home area network
handshaking, 522, 522f

hard disk drives (HDDs), 196, 218
    access time of, 225, 227
    capacity of, 228
    cookies and, 345
    data storage on, 225
    definition of, 65
    external, 65, 365
    how they work, 227
    internal, 65, 65f
    mechanical, 227f
    popularity of, 225
    sample requirements of, 228, 229f
    solid-state drive, 65
hard disk platter, 196f
hard drive, 66f
hardware, 42–43
    basic network, 258, 258f, 259f
    firewalls, 353
    open source, 240
    operating system coordination for, 173–175
Harvard Mark I, A8, A8f
HD (high definition), 301
HDDs. See hard disk drives
HDMI (high-definition multimedia interface) ports, 70, 70f, 301
head crash, 227
headphones, 56
health care, technology and, 5
heart rate monitor, 54
helpdesk analysts, B10
hexadecimal digit, 520
hexadecimal notation, 133
Hibernate option, 72
high definition (HD), 301
high-definition multimedia interface (HDMI) ports, 70, 70f, 301
History list, in web browser, 110
hoaxes, 317–318, 318f, 319f
Hoax-Slayer, 317
Hollerith, Herman, A7
Hollerith Tabulating Machine, A7
holograms, 165
HoloLens, 165
home area network (HAN), 252f, 253, 475f
    analyzing problems in, 273
    connecting devices to, 269–272, 269f, 270f, 271f, 272f
    planning, 268–269
    port limits in, 269–270, 270f
    setting up basic, 269, 269f
    software configuration for, 273–275, 273f, 274f
    specialized devices in, 271–272
    wireless device limits for, 270
HomeGroup, in Windows 10, 274, 274f, 488
home network servers, 271–272, 272f
home planning software, 149, 149f
home recording studio, 236f
honey pot, 503
Hopper, Grace, A8, A8f
hosts, 107
H&R Block Tax Software, 147
HTML (Hypertext Markup Language), 409–410, 410f, 412f, 413f
    CSS and, 531–532, 531f
    current standard for, 531

elements in, 529
    viewing source code of, 530, 530f
    web development and, 529–532
HTML embedded scripting language, 534
HTML tags, 529
HTTP (Hypertext Transfer Protocol), 87, 87f, 107, 338, 519f, 532–533
HTTPS (Hypertext Transfer Protocol Secure), 519f, 533
human errors, mistakes, 498
human-implantable data chips, 117f
Hushmail, 538
hybrid topology, 486
hyperlinks, 108
Hypertext Markup Language. See HTML
Hypertext Transfer Protocol (HTTP), 87, 87f, 107, 338, 519f, 532–533
Hypertext Transfer Protocol Secure (HTTPS), 519f, 533
hyperthreading, 214, 214f

I

IAB (Internet Architecture Board), 514f
IBM PC, A1f, A3
IC3 (Internet Crime Complaint Center), 334
ICANN (Internet Corporation for Assigned Names and Numbers), 514f, 519, 524
IDE (integrated development environment), 398–399, 398f
identity theft, 9f, 334–335
Identity Theft Resource Center, 502
IEEE (Institute of Electrical and Electronics Engineers), 406, 499, B13f
IETF (Internet Engineering Task Force), 514f
"if else" keywords, 392
IFTTT (If This Then That) app, 13, 151, 260
illustration (drawing) software, 152, 153f
IM (instant messaging), 96, 97f, 537, 538f
image backups, 365–366, 367f
image-editing desktop software, 151, 152f
images. See also digital photography
    analog photography, 296–297
    input devices for, 52
    output devices for, 54–56
    search engines for, 112
inappropriate data, 428, 428f
Inbox, Gmail, 537
incomplete data, 428, 428f
incremental backups, 364
Indiegogo, 296
information
    data compared to, 40
    storage options for, 65–68
information assurance, 502
information services careers, B10, B10f
information systems
    business, 455–460
    business intelligence systems, 460
    data-flow diagrams and, 383, 383f
    decision support systems, 458–459, 458f
    definition of, 382, 455–456, 455f
    enterprise resource planning systems, 460
    management information systems, 457, 458f
    purpose of developing, 382
    system development life cycle and, 382–384, 383f
    transaction-processing systems, 456, 457f

Information Systems Security Association (ISSA), B13f
information technology (IT). *See also* artificial intelligence; IT careers
  careers in, B1–B13
  ethics in, 17, 67, 118, 135, 171, 323–324, 348, 406, 502, 540
  explanation of, 17
  green, 68, 68f
  working with, 18–22
inheritance, 391
initial value, 389
injuries, avoiding, 73f
inkjet printers, 57, 57f
inoculation, 357
input devices
  definition of, 48
  games and, 52
  for image, sound, and sensor, 52–54
  keyboards and touch screens, 48–49
  mice/pointing devices, 50, 52
input forms, 438, 438f
Instagram, 4
installing software, 131–132
instant messaging (IM), 96, 97f, 537, 538f
Institute of Electrical and Electronics Engineers (IEEE), 406, 499, B13f
intangible personal property, 306
integrated circuits, 41, A10
integrated development environment (IDE), 398–399, 398f
integrated physical keyboard, 50f
integrity, data, 430
intellectual property (IP)
  corporate authorship and, 308
  definition of, 306
  ethics and, 26–27
  permission requests for, 314
  types of, 306–307
intelligence, 14
intelligent personal assistants (IPAs), 19, 19f, 53, 53f, 111
interactive white boards, 56, 56f
interface designers, A8
internal drive bays, 65
internal hard drives, 65, 65f
International Game Developers Association, B11
Internet
  accessing and moving around, 105–110
  backbones, 88
  Boom, A6
  broadband, 260–263, 261f
  business conducted on, 97–101
  cable, 261, 261f
  censorship and, 28, 29f
  circuit switching and, 517
  collaboration on, 89–94, 97f, 150, 150f
  communication over, 94–96, 97f, 535–541
  connecting to, 260–263
  connection speed tests for, 266
  data transmission on, 516–518
  dial-up connection to, 264
  digital music streaming on, 296, 437
  digital video broadcasting on, 300–301
  DSL, 261, 261f
  ethics and, 115–118

fiber-optic service for, 261, 261f
  hoaxes and, 317–318, 319f
  identification, 519–525
  management of, 514, 514f
  navigating, 108–110
  net neutrality and, 262
  networking components of, 515–516, 515f
  online reputation and, 320–322
  origin of, 86–88, 87f
  packet switching and, 517–518, 518f
  personal computers and origin of, A6
  personal information protection on, 363–364, 364f
  privacy and, 124, 264, 361
  process of, 88–89, 88f
  protocols, 516–517
  satellite, 261
  searching effectively on, 110–113
  side hustles on, 99
  Wi-Fi, 249, 254–255, 262–263
Internet Architecture Board (IAB), 514f
Internet Archive, 320, 321f
Internet backbone, 515, 515f
Internet cache, domain names and, 525
Internet Corporation for Assigned Names and Numbers (ICANN), 514f, 519, 524
Internet Crime Complaint Center (IC3), 334
Internet Engineering Task Force (IETF), 514f
Internet exchange point (IXP), 515
Internet Explorer, A6
Internet of Things (IoT), 249, 258, 259f, 264, 520, A9
Internet Protocol (IP), 518, 519f, 522–523
Internet Protocol (IP) addresses. *See* IP addresses
Internet Protocol version 4 (IPv4), 520–521
Internet Protocol version 6 (IPv6), 520–521
Internet service providers (ISPs), 260, 262, 266, 355, 515, 516f
Internet Society, 514f
interpreter, 397
interrupt, 173
interrupt handler, 173
intranet, 475
Intuit QuickBooks, 148
Intuit TurboTax, 147, 147f
IoT (Internet of Things), 249, 258, 259f, 264, 520, A9
IP. *See* intellectual property
IP (Internet Protocol), 518, 519f, 522–523
IP addresses, 88, 270, 271f
  definition of, 519
  dynamic addressing for, 521–522, 521f
  example of typical, 519
  expansion of, 520–521
  Google finding your, 520, 520f
  MAC addresses compared to, 494
  need for, 520
  running out of, 520
  static addressing for, 521
IPAs (intelligent personal assistants), 19, 19f, 53, 53f, 111
iPhone, 51
IPv4 (Internet Protocol version 4), 520–521
IPv6 (Internet Protocol version 6), 520–521
iris scanning, 333

ISPs (Internet service providers), 260, 262, 266, 355, 515, 516f
ISSA (Information Systems Security Association), B13f
IT. *See* information technology
IT careers, B1
  certifications for, B12
  challenges of, B5–B6
  chief information officer and, B6–B7
  demand, growth in, B2, B2f
  department structure in, B7f
  in game development, B11
  in information services, B10, B10f
  lifelong learning in, B6
  math skills and, B4
  organizational chart in, B6, B7f
  outsourcing, offshoring protection in, B3–B4, B3–B4f
  preparation for, B11–B12
  resources for, B12–B13, B13f
  salaries in, B2–B3, B3f
  stress and, B5–B6, B6f
  in support services, B10–B11
  in systems development, B10, B10f
  teamwork in, B4
  in technical services, B9–B11
  training for, B12–B13, B13f
  transferable skills in, B5
  trends in, B11
  in web development, B7–B8, B8f
  women in, B4, B6, B12, B13f
  work settings in, B4, B5f
iTunes, 93f, 129
IXP (Internet exchange point), 515
Izzy Video podcasts, 299

J

Jacquard, Joseph, A6–A7
Jacquard Loom, A6–A7, A7f
jam signal, 484, 485f
Java, 404, 408–409, 408f, 413f
Java applet, 409, 534, 534f
JavaScript, 410–411, 534–535
JavaScript Object Notation (JSON), 413, 413f, 532
JavaServer Pages (JSP), 411
Jobs, Steve, A1f, A2–A3
join query, 444, 444f
Journey Education Marketing, 130
JPEG (Joint Photographic Experts Group), 297
JSON (JavaScript Object Notation), 413, 413f, 532
JSP (JavaServer Pages), 411
jump drives, 66

K

Kahn, Robert, 87
Kaspersky Mobile Security, 340
KB (kilobyte), 41, 42f
KeepVid Video Downloader, 139
kernel (supervisor program), 178–179
Kernighan, Brian, 407
keyboards
  with Bluetooth technology, 49, 50f
  definition of, 48
  Dvorak, 48, 48f

efficient use of, 49, 49f
flexible, 49
integrated physical, 50f
laser-projection, 50f
QWERTY, 48
virtual, 48–49, 48f, 49
key pair, 539
keystroke logger (keylogger), 336, 344
keywords, 110, 392
Kickstarter, 7, 35–36
kilobytes (KB), 41, 42f
Kindle Direct Publishing, 293
Kingston Personal Flash Drives, 361
Kiva, 35–36
knowledge-based system, 459
knowledge representation, 15, 15f
Kodi, 302

L

LaaS (Lighting as a Service), 497
LAlarm, 369
LAN (local area network), 252f, 253, 474, 475f, 476f
landscape planning software, 149, 149f
language, of computers, 41–42, 432. See also programming languages
laptop computers, 44–45, 44f, 45f
laptop speakers, 236
large format printers, 58, 58f
laser printers, 57, 57f
laser-projection keyboard, 50f
latency, 227
law enforcement, artificial intelligence for, 20–21, 20f
LCD (liquid crystal display), 54–55, 55f
learning, 15, 15f, B6
Learn the Net, 409
LED (light-emitting diode) displays, 54
liability, ethics and, 28, 28f
Libby app, 292
LibreOffice, 140
LibreOffice Calc, 141
light-emitting diode (LED) displays, 54
Lighting as a Service (LaaS), 497
light sensor, 54
Lilypad, 207
LimeWire, 35
linked data, 114, 114f
Linking Open Data project, 114
links, 113
Linux, 167, 167f, 362
acquiring, 168
explanation of, 168
user interface of Windows 10, MacOS compared to, 186, 186f
liquid cooling, 215, 215f
liquid crystal display (LCD), 54–55, 55f
Lisa, A5, A6f
lists, databases compared to, 427–428, 427f, 428f
local administration, of networks, 253f, 254
local area network (LAN), 252f, 253, 474, 475f, 476f
locally installed software, 128
Location Sensor, in App Inventor, 224
lock screen, in Windows 10, 185
logical errors, 399
logical port blocking, 354, 355f

logical ports, 338, 338f, 354, 354f, 355f
logic bombs, 341, 342f
loops, 389, 389f
loop topology, 482–483, 483f
Lotus 1-2-3, A4, A5f
Lovelace, Ada, A7
low-level formatting, 227
Lulu, 293
Lumosity, 156

M

MAC (media access control) address. See media access control (MAC) address
MACH (My Automated Conversation coacH), 21, 21f
machine cycle, 211–212, 212f
decode stage of, 217
execute stage of, 218
fetch stage of, 217
store stage of, 218
machine learning (ML), 16
machine(s)
historical development of personal computer and, A6–A10
language, 217, 394, 394f
learning, 176–177
OS for, 169
Macintosh, A5, A6f
MacOS, 166–167, 167f
backups for, 366–367
safety of Microsoft Windows compared to, 171
Time Machine in, 198, 238, 238f
user interface of Windows 10 and Linux compared to, 186, 186f
viruses and, 339
wireless routers for, 270
macros, 146, 382
macro viruses, 341, 342f
Mad Dragon Music Group, 245
Magmito, 414
magnetometer, 54
mainframe computers, 46
MakeTechEasier.com, 139
malicious human activity, 498
malware, 171, 343
MAN (metropolitan area network), 252f, 253, 475f
management information systems (MIS), 457, 458f
Mann, Stephen, 22
many-to-many relationship, 431
marketing strategies, 7
Massive Open Online Courses (MOOCs), 3
master boot record, 341
MB (megabytes), 41, 42f
Mbps (megabits per second), 251
McAfee Internet Security, 340, 353
m-commerce (mobile commerce), 99, 130
mechanical internal hard drive, 66f, 227f
media access control (MAC) address, 278
definition of, 494
frames and, 495
IP addresses compared to, 494
media sharing, through social media, 93–94, 97f
media subsystems, 231–236
medicine, 21, 21f

megabits per second (Mbps), 251
megabytes (MB), 41, 42f
memory
cache, 213
cards, 64, 219
modules, 219
motherboard and, 63–64, 63f
OS management of, 174–175
physical, 219
RAM, 63–64
resident, 178
ROM, 64
types of, 219f
video, 231
for video cards, 231
virtual, 174, 175f
memory subsystem, 218–221
menu-driven interface, 173, 173f
mesh networks, 270
messaging apps, 91
metadata, 438
metasearch engines, 112
metropolitan area network (MAN), 252f, 253, 475f
microblogs, 92
microchips, 21, 21f
microphones (mics), 53, 53f
microprocessor chip, A10, A10f
microprocessors, 41
micro SD flash cards, 66f
Microsoft, A2, A4, A4f
Microsoft Access, 144
Microsoft account, 179
Microsoft Disk Operating System (MS-DOS), 172–173, A4–A5, A4f, A5f
Microsoft Edge, 105–107, 105f, 109, 360f
Microsoft Excel, 141, 142f, 447, A4, A5f
Microsoft HoloLens, 22f
Microsoft Home 2.0, 260
Microsoft Knowledge Base, 238
Microsoft .NET Framework, 407
Microsoft Office, 92f
Microsoft Office Mix, 144, 144f
Microsoft Office Online, 90, 98, 129
Microsoft OneNote, 145, 145f
Microsoft Outlook, 95, 146, 146f
Microsoft PowerPoint, 143–144, 143f, 173
Microsoft Sway, 144
Microsoft Upgrade Your World project, 204
Microsoft Video for Windows, 300f
Microsoft Windows, 166–167, 167f, 171
Microsoft Windows 10. See Windows 10
Microsoft Word, 91, 92f, 140
MIME (Multipurpose Internet Mail Extensions), 536
Mint site, 147, 147f
mirror sites, 155
MIS (management information systems), 457, 458f
ML (machine learning), 16
MLA (Modern Language Association), 317
MMS (Multimedia Message Service), 96
mobile application development, 413–414, 414f
mobile broadband, 262–263
mobile business intelligence, 461, 461f
mobile commerce (m-commerce), 99, 130
mobile hotspots, 262, 262f

mobile operating system, 167, 205
mobile payment apps, 130
model management system, 459
model releases, for photography, 312
modem, 258
Modern Language Association (MLA), 317
monitors
    backlit, 292, 292f
    internal factors of, 55
    size of, 55
    3D, 232, 232f
    types of, 54–55
    Ultra HD, 56
MOOCs (Massive Open Online Courses), 3
Moore, Gordon, 208–209
Moore's law, 208–209, 208f
Mosaic, 88, A6
motherboard, memory and, 63–64, 63f
mouse, 50, 52
Movie Blog, 91
MP3 (MPEG-1 Audio Layer 3), 152–153, 294
MPEG (Moving Picture Experts Group), 300, 300f
MPEG-1 Audio Layer 3 (MP3), 152–153, 294
MS-DOS (Microsoft Disk Operating System), 172–173, A4–A5, A4f, A5f
multidimensional databases, 432, 432f
multi-factor authentication, 363, 363f
Multimedia Message Service (MMS), 96
multimedia software, 150–152, 151f, 152f
multipartite viruses, 342
Multipurpose Internet Mail Extensions (MIME), 536
multishirking, 348
multitasking operating systems, 166
multitouch screens, 51, 51f
multiuser operating system, 169–170
Museum of Hoaxes, 317
My Automated Conversation coacH (MACH), 21, 21f
MyBookmarks, 109
MySQL, 144, 430, 430f

N

NAK (negative acknowledgment), 522, 523f
NASA, 313f, 314
NAS (network-attached storage) devices, 271, 271f, 365
NAT (network address translation), 355
National Center for the Analysis of Violent Crime database, 20
National Science Foundation (NSF), 514
National White Collar Crime Center (NW3C), 334
natural events and disasters, 498
natural language processing, 15, 15f, 176–177
natural language processing (NLP) system, 459
Nay, Robert, 414
near field communication (NFC), 56, 56f, 130, 167
negative acknowledgment (NAK), 522, 523f
NEI (Next Einstein Initiative), 6f
Nest thermostat, 260
Netflix, 262

net neutrality, 262
Netscape Navigator, 88, A6
network adapters. *See also* network interface card
    definition of, 492
    device drivers and, 494
    functions of, 493, 493f
    types of, 493
    viewing installed, 269, 269f
    wireless, 493, 494f
network address translation (NAT), 355
network administration, 251, 253–254, 253f
network administrators, 473, B9–B10, B10f
network architectures
    administration levels defining, 253–254, 253f
    definition of, 252
    distance between nodes defining, 252–253, 252f
network-attached storage (NAS) devices, 271, 271f, 365
network interface card (NIC), 64, 258, 492, 493f
network navigation devices, 258
network operating system (NOS), 169–170, 259, 497
network protocols, 481
network-ready devices, 272
networks. *See also* client/server networks; peer-to-peer (P2P) network
    basic hardware for, 258, 258f, 259f
    benefits of, 251
    business advantages, disadvantages of, 472–473, 472f
    central administration of, 253, 253f
    components of, 255–259, 256f
    data transfer rate in, 251
    definition of, 250
    disadvantages of, 251
    Ethernet, 254–255
    hacking car, 477
    home, 250f
    local administration of, 253f, 254
    mesh, 270
    software of, 259
    transmission media in, 255–257
    understanding, 250–251
    wired, 255–257
    wireless, 255–257, 275–278
network topologies
    bus topology, 481–482, 482f, 486f
    comparing, 485–486, 486f
    definition of, 481
    hybrid topology, 486
    ring topology, 482–483, 483f, 486f
    star topology, 483–485, 484f, 486f
neural networks, in AI, 16, 16f
New York Times, 107, 407f
"Next" command, 392
Next Einstein Initiative (NEI), 6f
NFC (near field communication), 56, 56f, 130, 167
NIC (network interface card), 64, 258, 492, 493f
Nieuwenhuijsen, Mark, 5–6
99 Bottles of Beer site, 400
NLP (natural language processing) system, 459

nodes, 250, 252–253, 252f, 276
No Film School, 299
non-auction/non-delivery scams, 334
nonvolatile storage, 64, 218
normalization, data, 430
Norton Security, 237, 353
NOS (network operating system), 169–170, 259, 497
Notability, 145f
notebook computers, 44–45, 44f
note-taking software, 145, 145f
Notifier, of App Inventor, 183
NSF (National Science Foundation), 514
number systems, 132–133
numeric check, 439
NVIDIA, 232
NW3C (National White Collar Crime Center), 334

O

Objective C, 409, 413f
object-oriented analysis, for algorithms, 391, 391f
object-oriented databases, 432
Object Query Language (OQL), 432
objects, 391, 391f
OC (optical carrier) line, 515
OCR (optical character recognition) software, 52
octet, 519
offshoring, B3–B4, B4f
Ogg Vorbis, 153
Okolloh, Ory, 4
OLAP (online analytical processing), 451
OLED (organic light-emitting diode) displays, 54–55, 55f
OLTP (online transaction processing), 456
Omaha Paper Company, 99
omnidirectional microphones, 53f
OmniFocus, 146
1GL (first-generation language), 394, 394f
OneDrive, 67, 98, 103, 189, 189f
Onenote, 106
one-to-many relationship, 431, 431f
one-to-one relationship, 431, 431f
online analytical processing (OLAP), 451
online annoyances, 343–345
online reputation, 320–322
online shopping precautions, 100f
online store, 411f
online transaction processing (OLTP), 456
Open Data initiatives, 381
openHAB, 260
opening unknown file types, 140
open source hardware, 240
open source software, 128–129, 129f, 162, 240
open system protocol, 517
Open Systems Interconnection (OSI) model, 499–500, 499f
operating system (OS), 42–43
    application software coordination with, 175
    basics of, 166–167
    in cloud computing, 167–168
    definition of, 166
    in early personal computers, A4, A4f
    file management and, 187–192

functions of, 166
hardware coordination for, 173–175
having multiple, 168–169
loading, 178–179, 178f
for machinery, networks, businesses, 169–170
memory management of, 174–175
mobile, 167, 205
multitasking, 166
multiuser, 169–170
peripheral device management of, 175
for personal use, 167–169
processor management of, 173
real-time, 169, 170f
specificity of, 168
updating, 169, 357–358
user interface for, 166, 172–173, 172f
operators, 393
optical carrier (OC) line, 515
optical character recognition (OCR) software, 52
optical drives, 67–68, 68f, 129, 226–227
optical media, 226
optical mouse, 50
OQL (Object Query Language), 432
Oracle, 144
Oracle Beehive, 96
organic light-emitting diode (OLED) displays, 54–55, 55f
organizational chart, for IT departments, B6, B7f
ORLive, 93
OS. See operating system
Osborne, A1f, A3
OSI (Open Systems Interconnection) model, 499–500, 499f
output devices
    definition of, 54
    for images, 54–56
    printers, 57–59
    for sound, 56
outsourcing, B3–B4, B4f
overclocking, 213
ownership, access versus, 7–9, 8f

P

P2P network. See peer-to-peer (P2P) network
packet analyzer (sniffer), 336
packet filtering, 354, 355f
packets, 517
packet screening, 503
packet switching, 517–518, 518f
page file, 174
paging, 174
PAN (personal area network), 252, 252f, 475f
Pandora, 295
Panjiva, 433
paparazzi, 322
paper mills, 316
parallel processing, 213
Pascal, Blaise, A6
Pascalene, A6
passive topology, 481
passphrases, 277
Password Meter, 359
passwords, 277

computer protection with, 358
    managing, 360, 360f
    strength of, 358–360, 359f
patents, 307
path, 107–108
path separator, 188
PayPal, 100
PB (petabytes), 41, 42f
PDLC. See program development life cycle
pedometer, 54
peer-to-peer (P2P) network, 253f, 254
    businesses and, 473, 474f
    centralized, 473
    client/server network compared to, 473–474, 474f
    decentralized, 473
    NOS and, 497
    sharing, 35, 275, 275f
Pendrivelinux, 362
PennApps Hackathon, 390
perception, 15, 15f
Performing Rights Organizations (PROs), 311
peripheral device, 46, 175
persistence of information, 320
personal area network (PAN), 252, 252f, 475f
personal computers. See also computers
    BASIC and, A4, A4f
    early development of, A1–A3, A1f, A2f
    early machines leading to, A6–A10
    GUI and early, A5, A5–A6
    history of, A1
    Internet boom and, A6
    operating systems in early, A4, A4f
    software for early, A4–A5, A5f
personal ethics, 25–26, 26f
personal finance, 19
personal firewall, 353
personal information, protecting, 363–364, 364f
personal information manager (PIM) software, 146, 146f
personal property, 306
personal video recording (PVR), 302
petabytes (PB), 41, 42f
PGP (Pretty Good Privacy), 539
phablets, 44
pharming, 346–347
phishing, 346–347, 347f, 349
photo printers, 298
photo-printing services, 298
PHP (PHP: Hypertext Processor), 411
physical memory, 219
physical protection measures, 501
picture element. See pixels
piggybacking, 276, 510
PIM (personal information manager) software, 146, 146f
Ping, 267
ping command, in Windows 10, 527
pinning, in Windows 10, 185
Pinterest, 110
pipelining, 213–214, 214f
piracy, 26, 35, 135, 311–312
pixels, 55, 297
placeholder, 113
plagiarism, 315–317, 317f

planning, 15, 15f
platform, 168
platters, 225
play testing, B11
Plug and Play, 175
podcasts, 92–93, 93f, 97f
Podfeed, 93f
PoE cameras, 22
pointing devices, 50, 52
point of eye (PoE) cameras, 22
point of presence (POP), 515, 516f
political change
    cell phone cameras and, 330
    social media and, 4
polymorphic viruses, 342
POP (point of presence), 515, 516f
portability, programming languages and, 395
portable storage devices, 66, 66f, 257
ports, 69–70, 69f, 70f, 269–270, 270f
positive acknowledgment (ACK), 522, 523f
possessed object, 498
power-on self-test (POST), 178, 178f
Power Options Systems Settings, 72f
PowerPoint, 91, 92f
power supply, for computers, 70–72
power surges, 368
PowToon, 144
predictive policing, 27, 27f
preemptive multitasking, 173, 174f
presentation software, 143, 143f
pretexting, 346
Pretty Good Privacy (PGP), 539
Prezi, 144
primary key field, 436
primary keys, in databases, 436–437
printers. See also 3D printers
    all-in-one, 58, 58f
    attributes of, 59f
    choosing best, 59, 59f
    cloud-ready, 58, 58f
    definition of, 57
    inkjet, 57, 57f
    large format, 58, 58f
    laser, 57, 57f
    photo, 298
    wireless, 57–58
print queue, 479
print servers, 478f, 479
privacy, 9f, 10
    cloud computing, considerations with, 98
    cookies and, 345
    e-mail and, 94
    ethics and, 27
    ethics of public databases and, 468
    facial recognition and, 85
    geolocation and, 116, 117f
    Internet and, 124, 264, 361
    at school, 548
    searching web, 109
    on shared computers, 361
    web surfing and, 361–362
privacy browsing, 106, 106f
Privacy Rights Clearinghouse, 502
private key, 539–540
private-key encryption, 539–540, 539f
problem solving, 15, 15f

problem statement, in PDLC, 385–386, 386f
processing, 40, 40f, 64–65, 212–214, 404
processors, 41, 173
productivity software
    choosing, 139, 140f
    database software, 144–145, 144f
    definition of, 139
    features of, 146
    financial planning software, 147, 147f
    note-taking software, 145, 145f
    personal information manager software,
       146, 146f
    presentation software, 143, 143f
    spreadsheet software, 141–142, 142f,
       143f
    tax preparation software, 147, 147f
    tips, tricks for, 139
    word processing software, 140, 141f
program development life cycle (PDLC)
    algorithm development in, 387–391,
       387f–391f
    coding in, 392–399
    debugging in, 399–400, 399f
    documentation, testing in, 400
    problem statement in, 385–386, 386f
    stages of, 384–385, 385f
program files, backups for, 364
programmers, A9
programming
    agile methodology and, 384
    completed example of, 395–396, 396f
    definition of, 384
    error handling and, 386
    ethics and, 406, 422
    importance of, 382
    mobile application development and,
       413–414, 414f
    objectives of, 404
    object-oriented analysis in, 391, 391f
    reusability and, 391, 396–397, 397f
    system development life cycle and,
       382–384, 383f
    testing plan for, 386
    top-down design in, 390–391, 390f
    video games, 415
programming languages
    AJAX, 412, 413f
    ASP, 411–412, 412f
    building blocks of, 392–393, 392f, 393f
    C, 413f
    C#, 408, 413f
    C++, 413f
    C, C++, 404
    C and C++, 407–408
    categories and evolution of, 394, 394f
    comments and, 395
    future of, 415–416
    HTML, 409–410, 410f, 413f
    Java, 404, 408–409, 408f, 413f
    JavaScript, 410–411
    JSON, 413, 413f
    JSP, 411
    Microsoft .NET Framework and, 407
    modern, 407–414
    Objective C, 409, 413f
    PHP, 411
    popular, 404
    portability and, 395

scripting languages, 410–411
    selecting, 404–405, 405f
    studying, 404
    Swift, 409
    variable declarations and, 395
    VBScript, 411, 413f
    visual, 406, 415–416
    Visual Basic, 407, 413f
    XML, 412–413, 413f
programs, 128
    executable, 397
    life cycle of, 384–400
    reasons for creating, 382
program specification, 383
Project Gutenberg, 293
project management tools, 91
project managers, A9
Project Morpheus, 23
projectors, 56
proprietary software (commercial software),
    128, 129f, 162
proprietary system protocol, 517
PROs (Performing Rights Organizations), 311
prosthetic devices, 21, 21f
protocols, network, 481
Proto.io, 414
prototypes, 407
proximity sensor, 54
proxy servers, 504
pseudocode, for algorithms, 387
psychology, computer technology and, 21
public domain, 308
public key, 539
public-key encryption, 539
PVR (personal video recording), 302
Python, 404

Q

QR (quick response) codes, 7
quad-core processing, 213, 213f, 214f
quarantining, 357
queries, in database, 441–442, 441f, 442f
query language, 432
Quicken, 147
quick response (QR) codes, 7
QuickTime, 300, 300f
QWERTY keyboards, 48

R

RAD (rapid application development), 407
radio frequency interference (RFI), 490
RAID (redundant array of independent
    disks), 228
RAID 0, 229, 229f
RAID 1, 230
Rails for Zombies, from Code School, 405
random access memory (RAM), 63–64,
    174, 217
    adding, 220–221
    cost, difficulty of adding, 221, 221f
    definition of, 218
    determining amount needed, 220, 221f
    determining amount of installed, 219
    determining usage of, 219, 220f
    reasons for using, 218
    sample allocation of, 221f
    types of, 219, 219f

random numbers, for encryption, 539
range check, 438, 439f
rapid application development (RAD), 407
Raspberry Pi, 240
raw uncompressed data (RAW)
    files, 297
read-only memory (ROM), 64, 218
read/write heads, 227
Really Simple Syndication (RSS), 92–93
real property, 306
real-time operating system (RTOS), 169,
    170f
real-time processing, 456
Real-time Transport Protocol (RTP), 519f
recommendation engines, 19, 19f
records, 434, 434f
recovery drive, 131–132
Recycle Bin, 191
recycling old computers, 239, 239f
Reddit, 110
Red Hat, 168
redundant array of independent disks
    (RAID), 228
referential integrity, 437
RefSeek, 318f
registers, 211
registry, 179
relational algebra, 443
relational databases, 431, 431f
relationships, data, 431, 431f
relativism, 24, 24f
release to manufacturers (RTM), 400
reliable sources
    for academic research, 318, 318f
    citation and, 137, 317
    website evaluation for, 113
    Wikipedia as, 115, 318
render farm, 233
rendering graphics, 233
Reset this PC, 179, 180f
resistive touch screen system, 51
resolution, 55, 297
Resource Monitor, 219, 220f
restarting computer, 71
restore point, 131
retail, computer technology and, 17–18
reusability, programming and, 391, 396–
    397, 397f
ReverbNation, 296
RFI (radio frequency interference), 490
Rift, by Oculus, 23, 23f
ring topology, 482–483, 483f, 486f
Ritchie, Dennis, 407
RJ-45 connectors, 257
robotic machinery, ethics and, 30, 30f
robots, 19, 19f
Roll Back Driver, 176f
ROM (read-only memory), 64, 218
root directory, 187
root DNS servers, 524
rootkits, 336
Rosetta Code wiki, 400
rotational delay, 227
routers, 258, 268, 270, 277, 496
RSS (Really Simple Syndication), 92–93
RTM (release to manufacturers), 400
RTOS (real-time operating system),
    169, 170f

RTP (Real-time Transport Protocol), 519f
rules-based systems, 16
runtime errors, 399

S

SaaS (Software as a Service), 497
Safari, 105f
salaries, for IT careers, B2–B3, B3f
Salary.com, B3, B3f
sampling rate, 294
Samsung Pay, 130
SANS Investigative Forensic Toolkit (SIFT), 370
satellite Internet, 261
scalability, of client/server network, 474
scareware, 171, 347–348, 347f
science, computer technology and, 21
scope creep, 384
Scribblar, 150
scripting languages, 410–411
script viruses, 341, 342f
SDLC (system development life cycle), 382–384, 383f
search engines
    Boolean operators refining, 113
    components of, 110
    customizing, 112–113, 112f
    definition of, 110
    for images and videos, 112
    specialized, 111–112
    uniqueness of different, 111
Search Engine Watch, 111
second-generation computers, A10
second-generation language (2GL), 394, 394f
second-level domains, 524
sectors, 196, 227
secure erase, 240
Secure Network Technologies, 500
Secure Sockets Layer (SSL), 99, 533
security, 99–100, 100f, 498–504. See also privacy
seek time, 227
select query, 443
self-driving cars, 30
semantic web, 114, 114f
semiconductors, 41
sensors, input devices for, 54
serial numbers, 278
Serval Mesh, 270
server-based network. See client/server network
servers, 88, 478–481, 478f, 516
server-side programs, 533
service marks, 307
Service Message Block (SMB), 274
service packs, 400
service set identifier (SSID), 277, 277f
Session Restore, 106
shared computers, privacy on, 361
Sharing, in App Inventor, 489
sharing economy, 8f, 9
shielded twisted-pair (STP) cable, 491, 491f
Short Message Service (SMS), 96
ShouldIRemoveIt, 131
Shutterfly, 298
shutting down computers, 71
side hustles, on Internet, 99

SIFT (SANS Investigative Forensic Toolkit), 370
Signal, 91
Simple Mail Transfer Protocol (SMTP), 519f, 535
Simplenote, 145f
Simple Query Wizard, 442
simulation programs, 156
single-lens reflex (SLR) cameras, 296–297
Siri, 111
SketchUp Make, 149, 149f
Skype, 12, 96
Slack, 150
Sleep mode, 71
Slingbox, 302, 302f
SLR (single-lens reflex) cameras, 296–297
smart homes, 260, 260f, 497
smartphones, 43–44, 43f, 45f
    biosensors for, 127
    ergonomics and, 73–74, 74f
    iris scanning and, 333
    storage capacity of, 66
    viruses and, 340
smart TVs, 272, 272f
smartwatches, 254
Smashwords, 293
SMB (Service Message Block), 274
SMS (Short Message Service), 96
SMTP (Simple Mail Transfer Protocol), 519f, 535
Snapchat, 89, 300
snapping windows, in Windows 10, 185
sniffer (packet analyzer), 336
Snipping Tool, in Windows 10, 185
Snopes, 317
social activism, hacktivism and, 29, 29f
social bookmarking, 110
social commerce, 99
social engineering, 346–348, 347f
social justice, ethics and, 27, 27f
social media, 89
    digital activism and, 115–116, 116f
    employees expressing views on, 284, 321
    hoaxes and, 317–318, 319f
    media sharing through, 93–94, 97f
    online reputation and, 320–322
    political change and, 4
social media directors, A8
SocialMention, 322, 322f
social networking, 89–90, 90f, 97f
software, 10, 42
    accounting, 148
    app creation, 154–155, 154f
    application, 128, 139–156, 166, 175
    audio-editing, 153
    beta versions of, 130, 400
    business, 148–149, 149f
    commercial, 128, 129f, 162
    computer-aided design, 148–149, 149f
    course management, 156
    database, 144–145, 144f
    definition of, 128
    desktop publishing, 148
    digital audio, 152–153
    digital video-editing, 151–152, 152f
    distributing, 128–129
    drawing, 152, 153f

    for early personal computers, A4–A5, A5f
    educational and reference, 155–156, 155f
    education discounts for, 130
    financial planning, 147, 147f
    freeware, 130
    home and landscape planning, 149, 149f
    home area network configuration of, 273–275, 273f, 274f
    image-editing desktop, 151, 152f
    installing and uninstalling, 131–132
    licenses, 134, 134f
    locally installed, 128
    mirror sites and, 155
    multimedia, 150–152, 151f, 152f
    of networks, 259
    note-taking, 145, 145f
    open source, 128–129, 129f, 162, 240
    personal information manager, 146, 146f
    piracy, 135, 311–312
    presentation, 143, 143f
    productivity, 139–147
    purchasing, 129–130
    SaaS, 128–129
    spreadsheet, 141–142, 142f, 143f
    subscription, 129
    system, 128, 166
    system reliability and, 238
    tax preparation, 147, 147f
    updates, 238, 357–358
    upgrading, 132–133
    vertical market, 148
    virtualization, 480, 480f
    web authoring, 148
    word processing software, 140, 141f
Software as a Service (SaaS), 128–129, 497
software firewalls, 353
SolarRoad, 6f
solid-state drive (SSD), 65, 66f, 217–218, 226–227, 226f
solid-state hybrid drive (SSHD), 226–227, 226f
Son of Citation Machine, 137
Sonos, 295, 295f
sound
    digital audio software, 152–153
    input devices for, 53
    output devices for, 56
sound cards, 64
    audio MIDI interface and, 236, 236f
    definition of, 235
    laptop speakers and, 236
    surround sound and, 235–236, 235f
    3D, 235
SoundCloud, 93–94, 296
source code, 397, 530, 530f
spam, 9f, 10
    blogs, 92
    filters, 344–345, 344f
    folder, 345f
speakers, 56, 236, 236f
spear phishing, 349, 349f
splogs, 92
spooler, 174
Spotify, 295–296, 295f, 437, 437f
spreadsheet software, 141–142, 142f, 143f
spyware, 9f, 100, 343–344

SQL (Structured Query Language), 394, 394f, 432, 442f, 443–444, 443f, 444f
Squarespace, 410
SSD (solid-state drive), 65, 66f, 217–218, 226–227, 226f
SSHD (solid-state hybrid drive), 226–227, 226f
SSID (service set identifier), 277, 277f
SSL (Secure Sockets Layer), 99, 533
stack, 173
Starbucks, 130f
Start menu, in Windows 10, 184–185, 184f
star topology, 483–485, 484f, 486f
statements, code, 392
static addressing, for IP addresses, 521
stealth viruses, 342
Stitcher, 93f
storage capacity, 228–230, 228f, 230f
storage devices, 65–68
storage drives, 225–227
store stage, of machine cycle, 218
STP (shielded twisted-pair) cable, 491, 491f
stress, IT careers and, B5–B6, B6f
Strong Password Generator, 358, 359f
Stroustrup, Bjarne, 408
structured data, 114, 432
Structured Query Language (SQL), 394, 394f, 432, 442f, 443–444, 443f, 444f
Stuffit, 192
StumbleUpon, 110
stylus, 48
subdirectory, 107–108
subscription software, 129
subsystems
    audio, 236f
    of computers, 210f
    CPU, 211–216
    media, 231–236
    memory, 218–221
    storage, 225–229
summary report, 458, 458f
Sunway TaihuLight, 47, 47f
supercomputers, 46–47
SuperFetch, 219
supervised learning, 15
supervisor program (kernel), 178–179
support services careers, B10–B11
surface acoustic wave touch screen system, 51
surfing, web, 361–362, 362f
surge protectors, 368, 368f
surround sound, 235–236, 235f
surround-sound system, 56
SUSE Linux Enterprise Server, 259
Swap.com, 9
swap file, 174
Swift, 154, 409
switches, 258, 258f, 495–496, 495f
syntax, 392
syntax errors, 392
System About window, 211f
system development life cycle (SDLC), 382–384, 383f
system evaluation, for computers, 210, 223
system files, 178
system reliability, 236–238, 236f, 237f, 238f
system requirements, 131
System Restore, 197, 197f, 236–237
system restore point, 197

systems analysts, A9
systems development careers, A9, A10f
system software, 42, 128, 166. See also operating system
system unit, 46, 46f

T
tabbed browsing, 105, 106f
tab isolation, 106
tables, 434, 434f
tablet computers, 43f, 44, 45f
tagging, 110, 320
tangible personal property, 306
Target, 97, 298
taskbar, in Windows 10, 184
Task Manager utility, 195, 195f
TaskRabbit, 99
Task Scheduler, 237
Task View, in Windows 10, 185
tax preparation software, 147, 147f
TB (terabytes), 41, 42f
TCP (Transmission Control Protocol), 518, 519f
TCP/IP protocol, 87f, 518, 519f
tear-off tabs, 106
technical services careers, B9–B11
technical writers, B9
technology. See also information technology; IT careers
    careers and, 18–21
    in collaboration, 7
    in consumption, 7–9
    environment and, 5–6
    ethics and, 17, 23–30
    health care and, 5
    users, 209f
    wearable, 207, 254
    on world stage, 4–6
TED, 6
telecommunications technicians, B10
Telnet, 267, 519f
templates, 146
terabytes (TB), 41, 42f
terminators, 481, 482f
terms of use, 312–313, 313f
Tesla S, 288f
test condition, 389
testing, in PDLC, 400
testing plan, 386
tethered downloads, 296
texting, 96, 97f
theft, computers and, 368–371, 369f, 371f
thermometer, 54
theSkyNet, 52
Thingiverse, 287
3GL (third-generation language), 394, 394f
third-generation computers, A10
third-generation language (3GL), 394, 394f
thrashing, 174
3D monitors, 232, 232f
3D printers, 21, 21f, 58f, 287
    medical uses of, 59
    regulation of, 28, 28f
    uses of, 58
3D sound cards, 235
3G service, 262–263
360-degree images, 39
three-way handshake, 522, 522f

throughput, 251
thumb drives, 66
thumbnail previews, 106
thunderbolt ports, 69, 69f, 234
time bombs, 341, 342f
time cards, automating, 423
Time Machine utility, 198, 238, 238f
time to live (TTL), 525
time-variant data, in data warehouses, 450
TinyDB, in App Inventor, 352
TinyWebDB, in App Inventor, 448
tissue-rendering programs, 20f
TiVo, 302
T line, 515
TLS (Transport Layer Security), 533
tokenization, 130
token method, 482
tokens, 482
Tomlinson, Ray, 87f, 535
Toodledo, 146
top-down design, for algorithms, 390–391, 390f
top-level domains, 107, 108f
touchpad, 52
touch screens, 48–49, 51
TPS (transaction-processing systems), 456, 457f
tracert command, in Windows 10, 527
trackpad, 52
tracks, 196, 227
Trackur, 322
trade dress, 307
trademarks, 307
transaction-processing systems (TPS), 456, 457f
transistors, 41, A10, A10f
Transmission Control Protocol (TCP), 518, 519f
transmission media, 255–257, 490–492
transportation industries, 19
Transport Layer Security (TLS), 533
Trello, 150, 150f
Trend Micro Internet Security Suite, 353, 356, 356f
Trojan horses, 336, 336f, 503
trolling, 118
TRS-80, A1f, A3
TRUSTe, 100
TruStealth test, 351
TTL (time to live), 525
Tumblr, 92
TuneCore, 296
tunneling, 476, 476f
Turing, Alan, A9
Turing Machine, A9
Turing test, 20, 20f
Turnitin, 316, 316f
twisted-pair cable, 255–256, 490–491, 490f, 491f
Twitter, 4, 89–90, 92, 116, 320
2GL (second-generation language), 394, 394f
2-in-1 PC, 44, 44f, 45f
typical installation, 131

U
Uber, 99
UberConference, 150

Ubuntu, 186, 186f
UDP (User Datagram Protocol), 519f, 522
UHDTV (ultra-high-definition television), 301, 301f
ultrabooks, 45, 45f
Ultra HD monitors, 56
ultra-high-definition television (UHDTV), 301, 301f
unethical behavior, 25
Unicode, 133
unidirectional microphones, 53f
Uniform Resource Locator (URL), 107, 107f, 310
uninstalling software, 131–132
United Nations, 6f
Unity, 415
Universal Automatic Computer (UNIVAC), A9, A9f
universal serial bus (USB) ports, 69, 69f
University of California at Berkeley, 107
UNIX, 170
unknown file types, opening, 140
unshielded twisted-pair (UTP) cable, 255–257, 256f, 257f
unstructured data, 432
unsupervised learning, 15
upgrading software, 132–133
urban legends, 317
URL (Uniform Resource Locator), 107, 107f, 310
USB 3.0, 234f
USB 3.1, 234
USB-C, 234, 234f
USB drives, 66, 234, 234f
USB (universal serial bus) ports, 69, 69f
User Datagram Protocol (UDP), 519f, 522
user interfaces, 166
    command-driven, 172–173, 173f
    graphical, 173, A5–A6, A5f, A6f
    of Linux, Windows 10, MacOS
        compared, 186, 186f
    menu-driven, 173, 173f
Ushahidi (testimony), crisis-mapping tool, 4–5, 5f
Ustream, 299
utilitarianism, 24, 24f
utility programs, 166
    accessibility, 198, 198f
    Disk Cleanup, 194, 194f
    disk defragmentation, 195–196
    File History, 196–197, 197f, 365, 366f
    System Restore, 197, 197f, 236–237
    Task Manager, 195, 195f
    Time Machine, 198, 238, 238f
    types of, 193, 193f
    Windows administrative, 194–198
UTP (unshielded twisted-pair) cable, 255–257, 256f, 257f

V

validation, of data, 438–439, 439f
validation rule, 438
variable declarations, programming
    languages and, 395
variables, 395
VB (Visual Basic), 407, 413f
VBScript, 411, 413f
vertical market software, 148

video cards, 64
    capacity of, 233, 233f
    definition of, 231
    GPU and, 231–232, 231f
    memory for, 231
    using multiple, 232
videoconferencing, 52f, 56
video games, 154–155, 415, B11, B11f
video memory, 231
Video Player, of App Inventor, 305
video producers, A8
Vimeo, 299, 301
virtual agents, 456
virtual assistant, 13
virtual desktops, 182, 185–186, 186f
virtualization software, 480, 480f
virtual keyboard, 48–49, 48f
virtual memory, 174, 175f
virtual private networks (VPNs), 362, 476
virtual reality (VR), 22, 23f
virtue ethics, 24, 24f
viruses, 9f, 10
    antivirus software preventing, 355–357
    on cell phones, 357
    definition of, 339
    MacOS and, 339
    passage of, 339, 340f
    smartphones and, 340
    software updates preventing, 357–358
    symptoms of, 340
    types of, 341–342, 342f
virus signature, 356
VisiCalc, A4, A5f
Visual Basic (VB), 407, 413f
visual programming languages, 406, 415–416
vlogs, 91
voice-activated digital assistants, 53, 53f, 111
Voice over Internet Protocol (VoIP), 12, 96, 96f, 97f
voice recognition software, 53
volatile storage, 64, 218
VoIP (Voice over Internet Protocol), 12, 96, 96f, 97f
VPNs (virtual private networks), 362, 476
VR (virtual reality), 22, 23f

W

W3C (World Wide Web Consortium), 514f
W3 Schools, 409
WAN (wide area network), 252f, 253, 474–475, 475f
WANK (Worms Against Nuclear Killers), 29
WAP (wireless access point), 493, 494f
warm boot, 71
wearable technology, 207, 254
Web 2.0, 7, 89
web application architecture, 533–535
web authoring software, 148
web-based e-mail, 95, 95f
web browsers, 87–88
    accessibility of, 107
    Bookmarks and Favorites in, 109
    definition of, 105
    features of, 105–106, 106f
    History list in, 110
    navigation on, 108–110

webcams, 52
webcasts, 93, 97f
web content creators, A8
web development
    careers, B7–B8, B8f
    HTML and, 529–532
    HTTP and, 532–533
    JSON and, 532
    XML and, 532, 532f
weblogs, 91–92
web programmers, A8
web server administrators, B10
web servers, 478f, 480, 516
web services, 407, 407f, 528
websites
    bookmarking, 110
    citation of, 137, 317
    creation of, 513
    evaluating reliability of, 113
    navigating, 108–110, 109f
web surfing, 361–362, 362f
WebViewer, in App Inventor, 104
WEP (Wired Equivalent Privacy), 277
WhatsApp, 91, 96
white-hat hackers, 335
whole-house surge protector, 368, 368f
wide area network (WAN), 252f, 253, 474–475, 475f
Wi-Fi, 249, 254–255, 262–263
Wi-Fi Alliance, 249
Wi-Fi-FreeSpot, 262
Wi-Fi Protected Access (WPA), 277
Wi-Fi Protected Access Version 2 (WPA2), 277
WiGig standard, 255, 268
WikiLeaks, 27
Wikipedia, 115, 318
wikis, 90–91
Wikispaces, 91
wild card, 113
Windows 10, 166
    desktop in, 184–185
    File Explorer in, 187, 188f, 189f, 193f
    File History in, 196–197, 197f, 365, 366f
    HomeGroup in, 274, 274f, 488
    lock screen in, 185
    ping command in, 527
    pinning in, 185
    power conservation in, 71, 71f
    Reset this PC in, 179, 180f
    setting up, 273–275, 273f, 274f
    snapping windows in, 185
    Snipping Tool in, 185
    Start menu in, 184–185, 184f
    System About in, 211f
    System Restore in, 197, 197f, 236–237
    taskbar in, 184
    Task Scheduler in, 237
    Task View in, 185
    tracert command in, 527
    user interface of MacOS and Linux
        compared to, 186, 186f
    using, 184–186
    virtual desktops in, 185–186, 186f
    wireless routers for, 270
Windows 95, A6
Windows administrative utilities, 194–198
Windows Defender, 344f

Windows Device Manager, 269f
Windows Firewall, 353, 354f
Windows Hello, 361f
Windows Media Video, 300, 300f
Windows Server, 259, 271–272, 272f
WinZip, 192
Wired Equivalent Privacy (WEP), 277
wired networks, 255–257
Wired site, 113
wireless access point (WAP), 493, 494f
wireless data, 5G, 263
wireless Internet, 262–263
wireless Internet service provider (wireless ISP), 262
wireless mice, 50
wireless network adapters, 493, 494f
wireless network interface card (wireless NIC), 493, 494f
wireless networks, 255–257
    mobile devices connecting to, 275
    securing, 276–278
    troubleshooting problems with, 275–276
wireless range extender, 276, 276f

wireless routers, 268, 270
WITI (Women in Technology International), B13f
The Witness Project, 6f
Wix, 410
wizards, 146
women, in IT careers, B4, B6, B12, B13f
Women in Technology International (WITI), B13f
Word for MS-DOS, A5, A5f
WordPerfect, A5, A5f
WordPress, 92
word processing software, 140, 141f
WordStar, A4–A5, A5f
work settings, in IT careers, B4, B5f
worksheets, 142
World Food Programme, United Nations, 6f
World Wide Web (WWW), 87, 87f
World Wide Web Consortium (W3C), 514f
worms, 341, 342f
Worms Against Nuclear Killers (WANK), 29
Wozniak, Steve, A1f, A2–A3
WPA (Wi-Fi Protected Access), 277
WPA2 (Wi-Fi Protected Access Version 2), 277

Writer, 140
Wunderground API, 407f
WWW (World Wide Web), 87, 87f

X
Xcode, 409, 409f
Xerox, A5
XML (eXtensible Markup Language), 412–413, 413f, 532, 532f

Y
Yahoo Finance API, 407f
Yahoo! Mail, 95
Yahoo! Messenger, 96
Yahoo! search, 112, 321f
YouTube, 91, 93–94, 93f, 301, 304, 311, 311f

Z
Z1, A8
Zipcar, 7
Zirko, Steven, 21
zombies, 336, 337f